D1299861

Futures, Options, and Swaps

Futures, Options, and Swaps

Fifth Edition

Robert W. Kolb and James A. Overdahl

Blackwell
Publishing

© 2007 by Robert W. Kolb and James A. Overdahl

BLACKWELL PUBLISHING
350 Main Street, Malden, MA 02148-5020, USA
9600 Garsington Road, Oxford OX4 2DQ, UK
550 Swanston Street, Carlton, Victoria 3053, Australia

The right of Robert W. Kolb and James A. Overdahl to be identified as the Authors of this Work
has been asserted in accordance with the UK Copyright, Designs, and Patents Act 1988.

All rights reserved. No part of this publication may be reproduced, stored in a retrieval system,
or transmitted, in any form or by any means, electronic, mechanical, photocopying, recording
or otherwise, except as permitted by the UK Copyright, Designs, and Patents Act 1988, without
the prior permission of the publisher.

First published 2007 by Blackwell Publishing Ltd

1   2007

Library of Congress Cataloging-in-Publication Data

Kolb, Robert W.
    Futures, options, and swaps / Robert W. Kolb and James A. Overdahl. — 5th ed.
        p. cm.
    Includes bibliographical references and index.
    ISBN 978–1–4051–5049–1 (alk. paper)
    1. Derivative securities. 2. Futures. 3. Options (Finance) 4. Swaps (Finance)
I. Overdahl, James A. II. Title.

    HG6024.A3K649 2007
    332.64′5—dc22

                                                    2006103248

A catalogue record for this title is available from the British Library.

Set in 10/12pt Times
by Graphicraft Limited, Hong Kong
Printed and bound in the United States
by Sheridan Books Ltd.

The publisher's policy is to use permanent paper from mills that operate a sustainable
forestry policy, and which has been manufactured from pulp processed using acid-free
and elementary chlorine-free practices. Furthermore, the publisher ensures that the text paper
and cover board used have met acceptable environmental accreditation standards.

For further information on
Blackwell Publishing, visit our website:
www.blackwellpublishing.com

Robert W. Kolb: *To my brothers, Stephen Register Kolb and Andrew Cooper Kolb*
James A. Overdahl: *For Jennifer, forever and for always*

Contents

Preface

The fifth edition of *Futures, Options, and Swaps* brings together in one text a comprehensive treatment of the three most important types of financial derivatives. These three types of derivatives are linked by a common pricing framework—the proposition that rational prices preclude arbitrage profits. This guiding principle is introduced in the first chapter and pursued throughout the text.

The text also emphasizes the use of futures, options, and swaps in risk management. While the book features numerous examples of speculative strategies that can be implemented with these instruments, the focus of the application examples is the management of preexisting risk.

To integrate the understanding of these instruments, the discussion emphasizes the relationships among futures, options, and swaps. For example, various parity conditions are derived and illustrated. As a second example, an interest rate swap is analyzed as a portfolio of bonds, as a portfolio of forward rate agreements, and as a portfolio of futures contracts.

This edition of *Futures, Options, and Swaps* has been substantially revised. Although the basic outline of the text remains the same, new material has been added to every chapter. The chapters have been updated to include market developments and regulatory changes that have taken place since the fourth edition appeared in 2003. The role of international competition is emphasized throughout, as is the role of electronic trading systems. The Commodity Futures Modernization Act of 2000, which thoroughly changed the regulatory landscape for futures trading in the United States, is examined in detail. This edition also includes two new features. First, standalone text boxes have been added, containing anecdotes or vignettes related to various topics discussed more formally in the text. Second, product profiles have been added to describe some of the more successful contracts around the world, as well as to highlight innovative or unusual features of traded contracts.

The treatment in this text emphasizes financial derivatives, but it does not neglect traditional commodity futures. From years of teaching this material, we have found that futures can be understood best when the discussion begins with a tangible good having no cash flows, such as gold. Accordingly, the book is organized as follows.

The organization of the text

Chapter 1, *Introduction*, introduces the key concept of arbitrage, which will be used in all subsequent pricing discussions. The chapter also defines and illustrates the various derivatives that will be considered in the text and explains the various uses of these instruments.

Futures

Chapters 2–9 focus on futures markets. Chapter 2, *Futures Markets*, provides an introduction to the institutional framework of the market, including margin, the clearinghouse, and daily settlement. Chapter 3, *Futures Prices*, explores the cost-of-carry model in depth, relating it to the no-arbitrage principle introduced in Chapter 1. Chapter 4, *Using Futures Markets*, discusses the role of speculators in providing market liquidity and in aiding price discovery. Chapter 4 also explores techniques of hedging with futures. Chapters 2–4 provide a comprehensive overview of the market and set the stage for the explicit discussion of financial futures.

Chapters 5–9 consider interest rate futures, stock index futures, and foreign currency futures. Chapter 5, *Interest Rate Futures: An Introduction*, and Chapter 6, *Interest Rate Futures: Refinements*, provide detailed coverage of interest rate futures. Chapter 5 introduces the contracts and covers the basic pricing principles, while Chapter 6 explores key issues (such as the features of the Treasury bond contract and the implicit options in the contract) in more detail. Chapter 6 can be omitted without loss of continuity. Chapter 7, *Stock Index Futures: An Introduction*, and Chapter 8, *Stock Index Futures: Refinements*, follow a similar strategy in treating stock index futures. Chapter 9, *Foreign Currency Futures*, discusses the contracts, pricing principles, and applications of foreign exchange futures. It also includes basic material on interest rate parity and purchasing power parity conditions.

Options

Chapters 10–19 cover options in detail. Chapter 10, *The Options Market*, introduces the essential institutional features of the U.S. options market, while Chapter 11, *Option Payoffs and Option Strategies*, begins the analytic treatment of options by exploring popular trading strategies and their payoffs at expiration, using familiar no-arbitrage conditions. Chapter 12, *Bounds on Option Prices*, continues to use no-arbitrage arguments to place rational bounds on option prices before expiration.

To specify the exact price that an option should have requires a model of how stock prices can move. Chapter 13, *European Option Pricing*, develops formal pricing models for European options. The price of an option depends on the characteristics of the underlying instrument, notably upon the way in which the price of the underlying instrument can vary. We consider the binomial model and eventually elaborate this model into the Black–Scholes model. Chapter 13 also explores the Merton model. Chapter 14, *Option Sensitivities and Option Hedging*, is a companion to Chapter 13 in that it explores the option sensitivities of the Black–Scholes and Merton models. These sensitivities (DELTA, THETA, VEGA, GAMMA, and RHO) are extremely important in using options to hedge or in controlling the risk of speculative strategies.

Chapter 15, *American Option Pricing*, develops an extensive treatment of American options. It includes coverage of American puts, the exact American call option pricing formula, the analytic approximation approach to pricing American options, and the binomial model as it applies to options with and without dividends. Chapter 16, *Options on Stock Indexes, Foreign Currency, and Futures*, explores stock index options, foreign currency options, and options on futures for both European and American options. Chapter 17, *The Options Approach to Corporate Securities*, shows that the principles of option pricing can be extended to analyze corporate securities. The chapter considers the option features of common stock, straight bonds, convertible bonds, callable bonds, and warrants. One of the most useful features of this chapter is to illustrate the power of the option approach to the world of finance. Chapter 18, *Exotic Options*, details the payoffs for a wide variety of exotic options, presents the valuation formulas, and includes a detailed computational example. Chapter 19, *Interest Rate Options*, focuses on European style interest rate options and emphasizes the Black model for pricing options on LIBOR. As such, Chapter 19 provides an introduction to the fundamentals necessary for understanding the swaps market.

Swaps

Coverage of swaps is contained in Chapters 20–22. Chapter 20, *The Swaps Market: An Introduction*, discusses the institutional features of the market, the application of swaps in risk management, and an intuitive approach to pricing. As such, it provides a self-contained introduction to swaps. It also lays the foundation for the detailed treatment in Chapters 21 and 22. Chapter 21, *Swaps: Economic Analysis and Pricing*, deals with two basic themes. First, the chapter shows how swaps may be analyzed as portfolios of other instruments, such as bonds and forward contracts. Second, the chapter shows how no-arbitrage principles can be used to price interest rate and currency swaps. Chapter 22, *Swaps: Applications*, provides a number of extended, self-contained, and independent application examples for swap risk management and pricing. For example, there is an extended discussion of using interest rate swaps to manage the duration gap of a financial institution.

OPTION! software

This text is accompanied by an IBM PC-compatible program, **OPTION!**, that can compute virtually every option and swap value discussed in this book, including a comprehensive module for pricing exotic options. Further, **OPTION!** can graph many of the relationships among different option prices discussed in the chapters that follow. Exploring the option concepts of the text with the software can greatly enhance an understanding of option pricing. The **OPTION!** software program and the operating instructions can be found online at www.blackwellpublishing.com/kolb. The website includes more than 80 exercises designed to enhance the understanding of option pricing principles and applications. These exercises can all be solved using the **OPTION!** software. **OPTION!** runs under Windows 98 and later versions, including Windows XP.

Robert W. Kolb
Boulder, Colorado
Bob@RobertWKolb.com

James A. Overdahl
Arlington, Virginia
Joverdahl@comcast.net

Acknowledgments

This fifth edition of *Futures, Options, and Swaps* has a long pedigree. It grew out of two earlier texts, *Understanding Futures Markets* and *Options*. *Understanding Futures Markets* was first published in the early 1980s and is now in its sixth edition. *Options* came on the scene in the early 1990s and is now in its third edition. Thus, the overwhelming bulk of this material has been extensively classroom-tested in many universities and corporations.

Over all of these editions, we have received the assistance of numerous people, ranging from hundreds of professors to a multitude of students. This book has grown out of their contributions and insights, and we are deeply grateful for their efforts. For their assistance with earlier editions, we would like to especially mention the following individuals: Gerry Gay of Georgia State University, John Polonchek and Tom Gosnell of Oklahoma State University, Don Smith of Boston University, Bob Johnson of the CFA Institute, Marcelle Arak of the University of Colorado at Denver, Jay Marchand of Mercer University, David P. Echevarria of St. Joseph's University, and Thomas William Miller, Jr. of the St. Louis University.

For the fifth edition, we would like to thank Xinlei Zhao of Kent State University, Peter Moles of the University of Edinburgh, Lyn Wu of the University of Memphis, Terrence Martell of Baruch College, Frank Rose of Lewis University, and Eric Terry of Ryerson University.

As other authors know, the completion of a manuscript is just one way station on the path to a finished book. We would like to thank our editor, George Lobell, for his assistance in all steps of the process of preparing this edition. Also, special thanks go to George's editorial assistant, Laura Stearns, for making our plans happen. We would also like to thank Geoffrey Palmer and Simon Eckley and the production team at Blackwell Publishing for helping bring this fifth edition to fruition.

Robert W. Kolb
James A. Overdahl

1

Introduction

Overview

This chapter begins by defining a derivative instrument. As the term implies, a **derivative instrument** is one whose principal source of value depends on the value of something else, such as an underlying asset, reference rate, or index.

The major types of derivatives considered in this book are forward contracts, futures contracts, options contracts, options on futures, and swap contracts. This chapter briefly introduces each of these instruments and explains their key features. Later chapters consider each type of instrument in detail.

After introducing the major types of derivatives, this chapter gives a brief explanation of why derivative instruments have grown to play such a critically important role in modern finance. As we will see, when used prudently, derivative instruments offer an efficient mechanism for financial institutions, commercial enterprises, governments, and individuals to "hedge" preexisting risk exposures; that is, to transfer risk from those who do not want it to those who are willing to accept it for a price. In addition, derivatives serve an important "price discovery" role, meaning that the prices of derivative instruments are useful for accurately assessing the future prospects of the underlying asset prices, reference rates, and price indexes from which derivative contracts inherit their value.

Although derivative instruments offer many benefits to our economy, they also hold the potential for being misused. A look at recent history reveals several instances in which derivative instruments were allegedly involved in financial scandals. For example, in 2002, the Allfirst unit of Allied Irish Bank (AIB) lost $750 million due to the unauthorized derivatives trading of a single rogue employee. In 1995, Barings Bank, an institution that had epitomized prudent financial management throughout its 200-year history, was brought down by the actions of an unsupervised employee who had placed large bets on Barings' behalf using derivative instruments written on Japanese equities. Because of their potential for misuse, derivatives have become inviting targets for criticism. For example, Berkshire Hathaway Chairman Warren Buffet has referred to derivatives as "time bombs" and "financial weapons of mass destruction."[1]

Compared with the fundamental asset price, reference rates, or indexes upon which they are based, derivatives afford numerous benefits to both speculators and risk managers. In addition, derivatives offer some surprising advantages in reducing transaction costs and other forms of trading efficiency.

Throughout this text, we will be concerned with the principles that determine the prices of the derivative instruments we consider. The text consistently employs a no-arbitrage principle to illuminate the pricing principles for each instrument. An arbitrage opportunity is a chance to make a riskless profit with no investment. In essence, finding an arbitrage opportunity is like finding free money, as we explain in more detail later in this chapter. The no-arbitrage principle states that any rational price for a financial instrument must exclude arbitrage opportunities. This is a minimal requirement for a feasible or rational price for any financial instrument. As we will see in detail in the chapters that follow, this no-arbitrage principle is extremely powerful in helping us to understand what prices can reasonably prevail for forwards, futures, options, options on futures, and swaps. The chapter then turns to explaining how the text is organized.

A computer program called **OPTION!** accompanies this text, and is available for download at www.blackwellpublishing.com/kolb. **OPTION!** allows the user to compute option prices with ease and provides modules for pricing swaps.

Derivatives defined

First and foremost, a derivatives instrument is a contract, or agreement, between two contract counterparties. Unlike many market transactions where ownership of an underlying asset is immediately transferred from the seller to the buyer, a derivatives transaction involves no actual transfer of ownership of the underlying asset at the time the contract is initiated. Instead, a derivative contract simply represents a promise, or an agreement, to transfer ownership of the underlying asset at a specific place, price, and time specified in the contract. In fact, most derivative contracts are settled without transfer of ownership ever occurring. The counterparty that contracts to buy is said to have established a **long position**. A counterparty that contracts to sell is said to have established a **short position**. Because of the bilateral nature of a derivative contract, the value of the contract depends not only on the value of its underlying asset but also on the creditworthiness of the counterparties to the contract.

Derivative contracts are characterized by the fact that for every long position, there is a corresponding short position. Prior to the agreement of the long and the short, the contract defining the terms of future exchange for that asset did not exist. This means that the aggregate net value of derivatives in the economy is zero.

Another characteristic of a derivative contract is that it must be based on at least one "underlying." An **underlying** is the asset, reference rate, or index from which a derivative derives its principal source of value. In practice, derivatives cover a diverse spectrum of underlyings, including stocks, bonds, exchange rates, interest rates, credit characteristics, weather outcomes, political events, or stock market indexes. Practically nothing limits the assets, financial instruments, reference rates, or indexes that can serve as the underlying for a derivative contract. Moreover, some derivatives can be based on multiple underlyings. For example, the value of a derivative may depend on the difference between a domestic interest rate and a foreign interest rate.

Consistent with the characteristics described above, we can define a **derivative** as a "zero net supply, bilateral contract that derives its principal source of value from some underlying asset, reference rate, or index."[2] The reader should be aware, however, that there are many competing definitions of derivatives. Economists, accountants, lawyers, and government regulators have struggled to develop a precise, universal definition. That the term "derivatives" is difficult to define arises from the fact that derivatives are not fundamentally different from other financial instruments. The difficulty of defining derivatives is thus traced to their basic similarity to other instruments of finance.

Falling within our definition are several types of derivatives, including commodity derivatives and financial derivatives. A **commodity derivative** is a derivative contract specifying a commodity or commodity index as the underlying. For example, a crude oil forward contract specifies the price, quantity, and date of a future exchange of the grade of crude oil that underlies the forward contract. Because oil is a commodity, a crude oil forward contract would be a commodity derivative. A **financial derivative** is a derivative contract specifying a financial instrument, interest rate, foreign exchange rate, or financial index as the underlying. For example, a call option on IBM stock gives the owner the right to buy the IBM shares that underlie the option at a predetermined price. In this sense, an IBM call option derives its value from the value of the underlying shares of IBM stock. Because IBM stock is a financial instrument, the IBM call option is a financial derivative. Similarly, a futures contract on a Treasury bond is a financial derivative, because the value of the T-bond futures depends on the value of the underlying Treasury bond.

This book considers five types of derivatives: forwards, futures, options, options on futures, and swaps. In this section, we briefly introduce each type of instrument and discuss its basic features. Subsequent chapters focus on futures, options, options on futures, and swaps in detail, while forward contracts are considered in passing throughout the text.

Forwards

A **forward contract** is an agreement negotiated between two parties for the delivery of a physical asset (e.g., oil or gold) at a certain time in the future for a certain price, fixed at the inception of the contract. The parties agreeing to the forward contract are known as counterparties. No actual transfer of ownership occurs in the underlying asset when the contract is initiated. Instead, there is simply an agreement to transfer ownership of the underlying asset at some future delivery date.

The following example illustrates a very simple, yet frequently occurring, type of forward contract. Having heard that a highly prized St. Bernard has just given birth to a litter of pups, a dog fancier rushes to the kennel to see the pups. After inspecting the pedigree of the parents, the dog fancier offers to buy a pup from the breeder. However, the exchange cannot be completed at this time, since the pup is too young to be weaned. The fancier and breeder thus agree that the dog will be delivered in six weeks and that the fancier will pay the $400 in six weeks upon delivery of the puppy. This contract is not a conditional contract; both parties are obligated to complete it as agreed.[3] The puppy example represents a very basic type of forward contract. The example could have been made more complicated by the breeder requiring a deposit, but that would not change the essential character of the transaction. In this example, there is a buyer and a seller.

From the simplicity of the contract and its obvious usefulness in resolving uncertainty about the future, it is not surprising that such contracts have had a very long history, that likely dates to the very beginning of the development of commercial markets. Some authors trace the origins of forward contracts to the commodity-lending activities of ancient Babylonian temples. These examples date from the time of the First Babylonian Dynasty (1894 B.C. to 1595 B.C.). Other authors trace the practice to Roman and even classical Greek times. Strong evidence suggests that Roman emperors entered into forward contracts with their suppliers of Egyptian grain. Still others have traced the origin of forward contracting to India.[4]

While there may not be much agreement about the origins of forward contracting, it is clear that trading originated with contracts similar in form to that of the puppy example. In fact, such contracts continue to be important today, not only among dog lovers, but in markets for commodity and foreign exchange as well. For example, hundreds of billions of dollars of foreign currencies change hands daily through forward contracts between money center banks. These contracts are very similar in structure to the puppy contract.

Forward contracts on both foreign exchange and physical commodities involve physical settlement at maturity. A contract to purchase Japanese yen for British pounds three months hence, for example, involves a physical transfer of sterling from the buyer to the seller, in return for which the buyer receives yen from the seller at the negotiated exchange rate. Many forward contracts, however, are cash-settled forward contracts. At the maturity of such contracts, the long receives a cash payment if the spot price on the underlying prevailing at the contract's maturity date is above the purchase price specified in the contract. If the spot price on the underlying prevailing at the maturity date of the contract is below the purchase price specified in the contract, then the long makes a cash payment.

Futures

A **futures contract** is a type of forward contract with highly standardized and precisely specified contract terms. As in all forward contracts, a futures contract calls for the exchange of some good at a future date for cash, with the payment for the good to occur at that future date. The purchaser of a futures contract undertakes to receive delivery of the good and pay for it, while the seller of a futures contract promises to deliver the good and receive payment. The price of the good is determined at the initial time of contracting.

The precise origins of futures trading are unclear. The answer depends on which attributes are considered essential for a contract to be called a modern-day futures contract. Perhaps the first organized exchange to trade futures contracts was the Dōjima Rice Market in Osaka, Japan.

As early as 1730, the Dōjima Rice Market was trading what were essentially rice futures, with standardized contractual definitions for product quality, delivery time, and delivery location. The contracts traded on a central trading floor, used a standardized clearing system, and the exchange provided a mechanism for determining official settlement prices.

In the Western world, the antecedents to modern futures contracts can be found in a type of forward contract known as a "to-arrive" contract. In a "to-arrive" contract, traders agree to terms for a transaction before the arrival of the goods. To-arrive contracts became popular, particularly in the Chicago grain trade, from the 1840s onward. In 1848, the Chicago Board of Trade (CBOT) was founded to facilitate the exchange of "to-arrive" contracts. In 1865, the CBOT listed a new type of standardized contract that they called "futures." By all accounts, this is the first time the term had been used.[5] Since then, the basic structure of futures contracts has been adopted by a number of other exchanges, both in the United States and abroad.

To see why futures contracts evolved from forward contracts, it is important to understand the main distinctions between the two types of contracts.[6] First, futures contracts are traded on an organized futures exchange, such as the CBOT. In contrast, forward contracts are privately negotiated in the over-the-counter market. Second, the terms of futures contracts are standardized across all contracts of the same type, whereas the terms of forward contracts are individually negotiated to suit the needs of each party to the contract. Third, futures contracts are cleared through a central clearinghouse, whereas forward contracts are not. Fourth, futures contracts rely on a system of margins and daily settlement to protect the financial integrity of the contract. Forward contracts generally do not rely on such a system. Fifth, users of futures contracts can easily and cheaply offset and close a position prior to contract expiration. Users of a forward contract can close their position only if they separately negotiate a termination agreement—something that may be costly to do. Finally, the regulatory structure governing the two types of contracts differs. Futures contracts are regulated by the CFTC, an agency of the federal government. Forward contracts are self-regulating in accordance with ordinary commercial contract law and, if things go badly, bankruptcy law.

While these important features of futures markets will be explored in more detail in Chapter 2, we must bear in mind that forwards and futures are essentially similar contracts. In fact, futures and forwards differ mostly in the institutional setting in which they trade; the principles for pricing and the use of forwards and futures are almost identical.

Options

Everyone has options. When buying a car, we can add more equipment to the automobile that is "optional at extra cost." In this sense, an option is a choice. This book examines options in financial markets. These are a very specific type of option—an option created through a financial contract.

Options have played a role in security markets for many years, although no one can be certain how long. Initially, options were created by individualized contracts between two parties. However, until recently, there was no organized exchange for trading options. In 1973, the Chicago Board Options Exchange (CBOE) began trading options on individual stocks. Since that time, the options market has experienced rapid growth, with the creation of new exchanges and many different kinds of new option contracts. Contracts include options written on individual stocks and bonds, foreign currencies, stock indexes, exchange-traded funds (ETFs), and futures contracts. The development of option exchanges stimulated greater interest and more active trading of options. In many respects, the recent history of option trading can be regarded as an option revolution.

There are two major classes of options: call options and put options.[7] The owner of a call option has the right to purchase the underlying good at a specific price, and this right lasts until a specific date. The owner of a put option has the right to sell the underlying good at a specific price, and this right lasts until a specific date. In short, the owner of a call option can call the underlying good away from someone else. Likewise, the owner of a put option can put the good to someone else by making the opposite party buy the good. To acquire these rights, owners of options buy them from other traders by paying the price, or premium, to a seller.

Like other forms of derivatives, for every option, there is both a buyer and a seller. The seller of an option is also known as an **option writer**. The seller receives payment for an option from the purchaser. In exchange for the payment received, the seller confers rights to the option owner. The seller of a call option receives payment and, in exchange, gives the owner of a call option the right to purchase the underlying good at a specific price, with this right lasting for a specific time. The seller of a put option receives payment from the purchaser and promises to buy the underlying good at a specific price for a specific time, if the owner of the put option chooses.

In these agreements, all rights lie with the owner of the option. In purchasing an option, the buyer makes payments and receives rights to buy or sell the underlying good on specific terms. In selling an option, the seller receives payment and promises to sell or purchase the underlying good on specific terms—at the discretion of the option owner. With put and call options and buyers and sellers, four basic positions are possible. Notice that the owner of an option has all the rights. After all, that is what the owner purchases. The seller of an option has all the obligations, because the seller undertakes obligations in exchange for payment.

Options on futures

An **option on a futures** contract or a **futures option** is an option that takes a futures contract as its underlying good. It contrasts with an **option on the physical**—an option on the good itself rather than an option on a futures contract. For example, in the gold market, the physical gold trades. In addition, options on gold and futures contracts on gold trade as well. The option on gold itself is an option on the physical, while the option on the gold futures contract is a futures option. Similarly, in the equity market, options trade on a stock index (an option on a physical) and options trade on stock index futures (a futures option).

The structure of a futures option is very similar to that of an option on the physical. For both instruments, the option owner has the right to exercise, and the seller has a duty to perform upon exercise. Upon exercising a futures option, however, the call owner receives a long position in the underlying futures at the settlement price prevailing at the time of exercise. The call owner also receives a payment that equals the settlement price minus the exercise price of the futures option. (The call owner would not exercise if the futures settlement price did not exceed the exercise price.) When a call option is exercised against her, a call seller receives a short position in the underlying futures at the settlement price prevailing at the time of exercise. In addition, the short call trader pays the long trader the futures settlement price minus the exercise price.

When the owner of a futures put option exercises, he receives a short position in the underlying futures contract at the settlement price prevailing at the time of exercise. In addition, the put owner receives a payment that equals the exercise price minus the futures settlement price. (The put owner would not exercise unless the exercise price exceeded the futures settlement price.) Upon exercise, the put seller receives a long position in the underlying futures contract, and the put seller must pay the exercise price minus the settlement price.

Swaps

A **swap** is an agreement between two or more parties to exchange sequences of cash flows over a period in the future. For example, Party A might agree to pay a fixed rate of interest on

$1 million each year for five years to Party B. In return, Party B might pay a floating rate of interest on $1 million each year for five years. The parties that agree to the swap are known as **counterparties**. There are five basic kinds of swaps, **interest rate swaps**, **currency swaps**, **equity swaps**, **commodity swaps**, and **credit swaps**. Swaps can also be classified as "plain vanilla" or "flavored." An example of a plain vanilla swap is the fixed-for-floating swap described above. Some types of plain vanilla swaps can be highly standardized, not unlike the standardization of contract terms found on an organized exchange. With flavored swaps, numerous terms of the swap contract can be customized to meet the particular needs of the swap's counterparties.

As we will see in considerable detail, futures and options contracts are generally traded on organized exchanges. These contracts are highly standardized and are limited to relatively few goods, with only a few fixed contract expirations per year. In addition, the horizon over which they trade is often much shorter than the risk horizon that businesses face.

In contrast, swaps are privately negotiated, over-the-counter derivatives that can be custom-tailored to the needs of the counterparties. If they wish, the potential counterparties can start with a blank sheet of paper and develop a contract that is completely dedicated to meeting their particular needs. Thus, swap agreements are more likely to meet the specific needs of the counterparties than exchange-traded instruments. The counterparties can select the dollar amount that they wish to swap, without regard to some fixed contract terms, such as those that prevail in exchange-traded instruments. Similarly, the swap counterparties choose the exact maturity that they need, rather than having to fit their needs to the offerings available on an exchange. This is very important in the swap market, because this flexibility allows the counterparties to deal with much longer horizons than can be addressed through exchange-traded instruments. Because the market does not operate on an exchange, participants have far greater privacy, and are not subject to the rules and regulations governing transactions within an exchange environment.

Swap transactions are facilitated by dealers, who act as financial intermediaries in swap transactions. Dealers must have a strong credit rating, be heavily capitalized, have good access to information about a variety of customers, and have relatively low costs of managing the risks related to dealing activities. Firms already active as financial intermediaries are natural candidates for being swap dealers. Most dealers, in fact, are commercial banks, investment banks, and other financial enterprises such as insurance company affiliates.

Swap customers, called **end users**, usually enter into a swap to modify an existing or anticipated risk exposure. End users of swaps include commercial banks, investment banks, thrifts, insurance companies, manufacturing and other nonfinancial corporations, institutional funds (e.g., pension funds, mutual funds, and hedge funds), and government-sponsored enterprises (e.g., Federal Home Loan Banks). Dealers, moreover, may use derivatives in an end-user capacity when they have their own demand for derivatives exposure. Bank dealers, for example, often have a portfolio of interest rate swaps separate from their dealer portfolio in order to manage the interest rate risk they incur in their traditional commercial banking practice.

The origins of the swaps market can be traced to the late 1970s, when currency traders developed currency swaps as a technique to evade British controls on the movement of foreign currency. The first interest rate swap occurred in 1981 in an agreement between IBM and the World Bank. Since that time, the market has grown rapidly. By the end of 2005, swaps with $285 trillion in underlying notional principal were outstanding. Over 90 percent of this amount was due to interest rate swaps and currency swaps. The swaps market has grown at a compounded annual rate exceeding 40 percent over the 1987–2005 period. In short, the growth of the swaps market has been the most rapid for any financial product in history.

As we will see, the swaps market is growing so rapidly because it provides firms facing financial risks a flexible way to manage that risk. We will explore the risk management motivation that has led to this phenomenal growth in some detail.

Applications of financial derivatives

Financial derivatives have attained their overwhelming popularity and rapid growth for a variety of reasons. This section briefly introduces some of the main benefits that financial derivatives bring to the market. Not all financial derivatives have the same virtues or the same limitations. Therefore, the benefits of derivatives explored in this section do not apply equally to all of the instruments that we will consider. However, subsequent chapters explore the specific applications of forwards, futures, options, and swaps in detail. Here we consider how financial derivatives help to make markets more nearly complete, how speculators and risk managers can use derivatives for their specific ends, and how many traders have been attracted to financial derivatives because of their trading efficiency, particularly their low transaction costs and highly liquid markets.

Market completeness

In the theory of finance, a **complete market** is a market in which any and all identifiable payoffs can be obtained by trading the securities available in the market. For example, a complete market would allow a trader to purchase a security or set of securities that would pay off if and only if the Dow Jones Industrial Average were to rise by 99–100 points over the next month, or if crude oil prices at the end of the year were to lie between $60 and $70 per barrel. It is quite difficult to trade any combination of stocks and bonds that would have a payoff in this circumstance and no other. If the financial instruments available in a market were not sufficiently rich and diverse to permit such a speculation, the market would be deemed incomplete.

From this definition of market completeness, we see that a complete market is an idealization that is most likely always unobtainable in practice. Nonetheless, completeness is a desirable characteristic of a financial market, because it can be shown that access to a complete market increases the welfare of the agents in the economy. Even if an actual market can never be truly complete, the more closely the market approaches completeness, the better off are the economic agents in the economy.

Financial derivatives play a valuable role in financial markets because they help to move the market closer to completeness. If we consider two financial markets that are the same, except that one includes financial derivatives, the market with financial derivatives will allow traders to more exactly shape the risk and return characteristics of their portfolios, thereby increasing the welfare of traders and the economy in general.

Speculation

Financial derivatives have a reputation for being risky. Without doubt, these instruments can prove tremendously risky in the hands of uninformed traders. However, the risks associated with financial derivatives are not necessarily evil, because they provide very powerful instruments for knowledgeable traders to expose themselves to calculated and well-understood risks in pursuit of profit.

In the hands of a knowledgeable trader, a position in one or more financial derivatives can permit a careful and artful speculation on a rise or fall in interest rates, on a change in the riskiness of the entire stock market or a single stock, on changing values of the euro versus the Japanese yen, or on a host of other specific propositions.

The precision and speculative power of derivatives stems largely from the fact that financial derivatives help to make the financial market more nearly complete. Although serving as a speculative tool is not the only use, and probably not the most important use, of financial derivatives, they are ideally suited for this purpose.

Risk management

While financial derivatives are undeniably risky in some applications, they also provide a powerful tool for limiting risks that individuals and firms face in the ordinary conduct of their business. For example, a corporation that is planning to issue bonds faces considerable interest rate risk. If interest rates rise before the bond is issued, the firm will have to pay considerably more over the life of the bond. As we will see, such a firm could use interest rate futures to control its exposure to this risk. Similarly, a pension fund with widely diversified holdings in the stock market faces considerable risk from general fluctuations in stock prices. The pension fund manager could use options on a stock index to reduce or virtually eliminate that risk exposure.

Even though financial derivatives are risky in the sense that their prices are subject to substantial fluctuations, they can be extremely powerful tools for limiting risk as well. While we consider some of the speculative strategies that financial derivatives facilitate, the text emphasizes using financial derivatives to control risk in the types of situations just discussed. Successful risk management with derivatives requires a thorough understanding of the principles that govern the pricing of financial derivatives.

Trading efficiency

In many applications, traders can use a position in one or more financial derivatives as a substitute for a position in the more fundamental underlying instruments. For example, we will see that an option position can mimic the profit or loss performance of an underlying stock index. Similarly, an interest rate futures contract can serve as a substitute for investment in a portfolio of Treasury securities.

In many instances, traders find financial derivatives to be a more attractive instrument than the more fundamental underlying security. Often, the transaction costs associated with trading a financial derivative are substantially lower than the costs of trading the underlying instrument. For example, a corporation might use the futures market to take a million dollar position in Treasury bonds for a transaction cost of about $100. In other situations, financial derivatives might be more attractive than the underlying assets because of greater liquidity in the market for financial derivatives. For example, a trader might want to hold a well-diversified stock market position. One way of obtaining such a position might be to buy a variety of stocks. Such a strategy would surely incur substantial transaction costs, but might involve the trader in buying or selling some stocks that were not very liquid. (A **liquid market** is a market with enough trading activity to allow traders to readily trade a good for a price that is close to its true value.) Faced with such a situation, the trader might prefer to use a stock index futures contract or options on a stock index to save on transaction costs and to enjoy the benefits of trading in a liquid market.

The concept of arbitrage

There are many alternative definitions of *arbitrage*. We begin our analysis with a strict definition of what we call **academic arbitrage**. In academic arbitrage, it is possible to trade to generate a riskless profit without investment. An **arbitrageur** is a person who engages in arbitrage. For example, shares of IBM trade on both the New York Stock Exchange and the Boston Stock Exchange. Suppose that shares of IBM trade for $110 on the New York market and for $105 on the Boston Exchange. A trader could make the following two transactions simultaneously:

> Buy one share of IBM on the Boston Exchange for $105.
> Sell one share of IBM on the New York Exchange for $110.

These two transactions generate a riskless profit of $5. Because both trades are assumed to occur simultaneously, there is no investment. Therefore, such an opportunity qualifies as an academic arbitrage opportunity—it affords riskless profits without investment.

In a well-functioning market, such opportunities cannot exist. If they did exist, they would make all of us fabulously wealthy. The existence of such academic arbitrage opportunities is equivalent to money being left on the street without being claimed. (If you have ever been to Wall Street, you know that there is no money lying on that street.) To understand the pricing of derivative instruments, we assume that there are no arbitrage opportunities. This is our no-arbitrage principle. We apply this principle to determine what we can about prices of financial derivatives on the assumption that there are no arbitrage opportunities.

In our example of the IBM share, we assume that there are no transaction costs. We always begin our exploration of pricing relationships under this assumption of perfect markets, so we assume there are no taxes, no transaction costs, and no frictions of any kind. After developing an understanding of pricing relationships in this simple environment, we go on to consider the more realistic world of transaction costs and other market imperfections.

The organization of the text

The remainder of this text is organized as follows. Chapters 2–9 focus on futures, Chapters 10–19 consider options and options on futures, and Chapters 20–22 discuss the swaps market.

Futures

Chapter 2 introduces the futures market and discusses the types of futures available. Although the text mentions futures on physical commodities, the text emphasizes financial futures. Chapter 3 considers the no-arbitrage pricing principles that govern futures in general and financial futures in particular. Chapter 4 discusses the variety of futures market participants and shows how they use the futures market for speculation and risk management.

Chapters 5–9 focus on specific financial futures. Interest rate futures are the focus of Chapters 5–6, while Chapters 7–8 analyze stock index futures, and Chapter 9 considers foreign currency futures.

Options and options on futures

Chapter 10 introduces the institutional framework of the options market in the United States. Chapter 11 analyzes a variety of option strategies and shows the power of options for tailoring risk to specific expectations. Chapter 12 approaches option pricing by asking the question "What option prices are consistent with the absence of arbitrage opportunities?" This key idea of no-arbitrage pricing turns out to be an extremely powerful analytical tool that we employ throughout the text.

Option pricing inescapably involves some rather complicated mathematics. But the mathematics are much simpler for a **European option**, an option that can be exercised only at its expiration. Chapter 13 extends the no-arbitrage approach to analyze the pricing of European options and explains the famous Black–Scholes option pricing model. As we will see, it gives extremely accurate results. Chapter 14 explores in detail the exact way in which option prices respond to the various parameters in the Black–Scholes model. These sensitivities can be used to shape the risk and return characteristics of option positions with great precision.

Chapter 15 explores the pricing of American options. An **American option** is an option that can be exercised at any time prior to expiration. The principles of European option pricing still hold, but American option pricing involves some special considerations. Chapter 16 applies the conceptual apparatus developed in earlier chapters to three special instruments: options on indexes, options on foreign currencies, and options on futures. The pricing of these instruments requires applying the concepts already developed to the particular institutional features of these underlying goods. Chapter 17 shows the power of option pricing and analysis in a very different application. The concepts of option pricing can be used to analyze corporate securities as having option characteristics. Therefore, the option approach to corporate securities gives a totally new and very powerful way of thinking about common stock, bonds, convertible debt, and other corporate securities.

Chapter 18, *Exotic Options*, considers a newly emerging class of more complex options. Exotic options typically have very complex payoff characteristics. For example, a **lookback option** has a payoff at expiration that is tied to the maximum or minimum price of a particular good over the life of the option. Chapter 19 focuses on interest rate options. For example, there is an active market for options on bonds and money market interest rates. These markets are organized both as exchanges and as over-the-counter markets. Most models of option prices assume that the interest rate is constant over the life of the option. For interest rate options, changes in interest rates primarily determine the payoffs on this class of options. Therefore, it is not appropriate to assume that the interest rate is constant. This discussion of interest rate options paves the way to a discussion of the swaps market. As we will see in some detail, an interest rate swap can be analyzed as a portfolio of interest rate options.

Swaps

Chapters 20–22 are specifically directed toward swaps. Chapter 20, "The Swaps Market: An Introduction," discusses the basic features of the swap agreement and the swap market. The chapter also provides an introduction to how swaps can be used to transform cash flow patterns in risk management applications and the rudiments of swap pricing. These issues of pricing and risk management applications are explored in detail in Chapters 21 and 22. Chapter 21, *Swaps: Economic Analysis and Pricing*, shows that swaps are equivalent to portfolios of more familiar instruments. For example, an interest rate swap can be analyzed as a simple portfolio of a coupon bond and a floating rate bond. Being able to analyze swaps in terms of other instruments has two significant benefits. First, the analysis of swaps provides a heightened understanding of the economics of the swap contract. Second, analyzing swaps in terms of other instruments leads directly to an understanding of arbitrage relationships among swaps and other instruments, and provides a direct way of pricing swaps. Chapter 22, *Swaps: Applications*, provides a series of examples showing how swaps can be used to manage a tremendous variety of financial risks, and how swaps can be used to take risk deliberately. These applications range from the simple and short to the long and complex.

OPTION! software

As we have mentioned, option pricing is mathematically challenging. Swap pricing is less complex mathematically, but is computationally intensive. While it is critical to understand the formulas (and to compute each different formula by hand at least once!), it is not necessary or useful to compute repeatedly the same formulas. **OPTION!** software can compute virtually every option value discussed in this book. Further, **OPTION!** can graph many of the relationships among different option prices discussed in the chapters that follow. **OPTION!** also features similar support for swap pricing. Exploring the option concepts of the text with the software can greatly enhance an understanding of option and swap pricing. Instructions for **OPTION!** are found on the web site that accompanies this book (see www.blackwellpublishing.com/kolb).

Exercises for **OPTION!**

The accompanying web site features more than 70 exercises designed to enhance your understanding of option and swap pricing principles and applications. These exercises can all be solved using the **OPTION!** software.

Exercises

1 If an arbitrage opportunity did exist in a market, how would traders react? Would the arbitrage opportunity persist? If not, what factors would cause the arbitrage opportunity to disappear?
2 Explain why it is reasonable to think that prices in a financial market will generally be free of arbitrage opportunities.
3 Explain the difference between a derivative instrument and a financial derivative.
4 What is the essential feature of a forward contract that makes a futures contract a type of forward contract?
5 Explain why the purchaser of an option has rights and the seller of an option has obligations.
6 In a futures contract, explain the rights and obligations of the buyer or seller. How does this compare with an option contract?
7 Explain the difference between an option on a physical good and an option on a futures transaction.
8 What is the essential feature of a swap agreement?
9 Distinguish between interest rate swaps and currency swaps.
10 What is a complete market? Can you give an example of a truly complete market? Explain.
11 Explain how the existence of financial derivatives enhances speculative opportunities for traders in our financial system.
12 If financial derivatives are as risky as their reputation indicates, explain in general terms how they might be used to reduce a preexisting risk position for a firm.
13 Consider the following three securities. Let us assume that at one period in the future the market will move either up or down. This movement in the market produces the following payoffs for the three securities:

Security	Current price	Payoff when the market moves down	Payoff when the market moves up
A	$35	$25	$50
B	$30	$15	$60
C	$40	$19	$56

(Note: This is a challenge exercise and it presumes some familiarity with arbitrage concepts. The issues raised by this exercise are explored directly in Chapter 13.)

A Construct a portfolio consisting of securities A and B that replicates the payoffs on security C in both the up and down states subject to the constraint that the sum of the commitments to the two securities (A and B) is one. In other words, construct a synthetic share of security C. Assume that there are no restrictions associated with short selling any of the securities.
B What are the commitments to securities A and B?
C How much does it cost to construct a synthetic share of security C? Compare this cost with the market price of security C. Which security is cheaper?
D Explain the transactions necessary to engage in riskless arbitrage. Explain why these transactions constitute a riskless arbitrage opportunity. How much profit can an investor make in this riskless arbitrage?
E Explain why we do not have to worry about future obligations in a properly constructed riskless arbitrage transaction.

F Explain why we would not expect such a structure of prices to exist in the marketplace.

G Explain the purpose of short selling in riskless arbitrage. Discuss the impact on the investor's ability to engage in riskless arbitrage of regulations that limit an investor's access to the proceeds from a short sale transaction.

H Construct a portfolio consisting of securities B and C that replicates the payoffs on security A in both the up and down states subject to the constraint that the sum of the commitments to the two securities (B and C) is one. In other words, construct a synthetic share of security A. Assume that there are no restrictions associated with short selling any of the securities.

I What are the commitments to securities B and C?

J How much does it cost to construct a synthetic share of security A? Compare this cost with the market price of security A. Which security is cheaper?

K Explain the transactions necessary to engage in a riskless arbitrage. How much profit can an investor make in this riskless arbitrage? Assume that one trades ten shares of security A in constructing the arbitrage transactions.

L Discuss the differences between the transactions necessary to capture the arbitrage profit when creating a synthetic share of security A and the arbitrage transactions undertaken to capture the arbitrage profit when creating a synthetic share of security C.

Notes

1 See Annual Report to Shareholders, Berkshire Hathaway Corporation, April 2003.

2 This definition comes from "An Overview of Derivatives: Their Mechanics, Participants, Scope of Activity and Benefits," by Christopher L. Culp and James A. Overdahl, in *The Financial Services Revolution*, Clifford E. Kirsch, editor (Chicago: Irwin Professional Publishing, 1997).

3 The mutual obligation of both buyer and seller of a futures contract is an important feature of the futures market that helps to distinguish futures contracts from options. If you buy a call option, then you buy the right to obtain a good at a certain price, but the buyer of a call has no obligation. Instead, as the term implies, he has an option to buy something but no obligation to do anything. The buyer of a futures contract, by contrast, undertakes an obligation to make a payment at a subsequent time and to take delivery of the good that is contracted. The initiation of any futures contract implies a set of future obligations.

4 For a discussion of the historical origins of forward contracting and futures markets, see C. Culp, *Risk Transfer: Derivatives in Theory and Practice*, Hoboken, NJ: John Wiley and Sons, 2004; A. Loosigian, *Interest Rate Futures*, Princeton, NJ: Dow Jones Books, Inc., 1980; L. Venkataramanan, *The Theory of Futures Trading*, New York: Asia Publishing House, 1965; J. C. Williams, "The Origin of Futures Markets," *Agricultural History*, 56:1, 1982, pp. 306–25; and U. Schaede, "Forwards and Futures in Tokugawa-Period Japan: A New Perspective on the Dōjima Rice Market," *Journal of Banking and Finance*, 13, 1989, pp. 487–513.

5 For an account of the early days of the Chicago Board of Trade, see *The Commodity Trading Manual*, Chicago: Chicago Board of Trade, 1989. It was not until 1925 that the CBOT adopted a central counterparty clearinghouse structure to make their contracts truly a futures option in the modern sense.

6 More precise legal distinctions are offered in a later section.

7 There are also some other more complicated types of options that are not traded on exchanges. For example, an **exchange option** is an option to exchange one asset for another. As we will see in Chapter 5, Treasury bond futures contracts allow the trader with a short futures position to choose which Treasury bond to deliver, from among several eligible bonds. The ability to choose which bond to deliver has been described as a **delivery option**. There are still other types of options, but the most important market for options is the option exchange, where just put and call options trade.

2

Futures Markets

Overview

This chapter lays the foundations that are essential to understanding how futures markets function. Futures markets originated to trade agricultural commodities, and it is only in the past few decades that financial futures have come to play an important role in these markets. Accordingly, this chapter considers financial futures in the broad context of the futures markets, while later chapters focus on financial futures more exclusively.

We focus on futures markets in the United States because U.S. futures markets have served as a model for newer futures markets found around the world. Although our focus is on U.S. markets, we also describe markets outside of the United States that have been growing rapidly in recent years.

Before entering the arena of the futures market, a prospective trader must understand the institutions that facilitate futures trading. These institutions include futures exchanges and futures clearinghouses. In this chapter we examine the ways in which futures exchanges are structured and the ways they compete with each other for business. We describe how the clearinghouse serves to guarantee the performance of all futures transactions and to protect the financial integrity of the marketplace. The chapter also describes the various types of futures contracts that are traded.

This chapter discusses the two key social benefits that futures markets provide: price discovery and risk transference through hedging. Because regulation is important in determining whether futures markets can serve their social functions and the interests of the trading parties, the chapter next discusses the regulatory framework, and provides a description of the taxation of futures markets.

A large industry such as the futures industry requires specialization of its participants. In this chapter, we examine the specialized role of brokers, trading advisors, and other professionals within the futures industry to show more completely how futures trading works. These specialists, collectively called "intermediaries," provide the interface between customers and the exchange. We will explore the function of each group and how they fit into the regulatory structure of the futures industry.

Futures were once a virtual U.S. monopoly. Now, non-U.S. markets are major players and compete with markets in the United States for global primacy. Starting from relative obscurity in the 1980s, non-U.S. markets are now collectively larger than markets in the United States. The process of globalization will continue to shape the futures industry in the years ahead. We consider the impact of globalization on the futures industry in this chapter.

Globalization is intimately tied to electronic trading. As recently as 1998, electronic trading accounted for only a small percentage of total trading volume. Today, well over half of all futures trades, and an overwhelming percentage of financial futures trades, occur on electronic systems. These systems allow traders in New York to trade in Japanese markets as if they were sitting in Tokyo. Worldwide electronic trading through the Chicago Mercantile Exchange's (CME's) Globex system began in 1992. Eurex, a pioneer in electronic trading that began operations in 1997, has seen trading volume on its all-electronic exchange surpass the volume of the world's largest futures exchanges within the first five years of operation. This chapter addresses the key issues associated with electronic trading.

Futures markets

Figure 2.1 shows the growth of trading volume on U.S. futures exchanges. When a contract is first listed for trading, there has been no volume. Assume that the first trade is for one contract, leaving one trader long one contract and one trader short one contract. In this example, there is a buyer and a seller. The buyer is said to have a **long position**, while the seller has a **short position**. The act of buying is also called **going long**, and the act of selling is called **going short**. For the contract to trade, there must be a long position and a short position. When one trader buys and another sells a forward contract, the transaction generates one contract of

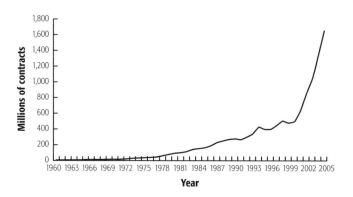

Figure 2.1   The growth of trading volume on U.S. futures exchanges

trading **volume**. At any moment in time, there is some number of futures contracts obligated for delivery; this number is called the **open interest**. (As we will see later in this chapter, most futures contracts do not actually lead to delivery.)

The organized exchange

As we have noted, futures contracts almost always trade on an organized exchange. (Some specialized instruments, such as some privately negotiated swaps, are technically futures, but these are limited to market sophisticates, such as large financial firms, and are excluded from futures regulation.) The organization of the Chicago Board of Trade, the oldest and, until recent times, largest futures exchange in the world, is typical. The exchange began as a nonprofit association of its members in the mid-nineteenth century. In recent years, however, there has been a movement away from the nonprofit form of organization, with both the Chicago Mercantile Exchange (CME) and the Chicago Board of Trade becoming for-profit corporations with publicly listed stock. The New York Mercantile Exchange (NYMEX) is also a for-profit corporation, although it does not currently have publicly traded stock.

In the not-for-profit organizational structure, individuals hold **exchange memberships**, also called **seats**. These memberships are equity shares held by individuals, and trade in an active market among qualified individuals in much the same way that equity shares are traded in other markets.

When an exchange converts to for-profit status (that is, it "demutualizes"), the members receive shares of stock in the new corporation. In the conversion of the CME, for example, members holding seats in the not-for-profit association received two classes of stock in the new for-profit corporation. One class of stock represents ownership in the corporation, while the other carries the right to trade on the exchange. In December 2002, The CME held an initial public offering (IPO) of its shares. These shares are now traded on both the New York Stock Exchange and NASDAQ under the ticker symbol CME. In July 2006, the market capitalization of Chicago Mercantile Exchange Holdings, Inc. was approximately $16 billion, a figure more than ten times the market capitalization at the time of the IPO.

Demutualized exchanges continue to have several classes of membership. These classes differ in the extent of trading privileges. For example, a full membership may grant trading

Table 2.1 Membership prices of major U.S. futures exchanges

Exchange	Full membership price
Chicago Mercantile Exchange (1 class B share)	$ 425,000
Chicago Board of Trade (no stock)	290,000
New York Mercantile Exchange (90,000 shares)	4,100,000
New York Board of Trade (equity membership)	825,000

Source: Exchange web sites; prices represent the last sale in June 2006

privileges in any exchange product, while other classes of membership may allow trading in a smaller set of products. Importantly, membership classes in demutualized exchanges can differ by the value of the exchange's stock that is attached to the membership. For example, at the Chicago Board of Trade a full membership can be purchased with stock or without. In June 2006, a CBOT full membership that included 18,224 shares of stock sold for $1,850,000 while a full membership without stock sold for $290,000. Full members of an exchange have the right to trade on the exchange and to have a voice in the exchange's operation. Members also serve on committees to regulate the exchange's operations, rules, audit functions, and public relations, and the legal and ethical conduct of members. Often, administrative officers of the exchange manage the ordinary operation of the exchange and report to the membership.

Table 2.1 shows recent membership prices for major futures exchanges in the United States. Although the value of trading privileges can explain some of the differences in membership prices, the biggest difference results from the equity stake in the exchange that the memberships represent. In the case of the CME, the membership reflects the value of trading privileges and a single share of Class B stock in CME Holdings, Inc. In the case of the CBOT, the membership includes full exchange trading privileges. For the New York Mercantile Exchange, the membership price reflects the combined value of trading privileges and the value of 90,000 shares in NYMEX Holdings, Inc. For the New York Board of Trade, the membership price includes the combined value of trading privileges and an equity share in the exchange.

Traditionally, futures contracts have traded by a system called **open outcry**, in which the central marketplace is a trading room where traders literally "cry out" their bids to go long and offers to go short. In this system, trading occurs face to face in a designated trading area called a **pit** or **ring**. This is a physical location on the floor of the exchange, with each commodity trading in a designated pit. A trader makes an offer to buy or sell to all other traders present in the pit. Traders also use an unofficial, but highly developed, system of hand signals to express their wishes to buy or sell.

Traders in the pit fall into two groups that we can distinguish by their function. First, a trader can trade for his or her own account and bear the losses or enjoy the profits stemming from this trading. Second, a trader can be a broker acting on behalf of his or her own firm or on behalf of a client outside the exchange. For example, the brokers trading on the exchange often represent large brokerage houses such as Merrill Lynch or Prudential Bache. Having distinguished between traders who execute trades for their own accounts and those who execute trades for others, we must realize that certain individuals exercise both functions simultaneously.

As recently as 1990, futures trading was conducted exclusively through open outcry. Although open-outcry trading volume has been growing, it now accounts for less than half of all futures trading volume. A substantial majority of futures trading volume now occurs on electronic trading platforms. These trading platforms are owned and operated by the futures exchanges. Some exchanges, such as the CME, the NYMEX, and the CBOT, use side-by-side trading—that is, both open-outcry trading and electronic trading—for some products. Other exchanges, such as Eurex, offer electronic trading exclusively.

Members of the exchange who trade in the pits are typically speculators. A **speculator** is a trader who enters the futures market in pursuit of profit, accepting risk in the endeavor. Some of the traders in the pit who trade for their own accounts may not be full exchange members themselves. It is possible to lease a seat on the exchange from a full member. Also, some exchanges have created special licenses allowing nonmembers to trade in certain contracts in which the exchanges are anxious to build volume. For the most part, a trader in the pit trading for his or her own account is a speculator.

In addition to speculators, many traders are **hedgers**, traders who trade futures to reduce some preexisting risk exposure. Hedgers are often producers or major users of a given commodity. For example, hedgers in wheat might include wheat farmers and large baking firms. Notice that these hedgers do not necessarily need to own the wheat when they hedge. A farmer might hedge by selling his anticipated harvest through the futures market. This could occur even before the farmer plants. Similarly, the baker who will eventually bake the farmer's wheat harvest into bread may hedge an expected need for wheat months before the wheat is actually required. Therefore, hedging is the purchase or sale of futures as a temporary substitute for a transaction in the cash market. For the most part, hedgers are not themselves located on the floor of the exchange. Instead, they trade through a brokerage firm. The brokerage firm communicates the order to the pit and has it executed by a broker in the pit.

Thus, there are two different kinds of brokers. An account executive for a brokerage firm is often called a broker. The account executive could be located in any town or city and the account executive deals with his or her customers, conveying their orders to the exchange. A second type of broker is a floor broker, a broker on the floor of the exchange who executes orders for other customers. For a typical transaction entered by a trader off the floor of the exchange, the order will be given to the customer's broker (account executive), who will transmit the order to the brokerage firm's representatives at the exchange. There a floor broker (FB), often employed by the brokerage firm, will execute the order on the floor of the exchange.

The advent of electronic trading platforms has reduced the role of FBs. The electronic trading environment has produced a new type of trader, called an "e-local," who performs many of the same tasks that FBs performed in an open-outcry trading environment. These traders also form associations, called **trading arcades**, that allow e-locals to trade in the company of other e-locals and share in office overhead expenses for such things as computer systems and real-time news feeds. Other e-locals associate through a **prop shop**; that is, a proprietary trading firm that pays the e-local a salary and a share of the firm's profits.

This organized structure for trading futures contracts differs from the organization of forward markets. Forward markets are loosely organized and have no physical location devoted to the trading.[1] Perhaps the best-developed forward market is the market for foreign exchange. It is a worldwide network of participants, largely banks and brokers, who communicate with each other electronically. In the forward market for foreign exchange, there is no organized exchange and no central trading point.

Standardized contract terms

Futures contracts are highly uniform and well-specified commitments for a carefully described good to be delivered at a certain time and in a certain manner. Generally, the futures contract specifies the quantity and quality of the good that can be delivered to fulfill the futures contract.

The contract also specifies the delivery date and method for closing the contract, and the permissible minimum and maximum price fluctuations permitted in trading.

As an example, consider the Chicago Board of Trade wheat contract. One wheat contract consists of 5,000 bushels of wheat that must be of one of the following types: No. 2 Soft Red, No. 2 Hard Red Winter, No. 2 Dark Northern Spring, or No. 1 Northern Spring. The wheat contract trades for expiration in the following months of each year: July, September, December, March, and May. The Board of Trade also stipulates the delivery terms for completing the contract. To deliver wheat in completion of the contract, the wheat must be in a warehouse approved by the Chicago Board of Trade. These warehouses must be in the Chicago Switching District or the Toledo, Ohio, Switching District. The buyer transmits payment to the seller, and the seller delivers a warehouse receipt to the buyer. The holder of a warehouse receipt has title to the wheat in the warehouse. Delivery can occur on any business day in the delivery month.

The contract also stipulates the minimum price fluctuation, or **tick** size. For wheat, one tick is 0.25 cents per bushel. With 5,000 bushels per contract, this gives a tick size of $12.50 per contract. The contract also specifies a **daily price limit**, which restricts the price movement in a single day. For wheat, the trading price on a given day cannot differ from the preceding day's closing price by more than 30 cents per bushel, or $1,500 per contract. When the contract is trading in its delivery month (called the spot month), this price limit is not in effect. Also, when a commodity enters a particularly volatile period, price limits are generally expanded over successive days. For example, when "mad cow disease" (bovine spongiform encephalopathy, or BSE) was discovered in the United States for the first time, live cattle futures prices dropped dramatically. On the first day, the futures price was allowed to fall only by the limit. Because the price fell to the limit in one day, the price limit was expanded for the next day and for the following days. For most commodities, price limits expand over several days until there is no limit on how much the price can change in a day. Also, some commodities do not have price limits.[2] Finally, the exchange also controls the trading times for each futures contract. Wheat trades from 9:30 a.m. to 1:15 p.m. Chicago time on each trading day, except for the last day of trading, when trading in the expiring contract ceases at noon. The last trading day for the wheat contract is seven business days before the last business day of the delivery month.

Although these rules may appear highly restrictive, they actually stimulate trading. Because the good being traded is so highly standardized, all the participants in the market know exactly what is being offered for sale, and they know the terms of the transactions. This uniformity helps to promote liquidity. All futures contracts have such a highly developed framework, which specifies all phases of the transaction. As we saw for wheat, these rules regulate all phases of the market, from the amounts the prices can move to the appropriate ways of making delivery. The prospective trader should consult a given contract for these exact details before initiating any trading. Each exchange publishes contract terms.

The clearinghouse

To ensure that futures contracts trade in a smoothly functioning market, each futures exchange has an arrangement with a futures clearinghouse. The clearinghouse may be organized as a separate corporation that offers futures clearing services, possibly in addition to other services, to multiple exchanges. Alternately, the clearinghouse may be organized as a division of a futures exchange. In either case, each exchange will be closely associated with a particular clearinghouse. Clearing arrangements vary across the industry, largely as a result of the Commodity Futures Modernization Act (CFMA) of 2000, which regulates clearinghouses as a line of business separate from the trade execution services offered by exchanges. The variety of clearing arrangements can best be observed in Chicago, where under a clearing service agreement between the CBOT and the CME that was implemented in 2004, most clearing functions for CBOT contracts are performed by the CME clearinghouse. Also in Chicago, the Clearing Corporation (CCorp) (formerly known as the Board of Trade Clearing Corporation) clears trades for Eurex U.S. and the Merchants Exchange of St. Louis.

The clearinghouse guarantees that all of the traders in the futures market will honor their obligations. The clearinghouse serves this role by adopting the position of buyer to every seller and seller to every buyer. This means that every trader in the futures markets has obligations only to the clearinghouse and has expectations that the clearinghouse will maintain its side of the bargain as well. Thus, the clearinghouse substitutes its own credibility for the promise of each trader in the market. The clearinghouses can make these promises believable because of their financial safeguard system. Two types of clearinghouse financial safeguard systems are observed across the market. The first type is called **good to the last drop**, meaning that the clearinghouse commits its capital to satisfy any default obligations not covered by (1) the margin posted by clearing members on behalf of customers and the member's proprietary accounts, or (2) a separately capitalized guarantee fund. In the good-to-the-last-drop model, the clearinghouse commits to satisfying all obligations to the point at which the clearinghouse itself is insolvent. The NYMEX clearinghouse and the London Clearing House (LCH) are examples of clearinghouses that use the good-to-the-last-drop model.

The second type of financial safeguard model is the **live another day** model. In this model, clearing members are protected primarily with guarantee funds. The core capital of the clearinghouse is not committed to satisfying all obligations. In this model, a primary objective is to sustain the clearinghouse so that it can continue to perform its risk-mitigating role during times of crisis, when it is needed the most. In this model, default obligations are ultimately borne by clearing members, who must absorb unpaid invoices. There are many ways in which this model can be implemented. For example, the CCorp makes no commitments beyond the guarantee fund. Other clearinghouses that use this safeguard model employ several lines of defense to protect the clearinghouse and ensure that all obligations are met.

A clearinghouse's first line of defense against clearinghouse default is the margin money deposited by clearing member firms on behalf of their customers and their own proprietary accounts. For example, in January 2005, the CME clearinghouse held $44.1 billion in margin money, although only the margin deposits of the defaulting clearing member could be claimed by the clearinghouse. A second line of defense is the value of pledged exchange memberships, which at the CME are attached to shares of stock in CME Holdings, Inc. In 2006, the aggregate value of these pledged memberships was approximately $1.7 billion, although the clearinghouse would claim only the membership of the defaulting clearing member. A third line of defense is the capital of the clearinghouse in excess of the working capital required for continuing clearinghouse operations. At the beginning of 2005, the value of this capital amounted to approximately $124 million at the CME clearinghouse. Another line of defense comes from the guarantee fund maintained by clearing members at the clearinghouse. The money in the fund comes from a volume-based assessment on members, so that the fund accrues value over time. At the beginning of 2005, the value of this guarantee fund totaled $913 million at the CME clearinghouse. If all of these funds are exhausted, the clearinghouse has the right to assess clearing members for unsatisfied obligations. The value of this assessment power totaled $2.5 billion at the beginning of 2005, at the CME clearinghouse. The clearinghouse also holds credit lines to ensure that funds are immediately available in the case of an emergency. Finally, the clearinghouse performs periodic risk evaluations of clearing members in an attempt to detect potential weaknesses in financial condition or risk controls.

Volume Investors

The March 1985 failure of Volume Investors, a futures broker and clearing member of the Commodities Exchange, Inc. (now a division of the NYMEX) illustrates the contractual relationships among the customer, the broker, and the clearinghouse. Some customers of Volume defaulted on a margin call, causing Volume to default on the clearinghouse's margin call. This clearinghouse's margin call exceeded Volume's assets. The clearinghouse seized all of the accumulated margin previously posted by Volume on behalf of its customers in order to pay the other clearing members. This left the nondefaulting customers of Volume with no margin at the clearinghouse and no timely means of obtaining from the failed broker their margin receipts or other funds held in their accounts. Thus, arm's-length customers of Volume, whose only connection with the individuals who defaulted was simply the use of a common broker, found that they had substantial sums at risk.[3]

In May 2000, a similar failure occurred when a customer of Klein and Co. Futures Inc. incurred substantial losses at the New York Board of Trade's New York Futures Exchange (NYFE) subsidiary. The losses caused the New York Clearing Corporation to liquidate Klein's customer margin account, which consisted of the commingled margins for all customers. Once again, arm's-length customers of the broker, whose only connection with the individual who defaulted was simply the use of a common broker, found that they had substantial sums at risk.

The clearinghouse takes no active position in the market, but interposes itself between the buyer and seller in each transaction. (As we will see, the clearinghouse works directly with brokerage houses that are *clearing members* and indirectly with the ultimate traders, who must go through a brokerage house that is a clearing member.) In the futures market, the number of contracts bought must always equal the number of contracts sold. So, for every party expecting to receive delivery of a commodity, the opposite trading partner must be prepared to make delivery. If we sum all outstanding long and short futures market positions, the total always equals zero.[4]

Table 2.2 shows the typical trading situation. In the table, we assume that all transactions occur on a single day—say, May 1. Party 1 trades on the futures exchange to buy one oats contract of 5,000 bushels for delivery in September. In order for Party 1 to buy the contract, some other participant must sell. In panel (a) of the table it is apparent that Parties 1 and 2 have

---

Table 2.2 Futures market obligations

The oat contract is traded by the Chicago Board of Trade. Each contract is for 5,000 bushels, and prices are quoted in cents per bushel.

(a) **Party 1**	**Party 2**
Buys one SEP contract for oats at 171 cents per bushel	Sells one SEP contract for oats at 171 cents per bushel
(b) **Party 1**	**Clearinghouse**
Buys one SEP contract for oats at 171 cents per bushel	Agrees to deliver to Party 1 a SEP contract for oats at a price of 171 cents per bushel
(c) **Party 2**	**Clearinghouse**
Sells one SEP contract for oats at 171 cents per bushel	Agrees to receive from Party 2 one SEP contract for oats and to pay 171 cents per bushel

Figure 2.2   The function of the clearinghouse in futures markets

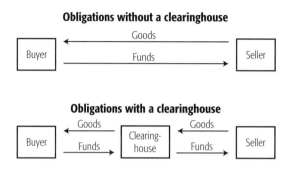

exactly complementary positions in the futures market. One party has bought exactly what the other has sold. Notice that the time of delivery, the amount of oats to be delivered, and the price all match. Without a perfect match in all these respects, there could not have been a transaction. In all probability, the two trading parties will not even know each other. It is perfectly possible that each will have traded through a broker from different parts of the country. In such a situation, problems of trust may arise. How can either party be sure that the other will fulfill the agreement? The clearinghouse exists to solve that problem. As panels (b) and (c) indicate, the clearinghouse guarantees fulfillment of the contract to each of the trading parties. After the initial sale is made, the clearinghouse steps in and acts as the seller to the buyer and acts as the buyer to the seller. In panel (b), the clearinghouse guarantees the buyer of the futures contract, Party 1, that it will deliver at the initially agreed upon time and price. To the seller, Party 2, the clearinghouse guarantees that it will accept delivery at the agreed upon time and price, as panel (c) shows. Figure 2.2 illustrates the same idea graphically. Without a clearinghouse, both parties must deal with each other, and they have direct obligations to one another. With a clearinghouse, each party has obligations to the clearinghouse and the clearinghouse will ensure that they perform.

Because of the clearinghouse, the two trading parties do not need to trust each other or even know each other's identity. Instead, the two traders only have to be concerned about the reliability of the clearinghouse. However, the clearinghouse is a large, well-capitalized financial institution. Its failure to perform on its guarantee to the two trading parties would bring the futures market to ruin. In the history of U.S. futures trading, the clearinghouse has always performed as promised, so the risk of a future default by the clearinghouse is very small.

A more careful examination of panels (b) and (c) in Table 2.2 gives further confidence that the clearinghouse will perform as promised. In total, the clearinghouse has no independent position in oats. It is obligated to receive oats and pay 171 cents per bushel, but it is also obligated to deliver oats and receive 171 cents per bushel. These two obligations net out to zero. Since it maintains no futures market position of its own, the riskiness of the clearinghouse is less than it may appear.[5]

Margin and daily settlement

In addition to the clearinghouse, there are other safeguards for the futures market. Chief among these are the requirements for margin and daily settlement. Before trading a futures contract, the prospective trader must deposit funds with a broker. These funds serve as a good-faith deposit, or performance bond, by the trader and are referred to as **margin**. The main purpose of margin is to provide a financial safeguard to ensure that traders will perform on their contract obligations. The margin requirement restricts the activity of traders, so the exchanges and brokers are anxious that the margin requirements not be unreasonably high. The amount of this margin varies from contract to contract and may vary by broker as well. The margin may be posted in cash, a bank letter of credit, or in short-term U.S. Treasury instruments. The trader who posts this margin retains title to it in a **segregated account** held at the brokerage. In a segregated account, customer margin money cannot be commingled with the brokerage house's own money. This is to prevent the brokerage from trading for its own account using customer money. Although customer money is segregated from the brokerage house's money, customer money is not individually segregated from the money of other customers. This means that customers can potentially be at risk to defaults by other customers, as we saw in the case of Volume Investors.

Types of margin
In this section, we consider the different types of margins and show how margin requirements would affect a trader holding a single futures position. In the next section, we consider margin rules for more complicated positions.

There are three types of margin. The initial deposit just described is the **initial margin**—the amount a trader must deposit before trading any futures. The initial margin approximately equals the maximum daily price fluctuation permitted for the contract being traded. Upon proper completion of all obligations associated with a trader's futures position, the initial margin is returned to the trader. If one has deposited a security as the margin, then the trader earns the interest that accrues while the security has served as the margin.

For most futures contracts, the initial margin may be 5 percent or less of the underlying commodity's value. It may seem strange that the initial margin is so small relative to the value of the commodity underlying the futures contract. The smallness of this amount is reasonable, however, because there is another safeguard built into the system in the form of **daily settlement** or **marking-to-market**. In the futures market, traders are required to realize any losses in cash on the day they occur. In the parlance of the futures market, the contract is marked-to-the-market.

To understand the process of daily settlement, consult Table 2.2 again and consider Party 1, who bought one contract for 171 cents per bushel. Assume that the contract closes on May 2 at 168 cents per bushel. This means that Party 1 has sustained a loss of 3 cents per bushel. Since there are 5,000 bushels in the contract, this represents a loss of $150, which is deducted from the margin deposited with the broker. When the value of the funds on deposit with the broker reaches a certain level, called the **maintenance margin**, the trader is required to replenish the margin, bringing it back to its initial level. This demand for more margin is known as a **margin call**. The additional amount the trader must deposit is called the **variation margin**. The maintenance margin is generally about 75 percent of the amount of the initial margin. For example, assume that the initial margin was $1,400, that Party 1 had deposited only this minimum initial margin, and that the maintenance margin is $1,100. Party 1 has already sustained a loss of $150, so the equity in the margin account is $1,250. The next day, assume that the price of oats drops 4 cents per bushel, generating an additional loss for Party 1 of $200. This brings the value of the margin account to $1,050, which is below the level of the required maintenance margin. This means that the broker will require Party 1 to replenish the margin account to $1,400, the level of the initial margin. To restore the margin account, the trader must pay $350 variation margin. Variation margin must always be paid in cash.

Figure 2.3 uses the initial margin level of $1,400 and the maintenance margin level of $1,100 to illustrate this process. At the outset, the value of the margin deposited with the broker is

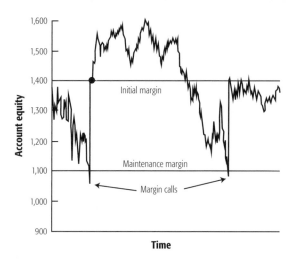

Figure 2.3 Account equity and margin requirements

$1,400. First, the trader has mixed results with some small gains and small losses, with losses predominating. Before long, losses drop the value of the account below $1,100. As the figure shows, the trader must then restore the value, or equity, in the account to $1,400. This is shown in Figure 2.3 by the large dot. After this first margin call, the trader has mixed results for a while, followed by large losses. These losses generate a second margin call. Figure 2.3 shows only the required cash flows. The trader could have withdrawn cash whenever the value of the equity exceeded $1,400. However, a trader cannot withdraw funds that would leave the account's equity value below the level of the initial margin.

Because futures prices change almost every day, each account will have frequent gains and losses. The losses can require a variation margin payment, and the gains may entitle the trader to withdraw cash. For convenience, traders do not want to face a daily margin call in many cases. There are two basic ways to avoid a margin call. First, a trader can deposit securities with a value well in excess of the initial margin. Second, a trader can deposit funds in excess of the initial margin into an interest-bearing account. In either case, such a deposit provides a liquidity pool that will protect the trader from untimely demands for variation margin payments. Similarly, the trader can instruct the broker to sweep profits from his account into an interest-bearing investment. Those funds can be held ready to meet margin calls as required.

This practice of posting maintenance or variation margin and daily settlement helps make the futures market safer. Assume that Party 1 in Table 2.2 posted only the initial margin, the bare minimum to have the trade executed. Also assume that the trader suffered a loss requiring more margin and that the trader was unable or refused to post the required additional margin. The broker in such a situation is empowered to close the futures position by deducting the loss from the trader's initial margin and returning the balance, less commission costs, to the trader. The broker would also close the trader's entire brokerage account as well. Failure to post the required maintenance margin is a violation of a trader's agreement with the broker. Now it becomes apparent why the initial margin is so small. The initial margin needs to cover only one day's price fluctuation, because any losses will be covered by the posting of additional variation margin. Failure to pay variation margin will lead to the futures position being closed out. If the

Figure 2.4 Margin cash flows

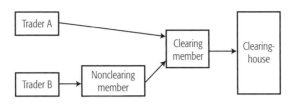

futures position cannot be immediately closed out (e.g., if trading is halted due to a limit price move), the broker takes over the position and manages it as a proprietary (broker-owned) position. Eventually, the broker will close out the position when it is possible to do so.

Margin cash flows

This section traces the flow of margin funds from the trader to the clearinghouse. The margin system functions through a hierarchy of market participants that links the clearinghouse with the individual trader. The members of an exchange may be classified as clearing members or nonclearing members. A **clearing member** is a member of the exchange who is also a member of the clearinghouse associated with the exchange. The clearinghouse deals only with clearing members. As a consequence, any nonclearing member must clear his or her trades through a clearing member.

The clearinghouse demands margin deposits from clearing members to cover all futures positions that are carried by that clearing member. For example, a clearing member might be a large broker who executes orders for individual traders and who provides clearing services for some nonclearing members of the exchange. Therefore, the clearing member will impose margin requirements on all of the accounts that he or she represents to the clearinghouse.

Figure 2.4 shows the margin flows for an individual trader who might trade through a clearing member or a nonclearing member. In the figure, Trader A trades through a broker who is a clearing member. In this case, Trader A deposits margin funds with the clearing member, who makes margin deposits with the clearinghouse. As a second alternative in Figure 2.4, Trader B trades through a broker who is a nonclearing member of the exchange. This broker must arrange to clear all trades with a clearing member. In this situation, Trader B deposits margin funds with his or her broker. This broker deposits margin funds with a clearing member, and the clearing member deposits margin funds with the clearinghouse.

It is not very important whether Traders A and B trade directly through a clearing member or a nonclearing member. Most large brokerage firms are clearing members, so most individual traders who trade through their local broker will be trading through a clearing member. However, many members of each exchange trade for their own account as speculators. Few of them are clearing members, so they need to clear their trades through a clearing member.

Closing a futures position

Initially, we discussed the completion of a futures contract through delivery. However, in the discussion of variation margin we noted that the broker might close the position after trading on May 2. The careful reader might remember that the initial trade shown in Table 2.2 called for a September delivery. In view of that fact, it may not seem that the futures position could be closed in May. There are, however, three ways to close a futures position: delivery, offset, and an exchange-for-physicals (EFP).

Delivery

Most futures contracts are written to call for completion of the futures contract through the physical delivery of a particular good. As we have seen in our discussion of the wheat contract, delivery takes place at certain locations and at certain times under rules specified by a futures exchange. In recent years, exchanges have introduced futures contracts that allow completion through **cash settlement**. In cash settlement, traders make payments at the expiration of the contract to settle any gains or losses, instead of making physical delivery. Cash settlement is now being used in a number of financial contracts and in a few contracts for physical commodities. Both physical delivery and cash settlement close the contract in the expiration period. However, few futures contracts are actually closed through either physical delivery or cash settlement. For example, in the fiscal year ending September 30, 2005, less than 1 percent of all contracts traded were settled by either physical delivery or cash settlement. Table 2.3 shows the commodity groups and the percentage of contracts completed by delivery or cash settlement within each group. Only currencies had more than 2 percent of its contracts settled by delivery or cash settlements, but these are each less than 2 percent. In the energy, livestock, and wood groups, delivery is extremely rare. Therefore, the vast majority of all contracts initiated must be completed by some means other than delivery or cash settlement.

A well-designed futures contract must ensure that adequate supplies of the contract's underlying cash commodity are available at delivery in order to prevent manipulation of the delivery process. One method that futures exchanges use to ensure the availability of adequate deliverable supplies is to allow shorts the option of delivering nonstandard commodities at nonstandard delivery points. When shorts choose this option, they often must pay a surcharge, or **delivery differential**, relative to what they would have paid if they had delivered standard stocks at standard delivery points. These differentials are fixed as standard terms within the futures contract.

There are two types of delivery differentials: **quality differentials** and **location differentials**. Quality differentials are also referred to as **grade differentials**, and location differentials are

Table 2.3 Completion of futures contracts via delivery or cash settlement, October 1, 2004–September 30, 2005

Commodity group	Volume	Delivered or settled in cash	
		Contracts	Percentage
Grains	41,758,271	79,462	0.19
Oilseeds	36,218,509	44,520	0.12
Livestock	10,583,505	42,672	0.40
Other agricultural	23,633,509	92,916	0.39
Energy/wood	134,878,082	3,310,330	2.45
Metals	26,433,443	151,313	0.57
Financial instruments	1,204,903,878	11,846,931	0.98
Currencies	75,530,356	1,160,747	1.54
All commodities	1,553,939,553	16,728,891	1.08

Source: Commodity Futures Trading Commission, Annual Report, 2005

sometimes referred to as **territorial differentials**. Some contracts also specify delivery **timing differentials**.

Quality differentials are based on the standard, or "par" delivery grade. The **par grade** is specified as part of the futures contract. For example, the CBOT's corn contract specifies No. 2 Yellow Corn as the par grade. However, No. 3 Yellow Corn is eligible for delivery at a 1.5 cents per bushel differential. In other words, if the cash price for the par grade at delivery were $3.00 per bushel, a short delivering a shipping certificate for No. 3 Yellow Corn would receive $2.985 per bushel. The CBOT's corn contract also allows delivery of No. 1 Yellow Corn, a premium grade to the par grade, for a 1.5 cents per bushel premium differential. Continuing with our example, a short delivering a shipping certificate for No. 1 Yellow Corn would receive $3.015 per bushel.

Location differentials are defined relative to the standard delivery point or points specified in the futures contracts. For example, the CBOT's corn contract specifies delivery at approved terminals along the Illinois River between Chicago and mile marker number 151 in Pekin, Illinois. Corn delivered at approved terminals between Chicago and Burns Harbor, Indiana, will also receive the par price. Corn delivered at terminals between Lockport, Illinois, and Seneca, Illinois, receive a 2 cents per bushel premium to par. This premium accounts for the fact that it is cheaper to transport corn to the Gulf of Mexico from locations near the Mississippi River than from locations closer to Chicago. Corn delivered to terminals between Ottawa, Illinois and Chilicothe, Illinois receives a 2.5 cents per bushel premium to par. Corn delivered to terminals between Peoria and Pekin receives a 3 cents per bushel premium to par.

For any given futures contract, delivery differentials are fixed as part of the contract's specifications. These fixed differentials are periodically reviewed by the exchanges to determine whether they adequately reflect current market conditions. At any point in time, however, the fixed differentials in the futures contract may not reflect the current market. Both longs and shorts will carefully calculate the current "true" delivery differential and compare it with the delivery differential fixed in the contract. The longs expect that shorts will choose to deliver the cheapest-to-deliver grade at the cheapest-to-deliver location.

A delivery process that couples delivery differentials with nonpar grades and locations greatly expands the potential deliverable supply for the futures contract. This is desirable for reducing the contract's susceptibility to manipulation. But expanding the deliverable supply can diminish the contract's usefulness as a hedging instrument by reducing the correlation between the futures contract and the par grade. Evaluating this tradeoff between reduced susceptibility to manipulation and reduced hedging effectiveness is a business decision of the exchange.

Offset

By far, most futures contracts are completed through **offset** or via a **reversing trade**. To complete a futures contract obligation through offset, the trader transacts in the futures market to bring his or her net position in a particular futures contract back to zero. Consider again the situation depicted in Table 2.2. The first party has an obligation to the clearinghouse to accept 5,000 bushels of oats in September and to pay 171 cents per bushel for them at that time. Perhaps the trader does not wish to actually receive the oats and wants to exit the futures market earlier—say, May 10. The trader can fulfill the commitment by entering the futures market again and making the reversing trade depicted in Table 2.4.

The first line of Table 2.4 merely repeats the initial trade that was made on May 1. On May 10, Party 1 takes exactly the opposite position by selling one SEP contract for oats at the current futures price of 180 cents per bushel. This time the trader transacts with a new entrant to the market, Party 3. After this reversing trade, Party 1's net position is zero. The clearinghouse

Table 2.4 The reversing trade		
	Party 1's initial position	**Party 2**
May 1	Bought one SEP contract for oats at 171 cents per bushel	Sold one SEP contract for oats at 171 cents per bushel
	Party 1's reversing trade	**Party 3**
May 10	Sells one SEP contract for oats at 180 cents per bushel	Buys one SEP oats contract at 180 cents per bushel

recognizes this, and Party 1 is absolved from any further obligation. In this example, the price of September oats rose 9 cents per bushel during this period, happily yielding Party 1 a profit of $450. Party 2, the original seller, is not affected by Party 1's reversing trade. Party 2 still has the same commitment, because the clearinghouse continues to stand ready to complete this transaction, which is described in Table 2.2. Now the clearinghouse also assumes a complementary obligation to the new market entrant, Party 3. Note that the position of the clearinghouse has not really changed due to the transactions on May 10. Also, Parties 2 and 3 have complementary obligations after the new trades, just as Parties 1 and 2 had complementary obligations after the initial transactions on May 1.

In entering the reversing trade, it is crucial that Party 1 sell exactly the same contract that was bought originally. Note in Table 2.4 that the reversing trade matches the original transaction in the good traded, the number of contracts, and the maturity. If it does not, then the trader undertakes a new obligation instead of canceling the old one. If Party 1 had sold one DEC contract on May 10 instead of selling the SEP contract, for example, he or she would be obligated to receive oats in September and to deliver oats in December. Such a transaction would result in holding two positions instead of a reversing trade.

Exchange-for-physicals (EFP)

A trader can complete a futures contract by engaging in an EFP. In an EFP, two traders agree to a simultaneous exchange of a cash commodity and futures contracts based on that cash commodity. The price and other terms of the transaction are privately negotiated by the parties involved. For example, assume that Trader A is long one wheat contract and genuinely wishes to acquire wheat. Also, assume that Trader B is short one wheat contract and owns wheat. The two traders agree on a price for the physical wheat and agree to cancel their complementary futures positions against each other. Table 2.5 shows this initial position in the first panel. Trader A buys the wheat from Trader B and they report their desire to cancel their futures position to the futures exchange. The exchange notes that their positions match (one short and one long) and cancels their futures obligations. The bottom panel of Table 2.5 illustrates the positions of Traders A and B in completing the EFP.

In this example, the result is much like an offsetting trade, because both futures traders have completed their obligations and are now out of the market. Traders like to use EFPs when price certainty is important. However, the EFP differs in certain respects from an offsetting trade. First, the traders actually exchange the physical good. Second, the futures contract was not closed by a transaction on the floor of the exchange. Third, the two traders privately negotiated the price and other terms of the transaction. Because an EFP transaction takes place away from the trading floor of the exchange, it is sometimes known as an **ex-pit** transaction. Federal law and exchange rules generally require all futures trading to take place in the pit or on an electronic

Table 2.5   An exchange-for-physicals transaction

Before the EFP

Trader A	Trader B
Long one wheat futures	Short one wheat futures
Wants to acquire actual wheat	Owns wheat and wishes to sell

EFP transaction

Trader A	Trader B
Agrees with Trader B to purchase wheat and cancel futures	Agrees with Trader A to sell wheat and cancel futures
Receives wheat; pays Trader B	Delivers wheat; receives payment from Trader A
Reports EFP to exchange; exchange adjusts books to show that Trader A is out of the market	Reports EFP to exchange; exchange adjusts books to show that Trader B is out of the market

trading platform. However, the EFP is the one recognized exception to this general rule. EFPs are also known as **against actuals** or **versus cash** transactions.

Exchanges and types of futures

Since the founding of the Chicago Board of Trade in 1848, futures markets have flourished. The past three decades have been a period of extraordinary growth for futures markets, due largely to the development of entirely new types of contracts in foreign exchange, interest rates, stock indexes, economic indicators, and weather.

Worldwide exchanges

Table 2.6 lists the major futures exchanges in the world and their trading volume for 2005. Eurex, a pioneer in electronic trading that began operations in 1997, has seen trading volume on its all-electronic exchange surpass the volume of most of the world's largest futures exchanges within the first five years of operation. The Chicago Mercantile Exchange and the Chicago Board of Trade, two of the three largest exchanges in the world, announced their intention to merge in the fall of 2006. The U.S. exchanges, which once dominated global futures trading, now face formidable competition from around the world.

Recent years have seen considerable restructuring in the industry. One of the largest mergers occurred in 2003, when Eurex U.S., through its holding company, U.S. Futures Exchange, offered a 20 percent stake to the owners of BrokerTec, an all-electronic futures exchange that had suspended its operations shortly before the merger. Another noteworthy exchange merger occurred in 1998, when the Coffee, Sugar, and Cocoa Exchange merged with the New York Cotton Exchange to form the New York Board of Trade. Four years earlier, two other New York exchanges, the Commodity Exchange of New York (COMEX) and the NYMEX, merged under the NYMEX name, with separate NYMEX and COMEX divisions. In 1986, prior to the recent merger activity in New York, a merger occurred in Chicago when the CBOT acquired the MidAmerica Commodity Exchange (MidAm) and converted all MidAm contracts to CBOT "mini" contracts. The CBOT decommissioned the MidAm in 2001 and closed it entirely in 2003. U.S. exchanges have also been active in joint ventures and other affiliations. For example, in 2001 the CME, the CBOT, and the Chicago Board Options Exchange (CBOE) formed OneChicago to trade single stock futures.

Table 2.6   Major futures exchanges in the world for 2005

Exchange	2005 Volume (futures only)	Percentage of top 20 volume
Chicago Mercantile Exchange (U.S.A.)	883,118,526	23.83
Eurex (Germany)	784,896,954	21.18
Chicago Board of Trade (U.S.A.)	561,145,938	15.14
Euronext-Liffe (U.K.)	309,788,907	8.36
Bolsa de Mercadorias e Futuros (Brazil)	199,446,464	5.38
New York Mercantile Exchange (U.S.A.)	166,608,642	4.50
National Stock Exchange of India (India)	116,286,968	3.14
Mexican Derivatives Exchange (Mexico)	107,989,126	2.91
Dalian Commodity Exchange (China)	99,174,714	2.68
London Metals Exchange (U.K.)	70,444,665	1.90
Tokyo Commodities Exchange (Japan)	61,780,446	1.67
Sydney Futures Exchange (Australia)	60,091,807	1.62
Korea Exchange (South Korea)	57,883,098	1.56
ICE Futures (U.K.)	41,936,690	1.13
SAFEX (South Africa)	36,456,767	0.98
OM Stockholm Exchange (Sweden)	34,142,225	0.92
Shanghai Futures Exchange (China)	33,789,754	0.91
New York Board of Trade (U.S.A.)	29,013,416	0.78
SIMEX (Singapore)	25,867,661	0.70
Tokyo Grain Exchange (Japan)	25,573,238	0.69
Total top 20 2005 futures volume	3,705,436,006	100

Source: Futures Industry Association

Types of futures contracts

The types of futures contracts that are traded fall into five fundamentally different categories. The underlying good traded may be a physical commodity, a foreign currency, an interest-earning asset, an index—usually a stock index—or an individual stock. Contracts for nearly 400 different goods are currently available worldwide. While Chapters 5–9 deal specifically with each of the different groups of underlying goods, it is useful to have some appreciation of the range of goods that are traded on the futures market.

Physical commodity contracts
Contracts on physical commodities include agricultural contracts, metallurgical contracts, and energy contracts. In the agricultural area, contracts are traded in grains (corn, oats, rice, and wheat), oil and meal (soybeans, soymeal, and soyoil, and sunflower seed and sunflower oil), livestock (lean hogs, cattle, and pork bellies), forest products (lumber and plywood), textiles (cotton), and foodstuffs (cocoa, coffee, orange juice, and sugar). For many of these commodities, several different contracts are available for different grades or types of the commodity. For most of the goods, there are also a number of months for delivery. The months chosen for delivery of the seasonal crops generally fit their harvest patterns. The number of contract months available for each commodity also depends on the level of trading activity. For some relatively inactive futures contracts, there may be trading in only one or two delivery months in the year. By contrast, an active commodity, such as soybean meal, may have trading in eight delivery months.

The metallurgical category includes contracts traded on gold, silver, aluminum, platinum, palladium, lead, nickel, tin, zinc, and copper. Metals futures contracts are traded primarily at the COMEX Division of the NYMEX and the London Metals Exchange.

The energy category includes contracts written on heating oil, crude oil, natural gas, unleaded gasoline, coal, propane, and electricity. Energy futures are traded primarily at the NYMEX and ICE Futures (a subsidiary of the Intercontinental Exchange, or ICE).

With few exceptions (such as electricity), these commodities share two important common characteristics: they are physically settled and are highly storable.

Foreign currencies
Active futures trading of foreign currencies dates back to the inception of freely floating exchange rates in the early 1970s. U.S. dollar based contracts trade on an ever-expanding list of currencies that includes the Australian dollar, the Brazilian real, the Russian ruble, the New Zealand dollar, the Swedish krona, the South African rand, the Norwegian krone, the British pound, the Canadian dollar, the Japanese yen, the Swiss franc, the Mexican peso, the Czech koruna, the Hungarian forint, and the European Monetary Union euro. In addition, contracts based on several different currency cross-rates are traded. For example, contracts trade on the euro–pound exchange rates and the Australian dollar—Japanese yen exchange rates. The foreign exchange futures market represents the one case of a futures market that exists in the face of a truly active forward market. The forward market for foreign exchange is many times larger than the futures market. Many people believe that the presence of the forward market deterred the introduction and slowed the growth of futures trading in foreign exchange.

Interest-earning assets
Futures trading on interest-bearing assets started only in 1975, but the growth of this market has been tremendous. Contracts are now traded on Treasury notes and bonds, Eurodollar deposits, interest rate swaps, Fed funds, and municipal bonds. The existing contracts span almost the entire U.S. yield curve, so it is possible to trade instruments with virtually every maturity. Many of these contracts are physically settled, but some, such as the Eurodollar futures contract traded at the CME, are cash settled to a reference rate. In addition to U.S. products, contracts on foreign debt instruments are traded on foreign futures exchanges. For example, futures contracts on three-month Euribor are traded in London at Euronext.liffe, and futures contracts on the ten-year German government bond (called the Bund) are traded in Frankfurt on the Eurex exchange.

Indexes
Most, but not all, index-based futures contracts are stock index futures. Prior to 1982, these contracts could not trade in the United States, because stock market regulators feared that stock index futures trading would harm the market for underlying stocks. In addition, a regulatory prohibition on the cash settlement of futures contracts constrained the launch of index-based futures contracts, which must be cash settled. After much controversy, index-based futures contracts began trading in 1982 and have been extremely successful. U.S. exchanges trade contracts on many different broad-based stock indexes: the Standard and Poor's 500, the Dow Jones Industrial Average, the Russell 2000, and the NASDAQ 100. These exchanges also trade futures contracts on style-based indexes, such as the Standard and Poor's Barra Growth Index and the Standard and Poor's Barra Value Index. Futures on narrow-based indexes, such as industry sector indexes, have been tried but have failed to generate significant volume. Outside of the United States, foreign exchanges trade futures on foreign stock indexes such as the British FTSE 100, the French CAC 40, the Dow Jones Euro Stoxx 50, the German DAX, the Brazilian

Bovespa stock index, the Japanese Nikkei 225 index, and the Korean KOSPI 200. We discuss stock index futures in detail in Chapters 7 and 8.

Index-based contracts do not permit physical delivery. A trader's obligation must be fulfilled by a reversing trade or a cash settlement at the end of trading. In addition to stock indexes, futures contracts have been written on other types on indexes as well, including a foreign exchange index, an index of municipal bonds, the consumer price index, a price variance index, and weather indexes based on heating degree days, cooling degree days or snowfall in major cities.

One of the more unusual index-based contracts can be found at the CME. The CME has constructed a futures contract based on the Goldman Sachs Commodity Index (GSCI). The GSCI is an index composed of the prices of 24 commodity futures contracts. The index provider selects the components and their weighting within the index. The index uses only the prices from nearby futures contracts. Essentially, this product is a futures contract on a basket of futures contracts.

Individual stocks

The last major group of futures contracts is for individual stocks, such as shares of IBM. These contracts are called "single stock futures" in the United States and "universal futures" in the United Kingdom. Although futures contracts written on broad-based stock market indexes have been traded since 1982, it was not until the passage of the CFMA of 2000 that trading of futures contracts on individual stocks was permitted in the United States. Outside of the United States, single stock futures have been traded for nearly a decade on various European and Asian exchanges. In Sweden and Finland, the products have been traded since the early 1990s. We discuss single stock futures in Chapters 7 and 8.

Relative importance of commodity types

Figure 2.5 presents another division of futures contracts into eight categories and shows the relative importance of trading in these different categories in the United States in 2005. As Figure 2.5 shows, the overwhelming majority of trading volume stems from financial instruments. These include futures contracts based on underlying instruments such as Treasury securities and stock indexes. As we have noted, trading in these contracts began in 1975, so growth in this

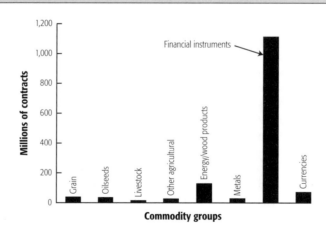

Figure 2.5 Market share by commodity type

Figure 2.6 Changing commodity trading volume

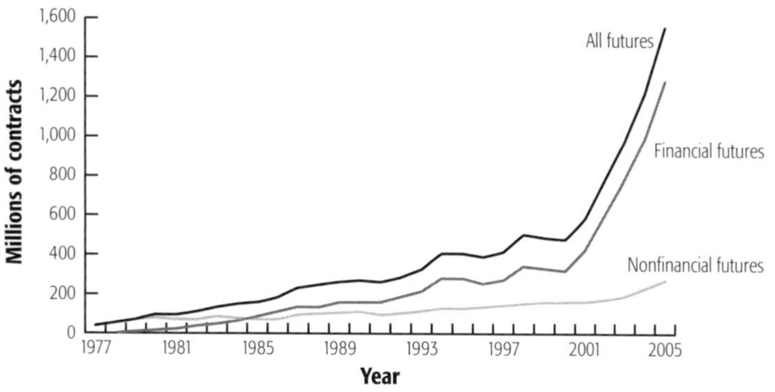

area has been dramatic. Figure 2.6 shows how the portions of futures trading volume have shifted among these commodity groups over recent years. Financial futures clearly dominate all other categories combined.

Purposes of futures markets

Any industry as old and as large as the futures market must serve some social purpose. If it did not, it would most likely have passed from existence some time ago. Traditionally, futures markets have been recognized as meeting the needs of three groups of futures market users: those who wish to discover information about future prices of commodities, those who wish to speculate, and those who wish to hedge. While Chapter 4 discusses the uses that these three groups make of futures markets in detail, it is important to have some understanding of the social function of futures markets before proceeding. Traditionally, speculation is not regarded as socially useful by itself, although it may have socially useful by-products. Thus, there are two main social functions of futures markets—price discovery and hedging.

Price discovery

Price discovery is the revealing of information about future cash market prices through the futures market. As discussed earlier, in buying or selling a futures contract, a trader agrees to receive or deliver a given commodity at a certain time in the future for a price that is determined now. In such a circumstance, it is not surprising that there is a relationship between the futures price and the price that people expect to prevail for the commodity at the delivery date specified in the futures contract. While the exact nature of that relationship will be considered in detail in Chapter 3, the relationship is predictable to a high degree. By using the information contained in futures prices today, market observers can form estimates of what the price of a given commodity will be at a certain time in the future. The forecasts of future prices that can be drawn from the futures market compare in accuracy quite favorably with other types of forecasts. Futures markets serve a social purpose by helping people make better estimates of future prices, so that they can make their consumption and investment decisions more wisely. Futures prices also assist in price discovery for some commodities where cash markets are not well developed.

As an example of price discovery and its benefits, consider a mine operator who is trying to decide whether to reopen a marginally profitable silver mine. The silver ore in the mine is not of the best quality, so the yield from the mine will be relatively low. The financial wisdom of operating the mine will depend on the price the miner can obtain for the silver once it is mined and refined. However, the miner must make the decision about the mine today, and the silver will not be ready for market for 15 months. The crucial element in the miner's decision is the future price of silver.

While the price of silver 15 months from now cannot be known with certainty, it is possible to use the futures market to estimate that future price. The price quoted in the futures market today for a silver futures that expires in 15 months can be a very useful estimate of the future price. As we will see in Chapter 3, for some commodities an estimate of the future price of the commodity can be derived from an examination of futures price. These estimates are generally regarded as being the best, or one of the best, estimates possible. In our example, let us assume that the futures price for silver is high enough to justify starting to operate the mine again. The miner figures that the new mine will be profitable if he can obtain the futures price for the silver when it becomes available in 15 months. In this situation, the miner has used the futures market as a vehicle of price discovery. Farmers, lumber producers, cattle ranchers, and other economic agents can use futures markets in the same way. They all use futures market estimates of future cash prices to guide their production or consumption decisions.

Hell and high water

The Great Chicago Fire started on October 6, 1871 and destroyed a large portion of the financial district of Chicago. Six of the 17 grain elevators used as delivery points for CBOT contracts were destroyed. In addition, the CBOT's headquarters building was destroyed and all records were lost.

Chicago was the setting for another disaster in 1992. This time, however, the disaster involved water rather than fire. The Great Chicago Underground Flood began on April 13, 1992, when construction workers on the Chicago River drove a support pillar into the bottom of the river and through the ceiling of an abandoned railway tunnel, built in 1899 to haul coal and to remove ashes from buildings in downtown Chicago. Workers attempted to plug the hole with rocks and mattresses, but massive amounts of river water poured into the maze of underground tunnels. The CBOT and the CME ceased operations as 250 million gallons of river water rushed into the basements and sub-basements of the exchange halls, causing a power outage and forcing the evacuation of the entire downtown area. Because the flood affected the heart of Chicago's financial district, it proved to be an exceptionally costly business disaster. Other markets were impacted by the closure of Chicago's futures exchanges. Country elevators throughout the Midwest, which relied on the price discovery role of the futures market as the basis for their cash market pricing, pulled bids and refused to post new bids for local farmers.

Hedging

Many futures market participants trade futures as a substitute for a cash market transaction. For example, we considered a farmer who sold wheat futures in anticipation of a harvest, and we noted that the farmer used futures as an alternative to the sale of wheat through the cash market. We now consider this classic kind of hedge in more detail. At planting time, the farmer bears a risk associated with the uncertain harvest price his wheat will command. The farmer might use the futures market to hedge by selling a futures contract. If the farmer expects to harvest 100,000 bushels of wheat in nine months, he could establish a price for that harvest by selling 20 wheat futures contracts (each wheat contract is for 5,000 bushels). By selling these futures contracts, the farmer seeks to establish a price today for the wheat that will be harvested in the future. With certain qualifications, this futures transaction protects the farmer from wheat price fluctuations that might occur between the present and the future harvest. The futures transaction serves as a substitute for a cash market sale of wheat. A cash market sale is impossible, because the wheat does not actually exist. In this example, the farmer sells wheat in the futures market as a temporary substitute for a future anticipated cash market transaction. Therefore, **anticipatory hedging** is a futures market transaction used as a substitute for an anticipated future cash market transaction.

Hedging transactions can take other forms. For example, consider an oil wholesaler who holds a substantial inventory of gasoline. The wholesaler needs the inventory as a stock from which to service retail customers. If the wholesaler simply holds the stock of gasoline, she must bear the price risk of fluctuating gasoline prices. As an alternative, she can sell gasoline futures as a substitute for selling the gasoline itself. By holding gasoline in her business inventory and selling gasoline futures to offset the risk associated with the gasoline, the wholesaler can reduce her business risk. The wholesaler could have used the cash market directly to reduce risk by simply selling her entire inventory in the cash market. Unfortunately, this method of reducing business risk eliminates the business, because the wholesaler would no longer have the gasoline inventory that is essential to her entire business. Selling futures substitutes for the risk-reducing transaction of selling her entire inventory.

For both of our examples, the hedger uses the futures market as a substitute for a cash market transaction. Both hedgers had a preexisting risk associated with the commodity being sold. The farmer anticipated harvesting and selling wheat, and he used the futures market as a substitute for a cash market sale of wheat. Even though the farmer did not have wheat on hand when he sold futures, he did have a preexisting risk in wheat. The risk arose from the anticipated holding of the cash wheat at harvest. For the oil wholesaler, the risk was immediate. As prices of gasoline fluctuate, the value of her gasoline inventory would fluctuate as well. Thus, the wholesaler had a preexisting risk associated with the price of gasoline, and she used the futures market transaction to reduce that risk.

Because hedgers are traders that use futures transactions as substitutes for cash transactions, hedgers are almost always business concerns that deal with a specific commodity. Almost without exception, individual traders are speculators, because they enter the futures market in pursuit of profit and increase their risk in the process. By contrast, hedgers have a preexisting risk exposure of some form that leads them to use futures transactions as a substitute for a cash market transaction. Hedging is the prime social rationale for futures trading and, therefore, we will give hedging a great deal of attention throughout the discussion of futures. Chapter 4 explains the use that the hedger makes of the futures markets, while the techniques and applications of hedging are elaborated for specific markets in Chapters 5–9.

Traders in the futures markets are either speculators or hedgers, or the agents of one of these two groups. Yet the benefits provided by the futures market extend to many other sectors of society. The individual interested in forecasts of future prices need not enter the market to benefit. For example, our silver miner did not need to trade any futures to capture the benefits of price discovery. The forecasts are available for the price of a daily newspaper. The chance for hedgers to avoid unacceptable risks by entering the futures market also has wide implications for social welfare. Some individuals would not engage in certain clearly beneficial forms of economic activity if they were forced to bear all of the risk of the activity themselves. Being able to transfer risk to other parties via the futures market enhances economic activity in general. Of course, a general stimulation of economic activity benefits society as a whole.

Regulation of futures markets

Federal regulation of futures markets dates to the enactment of the Grain Futures Act of 1922. This statute was superseded by the Commodity Exchange Act (CEA) of 1936. The CEA has been amended several times, most recently with the passage of the Commodity Futures Modernization Act of 2000 (CFMA). The aim of federal regulation is to provide a marketplace in which the social functions of futures markets can be fulfilled. Futures market regulations are designed to deter manipulation, abusive trading practices, and fraud, because these activities interfere with the process of price discovery or the efficient transfer of unwanted risk. For example, practices that make futures prices behave as poor indicators of future spot prices reduce the usefulness of the futures market for price discovery. Also, practices that distort prices can increase the cost of transferring risk. Congress created the CFTC in 1974 to administer the federal laws governing futures markets.

Onions

One curiosity embedded in the federal laws governing futures markets in the United States, is that futures trading in onions is illegal. Onion futures traded at the CME and the NYMEX between 1942 and 1959.[6] Due to concerns by onion growers of futures-related speculation and volatile prices, Congress passed public Law 85–839 (7 USC 13–1) in August 1958, which prohibited dealings in onion futures. As a result, onions were excluded from the definition of the term "commodity" in the Commodity Exchange Act. The definition of "commodity" in the CEA now reads as follows:

> The term "commodity" means wheat, cotton, rice, corn, oats, barley, rye, flaxseed, grain sorghums, mill feeds, butter, eggs, *Solanum tuberosum* (Irish potatoes), wool, wool tops, fats and oils (including lard, tallow, cottonseed oil, peanut oil, soybean oil, and all other fats and oils), cottonseed meal, cottonseed, peanuts, soybeans, soybean meal, livestock, livestock products, frozen concentrated orange juice, and all other goods and articles, except onions as provided in Public Law 85–839 (7 USC 13–1), and all services, rights, and interests, in which contracts for future delivery are presently or in the future dealt in.

Careful reading of the definition (especially the part about all services, rights, and interests) reveals that almost anything one can think of in the universe qualifies as a commodity–except onions. If a futures exchange were to offer a futures contract on a noncommodity such as onions, traders on the losing end of transactions could simply walk away from their obligations by claiming that the contract is illegal and therefore unenforceable. In addition, the statute specifies monetary penalties for anyone who trades onion futures. To date, no futures exchange has attempted to evade the onion prohibition by offering shallot, scallion, or leek futures.

In addition to direct regulation by the federal government, the laws and regulations governing futures trading at organized exchanges impose self-regulatory duties on industry members who interact with public customers. In other words, industry members themselves must perform a regulatory role. The CFTC oversees the entire regulatory structure to make sure that industry members perform their self-regulatory duties. There are four identifiable levels of regulation in the futures market: the broker; the exchange and clearinghouse; an industry self-regulatory body, the National Futures Association (NFA); and a federal government agency, the CFTC. To a large extent, these levels overlap, but each regulatory body has its specific duties.

The broker

As we have seen in our discussion of the margin system, the broker essentially represents his or her customers to the exchange and clearinghouse. In the margin system, the clearinghouse holds the clearing member responsible for all of the accounts that a clearing member carries. Because of the representations to the industry that the broker makes on behalf of its client, the broker has a duty to keep informed about the activities of its customer and to ensure that those activities are proper. Among futures market participants, the often-repeated rule for brokers is "Know your customer." The broker is the industry representative in the best position to know a given customer, because the customer gains access to trading directly through the broker.

As we will see in more detail, some kinds of futures trading are not permitted to any traders. Other traders have restrictions on the kind of trading in which they should engage. As an example, let us consider a position limit. For a commodity with a position limit, no single trader is allowed to hold more than a certain number of contracts. This rule limits the influence of a single trader on the market and aims to prevent the trader from controlling the futures price.[7] On occasion, some traders have tried to circumvent this rule by trading through different accounts. Often, the broker can detect such a maneuver and has a duty to report such activity. As this example shows, the broker is often in the best position to detect some abuses, because he or she is closest to the customer. The trading of some customers is restricted due to the nature of the customer's business. For example, some financial institutions are allowed to trade only certain types of futures for hedging purposes. The broker for such an institution should not allow prohibited trading.

In general terms, the broker is responsible for knowing the customer's position and intentions, for ensuring that the customer does not disrupt the market or place the system in jeopardy, and for keeping the customer's trading activity in line with industry regulations and legal restrictions.

Futures exchanges and clearinghouses as regulators

The futures exchanges and clearinghouses have specific self-regulatory duties. As a result of these duties, exchanges and clearinghouses are referred to as **self-regulatory organizations**, or **SRO**s. Many of these self-regulatory duties require the exchange and clearinghouse to control the conduct of the exchange and clearing members. To do so, the exchanges and clearinghouses formulate and enforce rules for their members. Generally, these rules are designed to create a smoothly functioning market in which traders can feel confident that their orders will be executed and cleared properly and at a fair price. Thus, all exchanges prohibit fraud, dishonorable conduct, and defaulting on contract obligations. Clearinghouse rules set minimum financial requirements for clearinghouse members in order to ensure the financial integrity of the clearing system.

More specifically, exchange rules prohibit **fictitious trading**—trading that merely gives the appearance of transacting without actually changing ownership.[8] Exchange rules prohibit circulating rumors to affect price, disclosing a customer's order, trading with oneself, taking the opposite side of a customer's order, making false statements to the exchange, and failing to comply with a legitimate order by the exchange.

The rules also prohibit **prearranged trading**. A prearranged trade occurs when two futures market participants consult in advance and agree to make a certain trade at a given price. Instead, the rules require that all orders be offered to the entire market through open outcry. The rules prohibit prearranged trading because a prearranged trade is noncompetitive and can be abusive. For example, assume that a floor broker receives an order to buy wheat and that the fair market price for the wheat contract is $4.20 per bushel. In a prearranged trade, the floor broker might agree with a friendly floor trader to buy the contract from him or her at $4.21. With the true market value at \$4.20, this practice cheats the customer by \$0.01 per bushel, or \$50 per contract. Had the order been offered to the market as the rules require, the order would have been filled at the prevailing price of \$4.20. Thus, the prohibition of prearranged trading aims at ensuring that each order is executed at a fair market price.

The rules also prohibit a broker from trading for his or her own account at the customer's requested price before filling a customer's order. The broker who trades for himself or herself before filling a customer's order engages in the prohibited practice called **front running**. To see why this practice is prohibited, assume that market prices are rising rapidly due to some new information. Assume also that the broker holds a customer order to buy. If the broker executes his or her own order first, the broker's own order will be executed at a more favorable price, because of the quickly rising prices. Thus, front running gives the broker an unfair advantage. As a second example, assume that a broker receives a very large customer order to sell. The broker knows that placing this order will depress the futures price temporarily. The front-running broker would enter his or her own order to sell first. The broker's order would be executed at the high price, and the broker would then execute the customer's order. Upon execution of the customer's order, the price falls as the broker anticipated. Now the broker can buy and close his or her position. This gives the broker a profit from front running. In front running, the broker uses his or her special knowledge of order flow or market movement to obtain an unethical and prohibited personal advantage.

In **dual trading**, a single individual fulfills the function of a floor trader and a floor broker simultaneously. That is, a single individual trades for his or her own account, while executing orders for traders off the floor of the exchange. Although permitted for many decades, dual trading does offer potential for abuse, and the practice has come under heightened scrutiny. Because dual trading creates a situation in which a single individual has his or her own orders in hand along with orders from an outside customer, dual trading can also facilitate front running and other questionable trading practices.

Traders maintain that dual trading serves the market in several ways. First, defenders maintain that dual trading helps promote liquidity in the market. If a trader can only execute orders for his or her own account or only execute orders for others, there will be less potential trading volume at any given time. Second, this lack of liquidity may lead to larger spreads between bid and asked prices, thereby making the market less efficient than it would be otherwise. Finally, defenders of dual trading maintain that the practice keeps trading costs low, because a dual trader needs to make only a portion of his or her income by acting as a floor broker.

In late 1993, the CFTC banned dual trading, but allowed a number of significant exceptions. For example, dual trading continues to be permitted for commodities with a daily trading volume of less than 8,000 contracts, for exchanges with very well developed audit systems, and where the banning of dual trading would adversely affect the public interest. In recent years, it appears that formerly dual traders on the CME have not gained a greater share of customers now that the trader's personal trading is restricted, and these traders have not shifted their trading to other commodities.[9]

Futures exchanges also set daily price limits, margin requirements, and position limits. They may also set position accountability levels. A position accountability level refers to the right of the exchange to have access to all information regarding the nature of a trader's position, trading strategy, and hedging information. Position limits and position accountability levels can be defined for any single contract month, or for all contract months combined. Exchanges are required by federal regulations to have position limits or position accountability levels for contracts as they enter the delivery month, in order to deter would-be manipulators. Some exchanges also have rules to set trading volume limits, although these rules have rarely been used in recent years. In addition, each exchange has rules that govern membership on the exchange. For example, exchange rules establish membership requirements and specify how customer complaints are to be resolved. For each of these categories, the rules of the exchange are subject to oversight by the CFTC. The federal law administered by the CFTC provides a set of core principles, or standards, that are meant to allow futures exchanges to use methods of their choice to achieve the federal requirements.

The National Futures Association (NFA)

In 1974, Congress passed a new law for the regulation of futures markets. Part of that law authorized the futures industry to create one or more self-regulatory bodies ". . . to prevent fraudulent and manipulative acts and practices, to promote just and equitable principles of trade, in general, to protect the public interest, and to remove impediments to and perfect the mechanism of free and open futures trading." While the law has contemplated more than a single self-regulatory body, the National Futures Association is the only such body in existence.

The following parties are required to be members of the NFA: futures commission merchants (FCMs), commodity pool operators, introducing brokers, commodity trading advisors, and associated persons. Exchanges, banks, and commodity business firms may join the NFA, but membership is not compulsory. Floor traders and floor brokers are not required to be members, because they are subject to exchange regulation. One must be a member of the NFA in order to do commodity-related business with the public.

The NFA screens and tests applicants for registration, and reviews personal background information before allowing individuals to register in the various categories of futures professionals. The NFA also requires FCMs and introducing brokers to maintain adequate capital and accurate trading records. Finally, the NFA can audit member firms' records and capital adequacy. For serious violations, the NFA can suspend or expel violators from the futures industry. Finally, the NFA operates an arbitration process for resolving trading disputes.

As the NFA states, it seeks to prevent infractions before they occur. By doing so, the NFA helps the futures industry to remain viable by keeping the public trust. However, in assessing the NFA, it is wise to remember that it is an industry self-regulatory body, designed to protect the integrity of the industry and to promote the interests of the industry.

The NFA also assists exchanges in carrying out their self-regulatory responsibilities with respect to market surveillance, compliance, and rule enforcement. It has entered into regulatory service agreement with the United States Futures Exchange (USFE), the Merchants' Exchange, OnExchange, Island Futures Exchange, and (the now defunct) BrokerTec. The NFA performed the market surveillance function for BrokerTec between 2001 and 2003 and entered into a similar agreement with the USFE in 2004.

The NFA plays a key role in the regulation of security futures products. The CFMA Act of 2000 requires the NFA to monitor futures market participants for compliance with the applicable securities laws. The statute recognizes the NFA as a "limited purpose national securities association."

The Commodity Futures Trading Commission (CFTC)

The CFTC was created by Congress in 1974 as an independent agency of the federal government to administer the Commodity Exchange Act (CEA). Prior to the creation of the CFTC, the CEA was administered by the U.S. Department of Agriculture. In its role as administrator of the CEA, the CFTC has exclusive federal jurisdiction over commodity futures and futures option markets in the United States. One of the CFTC's main missions is to protect market participants from manipulation, abusive trade practices, and fraud. The CFTC also has regulatory oversight of futures exchanges, futures clearinghouses, and other self-regulatory organizations such as the NFA. Congress also gave the agency authority to address market emergencies that could prevent markets from performing their price discovery and risk shifting roles.

The regulatory role of the CFTC changed greatly as a result of the passage of the CFMA of 2000.[10] While retaining prohibitions against fraud and market manipulation, the CFMA replaced many of the prescriptive rules and regulations for exchanges and clearinghouses with a broad set of core principles. These core principles give the CFTC flexibility to tailor regulation to the type of market, product, and participant, and to keep better pace with change. One result of the CFMA can be seen in the way the CFTC regulates exchanges wishing to list new contracts for trading. Prior to the CFMA, the CFTC required that futures exchanges submit new contracts to the CFTC for approval. The approval process took on average 90 days to complete and U.S. futures exchanges complained bitterly that the process hampered their ability to respond quickly to rapid market developments—constraints not faced by the exchanges' competitors overseas and in the OTC market. The burden of proof fell on the exchanges to demonstrate that a new contract met all regulatory requirements. Now, as a result of the CFMA, an exchange wishing to list a new contract can do so almost instantly if it can certify that the contract complies with the core principles and the CFTC's regulations, including the requirement that the contract not be readily susceptible to manipulation. In other words, the CFMA shifted the burden of proof to the CFTC to demonstrate that a contract does not comply with regulatory requirements. The CFTC's authority to level severe sanctions deters exchanges from falsely certifying their products. Exchanges have taken advantage of their new authority by certifying 438 new products in the three years following the enactment of the CFMA, a sizeable jump from the 175 new contracts approved by the CFTC in the three years leading up to the passage of the CFMA.[11]

The CFMA also changed the way in which the CFTC monitors exchange compliance with federal regulations. Rather than conducting detailed compliance reviews of exchange members, the CFTC now relies on rule-enforcement reviews of the exchange. The purpose of these reviews is to ensure that the exchanges are adhering to their own rules and procedures. In this way, the CFTC has more of an oversight role as opposed to a direct role in monitoring compliance. The exchange, through its self-regulatory obligations, has the primary responsibility for enforcing member compliance with rules. The CFTC's rule enforcement reviews ensure that the exchange is adequately performing its obligations.

The CFTC is based in Washington, D.C., with branch offices in New York City, Chicago, Kansas City, and Minneapolis. The Commission itself consists of five commissioners, one of whom serves as the CFTC's Chairman. The commissioners are appointed by the president and confirmed by the senate for staggered five-year terms. No more than three members of the CFTC can be from a single political party. Major policy decisions, the adoption of agency rules and regulations, and the authorization of enforcement proceedings must be approved by a majority vote of the Commissioners.

The CFTC employs a staff of approximately 500 people nationwide. The CFTC has three main operating divisions: the Division of Clearing and Intermediary Oversight, which oversees clearing organizations and activities related to market intermediaries; the Division of Market Oversight, which conducts daily market surveillance and oversees futures exchanges; and the Division of Enforcement, which investigates and prosecutes alleged violations of the CEA and CFTC regulations. The CFTC also has three supporting offices: the Office of the Chief Economist, which provides economic advice to the commission; the Office of the General Counsel, which serves as the commission's legal advisor; and the Office of the Executive Director, which handles the commission's administrative functions. Regulatory initiatives and commission decisions are announced on the CFTC's web site (www.cftc.gov).

The CFTC's large-trader reporting system

The heart of the CFTC's market surveillance program is its large-trader reporting system, which collects position-level data from large traders who own or control a position in a U.S. futures market above specific reporting thresholds. The purpose of this surveillance program is to help the CFTC identify potential concentrations of market power within a market and to enforce speculative position limits. Under the large-trader reporting system, clearing members, FCMs, and foreign brokers file daily electronic confidential reports with the CFTC showing the entire futures and option positions of large traders.

Reporting thresholds are set so that the CFTC has information representing 70–90 percent of the total open interest in any given market. The reporting level varies from market to market, depending on the size of the market and the size of deliverable supplies. Reporting thresholds are specified in the CFTC's regulations and are posted on its web site (www.cftc.gov).

The CFTC uses various means to ensure the accuracy of its large-trader data. If a trader holds positions at more than one brokerage firm, his positions are aggregated across the various firms to determine the trader's aggregate position. Aggregating positions is necessary for the CFTC's surveillance staff to make a thorough assessment of a trader's potential market impact and a trader's compliance with speculative position limits.

The CFTC transforms the raw large-trader data into analytical reports. Using these reports, the CFTC's surveillance staff monitors the largest traders in each market. CFTC staff members also monitor traders' position across markets. For contracts that settled at expiration through physical delivery, the CFTC's surveillance staff uses the large trader information to determine the adequacy of the potential deliverable supply.

The CFTC publishes a weekly report based on the confidential large trader report. The published report, called the *Commitments of Traders* report, shows the aggregate positions held by the largest reportable traders.

New regulatory initiatives

In the late 1990s and early 2000s, significant changes in the regulation of futures markets occurred, both in an amendment to the Commodity Exchange Act and in accounting rules.

Commodity futures

As mentioned earlier in this chapter, the CFMA of 2000 made sweeping changes to the way futures markets had previously been regulated. Although the law was passed by Congress in 2000, much of it required detailed rulemakings and interpretations before it could be fully implemented. As a result, many of the key features of the law have only recently become apparent. These key features, some of which have been discussed above, are more fully described below and include:

- Permitting futures trading on individual stocks and narrow-based stock indexes.
- Clarifying the legal status of privately negotiated swap transactions.
- Promoting competition and innovation in futures markets.
- Providing a predictable and calibrated regulatory structure tailored to the product, the participant, and the trading platform.
- Allowing exchanges to bring new contracts to market without prior regulatory approval.
- Establishing a set of core principles, or standards, that permit futures exchanges and clearing-houses to use different methods to achieve federal requirements.

- Giving the CFTC clear authority to stop certain illegal foreign exchange transactions aimed at defrauding small investors.
- Giving the CFTC separate oversight authority with respect to clearinghouse organizations.

One purpose of the CFMA was to promote competition and innovation in futures markets and to provide a predictable and calibrated regulatory structure tailored to the product, the participant, and the trading platform (i.e., the method of trading). These "three P's"—that is, product, participant, and platform—dictate the level of regulatory oversight the market receives. A soybean producer in Iowa will receive more regulatory protection than a bond trader representing a Wall Street financial institution. Transactions on an organized futures exchange will be subject to greater regulatory oversight than privately negotiated transactions between sophisticated traders. Products that are susceptible to manipulation will receive greater regulatory scrutiny than those products that are less susceptible to manipulation.

The CFMA laid out three tiers of regulation for futures exchanges depending on the types of products being traded, the level of sophistication of the participants using them, and the type of trading platform. The first tier is the most heavily regulated and includes futures on commodities that Congress judged to be potentially susceptible to manipulation and that are also offered to members of the public. This tier includes futures contracts on agricultural commodities. Futures contracts in the first tier must be traded on an organized futures exchange such as the CBOT, where trading can be continually monitored by exchange officials and CFTC staff.

In the second tier are exempt futures contracts; that is, futures contracts on instruments that are judged to be less susceptible to manipulation and are offered only to sophisticated investors, financial institutions, commercial users, and professional traders. These contracts, which include metals and energy products, are exempt from most federal regulations, except for those regulations concerning fraud and manipulation. These contracts need not be traded on an organized futures exchange. These exempt products can be traded on a set of separately regulated exchanges called "exempt commercial markets." They are also referred to by industry insiders as "2(h)(3)" markets, from the section of the CEA that governs their regulation. These exchanges are not required to conduct market surveillance to prevent market disruptions. Instead, fraud and manipulation are deterred by the certain knowledge that stiff monetary penalties, or possibly criminal penalties, await those market participants who commit fraudulent or manipulative acts. Congress granted regulatory exemptions to these exchanges as a way of promoting exchange competition by encouraging the development of new exchanges. As the exempt exchange gains trading volume, it becomes subject to additional regulatory requirements. Individual investors (so-called "retail customers") are, for their own protection, excluded from trading in exempt commercial markets.

In practice, products in this second tier are traded on both highly regulated exchanges such as the NYMEX and through exempt commercial markets such as the ICE. If exchanges choose to offer these products in a fully regulated environment, then these products can be offered to retail customers.

The third tier includes contracts on financial products that are traded on a principal-to-principal ("P2P") basis. These contracts are privately negotiated between large, sophisticated contract counterparties. These contracts, better known as "swaps," are transacted in the OTC market or on an electronic trading facility that facilitates principal-to-principal trades that are excluded from futures trading laws. Congress believed that products in the third tier were not susceptible to manipulation, and that participants had the sophistication and resources to fend for themselves and did not require protection through government regulation. In practice, some products in this category, such as interest rate products, are traded both on highly regulated organized exchanges and on a principal-to-principal basis.

The CFMA also greatly affected the way in which futures clearinghouses are regulated. Prior to the CFMA, regulations embodied the assumption that trade execution and clearing were necessarily a single, integrated activity. The result of these regulations was that an "exchange clearinghouse" was assumed to exist as part of the exchange. The CFMA recognizes clearing as a separate line of business from trade execution, and therefore regulates clearing separately from the way trade execution is regulated. The CFMA directs the CFTC to recognize "derivatives clearing organizations." Like exchanges, clearing organizations must abide by a set of core principles, which are tailored to the specific risks associated with clearing. The CFMA also enables clearing organizations to clear OTC derivatives in an effort to reduce counterparty risk and systemic risks associated with these transactions. It is important to note that, despite authorization to clear OTC products through a clearing organization, the underlying OTC transactions are outside the jurisdiction of the CFTC.

Who is a sophisticated trader?

In futures market regulation, a sophisticated trader is referred to as an eligible contract participant, or "ECP." The significance of this term is that it legally defines who can engage in transactions that are exempt or excluded from federal laws and regulations protecting futures market customers. For example, counterparties to a privately negotiated swap transaction must meet the legal standard of an ECP. The term applies to financial institutions, investment companies, corporations, pension plans, government entities, broker dealers, FCMs, insurance companies, floor brokers, traders, commodity pools, or wealthy individuals. Each entity has its own set of very detailed requirements to be considered eligible. ECPs who enter into privately negotiated derivatives transactions with other ECPs are presumed to be sophisticated traders who can fend for themselves, without the protection of the federal government. If there is a dispute between ECPs, they are on their own to resolve it through the courts. The qualification standards for asset size and wealth are used as proxies for the sophistication of the entity.

Accounting rules

In 1998, the Financial Accounting Standards Board (FASB) adopted a new set of rules governing the accounting practices for futures and other derivative instruments. These rules are contained in the FASB's Statement of Financial Accounting Standards No. 133, "Accounting for Derivative Instruments and Hedging Activities," also known as FAS 133.

Before the issuance of FAS 133, accounting rules for derivatives transactions were unclear and not uniform. The issuance of FAS 133 supersedes many previous FAS statements pertaining to derivatives (FAS 80, FAS 105, and FAS 119). FAS 133 also amends FAS 80 ("Foreign Currency Translation") and FAS 107 ("Disclosures about Fair Value of Financial Instruments"). As such, FAS 133 provides a new and uniform treatment of accounting for derivatives. Originally scheduled to come into effect in 1999, implementation of FAS 133 was delayed due to protests by affected firms. The FASB also issued FAS 138 to modify the terms of implementation in response to complaints, but FAS 138 does not significantly modify the principles of FAS 133. In 2000, FAS 133/FAS138 became fully operational and now forms the basic framework for derivatives accounting in the United States. The entire document is 245 pages long. Appendix A provides an overview of these accounting rules. Application of the principles of FAS 133 will require familiarity with the statement itself.

Taxation of futures trading

In 1981, Congress passed a law regarding the taxation of gains and losses in futures trading that had dramatic effects on the ways in which futures contracts could be used. The new law stipulated that all paper gains and losses on futures positions must be treated as though they were realized at the end of the tax year. For tax purposes, this new law meant that the futures positions must be marked-to-market at the end of the year. Forty percent of any gains or losses had to be treated as short-term gains and 60 percent as long-term capital gains or losses. Over the years, Congress has considered many proposals to change the tax treatment of futures contracts, but the 60/40 treatment has prevailed.

Brokers, advisors, and commodity fund managers

We have already seen that speculators and hedgers are traders who trade for their own accounts. Also, we have mentioned that the market utilizes brokers, individuals who execute trades for a customer, whether a speculator or a hedger. In this section, we consider brokers in more detail, because there are a number of different types of brokers.

In discussing brokers earlier in this chapter, we focused on an individual who executes orders on the floor of the exchange. We mentioned that such a broker is often the employee of a brokerage firm, such as Merrill Lynch. In the futures market, there are special names for the individuals and firms that execute orders on behalf of others.

The floor broker

When an individual trader, who is not a member of the exchange, places an order, he or she usually does so through an account executive with a brokerage firm. The order is transmitted to the floor of the exchange, where it is executed by a **floor broker** (**FB**), an individual who executes an order for the purchase or sale of a futures contract for another person. There are about 8,500 FBs registered across all exchanges in the United States.

Many FBs are members of **broker associations** or **broker groups**. A broker group is an association of FBs who band together to fill orders for their customers. The group might be as small as two brokers who cover for each other during vacations or as large as groups of brokers that operate in several markets and who share profits and expenses. These broker groups have become an important force among the trading community. For example, there are more than 200 broker groups at the CME and more than 100 at the NYMEX.

Broker groups provide some services to the futures community. First, they provide a training ground for new brokers. Second, they provide a flexible pool of manpower to respond to radical fluctuations in trading volume. Third, they provide an easy way for large brokerage houses to achieve execution in several pits simultaneously. Fourth, the capital of the association stands behind each of the members of the group. Thus, there is less chance of any single broker defaulting.

These broker groups have become the object of criticism for several reasons. First, the existence of an association might encourage members to trade with each other preferentially, instead of offering a trade to the entire market as the rules require. Second, broker groups were accused of dishonesty in fulfilling customer orders in some important legal actions during the 1990s. For example, one member of a broker group might trade for his own account, while another member of the same group might act as a FB in executing an order for someone outside the broker group. The temptation exists to give a preferential price to the other member of the broker group at the expense of the outside party. In 1993, the CFTC increased its monitoring of these broker groups and required identification of such cooperative relationships.

The futures commission merchant

A **futures commission merchant** (**FCM**) is a brokerage firm that accepts orders to trade futures on behalf of public customers and that accepts money to support such an order. In many cases, the FCM will be a large firm with offices in many cities, that accepts orders from individuals and other firms. The FCM transmits these orders to the floor of the exchange, where they are executed by a FB. The FB may be an employee of the FCM, although this is not always the case. Since the mid-1980s, the number of FCMs has declined due to consolidation in the industry and very stiff competition. In 1984, there were approximately 400 FCMs, but that number had declined to 211 by 2006. FCMs must be registered with the NFA. FCMs are periodically audited for regulatory compliance by the NFA, with oversight by the CFTC.

Within the futures industry, FCMs are sometimes called **carrying firms**, or **commission houses**. The FCM earns a commission for executing orders and for performing other services, such as clearing, on behalf of customers. Customer margin balances that are not forwarded to the clearinghouse can be invested by the FCMs in safe financial instruments from which the FCM can earn investment income. In this respect, FCMs play a role similar to that of a bank.

Over the past decade, mergers within the financial services industry have reduced the number of stand-alone FCMs. Although stand-alone FCMs still make up the majority of FCMs, many FCMs today are also broker/dealers who are registered with both the CFTC and the Securities and Exchange Commission (SEC). These broker/dealer–FCMs trade securities in addition to futures. FCMs are often part of a financial services holding company that offers a variety of services to customers. For example, Fimat, a wholly owned subsidiary of Société Générale in France, is one of the world's largest global brokers. It offers clearing and execution services on exchange-traded financial and commodities futures and options contracts across 21 marketplaces.

With few exceptions, public customers must use an FCM to place a trade at an organized futures exchange. Two small exchanges, FutureCom and HedgeStreet, allow customers to trade without an intermediary, but these are exceptions to the general rule.

Churning

Churning refers to the actions of brokers who execute trades on behalf of investors with the intent of generating commissions at the expense of the investors' interests. Churning is really a form of fraud, because the broker misrepresents how she would trade the investor's money. Churning is also a form of unauthorized trading, because the broker trades the account beyond the limits to which the investor has agreed.

To establish a claim for churning in futures markets, an investor must be able to demonstrate three elements by a preponderance of the evidence: (1) that the broker (or advisor) controlled the level and frequency of trading in the account; (2) that the overall volume of the broker's trading was excessive in light of the investor's trading objective; and (3) that the broker acted with the intent to defraud the investor, or acted with a reckless disregard for the investor's interests.

One way to satisfy the "excessive trading" element of proof is to compare the trading activity in an investor's account with professionally managed accounts (with similar investment objectives), where the account operators receive compensation based on performance and not on commissions. Because compensation is based on performance, these accounts do not have an incentive to churn. One study found the commission-to-equity ratio in actively managed commodity pools to be close to 19 percent annually.[12] Of course, this ratio can vary greatly depending on the fund's investment objective.

The introducing broker

An **introducing broker** (**IB**) is an individual or firm that accepts orders to trade futures, but that does not accept the funds from customers. Instead, the IB will have an established relationship with one or more FCMs, where the FCM processes the customer's trade, holds the customer's margin deposit, and provides accounting and documentation of the trades to the customer. Such an FCM is called the **carrying broker**. Customers of the IB must open accounts that are carried separately on the FCM's books. Essentially, the IB finds a customer, solicits that customer's business, and is responsible for maintaining customer relationships and servicing customer accounts. However, the IB does not process the trade or hold margin deposits. The IB and carrying broker share the commissions earned for executing trades. In 1989, the number of IBs peaked at about 1,800. By 2006, the number of IBs had fallen to about 1,700.

A 2004 survey of IB firms offers a business profile of a typical IB. Although some IBs operate on a large scale, the typical IB is a small, one-office operation with 50 active accounts and gross commissions of less than $200,000 per year. Customers of IBs tend to trade agricultural commodities and the primary reason they choose their IB is for service. Half the IBs surveyed had maintained a relationship with a single FCM for more than three years.[13]

The associated person

An **associated person** (**AP**) is an individual who solicits customer orders, customer funds, or customer participation in a commodity pool, or an individual who supervises anyone who makes such solicitations. Associated persons are the account executives and sales people who deal directly with customers on behalf of an FCM or IB. This broad category includes most of the professional individuals who make their livings in the futures industry. There were more than 55,000 APs in 1990, and slightly fewer than 52,000 by 2006.

The commodity trading advisor

A **commodity trading advisor** (**CTA**) is a person who directly or indirectly advises others regarding their futures trading. This category also applies to individuals who advise the public through written publications or other mass media. Thus, the writer of a futures newsletter who recommends certain positions in the futures market would be a CTA. In 2006, there were more than 2,600 CTAs registered in the United States.

The commodity pool operator

A **commodity pool operator** (**CPO**) is an individual or firm that pools together the funds of many investors into a single account for the purpose of trading futures and futures options. A **commodity pool** is the futures market analog to the securities market's mutual fund, in which individuals contribute funds for investment in stocks and bonds. Typically, a number of individuals contribute funds to form the commodity pool. The pool operator uses those funds to engage in futures trading designed to achieve a predetermined trading objective. The individuals who contributed funds to the pool own a share of the entire pool. There are nearly 1,800 CPOs in the United States.

Bunched orders and post-trade allocations

It is common practice for an account manager, such as a commodity trading advisor (CTA), to adminis-ter a single trading program for several clients. For good business reasons, the CTA may choose to place a single large order on behalf of all customers using the same trading program, as opposed to placing individual trades on behalf of each separate client. In the jargon of the futures industry, a collective trade on behalf of several accounts is called a bunched order. In placing a bunched order, the CTA may not be able to fill the entire order at a single price. In other words, the CTA may receive "split fills" on his order. This means that the CTA will have to allocate the filled trades among the various accounts after the trade has been executed. Inevitably, some customers will receive more favorable, and some less favorable, fills because of the fact that portions of the order were executed at different prices. Although there is nothing wrong with this practice *per se*, it presents the CTA with the opportunity to favor some accounts over others by allocating the more profitable trades to favored accounts. It is for this reason that federal commodities laws prohibit brokers, advisors, and other market professionals, except in specific instances, from allocating orders among accounts after trades have been executed. This prohibition is aimed at preventing such persons from abusing their discretion in allocating trades.

The CFTC regulations require that customers provide written instructions to account managers for bunched orders. Regulations require that post-trade allocations be fair and equitable, that they occur as soon as practicable after the entire transaction is executed, and that no account (or group of accounts) receives consistently favorable or unfavorable treatment. In addition, post-trade allocations must be completed "no later than a time sufficiently before the end of the day the order is executed to ensure that clearing records identify the ultimate customer for each trade." Regulations also require that the allocation method be sufficiently transparent so that regulators and outside auditors can verify the allocations.

The changing environment of futures markets

Rapid changes confront the futures markets in the United States. Most notable among these are the globalization of futures markets, the emergence of electronic trading systems, competition between exchanges, and the emergence of new products.

The globalization of futures markets

For decades, the United States has dominated the futures industry. Until recently, the totality of foreign exchanges generated a relatively insignificant trading volume compared to that of the United States. That has changed in the past 15 years, and all indications suggest that for-eign futures exchanges will continue to grow rapidly. Figure 2.7 shows how non-U.S. markets have grown more rapidly than U.S. markets in recent years. While U.S. exchanges continue to enjoy a commanding lead over the exchanges of any other nation, U.S. futures volume now accounts for less than half of the total world volume. Only a few years ago, the United States accounted for much more than half of the world futures volume. For example, in 1988 U.S. volume was 69.11 percent of the world total.

Most foreign exchanges are quite new. In spite of their recent start and relatively small size, the foreign exchanges present new competitive challenges to U.S.-based exchanges. This com-petition arises in virtually all types of futures contracts. Table 2.7 lists the ten most successful contracts traded worldwide by volume. It should be noted that the value of different contracts can vary greatly, and volume statistics do not account for this variation. From this table it can be seen that five of the top ten contracts are traded on foreign exchanges.

Figure 2.7   The U.S. and non-U.S. shares of the world volume of exchange-traded futures contracts

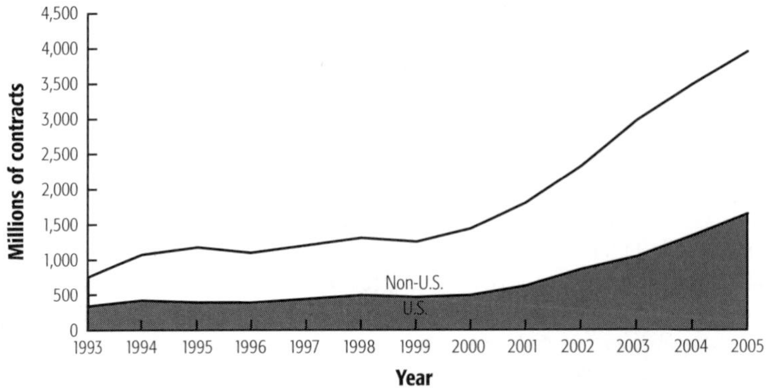

Table 2.7   The top ten futures contracts worldwide

Contract	Exchange	2005 Volume (millions of contracts)
Three-month Eurodollar	Chicago Mercantile Exchange	410.4
Euro Bund	Eurex	299.3
U.S. ten-year T-note	Chicago Board of Trade	215.9
E-mini® S&P 500®	Chicago Mercantile Exchange	207.1
Three-month Eurodollar	Euronext.liffe	166.8
Euro BOBL	Eurex	158.3
Euro Schatz	Eurex	141.2
DJ Euro Stoxx 50	Eurex	140.0
U.S. five-year T-note	Chicago Board of Trade	121.9
One-day interbank deposits	BM&F	121.3

Source: Futures Industry Association for the calendar year 2005

In 2003, international competition took a new form when Eurex announced that they were forming a subsidiary exchange in the United States, called Eurex U.S., to compete directly with U.S. exchanges.

A decade ago it was an easy task to determine whether a firm was domestic or foreign. One simply had to look for the physical location of the exchange's trading floor. Today, because of changes in communications technology and exchange ownership structures, the distinction between foreign and domestic exchanges has become blurred. Does the exchange reside where its computer server resides, where its corporate headquarters are located, where it is legally incorporated, or where its investors reside?

Today, we see many examples of exchanges that are truly global enterprises that cannot be easily classified by geography. For example, Eurex U.S. is headquartered in Chicago and is owned by a Delaware limited liability corporation called United States Futures Exchange, which is in turn 80 percent owned by a holding company that is ultimately owned by the SWX Swiss

Exchange and Deutsche Boerse AG, a publicly traded corporation. ICE Futures (formerly the International Petroleum Exchange) operates in London but is a wholly owned subsidiary of the Intercontinental Exchange, a Delaware corporation, headquartered in Atlanta. The CME is headquartered in Chicago but has Globex electronic trading terminals throughout the world. Likewise, Eurex is headquartered in Germany but has its terminals distributed globally. Many mutually owned U.S. futures exchanges have foreign members who own seats and who participate in exchange governance. For demutualized stockholder-owned exchanges such as the CME, and its parent CME Holdings, there is no way to know the nationality of shareholders.

U.S. trading of foreign products

For many years, the U.S. futures products have been traded globally. Since 1992, the year in which the CME launched its Globex trading system, traders around the globe have had direct electronic access to certain U.S. markets. Foreign futures products have also been available for trading by U.S. participants.

In general, U.S. laws and regulations do not restrict the offer and sale of foreign exchange-traded futures products in the United States. However, certain restrictions do apply for the offer and sale of futures on foreign stock indexes and futures on foreign government debt. The U.S. law requires that the CFTC approve foreign stock index futures products before they can be offered for sale in the United States. In 2006, 42 foreign stock index futures products had been approved for U.S. customers, including index futures based on the Dow Jones Euro STOXX 50, the FTSE 100, and the Nikkei 225. Futures contracts based on the debt obligations of the following countries have been approved for offer and sale to U.S. participants as of 2006: the United Kingdom, Canada, Japan, Australia, France, New Zealand, Austria, Denmark, Finland, the Netherlands, Switzerland, Germany, Italy, Ireland, Spain, Mexico, Brazil, Argentina, Venezuela, Belgium, and Sweden.

The U.S. futures exchanges also offer their own contracts based on foreign instruments. For example, the CME offers a futures contract on the Nikkei 225 and the CBOT offers futures contracts on the two-year and five-year German government notes (called the Schatz and BOBL, respectively), and the ten-year German Bund.

International competition in trading costs

With the ability of many traders to choose the country in which they wish to trade, exchange fees have become a matter of competitive concern. For example, we have seen that Eurodollars trade in a number of markets worldwide. As a result, exchanges compete for Eurodollar trading volume. One element of this competition is the fee that the exchange charges for executing an order. The large exchanges with well-established contracts have the most latitude in setting fees. Traders need those contracts and face powerful incentives to pay high fees in order to trade in those markets.

Ironically, the largest exchanges, those in the United States, have the lowest fees. These lower fees may reflect economies of scale in operating a futures exchange. The fees of European exchanges are somewhat higher, while the highest fees are found in Asian markets. For example, a member of the CBOT can trade a contract for 10 cents per side or less, depending on the commodity and trading platform. By contrast, a member of the Tokyo Commodity Exchange may face a fee as high as $1.5. Many observers see exchange fees as an important point of future competition among exchanges. Nonmember fees are typically much higher (e.g., five or six times higher) than member fees.

In the uncertain U.S. budget environment of recent years, some government officials floated the idea of a tax on futures transactions. However, representatives of the futures industry prevailed in their argument that such a tax would harm the competitiveness of U.S. markets by raising trading costs on U.S. futures products relative to the costs of futures products offered by foreign competitors.

Electronic futures trading

From the beginning of organized futures exchanges in the mid-1800s until a few years ago, the system of open outcry was the only method of futures trading. However, since the late 1990s, the dominance of open-outcry trading has been challenged by electronic trading systems. As Figure 2.8 shows, in 1998 open-outcry trading accounted for over 95 percent of all U.S. futures trading volume: by 2005, open-outcry trading accounted for just over half of all U.S. futures trading volume. For many financial futures, open outcry accounts for only a small percentage of trades. Although the volume of open-outcry trading has declined *relative* to electronic trading volume since 1998, Figure 2.8 also shows that it has been growing in *absolute* terms. Many knowledgeable observers expect the role of open-outcry trading to continue its decline relative to electronic trading in coming years. However, open-outcry trading has many proponents, and it may continue as a viable trading mechanism in some markets even as electronic trading volume grows. It is fair to say that electronic trading systems are rapidly changing the entire face of the futures markets around the world.

The advent of electronic trading systems also promises to be an important element in determining how futures exchanges are structured. One motive for the conversion of not-for-profit mutual exchanges to shareholder-owned exchanges is to create an institutional structure that can rapidly accommodate technological change. The problem exchanges face in adopting new technology can best be seen in the Chicago markets, where a high proportion of members are individuals who trade for their own accounts. Their livelihoods depend upon the trading acumen that they have developed through their years in the trading pits. Electronic trading systems threaten to make those open-outcry skills obsolete. Not surprisingly, these members

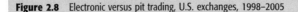

Figure 2.8   Electronic versus pit trading, U.S. exchanges, 1998–2005

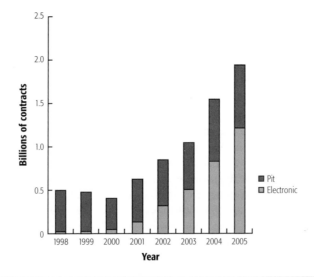

have resisted any threats to the system of open outcry. Having the exchange organized as a shareholder-owned for-profit enterprise provides a means of coping with traders who, for their own private reasons, do not want to adopt new technology that would enhance the profitability of the exchange: the buyout.

Compared to open-outcry pit trading, launching new contracts on an electronic trading platform is definitely cheaper. Many traders also believe that electronic systems are operationally superior to pit trading. Further, there are many different electronic trading systems, all of which have their own features. No matter what one believes about the virtues of open outcry versus electronic trading, it is clear that electronic trading is here to stay. Because electronic trading is largely driven by rapidly evolving technology, we can expect further change in this area in the coming years.

In 1992 the CME launched Globex, its electronic trading platform for futures. The trading volume on Globex during its first decade was small compared to the open-outcry trading volume. However, Globex trading now plays a significant role in the CME's overall operation. Some of the CME's most successful contracts, such as the E-mini® version of its S&P 500® futures contract, trade exclusively on Globex throughout the day and evening. Other Globex contracts, such as the three-month Eurodollar contract, trade side-by-side with open-outcry contracts, with pit traders monitoring Globex prices using handheld devices. Still other Globex contracts trade only after open-outcry trading hours.

The CBOT was originally a partner in Globex but eventually decided to form its own electronic system. Throughout the 1990s, the CBOT tried to create its own electronic trading platform, without success. In August 2000, the CBOT entered into a joint venture alliance with Eurex to create a/c/e (Alliance/Chicago/Eurex). This alliance was abandoned three years later and in November 2003 the CBOT entered into a licensing agreement to use the Liffe Connect electronic trading platform. Liffe Connect is designed and built by the Euronext.liffe exchange. The vast majority of trades in financial futures contracts at the CBOT now take place electronically. The CBOT also serves as the host for other North American futures exchanges using the Liffe Connect platform.

Outside the United States, electronic trading dominates open-outcry trading. For example, in 2004, Eurex was the world's largest derivatives exchange, and it only trades electronically. Similarly, in 1998 the LIFFE, now a subsidiary of Eurnext Liffe, decided to abandon pit trading for its financial futures and move to a totally electronic trading system.

With the development of electronic trading systems, futures trading on some contracts continue almost 24 hours a day. For example, Eurex U.S. trades futures contracts on U.S. Treasury products in a daily session that runs from 7 p.m. Central time to 4 p.m. the next day. At the CME, Eurodollar futures begin trading on Globex at 5 p.m. Chicago time, and trading continues until 4 p.m. the next day. During the Globex trading session, open-outcry trading of Eurodollar futures occurs between 7:20 a.m. and 2:00 p.m.

Increasingly, the intellectual property associated with new electronic trading technology has become an important asset for exchanges to hold as they develop and license their products to other exchanges. For example, Euronext.liffe developed its Liffe Connect electronic trading platform and licenses its use to the CBOT, the KCBT, the MGEX, and the Tokyo International Futures Exchange. For Euronext.liffe, their trading platform is one of their most important products. In order for futures exchanges to protect their investments in new trading technology, and to protect the licensing potential of their inventions, exchanges have become increasingly attentive to possibilities for the patenting, trademarking, or copyrighting of their intellectual property. In the late 1990s a new type of business model emerged in the futures industry, with exchanges holding intellectual property related to trading technology, with an eye toward licensing the use of the property to others or suing infringers for damages. Futures exchanges

Figure 2.9   The Jennings Trading Pit Patent, 1878

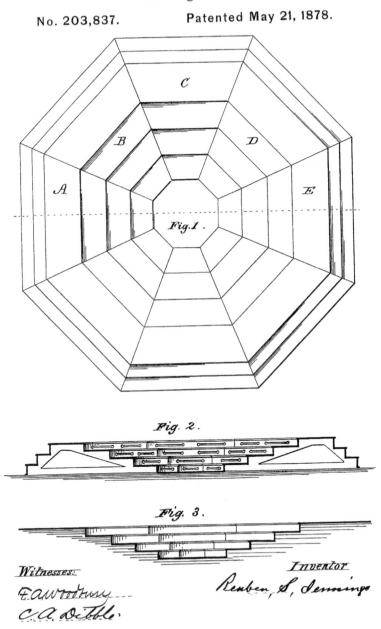

Source: Reproduced, with thanks, from the United States Patent and Trademark Office

are being forced to think more carefully about intellectual property law and its potential application to their trading technology.

Perhaps the most noteworthy example of this business model is eSpeed, Inc., a subsidiary of Cantor Fitzgerald L.P. and an operator of a number of electronic trading platforms. eSpeed has acquired a portfolio of patents used to support its technology licensing business. In April 2001, eSpeed paid $1.75 million to acquire the rights to U.S. patent number 4,903,201 covering automated futures trading systems, also known as the Wagner patent. In August 2001, eSpeed sued the CME, the CBOT, and the NYMEX for patent infringement. In August 2002, the CME and the CBOT settled the eSpeed patent litigation by each agreeing to pay eSpeed $15 million over a five-year period. In December 2003, the NYMEX resolved its share of the dispute by agreeing to pay eSpeed $8 million over a three-year period.

In 2004, eSpeed found itself being sued for patent infringement by Trading Technologies International, a Chicago-based company that holds a patent on a software platform that allows screen traders to see a range of bids and offers in the market before placing an order.

Patents on trading technology are nothing new to the futures industry. In 1877, Reuben S. Jennings of Chicago submitted to the U.S. Patent Office his claim for the invention of the trading pit. The invention was patented on May 21, 1878, as U.S. patent number 203,837. The patent states that the pit "furnishes sufficient standing-room, where persons may stand and conveniently trade with persons in any other part of the pit or platforms. It has great acoustic advantages over a flat floor . . ." Immediately after receiving his patent, Jennings served notice to futures exchanges, demanding a royalty payment from those using the trading-pit technology. A copy of Jennings' patent diagram is shown in Figure 2.9.

Out trades

An "out trade" occurs when a discrepancy exists between the trade data submitted by the broker representing the buyer and the trade data submitted by the broker representing the seller. Out trades are discovered when a clearinghouse matches trades—the first step in the clearing process. Brokers will attempt to reconcile the discrepancy and resubmit the trade for clearing before the opening of the next trading session. If an agreement cannot be reached between the two brokers, then the dispute will be settled by an appropriate exchange committee or by a predetermined procedure. Out trades are common and traders maintain error accounts to handle positions they may acquire as a result of out trades. Out trades are often resolved by brokers compromising and exchanging money to resolve their disputes. Traders who consistently use out-trade procedures to their advantage face a powerful sanction: other traders will refuse to trade with them.

There are two types of out trades: those caused by a discrepancy in the reported price and those caused by a discrepancy in the reported quantity. Exchange rules usually require the brokers to choose between the trade data submitted by the buyer and that submitted by the seller. Any compromises or adjustments are handled by side payments between the brokers. If the brokers cannot resolve the discrepancy, exchange rules may enforce a predetermined solution. For example, at the CBOT, in cases in which there is an unresolved discrepancy about quantity, the higher of the quantity figures will be used for clearing. In cases in which there is an unresolved discrepancy about price, by rule the buyer's price will be used. Exchange rules only facilitate timely clearing—they do not make the dispute go away. Brokers often split the difference with cash side payments, or bring the dispute to arbitration before an exchange committee designed to handle member disputes.

An out trade is part of the "frictions" of trading. It is costly for all involved and great effort is expended to economize on this cost. Some exchanges use cameras, which may help in resolving disputes. The exchange committees assigned to resolving disputes between members are another mechanism for economizing on this cost of using the market. An out trade is a feature of open-outcry trading. As trading volume continues to migrate from open-outcry trading to electronic trading platforms, out trades should diminish. In an electronic trading environment, out trades should be impossible.

However, even though out trades may be impossible in an electronic trading environment, other kinds of trading mistakes can occur. So-called "fat finger" errors may result from a trader mistakenly adding an extra zero to an order before hitting the "send" button. Sometimes these inadvertent trades can roil markets. Therefore, supervisors of electronic trading platforms have devised "error trade" policies and procedures for "busting," or canceling, transactions that are the result of clear error. The rules require that a transaction be challenged immediately after it has occurred. If the trade is busted, the party that committed the error may still be liable for any costs incurred by other traders as a result of the error. These disputes are handled by exchange committees devoted to hearing membership disputes.

Exchange competition

Within the futures industry there are two levels of exchange competition. The first level is competition between traders on the exchange floor, or electronic trading system, who make bids and extend offers for futures contracts. This type of competition is often cited as an example of unfettered free enterprise and pure competition. This view was memorably expressed in a scene from Paramount Studio's 1983 hit movie *Trading Places*. In the scene, Dan Ackroyd's character remarks to Eddie Murphy's character, as they prepare to enter the exchange floor, that futures trading represents "the last bastion of pure capitalism left on Earth." Yet it is important to note that transactions in these markets are highly regulated—and in a manner quite different from any government regulation there might be. Futures exchanges regulate in great detail trading practices, what can be traded, the terms of clearance and settlement, and standards of business conduct. Futures exchanges also impose sanctions against those who infringe upon exchange rules. Apparently, for perfect competition to exist, an intricate system of rules and regulations is needed to lower the cost of trading, to increase trading volume, and to promote overall trading efficiency. Futures exchanges adopt rules and regulations necessary to promote vigorous competition in the markets that they host.

The second level of competition exists between futures exchanges to become the market host. Although several exchanges may launch similar contracts in direct competition with each other, typically only one (if any) exchange succeeds in establishing a viable market for the product. Once a market is established at a particular exchange, the cost of switching from the established, liquid market to a new, illiquid market can be prohibitively high. There are only a few instances in futures market history in which an established contract has been pulled away to be hosted by a competing exchange.[14] We rarely see multiple exchanges offering similar contracts and competing head-to-head. Trading volume tends to migrate to one exchange and stay there. Because exchanges know that switching costs are high, there are tremendous advantages to being the first exchange to offer a contract.

Occasionally, direct exchange competition does result in trading volume migrating from one exchange to another. But such occurrences are rare and noteworthy when they do occur. Perhaps the most well-known episode of trading volume migrating from an established exchange occurred in 1998, in the case of the ten-year German bond contract (called the Bund). Prior to 1998, Bund futures were the flagship contract of the LIFFE (now Euronext.liffe), where nearly all Bund futures were traded. Starting in 1997, Eurex launched its own Bund futures contract, and by August 1998 nearly 100 percent of Bund futures trading volume resided at Eurex. The pace of migration away from LIFFE to Eurex accelerated as Eurex's share of trading volume approached the 50 percent mark. At that point the market "tipped," meaning that Eurex had now become the more liquid market, and trading volume quickly migrated away from LIFFE and toward Eurex. As a result, Eurex trading accounted for nearly 100 percent of volume and LIFFE's volume dwindled to nothing.

Eurex was able to win the competition for the Bund contract for four reasons. First, Eurex, as a German-based exchange, already had substantial trading volume in futures contracts on other German debt instruments. The Bund contract complemented these other contracts. Second, Eurex introduced a new fee structure that gave volume discounts to brokers who directed trading volume to the exchange. LIFFE responded with competing volume discounts of its own, but only after it was too late. Third, Eurex, an all-electronic exchange, had recently gained regulatory approval to install trading terminals in the United States. Trading volume from the United States formed a substantial share of Eurex's volume. Finally, German banks held a substantial stake in Eurex and directed their substantial trading volume in Bund futures to Eurex.[15]

As demonstrated by the competitive advantage that Eurex enjoyed as a result of offering an array of German debt instruments, one way for exchanges to compete is by trading contracts in a group of related, complementary, contracts. The CBOT trades contracts in the soybean complex, offering contracts on soybeans, soymeal, and soyoil. Trading contracts on all three gives traders the opportunity to trade one contract against the others. With all three contracts trading, there is little opportunity for another exchange to enter the field. If the CBOT traded only the soybean contract, then other exchanges might try to enter the market by offering contracts on soymeal or soyoil in an effort to draw away the business from the CBOT. To date, the CBOT has been successful in maintaining its dominant position in the soybean complex. No other exchange has been successful in this area, although the MidAmerica Commodity Exchange at one time tried to compete in soybeans by offering smaller (1,000-bushel versus 5,000-bushel) contracts.

Another example of the grouping phenomenon can be drawn from the interest rate futures market. Successful contracts are traded on interest rate futures at the CBOT and the International Monetary Market (IMM) of the Chicago Mercantile Exchange. The IMM trades contracts on only very short maturity instruments, such as three-month Eurodollar time deposits. The CBOT, by contrast, trades contracts on instruments of longer maturities, such as ten-year Treasury notes.

Another way in which exchanges compete is through specializing and attempting to develop market niches. For some commodities, futures contracts trade on a number of exchanges. In such cases, some product differentiation usually makes the competition less than direct. A good example of this occurs in the case of wheat. Wheat contracts are traded on the CBOT, the Kansas City Board of Trade (KCBT), and the Minneapolis Grain Exchange (MGEX). These futures contracts, however, specify somewhat different kinds of wheat. By specifying different deliverable grades of wheat, the exchanges may carve out their own market niches. For example, the Kansas City contract is written for No. 2 Hard Winter wheat, the MGEX contract is for U.S. No. 2 Northern Spring wheat, and the CBOT contract calls for delivery of one of the following types of wheat: No. 2 Soft Red, No. 2 Hard Red Winter, No. 2 Dark Northern Spring, or No. 1 Northern Spring. Since the kind of wheat differs slightly in each case, the exchanges avoid direct competition.

For wheat, another important factor in keeping contracts alive on three exchanges is the geographic distance. Each contract must specify how and where delivery can occur. The CBOT, Kansas City, and Minneapolis contracts all call for delivery at different places. If we actually consider the cost of taking delivery, the difference between a Kansas City and a Minneapolis delivery is very important, since the bulk of wheat makes its transportation quite expensive.

Futures exchanges also compete with related markets. For example, in many cases OTC swap contracts are economically identical to exchange-traded futures contracts. In fact, many dealers advertise the fact that the swaps they are offer are "lookalike" swaps, meaning that the swap's contract terms closely correspond with the contract terms of futures contracts. Although exchanges often view swap contracts as substitutes for exchange-traded futures contracts, the relationship can be complementary as well. Oftentimes, swap dealers turn to the futures market to hedge the risk in their swap portfolios. The best example of this is found with dealers of interest rate swaps who hedge the risks of their deal-making in the Eurodollar futures market. One reason why the CME's Eurodollar contract has been so successful is that swap dealers can rely on it to hedge their risks.

Another example of where futures exchanges compete with other (nonfutures) markets is in stock index products. For many years, the cheapest way to trade an entire stock index was to use a futures product based on a stock index. However, the development of the market for exchange-traded funds (ETFs) in the late 1990s means that there is now another avenue for investors to trade an entire stock index. An ETF is a transferable trust certificate that represents the shares of stock in an index. For example, a SPDR (Standard and Poor's Depository Receipt) is an ETF on the S&P 500. ETFs are offered by securities exchanges.

Futures exchanges also compete with some commodity price stabilization programs and crop insurance programs offered by the federal government. In recognition of this possibility, the 1996 Federal Agricultural Improvement and Reform (FAIR) Act authorized the United States Department of Agriculture (USDA) to determine whether futures and options could provide producers with reasonable protection from the financial risks of fluctuations in price, yield, and income inherent in the production and marketing of agricultural commodities.

To understand how exchanges compete, it is helpful to understand the economic incentives to which futures exchanges are responding. First, we must recognize that a futures exchange is a business firm that creates markets. The creation of markets is an entrepreneurial activity that entails substantial costs, such as gathering information, searching for trading partners, bargaining, and enforcing contracts. Futures exchanges economize on these costs by specifying the rules of trading, the terms of exchange contracts, the conditions of exchange membership, and the technology employed for order entry and trade execution.

By viewing futures exchanges as firms that create markets, we can see more clearly some of the ways in which exchanges compete, amongst which are innovation in the design of the contracts they offer, the technology they employ, the fees they charge, the business models they adopt, and the quality of trading information they provide to investors.

Exchanges also compete directly for the exclusive right to trade particular contracts. For example, exchanges bid for the exclusive right to use the S&P name in the creation of S&P stock index futures contracts in North America. For more than 20 years, the CME has prevailed in this competition. Likewise, the CBOT outbid its competitors to win the exclusive right to create Dow Jones futures contracts based on the Dow Jones trademarks. Exclusivity rights come up for bid periodically. Bidding for the exclusive right to trade is true competition, even though the exclusivity embedded in the agreement will necessarily mean that the contract will trade at only a single exchange. The "franchise-bidding model" is a credible way for competition to exist and flourish.

Still, if the final result of competition between exchanges is that trading volume migrates to a single exchange, isn't this bad? The answer is "Not necessarily." Centralized trading—that is, trading on a single exchange—can actually be efficient in the sense that it reduces the economy-wide costs of producing the service. In futures markets, the network effects of centralized trading lower trading costs to everyone by increasing liquidity and reducing so-called transaction costs; that is, the costs of searching for trading partners, bargaining, enforcing contracts, resolving disputes, and so on.

Having trading volume migrate to a single, dominant exchange raises antitrust concerns. However, antitrust law is aimed at deterring market dominance that is achieved or extended through anticompetitive conduct. Under antitrust law, the important question is whether an exchange's dominant position was achieved through open market competition; that is, by offering a superior product, service, or business model. Anticompetitive conduct refers to the creation of artificial barriers to prevent potential competitors from entering the industry. Oftentimes, these artificial barriers are created by government as a result of lobbying by aspiring monopolists. In other words, under antitrust law there is nothing wrong with being the dominant futures exchange as long as the exchange's dominant position was achieved through open competition.

Is it possible that the dominant position of futures exchanges in trading particular contracts reduces their incentive to innovate? This does not appear to be the case, as one of the most fertile areas of exchange competition is through innovation, particularly innovation in contract design and other forms of intellectual property. Exchanges know that if they are successful in launching a new product they will likely have a dominant position for many years to come. If this is so, exchanges will have a powerful incentive to innovate, because they know they will reap the exclusive reward from their efforts if they are successful.

Market transparency and competition

The word "transparency" can mean different things to different people. In the corporate finance world, people use the term to refer to the degree to which a firm's accounting choices help investors understand the true value of items on the firm's balance sheet. In the world of futures markets, "transparency" refers to the degree to which a futures exchange publicly disseminates real-time information on transaction prices, quotations, order flow, and other market variables. In the United States, the United Kingdom, and other domains, the level of government-mandated market transparency has become a source of contentious public debate. A central element of this debate is the extent to which market forces can be relied upon to supply the level of transparency demanded by the public. The debate has intensified due to recent innovations in trading technology that allow for the capture and dissemination of vast amounts of market information at low cost.

Transparency can be viewed as one dimension of competition between competing marketplaces. Futures exchanges compete in many other dimensions too: through their contract offerings, their technology employed for order entry and trade execution, their fee structure, and their business models. As an example of how futures exchanges compete based on their transparency, consider the experience of the New York Mercantile Exchange (NYMEX), the world's major market for energy futures and options. Following the collapse of Enron, many participants in the off-exchange, OTC derivatives market (in which Enron had been a major player) complained about the lack of transparency in the OTC market. At the same time, the NYMEX saw its trading volumes soar 35 percent in the first six months following the Enron collapse. The then-president of the NYMEX, Robert Collins, explained the rise in volume this way: "People are looking at us as a flight to quality. We give customers the benefit of transparency."[16] In other words, traders in the energy market who valued transparency voted with their feet and moved their trading volume from the OTC to the NYMEX.

Product innovation and contract success

We have seen that exchanges tend to specialize in certain groups of commodities. Yet they also compete in fringe areas where their successful contracts overlap. Relatively little is known about what makes a contract succeed or fail. This is an important question for the exchanges, because the introduction of a new futures contract requires substantial expense. The contract must be designed, trading must be organized, and the contract must be promoted through advertising. To commit all of these resources and still fail is very frustrating. Yet, by recent estimates, less than 50 percent of new futures contracts remain viable after three years and only 20 percent remain viable after ten years.[17] This low success rate for new contracts indicates how much remains to be learned in the areas of contract design and competition.

There are at least ten factors that increase the chance of a contract's success. First, there needs to be a large cash market. Usually, futures trading starts only for goods for which there is a well-established market for the cash good. For example, stock index futures trading was attractive because of the active market in stocks. Second, there must be price volatility. If the price does not fluctuate, there can be little interest in trading on the future price of the underlying good. In 1984, a futures contract on the Consumer Price Index (CPI) was launched. It failed in two years, perhaps due to a lack of volatility. Even in periods of high inflation, the CPI may not be particularly volatile. However, the contract launch occurred at an unlucky time of low and stable inflation. Third, there needs to be good information on cash market prices. As we discuss in Chapter 3, there is an intimate relationship between cash market prices and futures market prices. Traders in both markets look to the other for information about the present and future direction of prices. In essence, traders trade futures contracts against the cash market goods. This makes good information about cash prices essential. Fourth, there must be a lack of close substitutes for the new futures contract. If a successful contract already exists for a particular good, traders will not want to switch to a new and untried similar contract. Traders like to trade in liquid contracts, so they will likely stay with a liquid existing contract rather than try an unproven and illiquid similar futures contract.

Fifth, traders not only trade the futures contract in relation to the cash market, but they also trade one futures against another. Therefore, a contract has an improved chance of success if there is already a similar, but not too similar, existing contract. For example, the CBOT lists futures contracts on ten-year Treasury notes and five-year Treasury notes. The two are closely related, so the presence of both stimulates spread trading. However, they are sufficiently distinct so that each contract is viable on its own. Sixth, the contract must be designed well. In 1975, the CBOT listed a contract on mortgage interest rates, the Government National Mortgage Association (GNMA) contract. The contract suffered from poor design, because one set of traders was interested in high-coupon GNMAs while a second group wanted to use the market for low-coupon GNMAs. This conflict of trading interest contributed to the demise of the contract.[18] Seventh, there must be strong support from exchange members. When an exchange launches a contract, the exchange members need to support the new contract with active trading. If the members of the exchange are unwilling to trade the contract, the market will lack the liquidity necessary to attract traders from outside of the exchange. Other factors on the list, such as price volatility, the potential for spread trading, and an active cash market, help to stimulate floor trader interest. Eighth, there should be a large deliverable supply of the cash market good. With a large deliverable supply, no one party can control the cash good and affect price. Ninth, there should be an absence of legal barriers. In the early 1980s, the CBOT attempted to list a futures contract based on the Dow Jones Industrial Average of 30 blue chip stocks. Dow Jones successfully sued to prevent the listing altogether. It was not until 1997 that the CBOT was able to gain the permission of Dow Jones to form futures products based on the Dow Jones stock indexes. Finally, the underlying good should be homogenous, or "fungible." Fungibility is important for ensuring a uniform and large deliverable supply. If the underlying good varies tremendously in quality, for example, the delivery process will be impaired.

In spite of these apparent determinants of futures market success, much is still unknown.[19] Among the exchanges themselves there is considerable consternation about what makes a futures contract succeed. More often than not, new contracts fail in spite of the best efforts of the exchanges. Other times, exchanges inadvertently stumble onto successful contracts. For example, in 1998 the CME created a smaller version of its successful S&P 500 futures contract. This smaller contract, called the E-mini, was one-fifth the size of the regular S&P 500 futures contract and was aimed at individual investors. It was traded exclusively on the CME's Globex electronic trading system. The CME did not have great hopes for this contract, but figured it would bring in some additional retail trades. The CME fully expected that institutional investors would continue to use the larger floor-traded contract. To their amazement, institutional volume migrated to the smaller contract and the E-mini became tremendously successful, while the established S&P 500 futures contract withered.

   The story of the CME's Eurodollar futures market points out another path to success. Initially, the CME viewed OTC interest rate swap transactions based on the London Inter Bank Offering Rate (LIBOR) as pure substitutes for the Eurodollar contract. As a result of this view, the CME viewed interest rate swaps as a threat to the survival of the Eurodollar futures contract. However, the exchange soon discovered that swap dealers used the Eurodollar futures markets as a way to hedge the risks from their dealing activities. In fact, the two markets were complementary and swap activity spawned new trades in the Eurodollar futures pit. Largely because of the participation of swap dealers, the CME's Eurodollar futures contract is now viewed as one of the most successful futures contracts ever developed.

How does a futures exchange make money?

A futures exchange is a business. Although many exchanges are organized as "not-for-profit" businesses, this does not mean that the owners of the exchange—that is, the members—are unconcerned about making money. The term "not-for-profit" simply means that earnings are not distributed as cash dividends to the members. Instead of distributing earnings, not-for-profit exchanges invest the retained earnings in a variety of ways to improve the productivity and comforts of their members. The earnings are invested in improving the quality of the trading facilities, hiring professional staff to run the exchanges' day-to-day operations, and investing in the development of new futures contracts. In the past there have been numerous productive uses for the retained earnings, so that the not-for-profit structure of the exchanges was not a constraint on wealth maximization. Over the past decade, however, exchange members have become more skeptical about investing more retained earnings into exchange operations. More and more exchanges are "demutualizing" and becoming "for profit" businesses, so that free cash flows can be returned to the members. In December 2002, the CME, which had already demutualized, conducted the first initial public offering of shares by a futures exchange. These shares are traded at both the New York Stock Exchange (NYSE) and NASDAQ under the ticker symbol CME.

   Shown below are excerpts from the 2005 consolidated statement of income for the CME. The sources of income and revenue are characteristic of most major exchanges. In particular, notice that the sale of real-time data—that is, the quotation data fees—represents the second largest source of income. At other exchanges, such as the CBOT and the MGEX, rent from real estate holdings is a major contributor to revenue.

Revenues	
Clearing and transaction fees	$696,201,000
Quotation data fees	68,730,000
Globex access fees	18,866,000
Communication fees	8,964,000
Investment income	31,441,000
Securities lending interest income	58,725,000
Other	22,628,000
Expenses	
Compensation and benefits	$179,594,000
Occupancy	22,525,000
Professional fees and licenses	44,832,000
Communications and computers and software maintenance	57,935,000
Depreciation and amortization	64,917,000
Marketing, advertising, and public relations	13,278,000
Other	23,054,000

Market manipulation

The most dramatic dislocation in a futures market occurs in a market manipulation. Manipulating the price of a futures contract is a violation of the CEA. Section 9(a) of the CEA makes it a felony punishable by a fine of up to $1 million ($500,000 for individuals) and imprisonment of not more than five years, for any person found to "manipulate or attempt to manipulate the price of any commodity in interstate commerce, or for future delivery on or subject to the rules of any contract market, or to corner or attempt to corner any such commodity . . ." Market manipulation not only cheats other traders, but it also impairs the marketplace. First, other traders are cheated because the manipulation forces them to trade at a price that is not economically justified. In general, markets function properly when prices in the market represent the true equilibrium value of the good being traded. By definition, if the price is manipulated it cannot be at its equilibrium level. Second, a manipulation also impairs the market because honest traders flee markets in which prices do not correspond to the true economic value of the good being traded. If honest traders abandon the futures market, the market cannot serve its social functions. The market will not serve its price discovery function because the prices in the market are manipulated prices. Also, the market does not provide a means for transferring risk, because honest traders are afraid to participate in the market. For these reasons, manipulation is among the worst fates that can befall a market.[20]

Since 1922, futures markets in the United States have been subject to federal regulation, a primary purpose of which is to deter manipulation in futures markets. One curious feature of the Commodity Exchange Act, and the regulations promulgated under the Act, is that "manipulation" is referred to nearly 100 times without ever once being defined. The lack of a definition is not surprising, because the meaning of the word is so broad. Attempts to precisely define the term inevitably dissolve into circular logic: a manipulated price is an artificial price; an artificial price is one that has been manipulated.

Deterring manipulation in Tudor England

Throughout the history of financial markets, one can find attempts to deter market manipulation.[21] The Bible (Proverbs 11: 26) condemned grain traders who withheld corn from the market in an attempt to gain advantage.[22] In Tudor England, the Statute of Victuals required all sellers of commodities to sell for a reasonable price. Royal decrees prohibited trading practices that were deemed to be manipulative. Prohibited practices included "forestalling," "regrating," and "engrossing" in the sale of grain or other "victuals." Forestalling was the practice of hoarding grain in order to cause the price to rise. Regrating was the practice of a trader buying goods and reselling them in the same market at a higher price. Engrossing was the practice of buying up a significant amount of a commodity in order to drive up its price. Violators were prosecuted and punished by the Star Chamber, the institution that had the authority to enforce manipulation prohibitions. Violators were fined and pilloried. The prohibitions were repealed by Parliament in 1844, but the repeal did not apply to "the offence of knowingly and fraudulently spreading or conspiring to spread any false rumour with intent to enhance or decry the price of any goods or merchandise . . ."

Because the statute does not define manipulation, it has been left to the federal courts to identify the characteristics and attributes of an unlawful manipulation. Federal courts use a four-pronged test, which has evolved though the common law, to determine by a preponderance of the evidence whether a set of facts are consistent with an alleged manipulation. The four elements of proof in manipulation cases are:

(1)   that the accused had the ability to influence market prices;
(2)   that the accused specifically intended to do so;
(3)   that an artificial price occurred; and
(4)   that the accused caused an artificial price.

   Some critics have argued that the real-world use of this four-part test by courts and the CFTC makes it extremely difficult to meet any one of these standards, let alone all standards simultaneously.[23] The cost and difficulty of meeting these elements of proof diminishes the effectiveness of what should (in theory at least) be one of the most effective and efficient tools for deterring manipulation: the certain application of after-the-fact sanctions for anyone caught manipulating or attempting to manipulate a futures market. In addition to after-the-fact sanctions, there are other methods that regulators use to achieve deterrence. For example, the CFTC employs a staff of economists and futures market specialists who conduct real-time market surveillance of the positions of traders. The CFTC also has emergency powers to force would-be manipulators to liquidate their positions. Other anti-manipulation tools of regulators and the exchanges (which are self-regulatory organizations) include position limits and contract design elements that make manipulation more costly for the would-be manipulator. Futures exchanges also conduct surveillance of their markets in order to deter manipulation before it occurs.
   The history of futures markets has revealed many imaginative attempts to manipulate markets. We discuss three types of manipulation below: market power manipulation, false report manipulation, and micromanipulation.

Market power manipulation: corners, squeezes, and hugs

   In a market power manipulation, the trader has control of the underlying commodity and a large futures position that enables his actions to corner or squeeze the market. While various commentators use somewhat different definitions, we will define a **corner** as a successful effort by a trader or group of traders to influence the price of a futures contract by intentionally acquiring market power in the deliverable supply of the underlying good while simultaneously acquiring a large long futures position. If the deliverable supply is captured by long futures traders, it becomes unavailable to shorts for delivery. This means that the shorts will be forced to settle their contracts with the longs at inflated prices.
   In a market **squeeze**, a trader achieves effective control over the price of a futures contract due to disruptions in the supply of the cash commodity. The manipulative part of a squeeze arises when the trader uses this circumstance to create artificially high prices. The disruptions that create the squeeze need not be due to actions of the controlling trader, but might originate from other natural forces, such as the weather. A **hug** is a mild squeeze.
   Corners, squeezes, and hugs boil down to instances of exercising market power. In theory, this market power can be exercised on either the long side or the short side of the market. In practice, however, market power is almost exclusively used to drive prices up so as to benefit the holder of a long position.
   Exchanges design futures contracts with large deliverable supplies to lessen the chances of corners, squeezes, or hugs. Exchanges may use a system of delivery price differentials to expand the supply eligible for delivery. Exchanges also use position limits to reduce the chances that a trader can acquire enough market power to move the price to an artificial level. Corners, squeezes, and hugs are bad for business and contracts prone to these dislocations have little chance for success.
   As a practical matter, the costs and risks associated with a market power manipulation can be formidable for the manipulator. To begin with, buying up large quantities of the underlying stocks of the cash commodity requires considerable investment. If the manipulation is not

successful, the manipulation strategy will yield only costs and no benefits. Even if the manipulation is successful, the costs to the manipulator can be high. After the manipulation has run its course, the manipulator must dispose of the stocks he has acquired to corner the market; that is, he must **bury the corpse**. If the manipulation is successful, stocks of the underlying commodity will flow to the delivery point in response to the high price. This means that the price at the delivery point will plunge once the manipulator sells his stocks into the glutted market. Burying the corpse can be the most significant cost of executing a manipulation and can make an attempted manipulation self-defeating. A foresighted manipulator might attempt to solve this problem by selling distant contracts at the artificially high price to dispose of the corpse.

A successful market power manipulation leaves telltale footprints that are characteristic of a manipulation episode. The burying-the-corpse effect—that is, the collapse of spot prices (both in absolute terms and in relation to deferred contracts and spot prices at other locations) following the termination of manipulative actions—is one such characteristic footprint. Investigators, and the courts, will use the collapse in prices to help prove that the price during the alleged manipulation was artificial.

Stephen Craig Pirrong has identified other characteristics of a successful (long) market power manipulation, which include the following:[24]

(1) The cash market price at delivery locations specified in the futures contract is abnormally high relative to prices at nondelivery locations.
(2) The price of the delivery-eligible grade of a commodity rises relative to the prices of nondelivery grades of the same commodity.
(3) The spread relationship between related commodities (e.g., corn versus soybeans) is distorted.
(4) Unusually large shipments of the commodity are diverted to the delivery point immediately prior to and during the delivery period; and shipments from the delivery point are unusually small as traders amass stocks to make delivery.

The case of the shortsighted shorts

Do shorts have an obligation to avoid being victims of market squeezes? Possibly, or at least according to one court ruling. In October 1957, Volkart Brothers Inc., a large cotton dealer and a member of the New York Cotton Exchange (NYCE) and the New Orleans Cotton Exchange, held long futures positions in delivery month contracts at both exchanges exceeding all certified stocks of cotton eligible for delivery against the contracts by almost 100 percent. Volkart held its long position throughout the delivery month, and on the last trading day shorts found that they either had to pay a substantial premium to Volkart in order to offset their futures positions or pay a huge premium in the cash market in order to obtain the cotton they needed to fulfill their delivery obligations. The squeezed shorts alleged that Volkart had manipulated the delivery process and the case went to court.

In its defense, Volkart argued that the shorts only had themselves to blame for being placed in such a vulnerable position. Volkart noted that there were great quantities of cotton stocks at delivery locations and that shorts could have had these stocks certificated in preparation for fulfilling their delivery obligations. Under this expanded definition of deliverable supply, Volkart's long position did not dominate the deliverable stocks, meaning that there could be no manipulation. The Court of Appeals held that the squeeze occurred only because the shorts were negligent in failing to seek certification of cotton stocks in a timely matter.[25] Volkart was exonerated.

In other cases, courts have not accepted the expanded definition of deliverable stocks beyond certificated stocks, meaning that the value of the Volkart case as a precedent is unclear.

(5)   There are unusually large shipments of the commodity away from the delivery point at the end of a manipulation and unusually small inflows to the delivery location.

(6)   The price of the manipulated contract is abnormally high relative to the price of adjacent and deferred contacts (e.g., the price of the front-month contract versus the prices of back-month contracts).

Below, we discuss one proven market power manipulation and one alleged market power manipulation. First, we consider a manipulation in silver by the Hunt brothers of Dallas and their co-conspirators: this manipulation occurred in 1979–80. Second, we examine an alleged manipulation of soybeans that occurred in 1989. At that time, the large grain-trading firm Ferruzzi Finanziaria held 7 million bushels of soybeans, and the exchanges and the CFTC moved to force Ferruzzi to liquidate. In federal court, the Hunt brothers were found to have manipulated silver prices. However, Ferruzzi has never been brought to trial, and the manipulation in soybeans has not been proven, although Ferruzzi has paid the Chicago Board of Trade in settlement of the dispute.

The Hunt silver manipulation

With little doubt, the Hunt manipulation of silver in 1979–80 was the grandest futures manipulation of the twentieth century. At one time, the Hunts and their co-conspirators controlled silver worth more than $14 billion. Figure 2.10 shows the price of silver for 1979 and 1980. At the beginning of 1979, an ounce of silver was worth about $6. In January 1980, the price briefly exceeded $50 during one trading day. In March 1980, the price of silver crashed, and fell to the $12 per ounce range. In 1993, silver traded for about $5 per ounce.

In some ways the silver manipulation was very simple, while in other ways it was incredibly complex. The manipulative efforts involved many other participants besides the flamboyant and well-known Hunts. These other conspirators included a number of very wealthy Saudis. In outline, the Hunts operated a corner on the silver market. They amassed gigantic futures positions

Figure 2.10   Silver prices in 1979–80

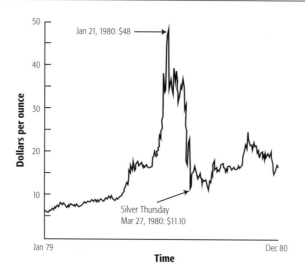

and demanded delivery on those contracts as they came due. At the same time, they bought tremendous quantities of physical silver and held the physical silver off the market. Thus, they accelerated demand through the futures market as they restricted supply through the cash market. As a result, the price of silver shot up.

As silver approached $50 per ounce in January 1980, the exchanges and the CFTC took effective action by imposing **liquidation-only trading**. Under liquidation-only trading, traders are allowed to trade only to close an existing futures position; they are not allowed to establish any new positions. (This rule forces traders to exit the market as any existing positions come to expiration; they cannot roll those positions forward to a later contract maturity.) The next day, the price of silver dropped by $12 per ounce in one day. From January through February and into March, the manipulators struggled to support the price of silver. However, the exchanges also increased margins on silver. On March 19, the Hunts defaulted on their margin obligations. In a final desperate attempt to support the price of silver, on March 26, 1980, the manipulators announced a plan to issue bonds backed by their physical silver holdings. The market interpreted this ploy as an act of desperation and it crashed again the next day. March 27, 1980, has become known as Silver Thursday because of this famous crash that ended the Hunts' effective domination of silver.

Minpeco, SA, a Peruvian government-sponsored minerals marketing firm, was a major short trader in the silver market during 1979–80. They sued the Hunts, their co-conspirators, and their brokers for $90 million of actual losses plus interest, plus trebled punitive damages. Minpeco won about $200 million in settlements and judgments against the defendants. This sum included a prejudgment settlement payment of $34 million by Merrill Lynch and Bache, two of the conspirators' largest brokers. The jury found that the three Hunt brothers, Bunker, Herbert, and Lamar, had indeed manipulated the silver market. After the verdict, Lamar Hunt, owner of the Kansas City Chiefs NFL team, paid $17 million in settlement. The full settlement was never collected from Bunker and Herbert, who sought protection in bankruptcy. Thus, these two brothers, who began the 1980s among the world's richest men, were bankrupt by 1990.

The alleged soybean manipulation of 1989

The soybean crisis of 1989 had its origins at least as far back as the preceding year. In 1988, the Midwest suffered a severe drought, which greatly reduced soybean yields. Thus, the market entered the 1989 crop year with greatly diminished supplies. Figure 2.11 shows the price of soybeans for 1989. Through early 1989, Central Soya, a wholly owned grain subsidiary of the Italian firm Ferruzzi, amassed large holdings of physical soybeans and took large long positions in the May 1989 soybean contract. As late as May 16, Ferruzzi held 16.2 million bushels of May soybean futures. The Chicago Board of Trade revoked Ferruzzi's status as a hedger on May 18. This meant that Ferruzzi was forced to reduce its futures position to the 3 million bushel speculative position limit. As a result, the May contract liquidated in an orderly manner.

However, instead of merely offsetting its May positions, Ferruzzi **rolled its position forward**; that is, Ferruzzi sold May contracts and bought July soybean futures. This action set the stage for a larger problem in July. By early June, Ferruzzi held a long position of 32 million bushels in the July futures contract. In addition, by July 1, Ferruzzi had achieved effective control over the deliverable supply of soybeans. Ferruzzi controlled 7 million bushels, while all other traders controlled only 1.6 million. With Ferruzzi holding 32 million bushels in long futures and only 1.6 million bushels available for delivery by other traders, Ferruzzi clearly had a dominant market position.

On July 11, 1989, the Chicago Board of Trade declared that an emergency existed. Effective on July 12, the Board of Trade revoked Ferruzzi's status as a hedger. This meant that Ferruzzi

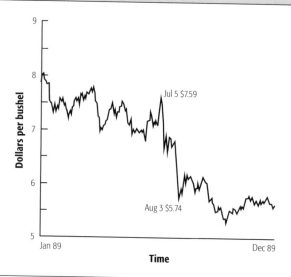

Figure 2.11   Soybean prices in 1989

was once again subject to the 3 million bushel position limit. Further, the CBOT ordered liquidation of at least 20 percent of futures positions for each of the next several trading days, down to an absolute limit of no more than 1 million bushels at the close of trading on July 20. These actions helped to avert the crisis, and the July contract traded without further disruptions. On September 15, 1989, Ferruzzi announced that its major grain and oilseed traders in Paris had resigned due to "differences over trading strategies."[26]

Ferruzzi later filed suit against the CBOT, and the CBOT imposed fines on Ferruzzi. In 1992, the dispute was laid to rest when Ferruzzi paid $2 million to the CBOT and dropped its suit. The CBOT viewed this payment as a fine, but Ferruzzi has disputed this characterization. The aftermath of this mess lingered into 1993, when the chairman of Ferruzzi committed suicide and deep losses of about $350 million, apparently stemming from the trading debacle, were discovered.[27]

False report manipulation

Section 9(a)(2) of the CEA makes it illegal for "anyone to knowingly make false communications or misleading or inaccurate reports concerning crop or market information or conditions that affect or tend to affect the price of any commodity in interstate commerce." Between 2002 and 2005 the CFTC settled enforcement proceedings for $297 million against 25 energy-trading firms alleged to have manipulated or attempted to manipulate the cash natural gas market when they provided false reports to the publishers of the natural gas price indexes *Platts Gas Daily* and *Inside FERC Gas Market Report*. The index providers published price indexes that tend to affect futures prices. The false reports involved the altering of price and volume information for actual trades. The false reports also involved the reporting of nonexistent trades.

Micromanipulation

A micromanipulation results from a momentary rigging of a futures contract's settlement price. It involves the intent to trade in a way that creates an artificial price that may last only an instant.

A trader may find it profitable to conduct this type of manipulation if it has an OTC derivatives position that is valued using the futures price as a reference price. In 2001, the CFTC settled allegations of a micromanipulation with Avista Energy, Inc.[28] The CFTC alleged that Avista had manipulated the settlement prices of NYMEX Palo Verde and California–Oregon–Border electricity futures contracts between April 1988 and July 1988 to benefit cash-settled OTC options positions that were tied to daily settlement prices of the NYMEX electricity futures contracts. The CFTC alleged that Avista had been able to raise and lower settlement prices by placing large orders ahead of the market close. The CFTC alleged that the before-the-close trading had no business or economic purpose, and had been undertaken for the sole purpose of manipulating settlement prices to benefit Avista's OTC positions.

Old Hutch

Benjamin Hutchinson (1829–99) was a legendary Chicago trader, whose career spanned nearly 40 years during the second half of the nineteenth century. His many attempts to corner the CBOT's grain markets earned him a fortune, a reputation, and the nicknames "King of the Corner" and "Old Hutch."

Perhaps the most memorable of his corners was aimed at the CBOT's September 1888 wheat contract. As early as January 1888, when wheat was trading for around 85 cents per bushel, Old Hutch began to secretly accumulate cash market inventories of wheat, while at the same time he began to build a long futures position. In the midst of his accumulation of cash wheat, rumors circulated that Old Hutch had died. This depressed prices and allowed Old Hutch, who was in fact very much alive, to accumulate additional stocks of wheat at even lower prices. In July and August, he shipped large amounts of wheat out of Chicago to East Coast markets on boats he had chartered. By chartering these vessels, he impeded the ability of the shorts to quickly increase the deliverable supply once his position was disclosed. His ownership of all cash wheat in Chicago and other cities became public knowledge on August 31. It is estimated that he acquired his cash position for an average price of 87 cents per bushel. His corner increased prices considerably and made him popular with farmers. One report from the time mentions that farmers were "blessing Old Hutch and that his name was being mentioned at rural prayer meetings."[29]

Old Hutch also increased his cash position during the expiring months. Prices continued to rise as crop reports worsened. On September 27, cash wheat reached $1.28. Some shorts now had trouble making delivery. Old Hutch settled with some shorts for $1.25. On the last trading date of the contract, the cash price rose to $2.08.

Old Hutch set the price of the contract at $2.00, which became the settlement price. Chicago newspapers reported that some shorts committed suicide to avoid their obligation to deliver. Reports from the period estimate that Old Hutch made as much as $8 million from the corner.

In 1889, Old Hutch's career came to an end the same way it began: by attempting a massive corner. He ventured millions attempting to corner the July 1890 corn contract, an unforeseen disruption in the markets led to a decline in the price of corn, and Old Hutch suffered heavy losses. Within a year, Old Hutch's fortune and reputation were gone and he left the markets permanently. Afterwards, he was occasionally seen in the galleries of the CBOT, but he never traded again. He spent his last years alone in rural Wisconsin and died in 1899.[30]

Conclusion

This chapter has explored the basic institutional features of the futures markets, focusing on the United States. We have seen that futures contracts are a type of forward contract traded on organized exchanges and featuring highly standardized contract terms. The institutional environment includes a clearinghouse to guarantee performance to all trades and a margin system designed to protect the financial integrity of the marketplace. This system allows the futures market to provide two key social benefits: price discovery and risk transference through hedging.

Futures markets trade contracts on a variety of goods, ranging from the traditional agricultural commodities to metals, interest rate contracts, contracts on stock indexes, and foreign currency futures. The market has a complex regulatory environment, with brokers, exchanges, an industry organization, and a federal agency all playing a role. These regulatory bodies govern the activities of a variety of futures market participants, including floor brokers, introducing brokers, futures commission merchants, advisors, and commodity pool operators.

Today, the futures industry in the United States faces challenges from emerging foreign futures markets and a movement toward electronic trading accelerated by technological change. These trends in the market not only threaten to end, but are ending, the dominance of futures trading long enjoyed by U.S. exchanges. However, these same developments broaden the range and scope of futures trading available in the increasingly worldwide economy.

Exercises

1   Explain the different roles of a floor broker and an account executive.

2   At a party, a man tells you that he is an introducing broker. He goes on to explain that his job is introducing prospective traders such as yourself to futures brokers. He also relates that he holds margin funds as a service to investors. What do you make of this explanation?

3   Assume that you are a floor broker and a friend of yours is a market maker who trades soybeans on the floor of the Chicago Board of Trade. Beans are trading at $6.53 per bushel. You receive an order to buy beans and you buy one contract from your friend at $6.54, one cent above the market. Who wins, who loses, and why? Explain the rationale for making such a practice illegal.

4   Back at the party after several more hours . . . your buddy from Exercise 2 buttonholes you again and starts to explain his great success as a dual trader, trading both beans and corn. What do you think?

5   You are having trouble escaping from your friend in Exercise 4. He goes on to explain that liquidation-only trading involves trading soybeans against soyoil to profit from the liquidation that occurs when beans are crushed. Explain how your understanding of "liquidation-only trading" differs from that of your friend.

6   In purchasing a house, contracting to buy the house occurs at one time. Typically, closing occurs weeks later. At the closing, the buyer pays the seller for the house and the buyer takes possession. Explain how this transaction is like a futures or forward transaction.

7   In the futures market, a widget contract has a standard contract size of 5,000 widgets. What advantage does this have over the well-known forward market practice of negotiating the size of the transaction on a case-by-case basis? What disadvantages does the standardized contract size have?

8   What factors need to be considered in purchasing a commodity futures exchange seat? What are all the possible advantages that could come from owning a seat?

9   Explain the difference between initial and maintenance margin.

10   Explain the difference between maintenance and variation margin.

11   On February 1, a trader is long the JUN wheat contract. On February 10, she sells a SEP wheat futures, and she sells a JUN wheat contract on February 20. On February 15, what is her position in wheat futures? What is her position on February 25? How would you characterize her transaction on February 20?

12   Explain the difference between volume and open interest.

13   Define "tick" and "daily price limit."

14   A trader is long one SEP crude oil contract. On May 15, he contracts with a business associate to receive 1,000 barrels of oil in the spot market. The business associate is short one SEP crude oil contract. How can the two traders close their futures positions without actually transacting in the futures market?

15   Explain how a trader closes a futures market position via cash settlement.

16   Explain "price discovery."

17   Contrast anticipatory hedging with hedging in general.

18   What is "front running"?

19 Explain the difference between the roles of the National Futures Association and the Commodity Futures Trading Commission.

20 What are the two types of financial safeguard models used by futures clearinghouses?

21 What does it mean for an exchange to "demutualize?"

22 How did the CFMA of 2000 alter the regulation of the futures industry?

23 In what ways do futures exchanges compete?

24 How do futures exchanges make money?

25 What are bunched orders? What issues are involved in the post-trade allocation of bunched orders?

26 What is an "out trade?" How do futures exchanges facilitate the reconciliation of out trades?

27 What are the four elements of proof required for a futures market manipulation claim?

28 What does it mean for a futures market to be *transparent*?

29 What is *churning*?

Notes

1 There are some exceptions to this general rule. For example, the London Metals Exchange trades metals forwards, but has a physical trading floor.

2 In general, futures on financial products tend to have few if any price limits. This means that price limits are restricted mainly to physical commodities. Michael J. Brennan, "A Theory of Price Limits in Futures Markets," *Journal of Financial Economics*, 16:2, 1986, pp. 213–33, provides an argument to explain why price limits are observed in some markets but not in others. Brennan argues that price limits serve to restrict the flow of information available to traders in the event of dramatic changes in the true economic value of the commodity. If the futures price has moved the limit, the traders' information about the true value of the good is restricted because the trader cannot observe the market price for the good. Therefore, the trader has a stronger incentive to meet his margin call than he or she might have if the true equilibrium price was known. Price limits do not restrict the trader's information if information is available from sources outside the futures market. For example, in financial markets there are good sources of information beyond the futures markets about the prices of goods. For agricultural markets, Brennan notes, the sources of information beyond the futures market are not as valuable. Thus, we would expect to find few price limits on financial futures, because price limits would not be effective in limiting the traders' information. Correlatively, price limits should be observed on agricultural commodities where the trader's information flow is poorer. Brennan notes that the pattern of price limits on futures is broadly consistent with this observation. Price limits are more popular on agricultural futures than on financial futures.

Price limits allegedly provide a "cooling-off period" when prices are very volatile. Others have argued that price limits prevent markets from "over-shooting" the true market price. Evidence from the academic literature for either proposition is mixed at best. For example, Chul Woo Park, "Examining Futures Price Changes and Volatility on the Trading Day After a Limit-Lock Day," *Journal of Futures Markets*, 20, 2000, pp. 445–66, finds that prices continue to rise on average after an up-limit day and that volatility is influenced in some markets but not others. Ma, R. Rao, and R. Sears, "Volatility, Price Resolution, and the Effectiveness of Price Limits," *Journal of Financial Services Research*, 3:3, 1989, pp. 165–99, find that volatility the next day is lower and that the price tends to reverse direction after it hits the price limit. This issue remains highly controversial, as the comments on the Ma, Rao, and Sears articles by M. Miller and S. Lehmann indicate. For other studies of price limits see: Henk Berkman and Onno W. Steenbeek, "The Influence of Daily Price Limits on Trading in Nikkei Futures," *Journal of Futures Markéts*, 18:3, 1998, pp. 265–79; Joan Evans and James Mahoney, "The Effects of Daily Price Limits on Cotton Futures and Options Trading," *Federal Reserve Bank of New York*, 1996; Laura E. Kodres and Daniel P. O'Brien, "The Existence of Pareto-Superior Price Limits," *American Economic Review*, 84:4, 1994, pp. 919–32; and Lucy F. Ackert and William C. Hunter, "Rational Price Limits in Futures Markets: Tests of a Simple Optimizing Model," *Review of Financial Economics*, 4:1, 1994, pp. 93–108.

3 For more information on the customer–broker relationship, see James V. Jordan and George Emir Morgan, "Default Risk in Futures Markets: The Customer Broker Relationship," *Journal of Finance*, 45, 1990, pp. 909–33.

4 Notice that this is different from the stock market. Stocks represent title to the real assets of the firms, and these are owned by someone at every point in time. The long and short positions in the stock market, when "netted out," always equal the number of shares

actually in existence, not zero, as in the futures market.

5   We might say that the clearinghouse is "perfectly hedged." No matter whether futures prices rise or fall, the wealth of the clearinghouse will not be affected. This is the case since the clearinghouse holds both long and short positions that perfectly balance each other.

6   See Roger W. Gray, "Onions Revisited," *Journal of Farm Economics*, 45:2, 1963, pp. 273–6. Onion futures commenced trading at the CME on September 8, 1942, and at the New York Mercantile Exchange on October 14, 1946. Although onion futures were banned in 1958, trading was permitted in already existing contracts with open interest. The last trade in onion futures occurred on November 5, 1959.

7   Position limits do not apply in the same way to hedgers. For many contracts, position limits only apply during the delivery month.

8   One form of fictitious trading called "wash trading" refers to two traders who have prearranged the purchase and sale of a contract without exposing either trader to risk. In some isolated instances, it is possible for a wash sale to have an economic purpose. For example, a trader who currently has a position established in the market may wish to avoid standing for delivery, where the position in the delivery queue depends on when the position was established. A trader may be tempted to engage in a wash transaction in order to move to the end of the delivery queue; that is, to "refresh" his position. Such a transaction, even though it arguably has an economic purpose, would be prohibited because all wash trades are *per se* prohibited.

9   See Eric. C. Chang, Peter R. Locke, and Steven C. Mann, "The Effect of CME Rule 552 on Dual Traders," *Journal of Futures Markets*, 14:4, June 1994, pp. 493–510. Other studies are quite skeptical regarding the benefits of restrictions on dual trading: Tom Smith and Robert E. Whaley, "Assessing the Costs of Regulation: The Case of Dual Trading," *Journal of Law & Economics*, 37:1, April 1994, pp. 215–46; Sugato Chakravarty, "Should Actively Traded Futures Contracts Come under the Dual-Trading Ban?," *Journal of Futures Markets*, 14:6, September 1994, pp. 661–84. Hun Y. Park, Asani Sarkar, and Lifan Wu, "The Costs and Benefits of Dual Trading," Federal Reserve Bank of New York, *Staff Reports*, Number 2, June 1995, find that dual traders attain better execution for their customers than pure brokers. But they also find that this performance is pit-specific, with this superior performance not being characteristic of trading in all commodities.

10 For a thorough survey of the CFMA, see Walter L. Lukken and James A. Overdahl, "Derivative Contracts and Their Regulation," in Clifford E. Kirsch (ed.), *Financial Product Fundamentals*, New York: Practicing Law Institute, February 2004, 18-31–18-33.

11 The pre-CFMA and post-CFMA numbers may be a bit misleading due to the fact that many of the new post-CFMA contracts were single-stock futures.

12 Scott H. Irwin, Terry R. Krukemeyer, and Carl R. Zulauf, "Investment Performance of Public Commodity Pools: 1979–1990," *Journal of Futures Markets*, 13:7, 1993, pp. 799–820.

13 David K. Bruderle, "Introducing Brokers: Small and Ag-Focused but Tech Savvy," *Futures Industry Magazine*, 25, 2004, pp. 62–5.

14 For examples of direct competition between exchanges, see M. E. Holder, M. J. Tomas III, and R. L. Webb, "Winners and Losers: Recent Competition Among Futures Exchanges for Equivalent Financial Contract Markets," *Derivatives Quarterly*, 5:2, 1999, pp. 19–27.

15 See Craig Pirrong, "Bund for Glory, or It's a Long Way to Tip a Market," working paper, University of Houston, 2003.

16 Quoted in an article by Mary Chung, "NYMEX is Boosted by Enron Backlash," *Financial Times*, May 31, 2002.

17 In an exhaustive study of the successes and failure of futures contracts, CFTC economist Michael Penick finds that of the 632 new futures contracts listed since 1940, 72 percent survive for one year, 44 percent survive for three years, and 20 percent survive for 10 years. He also finds that the rate of survival varies greatly across exchanges and across product types. Contracts developed by the old Mid-America Exchange had high survival rates (86 percent after three years), although the exchange itself did not survive as a stand-alone entity. The CBOT survival rate was a much lower 36 percent after three years. Contracts based on metals had the highest survival rates, while contracts based on energy had the lowest. See Michael A. Penick, "The Life Cycle of Futures Contracts: The Success and Failure Rates of Futures Contracts in the United States," Working paper, CFTC, Washington, DC: 2004.

18 Elizabeth Tashjian Johnston and John J. McConnell, "Requiem for a Market: An Analysis of the Rise and Fall of a Financial Futures Contract," *The Review of Financial Studies*, 2:1, 1989, pp. 1–23, conclude that the contract failed due to its poor design. See also K. Pierog and J. Stein, "New Contracts: What Makes Them Fly or Fail?" *Futures*, September 1989.

Subsequently, the CBOT has tried to introduce improved contracts on mortgage interest rates.

19   See, for example, D. Carlton, "Futures Markets: Their Purpose, Their History, Their Growth, Their Successes and Failures," *The Journal of Futures Markets*, 4:3, 1984, pp. 237–71. See also R. W. Anderson, *The Industrial Organization of Futures Markets*, Lexington, MA: D. C. Heath, 1984. Anderson's book contains a number of articles on different aspects of the industrial organization of futures markets.

20   Praveen Kumar and Duane J. Seppi, "Futures Manipulation with Cash Settlement," *Journal of Finance*, 47:4, 1992, pp. 1485–502, argue that cash settlement, rather than actual delivery of the underlying good, will prevent corners and squeezes. Stephen Craig Pirrong, "Mixed Manipulation Strategies in Commodity Futures Markets," *Journal of Futures Markets*, 15:1, 1995, pp. 13–38, develops a formal model of manipulation. Robert A. Jarrow, "Derivative Securities Markets, Market Manipulation, and Option Pricing Theory," *Journal of Financial & Quantitative Analysis*, 29:2, 1994, pp. 241–61, argues that the introduction of derivative markets enriches opportunities for manipulation.

21   Information in this section comes from an excellent essay on the history of market manipulation by J. W. Markham, L. H. Hunt, Jr., and M. S. Sackheim, "Market Manipulation—from Star Chamber to Lone Star," *Futures & Derivatives Law Report*, 2003, pp. 7–18.

22   "He that withholdeth corn the people shall curse him; but blessing shall be upon the head of him that selleth it." *The Bible*, King James version.

23   See Craig Pirrong, "Squeezes, Corpses, and the Anti-Manipulation Provisions of the Commodity Exchange Act," *Regulation*, 17:4, 1994; and Jerry W. Markham, "Manipulation of Commodity Futures Prices—the Unprosecutable Crime," *Yale Journal on Regulation*, 8:2, 1991, pp. 281–390.

24   See Stephen Craig Pirrong, "Manipulation of the Commodity Futures Market Delivery Process," *Journal of Business*, 66:3, 1993, pp. 335–69.

25   *Volkart Bros. Inc v. Freeman*, 311 F.2d.52, 58 (5th Cir. 1960).

26   This account relies on F. Bailey, "Emergency Action: July 1989 Soybeans," Chicago: Chicago Board of Trade, 1990. See also K. Schap and C. Flory, "Ferruzzi vs. CBOT: Who Is Right?" *Futures*, September 1989, and K. Pierog, "Report Vindicates CBOT Action in July Soybeans," *Futures*, October 1989.

27   See "Ferruzzi's Problems May Be Italy's Too," *The Wall Street Journal*, August 12, 1993.

28   *In re Avista Energy, Inc., et al.* [2000–2002 Transfer Binder], *Commodity Futures Law Reporter* (CCH) ¶ 28,623 (CFTC, August 21, 2001).

29   E. J. Dies, *The Plunger, A Tale of the Wheat Pit*, New York: Arno Press, orig. pub. 1929, pp. 137–8.

30   For more on the era of Old Hutch, see Jonathan Lurie, *The Chicago Board of Trade 1859–1905*, Urbana, IL: University of Illinois Press, 1979.

3

Futures Prices

Overview

Having explored the basic institutional features of the futures market in Chapters 1 and 2, we now consider futures prices. In an important sense, the study of the prices in a market provides the essential key to understanding all features of the market. Prices and the factors that determine those prices will ultimately influence every use of the market.

This chapter examines the fundamental factors that affect futures prices in general. There is little doubt that the determinants of foreign exchange futures prices and orange juice futures prices, for example, are very different. We must also recognize, however, that a common thread of understanding links futures contracts of all types. This chapter follows that common thread, while subsequent chapters explore the individual factors that affect prices for particular commodities. Perhaps the most basic and common factor affecting futures prices is the way in which their prices are quoted. Our discussion of futures prices begins with reading the price quotations that are available every day in *The Wall Street Journal*.

Futures market prices also bear economically important relationships to other observable prices. An important goal of this chapter is to develop an understanding of those relationships. The futures price for delivery of coffee in three months, for example, must be related to the spot price, or the current cash price, of coffee at a particular physical location. The **spot price** is the price of a good for immediate delivery. In a restaurant, for example, you buy a cup of coffee at the spot price. The spot price is also called the **cash price** or the **current price**.

This important difference between the cash price and the futures price is called the **basis**. Likewise, the futures price for delivery of coffee in three months must be related in some fashion to the futures price for delivery of coffee in six months. The difference in price for two futures contract expirations on the same commodity is an intracommodity spread. As we will see, the time spread can also be an economically important variable.

Because futures contracts call for the delivery of some good at a particular time in the future, we can be sure that the expectations of market participants help to determine futures prices. If people believe that gold will sell for $50 per ounce in three months, then the price of the futures contract for delivery of gold in three months cannot be $100. The connection between futures prices and expected future spot prices is so strong that some market observers believe that they must be, or at least should be, equal.

Similarly, the price for storing the good underlying the futures contract helps to determine the relationships among futures prices and the relationship between the futures price and the spot price. By storing goods, it is possible, in effect, to convert corn received in March into corn that can be delivered in June. The difference in price between the March corn futures and the June corn futures must, therefore, be related to the cost of storing corn.

All of these futures pricing issues are interconnected. The basis, the spreads, the expected future spot price, and the cost of storage all form a system of related concepts. This chapter describes the linkages among these concepts that are common to all futures contracts. The discussion begins with the futures prices themselves.

Reading futures prices

One of the most complete and widely available sources for futures prices is *The Wall Street Journal*, which publishes futures prices daily. These prices are reported in a standardized format, as shown in Figure 3.1. A listing in the regular section is a mark of some success for a futures contract. *The Wall Street Journal* also lists some less active contracts. More complete listings are available on a real-time basis from exchange web sites and from market data vendors such as Bloomberg.

The date shown near the top of Figure 3.1 is the day for which the prices were recorded. The publication date of *The Wall Street Journal* is the next business day. As the heading states,

Figure 3.1 Futures price quotations

FUTURES PRICES

Thursday, March 30, 2006

Agriculture Futures

	Open	High	Low	Settle	Change	Lifetime High	Lifetime Low	Open interest
Corn (CBT)-5,000 bu.; cents per bu.								
May	224.00	228.00	223.75	227.75	3.50	276.50	208.75	421,628
July	235.00	239.00	234.75	238.75	3.25	279.00	217.25	270,275
Oats (CBT)-5,000 bu.; cents per bu.								
May	171.25	173.00	169.00	172.25	1.00	200.75	154.00	5,986
Dec	166.50	166.50	166.00	166.00	−1.00	170.75	157.00	2,218
Soybeans (CBT)-5,000 bu.; cents per bu.								
May	581.50	589.00	581.00	587.75	5.25	742.00	530.25	179,961
July	595.00	601.25	593.00	601.00	5.75	736.00	535.00	92,435
Soybean Meal (CBT)-100 tons; $ per ton								
May	178.70	181.00	178.00	179.40	.70	230.50	164.80	60,344
July	180.80	182.80	180.10	181.60	.70	227.00	166.00	42,054
Soybean Oil (CBT)-60,000 lbs.; cents per lb.								
May	22.97	23.25	22.83	23.17	.20	26.35	20.00	100,486
July	23.40	23.64	23.25	23.57	.17	25.55	20.25	52,456
Rough Rice (CBT)-2,000 cwt.; cents per cwt.								
May	830.00	837.00	830.00	836.00	4.50	901.00	719.00	5,196
July	860.00	865.00	858.00	864.00	6.00	921.00	738.00	2,642
Wheat (CBT)-5,000 bu.; cents per bu.								
May	341.25	345.75	340.25	344.50	2.75	390.50	316.50	187,238
July	354.25	358.00	352.50	357.25	2.75	400.00	325.50	94,151
Wheat (KC)-5,000 bu.; cents per bu.								
May	406.25	412.00	405.50	410.75	4.25	456.00	344.25	39,605
July	411.75	417.00	410.25	415.75	4.00	462.50	342.00	39,216
Wheat (MPLS)-5,000 bu.; cents per bu.								
May	396.00	399.00	396.00	398.25	2.50	440.00	347.00	12,103
July	401.00	404.50	401.00	403.25	2.50	444.00	353.00	13,157
Cattle-Feeder (CME)-50,000 lbs.; cents per lb.								
Mar	103.550	103.550	103.300	103.350	−.150	116.100	96.000	2,575
May	103.750	104.450	103.125	104.400	.825	114.300	96.000	15,612
Cattle-Live (CME)-40,000 lbs.; cents per lb.								
Apr	80.750	81.175	80.525	81.000	.375	95.550	80.350	32,105
June	74.800	76.025	74.700	75.900	1.150	88.000	74.550	114,889
Hogs-Lean (CME)-40,000 lbs.; cents per lb.								
Apr	57.400	58.300	57.250	58.125	.625	71.325	55.000	12,599
June	66.250	66.900	65.800	66.750	.600	73.450	59.500	82,554
Pork Bellies (CME)-40,000 lbs.; cents per lb.								
May	83.300	83.650	81.250	81.775	−1.925	99.900	73.850	1,093
July	84.250	84.500	82.400	83.500	−1.700	99.900	75.300	450
Lumber (CME)-110,000 bd. ft., $ per 1,000 bd. ft.								
May	328.00	328.00	322.70	322.90	−1.10	382.80	293.00	3,070
July	334.60	335.70	332.70	335.40	.60	374.50	299.60	756
Milk (CME)-200,000 lbs., cents per lb.								
Mar	...	...	...	11.12	...	13.21	10.92	2,609
May	10.89	10.99	10.85	10.85	...	13.20	10.70	3,294
Cocoa (NYBOT)-10 metric tons; $ per ton								
May	1,491	1,513	1,491	1,509	22	1,810	1,366	47,870
July	1,519	1,536	1,517	1,533	22	1,782	1,390	24,425
Coffee (NYBOT)-37,500 lbs.; cents per lb.								
May	104.65	109.60	104.50	108.60	4.25	148.50	92.10	57,460
July	107.80	112.00	107.40	111.40	4.25	147.30	89.00	25,714
Sugar-World (NYBOT)-112,000 lbs.; cents per lb.								
May	18.08	18.48	18.08	18.27	.07	19.65	7.65	208,762
July	18.09	18.40	18.09	18.21	.09	18.71	7.70	112,000
Sugar-Domestic (NYBOT)-112,000 lbs.; cents per lb.								
May	23.65	24.00	23.65	24.00	.40	25.25	20.65	1,490
July	23.60	23.90	23.60	23.90	.32	25.20	20.88	4,244
Cotton (NYBOT)-50,000 lbs.; cents per lb.								
May	53.50	53.90	53.35	53.70	.54	61.20	49.25	87,342
July	54.90	55.35	54.90	55.35	.61	62.13	50.40	25,990
Orange Juice (NYBOT)-15,000 lbs.; cents per lb.								
May	147.00	150.25	146.55	148.75	1.30	151.50	95.30	22,737
July	144.00	146.70	144.00	146.05	1.35	147.80	98.00	7,860

Metal & Petroleum Futures

	Open	High	Low	Settle	Change	Lifetime High	Lifetime Low	Open interest
Copper-High (CMX)-25,000 lbs.; cents per lb.								
Apr	246.90	250.60	246.50	250.35	4.70	250.60	113.00	4,589
May	243.50	249.40	243.50	248.45	4.60	249.40	100.00	60,765
Gold (CMX)-100 troy oz.; $ per troy oz.								
Apr	572.60	587.40	571.30	586.70	13.40	587.40	418.00	33,999
June	578.00	592.00	576.50	591.80	13.20	592.00	312.00	233,541
Aug	583.90	598.00	581.90	597.10	13.30	598.00	435.50	9,542
Oct	588.40	603.00	587.10	602.50	13.40	603.00	436.50	10,459
Dec	593.80	608.50	592.60	607.80	13.50	608.50	338.00	17,758
Dc07	631.00	638.50	631.00	640.20	14.70	638.50	368.00	10,273
Platinum (NYM)-50 troy oz.; $ per troy oz.								
Apr	1076.90	1095.00	1076.00	1090.70	13.80	1095.00	815.00	889
July	1088.00	1104.80	1084.00	1102.70	14.80	1104.80	985.00	8,243
Silver (CMX)-5,000 troy oz.; cents per troy oz.								
Apr	1114.0	1142.0	1114.0	1161.8	54.5	1142.0	920.0	150
May	1110.0	1171.5	1110.0	1166.0	54.5	1171.5	685.5	83,288
Crude Oil, Light Sweet (NYM)-1,000 bbls.; $ per bbl.								
May	66.51	67.30	66.05	67.15	0.70	70.33	36.86	250,120
June	67.50	68.50	67.11	68.33	0.86	70.80	23.75	132,805
July	68.10	69.10	67.78	69.02	0.95	71.10	30.05	52,456
Dec	68.95	70.00	68.75	69.89	0.87	71.70	19.10	90,677
Dc07	68.55	69.35	68.55	69.49	0.77	70.80	19.50	65,963
Dc08	67.81	67.81	67.65	68.20	0.68	68.60	19.75	38,881
Heating Oil No. 2 (NYM)-42,000 gal.; $ per gal.								
Apr	1.8542	1.8890	1.8425	1.8843	.0323	2.1160	1.0954	11,012
May	1.8510	1.8850	1.8396	1.8793	.0299	2.0300	1.0600	66,907
Gasoline-NY Unleaded (NYM)-42,000 gal.; $ per gal.								
Apr	1.9525	2.0025	1.9465	1.9957	.0415	2.0760	1.4475	10,559
May	1.9050	1.9250	1.8935	1.9101	.0027	2.0700	1.4710	69,209
Natural Gas (NYM)-10,000 MMBtu.; $ per MMBtu.								
May	7.480	7.562	7.370	7.487	.031	11.266	3.571	108,520
June	7.680	7.748	7.580	7.674	.033	11.285	3.601	30,745
July	7.839	7.925	7.760	7.859	.043	11.300	3.580	27,545
Oct	8.244	8.290	8.150	8.252	.051	11.390	3.732	38,076
Nov	9.409	9.440	9.300	9.330	−.051	11.765	3.950	28,423
Ja07	11.034	11.060	10.850	10.890	−.141	12.600	4.823	46,332

Interest Rate Futures

	Open	High	Low	Settle	Change	Lifetime High	Lifetime Low	Open interest
Treasury Bonds (CBT)-$100,000; pts 32nds of 100%								
June	109-22	109-28	108-26	109-06	−16	117-24	108-26	624,046
Sept	109-20	109-20	108-26	109-07	−16	115-16	108-26	2,978
Treasury Notes (CBT)-$100,000; pts 32nds of 100%								
June	106-210	106-240	106-040	106-100	−9.5	110-130	106-040	1,960,846
Sept	106-160	106-210	106-065	106-110	−10.5	109-280	106-065	65,241
5 Yr. Treasury Notes (CBT)-$100,000; pts 32nds of 100%								
June	104-180	104-215	104-095	104-125	−5.5	106-250	104-095	1,160,470
Sept	104-195	104-195	104-120	104-120	−6.0	106-220	104-120	9,448
2 Yr. Treasury Notes (CBT)-$200,000; pts 32nds of 100%								
Mar	...	...	...	101-290	−1.5	102-272	101-295	1,028
June	101-305	101-315	101-282	101-287	−1.5	102-265	101-280	454,522
30 Day Federal Funds (CBT)-$5,000,000; 100 − daily avg.								
Mar	95.415	95.415	95.410	95.415	...	96.285	95.400	93,351
Apr	95.230	95.235	95.230	95.235	...	95.985	95.230	174,852

	Open	High	Low	Settle	Change	Yield	Change	Open interest
1 Month Libor (CME)-$3,000,000; pts of 100%								
Apr	95.1050	95.1050	95.0950	95.0975	−.0025	4.9025	.0025	22,165
May	94.9750	94.9750	94.9575	94.9650	−.0050	5.0350	.0050	41,500
Eurodollar (CME)-$1,000,000; pts of 100%								
Apr	94.9600	94.9600	94.9450	94.9500	−.0125	5.0500	.0125	44,588
June	94.8250	94.8400	94.7900	94.7950	−.0300	5.2050	.0300	1,365,087
Sept	94.7700	94.7900	94.7150	94.7250	−.0400	5.2750	.0400	1,340,598
Dec	94.7850	94.8100	94.7250	94.7400	−.0400	5.2600	.0400	1,388,203

Currency Futures

	Open	High	Low	Settle	Change	Lifetime High	Lifetime Low	Open interest
Japanese Yen (CME)-¥12,500,000; $ per 100¥								
June	.8578	.8630	.8568	.8614	.0034	.9949	.8455	161,932
Sept	.8706	.8736	.8678	.8721	.0035	.9435	.8572	18,741
Canadian Dollar (CME)-CAD 100,000; $ per CAD								
June	.8545	.8647	.8544	.8634	.0090	.8879	.7950	82,915
Sept	.8574	.8666	.8574	.8657	.0090	.8912	.7970	2,320
British Pound (CME)-£62,500; $ per £								
June	1.7364	1.7502	1.7361	1.7485	.0126	1.8120	1.7076	75,545
Sept	1.7438	1.7530	1.7410	1.7511	.0127	1.7941	1.7282	252
Swiss Franc (CME)-CHF 125,000; $ per CHF								
June	.7697	.7781	.7695	.7771	.0075	.8635	.7633	88,067
Sept	.7835	.7852	.7822	.7842	.0076	.8134	.7712	252
Australian Dollar (CME)-AUD 100,000; $ per AUD								
June	.7055	.7150	.7055	.7140	.0079	.7760	.7006	66,866
Sept	.7090	.7140	.7069	.7132	.0079	.7700	.7001	143
Mexican Peso (CME)-MXN 500,000; $ per 10MXN								
Apr	...	...	...	.91375	.00275	.94950	.90700	20
June	.90750	.91250	.90550	.90975	.00275	.95000	.84500	43,780
Euro (CME)-€125,000; $ per €								
June	1.2087	1.2230	1.2081	1.2213	.0131	1.3795	1.1798	136,658
Sept	1.2157	1.2292	1.2157	1.2277	.0132	1.2770	1.1864	2,080

Index Futures

	Open	High	Low	Settle	Change	Lifetime High	Lifetime Low	Open interest
DJ Industrial Average (CBT)-$10 × index								
June	11266	11320	11172	11204	−63	11410	10363	37,753
Sept	11310	11310	11281	11281	−63	11445	10891	58
Mini DJ Industrial Average (CBT)-$5 × index								
June	11265	11320	11172	11204	−63	11413	10600	66,550
Sept	11300	11305	11300	11281	−63	11470	11300	10
S&P 500 Index (CME)-$250 × index								
June	1310.30	1319.00	1305.00	1307.50	−2.60	1321.30	1080.00	645,025
Sept	1320.00	1329.30	1316.00	1318.30	−2.50	1331.40	1112.60	6,275
Mini S&P 500 (CME)-$50 × index								
June	1310.50	1319.25	1304.75	1307.50	−2.50	1321.50	1261.25	1,159,253
Sept	1330.00	1330.00	1316.00	1318.25	−2.50	1331.75	1311.25	777
Nasdaq 100 (CME)-$100 × index								
June	1720.50	1737.50	1715.50	1725.00	4.50	1791.50	1576.50	57,932
Mini Nasdaq 100 (CME)-$20 × index								
June	1720.5	1737.5	1715.5	1725.0	4.5	1.793.0	1652.5	275,210
Sept	1757.0	1757.0	1736.5	1744.5	4.5	1757.0	1693.5	74
Russell 1000 (NYBOT)-$500 × index								
June	714.50	715.50	712.60	713.00	−1.50	719.00	695.75	87,433
U.S. Dollar Index (NYBOT)-$1,000 × index								
June	89.90	89.90	89.01	89.06	−.84	91.65	86.23	25,202

Source: From "Futures," *The Wall Street Journal*, March 31, 2006, p. C10. Futures prices reflect day and overnight trading. Open interest reflects previous day's trading. Reprinted by permission of *The Wall Street Journal*, © 2006 Dow Jones & Company, Inc. All rights reserved worldwide.

the open interest, to be discussed later, pertains to the preceding trading day. Figure 3.1 shows quotations for agricultural and metallurgical futures. In later chapters, we present quotations for other kinds of futures. For each contract, the listing shows the commodity, the exchange on which it is traded, the amount of the good in one contract, and the units in which prices are quoted. For example, the very first contract is for the corn contract traded by the Chicago Board of Trade (CBOT). One contract is for 5,000 bushels and the prices are quoted in cents per bushel.

At this point, a word of warning is appropriate. The information about the contracts shown with the prices is useful, but incomplete. For corn, the type of corn that is traded is not mentioned, nor is the delivery procedure. Further, *The Wall Street Journal* does not give information about daily price limits and it does not report the tick size. With so much information omitted, a trader should not trade based on just what *The Wall Street Journal* shows. To have a good insight into the price behavior and the price fluctuations of a contract requires additional information, such as that found in the *Commodity Trading Manual* published by the CBOT.

For each of the delivery months, the price listings have a row of data, with the first line going to the contract that matures next, also called the **nearby contract** or **prompt month contract**. Each succeeding line pertains to another maturity month. Contracts that mature later are called **distant**, **deferred**, or **back-month** contracts. For example, the first contract following the nearby contract is called the **first-deferred contract** and the contract following that is called the **second-deferred contract**. The first three columns of prices give the opening, high, and low prices for each contract for the day of trading being reported.

The next price column records the **settlement price**, which is the price at which contracts are settled at the close of trading for the day. The settlement price is not always the last trade price of the day, as it would be with stocks. In Chapter 1, we examined the feature of daily settlement. The rules adopted by a futures exchange to determine the settlement price of a contract at the end of a trading session are critical, because it is this price that is used by the clearinghouse to mark traders' positions to market. All margin flows are based on the settlement price. If the settlement price brings a trader's equity below the level required for the maintenance margin, then the trader will receive a margin call and will have to pay variation margin.

Exchanges adopt rules to ensure that the settlement price reflects the market price at the end of a trading session. The rules for setting settlement prices vary among exchanges and clearinghouses. In a highly liquid market, determination of the settlement price may be a trivial exercise, but as markets become less liquid, exchanges must use other means to ensure that the settlement price is reasonable, and is not being distorted by the actions of traders who may benefit from not having the settlement price reflect the market price. As futures markets have moved to round-the-clock trading, additional issues arise in determining a reasonable settlement price.

Most exchanges have a settlement committee (also called the pit committee) for each pit or ring, usually comprised of members of the exchange who trade in that pit.[1] Members who are active in the market for which the settlement prices are being set are generally more active in contributing to the process. This committee meets immediately at the close of a trading session to establish the settlement price. When trading is active and prices are stable at the end of the day, the settlement committee has an easy job. The prices recorded from trades will be continuous, with slight fluctuations from trade to trade. In such cases, the committee may simply allow the final trading price to be the settlement price. Therefore, in many cases the price for the last trade and the settlement price are the same, but they are conceptually distinct.

Difficulties arise for the settlement committee, however, when a contract has little trading activity. Imagine that the last trade for a particular contract occurred three hours before the close of trading and that significant information pertaining to that contract was discovered after that last trade. In this example, the last actual trade price for the contract does not represent what

the true economic price would be at the close of trading. In such a case, the settlement committee performs an important function by establishing a settlement price that differs from the
price on the last recorded trade.

To establish a settlement price for a contract, the members will look to the best available
information, which will often reside in the prices of adjacent month contracts. The difference
between prices of contracts for different delivery months is very stable, at least relative to the
futures prices themselves. So the settlement committee will use that price difference, or spread,
to establish the settlement price on the contract that was not recently traded. Situations that are
even more drastic might arise from time to time, but the settlement committee must establish
a settlement price even when there is very little information to go on. Having this function performed by a committee helps rule out the possibility that an inaccurate settlement price might
be chosen to generate a windfall gain for the person choosing the settlement price. To further
guard against conflicts of interest in setting the settlement price, exchange and clearinghouse
staff will independently validate the prices recommended by the settlement committee.

An aside on settlement prices

History records various means of determining the settlement price. Ulrike Schaede, in a study of the
eighteenth-century Dōjima Rice Market in Japan,[2] recounts how the closing price at this exchange was
determined by placing a fuse cord in a wooden box, which was then hung within the sight of traders.
The fuse cord was then lit. Exchange officials allowed trading to continue as long as the fuse cord was
burning. The price at the moment the fire went out became the day's official price, called the "fuse cord
price." However, some traders would continue to trade after the official market close. To stop them from
trading, the exchange employed "watermen," who splashed water all over the marketplace in order to
disperse the trading crowd. If trading continued, the watermen used whole buckets of water to douse
traders until trading ceased. The prevailing price at this time was called the "bucket price." The bucket
price was used for settlement and the fuse cord price became the opening price of the next day's
trading session.

In some jurisdictions, government regulators can play a direct role in determining the settlement price.
On August 28, 1992, the futures contract on the Nikkei stock index traded at the Osaka Stock Exchange
closed at 17,760, or 210 points below the Nikkei index itself. This price was not to the liking of an official
in Japan's Ministry of Finance. After the close of trading, the government official moved up the price of
the Nikkei contract to 17,970. The point of this bureaucratic maneuver was to prevent downward pressure on the stock market when trading reopened on August 31.

As futures markets have moved to round-the-clock trading, the term "daily settlement price" has lost
its meaning. The term "trading session settlement price" is now used to reflect the fact that even with
round-the-clock trading, predetermined timeouts occur to allow the clearinghouse to mark positions to
market and collect variation margin, and to allow the exchange to perform maintenance on the operating system of its electronic trading platform.

The next column, after the settlement price, is denoted as "Change." The value in this column is the change in the settlement price from the preceding day to the current day, the day
for which prices are reported. The next two columns show the lifetime high and low prices for
each contract. Figure 3.1 indicates how prices may differ radically for some contracts over their
lives. For the contracts that are about to mature, the difference between the lifetime high and
low prices can be enormous. On the other hand, for contracts that have just been listed, there
has been little time for the lifetime high and low prices to diverge radically.

Table 3.1 How trading affects open interest

Time	Action	Open interest
$t = 0$	Trading opens for the popular widget contract	0
$t = 1$	Trader A buys and Trader B sells one widget contract	1
$t = 2$	Trader C buys and Trader D sells three widget contracts	4
$t = 3$	Trader A sells and Trader D buys one widget contract	3
	(Trader A has offset one contract and is out of the market; Trader D	
	has offset one contract and is now short two contracts)	
$t = 4$	Trader C sells and Trader E buys one widget contract	3

Ending positions

Trader	Long position	Short position
B		1
C	2	
D		2
E	1	
All traders	3	3

The final column in Figure 3.1 is called "Open Interest," and shows the total number of contracts outstanding for each maturity month. **Open interest** is the number of futures contracts for which delivery is currently obligated. To understand the meaning of this more clearly, assume that the December 2006 widget contract has just been listed for trading, but that the contract has not traded yet. At this point, the open interest in the contract is zero. Trading begins and the first contract is bought. This purchase necessarily means that some other trader sold. This transaction creates one contract of open interest, because there is one contract now in existence for which delivery is obligated.

Subsequent trading can increase or decrease the open interest, as Table 3.1 shows for trading in the incredibly popular widget contract. At $t = 0$, trading opens on the widget contract. The open interest is zero as is volume to date. At $t = 1$, Trader A buys and Trader B sells one widget contract. This transaction creates one contract of volume. After the transaction, the open interest is one contract, because one contract is obligated for delivery. At $t = 2$, Trader C buys and Trader D sells three widget contracts. The volume resulting from these trades is three contracts and the open interest is now four contracts. At $t = 3$, Trader A sells and Trader D buys one widget contract, creating one more contract of volume. Notice here that Trader A offsets his one contract through a reversing trade. After this offsetting transaction, Trader A is out of the market. Trader D has reversed one of her three contracts. This reduces the open interest by one contract. At $t = 4$, Trader C sells and Trader E buys one widget contract, for one contract of volume. With this transaction, Trader C reverses one contract, but Trader E enters the market. Because Trader E, in effect, takes the place of Trader C for this one contract, the open interest remains at three. The bottom panel of the table summarizes each trader's position and shows how the open interest remains at three contracts.

When a contract is distant from maturity, it tends to have relatively little open interest. As the contract approaches maturity, the open interest increases. Most often, the contract closest

Figure 3.2 The DEC 1989 S&P 500® futures open interest

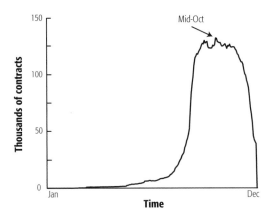

Figure 3.3 The DEC 1989 S&P 500® futures trading volume

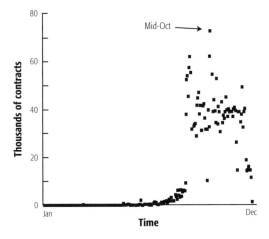

to delivery, the nearby contract, has the highest level of open interest. As the nearby contract comes very close to maturity, however, the open interest falls. This is due to the fact that traders close their positions to avoid actual delivery. As we saw in Chapter 1, actual delivery is fairly unusual. When the futures contract matures, all traders with remaining open interest must make or take delivery, and the open interest goes to zero. Recall also that the open interest figures reported in *The Wall Street Journal* pertain to the day preceding the one for which prices are reported. Figure 3.2 shows the pattern of open interest for the December 1989 S&P 500® futures contract over its life, and Figure 3.3 shows the pattern of trading volume for the same contract. The open interest and volume of trading follow a predictable pattern, such as the one shown in these two figures. Notice that the peak open interest occurs when the contract has about two or three months remaining until expiration.

In Figure 3.1, beneath the lines for each of the contract maturities, *The Wall Street Journal* reports more trading information. The figure shows the estimated volume for all maturities for a given commodity, followed by the actual volume for the preceding day. Next, the open interest for all contract maturities is shown. (This amount should equal the sum of the open interest figures shown for the individual contracts.[3]) Finally, the last number reports the change in the open interest since the preceding day. We may also note that it is possible for the volume of trading to exceed the number of contracts of open interest. This occurs when trading activity is particularly heavy for a given commodity on a certain day. Chapter 4 considers the different trading parties who give rise to the trading volume and open interest.

Prices are property[4]

The sale of real-time transaction prices, quotations, and other market data is a huge source of revenue for financial exchanges such as the Chicago Mercantile Exchange (CME) and the CBOT. However, had it not been for a series of nineteenth-century lawsuits, the exchanges may not have established property rights to information generated through the trading process and therefore may have been unable to sell these data.

In the late nineteenth century, transaction prices and market quotations were disseminated via the advanced trading system of that day—the telegraph. Just as the Internet revolutionized trading in the 1990s, so did the telegraph for the traders of its day: it increased the speed of communication, lowered the costs of disseminating quotations, and offered both costs and benefits to the exchanges. On the one hand, it allowed exchange members to receive and transmit customer orders over a vast geographic area, expanding the market for potential users of exchange instruments. On the other, the rapid transmission of up-to-the-minute quotations made it easier for off-exchange traders to "free-ride" off of the exchange-generated quotations. Off-exchange free-riders were labeled "bucket shops." To prevent free-riding by bucket shops, the exchanges devised new rules and contractual arrangements to define and enforce property rights to the information content of their quotations.

At one point during the exchanges' battle with the bucket shops, the CBOT was ordered by the courts to either refrain from disseminating quotations altogether or furnish quotations to all those who desired them. As a result, the CBOT decided to discontinue the dissemination of market reports and quotations. William Baker, president of CBOT, ordered all telegraph instruments and telegraph employees removed from the trading area, making it impossible for members to communicate from the exchange floor. During the resulting "Baker Blackout," the CBOT soaped the windows of the exchange hall to prevent the transmission of quotations from the exchange floor to outsiders through hand signals.[5]

The CBOT and other exchanges were ultimately successful in establishing a property right to the prices generated on the exchange floor. In 1905, the CBOT, as plaintiff, won a U.S. Supreme Court decision with Justice Holmes writing that, "the plaintiff's collection of quotations is entitled to the protection of the law.[6] It stands like a trade secret." Continuing, the court said that, "The plaintiff has the right to keep the work which it has done, or paid for doing, to itself. The fact that others might do similar work, if they might, does not authorize them to steal the plaintiff's." Following this decision, the courts made similar rulings regarding other financial exchanges.

The basis and spreads

In this section, we analyze relationships between two prices. The **basis** is the relationship between the cash price of a good and the futures price for the same good. We also consider spreads. A **spread** is the difference between two futures prices. If the two prices are for futures contracts on the same underlying good, but with different expiration dates, the spread is an **intracommodity spread**. If the two futures prices that form a spread are futures prices for two underlying goods, such as a wheat futures and a corn futures, then the spread is an **intercommodity spread**.

The basis

The basis receives a great deal of attention in futures trading. The **basis** is the current cash price of a particular commodity at a specified location minus the price of a particular futures contract for the same commodity:

basis = current cash price – futures price

Several features of this definition require explanation. First, the definition of the basis depends upon a cash price of a commodity at a specific location. The cash price of corn, for example, might differ between Kansas City and Chicago, so the bases for those two locations will also differ. Normally, one good cannot sell for different prices in two markets. If such a good had two prices, a trader could buy the commodity in the cheaper market and sell it in the market with the higher price, thereby reaping an **arbitrage profit**—a sure profit with no investment. Prices for corn in Chicago and Kansas City can differ, of course, because of the expense of transporting corn from one location to another. If corn is grown near Chicago, then we might reasonably expect the price of corn in Chicago to be lower than the price in Kansas City. Therefore, the basis calculated in considering futures prices may differ, depending upon the geographic location of the spot price that is used to compute the basis.

Usually, people speaking of the basis are referring to the difference between the cash price and the nearby futures contract. However, there is a basis for each outstanding futures contract, and these bases will often differ in systematic ways, depending upon the maturities of the individual futures contracts. Table 3.2 shows spot and futures gold prices for July 11 and illustrates this phenomenon. The cash, or spot, price is the London a.m. fix, or morning quotation, so the basis pertains to London. The futures prices are from the Commodities Exchange (COMEX) division of the New York Mercantile Exchange. The right-hand column shows the basis for

Table 3.2   Gold prices and the basis (July 11)

Contract	Prices	The basis
CASH	353.70	
JUL (this year)	354.10	−0.40
AUG	355.60	−1.90
OCT	359.80	−6.10
DEC	364.20	−10.50
FEB (next year)	368.70	−15.00
APR	373.00	−19.30
JUN	377.50	−23.80
AUG	381.90	−28.20
OCT	386.70	−33.00
DEC	391.50	−37.80

each futures contract. The basis is negative for all delivery months in this example. The chart of the basis shows that it is possible to contract for the future sale or purchase of gold at a price that exceeds the current cash price. The difference between the current cash price of $353.70 per ounce and the price of the more distant futures contracts is striking, as much as $37.80 per ounce for the most distant DEC contract.

Futures markets can exhibit a pattern of either normal or inverted prices. In a **normal market**, prices for more distant futures are higher than for nearby futures. For example, the gold prices in Table 3.2 represent a normal market. In an **inverted market**, distant futures prices are lower than those of contracts nearer to expiration. The interpretation of the basis can be very important, particularly for agricultural commodities. For many commodities, the fact that the harvest comes at a certain time each year introduces seasonal components into the series of cash prices.[7] Many traders believe that understanding these seasonal factors can be very beneficial for speculation and hedging. Moreover, the basis, such as that shown in Table 3.2, can be used as a valuable source of information to predict future spot prices of the commodities that underlie the futures contracts.

A further point about the basis emerges from a consideration of Table 3.2. Note that the basis for the nearby contract is only −$0.40, about one-thousandth of the cash price. There is good reason why it should be so small. The JUL contract is extremely close to delivery on the date in question, July 11. At delivery the futures price and the cash price must be equal, except for minor discrepancies due to transportation and other transaction costs. If someone were to trade the JUL contract on July 11, the trade would be for the delivery of gold within three weeks. The price of gold for delivery within three weeks must closely approximate the current spot price of gold.

When the futures contract is at expiration, the futures price and the spot price of gold must be the same. The basis must be zero, again subject to the discrepancy due to transaction costs. This behavior of the basis over time is known as **convergence**, as Figures 3.4 and 3.5 illustrate. In Figure 3.4, the cash price lies above the futures price. As time progresses and the futures contract approaches maturity, the basis narrows. At the maturity of the futures contract, the basis is zero, consistent with the no-arbitrage requirement that the futures price and cash price be equal at the maturity of the futures contract. Convergence should occur for the cash commodity

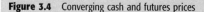

Figure 3.4 Converging cash and futures prices

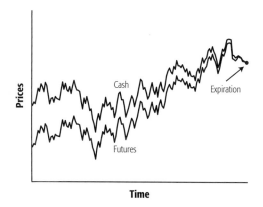

Figure 3.5 Convergence of the basis to zero

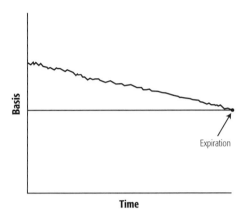

specified in the futures contract, but one would not expect the futures price to converge to cash prices from nondelivery locations or to cash prices for grades of the cash commodity that differ from the delivery specifications in the futures contract. Figure 3.5 shows the basis itself, corresponding to the prices in Figure 3.4. The basis is positive, but declines to zero as the futures contract approaches maturity.

Figure 3.6 illustrates one other feature of the basis that is very important for futures trading. The upper portion of the figure shows prices for the MAR S&P 500 futures contract. The graph covers the range from 300 to 380, an 80-point range within which the contract traded between July and its expiration in March of the next year. The bottom portion of Figure 3.6 illustrates how the basis for this contract behaved over the same time interval. To make the two graphs comparable, this bottom panel also covers a 100-point scale.

As the graph dramatically reveals, the fluctuation in the basis was much less than the range of fluctuation in the futures price itself. This is almost always the case. The basis is almost always much more stable than the futures price or the cash price, when those prices are considered in isolation. The futures price may oscillate and the cash price may swing widely, but the basis (cash minus futures price) tends to be relatively steady. The relatively low variability of the basis is very important for hedging and for certain types of speculation, as will be discussed in Chapter 4.

Spreads

Just as there is an important relationship between each futures contract and the cash price of the commodity, the relationships among futures prices on the same good are also important. As we discussed in Chapter 1, there are intracommodity spreads and intercommodity spreads. An intracommodity spread is the difference in price between two futures contracts of different maturity dates on the same commodity, and these spreads are important because they indicate the relative price differentials for a commodity to be delivered at two points in time. As we will see, there are strong economic relationships that govern the permissible time spreads that may exist between any two futures contracts.

Figure 3.6 The S&P 500® cash and basis: (a) the cash market value of the S&P 500; (b) the S&P 500 basis

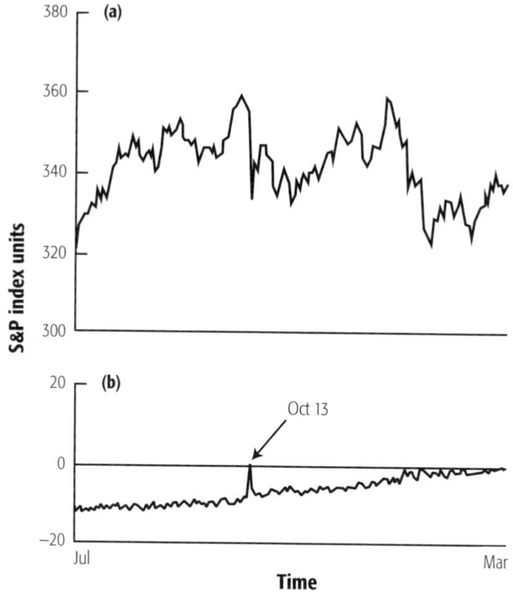

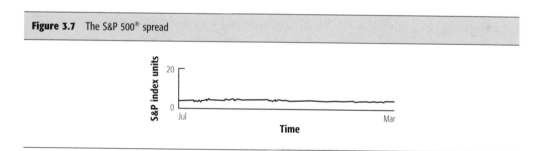

Figure 3.7 The S&P 500® spread

Spread relationships are important for speculators. Much speculation involves some kind of spread position—the holding of two or more related futures contracts. These traders form spread positions that they hope will profit from correctly predicting whether the price spread between related contracts will narrow or widen. If a trader hopes to use futures markets to earn speculative profits, an understanding of spread relationships is essential. Since most speculation uses spreads, the search for a profit turns on an ability to identify spread relationships that are economically unjustified. While the understanding of the spread relationships in a particular commodity requires considerable knowledge about the commodity itself, certain general principles apply to all spreads.

Figure 3.7 shows the spread between the S&P 500 futures contracts for JUN of the current year and MAR of the next year, computed here as the June price minus the March price. The time period here is the same used in Figure 3.6. Thus, we can see the stability of the spread in Figure 3.7 compared to the price itself in Figure 3.6.[8]

Limit orders

Traders will often submit orders with the condition that the order not be executed unless the price reaches a predetermined level. These conditioned orders are called "limit orders." For example, a corn producer may give instructions to his broker to sell March corn only if the price reaches $2.70 per bushel. On the other hand, a buyer may give instructions not to buy March corn unless the price falls below $2.50 per bushel. Limit orders are used by traders as a means of communicating their instructions to their broker. The broker monitors the market to make sure he is abiding by his customer's trading instructions.

Traders who submit limit orders give other traders the choice of whether or not to trade with the order. This choice can be characterized as an option to trade. For example, a limit order to sell gives other traders the option to buy at the limit price. The option to buy a set quantity at a set price is by definition a call option. A limit order to buy gives other traders the option to sell at the limit price. The option to sell a set quantity at a set price is by definition a put option.

Like any other option, the option to trade is valuable. Traders who write limit orders, however, do not get paid a premium as in the case of the other types of options that are traded in the market. Instead, traders who submit limit orders give away the option for free to the market. Any trader who wants to exercise the option may do so by submitting a market order. The option to trade will become more valuable the more volatile the market is, and the closer the limit price is to the current market price. To reduce the option value that they are giving away, traders often post-limit orders that are far from the market price when the market is volatile.

Models of futures prices

In this section, we consider two models of futures prices. The first of these is the cost-of-carry model. According to this model, futures prices depend on the cash price of a commodity and the cost of storing the underlying good from the present to the delivery date of the futures contract. The second model is the expectations model. According to this view, the futures price today equals the cash price that traders expect to prevail for the underlying good on the delivery date of the futures contract. For example, the futures price in January for the JUL contract is the market's January estimate of what the price of corn will be in July when the futures contract expires.

To explore these models, we employ the concept of arbitrage. We begin by assuming that prices in the market do not allow any arbitrage profits. Under this assumption, we ask whether or not futures pricing relationships are permissible. For the sake of simplicity, we begin by assuming that futures markets are perfect. A **perfect market** is a market with no transaction costs and no restrictions on free contracting between two parties. Thus, the analysis begins under the assumptions of an idealized world—a world that allows no arbitrage and that includes no market frictions. Gradually, we develop a more realistic analysis by relaxing these assumptions. This approach allows us to start the analysis within a fairly simple environment and to add complications after we explore the most essential features of the pricing relationships.

The cost-of-carry model in perfect markets

In this section, we use the concept of arbitrage that we have just explained to explore the cost-of-carry model, or the carrying charge theory of futures prices. The **cost of carry**, or **carrying charge**, is the total cost to carry a good forward in time. For example, wheat on hand in June can be carried forward to, or stored until, December.

Carrying charges fall into four basic categories: storage costs, insurance costs, transportation costs, and financing costs. Storage costs include the cost of warehousing the commodity in the appropriate facility. While storage seems to apply most clearly to physical goods, such as wheat or lumber, it is also possible to store financial instruments. In many cases, the owner of a financial instrument will leave the instrument in a bank vault. For many goods in storage, insurance is also necessary. For example, stored lumber should be protected against fire, and stored wheat should be insured against water damage.[9]

In some cases, the carrying charges also include transportation costs. Wheat in a railroad siding in Kansas must be carried to delivery in two senses. It must be stored until the appropriate delivery time for a given futures contract, but it must also be physically carried to the appropriate place for delivery. We will see that transportation costs between different locations determine price differentials between those locations. Without question, transportation charges play different roles for different commodities. Transporting wheat from Kansas to Chicago could be an important expense. By contrast, delivery of Treasury notes against a futures contract is accomplished by a wire transfer costing only a few dollars. In almost all cases, the most significant carrying charge in the futures market is the financing cost. For most situations, financing the good under storage overwhelms the other costs.

The carrying charge reflects only the charges involved in carrying a commodity from one time or one place to another. The carrying charges do not include the value of the commodity itself. Therefore, if gold costs $400 per ounce and the financing rate is 1 percent per month, the financing charge for carrying the gold forward is $4 per month (1 percent × $400).

Most participants in the futures markets face a financing charge on a short-term basis that is equal to the **repo rate**, the interest rate on repurchase agreements. In a **repurchase agreement**, a person sells securities at one point in time with the understanding that these will be repurchased at a certain price at a later time. Most repurchase agreements are for only one day and are known, accordingly, as overnight repos. The repo rate is relatively low, exceeding the rate on Treasury bills by only a small amount.[10] The financing cost for such goods is so low because anyone wishing to finance a commodity may offer the commodity itself as collateral for the loan. Further, most of the participants in the market tend to be financial institutions of one type or another that have low financing costs anyway, at least for very short-term obligations.

Cash and futures pricing relationships

The carrying charges just described are important because they play a crucial role in determining pricing relationships between spot and futures prices, as well as the relationships among prices of futures contracts of different maturities. As of now, let us assume that the only carrying charge is the financing cost at an interest rate of 10 percent per year. As an example, consider the prices and accompanying transactions shown in Table 3.3.

The transactions in Table 3.3 represent a successful cash-and-carry arbitrage. This is a **cash-and-carry arbitrage** because the trader buys the cash good and carries it to the expiration of the futures contract. In this example, we assume for simplicity that a futures contract is written on one ounce of gold. This assumption differs from actual futures contracts that are based on 100 ounces of gold. The trader traded at $t = 0$ to guarantee a riskless profit without investment. There was no investment, because there was no cash flow at $t = 0$. The trader merely borrowed funds to purchase the gold and to carry it forward. The profit in these transactions was certain once the trader made the transactions at $t = 0$. As these transactions show, to prevent arbitrage the futures price of the gold should have been $440 or less. With a futures price of $440, for example, the transactions in Table 3.3 would yield a zero profit. From this example, we can infer the following general rule:

Table 3.3 Cash-and-carry gold arbitrage transactions		
Prices for the analysis	Spot price of gold	$400
	Future price of gold (for delivery in one year)	$450
	Interest rate	10%
Transaction		*Cash flow*
$t = 0$	Borrow $400 for one year at 10%	+$400
	Buy one ounce of gold in the spot market for $400	−400
	Sell a futures contract for $450 for delivery of one ounce	
	in one year	0
	Total cash flow	$0
$t = 1$	Remove the gold from storage	$0
	Deliver the ounce of gold against the futures	
	Contract	+450
	Repay loan, including interest	−440
	Total cash flow	+$10

Cost-of-carry rule 1

The futures price must be less than or equal to the spot price of the commodity plus the carrying charges necessary to carry the spot commodity forward to delivery.

We can express rule 1 mathematically as follows:

$$F_{0,t} \leq S_0(1 + C) \tag{3.1}$$

where $F_{0,t}$ is the futures price at $t = 0$ for delivery at time t, S_0 is the spot price at $t = 0$, and C is the cost of carry, expressed as a fraction of the spot price, necessary to carry the good forward from the present to the delivery date on the futures.

As we have seen, if prices do not conform to cost-of-carry rule 1, a trader can borrow funds, buy the spot commodity with the borrowed funds, sell the futures contract, and carry the commodity forward to deliver against the futures contract. These transactions would generate a certain profit without investment, or an arbitrage profit. There would be a certain profit because it is guaranteed by the sale of the futures contract. Moreover, there would be no investment, since the funds needed to carry out the strategy were borrowed and the cost of using those funds was included in the calculation of the carrying charge. Such opportunities cannot exist in a rational market. The cash-and-carry arbitrage opportunity arises because the spot price is too low relative to the futures price.

We have seen that an arbitrage opportunity arises if the spot price is too low relative to the futures price. As we now see, the spot price might also be too high relative to the futures price. If the spot price is too high, we have a reverse cash-and-carry arbitrage opportunity. As the name implies, the steps necessary to exploit the arbitrage opportunity are just the opposite of those in the cash-and-carry arbitrage strategy. As an example of the reverse cash-and-carry strategy, consider the prices for gold and the accompanying transactions in Table 3.4.

In these transactions, the arbitrageur sells the gold short. As in the stock market, a short seller borrows the good from another trader and must later repay it. Once the good is borrowed, the short seller sells it and takes the money from the sale. (The transaction is called short selling because the seller sells a good that he or she does not actually own.) In this example, the short

Table 3.4   Reverse cash-and-carry gold arbitrage transactions

Prices for the analysis	Spot price of gold	$420
	Future price of gold (for delivery in one year)	$450
	Interest rate	10%

Transaction		Cash flow
$t = 0$	Sell one ounce of gold short	+$420
	Lend the $420 for one year at 10%	−420
	Buy one ounce of gold futures for delivery in one year	0
	Total cash flow	$0
$t = 1$	Collect proceeds from the loan ($420 × 1.1)	+462
	Accept delivery on the futures contract	−450
	Use gold from futures delivery to repay short sale	0
	Total cash flow	+$12

Table 3.5   Transactions for arbitrage strategies

Market	Cash and carry	Reverse cash and carry
Debt	Borrow funds	Lend short sale proceeds
Physical	Buy asset and store; deliver against futures	Sell asset short; secure proceeds from short sale
Futures	Sell futures	Buy futures; accept delivery; return physical asset to honor short sale commitment

seller has the use of all of the proceeds from the short sale, which are invested at the interest rate of 10 percent. The trader also buys a futures contract to ensure that he or she can acquire the gold needed to repay the lender at the expiration of the futures in one year.

Notice that these transactions guarantee an arbitrage profit. Once the transactions at $t = 0$ are completed, the $12 profit at $t = 1$ year is certain. Also, the trader had no net cash flow at $t = 0$, so the strategy required no investment. To make this arbitrage opportunity impossible, the spot and futures prices must obey cost-of-carry rule 2.

Cost-of-carry rule 2
The futures price must be equal to or greater than the spot price plus the cost of carrying the good to the futures delivery date.

Expressing this rule mathematically, with the notation we introduced above,

$$F_{0,t} \geq S_0(1 + C) \tag{3.2}$$

If prices do not obey this rule, there will be an arbitrage opportunity. Table 3.5 summarizes the transactions necessary to conduct the cash-and-carry and the reverse cash-and-carry strategies.

To prevent arbitrage, we have seen that the following two rules must hold:

To prevent cash-and-carry arbitrage:	$F_{0,t} \leq S_0(1 + C)$	(3.1)
To prevent reverse cash-and-carry arbitrage:	$F_{0,t} \geq S_0(1 + C)$	(3.2)

Table 3.6   Gold forward cash-and-carry arbitrage

Prices for the analysis	Futures price for gold expiring in one year	$400
	Futures price for gold expiring in two years	$450
	Interest rate (to cover from year 1 to year 2)	10%

Transaction		Cash flow
$t = 0$	Buy the futures expiring in one year	+$0
	Sell the futures expiring in two years	0
	Contract to borrow $400 at 10% for year 1 to year 20	0
	Total cash flow	$0
$t = 1$	Borrow $400 for one year at 10% as contracted at $t = 0$	+$400
	Take delivery on the futures contract	−400
	Begin to store gold for one year	0
	Total cash flow	$0
$t = 2$	Deliver gold to honor futures contract	+$450
	Repay loan ($400 × 1.1)	−440
	Total cash flow	+$10

Together, Equations 3.1 and 3.2 imply cost-of-carry rule 3:

Cost-of-carry rule 3
The futures price must equal the spot price plus the cost of carrying the spot commodity forward to the delivery date of the futures contract.

Expressing rule 3 mathematically, we have

$$F_{0,t} = S_0(1 + C) \tag{3.3}$$

Notice that the relationship of Equation 3.3 was derived under the following assumptions: Markets are perfect; that is, they have no transaction costs and no restrictions on the use of proceeds from short sales. It must be acknowledged that this argument explicitly excludes transaction costs. Transaction costs exist on both sides of the market, for purchase or sale of the futures. However, in many markets, transaction costs for short selling are considerably more expensive, which limits the applicability of the reverse cash-and-carry strategy.

Spreads and the cost of carry
These same cost-of-carry relationships also determine the price relationships that can exist between futures contracts on the same good that differ in maturity. As an example, consider the prices and accompanying arbitrage transactions shown in Table 3.6.

As this example shows, the spread between two futures contracts cannot exceed the cost of carrying the good from one delivery date forward to the next, as cost-of-carry rule 4 states:

Cost-of-carry rule 4
The distant futures price must be less than or equal to the nearby futures price plus the cost of carrying the commodity from the nearby delivery date to the distant delivery date.

Table 3.7   Gold forward reverse cash-and-carry arbitrage

Prices for the analysis	Futures price for gold expiring in one year	$440
	Futures price for gold expiring in two years	$450
	Interest rate (to cover from year 1 to year 2)	10%
Transaction		*Cash flow*
$t = 0$	Sell the futures expiring in one year	+$0
	Buy the futures expiring in two years	0
	Contract to lend $440 at 10% from year 1 to year 2	0
	Total cash flow	$0
$t = 1$	Borrow one ounce of gold for one year	$0
	Deliver gold against the expiring futures	+440
	Invest proceeds from delivery for one year	440
	Total cash flow	$0
$t = 2$	Accept delivery on expiring futures	−$450
	Repay one ounce of borrowed gold	0
	Collect on loan of $440 made at $t = 1$	+484
	Total cash flow	+$34

Expressing rule 4 mathematically, we have

$$F_{0,d} \le F_{0,n}(1 + C), \quad d > n \tag{3.4}$$

where $F_{0,d}$ is the futures price at $t = 0$ for the distant delivery contract maturing at $t = d$, $F_{0,n}$ is the futures price at $t = 0$ for the nearby delivery contract maturing at $t = n$, and C is the percentage cost of carrying the good from $t = n$ to $t = d$.

As we have seen, if this relationship did not hold, a trader could buy the nearby futures contract and sell the distant contract. The trader would then accept delivery on the nearby contract and carry the good until the delivery of the distant contract, thereby making a profit.

To complete our argument, we analyze what happens if the nearby futures price is too high relative to the distant futures price. To conduct the arbitrage in this case, consider the gold prices and arbitrage transactions shown in Table 3.7.

Thus, forward reverse cash-and-carry arbitrage is possible if the nearby futures price is too high relative to the distant futures price. To exclude this arbitrage opportunity, prices must conform to cost-of-carry rule 5:

Cost-of-carry rule 5
The nearby futures price plus the cost of carrying the commodity from the nearby delivery date to the distant delivery date cannot exceed the distant futures price.

Expressing rule 5 mathematically, we have

$$F_{0,d} \ge F_{0,n}(1 + C), \quad d > n \tag{3.5}$$

From our two-arbitrage arguments in Tables 3.6 and 3.7, we have derived the rules expressed in Equations 3.4 and 3.5. To exclude forward:

Cash-and-carry arbitrage: $\qquad F_{0,d} \leq F_{0,n}(1 + C), \quad d > n$ $\qquad$ (3.4)

Reverse cash-and-carry arbitrage: $\quad F_{0,d} \geq F_{0,n}(1 + C), \quad d > n$ $\qquad$ (3.5)

Following the same pattern of argument that we used for spot prices and futures prices, we see that Equations 3.4 and 3.5 imply cost-of-carry rule 6:

Cost-of-carry rule 6
The distant futures price must equal the nearby futures price plus the cost of carrying the commodity from the nearby to the distant delivery date.

We can express rule 6 mathematically as follows:

$$F_{0,d} = F_{0,n}(1 + C), \quad d > n \qquad (3.6)$$

If these relationships were ever violated, profit-hungry traders would immediately recognize the chance and trade until prices adjusted to eliminate all of the arbitrage opportunities.

Summary
All of the cost-of-carry relationships explored up to this point have been based on assumptions that markets are perfect. In particular, we have assumed that they allow unrestricted short selling. For example, we have assumed that the borrowing and lending rates are equal, that we can sell gold short and use 100 percent of the proceeds from the short sale, and that it is possible to contract to borrow and lend at forward rates. All of these assumptions require qualifications, which will be developed in the next section.

The basic rules developed in this section provide a very useful framework for analyzing relationships between cash and futures prices on the one hand, and spreads between futures prices on the other. Cost-of-carry rule 3 and Equation 3.3 express the basic cash–futures relationship:

$$F_{0,t} = S_0(1 + C) \qquad (3.3)$$

Cost-of-carry rule 6 and Equation 3.6 express the relationship for two futures prices:

$$F_{0,d} = F_{0,n}(1 + C), \quad d > n \qquad (3.6)$$

Notice that these two equations have the same form. We therefore use Equation 3.3 to make a final point to summarize the cost-of-carry model in perfect markets. Equation 3.7 implies that the cost of carry in the perfect market we have been considering equals the ratio of the futures price to the spot price minus 1. In Equation 3.7, the "C" is the **implied repo rate**—the interest rate implied by the difference between the cash and futures prices. Solving Equation 3.3 for the cost of carry C, we have

$$C = \frac{F_{0,t}}{S_0} - 1 \qquad (3.7)$$

In a well-functioning market, the implied repo rate must equal the actual repo rate. As we have seen in this section, deviations from this relationship lead to arbitrage opportunities in a perfect market. We now turn to considering the qualifications to the basic conclusion that are required by market imperfections.

The cost-of-carry model in imperfect markets

In real markets, four market imperfections operate to complicate and disturb the relationships of Equations 3.3 and 3.6. First, traders face transaction costs. Second, restrictions on short selling frustrate reverse cash-and-carry strategies. Third, borrowing and lending rates are not generally equal, as the assumption of perfect markets would imply. Finally, some goods cannot be stored, so they cannot be carried forward to delivery. This section considers each of these in turn.

The main effect of these market imperfections is to require adjustments in the identities expressed by Equations 3.3 and 3.6. Market imperfections do not invalidate the basic framework we have been building. Instead of being able to state an equality, as we did in the perfect markets framework leading to Equations 3.3 and 3.6, we will find that market imperfections introduce a certain indeterminacy to the relationship.

Direct transaction costs

In actual markets, traders face a variety of direct transaction costs. First, the trader must pay a fee to have an order executed. For a trader off the floor of the exchange, these fees include brokerage commissions and various exchange fees. Even members of the exchange must pay a fee to the exchange for each trade. Second, in every market, there is a bid–ask spread. A market maker on the floor of the exchange must try to sell at a higher price (the **asked price**) than the price at which he or she is willing to buy (the **bid price**). The difference between the asked price and the bid price is the **bid–ask spread**. In our discussion, let us assume that these transaction costs are some fixed percentage of the transaction amount, T. For simplicity, we assume that the transaction costs apply to the spot market, but not to the futures market.[11]

To illustrate the impact of transaction costs, we use the same prices with which we began our analysis in perfect markets. Now, however, we consider transaction costs of 3 percent. With transaction costs, our previous arbitrage strategy of buying the good and carrying it to delivery will not work. Table 3.8 shows the results of this attempted arbitrage. With transaction costs, the attempted arbitrage results in a certain loss, not an arbitrage profit.

We would have to pay \$400 as before to acquire the good, plus transaction costs of 3 percent for a total outlay of $\$400(1 + T) = \$412$. We would then have to finance this total amount until delivery for a cost of $\$412 \times 1.1 = \$453.20$. In return, we would only receive \$450 upon the delivery of the futures contract. Given these prices, it clearly does not pay to attempt this "cash-and-carry" arbitrage. As Table 3.8 shows, these attempted arbitrage transactions generate a certain loss of \$3.20. With transaction costs of 3 percent and the same spot price of \$400, the futures price would have to exceed \$453.20 to make the arbitrage attractive. In order to check this, consider the cash outflows and inflows. We pay the spot price plus the transaction costs, $S_0(1 + T)$, to acquire the good. Carrying the good to delivery costs $S_0(1 + T)(1 + C)$. These costs include acquiring the good and carrying it to the delivery date of the futures. In our example, the total cost is

$$S_0(1 + T)(1 + C) = \$400 \times 1.03 \times 1.1 = \$453.20$$

Thus, to break even, the futures transaction must yield \$453.20. We can write this more formally as follows:

$$F_{0,t} \le S_0(1 + T)(1 + C) \tag{3.8}$$

If prices follow Equation 3.8, the cash-and-carry arbitrage opportunity will not be available. Notice that Equation 3.8 has the same form as Equation 3.1, but Equation 3.8 includes transaction costs.

Table 3.8   Attempted cash-and-carry gold arbitrage transactions

Prices for the analysis	Spot price of gold	$400
	Future price of gold (for delivery in one year)	$450
	Interest rate	10%
	Transaction cost (T)	3%

Transaction		Cash flow
t = 0	Borrow $412 for one year at 10%	+$412
	Buy one ounce of gold in the spot market for $400 and pay 3% transaction costs, to total $412	−412
	Sell a futures contract for $450 for delivery of one ounce in one year	0
	Total cash flow	$0
t = 1	Remove the gold from storage	$0
	Deliver the ounce of gold to close futures contract	+450.00
	Repay loan, including interest	−453.20
	Total cash flow	−$3.20

Table 3.9   Attempted reverse cash-and-carry gold arbitrage

Prices for the analysis	Spot price of gold	$420
	Future price of gold (for delivery in one year)	$450
	Interest rate	10%
	Transaction costs (T)	3%

Transaction		Cash flow
t = 0	Sell one ounce of gold short, paying 3% transaction costs; receive $420 × 0.97 = $407.40	+$407.40
	Lend the $407.40 for one year at 10%	−407.40
	Buy one ounce of gold futures for delivery in one year	0
	Total cash flow	$0
t = 1	Collect loan proceeds ($407.40 × 1.1)	+$448.14
	Accept gold delivery on the futures contract	−450.00
	Use gold from futures delivery to repay short sale	0
	Total cash flow	−$1.86

In our discussion of the cost-of-carry model in perfect markets, we saw that futures prices could not be too high relative to spot prices. Otherwise, arbitrage opportunities would be available, as we saw in Table 3.4. We now explore the transactions as shown in Table 3.4, except that we include the transaction costs of 3 percent. Table 3.9 shows these transactions.

The inclusion of transaction costs in the analysis gives a loss on the same transactions that were profitable with no transaction costs. In the original transactions of Table 3.4 with the same prices, the profit was $12. For perfect markets, Equation 3.2 gave the no-arbitrage conditions for the reverse cash-and-carry arbitrage strategy:

$$F_{0,t} \geq S_0(1 + C) \tag{3.2}$$

Table 3.10   An illustration of no-arbitrage bounds

Prices for the analysis		
	Spot price of gold	$400
	Interest rate	10%
	Transaction costs (T)	3%

No-arbitrage futures price in perfect markets
$F_{0,t} = S_0(1 + C) = \$400 \times 1.1 = \$440$

Upper no-arbitrage bound with transaction costs
$F_{0,t} \leq S_0(1 + T)(1 + C) = \$400 \times 1.03 \times 1.1 = \$453.20$

Lower no-arbitrage bound with transaction costs
$F_{0,t} \geq S_0(1 - T)(1 + C) = \$400 \times 0.97 \times 1.1 = \$426.80$

Including transaction costs, we have

$$F_{0,t} \geq S_0(1 - T)(1 + C) \tag{3.9}$$

Combining Equations 3.8 and 3.9 gives

$$S_0(1 - T)(1 + C) \leq F_{0,t} \leq S_0(1 + T)(1 + C) \tag{3.10}$$

Equation 3.10 defines the **no-arbitrage bounds**—the bounds within which the futures price must remain to prevent arbitrage. In general, transaction costs force a loosening of the price relationship in Equation 3.3. In perfect markets, Equation 3.3 gave an exact equation for the futures price as a function of the spot price and the cost of carry. If the futures price deviated from that no-arbitrage price, traders could transact to reap a riskless profit without investment. For a market with transaction costs, Equation 3.10 gives bounds for the futures price. If the futures price goes beyond these boundaries, arbitrage is possible. However, the futures price can wander within the bounds without offering arbitrage opportunities. As an example, consider the bounds implied by the transactions in Table 3.8. If there are no transaction costs, the futures price must be exactly $440 to exclude arbitrage. With the 3 percent transaction costs on spot market transactions, the futures price is free to wander within the range $426.80–453.20 without creating any arbitrage opportunity, as Table 3.10 shows.

Figure 3.8 illustrates the concept of arbitrage boundaries. The vertical axis graphs futures prices and the horizontal axis shows the time dimension. The solid horizontal line in the graph shows the no-arbitrage condition for a perfect market. In a perfect market, the futures price must exactly equal the spot price times one plus the cost of carry, $F_{0,t} = S_0(1 + C)$. With transaction costs, however, we have a lower and an upper bound. If the futures price goes above the upper no-arbitrage bound, there will be a cash-and-carry arbitrage opportunity. This occurs when $F_{0,t} > S_0(1 + T)(1 + C)$. Likewise, if the futures price falls too low, it will be less than the lower no-arbitrage bound. Futures prices that are too low relative to the spot price give rise to a reverse cash-and-carry arbitrage. This opportunity arises when $F_{0,t} < S_0(1 - T)(1 + C)$. Figure 3.8 shows these no-arbitrage boundaries as dotted lines.

If the futures price stays between the bounds, no arbitrage is possible. If the futures price crosses the boundaries, arbitrageurs will flock to the market to exploit the opportunity. For example, if the futures price is too high, traders will buy the spot commodity and sell the futures.

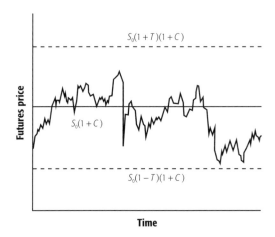

Figure 3.8   No-arbitrage bounds

This action will raise the price of the spot good relative to the futures price, thereby driving the futures price back within the no-arbitrage boundaries. If the futures price stays within the boundaries, no arbitrage is possible, and the arbitrageurs will not be able to affect the futures price.

From Figure 3.8, we note three important points. First, the greater the transaction costs, T, the farther apart will be the bounds. With higher transaction costs, the arbitrage relationships we have been exploring are less binding on possible prices. Second, we have been assuming that all traders in the market face the same percentage transaction costs, T. Clearly, different traders face different transaction costs. For example, a retail trader, who is not an exchange member, can face transaction costs that are much higher than those for a floor trader. It is easily possible for the retail trader to pay as much as 100 times the exchange and brokerage fees paid by a floor trader. Therefore, Figure 3.8 really pertains to a particular trader, not to every trader in the market. Consider a trader facing higher transaction costs of $2T$ instead of T. For this trader, the no-arbitrage bounds would be twice as wide as those in Figure 3.8. Third, we have seen that market forces exist to keep the futures price within the no-arbitrage bounds, and that each trader faces his or her own particular bounds, depending on that trader's transaction costs.

Differences in transaction costs give rise to the concept of **quasi-arbitrage**. Some traders, such as small retail customers, face full transaction costs. Other traders, such as large financial institutions, have much lower transaction costs. For example, exchange members pay much lower transaction costs than do outside traders. Therefore, the quasi-arbitrageur is a potential cash-and-carry or reverse cash-and-carry trader with relatively lower transaction costs. The futures price should stay within the bounds of the trader with the lowest transaction cost. Once the futures price drifts beyond the bounds of the trader with the lowest transaction cost, he or she will exploit the arbitrage opportunity. As we have seen, arbitrage activity will drive the futures price back within the no-arbitrage bounds for that trader.

Thus, in the actual market, we expect to see futures prices within the no-arbitrage bounds of the trader with the lowest transaction cost. This means that traders with higher transaction costs will not be able to exploit any arbitrage opportunities. If prices start to drift away from

---

Table 3.11   An illustration of no-arbitrage bounds with differential borrowing and lending rates

Prices for the analysis		
	Spot price of gold	$400
	Interest rate (borrowing)	12%
	Interest rate (lending)	8%
	Transaction costs (T)	3%

Upper no-arbitrage bound with transaction costs and a borrowing rate
$F_{0,t} \le S_0(1 + T)(1 + C_B) = \$400 \times 1.03 \times 1.12 = \$461.44$

Lower no-arbitrage bound with transaction costs and a lending rate
$F_{0,t} \ge S_0(1 - T)(1 + C_L) = \$400 \times 0.97 \times 1.08 = \$419.04$

---

the perfect markets equality of Equation 3.3, they will be exploited first by the traders with low transaction costs. This exploitation will take place through quasi-arbitrage, because the low transaction cost trader does not face the full transaction costs of an outside trader.

Unequal borrowing and lending rates
In perfect markets, all traders can borrow and lend at the risk-free rate. This is not true in real markets. Generally, traders face a borrowing rate that exceeds the lending rate. In our examples of cash-and-carry and reverse cash-and-carry arbitrage, we have assumed that the two rates are the same. For the cash-and-carry arbitrage, the trader borrows funds, while the trader lends funds in the reverse cash-and-carry arbitrage. Throughout our examples, we have assumed that traders can borrow as well as lend at a rate of 10 percent. If the borrowing and lending rates are not equal, Equation 3.10 requires adjustment to reflect that fact. In Equation 3.10, the upper bound on the futures price comes from the cash-and-carry arbitrage possibility, as shown in Figure 3.8. In the cash-and-carry arbitrage, the trader borrows funds, so the borrowing rate is the appropriate rate in the expression for the upper bound. Analogously, the reverse cash-and-carry trade uses a strategy of lending to fix the lower bound. Thus, the lending rate is appropriate for the expression that gives the lower bound. The following equation reproduces Equation 3.10, but reflects the different borrowing and lending rates:

$$S_0(1 - T)(1 + C_L) \le F_{0,t} \le S_0(1 + T)(1 + C_B) \tag{3.11}$$

where C_L is the lending rate and C_B is the borrowing rate.[12]

These differential borrowing and lending rates serve to widen the no-arbitrage boundaries that we have been exploring, because generally $C_L > C_B$. We can illustrate the effect of the differential rates by extending the example of Table 3.10 to include unequal borrowing and lending rates. Table 3.11 illustrates the effect of these unequal rates on the no-arbitrage bounds. As the table shows, including differential borrowing and lending rates widens the no-arbitrage boundaries.

Restrictions on short selling
In our analysis, so far we have assumed that traders can sell assets short and use the proceeds from the short sale. In all of our examples, we have also assumed that the short seller has the unrestricted use of all funds arising from the short sale. However, for a moment, consider the position of the broker who facilitates a short sale. In the stock market, for example, the prospective short seller asks his or her broker to borrow a share from another customer and to sell it on behalf of the short seller. If the short seller received all of the funds from the short sale,

the broker would be in a precarious position. The broker has borrowed the share from another customer and must return the share upon demand. If the broker allows the short seller to have all of the proceeds of the short sale, the broker runs a significant risk. The short seller might, for instance, take all of the funds and abscond. Alternatively, the price might move against the short seller, and the short seller might not be able to pay to reacquire the stock.

Because of these inherent risks, there are restrictions on short selling in virtually all markets. These restrictions are important, because we have found that short selling is a necessary technique for the reverse cash-and-carry arbitrage strategy. If a trader sells the spot good short, Equation 3.2 must hold to prevent arbitrage. Further, from Equations 3.1 and 3.2, we were able to derive the no-arbitrage condition of Equation 3.3 for a perfect market.

In actual markets, there are serious impediments to short selling. First, for some goods, there is virtually no opportunity for short selling. This is particularly true for many physical goods. Second, even when short selling is permitted, restrictions limit the use of funds from the short sale. Often, these restrictions mean that the short seller does not have the use of all of the proceeds from the short sale. A typical percentage for the broker to retain is 50 percent, meaning that the short seller would have the use of only 50 percent of the funds.

In the arbitrage relationship of Equation 3.2, we concluded that

$$F_{0,t} \geq S_0(1 + C)$$

This result assumes unrestricted short selling, so that the short seller had full use of the short sale proceeds, S_0. As discussed earlier, the reverse cash-and-carry transaction employs the short sale, and this arbitrage strategy determines the lower bound for the futures price. To reflect the fact that the short seller does not have use of the proceeds, but only some fraction f, we can recast Equation 3.2 to read

$$F_{0,t} \geq S_0(1 + fC)$$

where f is the fraction of usable funds derived from the short sale.

This fraction must lie between zero and one. In a perfect market, $f = 1.0$, and it effectively drops out of the equation. With restricted short selling, we can now rewrite our no-arbitrage conditions. First, for a market that is perfect except for restricting short sales, we have a modification of Equation 3.3:

$$S_0(1 + fC) \leq F_{0,t} \leq S_0(1 + C) \tag{3.12}$$

We can also integrate restricted short selling into our imperfect markets framework of Equation 3.11. Taking into account transaction costs, differential borrowing and lending rates, and restricted short selling, the no-arbitrage bounds are as follows:

$$S_0(1 - T)(1 + fC_L) \leq F_{0,t} \leq S_0(1 + T)(1 + C_B) \tag{3.13}$$

The restrictions on short selling widen the no-arbitrage bounds. Notice now, however, that restricted short selling affects only the reverse cash-and-carry strategy, so restricted short selling affects only the lower bound. The effects are substantial. Table 3.12 shows the lower no-arbitrage bounds for restrictions on the use of short sale proceeds. When traders face large restrictions on short selling, there is little chance for reverse cash-and-carry arbitrage. If traders can use only half of the short sale proceeds, the lower no-arbitrage bound is so low that it can have little effect on the futures price. We will see that different traders face different restrictions on using

| **Table 3.12** An illustration of no-arbitrage bounds with various short selling restrictions |

Prices for the analysis	Spot price of gold	$400
	Interest rate (borrowing)	12%
	Interest rate (lending)	8%
	Transaction costs (T)	3%

Upper no-arbitrage bound with transaction costs and a borrowing rate
$F_{0,t} \le S_0(1 + T)(1 + C_B) = \$400 \times 1.03 \times 1.12 = \$461.44$

Lower no-arbitrage bound with transaction costs and a lending rate, $f = 1.0$
$F_{0,t} \ge S_0(1 - T)(1 + fC_L) = \$400 \times 0.97 \times (1 + 1.0 \times 0.08) = \$419.04$

Lower no-arbitrage bound with transaction costs and a lending rate, $f = 0.75$
$F_{0,t} \ge S_0(1 - T)(1 + fC_L) = \$400 \times 0.97 \times (1 + 0.75 \times 0.08) = \$411.28$

Lower no-arbitrage bound with transaction costs and a lending rate, $f = 0.5$
$F_{0,t} \ge S_0(1 - T)(1 + fC_L) = \$400 \times 0.97 \times (1 + 0.5 \times 0.08) = \$403.52$

proceeds from a short sale. The differential use of these short sale proceeds is related to the concept of quasi-arbitrage. Traders with better access to short sale proceeds have less than full transaction costs to pay when they engage in cash-and-carry or reverse cash-and-carry trading strategies.

Equation 3.13 expresses the final results of our cost-of-carry model analysis, and includes transaction costs, differential borrowing and lending rates, and restrictions on short selling. In complexity, it is a far cry from our simple perfect markets no-arbitrage relationship of Equation 3.3. However, the two are closely related. In terms of Equation 3.13, the perfect markets assumptions can be expressed as follows:

$T = 0$, so there are no transaction costs.
$C_B = C_L = C$, so borrowing and lending rates are equal.
$f = 1.0$, so traders have full use of short sale proceeds.

If these three conditions hold, we are back to our perfect market assumptions, and Equation 3.13 becomes

$$1.0 \times S_0(1 - 0)(1 + C) \le F_{0,t} \le S_0(1 + 0)(1 + C)$$

which reduces to

$$S_0(1 + C) \le F_{0,t} \le S_0(1 + C)$$
$$F_{0,t} = S_0(1 + C)$$

This final expression is simply Equation 3.3, the perfect markets version of our cost-of-carry model.

Limitations to storage
Of all commodities, gold is perhaps the most storable. It is chemically stable, it has a high value relative to weight and volume, and so on. Some other commodities cannot be stored very well at all. The storability of a commodity is important to futures pricing, because the arbitrage

strategies that we have been considering depend on being able to store the underlying good. For example, the cash-and-carry arbitrage strategy assumes that a trader can buy a commodity today and store it until a later delivery date on a futures contract. If a commodity cannot be stored, some of the arbitrage strategies that we have been considering will not be available. Therefore, the no-arbitrage bounds we have developed will have to be altered to reflect the actual limitations to storage.

In the cash-and-carry arbitrage strategy, the ability to store the commodity limits the futures price relative to the cash price. As seen in Equation 3.1, the futures price cannot exceed the cash price by more than the cost of carry. To see the importance of this point, imagine a tasty tropical fruit that can be harvested on only one day per year, and assume that the fruit spoils in one day if it is not eaten. These physical characteristics of the fruit make it impossible to store. This limitation to storage means that a cash-and-carry strategy cannot link futures and cash prices. Because the fruit is not storable, we could say that the storage cost is infinite. Thus, Equation 3.1 would merely say that the futures price must be less than infinity. This we already know without a business degree.

While the tropical fruit example is quite fanciful, there are also commodities with very practical limits to storage. The CME traded a futures contract on fresh eggs for many years. While eggs can be stored for a while, there are definite limits that cannot be exceeded. Grains and oilseeds play an important role in agricultural futures. While wheat, oats, corn, soybeans, soymeal, and soyoil all store well, they cannot be stored indefinitely. Therefore, when storage is limited, the cash-and-carry strategy is also limited. The importance of these limitations to storage varies across commodities. As we noted, they are not important for gold, but they can be important for perishable assets.

How traders deal with market imperfections

We have seen that transaction costs, differential borrowing rates, and restrictions on short selling all act to widen the no-arbitrage bounds that link cash and futures prices. It is also important to realize that these factors have vastly different effects on different traders. They also differ widely across markets. This section considers these market imperfections in a practical light.

There are two critical points about transaction costs. First, every trader faces transaction costs on every trade. Second, these costs differ widely across traders. Let us consider two extreme cases. In both instances, we are interested in the marginal transaction cost, because the marginal transaction cost determines whether or not the trade takes place. Imagine a professor in Colorado who occasionally dabbles in the futures market. Such a trader will trade through a brokerage firm. The broker will charge a commission, the floor broker who executes the order will face a bid–ask spread, and the trader will have to pay exchange fees as well. Together, these costs could be as low as $15–20 or they could be much higher. In addition, the professor incurs substantial search costs to determine how to trade. These are difficult to quantify. In contrast with our dabbling professor, consider a major gold trading firm, such as Handy and Harmon or Engelhard. Such firms refine silver and gold and trade it worldwide. As part of their commercial enterprise, they operate a futures trading desk to hedge their own risk exposure in the gold market. In addition, the traders on the desk actively trade in the market, searching for the arbitrage opportunities that we have been considering. A large trading firm faces a very low marginal transaction cost.

These differences in transaction costs stem from several sources. First, the firm is already in the market for other business purposes. Unlike the professor, who studies the market merely looking for a good trading opportunity, these commercial concerns are already in the market in support of their physical metals business. This presence makes their information-gathering cost much lower than that faced by the professor, who trades only occasionally. Second, the commercial concern will typically own an exchange membership and have its own people on the floor. If so, the firm faces no brokerage commission, which is a large proportion of the cost of each trade for the professor.

A third and major factor is the difference in the chance to sell short. Short selling of metals is effectively closed to the professor, but it is virtually wide open for the metals trading firm. For the professor, selling short, if it is at all possible, will involve substantial limitations on the use of the short sale proceeds. The metals trading firm, by contrast, will hold an inventory of gold. Thus, the trading firm can simulate short selling by merely selling some of its inventory. From a trading perspective, the sale of the gold that the firm already owns is identical to selling gold short. As long as the firm has access to a supply of gold that it can sell, it can replicate the trading effect of selling short. For firms with substantial gold stocks, there is virtually no limitation to replicating a short sale. In sum, for many markets, large commercial concerns in the business face very low transaction costs. For them, the market imperfections we have examined are of little practical importance. Thus, in some markets, prices closely approximate the perfect markets pricing relationship of Equation 3.3.

The concept of a full carry market

In the price quotations of Figure 3.1, we readily observe different patterns of prices for different commodities. In general, for some commodities, the futures price rises with the maturity of the futures contract. For some commodities, the prices are inversely related to the futures maturity. For yet other commodities, the prices rise and fall, showing no obvious relationship to maturity.

We can group commodities into different types by the degree to which their prices approximate full carry. In a **full carry market**, futures prices conform to Equations 3.3 and 3.6. If prices match the relationships specified in the equation, the market is said to be at full carry. If the futures price is higher than Equations 3.3 and 3.6 indicate, then the market is **above full carry**. If it is less than the full carry price, the market is **below full carry**.

As an example, consider the following data for August 16:

Gold September	410.20
Gold December	417.90
Banker's acceptance rate—90 days[13]	7.80 percent

Is gold at full carry? In addition to financing, the warehousing and insurance of gold have costs. These amounts are negligible for gold in percentage terms, so we ignore them for the present. We begin by annualizing the percentage difference between the two gold prices:[14]

$$\left(\frac{F_{0,d}}{F_{0,n}}\right)^4 = 1.0772$$

Thus, the implied annual percentage difference between the two gold prices is 7.72 percent. This corresponds almost exactly to our interest rate estimate. In fact, this is not surprising, because gold is almost always at full carry. From this example, we can see that in a full carry market, prices should be normal. That is, the more distant futures price should exceed the nearby price. Other markets are not at full carry. Some markets are normal at times and near full carry, while they diverge radically at other times.

We have already seen that a well-developed market for short sales is important in keeping the no-arbitrage bounds tight, so that prices will more closely conform to the full carry relationship. There are five main factors that affect market prices and move them toward or away from full carry: short selling conditions, supply, seasonality of production, seasonality of consumption, and ease of storage.

Ease of short selling

We have already seen in our discussion of the cost-of-carry model that short selling restrictions widen the no-arbitrage bounds on futures prices. In the extreme case, where short selling is not permitted, there can be no reverse cash-and-carry arbitrage, so the futures price has no lower no-arbitrage bound. In markets for physical goods, short selling is highly restricted, even though some commercial interests can replicate short selling by reducing their inventories. By contrast, it is very easy to sell financial assets short. For this reason, and for others, financial assets tend to be full carry assets.

Large supply

If the supply of an asset is large relative to its consumption, the market for the good will more closely approximate a full carry market. On the side of cash-and-carry arbitrage, a large supply makes it easier for traders to acquire the physical good to store for future delivery. Relative to consumption for jewelry or industrial uses, for example, the supply of gold is very large. This factor helps to keep gold near full carry. By contrast, the world supply of copper is low relative to consumption. Typical supplies of copper on hand roughly equal three months of production.[15] Markets for copper and other industrial metals are not full carry markets.

Nonseasonal production

Temporary imbalances in supply and demand tend to cause distortions in normal price relationships. If production is highly seasonal, the stock of a good will be subject to large shifts. Many agricultural commodities have highly seasonal production due to their harvest cycles. In these markets, prices tend to be high for periods immediately prior to the harvest and low for the post-harvest months.

Nonseasonal consumption

Foodstuffs such as soybeans may have seasonal production, but consumption is fairly steady. People like to eat all year. For other goods, production is fairly continuous, but consumption is highly seasonal. For example, contract prices for heating oil often show a seasonal pattern of high prices in winter, while gasoline prices are often relatively high for the summer months.

High storability

In the example of the tropical fruit that must be harvested and eaten in a single day, we have the perfect example of a nonstorable commodity. If the good is nonstorable, cash-and-carry arbitrage strategies cannot link the cash price with the futures price. Thus, the cost-of-carry model is unlikely to apply to a good with poor storage characteristics. To a great extent, most physical commodities traded on futures exchanges have good storage characteristics. Some commodities that were less storable—such as fresh eggs and potatoes—have passed from futures trading. To the extent that a commodity has poor storage characteristics, however, the cost-of-carry model is unlikely to apply.

Convenience yield

We have seen in the preceding section that various factors cause the array of futures prices to vary from full carry for many commodities. In general, the cost-of-carry model fails to apply when an asset has a **convenience yield**—a return on holding the physical asset. When holding an asset has a convenience yield, the futures price will be below full carry. In an extreme case, the market can be so far below full carry that the cash price can exceed the futures price. When the cash price exceeds the futures price, or when the nearby futures price exceeds the distant futures price, the market is in **backwardation**. An asset has a convenience yield when traders are willing to pay a premium to hold the physical asset at a certain time. For example, natural gas prices tend to be high in the winter—just when people need heat. Likewise, soybean prices are high just before harvest—just when supplies are low and people still want to eat.

To further explore the concept of the convenience yield, assume that this is October and the cash price of soybeans is $6.00 per bushel. Harvest is one month away and a trader owns 5,000 bushels of soybeans. The futures price of soybeans for November is $5.50. In this example, the market is in backwardation, because the cash price exceeds the futures price. Under these circumstances, the trader will hold the soybeans from October to November only if he or she has some clear need for owning the beans during this period.

If the trader does not need the physical beans for the next month, he or she can sell the beans and buy a NOV futures contract. This strategy will yield a profit of $0.50 per bushel, and it will save a month of carrying costs. Clearly, given the price structure, only a person with a need for physical beans will hold them. For example, consider a food processor who still wants beans in October. The food processor might derive a convenience yield from owning beans, but only persons with a business need for the beans, such as a food processor, could derive a convenience yield.[16]

If the bean market is below full carry, it might seem that there is an opportunity for a reverse cash-and-carry arbitrage. This strategy requires selling beans short, but it is clear that short selling will not be possible. Short selling involves borrowing beans from someone else. Because the market is below full carry, no one will lend beans without cost. Anyone who owns the beans holds them because of the convenience yield they derive. If they owned the beans and received no convenience yield, they would sell them outright in the market, and buy the cheaper SEP futures to replace their beans in two months. Lending the beans to someone else so that other party can make money is the last application the holder of the physical beans would consider. Thus, if an asset has a convenience yield, the market can be below full carry, or even in backwardation. Such a situation will not provide a field day for reverse cash-and-carry arbitrage strategies, however, because short-selling opportunities will not be available.

Summary

In our exploration of the cost-of-carry model, we have seen that cash-and-carry and reverse cash-and-carry strategies place no-arbitrage bounds on futures prices. Transaction costs, differential borrowing and lending rates, restrictions on short selling, and limitations to storage all act to widen those bounds. Therefore, while the cost-of-carry model reveals much about the determinants of futures prices, it does not provide a complete determination of futures prices.

As we have seen, some commodities have characteristics that promote full carry. These include easy short selling, a large supply of the good, nonseasonal production and consumption, and high storability. Related to these, and also contributing to the applicability of the cost-of-carry model, is the lack of a convenience yield. Because market imperfections and the characteristics of the commodities themselves sometimes combine to force the no-arbitrage bounds apart, other factors help to determine as to where within the no-arbitrage bounds the futures price will lie. Within the no-arbitrage bounds, the market's expectation plays a large role in futures price determination.

Futures prices and expectations

Earlier, we considered a tropical fruit that can be harvested on only one day per year, July 4. The fruit is so delicate that it must also be consumed on that day or it will spoil. How would a futures contract on such a fruit be priced? As we explore in this section, the cost-of-carry model breaks down for the pricing of such a futures contract.

Cash-and-carry arbitrage strategies do not apply to this fruit, because it cannot be carried. The fruit spoils in one day. Therefore, the cash price and the futures price are not linked by the opportunity to carry the fruit forward. Another way of making the same point is to say that the cost of carry is infinite. Thus, any positive cash price is consistent with any positive futures price, no matter how high.

Reverse cash-and-carry strategies also do not apply. For example, assume that the cash price of the fruit is currently $2 and that the futures price for delivery in one year is $1. From our discussion of convenience yield, we know that this backwardation is due to the benefit that holding the cash fruit conveys. Therefore, no one would lend the fruit for short selling. Anyone who does not need the fruit for immediate consumption would merely sell it in the cash market and buy the cheaper futures. In sum, short selling would not be possible, so reverse cash-and-carry strategies will not serve to link the cash and futures prices. Because both the cash-and-carry and reverse cash-and-carry strategies fail for this fruit, they impose no-arbitrage bounds on the futures price.

The role of speculation

What does determine the futures price? Assume that market participants expect the price of the fruit in the next harvest to be $10 each. This price is the **expected future spot price**. In this event, the futures price must equal, or at least closely approximate, the expected future spot price. If this were not the case, profitable speculative strategies would arise.

As an example, if the futures price were $15, exceeding the expected future spot price of $10, speculators would sell the futures contract and then plan to buy the fruit for $10 on the harvest date. They would then be able to deliver the fruit and collect $15, for a $5 profit, if all went according to plan. By contrast, if the futures price were below the expected future spot price, say at $7, speculators would buy the futures contract, take delivery on the harvest date paying $7, and plan to sell the fruit at the market price of $10.

In short, the presence of speculators in the marketplace ensures that the futures price approximately equals the expected future spot price. Too great a divergence between the futures price and the expected future spot price creates attractive speculative opportunities. In response, profit-seeking speculators will trade as long as the futures price is sufficiently far away from the expected future spot price. We can express this basic idea by introducing the following notation:

$$F_{0,t} \approx E_0(S_t) \tag{3.14}$$

where $E_0(S_t)$ is the expectation at $t = 0$ of the spot price to prevail at time t. Equation 3.14 states that the futures price approximately equals the spot price currently expected to prevail at the delivery date. If this relationship did not hold, there would be attractive speculative opportunities.

Limits to speculation

With Equation 3.14, we have said that the futures price and the expected future spot price should be approximately equal. Why does this relationship hold only approximately? There are two basic answers to this question, one of which is fairly obvious and the second of which is fairly profound. First, the relationship holds only approximately because of transaction costs. Second, if some participants in the market are more risk averse than others, the futures price can diverge sharply from the expected future spot price.

Transaction costs

Assume that the fruit has a futures price of $9 and an expected future spot price of $10, and assume that the cost of transacting to take advantage of this discrepancy is $2. With these prices, a trader cannot buy the futures for $9 and plan to make a $1 profit by selling the fruit at its expected future spot price. This opportunity is not profitable with the transaction costs, because the total cost of acquiring the fruit would be the $9 delivery on the futures plus the $2 transaction cost. Transaction costs can keep the futures price from exactly equaling the expected future spot price. This parallels our discussion of transaction costs and their effect on the cost-of-carry model.

Risk aversion

Traders in futures markets can be classified, at least roughly, into hedgers and speculators. Hedgers have a preexisting risk associated with a commodity and sometimes enter the market to reduce that risk, while speculators trade in the hope of profit. Entering the futures market as a speculator is a risky venture. If people are risk averse, however, they incur risk willingly only if the expected profit from bearing the risk will compensate them for the risk exposure. Without doubt, most participants in financial markets are risk averse, so they seek compensation to warrant in taking a risky position.[17] In the futures markets, speculative profits can come only from a favorable movement in the price of a futures contract.

Assume that the expected future spot price of the fictional fruit is $10.00 and that the corresponding futures price is $10.05. Assume also that there is tremendous uncertainty about what the actual price of the fruit will be. The market expects a cash price of $10 upon harvest, but the fruit is very susceptible to weather conditions and it is also subject to the dreaded fictional fruit weevil. For a speculator, there appears to be a $0.05 profit available from the strategy of selling the futures, buying fruit for $10.00 at harvest, and delivering against the futures contract. However, this strategy subjects the speculator to considerable risk if the weather is bad or if the weevil strikes. Speculators may decide that the expected profit of $0.05 is not worth the risk exposure. If the speculators do not pursue the $0.05 expected profit, there will be no market forces to drive the futures price into exact equality with the expected future spot price. Thus, the futures price can differ from the expected future spot price if traders are risk averse.

Summary

The strong principles of the cost-of-carry model place no-arbitrage bounds on futures prices in many instances. In some cases those bounds are very wide, or even nonexistent, due to transaction costs, restrictions on short selling, or the characteristics of the physical commodity. Within the bounds placed by the cash-and-carry and reverse cash-and-carry strategies, expectations play a major role in establishing futures prices. We have seen that speculative strategies are available when the futures price does not equal the expected future spot price. Still, these speculative strategies do not ensure exact equality between the futures price and the expected future spot price. The futures price can diverge from the expected future spot price due to either transaction costs or risk aversion on the part of traders. Of the two, risk aversion is much more important and deserves extended consideration.

Futures prices and risk aversion

In this section, we explore in detail two theories of how risk aversion can affect futures prices. We have already seen that risk aversion among speculators can allow the futures price to diverge from the expected future spot price. According to the theory of normal backwardation, this divergence occurs in a systematic way. As a second theory, the capital asset pricing model (CAPM) relates market prices to a measure of systematic risk. Some scholars have applied the CAPM to futures markets to understand the differences that might exist between futures prices and expected future spot prices. We consider the two theories first, and conclude this section by examining the empirical evidence regarding the two theories.

The theory of normal backwardation

Assume for the moment that speculators are rational; that is, they make assessments of expected future prices based on available information. In assessing this information, rational speculators occasionally make mistakes, but on the whole, they process the information efficiently. As a result, on average, their expectations are realized. This does not imply that they are mistake free. Instead, they make errors of assessment that are not biased.[18] The expectational errors are randomly distributed around the true price that the commodity will have in the future. Assume also that speculators have "homogeneous expectations"; that is, they expect the same future spot price.

Such a group of speculators might confront the prices prevailing in a futures market and find that those prices match the expected future spot prices. If the futures price reaches the expected price of the commodity when the futures contract matures, then there is no reason to speculate in futures. If the futures price matches a speculator's expectation of subsequent cash prices for the commodity, then the speculator must expect neither a profit nor a loss by entering the futures market. Yet, by entering the market under such conditions, the speculator would certainly incur additional risk. After all, the trader's expectations might be incorrect. Faced with such a situation, no risk-averse speculator would trade, because the speculator would face additional risk without compensation.

Hedgers, taken as a group, need to be either long or short in the futures market to reduce the risk they face in their businesses. For example, a wheat farmer has a long position in cash wheat because he or she grows wheat. The farmer can reduce risk by selling wheat futures. If hedgers are net short, for example, speculators must be net long. For the sake of simplicity, consider a single speculator who is considering whether to take a long position. As just noted above, the rational speculator takes a long futures position only if the expected future spot price exceeds the current futures price. Otherwise, the speculator must expect not to make any profit.

The hedger, we assume, needs to be short to avoid unwanted risk. According to this line of reasoning, he must be willing to sell the futures contract at a price below the expected future spot price of the commodity. Otherwise, the hedger cannot induce the speculator to accept the long side of the contract. In effect, from this point of view, he buys insurance from the speculator. The hedger transfers his unwanted risk to the speculator and pays an expected profit to the speculator for bearing the risk. The payment to the speculator is the difference between the futures price and the expected future spot price. Even then, the speculator does not receive any guaranteed payment. The speculator must still wait for the expected future spot price to materialize to capture the profit expected for bearing the risk.

So far, the discussion has focused on a single hedger and a single speculator. It is necessary, however, to try to do justice to the fact that the marketplace is peopled by many individuals

Figure 3.9   Hypothetical net positions

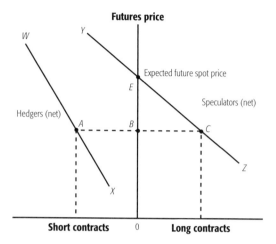

with different needs, different levels of risk aversion, and different expectations (heterogeneous expectations) about future spot prices.

Figure 3.9 depicts the situation that might prevail in the futures market for a commodity. It shows the relevant positions of hedgers and speculators as two groups. As the futures price varies, the number of contracts desired by the two groups will vary as well. We assume that hedgers are net short. At no futures price will hedgers, taken as a group, desire a long position in the futures.[19] This is reasonable given the definition of a hedger as one who enters the futures market to reduce a preexisting risk. Line WX shows the hedgers' desired position in the futures market for various futures prices. At higher prices, hedgers want to sell more futures contracts, as the downward slope for line WX indicates. Lines WX and YZ are drawn as straight lines, but that is only for convenience. Also, note that the hedgers hedge different amounts depending on the futures price. With low prices, they sell fewer contracts, thereby hedging less of their pre-existing risk than they would if futures prices were high.

In Figure 3.9, speculators are willing to hold either long or short net positions as the situation demands. Assuming that the speculators, as a group, correctly assess the appropriate expected future spot price, they will be neither long nor short when the futures price equals the expected future spot price. At that point, speculators hold a zero net position in the futures market. (In such a situation, some speculators would be long and others short, reflecting their divergent opinions. But, in the aggregate, they would hold a net zero position.) Line YZ shows the speculators' desired positions as a function of the futures price. If the futures price exceeds the expected future spot price, the speculators as well as the hedgers will desire to be net short. If the futures price lies below the expected future spot price, speculators will want to be net long, holding some position between E and Z on line YZ.

Not all positions shown on the graph are feasible. If the futures price lies above point E, then both the hedgers and speculators desire to be short. Yet, the number of outstanding short contracts must equal the number of long contracts. As the figure is drawn, there is only one price at which the market can clear: point B. With a price of B, the net short position desired by the hedgers exactly offsets the net long position desired by the speculators. This is graphically reflected by the fact that the distance AB equals the distance BC. Through the typical process by which markets reach equilibrium, the futures market may reach an equilibrium price at B, with the futures price lying below the expected future spot price.

Notice that the slope of WX (the hedgers' line) is steeper than that of YZ (the speculators' line). The more gentle slope of YZ expresses the greater risk tolerance of the speculators. For any drop in the futures price below the expected future spot price, E, the increase in the speculators' demand for long contracts exceeds the drop in the hedgers' desire to hold the short contracts. Indeed, this must be the case. Economically, the speculators must be more risk tolerant than the hedgers, because the speculators in this model accept the risk that the hedgers are unwilling to bear.[20]

This account explains how the futures price can diverge from the expected future spot price, even with no transaction costs. Likewise, if hedgers want to be net long, speculators must be net short, in which case they can hope to earn a return for their risk-bearing services only if the futures price lies above the expected future spot price. Again, the futures price need not equal the expected future spot price. Instead, the relationship between the futures price and the expected future spot price depends in part on whether the hedgers need to be net short or net long.

Clearly, in this model, the futures price will be below the expected future spot price if the hedgers are net short, as in Figure 3.9. The amount of the discrepancy depends upon the risk aversion of the two groups. For example, assume that the speculators are more risk averse than Figure 3.9 depicts. Higher risk aversion is represented in the graph by the steepness of the hedgers' or the speculators' line. If the speculators were more risk averse, their line would be steeper. As a result, at price B the speculators would be willing to hold fewer long contracts and the market would not clear at that price. Instead, the market clearing price would be below B, the exact price depending upon the steepness of the speculators' line. In that case, the market clearing price would be below B and fewer hedgers would be able to hedge.

This approach to determining futures prices originated with John Maynard Keynes and John Hicks. The view that hedgers are net short, as shown in Figure 3.9, is associated with Keynes and Hicks. Over the life of the futures contract, the futures price must move toward the cash price. (This is already clear, since the basis must equal zero at the maturity of the futures contract, as was discussed earlier.) If expectations about the future spot price are correct and hedgers are net short, then the futures price must lie below the expected future spot price. In such a case, futures prices can be expected to rise over the life of a contract.

The view that futures prices tend to rise over the contract life due to the hedgers' general desire to be net short is known as **normal backwardation**. (Normal backwardation should not be confused with a market that is in backwardation. A market is in backwardation at a given moment if the cash price exceeds the futures price or if a nearby futures price exceeds a distant futures price.) Conversely, if hedgers are net long, then the futures price would lie above the expected future spot price, and the price of the futures contract would fall over its life. This pattern of falling prices is known as a **contango**. Figure 3.10 depicts these price patterns.[21]

Figure 3.10 illustrates the price patterns for futures that we might expect under different scenarios. In considering the figure, assume that market participants correctly assess the future spot price, so that the expected future spot price in the figure turns out to be the actual spot price at the maturity of the futures contract. If the futures price equals the expected future spot price, then the futures price will lie on the dotted line, which equals the expected future spot price. With initially correct expectations, and no information causing a revision of expectations, the futures price should remain constant over its entire trading life.

Alternative concepts certainly exist, such as the theory of normal backwardation and the contango. If speculators are net long, as Keynes and Hicks believed, then futures prices must rise over the life of the contract if the speculators are to receive their compensation for bearing risk. Prices then follow the path that is labeled "Normal backwardation" in Figure 3.10. With the

Figure 3.10   Patterns of futures prices

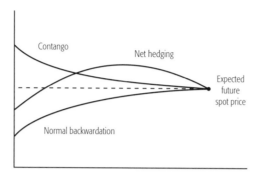

futures price rising over its life, the speculator earns a return for bearing risk. Notice that the line for normal backwardation terminates at the expected future spot price. This is necessary since the futures price and the spot price must be equal at the maturity of the futures contract, and the figure is drawn assuming that the expected future spot price turns out to be the subsequently observed spot price.

If speculators are net short and are to receive compensation for bearing risk, futures prices must follow a contango, as Figure 3.10 also illustrates. The fall in futures prices, as the contract approaches maturity, gives the short speculators the compensation that induced them to enter the market.

One final possibility is also shown in Figure 3.10, and it is known as the **net hedging hypothesis**. According to this view, the net position of the hedgers might change over the life of the futures contract. When the contract begins trading, the hedgers are net short and the speculators are net long. In such a situation, the futures price lies below the expected future spot price. Over time, the hedgers gradually change their net position. Eventually, the hedgers are net long, requiring the speculators to be net short. For the speculators to receive their compensation in this case, the futures price must lie above the expected future spot price, as it did in the contango.[22]

Perhaps this account of hedgers changing from being net short to net long over the life of the contract appears dubious, but it is certainly conceivable. Consider grain farmers who wish to hedge the crop that they will produce. To hedge the price risk associated with harvest, they need to be short. Cereal producers have a need for the grain, and they hedge their price risk by being long. To show how the price could follow the pattern suggested by the net hedging hypothesis, imagine that the farmers hedge first. This makes the hedgers net short. Later, the cereal producers begin to hedge their future need for the grain, and the net hedging position of the farmers and cereal producers taken together begins to move toward zero. When it reaches zero, the farmers and cereal producers in the aggregate are neither short nor long. Time passes, and still more cereal producers hedge by going long. Eventually, the long hedgers come to predominate and all hedgers taken together are net long. Under such a condition, the futures price must lie above the expected future spot price if the speculators are to receive compensation for bearing risk.

Futures prices and the CAPM

The CAPM has been widely applied to all kinds of financial instruments, including futures contracts. The following equation expresses the basic relationship of the CAPM:

$$E(R_j) = r + \beta_j[E(R_m) - r] \tag{3.15}$$

where r is the risk-free rate, $E(R_j)$ is the expected return on asset j, $E(R_m)$ is the expected return on the market portfolio, and β_j is the "beta" of asset j. The CAPM measures the systematic risk of an asset by the beta, which is usually estimated from a regression equation of the following form:

$$r_{j,t} = \alpha_j + \beta_j r_{m,t} + \varepsilon_{j,t} \tag{3.16}$$

where $r_{j,t}$ is the return on asset j in period t, $r_{m,t}$ is the return on the market portfolio m in period t, α_j is the constant term in the regression, and $\varepsilon_{j,t}$ is the residual error for day t. According to the CAPM, only unavoidable risk should be compensated in the marketplace, and traders can avoid much risk through diversification. Even after diversification, risk remains for some assets because the returns of the asset are correlated with the market as a whole. This remaining risk is systematic. In essence, β_j measures the systematic risk of asset j relative to the market portfolio. According to Equation 3.15, an asset with $\beta = 1$ has the same degree of systematic risk as does the market portfolio and the asset should earn the same return as the market. The risk-free asset has $\beta = 0$, and it should earn the risk-free rate of interest.

As we have seen, futures market trading does not require any investment. However, trading futures does require margin payments, but these are not investments. With no funds invested, there is no capital to earn the risk-free interest rate. Therefore, a futures position should have zero return if $\beta = 0$. If the beta of a futures position exceeds zero, a long position in the futures contract should earn a positive return. For example, for futures position j, assume that the following values hold: $E(R_m) = 0.09$; $r = 0.06$; $\beta_j = 0.7$. According to Equation 3.15, a long position in futures contract j should earn

$$E(R_j) = \beta_j[E(R_m) - r] = 0.7 \times (0.09 - 0.06) = 0.021$$

Thus, positive betas for futures contracts lead to the expectation of rising futures prices. Zero betas would be consistent with futures prices that neither rise nor fall. A negative beta would imply that futures prices should fall.

As with the theory of normal backwardation, approximately equal numbers of studies support and oppose the CAPM as it applies to futures markets. This untidy irresolution may be due to the fact that futures returns are very close to zero. Thus, some studies find average returns significantly different from zero, while others do not. Most studies do seem to find that futures contracts have betas near zero, at least when these betas are measured using conventional techniques. Final resolution of these issues will require more comprehensive data sets and analysis than have been employed to date.

Characteristics of futures prices

In this section, we consider four characteristics of futures prices and changes in futures prices. First, we consider the relationship between futures prices and forward prices for the same good. Theoretically, these prices could differ even when they depend on the same underlying good. This is possible because of the feature of daily settlement on the futures contract, but not on the forward contract. Second, we consider the forecasting ability of futures prices. If futures prices equal expected future spot prices, the process of price discovery is aided substantially. Third, we consider the distribution of futures price changes. If the distribution of price changes is nonnormal, statistical tests become more difficult, because most popular tests assume that the distribution of price changes is normal. As we will see, the distribution is generally not normal. This has important implications in many areas: For example, a test as to whether or not the average change in futures prices is positive depends on the normality of the changes being tested. Fourth, we consider the volatility of futures prices and the effect of this volatility on the volatility of cash market prices.

Futures prices versus forward prices

In Chapter 1, we considered the differences between forward and futures markets. Here, we analyze the factors that can cause forward and futures prices to diverge, even when the contracts have the same underlying commodities and the same time to expiration. Forward and futures prices can differ because of different tax treatments, different transaction costs, or different margin rules. Also, the chance of a default may be higher on a forward contract, due to the lack of a clearinghouse in forward markets. The main conceptual reason for a possible difference in prices stems from the daily settlement that characterizes futures markets.

To see the potential difference between forward and futures prices, consider the following example. A gold futures and a gold forward both expire in one year, and the current price of both contracts is $500. We assume that the spot price of gold in one year will also be $500. Thus, there will be no profit or loss on either contract. Moreover, when the contracts expire, the forward price, the futures price, and the cash price must all be equal. We have explored arbitrage arguments to show that this result must be obtained. There are about 250 trading days in a year, so we consider two very simple possible price paths that gold might follow over that year. First, we assume that the futures price rises by $2 each day for 125 days and then falls by $2 per day for 125 days. Second, we assume that the gold price falls by $2 per day for 125 days and then rises by $2 per day for 125 days. Figure 3.11 illustrates the two price paths. Under either scenario, the price will be $500 at expiration in one year. Thus, there is no profit or loss on either contract.

The forward trader is indifferent between the two possible price paths. The forward trader has no cash flow at the beginning and none at the end. Because of daily settlement, however, the futures trader has definite preferences. For example, a long futures trader would much prefer the price to rise first and fall later. Each day the price rises, the long futures trader receives a settlement payment that can be invested. Getting the cash inflows early in the holding period means that the futures trader can earn more interest than otherwise.

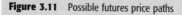

Figure 3.11   Possible futures price paths

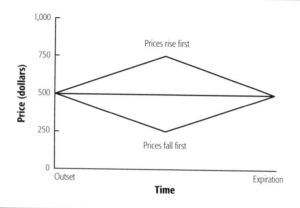

Assuming a 10 percent interest rate, the difference in these two price paths is about $25 for the futures trader. If the price rises first, the long futures trader receives payments that can be invested. However, later in the year the futures trader must make daily settlement payments. Nonetheless, in Figure 3.11, the trader makes $12.48 in interest by year-end if the price rises first.[23] Similarly, the trader loses $12.48 in interest if prices fall first. Notice that these differences stem strictly from the interest gains or losses on the daily settlement payments. This is clear from the example, because there are no profits or losses on the futures position. Therefore, we can see that the futures trader can be better or worse off than the forward trader.

Of course, traders do not know which will be more attractive until after the event, because no one knows what course prices will take. After all, interest rate movements are subject to chance. This makes it impossible to know at the outset which price path will occur, so the gold trader would not know which contract to take in our example, the forward or the futures.

It is possible to draw a general rule from this analysis. If the futures price is positively correlated with interest rates, then a long trader will prefer a futures position over a forward position. This result has been proven rigorously in a number of studies.[24] While the proof of this proposition is quite mathematical, we can follow the intuition that underlies it.

If the futures price and interest rates rise together, then the long futures trader will receive settlement payments that can be invested at the higher interest rate. If futures prices and interest rates both fall, the futures trader must make settlement payments, but the trader can finance those payments at the new lower interest rate. In this argument, the trader does not need to forecast interest rates to have a preference for futures over forwards. Instead, the preference for a futures over a forward depends only on the correlation between the futures price and the interest rate.

Both the futures and the forward will have the same profit in the end, exclusive of the settlement payments. If the futures position is likely to have more favorable interim cash flows due to its positive correlation with interest rates, the futures price should exceed the forward price. By the same token, if the futures price is negatively correlated with interest rates, then the futures price should be lower than the forward price. This conclusion follows because the long futures trader will then tend to experience losses just as interest rates rise. Finally, if the price of a commodity is uncorrelated with interest rates, then the forward and futures prices should be equal. Notice that all of these conclusions arise strictly from economic reasoning. We now turn to an examination of the evidence.

While most studies find a statistical difference between forward and futures prices, the difference is generally too small to be important economically. Thus, we can generally assume that forward and futures prices are approximately equal for most practical purposes.

Statistical characteristics of futures prices

This section considers four statistical characteristics of futures prices. First, we explore whether the price changes of futures contracts are normally distributed. Second, we consider whether successive price changes are correlated. Third, we examine the statistical properties of commodity futures as an asset class. Finally, we consider whether the volatility of futures contracts varies with the time remaining until the contract expires.

The distribution of futures prices

As we noted earlier, most statistical tests of futures prices rely on the assumption that the underlying price changes are normally distributed. If futures price changes are not normally distributed, then these tests become more difficult to conduct. Almost all studies in this area agree that changes in futures prices are not normally distributed, but that the distribution of percentage changes in

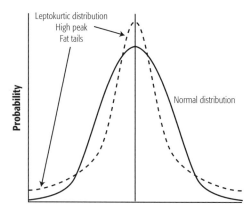

Figure 3.12   Normality and leptokurtosis

futures prices is leptokurtic. Figure 3.12 illustrates **leptokurtosis**—the tendency for a distribution to have too many extreme observations relative to a normal distribution. In the figure, the solid line shows a normal distribution. The dotted line shows a leptokurtic distribution. The greater frequency of extreme observations makes the tails of a leptokurtic distribution have "fat tails." As a second major theme, many of these empirical studies try to determine what distribution futures prices will follow if they are not normal. Two candidates dominate. First, the distribution may be stable Paretian. This distribution is symmetrical, like the normal distribution, but it is leptokurtic relative to a normal distribution. Second, some studies find that the distribution of futures price changes seems to be similar to a mixture of two or more normal distributions. Thus, these studies find that the distribution is not normal, but that it can be approximated by a mixture of normal distributions. Both camps agree that this nonnormalcy requires extra caution in making statistical inferences about futures prices.

Autocorrelation

In addition to testing the distribution of futures price changes, several studies have examined whether the times series of futures price changes is autocorrelated. A time series is **autocorrelated** if the value of one observation in the series is statistically related to another. In **first-order autocorrelation**, for example, one observation is related to the immediately preceding observation. This question has considerable practical importance. For example, if futures prices exhibit positive first-order autocorrelation, then positive returns in one period tend to be followed by positive returns in the next period. Similarly, negative returns tend to be followed by subsequent negative returns.

If the correlation were strong enough, it would be possible to devise trading strategies to profit from this follow-on tendency. For example, with positive first-order autocorrelation, one could devise a trading rule to buy the futures immediately following a price rise. Then, the second price rise would generate a profit.

Almost all studies have found that futures prices exhibit statistically significant first-order autocorrelation. While the autocorrelation appears to be significant statistically, it does not appear to be important economically. In other words, the autocorrelation is not strong enough to allow profitable trading strategies after we consider transaction costs.

Market microstructure

Market microstructure is a branch of financial economics that analyzes how trading technology influences the trading characteristics of a financial market. For example, market microstructure techniques can be applied to the futures market to determine whether the information content of prices formed in an open-outcry trading environment differs from the information content of prices formed in an electronic trading environment. Trading technology defines what traders can do and what they can know. Broadly defined, trading technology includes such things as the physical layout of a market, trading protocols and rules, market governance, and the information systems available to traders. Trading characteristics include the determinants of the market price, market liquidity, transaction costs, volatility, and trading profits. An understanding of a market's microstructure is valuable for understanding the behavior of prices and markets. This has immediate application for the regulation of markets, the formulation of new trading mechanisms, and the determination of optimal trade execution strategies. The value of market microstructure research has been enhanced over the past two decades by the availability of transactional datasets across many different market institutions. These datasets include observations on market transactions, quotations, order flow, and the inventory of market makers. Related reductions in the costs of computation and storage have also promoted market microstructure analysis.[25]

The statistical properties of commodity futures as an asset class

Hedge funds, pension funds, and other investment funds often look to commodity futures (as opposed to financial futures) as a separate asset class to diversify portfolios consisting of stocks, bonds, and other holdings. Whether or not commodity futures represent a separate asset class depends on the correlation of commodity futures prices with the prices of other financial instruments. In a study of the statistical properties of commodity futures prices between 1959 and 2004, Gary Gorton and K. Geert Rouwenhorst find that an equally weighted portfolio of commodity futures contracts has been effective in diversifying stock and bond portfolios.[26] The authors find that the correlation between commodity futures prices and the prices of stocks and bonds is negative over most time horizons, with stronger negative correlation over longer holding periods. The authors also find that commodity futures diversify cyclical variation in stock and bond returns. One reason for the diversification performance of commodity futures is that commodity futures prices are positively correlated with unexpected inflation, whereas stocks and bonds are negatively correlated with this factor.

To accommodate the demand of investment managers seeking exposure to commodity futures as an asset class, Goldman Sachs created the Goldman Sachs Commodity Index (GSCI). As mentioned in Chapter 1, the GSCI is an index composed of the prices of 24 commodity futures contracts. The index provider selects the components and their weighting within the index. The index uses only the prices from nearby futures contracts. Many funds establish futures positions to track this index. Others use the CME's GSCI futures contract to gain the exposure to commodities they desire.

The volatility of futures prices

In this section, we examine two dimensions of futures price volatility that have received considerable attention from scholars. First, we consider the relationship between futures trading and the volatility of prices for the underlying good. Usually, this issue has been addressed in the following form: "Does the introduction of futures trading make the underlying commodity price more volatile?" Typically, volatility is measured as the variance of price changes. Price volatility by itself is neither good nor bad. Volatility can be good if it occurs as the result of new information being incorporated into market prices. In this case, an increase in volatility is simply a reflection of the market doing its job. Volatility can be bad if it is driven by "noise" as opposed to the arrival of new information. In this case, an increase in volatility simply adds to the cost of trading. A second issue focuses on patterns in the volatility of futures prices themselves. As we will see, evidence suggests that futures prices become more volatile as they approach the expiration date.

Futures trading and cash market volatility

Some market observers allege that futures trading makes prices for the underlying good more volatile. Most recently, this claim has been alleged for equities. These critics of futures markets allege that recent stock market volatility can be traced to the introduction of stock index futures trading.[27] Often, these claims are accompanied by proposals for tighter regulation of futures trading. Therefore, the question has important public policy implications.

Most studies of the effect of futures trading on the cash market compare the volatility of the cash market before and after the introduction of futures trading. While not quite unanimous, the weight of evidence seems to suggest that futures trading does not increase the volatility of the cash market. In fact, some studies even find that cash market volatility falls after futures trading starts. The results of these studies are summarized in Table 3.13.[28]

Table 3.13 Futures trading and cash market volatility

Study	Market	Key results
Emery (1896)	Cotton, wheat	Lower cash market volatility
Hooker (1901)	Wheat	Lower cash market volatility
Working (1960)	Onions	Lower cash market volatility
Gray (1963)	Onions	Lower cash market volatility
Powers (1970)	Pork bellies, cattle	Lower cash market volatility
Tomek (1971)	Wheat	Lower cash market volatility
Johnson (1973)	Onions	No effect
Taylor and Leuthold (1974)	Cattle	Lower cash market volatility
Cox (1976)	Several	Lower cash market volatility
Froewiss (1978)	GNMA	Lower cash market volatility
Figlewski (1981)	GNMA	Higher cash market volatility
Dale and Workman (1981)	T-bills	No effect
Simpson and Ireland (1982)	GNMA	No effect
Bortz (1984)	T-bonds	Lower cash market volatility
Corgel and Gay (1984)	GNMA	Lower cash market volatility
Simpson and Ireland (1985)	T-bills	No effect
Moriarty and Tosini (1985)	GNMA	No effect
Santoni (1987)	S&P 500®	No effect
Edwards (1988)	T-bills, S&P 500	Lower cash market volatility
Harris (1989)	S&P 500	No effect
Brorsen et al. (1989)	Cattle	Higher cash market volatility
Weaver and Banerjee (1990)	Cattle	No effect
Damodaran (1990)	S&P 500	Lower cash market volatility
Antoniou and Foster (1992)	Crude oil	No effect
Netz (1996)	Wheat	Lower cash market volatility
Kocagil (1997)	Metals	No effect

Time to expiration and futures price volatility

In a paper now regarded as a classic, Paul Samuelson[29] argued that the volatility of futures prices should increase as the contract approaches expiration. This is the **Samuelson hypothesis**. In his analysis, Samuelson assumed that competitive forces in the futures market keep the futures price at a level equal to the expected future spot price at the contract's termination. Under this assumption, futures prices should follow a **martingale**—a price process in which the expected value of the next price equals the current price, so the expected price change is zero. Therefore, this conclusion implies that the futures price equals the expected future spot price.

While the mathematics of Samuelson's model are somewhat complex, the intuition is clear. High price volatility implies big price changes. Price changes are large when more information is being revealed about a commodity. Early in a futures contract's life, little information is known about the future spot price for the underlying commodity. Later, as the contract nears maturity, the rate of information acquisition increases. For example, little is known about a corn harvest a full year before harvest time. As the harvest approaches, the market gets a much better idea of the ultimate price that corn will command. For a futures contract expiring near the harvest, Samuelson's model implies that the futures price should be more volatile as the harvest approaches, and most studies support the hypothesis.

News versus noise

Politicians and market commentators often complain about market volatility and encourage regulators to take actions to address it. For example, in the early 1990s, several members of Congress condemned stock index arbitrage for its alleged role in contributing to stock market volatility and urged the Securities and Exchange Commission (SEC) to restrict the practice.

Financial economists, however, are more circumspect in condemning market volatility. This is because financial economists know that volatility can simply be a reflection of the market doing its job. Financial economists distinguish between fundamental volatility and transitory volatility. Fundamental volatility is caused by the actions of informed traders who base their trades on the arrival of new fundamental information. As informed traders conduct their trades, market prices change to reflect the new information. Fundamental volatility can be good for the economy because it helps investors to allocate scarce capital to its highest valued use. Transitory volatility is caused by the trading decisions of speculators who are uninformed about market fundamentals and trade instead off information they glean from the trading process itself. These speculators are sometimes called "noise traders." Financial economists are wary of transitory volatility, because it causes prices to deviate from fundamental value.

Even though economists are often critical of transitory volatility, it is essential for the existence of well-functioning markets. This is because the existence of transitory volatility makes it profitable for those with information to trade. It even becomes profitable for people to seek out costly information upon which they can base their trades. Over time, one would expect uninformed noise traders as a group to lose money by trading, and informed traders as a group to make money.[30]

Although, by definition, noise traders are uninformed about market fundamentals, they may still possess useful information gleaned from the noise of the trading process. Joshua Coval and Tyler Shumway studied the information content of actual noise measured by the ambient noise level in the trading pit for Treasury bond futures at the CBOT. Coval and Shumway controlled for market variables other than noise and were able to analytically isolate the effect of the noise level itself. These authors found that after a rise in the sound level, prices become more volatile–information that is useful for a trader to know. The study found that in addition to volatility, the sound level conveys other useful information to traders.[31] One implication of this study is that information gleaned from open-outcry trading may be hard to replicate in an electronic environment. Some electronic systems have attempted to address this issue by installing "artificial noise" in an attempt to replicate the noise level of pit trading.

Conclusion

While futures markets have a reputation for high risk and wild price swings, this chapter has stressed the underlying rationality of futures prices. We cannot deny that prices vary suddenly and sharply in the futures market, but it is quite possible that these price movements accurately reflect the arrival of new information at the market. Further, it is also apparent that futures prices observe the economic laws detailed earlier. Both the cost-of-carry model and the expected future price framework provide rational procedures for thinking about the behavior of futures prices. It must also be admitted that futures prices, on the whole, conform to these theories.

If the above conclusions are correct, then a picture of the usefulness of the market begins to emerge. If prices react rationally to new information, if spread relationships are strongly interconnected, and if futures prices are good estimates of expected future spot prices, it is possible to understand the uses that can be made of the market by different elements of society. These different groups in society were identified as those who wish to discover price information by observing futures markets, as speculators and as hedgers. If futures prices closely approximate expected future spot prices, then the price discovery function is well served. Speculators, on the other hand, will have a difficult life, because profitable opportunities will not be abundant. Hedgers, for their part, have an apparent opportunity to reduce their risk exposure with relatively little cost.

The next chapter explores how these different groups use the futures market. The difficulties faced by speculators are examined more closely, along with the benefits that the futures markets provide to hedgers and to society as a whole.

Hand signals

Because of the number of people on the trading floor and the general noise level, traders often use hand signals to communicate with their order desks and with other traders in the pit or with traders in other pits. There is no standard set of hand signals—it can vary from exchange to exchange and from pit to pit within an exchange. Readers interested in a more complete description should see the CME's web site (www.cme.com), which offers an illustrated guide to signals used at the CME.

Some hand signals are universal. For example, when a trader wants to signal a bid, he will extend his hand with his palm facing toward him. To signal an offer, he will extend his hand with his palm facing away from him. To signal price, traders will use their fingers to place quotes based on the last digit of the current bid or offer. For example, a hand with the palm facing away and two fingers extended may represent a "52" offer. A clenched fist represents zero. The system used to indicate the quantity of the bid or offer is a bit more complex. To place bids and offers on single contracts, traders touch their fingers to their chin. One finger placed to the chin means a bid or offer of one contract. To place a bid or offer on quantities in multiples of ten contracts, traders place their fingers to their forehead. To place bids on quantities in multiples of 100 contracts, traders place their closed fist to their forehead. For example, to place a bid on 500 contracts, a trader would raise his hand to his forehead, flash five fingers in the bid position, and then tap his forehead with his closed fist.

To signal expiration months, traders use another set of hand signals. January contracts are typically represented by a hand to the throat; February by the thumb down with the index and middle finger out; March by a tucked-in thumb and wiggling of the fingers; April by wiggling of the fingers while making a downward motion with the hand; May by holding the lapel of the jacket; June by pointing the "pinky" finger and index finger downward; July by pointing to an eye; August by rubbing the forehead; September by an open palm pointing up; October by a "V" sign made with the index finger and the middle finger; November by an "X" motion made across the face; and December by crossing the index finger with the middle finger.

Traders also must signal the "pack," or expiration cycle, of the contract. At the CME, the "whites" or front months do not use hand signals. Expiration months in the next year (the "reds") are signaled with a touch to the shoulder. Expiration months two years (the "greens") out are signaled with the "OK" symbol of the thumb and index finger joined in a loop. Wiggling the fingers back and forth represents an expiration month three years out (the "blues"), and a thumb to the ring finger signals an expiration month four years out beyond the current year's expirations (the "golds").

Other hand signals are used to communicate information on the status of orders. The "thumbs up" sign means that the order has been filled. Rotating the index finger means that the trader is working the order. A fist to the palm on the hand means that the order is a stop order and a hand motion across the throat means that the order has been cancelled.

Exercises

1 Explain the function of the settlement committee. Why is the settlement price important in futures markets in a way that the day's final price in the stock market is not so important?

2 Open interest tends to be low when a new contract expiration is first listed for trading, and it tends to be small after the contract has traded for a long time. Explain.

3 Explain the distinction between a normal and an inverted market.

4 Explain why the futures price converges to the spot price and discuss what would happen if this convergence failed.

5 Is delivery, or the prospect of delivery, necessary to guarantee that the futures price will converge to the spot price? Explain.

6 As we have defined the term, what are the two key elements of "academic arbitrage"?

7 Assume that markets are perfect in the sense of being free from transaction costs and restrictions on short selling. The spot price of gold is $370. Current interest rates are 10 percent, compounded monthly. According to the cost-of-carry model, what should the price of a gold futures contract be if expiration is six months away?

8 Consider the information in Exercise 7. Round trip futures trading costs are $25 per 100 ounce gold contract, and buying or selling an ounce of gold incurs transaction costs of $1.25. Gold can be stored for $0.15 per month per ounce. (Ignore interest on the storage fee and the transaction costs.) What futures prices are consistent with the cost-of-carry model?

9 Consider the information in Exercises 7 and 8. Restrictions on short selling effectively mean that the reverse cash-and-carry trader in the gold market receives the use of only 90 percent of the value of the gold that is sold short. Based on this new information, what is the permissible range of futures prices?

10 Consider all of the information about gold in Exercises 7–9. The interest rate in Exercise 7 is 10 percent per year, with monthly compounding. This is the borrowing rate. Lending brings only 8 percent, compounded monthly. What is the permissible range of futures prices when we consider this imperfection as well?

11 Consider all of the information about gold in Exercises 7–10. The gold futures expiring in six months trades for $375 per ounce. Explain how you would respond to this price, given all of the market imperfections we have considered. Show your transactions in a table similar to Tables 3.8 or 3.9. Answer the same question, assuming that gold trades for $395.

12 Explain the difference between pure and quasi-arbitrage.

13 Assume that you are a gold merchant with an ample supply of deliverable gold. Explain how you can simulate short selling and compute the price of gold that will bring you into the market for reverse cash-and-carry arbitrage.

14 Assume that silver trades in a full carry market. If the spot price is $5.90 per ounce and the futures that expires in one year trades for $6.55, what is the implied cost of carry? Under what conditions would it be appropriate to regard this implied cost of carry as an implied repo rate?

15 What is "normal backwardation"? What might give rise to normal backwardation?

16 Assume that the CAPM beta of a futures contract is zero, but that the price of this commodity tends to rise over time very consistently. Interpret the implications of this evidence for normal backwardation and for the CAPM.

17 Explain why futures and forward prices might differ. Assume that platinum prices are positively correlated with interest rates. What should the relationship be between platinum forward and futures prices? Explain.

18 Consider the life of a futures contract from inception to delivery. Explain two fundamental theories on why the futures prices might exhibit different volatility at different times over the life of the contract.

19 What is a limit order? How does placing a limit order provide an option to other traders?

20 What is market microstructure?

21 What is the difference between fundamental volatility and transitory volatility?

22 What is the implied repo rate? What information does the implied repo provide about the relationship between cash and futures prices?

Notes

1　Traders in Chicago use the term "pit," whereas traders in New York prefer the term "ring."

2　See Ulrike Schaede, "Forwards and Futures in Tokugawa-Period Japan: A New Perspective on the Dojima Rice Market," *Journal of Banking and Finance*, 13, 1989, pp. 487–513. The anecdote recounted here comes from pages 503 and 504 of her paper.

3　Sometimes the total open interest does not equal the sum of the open interest reported for each contract. This occurs because *The Wall Street Journal* does not report trading in some of the most distant contract maturities, yet these distant contracts are included for the total volume figure.

4　See J. Harold Mulherin, Jeffry Netter, and James A. Overdahl, "Prices are Property: The Organization of Financial Exchanges from a Transaction Cost Perspective," *Journal of Law and Economics*, October 1991, pp. 591–644.

5　A similar example was cited in *The Wall Street Journal*, May 13, 1992. The article states: "in the spring of 1837, brokers at the New York Stock & Exchange Board noticed a small hole in the brick wall of their building. They discovered that it had been bored by a broker who wasn't a member and was speculating in stocks on a street curb outside the exchange. The broker, like countless investors before and since, wanted desperately to know what was going on inside. The exchange, just as determined to keep out the broker and his ilk, filled the hole and continued trading behind closed doors."

6　*Board of Trade of the City of Chicago v. Christie Grain and Stock Company* 198 U.S. 236 (1905).

7　As will be explained in Chapter 4, we expect the price of seasonal goods to be relatively high just before harvest and relatively low just after harvest. It is this kind of consideration that leads futures market observers to expect systematically fluctuating differences in basis over the year.

8　The stability is even more dramatic when we take the difference in scale on the vertical axis into account.

9　In many cases, the owner of these goods will choose to insure these goods for himself or herself. Nonetheless, there is an implicit cost of insurance even when the owner self-insures.

10　For a very informative and readable account of repurchase agreements, see M. Bowsher, "Repurchase Agreements," *Instruments of the Money Market*, Richmond, VA: Federal Reserve Bank of Richmond, 1981.

11　In general, the bid–ask spread is greater if liquidity is low, volatility is higher, and uncertainty is great. Moreover, during the trading day, the bid–ask spread is generally higher at the start and at the end of the trading day due to increased uncertainty about the true price at those times. See Henry L. Bryant and Michael S. Haigh, "Bid–Ask Spreads in Commodity Futures Markets," *Applied Financial Economics*, 14, 2004, pp. 923–36. Bryant and Haigh use observed nominal spreads from LIFFE's electronic order book for commodity futures to compare to estimated spreads from open-outcry markets where spreads are not directly observable. Other authors, also using data from open-outcry markets, have attempted to estimate the bid–ask spread. See for example, C. K. Ma, R. L. Peterson, and S. R. Sears, "Trading Noise, Adverse Selection, and Intraday Bid–Ask Spreads in Futures Markets," *Journal of Futures Markets*, 12:5, 1992, pp. 519–38. See also Tom Smith and Robert E. Whaley, "Estimating the Effective Bid/Ask Spread from Time and Sales Data," *Journal of Futures Markets*, 14:4, 1994, pp. 437–55.

12　Recall that we are abstracting from all noninterest carrying charges under our assumption of zero transaction costs.

13　Rates on term repurchase agreements are generally not available in the financial press. A banker's acceptance is a negotiable instrument used in international trade that is guaranteed by a bank. In addition, the rates quoted in the "Money Rates" section of *The Wall Street Journal* are intended to offer only an indication of the prevailing rates.

14　The ratio of the distant to the nearby futures price defines the interest rate between the two dates $t = n$ and $t = d$. In this example, $d - n$ is 90 days, so we raise the expression to the fourth power to account for the quarterly compounding.

15　See for example, Table 31-1 in M. J. Pring, *The McGraw-Hill Handbook of Commodities and Futures*, New York: McGraw-Hill, 1985.

16　B. Wright and J. Williams, "A Theory of Negative Prices for Storage," *Journal of Futures Markets*, 9:1, 1989, pp. 1–13, explores the convenience yield more rigorously.

17　In his book, *Risk and Risk Bearing*, Chicago, IL: University of Chicago Press, 1940, Charles O. Hardy gives a different interpretation of the behavior of speculators. He compares the futures market to a gambling casino. In Hardy's view, if we ignore transaction costs in the futures market, the expected outcome of any trade is no gain and no loss. If transaction costs are considered, then the expected outcome is slightly negative. This, Hardy suggests, makes the futures market like a gambling casino, since people play even when they should expect to lose money.

18 An estimator is unbiased if and only if the expected value of the estimator equals the actual value of the parameter being estimated. Rational expectations theory has been applied to the commodities markets in this context. See T. J. Sargent, "Commodity Price Expectations and the Interest Rate," *Quarterly Journal of Economics*, 83, 1969, pp. 126–40, and J. F. Muth, "Rational Expectations and the Theory of Price Movements," *Econometrica*, 29, 1961, pp. 315–35.

19 By assuming that hedgers will be net short no matter what the futures price, we are merely assuming that their preexisting risk requires a short position. Some potential hedgers would, of course, abandon their risk-reducing short position if the futures price were low enough. However, in so doing, the potential hedger would have abandoned the intention of hedging and would be speculating. This is clear if we recall that the risk-reducing futures trade is to go short.

20 The idea for Figure 3.9 was suggested by a presentation by Hans Stoll.

21 A normal market gives rise to "normal backwardation" and an inverted market is consistent with prices following a "contango." (In the French futures market, you may sometimes encounter the "Last Contango in Paris." Sorry.)

22 Figure 3.10 was originally adapted from William Sharpe's book, *Investments*, Englewood Cliffs, NJ: Prentice Hall, 1981.

23 This calculation assumes that the interest rate is 10 percent per year and there are 250 trading periods, for a daily interest factor of 1.000381. Thus, the first day, the price rises by $2, so this gives interest of $2 \times 1.000381 \times 250 - $2 = 0.20, and so on. Later, when the losses start, they must also be compounded out to the horizon.

24 Several papers have appeared to argue against the necessary equality of forward and futures prices. See, for example, G. E. Morgan, "Forward and Futures Pricing of Treasury Bills," *Journal of Banking and Finance*, December 1981, pp. 483–96; R. Jarrow and G. Oldfield. "Forward Contracts and Futures Contracts," *Journal of Financial Economics*, 19, 1981, pp. 373–82; J. Cox, J. Ingersoll, and S. Ross, "The Relation between Forward Prices and Futures Prices," *Journal of Financial Economics*, 19, 1981, pp. 321–46; and S. Richard and M. Sundaresan, "A Continuous Time Equilibrium Model of Forward Prices and Futures Prices in a Multigood Economy," *Journal of Financial Economics*, 19, 1981, pp. 347–71.

25 For more information on market microstructure, see Maureen O'Hara, *Market Microstructure Theory*, Cambridge, MA: Blackwell, 1995.

26 Gary Gorton and K. Geert Rouwenhorst, "Facts and Fantasies about Commodity Futures," Working Paper number 04-20, International Finance Center, New Haven: Yale University, February 28, 2005.

27 We consider the specific evidence for equities in Chapters 8 and 9.

28 The studies listed in Table 31.3 are as follows: H. C. Emery, *Speculation on the Stock and Produce Exchanges of the United States*, Columbia University, 1896; R. H. Hooker, "The Suspension of the Berlin Produce Exchange and its Effect upon Corn Prices," *Journal of the Royal Statistical Society*, 64, 1901, pp. 574–604; H. Working, "Price Effects of Futures Trading," *Food Research Institute Studies*, 1, 1960; R. Gray, "Onions Revisited," *Journal of Farm Economics*, 45:3, May 1963, pp. 273–6; M. Powers, "Does Futures Trading Reduce Price Fluctuations in the Cash Markets?" *American Economic Review*, 60:3, June 1970, pp. 460–4; W. G. Tomek, "A Note on Historical Wheat Prices and Futures Trading," *Food Research Institute Studies*, 110:1, 1971, pp. 109–13; A. C. Johnson, "Effects of Futures Trading on Price Performance in the Cash Onion Market, 1930–68," U.S. Department of Agriculture Economic Research Service Technical Bulletin No. 1470, Washington, D.C., U.S. Government Printing Office, February 1973; G. Taylor and R. Leuthold, "The Influence of Futures Trading on Cash Cattle Price Variations," *Food Research Institute Studies*, 13:1, 1974, pp. 29–35; C. C. Cox, "Futures Trading and Market Information," *Journal of Political Economy*, 84, 1976, pp. 1215–37; K. C. Froewiss, "GNMA Futures: Stabilizing or Destabilizing?" *Federal Reserve Bank of San Francisco* Economic Review, Spring 1978, pp. 20–9; S. Figlewski, "Futures Trading and Volatility in the GNMA Market," *Journal of Finance*, 36:2, May 1981, pp. 445–56; C. Dale and R. Workman, "Measuring Patterns of Price Movements in the Treasury Bill Futures Market," *Journal of Economics and Business*, 33, 1981, pp. 81–7; W. G. Simpson and T. C. Ireland, "The Effect of Futures Trading on the Price Volatility of GNMA Securities," *Journal of Futures Markets*, 2:4, 1982, pp. 357–66; G. A. Bortz, "Does the Treasury Bond Futures Market Destabilize the Treasury Bond Cash

Market?" *Journal of Futures Markets*, 4:1, 1984, pp. 25–38; J. B. Corgel and G. D. Gay, "The Impact of GNMA Futures Trading on Cash Market Volatility," *Journal of the American Real Estate and Urban Economics Association*, 12, 1984, pp. 176–90; W. G. Simpson and T. C. Ireland, "The Impact of Financial Futures on the Cash Market for Treasury Bills," *Journal of Financial and Quantitative Analysis*, 20, 1985, pp. 371–9; E. J. Moriarty and P. A. Tosini, "Futures Trading and the Price Volatility of GNMA Certificates—Further Evidence," *The Journal of Futures Markets*, 5:4, Winter 1985, pp. 633–41; G. Santoni, "Has Programmed Trading Made Stock Prices More Volatile?" *Review*, Federal Reserve Bank of St. Louis, May 1987, pp. 18–29; F. Edwards, "Does Futures Trading Increase Stock Market Volatility?" *Financial Analysts Journal*, 44:1, January–February 1988, pp. 63–9; L. Harris, "S&P 500 Cash Stock Price Volatilities," *Journal of Finance*, 44:5, December 1989, pp. 1155–75; B. W. Brorsen, C. M. Oellermann, and P. L. Farris, "The Live Cattle Futures Market and Daily Cash Price Movements," *Journal of Futures Markets*, 9:4, 1989, pp. 273–82; R. D. Weaver and A. Banerjee, "Does Futures Trading Destabilize Cash Prices? Evidence for U.S. Live Beef Cattle," *Journal of Futures Markets*, 10:1, 1990, pp. 41–60; A. Damodaran, "Index Futures and Stock Market Volatility," *Review of Futures Markets*, 9:2, 1990, pp. 442–57; A. Antoniou and A. J. Foster, "The Effect of Futures Trading on Spot Price Volatility: Evidence for Brent Crude Oil Using GARCH," *Journal of Business Finance and Accounting*, 19:4, 1992, pp. 473–84; J. S. Netz, "The Effect of Futures Markets and Corners on Storage and Spot Price Variability," *American Journal of Agricultural Economics*, 77:1, 1995, pp. 182–92; and A. A. Kocagil, "Does Futures Speculation Stabilize Spot Prices? Evidence from Metals Markets," *Applied Financial Economics*, 7, 1997, pp. 115–25.

29 P. Samuelson, "Proof that Properly Anticipated Prices Fluctuate Randomly," *Industrial Management Review*, 6:2, 1965, pp. 41–9.

30 See Larry Harris, *Trading and Exchanges: Market Microstructure for Practitioners*, Oxford: Oxford University Press, 2003, p. 328.

31 See Joshua D. Coval and Tyler Shumway, "Is Sound Just Noise?" *The Journal of Finance*, 56:5, 2001, pp. 1887–910.

4

Using Futures Markets

Overview

In the three preceding chapters, we have discussed the institutional setting of futures markets and the determination of futures prices. This chapter explores three different ways in which futures markets serve different elements of society. As we have already noted, futures markets provide a means of price discovery. Second, futures markets provide an arena for speculation. Third, futures markets provide a means for transferring risk, or hedging. This chapter explores each of these contributions of futures markets.

First, we will analyze the function of **price discovery**—the revelation of information about the prices of commodities in the future. Because prices in the futures markets provide information that is not readily available elsewhere, the markets serve societal needs. We note that price discovery is open to everyone, even nontraders. Futures market price information is available to anyone for the price of a newspaper.

Second, we will examine the role of speculators in the futures market. A **speculator** is a trader who enters the futures market in pursuit of profit, thereby accepting an increase in risk. It may seem strange to list an opportunity for speculation as a service to society, but consider the following examples. Casinos provide speculative opportunities for citizens, and that might be reckoned as a public service. Professional and college sports teams also provide a way for people to speculate by betting, illegally in some U.S. states and legally in others.

Clearly, sports teams do not exist so that people can bet on them, but the chance to bet is a side effect, and perhaps a side benefit, of the existence of sports. The situation is similar in the futures markets. Futures markets do not exist in order to provide the chance to specu-

late, but they do provide speculative opportunities. Less obvious is the way in which speculators themselves contribute to the smooth functioning of the futures market. As we will show, the speculator pursues profits. As a side effect, the speculator provides liquidity to the market, which helps the market to function more effectively.

Third, we will analyze the role of hedgers. A **hedger** is a trader with a preexisting risk, who enters the futures market in order to reduce that risk. For example, a wheat farmer has price risk associated with the future price of wheat at harvest. By trading in the futures market, the farmer may be able to reduce that preexisting risk. This opportunity to transfer risk is perhaps the greatest contribution of futures markets to society. In many cases, businesses face risks that result from the ordinary conduct of business. Often, these risks are undesired, and the futures market provides a way in which risk may be transferred to other individuals who are willing to bear it. If people know that unwanted risks may be avoided by transacting in the futures market at a reasonable cost, then they will not be afraid to make decisions that will expose them initially to certain risks. They know that they can hedge that risk.

From the point of view of society, hedging has important advantages. Enterprises that are profitable but involve more risk than their principals wish to bear can still be pursued. The unwanted risk can then be transferred in the futures market and society benefits economically. This is the strongest argument for the existence of futures markets. By providing an efficient way of transferring risk to those individuals in society who are willing to bear it cheaply, futures markets contribute to the economy.[1]

Price discovery

In Chapter 3, we explored the connection between futures prices and expected future spot prices in some detail. In particular, we considered evidence on the relationship between futures prices and expected future spot prices. This relationship is crucial for the ability of the futures market to fulfill the social function of price discovery. In this section, we consider this issue in more detail.

Students of futures markets acknowledge a close connection between futures prices and expected future spot prices. The question is how the futures market can be used to reveal information about subsequent commodity prices. The usefulness of price forecasts based on futures prices depends on three factors:

(1) The need for information about future spot prices.
(2) The accuracy of the futures market forecasts of those prices.
(3) The performance of futures market forecasts relative to alternative forecasting techniques.

Information

Many individuals and groups in society need information about the future price of various commodities. For example, with information about the price of gold one year from now, it would be relatively simple to make a fortune. Certainly, speculation would be much more rewarding if one had a private and infallible source of information about future spot prices. Aside from such dreams of wealth, information about future spot prices is also needed for more mundane purposes, such as the planning of future investment and consumption by individuals, corporations, and governmental bodies.

Consider an underpaid college professor who wants to buy a house. Interest rates are high, so taking a long-term mortgage in such times would commit him to a lifetime of large payments. On the other hand, if he does not buy a house, then he cannot take advantage of the tax deduction that the interest portion of the house payments would provide. If interest rates were to drop soon, then it would be reasonable to wait to buy the house. By consulting the financial pages of the newspaper, the professor could find out what the market believed about the future level of interest rates. Futures contracts on long-term Treasury bonds are traded on the Chicago Board of Trade (CBOT). If the interest rate for a bond to be delivered in six months is three percentage points lower than current interest rates, then there is good reason to expect interest rates will fall over the next six months. In such a situation, the college professor might do well to wait a few months to buy his house.

Another example concerns a furniture manufacturer who makes wooden furniture. Assume that she is printing her catalog now for the next year and must include the prices of the different items of furniture. Setting prices in advance is always a very tricky affair. In addition to other problems, the price she charges will depend upon the expected future price of lumber. The cost of lumber varies greatly, depending largely on the health of the construction industry, so it is difficult for her to know how to include that cost factor in her calculations. One way in which she might deal with this is to use the prices from the lumber futures market to estimate the costs of the wood that she will have to purchase later on. In doing so, she uses the futures markets for their **price discovery** benefit.[2]

In both of these examples, individuals used futures prices to estimate the spot price at some future date. The advisability of such a technique depends on the accuracy of the forecasts drawn from the futures market. Futures prices may, of course, differ from subsequently observed spot prices. If there is a large discrepancy, the futures forecasts may not be very useful. Errors could result from two sources: inaccurate but unbiased forecasts and bias in the forecast itself.

Accuracy

A forecasting estimator is unbiased if the average value of the forecast equals the value of the variable to be forecasted.[3] Thus, futures prices might provide unbiased forecasts with very large errors. The situation is reminiscent of the joke about the two economists who predicted the unemployment rate for the next year. The first economist predicted that 12 percent of the workforce would be unemployed, while the second put the figure at full employment, or zero percent unemployed. The actual rate turned out to be 6 percent, from which the economists cheerfully concluded that, on average, they were exactly right. In forecasting the unemployment rate, one could say that the economists had provided an unbiased forecast, but one that had large errors.

As is typical for many commodities, the forecasts from the futures market have large errors. Futures prices fluctuate radically, which means that most of the time they provide an inaccurate forecast of the underlying commodity's spot price at the time of delivery. Without question, the large size of the forecast errors from the futures markets limits the reliability of the forecasts.[4]

One might reasonably wonder why there should be such large errors. According to the theory of finance, prices in well-developed markets reflect all available information. As new information becomes available, futures prices adjust themselves very swiftly. As a consequence, futures prices tend to exhibit radical fluctuations, which means that the prices will be inaccurate as estimates of subsequent spot prices.

In addition to the large errors that one can observe in futures market forecasts, futures prices may be biased. One possible reason for this was considered in Chapter 3. Futures prices may embody a risk premium that keeps the futures price from equaling the expected future spot price. In general, the possibility of bias is not too great a concern, at least for practical matters. Further, while there is still no real agreement about their existence, there is agreement that if biases do exist, they are small. In general, the errors in futures forecasts are so large that they tend to drown out any biases that may also be present.

Performance

Since forecasts based on futures prices seem to be so poor, why would anyone care about them? Before discarding the forecasts, consider the alternatives. What other forecast might be more accurate? A considerable amount of study on this topic has failed to lead to any final answer. Nonetheless, evidence suggests that forecasts based on futures prices are not excelled by other forecasting techniques. Futures forecasts have been compared to other techniques and have not been found to be inferior. The current situation in forecasts of the foreign exchange rate is typical. For example, compared to professional foreign exchange forecasting firms, some of which charge large fees, the futures price of foreign currency predicts very well. Many professional firms have recently turned in forecasting records with results worse than those of chance.[5]

In spite of the large errors in forecasts based on futures market prices, the futures market seems better than the alternatives. To summarize, the accuracy of futures forecasts is not that good, but it is certainly better than the alternatives, and futures market forecasts are free. Someone needing a forecast of future spot prices should not rely too heavily on any forecast. When relying on some forecasting technique, however, it should be the forecast that is freely available in the futures market.

Orange juice and weather

In the early 1980s, Richard Roll, a finance professor at UCLA, was visiting central Florida when a freeze hit the area and devastated the orange crop, which comprised the major source of oranges used for the production of frozen concentrated orange juice.[6] This incident got Roll thinking about the information content of futures prices. Surely, Roll figured, professional traders had powerful incentives to spend considerable resources to obtain accurate information about weather–and especially freezes in central Florida, since this information could be put to profitable advantage by trading futures contracts on frozen concentrated orange juice at the Citrus Associates of the New York Cotton Exchange (NYCE) (now part of the New York Board of Trade, NYBOT). In fact, the more Roll thought about it, the more he realized that futures traders had a more powerful incentive to get accurate weather forecasts than did the salaried forecasters employed by the U.S. Weather Service. With the cooperation of the U.S. Weather Service, Roll designed a test of the hypothesis that the futures market did a better job of predicting freezes than the Weather Service. The results of this test were consistent with this hypothesis. Since Roll's study was published, others have tried to construct more powerful tests without any change in the basic result: the market does a better job of forecasting than forecasters.

Perhaps one reason futures markets do a better job of forecasting weather than meteorologists is because meteorologists are saving their best forecasts for their own private transactions in the futures market. In 1993, *The Wall Street Journal* reported that many television meteorologists were moonlighting as commodities traders.[7] The article quoted one meteorologist as saying, "More and more meteorologists are realizing how much money can be made or lost trading commodities and are getting involved." Another is quoted as saying, "If you have a position, it does color what you say." Apparently, some television weathermen have turned their moonlighting into a full-time job, leaving television meteorology to trade commodities and to sell consulting services to other traders.

Speculation

Defining speculation or identifying the speculator in the futures market is always difficult. For our purposes, the following definition of a speculator will prove useful. A **speculator** is a trader who enters the futures market in search of profit and, by so doing, willingly accepts increased risk.[8]

Most individuals have no heavy risk exposure in most commodities. Consider an individual who is neither a farmer nor a food processor, but who has an interest in the wheat market. If she trades a wheat futures contract, then she most likely is speculating in the sense defined previously. She enters the futures market, willingly increases her risk, and hopes for profit.

One might object that this individual does not have a preexisting risk exposure in wheat. In fact, everyone who eats bread does. One's plans for consuming bread may change if wheat prices rise too high. This objection makes a good point. In order to know whether a particular action in the futures market is a speculative trade requires knowledge about the trader's current assets and future consumption plans. For an individual, however, entry into the futures market is most likely to be for speculation. For the woman who is trading a wheat futures contract, the size of the wheat contract (5,000 bushels) is so large relative to her needs for wheat that the transaction increases her overall risk. Assuming that she, like most people, is risk averse, she will not expose herself to the additional risk of entering the futures market unless she hopes to profit by doing so. This is what classifies her as a speculator.

Earlier, we also noted that speculators use futures transactions as a substitute for a cash market transaction. For an individual, trading a 5,000-bushel futures contract is unlikely to be a substitute for a cash market transaction, and this criterion also identifies the individual trading wheat as a speculator.

Different types of speculators may be categorized by the length of time they plan to hold a position. Traditionally, there are three kinds of speculators: scalpers, day traders, and position traders.

Scalpers

Of all speculators, scalpers have the shortest horizon over which they plan to hold a futures position. Scalpers aim to foresee the movement of the market over a very short interval, ranging from the next few seconds to the next few minutes. Many scalpers describe themselves as psychologists trying to sense the feel of the trading among the other market participants. In order to do this, they must be in the trading pit; otherwise, they could not hope to see buying or selling pressure building up among the other traders.[9]

Since their planned holding period is so short, scalpers do not expect to make a large profit on each trade. Instead, they hope to make a profit of one or two ticks—the minimum allowable price movement. Many trades by scalpers end in losses or in no profit. If the prices do not move in the scalper's direction within a few minutes of assuming a position, the scalper will likely close the position and begin looking for a new opportunity.

This type of trading strategy means that the scalper will generate an enormous number of transactions. Were he or she to make these transactions through a broker as an off-the-floor participant, the scalper would lose any anticipated profit through high transaction costs. Since scalpers are members of the exchange, or lease a seat from a member, their transaction costs are very low. Scalpers probably pay less than a dollar per round-turn in most futures markets, compared to about $25–80 for an off-the-floor trader who trades through a regular broker.[10] Without these very low transaction costs, the scalper's efforts would be hopeless. To sense the direction of the market and to conserve on transaction costs, a scalper needs to be on the floor of the exchange.

In his book, *The New Gatsbys*, Bob Tamarkin explores the personalities of futures traders based on his own experience. Writing about scalpers, he says that:

> Many traded by feel rather than by fundamentals, forgetting about things like leading economic indicators, government policies, and even supplies of commodities. They simply tried to catch the market on the way up and ditch it on the way down. In the trading pits they could do it faster and better than any outside speculators because they were squarely in the heart of the action.[11]

Discussing scalpers in general and describing an individual scalper named Paul, Tamarkin tells us that:

> Each trader had a theory about what was happening in the next five minutes. If everyone thought the market was going to open higher, but it opened lower, the psychology in the pit changed immediately. It was a herd mentality fed on raw emotion. It was the easy way. Get the trading feel of the crowd in the pit; then jump on board for the move. By the time the public got in, the market ticked that quarter or half cent, and Paul had his profit. The ultimate price of a commodity may have been determined by supply and demand, Paul thought, but in the interim, emotional factors reigned supreme.[12]

Although it may not be apparent at first glance, scalpers provide a valuable service to the market by their frenzied trading activity. By trading so often, scalpers help supply the market with liquidity. Their trading activity increases the ease with which other market participants may find trading partners. Without high liquidity, some outside traders would avoid the market, which would decrease its usefulness. A high degree of liquidity is necessary for the success of a futures market and scalpers play an important role in providing this liquidity.[13] We might say that scalpers provide the opportunity for other traders to trade immediately.

To illustrate the role played by scalpers in providing liquidity, consider the following example. An off-the-floor trader might see the most recently quoted price on a ticker machine and desire to trade at that price. If the market is not liquid, then it may be difficult to trade at or near that price for at least two reasons. First, if the market is not liquid, the observed transaction might have occurred some time ago and there may not be anyone willing to trade at that

Table 4.1 Mr. X's trades over 31 trading days

Total transactions	2,106
Number of contracts traded (round-turns—buy and sell one contract)	2,178
Number of trades (zero net position to a zero net position)	729
Profitable	353 (48%)
Unprofitable	157 (22%)
Scratch	219 (30%)

Source: William L. Silber, "Marketmaker Behavior in an Auction Market: An Analysis of Scalpers in Futures Market," *Journal of Finance*, 39:4, 1984, pp. 937–53. Reprinted by permission from Blackwell Publishing

last reported price. Second, without the willing pool of potential traders represented by the scalpers in the pit, the bid–ask spread could be quite wide, making it difficult to trade near the last reported price. The scalpers in the pit are there to seek profit, but they compete with each other to trade. As a result, the presence of the scalpers helps to keep the bid–ask price narrow, to keep the market more active and price quotations more current, and to attract outside traders to the market because they know that their orders can be executed near the equilibrium price for the commodity.

In an interesting article, Professor William Silber explores the behavior of scalpers. He arranged to observe all of the transactions of a scalper who he identifies only as Mr. X. This Mr. X was a trader on the New York Futures Exchange (NYFE), trading New York Stock Exchange Composite Index futures. For 31 trading days in late 1982 and early 1983, Silber tracked all of Mr. X's trading. Table 4.1 presents some of Silber's results. During this period, Mr. X traded 2,106 times, or about 70 times each day. These transactions involved the purchase and sale (round-turn) of 2,178 contracts.

Table 4.1 also shows the number of trades, which Silber defines as going from a zero net position and returning to a zero net position. Fewer than half (48 percent) of these trades were profitable, while 22 percent generated losses. Thirty percent were scratch trades—trades with neither a profit nor a loss. The trades generated an average profit of $10.56, or a total trading profit of $7,698.24, over the period. On average, a trade took 116 seconds; so the average length of time for which Mr. X had a risk exposure was two minutes. The longest trade, and hence the longest period of risk exposure, took 547 seconds, or a little over nine minutes. Clearly, Mr. X was reluctant to maintain positions for very long.

Table 4.2 presents one half-hour of Mr. X's trading. During this period, Mr. X made 19 transactions. Notice how Mr. X opens a position, either long or short, and then moves quickly back to a zero position in the market. During this half-hour, Mr. X goes through five trading cycles, beginning and ending the half-hour with a net zero position.

As Silber concludes, the major function that Mr. X provides to the market is liquidity. As a scalper, Mr. X takes the other side of trades coming in from traders off the floor of the exchange. Also, Silber found that Mr. X's trades tended to be more profitable when they were held for a shorter time. For instance, Mr. X's trades taking longer than three minutes were losing trades on average. As Silber concludes: "Scalper earnings compensate for the skill in evaluating market conditions in the very short run and for providing liquidity to the market over the time horizon."[14] This accords with the excerpts from Tamarkin.[15]

Table 4.2 One half-hour of Mr. X's trading

Transaction	Time	Contracts traded (buy +/sell −)	Net position
1	10:05:29	2	2
2	10:06:47	−2	0
3	10:08:10	5	5
4	10:09:15	−1	4
5	10:09:49	−2	2
6	10:10:25	−1	1
7	10:11:20	−1	0
8	10:12:56	6	6
9	10:13:29	−3	3
10	10:15:38	−1	2
11	10:16:58	−1	1
12	10:17:23	−1	0
13	10:22:25	−5	−5
14	10:23:11	3	−2
15	10:23:23	2	0
16	10:25:26	5	5
17	10:26:12	−1	4
18	10:26:18	−1	3
19	10:28:12	−3	0

Source: William L. Silber, "Marketmaker Behavior in an Auction Market: An Analysis of Scalpers in Futures Market," *Journal of Finance*, 39:4, 1984, pp. 937–53. Reprinted by permission from Blackwell Publishing

Futures traders in the laboratory

Experimental economics is a branch of economics that attempts to perform controlled experiments to test economic propositions. The approach has gained wide acceptance in the economics profession, culminating with the awarding of the 2002 Nobel Prize in Economics to George Mason University professor Vernon Smith, a pioneer in the field. In 2004, Michael Haigh and John List published results of an experimental study they conducted with 54 pit traders from the Chicago Board of Trade (CBOT).[16] Specifically, the study was designed to test the "myopic loss aversion" conjecture. A trader who displays myopic loss aversion is more acutely aware of losses than gains of equal size and makes short-term (myopic) choices. Haigh and List expected to find that myopic loss aversion would be less pronounced among a group of professional traders when compared to a control group of ordinary people who are not professional traders. Instead, Haigh and List found that while both CBOT traders and the control group of ordinary people exhibited trading behavior consistent with the myopic loss aversion conjecture, professional CBOT traders exhibited this behavior to a greater extent than the other subjects in the study. Apparently, professional futures traders think differently than ordinary individuals who are not professional traders. The implication of this finding for market researchers is that the models used to describe the economic behavior of individuals may not work as well for describing the behavior of professional traders.

Day traders

Compared to scalpers, day traders take a very farsighted approach to the market. Day traders attempt to profit from the price movements that may take place over the course of one trading day. The day trader closes his or her position before the end of trading each day, so that he or she has no position in the futures market overnight. Day traders may trade on or off the floor.

A day trader might follow a strategy such as concentrating activity around announcements from the U.S. government. The Department of Agriculture releases production figures for hogs at intervals that are well known in advance. The day trader may think that the hog figures to be released on a certain day will indicate an unexpectedly high level of production. If so, such an announcement will cause the futures prices for hogs to fall, due to the unexpectedly large future supply of pork. To take advantage of this insight, the day trader would sell the hog contract prior to the announcement and then wait for prices to fall after the announcement. Such a strategy could be implemented without holding a futures market position overnight. Therefore, it is a suitable strategy for a day trader to pursue. (To avoid drastic effects on markets, government announcements are often made late in the day, after the affected market closes.)

The scalper's strategy of holding a position for a very short interval is clearly motivated, but it is not so apparent why day traders limit themselves to price movements that will occur only during the interval of one day's trading. The basic reason is risk. Day traders believe that it is too risky to hold a speculative position overnight; too many disastrous price movements could occur.

To see the danger of maintaining a position overnight, consider a position in orange juice concentrate traded on the NYBOT. In late November, a trader holds a short position in orange juice futures. The weather in Florida is crucial for orange juice prices, and the trader checks the weather forecast for Florida that day before trading closes. There seems to be no possibility of damaging weather in the next few days, so he maintains his position overnight. Unexpectedly, a strong cold front pushes into Florida and destroys a large portion of the orange crop—which, in November, is still on the trees and not yet mature. Naturally, futures prices soar on the opening of trading the next day, and the trader who held his position overnight suffers a large loss. In fear of such sudden developments, day traders close their positions each day before trading stops.

The overwhelming majority of speculators are either scalpers or day traders, which indicates just how risky it can be to take a position home overnight. As the close of trading approaches each day, the pace of trading increases. Typically, 25 percent of the day's trading volume occurs in the last half-hour of trading. The last five minutes are particularly frenetic, as traders attempt to close all of their open positions.[17]

Position traders

A **position trader** is a speculator who maintains a futures position overnight. On occasion, they may hold them for weeks or even months. There are two types of position traders, those holding an **outright position** and those holding a **spread position**. Of the two strategies, the outright position is far riskier.

Outright positions

An outright position trader might adopt the following strategy if she believed that long-term interest rates were going to rise more than the market expected over the next two months. As interest rates rise, the futures prices, representing the price of bonds, must fall. However, the trader does not really know when during the next two months the rise in rates will occur. To take advantage of her belief about the course of interest rates, she could sell the futures contract on U.S. Treasury bonds traded at the CBOT and hold that position over the next two months. If she is correct, there will be a sharp rise in rates, not correctly anticipated by the market, and futures prices will fall. She can then offset and reap her profit.

The danger in this trader's outright position is clear. If she has made a mistake, and interest rates fall unexpectedly, then she will suffer a large loss. The outright position offers a chance for very large gains if she is correct, but it carries with it the risk of very large losses as well. For most speculators, the risks associated with outright positions are too large. The expected trading life of a new trader is about six months, but it is much shorter for outright position traders.

Spread positions

More risk-averse position traders may trade spreads. Intracommodity spreads involve differences between two or more contract maturities for the same underlying deliverable good. In contrast, intercommodity spreads are price differences between two or more contracts written on different, but related, underlying goods. For example, the difference between the July wheat and corn contracts would be an intercommodity spread. The spread trader trades two or more contracts with related price movements. The goal is to profit from changes in the relative prices.

Consider the case of a spread speculator who believes that the difference between the futures price of wheat and corn is too high. Such a trader believes that the intercommodity spread between wheat and corn is inconsistent with the justifiable price differential between the two goods. Wheat normally sells at a higher price per bushel than corn, but for this trader the differential in prices is too large. On February 1, the following closing prices could be observed for the JUL wheat and corn contracts, quoted in cents per bushel:

JUL wheat	329.50
JUL corn	229.00

The trader believes that this difference of more than one dollar is too large and is willing to speculate that the price of corn will rise relative to the price of wheat. Accordingly, the trader transacts as shown in the top panel of Table 4.3.

Table 4.3 An intercommodity spread: the wheat and corn contracts are both for 5,000 bushels

Date	Futures market
February 1	Sell one JUL wheat contract at 329.50 cents per bushel Buy one JUL corn contract at 229.00 cents per bushel

June 1	Buy one JUL wheat contract at 282.75 cents per bushel
	Sell one JUL corn contract at 219.50 cents per bushel
	Corn loss:
	    −$0.095 per bushel × 5,000 bushels = −$475.00
	Wheat profit:
	    $0.4675 per bushel × 5,000 bushels = $2,337.50
	Total profit: $1,862.50

Figure 4.1   July wheat and corn futures prices (February 1 – June 1)

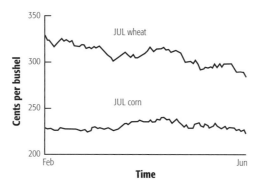

Figure 4.2   Wheat/corn spread profits (February 1 – June 1)

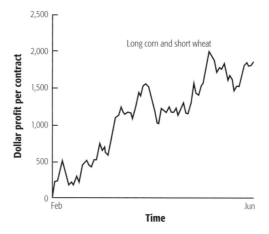

Figure 4.1 shows the prices for the JUL corn and wheat contracts for the relevant period. Prices are expressed in cents per bushel. As the figure shows, the prices of both corn and wheat did not change dramatically, but both prices fell after February 1, with wheat prices falling more than corn. Because the trader was short wheat and long corn, the price movements gave a profit on the wheat side of the trade and a loss on the corn side. However, the drop in wheat prices was greater than the drop in corn prices, giving an overall profit on the spread position. Figure 4.2 tracks the profits that the trader enjoyed from February 1 to June 1.

In this example, the trader correctly bet that the price of corn would rise relative to the price of wheat. As it happened, both prices fell, but the price of wheat fell more, giving an overall profit on the transaction. However, this result is not necessary for the trader to have a profit.

Table 4.4 Copper futures prices on November 10	
Delivery month (of following year)	Price (cents per lb)
JUL	67.0
SEP	67.5
DEC	70.5

For example, if wheat and corn both rose, but corn rose more, the trade would still be profitable. In a spread trade, only the relative prices matter, not the absolute prices.

Other types of spread strategies are also possible. In an intracommodity spread, a trader takes a position in two or more maturity months for the same good. The belief behind this strategy is that the relative prices between delivery dates for the same commodity will change, generating a profit for the trader. Whereas an outright position only requires a belief about the price movement of one commodity, a spread position focuses on the relative price movements between two or more commodities, or contract maturities.

The spread example considered previously was relatively simple, but spreads can be quite complex. One frequently mentioned complex spread is known as a **butterfly spread**, which is best illustrated by an example. Assume that today is November 10 and the prices for copper are as shown in Table 4.4. In comparing the price for September delivery, 67.5 cents per lb, with the prices on the adjacent delivery months of July and December, it seems that the September price is out of line. To this speculator, it appears that the September price should be about halfway between the July and December prices, but it is seriously below that level. Since the speculator does not really know whether copper prices are going to rise or fall in general, she only wants to attempt to take advantage of this apparent pricing discrepancy between different maturities.

To do this, she initiates a futures transaction in the form of a butterfly spread, such as the one illustrated in Table 4.5. Since she expects the price of the September contract to rise relative to the July and December contracts, she sells one contract of each of the July and December maturities. To offset the sale of these two contracts, she buys two contracts for the September delivery. By April 15, the prices of all of the contracts have fallen, but their price relationships are much closer to what the speculator believed was correct. On April 15, the September price has risen, relative to the other contracts, to a point about halfway between them. This is exactly what she expected to happen. The wings of the butterfly spread (the July and December contracts) have flapped, bringing all of the prices into line. As Table 4.5 reveals, this generates a total profit of $750 on the spread.

The classification of speculators into scalpers, day traders, and position traders is useful, but it should not obscure the fact that individuals can have multiple speculative strategies. A particular trader can easily merge his or her activities as a scalper and a position trader. Those individuals actively trading in the pits would be expected to take advantage of all types of opportunities that might become available.

Table 4.5   A butterfly spread in copper

Date	Futures market
November 10	Sell one JUL copper contract at 67 cents per lb Buy two SEP copper contracts at 67.5 cents per lb Sell one DEC copper contract at 70.5 cents per lb
April 15	Buy one JUL copper contract at 65 cents per lb Sell two SEP copper contracts at 67 cents per lb Buy one DEC copper contract at 68.5 cents per lb Profits and losses: JUL: $+\$0.02 \times 25{,}000$ lbs $= +\$500$ SEP: $-\$0.005 \times 2$ contracts $\times 25{,}000$ lbs $= -\$250$ DEC: $+\$0.02 \times 25{,}000$ lbs $= +\$500$ Total profit: $750

Note: The copper contract trades on the Commodity Exchange, Inc., a division of the NYMEX. Each contract is for 25,000 lbs.

The O'Hare spread

Chicago traders use the term "O'Hare spread" to refer to an insanely large futures position held in conjunction with a one-way plane ticket to an exotic foreign destination (preferably a place without an extradition treaty with the United States). If the trader wins his futures bet, then he keeps the money and flies away to live happily ever after. If he loses the bet, then the trader quickly grabs his bags, dashes off a note to his wife and kids, and hops the "L" for Chicago's O'Hare Airport in order to flee the country. The O'Hare spread is supposed to be a humorous anecdote about what a desperate trader might do. However, in 1992 two traders put on a real-life O'Hare spread.

Darrell Zimmerman and his friend Anthony Catalfo were floor brokers in the Treasury bond pit at the CBOT. They were authorized to trade Treasury bond futures and to take futures options positions as required to hedge their futures position. In October 1992, Zimmerman and Catalfo deposited approximately $30,000 into a trading account at Stern and Co., a clearing member of the Board of Trade Clearing Corporation (BOTCC), who authorized the pair to trade up to the amount of their deposit. Zimmerman and Catalfo then proceeded to place hundreds of trades beyond their authorized limits. They bought a massive number of put options on bond futures and simultaneously sold thousands of futures to try to influence the price of the put options. The net result of their trading was a loss of over $8 million. The pair headed to O'Hare Airport, leaving Stern and Co. stuck to handle the margin call. Stern and Co. was unable to meet the call, and was declared in default by the BOTCC. To resolve the matter, Lee Stern wrote a personal check for more than $7 million to make good on his company's obligations. Catalfo and Zimmerman became the targets of numerous civil and criminal proceedings. In addition, they faced disciplinary proceedings at the exchange and arbitration proceedings with Stern and Co. However, the pair fled to Canada. Eventually, Catalfo returned to the United States and was convicted and sent to prison. Zimmerman, however, remains in Canada, where he lives as a squatter in a British Columbia park, supporting himself as a street musician.

Speculative profits

In this section, we review several dimensions of speculative trading. First, we consider the evidence that is available on speculator success and failure for individuals. We have already seen that scalpers seem to make speculative profits. Here, we examine the results of several studies of overall trader performance. Second, we evaluate the practices and profits for some technical trading systems. Third, we consider the aims and performance of commodity pools. Finally, we analyze speculative profits in an efficient markets setting.

Evidence on speculative profits

For the most part, speculative profits and losses are difficult to observe. Most traders cherish the privacy of their brokerage accounts. This privacy allows them to enjoy their profits and lick their trading wounds in private, and also to tell "fish stories" about their trading prowess. Nonetheless, there are several studies that assess the trading results of speculators. A prime source of this information comes from the Commodity Futures Trading Commission's (CFTC's) large trader reports, in which traders with large positions are required to report those positions. This information is made public in the form of the Commitments of Traders report, which summarizes the large trader reports in aggregate form. Therefore, it is possible to determine what large (above the reporting requirements) and small (below the reporting requirements) traders are doing in the aggregate. Note that this is not the same as being able to examine a sample of actual trading for particular individuals.

The studies on the magnitude of speculative profits do not reach a consensus, and some of the methodologies employed have been criticized. Nonetheless, there appears to be little reason to think that speculators make large profits, particularly after considering transaction costs. Rather, the results of some gains and some losses might be broadly consistent with speculators trading futures contracts that are fairly priced.[18]

Technical trading systems

In futures markets, more than any other segment of the financial markets, technical trading systems seem to find favor. This can be verified by browsing through a recent issue of *Futures* and noting the many advertisements for various technical trading systems. **Technical analysis** is a method of analyzing markets that uses only market data (prices, volume, open interest, and similar information) to predict future price movements. For example, technical analysts believe certain price formations suggest that futures prices will rise. Other formations, according to technical analysis, portend a price decline. We do not explore the methods of technical analysis here, but many books cover the subject.[19] Instead, we want to explore the evidence on whether technical analysis can generate speculative profits.

To have any chance of success, technical analysis depends on the existence of patterns in futures prices. In most markets, scholars find that price patterns do exist, but that these patterns are not sufficiently strong to permit technical trading strategies to generate a profit. To make a trading profit, including covering transaction costs, would require very significant patterns. Many studies are based on simulations of trading systems, instead of systems that are in actual use. While many of these studies suggest that technical analysis may have some merit, this is a very controversial area and the final word has not yet been written on this subject. If technical analysis is useful in futures trading, that result would stand in contrast to findings for other financial markets.[20]

Commodity funds

A **commodity fund** or a **commodity pool** is a financial institution that accepts funds from a variety of participants and uses those funds to speculate in the futures market. As such, its organization is similar to a mutual fund. We have noted that trading futures does not require investment as such. Thus, the commodity funds use their customers' funds for two purposes: margin deposits and earning interest. The interest-earning portion provides a pool of funds for future margin calls. Gains and losses for the funds come from futures trading and from the interest that is being earned. Most funds rely strongly on technical analysis for their trading strategies.

What performance can we expect from commodity funds? To analyze this question, we make two initial assumptions. First, we assume that patterns in futures prices are not sufficient to allow technical analysis to generate profits. Second, we assume that the futures price equals the expected future spot price. Under these two restrictions, we would expect the futures trading portion of the commodity fund to neither lose nor profit. Under our assumptions, the fund might trade, but the expected payoff on each trade would be zero. For the interest-earning portion of their assets, we would expect the invested assets to earn the money market rate of interest. Under these assumptions, we expect a commodity fund to underperform a buy-and-hold money market investment, due to the transaction costs that the fund incurs in its trading strategy. To succeed, the commodity fund must be able to earn speculative profits, presumably through technical trading systems, since most funds rely largely on those systems.

Typically, commodity funds use only about 30 percent of invested funds as margin deposits. Thus, the bulk of the money received sits in a money market investment. Second, returns are often negative. Third, even when funds earn positive returns, they typically do not outperform their inherent level of systematic risk. That is, they do not beat the market. Fourth, even if funds are not attractive as investments in themselves, they might be useful in reducing risk when added to a portfolio of stocks and bonds. Evidence on this point is mixed. Fifth, past performance is not a good guide to future performance. In sum, the evidence seems fairly consistent with an efficient markets perspective. Funds do not seem to be an exciting investment vehicle, but may be a useful tool in some circumstances.

Many commodity funds are organized as hedge funds. The operators of these hedge funds are registered with the CFTC as Commodity Pool Operators, or CPOs, because they intend to trade futures contracts. Hedge funds operated by CPOs must provide end-of-year financial reports to the National Futures Association (NFA), provide written disclosure to prospective investors, subject themselves to periodic inspections by the NFA, adhere to recordkeeping and reporting requirements, abide by restrictions on advertising, and satisfy requirements on the handling of customer funds.

What are hedge funds?

A hedge fund[21] is a term used to describe a wide range of pooled investment vehicles that are privately organized and not widely available to the public. Hedge funds are accessible only to wealthy individuals and institutional investors. Hedge funds can employ any trading strategy they choose, including highly risky strategies; hence the term "hedge" is misleading in describing the risk appetite of the fund's investors. Many investors are attracted to certain hedge funds because they represent a separate asset class that fits well into an overall portfolio diversification strategy.

Although there is no single organizational form for hedge funds, most structure their operations in such a way that they are exempt from the laws and regulations that apply to more traditional investment vehicles such as mutual funds. To be exempt from the Investment Company Act of 1940 and the Investment Advisors Act of 1940 (the statues that regulate mutual funds and their investment advisors), hedge funds must be offered through "private placements," with shares sold to fewer than 100 "accredited investors." An accredited investor is an individual or institution that meets either net worth or income thresholds. For an individual to qualify as an accredited investor, he or she must have income in each of the two preceding years exceeding $200,000 (or $300,000 in joint income with a spouse). The individual must have a reasonable expectation of reaching the same level of income in the current year. An individual can also qualify as an accredited investor if he or she has a net worth (or joint net worth with a spouse) exceeding $1 million at the time of purchase. An institutional investor must have assets that exceed $5 million. The purpose of these restrictions is to limit hedge fund investors to wealthy (and presumably sophisticated) investors, who can fend for themselves and who do not need the federal government's investor-protection laws and regulations. If disputes arise, these investors can sue under existing contract law.

Hedge funds are subject to various regulatory reporting requirements that any other investment fund must meet. For example, if a hedge fund holds positions in futures or futures options, they are subject to the CFTC's large trader requirements.

Amaranth Advisors LLC

For several years leading up to 2006, Amaranth Advisors LLC, a hedge fund firm named for an imaginary flower that never fades, made investments that seemed to always bloom. At its peak, in August 2006, Amaranth managed about $9.5 billion in assets, but on Monday September 18, 2006 the bloom suddenly faded. A letter delivered to investors on that day announced that two Amaranth funds, Amaranth Partners and Amaranth International, had sustained significant losses resulting from transactions involving natural gas futures and futures option contracts. The firm eventually reported losing approximately $6 billion and in late September announced that it was liquidating all remaining assets.

Reports circulated that a large share of the losses resulted from a speculative calendar spread position that would make money if natural gas futures prices for March 2007 rose relative to April 2007 prices. Instead of rising, in just a few short weeks, the spread fell precipitously from $2.25 per million British thermal units (mmBtu) to less than $0.75.

As its trading losses mounted, Amaranth scrambled to quickly sell, at a steep discount, its energy portfolio to J P Morgan Chase & Co. and the hedge fund Citadel Investment Group, LLC. The new owners were better capitalized than Amaranth and could afford to hold the illiquid energy investments until they could be liquidated at favorable prices.

Although Amaranth's ability to lose so much money so quickly was remarkable, even more remarkable was that the episode caused barely a ripple in the natural gas futures markets. Amaranth's losses were large, but the market discipline exhibited by the futures clearinghouse, the futures commission merchant carrying Amaranth's positions, lenders, and other creditors kept the losses confined to the investors in the Amaranth funds. Amaranth met all of its margin calls and the financial safeguard system worked as it was designed to work.

"Normal" speculative returns

We have seen several examples of apparently successful speculation. First, we saw that Mr. X in Silber's study earned positive returns by scalping. Second, we considered several studies that reported on speculative profits. Third, we noted that some technical trading systems seem to earn positive returns, while evidence suggests that other systems do not. Finally, we examined commodity pools and found some evidence that some pools make speculative profits. In this section, we want to consider futures market speculation from an efficient markets perspective. To do this, we will review the concept of a "normal profit," and then consider Mr. X's trading in more detail.

An **efficient market** is a market in which prices fully reflect the information contained in a specified information set. To differentiate versions of the efficient markets hypothesis, we can specify different information sets. The traditional versions of the efficient markets hypothesis are known as the weak, semistrong, and strong versions.[22] The **weak form** claims that prices in a market fully reflect all information contained in the history of volume and price. The **semistrong** version claims that market prices fully reflect all publicly available information. The **strong** version states that market prices reflect all information, whether public or private. Private information includes information possessed only by corporate insiders and governmental officials. The strong version is almost certainly false, so we will be concerned only with the weak and semistrong forms.

If the weak-form version is true, then no information about past or present prices or volume is useful for guiding a speculative strategy. If the futures market is weakly efficient, there will be no cash-and-carry arbitrage opportunities of the type we analyzed in Chapter 3. Additionally, technical trading strategies will not work. If the semistrong version is true, then studying information about the determinants of prices will also not be useful in guiding a trading strategy.

Unlike investing in stocks or bonds, trading futures requires no actual investment, because of the system of margin and daily settlement. This suggests that any steady profits in futures trading would be inconsistent with an efficient market. Thus, the scalping profits of about $10 per contract reviewed earlier seem to fly in the face of the efficient markets hypothesis. We now want to examine some additional costs that the scalper faces.

To trade futures on a major exchange, one must own a seat, or secure the use of a seat from one who does own one. Second, trading on the exchange involves a commitment of time and energy. Since the time and energy is being committed to trading, it cannot be applied elsewhere to earn a return. Third, trading futures necessarily involves risk. Most people are unwilling to risk money unless the expected returns from those risks are high enough to justify the risk. With these ideas in mind, consider Mr. X, whom we assume owns a seat on a major exchange. What income does he need to make trading worthwhile from a financial point of view, and how does this compare with his actual trading results?

The first consideration is the value of the seat that is required in order to trade. As mentioned in Chapter 1, seats on the exchanges are bought and sold in a market, and Chicago Mercantile Exchange (CME) and CBOT seats have recently sold in the range of $400,000–935,000.[23] Taking a conservative figure of $500,000, it is clear that our trader loses the use of $500,000 by virtue of buying his seat. Assume that an equally risky investment would return a modest 10 percent. To cover the cost of his seat, Mr. X must make $50,000 per year. Second, Mr. X commits his time to trading, whereas if he were not trading he could hold another job. Most of the traders are people of competence and executive ability, and trading is grueling and nerve-wracking work with long hours that go beyond the limited trading times. Mr. X, having exhibited a willingness to work as hard as a trader must work and with the talents necessary to succeed as a trader, could expect to earn a relatively handsome salary in some other capacity. Perhaps $60,000 per year would be a conservative figure. As most salaried positions have fringe benefits for medical, dental, and life insurance, this is extremely conservative.

In addition to the foregone opportunities of investing the price of his seat elsewhere and of taking alternative employment, the high risk of trading must also be acknowledged. Relative to trading, a salaried position is very secure. Being risk averse, Mr. X would reasonably expect some compensation for his additional risk exposure. The amount of compensation is very difficult to quantify and clearly depends on his personal risk tolerance. Finally, the character of a trader's work needs to be considered somewhat more fully. Trading is extremely demanding—physically, emotionally, and mentally. A casual survey of the trading pits reveals few elderly participants. From conversations with many traders, it is clear that they do not generally expect to be trading past the age of 40.[24] As another indicator of the level of stress, one need only consult *The Wall Street Journal*, which has frequent articles on the problems of traders. They lose their voices from shouting and need voice coaches, they occasionally sustain physical injuries, and they sometimes suffer anxiety as a result of the stress in their work.[25] While many traders are attracted by the excitement of the pits, many people would demand high compensation for working under such conditions. The extreme physical and psychological demands are difficult to value in terms of dollars, but they are real costs.

Table 4.6 shows that Mr. X should make at least $110,000 per year without there being the slightest hint that supernormal profits are being captured. Many traders make very handsome incomes and live quite well—when they are not on the trading floor. This fact alone does not warrant the conclusions that trading futures contracts is an easy way to get rich quickly. The traders have high costs to cover before they reach the point at which they start to make supernormal profits. The chance to speculate on futures may not be the way to easy street.

Trading Places

> Think big, think positive, never show any sign of weakness. Buy low, sell high. Fear? That's the other guy's problem.
>
> Trading advice from Louis Winthorpe III to Billy Ray Valentine in *Trading Places*

Although over 20 years has elapsed since Paramount's 1983 hit film *Trading Places*, it remains a favorite of futures market professionals everywhere. For students just beginning to learn about futures trading and trading institutions, the film provides several excellent lessons. One useful lesson is that profitable trades result from buying low and selling high even when one holds a short position. Another lesson relates to the concept of market efficiency and the value of private information.

The film's plot centers around a scheme by the Duke brothers (played by Ralph Bellamy and Don Ameche) to use inside information to trade Frozen Concentrated Orange Juice (FCOJ) futures ahead of the orange crop report. Unbeknownst to the Duke brothers, Winthorpe and Valentine (played by Dan Ackroyd and Eddie Murphy) have discovered the scheme and have replaced the true crop report with a fake. Based on the fake crop report, the Duke brothers think that bad weather has affected the orange crop harvest and will result in higher prices when the report is made public. Trading on this information, the Duke brothers tell their floor trader to buy (go long) April FCOJ contracts. As the Duke brothers' trader executes his trades the price rises from an opening price of 102, topping out at 142. At a price of 142, Winthorpe and Valentine, who have access to the true crop report and know that the report shows that bad weather did not affect the orange harvest, begin to build a short April FCOJ futures position. When the crop report is made public, the price drops like a rock, all the way to 29. Valentine and Winthorpe then cover their short position by buying April contracts. The net result is that Valentine and Winthorpe bought at 29 and sold at 142. The Duke brothers bought in a price range between 102 and 142 and sold at prices approaching 29. The bottom line: Valentine and Winthorpe get rich and the Duke brothers end up in the poor house.

Careful observers of the film will notice that during the climactic trading session, the displayed prices for the April contract move rapidly while the prices for contracts expiring in the adjacent and deferred months remain constant. In reality, cost-of-carry arbitrage will force prices for other delivery months to move as well.

Table 4.6   Hypothetical alternative income for Mr. X

Resource	Annual amount
Use of money to secure seat	$50,000
Foregone alternative employment	$60,000
Additional risk undertaken	?
Additional stress and strain	?
Total:	$110,000+?

The real-world data from Silber's study reveals the difficulties that traders face. As Silber notes, Mr. X earned relatively little during this period. During the 31 trading days of Silber's sample, Mr. X had average profits of $742 per day. This was before commissions, which averaged $1.22 per contract traded. After commissions, Mr. X had daily profits of $672. With approximately 250 trading days per year, Mr. X would earn about $168,000 per year. Silber reports that these results place Mr. X in the upper quartile of scalpers on the NYFE. When we compare these results with the opportunity cost computed in Table 4.6, we can see that Mr. X does well, but not wonderfully. If we consider the risks he takes, the stress and strain he bears, and the out-of-pocket costs he faces, Mr. X will have to do better than he did in this period to convince us that he can beat the market.

Hedging

In contrast to the speculator, the **hedger** is a trader who enters the futures market in order to reduce a preexisting risk.[26] If a trader trades futures contracts on commodities in which he or she has no initial position, and in which he or she does not contemplate taking a cash position, then the trader cannot be a hedger. The futures transaction cannot serve as a substitute for a cash market transaction. Having a position, in this case, does not mean that the trader must actually own a commodity. An individual or firm that anticipates the need for a certain commodity in the future or a person who plans to acquire a certain commodity later also has a position in that commodity. In many cases, a hedger has a certain **hedging horizon**—the future date on which the hedge will terminate. For example, a farmer can anticipate that he or she will want to hedge from planting to the harvest. In other cases, there will be no specific horizon. We begin with two examples in which hedgers have definite hedging horizons.

A long hedge

The idea that you may be at risk in a certain commodity without actually owning it may be confusing to some, but consider the following example. Silver is an essential input for the production of most types of photographic films and papers, and the price of silver is quite volatile. For a manufacturer of film, there is a considerable risk that profits could be dramatically affected by fluctuations in the price of silver. If production schedules are to be maintained, it is absolutely essential that silver be acquired on a regular basis in large quantities. Assume that the film manufacturer needs 50,000 troy ounces of silver in two months and confronts the silver prices shown in Table 4.7 on May 10. The current spot price is 1,052.5 cents per ounce, and the price of the JUL futures contract lies above that at 1,068.0, with the SEP futures contract trading at 1,084.0.

Table 4.7   Silver futures prices on May 10

Contract	Price (cents per troy ounce)
Spot	1,052.5
JUL	1,068.0
SEP	1,084.0

Note: The COMEX division of the NYMEX trades a silver contract for 5,000 troy ounces.

Table 4.8   A long hedge in silver

Date	Cash market	Futures market
May 10	Anticipates the need for 50,000 troy ounces in two months and expects to pay 1,068 cents per ounce, or a total of $534,000	Buys ten 5,000 troy ounce JUL futures contracts at 1,068 cents per ounce
July 10	The spot price of silver is now 1,071 cents per ounce; the manufacturer buys 50,000 ounces, paying $535,500	Since the futures contract is at maturity, the futures and spot prices are equal, and the ten contracts are sold at 1,071 cents per ounce
	Opportunity loss: −$1,500	Futures profit: $1,500
	Net wealth change = 0	

Fearing that silver prices may rise unexpectedly, the film manufacturer decides that the price of 1,068.0 is acceptable for the silver that he will need in July. He realizes that it is hopeless to buy the silver on the spot market at 1,052.5 and to store the silver for two months. The price differential of 15.5 cents per ounce would not cover his storage costs. Also, the manufacturer will receive an acceptable level of profits even if he pays 1,068.0 for the silver to be delivered in July. To pay a price higher than 1,068.0, however, could jeopardize profitability seriously. With these reasons in mind, he decides to enter the futures market to hedge against the possibility of future unexpected increases in prices and, accordingly, he enters the trades shown in Table 4.8.

Taking the futures price as the best estimate of the future spot price, the manufacturer expects to pay 1,068.0 cents per ounce for silver in the spot market two months from now, in July. At the same time, he buys ten 5,000-ounce JUL futures contracts at 1,068.0 cents per ounce. Since he buys a futures contract in order to hedge, this transaction is known as a **long hedge**. The trader is also purchasing a futures contract in anticipation of needing the silver at a future date, so these transactions also represent an **anticipatory hedge**. Time passes, and by July the spot price of silver has risen to 1,071.0 cents per ounce, 3 cents higher than expected. Needing the silver, the manufacturer purchases the silver on the spot market, paying a total of $535,500. This is $1,500 more than expected. Since the futures contract is about to mature, the futures price must equal the spot price, so the film manufacturer is able to sell his ten futures contracts at the same price of 1,071.0 cents per ounce, making a 3 cent profit on each ounce, and a total profit of $1,500 on the futures position. The cash and futures results net to zero. In the cash market, the price was $1,500 more than expected, but there was an offsetting futures profit of $1,500, which generated a net wealth change of zero.

The reversing trade and hedging

One peculiar feature of these transactions is that the manufacturer did not accept delivery on the futures contract, but offset the contract instead. Rather than accepting delivery on a contract, it usually is better to reverse the trade, because offsetting saves on transaction costs and administrative difficulties. The short trader has the right to choose the delivery destination and the long trader must fear that the short trader will select an unpalatable destination. Instead of taking delivery, the long trader can acquire the physical commodity from normal suppliers. The hedger in this example could have achieved the same result by accepting delivery. If delivery were accepted on the futures contract, the silver would have been secured at a price of 1,068.0 cents per ounce, which is what happened when the reversing trade was used.

A short hedge

Although the long silver hedge involved the purchase of a futures contract, hedges do not necessarily involve long futures positions. A **short hedge** is a hedge in which the hedger sells a futures contract. As an example, we assume the same silver prices and a date of May 10, as shown in Table 4.7. A Nevada silver mine owner is concerned about the price of silver, since she wants to be able to plan for the profitability of her firm. If silver prices fall, she may be forced to suspend production. Given the current level of production, she expects to have about 50,000 ounces of silver ready for shipment in two months. Considering the silver prices shown in Table 4.7, she decides that she would be satisfied to receive 1,068.0 cents per ounce for her silver.

To establish the price of 1,068.0 cents per ounce, the mine owner decides to enter the silver futures market. By hedging, she can avoid the risk that silver prices might fall in the next two months. Table 4.9 shows the mine owner's transactions. Notice that these are exactly the mirror image of the film manufacturer's transactions. Anticipating the need to sell 50,000 ounces of silver in two months, the mine owner sells ten 5,000-ounce futures contracts for July delivery at 1,068.0 cents per ounce. On July 10, with silver prices at 1,071.0 cents per ounce, the mine owner sells the silver and receives $535,000. This is $1,500 more than she originally expected. In the futures market, however, the mine owner suffers an offsetting loss. The futures contracts

Table 4.9 A short hedge in silver		
Date	Cash market	Futures market
May 10	Anticipates the sale of 50,000 troy ounces in two months and expects to receive 1,068 cents per ounce, or a total of $534,000	Sells ten 5,000 troy ounce July futures contracts at 1,068 cents per ounce
July 10	The spot price of silver is now 1,071 cents per ounce; the mine owner sells 50,000 ounces, receiving $535,500	Buys ten contracts at 1,071 cents per ounce
	Profit: $1,500	Futures loss: −$1,500
	Net wealth change = 0	

she sold at 1,068.0 cents per ounce, she offsets in July at 1,071.0 cents per ounce. Once again, the profits and losses in the two markets offset each other, and produce a net wealth change of zero.

Viewing the results from the vantage point of July, it is clear that the mine owner would have been $1,500 richer if she had not hedged. She would have received $1,500 more than originally expected in the physicals market, and she would have incurred no loss in the futures market. However, it does not follow that she was unwise to hedge. The mine owner knew before establishing her hedge that she might have a higher profit margin in certain market conditions if her position was left unhedged. However, she knew that she definitely wanted to avoid a lower profit margin and therefore chose to establish a hedged position with futures contracts. In hedging, the mine owner and the film manufacturer both decided that the futures price was an acceptable price at which to complete the transaction in July.

Do hedgers need speculators?

Hedging is often viewed as the purchasing of insurance. According to this view, hedgers trade in the futures market and speculators bear the risk that the hedgers try to avoid. Naturally, the speculators demand some compensation for this service. In Chapter 3, the theories of normal backwardation and the contango were considered as explanations of the way in which speculators might receive compensation for bearing risk. In considering the two sides of the silver example, however, no speculators were needed to assume position trades. The long and short hedgers balanced each other out perfectly.

While the example is artificial, it illustrates an important point. Hedgers, as a group, need speculators to take positions and bear risk only for the mismatch in contracts demanded by the long and short hedgers. To the extent that their positions match, position-trading speculators are not needed for the job of bearing risk. This helps explain why the risk premiums, if there are any, are not large. In this example, the hedgers do not need speculators to act as position traders. However, even if long and short hedgers were always in balance, the market would still need the liquidity provided by scalpers, such as Mr. X, the scalper we studied earlier.

Cross-hedging

In the examples of a long and short hedge in silver, the hedgers' needs were perfectly matched with the institutional features of the silver markets. The goods in question were exactly the same goods traded on the futures market, the cash amounts matched the futures contract amounts, and the hedging horizons of the mine owner and film manufacturer matched the delivery date for the futures contract. In actual hedging applications, it will be rare for all factors to match so well. In most cases the hedged and hedging positions will differ in (1) the time span covered, (2) the amount of the commodity, or (3) the particular characteristics of the goods. In such cases, the hedge will be a **cross-hedge**—a hedge in which the characteristics of the spot and futures positions do not match perfectly.

As an example, consider the problem faced by a film manufacturer that uses silver, a key ingredient in manufacturing photographic film. Film production is a process industry, with more or less continuous production. However, silver futures, listed at the Commodity Exchange, Inc. COMEX Division of the New York Mercantile Exchange (NYMEX), trade for delivery in January, March, May, July, September, and December. The film manufacturer will also need silver in February, April, and so on. Thus, the futures expiration dates and the hedging horizon for the film manufacturer do not match perfectly. Second, consider the differences in quantity between the futures contract and the film manufacturer's needs. The COMEX contract is for 5,000 troy ounces of silver. The film manufacturer will likely need many thousands of ounces, so it will be fairly easy for the manufacturer to choose and trade a number of contracts that will bring the quantity of silver futures close to the actual need. However, if a hedger needed to hedge 7,500 ounces, he or she might have a problem choosing between one or two contracts. Finally, consider the differences in the physical characteristics of the silver underlying the futures contract and the silver used in manufacturing film. To produce film, silver needs to be in pellet form and it does not need to be as pure as silver bullion. Also, the pellets contain other metals besides silver. The COMEX silver contract specifies that deliverable silver must be in 1,000-ounce ingots that are 99.9 percent pure. In other words, the silver in the futures contract is extremely pure and refined, not like the adulterated silver products that are typically used in industry. Thus, the film manufacturer will have to hedge his or her industrial silver with pure silver bullion. Cross-hedging is often particularly problematic in the interest rate futures market. Financial instruments are extremely varied in their characteristics, such as risk level, maturity, and coupon rate. By contrast, really active futures contracts are only traded on a few different types of interest-bearing securities.

When the characteristics of the position to be hedged do not perfectly match the characteristics of the futures contract used for the hedging, the hedger must be sure to trade the right number and kind of futures contract to control the risk in the hedged position as much as possible. In general, we cannot expect a cross-hedge to be as effective in reducing risk as a direct hedge. We consider cross-hedging in more detail in later chapters.

Micro-hedging versus macro-hedging

Hedges can also be characterized by the scope of the underlying risks subject to the hedge. The term **micro-hedge** describes the case in which a futures position is matched against a specific asset or liability item on the balance sheet. An example of a micro-hedge would be a bank hedging rates on one-year certificates of deposit from the liability side of its balance sheet. The term **macro-hedge** describes the case in which the hedge is structured to offset the net (i.e., combined) risk associated with the hedger's overall asset/liability mix. An example of a macro-hedge would be a bank that uses interest rate futures to equate the interest rate exposure of its assets with the interest rate exposure of its liabilities.

Stack hedges versus strip hedges

Some situations require hedges of cash flow over extended periods. A hedge for this type of long-term risk can be implemented in two different ways. First, futures positions can be established in a series of futures contracts of successively longer expirations. This is called a **strip hedge**. Second, the entire futures position can be stacked in the front month and then rolled forward (less the portion of the hedge that is no longer needed) into the next front month contract. This is called a **stack hedge**.

Each strategy involves tradeoffs. The strip hedge has a higher correlation with the underlying risks than the stack hedge (i.e., has lower **tracking error**), but may have higher liquidity costs because the more distant contracts may be very thinly traded and may have high bid–ask spreads accompanied by high trade-execution risk. The stack hedge has lower liquidity costs but has higher tracking error. The stack hedge made news in 1993 when Metallgesellschaft's U.S. subsidiary, MG Refining and Manufacturing, was forced to unwind a substantial stack hedge in energy futures, with disastrous results. We will examine the Metallgesellschaft fiasco later in this chapter.

Risk-minimization hedging

In our first examples, we considered hedges when the hedger had a definite horizon in view. Often, the hedger will not want to hedge for a specific future date. Instead, the hedger may

Figure 4.3 Soybean cash prices

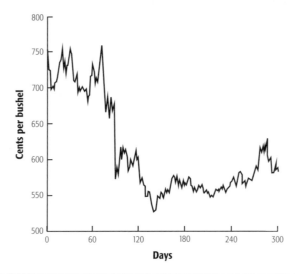

want to control a continuing risk on an indefinite basis. Consider, for example, a soy dealer who holds an inventory of soybeans. From this inventory, the dealer meets orders from her customers. As her inventory becomes low, she periodically replenishes her own inventory from cash market sources. The inventory that she holds will fluctuate in value with the price of soybeans. However, she can reduce the fluctuations in the value of her inventory by selling futures contracts, as the following case study shows.

Figure 4.3 shows 300 days of historical soybean cash prices. For this case, we assume that the present is day 60, and soybeans are near their recent high, closing today at 719.5 (719.5 cents per bushel). As Figure 4.3 shows, soybeans have been quite volatile in the preceding 60 days. Therefore, the dealer decides to hedge her inventory of 1 million bushels of soybeans by selling soybean futures. After she sells futures, she will be long the physical soybeans in her inventory and short soybean futures. If the hedge works, the risk of the combined cash/futures position should be less than the cash position alone.

With an inventory of 1 million bushels, and a soybean contract calling for 5,000 bushels, it might seem wise to sell one bushel in the futures market for each bushel in the cash market. This would call for selling 200 soybean contracts. However, a 1 : 1 hedge may not be optimal. In our example, the dealer wants to minimize her preexisting risk, which comes from holding her soybean inventory. We assume that she holds a given bean inventory for business reasons, and we treat that inventory decision as fixed. The dealer's problem is to choose the number of futures contracts that will minimize her risk. Thus, we define the **hedge ratio** (HR) as the number of futures contracts to hold for a given position in the commodity:

$$HR = -\frac{\text{futures position}}{\text{cash market position}} \qquad (4.1)$$

The dealer will trade HR units of the futures to establish the futures market hedge. After establishing the hedge, the trader has a portfolio, P, that consists of the spot position plus the futures position. The profits and losses on the portfolio for one day will be

$$p_{t+1} - p_t = S_{t+1} - S_t + HR(F_{t+1} - F_t) \tag{4.2}$$

Note that in our initial discussion we considered that the dealer might hedge each bushel in her cash position with one bushel of futures. In that case, the hedge ratio would be -1.0, the negative sign indicating a short position. Generally, if the trader is long the cash commodity, the futures position will be short. Likewise, if the trader is short the cash good, the futures position will be long.

   Now, however, the dealer wants to choose the hedge ratio that will minimize the risk of the portfolio of the spot beans and the futures position. The variance of the combined position depends on the variance of the cash price, the variance of the futures price, and the covariance between the two prices. It is a basic statistical rule that the variance of returns on a portfolio, P, of one unit of the spot asset and HR units of a futures contract is given by the following equation:

$$\sigma_P^2 = \sigma_S^2 + HR^2\sigma_F^2 + 2HR\rho_{SF}\sigma_S\sigma_F \tag{4.3}$$

where σ_P^2 is the variance of the portfolio, P; σ_S^2 is the variance of S_t; σ_F^2 is the variance of F_t; and ρ_{SF} is the correlation between S_t and F_t. The dealer minimizes the variance by choosing a hedge ratio defined as follows:[27]

$$HR = -\frac{\rho_{SF}\sigma_S\sigma_F}{\sigma_F^2} = -\frac{COV_{SF}}{\sigma_F^2} \tag{4.4}$$

where COV_{SF} is the covariance between S_t and F_t. As a practical matter, the easiest way to find the risk-minimizing hedge ratio is to estimate the following regression:

$$S_t = \alpha + \beta F_t + \varepsilon_t \tag{4.5}$$

where α is the constant regression parameter, β is the slope regression parameter, and ε is an error term with zero mean and standard deviation of 1.0. The **negative** of the estimated beta from this regression is the risk-minimizing hedge ratio, because the estimated beta equals the sample covariance between the independent (F_t) and dependent (S_t) variables divided by the sample variance of the independent variable. This is exactly the definition we gave of the risk-minimizing hedge ratio in Equation 4.4.

   From the regression estimation, we also obtain a measure of hedging effectiveness. The coefficient of determination, or R^2, is provided by the regression estimate. Conceptually:

   R^2 = portion of total variance in the cash price changes statistically related to the futures price changes

Thus the R^2 will always be a number between 0 and 1.0. The closer it is to 1.0, the better will be the degree of fit in the regression between the cash and the futures and the better will be the chance for our hedge to work well.

   There are at least three possible measures of S_t and F_t that we might be tempted to employ in the regression of Equation 4.5: price levels, price changes, and percentage price changes.

There has been considerable controversy regarding the proper measure.[28] While this controversy is not fully resolved, we recommend using either the change in price or the percentage change in price, but not the price level. If the general range of prices over the estimation period is fairly stable, the price change measure will be satisfactory. If the price changes dramatically, the use of percentage price changes will give better results.[29]

We now apply this regression approach to the problem of our soybean dealer, using the immediately previous 60 days of daily data to estimate the following regression equation:

$$\Delta C_t = \alpha + \beta \Delta F_t + \varepsilon_t$$

where ΔC_t is the change in the cash price on day t and ΔF_t is the change in the futures price on day t. Estimating the regression gives the following parameter estimates: $\alpha = 0.6976$; $\beta = 0.8713$; $R^2 = 0.56$. With the estimated $\beta = 0.8713$, the model suggests selling 0.8713 bushels in the futures market for each bushel in inventory. With 1 million bushels in inventory and a futures contract of 5,000 bushels, the model suggests selling 174 contracts, because

$$0.8713 \times (1,000,000/5,000) = 174.26 \text{ contracts}$$

From the estimation of the model, we see that the regression accounts for 56 percent of the variance of the cash price change during our sample period. This is an important point, because the regression chose an estimate of beta to maximize the R^2. This provides no certainty that we can expect similar results beyond the estimation period. To this point in our example, we have used the data that would actually be available to a trader on day 60. We assume that our soybean dealer estimated her hedge ratio and placed the hedge at the close of the next business day. Next, we want to evaluate the performance of the hedge.

Figure 4.4 shows how soybeans performed from day 61 through day 300, approximately over the next year, when we assume that the dealer offset in the futures market, thereby ending the hedge.[30] The graph in Figure 4.4 shows the wealth change from day 61 onward for one contract of cash soybeans and for a contract (5,000 bushels) of cash soybeans hedged with 0.8713 futures contracts. As the figure shows, soybean prices fell dramatically over the next year (240 trading days). From the time the hedge was placed until about day 150, soybean prices fell about $2.00 per bushel. During the same interval, the hedge position lost about $1.00 per bushel. From about day 150 to day 300, prices drifted somewhat higher.

Comparing the unhedged and the hedged strategies, we see that both lost money. However, the hedged strategy avoided about 50 percent of the loss associated with the drop in cash prices. Over the life of the hedge, the unhedged bushel of soybeans lost $1.56 and the hedged bushel lost $0.71. On the inventory of 1 million bushels, this represents a benefit of $850,000 from hedging. From Figure 4.4, we can also see that the hedged position had much less variance than the cash position. For an unhedged bushel, the standard deviation of the price change was $0.0815 per day. For the hedged position, the standard deviation was $0.0431.

Several special points need to be made about this particular hedge. First, we see that the hedge made money because the short position in the futures gave profits as soybean prices fell. We must realize that bean prices could just as easily have risen. In that event, the futures position in the hedge would have lost money. This brings us to the second point. Hedging aims at reducing risk, not generating profits. In this case, the goal was to reduce variance, which the hedge did. Had bean prices risen, the hedge would also have reduced variance, and would have been successful in attaining its goal. Thus, the hedger must expect an equal chance of monetary gains and losses from placing a hedge. However, with a good hedge, the variance can be reduced substantially.

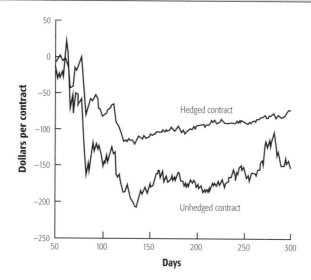

Figure 4.4   The performance of the hedged and unhedged soybean positions

Hedging and quantity risk

One problem in implementing a hedge is identifying the quantity to be hedged. Consider the case of a farmer interested in hedging the price of a farm crop. To be effective, the hedge must be done before the harvest. This means that the farmer is exposed to **quantity risk**. The size of the futures position used in the hedge depends on the farmer's expectation of the size of the crop. But there are many factors that can influence the size of the crop—for example, weather—that are outside the farmer's control.

Another type of risk in implementing a hedge can be traced to the delivery specifications of the futures contract used to construct the hedge. As we have seen, nearly all futures contracts allow delivery of any of several qualities of the underlying good. Location differences are also permitted. Consequently, the price of the futures contract will be more closely associated with the price of the deliverable variety that is cheapest to deliver as opposed to the price of the par variety.[31]

The costs and benefits of hedging

We have defined a hedger as a futures trader with a preexisting risk, who enters the futures market to reduce that risk. We have also seen that this definition implies that hedging activities will be restricted to commercial concerns generally. In this section, we explore the rationale for hedging by corporations.

Because the analysis is simpler, we begin by considering the incentives for hedging in a perfect market. As we have seen, hedging is essentially a transaction in a financial market. From the point of view of the firm, the decision to hedge is essentially a financing decision. In perfect markets, the financial policy of the corporation is irrelevant, because shareholders can always transact to undo the actions of the firm's managers. For example, as Miller and Modigliani have shown,[32] managerial decisions regarding the mixture of debt and equity can be unwound by the shareholders to create any capital structure the shareholder desires. Thus, if the firm issues no debt, the shareholder can create homemade leverage by issuing debt on his or her personal account.

In futures hedging, the situation is similar. If the firm fails to hedge, the shareholder in a perfect market can effectively hedge his or her stake in the firm by trading a fractional share in the futures market.[33] Similarly, if the firm hedges by selling futures, for instance, the shareholder can create an unhedged personal stake in the firm by buying a fractional futures contract. While hedging in a perfect market cannot increase the value of the firm, it cannot decrease it either, because shareholders can always transact to offset the firm's action. If corporate hedging in a perfect market is pointless, as this argument suggests, then any real benefit to hedging must come from market imperfections.

We consider six market imperfections that can make hedging important and that may impose real costs on firms: taxes, costs of financial distress, transaction costs, principal–agent problems, the costliness of diversification, and differences between internal and external financing costs.

Taxes as an incentive to hedge

In a perfect market, there are no taxes. In real markets, when taxes are levied on annual accounting income, they can provide an incentive for a firm to hedge. Consider a firm that will mine 1,000 ounces of gold bullion this year at a cost of $300 per ounce. The futures price for gold, and thus the firm's expected sales price, is $400 per ounce. This price will give a profit of $100,000. However, this is only an expected price, and the actual price may be $300 or $500 per ounce with equal probability, we assume. We also assume that the tax rate is 20 percent and that the firm has a tax credit of $20,000 that it can apply to offset income taxes. To hedge, the firm would sell futures for its 1,000 ounces of production at the $400 per ounce futures price. Table 4.10 shows the different outcomes depending on the sale price of gold and the firm's decision to hedge or not to hedge.

For both the hedged and the unhedged firm, revenues from selling gold will be either $300,000 or $500,000, depending on whether the gold price is $300 or $500. For the unhedged firm, there is no futures result. If the gold price is $300, the hedged firm has a futures gain of $100,000,

Table 4.10 How taxes provide an incentive to hedge

Sale price of gold	Unhedged firm		Hedged firm	
	Outcome 1	Outcome 2	Outcome 1	Outcome 2
	$300	$500	$300	$500
Gold revenue	$300,000	$500,000	$300,000	$500,000
Futures result	0	0	+100,000	−100,000
Less production cost	−300,000	−300,000	−300,000	−300,000
Pretax profit	0	200,000	100,000	100,000
Tax obligation	0	−40,000	−20,000	−20,000
Add tax credit (if applicable)	0	+20,000	+20,000	+20,000
Net income	0	$180,000	$100,000	$100,000
Expected after-tax net income	$90,000		$100,000	

because the hedge involved selling 1,000 ounces in the futures market at $400. If the gold price is $500, the hedging firm loses $100,000 in the futures market, because it sold for a futures price of $400 when it could have received $500 by not hedging. Production costs are $300,000 for all scenarios. Pretax profits for the unhedged firm will be either zero or $200,000, depending on the price of gold. For the hedged firm, the pretax profit will be $100,000 in both cases, due to the hedging.

We can now consider the effect of taxes and the $20,000 tax credit. A tax credit can be used only if the firm owes taxes. For the unhedged firm, the $300 price means that the firm has zero net income and no taxes are due. Therefore, the firm cannot use the tax credit, and its after-tax net income is zero. If gold sells for $500, the unhedged firm can use its tax credit fully, and its after-tax net income is $90,000. Thus, the unhedged firm has a 50 percent chance of using its tax credit. For the hedging firm, pretax income will be $100,000 no matter what the price of gold may be. This means that its tax obligation will be $20,000 in both cases. Thus, the hedged firm uses its tax credit to honor its taxes. This leaves the hedging firm with $100,000 in after-tax net income, no matter what the price of gold may be.

The difference between the unhedged and hedged firms comes down to the following distinction. By hedging, the firm guarantees that it will be able to use its tax credit. By not hedging, the firm runs a 50 percent chance of not being able to use the $20,000 credit. Notice that the difference in the expected after-tax net income between the two firms exactly equals $10,000, which is exactly the expected loss on being unable to use the tax credit for the unhedged firm ($20,000 × 0.50). Therefore, in our example, taxes create a legitimate incentive to hedge. With hedging, the firm is able to increase its expected after-tax income. With taxes, hedging can increase the value of the firm.[34]

The empirical evidence on the relationship between taxes and hedging is mixed. A 1993 study found that firms that hedged faced more progressive tax structures. Other studies have suggested that taxes apparently do affect the hedging decisions of firms, but not for the reasons cited above. Instead, hedging allows firms to increase their debt capacity and acquire additional tax credits. Consistent with this result is other evidence showing that firms with higher amounts of financial leverage are more likely to hedge.[35]

Costs of financial distress as an incentive to hedge

In Table 4.10, the expected pretax profits are the same for both the no-hedging and the hedging strategies. However, hedging reduces the risk inherent in the pretax profits. In perfect markets, reducing risk has no value, as long as expected values remain the same. Under perfect market assumptions, investors can diversify without any cost to create any risk position they desire. If a particular firm follows a high-risk strategy and goes bankrupt, assets are immediately deployed in an equally useful role. In the real world, by contrast, there are real costs associated with bankruptcy and financial distress. Lawyers and accountants must be paid, for example. In addition, assets cannot be deployed instantly to earn the same return. Firms in financial distress may also lose customers if they are forced to reduce the quality of the goods and services they provide. Financial distress may also force firms to exit lines of business they would otherwise continue to operate. Other costs include the loss of tax shields. Therefore, a risk-reducing strategy can help avoid these costs of financial distress, and hedging can consequently increase the value of the firm.

By reducing the variability of an investment project's returns, hedging can reduce the probability of a corporation approaching bankruptcy. For corporations with both debt and equity, reducing the probability of bankruptcy may alter shareholder's incentives to invest. Because bondholders will be paid ahead of equity holders in the event of bankruptcy, equity holders know that the benefits of increased investment will be shared with bondholders. Because of this, equity holders have an incentive to pass up otherwise profitable investments. Hedging alters the incentive to underinvest by reducing the number of future scenarios in which default occurs and therefore increases the number of scenarios in which equity holders are the residual claimants.[36]

Transaction costs as a disincentive to hedge

We have reason to believe that futures prices closely approximate expected future spot prices. If the futures price equals the expected future spot price, the expected profit from trading a futures contract is zero. This holds for both hedging and speculating. Therefore, the expected cost of a hedging transaction is roughly the transaction costs associated with placing and managing the hedge. For any one hedge, the actual result can be wildly favorable or negative, but the expected result is to lose the transaction costs. For the firm that continuously hedges, the law of large numbers comes into play. On some hedges, the firm will win, while it will lose on others. Over many hedges, the law of large numbers assures us that the actual result will more and more closely approximate the theoretical result—no futures gain nor losses, but losses equal to the transaction costs. Therefore, a policy of consistent hedging can be expected to lose the transaction costs in the long run. This high probability of a slightly negative result provides a disincentive for hedging.

Principal–agent conflicts as an incentive to hedging

In perfect markets, managers of the firm act as pure agents of the shareholders. They operate the firm in the interests of the shareholders, just as the shareholders would run the firm for themselves. However, in real firms, managers and shareholders often have conflicting desires. These lead to conflicts between the principals (shareholders) and their agents (managers). For example, managers may like to have sumptuous offices. The shareholders pay for the offices, and the managers use them. In the hedging decision, shareholders may tolerate more risk than managers. Shareholders can hold a portfolio of stocks; so one company may be only a small fraction of the shareholder's portfolio. By contrast, the managers work full time for the firm and may have a very large portion of their wealth committed to the firm. In this situation, the managers are more anxious than the shareholders to reduce risk. Given the managers' higher risk aversion, they may hedge when shareholders would really prefer that the firm be unhedged.

Lack of owner diversification as an incentive to hedge

In addition to managers, some shareholders may not be as fully diversified as perfect market conditions would imply. If the shareholders have committed a substantial portion of their wealth to a single firm, they may be highly risk averse like managers. For example, a farmer may have his or her entire wealth committed to a farm. This lack of diversification on the part of the owner can also create an incentive to hedge.

Differences between internal and external financing costs as an incentive to hedge

Market imperfections may cause external financing of investment projects to be more costly than the internal financing of projects. External financing refers to borrowing, or issuing new securities, while internal financing refers to retained earnings and cash reserves. Hedging can play a role in reducing the probability of the corporation facing cash flow shortages. This means that hedging can increase the probability that the corporation can continue to fund profitable investment opportunities with internal financing. Without hedging, cash flow shortages may force the corporation either to use more expensive external financing or to forego profitable investment opportunities. Hedging helps ensure that a corporation has sufficient internal funds available to take advantage of profitable investment opportunities and to reduce the probability of using more expensive external funding.[37]

When do corporations have a duty to hedge?

In general, the "business judgment rule" protects ordinary business decisions from being second-guessed by shareholders and courts. In other words, shareholders and judges cannot substitute their judgment (with the benefit of hindsight) for the day-to-day business judgment of corporation's managers or board of directors. The business judgment rule provides a presumption that informed business decisions are made as the result of good faith and honest judgment.

In 1992, shareholders of an Indiana grain elevator cooperative sued the cooperative's directors, arguing that the directors had failed to adequately inform themselves about the hedging opportunities that could have prevented over $400,000 in grain sale losses. The shareholders argued that the director's failure constituted a breach of the fiduciary duty owed by the directors to the cooperative's shareholders. An Indiana appeals court agreed with the shareholders and held the directors of the cooperative personally liable for the losses incurred due to the management's failure to hedge. The court reasoned that since the cooperative derived 90 percent of its revenue from grain sales, its failure to properly hedge proved that the managers and directors were not adequately informed about the hedging opportunities provided by commodity futures markets. In essence, the court argued that, under Indiana law, the director of a corporation has a duty to hedge the corporation's exposure to changes in commodity prices if this exposure is an important part of the corporation's business.[38] Although the precedent value of this case may be limited to Indiana, it points out the potential liability that directors may be exposed to by not being adequately informed about hedging opportunities. To ensure that their hedging decisions enjoy the protection of the business judgment rule, directors need to become adequately informed about corporate risks and set up a structure to address those risks.

In a related case, shareholders of Compaq Computer Corporation sued the corporation's chief executive officer and the chairman of the board of directors based on alleged violations of federal securities laws. The shareholders alleged that Compaq lacked an adequate foreign exchange hedging program to insulate the corporation from appreciation in the value of the U.S. dollar in foreign currency markets, from which Compaq derived over half its revenue. In this case the shareholders did not allege that the corporation had a duty to hedge. Instead, they argued that Compaq's decision not to hedge was a material fact that should have been publicly disclosed, so that investors could make informed decisions on whether to buy or sell Compaq stock.[39]

Summary

In this section, we have considered some of the costs and benefits associated with hedging. We began by observing that, essentially, only firms can hedge, because only firms can reduce their risks by trading futures. In perfect markets, hedging would be pointless, because individual traders can effectively hedge instead of the firm. Therefore, incentives to hedge arise from market imperfections. We saw that both taxes and the costs of financial distress can create a situation in which hedging can increase firm value. We also considered the potential conflicts between owners and managers as principals and agents, which can lead the managers to hedge more than the shareholders desire. Finally, we saw that incomplete owner diversification can also create an incentive to hedge.

If futures prices equal expected future spot prices, the expected gain or loss from trading a futures contract is zero, except for the transaction costs that must be paid. This means that the expected monetary payoff from hedging is slightly negative. Persistent hedging is very likely to generate a loss equal to the costs of transacting and the costs of managing the hedge. These costs provide a strong disincentive for the firm to hedge.

Government hedging

Government entities are routinely exposed to exogenous shocks that can result in revenues falling short of expectations over a budgeting period. Coping with a revenue deficit normally requires costly adjustments, either in the form of increased taxes, curtailed or deferred expenditures, or the issuance of external debt to finance the shortfall. These costs are borne, to varying degrees, by those who govern (e.g., politicians and government bureaucrats) and the governed (e.g., the citizens of the government entity). Because of these costs, attempts have been made to find less costly means of coping with budgetary risks. One alternative, explored with increasing frequency in the past two decades, has been for government entities to hedge their exposure to revenue shortfalls by using futures and other derivatives. For example, in 1992 the state of Texas launched a pilot program (suspended in 2000) to hedge a portion of the state's tax revenues tied to prices of crude oil and natural gas using energy futures contracts and privately negotiated swap contracts.[40]

Louisiana is another state that uses commodity futures to establish a firm price for all or part of the anticipated mineral production that is subject to state severance taxes or royalty contracts. In 2004, the state of Alaska was in the process of drafting legislation to operate a futures hedging program for its North Slope (ANS) crude oil revenues. The purpose of the hedging program is to complement the state's Constitutional Budget Reserve Fund. The Canadian province of Alberta has also studied the use of futures for oil production on provincial lands. Several state utility commissions (including California, Missouri, New Jersey, New Mexico, New York, Texas, and Wisconsin) encourage utilities under their jurisdiction to implement futures hedging programs to mitigate the risk of natural gas price spikes.

The U.S. federal government has also studied the use of futures hedging programs for oil and minerals. The largest single purchaser of fuel in the world, the U.S. military, has studied the possibility of having its Defense Fuel Supply Center use futures contracts to hedge some of its $5 billion per year fuel expense.

Metallgesellschaft

In December 1993, MG Refining and Marketing, Inc. (MGRM), a subsidiary of Metallgesellschaft AG, a German conglomerate, revealed that it was responsible for losses of approximately $1.5 billion. MGRM committed to sell, at prices fixed in 1992, certain amounts of petroleum every month for up to ten years. These contracts initially proved to be very successful, since they guaranteed a price over the current spot petroleum prices. By September 1993, MGRM had sold forward contracts amounting to the equivalent of 160 million barrels. Embedded in MGRM's contracts was an option clause allowing counterparties to terminate the contracts early if the front-month New York Mercantile Exchange (NYMEX) futures contract was greater than the fixed price at which MGRM was selling the oil product. If the buyer exercised this option, MGRM would be required to pay in cash one-half of the difference between the futures price and the fixed prices times the total volume remaining to be delivered on the contract. This option would be attractive to a customer that was in financial distress or simply no longer needed the oil.

MGRM thought that their risk management expertise, combined with the financial backing of their parent company, gave them the ability to offer their customers guaranteed contracts with sell-back options. To manage the risk from offering these contracts, MGRM employed a stack hedge using the front-end month futures contracts on the NYMEX. Recall that a stack hedge involves establishing a large "stacked" futures position in the front month and then rolling the position forward (less the portion of the hedge that is no longer needed) into the next front-month contract. Recall also that this strategy involves risk.

The futures contracts that MGRM used to hedge customer contracts were written on unleaded gasoline and the No. 2 heating oil. MGRM also held an amount of West Texas Intermediate sweet crude contracts. MGRM went long in the futures and entered into privately negotiated swap agreements to receive-floating and pay-fixed energy prices. At one point, MGRM held a notional futures position of 55 million barrels of gasoline and heating oil. Their swap positions accounted for nearly 100 million additional barrels.

It is not clear that there was anything conceptually wrong with MGRM's hedging strategy. But it is clear that MGRM had not adequately communicated its intentions to its parent company and its financial backers. In late 1993, MGRM's futures positions lost money as spot energy prices fell, requiring additional funds to meet margin calls. Presumably, the value to MGRM of its long-term, fixed-rate customer contracts increased as the value of the energy prices fell, leaving the net position hedged as planned. But the gains on the long-term customer contracts were not realized, while the futures losses were marked to market daily. By the end of 1993, the heavy cash outflows required to maintain the stack hedge, combined with concern about the credit risk taken on with the large swap position, caused MGRM's parent to change its assessment of the potential risks involved in its forward delivery contracts with customers. After reviewing the program, MGRM's parent decided to end MGRM's participation in the hedge program. In December 1993, MGRM's futures positions were unwound and customer contracts were cancelled. Given that many of these contracts were in-the-money to MGRM, this cancellation was costly.

Liquidating such huge futures positions on short notice was also extremely costly. The average trading volume in the NYMEX's heating oil and unleaded gasoline futures contracts averaged around 25,000 contracts per day. With MGRM needing to liquidate 55,000 long futures contracts, other traders were able to extract a large premium from MGRM for providing liquidity. The net result of MGRM's actions was to lose on both legs of its hedge. By unwinding the hedge, MGRM lost on the futures leg of its hedge, while at the same time foregoing the unrealized gains in the forward customer contracts. In total, MGRM lost $1.5 billion in the disaster.

MGRM's parent blamed the management of MGRM for the massive buildup of MGRM's forward and hedge positions. But MGRM's parent was clearly not blameless. If it truly was ignorant of MGRM's positions, then it was not doing its job. On the other hand, if it knew of MGRM's positions and did not understand them, then it was not doing its job. Wherever the truth lies, MGRM's parent shares the blame for this situation.

Conclusion

In this chapter, we have explored the three major uses that observers and traders make of futures markets. We began by considering the function of price discovery, a service of futures markets that can be enjoyed by traders and nontraders alike. We considered the way in which producers could use information from the futures market to guide their production decisions. If futures prices provide a good guide to future spot prices, then futures markets reveal price information that helps society to allocate capital more efficiently. In our discussion of price discovery, we considered a case study of price discovery in the oil market and we summarized the forecast power that Fama and French found in diverse commodity markets.

The futures market attracts speculators—traders who enter the market in pursuit of profit, willingly increasing their risks to do so. We classified speculators according to the length of time they planned to hold a futures position, as scalpers, day traders, and position traders. We noted that spread trading is an important form of speculative trading and we considered different spread trading techniques.

We examined the available evidence on the profitability of speculative trading. We found that studies disagree considerably on the magnitude and even the existence of speculative trading profits. We briefly considered the performance of technical trading systems, where we once again found different conclusions in the academic literature. Commodity funds have become important speculative trading vehicles

in recent years. We analyzed the evidence on the performance of commodity funds, and again found no evidence of overwhelming trading acumen. Finally, we considered the concept of "normal" speculative profits. This was an effort to take into consideration the investment of funds and time that are necessary to speculate as a scalper or other floor trader. We found that the trader must make a substantial income to justify the investment and loss of other job opportunities.

Hedging is one of the most important social functions of futures markets. A hedger is a trader who enters the futures market in an effort to reduce a preexisting risk. We saw that traders can hedge by being either long or short in the futures market. Except for providing liquidity, we noted that hedgers needed speculative position traders only to absorb an imbalance between long and short hedgers. Much hedging activity involves an imperfect match between the characteristics of the asset being hedged and the asset underlying a futures contract. Hedging in such a situation is called cross-hedging. We gave examples of how traders might use the market to hedge in such a situation. In many instances, hedgers will want to employ risk-minimization techniques for a given position. We showed that it is possible to derive the correct futures position to minimize a given initial risk using a statistical analysis of historical data. Using actual soybean data, we followed a strategy from beginning to end for hedging soybeans over a one-year period. Finally, we considered the costs and benefits of hedging.

Exercises

1 Explain how futures markets can benefit individuals in society who never trade futures.

2 A "futures price" is a market quoted price today of the best estimate of the value of a commodity at the expiration of the futures contract. What do you think of this definition?

3 Explain the concept of an unbiased predictor.

4 If a predictor is unbiased, how are errors possible?

5 Scalpers trade to capture profits from minute fluctuations in futures prices. Explain how this avaricious behavior benefits others.

6 Assume that scalping is made illegal. What would the consequences of such an action be for hedging activity in futures markets?

7 A trader anticipates rising corn prices and wants to take advantage of this insight by trading an intra-commodity spread. Would you advise that she trade long nearby/short distant or the other way around? Explain.

8 Assume that daily settlement prices in the futures market exhibit very strong first-order serial correlation. How would you trade to exploit this strategy? Explain how your answer would differ if the correlation was statistically significant but, nonetheless, small in magnitude.

9 Assume that you are a rabid believer in efficient markets. A commodity fund uses 20 percent of its funds as margin payments. The remaining 80 percent is invested in risk-free securities. What investment performance would you expect from the fund?

10 Consider two traders. The first is an individual with his own seat, who trades strictly for his own account. The other trader works for a brokerage firm actively engaged in retail futures brokerage. Which trader has a lower effective marginal trading cost? Relate this comparison in marginal trading costs to quasi-arbitrage.

11 Consider the classic hedging problems of the farmer who sells wheat in the futures market in anticipation of a harvest. Would the farmer be likely to deliver his harvested wheat against the futures? Explain. If he is unlikely to deliver, explain how he manages his futures position instead.

12 A cocoa merchant holds a current inventory of cocoa worth $10 million at present prices of $1,250 per metric ton. The standard deviation of returns for the inventory is 0.27. She is considering a risk-minimization hedge of her inventory using the cocoa contract of the Coffee, Cocoa, and Sugar Exchange. The contract size is 10 metric tons. The volatility of the futures is 0.33. For the particular grade of cocoa in her inventory, the correlation between the futures and spot cocoa is 0.85. Compute the risk-minimization hedge ratio and determine how many contracts she should trade.

13 A service station operator reads this book. He wants to hedge his risk exposure for gasoline. Every week, he pumps 50,000 gallons of gasoline, and he is confident that this pattern will hold through thick and thin. What advice would you offer?

14 Describe the difference between a stack hedge and a strip hedge. What are the advantages and disadvantages of each?

15 Why may it be inappropriate for a corporation to hedge?

16 What is a hedge fund? Do hedge funds actually hedge?

Notes

1 This argument can be expressed more formally by using the theory of complete markets. A market is complete if we can transact for any desired pattern of payoffs. Complete market theory has often been developed by using a state-preference framework of analysis. In the state-preference approach, the objects of choice are defined as payoffs under certain states of nature. The states of nature are defined so that each possible occurrence falls under one, and only one, state of nature. In this framework, a market is complete if and only if we can contract for a payoff in any state, or combination of states, of nature. (For a development of the state-preference framework, see S. Myers, "A Time State-Preference Model of Security Valuation," *Journal of Financial and Quantitative Analysis*, 3:1, March 1968, pp. 1–33.) If markets are complete, then we can freely contract for the set of payoffs that best fits our needs. The more nearly complete markets are, the more society benefits from the ability to fit payoffs to individuals' desired outcomes. With this background, the argument for futures markets is clear: they contribute to the welfare of society by making financial markets more clearly complete. (For a highly mathematical development of complete markets under a state-preference approach, see G. Debreu, *Theory of Value*, New Haven, CT: Yale University Press, 1959.)

2   The furniture manufacturer might also take the step of attempting to "lock-in" these "discovered" prices by buying futures contracts for lumber. Such a step is a small one and emphasizes the intimate connection between price discovery and hedging.

3   For a more formal treatment of the property of un-biasedness in estimators, see J. Maddala, *Introduction to Econometrics*, New York: Macmillan, 1988.

4   For an assessment of the accuracy of futures prices as forecasts of expected future spot prices, see R. Kolb, G. Gay, and J. Jordan, "Futures Prices and Expected Future Spot Prices," *Review of Research in Futures Markets*, 2, 1983, pp. 110–23.

5   See R. Levich, "Currency Forecasters Lose Their Way," *Euromoney*, 1983, pp. 140–7. Chapter 11 discusses the forecasting accuracy of professional currency forecasters in more detail.

6   See Richard Roll, "Orange Juice and Weather," *American Economic Review*, 74, 1984, pp. 861–80.

7   See Warren Getler, "Some Meteorologists Reap Windfall From Crop Futures Markets," *Wall Street Journal*, 13, 1993, p. C1.

8   Some authors attempt to distinguish speculators from investors. The usual difference between the two definitions seems to lie in their respective attitudes toward risk and the length of time they expect to hold their positions. Speculators are contrasted only with hedgers, so any investor in the futures market, no matter how conservative, would be regarded as a speculator for the purposes of this book.

9   On the floor of the exchanges, different commodities are traded in different pits. A pit is really an area of the floor, surrounded by steps or risers, which are usually about five steps high. The arrangement allows traders to see and communicate with each other. The term "pit" is really synonymous with trading in futures, as indicated by the title of Frank Norris' novel, *The Pit*, which is the story of futures trading in wheat.

10   A round-turn is the initiation and closing of a futures position. For example, a trader buys a futures option and sells a futures contract to make one round-turn transaction. The round-turn transaction costs are the costs incurred to complete the entire transaction.

11   B. Tamarkin, *The New Gatsbys: Fortunes and Misfortunes of Commodity Traders*, New York: William Morrow, 1985, p. 26.

12   Ibid., p. 43.

13   As discussed in Chapter 2, high liquidity is also crucial in the survival of a particular futures contract. In competing contracts, the one with the initially greater liquidity has a much higher probability of success.

14   W. L. Silber, "Marketmaker Behavior in an Auction Market: An Analysis of Scalpers in Futures Markets," *Journal of Finance*, 39:4, 1984, pp. 937–53.

15   B. Wade Brorsen, "Liquidity Costs and Scalping Returns in the Corn Futures Market," *Journal of Futures Markets*, 9:3, 1989, pp. 225–36, simulated scalper's behavior using corn data. Using his trading rule, Brorsen estimates scalping profits at about $10.00 per trade. Brorsen comments that his results match those of Silber. Gregory J. Kuserk and Peter R. Locke, "Scalper Behavior in Futures Markets: An Empirical Examination," *Journal of Futures Markets*, 13:4, 1993, pp. 409–31, also find that scalping offers significant income opportunities.

16   See Michael S. Haigh and John A. List, "Do Professional Traders Exhibit Myopic Loss Aversion? An Experimental Analysis," *Journal of Finance*, 60:1, 2005, pp. 523–34.

17   In any event, visitors to the exchanges are allowed on the floor only for short periods of time and under the supervision of exchange personnel. Access to the floor near the close of trading is more restricted, because as the day's trading nears its close the level of activity increases dramatically.

18   The United States Department of Agriculture (USDA) makes regular forecasts of crop harvests, and these have been analyzed in a recent spate of papers. These three papers find that the forecasts are generally unbiased and efficient, and that there are few differences between USDA forecasts and futures-based forecasts. McNew and Espinosa find that the USDA forecasts help to reduce price uncertainty. See: Scott H. Irwin, Mary E. Gerlow, and Te-Ru Liu, "The Forecasting Performance of Livestock Futures Prices: A Comparison to USDA Expert Predictions." *Journal of Futures Markets*, 14:7, 1994, pp. 861–75; Robert F. Baur and Peter F. Orazem, "The Rationality and Price Effects of U.S. Department of Agriculture Forecasts of Oranges," *Journal of Finance*, 49:2, 1994, pp. 681–95; and Kevin P. McNew and Juan Andres Espinosa, "The Informational Content of USDA Crop Reports: Impacts on Uncertainty and Expectations in Grain Futures Markets," *Journal of Futures Markets*, 14:4, 1994, pp. 475–92.

19   See, for example, *Commodity Trading Manual*, Chicago, IL: Chicago Board of Trade, 1989, and Martin J. Pring (ed.), *The McGraw-Hill Handbook of Commodities and Futures*, New York: McGraw-Hill, 1985.

20   Another recently emerging facet of the debate on patterns in futures prices comes from chaos theory. Some process, whether in nature or in a social process such as a financial market, may appear to consist of

purely random behavior. According to chaos theory, this appearance of randomness may be an illusion. With the insights of chaos theory, it may be possible to find patterns in seemingly chaotic data. For an application of this theory to futures markets, see R. Savit, "When Random Is Not Random: An Introduction to Chaos in Market Prices," *Journal of Futures Markets*, 8:3, 1988, pp. 271–90.

21 See Franklin R. Edwards, "Hedge Funds: What Do We Know?" *Journal of Applied Corporate Finance*, 15:4, 2003, pp. 8–21.

22 These three versions of the efficient markets hypothesis were first articulated by E. Fama in "Efficient Capital Markets: Theory and Empirical Work," *Journal of Finance*, 1970, pp. 383–417. For a more recent survey of the efficient markets literature, see T. Copeland, F. Weston, and K. Shastri, *Financial Theory and Corporate Policy*, 4th edn, Reading, MA: Addison Wesley, 2005.

23 Traditionally, the most highly valued commodity exchange seats have been those on the CBOT. In late 1982, a seat on the CME cost more than a CBOT seat for the first time in history. In the mid-1990s, CME seats consistently cost more than CBOT seats. The prices of these seats are very volatile. The value of the seats responds very directly to the level of trading at the exchange, which in itself is quite variable. For a study of commodity exchange seat prices, see R. Chiang, G. Gay, and R. Kolb, "Commodity Exchange Seat Prices," *Review of Futures Markets*, 6:1, 1987, pp. 1–10.

24 The youthfulness of the traders is particularly apparent in the newer markets, such as the interest rate futures market. Relatively, the older, more traditional commodities are traded by older traders. In his book, *The New Gatsbys*, New York: William Morrow, 1985, Bob Tamarkin emphasizes the physical strains and the mental stresses that traders endure. For example, see Chapter 20, "Pit Falls."

25 Many traders will not leave the trading pit during the six- to seven-hour trading session, even to go to the bathroom. It is simply too risky to leave the trading floor for even a short period of time. This indicates the level of stress in the pits.

26 The theory of hedging is still the subject of much debate. See C. Smith and R. Stulz, "The Determinants of Firms' Hedging Policies," *Journal of Financial and Quantitative Analysis*, 20:4, 1985, pp. 391–405; and R. Stulz, "Optimal Hedging Policies," *Journal of Financial and Quantitative Analysis*, 19:2, 1984, pp. 127–40.

27 To find the risk-minimizing hedge ratio, we take the first derivative of the portfolio's risk in Equation 4.3

with respect to HR, set the derivative equal to zero, and solve for HR.

28 See, for example, J. Hill and T. Schneeweis, "A Note on the Hedging Effectiveness of Foreign Currency Futures," *Journal of Futures Markets*, 1:4, 1981, pp. 659–64; and H. Witt, T. Schroeder, and M. Hayenga, "Comparison of Analytical Approaches for Estimating Hedge Ratios for Agricultural Commodities," *Journal of Futures Markets*, 7:2, 1987, pp. 135–46.

29 H. Witt, T. Schroeder, and M. Hayenga, "Comparison of Analytical Approaches for Estimating Hedge Ratios for Agricultural Commodities," *Journal of Futures Markets*, 7:2, 1987, pp. 135–46, study this issue in detail. They believe that price level regressions can work satisfactorily unless certain adverse conditions prevail. One of these conditions is autocorrelation in the price series—the price level at one time varies systematically with the price level at another time. However, most financial price level series exhibit first-order autocorrelation. For this reason, it is often better to use one of the other approaches.

30 There is nothing special about this ending date. We chose this date because the July contract is approaching expiration and the open interest in the contract would be falling at this time. Choosing a different date a few weeks one way or the other would not change the results appreciably.

31 For means of coping with these risks, see Jacques Rolfo, "Optimal Hedging Under Price and Quantity Uncertainty," *Journal of Political Economy*, 88, 1980, pp. 100–16; and Avraham Kamara and Andrew F. Siegel, "Optimal Hedging in Futures Markets with Multiple Delivery Specifications," *The Journal of Finance*, 42:4, 1987, pp. 1007–21.

32 M. Miller and F. Modigliani, "The Cost of Capital, Corporate Finance, and the Theory of Investment," *American Economic Review*, 48:3, 1958, pp. 261–97.

33 Notice that the shareholder can hedge his or her own portion in a perfect market, due to being able to trade a fractional share. In real markets, individuals cannot generally hedge, because futures contracts are large relative to the wealth level and risk exposure of most individuals.

34 The unhedged firm does not necessarily lose its tax credit. Generally, the unhedged firm would be able to retain its tax credit and apply it in a year when it does have positive income and a tax liability.

35 Empirical evidence concerning taxes and hedging can be found in an article by D. Nance, C. Smith, and C. Smithson, "On the Determinants of Corporate Hedging," *Journal of Finance*, 48, 1993, pp. 267–84;

and in an article by J. R. Graham and D. A. Rogers, "Do Firms Hedge in Response to Tax Incentives?" *Journal of Finance*, 57:2, 2002, pp. 815–39. Other studies providing empirical evidence on the hedging choices of firms include G. D. Haushalter, "Financing Policy, Basis Risk, and Corporate Hedging: Evidence from Oil and Gas Producers," *Journal of Finance*, 55:1, 2000, pp. 107–52; G. D. Haushalter "Why Hedge? Some Evidence from Oil and Gas Producers," *The Bank of America Journal of Applied Corporate Finance*, 13:4, 2001, pp. 87–92; G. Allayannis and J. Weston, "The Use of Foreign Currency Derivatives and Firm Market Value," *Review of Financial Studies*, 14:1, 2001, pp. 243–76; G. M. Bodnar, G. S. Hayt, and R. C. Marston, "1998 Wharton Survey of Financial Risk Management by U.S. Non-Financial Firms," *Financial Management*, 27:4, 1998, pp. 70–91; C. Géczy, B. A. Minton, and C. Schrand, "Why Firms Use Currency Derivatives," *Journal of Finance*, 52:4, 1997, pp. 1323–54; M. A. Peterson and S. R. Thiagarajan, "Risk Management and Hedging: With and Without Derivatives," *Financial Management*, 29:4, 2000, pp. 5–29; and P. Tufano, "Who Manages Risk? An Empirical Analysis of Risk Management Practices in the Gold Mining Industry," *Journal of Finance*, 51:4, 1996, pp. 1097–138.

36 This argument was advanced in an article by H. Bessembinder, entitled "Forward Contracts and Firm Value: Investment Incentives and Contracting Effects," *Journal of Financial and Quantitative Analysis*, 26:6, 1991, 520.

37 This argument was advanced in an article by K. Froot, D. Scharfstein, and J. Stein, entitled "Risk Management: Coordinating Corporate Investment and Financing Policies," *Journal of Finance*, 48, 1993, pp. 1629–58.

38 *Brane versus Roth*, 590 N.E. 2d 587 (Ind. Ct. App. 1992).

39 *In re Compaq Securities Litigation*, 848 F. Supp. 1307 (S.D. Tex. 1993).

40 For more information on the Texas hedging program, see William Falloon, "Texas Parries," *Risk*, 5:8, 1992, pp. 105–6; and James A. Overdahl, "The Use of Crude Oil Futures by the Governments of Oil-Producing States," *Journal of Futures Markets*, 7:6, 1987, pp. 603–18.

5

Interest Rate Futures: An Introduction

Overview

This chapter explores one of the most successful and exciting innovations in the history of futures markets–the emergence of interest rate futures contracts. Since the first contracts were traded on October 20, 1975 on the Chicago Board of Trade (CBOT), the market has expanded rapidly. In spite of a number of relatively unsuccessful contracts that have been introduced, the market has been a huge success. Pioneered in the United States at the CBOT and the Chicago Mercantile Exchange (CME), interest rate futures have spread to the world's major financial markets. Some of the most successful contracts today are traded abroad, notably in the United Kingdom, on the European continent, and in Singapore. However, these wildly successful non-U.S. contracts are clearly based on the structures that were invented and proven in the United States.

Almost all of the activity in the U.S. interest rate futures is concentrated in two exchanges, the CBOT and the International Monetary Market (IMM) of the CME. The Board of Trade specializes in contracts at the longer end of the maturity spectrum, with active contracts on long-term Treasury bonds and two-, five-, and ten-year Treasury notes, and five-year LIBOR-based swaps,[1] where LIBOR stands for the London InterBank Offer Rate. By contrast, the CME has successful contracts with very short maturities, such as their contracts for one-month and three-month Eurodollar deposits. While this chapter discusses features of many different contracts, we focus on the U.S. Treasury contracts traded on the CBOT and the Eurodollar contract traded on the CME. As we will see, these contracts created the conceptual foundations for most major non-U.S. contracts.

Short-maturity interest rate futures contracts

To understand the interest rate futures market, we need to understand the specifications for the different contracts. This section focuses on interest rate futures based on money market instruments.

Eurodollar futures

Eurodollar deposits are U.S. dollar deposits held in a commercial bank outside the United States. These banks may be either foreign banks or foreign branches of U.S. banks. The deposits are normally nontransferable and cannot be used as collateral for loans. London dominates the Eurodollar deposit market, so rates in this market are often based on **LIBOR**, the **London Interbank Offer Rate**. LIBOR is the rate at which banks are willing to lend funds to other banks in the interbank market. It is an important rate in international finance. For example, many over-the-counter interest rate contracts use the three-month U.S. dollar LIBOR as the reference rate. In addition to London, Eurodollar deposit rates are quoted in Paris (PIBOR) and Tokyo (TIBOR). The Eurodollar futures contract is perhaps misnamed. A more descriptive name might be the "three-month dollar LIBOR contract," to emphasize that it is a LIBOR-based contract.

Eurodollar futures trade on the CME and on the Singapore Monetary Exchange. By far the most successful contract resides at the CME. Eurodollar futures now dominate the U.S. market for short-term interest rate (STIR) contracts. The instrument underlying the Eurodollar contract is a $1 million nontransferable three-month Eurodollar time deposit, held in a commercial bank. Because the underlying instrument is nontransferable, there is no actual delivery on the Eurodollar contract. Instead, the contract is fulfilled by cash settlement.

When the Eurodollar futures contract began trading in 1981, it became the first contract to use cash settlement rather than the delivery of an actual good for contract fulfillment. We have already noted that Eurodollar deposits are nontransferable, a feature that by itself precludes delivery. As a result, the IMM requires fulfillment of a contract by a cash payment based on a measure of Eurodollar rates. To establish the final settlement price at contract expiration, the IMM uses the British Bankers' Association Interest Settlement Rate (BBA LIBOR), based on a fixing process that uses data from a set of contributor banks. Since its inception in 1981, the IMM's cash settlement procedure has worked very well, with Eurodollar futures having grown into one of the most successful contracts ever listed and serving as a worldwide model for other similar futures contracts. Once the final settlement price is determined, traders with open positions settle with cash through the normal mark-to-market procedure. This fulfills their obligation and the contract expires.

Prior to the final trading day, the daily settlement price depends on the quotations in the futures market. In a sense, the futures price appears free to wander from the spot market values except on the final day of trading. However, this is an illusion. Consider, for example, the second-to-last trading day. Traders know that tomorrow the futures settlement price will be set equal to the average LIBOR actually available from banks. Therefore, the price today cannot be very different from its cash market LIBOR. If it did differ significantly, traders would enter the market to buy or sell futures, and would expect to reap their profit when the futures price is pegged to the cash market LIBOR. This same argument holds for every other day prior to expiration as well, so the Eurodollar futures contract must behave as though there will be an actual delivery at the contract's expiration. In other words, we expect the Eurodollar yield represented in the futures contract to equal the 90-day forward rate. We will see evidence of this relationship later.

For the Eurodollar contract, the contract size is for $1 million, with the yield being quoted on an add-on basis. The add-on yield is given by

$$\text{add-on yield} = \left(\frac{\text{discount}}{\text{price}}\right)\left(\frac{360}{\text{DTM}}\right) \tag{5.1}$$

where DTM is the days until maturity. For example, assume the discount yield is quoted at 8.32 percent. To get the price associated with this discount yield, we apply the following formula:

$$\text{price} = \$1,000,000 - \frac{\text{discount} \times \$1,000,000 \times \text{DTM}}{360} \tag{5.2}$$

Using Equation 5.2, we see that for this discount yield the price for a $1 million face value three-month instrument is $979,200. Therefore, the dollar discount is $20,800 and 90 days remain until the bill will mature. With these values, we have

$$\text{add-on yield} = \left(\frac{\$20,800}{\$979,200}\right)\left(\frac{360}{90}\right) = 0.0850$$

Add-on yields exceed corresponding discount yields. In our example, the discount yield is 8.32 percent, and the add-on yield equivalent is 8.5 percent. However, for both measures, a shift of one basis point (1/100 of 1 percent) is worth $25 on a $1 million contract. This amount is determined from the following equation:

$$\$1,000,000 \times 0.0001 \times \frac{90}{360} = \$25$$

Also note that these yields and relationships vary with maturity, so the statements made here hold only for three-month maturities.

Eurodollar futures contract prices are quoted using the IMM index, which is a function of the three-month LIBOR rate:

$$\text{IMM index} = 100.00 - \text{three-month LIBOR} \tag{5.3}$$

The IMM adopted this method of price quotation to ensure that changes in quoted prices moved in the same direction as changes in prices of the futures contract, which, due to the inverse relationship between prices and yield, would not happen if quotations were based on yield.

The Eurodollar futures contract plays an important role in allowing dealers of LIBOR-based swaps to hedge the interest rate risk they accrue in their dealing activities. Since the Eurodollar futures contract settles to the three-month U.S dollar LIBOR, it is an ideal candidate to hedge the interest rate risk associated with LIBOR-based swaps. This use by swap dealers helps to explain the incredibly distant maturities for the Eurodollar contract (a full ten years) and the enormous open interest (nearly 7 million contracts at year-end 2005, with an annual trading volume of over 400 million contracts).

Product profile: the CME's Eurodollar futures contract

Contract size: Eurodollar time deposit having a principal value of $1 million with a three-month maturity.

Deliverable grades: Cash settled to three-month dollar LIBOR.

Tick size: 0.01 = $25.00 months 11–40; 0.005 = $12.50 months 2–10; 0.0025 = $6.25 for the nearest expiring month.

Price quote: Price is quoted in terms of the IMM three-month Eurodollar index, 100 minus the yield on an annual basis for a 360-day year, with each basis point worth $25.

Contract months: March, June, September, and December cycle for ten years.

Expiration and final settlement: Eurodollar futures cease trading at 5:00 a.m. Chicago time (11:00 a.m. London time) on the second London bank business day immediately preceding the third Wednesday of the contract month; final settlement price is based on the British Bankers' Association Interest Settlement Rate.

Trading hours: Floor: 7:20 a.m. to 2:00 p.m.; Globex: Monday through Thursday, 5:00 p.m. to 4:00 p.m.; shutdown period from 4:00 p.m. to 5:00 p.m. daily; Sunday and holidays, 5:30 p.m. to 4:00 p.m. next day.

Daily price limit: None.

Euribor futures

The Eurodollar futures markets thrives in large part due to the participation of dealer banks that hedge risks they have acquired through their dealing in interest rate swaps based on the U.S. dollar LIBOR. However, many (in fact, most) interest rate swaps are denominated in euro rather than dollars. Dealers of euro-denominated interest rate swaps use the rate from euro-denominated time deposits, called Euribor, as the reference rates used to construct their swap contracts. These swap dealers use Euribor futures to hedge the risk resulting from their dealing activities.

Euribor futures are traded at predominately at Euronext.liffe. The design of the contract resembles the design of the Eurodollar futures contract, but there are some important differences. The Euronext.liffe contract is based on an underlying three-month time deposit with a notional value of €1 million. The contract is cash settled at expiration to the European Bankers Federation's Euribor Offered Rate (EBF Euribor) for three-month euro time deposits at 10:00 a.m. London time on the last trading day. The last trading day is two business days prior to the third Wednesday of the contract month. Euronext.liffe's Euribor contract traded nearly 167 million contracts during 2005, with a year-end open interest of over 3 million contracts.

Product profile: the Euronext.liffe Euribor futures contract

Contract size: $1 million with a three-month maturity.
Deliverable grades: Cash settled to European Bankers Federation's Euribor Offered Rate (EBF Euribor) for three-month euro time deposits.
Tick size: 0.005 percent representing 12.5.
Price quote: 100 minus the Euribor rate of interest carried out to three decimal places.
Contract months: March, June, September, and December and four serial months so that 24 delivery months are available for trading, with the nearest six expirations being consecutive calendar months.
Expiration and final settlement: The last trading day is two business days prior to the third Wednesday of the contract month. Final settlement is based on the EBF Euribor for three-month euro time deposits at 10:00 a.m. London time on the last trading day.
Trading hours: 7:00 a.m. to 6:00 p.m.
Daily price limit: None.

TIEE 28 futures

The TIEE 28 futures contract is based on short-term (28-day) Mexican interest rates. The contract is traded on the Mexican Derivatives Exchange (Mercado Mexicano de Derivados, or MexDer) and has become one of the world's largest contracts in terms of volume. Each 28-day TIIE futures contract covers a face value of 1 million Mexican pesos. The contract is cash settled based of the 28-day interbank equilibrium interest rate (TIIE), calculated by Banco de México based on quotations submitted by full-service banks using a mechanism designed to reflect conditions in the Mexican peso money market. At year-end 2005, this contract had an annual trading volume of nearly 100 million contracts, with open interest over 21 million contracts. The CME offers a competing version of this contract.

Product profile: The MexDer's TIEE futures contract

Contract size: Each 28-day TIIE futures contract covers a face value of 1 million Mexican pesos.

Deliverable grade: Cash settled based of the 28-day interbank equilibrium interest rate (TIIE), calculated by Banco de México based on quotations submitted by full-service banks using a mechanism designed to reflect conditions in the Mexican peso money market.

Tick size: One basis point of the annualized percentile rate of yield.

Price quote: Trading of 28-day TIIE futures contracts uses the annualized percentile rate of yield expressed in percentile terms, with two decimal places.

Contract months: MexDer lists different series of the 28-day TIIE futures contracts on a monthly basis for up to 60 months (five years).

Expiration and final settlement: The last trading day is the bank business day after Banco de México holds the primary auction of government securities in the week corresponding to the third Wednesday of the maturity month.

Trading hours: Bank business days from 7:30 a.m. to 3:00 p.m., Mexico City time.

Daily price limit: None.

Treasury bill futures

The T-bill futures contract was once the flagship contract traded at the IMM of the CME. Starting in the 1980s, however, trading volume in the contract declined until it was eclipsed by another short-term interest rate contract: the three-month Eurodollar contract. In spite of the fact that the contract no longer actively trades, we describe its features because this contract became the model upon which all other short-term interest rate contracts have been based.

The contract is written on an underlying T-bill with 90 days maturity at contract expiration and a face value of $1 million. The contracts trade for delivery in March, June, September, and December. The contract expiration dates are chosen to correspond with the U.S. Treasury's funding cycle. The expiration dates for the contracts will match up with newly issued 13-week T-bills as well as previously issued one-year T-bills that have 13 weeks of remaining life at contract expiration.

Price quotations for T-bill futures use the IMM index, which is a function of the discount yield (DY):

$$\text{IMM index} = 100.00 - \text{DY} \tag{5.4}$$

where DY is the discount yield (for example, 7.1 is 7.1 percent). As an example, a discount yield of 8.32 percent implies an IMM index value of 91.68.

Given the fact that the instruments are priced by using a discount yield and a contract size of $1 million, a one basis point movement in the interest rate generates a price change of $25.00.

In the days in which the contract required physical delivery, the futures invoice price (the price at which the short bills the long) was determined by the following equation, which gives the price as a function of discount yield and days to maturity:

$$\text{futures invoice price} = \$1,000,000 - \frac{\text{DY} \times \$1,000,000 \times 90}{360} \tag{5.5}$$

With a discount yield of 8.32 percent on the futures contract, the cash settlement price to be paid at the futures expiration date would be \$979,200:

$$\text{futures invoice price} = \$1,000,000 - \frac{0.832 \times \$1,000,000 \times 90}{360} = \$979,200$$

Many futures contracts have a daily price limit, a constraint on how much the futures price is allowed to move in a single day of trading. For example, on the Globex electronic trading system, the price limit for the T-bill contract is 200 basis points, or \$5,000, in either direction from the previous day's settlement price. The contract specifications call for no limit on the daily price fluctuation of the open-outcry version of the contract traded on the exchange floor.

The T-bill futures contract is cash settled. This means that no physical delivery of a T-bill occurs. Instead, long and short futures positions are marked to a final settlement price based on the highest bid accepted by the U.S. Treasury in their auction during the week of the third Wednesday of the contract expiration month. The final mark-to-market procedure fulfills the obligation of traders with open positions and the contract expires.

Other short-term interest rate futures

In addition to the contracts referenced above, exchanges around the world offer several other futures contracts written on short-term reference interest rates. For example, the CME trades a three-month Euroyen contract and a three-month Euroswiss contract. These non-U.S. money market futures contracts have a structure that is very similar to that of the Eurodollar and Euribor contracts discussed at length above. Each has an underlying 90-day time deposit, cash settlement only, and is based on quotations from a group of banks. Thus, an understanding of the Eurodollar and Euribor contracts provides a sound foundation for understanding these other similar contracts. The price quotations for the Euroyen and Euroswiss contracts have a similar structure to those of other short-term interest rate futures contracts. The CME also trades a one-month LIBOR contract. This contract is similar to the Eurodollar futures contract except that it is based on one-month Eurodollar time deposit rates as opposed to three-month rates.

Euronext.liffe offers a Short Sterling futures contract. This contract is based on the three-month Sterling LIBOR rate for Sterling time deposits. The contract has a notional value of \$500,000. The contract is structured in the same way as the Eurodollar and Euribor contracts. At year-end 2005, this contract had an annual trading volume of over 68 million contracts, with a year-end open interest of nearly 1.7 million contracts.

The CBOT trades a futures contract based on 30-day Federal Funds. This contract is unusual for the CBOT, which generally focuses on futures contracts based on longer-term interest rate products. This contract has a notional value of \$5 million and is cash settled at expiration based on the average daily Federal Funds overnight rate for the delivery month as reported by the New York Federal Reserve. The structure of this contract resembles the structure of other short-term interest rate contracts we have studied. At year-end 2005, this contract had an annual trading volume of over 6.5 million contracts, with a year-end open interest of approximately 455,000 contracts.

The demise of the CD futures market

For one brief shining moment during the early 1980s, futures contracts written on domestic bank certificates of deposits were among the most actively traded short-term interest rate contracts in the world. The contract traded at the CME from 1981 to 1987, with a peak volume year in 1982, when over 1.5 million contracts changed hands. The CBOT and the New York Futures Exchange also attempted to trade similar contracts in 1981 and 1982. The contracts at both exchanges called for the physical delivery of a three-month, large negotiable certificate of deposit from a list of top-tier money center banks. The contract was marketed primarily as a means for U.S. banks to hedge against unanticipated changes in their borrowing costs. The fact that the contract was based on private debt was viewed as a design advantage over the existing T-bill futures contract, which was based on public debt, because private debt accounted for the credit spread over treasuries that the banks themselves faced in their borrowing. A bank hedging its borrowing costs with T-bill futures had to worry about credit events that could trigger a "flight to quality," causing T-bill yields to fall faster than yields on more risky private debt. Banks hedging their private debt exposure with T-bills faced the possibility that their hedges could suddenly become less effective as the credit spread moved against them during flight-to-quality events.

Because it was based on private bank debt, the CD futures market was thought to be the perfect answer for banks requiring hedges against unanticipated changes in their borrowing costs. However, the physical settlement feature of the CD futures contract soon proved to be troublesome. Since shorts were permitted to deliver any CD from the list of bank CDs eligible for delivery, they naturally chose to deliver the cheapest-to-deliver CDs—that is, the CDs from the least creditworthy banks on the list. During normal times, there would be little variation in credit quality among top-tier banks, meaning that a futures contract price should track a single cheapest-to-deliver CD over the contract's life. However, during the first few years of the CD futures contract's life, credit problems materialized at one top-tier bank after another, meaning that the cheapest-to-deliver CD—and the credit quality associated with that CD—could suddenly change. Since the price of the futures contract would track the cheapest-to-deliver CD, a sudden deterioration in credit quality at a single bank whose CDs were on the list of eligible bank CDs could cause the credit spread between the cheapest-to-deliver CD and other top-tier CDs to widen. A bank attempting to hedge its borrowing costs with the CD futures contract faced the possibility that credit spreads could suddenly widen if the creditworthiness of the cheapest-to-deliver CD changed over the hedging period. The physical settlement feature of the contract impaired the hedging effectiveness of the contract. The 1984 liquidity crisis at Continental Illinois proved to be the death knell for the contract. The steep rise in the volume for the cash-settled Eurodollar futures contract in 1984 corresponded precisely with the decline in CD futures trading volume. The U.S. banks came to depend on the Eurodollar contract to hedge domestic borrowing costs.

Longer-maturity interest rate futures

This section explores the characteristics of interest rate futures with coupon-bearing debt instruments as the underlying good. For these instruments, their longer maturity and the presence of a coupon influence the construction of the futures contracts. As we will see, these futures generally require the delivery of an actual bond and the presence of the coupon introduces some interesting pricing complications.

Treasury bond futures

Of all futures contracts, the T-bond contract is one of the most complex and most interesting. The complexity of the contract stems from the delivery rules under which it is traded and from the wide variety of bonds that can be delivered to fulfill the contract. For the T-bond contract, which trades at the CBOT, delivery can take place on any business day during the delivery month.

In spite of its peculiarities, the T-bond contract is one of the most successful futures contracts ever introduced. Starting in August 1977, its success has been amazing. In 1986, for example, more than 52 million T-bond futures contracts were traded, and in 1995 this figure exceeded 88 million. In 1998, the contract traded more than 100 million contracts for the year. However, the contract fell on hard times after the U.S. Treasury discontinued auctioning 30-year bonds. This decision was reversed in 2005 and trading volume is once again increasing. Trading volume in 2005 was nearly 87 million contracts. Among interest rate futures, T-note trading volume has increased relative to that of T-bond trading volume, and some foreign long-term contracts now exceed the T-bond contract in volume and open interest. Figure 5.1 presents quotations for T-bond, T-note, and other interest rate futures from *The Wall Street Journal*. The

Figure 5.1   Price quotations for interest rate futures contracts

Interest Rate Futures

	Open	High	Low	Settle	Change	Lifetime High	Lifetime Low	Open Interest
Treasury Bonds (CBT)-$100,000; pts 32nds of 100%								
June	109–22	109–28	108–26	109–06	−16	117–24	108–26	624,046
Sept	109–20	109–20	108–26	109–07	−16	115–16	108–26	2,978
Treasury Notes (CBT)-$100,000; pts 32nds of 100%								
June	106–210	106–240	106–040	106–100	−9.5	110–130	106–040	1,960,846
Sept	106–160	106–210	106–065	106–110	−10.5	109–280	106–065	65,241
5 Yr. Treasury Notes (CBT)-$100,000; pts 32nds of 100%								
June	104–180	104–215	104–095	104–125	−5.5	106–250	104–095	1,160,470
Sept	104–195	104–195	104–120	104–120	−6.0	106–220	104–120	9,448
2 Yr. Treasury Notes (CBT)-$200,000; pts 32nds of 100%								
Mar	...	...	...	101–290	−1.5	102–272	101–295	1,028
June	101–305	101–315	101–282	101–287	−1.5	102–265	101–280	454,522
30 Day Federal Funds (CBT)-$5,000,000; 100 – daily avg.								
Mar	95.415	95.415	95.410	95.415	...	96.285	95.400	93,351
Apr	95.230	95.235	95.230	95.235	...	95.985	95.230	174,852

	Open	High	Low	Settle	Change	Yield	Change	Open Interest
1 Month Libor (CME)-$3,000,000; pts of 100%								
Apr	95.1050	95.1050	95.0950	95.0975	−.0025	4.9025	.0025	22,165
May	94.9750	94.9750	94.9575	94.9650	−.0050	5.0350	.0050	41,500
Eurodollar (CME)-$1,000,000; pts of 100%								
Apr	94.9600	94.9600	94.9450	94.9500	−.0125	5.0500	.0125	44,588
June	94.8250	94.8400	94.7900	94.7950	−.0300	5.2050	.0300	1,365,087
Sept	94.7700	94.7900	94.7150	94.7250	−.0400	5.2750	.0400	1,340,598
Dec	94.7850	94.8100	94.7250	94.7400	−.0400	5.2600	.0400	1,388,203

Source: The Wall Street Journal, March 31, 2006, p. C10. Reprinted by permission of *The Wall Street Journal*, © 2006 Dow Jones & Company, Inc. All rights reserved worldwide

structure of these quotations parallels the others that we have already examined. The first four columns of figures give the opening, high, low, and settlement prices for the contract, with the quotations in "points and 32nds of par." For example, a quoted price of 97–26 means that the contract traded for 97 and 26/32nds of par. The decimal equivalent of this value is 97.8125 percent of par. With a par value of $100,000 per contract, the cash price would be $97,812.50. The next two columns show the high and low prices for the life of the contract, while the final column of figures gives the open interest per contract. The final line in the quotations gives the usual volume and open interest information. For the T-bond contract, the tick size is 1/32nd of one full percentage point of face value. This means that the value of one tick per contract is $31.25 = (1/32) \times 0.01 \times $100,000.

Delivery against the T-bond contract is a several-day process that the short trader can trigger to cause delivery on any business day of the delivery month. Like the T-bill and Eurodollar contracts, the T-bond contract trades for delivery in March, June, September, and December. Delivery can be made on any business day of the delivery month, with the short trader choosing the exact delivery day. To effect delivery, the short trader initiates a delivery sequence that extends over three business days. Table 5.1 shows the delivery procedure for T-bond futures, a procedure that applies to other Board of Trade contracts, such as the T-note futures contracts.

Before the delivery process begins, each clearing firm reports to the clearing service provider—that is, the clearinghouse—all open long positions, ordered by the dates on which they were established. The positions are also identified as to whether they are held in customer accounts or proprietary accounts held by the firm. This declaration of long positions occurs on what is called the **first position day**. This day occurs two days prior to the first business day of the contract expiration month.

During the delivery month, the owner of a short position in an expiring futures contract has the right to decide when to initiate the three-day delivery process. The short can start the process at any time during the contract expiration month. The first day in the delivery sequence is called **intention day**, where the short instructs his clearing firm to notify the clearinghouse that he or she intends to make delivery. The first permissible day for the short trader to declare his or her intention to make delivery corresponds with the first position day for long position holders; that is, two days prior to the first business day of the contract expiration month.

Once the clearinghouse has instructions from the short's clearing firm, it matches the delivering short traders' positions with the oldest long positions. Once long and short positions are matched, the short trader is then obligated to make delivery to that particular long trader on the delivery day.

The second day of the three-day delivery sequence is called **notice of intention day**, or simply **notice day**. On this day, the short's clearing firm prepares an invoice for the long's clearing firm detailing the Treasury security, or securities, that the short will deliver. The invoice will include information about coupon rates, maturity dates, and the amount of payment required for delivery as determined by the futures contract price.

The third and final day of the delivery sequence is **delivery day**, when the actual transaction takes place. On this day, the short delivers the Treasury security to the long trader and receives payment. The long trader then has all rights of ownership in the Treasury securities that were delivered in fulfillment of the contract. The Chicago Board of Trade web site (www.cbot.com) features a detailed 35-page description of the Treasury futures delivery process.

For the T-bond futures contract, a wide variety of bonds may be delivered against the contract at any one time. The rules of the Board of Trade call for the delivery of $100,000 worth of T-bonds having at least 15 years remaining until maturity or to their first permissible call date. Table 5.2 shows the 21 T-bonds eligible for delivery on the March, June, and September 2006 contracts that existed in March 2006. The first two columns of Table 5.2 list the coupon

Table 5.1   The delivery timetable for CBOT Treasury futures

	Short	Clearing services provider	Long
First position day (two business days prior to the named delivery month)			By 8:00 p.m., two days prior to the first day allowed for deliveries in expiring futures, clearing firms report to the clearing services provider all open long positions, by origin (i.e., house or customer) and trade date
Day 1: intention day	By 8:00 p.m., the short clearing firm notifies the clearing services provider that it intends to make delivery on an expiring contract; once the clearing services provider has matched the short clearing firm with the long clearing firm(s), this declaration cannot be reversed	By 10:00 p.m., the clearing services provider matches the delivering short's clearing firm to the clearing firm (or firms) with long positions having the oldest trade date(s); each party—long and short—is informed of the opposite party's intention to make or take delivery	By 8:00 p.m., all clearing firms report to the clearing services provider all open long positions in expiring futures contracts, by origin (i.e., house or customer) and trade date
Day 2: notice day	By 2:00 p.m. (3:00 p.m. on last notice day), using calculations based on the expiring contract's intention day settlement price, the short clearing firm invoices the long clearing firm through the clearing services provider		By 4:00 p.m., the long clearing firm provides the short clearing firm with the name and location of its bank
Day 3: delivery day	The short and long clearing firms have until 9:30 a.m. to resolve invoice differences; by 10:00 a.m., the short clearing firm deposits Treasury securities for delivery into its bank account, and it instructs its bank to transfer the securities, via Fed wire, to the long clearing firm's account versus payment no later than 1:00 p.m.		By 7:30 a.m., the long clearing firm makes funds available and notifies its bank to remit the funds and accept Treasury securities; by 1:00 p.m., the long clearing firm's bank has accepted the Treasury securities and, at the same time, has remitted the invoice amount via Fed wire to the short clearing firm's account

Source: The Chicago Board of Trade web site (www.cbot.com). © The Chicago Board of Trade. Reprinted by permission from the Chicago Board of Trade

Table 5.2   Conversion factors for Treasury bond futures for March, June, and September 2006

Coupon	Maturity date	Mar-06	Jun-06	Sep-06
4 1/4	02/15/36	0.7930	0.7937	0.7943
5 1/4	11/15/28	0.9081	0.9084	0.9090
5 1/4	02/15/29	0.9075	0.9081	0.9084
5 3/8	02/15/31	0.9198	0.9203	0.9206
5 1/2	08/15/28	0.9389	0.9394	0.9396
6	02/15/26	0.9999	1.0000	0.9999
6 1/8	11/15/27	1.0150	1.0148	1.0148
6 1/8	08/15/29	1.0154	1.0155	1.0153
6 1/4	08/15/23	1.0265	1.0264	1.0261
6 1/4	05/15/30	1.0316	1.0313	1.0313
6 3/8	08/15/27	1.0446	1.0444	1.0441
6 1/2	11/15/26	1.0585	1.0580	1.0578
6 5/8	02/15/27	1.0735	1.0732	1.0726
6 3/4	08/15/26	1.0871	1.0867	1.0860
6 7/8	08/15/25	1.0990	1.0984	1.0976
7 1/8	02/15/23	1.1177	1.1168	1.1156
7 1/4	08/15/22	1.1285	1.1274	1.1261
7 1/2	11/15/24	1.1663	1.1649	1.1637
7 5/8	11/15/22	1.1687	1.1671	1.1657
7 5/8	02/15/25	1.1813	1.1801	1.1786
8	11/15/21	1.2000	1.1979	1.1960

Source: The Chicago Board of Trade web site (www.cbot.com). © The Chicago Board of Trade. Reprinted by permission from the Chicago Board of Trade

rate and maturity date for each of the bonds. The last three columns list conversion factors for each bond for March, June, and September 2006. (These conversion factors are explained below.) As Table 5.2 shows, coupons on these bonds range from 4.5 to 8 percent and the maturities range from 2021 to 2036. The total issue size of the 21 bonds was $262.4 billion, making it very difficult to corner the deliverable supply of T-bonds.

The fact that some bonds are cheap and some expensive suggests that there may be an advantage to delivering one bond rather than another. If there is such an advantage, why did the CBOT allow several bonds to be delivered against the contract? These considerations are intimately related and have an important impact on the design of the contract. The significant differences in maturity and coupon rates among these bonds cause large price differences. Because the short trader chooses whether or not to make delivery and which bond to deliver, we might expect that only the cheapest bond would ever be delivered.

To eliminate an incentive to deliver just one particular bond, the CBOT initiated a system of conversion factors, which alters the delivery values of different bonds as a function of their coupon rate and term to maturity. The conversion factors in Table 5.2 are based on a hypothetical bond with a 6 percent coupon rate. A quick glance at Table 5.2 shows only one 6 percent coupon bond. For purposes of delivery, the CBOT adjusts the price of every bond using a conversion factor that is specific to a given bond and a particular futures contract expiration. The invoice amount is calculated as follows:

$$\text{invoice amount} = \text{DSP} \times \$100,000 \times \text{CF} + \text{AI} \tag{5.6}$$

where DSP is the decimal settlement price (e.g., 96–16 = 0.965), CF is the conversion factor, and AI is the accrued interest. Each term requires comment. The **decimal settlement price** is simply the decimal equivalent of the quoted price, which is expressed in "points and 32nds of par." The $100,000 reflects the contract amount. The conversion factor attempts to adjust for differences in coupons and maturities among the deliverable bonds.

The conversion factor for any bond can be approximated quite accurately by the following two rules:

(1)   Assume that the face value of the bond to be delivered is $1.
(2)   Discount the assumed cash flows from the bond at 6 percent using the bond pricing equation.

The result approximates the conversion factor for the bond in question. Exact conversion factors are available in the form as shown in Table 5.2 from the CBOT.[2] Looking closely at the conversion factors in Table 5.2, we can note that the closer the coupon rate is to 6 percent, the closer the conversion factor will be to 1. For a bond with a 6 percent coupon, the conversion factor equals 1. This makes sense, because the conversion factor would be calculated by discounting a 6 percent coupon instrument at 6 percent. For bonds with coupon rates above 6 percent, the shorter the maturity, the closer the conversion factor will be to 1. Just the opposite holds for bonds with coupon rates below 6 percent. In general, if yields are 6 percent across all maturities, the conversion factors will be proportional to the bonds' market prices. This is exactly the desired situation, since the delivery value of a bond should be proportional to its market value.

With a flat term structure and yields at 6 percent, there is no advantage to delivering any one bond rather than another. The correlative of this proposition is somewhat disturbing and very important for T-bond futures. If the term structure is not flat, or if yields are not equal to 6 percent, then there is some bond that is better to deliver than the other permissible bonds. This bond is known as the **cheapest to deliver**. Among T-bond futures traders, the concept of the cheapest-to-deliver bond is well known. Most brokerage houses have computer systems that show the cheapest-to-deliver T-bonds on a real-time basis. Since this feature is well known, futures prices tend to track the cheapest-to-deliver bond, which may change over time.

The interplay of actual bond market prices and the conversion factor biases noted earlier determine which bond will be the cheapest to deliver at any given moment. Prior to actual delivery, some bond will be the cheapest to acquire and to carry to delivery. We have already noted that the cost-of-carry relationship considers the net financing cost of carrying an asset to delivery. In the T-bond futures market, the net financing cost is the price that must be paid for funds less the coupon rate obtained by holding the bond itself. Therefore, at any particular moment, the cheapest-to-deliver bond will be the bond that is most profitable to deliver. In Chapter 6, we explain how to find the cheapest-to-deliver bond in more detail.

Why did the CBOT adopt this cumbersome system of conversion factors, particularly since it introduces biases into the market? As we have seen, a substantial deliverable supply of the spot commodity is a necessary condition for a successful futures contract. If the supply of the deliverable commodity is insufficient, then opportunities for market corners and squeezes can arise. To ensure a large deliverable supply, the CBOT allowed a wide range of bonds to qualify for delivery. With many bonds eligible for delivery, it is necessary to adjust bond prices to reflect their varying market values.

In futures markets, the short trader usually has choices to make in the delivery process. For example, we have noted that the short trader chooses the exact delivery day in the delivery month and also on which deliverable bond to deliver. Therefore, the short trader has a number of options embedded in the futures position. These timing and quality options have a value to the seller, so they effectively reduce the prices that we observe in futures markets. Assessing the value of these options for the seller becomes quite complicated. We consider them briefly later in this chapter, and we focus on them in substantial detail in Chapter 6.

Product profile: the CBOT's 30-year Treasury bond futures contract

Contract size: One U.S. Treasury bond with a face value at maturity of $100,000.

Deliverable grades: U.S. Treasury bonds that, if callable, are not callable for at least 15 years from the first day of the delivery month or, if not callable, have a maturity of at least 15 years from the first day of the delivery month. The invoice price equals the futures settlement price times a conversion factor plus accrued interest. The conversion factor is the price of the delivered bond ($1 par value) to yield 6 percent.

Tick size: 1/32 of a point ($31.25 per contract); par is on the basis of 100 points.

Price quote: Points ($1,000) and 1/32 of a point; that is, 84–16 equals $84^{16.5}/_{32}$.

Contract months: March, June, September, and December

Expiration and final settlement: The last trading day is the seventh business day preceding the last business day of the delivery month. The contract is settled with physical delivery. The last delivery day is the last business day of the delivery month.

Trading hours: Open auction: 7:20 a.m. to 2:00 p.m., Central time, Monday–Friday. Electronic: 7:00 p.m. to 4:00 p.m. next day, Central time, Sunday–Friday. Trading in expiring contracts closes at noon, Chicago time, on the last trading day.

Daily price limit: None.

Treasury note futures

The T-bonds and T-notes share a very similar structure, but they differ in the term to maturity at which they are initially offered. Both instruments pay semiannual coupons. Just as the spot market instruments are very similar, the T-bond and T-note futures contracts are very similar as well.

There are three T-note futures contracts trading at the CBOT. While similar in structure, these contracts are based on notes of varying maturities. Nominally, the contracts are designated as two-, five-, and ten-year contracts. However, a range of maturities is deliverable against each contract, with maturity being measured on the first day of the delivery month. Deliverable maturities are: 21 months to two years for the two-year contract, four years three months to five years three months for the five-year contract, and six years six months up to ten years for the ten-year contract. The contract size for the five- and ten-year contracts is $100,000 of face value, but it is $200,000 for the two-year contract. By having a larger denomination for the two-year contract, the CBOT brings the volatilities of the contracts into the same range. This difference in the volatility of the underlying bonds leads to differences in price quotations. For the two-year contract, the tick size is one quarter of a 32nd, while the five-year contract has a one half of a 32nd tick size. Each contract allows for a range of deliverable maturities, thereby increasing the deliverable supply for each contract. The T-note and T-bond contracts use the same system of conversion factors as the T-bond contract, and they have the same delivery system. Each of the T-note contracts has substantial trading volume and open interest.

Product profile: the CBOT's ten-year Treasury note futures contract

Contract size: One U.S. Treasury note with a face value at maturity of $100,000.

Deliverable grades: U.S. Treasury notes maturing at least $6^1/_2$ years, but not more than 10 years, from the first day of the delivery month. The invoice price equals the futures settlement price times a conversion factor plus accrued interest. The conversion factor is the price of the delivered ($1 par value) to yield 6 percent.

Tick size: One half of 1/32nd of a point ($15.625 per contract) rounded up to the nearest cent; par is on the basis of 100 points.

Price quote: Points ($1,000) and one half of 1/32nd of a point; that is, $84–16 = 84^{16}/_{32}$, $84–165 = 84^{16.5}/_{32}$.

Contract months: March, June, September, and December

Expiration and final settlement: The last trading day is the seventh business day preceding the last business day of the delivery month. The contract is settled with physical delivery. The last delivery day is the last business day of the delivery month.

Trading hours: Open auction: 7:20 a.m. to 2:00 p.m., Central time, Monday–Friday. Electronic: 7:00 p.m. to 4:00 p.m. next day, Central time, Sunday–Friday. Trading in expiring contracts closes at noon, Chicago time, on the last trading day.

Daily price limit: None.

Non-U.S. longer-maturity interest rate futures

Futures contracts based on the long gilt, the Euro Schatz, Euro BOBL, and Euro Bund, represent the major non-U.S. longer-maturity futures contracts. A gilt is a long-term Treasury obligation of the United Kingdom, and the long gilt futures contract trades on the Euronext.liffe for a £50,000 contract amount. The Euro Schatz, Euro BOBL, and Euro Bund are, respectively, two-, five-, and ten-year obligations of the German government, denominated in euro. Futures on these instruments trade on Eurex and have contract amounts of €100,000. Volume and open interest for these contracts are substantial, and exceed the volume and open interest of T-note and T-bond futures in some cases.

Each of these contracts is similar in structure to the T-bond futures contract. Each requires actual delivery of a debt instrument to fulfill the contract, each contract allows for multiple delivery instruments, and each has a system of conversion factors based on a 6 percent nominal bond underlying the futures contract. An understanding of the T-bond futures contract provides a sound basis for understanding these other similar contracts.

Product profile: Eurex's Euro Bund futures contract

Contract size: One German bund with a par value of €100,000.

Deliverable grades: A long-term debt instrument issued by the German federal government, with a term of $8^1/_2–10^1/_2$ years and an interest rate of 6 percent. The invoice price equals the futures settlement price times a conversion factor plus accrued interest.

Tick size: 0.01 percent, representing €10.

Price quote: In a percentage of par value, carried out to two decimal places.

Contract months: The three successive months within the March, June, September, and December delivery cycle.

Expiration and final settlement: The last trading day is two trading days prior to the delivery day of the contract month. The delivery day is the tenth calendar day of the contract month, if this day is an exchange trading day; otherwise, the immediately following exchange trading day.

Trading hours: Eurex operates in three trading phases. In the pre-trading period, users may make inquiries or enter, change, or delete orders and quotes in preparation for trading. This period is between 7:30 a.m. and 8:00 a.m. The main trading period is between 8:00 a.m. and 7:00 p.m. Trading ends with the post-trading period between 7:00 p.m. and 8:00 p.m.

Daily price limit: None.

The pricing of interest rate futures contracts

Introduction

Interest rate futures trade in markets that are virtually always at full carry. In other words, the cost-of-carry model provides a virtually complete understanding of the price structure of interest rate futures contracts. To understand why the cost-of-carry model fits interest rate futures, recall our discussion of Chapter 3. We identified five features of the underlying good that promote full carry: ease of short selling, large supply of the underlying good, nonseasonal production, nonseasonal consumption, and ease of storage.

The goods that underlie the major interest rate futures contracts meet these conditions very well. First, bonds are created, which mature in a nonseasonal way, so the restrictions on seasonality are met virtually perfectly. Second, storage is virtually effortless. Most Treasury securities exist only in computer records, not even being committed to paper. Third, the supply is incredibly ample. For the most important contracts, the underlying instruments are highly liquid debt instruments. For the three T-note contracts, the T-bond contract, and the T-bill contract, the underlying instruments are all issues of the U.S. Treasury. These instruments are available in huge supply and trade in a highly liquid market. The Eurodollar contract deals with questions of deliverable supply by avoiding delivery completely and using cash settlement. Finally, short selling is very well developed in this market. Because futures market participants hold these securities in such large amounts, these traders can simulate short selling by selling some of their inventory of Treasury securities. Therefore, it appears that interest rate futures prices should behave like the cost-of-carry model in a perfect market; that is, interest rate futures markets should be at full carry.

In Chapter 3, we considered the cost-of-carry model in perfect markets and concluded that the futures price should equal the spot price plus the cost of carrying the spot good forward to delivery on the futures contract:

$$F_{0,t} = S_0(1 + C) \tag{3.3}$$

We also concluded that a similar relationship must hold between a nearby futures price and a distant futures price:

$$F_{0,d} = F_{0,n}(1 + C) \tag{3.6}$$

where $F_{0,t}$ is the current futures price for a contract that expires at time t, S_0 is the current spot price, C is the percentage cost of carry between two dates, $F_{0,n}$ is the nearby futures price, and

$F_{0,d}$ is the distant futures price. Finally, if we assumed that the only carrying cost is the financing cost, we also concluded that dividing the futures price by the spot price yielded an **implied repo rate**:

$$\frac{F_{0,t}}{S_0} = 1 + C \tag{3.7}$$

where C is the implied repo rate. As we will see, the model applies very well to interest rate futures. However, we must take account of some of the peculiarities of debt instruments.

The cost-of-carry model in perfect markets

In this section, we apply the cost-of-carry model to interest rate futures under the assumption of perfect markets. In addition, we assume that the only carrying charge is the interest rate to finance the holding of a good, and also that we can disregard the special features of a given futures contract. For example, we ignore the embedded options that sellers of futures contracts may hold, such as the option to substitute various grades of the commodity at delivery or the option to choose the exact delivery date within the delivery month, and we also ignore the differences between forward and futures prices that may result from the daily resettlement cash flows on the futures contract. In summary, we are assuming that:

(1) Markets are perfect.
(2) The financing cost is the only carrying charge.
(3) We can ignore the options that the seller may possess.
(4) We can ignore the differences between forward and futures prices.

Later in this chapter, we will relax these assumptions.

Each interest rate futures contract that we have considered specifies the maturity of the deliverable bond. For example, the T-bill futures contract requires that a deliverable T-bill must have a maturity of 90–92 days. This requirement applies on the delivery date. As we have seen in Chapter 3, the cash-and-carry strategy involves selling a futures contract, buying the spot commodity, and storing it until the futures delivery date. Then the trader delivers the good against the futures contract. For example, if the futures price of gold is too high relative to the cash market price of gold, a trader could engage in a cash-and-carry arbitrage. Part of this strategy would involve buying gold, storing until the futures expiration, and delivering the gold against the futures contract.

To apply this strategy in the interest rate futures market, we must be very careful. For example, if a T-bill futures contract expires in 77 days, we cannot buy a 90-day T-bill and store it for future delivery. If we attempt to do so, we will find ourselves with a 13-day T-bill on the delivery date. This will not be deliverable against the futures contract. Therefore, to apply a cash-and-carry strategy, a trader must buy a bond that will still have or come to have the correct properties on the delivery date. For our T-bill cash-and-carry strategy, the trader must secure a 167-day T-bill to carry for 77 days. Then, the bill will have the requisite 90 days remaining until expiration on the delivery date.

We illustrate the cash-and-carry strategy with an example. Consider the data in Table 5.3, which uses the discount yields of the IMM index. The example assumes perfect markets, including the assumption that one can either borrow or lend at any of the riskless rates represented by the T-bill yields. These restrictive assumptions will be relaxed for a while. The data presented in Table 5.3 and the assumptions just made mean that an arbitrage opportunity is

Table 5.3   Interest rate futures and arbitrage: today's date is January 5

Futures	Discount yield (%)	Price ($ millions face value)
MAR contract (matures in 77 days on March 22)	12.50	968,750
Cash bills:		
167-day T-bill (deliverable on MAR futures)	10.00	953,611
77-day T-bill	6.00	987,167

Handwritten annotations:
- (3) short — "sell as reg. by contract"
- (1) long — "we can equity buy future to follow-thru w/ contract"
- (2) short — "need equity to fin. buy future" — "6.00 borrowing rate"
- "only borrow $ for 77 days, b/c will be transferred when sell T-Bill in MAR."

Table 5.4   Cash-and-carry arbitrage transactions

January 5
Borrow $953,611 for 77 days by issuing a 77-day T-bill at 6%
Buy a 167-day T-bill yielding 10% for $953,611
Sell a MAR T-bill futures contract with a yield of 12.50% for $968,750

March 22
Deliver the originally purchased T-bill against the MAR futures contract and collect $968,750
Repay the debt on the 77-day T-bill that matures today for $966,008

Profit:

$968,750
−966,008
$2,742

present. Since the futures contract matures in 77 days, the spot 77-day rate represents the financing cost to acquire the 167-day T-bill, which can be delivered against the MAR futures contract on March 22. This is possible because the T-bill that has 167 days to maturity on January 5 will have exactly 90 days to maturity on March 22.

As the transactions presented in Table 5.4 indicate, an arbitrage opportunity exists because the prices and interest rates on the three instruments are mutually inconsistent. To implement a cash-and-carry strategy, a trader can sell the MAR futures and acquire the 167-day T-bill on January 5. The trader then holds the bill for delivery against the futures contract. The trader must finance the holding of the bill during the 77-day interval from January 5 to delivery on March 22. To exploit the rate discrepancy, the trader borrows at the short-term rate of 6 percent and uses the proceeds to acquire the long-term T-bill. Note that the trader borrows exactly the $953,611 necessary to purchase the 167-day T-bill, by issuing a 77-day T-bill in the required amount. This T-bill has a face value of $966,008, not $1 million, because

$$\$953,611 = \$966,008 - 0.06 \times \$966,008 \times \frac{77}{360}$$

At the maturity of the futures, the long-term T-bill has the exactly correct maturity and can be delivered against the futures contract. This strategy generates a profit of $2,742 per contract. Relative to the short-term rate, the futures yield and the long-term T-bill yield were too high. In this example, the trader acquires short-term funds at a low rate (6 percent) and reinvests those funds at a higher rate (10 percent). It may appear that this difference generates the arbitrage profit, but that is not completely accurate, as the next example shows.[3]

Consider the same values as shown in Table 5.3, but now assume that the rate on the 77-day T-bill is 8 percent. Now the short-term rate is too high relative to the long-term rate and the futures yield. To take advantage of this situation, we reverse the cash-and-carry procedure of Table 5.4, as Table 5.5 shows. In other words, we now exploit a reverse cash-and-carry strategy. With this new set of rates, the arbitrage is more complicated, since it involves holding the T-bill that is delivered on the futures contract. In this situation, the arbitrageur borrows $952,174 for 167 days at 10 percent and invests these funds at 8 percent for the 77 days until the MAR futures matures. The payoff from the 77 day investment of $952,174 will be $968,750, exactly enough to pay for the delivery of the T-bill on the futures contract. This bill is held for 90 days until June 20, when it matures and pays $1 million. On June 20, the arbitrageur's loan on the 167-day T-bill is also due, and equals $998,493. This trader repays this debt from the $1 million received on the maturing bill. The strategy yields a profit of $1,507. Notice in the second example that the trader borrowed at 10 percent and invested the funds at 8 percent temporarily. This shows that it is the entire set of rates that must be consistent and that arbitrage opportunities need not only involve misalignment between two rates.

From our analyses in Chapter 3, we know that the reverse cash-and-carry strategy involves selling an asset short and investing the proceeds from the short sale. In our example of Table 5.5, the short sale is the issuance of debt. By issuing debt, the arbitrageur literally sells a bond. In Chapter 3, we also noted that a trader could simulate a short sale by selling from inventory. The same is true for interest rate futures. For example, a bank that holds investments in T-bills can simulate a short sale by selling a T-bill from inventory.

To this point, we have considered a cash-and-carry strategy in Table 5.4 and a reverse cash-and-carry strategy in Table 5.5. These two examples show that there must be a very exact relationship among these rates on the different instruments to exclude arbitrage opportunities. If the yield on the MAR futures is 12.50 percent and the 167-day spot yield is 10 percent, there is only one yield for the 77-day T-bill that will not give rise to an arbitrage opportunity, and that rate is 7.3063 percent. To see why that is the case, consider two ways of holding a T-bill investment for the full 167-day period of the examples:

(1)   hold the 167-day T-bill, or
(2)   hold a 77-day T-bill followed by a 90-day T-bill that is delivered on the futures contract.

Since these two ways of holding T-bills cover the same time period and have the same risk level, the two positions must have the same yield to avoid arbitrage. To see this, let us assume a $1 million face value. In this situation, a 167-day T-bill with a discount yield of 10.00 percent has a price of $953,611. If arbitrage is to be impossible, this amount must also grow to $1 million over the same period by first holding a 77-day T-bill, and then holding a 90-day T-bill that is delivered on the futures contract at day 77, with the T-bill futures having been purchased at the beginning of the period. As shown in Table 5.3, a T-bill delivered on the futures will have a price of $968,750 if the discount yield on the futures contract is 12.50 percent. To prevent arbitrage, given the 10.00 percent discount yield on the 167-day T-bill and the 12.50 percent discount yield on the futures that expires in 77 days, the no-arbitrage 77-day T-bill discount yield is shown to be 7.3063 percent as follows:

$$\$953,611 = \$968,750 - 0.073063 \times \$968,750 \times \frac{77}{360}$$

Table 5.5 Reverse cash-and-carry arbitrage transactions

January 5
Borrow $952,174 by issuing a 167-day T-bill at 10%
Buy a 77-day T-bill yielding 8% for $952,174 that will pay $968,750 on March 22
Buy one MAR futures contract with a yield of 12.50% for $968,750

March 22
Collect $968,750 from the maturing 77-day T-bill
Pay $968,750 and take delivery of a 90-day T-bill from the MAR futures contract

June
Collect $1 million from the maturing 90-day T-bill that was delivered on the futures contract
Pay $998,493 debt on the maturing 167-day T-bill

$$\begin{array}{r} \text{Profit:} \\ \$1,000,000 \\ \underline{-998,493} \\ \$1,507 \end{array}$$

If the discount yield on the 77-day T-bill is lower than 7.3063 percent, then cash-and-carry arbitrage will be possible, as illustrated in Table 5.4. If the yield is higher, then the reverse cash-and-carry arbitrage will work, as shown in Table 5.5.

The financing cost and the implied repo rate
With these prices, and continuing to assume that the only carrying cost is the financing charge, we can also infer the implied repo rate. We know that the ratio of the futures price divided by the spot price equals one plus the implied repo rate. As we have seen, the correct spot instrument for our example is the 167-day bill, because this bill will have the appropriate delivery characteristics when the futures matures. Thus, we have

$$1 + C\frac{P_F}{P_{167}} = \frac{\$968,750}{\$953,611} = 1.015875$$

The implied repo rate, C, is 1.5875 percent. This covers the cost of carry for 77 days from the present to the expiration of the futures. Therefore, assuming that the interest cost is the only carrying charge, the cost of carry equals the implied repo rate.

This equivalence between the cost of carry and the implied repo rate also leads to two rules for arbitrage.

(1) If the implied repo rate exceeds the financing cost, then exploit a cash-and-carry arbitrage opportunity: Borrow funds; buy the cash bond; sell futures; hold the bond; and deliver against futures.
(2) If the implied repo rate is less than the financing cost, then exploit a reverse cash-and-carry arbitrage opportunity: Buy futures; sell the bond short and invest the proceeds until futures expires; take delivery on futures; and repay the short sale obligation.

The futures yield and the forward rate of interest

We have seen that the futures price of an interest rate futures contract implies a yield on the instrument that underlies the futures contract. We call this implied yield the futures yield. Now we continue to assume that the financing cost is the only carrying charge, that markets are perfect, that we can ignore the options that the seller of a futures contract may possess, and that the price difference between forward contracts and futures contracts is negligible. Under these conditions, we can show that the futures yield must equal the forward rate of interest.

We continue to use the T-bill futures contract as our example. The T-bill futures, like many other interest rate futures contracts, has an underlying instrument that will be delivered when the contract expires. If we consider a SEP contract, it calls for the delivery of a 90-day T-bill that will mature in December. The futures yield covers the 90-day time-span from delivery in September to maturity in December. Given the necessary set of spot rates, it is possible to compute a forward rate to cover any given period.

To illustrate the equivalence between futures yields and forward rates under our assumptions, we continue to use our example of a T-bill with a 167-day holding period. Let us assume the following spot discount yields:

| For a 167-day bill | 10.0000 percent |
| For a 77-day bill | 7.3063 percent |

We have already seen that a 77-day T-bill with a yield of 7.3063 percent will increase from $953,611 to $968,750, a ratio of $968,750/$953,611 = 1.015875. Similarly, the 167-day bill increases from $953,611 to $1 million for a ratio of $1,000,000/$953,611 = 1.048646. To avoid arbitrage, the forward rate of interest for the period from day 77 to day 167 must be such that the two investment strategies have the same overall investment rate. Assuming X to be the forward rate that must be experienced for the entire period from day 77 to day 167, we have 1.048646 = X × 1.015875. Therefore, X must equal 1.032259. Thus, the forward rate to cover this entire 90-day period is 3.2259 percent. Notice that this rate exactly matches the rate on the T-bill delivered on the futures contract priced at $968,750, because $1,000,000/$968,750 = 1.032259. With these 77- and 167-day spot rates, the futures rate to cover the period from day 77 to day 167 must be 12.50 percent on a discount yield basis to avoid arbitrage. In deriving this result, we must bear our assumptions in mind: markets are perfect, that the financing cost is the only carrying charge, that the seller's options are ignored, and that there is a difference between forward and futures prices.

The cost-of-carry model for T-bond futures

In this section, we apply the cost-of-carry model to the T-bond futures contract. In essence, the same concepts apply, with one difference. The holder of a T-bond receives cash flows from the bond. This affects the cost of carry that the holder of the bond actually incurs. For example, assume that the coupon rate on a $100,000 face value T-bond is 8 percent and the trader finances the bond at 8 percent. In this case, the net carrying charge is zero—the earnings offset the financing cost.

To illustrate this idea, let us assume that, on January 5, a T-bond that is deliverable on a futures contract has an 8 percent coupon and costs $100.00. The trader faces a financing rate of 7.3063 percent on a discount basis for the 77 days until the futures contract is deliverable. (We temporarily ignore the conversion factor and the complications it brings.) With an 8 percent coupon, the accrued interest from the date of purchase to the delivery date on the futures is

Table 5.6   Cash-and-carry transactions for a T-bond

January 5
Borrow $100,103 for 77 days at the 77-day rate of 7.3063%
Buy the 8% T-bond for $100,103
Sell one T-bond futures contract for $101,692

March 22
Deliver the T-bond; receive an invoice amount of $101,692
Repay the loan of $101,692

Profit: 0

$$(77/182) \times 0.04 \times \$100,000 = \$1,692$$

Therefore, the invoice amount will be $101,692 = $100,000 + $1,692. If this is the invoice amount in 77 days, the T-bond must cost the present value of that amount, discounted for 77 days at the 77-day rate of 7.3063 percent. This implies a cost for the T-bond of $100,103. If the price is less than $100,103, a cash-and-carry arbitrage strategy will be available. Under these circumstances, the cash-and-carry strategy would have the cash flows shown in Table 5.6.

The transactions in Table 5.6 show that the futures price must adjust to reflect the accrual of interest. The bond in Table 5.6 had no coupon payment during the 77-day interval, but the same adjustment must be made to account for cash throw-offs that the bondholder receives during the holding period.

The cost-of-carry model in imperfect markets

We now relax our assumption of perfect markets and see how the cost-of-carry model applies to interest rate futures. In particular, we will focus on the possibility that the borrowing and lending rates may differ. We continue to ignore the seller's options and the price differences between forward and futures contracts. Thus, in this section we analyze the cost-of-carry model for the situation in which:

(1)   The borrowing rate exceeds the lending rate.
(2)   The financing cost is the only carrying charge.
(3)   We can ignore the options that the seller may possess.
(4)   We can ignore the differences between forward and futures prices.

In Chapter 3, we saw that allowing the borrowing and lending rates to differ leads to an arbitrage band around the futures price. For example, let us assume that the borrowing rate is 25 basis points, or one-fourth of a percentage point, higher than the lending rate. Continuing to use our T-bill example, we have:

Instrument	Lending rate	Borrowing rate
77-day bill	7.3063	7.5563
167-day bill	10.0000	10.2500

Table 5.7   Cash-and-carry transactions with unequal borrowing and lending rates

January 5
Borrow $953,611 for 77 days at the 77-day borrowing rate of 7.5563%
Buy a 167-day T-bill yielding 10% for $953,611
Sell one T-bill futures contract with a yield of 12.29% for $969,275

March 22
Deliver the originally purchased T-bill against the MAR futures contract and collect $969,275
Repay the debt on the 77-day T-bill that matures today for $969,277

Profit: −$2 ≈ 0

These assumptions approximate real market conditions. For example, a bank might be able to lend funds to the government by buying a T-bill. To borrow, however, the bank might have to transact at a somewhat higher rate.

When it was possible to both borrow and lend at the same rate, our earlier examples showed that the futures yield must be 12.50 percent. Now, with these different borrowing and lending rates, we want to determine how the futures yield can vary from 12.50 percent. To do this, we apply the cash-and-carry and reverse cash-and-carry strategies. In both cases, we find the futures price that gives a zero gain or loss on the strategy, allowing for rounding to the nearest $25 tick on the futures.

In the cash-and-carry strategy, we sell the futures and borrow in order to buy a good that we can deliver on the futures contract. Table 5.7 details the transactions with unequal borrowing and lending rates. The table illustrates the highest futures yield and lowest futures price that gives a zero profit with the unequal borrowing and lending rates. From this example, we see that the futures yield can be as low as 12.29 percent without generating an arbitrage opportunity. This futures yield implies that the futures price can be as high as $969,275 and still not generate an arbitrage opportunity.

We now consider the reverse cash-and-carry strategy. Here, we borrow long term to finance a short-term investment and we purchase the futures contract. When the futures contract expires, we accept delivery and hold the delivered good until the bond matures. Table 5.8 illustrates the transactions that show how high the futures yield and how low the futures price can be without providing an arbitrage opportunity.

From the transactions in Table 5.8, we see that the futures yield can be as high as 12.97 percent without providing an arbitrage opportunity. Similarly, the corresponding futures price can be as low as $967,575 without creating an arbitrage opportunity.

With equal borrowing and lending rates in our earlier examples, we saw that the futures yield had to be exactly 12.50 percent and the futures price had to be $968,750. The unequal borrowing and lending rates create a no-arbitrage band for the futures. Now the futures yield must fall in the range from 12.29 to 12.97 percent, and the futures price must lie in the range $967,575 to $969,275. As long as the futures yield and futures price stay within these respective ranges, arbitrage will not be possible.

A practical survey of interest rate futures pricing

If markets are perfect, if the only carrying charge is the financing cost, if we ignore the seller's options, and if we ignore differences between futures and forward prices, we have seen how the cost-of-carry model specifies an exact futures yield and futures price. If we allow market

Table 5.8   Reverse cash-and-carry transactions with unequal borrowing and lending rates

January 5
Borrow $952,454 at the 167-day borrowing rate of 10.25%
Buy a 77-day T-bill yielding 7.3063% for $952,454
Buy one MAR futures contract with a futures yield of 12.97% for $967,575

March 22
Collect $967,575 from the maturing 77-day T-bill
Pay $967,575 and take delivery of a 90-day T-bill on the futures contract

June 20
Collect $1 million from the maturing 90-day T-bill that was delivered on the futures contract
Pay $1,000,003 debt on the maturing 167-day T-bill

Profit: −$3 ≈ 0

imperfections in the form of unequal borrowing and lending rates, we have seen that the cost-of-carry model leads to a no-arbitrage band of possible futures prices. Now, we provide a practical approach to include other market imperfections in our analysis.

In Chapter 3, we considered transaction costs, a typical market imperfection. There we saw that transaction costs lead to a no-arbitrage band of possible futures prices. In essence, transaction costs increase the no-arbitrage band just as unequal borrowing and lending rates do. In Chapter 3, we also considered impediments to short selling as a market imperfection that would frustrate the reverse cash-and-carry arbitrage strategy. From a practical perspective, restrictions on short selling are relatively unimportant in interest rate futures pricing. First, supplies of deliverable Treasury securities are plentiful and government securities have little (or zero) convenience yield. Second, because Treasury securities are so widely held, many traders can simulate short selling by selling T-bills, T-notes, or T-bonds from inventory. Therefore, restrictions on short selling are unlikely to have any pricing effect.

In our analysis of the cost-of-carry model, we found that the futures yield must equal the forward rate of interest, under our assumptions. By assuming that we could ignore the difference between forward and futures prices, we implicitly assumed that we could ignore the effect of daily resettlement cash flows on pricing. However, in Chapter 3, we saw that daily resettlement cash flows could affect pricing of the futures contract if the price of the cash commodity were correlated with interest rates. In the interest rate futures market, the underlying goods are highly correlated with interest rates. Therefore, we might expect to find differences between futures and forward prices, and between futures and forward yields. In Chapter 3, we saw that a negative correlation between the price of the cash commodity and interest rates would lead to a futures price that is less than the forward price. This is exactly the situation with interest rate futures, because bond prices fall as interest rates rise. Therefore, we would expect the futures price to be less than the forward price for this reason. However, most studies indicate that this is not a serious problem in general. From a practical point of view, this difference is unlikely to be critical. We consider the theoretical ramifications of this relationship in more detail in Chapter 6.

In the construction of interest rate futures contracts, we have seen that the seller of a futures contract possesses timing and quality options that may be valuable. For example, the seller of a T-bond futures contract possesses a timing option because she can decide on which day of the delivery month to deliver. Likewise, the seller possesses a quality option, because she can decide which bond to deliver. The buyer of the futures contract knows that the seller acquires these options by selling the futures. Therefore, the futures price must adjust to account for those options. This means that the futures price with the seller's options must be less than it would be if it had no options attached.

Studies have shown that the seller's options can have significant value. We consider this issue in detail in Chapter 6. Here, we note that these options have sufficient value to be of practical importance in using interest rate futures. We will also see that it is even possible that these options can account for 15 percent of the futures price.

Speculating with interest rate futures

In the interest rate futures market, it is possible to speculate by holding an outright position, or by trading a spread. An outright position, such as buying a T-note futures contract, is a simple bet on the direction of interest rates. More sophisticated speculative strategies involve trading spreads. As we discussed in Chapter 4, a spread speculation involves a bet on a change in the relationship between two futures prices. In this section, we consider some basic speculative strategies and illustrate them with examples.

The concept of a speculative profit is a very slippery notion, as we discussed in Chapter 4. A speculator might earn accounting profits that constitute a justifiable return to the application of his capital and energies. This is different from economic profit or an economic rent, which would be a profit in excess of return for the use of capital and the bearing of risk. Accounting profits are consistent with market efficiency, but economic profits are not. As the speculative strategies of this section are considered, it is important to keep these different conceptions of profit in mind.

Speculating with outright positions

For a speculator with an outright position in futures, the speculation is very simple. The long trader is betting that interest rates will fall so that the price of the futures will rise. The short trader is betting that interest rates will rise so that the futures price will fall.

As an example of an outright speculation, we consider a trader who anticipated rising interest rates on September 20, 2005. In particular, the trader believes that short-term rates will rise, so she trades the Eurodollar contract as shown in Table 5.9. To profit from rising rates, the trader must be short in interest rate futures. Accordingly, she sells one DEC 05 Eurodollar contract at 90.30. Five days later, interest rates have risen and the futures contract trades at 90.12. Satisfied with the profit, she buys, for a gain of 18 basis points. Because each basis point is worth $25, her total profit is $450.

Table 5.9   Speculating with Eurodollar futures

Date	Futures market
September 20	Sell one DEC 05 Eurodollar futures at 90.30
September 25	Buy one DEC 05 Eurodollar futures at 90.12

Profit: $90.30 - 90.12 = 0.18$

Total gain: 18 basis points $\times$ $25 = $450

Speculating with spreads

For the most part, speculation with interest rate futures relies on spread trading. An intracommodity spread is typically a speculation on the term structure of interest rates; for example, a spread between the nearby and distant Eurodollar futures. An intercommodity spread can be a speculation on the changing shape of the yield curve, or it can be a speculation on shifting risk levels between different instruments. For example, T-notes and T-bonds have the same default risk, so a bond/note spread is a yield curve speculation. Often, an intercommodity spread is a speculation on changing risk levels between different instruments—for example, a spread between T-bills and Eurodollars. Of course, a given spread could combine features of both term structure and risk structure speculations. This section illustrates various different types of spread speculation.

An intracommodity Eurodollar spread

Table 5.10 presents a series of spot rates and futures rates for Eurodollars. As the spot rates show, the yield curve slopes upward, with three-month bills yielding 10 percent and 12-month bills yielding 11.47 percent. The table shows three futures contracts, with the nearby contract maturing in three months. For the futures contracts, the futures yields are consistent with the term structure given by the spot rates, in the sense that the futures yields equal the forward rates from the term structure. Faced with such circumstances, particularly with a very steep upward-sloping yield curve, a speculator might believe that the term structure would flatten within six months. Even if one were not sure whether rates were going to rise or fall, the speculator could still profit from a Eurodollar futures spread by entering the transactions shown in Table 5.11.

Table 5.10   Spot and futures Eurodollar rates for March 20

Time to maturity or futures expiration	Add-on yield (%)	Futures contract	Futures yield (%)	IMM index
Three months	10.00	JUN	12.00	88.00
Six months	10.85	SEP	12.50	87.50
Nine months	11.17	DEC	13.50	86.50
Twelve months	11.47			

Table 5.11   Speculation on Eurodollar futures

Date	Futures market
March 20	Buy the DEC Eurodollar futures at 86.50
	Sell the SEP Eurodollar futures at 87.50
April 30	Sell the DEC Eurodollar futures at 88.14
	Buy the SEP Eurodollar futures at 89.02

Profits:

DEC	SEP
88.14	87.50
−86.50	−89.02
1.64	−1.52

Total gain: 12 basis points × $25 = $300

If the yield curve flattens, the yield spread between successively maturing futures contracts must narrow. Currently, the yield spread between the DEC and SEP futures contracts is 100 basis points. By buying the more distant DEC contract and selling the SEP contract, the trader bets that the yield differential will narrow. If the yield curve flattens, no matter whether the general level of rates rises or falls, then this spread strategy gives a profit. As Table 5.11 shows, yields have fallen dramatically by April 30. The yield on the DEC contract has fallen from 13.50 to 11.86 percent and the SEP yield has moved from 12.50 to 10.98 percent. For the profits on this speculative strategy, the important point is that the yield spread has changed from 100 basis points to 88 basis points. This generates a profit on the spread of 12 basis points, or $300, because each basis point change represents $25. The same kind of result could have been obtained in a market with rising rates, as long as the yield curve flattens.

This example shows that all interest rate futures intracommodity spreads are speculations on the changing shape of the yield curve. No matter what change in the shape of the yield curve is anticipated, there is a way to profit from that change by trading the correct interest rate futures spread.

A T-bill/Eurodollar (TED) spread

Another basic kind of speculation possible in the interest rate futures market is a speculation on the changing risk structure of interest rates. Given the continuing international debt crisis, this is a time of danger for banks that are heavily engaged in international lending, with great fear of widespread default on the part of many developing nations. A speculator might view this situation as offering potential opportunity. If the crisis developed, we might expect to find a widening of the yield spread between T-bill deposits and Eurodollar deposits, for example. This widening yield spread would reflect the changing perception of the risk involved in holding Eurodollar deposits in the face of potentially very large loan losses. In February, assume that yields for the DEC T-bill and Eurodollar futures contracts are 8.82 and 9.71 percent, respectively. If the full riskiness of the banks' position has yet to be understood, we might expect the yield spread to widen. This would be the case whether interest rates were rising or falling. To take advantage of this belief, a trader could sell the DEC Eurodollar contract and buy the DEC T-bill contract, as shown in Table 5.12.

Since the trader expects the yield spread to widen, he or she sells the Eurodollar contract and buys the T-bill contract for index values of 90.29 and 91.18, respectively. Later, on October

Table 5.12	Intercommodity spread in short-term rates
Date	Futures market
February 17	Sell one DEC Eurodollar futures contract with an IMM index value of 90.29
	Buy one DEC T-bill futures contract yielding 8.82% with an IMM index value of 91.18
October 14	Buy one DEC Eurodollar futures contract with an IMM index value of 89.91
	Sell one DEC T-bill futures contract yielding 8.93% with an IMM index value of 91.07

Profits:

Eurodollar	T-bill
90.29	91.07
−89.91	−91.18
0.38	−0.11

Total profit: 27 basis points × $25 = $675

14, the yield spread of the example has, in fact, widened, with T-bill yields having moved up slightly, so the spread has widened by 27 basis points, which means a profit of $675 on the speculation.

Perhaps the single most important point about speculation can be emphasized using this example. Virtually everyone is aware of the problems being faced by banks involved in international lending, with articles appearing almost daily in *The Wall Street Journal*. Therefore, the futures prices must have already embedded in them the market's expectation of the future yield spread between T-bills and Eurodollars. By engaging in the speculative strategy as discussed here, a trader speculates against the rest of the market. It was not enough to expect yield spreads to widen, but the trader must have expected them to widen more than the market expected. Therefore, the trader must have been right to make a profit. This spread relationship is so well known that it has a name—the TED (Treasury/Eurodollar) spread.[4]

The TED spreads can also be constructed with Treasury note futures and LIBOR-based swap futures. The CBOT has five- and ten-year versions of each contract that can be used to create five- and ten-year TED spreads. These are referred to as "term TED spreads." The interest rate underlying the LIBOR swap contract is based on Eurodollar bank deposit rates. Therefore, spread differences between equivalent maturity Treasury notes rates and swap rates should reflect bank credit risk, just like that in the T-bill/Eurodollar spread.

Notes over bonds

Like the TED spread, other strategies are also sufficiently popular to earn nicknames. **Notes over bonds** (**NOB**) is a speculative strategy for trading T-note futures against T-bond futures. As we have seen, prices of bonds and notes are strongly correlated. Because the T-bonds underlying the T-bond futures contract have a longer duration than the T-notes underlying the T-note futures contract, a given change in yields will cause a greater price reaction for the T-bond futures contract. The NOB spread is designed to exploit that fact. Thus, the NOB spread is essentially an attempt to take advantage of either changing levels of yields or a changing yield curve by using an intermarket spread.

If yields rise by the same amount on both instruments, one can expect a greater price change on the T-bond. Assume a trader is long the T-bond futures and short the T-note futures. An equal drop in rates will give a profit on the long T-bond futures that exceeds the loss on the T-note futures, giving a profit on the spread.

The NOB can also be used to trade based on expectations of a changing yield curve shape. For example, assume a trader expects the yield curve to become more steeply upward sloping. This implies that yields on the long maturities (T-bonds) would rise relative to yields on shorter maturities (T-notes). To take advantage of this belief, the trader should sell T-bond futures and buy T-note futures. If a trader expects the yield curve to become more downward sloping, the trader would buy T-bond futures and sell T-note futures. Notice that this speculation only concerns the relative yields, not the levels.

A variation on the NOB trade is the "tens under twos," or TUT, spread. This spread is structured as a NOB spread and is used for the same purpose. The only difference is that it is structured with the two-year note contract serving as the short-term instrument and the ten-year note contract serving as the long-term instrument.

Hedging with interest rate futures

In this section, we explore the concept of hedging with interest rate futures. We present a series of examples, progressing from simple cases to situations that are more complex. In essence, the hedger in interest rate futures attempts to take a futures position that will generate a gain to offset a potential loss in the cash market. This also implies that the hedger takes a futures position that will generate a loss to offset a potential gain in the cash market. Thus, the interest rate futures hedger is attempting to reduce risk, not make profits.

A long hedge example

A portfolio manager learns on December 15 that he will have $970,000 to invest in 90-day T-bills six months from now. Current yields on T-bills stand at 12 percent and the yield curve is flat, so forward rates are all 12 percent as well. The manager finds the 12 percent rate attractive and decides to lock it in by going long in a T-bill futures contract maturing on June 15, exactly when the funds come available for investment. As Table 5.13 shows, the manager anticipates the cash position on December 15 and buys one T-bill futures contract to hedge the risk that yields might fall before the funds are available for investment on June 15. With the current yield and, more importantly, the forward rate on T-bills of 12 percent, the portfolio manager expects to be able to buy $1 million face value of T-bills because

$$\$970,000 = \$1,000,000 - 0.1200 \times \$1,000,000 \times \frac{90}{360}$$

The hedge is initiated and time passes. On June 15, the 90-day T-bill yield has fallen to 10 percent, confirming the portfolio manager's fears. Consequently, the $1 million face value of 90-day T-bills is worth

$$\$975,000 = \$1,000,000 - 0.10 \times \$1,000,000 \times \frac{90}{360}$$

Table 5.13   A long hedge with T-bill futures

Date	Cash market	Futures market
December 15	A portfolio manager learns he will receive $970,000 in six months to invest in T-bills Market yield: 12% Expected face value of bills to purchase $1 million	The manager buys one T-bill futures contract to mature in six months Futures price: $970,000
June 15	Manager receives $970,000 to invest	The manager sells one T-bill futures contract maturing immediately
	Market yield: 10% $1 million face value of T-bills now costs $975,000	Futures yield: 10%
	Loss = −$5,000	Futures price: $975,000 Profit = $5,000
	Net wealth change = 0	

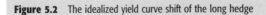

Figure 5.2   The idealized yield curve shift of the long hedge

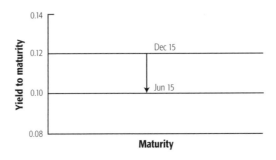

Just before the futures contract matures, the manager sells one June T-bill futures contract, making a profit of $5,000. But in the spot market, the cost of the $1 million face value of 90-day T-bills has risen from $970,000 to $975,000, generating a cash market loss of $5,000. However, the futures profit exactly offsets the cash market loss for a zero change in wealth. With the receipt of the $970,000 that was to be invested, plus the $5,000 futures profit, the original plan may be executed, and the portfolio manager purchases $1 million face value in 90-day T-bills.

By design, this example is extremely artificial in order to illustrate the long hedge. Notice that the yield curve is flat at the outset, and only its level changes. Figure 5.2 portrays the kind of yield curve shift that was assumed. This idealized yield curve shift is unlikely to occur. Moreover, the assumption of a flat yield curve plays a crucial role in accounting for the simplicity of this example. If the yield curve is flat, spot and forward rates are identical. When one "locks in" some rate via futures trading, it is necessarily a forward rate that is locked in, as the next example shows. We also assumed that the portfolio manager received exactly the right amount of funds at exactly the right time to purchase $1 million of T-bills. These unrealistic assumptions are gradually relaxed in the following examples.

A short hedge example

Interest rate futures can be used to hedge a variety of risks posed by fluctuating interest rates. For example, hedges constructed with interest rate futures are useful for banks facing an interest-sensitivity mismatch between their assets and liabilities. Suppose that in March a bank customer demands a $1 million fixed-rate loan for nine months. The problem the bank faces is estimating its cost of funds over the life of the loan. If the bank could issue a nine-month $1 million dollar fixed-rate certificate of deposit (CD), it would have a precise match between the interest sensitivity of its asset (the loan) and the interest sensitivity of its liability (the CD). However, suppose the bank can only lock in its funding for six months at 3.00 percent. To fund the loan for the entire nine months, the bank will need to issue a $1 million three-month CD in September at the interest rate prevailing at that time. The September Eurodollar futures yield quoted in March is 3.5 percent. This yield provides the bank with the market's assessment of the three-month CD rates that will prevail in September. This assessment is helpful to the bank in determining an expected cost of funds over the life of the loan, but still leaves the bank vulnerable to rates rising above the expected rate.

Table 5.14 Hedging a bank's cost of funds using interest rate futures

Date	Cash market	Futures market
March	Bank makes nine-month fixed rate loan financed by a six-month CD at 3.0% and rolled over for three months at an expected rate of 3.5%	Establish a short position in SEP Eurodollar futures at 96.5 reflecting a 3.5% futures yield
September	The three-month LIBOR is now at 4.5%; the bank's cost of funds are 1% above its expected cost of funds of 3.5%; the additional cost equals $2,500—i.e., 90/360 × 0.01 × $1 million	Offset one SEP Eurodollar futures contract at 95.5 reflecting a 4.5% futures yield; this produces a profit of $2,500—i.e., 100 basis points × $25 per basis point × one contract
	Total additional cost of funds: $2,500	Futures profit: $2,500
	Net interest expense after hedge: 0	

To hedge this risk, the bank can establish a short position in SEP Eurodollar futures in March. In constructing the hedge, the bank will use a single futures contract. If rates rise unexpectedly, the Eurodollar futures price will fall and the bank's short position will become more valuable. Suppose, in fact, that the three-month rate rises to 4.5 percent in September. We know that the Eurodollar futures yield must converge to the prevailing three-month rate at contract expiration. This means that the bank's Eurodollar futures position has gained $2,500. This amount precisely offsets the bank's increase in its cost of funds over and above the 3.5 percent rate it expected to prevail at the time the bank loan was priced and the hedge was constructed. Table 5.14 displays the cash flows associated with the construction of this hedge. Of course, by hedging, the bank has given up the opportunity to make extra money if its cost of funds had fallen unexpectedly. However, by hedging, and locking in its cost of funds, the bank is able to price the nine-month fixed rate loan with certainty and lock in an acceptable profit.

The cross-hedge

The financial vice-president of a large manufacturing firm has decided to issue $1 billion worth of 90-day commercial paper in three months. The outstanding 90-day commercial paper of the firm yields 17 percent, or 2 percent above the current 90-day T-bill rate of 15 percent. Fearing that rates might rise, the vice-president decides to hedge against the risk of increasing yields by entering the interest rate futures market.

He decides to hedge the firm's commercial paper in the T-bill futures market, since rates on commercial paper and T-bills tend to be highly correlated. Since one type of instrument is hedged with another, this hedge becomes a "cross-hedge." In general, a cross-hedge occurs when the hedged and hedging instruments differ with respect to (1) risk level, (2) coupon, (3) maturity, or (4) the time span covered by the instrument being hedged and the instrument deliverable against the futures contract. This means that the vast majority of all hedges in the interest rate futures markets are cross-hedges. The hedge contemplated by the vice-president is a cross-hedge, because the commercial paper and the T-bill differ in risk. Assuming that the commercial paper is to be issued in 90 days (and that the T-bill futures contract matures at the same time) ensures that the commercial paper and the T-bill delivered on the futures contract cover the same time span.

Table 5.15   A cross-hedge between T-bill futures and commercial paper

Time	Cash market	Futures market
$t = 0$	The financial vice-president plans to sell 90-day commercial paper in three months in the amount of $1 billion, at an expected yield of 17%, which should net the firm $957.5 million	The vice-president sells 1,000 T-bill futures contracts to mature in three months with a futures yield of 16%, a futures price per contract of $960,000, and a total futures price of $960 million
$t = 3$ months	The spot commercial paper rate is now 18%, the usual 2% above the spot T-bill rate; consequently, the sale of the $1 billion of commercial paper nets $955 million, not the expected $957.5 million	The T-bill futures contract is about to mature, so the T-bill futures rate = spot rate = 16%; the futures price is still $960,000 per contract, so there is no gain or loss
	Opportunity loss = ?	Gain/loss = 0
	Net wealth change = ?	

Therefore, the vice-president decides to sell 1,000 T-bill futures contracts to mature in three months. Table 5.15 shows the transactions. The futures price is $960,000, implying a futures yield of 16 percent. Notice that this differs by 1 percent from the current 90-day T-bill yield of 15 percent. Time passes, and in three months the futures yield has not changed, remaining at 16 percent. However, since the futures contract is about to mature, the spot and futures rates are now equal. Consequently, the trade incurs no gain or loss on the futures contract.

In the cash market, the 90-day commercial paper spot rate at the end of the hedging period has become 18 percent, not the 17 percent that was the original 90-day spot rate at the initiation date of the hedge. Since the vice-president thought he was "locking in" the 17 percent spot rate, he expected to receive $957.5 million for the commercial paper issue. But the commercial paper rate at the time of issue is 18 percent, so the firm receives only $955 million. This appears to be a loss in the cash market of $2.5 million. However, this is only appearance. The vice-president may have thought that he was locking in the prevailing spot rate of 17 percent at the time the hedge was initiated, but such a belief was unwarranted. By hedging the issuance of the commercial paper, the vice-president should have expected to lock in the three-month forward rate for 90-day commercial paper.

Figure 5.3 clarifies these relationships by presenting yield curves for T-bills and commercial paper based on bank discount yields. The yield curves are consistent with the data of the preceding discussion. At the outset of the hedge, the 90-day spot T-bill rate is 0.15, and the commercial paper rate equals 0.17. The 180-day spot rates are 0.152 and 0.171174 for T-bills and commercial paper, respectively. The shape of the yield curves gives sufficient information to calculate the forward, and hence the futures, rates for the time span covering the period from day 90 to day 180.

For the spot 90-day T-bill with a bank discount rate of 0.15, the price of a $1 million face value T-bill is $962,500. The growth in this investment over the 90-day horizon is 1.038961 = $1,000,000/$962,500. For the 180-day T-bill with a bank discount rate of 15.20 percent, the price is $924,000, and the growth would be 1.082251. The futures yield to cover from day 90

Figure 5.3   Hypothetical yield curves for T-bills and commercial paper

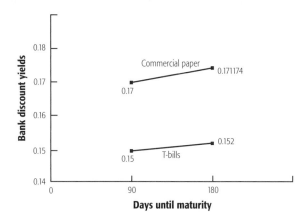

to 180 has been specified to be 16.00 percent, a price of $960,000 and an implied growth of 1.041667 = $1,000,000/$960,000. These values are mutually consistent because 1.082251 = 1.038961 × 1.041667.

Similarly, for the 90-day commercial paper with a rate of 0.17, the price of a $1 million face value instrument would be $957,500 with a growth of 1.044386 = $1,000,000/$957,500. For the 180-day commercial paper, the discount rate is 0.171174. This implies a price of $914,413 and a growth of 1.093598 = $1,000,000/$914,413. These commercial paper rates of 0.17 for the 90-day paper and 0.171174 for 180-day paper imply a forward bank discount rate of 0.18 for 90-day commercial paper for the period from day 90 to 180. For 90-day paper at a bank discount rate of 0.18, the price of a $1 million instrument is $955,000, which will grow by a factor of 1.047120 = $1,000,000/$955,000 over its life. These values are mutually consistent because 1.093598 = 1.044386 × 1.047120.

These forward rates, evaluated at time $t = 0$, are the expected future bank discount rates to prevail on three-month T-bills and commercial paper beginning in three months. Consequently, the implied yield on the commercial paper of this example is 0.18, not the 0.17 that the vice-president attempted to lock in.

Now, it is possible to understand exactly why the vice-president was unable to lock in 17 percent, even though it was the spot rate prevailing at the time the hedge was initiated. The reason is simply this: For the time period over which the commercial paper was to be issued (from three to six months into the future), the market believed that the 90-day commercial paper rate would be 18 percent in three months. The futures price and yield reflected this belief. Although the vice-president desired a 17 percent rate, the market's expected rate was 18 percent, and by entering the futures contract the vice-president locked in the 18 percent rate. Therefore, the opportunity loss of Table 5.15 is only apparent. The vice-president's expectation of issuing the commercial paper at 17 percent was completely unwarranted. Instead, the vice-president should have expected to issue the commercial paper at the market's expected bank discount rate of 18 percent. Then he would have expected to net $955,000,000 for the firm, which is exactly what happened in the example.

A cross-hedge with faulty expectations

In the preceding example, the vice-president misunderstood the nature of the futures market. If the vice-president had understood everything correctly, Table 5.15 would have shown a zero total wealth change. Thus far, all of the examples have been of perfect hedges—hedges leaving total wealth unchanged. Sometimes, however, even when the hedge is properly initiated with the appropriate expectations, those expectations can turn out to be false. In such cases, the hedge will not be perfect; total wealth will either increase or decrease.

To illustrate this possibility, assume the same basic hedging problem as in the cross-hedge example. In particular, assume that the vice-president wishes to hedge the same issuance of commercial paper and that the yield curves are as shown in Figure 5.3. The actions and expectations of the vice-president, shown in Table 5.16, are exactly correct. The yield curve implies that, in 90 days, the 90-day T-bill and commercial paper rates will stand at 16 and 18 percent, respectively.

However, in this instance, assume that these expectations formed are incorrect. During the 90-day period before the commercial paper was issued, the market came to view the commercial paper as being riskier than was previously thought, and the economy experienced a higher rate of inflation than anticipated. Historically, assume that the yield premium of commercial paper had been 2 percent above the T-bill rate, consistent with Figure 5.3. But now, due to the perception of increased risk for commercial paper, the yield differential widens to 2.25 percent. Then assume that in three months the T-bill rate happens to be 16.25 percent, rising due to greater than anticipated inflation. Under these assumptions, the commercial paper rate is 18.5 percent, not the originally expected 18 percent.

As Table 5.16 reveals, the total gain on the futures position is $625,000. Due to the commercial paper rate being 18.5 percent, and not the originally anticipated 18 percent, there is a loss on the commercial paper of −$1.25 million. Since the error in expectation was 0.5 percent on the commercial paper, but only 0.25 percent on the T-bills, the gain on the futures does not

---

Table 5.16   A cross-hedge with faulty expectations

Time	Cash market	Futures market
$t = 0$	The financial vice-president decides to sell 90-day commercial paper in three months in the amount of $1 billion, at an expected yield of 18%, which should net the firm $955 million	The vice-president sells 1,000 T-bill futures contracts to mature in three months, with a futures yield of 16%, a futures price per contract of $960,000, and a total futures price of $960 million
$t = 3$ months	The spot commercial paper rate was expected to be 18% at this time, but is really 18.5%; consequently, the sale of the $1 billion of commercial paper nets $953.75 million, not the expected $955 million	The T-bill futures contract is about to mature, so the T-bill futures rate = spot rate = 0.1625; the futures price is $959,375 per contract, so there is a gain per contract of $625, and a total gain on the 1,000 contracts of $625,000
	Opportunity loss = −$1,250,000	Gain = +$625,000
	Net wealth change = −$625,000	

offset the total loss of the commercial paper. This results in a net wealth change of −$625,000. However, the loss would have been −$1.25 million without the futures hedge.

In general, real-world hedges will not be perfect. Rates on both sides of the hedge tend to move in the same direction, but by uncertain amounts. On occasion, rates can even move in opposite directions, generating enormous gains or losses. In the example just discussed, assume that the commercial paper rate turned out to be 18.5 percent, but that the T-bill rate was 15.75 percent—below the expected 16 percent. In this case, the loss on the commercial paper would be −$1.25 million, and the loss on the futures would be −$625,000 for a total loss of −$1.875 million, because the firm loses on both sides of the hedge. Such an outcome is unlikely, but it is a possible result, of which hedgers should be aware.

Conclusion

In this chapter, we have considered the contract specifications of the most important interest rate futures contracts. We have explored the proper pricing of futures contracts using the cost-of-carry framework and have seen how interest rate futures are related to the term structure of interest rates.

We have noted some difficulties in applying the simplest form of the cost-of-carry relationship to interest rate futures, particularly to the T-bond futures contract. The breakdown of the arbitrage conditions gives expectations of future interest rates a role in the determination of interest rate futures prices.

If interest rate futures prices are not determined by strict cost-of-carry relationships, there may be ample reward to various speculative strategies. The chapter concluded by exploring some simple speculative strategies, as well as more complex relationships involving several instruments. In the next chapter, we continue our exploration of interest rate futures by considering the pricing performance and the hedging use of interest rate futures.

Exercises

1   A 90-day T-bill has a discount yield of 8.75 percent. What is the price of a $1 million face value bill?

2   The IMM index stands as 88.70. What is the discount yield? If you buy a T-bill futures at that index value and the index becomes 88.90, what is your gain or loss?

3   What is the difference between position day and first position day?

4   A $1 million face value T-bond has an annual coupon rate of 9.5 percent and paid its last coupon 48 days ago. What is the accrued interest on the bond?

5   What conditions are necessary for the conversion factors on the CBOT T-bond contract to create favorable conditions for delivering one bond instead of another?

6   The JUN T-bill futures IMM index value is 92.80, while the SEP has a value of 93.00. What is the implied percentage cost of carry to cover the period from June to September?

7   A spot 180-day T-bill has a discount yield of 9.5 percent. If the bank discount rate for the next three months is 9.2 percent, what is the price of a futures contract that expires in three months?

8   For the next three futures expirations, you observe the following Eurodollar quotations:

MAR	92.00
JUN	91.80
SEP	91.65

What shape does the yield curve have? Explain.

9   Assume that the prices in the preceding problem pertain to T-bill futures and the MAR contract expires today. What should be the spot price of a 180-day T-bill?

10   The cheapest-to-deliver T-bond is a 10 percent bond that paid its coupon 87 days ago and it is priced at 105–16. The conversion factor of the bond is 1.0900. The nearby T-bond futures expires in 50 days and the current price is 98–00. If you can borrow or lend to finance a T-bond for a total interest outlay of 2 percent over this period, how would you transact? What if you could borrow or lend for the period at a total interest cost of 3 percent? What if you could borrow for the period at a total interest cost of 3 percent and earn 2 percent on an investment over the whole period? Explain.

11 You expect a steepening yield curve over the next few months, but you are not sure whether the level of rates will increase or decrease. Explain two different ways you can trade to profit if you are correct.

12 The Canadian invasion of Alaska has financial markets in turmoil. You expect the crisis to worsen more than other traders suspect. How could you trade short-term interest rate futures to profit if you are correct? Explain.

13 You believe that the yield curve is strongly upward sloping and that yields are at very high levels. How would you use interest rate futures to hedge a prospective investment of funds that you will receive in nine months? If you faced a major borrowing in nine months, how would you use futures?

14 The spot rate of interest on a corporate bond is 11 percent, and the yield curve is sharply upward sloping. The yield on the T-bond futures that is just about to expire is 8 percent, but the yield for the futures contract that expires in six months is 8.75 percent. (You are convinced that this difference is independent of any difference in the cheapest-to-deliver bonds for the two contracts.) In these circumstances, a corporate finance officer wants to lock in the current spot rate of 11 percent on a corporate bond that her firm plans to offer in six months. What advice would you give her?

15 Helen Jaspers was sitting at her trading desk watching the T-bill spot and futures market prices. Her firm was very active in the T-bill market, and she was eager to make a trade. The quote on the T-bill having 120 days from settlement to maturity was 4.90 percent discount yield. This bill could be used for the September 20 delivery on the September T-bill futures contract, which was trading at 95.15. The quote on the T-bill maturing September 20, having 29 days between settlement and maturity, was 4.70 percent discount yield.

A Compute the T-bill and futures prices per dollar of face value.
B Compute the implied repo rate. Could the implied repo rate be used to tell Helen where arbitrage profits are possible? If so, how?
C What would be the arbitrage profit from a $1 million transaction?

16 Angela Vickers has the responsibility of managing Seminole Industries' short-term capital position. In three weeks, Seminole will have a cash inflow that will be rolled over into a $1 million 90-day T-bill. There is a T-bill futures contract that calls for delivery at the same time as the anticipated cash inflow.

It is trading at 94.75. There have been signs that the financial markets are calming and that interest rates might be falling.

A What type of hedge might Angela employ?
B Three weeks into the future, interest rates are actually higher. The 90-day T-bill discount yield is 6.00 percent. Calculate Seminole's net wealth change if the position is left unhedged.
C Calculate Seminole's net wealth change if the position is hedged.
D Was the hedge a mistake?

17 Fred Ferrell works for ABC Investments. As part of ABC's investment strategy, Fred is charged with liquidating $20 million of ABC's T-bill portfolio in two months. Fred has identified $20 million of T-bills that would be deliverable against the March T-bill futures contract at the time of liquidation. The price of the futures contract is 94.50. Fred is losing sleep at night over concerns about future economic uncertainty that could lead to a rise in interest rates.

A What action can Fred take to reduce ABC's exposure to interest rate risk?
B At the time of liquidation, the price of the 90-day T-bill has risen to 5.25 percent discount yield. Compute the change in ABC's net wealth that would have occurred if Fred had failed to hedge the position.
C Compute the change in ABC's net wealth that would have occurred assuming that Fred had hedged the position.

18 Alex Brown is a financial analyst for B.I.G. Industries. He has been given responsibility for handling the details of refinancing a $500 million long-term debt issue that will be rolled over in May (five months from today). The new 8 percent, 30-year debt, with a face value of $500 million, is anticipated to have a 75-basis-point default risk premium over the yield on the 30-year T-bond. The 30-year T-bond is currently trading at 5.62 percent. Alex sees this risk premium as typical for corporate debt of a quality similar to B.I.G.'s debt. Alex looks at the June T-bond and notices that it is trading at 123–25. He is concerned that changing interest rates between now and May could have a negative impact on the refinancing cash flow.

A Assuming no interest rate changes, what are B.I.G.'s anticipated proceeds from refinancing?
B What can Alex do to reduce the refinancing risks faced by B.I.G. Industries?

C   At the time of refinancing, the 30-year T-bond yield is 5.80 percent, the T-bond futures price is 121–09, and B.I.G.'s new debt issue is priced to yield 6.75 percent. Compute the realized proceeds from the refinancing.

D   Assuming that Alex sold $500 million in T-bond futures at 123–25 to hedge the refinancing and liquidated the futures position when the refinancing took place, find the profit from the futures trade, and evaluate the net wealth change due to the change in the refinancing rate and the futures trade.

E   Discuss possible reasons why the net wealth change is not zero.

Notes

1   The CBOT also trades a successful 30-day Federal Funds futures contract, a short-term interest rate contract.

2   The best way to secure a regular source of conversion factors, as well as much other useful information, is to visit the CBOT's web site (www.cbot.com).

3   For studies of this approach to pricing T-bill futures, see I. Kawaller and T. Koch, "Cash-and-Carry Trading and the Pricing of Treasury Bill Futures," *Journal of Futures Markets*, 4:2, 1984, pp. 115–23.

4   See the CME, "Market Perspectives," 5:1, February 1987, pp. 1–4. See also the CME, "The TED Spread," *Financial Strategy Paper*, 1987.

6

Interest Rate Futures: Refinements

Overview

Chapter 6 builds on the foundation of Chapter 5. Having already explored the fundamental features of interest rate futures, we now turn to refining our understanding of these important markets. Thus, Chapter 6 considers more closely some of the same issues addressed in Chapter 5. In addition, we examine some new issues, such as the informational efficiency of the interest rate futures market.

The T-bond contract is perhaps the most important futures contract ever devised. It also happens to be one of the most complicated. Further, it has provided the conceptual basis for many important interest rate futures contracts that trade in markets around the world. We begin this chapter with a detailed analysis of the T-bond contract. This analysis lays the foundation for a richer understanding on how to apply interest rate futures to speculate and manage risk. Next, we consider the informational efficiency of the interest rate futures markets. A market is efficient with respect to some set of information if prices in the market fully reflect the information contained in that set. There have been many studies of informational efficiency for interest rate futures and we review the results of those studies.

In Chapter 5, we saw that interest rate futures should be full carry markets. However, this conclusion requires some qualifications. Taking the T-bond contract as a model, we analyze the special features of the contract and show how these features can make full carry difficult to measure. For example, seller's options have important implications for the theoretically correct futures price.

Many traders use interest rate futures to manage risk. The techniques for risk management are quite diverse and increasingly sophisticated. Essentially two different sets of techniques apply, depending upon the nature of the risk. Therefore, we consider applications for short-term interest rate futures first and then conclude the chapter by examining the applications of long-term interest rate futures.

The T-bond futures contract in detail

In Chapter 5, we explored the basic features of the T-bond futures contract. In this section, we first review what we know about the contract from Chapter 5. Then, we develop a more complete analysis of the contract. This procedure provides a richer understanding of the contract that helps us to understand how to use interest rate futures for speculation and risk management.

Review of the T-bond contract

In our discussion of the T-bond futures contract in Chapter 5, we noted that the contract calls for the delivery of $100,000 principal amount of U.S. Treasury bonds that have at least 15 years to maturity or their first call date at the time of delivery. We noted that the delivery procedure stretched over three business days, with actual delivery occurring on the third day, which could be any business day of the delivery month.

For any particular futures contract expiration, a variety of bonds will be deliverable. These bonds can be of any coupon rate and any maturity above the minimum. In many cases, the bonds that are deliverable will include some recently issued Treasury bonds that may not even have existed when the contract was first listed for trading.

Without some adjustment, one of these bonds is likely to be much better to deliver than the others. For example, if the contract allowed the delivery of any bond without a price adjustment, every trader would want to deliver the cheapest bond. To make the variety of bonds permitted for delivery comparable, the Chicago Board of Trade (CBOT) uses a system of conversion factors. Essentially, the conversion factor for a given bond is found by assuming that the bond has a face value of $1 and discounting all of the bond's cash flows at 6 percent. While the conversion factors eliminate most of the inequalities between various bonds, they do not do a complete job. As a consequence, there is still a particular bond that is cheapest to deliver among the bonds permitted for delivery.

As another complication, we noted in Chapter 5 that the seller of the T-bond futures possesses several options. For example, the seller chooses which bond to deliver and which day to make delivery. These and other options have significant value, as we explore later in this chapter.

The cheapest-to-deliver bond

In this section, we show how to determine which bond will be cheapest to deliver, and we show how to find the exact invoice amount, including all the nuances in computing accrued interest. First, we analyze the cheapest-to-deliver bond when some time remains before expiration, but there will be no coupon payment before the expiration date. Second, we consider the case when a coupon payment intervenes between the beginning of the holding period and the futures expiration.

The case of no intervening coupons

Assume that today is Tuesday, March 14, 2006, and the MAR 06 T-bond futures settlement price is 107–16. A short trader decides today to deliver against the MAR 06 futures immediately. She selects today, March 14, as the Position Day, so actual delivery will occur on March 16, 2006. She is considering two bonds and wants to know exactly how much she will receive for each and which she should deliver. The two bonds are as follows:

Maturity	Coupon	Price	MAR 06 CF
November 15, 2028	5.25	93–15	0.9081
November 15, 2021	8.00	127–03	1.2000

We want to determine the exact invoice amount for each bond and which bond is cheapest to deliver.

To answer these questions, we first compute the cash price and invoice amounts for $100,000 face value of these bonds. The total price depends upon the quoted price plus the accrued interest. In Chapter 5, we saw that a bond accrues interest for each day based on the coupon rate and the principal amount. In the market, the actual calculation also depends upon the number of days in a half-year, as shown in Table 6.1.

Both bonds have the same coupon dates each year, May 15 and November 15, so both are on the May–November cycle. As shown in Table 6.1, for both a regular and a leap year, there are 181 days in the November–May half-year. From November 15 to March 14 is 119 days. Therefore, the accrued interest for each bond is as follows:

5.25 percent bond: AI = (119/181) × 0.5 × 0.0525 × $100,000 = $1,725.83
8.00 percent bond: AI = (119/181) × 0.5 × 0.08 × $100,000 = $2,629.83

Table 6.1 Days in half-years				
Interest period	Interest paid on 1st or 15th		Interest paid on last day	
	Regular year	Leap year	Regular year	Leap year
January–July	181	182	181	182
February–August	181	182	184	184
March–September	184	184	183	183
April–October	183	183	184	184
May–November	184	184	183	183
June–December	183	183	184	184
July–January	184	184	184	184
August–February	184	184	181	182
September–March	181	182	182	183
October–April	182	183	181	182
November–May	181	182	182	183
December–June	182	183	181	182
One year (any two consecutive half-years)	365	366	365	366

Source: Treasury Circular No. 300, 4th Rev.

where AI is the accrued interest. From Chapter 5,

$$0.9921 = \frac{1}{(1.1)^{30/360}}$$

where DFP is the decimal futures price (e.g., 96–16 = 0.965), CF is the conversion factor, and AI is the accrued interest.

With a March 14 futures settlement price on the MAR 06 futures of 107–16, the invoice amounts are as follows:

5.25 percent bond: $1.0750 \times \$100,000 \times 0.9081 + \$1,725.83 = \$99,346.58$
8.00 percent bond: $1.0750 \times \$100,000 \times 1.2000 + \$2,629.83 = \$131,629.80$

Thus, the two bonds have radically different invoice amounts; the 8.00 percent bond has an invoice amount that is 33 percent greater than that of the 5.25 percent bond.

To complete delivery, the short trader must deliver one bond and receive the invoice amount. Which should she deliver? The decision depends upon the difference between the invoice amount and the cash market price, which is the profit from delivery. The bond that is most profitable to deliver is the cheapest-to-deliver bond. In other words, the short trader will select the bond to deliver to maximize profit. For a particular bond i, the profit π_i is as follows:

$$\pi_i = \text{invoice amount} - (P_i + AI_i) = DFP_i \times \$100,000 \times CF_i + AI_i - (P_i + AI_i)$$

Because the AI is included in the invoice amount and subtracted as a payment being made by surrendering the bond, the profit simplifies to the following:

$$\pi_i = DFP_i \times \$100,000 \times CF_i - P_i \tag{6.1}$$

To find the cheapest-to-deliver bond, the short trader will compute the profitability for each deliverable bond. The bond with the maximum profit is the cheapest to deliver.[1] For the two bonds, the profit from delivery is as follows:

For the 5.25 percent bond: $\pi = 1.0750 \times \$100,000 \times 0.9081 - \$93,468.75 = \$4,152.00$
For the 8.00 percent bond: $\pi = 1.0750 \times \$100,000 \times 1.2000 - \$127,093.75 = \$1,906.25$

where \$93,468.75 is the decimal form of the price for the 5.25 percent bond quoted above as 93–15 and \$127,093.75 is the decimal form of the price for the 8 percent bond quoted above as 127–03. The profit from delivering the 5.25 percent bond is greater, so it is cheaper to deliver than the 8.00 percent bond. For the March 2006 futures, we saw in Chapter 5 that there were 21 bonds eligible for delivery as of March 2006. The cheapest-to-deliver bond is the one with the greatest profit from delivery, as computed using the method just illustrated.

Which bond is cheaper to deliver depends on the level of interest rates. As a general rule, when interest rates are below 6 percent, there is an incentive to deliver short-maturity/high-coupon bonds. When interest rates exceed 6 percent, there is an incentive to deliver long-maturity/low-coupon bonds. Expressing the same idea in terms of duration, a trader should deliver low-duration bonds when interest rates are below 6 percent and high-duration bonds when interest rates are above 6 percent.

The case of intervening coupons

So far, we have dealt with the cheapest to deliver bond when there are no coupon payments to consider. We now consider which bond is cheapest to deliver when a bond pays a coupon between the beginning of the cash-and-carry holding period and the futures expiration. To find the cheapest-to-deliver bond before expiration, we apply the cash-and-carry strategy. The bond with the greatest profit at delivery from following the cash-and-carry strategy will be the cheapest to deliver.

We assume that a trader buys a bond today and carries the bond to delivery. We compare the cash flows associated with that carry, relative to the invoice amount based on today's futures price. Of course, we cannot know the future cash flows with certainty. In particular, the futures price might change. However, we make our computation assuming that interest rates and futures prices remain constant. For this analysis, we must consider the estimated invoice amount plus our estimate of the cash flows associated with carrying the bond to delivery.

The estimated invoice amount depends on three factors:

(1) Today's quoted futures price.
(2) The conversion factor for the bond we plan to deliver.
(3) The accrued interest on the bond at the expiration date.

Acquiring and carrying a bond to delivery involves three cash flows as well:

(1) Pay today the quoted price plus accrued interest.
(2) Finance the bond from today until expiration.
(3) Receive and invest any coupons paid between today and expiration.

We can bring all of these factors together by considering the time line in Figure 6.1.

Today, we purchase a bond and finance it until delivery. Between today and delivery, we receive and invest a coupon. At delivery, we surrender the bond and receive the invoice amount. Thus, we have the following:

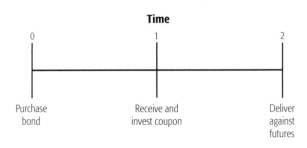

Figure 6.1   The time line for cash-and-carry arbitrage

estimated invoice amount = $\text{DFP}_0 \times \$100{,}000 \times \text{CF} + \text{AI}_2$

estimated future value of the delivered bond = $(P_0 + \text{AI}_0)(1 + C_{0,2}) - \text{COUP}_1(1 + C_{1,2})$

where P_0 is the quoted price of the bond today, $t = 0$; AI_0 is the accrued interest as of today, $t = 0$; $C_{0,2}$ is the interest factor for $t = 0$ to expiration at $t = 2$; COUP_1 is the coupon that will be received before delivery at $t = 1$; $C_{1,2}$ is the interest factor from $t = 1$ to $t = 2$; DFP_0 is the decimal futures price today, $t = 0$; CF is the conversion factor for a particular bond and the specified futures expiration; and AI_2 is the accrued interest at $t = 2$. The short trader will maximize profit by choosing to deliver the cheapest-to-deliver bond. For bond i, the expected profit from delivery is the estimated invoice amount less the estimated value of what will be delivered:

$$\pi = \text{DFP}_0 \times \$100{,}000 \times \text{CF} + \text{AI}_2 - \{(P_0 + \text{AI}_0)(1 + C_{0,2}) - \text{COUP}_1(1 + C_{1,2})\} \qquad (6.2)$$

As an illustration, assume that today is March 14, 2006, and we want to find the cheapest-to-deliver bond for the JUN 06 futures expiration. We illustrate the computation with the two bonds we have already considered.

Maturity	Coupon (%)	Price	JUN 06 CF
November 15, 2028	5.25	93–15	0.9084
November 15, 2021	8.00	127–03	1.1979

We assume that the bonds will be financed and the coupons invested at the repo rate of 7 percent simple interest and that the settlement price of the JUN 06 T-bond futures on March 14 is 106–23. We assume a \$100,000 face value and a target delivery date of June 30, 2006. Figure 6.2 shows the relevant dates and the number of days between them.

Both bonds paid their last coupons on November 15, 2005, 119 days ago. We have already seen that the accrued interest as of today (March 14, 2006) is \$1,725.83 for the 5.25 percent bond and \$2,629.83 for the 8.00 percent bond. These are the AI_0 values in Equation 6.2. The amount to be financed for each bond is as follows:

For the 5.25 percent bond: $P_0 + \text{AI}_0 = \$93{,}468.75 + \$1{,}725.83 = \$95{,}194.58$

For the 8.00 percent bond: $P_0 + \text{AI}_0 = \$127{,}093.75 + \$2{,}629.83 = \$129{,}723.58$

Figure 6.2 Dates for cash-and-carry arbitrage

Next, we consider the accrued interest that will accumulate from the next coupon date, May 15, 2006, to the planned delivery date, June 30, 2006. From May 15, 2006 to June 30, 2006 is 46 days in a half-year of 184 days. Therefore, the bonds will have the following accrued interest on June 30, 2006:

For the 5.25 percent bond: $AI_2 = (46/184) \times 0.5 \times 0.0525 \times \$100{,}000 = \$656.25$
For the 8.00 percent bond: $AI_2 = (46/184) \times 0.5 \times 0.08 \times \$100{,}000 = \$1{,}000.00$

With a futures price of 106–23 on March 14, 2006, $DFP_0 = 1.0671875$. The estimated invoice amounts for the two bonds are as follows:

For the 5.25 percent bond: $1.0671875 \times \$100{,}000 \times 0.9084 + \$656.25 = \$97{,}599.56$
For the 8.00 percent bond: $1.0671875 \times \$100{,}000 \times 1.1979 + \$1{,}000.00 = \$128{,}838.39$

Next, we compute the financing rates. On March 14, 108 days remain until the projected delivery date, so $C_{0,2} = 0.07 \times (108/360) = 0.0210$. From May 15, 2006 until June 30, 2006 is 46 days, so $C_{1,2} = 0.07 \times (46/360) = 0.008944$. Finally, we are in a position to compute the profits from delivery. Table 6.2 summarizes all of these intermediate calculations.

Using the values in Table 6.2, we compute the expected profit from delivering each bond. For the 5.25 percent bond:

$$\begin{aligned} \pi &= 1.06718750 \times \$100{,}000 \times 0.9084 + \$656.25 \\ &\quad - [(\$93{,}468.75 + \$1{,}725.83) \times 1.0210 - \$2{,}625 \times 1.008944] \\ &= \$3{,}054.37 \end{aligned}$$

Table 6.2 Data for cheapest-to-deliver bonds

Bond	P_0	AI_0	$C_{0,2}$	$C_{1,2}$	DFP_0	CF (JUN 06)	AI_2
5.25%	$93,468.75	$1,725.83	0.0210	0.008944	1.0671875	0.9084	$656.25
8.00%	$127,093.75	$2,629.83	0.0210	0.008944	1.0671875	1.1979	$1,000.00

For the 8.00 percent bond:

$$\pi = 1.06718750 \times \$100,000 \times 1.1979 + \$1,000.00$$
$$- [(\$127,093.75 + \$2,629.83) \times 1.0210 - \$4,000 \times 1.008944]$$
$$= \$426.39$$

For the 5.25 percent bond, the expected profit from delivery is \$3,054.37, but delivering the 8.00 percent bond generates only \$426.39. Therefore, the 5.25 percent bond is cheaper to deliver.

The cheapest-to-deliver bond and the implied repo rate

We can also analyze the same situation using the implied repo rate. Here, the implied repo rate for the given period equals the net cash flow at delivery divided by the net cash flow when the carry starts:

$$\text{implied repo rate} = \frac{\text{net cash flow over horizon}}{\text{net cash flow at inception}}$$

The numerator consists of cash inflows of the invoice amount, plus the future value of the coupons at the time of delivery, less the cost of acquiring the bond initially. The denominator consists of the cost of buying the bond. Therefore, in terms of our notation:

$$\text{implied repo rate} = \frac{\text{DFP}_0 \times \$100,000 \times \text{CF} + \text{AI}_2 + \text{COUP}_1(1 + C_{1,2}) - (P_0 + \text{AI}_0)}{(P_0 + \text{AI}_0)}$$

For the 5.25 percent bond, we have the following:

implied repo rate =

$$\frac{1.0671875 \times \$100,000 \times 0.9084 + \$656.25 + \$2,625 \times 1.008944 - (\$93,468.75 + \$1,725.83)}{\$93,468.75 + \$1,725.83}$$

$$= 0.053089$$

For the 8.00 percent bond:

implied repo rate =

$$\frac{1.067185 \times \$100,000 \times 1.1979 + \$1,000.00 + \$4,000 \times 1.008944 - (\$127,093.75 + \$2,629.93)}{\$127,093.75 + \$2,629.83}$$

$$= 0.024287$$

Annualizing these rates, we have, for the 5.25 percent bond, $0.053089 \times (360/108) = 17.6964$ percent and, for the 8.00 percent bond, $0.024287 \times (360/108) = 8.0956$ percent. Thus, the low-coupon 5.25 percent bond has a higher implied repo rate, suggesting that this bond is better than the 8.00 percent bond to carry to delivery. From this example, we can draw the following rule about the cheapest-to-deliver bond before expiration: the cheapest-to-deliver bond has the highest implied repo rate in a cash-and-carry strategy.

Table 6.3 Transactions showing implied repo rates

March 14, 2006
Borrow $129,723.58 for 108 days at an implied repo rate of 8.0956%
Buy $100,000 face value of 8.00 T-bonds maturing on November 15, 2021, for a total price of
$129,723.58, including accrued interest
Sell one JUN 06 T-bond futures contract at the current price of 106–23

May 15, 2006
Receive a coupon payment of $4,000 and invest for 46 days at 7.00%

June 30, 2006 (assuming futures is still at 106–23)
Deliver the bond and receive an invoice amount of $128,838.39
From the invested coupon, receive $4,000 + $4,000 \times 0.07 \times (46/360) = $4,035.78
Repay debt: $129,723.58 + $129,723.58 \times 0.080956 \times (108/360) = $132,874.17

Net profit = $128,838.39 + $4,035.78 − $132,874.17 = 0

If the implied repo rate equals the borrowing rate, the cash-and-carry arbitrage transaction leaves a zero profit. To illustrate this principle, we focus on the 8.00 percent bond and the cash-and-carry transactions of Table 6.3. As the example of Table 6.3 shows, financing a cash-and-carry arbitrage at the implied repo rate yields a zero profit.

To summarize, we state some general rules about how to conduct arbitrage if the cost of funds varies from the implied repo rate. The transactions we have considered assumed that the futures price did not change and that markets were perfect. In particular, for the reverse cash-and-carry arbitrage, the assumption that the trader has full use of the short sale proceeds was critical. Subject to these restrictions, and the elaboration of the next section, the general rules hold:

(1) Cash-and-carry arbitrage nets a zero profit if the actual borrowing cost equals the implied repo rate.
(2) If the effective borrowing rate is less than the implied repo rate, one can earn an arbitrage profit by cash-and-carry arbitrage; that is, by buying the cash bond and selling the futures.
(3) If the effective borrowing rate exceeds the implied repo rate and if one can sell bonds short, then one can earn an arbitrage profit by reverse cash-and-carry arbitrage; that is, by selling the bond short, buying the futures, and covering the short position at the expiration of the futures.

Why they call it risk arbitrage

In this section, we add more realism to our analysis of arbitrage by considering the peculiarities of the T-bond futures contract in still greater detail. As we will show, market realities add a risk component to both the cash-and-carry and reverse cash-and-carry arbitrage. These complications take our arbitrage framework out of the realm of "academic arbitrage" and show why all arbitrage in the T-bond futures market is really "risk arbitrage." The sources of risk are different for the cash-and-carry and reverse cash-and-carry strategies, and the risks stem from three sources: intervening coupon payments that must face reinvestment, the use of conversion factors, and the options that the seller possesses. In this section, we consider the risks generated by the reinvestment problem and the use of conversion factors. We also treat the seller's options in a general way.

Frustrations to cash-and-carry arbitrage

A closer examination of Table 6.3 shows some potentially risky elements of the cash-and-carry arbitrage. First, the debt was financed at a constant rate throughout the 108-day carry period. Second, the trader was actually able to invest the coupon at the expected reinvestment rate of 7 percent. Third, the futures price did not change over the horizon. We consider each of these problems in turn.

Assume that the trader in Table 6.3 finances the acquisition of the T-bond with overnight repos. The overnight repo rate changes each day, so the financing cost could drift upward. With an increasing financing cost, the transactions of Table 6.3 will not end in a zero profit. Instead, they will give a loss. Therefore, the transactions in Table 6.3 are potentially risky, depending upon the financing rate for the bond. Second, assume that the bond is financed for the entire period at the implied repo rate of 8.0956 percent. Also assume that short-term rates drift lower, so that the coupon can only be invested at 6 percent, not the 7 percent shown in Table 6.3. Now, the reinvested coupons will only grow to $4,031, not the $4,036 shown in the table. Therefore, the changing rate will generate a loss. These two examples illustrate the risks that remain inherent in a supposedly riskless cash-and-carry strategy. We now turn to a greater danger, a change in the futures price that can affect the cash flows from the cash-and-carry strategy.

In the transactions of Table 6.3, we assumed that the futures price did not change over the life of the contract. With the given financing rates, the cash-and-carry transactions yielded a zero profit. Now let us assume that the financing of the bond and the investment of the coupon work out exactly as shown in Table 6.3. However, now we consider a drop in the futures price from 106–23 to 104–23 that occurs between the time the contract is initiated and the expiration time. Such a change in the futures price is entirely feasible, and we need to consider the effect of this changing price on the cash flows from the cash-and-carry strategy.

Table 6.4 presents the same transactions as the zero profit cash-and-carry transactions of Table 6.3. The only difference between the two tables results from a drop in the futures price from 106–23 to 104–23 over the life of the contract. With a futures expiration price of 104–23, the actual invoice amount is as follows:

$$\text{invoice amount} = 1.047188 \times \$100,000 \times 1.1979 + \$1000.00 = \$126,442.59$$

Table 6.4   Transactions showing implied repo rates

March 14, 2006
Borrow $129,723.58 for 108 days at an implied repo rate of 8.0956%
Buy $100,000 face value of 8.00 T-bonds maturing on November 15, 2021, for a total price of $129,723.58, including accrued interest
Sell one JUN 06 T-bond futures contract at the current price of 106–23

May 15, 2006
Receive a coupon payment of $4,000 and invest for 46 days at 7.00%

June 30, 2006 (assuming futures has fallen to 104–23)
From March 14 to June 30, the futures price has fallen from 106–23 to 104–23, generating cash inflows of $2,000
Deliver the bond and receive an invoice amount of $126,442.59
From the invested coupon, receive $4,000 + $4,000 × 0.07 × (46/360) = $4,035.78
Repay debt: $129,723.58 + $129,723.58 × 0.080956 × (108/360) = $132,874.17

Net profit = $2,000 + $126,442.59 + $4,035.78 − $132,874.17 = −$395.80

Table 6.5   Transactions showing implied repo rates

March 14, 2006
Sell short $100,000 face value of 8.00 T-bonds maturing on November 15, 2021, for a total price of $129,723.58, including accrued interest
Buy one JUN 06 T-bond futures contract at the current price of 106–23
Lend $129,723.58 for 108 days at an implied repo rate of 8.0956%

May 15, 2006
Borrow $4,000 for 46 days at 7 percent and make a coupon payment of $4,000

June 30, 2006 (assuming futures is still at 106–23)
Collect investment: $129,723.58 + $129,723.58 × 0.080956 × (108/360) = $132,874.17
Accept delivery of the bond and pay invoice amount of $128,838.39
Pay debt from funds borrowed to make coupon payment: $4,000 + $4,000 × 0.07 × (46/360) = $4,035.78

Net profit = $132,874.17 − $128,838.39 − $4,035.78 = 0

The drop in the futures price has generated daily resettlement cash inflows of $2,000 over the life of the contract. With the reduced invoice amount, however, the cash-and-carry transactions generate a loss. As the transactions show, the reason for the loss is that futures price fluctuations generate gains or losses on a $1 basis. For example, a two-point drop in the futures price generates a gain of $2,000 in this case. However, when the futures price changes by $1, the delivery value of the bond changes by $1 times the conversion factor, which exceeds 1.0 in our example. This makes it possible for the supposedly riskless transaction to generate a loss. The dropping futures price generates $2,000 in daily resettlement profits, but it reduces the invoice amount from $128,838.39 to $126,442.59, a drop of $2,395.80. Thus, the changing price generates a new profit of $2,000 and a new loss of $2,395.80, for a net loss of $395.80, the value in Table 6.4.

Frustrations to reverse cash-and-carry arbitrage

In reverse cash-and-carry transactions, a trader sells an underlying good short and buys a futures contract. The trader then invests the proceeds from the short sale, planning to take delivery on the futures and return the borrowed commodity. Table 6.5 shows the reverse cash-and-carry transactions that are the mirror image of Table 6.3. In Table 6.5, the transactions generate a zero profit. The profit must be zero, because the transactions are exact complements to the transactions in Table 6.3.

We now consider the risk elements inherent in the reverse cash-and-carry transactions. First, all of the same risk elements that plagued the cash-and-carry strategy apply to the reverse cash-and-carry strategy as well. The trader of Table 6.5 could have lost if she had been forced to invest the short sale proceeds at less than the implied repo rate. If she had been forced to pay more than 7 percent on the borrowings to pay the coupon, the transactions would have resulted in a loss. Finally, if futures prices had risen, she would have had daily resettlement inflows that were less than the rise in the invoice amount, and these would have generated losses as well.

In addition to these sources of risk that plague cash-and-carry and reverse cash-and-carry strategies alike, the reverse cash-and-carry strategy faces other special risks that stem from the seller's options. In Table 6.5, we made several implicit assumptions. We assumed that the short futures trader delivered on June 30, 2006, and that the short trader delivered exactly the same bond that the trader of Table 6.5 sold short.

From Chapter 5, we know that the short trader of a T-bond futures has several options associated with the delivery. First, the short trader holds a **quality option**—the option to choose which bond to deliver. In Chapter 5, we noted that there are typically more than 20 deliverable bonds. The short trader can deliver any of these bonds. Therefore, the reverse cash-and-carry trader cannot be sure that she will receive a particular bond in the delivery. If the delivered bond is not the same bond that she sold short, she must go into the market to buy the bond that will allow her to cover the short sale. Of course, this exposes her to the risk that the price of the 8.00 percent bond could have changed. The seller of a T-bond futures contract also possesses a second important option. The **timing option** is the seller's option to choose the day of delivery. From Chapter 5, we know that delivery can occur on any business day in the delivery month. Therefore, the reverse cash-and-carry trader cannot be sure that delivery will occur on a particular date. This also exposes the trader of Table 6.5 to risk, because she cannot know that the delivery will occur on June 30. In addition to the quality and timing options, the short trader also possesses some other highly specialized options that add to the risk of the reverse cash-and-carry transactions. These options make the reverse cash-and-carry transactions extremely risky. As we discuss in the next section, these options have an important impact on the pricing of T-bond futures.

Seller's options in T-bond futures

The structure of the T-bond futures contract gives the seller timing and quality options. The timing option arises from the seller's right to choose the time of delivery. The quality option stems from the seller's right to select which bond to deliver. Certain features of the T-bond futures contract confer both types of options on the seller. We have already seen that the seller's ability to choose the delivery day impedes the long trader's reverse cash-and-carry trading strategies because the long trader can never know when the short will choose to deliver. However, besides frustrating the long trader, the quality and timing options have specific value for the short trader.

While we may distinguish timing and quality options conceptually, they become entangled in the actual specification of the T-bond futures contract. The two main seller's options in the T-bond futures market are the **wildcard option** and the **end-of-the-month option**. In this section, we discuss these options and analyze their effects on the pricing of the T-bond contract and optimal trading strategies to exploit these options.

The wildcard option

In the T-bond futures market, the futures seller chooses the position day by notifying the exchange of an intention to deliver. The actual delivery takes place two business days later. For example, if today is Monday, June 13, the trader may notify the exchange of his intention to deliver and June 13 becomes the position day. Actual delivery occurs in two business days on Wednesday, June 15. By making June 13 the position day, the short seller determines that the settlement price on June 13 will be the settlement price used to determine the invoice amount.

Under the rules of the exchange, the settlement price is determined at 2 p.m. On position day, the short trader has until 8 p.m. Chicago time to notify the exchange of an intention to deliver. The day of notification becomes the position day, with the invoice amount being based on the settlement price that day. Therefore, the short trader has a window from 2 p.m. to 8 p.m. for good luck to strike. If interest rates jump between 2 p.m. and 8 p.m., the short trader can

Table 6.6   Bond data at 2 p.m. on June 13

Bond	Coupon rate	Price	Conversion factor	Yield	Profit from delivery
A: 30-year	0.05	86.16	0.8616	0.0600	0
B: 20-year	0.09	134.67	1.3467	0.0600	0

notify the exchange of an intention to deliver and secure the 2 p.m. settlement price on the futures. The trader can then deliver the bond that fell in price due to a jump in interest rates.

The **wildcard option** is the option for the seller to lock in the 2 p.m. price by announcing an intention to deliver anytime before 8 p.m. In fact, the seller possesses a series of wildcard options. For example, on first position day, the second-to-last business day of the month preceding expiration, the seller has the wildcard option. If bond prices fall between 2 p.m. and 8 p.m. that day, the seller can announce an intention to deliver and capture the 2 p.m. price. If nothing happens between 2 p.m. and 8 p.m., the seller need not announce any intention to deliver. Instead, the seller can merely wait until the next day, hoping that something happens between 2 p.m. and 8 p.m. to cause a drop in bond prices. The seller can continue to play this game until the third-to-last business day of the month, which is the last position day. In buying T-bond futures, the long trader has conferred an option to the seller, and the long trader stands at risk each day. The value of the wildcard option depends on the chance that something will happen to cause a drop in bond prices between 2 p.m. and 8 p.m. on any possible position day.

Let us explore the effect of changes in interest rates on futures traders by using the June 13 data for two bonds in Table 6.6. Both bonds, we assume, will pay a coupon on June 15, so we ignore accrued interest. Bond A in the table has 30 years to maturity, pays a 5 percent coupon, and sells for 86.16 percent of par. It yields 6.00 percent and has a conversion factor for the June T-bond futures of 0.8616. Bond B has 20 years to maturity, pays a 9 percent coupon, and sells for 134.67 percent of par. It yields 6.00 percent and has a conversion factor of 1.3467. The settlement price on June 13 for the JUN futures is 100–00. For Bond A, the invoice amount is $86,160, and for Bond B it is $134,670. By construction, both bonds have zero profit from delivery.

Table 6.6 has been constructed so that neither bond is better to deliver than the other. Each gives a delivery profit of zero, because the price is proportional to the conversion factor and there is no accrued interest to consider. The price is proportional to the conversion factor, because we assume that both bonds yield 6 percent. Let us assume that this is the situation when trading ends on June 13. If yields remain unchanged, the trader will be indifferent about delivering one bond or the other.

We want to explore whether a change in interest rates can affect the desirability of delivering and whether changing rates can affect the choice of delivery instrument. Now assume that late in the Chicago afternoon of June 13, interest rates jump by 1 percent due to an invasion of a Middle Eastern principality. Bond A now yields 7.00 percent and its price falls to 75.06 percent of par. Now there is at least one beneficiary of the invasion, because the short trader can deliver this bond against the futures contract.

After the invasion, buying $100,000 principal amount of Bond A costs $75,060, and the trader can deliver this bond against the futures contract for the invoice amount of $86,160. This change in rates gives the short trader a profit from delivery of $11,100, the full amount of the bond's price fall. This results from the fact that the invoice amount was set at 2 p.m., but the bond price was free to fall between 2 p.m. and 8 p.m. on June 13. The short seller plays his wildcard

Table 6.7 Wildcard option results from sudden yield changes		
	Yields fall to 5%	Yields rise to 7%
Bond A		
Price	100.00	75.06
Dollar payoff to deliver	−$13,840	$11,100
Bond B		
Price	150.21	121.36
Dollar payoff to deliver	−$15,540	$13,310

and announces his intention to deliver. Table 6.7 summarizes this change for Bond A. For Bond B, also shown in Table 6.7, the rise in rates also causes the price to fall from 134.67 to 121.36. This gives a $13,310 profit from delivering Bond B after the rise in rates. Table 6.7 also shows the effect of a fall in rates from 6 to 5 percent. With this fall in rates, the trader shows a loss from delivering, so the trader defers delivery, hoping that rates will rise. In our example of rising rates, the wildcard option paid handsomely. Simply by the good luck of rates rising during the wildcard interval, the short trader was able to secure a delivery profit of $11,100 with Bond A or $13,310 with Bond B.

The chance to wait from 2 p.m. to 8 p.m. to play the wildcard is a timing option. However, the wildcard option also involves a quality option. At 2 p.m. on June 10, the trader is indifferent between delivering Bonds A and B in Table 6.6, because both have zero delivery profits. When rates rise due to the invasion, the two cash market prices change by different amounts, as Table 6.7 details. With the jump in rates, both bonds are profitable to deliver, but it is clearly better to deliver Bond B for a delivery profit of $13,310, rather than Bond A with a delivery profit of only $11,100. This example illustrates the quality option inherent in the wildcard option.

However, the quality component of the wildcard option is even better than it first appears. We have seen that the settlement price for computing the invoice amount is fixed at 2 p.m. on position day and that the short trader must announce an intention to deliver by 8 p.m. that same evening. However, the short trader has until 5 p.m. the next business day, notice of intention day, to declare which bond he or she intends to deliver. Thus, the trader has an extra business day to choose the bond that will be best to deliver.

The change in rates gives a clear preference for delivering one bond rather than another. As Table 6.7 shows, for a drop in yields to 5 percent, it is better to deliver Bond A. Of course, the short trader prefers not to deliver if yields fall, but if he must, he prefers to deliver Bond A. This example illustrates how changing interest rates can change the preferred delivery instrument, thereby creating a quality option.

The end-of-the-month option

As we have discussed, the seller of a T-bond futures contract may choose to deliver any deliverable bond on any business day of the delivery month. The last trading day for T-bond futures is the eighth to last business day of the delivery month. All contracts open after that time must be satisfied by delivery. The settlement price established on the final trading day is the settlement price used in all invoice calculations for all deliveries in the remainder of the month. The seller must deliver, but he can still make two choices. First, the seller can choose on which remaining day to deliver, and the seller can choose which bond to deliver.

Let us assume that interest rates are certain to be stable for those last few days. If so, the seller has a clear means of determining on which day to deliver. For each additional day the seller holds the bond, the bond accrues interest. However, for each such additional day, the seller must finance the bond, presumably at the overnight repo rate. Thus, the seller's choice is clear. If the coupon yield on the bond exceeds the financing rate to hold the bond, the seller should deliver on the last day. If the financing rate exceeds the coupon yield, the seller should deliver immediately. The choice of when to deliver, based on the rate of accruing interest, is a timing option and is known as the **accrued interest option**. It is a component of the end-of-the-month option.

In general, interest rates will not be constant over the last eight business days of the month. As interest rates change during this period, bond prices will change. However, for any given potential delivery day during this period, the invoice amount for a bond will not change. The invoice amount is determined by the settlement price on the last trading day and the amount of accrued interest to the delivery day. From the seller's point of view, the income to be received from delivery is known for each bond. The seller must deliver one of the deliverable bonds, but he still possesses a quality option. The seller can choose which bond to deliver.

The seller's options in the real market

While the seller's options may be interesting and may give a devilish twist to the T-bond and T-note futures contracts, it remains to be seen how important they really are. First, we will examine estimates of the value of the seller's options and their effects on futures prices. Second, we consider the extent to which traders seem to pay attention to these options in guiding their own trading.

The value of the seller's options

With all perfect market conditions in place, we are accustomed to the conclusion of the cost-of-carry model that the futures price should equal the spot price times one plus the cost of carry:

$$F = S(1 + C)$$

In discussing the seller's options, we have seen how they can have value. However, this formulation of the cost-of-carry model leaves no role for the seller's options. If the seller's options have value, then market equilibrium requires that the following equation should hold:

$$F + SO = S(1 + C)$$

where SO is the value of the seller's options. This implies that

$$F = S(1 + C) - SO \tag{6.3}$$

If this reformulation of the cost-of-carry model did not hold, the market would not be in equilibrium. This reformulation also implies that the futures prices observable in the market should be below the simple cost-of-carry price by the amount of the seller's options.

In other words, the market bids down the futures price because of the seller's options. The futures price must fall until the futures price plus the seller's options, $F + SO$, just equals the spot price times one plus the cost of carry, $S(1 + C)$. If the futures price were not bid down, then the seller would, in effect, get the options for free, and this would violate the principles of an efficient market.

This approach to the seller's options has been used by a number of scholars to estimate the value of the seller's options inherent in the T-bond futures contract. One difficulty with estimating the value of these options is that options generally have greater value the more the time that remains until expiration. In other words, the seller's options should be worth more one year from delivery than they are worth three months from delivery. Most studies indicate that the seller's options have considerable value.

The seller's options and trader behavior

Thus far, we have seen that the seller's options appear to have value. Possession of these options suggests that traders should behave in similar ways. Thus, we would expect to find traders delivering the same bonds on the same days and not delivering on the same days. Further, we expect short traders to be aware of, and follow, the optimal policy for delivering to take advantage of their options. To summarize the general pattern of deliveries in T-bond futures, we may note first that relatively few contracts are filled by delivery. As a general rule for the T-bond contract, there seems to be considerable attention paid to the characteristics of the bonds being delivered. Second, deliveries are infrequent in the early part of the month. Traders seem anxious to wait to exploit their end-of-the-month option. On occasion, however, significant deliveries do occur before the last few trading days. We might expect all traders to follow the exact same delivery strategy of delivering the same bond on the same day. In practice, we see departures from that behavior. Some of the early deliveries of just a few contracts appear to be motivated by other concerns. Also, even when deliveries are heavy, traders deliver different bonds. This suggests that some traders may find it cheaper to deliver a bond from their existing inventory rather than to buy the cheapest-to-deliver bond for the express purpose of making delivery. In general, however, deliveries are few, concentrated in the same bond, and occur near the end of the delivery month.

Gerald D. Gay and Steven Manaster examined the different strategies open to short T-bond traders to determine whether profits were available from optimal delivery strategies and to determine whether traders followed those optimal strategies.[2] They reached several important conclusions. First, delivery strategies during the 1977–83 period would have generated profits. This means that futures prices during this period did not fully reflect the value of the options available to the short sellers. Second, they compared an optimal delivery strategy with the actual deliveries during this period. They found that the actual deliveries exploited some, but not all, of the seller's options. In other words, the short traders took advantage of their options to some extent, but they did not fully exploit the options available to them. As Gay and Manaster note, these options may not have been fully understood by traders in this early period. This leaves open the possibility that futures prices will adjust to fully reflect the value of the seller's options as the market moves toward maturity.

The efficiency of the interest rate futures market

A market is informationally efficient if prices in that market fully reflect all information in a given information set. If the market is efficient with respect to some information set, then that information cannot be used to direct a trading strategy to beat the market. A trader beats the market by consistently earning a rate of return that exceeds the risk-adjusted market equilibrium rate of return. There are three commonly distinguished forms of the market efficiency hypothesis: the weak form, the semistrong form, and the strong form. These versions of market efficiency are distinguished by their information sets. The weak-form efficiency hypothesis asserts that information contained in the past history of price and volume data cannot be used to beat the market. The semistrong form asserts that traders cannot rely on public information to beat the market. The strong form asserts that even private information is insufficient to allow a trader to beat the market.

We have seen that cash-and-carry and reverse cash-and-carry arbitrage strategies rely only on observable prices. Thus, successful arbitrage strategies violate weak-form efficiency. For example, large divergences between forward and futures rates of interest would generate important academic arbitrage opportunities. Because the futures market is a zero-sum game, in the absence of transaction costs, one participant's profits implies the offsetting of losses for others.

For these reasons, users of any market should be concerned about market efficiency. This is true whether one is a speculator or hedger. Researchers have long recognized the importance of market efficiency. This section reviews the development of research on the efficiency of the interest rate futures market and draws conclusions about the efficiency based on the state of research to date. In spite of the attention that has been focused on the efficiency question, only T-bill and T-bond futures contracts have been explored well in published works. Almost all of these analyses focus on divergences between forward rates implied by spot market positions and futures market positions. This focus on rate discrepancies means that the tests have sought evidence of academic arbitrage opportunities in the interest rate futures market. Many early tests were based on a less than full understanding of the conditions under which market efficiency could be judged.

Early tests of futures market efficiency focused exclusively on differences between forward rates and futures rates on T-bills. Differences between these rates were sometimes interpreted without further ado as evidence of market inefficiency. Immediate difficulties with this conclusion arose because different researchers arrived at radically different conclusions, some finding efficiency and others finding gross inefficiencies. From preceding chapters, we know that forward and futures rates can differ for at least two basic reasons: market imperfections or the influence of daily resettlement. Many of the earliest researches into efficiency did not take these two factors into adequate consideration, yet both are important.

Attempts to evaluate academic arbitrage opportunities in the T-bill futures market involve taking complementary positions in the futures market and spot market. If there is to be genuine academic arbitrage, the difference between the futures and forward yields must be sufficiently large to cover considerable transaction costs. While many studies neglect the full magnitude of these transaction charges, more recent studies find potential for arbitrage even after transaction costs.

Depending on the exact way in which the arbitrage attempt is conducted, a trader must incur a variety of transaction costs. To see the full magnitude of these expenses, consider the misaligned futures and cash T-bill prices in Table 6.8. We explored these prices in Chapter 5. The transaction costs incurred to exploit this misalignment depend on the trader's initial position in the spot or futures market. With no position in either market, the trader must pay all transaction costs from the gross trading profits to capture an academic arbitrage profit. If an opportunity is attractive enough to show a profit, even after paying full transactions costs, it can be considered **pure arbitrage**.

If the trader already holds a portfolio of T-bills, for example, then some transaction costs can be avoided. Some of the costs have already been paid, and they should be considered as sunk costs for the analysis of the arbitrage. If a trader with an initial portfolio can successfully engage in arbitrage, then the profitable transaction is regarded as **quasi-arbitrage**.[3] In discussing pure arbitrage and quasi-arbitrage, we refer to academic arbitrage.

To exploit the rate discrepancies in Table 6.8 via pure arbitrage, the trader must be able to pay a variety of transactions costs:

Table 6.8   Interest rate futures and arbitrage: today's date is January 5

Futures	Bank discount yields (%)
MAR futures contract (matures in 77 days on March 22)	12.50
Cash bills	
167-Day T-bill (Deliverable on MAR futures)	10.00
77-Day T-bill	6.00

(1) Issuing a 77-day T-bill is equivalent to borrowing. The most creditworthy traders can borrow a T-bill for about 50 basis points above its current yield. For $953,611 for 77 days, the incremental borrowing cost due to a 50 basis point spread is $1,020. Consider also that the acquisition of the $953,611 might be through the issuance of a term repo agreement.

(2) To buy a 167-day T-bill, a trader must pay the asked price for the bill, even if he or she is a market participant, which could involve an additional cost of about $100. If not a participant in the spot T-bill market, the trader must trade through a broker and pay a commission as well.

(3) In selling the MAR futures contract, a trader can receive only the bid price, thereby increasing costs about $25. If he or she is not a trader on the IMM, the trader must pay commission costs as well.

(4) Delivering the T-bill also has costs, because the short trader in the futures market bears all costs of delivery. These costs might be about $50.

(5) Paying off the due bill also involves transactions costs of the wire transfer and record keeping, which might be $25.

This list of transaction charges is only an indication of the additional expenses that a trader might face in an arbitrage attempt. Many of the charges shown in the list are difficult to gauge, and different market participants face different levels of expense. Nonetheless, the expenses are large and can offset a substantial difference between forward and futures yields. In addition, a trader also faces a cost not shown in the list. To find an arbitrage opportunity, a trader must search for it, and the cost of searching for the opportunity must be included in the calculation of the arbitrage profit.

From the list of transaction costs, we see that some market participants are in a much better position than others. If a participant has a portfolio of spot T-bills, has a very good credit rating, is a trader on the futures exchange, and has a network of computerized information sources already in operation, then the transactions costs incurred in attempting to conduct an arbitrage operation are much smaller. This is the difference between pure arbitrage and quasi-arbitrage. For pure arbitrage, the yield discrepancy must be large enough to cover all transaction costs faced by a market outsider. For quasi-arbitrage, the trader faces less than full transaction costs.

Richard Rendleman and Christopher Carabini conducted one of the most thorough and careful studies of T-bill futures efficiency using daily data for the period from January 6, 1976 to March 31, 1978. The analysis focused on the three futures contracts closest to maturity at any moment. By a careful analysis of the transaction costs faced by a market outsider, Rendleman and Carabini defined a band of difference between the forward rate and the futures rate that would still not support pure arbitrage. In other words, if forward and futures rates diverged only slightly, by 50 basis points or less, the yield difference would not cover transaction costs and

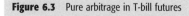

Figure 6.3 Pure arbitrage in T-bill futures

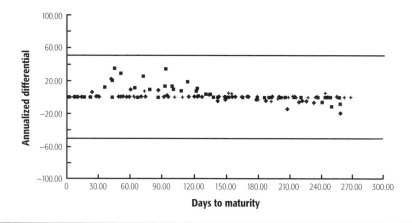

Source: R. Rendleman and C. Carabini, "The Efficiency of the Treasury Bill Futures Market," *Journal of Finance*, 34:4, 1979, pp. 895–914. Reprinted by permission from Blackwell Publishing

pure arbitrage would be impossible. Figure 6.3 shows their results. The divergences between actual and theoretical yields for T-bill futures always fall within the band of 50 basis points, which denotes the no-profit limits. This was true for all 1,606 observations in their sample, supporting their conclusion that the T-bill futures market was efficient—in the sense of excluding opportunities for pure arbitrage.

Regarding quasi-arbitrage opportunities, Rendleman and Carabini found occasions on which a trader could improve the return on a portfolio of spot T-bills. The quasi-arbitrage opportunities were found only infrequently, and no attempt was made to factor in the search costs needed to discover the opportunities. About these quasi-arbitrage opportunities, Rendleman and Carabini conclude that, "the inefficiencies in the Treasury bill futures market do not appear to be significant enough to offer attractive investment alternatives to the short-term portfolio manager."

In spite of the care with which the Rendleman and Carabini study was conducted, it is subject to one serious limitation; it relies on daily closing prices. In an evaluation of an arbitrage attempt, the purchase and sale of two related goods must be assumed to occur simultaneously. However, the spot and futures markets for T-bills close at different times. This means that the closing prices for each day will not be prices for the same moment on both markets. In academic jargon, the prices are nonsimultaneous, or exhibit nonsimultaneity.

To improve the test of T-bill futures efficiency, Elton, Gruber, and Rentzler (hereafter EGR) used intraday prices—prices from throughout the trading day. With intraday prices on futures and spot T-bills, they matched the times at which the trades occurred to determine simultaneous prices in both markets. Their dataset consisted of a sample of intraday spot prices spaced approximately an hour apart and every T-bill futures trade during the period from January 6, 1976 through December 22, 1982.

EGR divide the strategies they consider into those that involve immediate and delayed execution. For immediate execution, they assume that an arbitrage opportunity is identified from their simultaneous cash/futures price pairs and the trader enters arbitrage transactions at those prices. For delayed execution, EGR assume that an arbitrage opportunity is identified from one cash/

Table 6.9 Pure arbitrage results for T-bill futures

Size of filter ($)	Immediate execution				Delayed execution			
	Number of trades	Expected profit ($)	Actual profit ($)	Standard error ($)	Number of trades	Expected profit ($)	Actual profit ($)	Standard error ($)
0	2,304	894	889	15	1,725	893	880	18
100	2,093	980	975	16	1,569	977	964	19
200	1,902	1,064	1,058	16	1,428	1,059	1,041	19
300	1,738	1,142	1,135	16	1,301	1,137	1,117	20
400	1,595	1,212	1,206	17	1,206	1,199	1,176	20
500	1,469	1,279	1,271	17	1,107	1,267	1,244	21
600	1,332	1,352	1,346	18	1,005	1,339	1,315	22
700	1,190	1,437	1,432	18	890	1,429	1,401	23
800	1,063	1,519	1,516	18	789	1,517	1,490	24

Source: Edwin J. Elton, Martin. J. Gruber, and Joel Rentzler, "Intra-Day Tests of the Efficiency of the Treasury Bill Futures Market," *The Review of Economics and Statistics*, February 1984, 66:1, pp. 129–37. © 1984 the President and Fellows of Harvard College and the Massachusetts Institute of Technology. Reprinted by permission of MIT Press

futures price pair and the trade is executed at the prices of the next pair. This implies a delay of about one hour between identification and execution. According to EGR's analysis, the immediate execution strategy replicates the situation facing the floor trader, while the delayed execution strategy would be available to a market participant who is farther removed from the pit.

To analyze pure arbitrage strategies, EGR assume transaction costs on the arbitrage transactions of $175 plus an annual cost of 50 basis points to cover selling a T-bill short. As we have seen, a trader who enters such arbitrage transactions still faces daily resettlement cash flows. Therefore, any planned arbitrage profit can only be an expected profit. The actual profit may differ due to the effect of daily resettlement cash flows. Table 6.9 presents the key results of EGR's study of pure arbitrage for both immediate and delayed execution. EGR assume that these daily resettlement cash flows earn the overnight rate on a certificate of deposit.

The immediate execution results assume that transactions take place immediately upon finding an attractive opportunity, and the expected profit means that the effects of daily resettlement have not yet been considered. However, these results are net of transaction costs. The results are stratified by a filter rule that divides the opportunities by the size of the expected profit. For example, they found a total of 2,304 opportunities with some expected profit. The average expected profit across all of these trades was $894, assuming a transaction of one contract size.

Notice that they found many opportunities with very large discrepancies. For example, they found 1,063 opportunities with expected profits exceeding $800. The actual profit differs from the expected profit due to the interest gain or cost incurred on the daily resettlement cash flows. These differences are very small. If execution of the trades is delayed until the next cash market quotation, the expected profits diminish. Yet overall, EGR's results indicate that these arbitrage opportunities persist. Therefore, EGR conclude that the T-bill futures market is not efficient with respect to pure arbitrage opportunities.

In comparing the Rendleman and Carabini study with the later study by EGR, we must give greater weight to the results of EGR. The data employed by EGR are more complete, and they reduce the problems of nonsimultaneous pricing. Recent studies of T-bill futures market efficiency have tended to corroborate the results of EGR.

Having found frequent and significant departures from efficiency in the T-bill futures market, we now turn to the T-bond futures contract. The T-bond futures market has not received nearly the same attention devoted to the T-bill futures market. Part of the reason for this difference is the extreme complexity of the T-bond contract, particularly the diversity of deliverable instruments and the seller's options. Since the short trader chooses which bond to deliver in fulfillment of the contract, the long position has no opportunity for arbitrage, as we showed earlier in this chapter. For cash-and-carry arbitrage, the short trader could conduct arbitrage if it were profitable to:

(1)   buy a bond,
(2)   sell a futures contract on the bond, and
(3)   store the bond until delivery.

As we have seen, even such a strategy is limited in its effectiveness. The bond that the short trader might hold will pay a coupon, in most cases, on the 15th of the month preceding delivery. The investment rate for the coupon is uncertain, so the short trader cannot really count on an arbitrage profit if he or she must rely on the cash flow from the reinvested coupons. These conditions drastically restrict the possible arbitrage strategies. Further, we have seen that the futures price is bid down to reflect the seller's options. Capturing profits from the seller's options is risky. As a consequence, the reduction in futures prices to account for the seller's options makes successful arbitrage even less likely.

In their paper on T-bond futures efficiency, Kolb, Gay, and Jordan investigated the possibility of arbitrage for all T-bond futures contracts in existence from December 1977 through June 1981.[4] They analyzed just one day for each instrument, the last business day of the month preceding the delivery month. This is the first position day. For this date, and for any position day, arbitrage is possible because the trader knows what invoice amount will be received for a particular deliverable bond. The short trader receives the invoice amount upon delivery, with the invoice amount depending on the futures price, the conversion factor, and the accrued interest, as discussed earlier in this chapter. From this cash flow, the short trader must pay the cost of acquiring the bond and the financing cost of holding the bond from the time of acquisition until it can be delivered. Since the short trader chooses which bond to deliver, he needs to find only one deliverable bond that is profitable to secure an arbitrage opportunity. Figure 6.4 shows the profitability of delivery for all deliverable bonds for 15 contract maturities, as calculated for the last business day of the month preceding the delivery month.

Only three contract maturities had a bond that promised a positive cash flow: SEP 78, SEP 80, and MAR 80. For the SEP 78 contract, the positive cash flow was $49.07, and for the SEP 80 contract, the positive cash flow was $27.57. Out of these potential profits, the arbitrageur would have had to pay transaction and search costs, so these two occasions represent no chance for an arbitrage profit.

For the MAR 80 contract, one bond would have yielded a cash flow as large as $591.34. If there is to be hope of arbitrage, it must rest with this contract. This hope, however, appears to be illusory. Prices reported for this date vary widely from source to source, with reported futures prices differing by as much as $1,625. The uncertainty over the actual prices at which one could contract requires that this apparent arbitrage opportunity be regarded as spurious. Kolb, Gay, and Jordan conclude that their results, while limited, are fully consistent with the efficiency of the T-bond futures market.

Because of difficulty with specifying a tight arbitrage link between the cash market and the T-bond futures contract, most subsequent explorations of T-bond futures efficiency have focused on speculative strategies. Successful speculative strategies would constitute evidence against

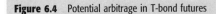

Figure 6.4   Potential arbitrage in T-bond futures

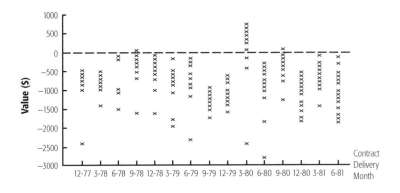

Source: R. Kolb, G. Gay, and J. Jordan, "Are There Arbitrage Opportunities in the Treasury-Bond Futures Market?" *The Journal of Futures Markets*, 2:3, 1987, pp. 217–29. Reprinted by permission from John Wiley & Sons, Inc.

efficiency if they were to earn a return too great for the level of speculative risk undertaken. However, the difficulty with evaluating such strategies lies in determining a market standard risk/expected return relationship. As a consequence, tests of speculative efficiency are always simultaneous tests of market efficiency and the adequacy of the risk/expected return measure used. Bearing this limitation in mind, we briefly consider some further tests of T-bond futures efficiency.

An important limitation of the Kolb, Gay, and Jordan methodology was the necessary restriction to a period within the delivery month. Bruce Resnick and Elizabeth Hennigar extend a similar analysis to periods outside the delivery month. Their results support the efficiency of the T-bond futures market.[5] In a separate study, Resnick evaluates the pricing relationship between T-bond futures of different maturities, in effect asking if the spread relationships are efficient. Resnick's findings also support a general conclusion of efficiency.[6]

R. Klemkosky and D. Lasser conduct a study similar to that of Resnick and Hennigar, but use a different time period and attempt to adjust for taxes. Noting that any kind of cash-and-carry arbitrage evaluation depends on the estimate of borrowing costs, Klemkosky and Lasser find inefficiencies. While they acknowledge that they are unable to fully adjust for risk, Klemkosky and Lasser judge the divergences between the spot and futures prices to be inconsistent with full efficiency. As they conclude: "either the borrowing costs are still being underestimated or the T-bond market was inefficient during periods of high interest rates, possibly because of an extraordinarily large risk premium being placed on the variable coupon reinvestment return."[7]

In a test of speculative efficiency, Don Chance examines speculative strategies based on the response of the futures market to announcements of changes in the consumer price index. Chance finds that T-bond futures prices rise following an announcement of lower inflation (measured against past inflation or against "expected" inflation). He also finds that the T-bond futures prices adjust slowly to this information, so that traders can react swiftly to the market and make a speculative profit as the market digests the information over the day following the announcement.[8]

How can we assess the variety of evidence on the efficiency of the interest rate futures market? Several years ago, it appeared that the weight of evidence favored efficiency, but today it appears that the weight is beginning to shift. The study by EGR is particularly persuasive. It is extremely rich in observations and every effort was made to adjust for potential discrepancies. Attempts to assess the efficiency of the T-bond futures markets are much more difficult, and the current state of evidence is inconclusive. In attempting to summarize this evidence in a single sentence, it appears that persistent inefficiencies continue to exist in these markets, but the size of the inefficiencies may not be large enough to reward a change in professions. Remember that none of these studies includes the search cost or the use of human capital required to find and exploit the alleged arbitrage opportunity.

We must also remember that most of these studies have focused on the existence of arbitrage opportunities. Arbitrage, however, is the grossest kind of inefficiency. A market may well have no arbitrage opportunities and still be inefficient. If risky positions can be taken in the futures market, and those risky positions earn returns in excess of a risk-adjusted normal return, then the futures market will still be inefficient. Few tests of such possibilities have been conducted, probably due to the difficulty in defining a risk-adjusted normal return. The ones that have been conducted reach divergent conclusions.

Applications: Eurodollar and T-bill futures

In Chapter 5, we considered speculative strategies and some hedging strategies. In this section we explore alternative risk management strategies using short-term interest rate futures. We proceed by considering a series of examples. Taken together, these examples provide a handbook of techniques for a variety of risk management strategies. All of these strategies turn on protection against shifting interest rates.

Changing the maturity of an investment

Many investors find themselves with an existing portfolio that may have undesirable maturity characteristics. For example, a firm might hold a six-month T-bill and realize that it will have a need for funds in three months. By the same token, another investor might hold the same six-month T-bill and fear that those funds might have to face lower reinvestment rates upon maturity in six months. This investor might prefer a one-year maturity. Both the firm and the investor could sell the six-month bill and invest for the preferred maturity. However, spot market transactions costs are relatively high, and many investors prefer to alter the maturities of investment by trading futures. The two examples that follow show how to use futures to accomplish both a shortening and lengthening of maturities.

Shortening the maturity of a T-bill investment

Consider a firm that has invested in a T-bill. Now, on March 20, the T-bill has a maturity of 180 days, but the firm learns of a need for cash in 90 days. Therefore, it would like to shorten the maturity so it can have access to its funds in 90 days, around mid-June.

For simplicity, we assume that the short-term yield curve is flat with all rates at 10 percent on March 20. For convenience, we assume a 360-day year to match the pricing conventions for T-bills. The face value of the firm's T-bill is $10 million. With 180 days to maturity and a 10 percent discount yield, the price of the bill is given by

$$P = FV - (DY \times FV \times DTM)/360$$

where P is the bill price, FV is the face value, DY is the discount yield, and DTM is the days until maturity. Therefore, the 180-day bill is worth $9.5 million. If the yield curve is flat

Table 6.10	Transactions to shorten maturities	
Date	Cash market	Futures market
March 20	Hold a six-month T-bill with a face value of $10 million, worth $9.5 million; wish for a three-month maturity	Sell ten JUN T-bill futures contracts at 90.00, reflecting the 10% discount yield
June 20		Deliver cash market T-bills against futures; receive $9.75 million

at 10 percent, the futures yield must also be 10 percent, and the 90-day T-bill futures price must be $975,000 per contract. Starting from an initial position of a six-month T-bill, the firm of our example can shorten the maturity by selling T-bill futures for expiration in three months, as shown in Table 6.10. On March 20, there was no cash flow, because the firm merely sold futures. On June 20, the six-month bill is now a three-month bill and can be delivered against the futures. In Table 6.10, the firm delivers the bills and receives the futures invoice amount of $9.75 million. (Although we have assumed that the futures price did not change, this does not limit the applicability of our results. No matter how the futures price changed from March to June, the firm would still receive a total of $9.75 million. We assume that this occurs in June instead of over the period.) The firm has effectively shortened the maturity from six months to three months.

Lengthening the maturity

Consider now, on August 21, an investor who holds a $100 million face value T-bill that matures in 30 days on September 20. She plans to reinvest for another three months after the T-bill matures. However, she fears that interest rates might fall unexpectedly. If so, she would be forced to reinvest at a lower rate than is now reflected in the yield curve. The SEP T-bill futures yield is 9.8 percent, as is the rate on the current investment. She finds this rate attractive and would like to lengthen the maturity of the T-bill investment. She knows that she can lengthen the maturity by buying a September futures contract and taking delivery. She will then hold the delivered bills until maturity in December.

With a 9.8 percent discount futures yield, the value of the delivery unit is $975,500. With $100 million being available on September 20, the investor knows she will have enough funds to take delivery of $100,000,000/$975,500 = 102.51 futures contracts. Therefore, she initiates the strategy presented in Table 6.11.

On August 21, she held a bill worth $99,183,333, assuming a yield of 9.8 percent. With the transactions of Table 6.11, she had no cash flow on August 21. With the maturity of the T-bill in September, the investor received $100 million and used almost all of it to pay for the futures delivery. We assume she invested the remainder, $499,000, at a bank discount rate of 9.8% for three months. In December, this investment would be worth $511,533. With the T-bills maturing in December, the total proceeds will be $102,511,533, from an investment that was worth $99,183,333 on August 21. This gives her a discount yield of about 9.8 percent over the four-month horizon from August to December.

Notice that this transaction "locked in" the 9.8 percent on the futures contract. In this example, this happens to match the spot rate of interest. However, the important point to recognize is that lengthening the maturity involves locking into the futures yield, no matter what that yield

Table 6.11 Transactions to lengthen maturities

Date	Cash market	Futures market
August 21	Hold a 30-day T-bill with a face value of $100 million; wish to extend the maturity for 90 days	Buy 102 SEP T-bill futures contracts, with a yield of 9.8%
September 20	The 30-day T-bill matures; receive $100 million; invest $499,000 in a money market fund at 9.8%	Accept delivery on 102 SEP futures, paying $99,501,000
December 19	T-bills received on SEP futures mature for $102 million; receive proceeds of $511,533 from investment	

may be. Thus, for the period covered by the T-bill delivered on the futures contract, the investment will earn the futures yield at the time of contracting.

Fixed and floating loan rates

In recent years, interest rates have fluctuated dramatically. These fluctuating rates generate interest rate risk that few economic agents are anxious to bear. For example, in housing finance, home buyers seek fixed-rate loans, because the fixed rate protects the borrower against rising interest rates. By the same token, lenders may be unwilling to offer fixed-rate loans, because they fear that their cost of funds might rise. With fixed-rate lending and a rising cost of funds, the lender faces a risk of paying more to acquire funds than it is earning on its fixed-rate lending. Therefore, many lenders want to make floating-rate loans.

In this section, we show how the borrower who receives a floating-rate loan can effectively convert this loan into a fixed-rate loan, thereby protecting against rises in interest rates. Similarly, for a lender who feels compelled to offer fixed-rate loans, we show how the lender can use the futures markets to make the investment perform like a floating-rate loan. Either the borrower or lender can bear the interest rate risk. Whichever party bears the interest rate risk can hedge the risk through the futures market. In a floating-rate loan, the borrower bears or hedges the risk. In a fixed-rate loan, the lender bears or hedges the risk.

In this section, we consider a single transaction from two points of view, those of the lender and the borrower. First, we assume that the loan is a floating-rate loan and that the borrower hedges the interest rate risk associated with the loan. Second, we consider a fixed-rate loan in which the lender hedges the interest rate risk.

Converting a floating-rate loan to a fixed-rate loan

A construction firm plans a project that will take six months to complete, at a total cost of $100 million. The bank offers to provide the funds for six months at a simple interest rate that is 200 basis points above the 90-day LIBOR rate. However, the bank insists that the loan rate for the second quarter will be 200 basis points above the 90-day LIBOR rate that prevails at that date. Also, the construction company must pay interest after the first quarter. Principal plus interest are due in six months.

Table 6.12	Synthetic fixed-rate borrowing	
Date	Cash market	Futures market
September 20	Borrow $100 million at 9.00% for three months and commit to extend the loan for three additional months at a rate 200 basis points above the three-month LIBOR rate prevailing at that time	Sell 100 DEC Eurodollar futures contracts at 92.70, reflecting the 7.3% yield
December 20	Pay interest of $2.25 million; LIBOR is now at 7.8%, so borrow $100 million for three months at 9.8%	Offset 100 DEC Eurodollar futures at 92.20, reflecting the 7.8% yield; produce profit of $125,000 = 50 basis points × $25 per point × 100 contracts
March 20	Pay interest of $2,450,000 and repay principal of $100 million Total interest expense: $4.7 million	Futures profit: $125,000
	Net interest expense after hedging: $4,575,000	

Today is September 20 and the current 90-day LIBOR rate is 7.0 percent. The DEC Eurodollar futures yield is 7.3 percent. Based on these rates and the borrowing plan, the construction company will pay 9 percent for the first three months and 9.3 percent for the second three months. These rates give the following cash flows from the loan:

September 20	Receive principal	+$100,000,000
December 20	Pay interest	−$2,250,000
March 20	Pay interest and principal	−$102,325,000

The cash flows for September and December are certain. However, the cash flow in March depends upon the LIBOR rate that prevails in December. The firm expects a 9.3 percent rate, which equals the futures yield for the DEC futures plus 200 basis points. However, between September and December, that rate could rise. For example, if the spot 90-day LIBOR rate in December is 7.8 percent, the firm will pay 9.8 percent and the total interest due in March will be $125,000 higher than expected.

The construction firm decides to lock into the 7.3 percent futures yield and its expected 9.3 percent borrowing rate, so that it will know its borrowing cost. Starting with a floating-rate loan and transacting to fix the interest rate is called a **synthetic fixed rate loan**. Table 6.12 shows how the construction company trades to protect itself from a jump in rates. At the outset, the firm accepts the floating-rate scheme for its loan and sells 100 DEC Eurodollar futures. If rates rise, the short futures position will give enough profits to pay the additional interest expense on the second quarter's loan.

As Table 6.12 shows, LIBOR rises by 50 basis points to 7.8 percent. This implies a borrowing rate of 9.8 percent for the second quarter, as the table shows. However, the rise in rates has created a futures profit of $125,000 = 50 basis points times $25 per basis point times 100 contracts. The table shows that the firm pays $125,000 more interest in the second quarter than anticipated due to the jump in rates. However, this is exactly offset by the futures profit.[9] In September, the firm expected to pay a total of $4,575,000 in interest for the loan. Counting the futures profit, this is exactly the interest that the firm pays because it hedged. By trading in the futures market, the construction firm changed its floating-rate loan into a fixed-rate loan.

Converting a fixed-rate loan to a floating-rate loan

We now consider the same transaction from the lender's point of view. If the construction company really wants a fixed-rate loan, let them have it, reasons the bank. We assume that the bank's cost of funds equals the 90-day LIBOR rate. The bank expects to pay 7.0 percent for funds this quarter and 7.3 percent next quarter, or an average rate of 7.15 percent over the six months of the loan. Therefore, the bank decides to make a fixed-rate six-month loan to the construction company at 9.15 percent. The bank's expected profit is the 200 basis point spread between the lending rate and the bank's LIBOR-based cost of funds. The bank expects to secure the funds by borrowing:

September 20	Borrow principal	+$100,000,000
	Make loan to construction company	−$100,000,000
December 20	Pay interest	−$1,750,000
March 20	Receive principal and interest from construction company	+$104,575,000
	Pay principal and interest	−$101,825,000

If all goes as expected, the bank's gross profit will be $1 million. Having made a fixed-rate loan, however, the bank is at risk of rising interest rates. For example, if LIBOR rises by 50 basis points to 7.8 percent for the second quarter, the bank will have to pay an additional $125,000 in interest. To avoid this risk, the bank transacts as shown in Table 6.13. Notice how they almost exactly match the transactions of the construction company, except that the bank has a lower borrowing rate. If interest rates rise, the bank's cost of funds rises, just as was the case for the construction company with a floating-rate loan. Both the construction company and the bank were able to hedge by selling Eurodollar futures.

With the rise in rates, the bank paid $125,000 more interest than it expected. However, this increased interest was offset by a futures market gain. Originally, the bank wanted to shift the interest rate risk to the construction company. However, as the transactions of Table 6.13 show, the bank is able to give the construction company the fixed-rate loan it desires and still avoid

---

Table 6.13   Synthetic floating-rate lending

Date	Cash market	Futures market
September 20	Borrow $100 million at 7.00% for three months and lend it for six months at 9.15%	Sell 100 DEC Eurodollar futures contracts at 92.70, reflecting the 7.3% yield
December 20	Pay interest of $1.75 million; LIBOR is now at 7.8%, so borrow $100 million for three months at 7.8%	Offset 100 DEC Eurodollar futures at 92.20, reflecting the 7.8% yield; produce profit of $125,000 = 50 basis points × $25 per point × 100 contracts
March 20	Pay interest of $1,950,000 and repay principal of $100 million Total interest expense: $3,700,000	Futures profit: $125,000
	Net interest expense after hedging: $3,575,000	

the interest rate risk. In essence, the bank creates a **synthetic floating rate loan**. For its customer, it offers a fixed-rate loan, but the bank transacts in the futures market to make the transaction equivalent to having given a floating-rate loan.

Strip and stack hedges

In the example of the synthetic fixed-rate loan and synthetic floating-rate lending, the interest rate risk focused on a single date. Often, the period of the loan covers a number of different dates at which the rate might be reset. For example, the construction company of our previous example makes a more realistic assessment of how long it will take to complete a project. Instead of six months, the construction firm realizes that the project will take a year.

The bank insists on making a floating-rate loan for three months at a rate that is 200 basis points above the LIBOR rate prevailing at the time of the loan. On September 15, the construction company observes the following rates:

Three-month LIBOR	7.00 percent
DEC Eurodollar	7.30 percent
MAR Eurodollar	7.60 percent
JUN Eurodollar	7.90 percent

For these four quarters, the firm expects to finance the $100 million at 9.00, 9.30, 9.60, and 9.90 percent, respectively. Therefore, the construction company expects to borrow $100 million for a year at an average rate of 9.45 percent. This gives a total expected interest cost of $9,450,000.

A stack hedge example

The construction firm decides to lock in this borrowing rate by hedging with Eurodollar futures. To implement the hedge, the firm sells 300 DEC Eurodollar futures. The firm hopes to protect itself against any changes in interest rates between September and December. In December, the futures will expire and the firm will offset the DEC futures and replace 200 of them with MAR futures. This is a **stack hedge**, because all of the futures contracts are concentrated, or stacked, in a single futures expiration.

We now consider how the construction firm fares with a single change in interest rates over the next year. Shortly after the firm enters the hedge, LIBOR rates jump by 50 basis points. Therefore, the firm's borrowing costs for the next three quarters are as follows:

December–March	9.80 percent
March–June	10.10 percent
June–September	10.40 percent

For simplicity, we consider only one interest rate change, so the firm secures these rates. Table 6.14 shows the construction firm's transactions and the results of the hedge. The firm hedges its $100 million loan with 300 contracts, or $300 million of underlying Eurodollars. After taking the loan, the first quarter's rate is fixed at 9.00 percent. Therefore, the firm is at risk for $100 million for three quarters. Because the maturity of the Eurodollars that underlie the futures is only one quarter, it requires three times as much futures value as its spot market exposure.

With the shift in rates, the firm must pay $9,825,000 in interest, which is more than the expected $9,450,000 when the firm took the loan. This difference is due to the across the board interest rate rise of 50 basis points. The same interest rate rise generates a futures trading profit of $375,000. Thus, the futures profit exactly offsets the increase in interests costs and the construction firm has successfully hedged its interest rate risk using a stack hedge.

Table 6.14 The results of a stack hedge

Date	Cash market	Futures market
September 20	Borrow $100 million at 9.00% for three months and commit to roll over the loan for three quarters at 200 basis points over the prevailing LIBOR rate	Sell 300 DEC Eurodollar futures contracts at 92.70, reflecting the 7.3% yield
December 20	Pay interest of $2,250,000; LIBOR is now at 7.8%, so borrow $100 million for three months at 9.8%	Offset 300 DEC Eurodollar futures at 92.20, reflecting the 7.8% yield; produce profit of $375,000 = 50 basis points × $25 per point × 300 contracts
March 20	Pay interest of $2,450,000 and borrow $100 million for three months at 10.10%	
June 20	Pay interest of $2,525,000 and borrow $100 million for three months at 10.40%	
September 20	Pay interest of $2,600,000 and principal of $100 million Total interest expense: $9,825,000	Futures profit: $375,000
	Interest expense net of hedging: $9,450,000	

Danger in using stack hedges

We now consider a potential danger in using a stack hedge of this type. In the example, the stack hedge worked perfectly because all interest rates changed by the same 50 basis points. As a result, the stack hedge gave a perfect hedge and the construction firm had no changes in its anticipated total borrowing cost. The same stack hedge might have performed very poorly if interest rates had changed in a somewhat different fashion.

For example, after the loan agreement is signed, the funds are received, and the same stack hedge is implemented, assume there is a single change in futures yields as follows. The DEC futures yield rises from 7.3 to 7.4 percent, the MAR futures yield rises from 7.6 to 8.3 percent, and the JUN futures yield jumps from 7.9 to 8.6 percent, as shown in Figure 6.5. With this change in rates, the construction firm will have the following borrowing costs and interest expenses:

September–December	9.00 percent	$2,250,000
December–March	9.40 percent	$2,350,000
March–June	10.30 percent	$2,575,000
June–September	10.60 percent	$2,650,000

This change in rates gives the same increase in borrowing costs from the initially expected level of $9,450,000 to $9,825,000. However, there is one important difference. The DEC futures yield changed by only ten basis points. Therefore, the futures profit on 300 DEC Eurodollar contracts is only $75,000, equal to ten basis points times $25 per basis point times 300 contracts. Now, the net borrowing cost after hedging is $9,750,000. This is $300,000 more than initially expected.

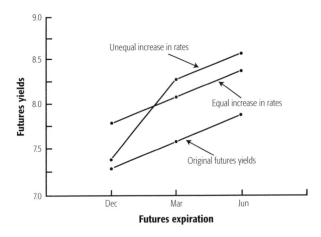

Figure 6.5   Yield curve shifts

The graph of Figure 6.5 shows the original position for the DEC, MAR, and JUN Eurodollar futures yields. In our first example of a stack hedge, we assumed that all futures yields rose by 50 basis points. The rates after this equal jump are shown in the graph. We then considered an unequal increase in rates and the effectiveness of the stack hedge. Figure 6.5 shows those unequal rates for which the stack hedge was so ineffective. With the unequal increase in rates, the futures yield curve has steepened considerably. The DEC futures yield increased slightly, but the MAR futures yield increased more, as did the JUN futures yield. The poor performance of the stack hedge was due to this unequal change in rates.

A strip hedge

The stack hedge of the previous example was really hedging against a change in the DEC futures yield, because all of the contracts were stacked on that single futures expiration. Instead of using a concentration of contracts on a single expiration, a **strip hedge** uses an equal number of contracts for each futures expiration over the hedging horizon.

For our example of a $100 million financing requirement at risk for three quarters, we have seen that a Eurodollar hedge requires 300 contracts. In a strip hedge, the construction firm would sell 100 Eurodollar contracts each of the DEC, MAR, and JUN futures. With the strip hedge in place, each quarter of the coming year is hedged against shifts in interest rates for that quarter. To illustrate the effectiveness of this strip hedge for an unequal increase in rates, Table 6.15 shows the results for the construction firm example.

The strip hedge of Table 6.15 works perfectly. The superior performance of the strip hedge results from aligning the futures market hedges with the actual risk exposure of the construction firm. Because the construction firm faced interest rate adjustments each quarter, it needed to hedge the interest rate risk associated with each quarter. This it could do through a strip hedge, but not through a stack hedge.

Strip versus stack hedges

From the example of the strip hedge, it appears that a strip hedge will always be superior to a stack hedge. While there are many circumstances in which a strip hedge will be preferred, it is

Table 6.15 The results of a strip hedge

Date	Cash market	Futures market
September 20	Borrow $100 million at 9.00% for three months and commit to roll over the loan for three quarters at 200 basis points over the prevailing LIBOR rate	Sell 100 Eurodollar futures for each of: DEC at 92.70, MAR at 92.40, and JUN at 92.10
December 20	Pay interest of $2,250,000; LIBOR is now at 7.4%, so borrow $100 million for three months at 9.4%	Offset 100 DEC Eurodollar futures at 92.60; produce profit of $25,000 = 10 basis points × $25 per point × 100 contracts
March 20	Pay interest of $2,350,000 and borrow $100 million for three months at 10.30%	Offset 100 MAR Eurodollar futures at 91.70; produce profit of $175,000 = 70 basis points × $25 per point × 100 contracts
June 20	Pay interest of $2,575,000 and borrow $100 million for three months at 10.60%	Offset 100 JUN Eurodollar futures at 91.40; produce profit of $175,000 = 70 basis points × $25 per point × 100 contracts
September 20	Pay interest of $2,650,000 and principal of $100 million Total interest expense: $9,825,000	Futures profit: $375,000

Interest expense net of hedging: $9,450,000

not always better than a stack hedge. Our earlier example of a firm that had a six-month horizon used a stack hedge with great success. Here, the stack hedge exactly matched the timing of the firm's interest rate exposure, whereas a strip hedge would not have worked so well. The important point is to use a strip or stack hedge as required to match the timing of the futures hedge to the timing of the cash market risk exposure.

There is also a practical consideration that often leads hedgers to use a stack hedge when theory might favor a strip hedge. To implement a strip hedge requires trading more distant contracts. In our example, the construction firm traded the nearby, second, and third contracts. There is not always sufficient volume and liquidity in distant contracts to make such a strategy viable. Strips work well with Eurodollar futures, because Eurodollar futures now have sufficient volume in distant contracts to make them attractive. This has not always been the case, however. When distant contracts lack liquidity, the hedger must trade off the advantages of a strip hedge with the potential lack of liquidity in the distant contracts. For the dominant interest rate futures contracts, strips work well because of the great liquidity in these markets.

Tailing the hedge

In Chapter 3, we considered the effect of daily resettlement cash flows on futures pricing and the performance of futures positions. There, we concluded that a correlation between the futures price and interest rates could justify a difference between forward and futures prices. A positive correlation between the futures price and interest rates will cause the futures price to exceed the forward price. By contrast, a negative correlation between the futures price and interest rates will cause the futures price to fall below the forward price. In interest rate futures, the futures price is strongly negatively correlated with interest rates, because rising interest rates generate falling interest rate futures prices.

Daily resettlement cash flows also have potential importance for hedging. If a futures hedge generates positive daily resettlement cash flows, those funds will be available for investment once they are received. This means that the futures market hedging gain may unintentionally exceed the cash market loss. While unintentional gains on a futures hedge may not seem to be a problem, it is also possible to have the contrary results. For a hedge that is functioning properly, but the futures position is losing money, the futures position may generate losses that exceed the complementary cash market gain.

In **tailing the hedge**, the trader slightly adjusts the hedge to compensate for the interest that can be earned from daily resettlement profits or paid on daily resettlement losses. Thus, the tail of the hedge is the slight reduction in the hedge position to offset the effect of daily resettlement interest. Tailing a hedge can work for any kind of hedging. However, because the daily resettlement cash flows are likely to be more important when the futures price is correlated with interest rates, tailing the hedge is most often observed in interest rate futures hedging.

To illustrate the principle behind tailing the hedge, consider the following idealized example. A large financial institution plans to buy $1 billion in 90-day T-bills 91 days from now. The T-bill futures that expires then has a yield of 10.00 percent, so the expected cost of those T-bills is $975 million. The institution hedges that commitment by buying 1,000 T-bill futures contracts. Overnight, interest rates fall by ten basis points. With this fall in rates, the expected cost of the T-bills increases to $975.25 million, for a cash market loss of $250,000. The drop in rates, however, generates a futures gain of $250 per contract for a total gain of $250,000. Thus, the futures market gain exactly offsets the cash market loss—or at least it does before we consider the interest on the $250,000 daily resettlement.

The $250,000 daily resettlement flow can be invested for the next 90 days over the hedging horizon. (The funds are available for investment for 90 days because we started with a 91-day horizon.) We assume an investment rate of 10 percent with daily compounding and a 360-day year. Therefore, the $250,000 will grow to $256,028 = $250,000 \times 1.1^{90/360}$ by the time the hedge is over. For simplicity, we assume that this is the only change in rates. At the end of the hedging period, the financial institution buys its T-bills and still has $6,028 left over. This is the interest from the daily resettlement cash flow.

Consider now the original hedged position and assume that rates rise by ten basis points instead of falling. This change in rates generates a $250,000 daily resettlement outflow that the institution will have to finance for the next 90 days. Under this scenario, the financial institution will not be able to buy the T-bills, because it will lack $6,028 at the termination of the hedge. The institution has to pay the $6,028 as interest to finance the $250,000 daily resettlement outflow. From this example, it is clear that the financial institution has traded too many futures contracts. The total effect on the futures—the daily resettlement cash flow plus interest—has exceeded the cash market effect. This is true whether rates rise or fall.

To reduce these errors in hedging, the financial institution could have traded slightly fewer futures contracts. With the 10 percent investment rate on the daily resettlement flow and a 90-day investment horizon, every dollar of daily resettlement flow will grow to $1.0241 = $1 \times 1.1^{90/360}$. Therefore, the financial institution can find the tailed hedge position by multiplying the untailed hedge position by the **tailing factor**. In our example, the tailing factor is $1/1.0241$. Notice, however, that the tailing factor is nothing other than the present value of $1 at the hedging horizon discounted to the present (plus one day) at the investment rate for the resettlement cash flows.[10] Thus, we define the tailing factor as the present value (as of tomorrow) of $1 to be received at the hedging horizon. The tailed hedge position is as follows:

$$\text{tailed hedge} = \text{untailed hedge} \times \text{tailing factor} \tag{6.4}$$

In the untailed hedge of 1,000 contracts in our example, the tailed hedge would be 976.45 = 1,000/1.0241 contracts. Had the institution traded exactly that number of contracts, the results of the ten basis point change in rates would have been a daily resettlement cash flow of $244,112.50, equal to ten basis points times 25 basis points per contract times 976.45 contracts. This daily resettlement flow would grow to $250,000 = $244,112.50 \times 1.1^{90/360}$ by the time the hedge was lifted. Now the futures market effect at the hedging horizon exactly matches the cash market effect. In summary, to tail the hedge, we discount the untailed hedge position from the hedging horizon date to the present.

Because the tailed hedge depends on the time from the present to the hedging horizon, the tailed hedge changes constantly even if there is no change in the futures price. In the example of the $1 billion T-bill hedge, assume that the investment rate for daily resettlement cash flows is still 10 percent, but assume that only 31 days remain until the hedge will be terminated. The daily resettlement cash flow will be available for investment over 30 days. The tailing factor in this case is

$$0.9921 = \frac{1}{(1.1)^{30/360}}$$

This implies that the tailed hedge position on this date would be 992 contracts. For this example, the tailed hedge grew from 976 to 992 contracts over 60 days. This growth in the tailing factor is just the familiar growth in the present value factor as the discounting period gets smaller. For a hedging horizon of one day, the tailing factor is the present value from the hedging horizon to the present (plus one day). This is no time at all, so the tailing factor one day before the hedging horizon is 1.0.

Because futures can only be traded in whole contracts, tailing the hedge requires a large position, such as the 1,000 contracts of our example, to be useful. Also, since the tail depends on the interest rate from the present to the hedging horizon, the tail adjustment can only be as good as the hedger's estimate of the term interest rate from the present to the hedging horizon. In most cases, the tail adjustment is fairly small in percentage terms. In our original example of a 10 percent interest rate and a 90-day horizon, the tailed hedge was only 2.35 percent smaller than the untailed hedge. The higher the interest rate and the more distant the hedging horizon, the greater will be the tailing factor. However, even in most illustrative examples, the tail is seldom more than 5 percent of the untailed position.[11]

Hedging with T-bond futures

This section begins with an example of a cross-hedge of AAA corporate bonds. The example shows that a simple hedging rule of using $1 of futures per $1 of bonds can lead to horrible hedging results. This example leads to a discussion of alternative hedging techniques, focusing on hedging with T-bonds.

In all previous hedging examples, the hedged and hedging instruments were very similar. Often, however, the need arises to hedge an instrument that is very different from those underlying in the futures contract. The effectiveness of a hedge depends on the gain or loss on both the spot and futures sides of the transaction. But the change in the price of any bond depends on the shifts in the level of interest rates, changes in the shape of the yield curve, the maturity of the bond, and its coupon rate.

To illustrate the effect of the maturity and coupon rate on hedging performance, consider the following example. A portfolio manager learns on March 1 that he will receive $5 million on June 1 to invest in AAA corporate bonds that pay a coupon rate of 5 percent and have ten years to maturity. The yield curve is flat and is assumed to remain so over the period from March 1 to June 1. The current yield on AAA bonds is 7.5 percent. Since the yield curve is flat, the forward rates are also all 7.5 percent, so the portfolio manager expects to acquire the bonds at that yield. However, fearing a drop in rates, he decides to hedge in the futures market to lock in the forward rate of 7.5 percent.

The next step is to select the appropriate hedging instrument. The manager considers two possibilities: T-bills or T-bonds. However, the AAA bonds have a 5 percent coupon rate and a ten-year maturity, which does not match the coupon and maturity characteristics of either the T-bills or T-bonds deliverable on the respective futures contracts. The deliverable T-bills have a zero coupon and a maturity of only 90 days, while the deliverable T-bonds have a maturity of at least 15 years and an assortment of semiannual coupons. For this example, we assume that the cheapest-to-deliver T-bond will have a 20-year maturity at the target date of June 1, and that this cheapest-to-deliver bond has a 6 percent coupon.

To explore fully the potential difficulties of this situation, we consider hedging the AAA position with T-bill and T-bond futures. We ignore T-notes to dramatize the need to match coupon and maturity characteristics. For the bills and bonds, we assume the yields are 6 and 6.5 percent, respectively. Assuming that yields remain at 7.5 percent, the bond in which the manager plans to invest will have a price of $826.30. With $5 million to invest, the manager anticipates buying 6,051 bonds.

Table 6.16 presents the hedging transactions and results for the T-bill hedge. Because $5 million is becoming available for investment, assume the manager buys $5 million face value of T-bill futures contracts. Time passes, and by June 1 yields have fallen by 42 basis points on

Table 6.16   A cross-hedge between corporate bonds and T-bill futures

Date	Cash market	Futures market
March 1	A portfolio manager learns he will receive $5 million to invest in 5%, ten-year AAA bonds in three months, with an expected yield of 7.5% and a price of $826.30; the manager expects to buy 6,051 bonds	The portfolio manager buys $5 million face value of T-bill futures (five contracts) to mature on June 1 with a futures yield of 6.0% and a futures price, per contract, of $985,000
June 1	AAA yields have fallen to 7.08%, causing the price of the bonds to be $852.72 and representing a loss, per bond, of $26.42; since the plan was to buy 6,051 bonds, the total loss is 6,051 × $26.42 = −$159,867	The T-bill futures yield has fallen to 5.58%, so the futures price = spot price = $986,050 per contract, for a profit of $1,050 per contract; since five contracts were traded, the total profit is $5,250
	Loss = −$159,867	Gain = $5,250
	Net wealth change = −$154,617	

Table 6.17   A cross-hedge between corporate bonds and T-bond futures

Date	Cash market	Futures market
March 1	A portfolio manager learns he will receive $5 million to invest in 5%, ten-year AAA bonds in three months, with an expected yield of 7.5% and a price of $826.30; the manager expects to buy 6,051 bonds	The portfolio manager buys $5 million face value of T-bond futures (50 contracts) to mature on June 1 with a futures yield of 6.5% and a futures price, per contract, of $94,448
June 1	AAA yields have fallen to 7.08%, causing the price of the bonds to be $852.72 and representing a loss, per bond, of $26.42; since the plan was to buy 6,051 bonds, the total loss is 6,051 × $26.42 = −$159,867	The T-bond futures yield has fallen to 6.08%, so the futures price = spot price = $99,081 per contract, for a profit of $4,633 per contract; since 50 contracts were traded, the total profit is $231,650
	Loss = −$159,867	Gain = $231,650
	Net wealth change = +$71,783	

both the AAAs and the T-bills, respectively. The price of the corporate bond is $852.72, or $26.42 higher than the anticipated price of $826.30. Since the manager expected to buy 6,051 bonds, this means that the total additional outlay will be 6,051 × $26.42 = $159,867, and this represents the loss in the cash market. In the futures market, rates have also fallen by 42 basis points, generating a futures price increase of $1,050 per contract. Because five contracts were bought, the futures profit is $5,250. However, the loss in the cash market exceeds the gain in the futures market, for a net loss of $154,617. Note that this loss results even though rates changed by the same amount on both investments.

Consider now the same hedging problem, but assume that we implement the hedge using a $5 million face value of T-bond futures. Table 6.17 presents the transactions and results. Again yields fall by 42 basis points on both instruments. Consequently, the effect on the cash market is the same, but the total futures gain is $231,650, more than offsetting the loss in the cash market and generating a net wealth change equal to +$71,783.

If the goal of the hedge is to secure a net wealth change of zero, a gain is appropriately viewed as no better than a loss. It is only by accident of rates moving in the appropriate direction that the gain was not a loss anyway. Recall that all of the simplifying assumptions were in place—a flat yield curve, with rates on both instruments moving in the same direction and by the same amount. However, as noted earlier, the coupon and maturity of the hedged and hedging instruments do not match. All three instruments—the bond, the T-bill futures, and the T-bond futures—have different durations, reflecting different sensitivities to interest rates. Consequently, for a given shift in yields (e.g., 42 basis points), the prices of the three instruments will change by different amounts. Therefore, a simple hedge of $1 in the futures market per $1 in the cash market is unlikely to produce satisfactory results.

Alternative hedging strategies

We have seen that simple approaches to hedging interest rate risk often give unsatisfactory results, due to mismatches of coupon and maturity characteristics. For the best possible hedges, we need strategies that take these coupon and maturity mismatches into consideration. This section chronicles some of the major strategies for hedging interest rate risk, starting from simple models and going on to more complex models.

The face value naive model

According to the face value naive (FVN) model, the hedger should hedge $1 face value of the cash instrument with $1 face value of the futures contract. For example, a hedger wishing to hedge $100,000 face value of bonds would use one T-bond futures contract. The example we just considered used this strategy. The FVN strategy neglects two critically important factors:

(1)   By focusing on face values, the FVN model completely neglects potential differences in market values between the cash and futures positions. Therefore, keeping face value amounts equal between the cash and futures market can result in poor hedges because the market values of the two positions differ.

(2)   The FVN model neglects the coupon and maturity characteristics that affect duration for both the cash market good and the futures contract.

Because of these deficiencies, we will not consider the FVN model further.

The market value naive model

The market value naive (MVN) model resembles the FVN model, except that it recommends hedging $1 of market value in the cash good with $1 of market value in the futures market. For example, if a $100,000 face value bond has a market value of $90,000 and the $100,000 face value T-bond futures contract is priced at 80–00, the MVN model would recommend hedging the cash bonds with $1.125 = 90/80$ futures contracts.

Because it considers the difference between market and face value, the MVN model escapes the first criticism lodged against the FVN model. However, the MVN model still makes no adjustment for the price sensitivity of the two goods. Therefore, we dismiss the MVN model without further consideration.

The conversion factor model

The conversion factor (CF) model applies only to futures contracts that use conversion factors to determine the invoice amount, such as T-bond and T-note futures. The intuition of this model is to adjust for differing price sensitivities by using the conversion factor as an index of the sensitivity.

In particular, the CF model recommends hedging $1 of face value of a cash market security with $1 of face value of the futures good times the conversion factor. As we have seen for T-bond and T-note futures, there are many deliverable instruments with different conversion factors. To apply the CF model, we must determine which instrument is cheapest to deliver and use the conversion factor for that instrument. Assuming we have identified the cheapest-to-deliver security, the hedge ratio (HR) is given by the following:

$$\text{HR} = -\left(\frac{\text{cash market principal}}{\text{futures market principal}} \right) \times \text{conversion factor} \qquad (6.5)$$

The negative sign indicates that one must take a futures market position opposite to the cash market position. For example, if the hedger is long in the cash market, the hedger should sell futures.

As an example, assume that a bond manager wishes to hedge a long position of $500,000 face value of bonds with T-bond futures. We assume the cheapest-to-deliver bond has a conversion factor of 1.2. In this situation, the manager should sell $600,000 worth of T-bond futures ($500,000 × 1.2) or six contracts, since the notional principal of each T-bond futures contract is $100,000. The CF model attempts to secure the same amount of principal value of bonds on both the cash and futures sides of the hedge. This method is useful principally when one contemplates delivering a cash market bond against a futures contract.

The basis point model

The basis point (BP) model focuses on the price effect of a one basis point change in yields. For example, we have seen that a change of one basis point causes a $25 change in the futures price of a T-bill or Eurodollar contract. Assume that today is April 2 and that a firm plans to issue $50 million of 180-day commercial paper in six weeks. For a one basis point yield change, the price of 180-day commercial paper will change twice as much as the 90-day T-bill futures contract, assuming equal face value amounts. In other words, on $1 million of 180-day commercial paper, a one basis point yield change causes a $50 price change. In an important sense, the commercial paper will be twice as sensitive to a change in yields.

To reflect this greater sensitivity, we can use the BP model to compute the following hedge ratio:

$$HR = -\frac{BPC_S}{BPC_F} \tag{6.6}$$

where BPC_S is the dollar price change for a one basis point change in the spot instrument, and BPC_F is the dollar price change for a one basis point change in the futures instrument. The ratio BPC_S/BPC_F indicates the relative number of contracts to trade. In our commercial paper example, the cash basis price change (BPC_S) is twice as great as the futures basis price change (BPC_F), so the hedge ratio is −2.0.

To explore the effect of this weighting, consider the following BP model hedge of the commercial paper. Planning to issue commercial paper, the firm will lose if rates rise, because the firm will receive less cash for its commercial paper. As it needs to sell the commercial paper, it is now long commercial paper and the firm must hedge by selling futures. With a −2.0 hedge ratio and a $50 million face value commitment in the cash market, the firm should sell 100 T-bill futures contracts.

Table 6.18 presents the BP model transactions. After rates on both sides of the contract move by 45 basis points, we have the following result. In the cash market, the firm receives $112,500 less than anticipated for its commercial paper. This loss, however, is exactly offset by the price movement on the $100 million of T-bills underlying the futures position. The BP model helped identify the correct number of futures to trade for each unit in the cash market. By contrast, the FVN model would have suggested trading only 50 futures, which would have hedged only half of the loss.

Sometimes the yields may not change by the same amount as they did in Table 6.18. In that case, the hedger may wish to incorporate the relative volatility of the yields into the hedge ratio. For example, assume that the commercial paper rate is 25 percent more volatile than the T-bill futures rate. In other words, a 100 basis point rise in the T-bill futures rate normally might be accompanied by a 125 basis point rise in the commercial paper rate. To give the same total price change in the futures market as in the cash position, we would need to consider the difference in volatility in determining the hedge ratio. In that case, the hedge ratio becomes

Table 6.18   Hedging results with the BP model for the issuance of commercial paper

Date	Cash market	Futures market
April 2	Firm anticipates issuing $50 million in 180-day commercial paper in 45 days at a yield of 11%	Firm sells 100 T-bill June futures contracts yielding 10% with an index value of 90.00
May 15	Spot market and futures market rates have both risen 45 basis points; the spot rate is now 11.45% and the futures market yield is 10.45%	
	Cash market effect Each basis point move causes a price change of $50 per million-dollar face value; firm will receive $112,500 less for the commercial paper, due to the change in rates (45 basis points × −$50 × 50 = −$112,500)	**Futures market effect** Each basis point increase gives a futures market profit of $25 per contract Futures profit = 45 basis points × +$25 × 100 contracts = +$112,500
	Net wealth change = 0	

$$HR = -\left(\frac{BPC_S}{BPC_F}\right)RV \tag{6.7}$$

where RV is the volatility of the cash market yield relative to the futures yield, normally found by regressing the yield of the cash market instrument on the futures market yield.

If we incorporate RV, assumed to be 1.25, into our commercial paper hedge, the transactions would appear as shown in the top portion of Table 6.19. Now the hedge ratio is as follows:

$$HR = -\left(\frac{\$50}{\$25}\right) \times 1.25 = -2.5$$

Consequently, the hedger sells 125 T-bill futures contracts. Assume again that the T-bill yields rise by 45 basis points. Also, true to its greater relative volatility, the commercial paper yield moves 56 basis points, 1.25 times as much. Because more T-bill futures were sold, the T-bill futures profit still almost exactly offsets the commercial paper loss.

The regression model

One way of calculating a hedge ratio for interest rate futures is the regression technique that we considered in Chapter 4. The hedge ratio found by regression minimizes the variance of the combined futures–cash position during the estimation period. This estimated ratio is applied to the hedging period.

For the regression (RGR) model, the hedge ratio is as follows:

$$HR = -\frac{COV_{S,F}}{\sigma_F^2} \tag{6.8}$$

Table 6.19 Hedging results with the BP model adjusted for relative yield variances for the issuance of commercial paper

Date	Cash market	Futures market
April 2	Firm anticipates issuing $50 million in 180-day commercial paper in 45 days at a yield of 11%	Firm sells 125 T-bill June futures contracts yielding 10% with an index value of 90.00
May 15	Spot market rates have risen 56 basis points to 11.56% and futures rates have risen 45 basis points to 10.45%	
	Cash market effect Each basis point move causes a price change of $50 per million-dollar face value; firm will receive $140,000 less for the commercial paper, due to the change in rates (56 basis points × −$50 × 50 = −$140,000)	**Futures market effect** Each basis point increase gives a futures market profit of $25 per contract Futures profit = 45 basis points × +$25 × 125 contracts = +$140,625
	Net wealth change = $625	

where $COV_{S,F}$ is the covariance between cash and futures, and σ_F^2 is the variance of futures. As noted in Chapter 4, this hedge ratio is the negative of the regression coefficient found by regressing the change in the cash position on the change in the futures position. These changes can be measured as dollar price changes or as percentage price changes:

$$\Delta S_t = \alpha + \beta \Delta F_t + \varepsilon_t$$

The RGR model finds the hedge ratio that gives the lowest sum-of-squares errors for the data used in the estimation. Using the estimated hedge ratio for an actual hedge assumes that the relationship between the price changes on the futures and cash instruments does not change dramatically between the sample period and the actual hedging period.

This is a practical assumption. If the relationship is basically unchanged, then the estimated hedge ratio will perform well in the actual hedging situation. Fundamental shifts in the relationship between the price of the futures contract and the cash market good can lead to serious hedging errors. This danger is present in all hedging situations, but may be exacerbated in interest rate hedging. Without doubt, the RGR Model has proven its usefulness in the market for the traditional futures contracts, and it has been adapted for use in the interest rate futures market by Louis Ederington, Charles Franckle, Joanne Hill, and Thomas Schneeweis.[12]

However, there are some problems in applying the RGR Model to interest rate hedging. First, since it involves statistical estimation, the technique requires a dataset for both cash and futures prices. This data may sometimes be difficult to acquire, particularly for an attempt to hedge a new security. In such a case, no cash market data would even exist, and a proxy would have to be used. Second, the RGR Model does not explicitly consider the differences in the sensitivity of different bond prices to changes in interest rates. As the examples of Tables 6.16 and 6.17 indicate, this can be a very important factor. The regression approach does include the different price sensitivities indirectly, however, since their differential sensitivities will be reflected in the estimation of the hedge ratio. Third, any cash bond will have a predictable price movement over time. The price of any instrument will equal its par value at maturity. The RGR Model does not consider this change in the cash bond's price explicitly, but the sample data should reflect this price movement tendency. Fourth, the hedge ratio is found by minimizing the variability in the combined futures–cash position over the life of the hedge. Since the regression hedge ratio depends crucially on the planned hedge length, one might reasonably prefer a hedging technique that focuses on the wealth position of the hedge when the hedge ends.[13] After all, the wealth change from the hedge depends on the gain or loss when the hedge is terminated, not on the variability of the cash–futures position over the life of the hedge. In spite of these difficulties, the RGR Model is a useful way to estimate hedge ratios, both for traditional commodities and, to a lesser extent, for interest rate hedging.

The price sensitivity model

The price sensitivity (PS) model has been designed explicitly for interest rate hedging.[14] The PS model assumes that the goal of hedging is to eliminate unexpected wealth changes at the hedging horizon, defined as follows:

$$dP_i + dP_F(N) = 0 \qquad (6.9)$$

where dP_i is the unexpected change in the price of the cash market instrument, dP_F is the unexpected change in the price of the futures instrument, and N is the number of futures to hedge a single unit of the cash market asset. Equation 6.9 expresses the goal that the unexpected change in the value of the spot instrument, denoted by I, and that in the futures position, denoted by F, should together equal zero. If this is achieved, the wealth change, or hedging error, is zero. Instead of focusing on the variance over the period of the hedge, the PS Model uses a hedge ratio to achieve a zero net wealth change at the end of the hedge.

The problem for the hedger is to choose the correct number of contracts, denoted by N in Equation 6.9, to achieve a zero hedging error. **Modified duration**, MD, is defined as Macaulay's duration divided by $1 + r$. Thus, for a debt instrument x, with Macaulay's duration D_x and yield r_x,

$$MD_x = \frac{D_x}{1 + r_x}$$

The correct number of contracts to trade (N) per spot market bond is as follows:

$$N = -\frac{P_i MD_i}{FP_F MD_F} \times RYC \qquad (6.10)$$

where FP_F is the futures contract price; P_i is the price of asset i expected to prevail at the hedging horizon; MD_i is the modified duration of asset i expected to prevail at the hedging horizon; MD_F is the modified duration of the asset underlying futures contract F expected to prevail at the hedging horizon; and RYC is, for a given change in the risk-free rate, the change in the cash market yield relative to the change in the futures yield, often assumed to be 1.0 in practice. In nontechnical terms, Equation 6.10 says that the number of futures contracts to trade for each cash market instrument to be hedged is the number that should give a perfect hedge, assuming that yields on the cash and futures instrument change by the same amount. To explore the meaning and application of this technique, consider again the AAA bond hedges of Tables 6.16

Table 6.20   Data for the price sensitivity hedge

Cash instrument		T-bill futures		T-bond futures	
P_i $826.30		FP_i	$985,000	FP_F	$94,448
MD_i 7.207358		MD_F	0.235849	MD_F	10.946953
		N	−0.025636	N	−0.005760
		Number of	−155.12	Number of	−34.85
		contracts to trade		contracts to trade	

Table 6.21   A performance analysis of the price sensitivity futures hedge

	Cash market	T-bill hedge	T-bond hedge
Gain/loss	−$159,867	+$162,876	+$161,460
Hedging error	–	$3,009	$1,593
Percentage hedging error		1.8822%	0.9965%

and 6.17. The large hedging errors resulted from the different price sensitivities of the futures instruments and the AAA bonds.

Table 6.20 presents the data needed to calculate the hedge ratios for hedging the AAA bonds with T-bill or T-bond futures. Here, we assume that the cash and futures market assets have the same volatilities, so that RYC = 1.0. For the T-bill hedge,

$$N = -\frac{\$826.30 \times 7.207358}{\$985,000 \times 0.235849} = -0.025636$$

The hedger should sell 0.025636 T-bill futures per AAA bond to be hedged. Because the portfolio manager plans to buy 6,051 bonds, he should hedge this commitment by trading 155.12 T-bill futures. (For this illustration, we assume that it is possible to sell fractional contracts.)
For the T-bond hedge,

$$N = -\frac{\$826.30 \times 7.207358}{\$94,448 \times 10.946953} = -0.005760$$

With 6,051 bonds to hedge, the portfolio manager should sell 34.85 T-bond futures.
With either of these hedges, the same shift in yields on the AAA bonds and the futures instrument should give a perfect hedge. Table 6.21 presents the performance of these two hedges for the same 42 basis point drop in rates used in Tables 6.16 and 6.17.
With the given hedges and the same drop in yields, the T-bill hedge gave a futures gain of 155.12 contracts × 42 basis points × $25 per basis point = $162,876 to offset the loss on the AAA bonds of $159,867. The futures gain on the T-bond hedge is 34.85 contracts × $4,633 per contract = $161,460. The next line of Table 6.21 shows the size of the hedging error for the T-bill and T-bond hedges, while the final line gives the percentage hedging error. The hedges worked quite well, both restricting the hedging error to less than 2 percent, and the hedging error

on the T-bond hedge being just under 1 percent. The hedging error is largely due to the large discrete change in interest rates. Also, for the T-bill hedge, part of the error is due to the difference between the bank discount yield on the T-bill and the bond yields on the corporate bond.

Conclusion

It is difficult to compare all of the hedging models reviewed in this section, because they differ so much in aim and complexity. The naive hedges, face value naive and market value naive, are probably appropriate only for hedging short-term instruments with short-term futures contracts. The CF model is essentially a naive model applicable to futures contracts with the structure of T-note or T-bond futures contracts.

The most widely used technique is some version of the PS model, although the RGR model is also often employed. In fact, it has been shown that the PS and RGR models are equivalent when the hedging horizon is instantaneous.[15] Because of the problems in acquiring data for the RGR model, the PS model appears to be preferred.

In a number of papers, Joanne Hill and Thomas Schneeweis find that the RGR model is an effective hedging tool.[16] However, D. Lasser finds the RGR model to perform no better than various naive models.[17] Raymond Chiang, Gerald Gay, and Robert Kolb find that the PS model is more effective than naive models in hedging the risk of corporate bonds.[18] A. Toevs and D. Jacob offer a useful comparison of a number of hedging strategies, including the naive models and the RGR model, in which they find the PS model to be the most effective.[19] Finally, Ira Kawaller argues that the regression approach is inferior to the basis point or price sensitivity approaches in hedging.[20] Table 6.22 summarizes the various approaches to hedging.

Table 6.22   A summary of alternative hedging strategies

Hedging model	Basic intuition
Face value naive (FVN)	Hedge $1 of cash instrument face value with $1 of futures instrument face value
Market value naive (MVN)	Hedge $1 of cash instrument market value with $1 of futures instrument market value
Conversion factor (CF)	Find the ratio of the cash market principal to the futures market principal; multiply this ratio by the conversion factor for the cheapest-to-deliver instrument
Basis point (BP)	For a one basis point yield change, find the ratio of the cash market price change to the futures market price change (sometimes weighted by the relative volatility of interest rates on the cash market instrument compared to the futures instrument interest rate)
Regression (RGR)	For a given cash market position, use regression analysis to find the futures position that minimizes the variance of the combined cash/futures position
Price sensitivity (PS)	Using duration analysis, find the futures market position designed to give a zero wealth change at the hedging horizon (sometimes weighted by the relative volatility of interest rates on the cash market instrument compared to the futures instrument interest rate)

Table 6.23 Instruments for the immunization analysis

	Coupon (%)	Maturity	Yield (%)	Price	Duration
Bond A	8	4	12	875.80	3.4605
Bond B	10	10	12	885.30	6.3092
Bond C	4	15	12	449.41	9.2853
T-bond futures[a]	6	20	12	548.61	9.0401
T-bill futures[a]	–	$1/4$	12	970.00	0.2500

[a]For comparability, face values of $1,000 are assumed for these instruments.

Immunization with interest rate futures

In bond investing, duration mismatches result in exposure to interest rate risk. For example, a financial institution, such as a bank or savings and loan association, might have an asset portfolio with a duration greater than its liability portfolio. A sudden rise in interest rates will cause the value of the assets to fall more than the value of the liability portfolio. As another type of risk, a bond portfolio might be managed to a certain future date, perhaps when a firm's pension liabilities become due. If the duration of the bond portfolio exceeds the time until the horizon date, a swing in interest rates will cause the present value of the bond portfolio to change more than the present value of the liabilities, leaving the entire bond portfolio/pension plan exposed to interest rate risk. By matching the duration of the assets and liabilities, it is possible for the financial institution to immunize itself against interest rate risk, which we call the bank immunization case. For the bond portfolio being managed to a horizon date, a similar immunization can be achieved by setting the duration of a bond portfolio equal to the length of the planning period. We call this the planning period case.[21]

Often, such immunization is very difficult to achieve. For example, banks cannot simply turn away depositors because they wish to lengthen the duration of their liabilities. With the development of interest rate futures markets, financial managers have a valuable new tool to use in immunization strategies. This section presents two examples of immunizing with interest rate futures, one for the planning period case and one for the bank immunization case. Table 6.23 presents data on three bonds we will use in the immunization examples, along with data for T-bill and T-bond futures contracts. The table reflects the assumption of a flat yield curve and instruments of the same risk level.

The planning period case
Consider a $100 million bond portfolio of Bond C with a duration of 9.2853 years. Assume now that a manager wants to shorten the portfolio duration to six years to match a given planning period. The shortening could be accomplished by selling Bond C and buying Bond A until the following conditions are met:

$$W_A D_A + W_C D_C = \text{six years}$$
$$W_A + W_C = 1$$

where W_i is the percentage of the portfolio funds committed to asset i. This means that the manager must put 56.39 percent of the $100 million in Bond A, the funds coming from the sale of Bond C. Call this Portfolio 1.

Alternatively, the manager could adjust the portfolio's duration to match the six-year planning period by trading interest rate futures. In Portfolio 2, the manager will keep $100 million in Bond C and trade futures to adjust the duration of the combined portfolio of Bond C and futures. If Bond C and T-bill futures comprise Portfolio 2, the T-bill futures position must satisfy the following condition:

$$P_P = P_C N_C + FP_{\text{T-bill}} N_{\text{T-bill}}$$

where P_P is the value of the portfolio, P_C is the price of Bond C, $FP_{\text{T-bill}}$ is the T-bill futures price, N_C is the number of C bonds, and $N_{\text{T-bill}}$ is the number of T-bills.

The following equation expresses the change in the price of a bond as a function of duration and the yield on the asset:

$$dP = -D[d(1 + r)/(1 + r)]P \qquad (6.11)$$

Applying Equation 6.11 to the portfolio value, Bond C, and the T-bill futures we have the following immunization condition:

$$-D_P\left(\frac{d(1 + r)}{1 + r}\right)P_P = -D_C\left(\frac{d(1 + r)}{1 + r}\right)P_C N_C - D_{\text{T-bill}}\left(\frac{d(1 + r)}{1 + r}\right)FP_{\text{T-bill}} N_{\text{T-bill}}$$

This can be simplified to the following:

$$D_P P_P = D_C P_C N_C + D_{\text{T-bill}} FP_{\text{T-bill}} N_{\text{T-bill}}$$

Because immunization requires mimicking Portfolio 1, which has a total value of $100 million and a duration of six years, it must be the case that $P_P = \$100$ million, $D_P = 6$, $D_C = 9.2853$, $P_C = \$449.41$, $N_C = 222{,}514$, $D_{\text{T-bill}} = 0.25$, and $FP_{\text{T-bill}} = \$970.00$.

Solving for $N_{\text{T-bill}} = -1{,}354{,}764$ indicates that this many T-bills (assuming $1,000 par value) must be sold short in the futures market. Because a T-bill futures contract has a $1 million face value, this technique requires selling 1,355 contracts. The same technique used to create Portfolio 2 can be applied using a T-bond futures contract, giving rise to Portfolio 3. Solving

$$D_P P_P = D_C P_C N_C + D_{\text{T-bond}} FP_{\text{T-bond}} N_{\text{T-bond}}$$

for $N_{\text{T-bond}}$ gives $N_{\text{T-bond}} = -66{,}243$. Since T-bond futures contracts have a face value denomination of $100,000, the trader must sell 662 T-bond futures contracts. For each of the three portfolios, Table 6.24 summarizes the relevant data.

To see how the immunized portfolio performs, assume that rates drop from 12 to 11 percent for all maturities. Assume also that all coupon receipts during the six-year planning period can be reinvested at 11 percent, compounded semiannually, until the end of the planning period. With the shift in interest rates the new prices are as follows: $P_A = \$904.98$, $P_C = \$491.32$, $FP_{\text{T-bill}} = \$972.50$, and $FP_{\text{T-bond}} = \$598.85$.

Table 6.25 shows the effect of the interest rate shift on portfolio values, terminal wealth at the horizon (year 6), and on the total wealth position of the portfolio holder. As Table 6.25 reveals, each portfolio responds similarly to the shift in yields. The slight differences are due to either rounding errors or the fact that the duration price change formula holds exactly only for infinitesimal changes in yields. The largest difference (between terminal values for

Table 6.24 Portfolio characteristics for the planning period case

		Portfolio 1 (bonds only)	Portfolio 2 (short T-bill futures)	Portfolio 3 (short T-bond futures)
Portfolio weights	W_A	56.39%	–	–
	W_C	43.61%	100%	100%
	W_{Cash}	~0	~0	~0
Number of instruments	N_A	64,387	0	–
	N_C	97,038	222,514	222,514
	$N_{\text{T-bill}}$	–	(1,354,764)	–
	$N_{\text{T-bond}}$	–	–	(66,243)
Value of each instrument	$N_A P_A$	56,390,135	–	–
	$N_C P_C$	43,609,848	100,000,017	100,000,017
	$N_{\text{T-bill}} FP_{\text{T-bill}}$	–	1,314,121,080	–
	$N_{\text{T-bond}} FP_{\text{T-bond}}$	–	–	36,341,572
	Cash	17	(17)	(17)
Portfolio value	$N_A P_A + N_C P_C + cash$	100,000,000	100,000,000	100,000,000

Source: Adapted from R. Kolb and G. Gay, "Immunizing Bond Portfolios with Interest Rate Futures," *Financial Management*, Summer 1982, pp. 81–9. Reprinted by permission of the author and the Financial Management Association

Table 6.25 The effect of a 1 percent drop in yields on realized portfolio returns

	Portfolio 1	Portfolio 2	Portfolio 3
Original portfolio value	100,000,000	100,000,000	100,000,000
New portfolio value	105,945,674	109,325,562	109,325,562
Gain/loss on futures	0	(3,386,910)	(3,328,048)
Total wealth change	5,945,674	5,938,652	5,997,514
Terminal value of all funds at $t = 6$	$201,424,708	$201,411,358	$201,523,267
Annualized holding period: Return over six years	1.120180	1.120168	1.120266

Source: Adapted from R. Kolb and G. Gay, "Immunizing Bond Portfolios with Interest Rate Futures," *Financial Management*, Summer 1982, pp. 81–9. Terminal values and holding period returns assume semiannual compounding at 11 percent. Reprinted by permission of the author and the Financial Management Association

Portfolios 2 and 3) is only 0.056 percent, which reveals the effectiveness of the alternative strategies.

The bank immunization case

Assume that a bank holds a $100 million liability portfolio in Bond B, the composition of which is fixed. The bank wishes to hold an asset portfolio of Bonds A and C that will protect the wealth position of the bank from any change as a result of a change in yields.

Five different portfolio combinations illustrate different means to achieve the desired result:

Portfolio 1: hold Bonds A and C (the traditional approach)
Portfolio 2: hold Bond C; sell T-bill futures
Portfolio 3: hold Bond A; buy T-bond futures
Portfolio 4: hold Bond A; buy T-bill futures
Portfolio 5: hold Bond C; sell T-bond futures

For each portfolio in Table 6.26, the full $100 million is put in a bond portfolio (and is balanced out by cash). Portfolio 1 exemplifies the traditional approach of immunizing by holding only bonds. Portfolios 2 and 5 are composed of Bond C and a short futures position. By contrast, the low volatility Bond A is held in Portfolios 3 and 4. In conjunction with Bond A, the overall interest rate sensitivity is increased by buying interest rate futures.

Now assume an instantaneous drop in rates from 12 to 11 percent for all maturities. Table 6.27 shows the effect on the portfolios. As the rows that report wealth change reveal, all five methods perform similarly. The small differences stem from rounding errors and the discrete change in interest rates.

One important concern in the implementation of immunization strategies is the transaction cost involved. In immunizing, commission charges, marketability, and liquidity of the instruments involved become increasingly important. These considerations highlight the practical usefulness of interest rate futures in bond portfolio management. Consider as an example the transaction costs associated with the different immunization portfolios for the planning period case. Starting from the initial position of $100 million in Bond C, and wishing to shorten the duration to six years, Table 6.28 shows the trades necessary and the estimated costs involved. To implement the "bonds only" traditional approach of Portfolio 1, one must sell 125,476 bonds of type C and buy 64,387 bonds of type A. Assuming a commission charge of $5 per bond, the total commission is $949,315. By contrast, one could sell 1,355 T-bill futures contracts to immunize Portfolio 2, or sell 662 T-bond futures contracts for Portfolio 3, at total costs of $27,100 and $13,240, respectively. (Additionally, one would have to deposit approximately $2 million margin for the T-bill strategy or $1 million for the T-bond strategy. But this margin deposit can be in the form of interest earning assets.) Table 6.28 presents these transaction costs calculations.

Clearly, there is a tremendous difference in transaction costs between trading the cash and futures instruments. In an extreme example of this type, the transaction costs for the "bonds only" case is prohibitive, amounting to almost 1 percent of the total portfolio value. It is practically impossible for another reason: the volume of bonds to be traded is enormous, exceeding any reasonable volume for bonds of even the largest issue. By contrast, today's robust futures volume makes it easy to implement the futures-based immunization strategies.[22]

Until recently, immunization strategies for bond portfolios have focused on all bond portfolios. Here it has been shown that interest rate futures can be used in conjunction with bond portfolios to provide the same kind of immunization. The method advocated here works equally well for the planning period case and the bank immunization case. Note that all of the examples assumed parallel shifting yield curves. If the change in interest rates brings about nonparallel shifts in the yield curve, then the "bonds only" and "bonds-with-futures" approaches will give different results. Which method turns out to be superior would depend upon the pattern of interest rate changes that actually occurred.

Table 6.26 A liability portfolio and five alternative immunizing portions

		Liability portfolio	Portfolio 1 (bonds only)	Portfolio 2 (short T-bill futures)	Portfolio 3 (long T-bond futures)	Portfolio 4 (long T-bill futures)	Portfolio 5 (short T-bond futures)
Portfolio weights	W_A	0	51.0936%	0	100%	100%	0
	W_B	100%	0	0	0	0	0
	W_C	0	48.9064%	100%	0	0	100%
	W_{Cash}	~0	~0	~0	~0	~0	~0
Number of instruments	N_A	0	58,339	0	114,181	114,181	0
	N_B	112,956	0	0	0	0	0
	N_C	0	108,824	222,514	0	0	222,514
	$N_{T\text{-bill}}$	0	0	(1,227,258)	57,440	1,174,724	(60,008)
	$N_{T\text{-bond}}$	0	0	0			
	$N_A P_A$	0	51,093,296	0	99,999,720	99,999,720	0
	$N_B P_B$	99,999,947	0	0	0	0	0
	$N_C P_C$	0	48,906,594	100,000,017	0	0	100,000,017
	Cash	53	110	(17)	280	280	(17)
	$N_{T\text{-bill}} P_{T\text{-bill}}$	0	0	(1,190,440,260)	31,512,158	1,139,482,280	0
	$N_{T\text{-bond}} P_{T\text{-bond}}$	0	0	0			(32,920,989)
Portfolio value		$100,000,000	$100,000,000	$100,000,000	$100,000,000	$100,000,000	$100,000,000

Source: Adapted from R. Kolb and G. Gay, "Immunizing Bond Portfolios with Interest Rate Futures," *Financial Management*, Summer 1982, pp. 81–9. Reprinted with permission of the author and Financial Management Association

Table 6.27   The effect of a 1 percent drop in yields on total wealth

	Liability	Portfolio 1	Portfolio 2	Portfolio 3	Portfolio 4	Portfolio 5
Original portfolio value	$100,000,000	$100,000,000	$100,000,000	$100,000,000	$100,000,000	$100,000,000
New portfolio value	$106,206,932	$106,263,146	$109,325,578	$103,331,521	$103,331,521	$109,325,579
Profit on futures	0	–	($3,068,145)	$2,885,786	$2,936,810	($3,014,802)
Total wealth change (portfolio and futures)	$6,206,932	$6,263,146	$6,257,416	$6,217,587	$6,268,611	$6,310,760
Total wealth change (asset-liability portfolio)	–	$56,214	$50,484	$10,655	$61,679	$103,828
% Wealth change	–	0.00056	0.00050	0.00011	0.00062	0.00104

Source: Adapted from R. Kolb and G. Gay, "Immunizing Bond Portfolios with Interest Rate Futures," *Financial Management*, Summer 1982, pp. 81–9. Reprinted by permission of the author and the Financial Management Association

Table 6.28   Transaction costs for the planning period case

	Portfolio 1	Portfolio 2	Portfolio 3
Number of instruments traded			
Bond A	64,387	–	–
Bond C	125,476	–	–
T-bill futures contracts		1,355	–
T-bond futures contracts	–	–	662
One-way transaction cost			
Bond A @ $5	321,935	–	–
Bond C @ $5	627,380	–	–
T-bill futures $20	–	27,100	–
T-bond futures @ $20	–	–	13,240
Total cost of becoming immunized	$949,315	$27,100	$13,240

Source: Adapted from R. Kolb and G. Gay, "Immunizing Bond Portfolios with Interest Rate Futures," *Financial Management*, Summer 1982, pp. 81–9. Reprinted by permission of the author and the Financial Management Association

Long-Term Capital Management

Philippe Jorion (2000) has provided an excellent review of the facts surrounding the 1998 collapse of Long-Term Capital Management (LTCM), a private hedge fund.[23] The following brief description of this case is excerpted from Jorion's study.

Although a derivatives trading strategy was not the initial cause of LTCM's downfall, LTCM did hold extremely large derivatives positions, including many privately negotiated swap contracts with some of Wall Street's largest financial institutions. The suddenness of LTCM's collapse left the fund's swap counterparties with credit risk exposures greatly in excess of their initial expectations. A bankruptcy by LTCM would have created large losses for its swap counterparties, lenders, and other creditors. In the judgment of the Federal Reserve's authorities, these losses were potentially large enough to impair not only these direct market participants, but also the economies of many nations.

Long-Term Capital Management was founded in 1993 by John Meriwether, who had previously headed up the highly profitable bond-arbitrage group at Salomon Brothers. At LTCM, Meriwether assembled a partnership consisting of former Salomon traders, two Nobel laureates (Robert Merton and Myron Scholes), and a former vice chairman of the Board of Governors of the Federal Reserve System (David Mullins). LTCM was set up as a hedge fund, employing the same trading strategies that had been used by Meriwether at Salomon Brothers.

In the early days of LTCM, the fund took little outright risk. The firm's goal was to limit the fund's risk to the same level of risk as the overall stock market. LTCM's core strategy involved trades designed to take advantage of small differences in prices of nearly identical bonds. In essence, the fund placed bets on small price differences that were likely to narrow as the nearly identical bonds converged to the same value. Based on an analysis of historical correlations, LTCM judged that convergence was likely to happen, barring default or market disruptions. The strategy worked well for the firm in 1995 and 1996, returning over 40 percent annually to investors after fees and expenses. By 1997, the firm had amassed investment capital of $7 billion and controlled $125 billion in assets.

During 1997, convergence trades had become less profitable, and LTCM produced a return of only 17 percent, compared to U.S. stocks, which gained 33 percent. Since the fund claimed to have the same overall level of risk as the stock market, producing lower returns than the stock market was embarrassing. The fund had to find a way to produce higher returns for its investors.

Part of LTCM's strategy to produce higher returns involved returning capital to investors. By shrinking the capital base to $4.7 billion while keeping assets at $125 billion, investors who remained in the fund, the thinking went, would see higher returns. Of course, a consequence of this action was that the leverage ratio of the fund went up.

LTCM enjoyed huge respect from Wall Street financial firms, many of which were clamoring to invest in the fund. But the firm was not seeking new investors, especially at a time when it was trying to shrink its capital base and increase leverage. However, some investors were allowed to participate in the fund under the condition, allegedly, that they also loaned funds to LTCM. Union Bank of Switzerland invested $266 and also loaned the fund $800 million. Credit Suisse Financial Products invested $33 million and loaned the fund $100 million.

In addition to increasing leverage, the fund also looked for new opportunities to exploit its trading strategy, adding new risks to the equation. LTCM applied its convergence arbitrage strategy to the swaps market, betting that the spread between swap rates and the most liquid Treasury bonds would narrow. It also applied the strategy to spreads between callable bonds and interest rate swaptions. The strategy was also applied to mortgage-backed securities and double-A corporate bonds. LTCM then ventured into equity trades, selling equity index options and taking speculative positions in takeover stocks with total return swaps. It became one of the largest players on the world's futures exchanges in debt and equity products. It had positions in futures, options, swaps, and other over-the-counter (OTC) derivatives totaling more than $1 trillion in notional principal.[24] Many of these trades offset each other, so the notional principal was not reflective of the fund's level of risk.

LTCM's troubles began in May and June 1998, when a downturn in the mortgage-backed securities market caused the value of the fund to drop about 16 percent. In August, Russia announced that it was defaulting on its bond payments–news that sent shock waves through the world's financial markets. The Russian bond default led the market to reassess credit risks in general, but credit risks on sovereign (i.e., government-issued) debt in particular. The Russian bond default caused credit spreads to increase sharply and stock markets to plunge. LTCM now found that it was on the losing side of the bets it had placed on the direction of swap spreads and stock market volatility.

By the end of August, LTCM's year-to-date loss exceeded 50 percent. In September, the portfolio's losses accelerated, with the investors losing a cumulative 92 percent of their year-to-date investment. The losses triggered huge margin calls on LTCM's losing T-bond futures positions. LTCM met the margin calls by depleting the fund's liquid resources. LTCM was now on the brink of bankruptcy, unable to meet further margin calls.

At the same time it was responding to margin calls on its futures positions, LTCM's 36 swap counterparties began to call for more collateral to cover the large credit exposure that LTCM now posed. Even with posted collateral, LTCM's swap counterparties feared that LTCM's collateral was insufficient to cover large losses. In addition, LTCM's counterparties feared that there was potential for losses to accrue before the collateral could be liquidated. While the counterparties monitored the credit risk of their individual positions with LTCM, it became clear in retrospect that they were unaware of the extent of LTCM's swap positions with other counterparties. Swap counterparties also failed to gauge the full extent of LTCM's leverage, resulting in a serious underestimate of the counterparty credit exposure posed by the fund.

By late September, lenders, swap counterparties, and other creditors began to sense the magnitude of the problem they faced. Bankruptcy, once thought to be a remote possibility, was now a distinct possibility. Because the fund was organized in the Cayman Islands, it was believed that LTCM would seek bankruptcy protection under Cayman law, as opposed to U.S. law. This fact added to the uncertainty faced by swap dealers, lenders, and other creditors.

In late September, the Federal Reserve Bank of New York organized a bailout for LTCM, by encouraging 14 banks to invest $3.6 billion in return for a 90 percent stake in the firm. The New York Fed was led to its action out of fear that an LTCM bankruptcy would trigger a contagion effect–that is a domino-like series of sequential defaults–spreading out across the globe. In addition, there was concern that an unknown number of other players in the market had positions similar to that of LTCM, and that any market disruptions caused by an LTCM bankruptcy would create a liquidity crisis as these other players rushed for the exits.

The bailout averted near-certain bankruptcy. But many commentators have questioned the wisdom of the New York Fed's actions. By intervening, it is argued, the New York Fed undermined the market discipline that is enforced by pain of failure. Allowing LTCM to fail, it is argued, would have provided powerful incentives for other hedge funds to more carefully examine their risk management practices. It also would have forced swap dealers and lenders to do a better job of accessing the true extent of their credit exposure to funds, such as LTCM.

By the end of 1999, all money had been paid back to investors and John Meriwether had started a new hedge fund. Because the possibility of bankruptcy was averted by the bailout, we will never know if the New York Fed's fears of a contagion effect were justified. Although derivatives were not the initial cause of the LTCM fiasco, the case still offers important lessons about potential dangers of using financial derivatives. The case highlights the importance of managing counterparty credit risk. The case also highlights the need for stress testing day-to-day risk management. The example of LTCM also illustrates the potential problems caused by model risk. LTCM's trading models contained assumptions about the historical correlation of assets that failed to account for the possibility of market disruptions.

Conclusion

Interest rate futures constitute one of the most exciting and complex financial markets. Only in recent years have the uses of the market begun to mature, and there remain many potential users who could benefit from the market. As we have seen, interest rate futures have many applications, including bond portfolio management. Interest rate futures can also be used to control foreign interest rate risk, to manage public utilities and insurance companies, to hedge mortgage financing risk, and to reduce risk in creative financing arrangements. Other uses abound and are just starting to be explored.

"White Auggie, Red Auggie"

Futures contracts are listed several years into the future. For example, the Eurodollar futures contract traded at the CME has contracts listed on a quarterly cycle (March, June, September, and December) extending ten years into the future. Each year of the quarterly expiration cycle is called a "pack." So, for the Eurodollar contract, at any one time there will be ten packs trading (40 contract months). To distinguish between the packs, information on the contracts is displayed according to a color coding system. On the floor of the exchange, the first year's contracts (called the front months) are displayed with a white line across the top of the board. For the next pack, red is used. Each pack has its own color identity:

Pack 1 (current year) = white
Pack 2 (contracts 1–2 years out) = red
Pack 3 (contracts 2–3 years out) = green
Pack 4 (contracts 3–4 years out) = blue
Pack 5 (contracts 4–5 years out) = gold
Pack 6 (contracts 5–6 years out) = purple
Pack 7 (contracts 6–7 years out) = orange
Pack 8 (contracts 7–8 years out) = pink
Pack 9 (contracts 8–9 years out) = silver
Pack 10 (contracts 9–10 years out) = copper

This color system has migrated from the trading floor to electronic trading screens. In addition, information vendors, such as Bloomberg, have adopted the custom in displaying market information.

Traders use slang terms to identify contract months. August is "Auggie" and December is "Dec" (pronounced "deese"). So, a "white Auggie" refers to this year's August contract and a "red Auggie" refers to next year's August contract.

Contract months are also identified by standard letter symbols when they are quoted. The assigned symbols are as follows:

January = F	April = J	July = N	October = V
February = G	May = F	August = Q	November = X
March = H	June = M	September = U	December = Z

So, for example, the December S&P 500® contract at the CME would combine the product symbol SP with the contract month symbol, Z, and be listed as "SPZ."

Exercises

1   Explain the risks inherent in a reverse cash-and-carry strategy in the T-bond futures market.

2   Explain how the concepts of quasi-arbitrage help to overcome the risks inherent in reverse cash-and-carry trading in T-bond futures.

3   Assume that the economic and political conditions are extremely turbulent. How would this affect the value of the seller's options on the T-bond futures contract? If they have any effect on price, would they cause the futures price to be higher or lower than it otherwise would be?

4   Explain the difference between the wildcard option and the end-of-the-month option.

5   Some studies have found that interest rate futures markets were not very efficient when they first began but that they became efficient after a few years. How can you explain this transition?

6   Assume you hold a T-bill that matures in 90 days, when the T-bill futures expires. Explain how you could transact to effectively lengthen the maturity of the bill.

7   Assume that you will borrow on a short-term loan in six months, but you do not know whether you will be offered a fixed-rate or a floating-rate loan. Explain how you can use futures to convert a fixed-rate loan to a floating-rate loan, and to convert a floating-rate loan to a fixed-rate loan.

8   You fear that the yield curve may change shape. Explain how this belief would affect your preference for a strip or a stack hedge.

9   A futures guru says that tailing a hedge is extremely important, because it can change the desired number of contracts by 30 percent. Explain why the guru is nuts. By how much can the tailing factor reasonably change the hedge ratio?

10   We have seen in Chapter 4 that regression-based hedging strategies are extremely popular. Explain their weaknesses for interest rate futures hedging.

11   You estimate that the cheapest-to-deliver bond on the T-bond futures contract has a duration of 6.5 years. You want to hedge your medium-term Treasury portfolio that has a duration of 4.0 years. Yields are 9.5 percent on the futures and on your portfolio. Your portfolio is worth $120 million and the futures price is 98–04. Using the PS model, how would you hedge?

12   Explain the relationship between the bank immunization case and hedging with the PS model.

13   Compare and contrast the BP and RGR models for immunizing a bond portfolio.

14   It is a hot day in August, and William has just completed the purchase of $20 million of T-bills maturing next March and $10 million of T-bills maturing in one month. The phone rings, and William is informed that the firm has just made a commitment to provide $30 million in capital to a client in mid-December. If William had known this 20 min earlier, he would have invested differently.

A   What risks does William face by using his present investments to meet the December commitment?

B   Using the futures markets, how can William reduce the risks of the December commitment? Show what transactions would be made.

15   Handcraft Ale, Ltd. has decided to build additional production capacity in the United States to meet increasing demand in North America. Uma Peele has been given the responsibility of obtaining financing for the project. Handcraft Ale will need $10 million to carry the firm through the construction phase. This phase will last two years, at which time the $10 million debt will be repaid using the proceeds of a long-term debt issue. Ms. Peele gets rate quotes from several different London banks. The best quote is as follows:

Variable: LIBOR + 150 basis points
Fixed: 8.5 percent

Each of these loans would require quarterly interest payments on the outstanding loan amount. Ms. Peele looks up the current LIBOR rate and finds that it is 5.60 percent. The variable rate of 7.1 percent (5.60 + 1.5) looks very attractive, but Ms. Peele is concerned about interest rate risk over the next two years.

A   What could Ms. Peele do to take advantage of the lower variable rate while at the same time have the comfort of fixed-rate financing?

B   Consider the following three-month Eurodollar quotes:

Delivery month	Rate
AUG 06	94.32
SEP	94.34
OCT	94.31
NOV	94.33
DEC	94.35
JAN 07	94.43
MAR	94.40
JUN	94.43
SEP	94.40
DEC	94.25
MAR 08	94.30
JUN	94.27
SEP	94.23
DEC	94.15

Handcraft Ale takes out a floating-rate note, with the first interest payment coming in December. LIBOR at the time of loan initiation is 5.70 percent. Design a strip hedge to convert the Handcraft Ale floating-rate note to a fixed-rate note. What is the anticipated fixed rate?

C   Suppose that Handcraft Ale's quarterly interest payments were in November, February, May and August. Would a strip hedge be possible? Design a hedge that Ms. Peele could use in this case.

16   Jim Hunter is preparing to hedge his investment firm's decision to purchase $100 million of 90-day T-bills 60 days from now in June. The discount yield on the 60-day T-bill is 6.1 percent, and the June T-bill futures contract is trading at 94.80. Jim views these rates as very attractive relative to recent history, and he would like to lock them in. His first impulse is to buy 100 June T-bill futures contracts, but his recent experience leads him to believe that he should be buying something less.

A   Why is a one-to-one hedge ratio inappropriate in Jim's situation?

B   Compute an appropriate hedge ratio given the market conditions faced by Jim.

C   Under what conditions might Jim need to adjust his hedge ratio between now and June?

17   Alex Brown has just returned from a seminar on using futures for hedging purposes. As a result of what he has learned, he reexamines his decision to hedge $500 million of long-term debt that his firm plans to issue in May. His current hedge is a short position of 5,000 T-bond futures contracts ($100,000 each). If the debt could be issued today, it would be priced at 119–22 to yield 6.5 percent. With its 8 percent coupon and 30 years to maturity, the duration of the debt would be 13.09 years. On the futures side, the futures prices are based on the cheapest-to-deliver bonds, which are trading at 124–14 to yield 5.6 percent. These bonds have a duration of 9.64 years.

A   List and briefly describe possible strategies Alex Brown could use to hedge his impending debt issue.

B   What strategy is Alex Brown currently using? What are the strengths and weaknesses of this strategy?

C   Based on the knowledge Alex gained at the hedging seminar, he feels that a price sensitivity hedge would be most appropriate for his situation. Design a hedge using the price sensitivity method. Assume that the relative volatility between the corporate interest rate and the T-bond interest rate, RV, is equal to one.

D   At the time of refinancing, the T-bond futures price is 121–27 and B.I.G.'s new debt issue is priced at 116–08. Compute the net wealth change resulting from the naive hedge.

E   Compute the net wealth change resulting from the price sensitivity hedge.

Notes

1   We ignore the differences between the three-day settlement process in futures markets and the one-day settlement procedures common in the cash market.

2   G. Gay and S. Manaster, "Implicit Delivery Options and Optimal Delivery Strategies for Financial Futures Contracts," *Journal of Financial Economics*, 16:1, 1986, pp. 41–72.

3   See R. Rendleman and C. Carabini, "The Efficiency of the Treasury Bill Futures Market," *Journal of Finance*, 34:4, 1979, pp. 895–914. In this article, they develop the idea of quasi-arbitrage.

4   See R. Kolb, G. Gay, and J. Jordan, "Are There Arbitrage Opportunities in the Treasury-Bond Futures Market?" *Journal of Futures Markets*, 2:3, 1982, pp. 217–30.

5   B. Resnick and E. Hennigar, "The Relationship between Futures and Cash Prices for U.S. Treasury Bonds," *Review of Research in Futures Markets*, 2:3, 1983, pp. 282–99.

6   B. Resnick, "The Relationship between Futures Prices for U.S. Treasury Bonds," *Review of Research in Futures Markets*, 3:1, 1984, pp. 88–104.

7   R. Klemkosky and D. Lasser, "An Efficiency Analysis of the T-Bond Futures Market," *Journal of Futures Markets*, 5:4, 1985, pp. 607–20. The quoted material is from page 620.

8   D. Chance, "A Semi-Strong Form Test of the Efficiency of the Treasury Bond Futures Market," *Journal of Futures Markets*, 5:3, 1985, pp. 385–405.

9   We ignore the daily resettlement feature and the interest that could have been earned on the $125,000 futures profit in the second quarter.

10   Strictly speaking, it is the discount factor from the hedging horizon to the present plus one day. For example, the hedge was initiated with 91 days to the horizon, the cash flow was generated on that day and became available for investment with 90 days to run until the hedging horizon.

11   For more on tailing, see I. Kawaller, "Hedging with Futures Contracts: Going the Extra Mile," *Journal of Cash Management*, 6, 1986, pp. 34–6; and I. Kawaller and T. Koch, "Managing Cash Flow Risk in Stock Index Futures: The Tail Hedge," *The Journal of Portfolio Management*, 15:1, 1988, pp. 41–4.

12   See L. Ederington, "The Hedging Performance of the New Futures Market," *Journal of Finance*, 34:1, 1979, pp. 157–70; C. Franckle, "The Hedging Performance of the New Futures Market: Comment," *Journal of Finance*, 35:5, 1980, pp. 1272–9; and J. Hill and T. Schneeweis, "Risk Reduction Potential of Financial Futures," in G. Gay and R. Kolb (eds), *Interest Rate Futures: A Comprehensive Introduction*, Richmond, VA: Robert F. Dame, Inc., 1982, pp. 307–24.

13   The dependence of the regression hedge ratio on the planned length of the hedging period was proven by C. Franckle, "The Hedging Performance of the New Futures Market: Comment," *Journal of Finance*, 35:5, 1980, pp. 1272–9.

14   See R. Kolb and R. Chiang, "Improving Hedging Performance Using Interest Rate Futures," *Financial Management*, 10:4, 1981, pp. 72–9; and "Duration, Immunization, and Hedging with Interest Rate Futures," *Journal of Financial Research*, 10:4, 1982, pp. 161–70.

15   A. Toevs and D. Jacob, "Futures and Alternative Hedge Ratio Methodologies," *Journal of Portfolio Management*, 12:3, 1986, pp. 60–70.

16   For an example, see J. Hill and T. Schneeweis, "Risk Reduction Potential of Financial Futures," in G. Gay and R. Kolb (eds), *Interest Rate Futures: Concepts and Issues*, Englewood Cliffs, NJ: Prentice Hall, 1982, pp. 307–24.

17   D. Lasser, "A Measure of *Ex-Ante* Hedging Effectiveness for the Treasury-Bill and Treasury-Bond Futures Markets," *Review of Futures Markets*, 6:2, pp. 278–95.

18   R. Chiang, G. Gay, and R. Kolb, "Interest Rate Hedging: An Empirical Test of Alternative Strategies," *Journal of Financial Research*, 6:3, 1983, pp. 187–97.

19   A. Toevs and D. Jacob, "Futures and Alternative Hedge Ratio Methodologies," *Journal of Portfolio Management*, 12:3, 1986, pp. 60–70.

20   See I. G. Kawaller, "Choosing the Best Interest Rate Hedge Ratio," *Financial Analysts Journal*, 48:5, 1992, pp. 74–7.

21   For a more complete explanation of bank immunization and planning period immunization, see R. Kolb, *Investments*, 4th edn, Miami, FL: Kolb Publishing, 1995.

22   This discussion of immunization with futures draws upon G. Gay and R. Kolb, "Immunizing Bond Portfolios with Interest Rate Futures," *Financial Management*, 11:2, 1982, pp. 81–9.

23   Philippe Jorion, "Risk Management Lessons from Long-Term Capital Management," *European Financial Management*, 6, 2000, pp. 277–300.

24   According to Jorion, the total futures positions amounted to over $500 billion, swaps over $750 billion, and options and other OTC derivatives over $150 billion.

7

Security Futures Products:
An Introduction

Overview

Everyone who follows the financial news hears predictions about the future of the stock market. Usually, these predictions refer to the future movement of some stock market index. With the advent of stock index futures trading in 1982, these pundits can now trade to take advantage of their insights (perhaps they should be required to do so). In addition to providing a chance to speculate, stock index futures also have a role in hedging various kinds of portfolio risk. In 2002, futures on individual stocks, called single stock futures, began trading at two exchanges in the United States. Together, stock index futures and single stock futures are called security futures products. Currently, dramatic changes in security futures products are under way. Previously successful contracts have greatly diminished in importance, while new contracts have begun to gain ascendancy. Stock index futures trading originated in the United States, but in recent years the real growth has been in foreign markets, with foreign indexes as the underlying good. Single stock futures originated outside of the United States, but is gaining a foothold in the United States.

This chapter begins our exploration of stock index futures and the indexes upon which they are based. Various indexes use different calculation methods to compute the index value, so we consider a few representative U.S. indexes to illustrate these methods. Successful trading of the index contracts requires a thorough understanding of the construction of the indexes. When the differences and interrelationships among the indexes are understood, it is easier to understand the differences among the futures contracts that are based on those indexes. The differences among the indexes should not be exaggerated, however. The kinds of risk and the expected changes in the levels of the indexes are predicted by the **capital asset pricing model** (**CAPM**). The CAPM, discussed in Chapter 3, expresses the relationship between the returns of individual stocks and partially diversified portfolios, on the one hand, and the broad indexes on the other. The chapter concludes with an exploration of single stock futures.

As is the case with all futures contracts, the exact construction of the contracts is very important for the trader. No-arbitrage conditions constrain the possible deviations between the price of the futures contract and the level of the underlying index. Cash-and-carry strategies keep the futures price from being too high relative to the price of the stock market index. Similarly, the availability of reverse cash-and-carry strategies keeps the futures price from being too low relative to stock prices. In other words, potential arbitrage strategies constrain the basis for stock index futures as these strategies do for other types of futures contracts.

The indexes

We can classify stock market indexes by the calculation method used to compute the index. Some indexes measure only price changes in the stock, while others include the total return to the shareholder—capital gains plus dividend as well. We can also distinguish between stock indexes that weight each share in the index by the price of a share or by the market value of the outstanding shares. For example, the Dow Jones Industrial Average (DJIA) and the Nikkei 225 are price-weighted indexes in which the weight given to each share is proportional to its price, and neither of these indexes includes dividends earned by the shares. By contrast, the S&P 500® index weights each stock in its index by the market capitalization of the shares, but it also does not reflect dividends.

Yet other indexes attempt to capture the total return from owning a portfolio, including capital gains, cash dividends, and all changes in ownership, such as stock dividends, spin-offs, mergers, and so on. For example, the DAX 30 is a "blue chip" index of 30 German stocks (DAX stands for "Deutscher Aktien Index," and "Aktien" is the German word for a share of stock). Similarly, the main French index, the CAC 40, employs the same type of calculation technique for the 40 shares in its index (CAC stands for "Compagnie des Agents de Change"). The new Dow Jones Stoxx family of indexes provide various measures of different portfolios. For example, the Dow Jones Euro Stoxx 50 is an index of this type that includes 50 major European firms based in countries that are in the European Monetary Union. We consider each of these types of indexes in turn.

Price-weighted indexes

The DJIA is the most widely followed index in the United States, and consists of 30 very large and prominent industrial firms. Another price-weighted index is the Nikkei 225, the most widely followed and quoted index for the Japanese stock market. It includes 225 of the largest Japanese companies, including firms such as Sony, Fuji Photo Film, Honda, Toyota, Yamaha, NEC, Citizen Watch, and Nippon Telephone and Telegraph. Changes in membership in the 225 stocks occur only due to special events such as mergers and liquidations. In the 1980s, for example, there were only eight substitutions. Shares in the Japanese stock market are classified as First Section or Second Section. Stocks in the First Section are the larger and more important firms in the economy, and all Nikkei shares are in the First Section. Neither the DJIA nor the Nikkei 225 includes dividends—they both reflect only on price changes.

For our discussion, we take the DJIA as a representative price-weighted index. The 30 stocks in the DJIA are shown in Table 7.1. While the list is quite stable, there are changes in the constituent stocks from time to time. The DJIA is computed by adding the share prices of the 30 stocks comprising the index and dividing by the DJIA divisor. The divisor is used to adjust for stock splits, mergers, stock dividends, and changes in the stocks included in the index.

The DJIA can be computed according to the following formula:

$$\text{index} = \frac{\sum_{i=1}^{N} P_i}{\text{divisor}} \tag{7.1}$$

where P_i is the price of stock i.

Table 7.1   Stocks in the Dow Jones Industrial Average

Alcoa	Exxon-Mobil	McDonald's
Altria Group	General Electric	Merck & Company, Inc.
American Express	General Motors	Minnesota, Mining, Mfg.
American International Group	Hewlett-Packard	Microsoft
AT&T	Home Depot	Pfizer, Inc.
Boeing	Honeywell	Procter & Gamble
Caterpillar	Intel	United Technologies
Citigroup	IBM	Verizon Communications
Coca-Cola	Johnson & Johnson	Wal-Mart Stores
DuPont	J P Morgan-Chase	Walt Disney

Source: Dow Jones web site, November 21, 2005. Reprinted by permission of Dow Jones, © 2006 Dow Jones & Company, Inc. All rights reserved worldwide.

Because the index depends on the number of dollars from summing all the prices, the DJIA does not reflect the percentage change in the price of a share. For example, consider a stock that doubles from $1 to $2, and contrast this price change with a stock that moves from $100 to $101. In the first case, a stock has increased 100 percent, while in the latter case a stock has increased just 1 percent. For the DJIA, both stock price changes have the same effect on the index, because the index depends on the sum of the prices, not the percentage price changes of the individual stocks.

The divisor used for computing the DJIA is designed to keep the index value from changing due to stock splits or stock dividends, or due to a substitution of one stock for another in the index. To see how the divisor functions, assume that Dow Jones decides to delete Boeing from the index and replace it with Dow Chemical. Assume that Boeing is priced at 6.00, Dow Chemical trades at 47.00, that the current value of the index is 1,900.31, with a divisor of 0.889, and that the sum of the 30 stock prices is $1,689.375. The substitution of Dow for Boeing will generate a new total of prices of $1,730.375, which equals the old sum ($1,689.375) plus the current price of the new stock ($47) minus the current price of the deleted stock ($6). If the divisor is not changed, the new index value will be 1,946.43. Thus, the substitution of one stock for another, with no change in the divisor, manufactures a jump in the DJIA of 46 points. Obviously, this cannot be permitted or the index will become meaningless as a barometer of stock prices.

For the index to reflect the level of prices in the market accurately, a simple substitution of one stock for another should not change the index. The same principle holds for stock dividends and stock splits. Therefore, the divisor must change to accommodate the change in stocks or the stock dividend or the stock split. In our example of substituting Dow Chemical for Boeing, the divisor must change to maintain a constant index value of 1,900.31 with the new total of prices of 1,730.375. Therefore, the new divisor must satisfy the following equation:

$$1,900.31 = \frac{1,730.375}{\text{new divisor}}$$

Thus, to keep the index value unchanged, the new divisor must be 0.9106. Generalizing from this example, we see that the following equation gives the value for the new divisor:

$$\text{new divisor} = \frac{1,730.375}{1,900.31} = 0.9106 \tag{7.2}$$

To find the new divisor, compute the new sum of prices that results from substituting one firm for another. Then divide this sum by the original index value. When the index was created, there were only 12 stocks in the index and the divisor was 12.0. Due to substitutions, stock dividends and other changes, the divisor today is less than 1.0. As noted above, the Nikkei 225 index is a price-weighted index like the DJIA and it is calculated in a virtually identical manner.

Market capitalization-weighted indexes

The S&P 500 index is the most widely followed index in the U.S. finance industry. For example, the performance of many money managers is judged by comparing their portfolio results to the performance of the S&P 500. The index is based on 500 firms from various industries, most of which are listed on the New York Stock Exchange.[1] Together, these 500 firms comprise approximately 80 percent of the total value of the stocks listed on the New York Stock

Table 7.2   The calculation of the S&P 500®

	Outstanding shares		Price		Value
Company ABC	100	×	$50	=	$5,000
Company DEF	300	×	40	=	$12,000
Company GHI	200	×	10	=	$2,000
	Current market valuation			=	$19,000

If the 1941–3 value were $2,000, then $19,000 is to $2,000 as X is to 10.

Current market valuation	$19,000/$2,000	=	$X/10$
1941–3 market valuation	$190,000	=	$2,000X$
	95.00	=	X

Source: Chicago Mercantile Exchange, "Inside S&P 500 Stock Index Futures." Reprinted by permission of the Chicago Mercantile Exchange. S&P 500® is a trademark of The McGraw-Hill Companies, Inc. © Standard & Poor's. Reprinted by permission

Exchange (NYSE). Another similar index is the principal index of the British stock market, the FT-SE 100 (pronounced "footsie"), including 100 stocks and computed by the FT-SE International and reported in the *Financial Times*. Each of the stocks in these indexes has a different weight in the calculation of the index, and the weight is proportional to the total market value of the stock (the price per share times the number of shares outstanding). Therefore, the S&P 500 and the FT-SE indexes are value-weighted. This contrasts with the composition of the DJIA and the Nikkei, which assign equal weight to each stock price.

For our discussion of the value-weighted indexes, we focus on the S&P 500 index, although almost every point holds for the FT-SE 100 as well. The value of the S&P 500 index is reported relative to the average value during the period of 1941–3, which was assigned an index value of 10. As a simplified example of the way the index is computed, assume that the index consists of only three securities, ABC, DEF, and GHI. Table 7.2 shows how the value of the three firms would be weighted to calculate the index. For each stock, the total market value of the outstanding shares is computed. In the table, the three firms' shares have a total value of $19,000. If the value in the 1941–3 period had been $2,000, the current level of the index would be calculated as shown in the table, where "X" is the current index level with a value of 95.00. Mathematically, the calculation of the index is given by

$$\text{S\&P index}_t = \left(\frac{\sum_{i=1}^{500} N_{i,t} P_{i,t}}{\text{O.V.}} \right) = 10 \tag{7.3}$$

where O.V. is the original valuation in 1941–3, $N_{i,t}$ is the number of shares outstanding for firm i, and $P_{i,t}$ is the price of shares in firm i.

The weights of each firm change as their prices rise and fall relative to those of other firms represented in the index. Firms such as Exxon-Mobil, AT&T, and IBM represent large shares of the index, while other firms have only a minuscule impact. The index is computed on a continuous basis during the trading day and reported to the public. There is considerable variability in the performance of the index over time, even though it is a large portfolio of the very largest and most stable firms. As we shall see in the next chapter, recent developments in the stock index futures market have given new importance to the volatility of stock market indexes.

Total return indexes

The third class of indexes measures the total return on a portfolio of the stocks in the index, including both dividends and price changes. The important total return indexes also employ market capitalization weighting schemes. As noted above, examples are the DAX 30 from Germany, the CAC 40 from France, and a variety of Dow Jones Stoxx indexes.

The idea behind these indexes is quite simple, but the computation is quite complex in its details. In essence, the index value at time t is given by

$$\text{index}_t = \frac{M_t}{B_t} \times \text{base value} \tag{7.4}$$

where M_t is the market capitalization of the index at time t; B_t is the adjusted base date market capitalization of the index at time t; and the base value is the original numerical starting value for the index, for example, 100 or 1,000. The idea is that the numerator reflects the total accumulated value of the portfolio and the denominator represents the initial value of the portfolio. So far, this is the same as the idea behind the value-weighted indexes that we have already considered. However, compared with the S&P 500 or the FT-SE 100, the total return indexes include many additional factors that affect the denominator and numerator. The numerator is affected by the price of the shares, the number of shares presently outstanding, and the exchange rate between the currency of the share price and the currency of the index. The denominator is affected by the many events in a firm's life that can change the number or values of the shares outstanding for each company. These include cash dividends, special cash dividends, splits and reverse splits, rights offerings, stock dividends, return of capital, mergers, share tenders and repurchases, and spin-offs of business units. In addition, stocks are frequently added and subtracted from the index. While all of these events make the accounting difficult, the concept is quite simple—the index reflects the total change in the value of the portfolio from inception to the current date.[2]

Stock index futures contracts

Table 7.3 summarizes the principal features of the stock indexes that we have discussed and the key features of the futures contracts that are based upon them. Futures also trade on many stock indexes that we have not discussed. However, the indexes covered here are major and representative. As Table 7.3 shows, the total value of a futures position depends on the currency, the multiplier, and the level of the index. For example, in early 2001, the DJIA was about 11,000, giving a contract value of about $110,000 ($10 × 11,000). The S&P 500 stood at about 1,400 for a value of about $350,000 ($250 × 1,400) for the open-outcry version of the CME's S&P 500 futures contract and a value of $70,000 ($50 × 1,400) for the E-mini® version of the contract. The Dow Jones Euro Stoxx 50 was in the range of 4,700, giving a contract value of €47,000 (10 × 4,700). With a euro being worth about $1.2, the dollar value of this contract was about $56,400. Thus, there is a considerable range of values for each of these different contracts. All of these futures trade on the March, June, September, and December cycle and all are settled in cash. Price changes for each futures contract depend on the contract size and volatility of the index. Some of these indexes are highly correlated (over 0.90) with each other, while some pairs exhibit very low correlations (less than 0.50).

Table 7.3   A summary of key stock index futures contracts

Contract	Exchange	Currency	Contract size	Index composition	Index calculation
DJIA	CBOT	U.S.	10 × Index	30 U.S. blue chip	Price weighting (no dividends)
Nikkei 225	CME	U.S.	5 × Index	225 Japanese First Section	Price weighting (no dividends)
NASDAQ 100 E-mini	CME	U.S.	20 × Index	100 NASDAQ stocks	Modified Market cap weighting
S&P 500®	CME	U.S.	250 × Index	500 mostly NYSE	Market cap weighting (no dividends)
S&P 500® E-mini®	CME	U.S.	50 × Index	500 mostly NYSE	Market cap weighting (no dividends)
FTSE 100	Euronext	British	10 × Index	100 large British	Market cap weighting (no dividends)
DAX 30	EUREX	Euro	25 × Index	30 German blue chip	Total return
CAC 40	Euronext	Euro	10 × Index	40 French blue chip	Total return
DJ Euro Stoxx 50	EUREX	Euro	10 × Index	50 European blue chip	Total return

Note: Some stock index futures trade on both U.S. and non-U.S. exchanges, and some non-U.S. markets dominate in certain contracts.

Product profile: The CME's E-mini® S&P 500® futures contract

Contract size: $50 times the S&P's 500 stock index.

Deliverable grades: Cash settled to the S&P's 500 stock index.

Tick size: 0.25 = $12.50.

Price quote: The price is quoted in terms of S&P's 500 index points. One S&P 500 index point = $50.

Contract months: At any time, the nearest two delivery months will trade from the March, June, September, and December cycle.

Expiration and final settlement: Trading ceases at 8:30 a.m. (Chicago time) on the third Friday of the contract month. The contract is settled on the morning of the expiration day based on the opening values of the component stocks, regardless of when those stocks open on expiration day. However, if a stock does not open on that day, its last sale price will be used.

Trading hours: Traded on Globex: Monday through Thursday, 3:30 p.m. to 3:15 p.m. next day; shutdown period from 4:30 p.m. to 5:00 p.m. nightly; Sunday and holidays, 5:30 p.m. to 3:15 p.m. next day.

Daily price limit: 5 percent increase or decrease from prior settlement price.

Product profile: The CME's E-mini NASDAQ 100 futures contract

Contract size: $20 times the NASDAQ 100 stock index.

Deliverable grades: Cash settled to the NASDAQ 100 stock index.

Tick size: 0.25 = $12.50.

Price quote: The price is quoted in terms of NASDAQ 100 index. One NASDAQ 100 index point = $20.

Contract months: At any time, the nearest two delivery months will trade from the March, June, September, and December cycle.

Expiration and final settlement: Trading ceases at 8:30 a.m. (Chicago time) on the third Friday of the contract month. The contract is settled on the morning of the expiration day based on the opening values of the component stocks, regardless of when those stocks open on expiration day. However, if a stock does not open on that day, its last sale price will be used.

Trading hours: Traded on Globex: Monday through Thursday, 3:30 p.m. to 3:15 p.m. next day; shutdown period from 4:30 p.m. to 5:00 p.m. nightly; Sunday and holidays, 5:30 p.m. to 3:15 p.m. next day.

Daily price limit: 5 percent increase or decrease from prior settlement price.

Product profile: Eurex's Dow Jones Euro STOXX 50 futures contract

Contract size: €10 per Dow Jones STOXX 50 index point.

Deliverable grades: Cash settled to the Dow Jones STOXX 50.

Tick size: One index point representing €10.

Price quote: The price is quoted in terms of Dow Jones STOXX 50 index points with no decimal places.

Contract months: At any time, the nearest three months will trade from the March, June, September, and December expiration cycle.

Expiration and final settlement: The last trading day is the third Friday of the expiration month, if that is a trading day; otherwise, the day immediately prior to that Friday. Trading ceases at 12:00 noon on the last trading day. The final settlement price is the average price of the Dow Jones STOXX 50 index calculated in the final ten minutes of trading on the last trading day.

Trading hours: Eurex operates in three trading phases. In the pre-trading period users may make inquiries or enter, change, or delete orders and quotes in preparation for trading. This period is between 7:30 a.m. and 8:50 a.m. The main trading period is between 8:50 a.m. and 8:00 p.m. Trading ends with the post-trading period between 8:00 p.m. and 8:30 p.m.

Daily price limit: None.

Stock index futures prices

Figure 7.1 presents price quotations for stock index futures. The organization of the quotations is similar to those of other commodities. Like most financial futures, stock index futures essentially trade in a full carry market. Therefore, the cost-of-carry model provides a virtually complete understanding of stock index futures pricing. When the conditions of the cost-of-carry model are violated, arbitrage opportunities arise. For a cash-and-carry strategy, a trader would

Figure 7.1   Quotations for stock index futures

Index Futures

	Open	High	Low	Settle	Change	Lifetime High	Lifetime Low	Open interest
DJ Industrial Average (CBT)-$10 × Index								
June	11266	11320	11172	11204	−63	11410	10363	37,753
Sept	11310	11310	11281	11281	−63	11445	10891	58
Mini DJ Industrial Average (CBT)-$5 × index								
June	11265	11320	11172	11204	−63	11413	10600	66,550
Sept	11300	11305	11300	11281	−63	11470	11300	10
S&P 500 Index (CME)-$250 × index								
June	1310.30	1319.00	1305.00	1307.50	−2.60	1321.30	1080.00	645,025
Sept	1320.00	1329.30	1316.00	1318.30	−2.50	1331.40	1112.60	6,275
Mini S&P 500 (CME)-$50 × index								
June	1310.50	1319.25	1304.75	1307.50	−2.50	1321.50	1261.25	1,159,253
Sept	1330.00	1330.00	1316.00	1318.25	−2.50	1331.75	1311.25	777
Nasdaq 100 (CME)-$100 × index								
June	1720.50	1737.50	1715.50	1725.00	4.50	1791.50	1576.50	57,932
Mini Nasdaq 100 (CME)-$20 × index								
June	1720.5	1737.5	1715.5	1725.0	4.5	1793.0	1652.5	275,210
Sept	1757.0	1757.0	1736.5	1744.5	4.5	1757.0	1693.5	74
Russell 1000 (NYBOT)-$500 × index								
June	714.50	715.50	712.60	713.00	−1.50	719.00	695.75	87,433

Source: *The Wall Street Journal*, March 31, 2006, p. c10. Reprinted by permission of *The Wall Street Journal*, © 2006 Dow Jones & Company, Inc. All rights reserved worldwide

buy the stocks that underlie the futures contract and sell the futures. The trader would then carry these stocks until the futures expiration. The cash-and-carry strategy is attractive when stocks are priced too low relative to the futures. In a reverse cash-and-carry strategy, the trader would sell the stocks short and invest the proceeds, in addition to buying the futures. The reverse cash-and-carry strategy is attractive when stocks are priced too high relative to the futures. Thus, any discrepancy between the justified futures and cash market prices would lead to a profit at the expiration of the futures, simply by exploiting the appropriate strategy. From Chapter 3, the basic cost-of-carry model for a perfect market with unrestricted short selling was given by the following equation:

$$F_{0,t} = S_0(1 + C) \tag{3.3}$$

where $F_{0,t}$ is the futures price at $t = 0$ for delivery at time t, S_0 is the spot price at $t = 0$, and C is the percentage cost of carrying the good from $t = 0$ to time t.

The Comex 500

The ever-increasing popularity of index investing, including index-based futures contracts, has made the business of creating and maintaining financial indexes a valuable enterprise for index producers such as the Standard & Poor's Corporation (S&P), a division of The McGraw-Hill Companies. Ultimately, the under-lying source of value for index producers resides in their claim that financial indexes possess certain prop-erty attributes afforded protection under various state and federal laws. As a result of numerous legal battles, index producers have established their right to authorize the terms by which other parties may use their indexes and to collect licensing fees from these parties. For example, S&P has negotiated a license with the Chicago Mercantile Exchange (CME) granting the CME exclusive rights to trade a futures con-tract based on the S&P 500 index.

Index producers have fought many legal battles to defend their indexes from unauthorized use. Some of these legal battles appear to have been sparked by a December 1981 requirement of the Commodity Futures Trading Commission (CFTC) permitting trading in stock index futures contracts only if the con-tracts were based on widely known and well-established stock indexes. As a result of the CFTC's require-ment, futures exchanges abandoned their efforts at creating their own independent indexes and focused their efforts on constructing futures contracts based on the most widely known and well-established stock indexes of the day: the S&P 500 and the Dow Jones Industrial Average.

In 1982, Comex sought a license from S&P to use the S&P 500 index as the basis for futures contracts to be traded at the Comex. However, S&P was unwilling to license its index because it had previously entered into an exclusive licensing agreement with the CME. Having failed to obtain a license, Comex constructed a "Comex 500 index" and linked it with the S&P 500 index without S&P's authorization. S&P sued and prevailed in the courts.

A related case involved Dow Jones and the Chicago Board of Trade (CBOT). In February 1982, the CBOT applied to the CFTC to trade stock index futures based on the Dow Jones averages. The CBOT indexes were identical to the Dow Jones averages, and when Dow Jones changed a component stock or revised the divisor, the CBOT would make the same change so that the CBOT indexes would remain identical to the Dow Jones averages. Dow Jones sought to stop the CBOT from trading their futures con-tracts, both by suing and by threatening to suspend publication of its stock averages. The courts ruled that the CBOT could not use the Dow Jones averages without the permission of Dow Jones.

The cost-of-carry model for stock index futures

The application of Equation 3.3 to stock index futures faces one complication—dividends. Holding the stocks gives the owner dividends, but most of the indexes reflect price changes only. Futures based on these indexes are tied directly to the index values, so the futures prices do not include dividends in these cases. To apply to stock index futures, Equation 3.3 must be adjusted to include the dividends that would be received between the present and the expiration of the futures. In essence, the chance to receive dividends lowers the cost of carrying the stocks. Carrying stocks requires that a trader finance the purchase price of the stock from the present until the futures expiration. However, the trader will receive dividends from the stock, which will reduce the value of the stocks. This contrasts directly with the cost of carry for holding a commodity such as gold. As we have seen, gold generates no cash flows, so the cost of carry for gold is essentially the financing cost. For stocks, the cost of carry is the financing cost for the stock, less the dividends received while the stock is being carried.

As an example, assume the present is time zero and that a trader decides to engage in a self-financing cash-and-carry transaction. The trader decides to buy and hold one share of Widget, Inc., currently trading for $100. Therefore, the trader borrows $100 and buys the stock. We

Table 7.4   Cash flows from carrying stock

$t = 0$
Borrow $100 for one year at 10%	+$100
Buy one share of Widget, Inc.	−$100

$t = 6$ months
Receive dividend of $2	+$2
Invest $2 for six months at 10%	−$2

$t = 1$ year
Collect proceeds of $2.10 from dividend investment	+$2.10
Sell Widget, Inc., for P_1	+P_1
Repay debt	−$110.00

Total profit: $P_1 + \$2.10 - \$110.00$

assume that the stock will pay a $2 dividend in six months and the trader will invest the pro-
ceeds for the remaining six months at a rate of 10 percent. Table 7.4 shows the trader's cash
flows. In Table 7.4, a trader borrows funds, buys and holds a stock, receives and invests a
dividend, and liquidates the portfolio after one year. At the outset, the stock costs $100, but its
value in a year, P_1, is unknown. From Table 7.4, the trader's cash inflow after one year is the
future value of the dividend, $2.10, plus the current value of the stock, P_1, less the repayment
of the loan, $110.

From this example, we can generalize to understand the total cash inflows from a cash-and-
carry strategy. First, the cash-and-carry strategy will return the future value of the stock, P_1, at
the horizon of the carrying period. Second, at the end of the carrying period, the cash-and-carry
strategy will return the future value of the dividends—the dividend plus interest from the time
of receipt to the horizon. Against these inflows, the cash-and-carry trader must pay the financing cost for the stock purchase.

We are now in a position to determine the futures price that is consistent with the cash-and-
carry strategy. From the arguments of Chapter 3, we know that Equation 3.3 holds as an equality with perfect markets and unrestricted short selling. The cash-and-carry trading opportunity
requires that the futures price must be less than or equal to the cash inflows at the futures expiration. Similarly, the reverse cash-and-carry trading opportunity requires that the futures price
must equal or exceed the cash inflows at the futures expiration. Therefore, the stock index futures
price must equal the cost of the stocks underlying the stock index, plus the cost of carrying
those stocks to expiration, $S_0(1 + C)$, minus the future value of all dividends to be received,
$D_i(1 + r_i)$. The future value of dividends is measured at the time the futures contract expires.
More formally,

$$F_{0,t} = S_0(1 + C) - \sum_{i=1}^{N} D_i(1 + r_i) \qquad (7.5)$$

where $F_{0,t}$ is the stock index futures price at $t = 0$ for a futures contract that expires at time t;
S_0 is the value of the stocks underlying the stock index at $t = 0$; C is the percentage cost of
carrying the stocks from $t = 0$ to the expiration at time t; D_i is the ith dividend; and r_i is the

Table 7.5 Computing fair value	
Today's date	July 6
Futures expiration	September 20
Days until expiration	76
Index	Price-weighted index of two stocks
Index divisor	1.80
Interest rates	All interest rates are 10% simple interest; 360-day year
Stock A	
Today's price	$115
Projected dividends	$1.50 on July 23
Days dividend will be invested	59
r_A	$0.10 \times (59/360) = 0.0164$
Stock B	
Today's price	$84
Projected dividends	$1.00 on August 12
Days dividend will be invested	39
r_B	$0.10 \times (39/360) = 0.0108$

interest earned on carrying the ith dividend from its time of receipt until the futures expiration at time t.

Fair value for stock index futures

A stock index futures price has its **fair value** when the futures price fits the cost-of-carry model. In this section, we consider a simplified example of determining the fair value of a stock index futures contract. We consider a futures contract on a price-weighted index, and for simplicity we assume that there are only two stocks. Table 7.5 provides the information that we will need.

Based on the data in Table 7.5, the index value is 110.56, as given by

$$\frac{P_A + P_B}{\text{index divisor}} = \frac{115 + 84}{1.8} = 110.56$$

The cost of buying the stocks underlying the portfolio is simply the sum of the prices of Stocks A and B, or $199. For carrying the stocks to expiration, the interest cost will be 10 percent for 76 days, or 2.11 percent. Thus, the cost of buying and carrying the stocks to expiration is $199 \times 1.0211 = \$203.20$. Offsetting this cost will be the dividends received and the interest earned on the dividends. For the stocks, the future value of the dividends at expiration will be:

For Stock A: $1.50 \times 1.0164 = \$1.52$
For Stock B: $1.00 \times 1.0108 = \$1.01$

Therefore, the entire cost of buying the stocks and carrying them to expiration is the purchase price of the stocks plus interest, less the future value of the dividends measured at expiration:

$203.20 - \$1.52 - \$1.01 = \$200.67$

In the cost-of-carry model, we know that the futures price must equal this entire cost of carry. However, the futures price is expressed in index units, not the dollars of the actual stock prices. To find the fair value for the futures price, this cash value of $200.67 must be converted into index units by dividing by the index divisor, 200.67/1.8 = 111.48. Thus, the fair value for the futures contract is 111.48. Because it conforms to the cost-of-carry model, this fair value for the futures price is the price that precludes arbitrage profits from both the cash-and-carry and reverse cash-and-carry strategies.

Index arbitrage and program trading

In the preceding section, we saw how to derive the fair value futures price from the cost-of-carry model. From Chapter 3, we know that deviations from the theoretical price of the cost-of-carry model give rise to arbitrage opportunities. If the futures price exceeds its fair value, traders will engage in cash-and-carry arbitrage. If the futures price falls below its fair value, traders can exploit the pricing discrepancy through a reverse cash-and-carry trading strategy. These cash-and-carry strategies in stock index futures are called **index arbitrage**. This section presents an example of index arbitrage using a simplified index with only two stocks. Because index arbitrage can require the trading of many stocks, index arbitrage is often implemented by using a computer program to automate the trading. Computer-directed index arbitrage is called **program trading**. We introduce program trading later in this section, but we reserve the fullest discussion for Chapter 8.

Index arbitrage

Table 7.5 gave values for Stocks A and B, and we saw how to compute the fair value of a stock index futures contract based on an index composed of those two stocks. With the values in Table 7.5, the cash market index value is 110.56, and the fair value for the futures contract is 111.48, where both values are expressed in index points. If the futures price exceeds the fair value, cash-and-carry index arbitrage is possible. A futures price below its fair value creates an opportunity for reverse cash-and-carry index arbitrage.

To illustrate cash-and-carry index arbitrage, assume that the data of Table 7.5 hold, but that the futures price is 115.00. Because this price exceeds the fair value, an index arbitrageur would trade as shown in Table 7.6. At the outset on July 6, the trader borrows the money necessary to purchase the stocks in the index, buys the stocks, and sells the futures. On July 23 and August 12, the trader receives dividends from the two stocks and invests the dividends to the expiration date at 10 percent. Like all stock index futures, our simple example uses cash settlement. Therefore, at expiration on September 20, the final futures settlement price is set equal to the cash market index value. This ensures that the futures and cash prices converge and that the basis goes to zero.[3]

The profits or losses from the transactions in Table 7.6 do not depend on the prices that prevail at expiration on September 20. Instead, the profits come from a discrepancy between the futures price and its fair value. To illustrate the profits, we assume that the stock prices do not change. Therefore, the cash market index is at 110.56 at expiration. As Table 7.6 shows, these transactions give a profit of $6.32.

This will be the profit no matter what happens to stock prices between July 6 and September 20. For example, assume the prices of Stocks A and B both rise by $5, to $120 and $89, respectively. The cash market cash flows will then come from the sale of the shares, the future value of the dividends, and the debt repayment:

Table 7.6   Cash-and-carry index arbitrage

Date	Cash market	Futures market
July 6	Borrow $199 for 76 days at 10%; buy Stocks A and B for a total outlay of $199	Sell one SEP index futures contract for 115.00
July 23	Receive dividend of $1.50 from Stock A and invest for 59 days at 10%	
August 12	Receive dividend of $1.00 from Stock B and invest for 39 days at 10%	
September 20	For illustrative purposes, assume any values for stock prices at expiration: we assume that stock prices did not change and, therefore, the index value is still 110.56	
	Receive proceeds from invested dividends of $1.52 and $1.01; sell Stock A for $115 and Stock B for $84; total proceeds are $201.53; repay debt of $203.20	At expiration, the futures price is set equal to the spot index value of 110.56, which gives a profit of 4.44 index units; in dollar terms, this is 4.44 index units times the index divisor of 1.8
	Loss: $1.67	Profit: $7.99

Total profit: $7.99 − $1.67 = $6.32

Sale of Stock A	+120.00
Sale of Stock B	+89.00
Future value of dividends on Stock A	+1.52
Future value of dividends on Stock B	+1.01
Debt repayment	−203.20
Futures profit/loss	−2.01

On the futures transaction, the index value at expiration will then equal $116.11 = (120 + 89)/1.8$. This gives a futures loss of 1.11 index points, or $2.01. Taking all of these cash flows together, the profit is still $6.32. The profit will be the same no matter what happens to stock prices.

If the futures price is too low relative to the fair value, arbitrageurs can engage in reverse cash-and-carry transactions. For example, assume that the futures price is 105.00, well below the fair value of 111.48. Now the arbitrageur will trade as shown in Table 7.7. Essentially, the transactions in Table 7.7 are just the opposite of those in Table 7.6. The most important difference is that the trader sells stock short. Having sold the stock short, the trader must pay the dividends on the stocks as they come due.

The transactions give the trader a net profit of $11.68. Again, this profit does not depend upon the actual stock prices that prevail at expiration. Instead, the profit comes from the discrepancy between the actual futures price of 105.00 and the fair value of 111.48. Once the trader initiates the transactions in Table 7.7, the profit will depend only on the discrepancy between the fair value and the prevailing futures price. The profit will equal the error in the futures price times the index divisor: $(111.48 − 105.00) \times 1.8 = \$11.68$.[4]

Table 7.7   Reverse cash-and-carry index arbitrage

Date	Cash market	Futures market
July 6	Sell Stocks A and B for a total of $199; lend $199 for 76 days at 10%	Buy one SEP index futures contract for 105.00
July 23	Borrow $1.50 for 59 days at 10% and pay dividend of $1.50 on Stock A	
August 12	Borrow $1.00 for 39 days at 10% and pay dividend of $1.00 on Stock B	
September 20	For illustrative purposes, assume any values for stock prices at expiration: we assume that stock prices did not change, and therefore, the index value is still 110.56	
	Receive proceeds from investment of $203.20; repay $1.52 and $1.01 on money borrowed to pay dividends on Stocks A and B; buy Stock A for $115 and Stock B for $84; return stocks to repay short sale	At expiration, the futures price is set equal to the spot index value of 110.56, which gives a profit of 5.56 index units; in dollar terms, this is 5.56 index units times the index divisor of 1.8
	Profit: $1.67	Profit: $10.01
	Total profit: $1.67 + $10.01 = $11.68	

Program trading

While we have illustrated the cash-and-carry and reverse cash-and-carry transactions with a hypothetical two stock index futures contract, real stock index futures trading involves many more stocks. The DJIA and DAX 30 are smallest with 30 stocks, while the S&P 500 contains (of course) 500 stocks, the Russell 2000 index has 2,000 underlying stocks, and the Nikkei has 225 stocks. To exploit index arbitrage opportunities with actual stock index futures requires trading the futures and simultaneously buying or selling the entire collection of stocks that underlie the index.

If we focus on the S&P 500 futures contract, we can see that the transactions of Tables 7.6 and 7.7 call for the buying or selling of 500 stocks. The success of the arbitrage depends upon identifying the misalignment between the futures price and the fair futures price. However, at a given moment the fair futures price depends upon the current price of 500 different stocks. Identification of an index arbitrage opportunity requires the ability to instantly find pricing discrepancies between the futures price and the fair futures price reflecting 500 different stocks. In addition, exploiting the arbitrage opportunity requires trading 500 stocks at the prices that created the arbitrage opportunity. Enter the computer!

Large financial institutions (and these days many individual traders) can communicate orders to trade stock via their computers for very rapid execution. Faced with a cash-and-carry arbitrage opportunity, one of these large traders could execute a computer order to buy each and every stock represented in the S&P 500. Simultaneously, the institution would sell the S&P 500 futures contract. The use of computers to execute large and complicated stock market orders is called **program trading**. While computers are used for other kinds of stock market transactions, index arbitrage is the main application of program trading. Often, "index arbitrage" and "program trading" are used interchangeably. Program trading has been blamed for much volatility in the stock market, including the crash of October 1987. Chapter 8 presents a real-world example of program trading and analyzes the hidden risks in this kind of index arbitrage. Chapter 8 also discusses the evidence on program trading and stock market volatility.

Predicting dividend payments and investment rates

In the example of computing fair value from Table 7.5, we assumed certainty about the amount, timing, and investment rates for the dividends on Stocks A and B. In the actual market, these quantities are highly predictable, but they are not certain. Dividend amounts and payment dates can be predicted based on the past policy of the firm. However, these quantities are far from certain until the dividend announcement date, when the firm announces the amount and payment date of the dividend. In practice, there is quite a bit of variability in the payment of dividends, depending on the time of year. Figure 7.2 shows a typical distribution of dividend payments through the year. Notice how dividends tend to cluster at certain days in early March, June, September, and December.

In actual practice, traders follow the dividend practices of firms to project the dividends that the stocks underlying an index will pay each day. This problem varies in difficulty from one index to the next. The DJIA has only 30 very large firms, with relatively stable dividend policies. By contrast, the Russell 2000 index has 2,000 firms. Many of these firms are small and may have irregular dividend payment patterns. Therefore, it is more difficult to predict the exact dividend stream for the Russell 2000 or the S&P 500 index. While the difficulties in predicting dividends may introduce some uncertainties into the cost-of-carry calculations, projections of dividends prove to be quite accurate in practice.

In our example of computing the fair value of a stock index futures contract and in our arbitrage examples, we also assumed that dividends could be invested at a known rate. In practice, it is difficult to know the exact rate that will be received on invested dividends. While knowing the exact rate to be received on invested dividends is difficult, good predictions are

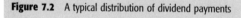

Figure 7.2   A typical distribution of dividend payments

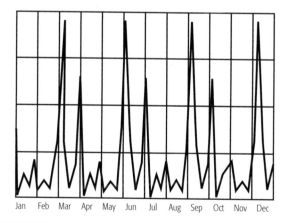

Source: Chicago Mercantile Exchange, "Using S&P 500 Stock Index Options and Futures." Reprinted by permission of the Chicago Mercantile Exchange. S&P 500® is a trademark of The McGraw-Hill Companies, Inc. © Standard & Poor's. Reprinted by permission

possible. For the most part, the futures expiration date is not very distant, so the current short-term interest rate can provide a good estimate of the investment rate for dividends.

Market imperfections and stock index futures prices

In Chapter 3, we saw that four different types of market imperfections could affect the pricing of futures contracts. Those market imperfections are direct transaction costs, unequal borrowing and lending rates, margins and restrictions on short selling, and limitations to storage. As we also saw in Chapter 3, the effect of these market imperfections is to create a band of no-arbitrage prices within which the futures price must fall. In this section, we consider these imperfections briefly in the context of stock index futures.

Direct transaction costs affect stock index futures trading to a considerable extent. Relative to many goods, transaction costs for stocks are low in percentage terms. Nonetheless, stock traders face commissions, exchange fees, and a bid–ask spread. In general, these costs may be about one-half of 1 percent for stock market transactions. Even with such modest transaction costs, we cannot expect the cost-of-carry model to hold as an exact equality. Instead, these trans-actions costs will lead to a no-arbitrage band of permissible stock index futures prices.

Unequal borrowing and lending costs, margins, and restrictions on short selling all play a role in stock index futures pricing. In the stock market, the restrictions on short selling are quite explicit. The Federal Reserve Board will not allow a trader to use more than 50 percent of the proceeds from a short sale. The short seller's broker may restrict that usage to an even smaller percentage. As we have seen in Chapter 3, these factors all force slight discrepancies in the cost-of-carry model. The pricing relationship of Equation 7.5 holds as an approximation, not with exactitude. Thus, these market imperfections create a no-arbitrage band of permissible futures prices. However, a highly competitive trading environment and low transaction costs keep this no-arbitrage band quite tight around the perfect markets theoretical fair value of Equation 7.5.

Because the stocks of the DJIA, Nikkei, S&P 500, FT-SE, DAX, CAC 40, and other indexes are so widely held by financial institutions with low transaction costs, quasi-arbitrage has often been a dominant feature of stock index futures trading. As an example of the importance of quasi-arbitrage, consider the differential use of short sale proceeds for a retail customer and a pension fund with a large stock portfolio. Assume that the retail customer must sell a stock short through her broker. This customer will be able to use only half of the proceeds of the short sale. By contrast, we will assume that the pension fund already owns the stocks neces-sary to sell short for the reverse cash-and-carry transaction. In this situation, the pension fund can simulate a short sale by selling a portion of its stock portfolio. Because the pension fund is actually selling stocks, not technically selling short, it receives the full use of its proceeds. However, selling stocks from a portfolio is a perfect substitute for an actual short sale. Thus, the pension fund faces substantially lower transaction costs than the retail customer for engag-ing in reverse cash-and-carry arbitrage. A similar conclusion emerges from considering pro-gram trading. A small retail trader faces enormous transaction costs in attempting to engage in index arbitrage. The quasi-arbitrage opportunities enjoyed by financial institutions ensure that no individual could ever engage in index arbitrage. In Chapter 8, we shall review the evidence on stock index futures pricing and show that these markets approximate full carry markets. This suggests that quasi-arbitrage is a dominant feature of stock index futures pricing.

Speculating with stock index futures

Speculating with stock index futures is exciting. Futures contracts allow the speculator to make the most straightforward speculation on the direction of the market, or to enter very sophisticated spread transactions to tailor the futures position to more precise opinions about the direction of stock prices. Further, the low transactions costs in the futures market make the speculation much easier to undertake than similar speculation in the stock market itself. With broad market indexes from many countries, the speculative opportunities are virtually endless.

One of the simplest speculative positions arises from a belief about impending market movements. If a trader anticipates a major market rally, he could simply buy a futures contract and hope for a price rise on the futures contract when the rally actually occurs. While this course of action is very simple, it does not do full justice to the complexity of the speculative opportunity. The trader might also consider which contract maturity is desirable as a trading vehicle and which of the four contracts to trade.

Some recent major market moves have been led by large firms, and a trader believes that another major advance, led by the largest firms again, is impending. Thus, the trader has a definite reason to prefer the DJIA index to the S&P 500 index. Comparing the DJIA and the S&P 500 indexes, she expects the DJIA to advance more rapidly, as it is more completely dominated by large firms.

With these differential responses in mind, one conservative speculation position strategy could use a spread between two indexes. If the trader anticipates a major market increase, but wishes to closely control her risk exposure, she might use a spread between the DJIA and the S&P 500 indexes. Assume that she anticipates a market rise in April. Consistent with this outlook, the transactions of Table 7.8 show how to initiate a spread to speculate on an anticipated market rally. The speculator first notes that the DJIA futures is 8,603.50, while the S&P 500 is 999.00. The speculator wants to take account of the difference in the dollar size of the two contracts. For example, consider a 1 percent increase in each index; this price rise gives about an $860 gain on each DJIA futures and about a $2,500 gain on each S&P 500 futures:

DJIA: 8,603.50 × 0.01 × $10 per point = $860.35
S&P 500: 999.000 × 0.01 × $250 per point = $2,497.50

To make the positions in the two futures roughly comparable requires about three DJIA contracts for each S&P contract. Since the speculator is anticipating a rise in the DJIA relative to

Table 7.8   A conservative intercommodity spread

Date	Futures market		
April 22	Buy 20 SEP DJIA futures contracts at 8,603.50 Sell five SEP S&P 500® futures contract at 999.00		
May 6	Sell 20 SEP DJIA futures contracts at 8,857.30 Buy five SEP S&P 500 futures contract at 1,026.45		
		DJIA	*S&P 500*
	Sell	8,857.30	999.00
	Buy	8,603.50	1,026.45
	Profit/loss (points)	253.80	−27.45
	× $ per contract point	× 10	× 250
	× number of contracts	× 20	× 5
	Profit/loss	$50,760.00	−$34,312.50
	Total profit: $16,447.50		

Table 7.9   A conservative intracommodity spread

Date	Futures market		
April 22	Buy one DEC S&P 500® contract at 1,085.70 Sell one JUN S&P 500 contract at 1,079.40		
May 6	Sell one DEC S&P 500 contract at 1,109.25 Buy one JUN S&P 500 contract at 1,102.50		

	June	*December*
Sell	1,079.40	1,109.25
Buy	−1,102.50	−1,085.70
Profit (points)	−23.10	23.55
× $250 per contract	−$5,775.00	$5,887.50

Total profit: $112.50

the S&P 500, she decides to go with a 4 : 1 ratio of DJIA to S&P 500 futures. Thus, this kind of a spread trade is called a **ratio spread**.

Our prescient speculator buys 20 SEP DJIA futures contract at 8,603.50 on April 22 and sells five SEP S&P 500 futures contract at 999.00. A few weeks later, prices have risen, with the DJIA futures trading at 8,857.30 and the S&P 500 futures at 1,026.45. Not wishing to be greedy, she elects to close her position on May 6. She sells the DJIA contracts at 8,857.30 and buys the S&P 500 contracts at 1,026.45. Her spread has worked perfectly. The DJIA futures has gained 2.95 percent while the S&P 500 index contract has gained only 2.75 percent. Therefore, the gain on the DJIA of 253.80 index points times $10 per point times 20 contracts is $50,760. This gain more than offsets the loss on the S&P 500 contract of $34,312.50, the product of −27.45 points times $250 per point times five contracts. The total gain is $16,447.50.

Contracts farther from expiration often respond to a given market move more than the nearby contracts and the index itself. The speculator could have initiated an intracommodity spread to take advantage of this same market rally. Table 7.9 shows one possible set of transactions using the S&P contract and the same dates. The speculator believes that the more distant contracts will be more responsive to a market move than the nearby contracts. Believing that the market will rise, she buys the more distant DEC contract at 1,085.70 on April 22, while simultaneously selling the nearby JUN contract at 1,079.40. By May 6, the rally has occurred, so she reverses her position by buying the JUN contract at 1,102.50 and selling the DEC contract at 1,109.25. As the table shows, the JUN contract has moved 23.10 points and the more sensitive DEC contract has moved 23.55 points. The strategy has worked, in a certain sense, because the more distant contract was more sensitive. However, the difference in the price changes was not very large. In fact, the gross profit on the spread was only $112.50, hardly enough to cover the transaction costs. This trade was, perhaps, too conservative. An outright long position in any contract would have worked well, but the conservative trader managed to protect herself completely out of the benefits that could have been obtained, given the major character of the market advance. For the speculator committed to spread trading, the stock index futures market presents a problem, because the different contracts tend to be so highly correlated.

The demise of Barings Bank

Theoretically, stock index arbitrage is risk free, and properly executed arbitrage transactions involve very low levels of actual risk. The risk is limited because of the close relationship between a stock index futures contract and the underlying stock index itself. Thus, as we have seen, arbitrage is a low-risk strategy that seeks to capture small and temporary pricing discrepancies between markets.

Nicholas Leeson, a trader for Barings Bank, stationed in Singapore, was supposed to be conducting arbitrage between Japanese stock index futures contracts traded in Japan and similar futures contracts traded on the Singapore exchange (SIMEX). Such trading involves buying the cheaper contract and simultaneously selling the more expensive one, then reversing the trade when the price difference has narrowed or disappeared.

However, Leeson apparently did exactly the opposite in late 1994 and early 1995. Through the futures markets and using options on futures, Leeson made very large one-sided bets that Japanese stocks would rise. The Kobe earthquake, however, rocked the entire Japanese economy and led to a dramatic drop in the Japanese stock market. The highly leveraged bets on a rising Japanese market turned out to be giant losers. These losses completely exhausted the capital of Barings, which declared bankruptcy and was acquired by the Dutch investment bank ING for £1.00.

When Barings filed for bankruptcy in February 1995, it was discovered that Leeson, in the name of Barings, had established (and concealed in an error account) outstanding notional futures positions on Japanese equities of $7 billion. In addition, he had outstanding notional futures positions on Japanese bonds and Euroyen totaling $20 billion.[5] Leeson had also sold Nikkei put and options with a nominal value of about $7 billion. The reported capital of Barings at the time was $615 million. In a short period, Leeson's trades lost about $1.4 billion. After the losses became public, Leeson was arrested, convicted, and sentenced to a six-and-a-half year prison term in Singapore. By 1999 Leeson was out of prison, giving speeches on the dangers posed by rogue traders at $100,000 per appearance, appearing in commercials on behalf of brokerage firms, playing celebrity online poker, and receiving numerous job offers in risk management. (Perhaps there really is no such thing as bad publicity!)

Leeson's rogue trading, while spectacular, is hardly an isolated incident. The 1990s witnessed a steady stream of staggering losses caused by rogue traders. In the mid-1990s, the Daiwa and Sumitomo corporations each lost over $1 billion from rogue traders in their employ. In 1997, Codelco lost $200 million, allegedly caused by a rogue trader. In February 2002, Allied Irish Banks (AIB) announced a $750 loss attributed to rogue trading. The threat of rogue trading highlights the need for corporations to adopt strict internal control procedures to monitor the derivatives positions taken by traders on the corporation's behalf.[6]

Single stock futures

Although futures contracts written on broad-based stock market indexes have been traded for over two decades, it was not until the passage of the Commodity Futures Modernization Act of 2000 (CFMA) that trading of futures contracts on individual stocks and narrow-based indexes was permitted in the United States. The CFMA repealed an 18-year-old government ban on single stock futures embedded in an agreement by the heads of the Securities and Exchange Commission (SEC) (John Shad) and the CFTC (Philip McBride Johnson) known as Shad/Johnson Accord (or the Johnson/Shad Accord at the CFTC). The Shad/Johnson Accord was a compromise solution to a disagreement over regulatory jurisdiction. The Accord permitted futures trading on broad-based, well-diversified indexes such as the S&P 500. However, no agreement was reached on single stocks and narrow-based indexes, and as a result they were effectively banned.

Worldwide, 20 exchanges currently trade single stock futures or have announced their intention to do so. Outside of the United States, single stock futures have been traded for nearly a decade on various European and Asian exchanges. In Sweden and Finland, the products have been traded since the early 1990s. In the United States, two exchanges, NQLX and One-Chicago, started trading single stock futures in the fall of 2002. NQLX began as a joint venture between Nasdaq and the London International Financial Futures Exchange (LIFFE), and was based in New York City before closing down in December 2004. OneChicago is a joint venture of the Chicago Board Options Exchange (CBOE), CBOT, and CME, based in Chicago. Single stock futures are traded exclusively on an electronic platform. Since the launch of these contracts, volume has been small, representing only a small fraction of total trading volume for financial futures. In the United States, trading venues for single stock futures are jointly regulated by the CFTC and SEC.

In the United States, single stock futures are generally settled with actual physical delivery. This means that at contract expiration, the holders of short positions in a futures contract on a single stock must deliver the requisite number of shares of stock to the holders of long positions. Physical settlement of SFPs is facilitated through the National Securities Clearing Corporation (NSCC). Cash settlement, though rare in the United States, is permitted and could therefore be used as the means for settling the futures contract if an exchange chose to do so. Cash settlement is an attractive feature in Europe because it facilitates cross-border settlement.

Like other futures contracts, single stock futures contracts specify the identity of the underlying security, delivery procedures, the contract size, margin, the trading environment, the minimum price fluctuation, daily price limits, the expiration cycle, trading hours, and position limits. Unlike other types of futures contracts, single stock futures contracts contain provisions for adjustments to reflect certain corporate events, such as stock splits and special dividends. Adjustments are made in a way that is consistent with adjustments made in the equity options market.

Single stock futures contracts are written on shares of common stock. In addition, single stock futures can be written on American Depository Receipts (ADRs), Trust Issued Receipts (TIRs), Exchange Traded Funds (ETFs), and shares of closed-end mutual funds. Single stock futures contracts expire on the third Friday of the delivery month.

Normally, single stock futures specify 100 shares of the underlying security as the contract size. This conforms to the round-lot structure of the securities and securities options markets. However, this is not a regulatory requirement, and an exchange is free to choose a larger or smaller contract size for futures contracts on single stocks. Not all market participants are pleased with the 100-share per contract feature. For many traders, particularly institutional traders, the transaction cost advantage of single stock futures over cash market securities becomes more pronounced the larger is the contract size. Smaller contract sizes lessen the transaction cost advantage of single stock futures over cash market securities.

The CFMA requires that margin requirements for single stock futures should be no lower than the lowest level of margin required for comparable option contracts. The CFMA also requires that futures margin rules be consistent with the Federal Reserve Board's Regulation T, the rule that governs the credit activities of broker–dealers. In joint decision, the SEC and CFTC set a minimum rate of 20 percent for retail accounts. Market makers are exempt from this requirement.

Single stock futures are priced using the cost-of-carry arbitrage relationship expressed in Equation 7.5. For example, consider the June futures contract on Wal-Mart stores observed today (February 20). The June futures contract will expire on June 18. The current price of Wal-Mart stock is $59.45 per share. Wal-Mart is expected to pay a regular quarterly dividend of 9 cents per share on April 7. The current financing cost is assumed to be 1.6 percent per year.

Since there is only a single dividend payment during the life of the futures contract, the cost-of-carry relationship from Equation 7.5 becomes simple:

$$F_{0,t} = 59.45 \times (1 + 0.016 \times 119/365) - 0.09 \times (1 + 0.016 \times 72/119)$$
$$= \$59.45 + 0.031 - 0.09$$
$$= \$59.67 \text{ per share}$$

In this example, the holding period between February 20 and June 18 is 119 days. The purchase of the underlying stock requires the use of dollars today with a financing cost of 1.6 percent per year (0.016 in decimal form). The period between the dividend payment date, April 7, and the futures expiration date, June 18, is 72 days and the interest earned on the cash dividend over this period is assumed to accrue at the financing rate of 1.6 percent.

Insider trading in futures markets

Under securities law, illegal insider trading refers to the buying or selling of a security, in breach of a fiduciary duty or other relationship of trust and confidence, while in possession of material, nonpublic information about the security. The SEC regularly brings cases against corporate officers, directors, and employees who trade the corporation's securities after learning of significant confidential corporate developments. The SEC also brings insider trading cases against other persons who have been "tipped" by corporate insiders. In addition, the SEC brings insider trading cases against individuals who were provided with confidential insider information in order to provide services to the corporation whose securities they traded.

In the futures market, the information that moves markets is generally related to global or macro-economic developments, as opposed to developments inside a corporation. Government reports are the most important source of market-moving macroeconomic information. Because government agencies are aware of the importance of the information they possess, great effort is expended to ensure that this information is held in strict confidence until it is released to all market participants at the same instant. For example, Federal Reserve announcements concerning open market committee meetings, Bureau of Labor Statistics announcements on jobs and unemployment, and United States Department of Agriculture crop reports are handled with extreme care to ensure that government information is released in a way that does not create advantages or disadvantages for any group of market participants.

When market-moving macroeconomic information is illegally disclosed by a government employee, this employee has breached a fiduciary duty to his employer. Various federal statutes establish severe penalties, including criminal penalties, for individuals who illegally disclose nonpublic government information.

One form of illegal insider trading in the futures market is called "front running." Front running is a prohibited trading practice whereby a broker places his own trades ahead of his client's orders based on privileged information that the broker possesses about the client's trading intentions.

Insider trading is a potential concern for single stock futures or futures based on narrow sector indexes. For this reason, these products are regulated jointly by futures regulators (the CFTC) and securities regulators (the SEC).

Risk management with security futures products

Hedging with stock index futures applies directly to the management of stock portfolios. The usefulness of stock index futures in portfolio management stems from the fact that they directly represent the market portfolio. Before stock index futures began trading, there was no comparable way of trading an instrument that gave a price performance that was so directly tied to a broad market index. Further, stock index futures have great potential in portfolio management due to their very low transaction costs. In this section, we consider some hedging applications of stock index futures.

A short hedge and hedge ratio calculation

As a first case, consider the manager of a well-diversified stock portfolio with a value of $40 million, and assume that the portfolio has a beta of 1.22, measured relative to the S&P 500. This implies that a movement of 1 percent in the S&P 500 index would be expected to induce a change of 1.22 percent in the value of the stock portfolio. The portfolio manager fears that a bear market is imminent and wishes to hedge his portfolio's value against that possibility. One strategy would be to liquidate the portfolio and place the proceeds in short-term debt instruments and then, after the bear market, return the funds to the stock market. Such a plan is infeasible. First, the transaction costs from such a strategy are quite high. Second, if the fund is large, liquidating the portfolio could drive down stock prices. This would prevent the portfolio manager from liquidating the portfolio at the prices currently quoted for the individual stocks.

As an obvious alternative to liquidating the portfolio, the manager could use the S&P 500 stock index futures contract. By selling futures, the manager should be able to offset the effect of the bear market on the portfolio by generating gains in the futures market. One kind of naive strategy might involve selling one dollar of the value underlying the index futures contract for each dollar of the portfolio's value. Assuming that the S&P index futures contract stands at 1,060.00, the advocated futures position would be given by

$$-\frac{V_P}{V_F} = -\frac{\$40,000,000}{1,060 \times \$250} = -150.94 \approx -150 \text{ contracts}$$

where V_P is the value of the portfolio and V_F is the value of the futures contract.

One problem with this approach is that it ignores the higher volatility of the stock portfolio relative to that of the S&P 500 index. As noted previously, the beta of the stock portfolio, as measured against the index, was 1.22. Table 7.10 shows the potential results of a hedge consistent with these facts. The portfolio manager initiates the hedge on March 14, selling 150 DEC futures contracts against the $40 million stock portfolio. By August 16, his fears have been realized and the market has fallen. The S&P index, and the futures, have both fallen by 4.43 percent to 1,013. The stock portfolio, with its greater volatility, has fallen 1.22 times as much (1.22×4.43 percent), generating a loss of $2,161,840. This leaves a net loss on the hedge of $399,340. The failure to consider the differential volatility between the stock portfolio and the index futures contract leads to suboptimal hedging results.

Table 7.10 A short hedge		
Date	Stock market	Futures market
March 14	Hold $40 million in a stock portfolio	Sell 150 S&P 500® December futures contracts at 1,060.00
August 16	Stock portfolio falls by 5.40% to $37,838,160 Loss: −$2,161,840	S&P futures contract falls by 4.43% to 1,013.00 Gain: 47 basis points × $250 × 150 contracts = $1,762,500
	Net loss: −$399,340	

The manager might be able to avoid this result by weighting the hedge ratio by the beta of the stock portfolio. According to this scenario, the manager could use the following equation to find the number of contracts to trade:

$$-\beta_p\left(\frac{V_p}{V_F}\right) = \text{number of contracts} \tag{7.6}$$

where β_p is the beta of the portfolio that is being hedged. Using this approach for our example, the manager would sell 185 contracts:

$$-1.22\left(\frac{\$40,000,000}{1,060 \times \$250}\right) = -184.15 \approx -185 \text{ contracts}$$

Had the manager traded 185 contracts, the futures gain reported in Table 7.10 would have been $2,173,750 instead of $1,762,500. This higher gain would have almost exactly offset the loss on the spot position of $2,161,840. Note, however, that these excellent results depend on two crucial assumptions. First, such results could be achieved only if the movement of the stock portfolio during the hedge period exactly corresponded to the volatility implied by its beta. Second, the technique of Equation 7.6 uses the beta of the stock portfolio as measured against the S&P 500 index itself. This assumes that the futures contracts move exactly in tandem with the spot index. This assumption is clearly violated by recent market experience, because the futures contracts for all of the indexes are more volatile than the indexes themselves. This is reflected by the fact that the futures contracts generally have betas above 1.0 when they are measured relative to the stock index itself. The methodology of Equation 7.6 does not take this into account, since it implicitly assumes the index and the futures contracts to have the same price movements, which would imply equal betas. We will consider more sophisticated approaches to this type of hedging problem in Chapter 8.

A long hedge

As with all other futures contracts, both long and short hedges are possible in stock index futures. Imagine a pension fund manager who is convinced that she stands at the beginning of an extended bull market in Japanese equities. The current exchange rate is $1 = ¥140. She anticipates that ¥6 billion = $42,857,143 ≈ $43,000,000 in new funds will become available in three months for investment. Waiting three months for the funds to invest in the stock market could mean that the bull market would be missed altogether. An alternative to missing the market move would be to use the stock index futures market. The pension manager could simply buy an amount of a stock index futures contract that would be equivalent in dollar commitments to the anticipated inflow of investable funds. On May 19, with the Nikkei index futures contract standing at 14,400, the CME futures contract represents an underlying cash value of $72,000 ($5 per index point). The pension manager can secure her position in the market by buying $43 million worth of futures. Since she expects the funds in three months, the SEP contract is a natural expiration to use, so she buys 600 SEP contracts, as shown in Table 7.11, because $43,000,000/$72,000 = 597.22 ≈ 600. By August 15, the Nikkei spot and futures have risen 2.5 percent or 360 points, to 14,760. Therefore, the ¥6 billion could not buy the same shares that would have been possible on May 19. To offset this fact, the pension manager has earned a futures profit of $1,080,000. This gain in the futures market helps offset the new higher prices that would be incurred in the stock purchase. Because the CME Nikkei contract is based on the Nikkei index but quoted in dollars, this strategy still leaves the trader exposed to exchange rate risk, which could be offset by an exchange rate hedge.

Table 7.11 A long hedge with stock index futures

Date	Stock market	Futures market
May 19	A pension fund manager anticipates having ¥6 billion to invest in Japanese equities in three months	Buys 600 SEP Nikkei futures on the CME at 14,400
August 15	¥6 billion becomes available for investment; stock prices have risen, so the ¥6 billion will not buy the same shares that it would have on May 19	The market has risen and the Nikkei futures stands at 14,760 Futures profit: 360 points × $5 × 600 contracts = $1,080,000

Hedging with single stock futures

Constructing hedges with single stock futures follows the same logic as with hedges constructed with stock indexes. An important difference, however, is that the hedger will not need to make adjustments to the hedge ratio to account is for correlation differences between the price of the stock being hedged and the price of the futures. If one is hedging a portfolio of Wal-Mart stock with Wal-Mart futures, the correlation in prices will be equal to one implying a one-to-one hedge ratio. One can think of a hedge constructed with stock index futures as a cross-hedge, requiring an adjustment to the hedge ratio to account for differing correlations.

As an example, consider a manager holding a portfolio of 1,000 shares of Wal-Mart stock on behalf of a client on February 20. Wal-Mart shares currently cost $59.45 per share. The manager plans to liquidate the stock in three months to meet the cash flow needs of his client. However, Wal-Mart will issue earnings guidance during this period and the manager fears that the price may decline. Instead of liquidating the stock today, the manager chooses to hedge by selling (going short) ten Wal-Mart single stock futures contracts. The manager selects ten futures contracts because each contract is written on 100 shares of Wal-Mart stock. The current price of June Wal-Mart futures is $59.67 per share.

With this hedged position, no matter what happens to the price of Wal-Mart stock, the manager is guaranteed to lock in the current price of $59.67 per share. Each $1.00 decline in the price of Wal-Mart shares will produce a gain of $1.00 per share in the futures position.

Conclusion

In this chapter, we have explored the major stock indexes on which futures contracts are traded. In addition, we have considered the structure of the futures contracts based upon them and the differences among the various futures contracts. We applied familiar cash-and-carry and reverse cash-and-carry arbitrage strategies to show that stock index futures prices should conform to the cost-of-carry model. However, we noted the cost-of-carry model must be adjusted to reflect cash dividends. In the context of the cost-of-carry model, we saw that index arbitrage and program trading are applications of cash-and-carry approaches to futures pricing.

The chapter considered some speculative trading strategies. In addition to speculative applications, stock index futures are useful for managing risk. We considered some examples of short and long hedges. In the short hedge example, we showed how a portfolio manager could protect against a potential bear market. With a long hedge example, we showed how a trader could capture a potential bull market by using futures as a substitute for actually buying shares. The chapter also discussed single stock futures.

Exercises

1   Assume that the DJIA stands at 8,340.00 and the current divisor is 0.25. One of the stocks in the index is priced at $100.00 and it splits 2 : 1. Based on this information, answer the following questions:

A   What is the sum of the prices of all the shares in the index before the stock split?
B   What is the value of the index after the split? Explain.
C   What is the sum of the prices of all the shares in the index after the split?
D   What is the divisor after the split?

2   What is the main difference in the calculation of the DJIA and the S&P 500 indexes? Explain.

3   For the S&P 500 index, assume that the company with the highest market value has a 1 percent increase in stock prices. Also, assume that the company with the smallest market value has a 1 percent decrease in the price of its shares. Does the index change, and if so, in what direction?

4   The S&P 500 futures is scheduled to expire in six months, and the interest rate for carrying stocks over that period is 11 percent. The expected dividend rate on the underlying stocks for the same period is 2 percent of the value of the stocks (the 2 percent is the half-year rate, not an annual rate). Ignoring the interest that it might be possible to earn on the dividend payments, find the fair value for the futures if the current value of the index is 945.00.

5   Consider a very simple index such as the DJIA, but assume that it has only two shares, A and B. The price of A is $100.00, and B trades for $75.00. The current index value is 175.00. The futures contract based on this index expires in three months, and the cost of carrying the stocks forward is 0.75 percent per month. This is also the interest rate that you can earn on invested funds. You expect Stock A to pay a $3 dividend in one month and Stock B to pay a $1 dividend in two months. Find the fair value of the futures. Assume monthly compounding.

6   Using the same data as in Exercise 5, now assume that the futures trades at 176.00. Explain how you would trade with this set of information. Show your transactions.

7   Using the same data as in Exercise 5, now assume that the futures trades at 174.00. Explain how you would trade with this set of information. Show your transactions.

8   For a stock index and a stock index futures constructed like the DJIA, assume that the dividend rate expected to be earned on the stocks in the index is the same as the cost of carrying the stocks forward. What should be the relationship between the cash and futures market prices? Explain.

9   Your portfolio is worth $100 million and has a beta of 1.08 measured against the S&P index, which is priced at 350.00. Explain how you would hedge this portfolio, assuming that you wish to be fully hedged.

10   You have inherited $50 million, but the estate will not settle for six months and you will not actually receive the cash until that time. You find current stock values attractive and you plan to invest in the S&P 500 cash portfolio. Explain how you would hedge this anticipated investment using S&P 500 futures.

11   William's new intern, Jessica, is just full of questions. She is particularly inquisitive about stock index futures. She notices that the futures price is consistently higher than the current index level and that the difference gets smaller as the contracts near their expiration dates.

A   Explain the relationship between the futures price, the spot price, interest rates, and dividends.
B   Jessica asks William to explain the Dow index to her. What type of index is the Dow? How is it constructed? How could she build a portfolio of stocks to replicate it?
C   Jessica wants a numerical example of the relationship between a price weighted index and the futures contract based on that index. She supposes the following example. A futures contract is based on a price-weighted index of three stocks, A, B, and C. The futures contract expires in three months. Stock A pays a dividend at the end of the first month, and Stock C pays a dividend at the end of month two. The term structure is flat over this time period, with the monthly interest rate equal to 0.5 percent. The stock prices and dividends are as follows:

Stock	Price ($)	Dividend ($)
A	30	0.11 in one month
B	50	0
C	40	0.15 in two months

Compute the index assuming a divisor of 3. How many shares of each stock should be bought to replicate the index?

D   Suppose the divisor had been 0.5. Compute the index. How many shares of each stock must be bought to replicate the index?

E   Assuming that the divisor is 0.5, compute the fair value for the three-month futures contract.

F   Right now, the DJIA is at 8,635. Its dividend yield is 1.76 percent. The 90-day T-bill rate is 5.6 percent bond equivalent yield. Compute a fair price today for the index futures contract expiring in 90 days.

12   Casey Mathers manages the $60 million equity portion of Zeta Corporation's pension assets. This past Friday, August 7, Zeta announced that it was downsizing its workforce and would be offering early retirement to many of its older employees. The impact on the portfolio Casey manages would be an anticipated $10 million withdrawal over the next four months. The stock market has been good for the past five years, but recently there have been signs of weakness. Casey is concerned about a drop in asset prices before the $10 million is withdrawn from the portfolio. Casey runs a fairly aggressive portfolio with a beta of 1.2, relative to the S&P 500 index. Casey sees the following S&P 500 index futures prices:

Expiration	Contract value $250 × index
SEP	1,088.50
DEC	1,100.00
MAR × 1	1,110.50

A   How much of the portfolio should Casey hedge? Justify your answer.

B   Design a hedge based on your answer to part A above.

13   Byron Hendrickson manages the $30 million equity portion of Fredrick and Sons' pension plan assets. Byron has been trying to get the management of Fredrick and Sons to move more of their assets from their fixed-income portfolio (market value of $60 million) to the equity portfolio in order to achieve the objectives that management had set forth for growth of the plan. The management has decided to invest the proceeds of several bond issues that will be maturing over the next three months. The total proceeds from the bond issues will be $10 million. It is now December 15. Byron believes that the January price run-up will be particularly strong this year. Since his portfolio is not particularly aggressive, with a beta equal to 0.85, he would really like to have that $10 million working for him in January. Design a hedge that will prevent Byron from missing the January action, based on the following current market prices for the S&P 500 index futures:

Expiration	Contract value $250 × index
MAR	1,157.00
JUN	1,170.80

Notes

1   In earlier times, the S&P 500 consisted of 400 industrial firms, 40 financial institutions, 40 utilities, and 20 transportation firms.

2   For more detail on the computation method, see http://www.stoxx.com/index_description/ind_calculation.html

3   As we will see in Chapter 8, trading for the S&P 500 and the NYSE futures contracts ends on one day, and the final settlement price is set at the next day's opening price.

4   These calculations are sometimes off by a penny or two due to rounding errors.

5   See the *Report of the Banking Supervision Inquiry into the Circumstances of the Collapse of Barings, Ordered by the House of Commons*, London: Her Majesty's Stationary Office, July 1995.

6   In an interesting approach to the problem of Barings, one calculation insists that Barings would have made a profit of $3 billion on its position had it simply held until the end of 1995. See Numa Financial Systems, Ltd., "Barings Theoretical P/L 1995," NumaWeb home page (www.numa.com). This would have been the eventual result, although the position would also have experienced a low of −$5 billion in June 1995. For a more sober assessment, see Bank of England, "Report of the Board of Banking Supervision Inquiry into the Circumstances of the Collapse of Barings," July 18, 1995. The affair has already given rise to a number of books: see Judith Rawnsley, *Going for Broke*, New York: HarperCollins, 1995; Nick Leeson, *Rogue Trader*, Boston, MA: Little Brown, 1996; Stephen

Fay, *The Collapse of Barings*, New York: Richard Cohen Books, 1996; Peter G. Zhang, *Barings Bankruptcy and Financial Derivatives*, Singapore: World Scientific, 1995; and Luke Hunt and Karen Heinrich, *Barings Lost: Nick Leeson and the Collapse of Barings plc.*, Singapore: Butterworth-Heinemann Asia, 1996. For a history of Barings as a force in world merchant banking, see Philip Ziegler, *The Sixth Great Power: A History of One of the Greatest of All Banking Families, the House of Barings, 1762–1929*, New York: A. A. Knopf, 1988. For a survey of several market disasters, including Barings, see Anatoli Kuprianov, "Derivatives Debacles," Federal Reserve Bank of Richmond, *Economic Quarterly*, 81:4, 1995, pp. 1–39.

8

Security Futures Products: Refinements

Overview

In Chapter 7, we saw that prices for stock index futures and single stock futures are governed by the cost-of-carry model. Because stocks often pay dividends, we saw how to tailor the cost-of-carry model to reflect the dividends on the stocks that underlie the stock index futures. In this chapter, we explore some of the empirical evidence on the relationship between theoretical and observed market prices. As in any violation of cost-of-carry principles, arbitrage opportunities should be possible if stock index futures prices do not correspond to theoretically determined prices.

Index arbitrage is the specific name given to attempts to exploit discrepancies between theoretical and actual stock index futures prices. As we also discussed in Chapter 7, index arbitrage usually proceeds through program trading. With the advent of program trading, there has been some evidence of a link between high index price variability and the style of trading used by program traders. This chapter considers some of the evidence on volatility and explores the market concern about volatility.

Because of the perception that futures trading is responsible for stock market volatility, new concern has focused on trading practices in the futures market, leading to some changes in trading rules. This chapter also considers some of the new trading practices rules recently implemented in the S&P 500® futures pit.

Chapter 7 considered some speculative and hedging applications of security futures products. This chapter explores some more sophisticated techniques for using stock index futures and single stock futures. By trading security futures products in conjunction with a stock portfolio, a portfolio manager can tailor the risk characteristics of the entire portfolio. These strategies have aspects of both speculation and hedging. Two of the most notable of these are asset allocation and portfolio insurance, which we consider in some detail.

Stock index futures prices

In this section, we consider a variety of issues related to stock index futures pricing. First, we examine the empirical evidence on stock index futures efficiency. Namely, do stock index futures prices conform to the cost-of-carry model? Evidence suggests that the market was not efficient when trading began, but that it is now efficient. Second, we consider the effect of taxes on stock index futures prices. A tax-timing option available to traders of stocks, but denied to stock index futures traders, might explain the discrepancy between theoretical and actual prices for stock index futures. Third, we consider the timing relationship between stock index futures prices and the cash market index. Does the futures price lead the cash market index, or does the cash market index lead the futures? Finally, we consider seasonal impacts on stock index futures pricing. Here "seasonal" refers not only to the time of year, but also to the time of the month, the time of the week, and even the time of day.

Stock index futures efficiency

In Chapter 7, we saw that cost-of-carry principles apply directly to the pricing of stock index futures. In particular, if the spot stock index price and the futures price are misaligned, cash-and-carry or reverse cash-and-carry arbitrage opportunities will become available. We considered examples of these kinds of transactions in Chapter 7. In this section, we consider whether the stock index futures market is informationally efficient. If it is efficient, then stock index futures prices should conform to the cost-of-carry model that we developed in Chapter 7. As we will see, the general conclusion suggests that the market was inefficient in the early days of trading, but that it now conforms well to the cost-of-carry model.

Exploring actual market data, David Modest and Mahadevan Sundaresan apply the carrying charges model to form permissible bounds for futures prices, and try to take into account the actual transaction costs that would be incurred in trading the futures and the stocks in the indexes.[1] The bounds depend critically on the assumptions of a $25 round-trip transaction cost for the futures contract and a $0.10 per share transaction cost for the stock itself. We must also assume that the T-bill rate is the appropriate interest rate for all calculations of carrying charges.

Modest and Sundaresan's analysis makes two additional assumptions. The first concerns the assumption that we make regarding the use of proceeds from short selling stocks. If a trader does not have full use of the proceeds from short sales due to margin requirements, then the interest on the proceeds that cannot be used has a marked impact on the analysis. We have already encountered this issue in our discussion of T-bill futures efficiency. Essentially, an arbitrage opportunity might require the short sale of the stock index, which means that the individual stocks comprising the index are sold short in the stock market. In this situation, the short seller may not receive full use of the proceeds from the short sale, because the broker will hold a significant fraction of those proceeds as protection against default by the short seller. Therefore, the success of any such arbitrage depends critically upon assumptions regarding the use of short sale proceeds. Modest and Sundaresan examine alternative assumptions about the use of short sale proceeds.

A second critical assumption concerns dividends. We have already seen in Chapter 7 that dividends are important to the pricing of stock index futures. In addition, the extreme intertemporal variation in dividends shown in Figure 7.2 means that their effect will vary dramatically from one time period to the next. For accuracy in pricing stock index futures, it is very important to take account of dividends.

We begin our discussion of this issue by focusing on David Modest and Mahadevan Sundaresan's paper "The Relationship Between Spot and Futures Prices in Stock Index Futures Markets: Some Preliminary Evidence," which examines the early history of trading. The paper addresses most of the issues that are necessary to determine the efficiency of prices in a market. For instance, we have seen that every real market has a range of permissible no-arbitrage prices. This no-arbitrage band arises because of transaction costs and restrictions on short selling. Therefore, tests of market efficiency depend critically on careful estimations of these transaction costs.

Modest and Sundaresan computed the no-arbitrage boundaries for the DEC 1982 futures contract under the assumptions outlined above and those results are presented in Figure 8.1. The graph tracks the futures prices from April 21 through September 15, 1982. The dotted lines on the graph show the bounds, which are adjusted for dividends and the assumption that half the proceeds from short sales are available. The solid line represents the actual futures price. Clearly, the futures price lies within the bounds except for near misses on two occasions. On the whole, these results are consistent with the rationality of futures pricing. In another part of their study, the bounds were also adjusted for dividends, but with the assumption that one has use of 100 percent of the proceeds from short sales. In this situation, arbitrage opportunities were consistently available.

In their study, Modest and Sundaresan did not attempt to include an estimate of the daily dividend payment from the S&P 500 index. Instead, they estimated the dividend rate on the

Figure 8.1   No-arbitrage bounds and futures prices

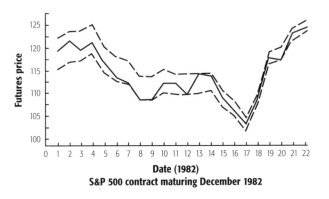

Date (1982)
S&P 500 contract maturing December 1982

Source: D. Modest and M. Sundaresan, "The Relationship Between Spot and Futures Prices in Stock Index Futures Markets: Some Preliminary Evidence," *The Journal of Futures Markets*, 3:2, 1983, pp. 15–41. © 1983. Reprinted by permission of John Wiley & Sons, Inc.

index using quarterly dividend data and then interpolated that into monthly dividend data. As a result, their study does not reflect the high variability in dividends on a daily basis. The graph of Figure 8.1 applies to the DEC 1982 contract for April 21 – September 15, 1982. Over that time, dividends had very sharp quarterly peaks. Had Modest and Sundaresan been able to take these daily fluctuations into account more accurately, we would expect observed prices to lie more consistently within the no-arbitrage bounds, and their paper would be even more valuable.

Perhaps of equal importance with regard to the exact treatment of dividends is the assumption made about the use of proceeds from short sales. In addition, we have seen that some traders face full transaction costs. By contrast, other traders face much lower transaction costs. For example, large institutions with significant portfolios can simulate short selling by selling part of their existing portfolio. In this simulated short selling, they retain full use of the proceeds. Throughout our discussion, we have referred to arbitrage activities by these low transaction cost traders as **quasi-arbitrage**.

Modest and Sundaresan's results clearly point to quasi-arbitrage opportunities. In the early days of stock index futures trading, it appears that significant quasi-arbitrage opportunities were available. However, after the seasoning of the market, prices tended to remain within the no-arbitrage bounds. While such conclusions depend upon estimates of transaction costs, other studies substantiate the conclusion reached by Modest and Sundaresan.

The Modest and Sundaresan paper covers most of the key issues involved in index arbitrage. However, their work dealt with the early period of stock index futures trading. Since that time, trading strategies have changed in some important ways, which have been studied by George Sofianos, in his paper "Index Arbitrage Profitability."[2] Sofianos found that mispricings were "narrow and short-lived, lasting on average about three minutes." He found that these mispricings were so small that transacting on them and holding them until expiration would earn less than investing in commercial paper. Because there were numerous mispricing reversals (first futures too high, then cash too high, for instance), an active arbitrageur could probably make returns somewhat in excess of her opportunity cost of funds. While Sofianos's best guess of the size of the returns for the active arbitrageur was about 5 percent above the commercial paper rate, he qualifies that finding because of uncertainty over transaction costs and certain technical measurement problems that he faced. He found that about 70 percent of arbitrage positions were closed before expiration.

Taxes and stock index futures

A difference in tax treatment between futures and the stocks themselves might justify a discrepancy from the cost-of-carry model. In such a case, the market might be efficient. Comparing a long position in the stocks underlying an index and a long position in the stock index futures contract shows that there is a difference in tax treatment. The owner of a stock may have a paper gain or loss on the stock as the end of the year approaches. For example, assume that a share was purchased for $100 and that the trader pays taxes at the rate of 30 percent. If the stock sells for $90 as the end of the year approaches, the trader has the option to sell the stock for $90, realizing a $10 loss. If he or she sells the stock, taxable income will be reduced by $10. With a 30 percent tax rate, selling the stock generates a tax saving of $3. By contrast, assume that as the end of the year approaches the stock price is $110 instead of $90. In this situation, the tax-saving strategy is to wait until after the turn of the year to take the gain, thereby deferring the taxes for a full year by just waiting a few days to make the trade.

Because futures prices are marked to market at year-end for tax purposes, the futures contract possesses no tax-timing option. In the futures markets, tax rules require all paper gains or losses to be recognized as cash gains or losses each year. The tax-timing option included with the stock, but lacking with the futures contract, implies that rational pricing must reflect the value of the tax-timing option in the relationship between the cash and futures prices of the stock index.

This possibility was first noted by Bradford Cornell and Kenneth French. They show how this tax-timing option can give extra value to the stocks relative to the futures. Cornell and French compute the value of the tax option as the difference between the observed market price and the price implied by the carrying charges model. While the tax option clearly has a value, the technique adopted by Cornell and French assumes that the stock index futures contract is priced rationally, and they compute the value of the option in accordance with that fundamental belief. For the purpose of trying to evaluate the price performance characteristics of the stock index futures contract, note that the tax-timing option would have a value, but that a trader cannot immediately assume that its value is equal to the discrepancy between the observed market price and the theoretically justified price assuming no tax-timing option. However, in an empirical study of the effect of the tax-timing option on futures prices, Cornell concludes that the tax-timing option does not appear to affect prices.[3] Cornell suggests that trading may be dominated by tax-free investors, or that other tax rules may prevent the tax-timing option from significantly affecting prices.

The day-of-the-week effect in stock index futures

It has been well documented that returns on many securities vary by the day of the week. There is nothing in the financial theory to explain why returns on Thursday should be different from returns on Tuesday or Wednesday. Nonetheless, a great deal of evidence shows that returns differ depending on the day of the week. In particular, Friday returns are generally high and Monday returns (the return from Friday close to Monday close) are even negative. These return differences are substantial and it may be possible for investors to earn a return that beats the market by timing their purchases to take advantage of these persistent differences. If so, the day-of-the-week effect would show either that the semistrong efficient market hypothesis (EMH) was not true or that the capital asset pricing model (CAPM) was not true, or both. If the CAPM is the correct pricing relationship in the market, then the EMH must be false, because it appears that prices do not adjust correctly to reflect all available information. If the EMH is true, it seems that the CAPM must be false, because there must be additional risk factors not recognized by the CAPM to explain the different returns depending on the day of the week.

The day-of-the-week effect has also been explored in the stock index futures market. Given the strong relationship that must hold between stock index futures and the stock index itself, we would expect to find an effect in the futures market if there is one in the stock market itself. Most studies find a weekend effect—price changes from the Friday close to the Monday open are low or negative.[4]

Leads and lags in stock index prices

We have seen that arbitrage seekers force stock index cash market and futures market prices to conform to the cost-of-carry model. Thus, a movement in one price must generate a movement in the other price to keep prices in conformance with the cost-of-carry model.

At first blush, it might seem that the index should lead the futures. For example, if new information arrives in the market about a particular stock, the price of that stock will change. The index value changes to reflect the new price of the constituent stock. To keep prices in conformance with the cost-of-carry model, the index futures price must change. Under this scenario, the cash market index changes first and the futures index price changes later. Thus, the cash index leads the futures price.

However, the dominant information affecting the stock market might be more general information. If the most important information affects the general level of stock prices, rather than the price of a single firm, there may be a different transmission of stock price changes. For example, assume that war breaks out in the Middle East and that this is bad news for stock prices. Traders may react to this information by trading in either the stock market or the stock index futures market. The choice of market will be affected by both the relative liquidity and the transaction costs in the two markets. If liquidity and transaction costs are most important, futures trading will be more attractive. Thus, with news of the invasion, traders might first sell index futures, driving down the futures price. The cash market index must then adjust to exclude arbitrage opportunities. Under this scenario, the futures price will lead the cash market index.

These leads and lags are most likely to occur on a minute-to-minute basis. If the leads or lags persisted over days, for example, they could well lead to arbitrage opportunities. Whether the cash market index leads the futures or vice versa is essentially an empirical question. The question of leads and lags has been explored in several studies, most of which find that futures prices lead cash market prices.

While stock index futures prices may lead the stock index, this differential movement does not necessarily create arbitrage opportunities. First, movements in the two prices are generally almost simultaneous. Quickly responding prices may not allow any arbitrage opportunities. Second, both prices vary continuously by small amounts as new information reaches the market. Even substantial lags would not create an arbitrage opportunity if the difference in prices is small. In other words, the futures price could always lead the cash market index. However, if the price difference is small, the difference in prices could always remain within the no-arbitrage bounds of the cost-of-carry model.

Real-world program trading

Chapter 7 explained the basic idea of index arbitrage through program trading. There, we considered an imaginary two-stock index and showed how to engage in cash-and-carry and reverse cash-and-carry strategies to exploit mispricing of the index versus the index futures. To provide a more realistic feel for real-world program trade in stock index futures, this section begins with an historical example of an actual program trade. We then consider the risks inherent in program trading that make the enterprise much more perilous than our historical example would seem to indicate. Finally, we conclude with some statistics on the extent of program trading in today's markets.

A real-world example of index arbitrage

As discussed in Chapter 7, the futures price that conforms to the cost-of-carry model is called the **fair-value futures price**. In this section, we consider an example of determining the fair value of the December 2001 S&P 500 stock index futures contract traded on November 30, 2001.

The December 2001 futures contract closed at 1,140.00 index points on November 30. The cash index price on this date was 1,139.45. The value of the compounded dividend stream expected to be paid out between November 30 and December 21, the expiration date of the December contract, totaled 0.9 index points.[5] The financing cost prevailing at the time for large, creditworthy borrowers was approximately 1.90 percent annualized over a 365-day year, or 0.1093 percent over the 21 days between November 30 and the December 21 expiration date for the futures contract. Using this information we can apply the cost-of-carry model to determine the fair-value futures price:

$$F_{0,t} = 1,139.45 \times (1 + 0.001093) - 0.9 = 1,139.80 \text{ index points}$$

This is the estimated fair value of the December 2001 futures contract at the close of trading on November 30, 2001. Given the way in which the S&P 500 futures contract is designed, each index point is worth $250. This means the expected invoice price of the contract is $284,950; that is, $250 per index point times 1,139.80 index points. Since the closing futures price on this day is 1,140, it would appear that an arbitrage opportunity does not exist. The **basis error** for this contract—that is, the actual futures price minus the fair-value futures price—is only 0.20 index points. The annualized rate of return from a cash-and-carry arbitrage strategy at these prices would only be 0.3054 percent, less than the financing cost of 1.90 percent. The annualized rate of return for this strategy is determined by calculating the rate of return over the 21-day arbitrage period and then annualizing the 21-day rate of return over a 365-day year (i.e., $(1,140/1,139.80)^{365/21} - 1$).

Suppose that the December 2001 futures price on November 30, 2001 had been 1,143.00 instead of the actual 1,140. In this case the rate of return on the strategy would be 4.99 percent annualized over a 365-day year (i.e., $(1,143/1,139.80)^{365/21} - 1$). This rate of return is well above the annualized financing cost of 1.90 percent. In this case, the futures price is above its fair market value as determined by the cost-of-carry model by 3.20 index points. To exploit this apparent arbitrage opportunity, the trader would simultaneously sell the relatively overvalued futures and buy the relatively undervalued cash index. In other words, the trader would buy low and sell high using a cash-and-carry arbitrage strategy. The cash flows for this cash-and-carry strategy are summarized in Table 8.1.

Now, suppose instead that the December 2001 futures price on November 30, 2001 had been 1,138.00. In this case, the rate of return from this strategy would be 2.78 percent annualized over a 365-day year (i.e., $(1,139.80/1,138)^{365/21} - 1$). This rate of return is above the trader's annualized financing cost of 1.90 percent. In this case, the futures price is below its fair market value as determined by the cost-of-carry model by −1.80 index points. To exploit this apparent arbitrage opportunity, the trader would simultaneously buy the relatively undervalued

Table 8.1 Cash-and-carry index arbitrage

Date	Cash market	Futures market
November 30	Borrow $284,862.5 (1,139.45 × $250) for 21 days at 1.9%; buy stocks in the S&P 500® for $284,862.5	Sell one DEC S&P 500 index futures contract for 1,143.00
December 21	Receive accumulated proceeds from invested dividends of $225 (0.9 index points × $250); sell stock for $285,000 (1,140 index points × $250); total proceeds are $285,225; repay debt of $285,173.9	At expiration, the futures price is set equal to the spot index value of 1,140.00, giving a profit of 3.00 index units; in dollar terms, this is 3.00 index points × $250 per index point
	Gain: $311.40	Gain: $750
	Total profit: $311.40 + $750 = $1,061.40	

Table 8.2 Reverse cash-and-carry index arbitrage

Date	Cash market	Futures market
November 30	Sell stock in the S&P 500® index for $284,862.5 (1,139.45 × $250); lend $284,862.5 for 21 days at 1.9%	Buy one DEC index futures contract for 1,138.00
December 21	Receive proceeds from investment of $285,173.9; buy stocks in the S&P 500 index for $285,000 (1,140.00 × $250); return stocks to repay short sale	At expiration, the futures price is set equal to the spot index value of 1,140.00, giving a profit of 2.00 index points; in dollar terms, this is 2.00 index points × $250 per index
	Gain: $173.9	Profit: $500
	Total profit: $173.9 + $500 = $673.9	

cash futures and sell the relatively overvalued cash index. The stocks would either be sold short or sold out of inventory. In other words, the trader would buy low and sell high using a reverse cash-and-carry arbitrage strategy. The cash flows for this cash-and-carry strategy are summarized in Table 8.2.

Identifying an apparent arbitrage opportunities does not depend on the prices that prevail at expiration on December 21 (which happens to be 1,140 index points). Instead, the arbitrage opportunities arise solely from a discrepancy between the current futures price and its fair value. The arbitrage gain is locked in no matter what happens to stock prices between November 30 and December 21.

The success of the arbitrage depends upon identifying the misalignment between the actual futures price and the fair value futures price. However, at a given moment the fair value futures price depends upon the current price of 500 different stocks. Identifying an index arbitrage opportunity requires the ability to instantly find pricing discrepancies between the futures price and the fair futures price reflecting 500 different stocks. In addition, exploiting the arbitrage opportunity requires trading 500 stocks at the prices that created the arbitrage opportunity.

Large financial institutions can communicate orders to trade stock via their computers for very rapid execution. Faced with a cash-and-carry arbitrage opportunity, one of these large traders could execute a computer order to buy each and every stock represented in the S&P 500. Simultaneously, the institution would sell the S&P 500 futures contract. The use of computers to execute large and complicated stock market orders is called **program trading**. While computers are used for other kinds of stock market transactions, index arbitrage is the main application of program trading. Often, "index arbitrage" and "program trading" are used interchangeably.

Viewers of early morning financial market news shows on cable television are aware that the concept of fair value can also apply to the underlying stock index. Because stock index futures trade around the clock, futures prices can be used as indicators of the opening price for the underlying stock index. For example, S&P 500 stock index futures are traded around the clock on Globex, whereas most S&P 500 stocks trade during regular trading hours at the New York Stock Exchange (NYSE). Given the futures price and cost-of-carry information, a "fair value stock index price" can be estimated. Some financial television networks track this fair value price in real time and display it on the bottom of the screen ahead of the market open. This fair value stock index price serves as an indicator of how the stock market will open.

For example, suppose that it is 7:00 a.m. EST on November 30 and the NYSE has not yet opened. The current price of the December S&P 500® E-mini® futures contract traded on the CME's Globex system is 1,139.80 index points. As in the example above, assume that the financing cost over the remaining 21 days of the futures contract is 0.1093 percent (reflecting an annual rate of 1.90 percent). The expected dividends over the remaining 21 days of the contract's life are expected to total 0.9 index points. Using this information and the cost-of-carry relationship, we can determine the fair value of the cash index:

$$\text{fair value cash index price} = (1{,}139.80 + 0.9)/(1 + 0.00193) = 1{,}139.45 \text{ index points}$$

If the closing S&P had been less than 1,139.45, then one could infer, based on information available at 7:00 a.m., that the stock market would open higher. If the previous closing price had been higher than 1,139.45, then one could infer that the stock market would open lower.

Real-world impediments to stock index arbitrage

The cost-of-carry model is an essential tool for determining whether arbitrage opportunities exist between the cash market and the futures market. However, the model needs to be refined to account for real-world impediments to arbitrage strategies. For example, our model assumes a known dividend stream between the date the arbitrage strategy is implemented and the date of futures expiration. Since most corporations have stable dividend policies and declare dividends well in advance of actual payment, treating dividends as known is justifiable. On occasion, however, dividend payments may be suspended or altered. For example, in the fall of 2001, Enron Corporation declared a quarterly dividend to be paid in December of that year. But between the date the dividend was declared and date it was to be paid, Enron filed for bankruptcy protection and suspended the dividend payment.

Another potential real-world problem of conducting stock index arbitrage is that the composition of the underlying index changes continuously through time. For arbitrage strategies of short duration, this is not much of a problem. But for strategies of longer duration, the composition of the index can change noticeably, especially during periods of frequent corporate takeovers and spin-offs.

Direct evidence on how index arbitrageurs actually behave in the real world can be found in the Sofianos study referred to earlier in the chapter. Sofianos examines 2,659 S&P 500 index arbitrage trades over a six-month period, explicitly accounting for commissions, margins, bid–ask spread costs and other factors, such as the **early closing option**. The early closing option accounts for the fact that in the real world index arbitrage strategies can be unwound prior to futures expiration when it is profitable to do so. The early closing option, like any option, is valuable to the option holder, and this value will be reflected in the arbitrageur's calculation of the profitability of the arbitrage strategy.

Sofianos finds that the existence of arbitrage opportunities depends on the level of transaction costs. As expected, lower transaction costs are associated with more frequent arbitrage opportunities. Sofianos finds that the duration of arbitrage opportunities range from 2.5 to 4.5 minutes. This means that arbitrage opportunities must be exploited quickly in order to be profitable.

Sofianos finds differences in profitability between cash-and-carry arbitrage and reverse cash-and-carry arbitrage. Because of stock exchange restrictions on short sales of stock, arbitrage strategies requiring short sales of stock can be more costly than an otherwise equivalent strategy requiring the purchase of stock or the sale of stock out of existing inventory. Orders requiring short selling of stocks take longer to fill, resulting in higher risks in trade execution. To compensate for this increased execution risk, reverse cash-and-carry strategies require higher expected returns before a profitable position can be established.

Sofianos finds that, rather than trading all the stocks in the index, arbitrageurs often use surrogate stock baskets containing a subset of the index stocks. He finds that the average number of stocks used in S&P 500 arbitrage strategies is only 280 out of the 500 members of the index. By using fewer stocks, arbitrageurs can reduce transaction costs, but they introduce the risk that the surrogate portfolio may not precisely track the entire index. This **tracking risk** means that the arbitrage strategy is no longer risk free. To compensate for tracking risk, arbitrageurs will use surrogate baskets only when the difference between the futures price and the fair value futures price is large.

Sofianos also finds that arbitrageurs frequently establish (or liquidate) their futures and cash positions at different times. In over one-third of the trades studied by Sofianos, arbitrageurs did not establish the cash and futures legs of the transaction simultaneously. This practice, known as **legging**, is risky, because until the arbitrageur establishes both legs, the arbitrage profit is not locked in.

Sofianos points out some other real-world problems of conducting stock index arbitrage. For example, the prices observed on trading screens may not reflect the actual state of the market at the time arbitrageurs make their decisions. The staleness problem is particularly pronounced at the opening. S&P starts reporting S&P 500 index values before all component stocks have opened for trading. For stocks that have not opened, the index uses the previous day's closing price. Apparent arbitrage opportunities may therefore be illusory. The cost associated with stale prices is really a subset of the execution risk problem.

Hedging with stock index futures

In Chapter 7, we considered the basic techniques for hedging with stock index futures. We presented examples of short and long hedges, and discussed a hedging strategy for hedging a portfolio with stock index futures that reflected the beta of the portfolio being hedged. The hedge position from Chapter 7 is as follows:

$$-\beta_P\left(\frac{V_P}{V_F}\right) = \text{number of contracts} \tag{7.6}$$

where V_P is the value of the portfolio, V_F is the value of the futures contract, and β_P is the beta of the portfolio that is being hedged. In this section, we analyze stock index futures hedging. We begin by showing that the hedge in Equation 7.6 gives the futures position to establish a combined stock and futures portfolio with the lowest possible risk. We illustrate this hedging technique with actual market data. It is also possible to use futures to alter the beta of an existing portfolio. For example, if a stock portfolio has a beta of 0.8 and the desired beta is 0.9, it is possible to trade stock index futures to make the combined stock and futures portfolio behave like a stock portfolio with a beta of 0.9.

The minimum risk hedge ratio

In Chapter 7, we studied the problem of combining a cash market position with futures to minimize risk. There, we took the cash market position as fixed and sought to find the futures hedge ratio, HR, that would minimize risk. From Equation 4.3, we saw that the risk of a combined cash and futures position is as follows:

$$\sigma_P^2 = \sigma_S^2 + HR^2\sigma_F^2 + 2HR\rho_{SF}\sigma_S\sigma_F \tag{4.3}$$

where σ_P^2 is the variance of the portfolio, P; σ_S^2 is the variance of S; σ_F^2 is the variance of F; and ρ_{SF} is the correlation between S_t and F_t. From Equation 4.3, the risk-minimizing hedge ratio, HR, is as follows:

$$HR = -\frac{\rho_{SF}\sigma_S\sigma_F}{\sigma_F^2} = -\frac{COV_{SF}}{\sigma_F^2} \tag{4.4}$$

where COV_{SF} is the covariance between S and F. As a practical matter, the easiest way to find the risk-minimizing hedge ratio is to estimate the following regression:

$$S_t = \alpha + \beta_{RM}F_t + \varepsilon_t \tag{8.1}$$

where S_t is the returns on the cash market position in period t, F_t is the returns on the futures contract in period t,[6] α is the constant regression parameter, β_{RM} is the slope regression parameter for the risk-minimizing hedge, and ε is an error term with zero mean and a standard deviation of 1.0. The negative of the estimated beta from this regression is the risk-minimizing hedge ratio, because the estimated β_{RM} equals the sample covariance between the independent (F) and dependent (S) variables divided by the sample variance of the independent variable. The R^2 from this regression shows the percentage of risk in the cash position that is eliminated by holding the futures position.

At this point, it is important to distinguish the beta in Equation 8.1 and the beta of the portfolio in the sense of the CAPM. The CAPM beta is the beta from regressing the returns of a given asset on the returns from the "true" market portfolio. However, the returns on the true market portfolio are unobservable. Therefore, as a practical measure, proxies are used for the market portfolio and the betas of assets are estimated by regressing the returns of a particular asset on the returns from the proxy of the market portfolio. The potential confusion becomes more dangerous because the S&P 500 spot index is one of the best-known proxies for the true market portfolio.

In Equation 7.6, we computed a hedge ratio using the beta for the portfolio. This beta is the estimated CAPM beta, because it is estimated by regressing the returns from a portfolio on the proxy for the market portfolio. By contrast, the beta in Equation 8.1 is the beta for a risk-minimizing hedge ratio and is not the same as the estimated CAPM beta. The beta in Equation 8.1 is found by regressing the returns of the portfolio on the returns from the futures contract. The estimated CAPM beta is found by regressing the returns of the portfolio on the returns of the spot market index being used as a proxy for the unobservable true market portfolio. Thus, the hedging position in Equation 7.6 is not a risk-minimizing hedge. Nonetheless, such hedges can be very useful. We might think of the hedge ratio in Equation 7.6 as a rough-and-ready approximation to risk-minimizing hedging.

Having found the risk-minimizing hedge ratio, $-\beta_{RM}$, we need to compute the number of contracts to trade. The solution to this problem almost exactly matches the hedging position in Equation 7.6, but we use the risk-minimizing hedge ratio, $-\beta_{RM}$, instead of the CAPM beta for the portfolio, β_P. Thus, the risk-minimizing futures position is as follows:

$$-\beta_{RM}\left(\frac{V_P}{V_F}\right) = \text{number of contracts}$$

A minimum-risk hedging example

In this section, we consider an example of a minimum-risk hedge in stock index futures using actual market data. Let us assume that a trader has a portfolio worth $10 million on November 28. The portfolio is invested in the 30 stocks in the Dow Jones Industrial Average (DJIA). The portfolio manager will hedge this cash market portfolio using the S&P 500 JUN futures contract. We consider each step that the portfolio manager follows to compute the hedge ratio and to implement the hedge.

Organize data and compute returns
The manager plans to hedge according to Equation 7.6. Therefore, she needs to find the beta for the hedge ratio. Accordingly, she collects data for her portfolio value for 101 days from July 6 through yesterday, November 27. She also finds the price of the S&P 500 JUN futures for each day. There is nothing magical about using 101 days, but these data are available and she believes that this procedure will provide a sufficient sample to estimate the hedging beta. From the 101 days of prices, she computes the daily percentage change in the value of the cash market portfolio and the futures price. This gives 100 paired observations of daily returns data.

Estimate hedging beta
With the data in place, the portfolio manager regresses the cash market returns on the returns from the futures contract as shown in Equation 8.1. From this regression the estimated beta is 0.8801, so $\beta_{RM} = 0.8801$. This indicates that each dollar of the cash market position should be hedged with $0.8801 in the futures position. The R^2 from the regression is 0.9263, and this high R^2 encourages the belief that the hedge is likely to perform well. Again, for emphasis, the estimated beta from regressing the portfolio's returns on the stock index futures returns is not the same as the portfolio's CAPM beta; β_P does not equal β_{RM}.

Compute futures position
The portfolio manager wants to hedge a $10 million cash portfolio with the S&P JUN futures contract. Having found the risk-minimizing hedge ratio, she needs to translate the hedge ratio into the correct futures position that takes account of the size of the futures contract. On November 27,

Figure 8.2   Hedged and unhedged portfolio values

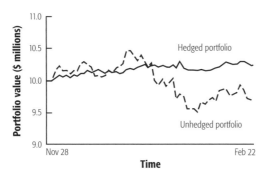

the S&P futures closed at 354.75. The futures contract value is for the index times $250. Therefore, applying Equation 7.6, she computes the number of contracts as follows:

$$-\beta_{RM}\left(\frac{V_P}{V_F}\right) = -0.8801 \times \left(\frac{\$10,000,000}{354.75 \times \$250}\right) = -99.2361$$

The estimated risk-minimizing futures position is −99.24 contracts, so the portfolio manager decides to sell 100 contracts.

Evaluate hedging results
Figure 8.2 shows the value of the unhedged and hedged portfolio for the next 60 days until February 22 of next year, when our trader decides to terminate the hedge. The unhedged portfolio's ending value is $9,656,090. The settlement price for the futures on February 22 is 330.60. Therefore, the futures profit is $100 \times \$250 \times (354.75 - 330.60) = \$603,750$. The futures profit results from trading 100 contracts with each index point being worth $250 and the index having fallen 24.15 points. The value of the hedged portfolio consists of the cash market portfolio plus the futures profit, so the hedged portfolio's terminal value is $10,259,840. In this example, the hedge protected the portfolio against a substantial loss.

In the real world, an institution hedging with stock index futures would use the CME's S&P 500 E-mini contract, in combination with the larger open-outcry version of the contract, to refine the hedge construction. The S&P 500 E-mini contract has the same terms as the regular S&P 500 futures contract except that each index point is worth $50 instead of $250. In this example, the hedge construction could be refined by selling 99 regular S&P 500 futures and one S&P 500 E-mini futures contract.

Ex-ante versus ex-post hedge ratios

In our risk-minimizing hedging example, we computed $\beta_{RM} = 0.8801$ using historical data and applied the hedge ratio to a future period. It is highly unlikely that the estimated hedge ratio would equal the hedge ratio that we would have used if we had perfect foresight about the behavior of the cash market position and the futures price. This is the difference between an ex-ante and an ex-post hedge ratio. **Ex ante**, or **before the fact**, the best hedge ratio we could find was −0.8801. **Ex post**, or **after the fact**, some other hedge ratio would be likely to perform better

Figure 8.3   Ex-ante versus ex-post hedging results

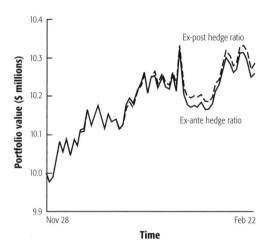

than the ex-ante hedge ratio of 20.8801. In this section, we consider the difference between ex-ante and ex-post hedge ratios in the context of our example.

The portfolio manager used historical returns from July 7 to November 27 to estimate the hedge ratio of -0.8801. She applied this hedge ratio on November 28, and maintained the hedged position until February 22 of the next year. The ex-post risk-minimizing hedge ratio was not available to her when she made her hedging decision on November 28. What would have been the ideal risk-minimizing hedge ratio have been, had she had complete knowledge about how prices would move from November 28 to February 22? To find this ex-post hedge ratio, we estimated Equation 8.1 using data from November to February and found an ex-post hedge ratio of -0.9154. This implies a futures position of 51.61 contracts. We round this to 52 contracts. Figure 8.3 shows the results of hedging with the ex-ante and ex-post hedge ratios.

In a world with perfect foresight, the ex-post hedge ratio is the risk-minimizing hedge ratio that we would like to use. However, the ex-ante hedge ratio is the best estimate we can make at the time the decision must be implemented. As Figure 8.3 shows, the ex-ante hedge ratio performs quite well. The terminal value of the hedge with the ex-ante hedge ratio is $10,259,840. With the ex-post hedge ratio, the terminal value is $10,283,990. While the ex-ante hedge ratio performed well, the ex-post hedge ratio would have been even better. This is exactly the result that we would expect.

Altering the beta of a portfolio

Portfolio managers often adjust the CAPM betas of their portfolios in anticipation of bull and bear markets. If a manager expects a bull market, she might increase the beta of the portfolio to take advantage of the expected rise in stock prices. Similarly, if a bear market seems imminent, the manager might reduce the beta of a stock portfolio as a defensive maneuver. If the manager trades only in the stock market itself, changing the beta of the portfolio involves selling some stocks and buying others. For example, to reduce the beta of the portfolio, the manager would sell high-beta stocks and use the funds to buy low-beta stocks. With transaction costs in the stock market being relatively high, this procedure can be expensive.

The portfolio manager has an alternative. She can use stock index futures to create a combined stock/futures portfolio with the desired response-to-market condition. In this section we consider techniques for changing the risk of a portfolio using stock index futures.

In the CAPM, all risk is either systematic or unsystematic. **Systematic risk** is associated with general movements in the market and affects all investments. By contrast, **unsystematic risk** is particular to a certain investment or a certain range of investments. Diversification can almost completely eliminate unsystematic risk from a portfolio. The remaining systematic risk is unavoidable. Studies show that a random selection of 20 stocks will create a portfolio with very little unsystematic risk. Therefore, in this section we restrict our attention to portfolios that are well diversified and consequently have no unsystematic risk.

Starting with a stock portfolio that has systematic risk only and combining it with a risk-minimizing short position in stock index futures creates a combined stock/futures portfolio with zero systematic risk. According to the CAPM, a portfolio with zero systematic risk should earn the risk-free rate of interest. Instead of eliminating all systematic risk by hedging, it is possible to hedge only a portion of the systematic risk to reduce, but not eliminate, the systematic risk inherent in the portfolio. Similarly, a portfolio manager can use stock index futures to increase the systematic risk of a portfolio.

A risk-minimizing hedge matches a long position in stock with a short position in stock index futures in an attempt to create a portfolio whose value will not change with fluctuations in the stock market. To reduce, but not eliminate, the systematic risk, a portfolio manager could sell some futures, but fewer than the risk-minimizing amount. For example, to eliminate half of the systematic risk, the portfolio manager could sell half of the number of contracts stipulated by the risk-minimizing hedge. The combined stock/futures position would then have a level of systematic risk equal to half of the stock portfolio's systematic risk.

It is also possible to trade stock index futures to increase the systematic risk of a stock portfolio. If a trader buys stock index futures, he increases his systematic risk. Therefore, if a portfolio manager holds a stock portfolio and buys stock index futures, the resulting stock/futures position has more systematic risk than the stock portfolio alone. For example, assume a portfolio manager buys, instead of selling, the risk-minimizing number of stock index futures. Instead of eliminating the systematic risk, the resulting stock/long futures position should have twice the systematic risk of the original portfolio.

We can illustrate this principle by considering the same data we used to illustrate the risk-minimizing hedge. In that example, the risk-minimizing futures position was to sell 52 contracts. Selling 52 contracts created a stock/futures position with zero systematic risk. By selling just 26 contracts, the portfolio manager could cut the systematic risk of the original portfolio in half. Similarly, by buying 52 contracts, the resulting stock/futures position would have twice the systematic risk of the original futures position.

Figure 8.4 shows the price paths of two portfolios over the 60-day hedging period from November 28 to February 22. First, the graph shows the unhedged portfolio. Its value begins at $10 million and terminates at $9,656,090, as we have seen. Over this period, the unhedged portfolio lost about $350,000. The graph also shows the portfolio created by holding the stocks and buying 52 futures contracts. In our analysis of the risk-minimizing hedge, we found that the trader could minimize risk by selling 52 futures contracts. Buying 52 contracts doubles the systematic risk. The new portfolio of stock plus a long position of 52 contracts increases the sensitivity of the portfolio to swings in the stock market. In effect, holding the stock portfolio and buying stock index futures simulates more than 100 percent investment in the stock index. Stock prices in general fell during this 60-day period. For example, the all stocks portfolio lost 3.44 percent of its value over this period.

By buying stock index futures, the portfolio manager would increase the overall sensitivity of the portfolio to changes in the stock market. Not surprisingly, then, the stock/long futures

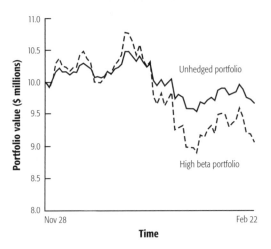

Figure 8.4   Price paths for hedged and unhedged portfolios

portfolio lost more than the pure stock portfolio. As Figure 8.4 shows, every move of the stock/long futures portfolio exaggerates the movement of the all stocks portfolio. For the portfolio of stock plus a long position of 52 index futures, the terminal value is $9,052,340. This portfolio lost 9.48 percent of its value. However, as Figure 8.4 shows, for periods when the stock prices advanced from their initial level, the stock/long futures position rose even more. This is just what we expected, because buying futures increases the systematic risk of the existing stock portfolio.

Asset allocation

In **asset allocation**, an investor decides how to divide funds among broad asset classes. For example, the decision to invest 60 percent in equities and 40 percent in T-bills is an asset alloca-tion decision. The choice between investing in General Motors and Ford Motors is not an asset allocation decision. Thus, asset allocation focuses on the macrolevel commitment of funds to various asset classes and the shifting of funds among these major asset classes. In this sec-tion, we use the basic cost-of-carry model to show how a trader can radically adjust an initial portfolio to move from equities to T-bills or from T-bills to equities by using stock index futures. Because these portfolio maneuvers radically change the type of asset the trader holds, the maneu-vers implement asset allocation decisions.

The basic cost-of-carry model we have used since Chapter 3 asserts that the futures price equals the spot price times one plus the cost of carry under suitable market conditions:

$$F_0 = S_0(1 + C) \tag{3.3}$$

where F_0 is the futures price at $t = 0$, S_0 is the spot price at $t = 0$, and C is the percentage cost of carrying the spot good from $t = 0$ to the futures expiration. The cost of carry includes the financing cost of purchasing the asset, plus storage, insurance, and transportation. As we have seen in Chapter 3, for financial futures the cost of carry essentially equals the financing cost, because storage, insurance, and transportation are negligible. Therefore, in a full carry market, a cash-and-carry strategy of selling a futures and buying and holding the spot good until the futures expires should earn the financing rate, which essentially equals the risk-free rate of interest. We can express this relationship as follows:

$$\text{short-term riskless debt} = \text{stock} - \text{stock index futures} \tag{8.2}$$

Creating a synthetic T-bill

From the analysis in the preceding section, we see that the basic cash-and-carry strategy of holding the stock and selling futures gives a resulting stock/futures portfolio that mimics a T-bill. Of course, it does not create a real T-bill. Instead, the stock/futures portfolio behaves like a T-bill. We might say that the trader creates a synthetic T-bill by holding stock and selling futures:

$$\text{synthetic T-bill} = \text{stock} - \text{stock index futures}$$

This synthetic T-bill is related to risk-minimizing hedging. In a minimum-risk hedge, a trader sells futures against a stock portfolio to create a combined stock/futures portfolio that has no systematic risk. A portfolio with no systematic risk has an expected return that equals the risk-free rate. Thus, the position created by risk-minimizing hedging is essentially the creation of a synthetic T-bill.

Consider the asset allocation decision of a trader with a stock portfolio. Assume the trader believes that a bear market is imminent and that the proper asset allocation decision is to hold no equities and to invest all funds in T-bills. The trader can sell all of the equities and invest the funds in T-bills. However, selling an entire portfolio can incur substantial transaction costs. Instead, the manager can implement the asset allocation decision by selling stock index futures against the portfolio. By implementing a risk-minimizing hedge, the manager creates a synthetic T-bill.

Creating a synthetic equity position

It is also possible to use stock index futures to create a synthetic stock market position. Consider now a trader who holds all assets in T-bills. We assume that this trader expects a stock market surge, and she would like to take advantage of the rising stock prices. However, she is reluctant to incur all of the transaction costs associated with buying stocks. She too can implement her asset allocation decision by using stock index futures. Rearranging Equation 8.2 shows how to create the risky stock position:

$$\text{synthetic stock portfolio} = \text{T-bill} + \text{stock index futures}$$

The trader can buy stock index futures and hold the futures in conjunction with T-bills to mimic a stock portfolio. Thus, she implements her asset allocation decision by trading stock index futures.

In our discussion of asset allocation, we have considered examples of using stock index futures to change from 100 percent stock investment to 100 percent T-bill investment, and vice versa. Of course, the change in the portfolio does not need to be so radical. When we considered hedging, we saw that a trader can implement a risk-minimizing hedge or a transaction that shapes the risk of the portfolio. For example, by trading half of the risk-minimizing futures position, a trader could cut the systematic risk of the stock position in half. Similarly, by holding stock and buying stock index futures, the trader could increase the systematic risk of the position. The same principles apply to asset allocation decisions. For the trader with an initial stock position, selling half of the risk-minimizing number of futures results in a portfolio that behaves like a portfolio that is invested half in stock and half in T-bills. Similarly, a trader with a long position in stock who buys stock index futures creates a combined stock/futures portfolio that behaves like a leveraged stock portfolio.

Hedge fund uses of stock index futures

One popular hedge fund strategy is to establish a portfolio consisting of long positions in some stocks and short positions in other stocks, with no net exposure to market risk. The goal of the strategy is to make money from speculating on individual stocks within the portfolio without worrying about the direction of the overall market. Hedge funds employing this strategy are sometimes called "long/short equity funds," "equity market neutral funds," "hedged equity funds," or "relative value funds." One version of the strategy is referred to as "pairs trading." The manager will position the portfolio to have approximately equal weights assigned to the long and short equity positions. Such a portfolio will be approximately market neutral (i.e., have a beta equal to zero), but typically the portfolio will exhibit some net market exposure. Long/short portfolio managers refer to this net market exposure as "deadweight." The manager may use a stock index futures contract, such as the S&P 500 futures contract, to establish a hedge to account for the remaining market exposure.

As an example, consider a hedge fund that believes that investors are on the verge of reallocating the sector weights within their portfolios. In particular, the hedge fund manager believes that investors will rotate their investments from the pharmaceutical sector to the retail sector. The hedge fund manager believes that as this sector rotation occurs, retail stocks will rise relative to pharmaceutical stocks. In other words, the hedge fund manager believes that stocks in the retail sector are undervalued relative to the pharmaceutical sector. To take advantage of this belief, the hedge fund manager goes long retail stocks while simultaneously going short pharmaceutical stocks.

Table 8.3 displays portfolio characteristics of the hedge fund under the long/short strategy. The weighted average beta of the pharmaceutical sector stocks within the portfolio is 0.39, with

Table 8.3   Hedge fund portfolio characteristics using a long/short strategy

Stock	Beta	Share value ($ millions)
Pharmaceutical stocks		
Bristol-Myers Squibb Co.	0.429	8.03
Eli Lilly & Co.	0.306	9.44
Johnson & Johnson	0.262	8.25
Merck & Co., Inc.	0.316	7.12
Pfizer, Inc.	0.378	9.24
Value-weighted beta	0.390	Total value = $42.08
Retail stocks		
Home Depot, Inc.	1.401	$10.64
Kohl's Corp.	1.008	7.35
Lowe's Cos.	1.061	10.24
Target Corp.	1.006	10.39
Wal-Mart Stores, Inc.	0.792	8.6
Value-weighted beta	1.07	Total value = $47.22
Net for entire portfolio	1.07	$5.14

an aggregate value of −$42.08 million. The negative sign reflects the fact that these stocks were sold short. The weighted average beta of the retail sector stocks within the portfolio is 1.07, with an aggregate value of $47.22 million. The net cash value of the portfolio (long position plus short position) is $5.14 million. The beta for the net value of the portfolio is 1.07, since the net amount results entirely from the overweighting of stocks in the retail sector, where the weighted beta was 1.07.

To make the portfolio market neutral, the hedge fund manager decides to establish a short position in S&P 500 stock index futures, which are currently trading at 1,154.25 index points. The manager uses Equation 7.6 to determine the number of contracts to trade:

$$-1.07[5,140,000/(1,154.25 \times \$250)] = -19.059 \approx -19 \text{ contracts}$$

Product profile: TRAKRS

TRAKRS (Total Return Asset Contracts) are futures contracts based on an index that is calculated on a total return basis.[6] In other words, the underlying index is calculated to include dividends and other distributions. TRAKRS are innovative products designed to allow futures customers to track an index of stocks, bonds, currencies, or other financial instruments.

The indexes used for TRAKRS are designed by Merrill Lynch, Pierce, Fenner & Smith (the index provider) and are listed at the CME. These indexes follow a predetermined rebalancing formula employed by the index provider to produce results in a target payoff structure. The rebalancing rules allow the index to mimic actively managed portfolios or trading strategies. As a result, these indexes are referred to as "strategy-based" or "actively managed" indexes. In general, such indexes can follow any rebalancing formula defined by the index provider as part of the construction of the index. Because a TRAKRS futures position mimics the payoff of an actual portfolio, some liken it to holding a "virtual portfolio." The TRAKRS product is designed to combine the trading efficiency of a futures contract with the investment characteristics of a fund managed with a well-defined strategy.

For example, one TRAKRS product is called the Long–Short Technology TRAKRS. This futures contract is based on an index that follows a rebalancing algorithm designed to mimic the long–short strategy often used by hedge funds. The index is based on 35 long positions in technology stocks and three short positions in technology-based, exchange-traded funds. The index also has a cash component. The index follows a predetermined rebalancing rule to adjust the index components and position weightings.

The margin requirements for TRAKRS differ from other futures products. Retail customers who hold long positions must post 100 percent margin at the time of purchase. For retail holders of short positions, there is a 50 percent margin requirement. Institutional holders operate with traditional margin for futures products. TRAKRS are electronically traded at the CME. Contract sizes are designed with small investors in mind. A contract position can be established for as little as $25 per contract. During 2003, nearly 20 million TRAKRS traded at the CME.

Portfolio insurance

As we have seen, traders can tailor the risk of a stock portfolio by trading stock index futures. For a given well-diversified portfolio, selling stock index futures can create a combined stock/ futures portfolio with reduced risk. Holding a stock portfolio and buying stock index futures results in a portfolio with greater risk and expected return than the initial portfolio.

Portfolio insurance refers to a collection of techniques for managing the risk of an underlying portfolio. With most portfolio insurance strategies, the goal is to manage the risk of a portfolio to ensure that the value of the portfolio does not drop below a specified level, while at the same time allowing for the portfolio's value to increase. Portfolio insurance strategies are often implemented using options, as we discuss in later chapters. However, stock index futures are equally important tools for portfolio insurance. Implementing portfolio insurance strategies using futures is called **dynamic hedging**. Although the mathematics of dynamic hedging are too complex for full treatment here, we can understand the basic idea behind portfolio insurance with stock index futures.

A portfolio insurance example

Consider a fully diversified stock portfolio worth $100 million. The value of this portfolio can range from zero to infinity. Many investors would like to put a floor beneath the value of the portfolio. For example, it would be very desirable to ensure that the portfolio's value never falls below $90 million. Portfolio insurance offers a way to control the downside risk of a portfolio. However, in a financial market there is no free lunch, so it is only possible to limit the risk of a large price fall by sacrificing some of the potential for a gain. Portfolio insurance, like life insurance, is not free, but it may be desirable for some traders.

We have seen that a risk-minimizing hedge converts a stock portfolio into a synthetic T-bill. By fully hedging our example stock portfolio, we can keep the portfolio's value above $100 million. A fully hedged portfolio will increase in value at the risk-free rate, although full hedging eliminates all of the potential gain in the portfolio beyond the risk-free rate. In dynamic hedging, however, the trader holds the stock portfolio and sells some futures contracts. The more insurance the trader wants, the more futures he or she will sell.

Let us assume that a stock index futures contract has an underlying value of $100 million and a trader sells futures contracts to cover $50 million of the value of the portfolio. Thus, in the initial position, the trader is long $100 million in stock and short $50 million in futures, so 50 percent of the portfolio is hedged. Table 8.4 shows this initial position in the time zero row. At $t = 0$, there has been no gain or loss on either the stock or futures. In the first period, we assume that the value of the stock portfolio falls by $2 million. The 50 futures contracts cover half of that loss with a gain of $1 million. Therefore, at $t = 1$, the combined stock/futures portfolio is worth $99 million. Now, the manager increases the coverage in the futures market by selling five more contracts. This gives a total of 55 short positions and coverage for 56 percent (55/99) of the total portfolio. In the second period, the stock portfolio loses another $2 million, but with 55 futures contracts, the futures gain is (55/99) × $2 million = $1.11 million. This gives a total portfolio value of $98.11 million.

By $t = 4$, the stock portfolio has fallen $10 million, but the futures profits have been $6.21 million. This gives a total portfolio value of $96.21 million. Also, the manager has increased the futures position in response to each drop in stock prices. At $t = 4$, the trader is short 80 contracts, hedging 83 percent of the stock market portfolio. At $t = 5$, the stock price drops dramatically, losing $35.86 million. The futures profit covers $30.65 million. This leaves a total portfolio value of $90 million. However, this is the floor amount of the portfolio, so the trader must now move to a fully hedged position. If the stock portfolio is only partially hedged, the next drop in prices can take the value of the entire portfolio below the floor amount of $90 million. At $t = 6$, the price of the stocks drops $10 million, but the futures position fully covers the loss. Therefore, the combined portfolio maintains its floor value of $90 million.

Table 8.4 shows the basic strategy of portfolio insurance with dynamic hedging. Initially, the portfolio is partially hedged. If stock prices fall, the trader increases the portion of the portfolio that is insured. Had the stock portfolio risen in value, the futures position would have lost money. However, the loss on the futures position would have been less than the gain on the

Table 8.4 Portfolio insurance transactions and results

Time, t	Gain/loss ($ millions)		Total value	Futures position	Portion hedged
	Stocks	Futures			
0	0.00	0.00	100.00	−50	0.50
1	−2.00	1.00	99.00	−55	0.56
2	−2.00	1.11	98.11	−60	0.61
3	−2.00	1.22	97.33	−70	0.72
4	−4.00	2.88	96.21	−80	0.83
5	−35.86	30.65	90.00	−90	1.00
6	−10.00	10.00	90.00	−90	1.00

stocks, because the portfolio was only partially hedged. As the stock prices rose, the manager would have bought futures, thereby hedging less and less of the portfolio. Less hedging would be needed if the stock price rose, because there would be little chance of the portfolio's total value falling below $90 million.

Implementing portfolio insurance

By design, Table 8.4 is highly simplistic. First, it does not show how the starting futures position was determined. Second, it does not show how the adjustments in the futures position were determined. Third, it considers only large changes in the value of the stock portfolio. For instance, the smallest change in the table is 2 percent of the stock portfolio's value. The exact answer to these questions is highly mathematical. However, we can explore these issues in an intuitive way.

Choosing the initial futures position depends on several factors. First, it depends on the floor that is chosen relative to the initial value of the portfolio. For example, if the lowest acceptable value of the portfolio is $100 million, then the manager must hedge 100 percent at $t = 0$. Thus, the lower the floor relative to the portfolio value, the lower is the percentage of the portfolio that the manager will need to hedge. Second, the purpose of the insurance strategy is to guarantee a minimum terminal portfolio value while allowing for more favorable results. As a consequence, the futures position must take into account the volatility of the stock portfolio. The higher the estimated volatility of the stock portfolio, the greater is the chance of a large drop in value that will send the total portfolio value below the floor. Therefore, the portion of the portfolio that is to be hedged depends critically on the estimated volatility of the stock portfolio. Of course, this will differ both across time and for portfolios of different risk.

Adjustments in the futures position depend upon the same kinds of considerations that determine the initial position. First, the value of the portfolio relative to the floor is critical. Second, new information about the volatility of the stock portfolio also affects the futures position. In Table 8.4, the volatility of the stock portfolio accelerates. Each percentage drop is larger than the previous one. Therefore, this increasing volatility will lead to a larger short futures position than would otherwise be necessary.

In Table 8.4, the drops in the stock portfolio's values are large. In actual practice, dynamic hedging works by continually monitoring the value of the portfolio. Small changes in the portfolio can trigger small adjustments in the futures position. For many portfolios, monitoring and updating can occur many times a month. This is why it is called dynamic hedging—the hedge is monitored and updated continuously, often with computerized trading programs. Table 8.4 does not show that continual monitoring. Instead, we might take the different rows in the table as snapshots of the portfolio's value at different times.

Table 8.4 abstracts from some of the cash flow issues that dynamic hedging will raise. For example, it does not explicitly consider the cash flows that come from daily settlement of the futures position. There are a host of technical issues such as these that actual dynamic hedging must face.

Index futures and stock market volatility

Stock index futures trading began in 1982 and quickly grew to importance. October 19, 1987 saw a huge stock market crash—the Dow Jones Industrial Average (DJIA) lost 22.61 percent that day. On October 13, 1989, there was a so-called mini-crash. Stock index futures trading is introduced and two market crashes follow: Just a coincidence? In the late 1980s and early 1990s, the influence of stock index futures on the stock market and stock market volatility was an important issue of public policy. Now, in the twenty-first century, concern focuses more on Internet stock volatility and the influence of day traders on stock market volatility. Even if concern over stock index futures has been abated, there is an intimate interaction between stock index futures and the stock market that could cause concern. This section briefly reviews stock market volatility and the interaction between futures and the underlying shares in the stock market.

The first question to be addressed is: Has stock market volatility increased since the introduction of stock index futures trading? Taking the long view (back to 1300), the conclusion seems to be that worldwide financial volatility has generally decreased.[7] Some of the greatest financial volatility has occurred in the twentieth century, however, notably in the 1920s and 1930s. Figure 8.5 shows how U.S. stock market volatility has varied over most of the twentieth

Figure 8.5   The index of stock market volatility, 1927–87

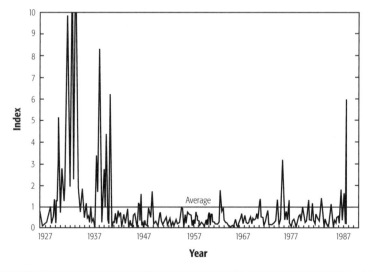

Source: P. Fortune, "An Assessment of Financial Market Volatility: Bills, Bonds, and Stocks," *New England Economic Review*, November/December 1989, p. 16. © 1989. Reprinted by permission from the author.

century. The decade of the 1990s was relatively low in volatility. Notice in Figure 8.5 the high volatility in 1987 due mainly to the October 19 "Black Monday" Crash.

We might also pose the following question: Even if it were proven that stock index futures trading did increase stock market volatility, is that bad? To most economists, price volatility results from the arrival of new information in the market. Traders receive new information that causes them to reassess the true value of the good being traded. In an efficient market, the price quickly adjusts to reflect this new information. One result of this process is volatility. Thus, economists often interpret volatile prices as evidence of a properly functioning and informationally efficient market. Under this view, volatility is good, not bad. Nonetheless, if stock index futures trading contributed to volatility in a way that was not tied to information or a properly functioning market, the futures trading could be deleterious to the market.

How could stock index futures cause market volatility?

There are two main practices in stock index futures trading that have been alleged to cause stock market volatility. These are index arbitrage (particularly program trading) and portfolio insurance. Both practices contribute to volatility, critics say, because they quickly dump large orders on the market at critical times. These large orders can reinforce existing trends in prices, thereby contributing to stock market volatility. We will consider each in turn.

Index arbitrage and stock market volatility

In index arbitrage, traders search for discrepancies between stock prices and futures prices. When the two prices differ from the cost-of-carry model enough to cover transaction costs, index arbitrageurs sell the overpriced side of the pair and buy the underpriced side. In the classic trade, the arbitrageur holds the combined stock/futures position until expiration. At expiration, the cash settlement procedures for index futures guarantee that the stock and futures prices will converge. This convergence is guaranteed to hold at the open of trading on the expiration day, because the last futures settlement price is set equal to the opening cash market index value on that day. Some stock index futures also use the closing price as the final settlement price. In that case, to take advantage of convergence, index arbitrageurs often unwind their positions by entering market-on-close orders for the last trading day of the futures. A market-on-close order sells or buys a stock at the market price prevailing at the close of trading.

Consider now an index arbitrageur who is long stock and short futures. We assume that the futures settles based on the closing price and that the trader enters a market-on-close order to sell the stocks. Additionally, assume that other arbitrageurs are also long stock and short futures and seek to unwind their positions in a similar manner. All of these stocks will come to market at the same time, so there could be an extremely large number of stocks to be sold all at once at the close of trading. Critics fear that this practice can lead to dramatic volatility in the market in a way that disrupts trading. In particular, they fear that such high volatility might scare away some investors.

Notice that this effect occurs only if there is a substantial order imbalance among index arbitrageurs. There may be a very high level of index arbitrage with no serious order imbalance. Assume for a moment that, over the life of the futures, the stock and futures prices vary in being high or low relative to the cost-of-carry model. Some traders will initiate their index arbitrage transactions by buying stocks, while others will arbitrage by selling stocks. At the expiration of the futures, the unwinding could result in roughly equal numbers of buy and sell orders for stocks. In such a situation, we would not expect index arbitrage to have any effect on prices, and it could not contribute to volatility. Furthermore, from the Sofianos study, we know that index arbitrageurs, at least in the post-Crash period, typically close their positions before expiration.

Portfolio insurance and stock market volatility

Portfolio insurance can also contribute to potential order imbalances that might affect stock prices. From our example of a portfolio insurance trade in Table 8.4, we see that a drop in stock prices requires the portfolio insurer to sell additional stock index futures. Similarly, when prices rise, the insurer buys stock index futures. A potential problem for market volatility arises because portfolio insurance generates trading in the same direction that the market happens to be moving. Thus, portfolio insurance can contribute to the existing momentum of the market.

To see the potential effects of portfolio insurance in exacerbating an existing trend, assume that the stock and futures prices are tightly linked by the cost-of-carry model. Due to this linkage, a drop in stock prices will quickly stimulate a drop in futures. The same transmission will occur from a drop in futures to a drop in stock prices. Now assume that there is a large drop in stock prices.

In response to the drop in stock prices, the futures price will have to fall. The cost-of-carry model requires this adjustment. However, the drop in stock prices also stimulates a large number of orders from portfolio insurers to sell index futures. This is clear from our example in Table 8.4. Critics fear that the sell orders from portfolio insurers might temporarily depress the futures price below the price justified by the cost-of-carry model. Assuming this happens, stock prices must again fall to match the depressed futures price. Now, with this next drop in stock prices, the portfolio insurers must again sell futures. Critics of portfolio insurance fear that this selling – price fall – selling scenario could create a spiral of falling prices and more sell orders, putting the entire market into a tailspin that could be disastrous.

Summary

According to critics, unrestricted stock index futures trading can contribute to stock market volatility, or even panics, by creating order imbalances that force stock prices below the prices justified by economic fundamentals. For index arbitrage, the feared order imbalance is most likely to occur at the expiration of the futures. Critics fear that portfolio insurers will respond to a sudden drop in stock prices by dumping sell orders onto the stock index futures market, thereby depressing prices. These depressed prices will feed into the stock market, causing another drop in prices. The portfolio insurer will again sell stock index futures, and perhaps help to create a downward price spiral. (On the other hand, if prices fall too much, the stocks will be cheap, and value-oriented investors will be attracted to buy. This buying would help to restore prices to their rational levels.)

Index futures and stock market crashes

In October 1987, the Crash led some to believe that the entire financial system was threatened. The events of October 19, 1987 touched off a series of debates and policy discussions that still continues, although the passage of time and the absence of crashes has muted the debate considerably. This section analyzes the relationship between stock index futures and stock prices during October 1987. Later, we consider the mini-crash of October 13, 1989.

The Crash of October 19, 1987 remains as controversial as it was dramatic. The DJIA lost 22.61 percent of its value that day. Trading volume was so heavy that it brought the trade processing divisions of brokerage houses to a virtual halt. During the day, it was often impossible to trade or even obtain accurate price quotations. In many respects, there was no stock market on that Black Monday. No sooner did trading cease than finger pointing started. Here are a few choice quotations. Anis C. Wallace: "Investors knew that stocks were overpriced by any traditional valuation measure such as price/earnings ratios and price to book value. They also knew that the combination of program trading and portfolio insurance could send prices plummeting." David E. Sanger: "On Monday, October 19, Wall Street's legendary herd instinct, now embedded in digital code and amplified by hundreds of computers, helped turn a sell-off into a panic." Former Treasury Secretary Donald Regan: "In my mind, we should start by banning index option arbitrage and then proceed with other reforms which will restore public confidence in the financial markets." Marshall Front: "Futures and options are like barnacles on a ship. They take their life from the pricing of stocks and bonds. When the barnacles start steering the ship, you get into trouble, as we saw last week."[8]

In the aftermath of the Crash, the government formed a presidential task force under Nicholas Brady, who later became Secretary of the Treasury, to study the Crash and its causes. The report of the task force is widely known as the Brady Report. While most observers agree that the inability of cash markets to handle the incredible order flow contributed to the market turmoil, the Brady Report attributed the fall in prices to index arbitrage and portfolio insurance. This view of the Crash has become known as the **cascade theory**. According to the Brady Report, portfolio insurers sought to liquidate their equity exposure by selling stock index futures. This selling action drove futures prices below their equilibrium price. In terms of the cost-of-carry model, the selling by portfolio insurers created a reverse cash-and-carry arbitrage. Seeing a profit opportunity, index arbitrageurs implemented reverse cash-and-carry strategies by buying futures and selling stocks. This action depressed prices further, and with new lower equity prices, portfolio insurers dumped more stock index futures, depressing prices still further. The vicious cycle had been started. The repeated action of index arbitrageurs and portfolio insurers caused a downward "cascade" in prices. Thus, the Brady Report maintained that "mechanical, price-insensitive selling" by institutions was a key cause of the Crash.[9]

The stock/futures basis on October 19, 1987

The cascade theory, and thus the conclusions of the Brady Report, rest on the view that the stock/futures basis on October 19 was disrupted by the actions of "mechanical, price-insensitive" trading systems. Specifically, the Brady Report alleges that futures prices that day were too low relative to stock values. Therefore, the stock/futures basis became a critical empirical issue. The price relationships between stocks and stock index futures have been studied on a minute-to-minute basis for both the S&P 500 and the MMI.[10] Both markets reveal a similar story. At first glance, the usually tight relationship of the cost-of-carry model apparently failed completely. However, in large part, this appearance was due to the inability to trade or even to know the current value of individual shares. For instance, even though the market opened at 9:30 a.m. New York time, some stocks did not trade for more than an hour. Among the MMI stocks, Exxon was the last one to start trading, at 11:23 a.m. With stocks failing to trade in New York, traders were forced to use Friday prices as guides to Monday values. Such an estimate was, to say the least, imprecise.

Figure 8.6 shows the spread between the cash and futures, using Chicago time. The extremely large difference at the open was due largely to the late opening of the individual stocks in New York. Until the stocks began to trade, there was no cash market for the traders in Chicago to use as a guide to proper values for the futures. However, it appears that the futures and stock did track each other with some accuracy during the middle of the day, when prices were somewhat more available. The situation in the S&P 500 was similar. Lawrence Harris summarizes: "Nonsynchronous trading explains part of the large absolute futures–cash basis observed during the Crash. The remainder may be due to disintegration of the two markets."[11] Thus, even in the madness, the cost-of-carry model was functioning with the available information. There was simply very little information flow. However, the stock/futures basis did seem to respond to the information that was available.

Figure 8.6   The MMI spread, October 19, 1987

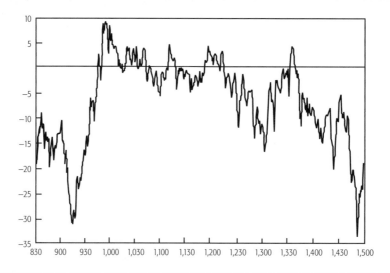

Source: G. Bassett, V. France, and S. Pliska, "The MMI Cash–Futures Spread on October 19, 1987," *The Review of Futures Markets*, 8:1, 1989, p. 119. © 1989. Reproduced by permission from *The Review of Futures Markets*

Order imbalance, index arbitrage, and portfolio insurance on October 19

Even if the basis held to the cost-of-carry model as well as one could expect, given the dramatic events on October 19, there is still a residual concern about the role of index arbitrage and portfolio insurance. On that day, 16 firms accounted for almost all stock index arbitrage and portfolio insurance trading. Twelve firms concentrated on index arbitrage, while four focused on portfolio insurance. About 9 percent of NYSE volume was generated by index arbitrage trading. For stock index futures, 12–24 percent of selling originated through portfolio insurance activity.[12] As a percentage of activity, these numbers suggest the possibility that futures-related activity was large enough to significantly affect the day's trading.

One interesting piece of evidence comes from comparing S&P 500 stocks with non-S&P 500 stocks. Blume, MacKinlay, and Terker found that S&P stocks fell about seven percentage points farther than non-S&P 500 stocks on October 19. By mid-morning during the recovery on October 20, the difference had been almost eliminated. In other words, stocks in the S&P 500 fell more during the Crash, but bounced back to parity with other stocks very quickly.[13] Also, Blume, MacKinlay, and Terker found that the fall in S&P 500 stock prices was positively correlated with order imbalances on October 19. With heavy sell orders awaiting execution, stock prices fell more than at other times. If this order imbalance was related to futures trading, then the futures market could share some responsibility for the drop in the market.

Some evidence appears to show that futures trading is not necessary to start a panic in a given market, but this theory does not really absolve futures of all responsibility. The Crash was a worldwide phenomenon, as Richard Roll points out.[14] Of 23 markets worldwide, 19 fell by more than 20 percent. Further, the Crash seems to have begun in non-Japanese Asian markets and spread to European markets, followed by North American markets and then Japanese markets. This progression took place around the clock as trading developed on October 19 and 20. Comparing market performance and the presence of computer-directed trading in isolation, Roll found that if computer trading had any impact at all, it actually helped to reduce the market decline.

The fact that the Crash started in markets with limited futures trading does appear to show that other factors besides futures trading were at work. This opens up the possibility of a **contagion theory** of the Crash. A crash develops in one country's market for some unknown reason. News arrives in other markets, carrying the crash "virus," which helps a crash to develop in the second market. This kind of contagion theory was developed by King and Wadhwani.[15]

Assume that the U.S. market is infected and a crash starts to develop. The U.S. crash is then intensified by order imbalance resulting from futures trading. Now, other countries could catch the crash "virus" from the United States in its more heightened and virulent form. Yet this does not seem to fit the facts for October 1987. First, the United States lost less than most other markets, both those that had crashed before and those that crashed later. Based on the version of the contagion theory just explained, we would expect the U.S. Crash to be deeper than those of countries that crashed earlier.

To summarize the portion of evidence related to futures, the Crash did not start in the United States, so the futures markets could not have been the original source of the problem. The Crash in the United States was not relatively more severe, even though futures markets are more developed in the United States than elsewhere. There was no tendency for the crashes in markets trading after the U.S. Crash to be more severe than crashes in markets trading before the U.S. Crash. Nonetheless, if futures contributed to the U.S. Crash and if the contagion theory has merit, then the U.S. Crash could have contributed to crashes that occurred later.

Thus, residual suspicion about the role of futures remains, even though there is no compelling evidence to show that futures trading, whether index arbitrage or portfolio insurance, caused the Crash.[16] Study continues and the issue remains controversial. However, there does seem to be fairly widespread rejection of the Brady Report's main conclusion that the Crash was caused by index arbitrage and portfolio insurance leading to a cascade in stock prices.[17]

Policy recommendations and changing trading rules

In proposals for reform, the Brady Report recommended that the regulatory system be modified to have a single agency, that there be a unified clearing system for all financial markets, that margins be consistent between cash and futures markets, and that information systems across markets be improved. The Report also recommended that exchanges implement **circuit breakers**—systems of planned trading halts—in times of volatility. There is continuing action on all of these fronts and much has already been implemented.

Since the Crash, circuit breakers have been put in place and refinements to the system continue. In essence, a circuit breaker is a planned decoupling of the stock index futures market and the stock market through price limits and trading halts. The system also permits delaying program trades. The idea is to halt trading when prices fall below their fundamental values. During the pause in trading, it is argued, the effect of mob psychology will dissipate, and when trading resumes, prices will return to rational levels. These circuit breakers are controversial and their value is unknown.

However, even if trading is halted, prices can continue to fall and traders will be stuck with additional losses. According to market lore, the worst fear of many traders is to be stuck in a position. Some scholars believe that trading halts may create more panic than calm and consequently assert that trading halts are unwise. Nonetheless, futures markets already embody something like circuit breakers in the form of daily price limits. Also, defenders of circuit breakers believed they performed well in the mini-crash of October 13, 1989.

In addition to circuit breakers, a rule on the NYSE also restricts or "collars" index arbitrage. The NYSE's trading collar requires that on days when the DJIA declines by 180 points or more from the previous day's closing value, all index arbitrage sell orders for stocks from the S&P 500 index be entered with the instruction "sell plus."[18] Conversely, on days when the DJIA advances by 180 points or more from the previous day's closing value, all index arbitrage buy orders for stocks from the S&P 500 are to be entered with the instruction "buy minus." The tick restrictions apply to all index arbitrage orders in component S&P 500 stocks traded at the NYSE, regardless of how the orders are routed to the specialist's post. The tick restrictions are removed at the end of the trading day, or sooner if the market rebounds to a level within 90 DJIA points of the previous day's close. The 180-point threshold is revaluated periodically.

Empirical research suggests that the NYSE's trading collars significantly curtail index arbitrage activity. Arbitrage subject to the collar is about one-third of what would be expected in the absence of the collar. Despite the significant curtailment of index arbitrage activity, the cash and futures markets remain linked, although evidence suggests that the collar weakens the linkage between cash and futures markets in that pricing discrepancies between the markets are eliminated less quickly. This finding suggests that information is conveyed from the futures market to the stock market by some means other that the order flow generated by arbitrage trades. It may be the case that the NYSE's specialists revise their quotes in anticipation of a heavy one-sided order flow. Quote revision by specialists can explain why the virtual elimination of index arbitrage volume does not eliminate market linkage. Finally, the NYSE's trading collars do not appear to affect trading costs in the stock market, as measured by the average bid–ask spread for S&P 500 stocks. In summary, the NYSE's trading collars appear to have had little impact on trading costs and intermarket arbitrage, despite significant curtailment of index arbitrage volume.[19]

Probably the most controversial recommendation of the Brady Report is that there be "consistent margins" between stock and futures markets. This has been interpreted as calling for a large increase in futures margins. Such a policy would destroy the futures market as it now exists. According to defenders of futures, this policy recommendation shows a complete lack of understanding of futures margins.[20] Futures margins are not a partial payment for a good, as they are in the stock market. Instead, futures margins serve as a security bond for the changes in the futures price that day. The bond is payable daily and renewable daily. In the ensuing debate, margin levels have become a political football in the struggle between the Commodity Futures Trading Commission (CFTC) and the Securities and Exchange Commission (SEC). Also, stock index margins have been raised by the futures exchanges in an apparent effort to deter any move for even higher margins. In defense of the futures margining system, it is important to realize that no customer funds were lost due to failure to meet margin calls and no clearinghouse failed because of the Crash.

The mini-crash of October 13, 1989

Almost exactly two years after the 1987 Crash, it seemed that history would repeat itself. On October 13, 1989, a Friday the 13th, stock prices began a sickening slide. That day, the Dow dropped 190 points, with a 135-point drop in the final hour of trading. This mini-crash provided an opportunity to test some of the procedures instituted after the 1987 Crash.

Falling prices triggered a circuit breaker at 2:15 p.m. for the MMI futures and at 3:07 p.m. for the S&P 500 futures. For both contracts, trading could resume only at prices above the price that triggered the circuit breaker. Trading resumed and the circuit breaker was hit again for the S&P 500. In assessing the performance of the circuit breakers, both the CFTC and the exchanges seem to feel that they performed well.[21] Further efforts to refine the system continue and the market awaits further, perhaps more severe, tests of the system. For now, with low volatility and markets that seem to be functioning well, we can rest easy—at least until we are rocked out of our beds by another Black Monday.

Conclusion

This chapter has reviewed a wide range of issues related to stock index futures. We began by examining stock index futures pricing. We considered the efficiency of the stock index futures markets, the effect of taxes on stock index futures prices, the influence of seasonal factors on prices, and leads and lags between the futures market and the stock market. Next, we considered a real-world example of program trading, focusing on an index arbitrage example. This example showed the hidden risks in the apparently riskless strategy of index arbitrage.

To extend the introduction to hedging in Chapter 7, we worked through an example of minimum risk hedging in detail, and we considered the difference between ex-ante and ex-post hedge ratios. We also saw how to use a hedging approach to adjust the beta of a portfolio. Adjusting the beta by a small amount may be a hedging activity, but we also explored

asset allocation using stock index futures. Using stock index futures, traders holding riskless bonds can simulate full investment in equities. Similarly, a trader fully invested in equities can use stock index futures to make the combined stock/futures portfolio behave like a riskless bond.

This chapter also focused on the connection between stock index futures and stock market volatility. As we saw, the main arguments for a connection rely on order imbalances that might be caused by index arbitrage or portfolio insurance. Finally, we considered the Crash of 1987 and the mini-crash of 1989. Although futures do not appear to be responsible for the price changes observed on these days, the events have been important in changing the institutional arrangements in the futures market and years of low volatility and high stock prices have led to a complacency about volatility.

Exercises

1   Explain the market conditions that cause deviations from a computed fair value price and that give rise to no-arbitrage bounds.

2   The No-Dividend Index consists only of stocks that pay no dividends. Assume that the two stocks in the index are priced at $100 and $48, and assume that the corresponding cash index value is 74.00. The cost of carrying stocks is 1 percent per month. What is the fair value of a futures contract on the index that expires in one year?

3   Using the same facts as in Exercise 2, assume that the round-trip transaction cost on a futures is $30. The contract size, we now assume, is for 1,000 shares of each stock. Trading stocks costs $0.05 per share to buy and the same amount to sell. Based on this additional information, compute the no-arbitrage bounds for the futures price.

4   Using the facts in Exercises 2 and 3, we now consider differential borrowing and lending costs. Assume that the 1 percent per month is the lending rate and assume that the borrowing rate is 1.5 percent per month. What are the no-arbitrage bounds on the futures price now?

5   Using the facts in Exercises 2–4, assume now that the short seller receives the use of only half of the funds in the short sale. Find the no-arbitrage bounds.

6   Consider the trading of stocks in an index and trading futures based on the index. Explain how different

transaction costs in the two markets might cause one market to reflect information more rapidly than the other.

7   For index arbitrage, explain how implementing the arbitrage through program trading helps to reduce execution risk.

8   Index arbitrageurs must consider the dividends that will be paid between the present and the futures expiration. Explain how overestimating the dividends that will be received could affect a cash-and-carry arbitrage strategy.

9   Explain the difference between the beta in the CAPM and the beta one finds by regressing stock returns against returns on a stock index.

10   Explain the difference between an ex-ante and an ex-post minimum risk hedge ratio.

11   Assume you hold a well-diversified portfolio with a beta of 0.85. How would you trade futures to raise the beta of the portfolio?

12   An index fund is a mutual fund that attempts to replicate the returns on a stock index, such as the S&P 500. Assume you are the manager of such a fund and that you are fully invested in stocks. Measured against the S&P 500 index, your portfolio has a beta of 1.0. How could you transform this portfolio into one with a zero beta without trading stocks?

13   You hold a portfolio consisting of only T-bills. Explain how to trade futures to create a portfolio that behaves like the S&P 500 stock index.

14 In portfolio insurance using stock index futures, we noted that a trader sells additional futures as the value of the stocks falls. Explain why traders follow this practice.

15 Casey Mathers, manager of the Zeta Corporation's equity portfolio, hires a new assistant called Alec. Being pretty sharp, Alec immediately questions Casey's decision to hedge an anticipated $10 million withdrawal. Casey had hedged the portfolio using the S&P 500 index futures contract. In calculating the hedge, Casey used the portfolio beta of 1.2 that was computed using the S&P 500 index.

A Explain to Casey why his hedge may not be a risk minimization hedge.
B Given Alec's results, is the S&P 500 futures index the most appropriate hedging vehicle? Be sure to justify your answer.
C Design a risk minimization hedge using Alec's results.
D Will Alec's hedging strategy turn out to be superior to Casey's hedging strategy? Justify your answer.

16 Raymond J. Johnson, Jr. manages a $20 million equity portfolio. It has been designed to mimic the S&P 500 index. Ray has a hunch that the market is going south during the coming month. He has decided that he wants to eliminate his exposure for the next month and take off for Montana to go fishing. Ray has the following information at hand:

S&P 500 index futures with one month to delivery	1,084.50
Dividend yield on Ray's portfolio	2.1 percent
S&P 500 index today	1,081.40

A Design a hedge to eliminate Ray's market risk for the next month.
B Compute the return he can expect to receive over the next month.

17 Remember Ray? He's the guy running the S&P 500 index fund who wanted to go fishing. Ray has changed his mind. The fishing reports from Montana were not favorable, so he has decided not to go. Since he is not leaving, he had decided to devise a portfolio insurance strategy for his $20 million portfolio. His objective is to not let his portfolio value fall below $18 million.

A Design a portfolio insurance strategy that applies no hedges for portfolio values at or above $20 million and is fully hedged at or below $18 million.
B On day one, the stock portfolio value falls from $20 million to $19.4 million, and the S&P 500 futures price falls to 1,052. What action should Ray take?
C On day two, the value of Ray's portfolio increases by 2 percent. The S&P 500 futures contract increases to 1,073. What would be the change in value of Ray's portfolio (including any hedges that may be in place)? What action should Ray take?
D Is Ray really protected against his portfolio value falling below $18 million in value? Explain.

18 What real-world complications can hinder the effectiveness of a stock index arbitrage strategy?

19 It's 7:00 a.m. and the New York Stock Exchange doesn't open until 9:30 a.m. The current S&P 500 E-mini nearby futures contract is trading on the CME's Globex system at 1,150.00 index points. There are 21 days remaining until contract expiration. You expect the underlying index to pay out dividend equivalent to 1.1 index points over the remaining life of the contract. You expect your financing cost to be 1.9 percent per year. If the closing price for the index from the previous day was 1,135.00, use the cost-of-carry relationship to determine whether you expect the stock market to open higher or lower based on current information.

Notes

1 D. Modest and M. Sundaresan, "The Relationship Between Spot and Futures Prices in Stock Index Futures Markets: Some Preliminary Evidence," *Journal of Futures Markets*, 3:1, 1983, pp. 15–41.
2 George Sofianos, "Index Arbitrage Profitability," *Journal of Derivatives*, 1:1, Fall 1993, pp. 6–20.
3 B. Cornell and K. French, "Taxes and the Pricing of Stock Index Futures," *Journal of Finance*, 38:3, 1983,

pp. 675–94; and B. Cornell, "Taxes and the Pricing of Stock Index Futures: Empirical Results," *The Journal of Futures Markets*, 5:1, 1985, pp. 89–101.
4 See, for example, E. Dyl and E. Maberly, "The Weekly Pattern in Stock Index Futures: A Further Note," *Journal of Finance*, 41:5, 1986, pp. 1149–52.
5 It can be a tedious task to obtain expected dividend information on the 500 individual stocks in the

underlying index. Standard and Poor's Index Services Division tracks this information and makes it available to its customers. A rough estimate of the dividend stream, based on the annualized dividend yield, can be found on the S&P web site (www.spglobal.com).

6 Strictly speaking, there is no return on a futures contract, because a position in a futures contract requires no investment. By the futures return, we mean the percentage change in the futures price.

7 See Alexander M. Ineichen, "Twentieth Century Volatility," *The Journal of Portfolio Management*, 27:1, Fall 2000, pp. 93–101.

8 All quoted in G. Santoni, "The October Crash: Some Evidence on the Cascade Theory," *Review*, Federal Reserve Bank of St. Louis, May/June 1988, pp. 18–33.

9 *Report of the Presidential Task Force on Market Mechanisms*, 1988, p. v. See also G. Santoni, "The October Crash: Some Evidence on the Cascade Theory," *Review*, Federal Reserve Bank of St. Louis, May/June 1988, pp. 18–33, for a thoughtful critique of the Brady Report. P. Tosini, "Stock Index Futures and Stock Market Activity in October 1987," *Financial Analysts Journal*, 44:1, 1988, pp. 28–37, also discusses the cascade theory.

10 See L. Harris, "The October 1987 S&P 500 Stock-Futures Basis," *Journal of Finance*, 44:1, 1989, pp. 77–99; G. Bassett, V. France, and S. Pliska, "The MMI Cash–Futures Spread on October 19, 1987," *The Review of Futures Markets*, 8:1, 1989, pp. 118–38; G. Santoni, "The October Crash: Some Evidence on the Cascade Theory," *Review*, Federal Reserve Bank of St. Louis, May/June 1988, pp. 18–33.

11 L. Harris, "The October 1987 S&P 500 Stock-Futures Basis," *Journal of Finance*, 44:1, March 1989, p. 77. This view is supported by A. Kleidon and R. Whaley, "One Market? Stocks, Futures, and Options During October 1987," *Journal of Finance*, 47:3, 1992, pp. 851–77. Kleidon and Whaley find that the market conformed well to cost-of-carry relationships in early October, but very poorly during the Crash.

12 These values are drawn from P. Tosini, "Stock Index Futures and Stock Market Activity in October 1987," *Financial Analysts Journal*, 44:1, 1988, pp. 28–37.

13 M. Blume, A. MacKinlay, and B. Terker, "Order Imbalances and Stock Price Movements on October 19 and 20, 1987," *Journal of Finance*, 44:4, 1989, pp. 827–48.

14 R. Roll, "The International Crash of October 1987," *Financial Analysts Journal*, 44:5, 1988, pp. 19–35.

15 M. King and S. Wadhwani, "Transmission of Volatility Between Stock Markets," *The Review of Financial Studies*, 3:1, 1990, pp. 5–33.

16 The Office of Technology Assessment, U.S. Congress, studied the Crash and reported on it in its study, "Electron Bulls & Bears: U.S. Securities Markets & Information Technology," September 1990. The study concluded that the responsibility of futures for the Crash could not be resolved by statistical analysis.

17 Among those who reject the Brady Report conclusions of a futures induced cascade are: G. Santoni, "The October Crash: Some Evidence on the Cascade Theory," *Review*, Federal Reserve Bank of St. Louis, May/June 1988, pp. 18–33; J. Hill, "Program Trading, Portfolio Insurance, and the Stock Market Crash: Concepts, Applications and an Assessment," Kidder Peabody, January 1988; R. Roll, "The International Crash of October 1987," *Financial Analysts Journal*, 44:5, 1988, pp. 19–35; D. Harrington, F. Fabozzi, and H. Fogler, *The New Stock Market*, Chicago: Probus, 1990; and M. Miller, B. Malkiel, M. Scholes and J. Hawke, "Stock Index Futures and the Crash of '87," *Journal of Applied Corporate Finance*, 1:4, 1989, pp. 6–17.

18 "Sell-plus" means that the order can be executed on a plus or zero-plus tick. A plus tick is a price above the price of the preceding sale. A zero-plus tick is a price equal to the preceding sale if the last transaction at a different price was at a lower price. "Buy-minus" means that the order can be executed on a minus or zero-minus tick. A minus tick is a price below the price of the preceding sale. A zero-minus tick is a price equal to the preceding sale if the last transaction at a different price was at a higher price.

19 See James Overdahl and Henry McMillan, "Another Day, Another Collar: An Evaluation of the Effects of NYSE Rule 80A on Trading Costs and Intermarket Arbitrage," *Journal of Business*, 1998, pp. 27–53.

20 See, for example, M. Miller, B. Malkiel, M. Scholes, and J. Hawke, "Stock Index Futures and the Crash of '87," *Journal of Applied Corporate Finance*, 1:4, 1989, pp. 6–17.

21 See "CFTC Reviews Friday the 13th," *Futures Industry Association Review*, November/December 1989, pp. 10–11.

9

Foreign Exchange Futures

Overview

Foreign currencies are traded in both a highly active forward market and a futures market. The foreign exchange market is the only one in which a successful futures market has grown up in the face of a robust forward market. The forward market for foreign exchange has existed for a long time, but the foreign exchange futures market developed only in the early 1970s, with trading beginning on May 16, 1972, on the International Monetary Market (IMM) of the Chicago Mercantile Exchange (CME). Without doubt, the presence of such a strong and successful forward market retarded the development of a futures market for foreign exchange. This dual market system means that the futures market cannot be understood in isolation from the forward market. The conceptual bond arises both from the similarity of the two markets and from the fact that the forward market continues to be much larger than the futures market. Because many traders are active in both markets, familiar cash-and-carry and reverse cash-and-carry strategies ensure that the proper price relationships between the two markets are maintained.

As discussed in Chapter 3, forward and futures markets for a given commodity are similar in many respects. Because of this similarity, specific price relationships must hold between the two markets to prevent arbitrage opportunities. While any observer might be more impressed by the similarities between the two markets, the forward and futures markets differ in several key respects. Particularly important are the differences in the cash flow patterns (due to daily resettlement in the futures market) and the different structures of the contracts with respect to their maturities.

To understand foreign exchange futures trading, this chapter begins with a brief discussion of the markets for foreign exchange: the spot, forward, and futures markets. Next, we review the most important factors in determining exchange rates between two currencies, including the exchange rate regimes of fixed versus floating rates, the question of devaluation, and the influence of the balance of payments. Against this institutional background, we analyze no-arbitrage pricing relationships, such as the interest rate parity (IRP) theorem and the purchasing power parity (PPP) theorem. These theorems essentially express the pricing relationship of the cost-of-carry model. We also examine the relationship between forward and futures prices and the accuracy of foreign exchange forecasting. As always in the futures market, the twin issues of speculation and hedging play an important role, and we consider them in detail.

Price quotations

In the foreign exchange market, every price, or exchange rate, is a relative price. To say that $1 is worth 0.8 euro (€0.8) also implies that €0.8 will buy $1.00, or that €1 is worth $1.25. All foreign exchange rates are related to each other as reciprocals, a relationship that is quite apparent in Figure 9.1, which shows the foreign exchange quotations, as they appear daily in *The Wall Street Journal*. The quotations consist of two double columns of rates, one for the U.S. dollar equivalent of the foreign currency and one set of two columns for the amount of foreign currency per U.S. dollar. Each set of quotations shows the rates for the current and the preceding business day. We focus only on the two columns of current quotations. The rate in one column has its reciprocal in the other column (sometimes these are not exact due to transaction costs). The value of the dollar per euro is just the reciprocal of the value of the euro per dollar. For some countries, such as Australia, the quotations show only the spot rate, the rate at which Australian and U.S. dollars may be exchanged at the moment.

Figure 9.1 Foreign exchange quotations

Exchange Rates   March 30, 2006

The foreign exchange mid-range rates below apply to trading among banks in amounts of $1 million and more, as quoted at 4 p.m. Eastern time by Reuters and other sources. Retail transactions provide fewer units of foreign currency per dollar.

Country	U.S. $ equivalent Thu	Wed	Currency per U.S. $ Thu	Wed
Argentina (Peso)-y	.3245	.3248	3.0817	3.0788
Australia (Dollar)	.7147	.7070	1.3992	1.4144
Bahrain (Dinar)	2.6534	2.6533	.3769	.3769
Brazil (Real)	.4564	.4530	2.1911	2.2075
Canada (Dollar)	.8614	.8524	1.1609	1.1732
1-month forward	.8621	.8531	1.1600	1.1722
3-months forward	.8637	.8546	1.1578	1.1701
6-months forward	.8659	.8568	1.1549	1.1671
Chile (Peso)	.001893	.001879	528.26	532.20
China (Renminbi)	.1246	.1246	8.0253	8.0259
Colombia (Peso)	.0004353	.0004368	2297.27	2289.38
Czech. Rep. (Koruna)				
Commercial rate	.04248	.04182	23.541	23.912
Denmark (Krone)	.1629	.1611	6.1387	6.2073
Ecuador (US Dollar)	1.0000	1.0000	1.0000	1.0000
Egypt (Pound)-y	.1742	.1742	5.7418	5.7418
Hong Kong (Dollar)	.1289	.1289	7.7597	7.7603
Hungary (Forint)	.004584	.004514	218.15	221.53
India (Rupee)	.02248	.02245	44.484	44.543
Indonesia (Rupiah)	.0001098	.0001094	9107	9141
Israel (Shekel)	.2144	.2129	4.6642	4.6970
Japan (Yen)	.008522	.008487	117.34	117.83
1-month forward	.008561	.008519	116.81	117.38
3-months forward	.008627	.008592	115.92	116.39
6-months forward	.008736	.008699	114.47	114.96
Jordan (Dinar)	1.4108	1.4108	.7088	.7088
Kuwait (Dinar)	3.4240	3.4240	.2921	.2921
Lebanon (Pound)	.0006634	.0006634	1507.39	1507.39
Malaysia (Ringgit)-b	.2710	.2706	3.6900	3.6955
Malta (Lira)	2.8316	2.8007	.3532	.3571
Mexico (Peso)				
Floating rate	.0915	.0913	10.9314	10.9553

Country	U.S. $ equivalent Thu	Wed	Currency per U.S. $ Thu	Wed
New Zealand (Dollar)	.6129	.6053	1.6316	1.6521
Norway (Krone)	.1526	.1507	6.5531	6.6357
Pakistan (Rupee)	.01666	.01668	60.024	59.952
Peru (new Sol)	.2987	.2991	3.3478	3.3434
Philippines (Peso)	.01953	.01950	51.203	51.282
Poland (Zloty)	.3085	.3044	3.2415	3.2852
Russia (Ruble)-a	.03611	.03598	27.693	27.793
Saudi Arabia (Riyal)	.2667	.2667	3.7495	3.7495
Singapore (Dollar)	.6180	.6168	1.6181	1.6213
Slovak Rep. (Koruna)	.03225	.03182	31.008	31.427
South Africa (Rand)	.1619	.1587	6.1767	6.3012
South Korea (Won)	.0010245	.0010255	976.09	975.13
Sweden (Krona)	.1293	.1276	7.7340	7.8370
Switzerland (Franc)	.7707	.7631	1.2975	1.3104
1-month forward	.7730	.7653	1.2937	1.3067
3-months forward	.7780	.7703	1.2853	1.2982
6-months forward	.7853	.7774	1.2734	1.2863
Taiwan (Dollar)	.03074	.03068	32.531	32.595
Thailand (Baht)	.02574	.02569	38.850	38.926
Turkey (New Lira)-d	.7410	.7381	1.3495	1.3548
U.K. (Pound)	1.7467	1.7343	.5725	.5766
1-month forward	1.7472	1.7348	.5723	.5764
3-months forward	1.7487	1.7363	.5719	.5759
6-months forward	1.7515	1.7390	.5709	.5750
United Arab (Dirham)	.2723	.2723	3.6724	3.6724
Uruguay (Peso)				
Financial	.04120	.04130	24.272	24.213
Venezuela (Bolivar)	.000466	.000466	2145.92	2145.92
SDR	1.4406	1.4378	.6942	.6955
Euro	1.2155	1.2024	.8227	.8317

Special Drawing Rights (SDR) are based on exchange rates for the U.S., British, and Japanese currencies. Source: International Monetary Fund.

a-Russian Central Bank rate. b-Government rate. d-Rebased as of Jan. 1, 2005. y-Floating rate.

Source: *The Wall Street Journal*, March 31, 2006, p. C10. Reprinted by permission of *The Wall Street Journal*, © 2006 Dow Jones & Company, Inc. All rights reserved worldwide

For many major currencies, such as those of European Union, the United Kingdom, Japan, and Canada, the quotations show forward rates for periods of one, three, and six months into the future. Sometimes rates are quoted by days, for a 30-, 60-, or 90-day horizon. The 30-day forward rate, for example, indicates the rate at which a trader can contract today for the delivery of some foreign currency 30 days later. If the trader buys the foreign currency, then he or she agrees to pay the 30-day forward rate in 30 days for the currency in question, with the actual transaction taking place in 30 days. This kind of transaction exactly fits the description of forward markets in Chapter 1.

The quotations shown in Figure 9.1 are drawn from a market dominated by large banks in the U.S. and abroad. This market is known as the **interbank market**. As Figure 9.1 notes, the quotations pertain to transactions in amounts of $1 million or more. As is typical of forward markets, there is no physical location where trading takes place. Instead, banks around the world are linked electronically with each other. The large banks in the market have trading rooms elaborately equipped with electronic communications devices. A trader in such a room may have access to 60 telephone lines, five or more video quotation screens, and a Globex trading screen.[1] The market has no regular trading hours and is open somewhere in the world 24 hours per day. In addition to banks, some large corporations and investment funds have access to the market through their own trading rooms.

Product profile: the CME's Euro FX futures contract

Contract size: €125,000.
Deliverable grades: N/A.
Tick size: 0.0001 = $12.50.
Price quote: U.S. dollars per euro.
Contract months: six months in the MAR, JUN, SEP, and DEC cycle.
Expiration and final settlement: Eurodollar futures cease trading at 9:16 a.m. Chicago time on the second business day immediately preceding the third Wednesday of the contract month. The contract is physically settled.
Trading hours: Floor, 7:20 a.m. to 2:00 p.m.; Globex, Monday through Thursday, 5:00 p.m. to 4:00 p.m. next day; shutdown period from 4:00 p.m. to 5:00 p.m. nightly; Sunday and holidays, 5:00 p.m. to 4:00 p.m. next day.
Daily price limit: None.

Regional banks are unlikely to have their own trading rooms. Instead, they clear their foreign exchange transactions through correspondent banks, with whom they have the appropriate arrangements. Corporations that are too small to have their own trading room, as well as individuals, make foreign exchange transactions through their own banks. As Figure 9.1 notes, the rates quoted are not available to small retail traders. Instead, retail transactions will be subject to a larger bid–ask spread that allows the bank providing the foreign exchange service to make a profit.

Geographic and cross-rate arbitrage

A number of pricing relationships exist in the foreign exchange market, the violation of which would imply the existence of arbitrage opportunities. The first two to be considered involve **geographic arbitrage** and **cross-rate arbitrage**. One of the best ways to learn about the relationships that must exist among currency prices is to explore the potential arbitrage opportunities that arise if the pricing relationships were violated.

Geographic arbitrage occurs when one currency sells for two prices in two different markets. Such pricing would be a simple violation of the law of one price. As an example, consider the following exchange rates between euros and U.S. dollars as quoted in New York and Frankfurt. These are 90-day forward rates.

Table 9.1   Geographic arbitrage

This is an arbitrage transaction since it yields a certain profit with no investment. Notice that the arbitrage is not complete until the transactions at t = 90 are completed

$t = 0$ (the present)
   Buy €1 in New York 90 days forward for $1.25
   Sell €1 in Frankfurt 90 days forward for $1.33

$t = 90$
   Deliver €1 in Frankfurt; collect $1.33
   Pay $1.25; collect €1

Profit:	$1.33
	−1.25
	$0.08

New York	$/€	1.25
Frankfurt	€/$	0.75

The New York price, quoted as dollars per euro, implies a euro-per-dollar price equal to the inverse of the dollar-per-euro price:

$$\frac{1}{1.25} = €/\$ = 0.8$$

In New York, the euro-per-dollar rate is 0.80, but in Frankfurt it is 0.75. Since these are not equal, an arbitrage opportunity exists. To test for a geographic arbitrage opportunity, simply take the inverse of the price prevailing in one market and compare it with the price quoted in another.

   To conduct the arbitrage, the trader purchases the currency where it is cheap and sells it where it is expensive. In New York, a trader receives €0.80 per dollar, but only €0.75 per dollar in Frankfurt. Therefore, the euro is cheaper in New York. To exploit this pricing discrepancy, the trader transacts as shown in Table 9.1. These transactions represent the exploitation of an arbitrage opportunity, since they ensure a profit with no investment. At the outset, there is no cash flow. The only cash flow involved in the transactions occurs simultaneously when the commitments initiated at $t = 0$ are completed at $t = 90$. The profit, however, was certain from the time of the initial transactions.

   Arbitrage is also possible to exploit misalignments in cross-rates. To understand a cross-rate, consider the following example. In New York, an exchange rate is quoted for the dollar versus the euro. There is also a rate quoted for the dollar versus the British pound. Together, these two rates imply an equilibrium exchange rate between the euro and the British pound. This implied exchange rate is a **cross-rate**. Therefore, the exchange rates in New York involving the dollar imply an exchange rate between the euro and pound that do not involve the dollar. Figure 9.2 shows quotations for cross-rates from *The Wall Street Journal*.

   If the direct rate quoted elsewhere for the euro versus the pound does not match the cross-rate in New York, an arbitrage opportunity exists. As an example, assume that the following rates are observed, where SF indicates the Swiss franc, and all of the rates are 90-day forward rates:

New York	$/€	1.25
	$/SF	0.77
Frankfurt	€/SF	0.630

Figure 9.2   Cross-rates

Key Currency Cross Rates					Late New York Trading Thursday, March 30, 2006		
	Dollar	Euro	Pound	SFranc	Peso	Yen	CdnDlr
Canada	1.1609	1.4111	2.0277	0.8947	.10620	.00989	...
Japan	117.34	142.63	204.96	90.437	10.735	...	101.080
Mexico	10.9314	13.2871	19.094	8.4248	...	.09316	9.4163
Switzerland	1.2975	1.5771	2.2664	...	.11870	.01106	1.1177
U.K.	.57250	.6959	...	.4412	.05237	.00488	.49316
Euro	.82270	...	1.4370	.63406	.07526	.00701	.70868
U.S.	...	1.2155	1.7467	.77070	.09148	.00852	.86140

Source: *The Wall Street Journal*, March 31, 2006, p. B5. Reprinted by permission of *The Wall Street Journal*, © 2006 Dow Jones & Company, Inc. All rights reserved worldwide

The exchange rates quoted in New York imply the following cross-rate in New York for the €/SF:

$$\text{€/SF} = \left(\frac{1}{\$/\text{€}}\right)(\$/\text{SF}) = \frac{1}{1.25} \times 0.77 = 0.616$$

Because the rate for the directly quoted euro per Swiss franc in Frankfurt differs from the cross-rate quoted in New York, an arbitrage opportunity exists. To exploit the arbitrage opportunity, one can trade only the exchange rates actually shown. For example, in New York there may not be a market for euros in terms of the Swiss franc.[2] To exchange euros for Swiss francs in the New York market involves two transactions. First, a trader sells euros for dollars and then buys Swiss francs with dollars.

To know how to trade, one must know which currency is relatively cheaper in a given market. In New York a person receives €0.616 per Swiss franc, but in Frankfurt one Swiss franc is worth €0.63. The euro, therefore, is cheaper in Frankfurt than in New York. Table 9.2 shows the transactions required to conduct the arbitrage.

Table 9.2   Cross-rate arbitrage transactions

$T = 0$ (the present)
  Sell SF 1 90 days forward in Frankfurt for €0.63
  Sell €0.63 90 days forward in New York for $0.788
  Sell $0.788 90 days forward in New York for SF 1.023

$T = 90$ (delivery)
  Deliver SF 1 in Frankfurt; collect €0.63
  Deliver €0.63 in New York; collect $0.788
  Deliver $0.788 in New York; collect SF 1.023

Profit: SF 1.023
                −1.000
         SF 0.023

Forward and futures market characteristics

The institutional structure of the foreign exchange futures market resembles that of the forward market, with a number of notable exceptions. While the forward market is a worldwide market with no particular geographic location, the principal futures market is the International Monetary Market (IMM) of the Chicago Mercantile Exchange (CME). In the futures market, contracts trade on the most important currencies, such as the euro, the British pound, the Canadian dollar, the Swiss franc, and the Japanese yen. All of the contracts trade on the MAR, JUN, SEP, and DEC cycle, with expiration on the third Wednesday of the expiration month. By contrast, forward market quotations are stated for a given number of days into the future.[3] In the futures market, the exchange determines the maturity date of each contract. With each passing day, the futures expiration comes one day closer. In the forward market, contracts for expiration 30, 90, and 180 days into the future are available each trading day. In the futures market, contracts mature on only four days of the year; in the forward market, contracts mature every day. In the forward market, contract size is negotiated. In the futures market, the rules of the exchange determine the contract size. Table 9.3 summarizes the differences between forward and futures markets for foreign exchange. The most important differences are the standardized contract, the standardized delivery dates, the differences in daily cash flows, and the differences in the ways contracts are closed. It is particularly interesting to note that less than 1 percent of all foreign exchange futures are completed by delivery, but delivery occurs on more than 90 percent of all forward contracts.

The forward market for foreign exchange dates back to beyond the reaches of history, while the futures market began only in the 1970s. The major center for the forward market continues to be London, but New York has been gaining in importance as the market for foreign exchange in the United States has grown rapidly. While foreign currency futures trading has grown dramatically, the forward market still dwarfs the futures market by a factor of about 20 to 1, as measured by the U.S. dollar volume of trading. Since banks are the major participants in the forward market, it is not too surprising that their level of activity in the futures market is rather limited.

Figure 9.3 shows foreign exchange futures price quotations. The columns of quotations follow the pattern set for other types of contracts, showing the open, high, low, and settlement prices, and the change in the settlement price since the preceding day. The next two columns present the high and low lifetime prices for each contract, while the final column shows the open interest in each contract. The final line of data for each contract shows the estimated volume of the current day, the actual volume of the preceding day, the current open interest across all contract maturities for each contract, and the change in the open interest since the preceding day.

While the price quotations for each currency are similar, there are some differences. First, different contracts trade a different number of units of the foreign currency. For instance, one contract is for ¥12.5 million but only €125,000. The difference in quantity reflects the vast difference in the value between a single euro and a single yen. In 2004, one U.S. dollar was worth about ¥110 but less than one euro. Notice also that the quotations for the yen have two zeroes suppressed.

Figure 9.4 shows the growth of foreign currency futures trading volume at U.S. exchanges. As the figure shows, the foreign exchange futures market grew rapidly until 1992, climbing from a level of only 199,920 contracts in 1975 to just over 38 million by 1992. During the mid-1990s, volume was flat at about 25 million contracts per year. Starting around the year 2001, trading volume began increasing again, due in part to the switch from pit trading to electronic

Table 9.3 Futures versus forward markets

	Forward	Futures
Size of contract	Tailored to individual needs	Standardized
Delivery date	Tailored to individual needs	Standardized
Method of transaction	Established by the bank or broker via telephone contract with limited number of buyers and sellers	Determined by open auction among many buyers and sellers on the exchange floor
Participants	Banks, brokers, and multinational companies; public speculation not encouraged	Banks, brokers, and multinational companies; qualified public speculation encouraged
Commissions	Set by "spread" between bank's buy and sell price; not easily determined by customer	Published small brokerage fee and negotiated rates on block trades
Security deposit	None as such, but compensating bank balances required	Published small security deposit required
Clearing operation (financial integrity)	Varies across individual banks and brokers; no separate clearinghouse function	Handled by exchange clearinghouse; daily settlements to the market
Marketplace	Over the telephone worldwide	Central exchange floor with worldwide communications
Economic justification	Facilitate world trade by providing hedge mechanism	Same as forward market; in addition, it provides a broader market and an alternative hedging mechanism via public participation
Accessibility	Limited to very large customers who deal in foreign trade	Open to anyone who needs hedge facilities, or has risk capital with which to speculate
Regulation	Self-regulating	April 1975—regulated under the Commodity Futures Trading Commission
Frequency of delivery	More than 90% settled by actual delivery	Less than 1% settled by actual delivery
Price fluctuations	No daily limit	No daily limit
Market liquidity	Offsetting with other banks	Public offset; arbitrage offset

Source: IMM, "Understanding Futures in Foreign Exchange Futures," pp. 6–7. Reprinted by permission from the Chicago Mercantile Exchange.

Figure 9.3   Foreign exchange futures quotations

Currency Futures

	Open	High	Low	Settle	Change	Lifetime High	Lifetime Low	Open interest
Japanese Yen (CME)-¥12,500,000; $ per 100¥								
June	.8578	.8630	.8568	.8614	.0034	.9949	.8455	161,932
Sept	.8706	.8736	.8678	.8721	.0035	.9435	.8572	18,741
Canadian Dollar (CME)-CAD 100,000; $ per CAD								
June	.8545	.8647	.8544	.8634	.0090	.8879	.7950	82,915
Sept	.8574	.8666	.8574	.8657	.0090	.8912	.7970	2,320
British Pound (CME)-£62,500; $ per £								
June	1.7364	1.7502	1.7361	1.7485	.0126	1.8120	1.7076	75,545
Sept	1.7438	1.7530	1.7410	1.7511	.0127	1.7941	1.7282	252
Swiss Franc (CME)-CHF 125,000; $ per CHF								
June	.7697	.7781	.7695	.7771	.0075	.8635	.7633	88,067
Sept	.7835	.7852	.7822	.7842	.0076	.8134	.7712	252
Australian Dollar (CME)-AUD 100,000; $ per AUD								
June	.7055	.7150	.7055	.7140	.0079	.7760	.7006	66,866
Sept	.7090	.7140	.7069	.7132	.0079	.7700	.7001	143
Mexican Peso (CME)-MXN 500,000; $ per 10MXN								
Apr	...	...	...	.91375	.00275	.94950	.90700	20
June	.90750	.91250	.90550	.90975	.00275	.95000	.84500	43,780
Euro (CME)-€125,000; $ per €								
June	1.2087	1.2230	1.2081	1.2213	.0131	1.3795	1.1798	136,658
Sept	1.2157	1.2292	1.2157	1.2277	.0132	1.2770	1.1864	2,080

Source: "Futures Price Quotations," *The Wall Street Journal*, March 31, 2006, p. B5. Futures prices reflect day and overnight trading. Open interest reflects previous day's trading. Reprinted by permission of *The Wall Street Journal*, © 2006 Dow Jones & Company, Inc. All rights reserved worldwide

trading. By 2005, trading volume had climbed to nearly 85 million contracts. Figure 9.5 shows the share of volume for key currencies in 2005.

The European Monetary Union

Tracing its origins to the 1957 Treaty of Rome, the European Union (EU) was created by the ratification of the Maastricht Treaty of 1993 and currently consists of 25 countries: Austria, Belgium, Cyprus, Czech Republic, Denmark, Estonia, Finland, France, Germany, Greece, Hungary, Ireland, Italy, Latvia, Lithuania, Luxembourg, Malta, Netherlands, Poland, Portugal, Slovakia, Slovenia, Spain, Sweden, and the United Kingdom. These countries have agreed to consolidate a wide range of economic and governmental functions. Most important for the currency market is the movement toward a common currency to replace the national currency unit (NCU) of individual countries.

In 1998, some members of the EU formed the European Monetary Union (EMU). Members of the EMU replaced their individual NCUs with a common currency, the euro. As of late 2004, the following members of the European Union are members of the EMU and have adopted the

Figure 9.4   Growth in trading in foreign exchange futures

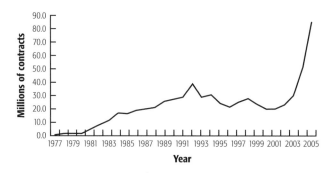

Figure 9.5   Market share for foreign currency futures in U.S. markets for 2005

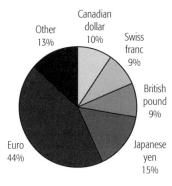

Source: Commodity Futures Trading Commission, *Annual Report*, 2005

euro as their official currency: Austria, Belgium, Finland, France, Germany, Greece, Ireland, Italy, Luxembourg, Netherlands, Portugal, and Spain. Other EU countries, most notably, the United Kingdom, do not participate in the EMU and have chosen to use their own national currencies for the present.

Determinants of foreign exchange rates

As with almost any good, fundamental factors shape the exchange rate that prevails between the currencies of two countries. These factors are numerous and quite complex, with entire books being written on the subject. Consequently, the brief discussion that follows merely indicates some of the most important influences on exchange rates. One way of thinking about currencies is to regard them as essentially similar to other assets, subject to the same basic laws of supply and demand. When a particular currency is unusually plentiful, its price might be expected to fall. Of course, the price of a given currency in terms of some other currency is merely the exchange rate between the two currencies. In foreign exchange, the flow of payments between residents of one country and the rest of the world gives rise to the concept of the balance of payments. The balance of payments is generally calculated on a yearly basis. If expenditures by a particular country exceed receipts, then that country has a deficit in its balance of payments; if receipts exceed expenditures, then the country has a surplus. The balance of payments encompasses all kinds of flows of goods and services among nations, including the movement of real goods, services, international investment, and all types of financial flows.

To illustrate how the balance of payments influences exchange rates, consider the following example. A country, Importeria, trades with other countries and always imports more goods than it exports. This means that there is always a net flow of real goods into Importeria. It must pay for these goods in some way, so we assume that the government of Importeria simply prints additional currency to pay for the excess goods that it imports. Such a practice must eventually cause a change in the exchange rates between Importeria and its trading partners. As the trading partners continue to send more and more goods to the country, they collectively have fewer and fewer real goods themselves, but a growing supply of the currency of Importeria.

As the world's supply of Importeria's currency swells, it becomes apparent that it has only a few uses. It can be used to acquire other currencies, or it can be used to purchase goods from Importeria. However, the accumulation of its currency continues until there is an excess supply at the prevailing exchange rate, so the value of Importeria's currency must fall. Just as Importeria cannot continually import more than it exports without causing the value of its currency to fall, no country can continually consume more than it creates without eventually causing a fall in the value of its currency.

Fixed exchange rates

The currency adjustment that Importeria might have to suffer depends on the international exchange rate system. For most of the history of the United States, there has been a system of **fixed exchange rates**. A fixed exchange rate is a stated exchange rate between two currencies at which anyone may transact. A country such as Importeria might import more than it exports for quite some time without causing a change in the fixed exchange rate. However, even fixed exchange rates are only fixed in the short run, and are subject to periodic adjustments. For Importeria, the continual excess of imports over exports puts pressure on the value of its currency as the world supply of its currency continues to grow. Eventually, the fixed exchange rate between Importeria's currency and that of other nations will be adjusted. For Importeria, the value of the currency will have to fall or be **devalued**. The value of other currencies will increase relative to Importeria's, so these currencies are said to have been **revalued**. Devaluations and revaluations, when they occur, are usually large in size. It is not uncommon for the value to change by 25–50 percent, or even more.

It may seem perplexing that the value of the currencies would not adjust smoothly over time, as Importeria continued its program of excess imports. A fixed exchange rate system, however, prevents gradual adjustment. Rates are fixed through the intervention of the central banks of Importeria and other countries. As excess supplies of Importeria's currency accumulate, central banks may use their reserves of other currencies to buy Importeria's currency, thereby easing the imbalance between supply and demand that would arise at the fixed level of rates. In effect, central banks would be absorbing the excess supply of Importeria's currency, which would otherwise exist at the fixed level of exchange rates. If the pressures against this currency are not too severe, purchases by central banks may succeed in maintaining the fixed level of exchange rates. Often, however, the excess supply of a currency may become excessive. Then central banks become unable, or unwilling, to purchase all of the currency that is supplied. When this happens, a country such as Importeria would be forced to devalue its currency and set a new rate of exchange as the official rate. If the value of the Importeria unit of currency was one-tenth of a U.S. dollar before the devaluation, it might be reset at one-twelfth of a dollar after the devaluation. After the devaluation, Importeria would try to maintain the new exchange rate. If Importeria continued to import much more than it exported, it would soon face another devaluation.

One obvious and apparently disadvantageous feature of a fixed exchange rate system is that changes in the exchange rates occur infrequently, but when they do, the changes are rather large. There are, however, considerable advantages to a fixed exchange rate system. First, fixed exchange rates make planning exchange transactions considerably easier. If businesses can depend on a fixed exchange rate for the next year, they will not face **exchange risk**—the risk that the value of a currency will change relative to other currencies. Freedom from exchange risk facilitates business planning and promotes international trade. Second, for firms engaged in international commerce, fixed exchange rates mean that accounting income is not sensitive to exchange rate fluctuations. Third, a fixed exchange rate may provide a form of discipline for economic policies by the participating countries. According to this argument, governments would realize that pursuing certain policies would be likely to lead to devaluation.

Perhaps for these reasons, and also as a signal of financial probity, the industrialized West pursued a fixed exchange rate policy from the end of World War II until 1971. During this period, the dollar was even convertible into gold at a rate of $35 per ounce, according to the Bretton Woods Agreement. Other major currencies fixed their value in terms of the U.S. dollar. In August 1971, faced with a weakening dollar and a soaring balance-of-payments deficit, the United States abandoned the gold standard. In spite of attempts to reestablish some semblance of a fixed rate system, notably the Smithsonian Agreement of 1971, March 1973 witnessed a new era in international foreign exchange. The fixed rate system was abandoned, with daily fluctuations in exchange rates becoming the norm.

Other exchange rate systems

This free market system of exchange rates prevails today, but there are a number of important exceptions and variations that the foreign exchange trader must consider. With the breakdown of the Bretton Woods system and the failure of the Smithsonian Agreement, countries were free to adopt a variety of strategies as far as their exchange rates were concerned. This freedom has led to strategies such as free floats, managed or dirty floats, pegs, and joint floats. A currency is **freely floating** if it has no system of fixed exchange rates and if the country's central bank does not attempt to influence the value of the currency by trading in the foreign exchange market. Few countries have truly freely floating exchange rates, because central banks seem unable to resist the temptation to intervene. When the central bank of a country engages in market transactions to influence the exchange value of its currency, but the rate is basically a floating rate, the country is following a policy of a **managed float** or a **dirty float**. Opposed to this floating system, a number of countries use a **pegged** exchange rate system. The value of one currency might be pegged to the value of another currency, which itself floats. For example, Importeria might try to maintain a fixed exchange rate with the dollar, but the dollar itself floats against most of the world's currencies. In such a situation, the currency of Importeria would be pegged to the dollar. Some pegged currencies may be pegged to a single currency, while others could be pegged to a basket, or portfolio, of currencies.

One other policy for exchange rate management—that of a joint float—is particularly important for the foreign exchange futures market. In a **joint float**, participating currencies have fixed exchange values relative to other currencies in the joint float, but the *group* of currencies floats relative to other currencies that do not participate. The prime example of the joint float technique comes from the European Community (EC) (formerly the European Economic Community, or Common Market). The member nations formed the European Monetary System (EMS) in 1979 and created the European Currency Unit (ECU). The basic strategy of the EMS agreement is to maintain very narrowly fluctuating exchange rates among the currencies of the participating countries. Currently, all of the individual currencies of the participating countries have been replaced by the euro.

In theory, a joint float system means that the values of the currencies of the participating countries will be fixed relative to one another but will float relative to those of external countries. This has important implications for speculation and hedging in all of these currencies, particularly where the futures market is concerned. Recent experience has shown that some countries may be forced to devalue their currency relative to those of the group.

Forward and futures prices for foreign exchange

As we discussed in Chapter 3, a distinction between forward and futures prices emerges from the daily resettlement feature of futures contracts. Consider forward and futures contracts on foreign exchange that have the same expiration. Both the futures and the forward will have the same profit in the end, exclusive of interest earned on the resettlement payments. If the futures position is likely to have more favorable interim cash flows due to its positive correlation with interest rates, the futures price should exceed the forward price. By the same token, if the futures price is negatively correlated with interest rates, then the futures price should be lower than the forward price. This conclusion follows because the futures trader will then tend to experience losses just as interest rates rise. Finally, if the price of a commodity is uncorrelated with interest rates, then the forward and futures prices should be equal. Notice that all these conclusions arise strictly from economic reasoning and hold if investors are risk neutral.

While futures and forward prices differ in theory, the magnitude and practical significance of that difference is an empirical question. In general, studies of this issue find very little difference between foreign exchange forward and futures prices. As one study concluded, "The foreign exchange data reveal that mean differences between forward and futures prices are insignificantly different from zero, both in a statistical and economic sense." In view of these findings, results based on research in the forward market will be regarded as holding for the futures market as well.

More futures price parity relationships

Earlier in this chapter, we noted the geographic or cross-rate arbitrage opportunities that occur when foreign exchange rates are improperly aligned among single contracts. The arbitrage examples of Tables 9.1 and 9.2 arose from a pricing discrepancy in the foreign exchange rates for a single maturity of 90 days forward. Other price relationships are equally important and determine the permissible price differences that may exist between foreign exchange rates for delivery at different times. These relationships are expressed as the **interest rate parity (IRP) theorem** and the **purchasing power parity (PPP) theorem**. As we will see, the IRP theorem is simply the cost-of-carry model in a very thin disguise.

<table>
<tr><td colspan="5">Table 9.4   Interest rates and exchange rates to illustrate interest rate parity</td></tr>
</table>

	Exchange rates ($/€)		Interest rates	
			U.S.	Germany
Spot	1.25		–	–
30-day	1.23		0.18	0.5760
90-day	1.20		0.19	0.3300
180-day	1.17		0.20	0.3697

The interest rate parity theorem

The interest rate parity theorem asserts that interest rates and exchange rates form one system. According to the IRP theorem, foreign exchange rates will adjust to ensure that a trader earns the same return by investing in risk-free instruments of any currency, assuming that the proceeds from investment are repatriated into the home currency by a forward contract initiated at the outset of the holding period. We can use the rates of Table 9.4 to illustrate interest rate parity. Faced with the rates in Table 9.4 and assuming interest rate parity holds, a trader must earn the same return by following either of the following two strategies:

Strategy 1:   Invest in the United States for 180 days.
Strategy 2:   (a) Sell dollar for euro at the spot rate.
                  (b) Invest euro proceeds for 180 days in Germany.
                  (c) Sell the proceeds of the German investment for dollars through a forward contract initiated at the outset of the investment horizon.

With our sample data, the following equation expresses the same equivalence:

$$\$1 \times (1.20)^{0.5} = [(\$1/1.25) \times (1.3697)^{0.5}] \times 1.17$$

In the equation, Strategy 1 is on the left-hand side. There, $1 is invested at the 20 percent U.S. rate for six months (0.5 years). For Strategy 2 on the right-hand side, the dollar is first converted into euros at the spot rate of $1.25 per euro. The trader invests these proceeds at the Euribor rate, which represents the German interest rate, for 0.5 years. This 180-day rate is 36.97 percent. Investment of the euros will pay 0.920174 in 180 days. The investment proceeds are sold for dollars using the 180-day forward rate of 1.17. For this 180-day horizon, the equivalence between the two strategies holds, so no-arbitrage opportunity is available. In this example, the IRP theorem holds.

Interest rate parity and the cost-of-carry model

In essence, the IRP theorem is simply the exchange rate equivalent of the cost-of-carry model. To see this equivalence, consider the cash-and-carry strategy for the interest rate market. In a cash-and-carry transaction a trader follows the following steps: borrow funds and buy a bond, carry the bond to the futures/forward expiration, and sell the good through a futures/forward contract arranged at the initial date. The cost of carry is the difference between the rate paid on the borrowed funds and the rate earned by holding the bond. Our familiar cash-and-carry strategy is known as **covered interest arbitrage** in the foreign exchange market. In covered interest arbitrage, a trader borrows domestic funds and buys foreign funds at the spot rate. The trader then invests these funds at the foreign interest rate until expiration of the forward/futures contract. The trader also initiates a futures/forward contract to convert the proceeds from the foreign investment back into the domestic currency. The cost of carry is the difference between the interest rate paid to borrow funds and the interest earned on the investment in foreign funds.

Thus, a trader borrows the domestic currency, DC, at the domestic rate of interest, r_{DC}, and exchanges these funds for foreign currency, FC, at the spot exchange rate. The trader receives DC/FC units of the foreign currency and invests at the foreign interest rate, r_{FC}. This rate, r_{FC}, is the interest rate applicable to the time from the present to the expiration of the forward or futures. At the outset of these transactions, $t = 0$, the trader also sells the forward or futures contract at price $F_{0,t}$ for the amount of funds $(DC/FC)(1 + r_{FC})$. With these transactions, the trader has no net cash flow at $t = 0$. At expiration, the trader receives $(DC/FC)(1 + r_{FC})$ units of the foreign currency from the investment of foreign funds. The trader delivers this foreign currency against the forward or futures contract and receives $F_{0,t}$ in the domestic currency. The trader must then pay the debt on the original borrowing, which is $DC(1 + r_{DC})$. If the IRP theorem, or equivalently, the cost-of-carry model, holds, the trader must be left with zero funds. Otherwise, an arbitrage opportunity exists.

Applying this notation to our previous example of the cost-of-carry transactions for the 180-day horizon, we can generalize this example to write an equation for the IRP theorem or the cost-of-carry model as it applies to foreign exchange. For convenience, we begin with $1 as the amount of the domestic currency, DC. Earlier, for our example, we wrote

$$\$1 \times (1.20)^{0.5} = [(\$1/1.25) \times (1.3697)^{0.5}] \times 1.17$$

In the new notation, this translates as follows:

$$DC(1 + r_{DC}) = (DC/FC)(1 + r_{FC})F_{0,t}$$

Remember that r_{DC} and r_{FC} are the interest rates for the specific period between the present, $t = 0$, and the expiration of the futures at time t.

Isolating the futures price on the left-hand side gives

$$F_{0,t} = \frac{DC(1 + r_{DC})}{\left(\dfrac{DC}{FC}\right)(1 + r_{FC})} = FC\left(\frac{(1 + r_{DC})}{(1 + r_{FC})}\right) \tag{9.1}$$

Equation 9.1 says that, for a unit of foreign currency, the futures price equals the spot price of the foreign currency times the quantity:

$$\left(\frac{(1 + r_{DC})}{(1 + r_{FC})}\right) \tag{9.2}$$

This quantity is the ratio of the interest factor for the domestic currency to the interest factor for the foreign currency. We can compare this to our familiar Equation 3.3 for the cost-of-carry model in perfect markets with unrestricted short selling:

$$F_{0,t} = S_0(1 + C) \tag{3.3}$$

where $F_{0,t}$ is the futures or forward price at $t = 0$ for a foreign exchange contract to expire at time t, S_0 is the spot price of the good at $t = 0$, and C is the percentage cost of carrying the good from $t = 0$ to time t. Equations 3.3 and 9.1 have the same form. Therefore, the quantity in Equation 9.2 equals one plus the cost of carry, $(1 + C)$. The cash-and-carry strategy requires borrowing at the domestic rate, r_{DC}, so this is an element of the carrying cost. However, the borrowed domestic funds are converted to foreign currency and earn at the foreign interest rate r_{FC}. Therefore, the foreign earnings offset the cost being incurred through the domestic interest rate. The net result is that the quantity of Equation 9.2 gives the value for one plus the carrying cost. As a simpler approximation, we note that

$$1 + \text{cost of carry} = \left(\frac{(1 + r_{DC})}{(1 + r_{FC})} \right) \approx 1 + (r_{DC} - r_{FC}) \tag{9.3}$$

Therefore, the cost of carry approximately equals the difference between the domestic and foreign interest rates for the period from $t = 0$ to the futures expiration. To complete this discussion, let us apply this equation for the 180-day horizon using the rates in Table 9.4. We have already seen that there is no arbitrage possible for this horizon. For this example, we have the following data: $F_{0,t} = 1.17$; $S_0 = 1.25$; $r_{DC} = 0.095445$ for the half-year; and $r_{FC} = 0.170347$ for the half-year. Applying Equation 9.1 to this data, we have

$$1.17 = 1.25 \times \frac{1.095445}{1.170347}$$

This equation holds exactly. The cost of carry -0.064. For this example, the approximate cost of carry for the half-year is

$$r_{DC} - r_{FC} = 0.095445 - 0.170347 = -0.0749$$

Thus, the cost of carry for the half-year is approximately -0.075. The cost of carry is negative because the cash-and-carry trader pays at the domestic rate but earns interest at the higher foreign rate. For the same reason, the futures price of the foreign currency must exceed the spot price. If the foreign rate of interest had been lower, the futures price of the foreign currency would have to be lower than the spot price to avoid arbitrage.

Exploiting deviations from interest rate parity

The analysis of the values in Table 9.4 shows that there is not an arbitrage opportunity in the 180-day contract. If the IRP theorem is to hold in general, there cannot be an arbitrage opportunity for any investment horizon. In Table 9.4, the rates allow an arbitrage opportunity in the 90-day contract. This is apparent when one realizes that the strategy of holding the U.S. dollar and euro investment does not yield the same 90-day terminal wealth in U.S. dollars when the euros are converted into dollars by issuing a forward contract. The following computation illustrates the different terminal dollar values earned by the two strategies:

Strategy 1:	Hold in the United States:
	$\$1 \times (1.19)^{0.25} = \$1.0444$
Strategy 2:	Convert to euros, invest, and use a forward contract:
	$(\$1/1.25) \times (1.33)^{0.25} \times 1.20 = \$1.030942$

Table 9.5   Covered interest arbitrage

$t = 0$ (present)
   Borrow €0.8 in Germany for 90 days at 33%
   Sell €0.8 spot for $1.00
   Invest $1.00 in the U.S. for 90 days at 19%
   Sell $1.030942 90 days forward for €0.804764

$t = 90$ (delivery)
   Collect $1.0444 on investment in the U.S.
   Deliver $1.030942 on forward contract; collect €0.804764
   Pay €0.804764 on €0.8 that was borrowed

	Profit:	$1.04444
		−1.03042
		0.01402

Strategy 1, investing in the United States, gives a higher payoff than converting dollars to euros and investing in Germany. This difference implies that an arbitrage opportunity exists.

This is also evident by applying the cost-of-carry model for foreign exchange to the 90-day values in Table 9.4. For this horizon, the values in Table 9.4 imply the following data: $F_{0,t} = 1.20$; $S_0 = 1.25$; $r_{DC} = 0.044448$ for the quarter-year; and $r_{FC} = 0.073898$ for the quarter-year. With these values, the futures price should be 1.215721:

$$FC\left(\frac{(1 + r_{DC})}{(1 + r_{FC})}\right) = 1.25 \times \frac{1.044448}{1.073898} = 1.215721$$

Because the futures price is less than this amount, an arbitrage opportunity exists. With our example data, it is clearly better to invest funds in the United States rather than Germany. Table 9.5 shows the transactions that will exploit this discrepancy, assuming that the transactions begin with $1.00.

This kind of arbitrage in foreign exchange is covered interest arbitrage. With these transactions, the trader uses a forward contract to cover the proceeds from the euro investment. The proceeds are covered, because the trader arranges through the forward contract to convert the euro proceeds into dollars as soon as the proceeds are received. The IRP theorem asserts that such opportunities should not exist. The section on market efficiency explores whether the IRP theorem actually holds.

The purchasing power parity theorem

The purchasing power parity theorem asserts that the exchange rates between two currencies must be proportional to the price level of traded goods in the two currencies. The PPP theorem is intimately tied to interest rate parity, as we discuss later. Violations of the PPP theorem can lead to arbitrage opportunities, such as the following example of "tortilla arbitrage."

For tortilla arbitrage, we assume that transportation and transaction costs are zero and that there are no trade barriers, such as quotas or tariffs. These assumptions are essentially equivalent to our usual assumptions of perfect markets. The spot value of the Mexican peso (MP) is $0.10 and the cost of a tortilla in Mexico City is MP 1, as Table 9.6 shows. In New York a tortilla sells for $0.15, so this price creates an arbitrage opportunity. A trader can exploit this

Table 9.6 Tortilla arbitrage	MP/$	Cost of one tortilla
Mexico City	10	MP 1
New York	10	$0.15

Arbitrage transactions
Sell $1 for MP 10 in the spot market
Buy ten tortillas in Mexico City
Ship the tortillas to New York
Sell ten tortillas in New York at 0.15 for $1.50

Profit: $1.50
−1.00
0.50

Table 9.7 Purchasing power parity over time		

Expected inflation rates from $t = 0$ to $t = 1$: $ 0.10
MP   0.20

	$t = 0$	$t = 1$
Exchange rates (MP/$)	10.00	10.91
Tortilla prices:		
Mexico City	MP 1.00	MP 1.20
New York	$0.10	$0.11

opportunity by transacting as shown in the bottom portion of Table 9.6. Given the other values, the price of a tortilla in New York must be $0.10 to exclude arbitrage.

Over time, exchange rates must also conform to the PPP theorem. The left column of Table 9.7 presents prices and exchange rates consistent with the PPP theorem at $t = 0$. The right column shows values one year later at $t = 1$, after a year of inflation in Mexico and the United States. During this year, Mexican inflation was 20 percent, so a tortilla now sells for MP 1.2. In the United States, inflation was 10 percent, so a tortilla is now $0.11. To be consistent with the PPP theorem, the exchange rates must also have adjusted to keep the relative value of the euro and dollar consistent with the relative purchasing power of the two currencies. As a consequence, the dollar must now be worth MP 10.91. Any other exchange rate would create an arbitrage opportunity. The requirement that the PPP theorem holds at all times means that the exchange rate must change proportionately to the relative price levels in the two currencies.

Purchasing power and interest rate parity

The intimate relationship that exists between the purchasing power parity theorem and the interest rate parity theorem originates from the link between interest rates and inflation rates. According to the analysis of Irving Fisher, the nominal, or market, rate of interest consists of two elements, the **real** rate of interest and the **expected** inflation rate. This relationship can be expressed mathematically as follows:

$$1 + r_n = (1 + r^*)[1 + E(I)] \tag{9.4}$$

where r_n is the nominal interest rate, r^* is the real rate of interest, and $E(I)$ is the expected inflation rate over the period in question. Since the expected inflation is the expected change in purchasing power, the PPP theorem expresses the linkage between exchange rates and relative inflation rates. A difference in nominal interest rates between two countries is most likely due to differences in expected inflation. This means that interest rates, exchange rates, price levels, and foreign exchange rates form an integrated system.

Foreign exchange futures prices and expected future exchange rates

Throughout this book, and particularly in Chapter 3, we have stressed the relationship between futures prices and expected future spot prices. If risk-neutral speculators are available in sufficient quantity, their profit-seeking activity will drive the futures price toward equality with the expected future spot price. The same process occurs in the foreign exchange market. The linkages among interest rates, price levels, expected inflation, and exchange rates merely emphasize the fundamental relationship that exists between forward and futures foreign exchange prices, on the one hand, and the expected future value of the currencies, on the other.

To investigate these relationships, consider the exchange rates and price levels of Table 9.8. In the left-hand panel, a set of consistent exchange rates, interest rates, expected inflation rates, and tortilla prices are presented for March 20, 2005. The right-hand panel presents the expected spot exchange rate for March 20, 2006, along with expected tortilla prices, consistent with the expected levels of inflation in Mexico and the United States.

Assume that all of these values hold and that the expected spot exchange rate in one year is MP 11 per dollar. With the MAR 2006 futures price of MP 10.45 per dollar, a speculative opportunity exists as follows. A speculator might buy a futures contract for the delivery of dollars in one year for MP 10.45 per dollar. If the expectation that the dollar will be worth MP 11 in one year is correct, the speculator will earn a profit that results from acquiring a dollar via the futures market for MP 10.45 and selling it for the price of MP 11. If we assume that avaricious risk-neutral speculators are present in the foreign exchange market, the discrepancy between the futures price of MP 10.45 per dollar and an expected spot exchange rate of MP 11 per dollar (at the time the futures contract matures) cannot exist. In fact, given a profusion of risk-neutral speculators, the only expected spot exchange rate to prevail on March 20, 2006 that

Table 9.8 Price levels, interest rates, expected inflation, and exchange rates

March 20, 2005		March 20, 2006	
Exchange rates		Expected spot exchange rate	
Spot	10.00 MP/$		10.45 MP/$
MAR 2006 futures	10.45 MP/$		
Interest rates (one-year maturities)			
U.S.	0.12%		
Mexico	0.17%		
Expected inflation rates (for the next year)			
U.S.	0.10%		
Mexico	0.15%		
Tortilla prices		Expected tortilla prices	
U.S.	$0.10	U.S.	$0.11
Mexico	MP 1.0	Mexico	MP 1.15

would eliminate the incentive to speculate would be MP 10.45 per dollar. Of course, different market participants have different expectations regarding inflation rates and expected future spot exchange rates, and this difference in expectations is the necessary requirement for speculation.

Foreign exchange forecasting accuracy

In this section, we examine the evidence on the accuracy of foreign exchange futures and forward prices as forecasts of future spot exchange rates. As we have just argued in the preceding section, the presence of risk-neutral speculators should drive the futures and forward prices into equality with the expected future spot rate of exchange. If today's expectation of future exchange rates is unbiased, and if the forward and futures prices equal that expectation, we would find that today's forward or futures exchange rate should, on average and in the long run, equal the subsequently observed spot exchange rate. Thus, there are two parts to this equivalence. First, does the forward or futures price equal the market's expectation of the future spot exchange rate? Second, is today's expectation of the future spot exchange rate unbiased? That is, does today's expectation of the future spot exchange rate, on average and in the long run, equal the actual subsequently observed spot rate?

Methodology for tests of forecasting accuracy

Unfortunately, there is no truly accurate way to observe today's market expectation of future exchange rates. Therefore, most tests assume that the market expectation is an unbiased estimate of the future spot exchange rate. Under this assumption, scholars test the relationship between the forward and futures price today and the subsequently observed spot rate. In our notation, they test the following equivalence:

$$F_{0,t} = S_t \qquad (9.5)$$

where $F_{0,t}$ is the forward or futures price at $t = 0$ for a contract expiring at time t and S_t is the spot exchange rate observed at time t. Testing the equivalence in Equation 9.5 determines whether the forward or futures price is a good estimate of the future spot rate of exchange. Even if there are large deviations between the two prices in Equation 9.5, it is still possible that the forward or futures price could provide an unbiased prediction of the future spot rate. An **unbiased predictor** is a predictor whose expected value equals the variable being predicted. In other words, if the quantity $F_{0,t} - S_t$ equals zero, on average, the forward or futures price would provide an unbiased estimate of the future spot rate of exchange.

No predictor is perfect. Therefore, it is possible that the forward or futures price may seem to be error ridden. However, the most relevant test of any predictor comes from testing the accuracy of the predictor against alternative predictors. As we will see, forward and futures prices do not provide very good predictions of future spot rates—unless we compare them to alternative forecasting schemes.

Earlier in this chapter, we reviewed the evidence on the relationship between futures and forward prices of foreign exchange. There we saw that the evidence strongly suggests that the two are equal. We rely on that equivalence in this section. In the discussion that follows, we speak of futures and forward prices in general, without distinguishing the two.

Tests of market-based forecasts

A **market-based forecast** is a forecast of a future economic value derived from an examination of current market prices. In the context of foreign exchange, we ask whether the current futures price provides a good market-based forecast of the future foreign exchange rate. As we have seen, this essentially amounts to testing the equivalence of futures prices and subsequently observed spot exchange rates.

While earlier studies generally found that futures prices were unbiased predictors of future spot rates, later studies clearly find bias and large errors in the futures forecasts of subsequent spot prices. However, most studies do not find biases that are sufficiently large or consistent to allow profitable trading strategies. In summary, the errors in forecasts of future exchange rates appear to be large, and biases do seem to exist in these forecasts, although the biases appear to be too small to allow profitable exploitation.[4]

Competitors of market-based forecasts

If we consider the futures price as a forecast of the future spot rate of exchange, we must conclude that the forecast is likely to have large errors, and we must acknowledge that the forecast may be biased. These two features do not appear to recommend market-based forecasts of future spot exchange rates. Perhaps some other type of forecast is better. The usefulness of market-based forecasts of future exchange rates depends on a whole range of factors, including availability, cost, extent of bias, the size of the forecast error, and the performance of the forecast relative to other methods. In this section, we compare market-based forecasts with the performance of commercial forecasting firms. As will become apparent, in spite of their limitations, the futures forecasts have important advantages.

Clearly, the futures forecast has an advantage in availability and cost. Both are readily available every day for the price of *The Wall Street Journal*. If forward and futures prices provide the best forecast of the future spot rate that is available, the biases in the forecasts are probably not too serious. Even if the biases are substantial, the futures forecast may still be the best forecast available. Perhaps the most severe challenge to the market-based forecasts comes from the forecasting services that prepare and disseminate forecasts of exchange rates. However, market-based forecasts appear to have smaller errors than forecasts from commercial firms.[5]

The efficiency of foreign exchange futures markets

The efficiency of the foreign exchange market has been explored by numerous researchers over an extended period of time. In spite of this attention, the efficiency of the market remains an open question. This situation is not unusual when a complex empirical issue in finance is at stake. If arbitrage opportunities such as geographic, cross-rate, or covered interest arbitrage exist, then the foreign exchange market is inefficient. Reflection on the structure of the market helps to support the case for efficiency. With a worldwide network of active traders, all of them linked by sophisticated information systems and all aware of the profits implied by arbitrage opportunities, we might expect any incipient arbitrage opportunities to be detected very early. As quasi-arbitrage opportunities appear, we would expect traders to adjust their trading patterns to exploit even the slightest opportunity. This activity, we expect, should eliminate any observable arbitrage opportunities.

On the other hand, the foreign exchange market is unique in attracting central bank intervention from a variety of countries. If central banks cannot keep their hands off the market and insist on managing floating rates, the character of the market could be affected. If the market is subject to the actions of well-capitalized governmental agencies with agendas that are not profit-determined, then we might expect profit opportunities to arise from betting against central banks. In this section, we explore the evidence on market efficiency, beginning with an example of interest rate parity.

Table 9.9 The percentage of deviations from interest parity within ±0.25 percent (all assets are for three-month maturities)

Country	Percentage within bounds
Canada	93.43
United Kingdom	96.68
Germany	98.82
Switzerland	78.59

Source: Richard M. Levich, "The Efficiency of Markets for Foreign Exchange: A Review and Extension." Reprinted in Kolb and Gay, *International Finance: Concepts and Issues*, Richmond, VA: Robert F. Dame, Inc., 1982. © 1982. Reprinted by permission from Richard M. Levich

We have seen that deviations from interest rate parity create opportunities for cash-and-carry and reverse cash-and-carry trading strategies. With transaction costs, slight deviations from interest rate parity are possible, because transaction costs make it unprofitable for traders to exploit minor discrepancies. The arbitrage opportunity depends upon finding deviations from interest rate parity that are large enough to cover all transaction costs and still leave a profit. As a result, one way of searching for the existence of violations of the IRP theorem is to look for the occurrence of large deviations from interest rate parity. Table 9.9 shows deviations from interest rate parity for some major currencies on which futures contracts trade. Richard M. Levich selected 0.25 percent as a permissible deviation from interest rate parity, which would still be consistent with the absence of arbitrage opportunities. He believed that this fourth of one percent would be a reasonable bound for transaction costs to form a no-arbitrage band around the price exactly consistent with the IRP theorem. As Table 9.9 shows, a high percentage of Levich's observations fall within that band. From this, Levich concludes that, "Therefore, the Euro-currency market is efficient in that there are few unexploited opportunities for risk-free profit through covered interest arbitrage."[6]

To what extent do deviations outside the band of 0.25 percent represent arbitrage opportunities? If we find only few opportunities, it may still be worthwhile to look for them. Based on Table 9.9, it seems potentially worthwhile to follow the Swiss franc, since over 20 percent of the observations appear to lie outside the stated boundaries. The critical question here is the selection of the no-arbitrage boundaries. If transactions costs exceed 0.25 percent, then the bounds are too narrow. By the same token, perhaps transactions costs are really less than 0.25 percent, and the no-arbitrage boundaries are too lax. These questions are not easy to answer, since it is virtually impossible to know what measure of transaction costs to use. The most striking feature of Table 9.9, however, appears to be the prevalent tendency for so many opportunities to fall within 0.25 percent of exact interest rate parity. While it may not be possible to say that no-arbitrage opportunities are to be found in the foreign exchange market, it is much more impressive to note how closely the observations tend to correspond to interest rate parity.[7]

Levich's study characterizes the earlier evidence on the efficiency of foreign exchange markets. Nonetheless, more recent evidence on forward and futures markets for foreign exchange suggests that the markets are not efficient. Most studies of foreign exchange market efficiency find significant departures from theoretical pricing relationships. Further, some studies find that speculative strategies can earn significant profits. Part of the findings may be due to intervention in the foreign exchange markets by central banks. As a tentative explanation, it seems possible that central banks intervene to stabilize currencies. In the process, they provide profits to savvy speculators. However, most of these opportunities appear to be quite small.[8]

Speculation in foreign exchange futures

We have seen that the market for foreign exchange has some significant inefficiencies. This inefficiency appears to open the door to speculative strategies. Nonetheless, we should not expect gross inefficiencies in the market. For example, it still appears that market-based forecasts outperform professional forecasts. This suggests that attempts to "beat the market" may still be hazardous. In this section, we illustrate strategies to speculate with foreign exchange. These strategies presume that the trader has well-developed expectations about the value of foreign exchange rates.

Speculating with an outright position

In speculation, the most important point to remember is that the trader opposes his or her wisdom to the opinion of the entire market, since prices available in the market reflect the consensus opinion of all participating parties. The dependence of speculative profits on superior estimation of future exchange rates is demonstrated in Tables 9.10 and 9.11. Imagine a speculator

Table 9.10   Foreign exchange prices: spot and futures, April 7

	$/€
Spot	1.2321
JUN futures	1.2449
SEP futures	1.2533
DEC futures	1.2756

Table 9.11   Speculation in foreign exchange

Date	Cash market		Futures market
April 7	Anticipates a fall in the value of the euro over the next eight months		Sell one DEC euro futures contract at 1.2756
December 10	Spot price $/€ = 1.2533		Buy one DEC euro futures contract at 1.2554
	Profit:	$1.2756 −1.2554	
	Profit per euro	$0.0202	
	Times euro per contract	× 125,000	
	Total profit	$2,525	

who confronts the exchange rates of Table 9.10 between the U.S. dollar and the euro on April 7. As an expression of the market's beliefs, these exchange rates imply that the euro will rise relative to the dollar. The speculator, however, strongly disagrees. She believes that the price of the euro, in terms of dollars, will actually fall over the rest of the year. Table 9.11 shows the speculative transactions she enters to take advantage of her belief.

Since the speculator expects the euro to fall, she sells the DEC futures contract for 1.2756. If the subsequent spot price is less, she makes a profit. The speculator does not actually need to be correct in the stated belief that the spot exchange value of the euro will fall over the next eight months. A profit is assured if the euro is worth less than the DEC futures price. On December 10, as Table 9.11 shows, the DEC futures is 1.2554 and the spot exchange rate is 1.2533. Notice that the belief that the euro would fall in value was incorrect. The December 10 spot price still exceeds the original spot price, as does the price of the DEC futures contract. Nonetheless, the drop in the futures price from 1.2756 to 1.2554 generates a profit of $0.0202 per euro. Since the euro futures contract calls for delivery of €125,000, the total profit is $2,525.

Speculating with spreads

In addition to outright positions, such as the position in the previous example, various spread strategies are also possible. These include intracommodity and intercommodity spreads. Some intercommodity spreads are important, because they allow positions that might not be easily attainable in other markets. The only U.S. futures market for individual foreign exchange contracts is the IMM, in which all prices are stated in terms of dollars. A speculator might believe that the Swiss franc will gain in value relative to the euro but might also be uncertain about the future value of the dollar relative to either of these currencies. It is possible to speculate on the SF/€ exchange rate by trading on the IMM futures market.

Table 9.12 presents market prices on the IMM for June 24 for the dollar per euro and dollar per Swiss franc spot and future exchange rates. The futures prices imply cross-rates between the euro and the Swiss franc as well, as shown in the right column. The structure of rates is peculiar, with the €/SF rate dipping first and then rising. In particular, a speculator finds the implied cross-rate for December to be too low. The speculator believes that the Swiss franc will tend to appreciate against the euro over the coming year. Even though it is impossible to trade the euro against the Swiss franc directly on the IMM, given the available rate quotations, the speculator can use a spread to achieve the desired speculative position.

Since the speculator believes that the value of the euro will fall relative to the Swiss franc, he must also believe that the value of the euro relative to the dollar will perform worse than the value of the Swiss franc relative to the dollar. In other words, even if the euro appreciates against the dollar, his belief about the relative value of the Swiss franc implies that the Swiss franc would appreciate even more against the dollar. Likewise, if the euro falls against the dollar,

Table 9.12 Spot and futures exchange rates, June 24			
	$/€	$/SF	Implied €/SF cross-rate
Spot	1.1467	0.7700	0.6715
SEP	1.1652	0.7761	0.6660
DEC	1.2247	0.7792	0.6363
MAR	1.2390	0.8095	0.6354
JUN	1.2240	0.8574	0.6892

Table 9.13   A speculative cross-rate futures spread

Date	Futures market
June 24	Sell one DEC euro futures contract at 1.2247
	Buy one DEC SF futures contract at 0.7792
December 11	Buy one DEC euro futures contract at 1.1628
	Sell one DEC SF futures contract at 0.7523

Futures trading results:

	Euro	SF
Sold	1.2247	0.7523
Bought	−1.1628	−0.7792
	$0.0619	$0.0269
× 125,000	= $7,737.5	= −$3,362.5
	Total profit: $4,375	

the speculator would believe that the Swiss franc would either gain or not fall as much as the euro. It is important to realize that the speculator need not have any belief regarding the performance of the dollar relative to either of the European currencies. He is merely going to trade through the dollar to establish a position in the €/SF exchange rate.

Table 9.13 shows the transactions necessary to exploit the belief that the December cross-rate is too low. If the speculator is correct, the euro will fall relative to the Swiss franc. Therefore, he sells one DEC euro contract at 1.2247 and buys one DEC Swiss franc contract at 0.7792. This spread is equivalent to speculating that the implied cross-rate of 0.6363 is too low, or that it will require more than €0.6363 to buy one Swiss franc by December. By December 11, the two contracts are approaching expiration, and the speculator offsets both contracts. He buys the DEC euro contract at 1.1628 and sells the SF contract at 0.7523. This generates a profit of $0.0619 per euro and a loss of $0.0269 per Swiss franc. Both contracts are written for 125,000 units of the foreign currency, so the net profit on the spread transaction is $4,375.

As a final example of currency speculation, consider the spot and futures prices for the British pound in Table 9.14. A speculator observes these relatively constant prices, but believes that the British economy is even worse than generally appreciated. Specifically, she anticipates that the British inflation rate will exceed the U.S. rate. Therefore, the trader expects the pound to fall relative to the dollar. One easy way to act on this belief is to sell a distant futures contract, but this position trader is very risk averse, and she decides to trade a spread instead of an outright position. She believes that the equal prices for the DEC and MAR contracts will not be

Table 9.14   Spot and futures prices, August 12

	$/BP
Spot	1.4485
SEP	1.4480
DEC	1.4460
MAR	1.4460
JUN	1.4470

Table 9.15   Time spread speculation in the British pound

Date	Futures market
August 12	Buy one DEC BP futures contract at 1.4460
	Sell one MAR BP futures contract at 1.4460
December 5	Sell one DEC BP futures contract at 1.4313
	Buy one MAR BP futures contract at 1.4253

	December	March
Sold	1.4313	1.4460
Bought	−1.4460	−1.4253
	−$0.0147	$0.0207
× 62,500	= −$918.75	+$1,293.75
	Total profit: $375	

sustained, so she trades as shown in Table 9.15, selling what she believes to be the relatively overpriced MAR contract and buying the relatively underpriced DEC contract. By December, the speculator's expectations have been realized and the pound has fallen relative to the dollar, with the more distant futures contract falling even more. The speculator then closes her position on December 5 and realizes a total profit of $375, as Table 9.15 shows. As a result of her conservatism, the profit is only $375. Had the trader taken an outright position by selling the MAR contract, the profit would have been $1,293.75. In these examples of successful speculations, it must be recognized that the speculator pits his or her knowledge against the collective opinion of the entire market, as that opinion is expressed in market prices.

Hedging with foreign exchange futures

Many firms, and some individuals, find themselves exposed to foreign exchange risk. Importers and exporters, for example, often need to make commitments to buy or sell goods for delivery at some future time, with the payment to be made in a foreign currency. Likewise, multinational firms operating foreign subsidiaries receive payments from their subsidiaries that may be denominated in a foreign currency. A wealthy individual may plan an extended trip abroad and may be concerned about the chance that the price of a particular foreign currency might rise unexpectedly. All of these different parties are potential candidates for hedging unwanted currency risk by using the foreign exchange futures market.

If a trader faces the actual exchange of one currency for another, the risk is called **transaction exposure**, because the trader will transact in the market to exchange one currency for another. Firms often face **translation exposure**, the need to restate one currency in terms of another. For example, a firm may have a foreign subsidiary that earns profits in a foreign currency. However, the parent company prepares its accounting statements in the domestic currency. For accounting purposes, the firm must translate the foreign earnings into the domestic currency. While this procedure does not involve an actual transaction in the foreign exchange market, the reported earnings of the firm expressed in the domestic currency can be volatile due to the uncertain exchange rate at which the subsidiary's foreign earnings will be translated into the domestic currency. In the examples that follow, we consider hedges of both transaction and translation exposure.

Table 9.16   Swiss exchange rates, January 12

	$/SF
Spot	0.4935
MAR	0.5034
JUN	0.5134
SEP	0.5237
DEC	0.5342

Table 9.17   Moncrief's Swiss franc hedge

	Cash market	Futures market
January 12	Moncrief plans to take a six-month vacation in Switzerland, to begin in June; the trip will cost about SF 250,000	Moncrief buys two JUN SF futures contracts at 0.5134 $/SF for a total cost of $128,350
June 6	The $/SF spot rate is now 0.5211, giving a dollar cost of $130,275 for SF 250,000	Moncrief delivers $128,350 and collects SF 250,000
	Savings on the hedge = $130,275 − 128,350 = $1,925	

Hedging transaction exposure

The simplest kind of example arises in the case of someone like John Moncrief, who is planning a six-month trip to Switzerland. Moncrief plans to spend a considerable sum during this trip, enough to make it worthwhile to attend to exchange rates, shown in Table 9.16. With the more distant rates lying above nearby rates, Moncrief fears that spot rates may rise even higher, so he decides to lock in the existing rates by buying Swiss franc futures. Because he plans to depart for Switzerland in June, he buys two JUN SF futures contracts at the current price of 0.5134. He anticipates that SF 250,000 will be enough to cover his six-month stay, as Table 9.17 shows. By June 6, Moncrief's fears have been realized, and the spot rate for the SF is 0.5211. Consequently, he delivers $128,350 and collects SF 250,000. Had he waited and transacted in the spot market on June 6, the SF 250,000 would have cost $130,275. Hedging his foreign exchange risk, Moncrief has saved $1,925, which is enough to finance a few extra days in Switzerland.

In this example, Moncrief had a preexisting risk in the foreign exchange market, since it was already determined that he would acquire the Swiss francs. By trading futures, he guaranteed a price of $0.5134 per Swiss franc. Of course, the futures market can be used for purposes that are even more serious than reducing the risk surrounding Moncrief's Swiss vacation.

Hedging import/export transactions

Consider a small import/export firm that is negotiating a large purchase of Japanese watches from a firm in Japan. The Japanese firm, being a very tough negotiator, has demanded that pay-

Table 9.18 $/yen foreign exchange rates, April 11

	$/¥
Spot	0.004173
JUN futures	0.004200
SEP futures	0.004237
DEC futures	0.004265

ment be made in yen upon delivery of the watches. (If the contract had called for payment in dollars, rather than yen, the Japanese firm would bear the exchange risk.) Delivery will take place in seven months, but the price of the watches is agreed today to be ¥2,850 per watch for 15,000 watches. This means that the purchaser will have to pay ¥42.75 million in about seven months. Table 9.18 shows the current exchange rates on April 11. With the current spot rate of 0.004173 dollars per yen, the purchase price for the 15,000 watches would be $178,396. If the futures prices on April 11 are treated as a forecast of future exchange rates, it seems that the dollar is expected to lose ground against the yen. With the DEC futures trading at 0.004265, the actual dollar cost might be closer to $182,329. If delivery and payment are to occur in December, the importer might reasonably estimate the actual dollar outlay to be about $182,000 instead of $178,000.

To avoid any worsening of his exchange position, the importer decides to hedge the transaction by trading foreign exchange futures. Delivery is expected in November, so the importer decides to trade the DEC futures. By selecting this expiration, the hedger avoids having to roll over a nearby contract, thereby reducing transaction costs. Also, the DEC contract has the advantage of being the first contract to mature after the hedge horizon, so the DEC futures exchange rate should be close to the spot exchange rate prevailing in November when the yen are needed.

The importer's next difficulty stems from the fact that the futures contract is written for ¥12.5 million. If he trades three contracts, his transaction will be for ¥37.5 million. If he trades four

Table 9.19   The importer's hedge

Date	Cash market	Futures market
April 11	The importer anticipates a need for ¥42.75 million in November, the current value of which is $178,396, and which has an expected value in November of $182,329	The importer buys three DEC yen futures contracts at 0.004265 for a total commitment of $159,938
November 1	Receives watches; buys ¥42.75 million at the spot market rate of 0.004273 for a total of $182.671	Sells three DEC yen futures contracts at 0.004270 for a total value of $160,125

	Spot market results:
	Anticipated cost $182,329
	– Actual cost −182.671
	                                      −$342
	            Net loss: −$155
		Futures market results:
		Profit = $187

contracts, however, he would be trading ¥50 million, when he really only needs coverage for ¥42.75 million. No matter which way he trades, the importer will be left with some unhedged exchange risk. Finally, he decides to trade three contracts. Table 9.19 shows his transactions. On April 11, he anticipates that he will need ¥42.75 million, with a current dollar value of $178,396 and an expected future value of $182,329, where the expected future worth of the yen is measured by the DEC futures price. This expected future price is the most relevant price for measuring the success of the hedge. In the futures market, the importer buys three DEC yen contracts at 0.004265 dollars per yen.

On November 18, the watches arrive, and the importer purchases the yen on the spot market at 0.004273. Relative to his anticipated cost of yen, he pays $342 more than expected. Having acquired the yen, the importer offsets his futures position. Since the futures has moved only 0.000005, the futures profit is only $187. This gives a total loss on the entire transaction of $155. Had there been no hedge, the loss would have been the full change of the price in the cash market, or $342. This hedge was only partially effective for two reasons. First, the futures price did not move as much as the cash price. The cash price changed by 0.000008 dollars per yen, but the futures price changed by only 0.000005 dollars per yen. Second, the importer was not able to fully hedge his position, due to the fact that his needs fell between two contract amounts. Since he needed ¥42.75 million and only traded futures for ¥37.5 million, he was left with an unhedged exposure of ¥5.25 million.

Hedging translation exposure

Many corporations in international business have subsidiaries that earn revenue in foreign currencies and remit their profits to a U.S. parent company. The U.S. parent reports its income in dollars, so the parent's reported earnings fluctuate with the exchange rate between the dollar and the currency of the foreign country in which the subsidiary operates. This necessity to restate foreign currency earnings in the domestic currency is translation exposure. For many firms, fluctuating earnings are an anathema. To avoid variability in earnings stemming from exchange rate fluctuations, firms can hedge with foreign exchange futures.

Table 9.20 shows euro exchange rates for January 2 and December 15. Faced with these exchange rates is the Schropp Trading Company of Neckarsulm, a subsidiary of an American firm. Schropp Trading expects to earn €12.8 million this year and plans to remit those funds to its American parent. With the DEC futures trading at 1.2533 dollars per euro on January 2, the expected dollar value of those earnings is $16,042,240. If the euro falls, however, the actual dollar contribution to the earnings of the parent will be lower.

The firm can either hedge or leave unhedged the value of the earnings in euros, as Table 9.21 shows. With the rates in Table 9.20, the €12.8 million will be worth only $15,302,400 on December 15. This shortfall could have been avoided by selling the expected earnings in euros in the futures market in January at the DEC futures price of 1.2533. Table 9.21 shows this possibility. With a contract size of €125,000, the firm could have sold 103 contracts at the January

Table 9.20   Exchange rates for the euro

	January 2	December 15
Spot	1.2598	1.1955
DEC futures	1.2533	1.1955

Table 9.21 The Schropp Trading Company of Neckarsulm		

January 2

Expected earnings in Germany for the year		€12.8 million
Anticipated value in U.S. dollars (computed @ 1.2533 $/€)		$16,042,240

Schropp Trading Company's contribution to its parent's income

	Unhedged	*Hedged*
Contribution to parent's income in U.S. dollars from €12.83 million earnings (assumes spot rate of 1.1955)	$15,302,400	$15,302,400
Futures profit or loss (closed at the spot rate of 1.1955)	0	$774,175
Total	$15,302,400	$16,046,575

2 price. This strategy would have generated a futures profit of $774,175 (103 contracts × €125,000 × $0.0578 profit per euro). This futures profit would have almost exactly offset the loss in the value of the euro, and Schropp Trading could successfully make its needed contribution to the American parent by remitting $16,046,575.

Conclusion

This chapter began by exploring the foreign exchange spot and forward markets. Of all goods with futures markets, the foreign exchange market is unique in the strength of the forward market. In fact, the forward market is much larger than the futures market. Nonetheless, as we discussed, forward prices and futures prices for foreign exchange are virtually identical.

Because foreign exchange rates represent the price of one unit of money in terms of another unit of money, every foreign exchange rate is clearly a relative price. Because of this unique character of foreign exchange markets, we considered the determinants of foreign exchange rates, such as the balance of payments. With modern money being a creation of governments, government intervention in the foreign exchange market is more dominant than in most other markets. Governments attempt to establish exchange rate systems that either fix the value of a currency in terms of another currency or allow the value of currencies to float. Even when the value of a currency is allowed to float, governments often intervene to manage the value of their currency.

As we have seen for all markets, no-arbitrage conditions constrain foreign exchange rates. One of the most famous of these relationships is the IRP theorem. As we have discussed in detail, the IRP theorem is just the cost-of-carry model for foreign exchange. Thus, foreign exchange pricing principles match the concepts that we have developed for other markets.

Compared to many other markets, there have been a number of studies of the forecasting accuracy of futures and forward exchange rates. These studies ask whether the futures price is a good forecast of the

spot price that will prevail at the futures expiration. In general, most of these studies find significant errors or biases in the futures-based forecast. However, compared with most professional forecasting services, the futures price still provides a superior forecast of future spot prices.

The evidence on the efficiency of the foreign exchange market is probably more negative than the evidence for any of the other markets we have considered. Most studies seem to agree in finding significant departures from efficiency. These range from violations of parity conditions to finding successful speculative strategies. The reason for this apparent inefficiency is unclear, but several studies point to central bank intervention as a possible explanation: Central banks enter the market to pursue policy objectives, thereby providing speculators with profit opportunities. Whether this tentative explanation can be sustained is not totally clear.

As with all futures markets, the foreign currency futures market has numerous hedging applications. We showed how to use foreign currency futures to hedge risk for importers and exporters. In addition, we considered the problems of transaction and translation exposure. In transaction exposure, a trader actually faces the exchange of one currency for another and wishes to hedge the future commitment of funds. In translation exposure, funds received in one currency will be restated for accounting purposes in another currency. Because it concerns only accounting, translation exposure need not require the actual exchange of one currency for another. Nonetheless, firms can hedge translation exposure to avoid the volatility of reported earnings in the home currency.

Exercises

1 The current spot exchange rate for the dollar against the Japanese yen is ¥146 per dollar. What is the corresponding U.S. dollar value of ¥1?

2 You hold the current editions of *The Wall Street Journal* and its U.K. equivalent, the *Financial Times*. In *The Wall Street Journal*, you see that the dollar per British pound 90-day forward exchange rate is $2.00 per pound. In the *Financial Times*, the 90-day dollar per pound rate is £0.45 per U.S. dollar. Explain how you would trade to take advantage of these rates, assuming perfect markets.

3 In Exercise 2, we assumed that markets are perfect. What are some practical impediments that might frustrate your arbitrage transactions in Exercise 2?

4 In *The Wall Street Journal*, you see that the spot value of the euro is $1.25 and that the Swiss franc is worth $0.72. What rate of exchange do these values imply for the Swiss franc and the euro? Express the value in terms of euros per Swiss franc.

5 Explain the difference between a pegged exchange rate system and a managed float.

6 Explain why covered interest arbitrage is just like our familiar cash-and-carry transactions from Chapter 3.

7 For covered interest arbitrage, what is the cost of carry? Explain carefully.

8 The spot value of the euro is $1.25, and the 90-day forward rate is $1.20. If the U.S. dollar interest factor to cover this period is 2 percent, what is the EMU rate? What is the cost of carrying a euro forward for this period?

9 The Swiss franc is worth $0.21 in the spot market. The Swiss franc futures that expires in one year trades for $0.22. The U.S. dollar interest rate for this period is 10 percent. What should the Swiss franc interest rate be?

10 Using the data of Exercise 9, explain which country is expected to experience the higher inflation over the next year. If the expected inflation rate in the U.S. is 7 percent, what inflation rate for the Swiss franc does this imply?

11 Using the data of Exercise 9, assume that the Swiss franc interest rate for the year is also 10 percent. Faced with these values, explain how you might transact.

12 Many travelers say that shoes are a big bargain in Italy. How can this be, given the purchasing power parity theorem?

13 For the most part, the price of oil is denominated in dollars. Assume that you are a French firm that expects to import 420,000 barrels of crude oil in six months. What risks do you face in this transaction?

Explain how you could transact to hedge the currency portion of those risks.

14 A financial comptroller for a U.S. firm is reviewing the earnings from a German subsidiary. This subsidiary earns €1 million every year with exactitude, and it reinvests those earnings in its own German operations. This plan will continue. The earnings, however, are translated into U.S. dollars for preparation of the U.S. parent's financial statements. Explain the nature of the foreign exchange risk from the point of view of the U.S. parent. Explain what steps you think the parent should take to hedge the risk that you have identified.

15 Joel Myers works for a large international bank. He has been watching the trading screen on this hot August morning and has been disappointed in the lack of trading activity. He is just about to take a break when a flurry of activity in the Swiss bond and currency markets catches his attention. He quickly pulls up the following quotes:

Spot exchange rate:	$0.1656 per SF
One-month forward:	$0.1659 per SF
Three-month forward:	$0.1665 per SF
Six-month forward:	$0.1673 per SF

T-bill yields (bond equivalent)

One-month:	4.95 percent
Three-month:	5.01 percent
Six-month:	5.11 percent

A Compute the one-month (30-day), three-month (91-day), and six-month (182-day) yields that Joel should expect to see in the Swiss money market.

B Suppose Joel sees that the six-month yield in the Swiss money market is 4 percent. Assuming there are no market frictions, is arbitrage possible? If so, show the arbitrage transactions and compute the profit for a $1 million arbitrage.

16 As the Fall semester starts, David McElroy is making arrangements for Oklahoma State University's (OSU) Summer in London program for the next summer. This is a program in which OSU faculty teaches courses to OSU students at Regents College in London, England. Room and board is £1,500 per participant, to be paid on May 15. The enrollment is capped at 42 people, and OSU always operates at the cap. In the past, the Summer in London program has been burned by adverse movements in exchange rates. This has happened because OSU has borne the exchange rate risk between the dollar-denominated room and board rate quoted to the students and the British pound rate paid to Regents College. David wonders if there is some way that OSU could pass this risk off to someone else.

A Does OSU face translation or transactions exposure?
B What could OSU do to reduce this exchange rate risk?
C David asks a finance professor for advice. The professor pulls up the following $/£ quotes on the £62,500 futures contract:

Delivery	$/£
SEP (this year)	1.6152
DEC (this year)	1.6074
MAR (next year)	1.6002
JUN (next year)	1.5936

What strategy might the professor recommend to reduce OSU's exchange rate exposure? (Make a recommendation.)
D May 15 arrives and the following situation is realized:

Number of participants	42
Dollar room and board rate	$2,400
$/£ exchange rate	$1.65
June futures contract	$1.6451 per pound

Compute OSU's gains and losses in the cash market and the futures market. Was the hedging strategy successful?

17 Viva Soda is an up-and-comer in the highly competitive sports drink market. Viva owns three regional bottling facilities in the U.S. and one Canadian subsidiary that meets the demand for Viva in the Canadian provinces. Great North Bottling, the Canadian subsidiary, accounts for 25 percent of Viva's total sales and net earnings at the present exchange rates. Dave Baker, CFO for Viva, is very

concerned about Viva's translation exposure. Viva will be in the debt refinancing market in one year. Dave is acutely aware of the relationship between the cost of debt and earnings results. Dave's assistant has made the following forecasts of Great North's earnings before taxes for the next four quarters:

Quarter	Great North earnings before taxes
DEC 98	CAN$ 10 million
MAR 99	CAN$ 7.5 million
JUN	CAN$ 8.5 million
SEP	CAN$ 12 million

A What risks does Viva face with regard to its Canadian operations? What could Dave Baker do to hedge the risk?
B Dave's assistant notes the following futures exchange rates for the Canadian dollar:

Delivery	U.S.$/CAN$
DEC 98	0.6603
MAR 99	0.6609
JUN	0.6615
SEP	0.6621

Design a hedge that will solve Dave's problem. Assume that one futures contract is for CAN$ 100,000.
C Assume that the spot prices shown in the following table are realized:

Month	U.S.$/CAN$
DEC 98	0.6271
MAR 99	0.6827
JUN	0.5961
SEP	0.7100

Compute the translated earnings each quarter and the net impact on Viva's results considering the hedging activities.

Notes

1 One such trading room was featured in the film *Rollover*, starring Kris Kristofferson and Jane Fonda. In this story of international financial intrigue and panic, Kristofferson played the brilliant hard-nosed manager of the trading room, who saves the world from financial collapse.

2 Actually, in major foreign exchange centers, such as New York, some traders will make markets in the major cross-rates. For many currencies in many markets, however, a separate quotation for cross-rates is not available.

3 Although maturities of 30, 90, and 180 days are normally listed, forward market transactions may be arranged with different maturities to suit the needs of the customer.

4 For representative studies in this area, see the following articles: L. Hansen and R. Hodrick, "Forward Exchange Rates as Optimal Predictors of Future Spot Rates: An Econometric Analysis," *Journal of Political Economy*, 88:5, 1980, pp. 829–53; R. Hodrick and S. Srivastava, "Foreign Currency Futures," *Journal of International Economics*, 22:1/2, 1987, pp. 1–24; L. Kodres, "Tests of Unbiasedness in Foreign Exchange Futures Markets: The Effects of Price Limits," *The Review of Futures Markets*, 7:1, 1988, pp. 139–66; S. Kohlhagen, "The Forward Rate as an Unbiased Predictor of the Future Spot Rate," *Columbia Journal of World Business*, 14:4, Winter 1979, pp. 77–85.

5 See, for example, R. Levich, "Evaluating the Performance of the Forecasters," in R. Ensor (ed.), *The Management of Foreign Exchange Risk*, 2nd edn, London, Euromoney Publications, 1982, pp. 121–34.

6 See R. Levich, "The Efficiency of Markets for Foreign Exchange: A Review and Extension," in G. Gay and R. Kolb (eds.), *International Finance: Concepts and Issues*, Richmond, VA: Robert F. Dame, 1982, p. 406.

7 Many other empirical tests tend to confirm the conclusion of efficiency reached by Levich, and a number of these are included in the bibliography to his article.

8 For studies of foreign exchange market efficiency, see K. Cavanaugh, "Price Dynamics in Foreign Currency Futures Markets," *Journal of International Money and Finance*, 6:3, 1987, pp. 295–314; and D. Glassman, "The Efficiency of Foreign Exchange Futures Markets in Turbulent and Non-Turbulent Periods," *The Journal of Futures Markets*, 7:3, 1987, pp. 245–67.

10

The Options Market

Overview

As we discussed in Chapter 1, options can be either call options or put options. A **call option** is a financial instrument that gives its owner the right to purchase an underlying good at a specified price for a specified time. A **put option** is a financial instrument that gives its owner the right to sell the underlying good at a specified price for a specified time. This chapter considers the options exchanges and the well-defined options contracts that trade on these exchanges.

In modern options trading, an individual can contact a broker and trade an option on an exchange in a matter of moments. This chapter explains how orders flow from an individual to the exchange, and it shows how the order is executed and confirmed for the trader. At first, the options exchanges only traded options on stocks. Now, exchanges trade options on a wide variety of underlying goods, such as bonds, futures contracts, and foreign currencies. The chapter concludes with a brief consideration of these diverse types of options.

The importance of options goes well beyond the profit-motivated trading that is most visible to the public. Today, sophisticated institutional traders use options to execute extremely complex strategies. For instance, large pension funds and investment banking firms trade options in conjunction with stock and bond portfolios to control risk and capture additional profits. Corporations use options to execute their financing strategies and to hedge unwanted risks that they could not avoid in any other way. Option research has advanced in step with the exploding option market. Scholars have found that there is an option way of thinking that allows many financial decisions to be analyzed using an option framework. Together, these developments constitute an options revolution.

An option example

Consider an option with a share of XYZ stock as the underlying good. Assume that today is March 1 and that XYZ shares trade at $110. The market, we assume, trades a call option to buy a share of XYZ at $100, with this right lasting until August 15 and the price of this option being $15. In this example, the owner of a call must pay $100 to acquire the stock. This $100 price is called the **exercise price**, or **strike price**. The price of the option, or the **option premium**, is $15. The option expires in 5.5 months, which gives 168 days until expiration.

If a trader buys the call option, he pays $15 and receives the right to purchase a share of XYZ stock by paying an additional $100, if he so chooses, by August 15. The seller of the option receives $15, and she promises to sell a share of XYZ for $100 if the owner of the call chooses to buy before August 15. Notice that the price of the option, the option premium, is paid when the option trades. The premium that the seller receives is hers to keep whether or not the owner of the call decides to exercise the option. If the owner of the call exercises his option, he will pay $100 no matter what the current price of XYZ stock may be. If the owner of the option exercises his option, the seller of the option will receive the $100 exercise price when she delivers the stock as she promised.

At the same time, puts will trade on XYZ. Consider a put with a strike price of $100 trading on March 1 that also expires on August 15. Assume that the price of the put is $5. If a trader purchases a put, he pays $5. In exchange, he receives the right to sell a share of XYZ for $100

Table 10.1   The disposition of equity options, 2002

Disposition	Percentage disposition	
	Calls	Puts
Exercise	9.6	24.8
Sale	46.4	45.8
Long expired worthless	45.0	29.4

Source: Chicago Board Options Exchange, *Market Statistics*, 2002, p. 5.
© 2002 Chicago Board Options Exchange. Reprinted by permission
from Chicago Board Options Exchange, Incorporated

at any time until August 15. The seller of the put receives $5, and she promises to buy the share of XYZ for $100 if the owner of the put option chooses to sell before August 15.

In both the put and call examples, the payment by the purchaser is gone forever at the time the option trades. The seller of the option receives the payment and keeps it, whatever the owner of the option decides to do. If the owner of the call exercises his option, then he pays the exercise price as an additional amount and receives a share. Likewise, if the owner of the put exercises his option, then he surrenders the share and receives the exercise price as an additional amount. The owner of the option may choose never to exercise. In that case, the option will expire on August 15. The payment that the seller receives is hers to keep whether or not the owner exercises. If the owner chooses not to exercise, the seller has a profit equal to the premium received and does not have to perform under the terms of the option contract. Table 10.1 shows the disposition of stock options for the year 2002, the last year such statistics were published. It gives a good guide to the frequency with which options are disposed of by exercise, by sale, or by expiring worthless. Most are sold, while many others expire worthless. Although exercise is common, it is the least common means of exiting the market for stock options.

Moneyness

The option concept of *moneyness* is as important as the word is awkward. It refers to the potential profit or loss from the immediate exercise of an option. An option may be **in-the-money**, **out-of-the-money**, or **at-the-money**.

A call option is in-the-money if the stock price exceeds the exercise price. For example, a call option with an exercise price of $100 on a stock trading at $110 is $10 in-the-money. A call option is out-of-the-money if the stock price is less than the exercise price. For example, if the stock is at $110 and the exercise price on a call is $115, the call is $5 out-of-the-money. A call option is at-the-money if the stock price equals (or is very near to) the exercise price.

A put option is in-the-money if the stock price is below the exercise price. As an example, consider a put option with an exercise price of $70 on a stock that is worth $60. The put is $10 in-the-money, because the immediate exercise of the put would give a $10 cash inflow. Similarly, if the put on the same stock had an exercise price of $55, the put would be $5 out-of-the-money. If the put had an exercise price equal to the stock price, the put would be at-the-money. Puts and calls can also be **deep-in-the-money** or **deep-out-of-the-money**, if the cash flows from an immediate exercise would be large in the speaker's judgment.

American and European options

There are two fundamental kinds of options: the American option and the European option. An **American** option permits the owner to exercise at any time before or at expiration. The owner of a **European option** can exercise only at expiration. Thus, the two kinds of options differ because the American option permits early exercise. To this point, we have considered option values only at expiration. If the option is at expiration, American and European options will have the same value. Both can be exercised immediately or be allowed to expire worthless. Prior to expiration, we will see that the two options are conceptually distinct. Further, they may have different values under certain circumstances. In this chapter, and through the remainder of this part of the book on options, we will need to distinguish the principles that apply to each kind of option.

Consider any two options that are just alike, except one is an American option and the other is a European option. By saying that the two options are just alike, we mean that they have the same underlying stock, the same exercise price, and the same time remaining until expiration. The American option gives its owner all the rights and privileges that the owner of the European option possesses. However, the owner of the American option also has the right to exercise the option before expiration if he desires. From these considerations, we can see that the American option must be worth at least as much as the European option.

The owner of an American option can treat it as a European option just by deciding not to exercise until expiration. Therefore, the American option cannot be worth less than the European option. However, the American option can be worth more. The American option will be worth more if it is desirable to exercise earlier. Under certain circumstances, which we will explore later, the right to exercise before expiration can be valuable. In this case, the American option will be worth more than the otherwise identical European option.

In some cases, the right to exercise before expiration will be worthless. For these situations, the American option will have the same value as the European option. In general, the European option is simpler and easier to analyze. In actual markets, however, most options are American options. This is true both in the United States and throughout the world. We should not associate the names *American* and *European* with geographic locations. In the present context, the names simply refer to the time at which holders can exercise these options.

Why trade options?

Today, options trading is more popular than ever before. For the investor, options serve a number of important roles. First, many investors trade options to speculate on the price movements of the underlying stock. Investors could, however, merely trade the stock itself. As we will see, trading the option instead of the underlying stock can offer a number of advantages. Call options are always cheaper than the underlying stock, so it takes less money to trade calls. Generally, but not universally, put options are also cheaper than the underlying goods. In relative terms, the option price is more volatile than the price of the underlying stock, so investors can get more price action per dollar of investment by investing in options instead of investing in the stock itself.

Options are extremely popular among sophisticated investors who hold large stock portfolios. Accordingly, institutional investors, such as mutual funds and pension funds, are prime users of the options market. By trading options in conjunction with their stock portfolios, investors can carefully adjust the risk and return characteristics of their entire investment. As we will see, a sophisticated trader can use options to increase or decrease the risk of an existing stock portfolio. For example, it is possible to combine a risky stock and a risky option to form a riskless combined position that performs like a risk-free bond.[1]

Many investors prefer to trade options rather than stocks in order to save transaction costs, to avoid tax exposure, and to avoid stock market restrictions.[2] We have already mentioned that some investors trade options to achieve the same risk exposure with less capital. In many instances, traders can use options to take a particular risk position and pay lower transaction costs than stocks would require. Likewise, specific provisions of the tax code may favor option trading over trading the underlying stock. If different traders face different tax schedules, one may find advantage in buying options and another may find advantage in selling options, relative to trading stocks. Finally, the stock and option markets have their own institutional rules. Differences in these rules may stimulate option trading. For example, selling stock short is highly restricted.[3] By trading in the option market, it is possible to replicate a short sale of stock and to avoid some stock market restrictions.[4]

The option contract

One of the major reasons for the success of options exchanges is that they offer standardized contracts. In a financial market, traders want to be able to trade a good quickly and at a fair price. They can do this if the market is **liquid**. A liquid market provides an efficient and cost-effective trading mechanism with a high volume of trading, and standardizing the options contract has helped promote liquidity. The standardized contract has a specific size and expiration date. Trading on the exchange occurs at certain well-publicized times, so traders know when they will be able to find other traders in the marketplace. The exchange standardizes the exercise prices at which options will trade. With fewer exercise prices, there will be more trading available at a given exercise price. This too promotes liquidity.

Each option contract is for 100 shares of the underlying stock. Exercise prices are specified at intervals of $10, $5, or $2.50, depending on the share price. For example, XYZ trades in the $100 range, and XYZ options have exercise prices spaced at $5 intervals. Every option has a specified expiration month. The option expires on the Saturday after the third Friday in the exercise month. Trading in the option ceases on the third Friday, but the owner may exercise the option on the final Saturday.

The options marketplace

In this section, we consider the most important facets of the options market in the United States. We begin by considering the exchanges where options trade. We then consider an extended example to see how to read option prices as they appear in *The Wall Street Journal*. We conclude this section by analyzing the market activity in the different types of options that are traded on the various exchanges.

Reading option prices

Table 10.2 shows typical price quotations for options on a common stock from a U.S. newspaper. Prices are for January 26 for trading options on the stock of XYZ Corporation. On that day, XYZ closed at $96^{1}/_{8}$ per share. The table shows listings for XYZ options with strike prices of $90, $95, $100, and $105. It would not be unusual for other strike prices to be represented as well. Options expire in February, March, and April of the same year, and the table shows option prices for both puts and calls. An "r" indicates that the option was not traded on the day for which prices are reported, while an "s" shows that the specific option is not listed for trading.[5]

Table 10.2 Option price quotations

XYZ	Strike price	Calls			Puts		
$96^7/_8$		FEB	MAR	APR	FEB	MAR	APR
	$90	$6^7/_8$	s	$9^1/_8$	$^5/_8$	s	$1^3/_8$
	95	$2^7/_8$	$4^3/_8$	$5^1/_2$	$1^5/_8$	$2^5/_8$	$3^1/_2$
	100	$^7/_8$	$1^7/_8$	$3^1/_8$	$4^5/_8$	r	$6^1/_4$
	105	$^1/_4$	$^{13}/_{16}$	$1^5/_8$	$9^1/_2$	r	11

As an example, consider the call option with a strike price of $100 that expires in March. This option has a price of 1^7/_8$, or $1.875. This is the price of the call for a single share. However, each option contract is written for 100 shares. Therefore, to purchase this option, the buyer would pay $187.50 for one contract. Owning this call option would give the buyer the right to purchase 100 shares of XYZ at $100 per share until the option expires in March.

We can learn much from a careful consideration of the price relationships revealed in the table. First, notice that option prices are generally higher the longer the time is until the option expires. This is true for both calls and puts. Other things being equal, the longer one has the option to buy or sell, the better. Thus, we expect options with longer terms to expiration to be worth more. Second, for a call, the lower the strike price, the more the call option is worth. For a call, the strike price is the amount the call holder must pay to secure the stock. The lower the amount one must pay, the better; therefore, the lower the exercise price, the more the call is worth. Third, for a put option, the higher the strike price, the more the put is worth. For a put, the strike price is the value the put holder receives when he exercises his option to sell the put. Therefore, the more the put entitles its owner to receive, the greater is the value of the put. A moment's reflection shows that these simple relationships make sense. The following chapters in this part of the book explore these and similar relationships in detail.

Option exchanges

Trading options undoubtedly grew up with the development of financial markets. In the nineteenth century, investors traded options in an informal market. However, the market was subject to considerable corruption. For example, some sellers of options would refuse to perform as obligated. In the twentieth century, the United States developed a more orderly market called the Put and Call Broker and Dealers Association. Member firms acted to bring buyers and sellers of options together. However, this was an over-the-counter market. The market had no central exchange floor, and standardization of option contract terms was not complete. If an investor wanted to buy or sell an option, he or she phoned one of the put and call dealers who advertised in the financial press and negotiated a contract. Because the market was highly customized, no secondary market existed. This meant that an investor wanting to terminate an option position would have to negotiate with the dealer who dealt the original contract. The lack of an exchange and imperfect standardization of the contracts kept this option market from flourishing.

In 1973, the Chicago Board of Trade, a large futures exchange, created the Chicago Board Options Exchange (CBOE). The CBOE is an organized options exchange that trades highly standardized option contracts. It opened on April 26, 1973, to trade calls; put trading began in 1977. By 1978, more than 100,000 options were being traded on an average day. By 2006, worldwide volume for options on individual equities and options on stock indexes averaged over 20 million contracts per day across more than 50 exchanges.

Trading of options on organized exchanges in the United States embraces a number of different underlying instruments. First among these is the stock option—an option on an individual share of common stock issued by a corporation. Although we focus most closely on this type of option for the majority of our discussion of options, there are other important classes of options with very different underlying instruments. Options trade on various financial indexes. These indexes can be indexes to measure the performance of groups of stocks, or precious metals, or any other good for which an index can be constructed as a measure of value. Options also trade on foreign currencies. For these foreign currency options, the underlying good is a unit of a foreign currency, such as the Japanese yen, and traders buy and sell call and put options on the yen, as well as on other currencies. Another major type of underlying good is a futures contract. For an option on futures, also known as futures options, the underlying good is a position in a futures contract. As we will see, this is an important class of options. Futures contracts are written on a wide variety of goods, such as agricultural products, precious metals, petroleum products, stock indexes, foreign currency, and debt instruments. Therefore, futures options by themselves embrace a tremendous diversity of goods.

Table 10.3 is divided into two panels: panel 1 lists the option exchanges in the United States, while panel 2 lists a sample of some of the most important non-U.S. option exchanges. The right-hand column of Table 10.3 indicates the kinds of options traded. For the United States, the CBOE was founded as an options exchange and trades options exclusively. The Philadelphia, American, and Pacific exchanges were originally exclusively stock exchanges and have expanded into option trading. The remaining U.S. exchanges are futures exchanges that mainly trade options on the futures listed on their own exchange. The non-U.S. exchanges were founded much later generally and tend to be organized more as purely derivatives exchanges.

Exchange diversity and market statistics

In this section, we consider the options market in more detail, focusing on the United States. Table 10.4 shows the volume of all exchange-traded options in the United States by the type of option—stock option, index option, foreign currency option, and options on futures.

Stock options

In the United States, options on individual stocks trade on the ISE, the CBOE, and four exchanges. These exchanges trade all options on individual stocks in the United States, but they also trade options on other instruments, as indicated in Table 10.3, panel 1.

Table 10.5 shows the relative importance of these exchanges—the Chicago Board Options Exchange (CBOE), the International Securities Exchange (ISE), the American Stock Exchange (AMEX), the Philadelphia Stock Exchange (PHLX), the Pacific Exchange (PCX), and the Boston Options Exchange (BOX)—in option trading of all kinds. The ISE and CBOE clearly dominate the trading volume. Table 10.6 shows the distribution of trading volume in stock options among the five exchanges. Again, the ISE and CBOE dominate.

Figure 10.1 shows a sample of the price quotations for options on individual stocks that appear each day in *The Wall Street Journal*. The first column lists the identifier for the stock and shows the closing stock price for the shares immediately beneath the identifier. The next two columns of data show the exercise price and the month in which the option expires. The option will expire on a specific date in the expiration month. For the call and the put separately, the quotations show the volume and the final price for the option. Options trade on hundreds of individual stocks.

Table 10.3   Principal option exchanges

Exchange	Key instruments on which options trade
Panel 1: option exchanges in the United States	
International Securities Exchange (ISE)	Individual stocks, stock indexes
Chicago Board Options Exchange (CBOE)	Individual stocks, stock indexes, Treasury securities
Philadelphia Stock Exchange (PHLX)	Individual stocks, stock indexes, currencies, precious metal index
American Stock Exchange (AMEX)	Individual stocks, stock indexes
Pacific Exchange (PCX)	Individual stocks, stock indexes
Boston Options Exchange (BOX)	Individual stocks
Chicago Board of Trade (CBOT)	Full range of futures traded on the CBOT: futures on agricultural goods, debt instruments, and stock indexes
Chicago Mercantile Exchange (CME)	Full range of futures traded on CME: futures on agricultural goods, stock indexes, debt instruments, and currencies
New York Board of Trade (NYBT)	Full range of futures traded on NYBT: futures on agricultural goods, currencies, debt instruments and stock indexes
Kansas City Board of Trade (KCBT)	Futures traded on KCBT: futures on agricultural goods
Minneapolis Grain Exchange (MGE)	Futures traded on MGE: futures on agricultural futures
New York Mercantile Exchange (NYME)	Full range of futures traded on NYME: Futures on agricultural goods, energy, precious and industrial metals
Panel 2: key option exchanges outside the United States	
Eurex—Germany and Switzerland	Individual stocks, stock index futures, interest rate futures
Euronext—Netherlands, Belgium, France, Portugal, and the United Kingdom	Individual stocks, stock indexes, and agricultural products
Euronext.liffe—the United Kingdom	Individual stocks, and a full range of futures traded on Euronext.liffe: futures on stock indexes, interest rates, and agricultural goods
ICE Futures—the United Kingdom	Full range of futures traded on ICE: futures on energy products

Index options

Table 10.7 shows the distribution of trading in index options by exchange. The lead of the CBOE is overwhelming. The most successful index options have stock indexes as the underlying good. Particularly important are options on the Dow Jones Industrial Average, the S&P 500®, and various NASDAQ indexes. Options on more narrow stock indexes are also successful. The Eurex and Euronext are particularly successful, with options on various European stock indexes. Figure 10.2 shows a sample of the quotations for index options from *The Wall Street Journal*. It also indicates the wide variety of indexes that underlie various options. Notice that these

Table 10.4   Listed option volume in the United States by type of option

Type of option	2005 Volume	
	Contracts (millions)	Percentage
Stock options	1,369.048	73.12
Options on futures	367.970	19.65
Index options	135.104	7.22
Foreign currency options	0.160	0.01
Total	1,872.282	100.00

Source: Compiled from the Options Clearing Corporation's *Daily Contract Volume Report*, found at www.theocc.com, and the Futures Industry Association's report entitled *Volume of Futures and Options Trading on U.S. Futures Exchanges, 1968–2005*

Table 10.5   Total option volume by exchange, 2005

Exchange	Contract volume (millions)	Percentage
Chicago Board Options Exchange	468.35	31.14
International Securities Exchange	448.70	29.83
American Stock Exchange	201.63	13.41
Philadelphia Stock Exchange	162.44	10.80
Pacific Exchange	144.78	9.63
Boston Options Exchange	78.20	5.20
Total	1,504.09	100.00

Source: The Options Clearing Corporation. © The Options Clearing Corporation. Reprinted by permission from the Options Clearing Corporation

Table 10.6   Equity option volume by exchange, 2005

Exchange	Contract volume (millions)	Percentage
International Securities Exchange	444.23	32.45
Chicago Board Options Exchange	352.53	25.75
American Stock Exchange	193.09	14.10
Philadelphia Stock Exchange	156.22	11.41
Pacific Exchange	144.78	10.58
Boston Options Exchange	78.20	5.71
Total	1,369.05	100.00

Source: The Options Clearing Corporation. © The Options Clearing Corporation. Reprinted by permission from the Options Clearing Corporation

include stock indexes for foreign stock markets. The quotations show the expiration month, the exercise price, whether the option is a call or a put, the volume, the closing price, the change since the previous day's close, and the open interest.

Figure 10.1 Price quotations for stock options from *Barron's*

Volume figures reflect Monday through Friday. Open interest figures as of close of business Thursday. Our list includes only the week's 500 most actively traded equity options and 50 most active XC-Composite p.Put.

Equity Options

Company / Exch Close	Strike Price	Sales Vol	Open Int	Week's High	Week's Low	Last Price	Net Chg

(Three-panel tabular listing of equity option quotations; representative rows below.)

Panel 1

ABB Ltd Jun 12.50 12121630 3054 1.00 0.60 0.95 + 0.25
AK Steel Sep 15.00 11327 11475 2.10 1.40 1.85 + 0.55
AMR May 25.00p 15102 17354 1.80 1.20 1.50 + 0.05
27.05 Apr 30.00 9664 10158 0.65 0.30 0.65 + 0.10
27.05 Aug 30.00 12123070 5160 2.55 1.90 2.30 + 0.05
Aft Tech Apr 15.00 12496 10856 2.70 0.60 2.20 + 1.50
17.18 Apr 17.50 21824 14849 0.75 0.05 0.45 + 0.35
AbtLab May 42.50 12121780 8899 2.35 1.20 1.30 − 0.80
42.47 May 45.00 12121694 6616 1.10 0.35 0.35 − 0.45
AberFitch Apr 50.00 12121332 328 9.30 5.40 9.30 + 2.90
AdobeS Apr 35.00p 10261 9187 0.85 0.40 0.80 + 0.35
34.95 Oct 40.00 24242607 349 2.25 1.75 1.75 − 0.35
AMD Apr 27.50p 12121506 3410 0.25 0.10 0.25 + 0.10
33.16 Apr 27.50 12121708 582 7.50 6.50 6.50
33.16 Apr 32.50p 10230 10001 1.60 0.65 1.45 + 0.75
33.16 Apr 35.00 24994 28540 2.65 1.05 1.15 − 1.55
33.16 Apr 37.50 13806 25049 1.45 0.50 0.60 − 0.75
33.16 May 37.50 12404 6789 2.15 1.00 1.15 − 0.15
33.16 Apr 37.50p 12121607 498 5.20 3.70 5.20 + 1.90
33.16 Apr 40.00 8569 26297 0.70 0.25 0.25 − 0.45
Aetna Apr 47.50 12121995 3360 3.40 2.30 2.30 − 1.10
49.14 Apr 50.00p 12122354 5777 1.75 0.75 1.55 + 0.45
Agilent May 32.50 12121208 8.39 5.38 4.40 5.38 + 0.98
AirPd Apr 65.00 12121251 660 2.60 1.45 2.60 + 0.80
Alcan May 45.00 12121510 301 3.80 2.30 2.85 + 0.25
Alcoa May 32.50p 12121519 311 2.71 1.75 1.75 − 1.85
50.56 Jul 35.00 10552 16425 0.50 0.35 0.40 + 0.05
30.56 Oct 35.00p 12121265 131 5.60 4.90 4.90
Alcon Aug 105.00p 12121253 273 8.00 7.20 7.50 + 2.50
Allergan May 110.00 12121242 19 5.70 3.40 3.70
Altria Apr 65.00 12038 37786 0.50 0.25 0.45 + 0.15
70.86 Jun 65.00p 8406 51635 1.75 0.30 0.70
70.86 Apr 70.00p 17829 59641 1.55 0.85 1.45 + 0.45
70.86 May 70.00p 8313 6126 2.50 1.65 2.45 + 0.85
70.86 Apr 75.00 37530 98771 1.25 0.55 0.60 − 0.55
70.86 Jun 80.00 9261 101795 0.90 0.55 0.55 − 0.30
Amazon Apr 27.50 12121238 53 9.40 8.10 9.40
36.53 Jul 30.00p 12123745 4329 0.70 0.50 0.50 − 0.20
36.53 Apr 32.50p 12121296 6495 0.20 0.05 0.10 − 0.10
36.53 May 32.50 12121313 429 0.95 0.55 0.55 − 0.25
36.53 Jul 32.50p 12121293 526 1.30 1.00 1.00 − 0.30
36.53 May 35.00p 12123045 4485 1.80 1.18 1.20 − 0.70
36.53 Apr 40.00p 12121468 12688 4.80 3.30 3.50 − 1.02
A Hess Apr 130.00p 12122254 1785 0.55 0.30 0.45
142.40 May 130.00p 12121674 1684 2.20 1.65 2.05 − 0.55
142.40 Apr 140.00p 12121616 1373 3.40 1.95 2.85
142.40 May 140.00p 12121990 5391 5.70 4.20 5.60 + 0.10
AEP May 30.00p 12121214 1 0.15 0.05 0.15
AmIntGp Apr 60.00p 24243298 6850 7.60 6.40 7.10 − 0.05
66.09 May 65.00 24243224 21228 3.30 2.15 2.45 − 1.05
66.09 Nov 65.00p 12121474 1623 2.70 2.25 2.45 + 0.05
66.09 Apr 70.00p 12122880 14322 0.20 0.05 0.05 − 0.15
66.09 Apr 75.00p 12121251 4 8.80 7.90 8.30
66.09 May 75.00 24243429 9953 0.15 0.05 0.05
66.09 Aug 75.00p 12121336 4712 0.60 0.40 0.45 − 0.20
Amererd Apr 25.00 12121245 286 6.50 6.00 6.40 + 0.40
Amgen Apr 72.50 12131140 5612 2.70 1.55 2.00 − 0.40
72.75 Jul 72.50 12121303 119 4.80 3.90 4.40 − 0.20
72.75 Apr 75.00 10716 25812 1.40 0.65 0.95 − 0.20
Apache Apr 70.00p 12121580 4185 5.33 3.34 4.70
142.40 May 32.50 10502 6272 4.60 2.30 4.20 + 1.55
62.72 Apr 37.50 12121417 849 25.60 21.20 25.60 + 2.90
62.72 Apr 50.00 11937 27515 0.55 0.05 0.15 − 0.15
62.72 Apr 55.00 11786 15001 9.10 4.30 8.51 + 2.31
62.72 May 55.00p 42857 46573 1.90 0.40 0.55 − 0.55
62.72 Jul 55.00p 9158 9950 2.55 0.85 1.00 − 0.80
62.72 Jul 55.00 11775 38565 3.90 2.00 2.15 − 1.05
62.72 Apr 57.50 8764 3317 7.00 3.31 6.50
62.72 Apr 57.50p 23131 9205 5.00 0.85 1.00
62.72 Apr 60.00 60126 32671 5.30 2.25 4.70 + 1.50
62.72 May 60.00 65892 53060 4.40 1.50 1.75 − 1.25
62.72 Jun 60.00 14934 7352 6.10 3.10 5.60 + 1.40
62.72 Jul 60.00p 8468 39589 6.30 3.70 3.80 − 1.60
62.72 Apr 60.00p 36529 21920 3.70 1.45 3.20 + 1.55
62.72 May 62.50 47021 35265 6.10 2.40 2.75 − 1.65
62.72 Apr 65.00 68014 54655 2.40 0.90 1.25 + 0.80
62.72 Apr 65.00p 14671 33554 8.00 3.70 4.07 − 2.13
62.72 May 65.00p 9564 8324 3.40 1.60 3.07 + 0.87
62.72 Jun 65.00 23551 26915 1.50 0.50 1.25 + 0.45
62.72 Apr 70.00 18570 35272 0.90 0.25 0.70 + 0.20
62.72 Apr 70.00p 12457 26700 0.50 0.15 0.40 + 0.10
62.72 May 75.00 12123 26983 0.25 0.10 0.15 − 0.10
62.72 Apr 80.00p 10684 3226 22.40 17.00 17.30 − 3.00
AppldMat Apr 12121 2630 2875 1.85 1.39 1.55 − 0.25
17.51 Oct 17.00p 24242535 555 1.09 0.92 1.05 + 0.10
17.51 Apr 17.50 9527 23361 0.55 0.24 0.30 − 0.15
17.51 May 18.00 24242551 390 1.68 1.40 1.56 − 0.09
17.51 May 20.00p 12121318 142 2.47 2.28 2.28
ArchCoal Oct 50.00p 12121262 264 1.80 1.55 1.85 − 0.55
75.94 Oct 60.00p 12121308 149 2.25 1.85 1.85 − 0.55
Autodesk Jul 35.00 8112 225 0.80 2.05 + 0.90
38.52 Jul 37.50p 12121390 453 2.75 2.20 2.20 + 0.10
AutoData May 12.50 12121585 12544 1.05 0.55 0.55 − 0.25
BEA Sys Jun 42.50 9099 28567 1.20 0.95 1.15 + 0.15
Bk of Am Aug 10766 52184 1.45 0.75 0.75 − 0.05
45.54 May 45.00 12721 44295 2.50 1.35 1.35 − 1.20
45.54 Apr 47.50 10327 24886 0.49 0.10 0.10 − 0.35
BankNY Apr 30.00 10801 17910 3.80 1.70 3.70 + 1.00
36.04 Apr 35.00 37180 16876 1.60 0.40 1.60 + 0.70
BestBuy Apr 55.00 13004 070 0.85 0.10 − 0.65
55.93 Apr 55.00 20861 10978 2.85 0.90 1.00 − 0.80
55.93 May 55.00 19936 14387 2.65 0.70 0.85 − 1.40
55.93 Apr 60.00 9982 9733 0.85 0.05 0.15 − 0.25
Blloyal Jul 25.00p 12124912 7914 2.25 1.80 2.15 − 0.08
BostSc Apr 30.00p 31140 7819 0.15 0.05 0.05
23.05 Apr 22.50p 15626 33881 0.45 0.15 0.40 + 0.15
23.05 Apr 25.00p 9427 26310 0.30 0.10 0.15 − 0.10
23.05 May 25.00p 12741 50770 0.65 0.39 0.45 − 0.15
Broadcm Apr 40.00 17293 8149 3.26 1.50 1.80 − 1.65
43.16 May 42.50 10807 11953 4.10 2.15 3.30 − 0.20
43.16 May 42.50p 10303 7163 3.50 2.10 2.20 + 0.30
43.16 Apr 45.00 24157 16094 1.95 0.50 0.70 − 1.15
43.16 May 45.00 8731 5725 2.80 1.30 2.20 − 0.20
CBS B Apr 11482 14859 0.35 0.15 0.50 − 0.05
ChesEng Apr 32.50 11092 30404 1.15 0.55 0.50 − 0.05
Clmarex Sep 50.00p 12121932 1442 1.40 0.75 0.95 − 0.30
Cisco Apr 20.00 14068 93579 2.10 1.35 1.80 + 0.30
21.67 Apr 22.50p 36479 79863 0.25 0.10 0.15 − 0.05
21.67 Apr 22.50 11499 10975 1.50 0.70 0.85 − 0.20
21.67 May 22.50 10125 20372 0.65 0.40 0.51 + 0.11
Citigrp Apr 45.00p 8400 11444 3.20 2.70 2.95 + 0.20
47.24 Jun 45.00 11784 34389 0.55 0.35 0.55 + 0.12
47.24 May 45.00p 11746 56790 1.55 1.15 1.50

Panel 2

Elan Apr 15.00 24719 67386 0.55 0.25 0.35 + 0.05
14.44 May 15.00 19917 13242 1.15 0.65 0.90 + 0.25
Emdeon Jul 12.50 12804 9088 0.70 0.30 0.65 + 0.20
EncysIveP Apr 7.50p 14758 12308 2.95 2.30 2.60 + 0.25
ExxonMob Apr 57.50 12122277 1514 4.90 4.23 4.30 − 0.10
60.86 May 57.50p 12121757 733 0.50 0.35 0.45 − 0.15
Fth Thrd May 40.00 8602 9964 2.10 1.05 1.10 − 0.55
FIData May 45.00p 12125666 10423 0.75 0.50 0.65 + 0.05
FordM Jun 10.00p 17525 13605 2.00 1.95 2.00 − 0.25
ForstL May 40.00p 9104 10664 1.25 0.60 0.85 − 0.25
44.63 Aug 40.00p 17381 5499 2.30 1.75 1.95 − 0.25
FormFact Apr 35.00p 12121342 254 0.75 0.40 0.45 − 0.15
Genentc Apr 85.00 8724 8397 3.30 2.00 2.35 − 0.60
Gen El Apr 32.50 12362 12686 2.65 1.25 2.40 + 0.70
34.78 Jun 32.50 16128 42221 2.95 1.75 2.80 + 0.60
34.78 Apr 35.00 41442 59553 0.60 0.10 0.45 + 0.25
34.78 Apr 35.00p 10552 9217 1.50 0.45 0.55 − 0.55
34.78 May 35.00 12753 9056 0.85 0.25 0.70 + 0.30
34.78 Jun 35.00 15137 98931 1.05 0.45 0.95 + 0.40
GenMotrs May 25.00 10727 10799 0.60 0.15 0.40 + 0.20
21.27 Apr 20.00 16449 17715 3.50 1.60 2.10 − 0.75
21.27 May 20.00p 49809 48589 1.30 0.25 0.85 + 0.55
21.27 Apr 20.00p 16605 68882 2.50 1.10 2.05 + 0.60
21.27 Apr 22.50 29328 41790 1.50 0.45 0.70 − 0.45
21.27 May 22.50p 24587 20638 2.60 0.75 1.90 + 0.85
21.27 Apr 25.00 10884 21203 0.45 0.10 0.10 − 0.25
21.27 May 25.00 12565 13334 0.80 0.35 0.45 − 0.15
GoldFLtd Apr 22.50 8407 6304 0.90 0.25 0.50 + 0.20
Goldcorp Apr 30.00 14157 11212 1.20 0.30 0.80 + 0.40
Google Jun 85.00 12121254 568 304.20 281.80 304.20 + 48.70
390.00 Jun 285.00 12121235 302 180.70 166.70 149.30 − 13.00
390.00 Jun 310.00p 10046 5683 2.25 0.80 1.05 − 1.20
390.00 Apr 320.00p 9187 7200 3.30 1.25 1.70 − 1.50
390.00 May 330.00p 9336 6359 4.80 1.90 2.50 − 2.20
390.00 Apr 340.00p 23699 5613 7.00 2.90 3.50 − 3.20
390.00 Apr 350.00p 17847 9016 10.00 4.20 4.80 − 4.90
390.00 Apr 360.00 17136 14356 46.20 19.90 34.20 + 14.10
390.00 Apr 360.00p 28784 11481 13.40 6.10 8.00 − 5.40
390.00 Apr 370.00 25846 13427 38.90 14.50 27.30 + 12.30
390.00 May 370.00p 27044 8132 18.30 8.80 11.00 − 7.10
390.00 Apr 380.00 25547 15809 32.00 10.50 21.10 + 10.50
390.00 Jun 380.00p 20775 7692 24.30 12.00 13.90 − 9.90
390.00 Apr 390.00 39716 19124 26.10 7.10 16.10 + 8.80
390.00 Jun 390.00p 15877 5694 31.00 16.00 19.40 − 11.00
390.00 Apr 400.00 38394 14019 20.90 4.80 11.20 − 6.20
390.00 Apr 410.00 18347 7882 16.50 3.10 8.00 + 4.70
390.00 Apr 420.00 18150 8992 12.40 1.95 5.10 + 3.10
430.00 Jun 430.00 11902 5038 9.20 1.20 3.40 + 0.40
440.00 Apr 440.00 11853 6263 6.70 0.75 2.10 + 1.30
390.00 May 450.00 13710 5368 4.80 0.40 1.05 + 0.55
460.00 Apr 460.00p 10980 5900 3.50 0.25 0.70 + 0.35
500.00 May 500.00 9000 3465 0.85 0.05 0.15 + 0.05
Guidant Apr 70.00p 11061 70096 0.90 0.60 0.70 − 0.35
Halbtn Apr 75.00 12365 17538 2.45 0.80 1.55 + 0.50
iShNqBio Apr 80.00p 18412 21745 1.05 0.70 0.75 − 0.10
82.38 Apr 85.00 15936 16714 0.50 0.35 0.45 − 0.20
iShRs2000 Aug 63.00p 15000 69547 0.10 0.10 0.10 − 0.10
75.97 Aug 65.00p 24560 28452 0.65 0.50 0.55 − 0.10
75.97 May 67.00p 12572 31172 0.30 0.15 0.17 − 0.08
75.97 May 69.00p 33550 72910 0.35 0.20 0.35 + 0.10
75.97 May 69.00p 18535 73646 0.50 0.30 0.30 − 0.10
75.97 May 70.00p 45588 121872 0.60 0.35 0.55 − 0.15
75.97 Apr 71.00p 14585 99965 0.40 0.15 0.20 − 0.05
75.97 May 71.00p 33574 49235 0.75 0.45 0.50 − 0.15
75.97 Jun 71.00p 22670 22319 1.80 0.75 1.40 − 0.65
75.97 May 72.00p 156102 144611 0.55 0.20 0.30 − 0.10
75.97 May 72.00p 64085 120589 1.00 0.60 0.60 − 0.35
75.97 Apr 72.00p 8806 32891 2.00 1.55 1.75 − 0.30
75.97 Apr 73.00p 37115 83334 0.75 0.30 0.35 − 0.35
75.97 May 73.00p 45966 48376 1.25 0.50 0.80 − 0.30
75.97 May 73.00p 15499 29550 2.30 1.75 1.85 − 0.85
75.97 Apr 74.00p 161733 129665 1.10 0.45 0.55 − 0.35
75.97 May 74.00p 27098 62904 3.30 2.40 3.00 + 0.50
75.97 Apr 74.00p 108378 84955 1.65 0.95 1.10 − 0.35
75.97 May 74.00p 15712 21902 4.20 4.10 4.20 + 0.80
75.97 Aug 74.00p 16490 23744 2.70 2.20 2.70 + 0.45
75.97 Apr 75.00 28913 25673 2.05 1.05 1.80 + 0.45
75.97 May 75.00 55813 61445 1.50 0.70 0.80 − 0.10
75.97 Jun 75.00 29882 55003 2.75 1.75 2.60 + 0.65
75.97 Apr 75.00p 38663 22416 2.05 1.25 1.35 − 0.45
75.97 Apr 76.00 32591 33999 1.40 0.60 1.25 + 0.50
75.97 Apr 76.00p 22156 16181 1.90 1.10 1.15 − 0.73
75.97 May 76.00p 17789 29119 2.10 1.25 1.85 + 0.40
75.97 Apr 76.00p 22215 22098 2.45 1.60 1.70 − 0.30
75.97 Apr 77.00p 25833 26986 0.85 0.55 0.75 + 0.35
75.97 Jun 78.00p 12818 25340 1.10 0.55 1.00 + 0.30
75.97 Apr 80.00p 22282 18990 1.65 1.20 1.55 + 0.15
Inco Apr 50.00 17764 17580 2.80 1.35 1.75
IndevusPh Sep 7.50 11002 11706 1.20 0.90 0.95 − 0.25
Intel Apr 17.50p 9277 10712 3.30 2.90 2.95 − 0.15
19.46 Oct 17.50p 79408 13052 3.30 2.90 0.95 + 0.20
19.46 Apr 20.00 91904 157286 0.95 0.55 0.60 − 0.35
19.46 May 20.00 50728 26731 0.95 0.60 0.65 − 0.30
19.46 Jul 20.00p 8603 13771 1.10 0.60 1.05 + 0.10
19.46 Jun 20.00 41871 62920 1.30 1.00 1.00 − 0.15
19.46 Apr 22.50 12645 54626 0.35 0.15 0.35 + 0.15
19.46 May 22.50 8288 10227 5.50 5.10 5.50
IBM Apr 80.00p 9066 35729 0.75 0.40 0.40 − 0.25
82.47 Apr 85.00 13182 46084 1.00 0.55 0.60 − 0.40
82.47 Oct 85.00p 8421 7661 4.60 3.90 4.00 − 0.20
90.00 Apr 90.00 9370 14655 2.15 1.65 1.65 − 0.50
JDS Uni Apr 4.00 10579 25527 0.55 0.20 0.30 + 0.10
Kohls Apr 55.00p 12345 18111 4.10 3.20 3.90 + 0.40
Level 3 Apr 5.00 10286 4909 0.30 0.05 0.05 − 0.25
5.18 Apr 5.00 22928 13834 0.70 0.10 0.20 − 0.40
5.18 May 5.00 12079 8941 1.00 0.20 0.55 − 0.40
5.18 Jun 5.00 9204 21937 1.05 0.25 0.60 − 0.40
5.18 Apr 5.00p 22963 15773 1.25 0.45 0.80 + 0.40
Lexmark May 45.00 11468 11924 2.30 1.20 1.30 − 0.25
Lilly Apr 50.00p 8373 15312 1.80 0.15 1.05 − 0.35
Lucent T Apr 2.50 8539 142655 0.20 0.10 0.15 − 0.05
MDC Hdg May 50.00p 10521 1483 0.05 0.50 + 0.20
64.31 May 40.00p 10559 10530 0.55 0.45 0.55 + 0.20
MEMC Apr 40.00 12121668 1714 0.95 0.35 0.40 − 0.45
MGM Mir Apr 45.00p 8366 8688 3.10 2.27 2.95 + 0.30
45.09 Apr 45.00 16308 9149 2.60 0.80 1.60 + 0.30
Marvell T Apr 50.00 12121296 343 7.70 6.90 7.60 + 0.90
Maxim Apr 30.00 12121278 1 0.30 0.10 0.10
Maytag Apr 15.00 8917 33288 0.75 0.15 0.75 + 0.10
21.33 Apr 17.50p 12569 26053 4.50 1.15 3.80 + 2.30
21.33 Jul 17.50p 9654 11624 4.15 1.60 4.20 + 2.10
Medtrn Apr 50.00p 14774 8883 0.65 0.15 0.55 + 0.45
Merck Apr 7.50 21338 19642 0.50 0.20 0.20 − 0.20

Panel 3

35.23 Apr 32.50p 11128 14097 0.25 0.10 0.20 + 0.05
35.23 Apr 35.00p 21532 30350 0.85 0.50 0.80 + 0.35
Microst Apr 25.00 44269 56551 2.60 1.95 2.38 + 0.23
27.21 Apr 27.50 36298 157635 0.40 0.15 0.30 + 0.09
27.21 May 27.50p 16169 52919 0.75 0.25 0.45 − 0.15
27.21 May 27.50 9439 17286 0.70 0.40 0.60 + 0.10
27.21 Apr 27.50p 12981 8164 0.95 0.60 0.95 + 0.15
MorgStan Apr 65.00 8590 16227 0.65 0.15 0.25 + 0.10
Motorola Apr 22.50 27896 62887 1.25 0.40 0.95 + 0.30
22.91 Apr 22.50p 11334 52634 0.20 0.05 0.11 + 0.03
22.91 Jul 25.00 15050 35218 0.90 0.50 0.75 + 0.20
Nabors Apr 70.00 11072 9822 4.63 1.25 3.12 + 1.62
71.58 Apr 75.00 9227 6780 1.60 0.30 0.90 + 0.55
Nasd100Tr May 36.00p 21808 24524 0.05 0.05 0.05 − 0.05
41.93 Apr 39.00p 11578 57456 0.15 0.05 0.05 − 0.05
41.93 Apr 40.00 15464 27427 2.45 1.35 2.15 + 0.50
41.93 May 40.00p 70509 266085 0.27 0.05 0.15 − 0.30
41.93 May 40.00p 16809 79845 0.50 0.24 0.30 − 0.15
41.93 Sep 41.00 32593 78142 1.17 0.80 0.90 − 0.20
41.93 Apr 41.00 56395 81095 1.60 0.75 1.35 + 0.40
41.93 Apr 41.00p 216567 412263 0.65 0.17 0.30 − 0.20
41.93 May 41.00p 62652 51230 1.96 1.11 1.70 + 0.35
41.93 May 41.00p 186168 161008 0.90 0.40 0.50 − 0.25
41.93 Jun 41.00p 25461 94839 1.10 0.60 0.70 − 0.30
41.93 Jun 42.00 196623 208201 0.85 0.30 0.65 + 0.25
41.93 May 42.00p 133788 157306 1.21 0.40 0.55 − 0.45
41.93 Apr 42.00p 49047 85416 1.25 0.60 1.10 + 0.30
41.93 May 42.00p 36515 38227 1.40 0.70 0.90 − 0.35
41.93 Jun 42.00p 10151 51982 1.56 0.95 1.40 + 0.25
41.93 Jun 42.00p 16232 48832 1.55 0.90 1.05 − 0.40
41.93 Apr 43.00 77733 58049 0.35 0.10 0.25 + 0.10
41.93 Apr 43.00p 30002 28013 2.00 0.94 1.20 − 0.55
41.93 May 43.00p 104481 170184 0.70 0.30 0.60 + 0.20
41.93 Apr 43.00p 13461 20053 2.10 1.15 1.40 − 0.50
41.93 Jun 43.00 22466 47931 1.05 0.60 0.85 − 0.15
41.93 May 43.00p 12125213 284 6.20 5.10 6.10 + 0.54
41.93 Apr 43.00p 13594 28580 0.35 0.15 0.30 + 0.10
Neteease Apr 25.00 10497 10215 1.15 0.30 0.70
NwCentFn May 30.00 28396 34 19.10 15.80 16.20 − 2.20
46.02 May 35.00 71721 85 14.10 11.10 11.60 − 1.90
46.02 May 40.00 629860 28886 9.00 6.30 7.10 − 0.60
NwmtMn Apr 50.00 19803 15271 4.70 1.60 2.85 + 1.25
51.89 May 52.50 36286 11782 2.80 0.70 1.45 + 0.75
51.89 May 55.00 30765 19193 1.40 0.25 0.60 + 0.32
51.89 May 55.00 19086 16059 2.50 0.95 1.55 + 0.65
NokiaCp Apr 15.00 53105 98 6.30 5.10 6.30 + 0.80
20.72 Jul 15.00p 12125213 284 6.20 5.10 6.10 + 0.54
20.72 Apr 17.50 12519989 7583 3.90 2.55 3.40 + 0.40
NokiaR Apr 20.00p 41265 39552 1.45 0.35 1.10 + 0.40
20.72 Apr 20.00p 10590 21586 0.80 0.30 0.35 − 0.15
Novavax Apr 7.50 12716 13127 1.10 0.35 0.80 + 0.10
7.98 May 10.00 10850 635 0.60 0.35 0.35 − 0.20
Nucor Apr 55.00 13275 878 51.00 50.00 50.00 + 25.50
104.79 Apr 60.00 22165 21 45.00 40.00 45.60 + 14.90
104.79 Apr 65.00 26169 45 41.00 40.00 40.60 + 9.50
104.79 Apr 75.00 14193 75 38.30 35.00 35.50 + 6.80
104.79 Apr 80.00 11430 65 32.70 30.00 32.70 + 10.60
104.79 Apr 85.00 15334 95 28.40 25.60 25.70 + 8.00
104.79 Apr 85.00p 16467 67 21.00 17.40 20.60 + 3.20
NyidiaCp Apr 55.00p 12591 7552 3.80 1.70 1.10 − 2.80
57.26 May 50.00p 10886 8997 5.00 2.50 2.64 − 2.86
OilSwfT Jul 135.00p 9296 28475 2.45 0.65 0.80 − 1.10
146.81 Apr 145.00p 15209 15709 4.30 1.25 1.75 − 1.55
146.81 Apr 145.00p 10893 13052 7.80 2.50 5.60 + 2.00
146.81 May 145.00p 27626 18649 7.00 2.30 3.20 − 2.30
146.81 Jun 150.00p 9428 11684 4.70 1.05 3.00 + 1.35
146.81 Apr 155.00p 8186 17899 10.60 4.00 5.70 − 3.10
146.81 Apr 155.00 14415 8537 2.40 0.45 1.50 + 0.85
OpnwrSys Jul 25.00p 12121291 427 5.10 4.20 4.20 − 0.10
Oracle Jun 14.00p 16055 13775 2.00 1.80 1.95
13.69 Apr 14.00p 12340 26810 0.25 0.10 0.20
palmOne Apr 20.00 34509 24672 3.42 1.10 3.20 + 2.20
23.16 Apr 22.50 27885 32245 1.35 0.20 1.25 + 0.95
23.16 May 22.50 18907 16792 1.90 0.55 1.80 + 1.16
23.16 Apr 25.00 9521 17684 0.35 0.05 0.30 + 0.20
23.16 May 25.00 15938 33181 0.81 0.20 0.80 + 0.51
PanAskv Apr 22.50p 12121562 889 0.25 0.10 0.25
PatrsEng Apr 30.00 8897 9700 3.40 0.60 2.32 + 1.57
PepsiCo Apr 60.00 11677 14185 0.45 0.10 0.15 − 0.45
Pfizer Apr 22.50p 8976 47778 0.20 0.10 0.15 − 0.05
24.92 Apr 25.00 18289 21293 1.25 0.40 0.85 − 0.25
24.92 Jun 25.00 19970 19148 0.45 0.10 0.45 + 0.30
24.92 Apr 25.00p 9016 11644 0.75 0.20 0.75 + 0.35
24.92 May 27.50 9051 46541 0.15 0.05 0.05 − 0.05
24.92 Jul 27.50 9842 79099 0.40 0.15 0.20 − 0.05
ProctGam Apr 55.00p 11011 43620 0.30 0.10 0.20 + 0.05
57.63 Oct 60.00p 12588 39899 3.80 3.10 3.40 + 0.30
57.63 Oct 60.00 13178 15817 3.80 3.10 3.40 + 0.30
Qualcom Apr 50.00 12121265 621 25.90 24.40 25.90 + 2.30
50.61 Apr 50.00p 12121285 344 22.00 20.80 22.00 + 2.80
50.61 Apr 50.00 12121561 1322 16.00 14.70 16.60 + 1.40
50.61 May 52.50 24242496 2101 13.50 11.30 13.50 + 1.90
50.61 Jun 52.50 12121889 8995 9.10 7.00 8.50 + 1.71
50.61 Apr 42.50 12121180 1187 9.10 7.40 9.00 + 1.90
50.61 Apr 45.00 12121305 11992 6.80 4.80 6.50 + 0.35
50.61 Apr 47.50 12121336 32660 4.60 2.60 3.60 + 0.40
50.61 Jun 50.00 12123708 1767 3.10 1.80 2.45 + 0.45
Rambus Jun 39.34 11799 15321 1.05 0.55 0.65 − 0.40
39.34 May 45.00 11799 13024 2.75 1.35 2.20 − 0.15
39.34 Apr 45.00 14201 17763 3.80 2.30 3.20 − 0.10
39.34 Apr 45.00p 8405 7751 1.55 0.30 1.45 + 0.15
RedHat Apr 25.00p 11599 15333 0.95 0.70 0.75 − 0.20
27.98 Apr 27.50 13408 17359 2.15 1.25 1.50 − 0.25
27.98 Apr 30.00 13299 18749 4.80 2.15 3.70 + 0.75
RschMot Apr 90.00 10259 25526 2.45 1.15 1.88 + 0.10
St JudeMd May 35.00p 9053 0.35 0.55 0.35 − 0.55
41.00 May 40.00 10011 2575 1.50 0.50 1.50 + 0.95
41.00 Apr 40.00p 9213 3299 1.50 0.60 0.70 − 0.30
SanDisk Apr 50.00 12121290 1 2.90 1.90 1.90 + 0.65
57.52 Jun 50.00 11744 22029 2.90 1.40 3.50 + 0.75
57.52 Jul 55.00p 11086 11772 4.10 3.10 3.40 − 0.30
57.52 Apr 57.50 12733 21050 4.30 2.40 3.50
57.52 Apr 60.00 10521 24811 3.30 1.80 2.40 − 0.10
SaraL Apr 17.50p 12121376 4624 0.65 0.50 0.55 − 0.15
SemiHTr Apr 35.00p 18422 49681 0.95 0.30 0.55 + 0.15
36.32 May 35.00p 20435 35127 1.95 0.85 1.30 + 0.15
36.32 Apr 37.50p 24630 58338 0.75 0.30 0.44 − 0.06

Source: Barron's, April 3, 2006, p. M26. Reprinted by permission of Barron's, © 2006 Dow Jones & Company, Inc. All rights reserved worldwide

Figure 10.2 Price quotations for index options from *Investor's Business Daily*

Index Options

Closing prices may vary due to after hour settlements/trading at time of data transmission.

P Strike C Price	Vol.	Last Price	Vol.	Last Price	Vol.	Last Price
Apr			**May**			
Bank Idx						Close 106.98 Jun
c107	157	1	....	....	....	....
DJ Inds						Close 111.41 Jun
c100	....	....	....	....	234	16^{20}
p100	....	....	....	....	40	0^{20}
c101	....	....	25	10^{80}	....	....
c103	50	8^{50}	63	8^{90}	....	....
c104	....	....	228	7^{90}	....	....
c105	....	....	166	7^{20}	....	....
c107	125	4^{60}	....	....	....	....
p108	50	0^{10}	....	....	10	0^{80}
p109	60	0^{20}	....	....	6	1
p110	42	0^{30}	34	0^{90}	114	1^{35}
c110	....	....	255	2^{55}	....	....
c111	1.1k	0^{95}	265	1^{95}	15	2^{80}
p111	315	0^{65}	35	1^{35}	35	1^{55}
c112	....	....	....	....	246	7^{90}
p112	128	1^{10}	377	1^{75}	12	2^{16}
c112	411	0^{55}	66	1^{35}	63	1^{95}
p113	86	1^{40}	95	1^{95}	....	....
c113	768	0^{20}	223	1	6	1^{50}
c114	....	....	201	0^{60}	....	....
c116	....	....	....	....	300	0^{60}
GS Idx						Close 144.91 Jun
c90	....	....	....	....	20	56^{70}
p100	....	....	20	0^{05}	....	....
p120	10	0^{05}	58	0^{60}	13	1^{25}
c125	40	19^{60}	10	22^{30}	42	22^{70}
p125	....	....	23	1	16	2
p127	50	0^{10}	30	1^{25}	....	....
p130	256	0^{20}	533	1^{70}	3	3^{10}
c130	....	....	10	17^{80}	26	18^{60}
p135	32	0^{60}	12	2^{90}	17	4^{10}
c135	30	11^{60}	....	....	1	15^{90}
p137	144	0^{80}	....	....	....	....
c140	563	6^{50}	2	9^{60}	19	12^{30}
p140	137	1^{55}	17	4^{40}	56	6^{30}
p142	97	2^{50}	3	5^{10}	....	....
c142	31	5^{50}	10	8^{40}	....	....
p145	349	3^{60}	115	6	55	8^{50}
c145	134	3^{30}	130	6^{80}	110	9^{90}
c147	227	2^{25}	51	6^{30}	....	....
p147	55	3^{90}	743	7^{30}	....	....
p150	47	6^{70}	266	8^{90}	40	10^{90}
c150	58	1^{40}	49	4^{80}	118	6^{80}
c152	8	0^{85}	43	4^{40}	....	....
c155	72	0^{45}	9	3^{10}	4	6^{90}
p155	21	11^{10}	....	....	....	....
c160	56	0^{20}	35	1^{85}	2	4^{40}
p165	....	....	....	....	30	22^{10}
c165	....	....	100	1	630	2^{75}
c177	25	0^{05}	....	....	....	....
c180	....	....	....	....	20	0^{90}
MidCap						Close 789.20 Jun
p760	200	1^{55}	....	....	....	....
MSHTc						Colse 551.36 Jun
p530	....	....	59	3^{90}	....	....
c560	....	....	25	8^{70}	5	12^{80}
Masd100						Close 1718.86 Jun
p1350	10	0^{05}	....	....	32	0^{90}
p1375	....	....	....	....	29	1
p1400	....	....	....	....	33	1^{30}
p1425	5	0^{10}	10	0^{75}	22	1^{55}
p1475	50	0^{10}	3	1	10	2^{50}
p1500	495	0^{15}	10	1^{40}	10	3^{80}
p1525	336	0^{30}	92	1^{90}	10	4^{90}

P Strike C Price	Vol.	Last Price	Vol.	Last Price	Vol.	Last Price
Apr			**May**			
p1550	783	0^{30}	131	2^{80}	55	6^{10}
p1560	70	0^{30}	....	....	....	....
p1575	200	0^{35}	159	3^{80}	1	8^{30}
p1585	30	0^{45}	....	....	....	....
p1590	35	0^{55}	....	....	....	....
p1600	110	0^{50}	133	5^{40}	6	11^{50}
p1625	1.2k	1	172	7^{80}	255	15^{60}
p1650	2.2k	1^{95}	123	11^{10}	....	....
c1650	117	72	....	....	....	....
p1675	1.2k	4^{40}	266	16^{70}	1	26^{20}
p1680	429	5^{30}	....	....	....	....
c1700	92	27^{40}	8	47	8	61^{50}
p1700	451	9	141	24^{10}	6	31
p1710	136	12^{60}	....	....	....	....
c1710	30	21	....	....	....	....
p1725	1.0k	19^{40}	580	35	240	43^{10}
c1725	910	15^{10}	67	33^{60}	258	49
p1750	231	34^{90}	44	46	2	52^{40}
c1750	1.7k	6	286	23^{10}	45	35^{80}
c1775	1.1k	1^{80}	96	13^{70}	....	....
c1790	327	0^{80}	....	....	....	....
c1800	1.4k	0^{45}	784	8	....	....
c1810	670	0^{35}	....	....	....	....
c1825	337	0^{20}	1.1k	4^{40}	....	....
c1835	25	0^{15}	....	....	....	....
c1850	139	0^{10}	291	2^{25}	10	8
c1875	....	....	119	1	3	4^{40}
c1900	....	....	65	0^{80}	....	....
c1975	....	....	30	0^{15}	....	....
c1995	....	....	....	....	30	0^{35}
NtGas						Close 407.06 Jun
c415	250	2^{05}	....	....	....	....
Oil Idx						Close 1112.93 Jun
p1040	....	....	25	8	....	....
p1080	....	....	35	17^{30}	....	....
c1170	....	....	20	9^{50}	....	....
OilSvc						Close 217.03 Jun
p190	....	....	26	1^{35}	....	....
p192	....	....	200	1^{70}	....	....
c210	....	....	70	12^{90}	1	15^{70}
c217	80	4^{30}	....	....	....	....
Rus2000						Close 752.95 Jun
p700	526	0^{60}	3.0k	4^{30}	....	....
p710	171	1^{20}	291	5^{40}	....	....
p720	37	1^{75}	1	7^{30}	....	....
c730	31	25^{30}	....	....	....	....
p730	291	2^{95}	10	9^{30}	5	13^{70}
p740	65	5^{50}	11	10^{60}	....	....
c740	21	18	2	26^{40}	....	....
p750	70	8^{50}	72	14^{60}	200	17^{30}
c750	142	10^{60}	126	20	....	....
p760	93	13^{40}	52	20^{70}	45	24^{80}
c760	815	5^{40}	10	17^{50}	....	....
c770	....	....	4	13	50	15^{60}
p770	....	....	20	26^{50}	....	....
c780	....	....	3	6^{50}	33	11^{90}
c790	....	....	45	3^{90}	....	....
c800	....	....	42	2^{40}	....	....
c810	106	0^{10}	145	1^{40}	....	....
Russ2000						Close 752.95 Jun
p660	33	0^{15}	40	1^{30}	5	3^{10}
p670	353	0^{15}	41	2	....	....
p680	82	0^{25}	654	2^{50}	....	....
p690	209	0^{40}	232	3^{10}	1.3k	5^{80}
SemiconEu						Close 510.86 Jun
p472	40	0^{55}	....	....	....	....

P Strike C Price	Vol.	Last Price	Vol.	Last Price	Vol.	Last Price
Apr			**May**			
p477	22	0^{90}	....	....	....	....
p507	35	6^{60}	....	....	....	....
c512	31	7	....	....	....	....
p517	24	11^{40}	....	....	....	....
c522	20	4	....	....	....	....
c527	20	2^{50}	....	....	....	....
c532	103	1^{65}	....	....	....	....
c562	20	0^{15}	....	....	....	....
SemiconIdx						Close 510.86 Jun
p465	2	0^{35}	25	3^{50}	....	....
p475	98	0^{85}	....	....	....	....
p480	5	0^{90}	141	5^{30}	....	....
p485	....	....	110	7^{50}	....	....
p495	....	....	50	9^{70}	....	....
p500	68	5	....	....	....	....
p505	38	6^{60}	....	....	....	....
p510	136	8^{70}	15	15^{50}	....	....
c510	92	9	24	19	....	....
c515	124	6^{10}	....	....	3	23^{30}
p515	36	11^{50}	....	....	....	....
c520	533	4^{70}	....	....	2	18^{90}
c525	27	3	....	....	....	....
c530	56	2	....	....	....	....
c535	28	1^{50}	....	....	....	....
c540	7	1	70	7^{40}	....	....
c550	12	0^{20}	20	5	....	....
c565	....	....	31	1^{90}	....	....
c570	....	....	34	1^{50}	....	....
SP100						Close 587.67 Jun
p535	150	0^{05}	....	....	....	....
p540	992	0^{15}	223	0^{45}	115	1^{30}
p545	5	0^{10}	30	0^{75}	....	....
p550	48	0^{10}	105	0^{95}	....	....
p555	225	0^{15}	66	1^{05}	....	....
c560	43	30^{30}	....	....	....	....
p560	1.3k	0^{25}	73	1^{65}	5	2^{70}
p565	1.5k	0^{30}	47	2	....	....
p570	749	0^{45}	194	2^{50}	....	....
c575	185	14^{10}	....	....	....	....
p575	326	0^{80}	44	3^{60}	....	....
c580	150	9^{50}	14	14	10	18^{70}
p580	3.4k	1^{55}	443	4^{90}	20	7^{40}
c585	919	6^{60}	43	10^{90}	....	....
p585	4.9k	2^{75}	118	6^{40}	....	....
p590	5.8k	4^{90}	156	8^{40}	....	....
c590	4.5k	3^{70}	91	7^{40}	....	....
p595	561	8^{80}	....	....	....	....
c595	5.5k	1^{70}	....	....	....	....
c600	3.5k	0^{65}	211	3^{10}	30	6
p600	119	13^{50}	52	15	40	15^{80}
c605	2.3k	0^{20}	....	....	....	....
c610	2.7k	0^{05}	334	1^{05}	....	....
c615	....	....	344	0^{60}	....	....
c620	40	0^{05}	232	0^{35}	76	1
c640	....	....	....	....	50	0^{20}
SP100 Eur						Close 587.67 Jun
p570	28	0^{50}	....	....	....	....
p575	24	0^{90}	....	....	....	....
c585	680	5^{80}	....	....	....	....
p585	655	3	1	6^{50}	....	....
c590	710	3^{50}	....	....	....	....
p590	600	5^{40}	....	....	....	....
c600	310	0^{60}	1	3^{30}	....	....
p605	22	16	....	....	....	....
p610	22	20^{60}	....	....	....	....
SPX500						Close 1296.61 Jun
p30	5.5k	6^{90}	....	....	....	....

P Strike C Price	Vol.	Last Price	Vol.	Last Price	Vol.	Last Price
Apr			**May**			
c30	97	14^{90}	....	....	....	....
p850	....	....	....	....	200	0^{05}
p950	....	....	....	....	120	0^{15}
p1100	....	....	20	0^{40}	....	....
c1125	....	....	100	174	....	....
p1125	....	....	50	0^{65}	....	....
p1150	5	0^{10}	1.6k	0^{80}	20	1^{80}
c1150	180	147	180	149^{40}	20	156^{10}
c1175	....	....	72	125^{30}	....	....
p1175	1.0k	0^{20}	45	1^{10}	60	2^{60}
p1190	....	....	627	1^{40}	....	....
c1200	....	....	2	102	40	108^{60}
p1200	11k	0^{25}	33	1^{75}	1.1k	3^{80}
p1205	....	....	34	1^{90}	....	....
p1215	....	....	167	2^{40}	....	....
p1220	15	0^{40}	122	2^{60}	....	....
c1220	....	....	72	83^{10}	....	....
p1225	20	0^{30}	....	....	418	6
p1230	45	0^{50}	309	3^{30}	....	....
p1235	1.3k	0^{50}	8	3^{70}	....	....
p1240	1.3k	0^{50}	182	4^{10}	....	....
p1245	24	0^{85}	17	4^{80}	....	....
c1250	50	52^{30}	2.0k	54^{20}	20	64^{40}
p1250	21k	1	24k	5^{50}	437	10
c1255	....	....	22	51	....	....
p1255	....	....	105	6^{10}	....	....
p1265	2.2k	1^{80}	277	8^{10}	....	....
p1270	483	2^{70}	651	9^{50}	....	....
c1275	269	29^{50}	72	34^{70}	....	....
p1275	2.1k	3	1.0k	10^{50}	401	13^{70}
p1280	1.2k	4	7	11^{70}	50	15
p1285	305	5^{20}	2.0k	13	1	16^{30}
c1285	50	18	....	....	....	....
p1290	....	....	1.3k	15^{20}	2	19^{20}
c1290	....	....	22	27^{50}	20	35^{20}
c1295	1.1k	12	87	21^{60}	....	....
p1295	1.7k	8^{40}	851	15^{20}	1	21
p1300	4.3k	11^{30}	2.9k	18^{80}	1.0k	24
c1300	7.7k	9^{30}	2.2k	18^{80}	845	27
c1305	363	6^{60}	2.4k	16^{40}	3.9k	23
p1305	3.3k	12^{90}	15	20^{20}	4.1k	25
c1310	1.2k	4^{80}	388	14	2.1k	21^{50}
p1310	198	17^{90}	179	23	1.6k	25
p1320	75	26	....	....	25	30^{90}
c1320	317	2^{15}	521	8^{90}	....	....
p1325	17	29	3	32^{50}	353	35
c1325	4.5k	1^{30}	8.1k	7^{50}	11	14^{70}
c1330	240	0^{90}	20	7	....	....
c1335	2.7k	0^{45}	....	....	....	....
c1340	304	0^{40}	53	4^{10}	735	9
c1345	1.0k	0^{30}	157	3^{30}	....	....
c1350	2.8k	0^{15}	4.5k	2^{45}	28	5^{70}
p1350	....	....	....	....	206	52^{50}
c1355	95	0^{15}	151	2^{10}	....	....
c1360	....	....	322	1^{30}	4	4^{50}
c1365	12	0^{15}	418	1^{45}	121	3^{70}
c1370	136	0^{95}	....	....	....	....
c1375	11	0^{95}	3.5k	0^{70}	162	2^{25}
c1400	....	....	2.0k	0^{20}	146	1
c1425	....	....	120	0^{15}	10	0^{40}
SPX500 st						Close 1296.61 Jun
p1285	275	2	....	....	....	....
c1300	631	4^{50}	....	....	....	....
p1300	67	7^{20}	....	....	....	....
c1315	195	0^{50}	....	....	....	....

Source: *Investor's Business Daily*, April 11, 2006, p. B10. Reprinted by permission of *Investor's Business Daily*, © 2006–2007 Investor's Business Daily, Inc. Republished with permission

Table 10.7   Index option contract volume by exchange, 2005

Exchange	Contract volume (millions)	Percentage
Chicago Board Options Exchange	115.819	85.76
American Stock Exchange	8.545	6.33
Philadelphia Stock Exchange	6.213	4.60
International Securities Exchange	4.465	3.31
Total	135.04	100.00

Source: Options Clearing Corporation

Distinctions between options on individual stocks and options on stock indexes have blurred in recent years with the popularity of exchange-traded funds (ETFs)—depository receipts that offer investment results that track the price and yield performance recognizable indexes such as the Dow Jones Industrial Average (under the product name DIAMONDS®), the NASDAQ 100 (under the product name "The Cube," from its QQQ ticker symbol) or the S&P 500 (under the product name SPDR®s, or "spiders"). The depositor receipts represent a claim on a unit trust holding a portfolio that tracks the specified index. These depository receipts trade like shares of stock, and options written on these depository receipts trade like stock options. The option contracts are cash settled. The cash payment is based on the index value at the end of the day on which exercise instructions are issued. An option on an ETF is classified as an option on an individual stock (the depository receipt) even though the ETF may be linked to a stock index.

The astonishing rise of the ISE

The International Securities Exchange, or ISE, began operations as a fully electronic U.S. options exchange on May 26, 2000. By 2006, the ISE was trading over half a billion contracts per year and had become the world's largest equity options exchange. The ISE's success derived from the fact that its screen-based business model enabled the exchange to offer customers lower fees and instantaneous executions in tight, liquid markets. The ISE's business model attracted many well-capitalized global financial institutions, whose purchase of exchange memberships provided initial development capital for the exchange.

Even before the ISE traded its first contract, its 1999 announcement that it intended to list the highest volume options traded on competing exchanges triggered an intense round of direct inter-exchange competition. The ISE announcement prompted the multiple listing of the most liquid options classes. As a result, bid–ask spreads fell dramatically for investors. These firms, which had previously viewed participation in the options market as costly and inefficient, have significantly increased the overall liquidity in the options market.

Going forward, the ISE's next challenge is to expand its product base into index options. Standing in the way of the ISE's plans are exclusive licensing agreements between index providers and other option exchanges–in many cases, agreements formed prior to the launch of the ISE. These exclusive licensing agreements periodically come up for bid in the open market, but in the meantime the ISE is shut out of the market for many of the most popular index products. The ISE has challenged these exclusivity agreements on anti-trust grounds. At the same time, index providers have been reevaluating the wisdom of exclusive licensing agreements.

The ISE's success has attracted competitors. In 2004, a rival all-electronic exchange, the Boston Options Exchange (BOX), began operations. In 2005 the ISE became a publicly traded corporation, with its shares traded on the New York Stock Exchange under the acronym ISE.

Table 10.8   Futures option volume by exchange, 2005

Exchange	Contracts traded	
	Number of contracts	Percentage
Chicago Mercantile Exchange	207,233,185	56.32
Chicago Board of Trade	113,505,455	30.85
New York Mercantile Exchange (including Comex Division)	38,002,895	10.33
New York Board of Trade	8,932,169	2.43
Kansas City Board of Trade	263,511	0.07
Minneapolis Grain Exchange	32,464	0.01
Total	367,969,679	100.00

Source: The Futures Industry Association's report entitled *Volume of Futures and Options Trading on U.S. Futures Exchanges, 1968–2005.* © Futures Industry Association. Reprinted by permission of the Futures Industry Association

Foreign currency options

Option trading on individual foreign currencies is concentrated at the Philadelphia Stock Exchange (PHLX).[6] Each option contract is written for a specific number of units of the foreign currency. For example, the Canadian dollar contract specifies an underlying of CAN$ 50,000. The market for foreign currency options is not flourishing. In fact, it has diminished greatly in the past ten years, due largely to the increasingly important over-the-counter market (covered in Chapters 19–22) and to the ascendancy of the euro as a replacement for many European national currencies.

Options on futures

In the United States, options on futures trade only on futures exchanges, and futures exchanges trade only options on futures. In general, each futures exchange trades options on its own active futures contracts. Therefore, the variety of options on futures is almost as diverse as futures contracts themselves.

Because the futures market is dominated by two large exchanges, the Chicago Mercantile Exchange (CME) and the Chicago Board of Trade (CBOT), these two exchanges have the largest share of trading of options on futures. Table 10.8 shows the relative volume of trading in options on futures by exchange. Together, the CME and CBOT have over 85 percent of all volume. Both of these exchanges trade options on agricultural commodities and financial instruments. The New York Mercantile Exchange is the third largest exchange for trading options on futures, largely because of its successful oil-related products. The other exchanges have only minor volume.

Table 10.9 shows the volume of trading in futures options by the type of the underlying futures. Interest rate products account for the majority of futures options. Options on energy futures constitute the second largest category, and this volume stems mainly from options on oil-related futures traded primarily at the New York Mercantile Exchange (NYMEX). Options on traditional agricultural futures are the third largest category.

Table 10.9   Futures option open interest and volume, 2005

Type of underlying futures contract	Millions of contracts	Percentage
Interest rates	284.42	77.30
Energy products	33.84	9.20
Agricultural commodities	26.25	7.13
Equity indexes	15.41	4.19
Precious metals	4.02	1.09
Foreign currency	3.22	0.87
Nonprecious metals	0.14	0.04
Other	0.67	0.18
Total	367.97	100.00

Source: The Futures Industry Association's report entitled *Volume of Futures and Options Trading on U.S. Futures Exchanges, 1968–2005*. © Futures Industry Association. Reprinted by permission of the Futures Industry Association

Option trading procedures

Every options trader needs to be familiar with the basic features of the market. This section explores the process by with option orders are placed and executed.

Like the futures exchanges discussed in earlier chapters, options exchanges are also moving rapidly toward electronic trading. As we have seen, the ISE, an all-electronic exchange, has in only a few short years become one of the dominant options exchanges in the United States. The discussion below describes both floor-based trading procedures, such as those found at the CBOE, and electronic trading procedures, such as those found at the ISE.

Floor-based market participants

From its image in the popular press and television, one gets the impression that the exchange floor is the scene of wild and chaotic action. Although the action may become wild, it is never chaotic. Understanding the role of the different participants on the floor helps dispel the illusion of chaos. Essentially, there are three types of people on the exchange floor: traders, clerical personnel associated with the traders, and exchange officials.

There are four different kinds of participants on the floor of the exchange: market makers, floor brokers, order book officials, and exchange officials. A market maker is a trader who trades for his or her own account. A floor broker trader is a trader who executes orders for another trader. The order book official is an employee of the exchange, who makes certain kinds of option trades and keeps the book of orders awaiting execution at specified prices. Exchange officials record and report prices and conduct surveillance of trading operations. The various types of participant are described below.

The market maker

The typical market maker owns or leases a seat on the options exchange and trades for his or her own account to make a profit. However, as the name implies, the market maker has an obligation to make a market for the public by standing ready to buy or sell options. Typically, a market maker will concentrate on the options of just a few stocks. Focusing on a few issues allows the market maker to become quite knowledgeable about the other traders who deal in options on those stocks.

Market makers follow different trading strategies, and they switch freely from one strategy to another. Some market makers are scalpers. The scalper follows the psychology of the trading crowd and tries to anticipate the direction of the market in the next few minutes. The scalper tries to buy if the price is about to rise and tries to sell just before it falls. Generally, the scalper holds a position for just a few minutes, trying to make a profit on moment-to-moment fluctuations in the option's price. By contrast, a position trader buys or sells options and holds a position for a longer period. This commitment typically rests on views about the underlying worth of the stock or movements in the economy. Both scalpers and position traders often trade option combinations. For example, they might buy a call at a strike price of 90 and sell a call with a strike price of 95. Such a combination is called a **spread**. A spread is any option position in two or more related options. In all such combination trades, the trader seeks to profit from a change in the price of one option relative to another.

The floor broker

Many option traders are located away from the trading floor. When an off-the-floor trader enters an order to buy or sell an option, the floor broker has the job of executing the order. Floor brokers typically represent brokerage firms, such as Merrill Lynch or Prudential Bache. They work for a salary or receive commissions, and their job is to obtain the best price on an order while executing it rapidly. Almost all brokers have support personnel who assist in completing trades. For example, major brokerage firms will have clerical staff who receive orders from beyond the trading floor. These individuals deal with all of the record keeping necessary to execute an order and assist in transmitting information to and from the floor brokers. In addition, many brokerage firms engage in proprietary trading—trading for their own account. Therefore, they have a number of trained people on the floor of the exchange to seek trading opportunities and to execute transactions through a floor broker.

The order book official

The order book official is an employee of the exchange, who can also trade. However, the official cannot trade for his or her own account. Instead, the order book official primarily helps to facilitate the flow of orders. The order book is the listing of orders that are awaiting execution at a specific price. The order book official discloses the best limit orders (highest bid and lowest ask) awaiting execution. In essence, the order book official performs many of the functions of a specialist on a stock exchange. The order book official also has support personnel to help keep track of the order book and to log new orders into the book as they come in.

Exchange officials

Exchange officials comprise the fourth group of floor participants. We have already noted that the order book official and his or her assistants are exchange employees. They serve the special function we described above. However, there are other exchange employees on the floor, such as price reporting officials and surveillance officials. After every trade, price reporting officials enter the order into the exchange's price reporting system. The details of the trade immediately go out over a financial reporting system, so that traders all over the world can obtain the information reflected in the trade. This process takes just a few seconds. Then traders and other interested parties around the world will know the price and quantity of a particular option that just traded. In addition to personnel involved with price reporting, the exchange has personnel on the floor to monitor floor activity. The exchange is responsible for providing an honest marketplace, so it strives to maintain an orderly market and to ensure that brokers and market makers follow exchange rules.

Electronic trading participants

Just as with floor-based trading systems, electronic trading systems have participants who play specific roles in the trading process. At the ISE, participants are defined by the roles and responsibilities they have in posting bids and offers, and improving the price received by the customer. The ISE defines three types of participant: primary market makers, competitive market makers, and electronic access members.

The primary market maker

Primary market makers have many important responsibilities. They must oversee the opening of the market. They must provide continuous quotations in all their assigned option classes and maintain orderly markets. They must also handle customer orders even when the exchange's price is not the best available price when compared to prices posted on competing option exchanges. Finally, they serve as a point of contact for customers to answer market questions. One primary market maker is appointed to each group of assigned option classes. At the ISE there are ten primary market makers.

The competitive market maker

Competitive market makers are required to provide continuous quotations in at least 60 percent of the option classes to which they are assigned. Up to 16 competitive market makers are appointed to each group of assigned option classes.

The electronic access member

An electronic access member is a broker–dealer who places orders on the exchange for his or her own account or for customer accounts. Each electronic access member pays an access fee that permits the firm to place orders in all the options traded on the exchange. Electronic access members cannot engage in market making activities on the exchange.

Other trading systems

The alignment of personnel described here follows the practice at the CBOE and the Pacific Exchange. Other exchanges, such as the American and Philadelphia Stock Exchanges, use a specialist instead of an order book official. In this system, the specialist keeps the limit order book but does not disclose the outstanding orders. Also, the specialist alone bears the responsibility for making a market, rather than relying on a group of market makers. In place of market makers, these exchanges have registered option traders, who buy and sell for their own account or act as brokers for others.

One of the most important differences between the two systems is the role of the market makers and registered option traders. At the CBOE and the Pacific Exchange, a market maker cannot act as a broker and trade for his account on the same day. The same individual can play different roles on different days, however. Restricting individuals from simultaneously acting as market makers and brokers helps avoid a conflict of interest between the role of market maker and broker. The system of allowing an individual simultaneously to trade for him- or herself (as a market maker) and to execute orders for the public (a broker) is called **dual trading**. Many observers believe that dual trading involves inherent conflicts of interest between the role of broker and market maker. For example, consider a dual trader who holds an order to execute as a broker. If this dual trader suddenly confronts a very attractive trading opportunity, he may well decide to take it for his own profit, rather than execute the order for his customer.

Types of orders

Every option trade falls into one of four categories. It can be an order to:

(1)   open a position with a purchase;
(2)   open a position with a sale;
(3)   close a position with a purchase; or
(4)   close a position with a sale.

For example, a trader could open a position by buying a call and later close that position by selling the call. Alternatively, he could open a position by selling a put and close the position by buying a put. An order that closes an existing position is an **offsetting order**.

As in the stock market, there are numerous types of orders in the options market. The simplest order is a market order. A market order instructs the floor broker to transact at whatever price is currently available in the marketplace. For example, one might place an order to buy one call contract for a stock on the market. The floor broker will fill this order immediately at the best price currently available. As in the stock market, the alternative to a market order is a limit order. In a limit order, the trader instructs the broker to fill the order only if certain conditions are met. For example, assume that an option trades for $5^{1}/_{8}$. In this situation, one might place a limit order to buy an option only if the price is $5 or less. In a limit order, the trader tells the broker how long to try to fill the order. If the limit order is a day order, the broker is to fill the order that day if it can be filled within the specified limit. If the order cannot be filled that day, the order expires. Alternatively, a trader can specify a limit order as being good-until-canceled. In this case, the order stays on the limit order book indefinitely.

Order routing and execution

To get a better idea of how an order is executed, let us trace an order from an individual trader. A college professor in Miami decides that today is the day to buy an option on XYZ. One way he can place his order is to call his local broker and give instructions to buy a call. The broker takes the order and makes sure she has recorded the order correctly. The broker then transmits the order to the brokerage firm's representatives at the exchange. Usually, this is done over a computerized system operated by the brokerage firm.

In a floor-based trading environment, the brokerage firm's clerical staff on the floor of the exchange receives the order and gives it to a runner. The runner quickly moves to the trading area and finds the firm's floor broker who deals in XYZ options. The floor broker executes the order by trading with another floor broker, a market maker, or an order book official. Then the floor broker records the price obtained and information about the opposite trader. The runner takes this information from the floor broker back to the clerical staff on the exchange floor. The brokerage firm clerks confirm the order to the Miami broker, who tells the professor the result of the transaction. In the normal event, the entire process takes about two minutes and the professor can reasonably expect to receive confirmation of his order in the same phone call used to place the order.

Instead of calling his broker, the professor could log onto his online trading account with his broker. The pull-down menus on the trading screen allow the professor to specify the quantity and type of option, as well as providing instructions on how the order is to be placed. Once the professor hits the "place trade" button, the order is immediately routed through the broker's systems to the trading venue that provides the best-quality execution for the professor's trade. The professor waits at his screen for a few seconds before receiving a message that his trade is confirmed.

The long bumpy road to the multiple listing of equity options

CBOE established a market for exchange-traded equity option contracts in 1973. Between 1973 and 1975, options traded only on CBOE. Within the next couple of years, the SEC approved stock options trading on the American Exchange (AMEX; December 19, 1974), the Philadelphia Exchange (PHLX; May 15, 1975), the Pacific Coast Exchange (PSE; March 30, 1976), and the Midwest Stock Exchange (MSE; December 8, 1976). At first, none of these exchanges chose to cross-list the same options as their competitors. The first multiple listing occurred in 1976, when CBOE began trading options that were also listed at PHLX. Between February 1976 and July 1977, 22 call option classes were listed on more than one exchange. In response to the growth in equity options trading, the questions surrounding trading on multiple exchanges, and reported sales and trading abuses, the SEC imposed a moratorium on options listings on July 18, 1977. After completing the study in 1978, the SEC decided to permit new listings of stock options, but not to permit multiple trading of any new listings. Instead, the SEC proposed a lottery system to allocate an exclusive, but not transferable right to trade a new option class to a single exchange. This plan, formally known at the SEC as "The Allocation Plan," but known on the street as "The Hat," was adopted by the SEC in May 1980.

This allocation plan, however, was not used for the trading on nonstock options or options on OTC stocks. In approving the CBOE's proposal to trade options on GNMA securities, the SEC did not grant CBOE an exclusive right to such options, ruling instead that the options could be traded on any authorized exchange. The SEC stated that "[c]ompetitive forces should be permitted to define the structure on the nonequity options markets to the maximum extent possible." Subsequently, the SEC granted approval for multiple trading of options on broad-based (November 22, 1982) and narrow-based (August 12, 1083) stock indexes, Treasury securities (October 14, 1982), foreign currencies (October 14, 1982), and OTC equities (May 8, 1985).

In May 1989, the SEC passed a rule (Rule 19c-5) that prohibited exchanges from restricting the multiple listing of any option class. This reversal in policy was based on the SEC's view that competition between exchanges would bring substantial benefits to investors in the form of better option prices, improved services, and innovative products. At the same time, the SEC mandated the creation of an intermarket order routing system to link the exchanges that were trading similar option products. The SEC was concerned that the absence of a linkage system would lead to disparate pricing of the same option on different exchanges. The intermarket linkage policy of the SEC regarding the multiple trading of stock options reflects the congressional mandate for a National Market System. After various delays, exchanges were free to list any option class by the end of 1994. At this time, all new option listings became immediately available for listing on multiple exchanges. Existing contracts whose trading rights had previously been allocated to a single exchange gradually became available for cross-listing. However, up until August 1999, less than 40 percent of option trading volume occurred in options listed on a more than one exchange. In mid-August 1999, U.S. options exchanges began a campaign to target each other's exclusively listed stock options. By the end of September 1999, 76 percent of option volume occurred in options that were listed on multiple exchanges. By August 2000, 85 percent of trading volume occurred in options that were listed on multiple exchanges and 63 percent occurred in options that were traded on four or more exchanges. De Fontnouville, Fishe, and Harris found that bid–ask spreads for options declined 30–40 percent following multiple listing.[7]

The clearinghouse

In executing the trade just described, the buyer of a call has the right to purchase 100 shares of XYZ at the exercise price. However, it might seem that the buyer of the call is in a somewhat dangerous position, because the seller of the call may not want to fulfill his part of the bargain if the price of XYZ rises. For example, if XYZ sells for $120, the seller of the call may be unwilling to part with the share for $100. The purchaser of the call needs a mechanism to secure his position without having to force the seller to perform.

The clearinghouse, the Options Clearing Corporation (OCC), performs this role. After the day's trading, the OCC first attempts to match all trades. For the college professor's transaction, there is an opposite trading party. When the broker recorded the purchase for the professor, she traded with someone else who also recorded the trade. The clearinghouse must match the paperwork from both sides of the transaction. If the two records agree, the trade is a matched trade. This process of matching trades and tracking payments is called **clearing**. Every options trade must be cleared. If records by the two sides of the trade disagree, the trade is an **outtrade** and the exchange works to resolve the disagreement.

Assuming that the trade matches, the OCC guarantees both sides of the transaction. The OCC becomes the seller to every buyer and the buyer to every seller. In essence, the OCC interposes its own credibility for that of the individual traders. This has great advantages. The college professor did not even know the name of the seller of the option. Instead of being worried about the credibility of the seller, the professor needs only to be satisfied with the credibility of the OCC. But the OCC is well capitalized and anxious to keep a smoothly functioning market. Therefore, the college professor can be assured that the other side of his option transaction will be honored. If an option trader fails to perform as promised, the OCC absorbs the loss and proceeds against the defaulting trader. Because the OCC is a buyer to every seller and a seller to every buyer, it has a zero net position in the market. It holds the same number of short and long positions. Therefore, the OCC has very little risk exposure from fluctuating prices.

Margins

Besides having a net zero position, the clearinghouse further limits its risk by requiring margin payments from its clearing members. A clearing member is a securities firm that has an account with the clearinghouse. All option trades must be channeled through a clearing member to the clearinghouse. Most major brokerage firms are clearing members. Individual market makers, however, are not clearing members, and they must clear their trades through a clearing member. In effect, the clearing member represents all of the parties that it clears to the clearinghouse. By demanding margin payments from its clearing members, the clearinghouse further ensures its own financial integrity. Each clearing member in turn demands margin payments from the traders it clears. The margin payments are immediate cash payments that show the financial integrity of the traders and help to limit the risk of the clearing member and the clearinghouse.

To understand margins, we recall that there are four basic positions: long a call, or long a put; and short a call, or short a put. The margin rules differ with the type of position. First, options cannot be bought on credit. The buyer of an option pays the full price of the option by the morning of the next business day. For example, the college professor in Miami who buys a call or put must pay his broker in full for the purchase. We may think of long option positions as requiring 100 percent margin in all cases.

For option sellers, margin rules become very important. The Federal Reserve Board sets minimum margin requirements for option traders. However, each exchange may impose additional margin requirements. Also, each broker may require margin payments beyond those required by the Federal Reserve Board and the exchanges. A single broker may also impose different margin requirements on different customers. Further, options on different underlying instruments are subject to different margin requirements. Because these option requirements may differ so radically and because they are subject to frequent adjustment, this section illustrates the underlying principles of margin rules for options on stocks.[8]

The seller of a call option may be required to deliver the stock if the owner of a call exercises his option. Therefore, the maximum amount the seller can lose is the value of the share. If the seller keeps money on deposit with the broker equal to the share price, then the broker, clearing member, and clearinghouse are completely protected. This sets an upper bound on the reasonable amount of margin that could be required. Sometimes the seller of a call has the share itself on deposit with the broker. In this case, the seller has sold a **covered call**—the call is covered by the deposit of the shares with the broker. If the call is exercised against the seller of a covered call, the stock is immediately available to deliver. Therefore, there is no risk to the system in a covered call. Accordingly, the margin on a covered call is zero.

If the seller of a call does not have the underlying share on deposit with the broker, the seller has sold an **uncovered call** or a **naked call**. We have just seen that the maximum possible loss is the value of the share. For the writer of a put, the worst result is being forced to buy a worthless stock at the exercise price. This worst case gives a loss equal to the exercise price. Therefore, if the margin equaled the exercise price, the broker, clearing member, and clearinghouse would be fully protected. Instead of demanding complete protection, the seller of a call or put must deposit only a fraction of the potential loss as an **initial margin**.

For a seller of an option, the margin requirement depends on whether the option is in-the-money or out-of-the-money. If the option is in-the-money, the initial margin equals 100 percent of the proceeds from selling the option plus an amount equal to 20 percent of the value of the underlying stock. For example, assume that a stock currently sells for $105 and a trader sells a call contract for 100 shares with a strike price of $100 on this stock for $6 per share. Ignoring brokerage fees, the proceeds from selling the call would be $600. To this, we add 20 percent of the value of the underlying stock, or $2,100 for the 100 shares. Therefore, the initial margin requirement is $2,700.

If the option is out-of-the-money, the rule is slightly different. The initial margin equals the margin sale proceeds plus 20 percent of the value of the underlying stock minus the amount the option is out-of-the-money. However, this margin rule could result in a negative margin, so the initial margin must also equal 100 percent of the option proceeds plus 10 percent of the value of the underlying security. Consider a call that is out-of-the-money, with the stock trading at $15 per share and the option having an exercise price of $20 and trading for $1. Based on a 100-share contract and ignoring any brokerage commissions, the margin must be the proceeds from selling the option ($100), plus 20 percent of the value of the underlying stock ($0.20 \times $15 \times 100 = 300), less the amount the option is out-of-the-money [($20 − $15) × 100 = $500]. This gives a margin requirement that is negative ($100 + $300 − $500 = −$100). Therefore, the second part of the rule comes into play. The minimum margin must equal the sale proceeds from the option ($100) plus 10 percent of the value of the underlying stock ($0.10 \times $15 \times 100 = 150). Therefore, the margin for this trade will be $250.

The margins we have been discussing are initial margin requirements. The trader must make these margin deposits when he or she first trades. If prices move against the trader, he or she will be required to make additional margin payments. As the stock price starts to rise and causes losses for the short trader, the broker requires additional margin payments, called maintenance margin. By requiring maintenance margin payments, the margin system protects the broker, clearing member, and clearinghouse from default by traders. This system also benefits traders, because they can be confident that payments due to them will be protected from default as well.

Many option traders trade option combinations. Margin rules apply to these transactions as well, but the margin requirements reflect the special risk characteristics of these positions. For many option combinations, the risk may be less than the risk of a single long or short position in a put or call.[9]

The Options Price Reporting Authority (OPRA)

OPRA (pronounced like the word "opera") is the options industry organization responsible for collecting, consolidating, and disseminating transaction prices, quotations, and other market information generated by the trading of securities options in the United States. OPRA is owned and governed by the six option exchanges in the United States, who provide the data and share in the revenue OPRA receives from selling the data to information vendors and other subscribers. OPRA was created in response to the 1975 National Market System amendment to the Securities Exchange Act of 1934, requiring that transaction and quotation information generated by option exchanges be consolidated into a single real-time database. In mandating a consolidated database, Congress hoped to promote competition between exchanges by ensuring that investors had single-source access to the best price and best quote information across all options exchanges.

Commissions

As we have seen, the same brokerage system that trades stocks can execute option transactions. In stocks, commission charges depend on the number of shares and the dollar value of the transaction. A similar system applies for call option contracts. The following schedule shows a representative commission schedule from a discount broker:

Dollar value of transaction	Representative commissions for broker-assisted trades
$0–2,500	$29 + 1.6% of principal amount
$2,500–10,000	$49 + 0.8% of principal amount
$10,000+	$99 + 0.3% of principal amount

Internet trading is considerably cheaper, perhaps $10 per transaction plus $1 for each contract traded. Fees for broker-assisted orders can be substantially higher.[10] In addition to these fees, each transaction can be subject to certain minimum and maximum fees. For instance, a broker might have a maximum fee per contract of $40.

As an example of commissions with this fee schedule, assume that you buy five contracts with a quoted price of $6.50. The cost of the option would be $650 per contract, for a total cost of $3,250. The commission would be $49 + 0.008 × $3,250 = $75. For the same dollar value of a transaction in stocks, the commission tends to be lower. However, once the dollar amount of the transaction approaches $10,000, commissions on stocks and options tend to be similar.

Even though the commission per dollar of options traded may be higher than for stocks, there can be significant commission savings in trading options. In our example, the option price is $6.50 per share of stock. The share price might well be $100 or more. If it were $100, trading 500 shares would involve a transaction value of $50,000. Commissions on a stock transaction of $50,000 would be much higher than commissions on our option transaction. Trading the option on a stock and trading the stock itself can give positions with very similar price actions. Therefore, option trading can provide commission savings over stock trading. This principle holds even though option commissions tend to be higher than stock commissions for a given dollar transaction.

Another way to see this principle is to realize that options inherently have more leverage than a share of stock. As an example, assume that the stock price is $100 and the option on the stock trades for $6.50. If the stock price rises 3 percent to $103, the option price could easily rise 30 percent to $8.45. On a percentage basis, the option price moves more than the stock price. Unfortunately for option traders, this happens for price increases and decreases. With this greater leverage, the same dollar investment in an option will give a greater dollar price movement than investment in the stock.

Taxation

Taxation of option transactions is no simple matter. We cannot hope to cover all of the nuances of the tax laws in this brief section. Therefore, we will attempt merely to illustrate the basic principles.

Disposition of an option, either through sale, exercise, or expiration, gives rise to a profit or loss. Profits and losses on options trading are treated as capital gains and losses. Therefore, option profits and losses are subject to all the regular rules that pertain to all capital gains and losses. Capital gains may be classified as either long term or short term. A capital gain is a long-term gain if the instrument generating the gain has been held longer than one year; otherwise, the gain or loss is short term. In general, long-term capital gains qualify for favorable tax treatment.

Capital losses offset capital gains and thereby reduce taxable income. However, capital losses are deductible only up to the amount of capital gains plus $3,000. Any excess capital loss cannot be deducted, but must be carried forward to offset capital gains in subsequent years. For example, assume that a trader has capital gains of $17,500 from securities trading. Unfortunately for the trader, he also has $25,000 in capital losses. Therefore, $17,500 of the losses completely offset the capital gains, freeing the trader from any taxes on those gains. This leaves $7,500 of capital losses to consider. The trader can then use $3,000 of this excess loss to offset other income, such as wages. In effect, this protects $3,000 of wages from taxation. The remaining $4,500 of losses must be carried forward to the next tax year, where it can be used to offset capital gains realized in that tax year.

Option transactions give rise to capital gains and losses, and the tax treatment differs for buyers and sellers of options. Further, the tax treatment becomes very complicated for combinations of options. Therefore, we consider only the four simplest stock option positions: long a call, short a call, long a put, or short a put.

Long a call
If a call is exercised, the price of the option, the exercise price, and the brokerage commissions associated with purchasing and exercising the option are treated as the cost of the stock for tax purposes. The holding period for the stock begins on the day after the call is exercised, so the stock must be held for a year to qualify for treatment as a long-term capital gain. If the call expires worthless, it gives rise to a short-term or long-term capital loss equal to the purchase price of the option plus any associated brokerage fees incurred in purchasing the option. If the option is sold before expiration, the capital gain or loss is the sale price of the option minus the purchase price of the option minus any brokerage fees incurred.

Short a call
When a trader sells a call, the premium that is received is not treated as immediate income. Instead, the treatment of this premium depends upon the disposition of the short call. If the call expires without being exercised, the gain on the transaction equals the price of the option less any brokerage fees, and this gain is always treated as a short-term gain, no matter how long the position was held. If the trader offsets the position before expiration, the capital gain or loss equals the sale price minus the purchase price minus any commissions, and this gain or loss is considered a short-term gain or loss without regard to how long the position was held. If the

call is exercised against the trader, the strike price plus the premium received minus any commissions becomes the sale price of the stock for determining the capital gain or loss. The gain or loss will be short-term or long-term depending upon how the stock that is delivered was acquired. For example, if the trader delivers stock that had been held for more than one year, the gain or loss would be a long-term gain or loss.

Long a put

If a put is purchased and sold before expiration, the gain or loss equals the sale price minus the purchase price minus any brokerage commissions, and the gain or loss will be short term or long term depending on how long the put was held. If the put expires worthless, the loss equals the purchase price plus the brokerage commissions, and the loss can be either short term or long term. If the trader exercises the put, the cost of the put plus commission reduces the amount realized upon the sale of the stock delivered to satisfy the exercise. The resulting gain or loss can be either short term or long term depending upon how long the delivered stock was held.

Short a put

The premium received for selling a put is not classified as income until the obligation from the sale of the put is completed. If the trader offsets the short put before expiration, the capital gain or loss equals the sale price minus the purchase price minus the brokerage commissions, and the resulting gain or loss is always a short-term gain or loss. If the put expires worthless, the capital gain equals the sale price less the brokerage commissions, and the capital gain is a short-term gain. If the put is exercised against the trader, the basis of the stock acquired in the exercise equals the strike price plus the commission minus the premium received when the put was sold. The holding period for determining a capital gain or loss begins for the stock on the day following the exercise.

There are other special and more complicated rules for taxing option transactions, so the account here is not definitive. Additional complications arise for some options on stock indexes, for example. Also, there are special tax rules designed to prevent option trading merely to manipulate taxes.[11] Appendix A discusses the new rules for accounting for derivatives, including options.

Option adjustments for corporate events

Stock splits, special dividends, spin-offs, and corporate mergers would seem to present perfect opportunities for option traders to make money. However, traders trying to cash in on such opportunities need to be aware of rules set by both the exchange and the clearinghouse that adjust the terms of outstanding option contracts in response to certain corporate events. These rules have been in place for many years and are well known by professional traders. However, adjustments to outstanding option contracts can sometimes surprise even experienced traders. The policies for adjusting outstanding option contracts are described in a joint publication of the U.S. options exchanges entitled "Characteristics and Risks of Standardized Options," which is available on each exchange's web site.

As a general rule, stock splits will trigger an adjustment in the option contract. For example, in the event of a two for one stock split, the strike prices of all outstanding puts and calls are automatically adjusted to one-half their original value and the number of shares covered by the options are automatically doubled.

As a general rule, adjustments for special cash dividends are made only if they exceed 10 percent of the aggregate market value of the security outstanding. For example, on July 20, 2004, Microsoft announced a $3.00 per share special cash dividend. The closing price for Microsoft stock that day was $28.32 per share, meaning that the cash dividend represented 10.59 percent of the per share value of the stock. Pursuant to OCC rules, the exchanges trading Microsoft options promptly announced that the strike prices of all outstanding Microsoft puts and calls would be adjusted downward by $3.00 per share, the amount of the special dividend, on the date the shareholder became entitled to the dividend (the ex-distribution date). If the Microsoft special dividend had represented less than 10 percent of the per share value of the stock, it would have been treated as an ordinary dividend and no adjustment to the outstanding options would have been made.

Adjustments to option contracts in response to some corporate events are not automatic. In these instances, the decision on whether and how to adjust outstanding option positions is left to the discretion of an adjustment panel consisting of representatives of the exchanges where the options trade. For example, suppose that the ACME corporation spins off its ZETA subsidiary by distributing to its shareholders 1.5 shares of ZETA stock for each share of ACME stock. In this case, outstanding ACME options might be adjusted to requite delivery of 100 shares of ACME stock plus 150 shares of ZETA stock. Alternatively, the exercise prices of outstanding options might be reduced by the value, on a per share basis, of the distributed ZETA shares, as determined by the adjustment panel.

As a general rule, adjustments are not made for tender offers. However, if all of the outstanding shares of an underlying security are acquired in a merger or consolidation, outstanding options will be adjusted to require delivery of the cash, securities, or other property payable to holders of the underlying security as a result of the acquisition. For example, if XYZ is acquired by PQR in a merger where each holder of XYZ stock receives $50 plus a half-share of PQR stock for each share of XYZ stock held, XYZ options might be adjusted to call for the delivery of $5,000 in cash and 50 shares of PQR stock instead of 100 shares of XYZ stock. When an underlying security is converted into a right to receive a fixed amount of cash, options on that security will generally be adjusted to require the delivery upon exercise of a fixed amount of cash, and the trading in the options will ordinarily cease when the merger becomes effective. As a result, after such an adjustment is made all options on that security that are not in the money will become worthless and all that are in the money will have no time value.

Sometimes the adjustment panel faces difficult choices in characterizing a corporate event. For example, in 1985 the management of Phillips Petroleum Corporation used a series of complicated maneuvers to fight off an unsolicited takeover bid by T. Boone Pickens and Carl Icahn. Phillips first arranged a recapitalization plan that would have swapped a package of debt securities and stock for each common share outstanding. Ordinarily, the adjustment panel would have automatically adjusted the outstanding Phillips option contracts to reflect the change in value of Phillips stock, since all shareholders would have been affected equally. But before the recapitalization plan became final, Phillips revised the plan's terms so that the offer applied to only 50 percent of the company's outstanding shares. As a result of the revision to the plan, the adjustment panel decided not to adjust the terms of the Phillips options contracts, since holders of Phillips stock would be affected in different ways depending on whether they chose to accept the offer. In effect, the adjustment panel determined that the revised plan was a tender offer rather than a recapitalization. The adjustment panel decision triggered lawsuits by those who had sold puts early in the Phillips deal. They were betting that the value of Phillips's stock would increase after the recapitalization and that they would be then able to cheaply cover their short put positions.

Instead, put prices soared when Phillips announced its final offer. This is because without adjustment to the option contracts, the puts could be settled with so-called when-distributed shares; that is, the shares reissued under the terms of the recapitalization offer. The when-distributed shares were worth much less than the original shares. Since a put option gives the holder the right to sell shares at the put's exercise price, a fall in the share price relative to the unadjusted strike price makes the puts more valuable to their holders and more costly to their sellers. Call options would continue to be priced on the higher-valued original shares that comprised the 50 percent of shares that were not tendered and therefore still trading. In addition to pointing out the dangers of trying to outguess the actions of the adjustment panel, this case also illustrates the fact that pricing relationships that normally prevail between puts and calls may fall by the wayside in the face of certain corporate events.

Two-tier tender offers also do not result in adjustments. A two-tier offer is structured so as to offer a high price for a "front end" of tendered shares (e.g., the first 60 percent of outstanding shares) and a lower price for the "back end" (i.e., the remaining shares). The purpose of structuring an offer this way is to create incentives for shareholders to tender their shares. If the expiration date of the tender offer precedes the expiration date of outstanding option contracts, then the calls will be priced based on the front end of the offer, and the puts will be priced off the back end. As an example, consider the case of American Medical International. Inverness Medical Innovations, Inc., or IMA, offered $26.50 per share of AMI for the first 63 million shares. The remaining shareholders would have their AMI shares converted to some number of unspecified IMA securities (probably junk bonds). After the expiration of the tender offer, the price of AMI stock dropped from $23^3/_4$ to $8 per share in one day. The market clearly valued the front end of the offer as more valuable than the back end. Obviously, such an event made life extremely challenging for those who had outstanding positions in AMI calls and puts, since the terms of these contracts were unadjusted.

Conclusion

This chapter has introduced the options market. In the short time since they started trading on the Chicago Board Options Exchange, options have helped to revolutionize finance. They permeate the world of speculative investing and portfolio management. Corporations use them in their financing decisions to control risk. Beyond their uses as trading vehicles, options provide a new way to analyze many financial transactions.

Exercises

1 State the difference between a call and a put option.
2 How does a trader initiate a long call position, and what rights and obligations does such a position involve?
3 Can buying an option, whether a put or a call, result in any obligations for the option owner? Explain.
4 Describe all of the benefits that are associated with taking a short position in an option.
5 What is the difference between a short call and a long put position? Which has rights associated with it, and which involves obligations? Explain.
6 Consider the following information. A trader buys a call option for $5 that gives the right to purchase a share of stock for $100. In this situation, identify the exercise price, the premium, and the strike price.
7 Explain what happens to a short trader when the option he or she has sold expires worthless. What benefits and costs has the trader incurred?
8 Explain why an organized options exchange needs a clearinghouse.
9 What is the difference between an American and a European option?
10 Assume that a trader does not want to continue holding an option position. Explain how this trader can fulfill his or her obligations, yet close out the option position.
11 A developer has purchased 60 acres of rural property just north of Augusta, Georgia, to develop a golf course. The golf course development will also include a housing development. In order to generate operating capital, the developer is selling rights. The rights give the holder of the contract the right to purchase lots in the housing development for a fixed price. Each lot in the housing development is half an acre. The agreements expire six months after they are signed. The developer is offering the following inducement. A potential homeowner can purchase a lot for $25,000 at the end of six months if the homeowner enters into the contract this week. The purchase price for a lot increases to $40,000 on all contracts signed after this week.

 A Describe the type of option being sold by the developer.

 B Describe the position held by the potential homeowner as an option.
 C Discuss the risks associated with this transaction.
 D Suppose you purchased the rights on a corner lot on the 18th hole during the inducement period, and you have just found out that legendary golfer Tiger Irons is building a house on the same block. Explain what you think will happen to the value of the right that you own. Is this contract in-the-money?
 E Suppose the developer was selling two contracts. One contract permits you to purchase a lot anytime during the six-month period, while the other allows you to purchase the lot only at the end of six months. Which of the two contracts is worth more? Explain why.
 F To reduce your cash outflows shortly before it became public knowledge that Tiger was going to build a house in the development, you signed a contract with a colleague. This contract gives you the right to sell the lot to your friend anytime in the next six months for $35,000. Describe your position and that of your friend.
 G Describe potential obligations associated with the options involving the developer and the two friends.
 H Suppose the contract that you signed required you to sell the property to your friend at the end of six months for $35,000. What type of contract would this be?
 I Suppose that you signed the contract that required you to sell the property to your friend, but once you found out that Tiger was going to be your neighbor, you did not want to sell the property. What recourse would be available to you?

12 When you purchase or sell an option on the Chicago Board of Options Exchange you contract with the Options Clearing Corporation. Discuss the advantages of this type of trading arrangement.

 A If all trades in a day match, describe the net position of the clearing corporation.

B When a retail customer makes a margin payment, to which organization is the margin paid? Trace the flow of margin funds from the retail customer to the ultimate recipient.

13 Describe the services provided by a market maker, floor broker, and order book official. Discuss the differences between a market maker and an order book official.

14 During an extended period of financial difficulty, a firm's CFO offers the firm's treasurer the following contract in lieu of 25 percent of her salary. The contract permits the treasurer to "clip up to ten coupons," which entitles her to convert each coupon into 10,000 shares of stock at no cost anytime during a three-year period. Suppose the treasurer chooses to accept the contract. Explain what type of contract the treasurer holds.

15 Explain the "rights" attached to a stock option contract traded on the CBOE. Discuss the economic motivation for exercising a stock option at expiration.

16 Explain the obligations associated with establishing a long position in an option contract.

17 Explain the obligations associated with a short position in call and put options.

18 A trader purchases an option for $6.50 that gives him the right to sell 100 shares of stock for $50 per share. Identify the type of option, the option's price, and the option's strike price.

19 Consider the following "opportunities." Determine if the opportunity is an option, and if it is an option, explain what type of option the opportunity represents. Describe positions of the parties involved in the opportunity.

A An old college classmate calls and offers you the opportunity to purchase automobile insurance. The insurance is renewable semiannually.

B You have just received your SAT scores from ETS. It turns out that you had a good day and scored a perfect 1,600. One week later, you receive the following offer in a letter from Private School University. If you enroll in PSU in the Fall, PSU will guarantee that your total annual cost of attending PSU will be $1. The offer applies only if you enroll at PSU for the upcoming Fall semester.

C The following day, your parents, who attended the local state-supported university, receive a letter from their alma mater, Basketball Power University. The letter makes the following offer. If their child enrolls in BPU for the Fall semester, BPU will guarantee that they can purchase ten courtside basketball seats for the face value of the tickets as long as their child is enrolled in BPU.

D A high school classmate calls during dinner from his firm, High Pressure Telemarketing. He offers you the opportunity to enter into a long-term, fixed price, noncancellable lease on a condo in Miami Beach. This opportunity is not a time share, and you cannot sublet the condo.

E You have just purchased 40 acres of heavily wooded land in the nearby hills. To minimize fire danger and relieve work-related stress, you plan to remove all the underbrush and dead trees from the property. The local hardware store is advertising a sale on chain saws. At the store, a sales consultant informs you that they are temporarily out of the saw that you are interested in. The salesperson offers you a rain check that gives you the "opportunity" to purchase the saw at the sale price for two weeks.

F As usual, things are running late. After work, you run home to get dinner. Arriving home, you frantically search for the telephone book. In the middle of the telephone book, you find a coupon from the local pizza parlor, My Pies, that gives you the opportunity to buy a large supreme pizza and two liters of pop for $15.99.

20 Compare the obligations associated with exercising stock index options and stock options.

21 An investor holds a long option position that she wishes to close. Explain the different means available to the investor to close this options position. Explain how your answer varies depending on whether the option position was entered on an exchange or over the counter.

22 Suppose that there are two call options written on the same share of stock, XYZ. Both options have the same expiration date and strike price. Explain why the American option is always worth at least as much as the European option.

23 Explain why the bid–ask spread quoted by the market maker on the floor of the CBOE represents a real cost to an investor trading options. Explain why the investor is willing to trade at the quoted spread prices in a competitive market.

24 Mr. Smith holds a certificate of deposit (CD) from his local bank that matures in three months. He is well aware of the current bull market for stocks, and the opportunity cost of having his money tied up in a CD earning 4.5 percent. When the CD matures, Mr. Smith is planning to invest in the stock market. He feels that the market will continue its strong bull run for the next three months, and he does not want to wait three months to invest in the market. Discuss how Mr. Smith may use options to invest in the market today. Explain the type of contracts and the positions Mr. Smith could use to undertake this investment.

25 It is late in the afternoon of the third Friday of the expiration month, and an investor has an open long position in a deep in-the-money European call option. The investor must decide whether to sell the option in the market while the market is open or to exercise the option at the close of the market. For an option contract, the one-way transaction cost is $25. The exercise fee for an option is $25, and the commission for selling 100 shares of stock is $20. Discuss the impact of transactions costs on the investor's decision to either exercise the option or sell the option.

26 Consider the following option quotations:

Option			Call		Put	
IBM	Strike	Exp.	Vol.	Last	Vol.	Last
$101^3/_8$	115	Sep	1,632	$^3/_{16}$	10	$13^1/_4$
$101^5/_8$	115	Oct	861	$1^1/_4$	10	$14^1/_4$
$101^5/_8$	115	Jan	225	4	3	14

A What is the cost of 15 IBM Oct 115 call options?

B Assume that the clearing corporation is using the following schedule for the calculation of margin requirements:

> The maximum of:
> 100% of the proceeds from the sale of the options plus 20% of the value of the underlying stock position minus the dollar amount the option's contract is out-of-the-money, or 100% of the proceeds from the sale of the options plus 10% of the value of the underlying stock position.

What are the initial margin requirements for the buyer and seller of three IBM Jan 115 call options? Explain how the answer changes if the seller owns 300 shares of IBM.

C Explain what happens to your option position if you are unable to meet a margin call.

Notes

1 Christopher K. Ma and Ramesh P. Rao, "Information Asymmetry and Options Trading," *The Financial Review*, 23:1, February 1988, pp. 39–51, discuss the different roles that options can play for informed and uninformed traders. The informed trader is one with special knowledge about the underlying stock; the uninformed trader has no special knowledge. In their analysis, the informed trader tends to take an outright position in the option, while the uninformed trader is likely to use options to reduce the risk of an existing stock position. Although these factors may benefit market participants, the same authors analyze the effect of a new listing of options on stock prices in "The Effect of Call-Option-Listing Announcement on Shareholder Wealth," *Journal of Business Research*, 15:5, October 1987, pp. 449–65. Ma and Rao show that the listing of an option on a stock that never had options before leads to stock price declines and thus to a loss of shareholder wealth. Apparently, this drop in stock prices reflects the market's view that new option trading is likely to make the stock more volatile. Ma and Rao also find, however, that stock prices rebound when the option actually begins to trade.

2 Consider an option position and a stock position designed to give the same profits and losses for a given movement in the stock price. If we consider a short-term investment horizon, the option strategy will almost always be cheaper and incur lower transaction costs. This is not necessarily true for a long-term investment horizon. All exchange-traded options are dated; that is, they expire within the next few months. Therefore, maintaining an option position in the long term involves trading to replace expiring options. By contrast, taking the stock position requires only one transaction, and the stock can be held indefinitely. Therefore, the repeated transaction costs incurred with the option strategy can involve greater transaction costs in the long term than the stock strategy.

3 Selling stock short involves borrowing a share, selling it, repurchasing the share later, and returning it to its owner. The short seller hopes to profit from a price decline by selling before the decline and repurchasing after the price falls. Rules on the stock exchange restrict the timing of short selling and the use of short sale proceeds.

4 Stephen A. Ross, "Options and Efficiency," *Quarterly Journal of Economics*, 90, February 1976, pp. 75–89, shows that options serve a useful economic role by completing markets. In a complete market, a trader can trade for any pattern of payoffs that he or she desires. The more nearly complete a market is, the greater is its likely efficiency. Thus, because options help to complete markets, they contribute to economic efficiency and thereby raise the welfare level of society as a whole.

5   The "r" and "s" have no specific meaning. However, this is the convention used by *The Wall Street Journal* for its option price reports.

6   The Chicago Mercantile Exchange trades foreign currency futures and options on those futures in a robust market. However, the CME trades no options on the foreign currencies themselves.

7   For a history of multiple listing of options, see Patrick De Fontnouvelle, Raymond P. H. Fishe, and Jeffrey H. Harris, "The Behavior of Bid–Ask Spreads and Volume in Options Markets during the Competition for Listings in 1999," *Journal of Finance*, 58:6, December 2003, pp. 2437–63.

8   George Sofianos, "Margin Requirements on Equity Instruments," *Federal Reserve Bank of New York Quarterly Review*, 13:2, Summer 1988, pp. 47–60, explains margin rules in more detail. Stephen Figlewski, "Margins and Market Integrity: Margin Setting for Stock Index Futures and Options," *Journal of Futures Markets*, 4:3, Fall 1984, pp. 385–416, argues that margins on stocks are set too high relative to margins on options and futures. According to his analysis, the margin requirements give different levels of protection for different instruments.

9   Margins can be devilishly complicated. Andrew Rudd and Mark Schroeder, "The Calculation of Minimum Margin," *Management Science*, 28, December 1982, pp. 1368–79, present a linear program to compute minimum margin under a variety of scenarios.

10 A discount broker executes unsolicited orders for its customers. It provides little or no research information, but seeks to offer fully competitive order execution at reduced prices. Charles Schwab and Quick and Reilly are two leading discount brokerage firms. By contrast, full discount brokers typically have account executives who actively solicit orders from their customer base. The full discount broker also maintains a research department.

11 When options markets were new, there was a substantial controversy over the impact of an option market on the underlying stock. Many economists feared that the existence of an option market would interfere with the market for the underlying good. With the success of the option market, that controversy has subsided substantially. In fact, it now appears that the existence of an option market helps the market for the underlying good. See Raman Kumar, Atulya Sarin, and Kuldeep Shastri, "The Impact of Options Trading on the Market Quality of the Underlying Security: An Empirical Analysis," *Journal of Finance*, 53:2, April 1998, pp. 717–32. These authors find the existence of the option market increases the accuracy of pricing, trading volume, trading frequency, and transaction size. The presence of the option market also leads to a decreased spread in the market for the underlying good.

11

Option Payoffs and Option Strategies

Overview

This chapter considers the factors that determine the value of an option at expiration and introduces the principal strategies used in options trading. When an option is about to expire, it is relatively easy to determine its value. Thus, we begin our analysis by considering option values at expiration. When we say that an option is at expiration, we mean that the owner has a simple choice: exercise the option immediately or allow it to expire as worthless. As we will see, the value of an option at expiration depends only on the stock price and the exercise price. We also give rules for whether an owner should exercise an option or allow it to expire.

With all assets, we consider either the value of the asset or the profit or loss incurred from trading the asset. The value of an asset equals its market price. As such, the value of an asset does not depend on the purchase price. However, the profit or loss on the purchase and sale of an asset depends critically on the purchase price. In considering options, we keep these two related ideas strictly distinct. We present graphs for both the value of options and the profits from trading options, but we want to be sure not to confuse the two. By graphing the value of options and the profits or losses from options at expiration, we develop our grasp

of option pricing principles. To focus on the principles of pricing, we ignore commissions and other transaction costs in this chapter.

Option traders often trade options with other options and with other assets, particularly stocks and bonds. This chapter analyzes the payoffs from combining different options and from combining options with the underlying stock. Many of these combinations have colorful names, such as spreads, straddles, and strangles. Beyond the terminology, these combinations interest us because they offer special profit-and-loss characteristics. We also explore the particular payoff patterns that traders can create by trading options in conjunction with stocks and bonds.

We can use **OPTION!**, the software available from the web site that accompanies this book, to explore the concepts we develop in this chapter. The first module of **OPTION!** analyzes values, profits, and losses of options and option combinations at expiration. **OPTION!** can prepare reports of outcomes, and it can graph profits and losses of all the combinations we explore in this chapter. Detailed instructions for using **OPTION!** are available on the web site www.blackwell-publishing.com/kolb.

Stocks and bonds

We begin our analysis with the two most familiar securities—common stock and a default-free bond. Figure 11.1 presents the graph of the value of a share of stock and the value of a bond at a certain date. At any time, the value of a risk-free pure discount bond is just the present value of the par value. The graph expresses the value of a share of stock and the value of a bond as functions of stock price. In other words, we graph the stock price, or stock value, against the stock price. In the graph, a line runs from the bottom left to the upper right corner. Also, the graph has a horizontal line that intersects the y-axis at $100.

The diagonal line shows the value of a single share of the stock. When the stock price on the x-axis is $100, the value of the stock is $100. The horizontal line reflects the value of a $100 face value default-free bond at maturity. The value of the bond does not depend on the price of the stock. Because it is default-free, the bond pays $100 when it matures, no matter what happens to the stock price. For convenience, we assume that the bond matures in one year, and we graph the value of the stock and bond on that future date. Notice that the value of these instruments does not depend in any way on the purchase price of the instruments.

Figure 11.1 The value of a stock and a bond

Figure 11.2 Profits and losses from a stock

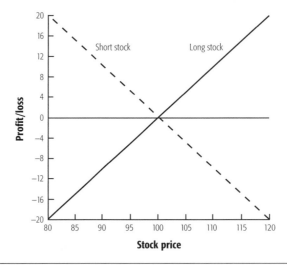

We now consider possible profits and losses from the share of stock and the risk-free bond. Let us assume that the stock was purchased for $100 at time t and that the pure discount (zero-coupon) risk-free bond was purchased one year before maturity at $90.91. This implies an interest rate of 10 percent on the bond. Figure 11.2 graphs the profits and losses from a long and short position in the stock. The solid line running from the bottom left to the top right of Figure 11.2 shows the profits and losses for a long position of one share in the stock, assuming

Figure 11.3   Profits from a bond

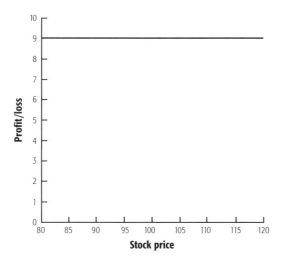

a purchase price of $100. When the stock price is $100, our graph shows a zero profit. If the stock price is $105, there is a $5 profit, which equals the stock price of $105 minus the purchase price of $100.

The dashed line in Figure 11.2 runs from the upper left corner to the bottom right corner and shows the profits or losses from a short position of one share, assuming that the stock was sold at $100. Throughout our discussion of options, we use dotted lines to indicate short positions in value and profit-and-loss graphs. If the stock is worth $105, the short position shows a loss of $5. The short trader loses $5 because he sold the stock for $100. Now with the higher stock price, the short trader must pay $105 to buy the stock and close the short trade. As Figure 11.2 shows, the short trader bets that the stock price will fall. For example, if the trader sells the stock short at a price of $100 and the stock price falls to $93, the short trader can buy the stock and repay the person from whom he borrowed the share, earning a $7 profit (+$100 − $93).

As a final point on stock values and profits, consider the profit-and-loss profile for a combination of a position that is long one share and short one share. If the stock trades at $105, the long position has a profit of $5 and the short position has a loss of $5. Similarly, if the stock trades at $95, the long position has a loss of $5 and the short position has a profit of $5. No matter what stock price we consider, the profits and losses from the long and short positions cancel each other. The profit or loss is always zero. Thus, taking a long and short position in exactly the same good is a foolish exercise.

Figure 11.3 graphs the profits from the bond that we considered. The purchase price of the bond is $90.91, and it matures in one year, paying $100 with certainty. The profit equals the payoff of $100 minus the cost of $90.91. Thus, the owner of the bond has a sure profit of $9.09 at expiration. Figure 11.3 shows this profit with the solid line in the upper portion of the graph. Similarly, the issuer of the bond will lose $9.09. The issuer receives $90.91, but pays $100. Presumably, the issuer has some productive use for the bond proceeds during the year that will yield more than $9.09.

Option notation

We now introduce some notation for referring to options. As we will see, in analyzing options we are often interested in the option price as a function of the stock price, the time until expiration, and the exercise price. The options may be either calls or puts, and the options may be either European or American. Therefore, we adopt the following notation:

S_t is the price of the underlying stock at time t;
X is the exercise price for the option;
T is the expiration date of the option;
c_t is the price of a European call at time t;
C_t is the price of an American call at time t;
p_t is the price of a European put at time t; and
P_t is the price of an American put at time t.

We will often write the value of an option in the following form:

$$c_t(S_t, X, T - t)$$

which means the price of a European call at time t given a stock price at t of S_t, for a call with an exercise price of X, that expires at time T, which is an amount of time $T - t$ from now (time t). For convenience, we sometimes omit the "t" subscript, as in

$$p(S, X, T)$$

In such a case, the reader may assume that the current time is time $t = 0$, and that the option expires T periods from now. In this chapter, we focus principally on the value of options at expiration, so we will be concerned principally with values such as

$$C_T(S_T, X, T)$$

which indicates the price of an American call option at expiration, when the stock price is S_T, the exercise price is X, and the option expires at time T, which happens to be immediately.

Golden Nugget

Does a company have the right to decide whether options can be traded on the stock it issues? In 1987, the American Stock Exchange (AMEX) commenced trading put and call options on Golden Nugget common stock without the firm's consent. Golden Nugget sued the AMEX for misappropriation of Golden Nugget property. The court recognized that the claims in the case were novel and stated, "To succeed on any of its claims, Golden Nugget must persuade us that it has a property or other protectable interest in Golden Nugget common stock owned by its shareholders." The court, however, found it "impossible to conceptualize a property right of the plaintiff that has been misappropriated." The court held that Golden Nugget had no right to stop options trading.

The Golden Nugget case became an important reference case in January 2005, when the International Securities Exchange (ISE) listed options on shares of exchange-traded funds (ETFs). What made this case interesting was that the ETFs were linked to stock indexes with trademark and service marks, and the ISE had not obtained a license from the index providers to list the index-linked ETFs. McGraw-Hill, the provider of the S&P 500® index underlying the SPDR® ETFs, and Dow Jones, the provider of the Dow Jones Industrial Average underlying the DIAMONDS® ETFs, sued the ISE for trademark infringement, misappropriation, and unfair competition. The Options Clearing Corporation (OCC), which cleared the ETFs for ISE, was also sued. Citing the Golden Nugget case, a federal district court held that the index provider did not retain a property interest in the options traded on ETFs linked to the providers' indexes. The court refused to halt ISE's trading of options on the ETFs, in essence agreeing with ISE's reasoning that an ETF trust certificates or depository receipts, even if linked to a stock index, fitted the fact pattern of the Golden Nugget case. Citing the Golden Nugget case, the district court concluded that options on index-linked ETFs were not new products, but conditional contracts to buy or sell an already existing product.

European and American option values at expiration

In general, the difference between an American and a European option concerns only the exercise privileges associated with the option. An American option can be exercised at any time, while a European option can be exercised only at expiration. At expiration, both European and American options have exactly the same exercise rights. Therefore, European and American options at expiration have identical values, assuming the same underlying good and the same exercise price:

$$C_T(S_T, X, T) = c_T(S_T, X, T) \quad \text{and} \quad P_T(S_T, X, T) = p_T(S_T, X, T)$$

Throughout this chapter, we focus on option values and profits at expiration. Therefore, we use the notation for an American option throughout, but the results hold perfectly well for European options as well.

Buy or sell a call option

We now consider the value of call options at expiration, along with the profits or losses that come from trading call options. At expiration, the owner of an option has an immediate choice: exercise the option or allow it to expire worthless. Therefore, the value of the option will either be zero or it will be the **exercise value** or the **intrinsic value**—the value of the option if it is exercised immediately. The value of a call at expiration (whether European or American) equals zero, or the stock price minus the exercise price, whichever is greater. At expiration, there is no question of early exercise, so the principles we explore pertain equally to both American and European calls. For our discussion of option values and profits at expiration, we use the notation for American options (C_T or P_T), but the principles apply identically to European options as well:

$$C_T = \text{MAX}\{0, S_T - X\} \tag{11.1}$$

To understand this principle, consider a call option with an exercise price of $100 and assume that the underlying stock trades at $95. At expiration, the call owner may either exercise the option or allow it to expire worthless. With the prices we just specified, the call owner must allow the option to expire. If the owner of the call exercises the option, he pays $100 and receives a stock that is worth $95. This gives a loss of $5 on the exercise, so it is foolish to exercise.

Instead of exercising, the owner of the call can merely allow the option to expire. If the option expires, there is no additional loss involved with the exercise, because the owner of the call avoids exercising. In our example,

$$S_T - X = \$95 - \$100 = -\$5$$

The call owner need not exercise. By allowing the option to expire, the option owner acknowledges that the call is worthless. With our example numbers, at expiration, we have

$$C_T = \text{MAX}\{0, S_T - X\} = \text{MAX}\{0, \$95 - \$100\} = \text{MAX}\{0, -\$5\} = 0$$

We can extend this example to any ending stock price we wish to consider. For any stock price less than the exercise price, the value of $S_T - X$ will be negative. Therefore, for any stock price less than the exercise price, the call will be worthless. If the stock price equals the exercise price, the value of $S_T - X$ equals zero, so the call will still be worthless. Therefore, for any stock price equal to or less than the exercise price at expiration, the call is worth zero.

If the stock price exceeds the exercise price, the call is worth the difference between the stock price and the exercise price. For example, assume that the stock price is $103 at expiration. The call option with an exercise price of $100 now allows the holder to exercise the option by paying the exercise price. Therefore, the owner of the call can acquire the stock worth $103 by paying $100. This gives an immediate payoff of $3 from exercising. Notice that this example conforms to our principle. Using these numbers, we find that

$$C_T = \text{MAX}\{0, S_T - X\} = \text{MAX}\{0, \$103 - \$100\} = \text{MAX}\{0, \$3\} = \$3$$

Figure 11.4 graphs the value of our example call at expiration. Here, the value of the call equals the maximum of zero or the stock price minus the exercise price. As the graph shows, the value of the call is unlimited, at least in principle. If the stock price were $1,000 at

Figure 11.4　The value of a call at expiration

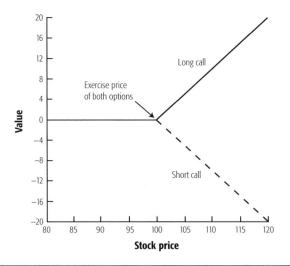

expiration, the call would be worth MAX$\{0, S_T - X\}$ = $900. This graph shows the characteristic shape for a long position in a call option.

Figure 11.4 also shows the value of a short position in the same call option. The dotted line graphs the short position. (For stock prices between 0 and $100, both graphs lie on the same line.) Notice that the short position has a zero value for all stock prices equal to or less than the exercise price. If the stock price exceeds the exercise price, the short position is costly. Using our notation, the value of a short call position at expiration is

$$-C_T = -\text{MAX}\{0, S_T - X\}$$

Assume that the stock price is $107 at expiration. In this case, the call owner will exercise the option. The seller of the call must then deliver a stock worth $107 and receive the exercise price of $100. This means that holding a short position in the call is worth −$7. The short position never has a value greater than zero, and when the stock price exceeds the exercise price, the short position is worse than worthless. From this consideration, it appears that no one would ever willingly take a short position in a call option. However, this leaves out the payments made from the buyer to the seller when the option first trades.

Continuing with our same example of a call option at expiration with a strike price of $100, we consider profit-and-loss results. We assume that the call option was purchased for $5. To profit, the holder of a long position in the call needs a stock price that will cover the exercise price and the cost of acquiring the option. For a long position in a call acquired at time $t < T$, the cost of the call is C_t. The profit or loss on the long call position held until expiration is

$$C_T - C_t = \text{MAX}\{0, S_T - X\} - C_t$$

The seller of a call receives payment when the option first trades. The seller continues to hope for a stock price at expiration that does not exceed the exercise price. However, even if the stock price exceeds the exercise price, there may still be some profit left for the seller. The profit or loss on the sale of a call, with the position being held until expiration, is

$$C_t - C_T = C_t - \text{MAX}\{0, S_T - X\}$$

Figure 11.5 graphs the profits and losses for the call option positions under the assumptions we have been considering. Graphically, bringing profits and losses into consideration shifts the long call graph down by the $5 purchase price and shifts the short call graph up by the $5 purchase price.

We can understand Figure 11.5 for both the long and short positions by considering a few key stock values. We begin with the long position. To acquire a long position in the call option, the trader paid $5. If the stock price is $100 or less, the value of the option is zero at expiration and the owner of the call lets it expire. Therefore, for any stock price equal to or less than the $100 exercise price, the call owner simply loses the entire purchase price of the option. If the stock price at expiration is above $100 but less than $105, the graph shows that the holder of the long call still loses, but loses less than the total $5 purchase price. For example, if the stock price at expiration is $103, the long call holder loses $2 in total. The call owner exercises, buying the $103 stock for $100, and makes $3 on the exercise. This $3 exercise value, coupled with the $5 paid for the option, gives a net loss of $2. As another example, if the stock price is $105 at expiration, the holder of the call makes $5 by exercising, a profit that exactly offsets the purchase price of the option, so there is no profit or loss. From this example, we see that the holder of a call makes a zero profit if the stock price equals the exercise price plus the

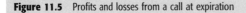

Figure 11.5 Profits and losses from a call at expiration

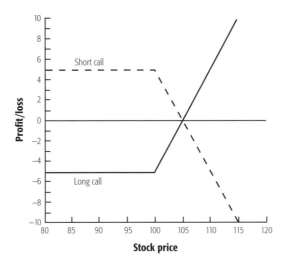

price paid for the call. To profit, the call holder needs a stock price that exceeds the exercise price plus the price paid for the call.

Figure 11.5 shows several important points. First, for the call buyer, the worst that can happen is losing the entire purchase price of the option. Comparing Figure 11.5 with Figure 11.2, we can see that the potential dollar loss is much greater if we hold the stock rather than the call. However, a small drop in the stock price can cause a complete loss of the option price. Second, potential profits from a long position in a call option are theoretically unlimited. The profits depend only on the price of the stock at expiration. Third, our discussion and graph show that the holder of a call option will exercise any time the stock price at expiration exceeds the exercise price. The call holder will exercise to reduce a loss or to capture a profit.

We now consider profit and loss on a short position in a call option. When the long trader bought a call, he paid $5 to the seller. As we noted in Chapter 10, the premium paid by the purchaser at the time of the initial trade belongs to the seller, no matter what happens from that point forward. As Figure 11.5 shows, the greatest profit the seller of the call can achieve is $5. The seller attains this maximum profit when the holder of the call cannot exercise. In our example, the seller's profit is $5 for any stock price of $100 or less, because the call owner will allow the option to expire worthless for any stock price at expiration at or below the exercise price.

If the call owner can exercise, the seller's profits will be lower and the seller may incur a loss. For example, if the stock price is $105, the owner of the call will exercise. In this event, the seller will be forced to surrender a share worth $105 in exchange for the $100 exercise price. This represents a loss for the seller in the exercise of $5, which exactly offsets the price the seller received for the option. So with a stock price of $105, the seller makes a zero profit, as does the call owner. If the stock price exceeds $105, the seller will incur a loss. For example, with a stock price of $115, the call owner will exercise. At the exercise, the seller of the call delivers a share worth $115 and receives the $100 exercise price. The seller thereby loses $15 on the exercise. Coupled with the $5 the seller received when the option traded, the seller now has a net loss of $10.

In summary, we can note two key points about the profits and losses from selling a call. First, the best thing that can happen to the seller of a call is never to hear any more about the transaction after collecting the initial premium. As Figure 11.5 shows, the best profit for the seller of the call is to keep the initial purchase price. Second, potential losses from selling a call are theoretically unlimited. As the stock price rises, the losses for the seller of a call continue to mount. For example, if the stock price went to $1,000 at expiration, the seller of the call would lose $895.

Figure 11.5 also provides a dramatic illustration of one of the most important and sobering points about options trading. The profits from the buyer and seller of the call together are always zero. The buyer's gains are the seller's losses and vice versa:

long call profits + short call profits
$$= (C_T - C_t) + (C_t - C_T) = (\text{MAX}\{0, S_T - X\} - C_t) + (C_t - \text{MAX}\{0, S_T - X\}) = 0$$

Therefore, the options market is a **zero-sum game**; there are no net profits or losses in the market.[1] The trader who hopes to speculate successfully must be planning for someone else's losses to provide his or her profits. In other words, the options market is a very competitive arena, with profits coming only at the expense of another trader.

A brief history of exchange-traded options

The Chicago Board Options Exchange (CBOE) opened for trading on April 26, 1973, becoming the first organized options exchange in the world. Prior to the exchange's formation, if an investor wanted to buy or sell an option he or she phoned one of the put and call dealers who advertised in the financial press and negotiated a contract. Because the market was highly customized, no secondary market existed. This meant that an investor wanting to terminate an option position would have to negotiate with the dealer who dealt the original contract.

CBOE started trading operations under a pilot program, agreed to in negotiations with the SEC, that limited trading to call options on 16 stocks that met the CBOE's listing requirements. By June 1973, CBOE was trading 2,500 options per day on 23 NYSE listed stocks. By March 1976, trading was expanded to 80 stocks, membership had grown from 400 members to 1,300, and seat prices had grown from $10,000 to $94,500. In June 1977, put options began trading. By 1978, more than 100,000 options were being traded on an average day. By 2006, global volume for options on individual equities and options on stock indexes exceeded 20 million contracts per day across more than 50 exchanges.

Call options at expiration and arbitrage

What happens if option values stray from the relationships we analyzed in the preceding section? In this section, we use the no-arbitrage pricing principle to show that call option prices must obey the rules we just developed.[2] If prices stray from these relationships, arbitrage opportunities arise. In the preceding section, we considered an example of a call option with an exercise price of $100. At expiration, with the stock trading at $103, the price of a call option must be $3. In this section, we show that any other price for the call option will create an arbitrage opportunity. If the price is too high, say $4, there is one arbitrage opportunity. If the call is too cheap, say $2, there is another arbitrage opportunity. To see why the call must trade for at least

$3, consider the arbitrage opportunity that arises if the call is only $2. In this case, the money-hungry arbitrageur would transact as follows:

Transaction	Cash flow
Buy one call	−$2
Exercise the call	−100
Sell the share	+103
Net cash flow	+$1

These transactions meet the conditions for arbitrage. First, there is no investment because all the transactions occur simultaneously. The only cash flow is a $1 cash inflow. Second, the profit is certain once the trader enters the transaction. Therefore, these transactions meet our conditions for arbitrage: they offer a riskless profit without investment. If the call were priced at $2, traders would follow our strategy mercilessly. They would madly buy options, exercise, and sell the share. These transactions would cause tremendous demand for the call and a tremendous supply of the share. These supply and demand forces would subside only after the call and share price had adjusted to prevent the arbitrage.

We now consider why the call cannot trade for more than $3 at expiration. If the call price exceeds $3, a different arbitrage opportunity arises. If the call were priced at $4, for example, arbitrageurs would simply sell the overpriced call. Then they would wait to see whether the purchaser of the call would exercise. We consider transactions for both possibilities—the purchaser exercises or does not exercise.

If the purchaser exercises, the arbitrageur has already sold the call and received $4. Now to fulfill his exercise commitment, the seller acquires a share for $103 in the market and delivers the share. Upon delivery, the seller of the call receives the exercise price of $100. These three transactions yield a profit of $1. If the purchaser foolishly neglects to exercise, the situation is even better for the arbitrageur. The arbitrageur has already sold the call and received $4. If the purchaser fails to exercise, the option expires and the arbitrageur makes a full $4 profit. The worst-case scenario still provides the arbitrageur with a profit of $1. Therefore, these transactions represent an arbitrage transaction. First, there is no investment. Second, the transactions ensure a profit.

With a $4 call price, an exercise price of $100, and a stock price at expiration of $103, traders would madly sell call options. The excess supply of options at the $4 price would drive down the price of the option. The process would stop only when the price relationships offered no more arbitrage opportunities. This would happen when the prices of the call and stock conformed to the relationships we developed in the preceding section. In other words, prices in financial markets must conform to our no-arbitrage principle by adjusting to eliminate any arbitrage opportunity.

The purchaser exercises

Transaction	Cash flow
Sell one call	+$4
Buy one share	−103
Deliver share and collect exercise price	+100
Net cash flow	+$1

The purchaser does not exercise	
Transaction	Cash flow
Sell one call	+$4
Net cash flow	+$4

Buy or sell a put option

This section deals with the value of put options and the profits and losses from buying and selling puts when the put is at expiration. Again, we use the notation for an American put (P_T), but all of the conclusions hold identically for European puts. In most respects, we can analyze put options in the same way we analyzed call options. At expiration, the holder of a put has two choices—exercise or allow the option to expire worthless. If the holder exercises, he surrenders the stock and receives the exercise price. Therefore, the holder of a put will exercise only if the exercise price exceeds the stock price. The value of a put option at expiration equals zero, or the exercise price minus the stock price, whichever is higher:

$$P_T = \text{MAX}\{0, X - S_T\} \tag{11.2}$$

We can illustrate this principle with an example. Consider a put option with an exercise price of $100 and assume that the underlying stock trades at $102. At expiration, the holder of the put can either exercise or allow the put to expire worthless. With an exercise price of $100 and a stock price of $102, the holder cannot exercise profitably. To exercise the put, the trader would surrender the stock worth $102 and receive the exercise price of $100, thereby losing $2 on the exercise. Consequently, if the stock price is above the exercise price at expiration, the put is worthless. With our example numbers, we have

$$P_T = \text{MAX}\{0, X - S_T\} = \text{MAX}\{0, \$100 - \$102\} = \text{MAX}\{0, -\$2\} = 0$$

Consider now the same put option with the stock trading at $100. Exercising the put requires surrendering the stock worth $100 and receiving the exercise price of $100. There is no profit in exercising and the put is at expiration, so the put is still worthless. In general, if the stock price equals or exceeds the exercise price at expiration, the put is worthless.

When the stock price at expiration falls below the exercise price, the put has value. In this situation, the value of the put equals the exercise price minus the stock price. For example, assume the stock trades at $94 and consider the same put with an exercise price of $100. Now the put is worth $6, because it gives its owner the right to receive the $100 exercise price by surrendering a stock worth only $94. Using these numbers, we find that

$$P_T = \text{MAX}\{0, X - S_T\} = \text{MAX}\{0, \$100 - \$94\} = \text{MAX}\{0, \$6\} = \$6$$

Figure 11.6 graphs the value of our example put option at expiration. The graph shows the value of a long position as the solid line and the value of a short position as the dashed line. For stock values equaling or exceeding the $100 exercise price, the put has a zero value. If the stock price is below the exercise price, however, the put is worth the exercise price minus the stock price. As our example showed, if the stock trades for $94, the put is worth $6. The graph reflects this valuation.

Figure 11.6   The value of a put at expiration

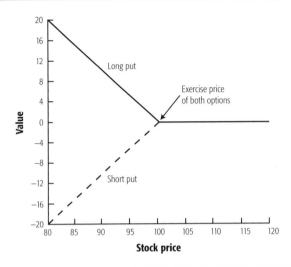

Figure 11.6 also shows the value of a short position in the put. For stock prices equaling or exceeding the exercise price, the put has a zero value. This zero value results from the fact that the holder of the long put will not exercise. However, when the stock price at expiration is less than the exercise price, a short position in the put has a negative value, which results from the opportunity that the long put holder has to exercise. For example, if the stock price is $94, the holder of a short position in the put must pay $100 for a stock worth only $94 when the long put holder exercises. In this situation, the short position in the put will be worth −$6.

Our analysis of put values parallels our results for call options in several ways. First, as we saw with the values of call options at expiration, the value of long and short positions in puts always sums to zero for any stock price. We noted in our discussion of call options that the option market is a zero-sum game. The same principle extends to put options with equal force. Second, we see for put options, as we noted for call options, that a short position can never have a positive value at expiration. The seller of a call or put hopes that nothing happens after the initial transaction, when he collects the option price. The best outcome for the seller of either a put or a call is that there will be no exercise and that the option will expire worthless. Third, noting that a short put position has a zero value at best, we might wonder why anyone would accept a short position. As we saw with a call option, the rationality of selling a put requires us to consider the sale price. This leads to a consideration of put option profits and losses.

We continue with our example of a put option with an exercise price of $100. Now we assume that this option was purchased for a price of $4. We consider how profits and losses on long and short put positions depend on the stock price at expiration. As we did for calls, we consider a few key stock prices.

First, we analyze the profits and losses for a long position in the put, where the purchase price is $4 and the exercise price is $100. If the stock price at expiration exceeds $100, the holder of the put cannot exercise profitably and the option expires worthless. In this case, the put holder loses $4, the purchase price of the option. Likewise, if the stock price at expiration equals $100, there is no profitable exercise. Exercising in this situation would only involve

Figure 11.7   Profits and losses from a put at expiration

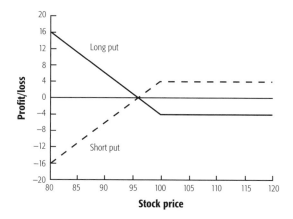

surrendering a stock worth $100 and receiving the $100 exercise price. Again, the buyer of the put option loses the purchase price of $4. Therefore, if the stock price at expiration equals or exceeds the exercise price, the buyer of a put loses the full purchase price. Figure 11.7 shows the profits and losses for long and short positions in the put.

If the stock price at expiration is less than the exercise price, there will be a benefit to exercising. For example, assume that the stock price is $99 at expiration. Then, the owner of the put will exercise, surrendering the $99 stock and receiving the $100 exercise price. In this case, the exercise value of the put is $1. With the $99 stock price, the holder of the put makes $1 on the exercise but has already paid $4 to acquire the put. Therefore, the total loss is $3. If the stock price is $96 at expiration, the buyer of the put makes a zero profit. The $4 exercise value exactly offsets the price of the put. When the stock price is less than $96, the put buyer makes a profit. For example, if the stock price is $90 at expiration, the owner of a put exercises. In exercising, he surrenders a stock worth $90 and receives the $100 exercise price. This gives a $6 profit after considering the $4 purchase price of the option.

Moneyness

In the preceding sections, we have explored the value of calls and puts at expiration. We noted that calls have a positive value at expiration if the stock price exceeds the exercise price, and puts have a positive value at expiration if the exercise price exceeds the stock price. We now introduce important terminology that applies to options both before and at expiration. Both calls and puts can be **in-the-money**, **at-the-money**, or **out-of-the-money**. The following table shows the conditions for puts and calls to meet these moneyness conditions for any time t:

	Calls	Puts
In-the-money	$S_t > X$	$S_t < X$
At-the-money	$S_t = X$	$S_t = X$
Out-of-the-money	$S_t < X$	$S_t > X$

In addition, options can be **near-the-money** if the stock price is close to the exercise price. Further, a call is **deep-in-the-money** if the stock price is considerably above the exercise price, and a put is deep-in-the-money if the stock price is considerably smaller than the exercise price.

How do exchanges select stocks for option listing?

In the stock market, firms apply to the exchange for listing. In the options market, however, decisions on which option contracts to list are made by the exchanges. Stewart Mayhew and Vassil Mihov conducted an empirical study of the listing choices of option exchanges in the United States between 1973 and 1996. Mayhew and Mihov identified a set of firms eligible for listing and then compared the characteristics of those actually selected with those that were eligible but not selected. They found that exchanges tend to list options on stocks with high trading volume, volatility, and market capitalization. They also found that the relative importance of the factors influencing the listing decision has changed significantly over time. When the options industry was young, exchanges selected large firms with high trading volume and volatility was not an important factor. As the industry matured, exchanges starting to select contracts with higher volatility. One implication of their results is that studies purporting to show the effect of option listing on the volatility of underlying stocks may be biased. If exchanges list options in response to or in anticipation of changing volatility, a spurious relation may be introduced between option listing and volatility.[3]

Option combinations

This section discusses some of the most important ways in which traders can combine options. By trading option combinations, traders can shape the risk and return characteristics of their option positions, which allows more precise speculative strategies. For example, we will see how to use option combinations to profit when stock prices move a great deal or when they stagnate.

The straddle

A **straddle** consists of a call and a put with the same exercise price and the same expiration. The buyer of a straddle buys the call and put, while the seller of a straddle sells the same two options.[4] Consider a call and put, both with $100 exercise prices. We assume that the call costs $5 and the put trades for $4. Figure 11.8 shows the profits and losses from purchasing each of these options. The profits and losses for buying the straddle are just the combined profits and losses from buying both options. If we designate T as the expiration date of the option and let t be the present, then C_t is the current price of the option and C_T is the price of the option at expiration. Similarly, P_t is the present price of the put and P_T is the price of the put at expiration. Using this notation, the cost of the long straddle is

$$C_t + P_t$$

and the value of the straddle at expiration will be

$$C_T + P_T = \text{MAX}\{0, S_T - X\} + \text{MAX}\{0, X - S_T\} \tag{11.3}$$

Figure 11.8 Profits and losses at expiration from the options in a straddle

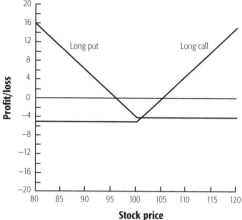

Similarly, the short straddle position costs

$$-C_t - P_t$$

so the short trader receives a payment for accepting the short straddle position. The value of the short straddle at expiration will be

$$-C_T - P_T = -\mathrm{MAX}\{0, S_T - X\} - \mathrm{MAX}\{0, X - S_T\}$$

Because the options market is always a zero-sum game, the short trader's profits and losses mirror those of the long position. Figure 11.9 shows the profits and losses from buying and selling the straddle. As the graph shows, the maximum loss for the straddle buyer is the cost of the two options. Potential profits are almost unlimited for the buyer if the stock price rises or falls enough. As Figure 11.9 also shows, the maximum profit for the short straddle trader occurs when the stock price at expiration equals the exercise price. If the stock price equals the exercise price, the straddle owner cannot exercise either the call or the put profitably. Therefore, both options expire worthless and the short straddle trader keeps both option premiums for a total profit of $9. However, if the stock price diverges from the exercise price, the long straddle holder will exercise either the call or the put. Any exercise decreases the short trader's profits and may even generate a loss. If the stock price exceeds the exercise price, the call owner will exercise, while if the stock price is less than the exercise price, the straddle owner will exercise the put.

Figure 11.9 shows that the short trader essentially bets that the stock price will not diverge too far from the exercise price, so the seller is betting that the stock price will not be too volatile. In making this bet, the straddle seller risks theoretically unlimited losses if the stock price goes too high. Likewise, the short trader's losses are almost unlimited if the stock price goes too low.[5] The short trader's cash inflows equal the sum of the two option prices. At expiration, the short trader's cash outflow equals the exercise result for the call and for the put. If the call is

Figure 11.9 Profits and losses at expiration from a straddle

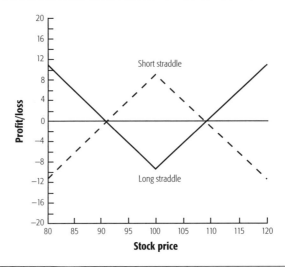

exercised against him at expiration, the short trader loses the difference between the stock price and the exercise price. If the put is exercised against him, the short trader loses the difference between the exercise price and the stock price.

The strangle

Like a straddle, a **strangle** consists of a put and a call with the same expiration date and the same underlying good. In a strangle, the call has an exercise price above the stock price and the put has an exercise price below the stock price. Let X_1 and X_2 be the two exercise prices, such that $X_1 > X_2$. Therefore, a strangle is similar to a straddle, but the put and call have different exercise prices. Let $C_{t,1}$ denote the cost of the call with exercise price X_1 at time t, and let $P_{t,2}$ indicate the cost of the put with exercise price X_2. The long strangle trader buys the put and call, while the short trader sells the two options. The cost of the long strangle is

$$C_t(S_t, X_1, T) + P_t(S_t, X_2, T)$$

Then the value of the strangle at expiration will be

$$C_T(S_T, X_1, T) + P_T(S_T, X_2, T) = \text{MAX}\{0, S_T - X_1\} + \text{MAX}\{0, X_2 - S_T\} \tag{11.4}$$

The cost of the short strangle is

$$-C_t(S_t, X_1, T) - P_t(S_t, X_2, T)$$

The value of the short strangle at expiration will be

$$-C_T(S_T, X_1, T) - P_T(S_T, X_2, T) = -\text{MAX}\{0, S_T - X_1\} - \text{MAX}\{0, X_2 - S_T\}$$

Figure 11.10 Profits and losses at expiration from the options in a strangle

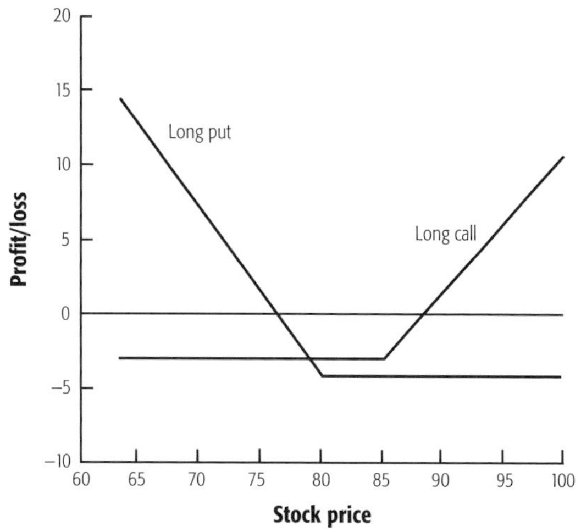

To illustrate the strangle, we use a call with an exercise price of $85 and a put with an exercise price of $80. The call price is $3 and the put price is $4. Figure 11.10 graphs the profits and losses for long positions in these two options. The call has a profit for any stock price above $88, and the put has a profit for any stock price below $76. However, for the owner of a strangle to profit, the price of the stock must fall below $76 or rise above $88. Figure 11.11 shows the profits and losses from buying and selling the strangle based on these two options. The total outlay for the two options is $7. To break even, either the call or the put must give an exercise profit of $7. The call makes an exercise profit of $7 when the stock price is $7 above the exercise price of the call. This price is $92. Similarly, the put has an exercise profit of $7 when the stock price is $73. Any stock price between $73 and $92 results in a loss on the strangle, while any stock price outside the $73–92 range gives a profit on the strangle.

Figure 11.11 shows that buying a strangle is betting that the stock price will move significantly below the exercise price on the put or above the exercise price on the call. The buyer of the strangle has the chance for very large profits if the stock prices move dramatically away from the exercise prices. Theoretically, the profit on a strangle is boundless. A stock price at expiration of $200, for example, gives a profit on the strangle of $108.

The profits on the short position are just the negative values of the profits for the long position. Figure 11.11 shows the profits and losses for the short strangle position as dotted lines. At any stock price from $80 to $85, the short strangle has a $7 profit. Between these two prices, the long trader cannot profit by exercising either the put or the call, so the short trader keeps the full price of both options. For stock prices below $80, the straddle buyer exercises the put, and for stock prices above $85, the straddle buyer exercises the call. Any exercise costs the short trader, who still has some profit if the stock price stays within the $73–92 range. However, for very low stock prices, the short strangle position gives large losses, as it does for very high stock prices. Therefore, the short-strangle trader is betting that stock prices stay within a fairly wide band. In essence, the short-strangle trader has a high probability of a small profit, but accepts the risk of a very large loss.

Figure 11.11   Profits and losses at expiration from a strangle

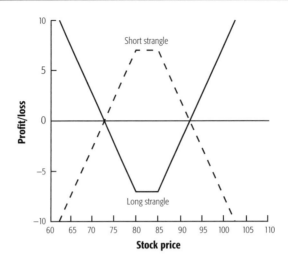

Bull and bear spreads with call options

A **bull spread** in the options market is a combination of options designed to profit if the price of the underlying good rises.[6] A bull spread utilizing call options requires two calls with the same underlying stock and the same expiration date, but with different exercise prices. The buyer of a bull spread buys a call with an exercise price below the stock price and sells a call option with an exercise price above the stock price. The spread is a *bull* spread because the trader hopes to profit from a price rise in the stock. The trade is a *spread* because it involves buying one option and selling a related option. Compared to buying the stock itself, the bull spread with call options limits the trader's risk, but the bull spread also limits the profit potential.

The cost of the bull spread is the cost of the option that is purchased, less the cost of the option that the trader sells. Letting $C_{t,1}$ be the cost of the first option that is purchased at time t with exercise price X_1, and letting $C_{t,2}$ be the cost of the second option with exercise price X_2, such that $X_1 < X_2$, the cost of the bull spread is

$$C_t(S_t, X_1, T) - C_t(S_t, X_2, T)$$

At expiration, the value of the bull spread will be

$$C_T(S_T, X_1, T) - C_T(S_T, X_2, T) = \text{MAX}\{0, S_T - X_1\} - \text{MAX}\{0, S_T - X_2\} \qquad (11.5)$$

To illustrate the bull spread, assume that the stock trades at $100. One call option has an exercise price of $95 and costs $7. The other call has an exercise price of $105 and costs $3. To buy the bull spread, the trader buys the call with the lower exercise price, and sells the call with the higher exercise price. In our example, the total outlay for the bull spread is $4. Figure 11.12 graphs the profits and losses for the two call positions individually. The long position profits if the stock price moves above $102. The short position profits if the stock price does

Figure 11.12 Profits and losses at expiration from the options in a bull spread

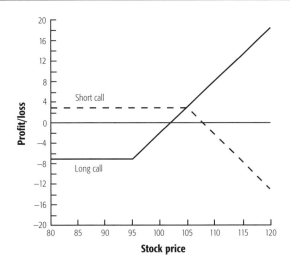

not exceed $108. As the graph shows, low stock prices result in an overall loss for the bull spread, because the cost of buying the call with the lower exercise price exceeds the proceeds from selling the call with the higher exercise price. It is also interesting to consider prices at $105 and above. For every dollar by which the stock price exceeds $105, the long call portion of the spread generates an extra dollar of profit, but the short call component starts to lose money. Thus, for stock prices above $105, the additional gains on the long call exactly offset the losses on the short call. Therefore, no matter how high the stock price goes, the bull spread can never give a greater profit than it does for a stock price of $105.

Figure 11.13 graphs the bull spread as the solid line. For any stock price at expiration of $95 or below, the bull spread loses $4. This $4 is the difference between the cash inflow for selling one call and buying the other. The bull spread breaks even for a stock price of $99. The highest possible profit on the bull spread comes when the stock sells for $105. Then the bull spread gives a $6 profit. For any stock price above $105, the profit on the bull spread remains at $6. Therefore, the trader of a bull spread bets that the stock price goes up, but he hedges his bet. We can see that the bull spread protects the trader from losing any more than $4. However, the trader cannot make more than a $6 profit. We can compare the bull spread with a position in the stock itself in Figure 11.2. Comparing the bull spread and the stock, we find that the stock offers the chance for bigger profits, but it also has greater risk of a serious loss.

A **bear spread** in the options market is an option combination designed to profit from falling stock prices. To execute a bear spread with call options requires two call options with the same underlying stock and the same expiration date. The two calls, however, have different exercise prices. To execute a bear spread with calls, a trader would sell the call with the lower exercise price and buy the call with the higher exercise price. In other words, the bear spread with calls is just the short position to the bull spread with calls.

The cost of a bear spread is

$$-C_t(S_t, X_1, T) + C_t(S_t, X_2, T)$$

Figure 11.13 Profits and losses at expiration from bull and bear spreads with calls

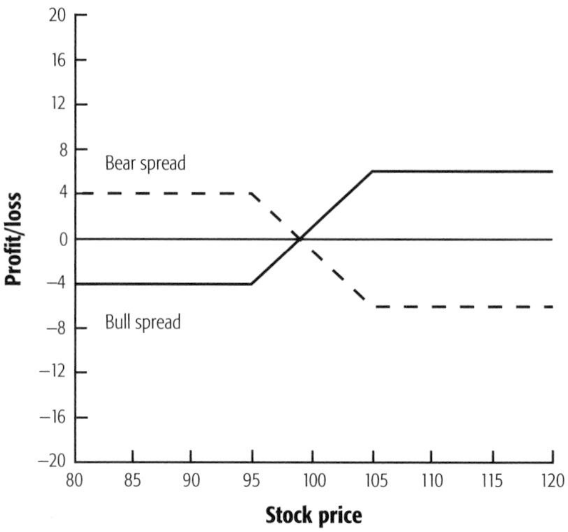

At expiration, the value of the bear spread will be

$$-C_T(S_T, X_1, T) + C_T(S_T, X_2, T) = -\text{MAX}\{0, S_T - X_1\} + \text{MAX}\{0, S_T - X_2\} \tag{11.6}$$

Figure 11.13 shows the profit-and-loss profile for a bear spread with the same options we have been considering. The dotted line shows how profit and losses vary if a trader sells the call with the $95 strike price and buys the call with the $105 strike price. In a bear spread, the trader bets that the stock price will fall. However, the bear spread also limits the profit opportunity and the risk of loss compared to a short position in the stock itself. We can compare the profit-and-loss profiles of the bear spread in Figure 11.13 with the short position in the stock shown as the dotted line in Figure 11.2.[7]

Bull and bear spreads with put options

It is also possible to execute bull and bear spreads with put options in a manner similar to the bull and bear spread with call options. The bull spread consists of buying a put with a lower exercise price and selling a put with a higher exercise price. The bear spread trader sells a put with a lower exercise price and buys a put with a higher exercise price. Consistent with our notation for call options, the cost of the bull spread with puts is

$$P_t(S_t, X_1, T) - P_t(S_t, X_2, T)$$

with exercise prices X_1 and X_2, respectively, such that $X_1 < X_2$. The value of the bull spread at expiration will be

$$P_T(S_T, X_1, T) - P_T(S_T, X_2, T) = \text{MAX}\{0, X_1 - S_T\} - \text{MAX}\{0, X_2 - S_T\} \tag{11.7}$$

It is also possible to initiate a bear spread with puts. The bear spread is just the opposite of a bull spread. For a put bear spread, the trader uses two options on the same underlying good that have the same time until expiration. The trader sells the put with the lower exercise price and buys the put with the higher exercise price. The bear spread with puts is simply the complementary position to the bull spread, and costs

$$-P_t(S_t, X_1, T) + P_t(S_t, X_2, T)$$

The value of the bear spread with puts at expiration is

$$-P_T(S_T, X_1, T) + P_T(S_T, X_2, T) = -\text{MAX}\{0, X_1 - S_T\} + \text{MAX}\{0, X_2 - S_T\}$$

To illustrate bull and bear spreads with put options, consider two puts with the same expiration date and the same underlying stock. Assume that one put has an exercise price of $90 and the other has an exercise price of $110. The put with an exercise price of $90 trades at $3, while the put with an exercise price of $110 trades at $9.

The bull trader would buy the put with $X = \$90$ and sell the put with $X = \$110$, for a total cash inflow of $6. Assume that the stock price at expiration is $90. The bull trader cannot exercise the put option with $X = \$90$. However, the put option with $X = \$110$ that the trader sold will be exercised, giving our trader an exercise loss of $20. Thus, the total loss for the bull trader will be $14, the initial cash inflow of $6 minus the $20 exercise loss. For any terminal stock price lower than $90, the bull trader will lose an additional dollar on the short put position. However, if the stock price falls below $90, the bull trader can exercise the long put with a strike price of $90. Thus, the gain on the long put will offset any further losses on the short put for stock prices lower than $90. Therefore, the maximum loss on the bull spread of $14 occurs with a stock price of $90 or lower.

If the stock price at expiration is $110 or higher, the short put cannot be exercised against the bull trader of our example. Also, the long put cannot be exercised, because it cannot be exercised at any price of $90 or higher. With no exercises occurring, the bull trader merely keeps the initial cash inflow that occurred when the position was assumed, and the bull trader nets a profit of $6.

For prices between $90 and $110, the short put will be exercised against the bull trader and will reduce the trader's profits or generate a loss. For example, if the stock price is $100 at expiration, the bull trader will lose $10 on the exercise of the put with $X = \$110$. This loss, coupled with the initial cash inflow of $6, gives a total loss on the trade of $4. Figure 11.14 shows the profits and losses from this bull trade with puts as the solid line, and it shows the bear spread with puts as a dashed line. As Figure 11.14 shows, the bear trader takes the opposite position from the bull trader.

In terms of our example, the bear trader would buy the put with $X = \$110$ and sell the put with $X = \$90$, for a total outlay of $6. For any terminal stock price less than $110, the bear trader can exercise the put with $X = \$110$, and will break even for a terminal stock price of $104. For any stock price below $90, the bear trader's short call will be exercised against her as well, giving an exercise loss on that option. This exercise loss will offset any further profits on the long put with $X = \$110$. As a result, the bear trader cannot make more than $14. This $14 profit occurs for any stock price of $90 or less. For example, if the terminal stock price is $85, the bear trader has an exercise profit of $25 on the long put with $X = \$110$ and an exercise loss of −$5 on the short put with $X = \$90$. This total exercise profit of $20 must be reduced by the $6 outlay required to assume the bear spread, for a net gain of $14. This gain of $14 when the stock price is $85 exactly equals the loss of $14 that the bull spread holder would incur.

Figure 11.14 Profits and losses at expiration from bull and bear spreads with puts

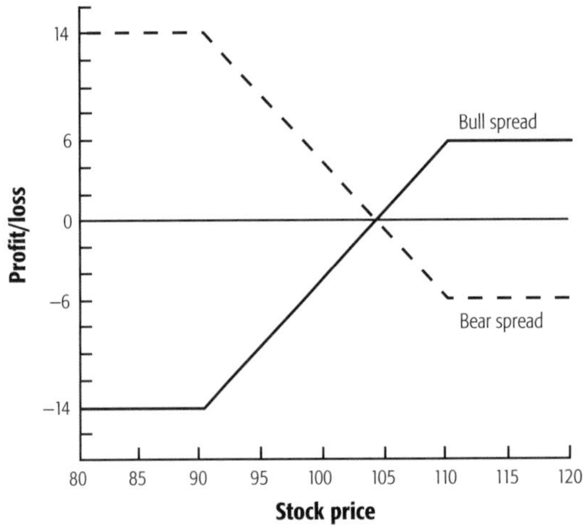

The box spread

A **box spread** consists of a bull spread with calls plus a bear spread with puts, with the two spreads having the same pair of exercise prices. In terms of our notation, the box spread costs

$$C_t(S_t, X_1, T) - C_t(S_t, X_2, T) - P_t(S_t, X_1, T) + P_t(S_t, X_2, T)$$

The value of the box spread at expiration is

$$C_T(S_T, X_1, T) - C_T(S_T, X_2, T) - P_T(S_T, X_1, T) - P_T(S_T, X_2, T)$$
$$= \text{MAX}\{0, S_T - X_1\} - \text{MAX}\{0, S_T - X_2\} - \text{MAX}\{0, X_1 - S_T\} + \text{MAX}\{0, X_2 - S_T\} \quad (11.8)$$

As an example, consider the following four transactions:

Transaction	Exercise price
Long one call	$95
Short one call	105
Long one put	105
Short one put	95

The value of the box spread at expiration will be

$$\text{MAX}\{0, S_T - \$95\} - \text{MAX}\{0, S_T - \$105\} + \text{MAX}\{0, \$105 - S_T\} - \text{MAX}\{0, \$95 - S_T\}$$

For a stock price of $102 at expiration, the payoff will be

$$\$7 - \$0 + \$3 - \$0 = \$10$$

For a stock price of $80, the payoff at expiration will be

$0 – $0 + $25 – $15 = $10

In fact, for any terminal stock price, the box spread will pay the difference between the high and low exercise prices, $X_2 - X_1$, which is $10 in this example. Thus, the box spread is a riskless investment strategy. To avoid potential arbitrage opportunities, the price of the box spread must be the present value of the certain payoff. Therefore, the cost of the box spread purchased at time t must be

$$\frac{X_2 - X_1}{(1 + r)^{(T-t)}}$$

Continuing with this example, let us assume that the options expire in one year and that the risk-free interest rate is 10 percent. Under these assumptions, the box spread must cost $9.09. Any other price would lead to arbitrage.

The butterfly spread with calls

A **butterfly spread** can be executed by using three calls with the same expiration date on the same underlying stock. The long trader buys one call with a low exercise price, buys one call with a high exercise price, and sells two calls with an intermediate exercise price. Continuing to let X_i represent exercise prices such that $X_1 < X_2 < X_3$, the cost of the long butterfly spread is

$$C_t(S_t, X_1, T) - 2C_t(S_t, X_2, T) + C_t(S_t, X_3, T)$$

The value of the butterfly spread at expiration is

$$C_T(S_T, X_1, T) - 2C_T(S_T, X_2, T) + C_T(S_T, X_3, T)$$
$$= \text{MAX}\{0, S_T - X_1\} - 2\,\text{MAX}\{0, S_T - X_2\} + \text{MAX}\{0, S_T - X_3\} \tag{11.9}$$

The short trader takes exactly the opposite position, selling one call with a low exercise price, selling one call with a high exercise price, and buying two calls with an intermediate exercise price. The cost of the short position is

$$-C_t(S_t, X_1, T) + 2C_t(S_t, X_2, T) - C_t(S_t, X_3, T)$$

The value of the short butterfly spread at expiration is

$$-C_T(S_T, X_1, T) + 2C_T(S_T, X_2, T) - C_T(S_T, X_3, T)$$
$$= -\text{MAX}\{0, S_T - X_1\} + 2\,\text{MAX}\{0, S_T - X_2\} - \text{MAX}\{0, S_T - X_3\}$$

For the long trader, the spread profits most when the stock price at expiration is at the intermediate exercise price. In essence, the butterfly spread gives a payoff pattern similar to a straddle. Compared to a straddle, however, a butterfly spread offers lower risk at the expense of reduced profit potential.

As an example of a butterfly spread, assume that a stock trades at $100 and a trader buys a butterfly spread by trading options with the prices shown in the following table:

Figure 11.15   Profits and losses at expiration for the options in a butterfly spread

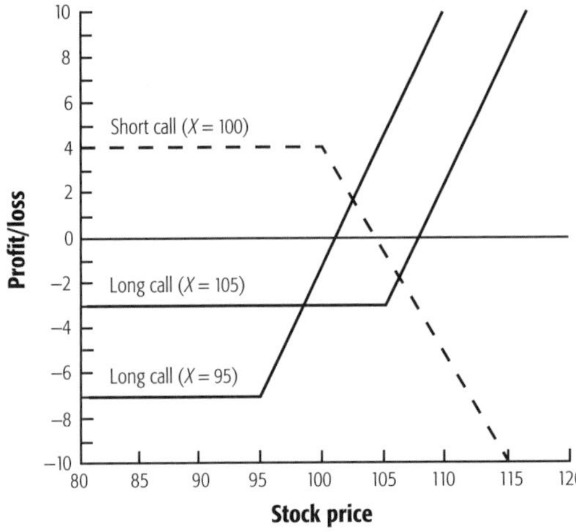

	Exercise price	Option premium
Long one call	$105	$3
Short two calls	100	4
Long one call	95	7

As the table shows, the buyer of a butterfly spread sells two calls with a strike price near the stock price and buys one each of the calls above and below the stock price. Figure 11.15 graphs the profits and losses from each of these three option positions. To understand the profits and losses from the butterfly spread, we need to combine these profits and losses, remembering that the spread involves selling two options and buying two, a total of four options with three different exercise prices.

Let us consider a few critical stock prices to see how the butterfly spread profits respond. The critical stock prices always include the exercise prices for the options. First, if the stock price is $95, the call with an exercise price of $95 is worth zero and a long position in this call loses $7. The long call with the $105 exercise price also cannot be exercised, so it is worthless, giving a loss of the $3 purchase price. The short call position gives a profit of $4 per option and the spread sold two of these options, for an $8 profit. Adding these values gives a net loss on the spread of $2, if the stock price is $95. Second, if the stock price is $100, the long call with a strike price of $95 loses $2 (the $5 stock profit minus the $7 purchase price). The long call with an exercise price of $105 loses its full purchase price of $3. Together, the long calls lose $5. The short call still shows a profit of $4 per option, for a profit of $8 on the two options. This gives a net profit of $3 if the stock price is $100. Third, if the stock price is $105 at expiration, the long call with an exercise price of $95 has a profit of $3. The long call with an exercise price of $105 loses $3. Also, the short call position loses $1 per option for a loss on two positions of $2. This gives a net loss on the butterfly spread of $2. In summary we have a $2 loss for a $95 stock price, a $3 profit for a $100 stock price, and a $2 loss for a $105 stock price.

Figure 11.16   Profits and losses at expiration for a butterfly spread with calls

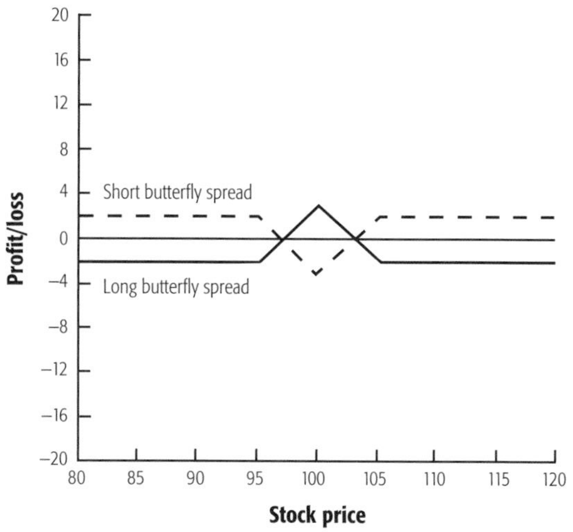

Figure 11.16 shows the entire profit-and-loss graph for the butterfly spread. At a stock price of $100, we noted a profit of $3. This is the highest profit available from the spread. At stock prices of $95 and $105, the spread loses $2. For stock prices below $95 or above $105, the loss is still $2. As the graph shows, the butterfly spread has a zero profit for stock prices of $97 and $103. The buyer of the butterfly spread essentially bets that stock prices will hover near $100. Any large move away from $100 gives a loss on the butterfly spread. However, the loss can never exceed $2. Comparing the butterfly spread with the straddle in Figure 11.9, we see that the butterfly spread resembles a short position in the straddle. Compared to the straddle, the butterfly spread reduces the risk of a very large loss. However, the reduction in risk necessarily comes at the expense of a chance for a big profit.

The butterfly spread with puts

The butterfly spread can also be initiated with a combination of put options. For a long position in a butterfly spread, the trader buys a put with a low exercise price, buys a put with a high exercise price, and sells two puts with an intermediate exercise price. The short trader sells a put with a low exercise price, sells a put with a high exercise price, and buys two puts with an intermediate exercise price.

For the long position in the butterfly spread with puts, the cost is

$$P_t(S_t, X_1, T) - 2P_t(S_t, X_2, T) + P_t(S_t, X_3, T)$$

The value at expiration is

$$P_T(S_T, X_1, T) - 2P_T(S_T, X_2, T) + P_T(S_T, X_3, T)$$
$$= \text{MAX}\{0, X_1 - S_T\} - 2\,\text{MAX}\{0, X_2 - S_T\} + \text{MAX}\{0, X_3 - S_T\} \tag{11.10}$$

For the short trader, the cost of the short position is

$$-P_t(S_t, X_1, T) + 2P_t(S_t, X_2, T) - P_t(S_t, X_3, T)$$

The value at expiration for the short butterfly spread with puts is

$$-P_T(S_T, X_1, T) + 2P_T(S_T, X_2, T) - P_T(S_T, X_3, T)$$
$$= -MAX\{0, X_1 - S_T\} + 2\,MAX\{0, X_2 - S_T\} - MAX\{0, X_3 - S_T\}$$

The long and short butterfly trades with puts give a profit pattern just like the butterfly trade with calls, as illustrated in Figure 11.16.

To explore these transactions more fully, consider the following transactions for a long butterfly spread with puts:

	Exercise price	Option premium
Long one put	$95	$5
Short two puts	100	7
Long one put	105	10

The total cost of this position is $1. If the stock price at expiration is exactly $95, the put with $X = \$95$ cannot be exercised. However, both puts with $X = \$100$ will be exercised against the long trader, for an exercise loss of $10. The long trader will be able to exercise the put with $X = \$105$, for an exercise profit of $10, so the long butterfly trader will experience no net gain or loss on the exercise. The same is true for any stock price lower than $95. Lower stock prices will generate larger losses on the exercise of the puts with $X = \$100$, but these will be exactly offset by higher exercise gains on the two long puts that constitute the long butterfly spread. Thus, for any stock price of $95 or lower, there is no exercise gain or loss and the trader loses the $1 cost of the butterfly spread. At a terminal stock price of $105 or higher, no put can be exercised, so there is no exercise gain or loss and the purchase of the butterfly spread loses the $1 cost of the position. Figure 11.17 shows these profits and losses as a solid line.

For a stock price at expiration between $95 and $105, the long trader has an exercise gain that will offset the $1 cost of the position and may even make the entire transaction profitable. For example, if the terminal stock price is $100, the puts with $X = \$95$ and $X = \$100$ cannot be exercised. In this situation, the trader can exercise the put with $X = \$105$ for a $5 exercise profit. This exercise profit, offset by the $1 cost of the position, gives a total gain on the trade of $4, and this is the maximum profit from the trade. For terminal stock prices between $95 and $100 or between $100 and $105, the gain will be less and may even be a loss. For a terminal stock price of $96, for example, the trader will exercise the put with $X = \$105$ for a $9 exercise profit. However, the two short puts with $X = \$100$ will be exercised against her, for an exercise loss of -$8. The net exercise gain will be $1, which exactly offsets the $1 cost of the position. Thus, the trade has a zero gain/loss at a terminal stock price of $96. The same occurs if the terminal stock price is $104. For a terminal stock price between $96 and $104, there is some profit, with the maximum profit of $4 occurring when the stock price is $100.

As we noted at the beginning of this section, it is also possible to initiate a short butterfly position with puts. With the options of this example, the short butterfly transaction would require selling a put with $X = \$95$, selling a put with $X = \$105$, and buying two puts with $X = \$100$, for a total cash inflow of $1. This short butterfly position would have profits and losses that exactly mirror those of the long position. Figure 11.17 shows the profits and losses for this short butterfly position with puts as a dashed line.

The condor with call options

A **condor** is a specialized position that involves four options on the same underlying good and with the same expiration date. The four options have different exercise prices. For a long condor entered with call options, a trader buys a call with a low exercise price, sells a call with a somewhat higher exercise price, sells a call with a yet higher exercise price, and buys a call with the highest exercise price. Notice that this is like a butterfly, in that the long trader buys two calls with extreme exercise prices, and sells two calls with intermediate exercise prices. In a butterfly, the intermediate exercise price is the same for the two calls, while a condor uses two different intermediate exercise prices. Thus, the cost of a long condor is

$$C_t(S_t, X_1, T) - C_t(S_t, X_2, T) - C_t(S_t, X_3, T) + C_t(S_t, X_4, T)$$

The value of the long condor at expiration is

$$C_T(S_T, X_1, T) - C_T(S_T, X_2, T) - C_T(S_T, X_3, T) + C_T(S_T, X_4, T)$$
$$= \text{MAX}\{0, S_T - X_1\} - \text{MAX}\{0, S_T - X_2\} - \text{MAX}\{0, S_T - X_3\} + \text{MAX}\{0, S_T - X_4\} \quad (11.11)$$

For the short condor position executed with calls, the cost of the position is

$$-C_t(S_t, X_1, T) + C_t(S_t, X_2, T) + C_t(S_t, X_3, T) - C_t(S_t, X_4, T)$$

For the short condor, the value at expiration is

$$-C_T(S_T, X_1, T) + C_T(S_T, X_2, T) + C_T(S_T, X_3, T) - C_T(S_T, X_4, T)$$
$$= -\text{MAX}\{0, S_T - X_1\} + \text{MAX}\{0, S_T - X_2\} + \text{MAX}\{0, S_T - X_3\} - \text{MAX}\{0, S_T - X_4\}$$

The following transactions illustrate a long condor position entered with call options:

	Exercise price	Option premium
Long one call	$90	$10
Short one call	95	7
Short one call	100	4
Long one call	105	2

The total cost of the condor is $1. If the terminal stock price is $90 or less, no call can be exercised and the position expires worthless for a total loss of $1. If the stock price at expiration is $95, for example, the long trader can exercise the call with $X = $90 for an exercise profit of $5. This gives a total profit on the position of $4. For any stock price above $95, the short call with $X = $95 will be exercised against the purchase of the condor, and for any stock price above $100, the short call with $X = $100 will also be exercised. For example, if the terminal stock price is $102, the transactions give the following result. The long call with $X = $90 will have a $12 exercise profit, the short call with $X = $95 will generate an exercise loss of $7, and the short call with $X = $100 will generate an exercise loss of $2. These exercise results, coupled with the $1 initial cost of the position, give a final profit of $2.

For higher terminal stock prices, those of $105 or higher, the exercise gains and losses are exactly offsetting. For example, if the terminal stock price is $107, the exercise gains and losses are $17 for the call with $X = $90, -$12 for the call with $X = $95, -$7 for the call with $X = $100, and $2 for the call with $X = $105, for a net exercise result of zero. This leaves a loss of $1, which was the original cost to enter the position. Figure 11.18 shows the short condor position with the dashed line. As usual, the results for the short position are a mirror image of those for the long position. In a zero-sum game, the winner's gains exactly match the loser's losses.

Figure 11.18   Profits and losses at expiration for a condor with calls

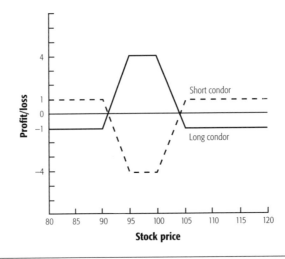

The condor with puts

As with the other strategies we have considered, it is also possible to initiate a condor with puts as well as with calls. Again, all options have the same underlying stock and the same expiration date. For a long condor with puts, the trader buys a put with the lowest exercise price, sells a put with a higher exercise price, sells a put with a yet higher exercise price, and buys a put with the highest exercise price. The short condor trader takes the opposite side of the long position, selling a put with the lowest exercise price, buying a put with a higher exercise price, buying a put with a yet higher exercise price, and selling a put with the highest exercise price.

The cost of a long condor with puts is

$$P_t(S_t, X_1, T) - P_t(S_t, X_2, T) - P_t(S_t, X_3, T) + P_t(S_t, X_4, T)$$

The value of the long condor with puts at expiration is given by

$$P_T(S_T, X_1, T) - P_T(S_T, X_2, T) - P_T(S_T, X_3, T) + P_T(S_T, X_4, T)$$
$$= MAX\{0, X_1 - S_T\} - MAX\{0, X_2 - S_T\} - MAX\{0, X_3 - S_T\} + MAX\{0, X_4 - S_T\} \quad (11.12)$$

The following transactions illustrate a long condor initiated with puts:

	Exercise price	Option premium
Long one put	$90	$2
Short one put	95	5
Short one put	100	9
Long one put	105	13

With these prices, the long condor position costs $1. For a terminal stock price of $105 or higher, none of these puts can be exercised, so the total loss on the position is $1. For a stock price of $90, three puts will be exercised, but there will be no net gain or loss on the exercise. The long trader will exercise the put with $X = \$105$ for an exercise gain of $15, but two puts will be exercised against the trader for an exercise loss of $5 on the put with $X = \$95$ and a loss of $10 on the put with $X = \$100$. This gives a zero result from the exercise, and the long trader loses the $1 cost of the position. For any stock price less than $90, the long condor trader can exercise the put with $X = \$90$, so the exercise result is zero for any stock price of $90 or less.

As with the long condor executed with calls, the long condor with puts pays best when the terminal stock price is between the two intermediate exercise prices. In our example, this range extends from $95 to $100. For a terminal stock price of $100, for example, the long trader can exercise the put with $X = \$105$ for an exercise gain of $5. Given the $1 cost of the position, the total profit on the transaction would then be $4. This is the same for any terminal stock price in the range of $95 to $100, as Figure 11.19 shows.

The short condor trader could use puts as well, again taking the mirror position of the long trader. Specifically, the short condor with puts requires selling the put with the lowest exercise price, buying a put with a higher exercise price, buying a put with a yet higher exercise price, and selling a put with the highest exercise price. Thus, the short condor executed with puts costs

$$-P_t(S_t, X_1, T) + P_t(S_t, X_2, T) + P_t(S_t, X_3, T) - P_t(S_t, X_4, T)$$

Figure 11.19   Profits and losses at expiration for a condor with puts

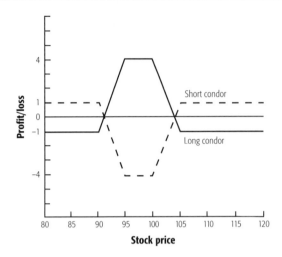

The value of the short condor with puts at expiration is given by

$$-P_T(S_T, X_1, T) + P_T(S_T, X_2, T) + P_T(S_T, X_3, T) - P_T(S_T, X_4, T)$$
$$= -\text{MAX}\{0, X_1 - S_T\} + \text{MAX}\{0, X_2 - S_T\} + \text{MAX}\{0, X_3 - S_T\} - \text{MAX}\{0, X_4 - S_T\}$$

With our example prices, that would involve selling a put with $X = \$90$, buying a put with $X = \$95$, buying a put with $X = \$100$, and selling a put with $X = \$105$. Figure 11.19 shows the profits and losses for the short condor position as a dashed line.

Ratio spreads

A **ratio spread** is a spread transaction in which two or more related options are traded in a specified proportion. For example, a trader might buy a call with a lower exercise price and sell three calls with a higher exercise price. As the ratio of one instrument to the other can be varied without limit, there are infinitely many different ratio spreads that are possible. Consequently, we will consider just one fairly simple ratio spread as a guide to the variety of ratio spreads available.

In a ratio spread, the number of contracts bought differs from the number of contracts sold to form the spread. For example, buying two options and selling one gives a 2 : 1 ratio spread. The spread can be varied infinitely by changing the ratio between the options that are bought and sold. Thus, it is impossible to provide a complete catalog of ratio spreads. Consequently, we illustrate the idea behind ratio spreads by considering a 2 : 1 ratio spread.

Earlier, we considered a bull spread using call options and illustrated this trade by considering two call options, one with an exercise price of $95 and costing $7, the other with an exercise price of $105 and costing $3. Figure 11.13 presented the profits and losses from that position. For comparison, consider a ratio spread in which a trader buys two calls with $X = \$95$ and sells one call with $X = \$105$. (In this case, the trader has utilized a 2 : 1 ratio.) The total cost of the position is $11. For any terminal stock price of $95 or less, neither call can be exercised and

Figure 11.20 Profits and losses at expiration for a 2 : 1 ratio spread

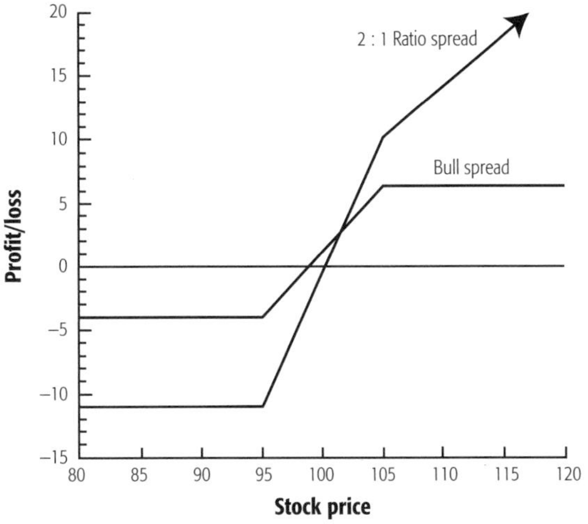

the trader loses $11. If the stock price exceeds $95, the trader can exercise both of the purchased calls. For example, with a stock price of $105, the trader exercises both calls for an
exercise profit of $20, giving a total gain on the trade of $9. For any stock price above $105,
the trader will exercise the two calls purchased with $X = \$95$, but the call sold with $X = \$105$
will be exercised against her as well. This partially offsets the benefits derived from exercising the two calls with $X = \$95$. For example, a stock price of $110 gives an exercise profit on
the two options with $X = \$95$ of $30. This gain is partially offset by the exercise against our
trader of the option with $X = \$105$, for an exercise loss of $5. The net gain at exercise is $25,
which more than compensates for the $11 cost of the position and gives a net profit of $14 on
the trade.

Figure 11.20 shows the profits and losses for the bull spread with call options, repeating the
information of Figure 11.13, and it shows profits and losses from the ratio spread we are considering. In comparing these two profit-and-loss patterns, we see that the ratio spread costs more
to undertake, but that it also offers higher profits if the stock price rises sufficiently.

As we observed, the profit on the ratio spread is $9 for a terminal stock price of $105. For
higher stock prices, the ratio call profits increase dramatically. By contrast, the bull spread we
have been considering reaches its maximum profitability of $4 at a terminal stock price of $105.
By varying the ratio between the options in a spread, it is possible to create a wide variety of
payoff patterns.

Summary

In this section, we have considered the wide variety of option combinations available when all
of the options have a common expiration date. As the variety of combinations shows, it is possible to construct a wide range of profit-and-loss profiles by choosing the correct combination
of options. Table 11.1 summarizes the variety of positions we have considered and tabulates
the cost to undertake the position, along with the value of the position at expiration. In addition, the table shows the condition that would make such a trade reasonable.

Table 11.1 Option combinations and their profits

Position	Cost	Value at expiration	Trader expects
Long call	C_t	$\text{MAX}[0, S_T - X]$	Rising stock price
Short call	$-C_t$	$-\text{MAX}[0, S_T - X]$	Stock price stable or falling
Long put	P_t	$\text{MAX}[0, X - S_T]$	Falling stock price
Short put	$-P_t$	$-\text{MAX}[0, X - S_T]$	Stock price stable or rising
Long straddle	$C_t + P_t$	$C_T + P_T$	Stock price volatile, rising or falling
Short straddle	$-C_t - P_t$	$-C_T - P_T$	Stock price stable
Long strangle	$C_t(S_t, X_1, T) + P_t(S_t, X_2, T)$	$C_T(S_T, X_1, T) + P_T(S_T, X_2, T)$	Stock price very volatile, rising or falling
Short strangle	$-C_t(S_t, X_1, T) - P_t(S_t, X_2, T)$	$-C_T(S_T, X_1, T) - P_T(S_T, X_2, T)$	Stock price generally stable
Bull spread with calls	$C_t(S_t, X_1, T) - C_t(S_t, X_2, T)$	$C_T(S_T, X_1, T) - C_T(S_T, X_2, T)$	Stock price rising
Bear spread with calls	$-C_t(S_t, X_1, T) + C_t(S_t, X_2, T)$	$-C_T(S_T, X_1, T) + C_T(S_T, X_2, T)$	Stock price falling
Bull spread with puts	$P_t(S_t, X_1, T) - P_t(S_t, X_2, T)$	$P_T(S_T, X_1, T) - P_T(S_T, X_2, T)$	Stock price rising
Bear spread with puts	$-P_t(S_t, X_1, T) + P_t(S_t, X_2, T)$	$-P_T(S_T, X_1, T) + P_T(S_T, X_2, T)$	Stock price falling
Box spread	$C_t(S_t, X_1, T) - C_t(S_t, X_2, T) - P_t(S_t, X_1, T) + P_t(S_t, X_2, T)$	$X_2 - X_1$	Riskless strategy
Long butterfly spread with calls	$C_t(S_t, X_1, T) - 2C_t(S_t, X_2, T) + C_t(S_t, X_3, T)$	$C_T(S_T, X_1, T) - 2C_T(S_T, X_2, T) + C_T(S_T, X_3, T)$	Stock price stable
Short butterfly spread with calls	$-C_t(S_t, X_1, T) + 2C_t(S_t, X_2, T) - C_t(S_t, X_3, T)$	$-C_T(S_T, X_1, T) + 2C_T(S_T, X_2, T) - C_T(S_T, X_3, T)$	Stock price volatile, rising or falling
Long butterfly spread with puts	$P_t(S_t, X_1, T) - 2P_t(S_t, X_2, T) + P_t(S_t, X_3, T)$	$P_T(S_T, X_1, T) - 2P_T(S_T, X_2, T) + P_T(S_T, X_3, T)$	Stock price stable
Short butterfly spread with puts	$-P_t(S_t, X_1, T) + 2P_t(S_t, X_2, T) - P_t(S_t, X_3, T)$	$-P_T(S_T, X_1, T) + 2P_T(S_T, X_2, T) - P_T(S_T, X_3, T)$	Stock price volatile, rising or falling
Long condor with calls	$C_t(S_t, X_1, T) - C_t(S_t, X_2, T) - C_t(S_t, X_3, T) + C_t(S_t, X_4, T)$	$C_T(S_T, X_1, T) - C_T(S_T, X_2, T) - C_T(S_T, X_3, T) + C_T(S_T, X_4, T)$	Stock price stable
Short condor with calls	$-C_t(S_t, X_1, T) + C_t(S_t, X_2, T) + C_t(S_t, X_3, T) - C_t(S_t, X_4, T)$	$-C_T(S_T, X_1, T) + C_T(S_T, X_2, T) + C_T(S_T, X_3, T) - C_T(S_T, X_4, T)$	Stock price volatile
Long condor with puts	$P_t(S_t, X_1, T) - P_t(S_t, X_2, T) - P_t(S_t, X_3, T) + P_t(S_t, X_4, T)$	$P_T(S_T, X_1, T) - P_T(S_T, X_2, T) - P_T(S_T, X_3, T) + P_T(S_T, X_4, T)$	Stock price stable
Short condor with puts	$-P_t(S_t, X_1, T) + P_t(S_t, X_2, T) + P_t(S_t, X_3, T) - P_t(S_t, X_4, T)$	$-P_T(S_T, X_1, T) + P_T(S_T, X_2, T) + P_T(S_T, X_3, T) - P_T(S_T, X_4, T)$	Stock price volatile
Ratio spreads	Too various to catalog		

Note: $X_1 < X_2 < X_3 < X_4$.

It is also possible to create an option combination with options that have different expiration dates. When an option combination has more than one expiration date represented in the options that constitute the spread, the combination is called a **calendar spread**. The absence of a uniform expiration date adds greater complication and requires that we consider calendar spreads in Chapter 14 after we introduce the pricing principles for options before expiration.

In this section, we have studied options combined with other options. However, it is also possible to combine options with other instruments to form additional profit-and-loss profiles. Most interestingly, options can be combined with the underlying stock and with the risk-free asset. We now turn to a consideration of combinations of options with bonds and stocks.

Combining options with bonds and stocks

Thus far, we have considered some of the most important combinations of options. We now show how to combine options with stocks and bonds to adjust payoff patterns to fit virtually any taste for risk and return combinations. These combinations show us the relationships among the different classes of securities. By combining two types of securities, we can generally imitate the payoff patterns of a third. In addition, this section extends the concepts we have developed earlier in this chapter. Specifically, we learn more about shaping the risk and return characteristics of portfolios by using options.

In this section, we consider five combinations of options with bonds or stocks. First, we consider the popular strategy of the **covered call**—a long position in the underlying stock and a short position in a call option. Second, we explore portfolio insurance. During the 1980s, portfolio insurance became one of the most discussed techniques for managing the risk of a stock portfolio. We illustrate some of the basic ideas of portfolio insurance by showing how to insure a stock portfolio. Third, we show how to use options to mimic the profit-and-loss patterns of the stock itself. For investors who do not want to invest the full purchase price of the stock, it is possible to create an option position that gives a profit-and-loss pattern much like the stock itself. Fourth, by combining options with the risk-free bond, we can synthesize the underlying stock. In this situation, the option and bond position gives the same profit-and-loss pattern as the stock, and it has the same value as the stock as well. Finally, we show how to combine a call, a bond, and a share of stock to create a synthetic put option.

The covered call: stock plus a short call

In a covered call transaction, a trader is generally assumed to already own a stock and writes a call option on the underlying stock. (The strategy is "covered" because the trader owns the underlying stock, and this stock covers the obligation inherent in writing the call.) This strategy is generally undertaken as an income enhancement technique. For example, assume a trader owns a share currently priced at $100. She might write a call option on this share with an exercise price of $110 and an assumed price of $4. The option premium will be hers to keep. In exchange for accepting the $4 premium, our trader realizes that the underlying stock might be called away from her if the stock price exceeds $110. If the stock price fails to increase by $10, the option she has written will expire worthless, and she will be able to keep the income from selling the option without any further obligation. As this example indicates, the strategy turns on selling an option with a strike price far removed from the current value of the stock, because the intention is to keep the premium without surrendering the stock through exercise.

Although writing covered calls can often serve the purpose of enhancing income, it must be remembered that there is no free lunch in the options market. The writer of the covered call is actually exchanging the chance of large gains on the stock position in favor of income from

Figure 11.21   Profits and losses at expiration for a covered call

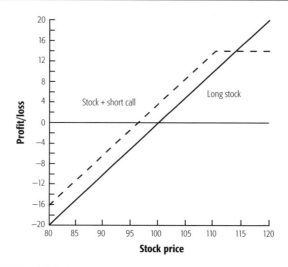

selling the option. For example, if the stock price were to rise to $120, the trader would not receive this benefit, because the stock would be called away from her.

Figure 11.21 graphs the profits and losses at expiration for the example we have been considering. The solid line shows the profits and losses for the stock itself, while the dashed line shows the profits and losses for the covered call (the stock plus short call). For any stock price less than or equal to $110, the written call cannot be exercised against our trader, and she receives whatever profits or losses the stock earns plus the $4 option premium. Thus, she is $4 better off with the covered call than she would be with the stock alone for any stock price of $110 or less. If the stock price exceeds $110, the option will be exercised against her, and she must surrender the stock. This potential exercise places an upper limit on her profit at $14. If the stock price had risen to $120 and the trader had not written the call, her profit would have been $20 on the stock investment alone. In the covered call position, she would have made only $14, because the stock would have been called away from her. The desirability of writing a covered call to enhance income depends upon the chance that the stock price will exceed the exercise price at which the trader writes the call.

Portfolio insurance: stock plus a long put

Along with program trading, portfolio insurance was a dominant investing technique developed in the 1980s. **Portfolio insurance** is an investment management technique designed to protect a stock portfolio from severe drops in value. Investment managers can implement portfolio insurance strategies in various ways. Some use options while others use futures, and still others use combinations of other instruments. We analyze a simple strategy for implementing portfolio insurance with options. Portfolio insurance applies only to portfolios, not individual stocks. Therefore, for our discussion we assume that the underlying good is a well-diversified portfolio of common stocks. We may think of the portfolio as consisting of the Standard & Poor's 100. This is convenient, because a popular stock index option is based on the S&P 100. Therefore, the portfolio insurance problem we consider is protecting the value of this stock portfolio from large drops in value.[8]

Figure 11.22   Profits and losses at expiration for a stock index and a long put

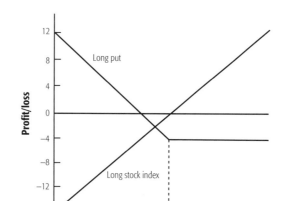

In essence, portfolio insurance with options involves holding a stock portfolio and buying a put option on the portfolio.[9] If we have a long position in the stock portfolio, the profits and losses from holding the portfolio consist of the profits and losses from the individual stocks. Therefore, the profits and losses for the portfolio resemble the typical stock's profits and losses.

Let S_t be the cost of the stock portfolio at time t, and let P_t be a put option on the portfolio. The cost of an insured portfolio is, therefore

$$S_t + P_t$$

Because the price of a put is always positive, it is clear that an insured portfolio costs more than the uninsured stock portfolio alone. At expiration, the value of the insured portfolio is

$$S_T + P_T = S_T + \text{MAX}\{0, X - S_T\} \tag{11.13}$$

As the profit on an uninsured portfolio is $S_T - S_t$, the insured portfolio has a superior performance when $S_T < X - P_t$.

As an example of an insured portfolio, consider an investment in the stock index at a value of 96.00. Figure 11.22 shows the profit-and-loss profiles for an investment in the index at 96 and for a put option on the index. The figure assumes that the put has a strike price of 96.00 and costs 4.00 (we are expressing all values in terms of the index). Figure 11.23 shows the effects of combining an investment in the index stocks and buying a put on the index. For comparison, Figure 11.23 also shows the profits and losses from a long position in the index itself.

The insured portfolio, the index plus a long put, cost 100.00, 96.00 for the stock index and 4.00 for the put. This insured portfolio offers protection against large drops in value. If the stock index suddenly falls from 96.00 to 80.00, for example, the insured portfolio loses only 4.00 and is still worth 96.00. No matter how low the index goes, the insured portfolio can lose only 4.00 points. However, this insurance has a cost. Investment in the index itself shows a

Figure 11.23   Profits and losses at expiration for an insured portfolio

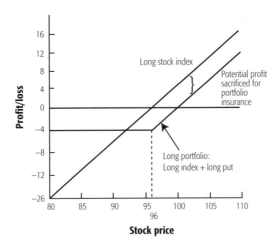

profit for any index value over 96.00. By contrast, the insured portfolio has a profit only if the index climbs above 100.00. In the insured portfolio, the index must climb high enough to offset the price of buying the insuring put option. Because the put option will expire, keeping the portfolio insured requires that the investor buy a series of put options to keep the insurance in force. In Figure 11.23, notice that the combined position of a long index and a long put gives a payoff shape that matches a long position in a call. Like a call, the insured portfolio protects against extremely unfavorable outcomes as the stock price falls. This similarity between the insured portfolio and a call position suggests that a trader might buy a call and invest the extra proceeds in a bond in order to replicate a position in an insured portfolio.

As a further comparison, we consider the likely returns profit from holding the stock portfolio and insured portfolios. Assume that the option expires in one year. The stock portfolio returns are normally distributed with a 10 percent expected return and a standard deviation of returns of 15 percent, as shown in Figure 11.24. There is an approximately 68 percent chance that the returns will lie between −5 percent and +25 percent, because in a normal distribution about 68 percent of all observations lie within one standard deviation of the mean.

For the insured portfolio we noted that the maximum loss is 4.00, so the terminal value must be at least 96.00, a loss of −4.00/100.00 = −4.00 percent. Figures 11.23 and 11.24 imply that there is a good chance that the insured portfolio will actually lose this 4.00 percent. Any return of zero or less on the stock portfolio gives a −4.00 percent return for the insured portfolio. The chance that the stock portfolio will have a zero or lower return equals the chance that the stock portfolio will have a return that is two-thirds of a standard deviation below its mean return of 10 percent. As a feature of the normal distribution, this probability is 25.25 percent. Therefore, there is a 25.25 percent probability that the insured portfolio will have a return of −4.00 percent.

Although the insured portfolio protects against large losses, it has a lower chance of large returns. For example, there is a 2.2750 percent chance that the stock portfolio will have a return of 40 percent or higher, which is two standard deviations above the mean return of 10 percent. For the insured portfolio to have a return of 40 percent or higher, the terminal value of the insured portfolio would have to be at least 140.00 = 100.00 × 1.40. This result for the insured

Figure 11.24   The probability distribution for a stock index's returns

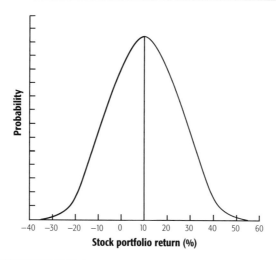

portfolio implies that the stock portfolio itself would have to be worth 140.00, which is a return of 45.8333 percent on the stock portfolio, or 2.388887 standard deviations above the mean return of 10 percent ($0.10 + 2.38887 \times 0.15 = 0.458333$). The chance of a return 2.388887 standard deviations above the mean is 0.8450 percent. Thus, there is a 2.2750 percent chance that the stock portfolio will have a return of 40 percent or higher, but only a 0.8450 percent chance that the insured portfolio will do so. This numerical example shows that there is a smaller chance of high returns on the insured portfolio compared to the stock portfolio, as the insured portfolio involves a tradeoff compared to investment in the stock index itself. The insured portfolio provides insurance against large losses at the expense of sacrificing large gains. Said another way, the insured portfolio has a truncated returns distribution at exactly −4.00 percent, which is purchased at the cost of sacrificing the chance of high returns.

Figure 11.25 illustrates the truncation of the returns distribution by comparing the cumulative distribution of returns for both portfolios, where the smooth line and kinked line pertain to the stock and insured portfolios, respectively. For the insured portfolio, the vertical line at −4.00 percent reflects the zero probability of a return below −4.00 percent and the 25.25 percent probability that the return on the insured portfolio will be exactly −4.00 percent. For the stock portfolio to have a return of −4.00 percent or worse, the return must be at least 14.00 percent below the expected return, which is 0.933333 standard deviations or more below the mean return. The probability of this occurring is 17.53 percent. Similarly, compared to the insured portfolio, there is a better chance that the stock portfolio will achieve any given return above −4.00 percent. For example, we have already seen that the chance of a return of 40 percent or better for the stock portfolio is 2.2750 percent, but only 0.8450 percent for the insured portfolio. This means that there is an 82.47 percent chance that the stock portfolio will outperform the insured portfolio, because there is an 82.47 percent chance that the stock portfolio will return more than −4.00 percent.

The cumulative distributions of the insured portfolio and the stock portfolio in Figure 11.25 dramatize the truncation of the returns distribution and the reduced potential for high returns for the insured portfolio. As such, Figure 11.25 echoes Figure 11.23, where the insured

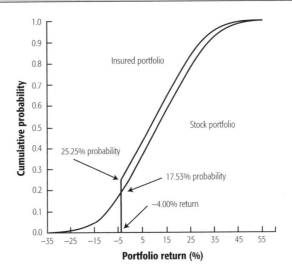

Figure 11.25   A comparison of returns distributions for an insured and an uninsured stock portfolio

portfolio has potential losses truncated at −4.00 and reduced profit potential compared to the stock index alone. In Figure 11.25, the insured portfolio has truncated distribution on the loss side at −4.00 percent, reflected by the vertical line at −4.00 percent. However, the insured portfolio also has a reduced chance for large positive gains, shown by the fact that the cumulative distribution line for the insured portfolio lies above that for the stock returns larger than −4.00 percent. As these cumulative distributions show, if stocks do well, the stock portfolio will outperform the insured portfolio. Thus, Figures 11.23 and 11.25 present two views of the same phenomenon.

This portfolio insurance example emphasizes the role of options in adjusting the returns distribution for the underlying investment. With options, we can adjust the distribution to fit our tastes—subject to the risk and return tradeoff governing the entire market.[10] Finally, we note that the insured portfolio has the same profits and losses as a call option with a strike price of 96.00 and a premium of 4.00. This does not mean, however, that the insured portfolio and such a call option would have the same value. At expiration, the call will have no residual value beyond its profit and loss at that moment. By contrast, the insured portfolio will include the value of the investment in the stock index. Therefore, for a particular time horizon, two different investments can have the same profit-and-loss patterns without having the same value.

Mimicking and synthetic portfolios

We now begin to study how European options can be combined with other instruments, notably the underlying stock and the risk-free bond, to create specialized payoff patterns at expiration. As we will see, it is possible to create portfolios of European options, the underlying stock, and the risk-free bond that simulate another instrument in key respects. We define two basic types of relationships: mimicking portfolios and synthetic instruments.[11]

A **mimicking portfolio** has the same profits and losses as the instrument or portfolio that it mimics, but it does not necessarily have the same value. A **synthetic instrument** has the same profits and losses, as well as the same value, as the instrument it synthetically replicates. For example, we will see that it is possible to create a portfolio of instruments that has the same value and the same profits and losses as a put. In this case, the portfolio would be known as a synthetic put.

Mimicking stock: long call plus a short put
By combining a long position in a European call and a short position in a European put, we can create an option position that has the same profit-and-loss pattern at expiration as does the underlying stock. This long call/short put position costs

$$c_t - p_t$$

At expiration, the payoff on this option combination is

$$c_t - p_T = \text{MAX}\{0, S_T - X\} - \text{MAX}\{0, X - S_T\} \tag{11.14}$$

Assume for the moment that the call and put are chosen so that the exercise price equals the stock price at the time the put is purchased. That is, assume $X = S_t$. Under this special condition, the payoff on the long call/short put position is

$$\text{MAX}\{0, S_T - S_t\} - \text{MAX}\{0, S_t - S_T\}$$

If the stock price rises, $S_T > S_t$, so the call is worth $S_T - S_t$ and the put is worth nothing. Notice that $S_T - S_t$ is just the profit on the stock portfolio alone. If the stock price falls, $S_t > S_T$. In this case, the call is worth zero, and the put is worth $S_t - S_T$. As the option combination includes a short position in the put, the payoff to the portfolio is $S_T - S_t$, which is the same as the stock portfolio. Thus, the long call/short put portfolio has a value that equals the profit or loss from investing in the underlying stock. Notice again that this special condition arises when the exercise price on the options equals the stock price at the time the option combination is purchased.

To illustrate this idea, consider a stock priced at $100 and call and put options with exercise prices of $100. Assume that the call costs $7 and the put costs $3. We want to compare two investments. The first investment is buying one share of stock for $100. The second investment is buying one call for $7 and selling one put for $3.

When the options expire, the two investments have parallel profits and losses. However, the profit on the stock will always be $4 greater than the profit on the option position. For example, assume the stock price is $110 at expiration. The stock has a profit of $10 and the option investment has a profit of $6. For the option position, the put expires worthless and the call has an exercise value of $10. From this exercise value we subtract the $4 net investment required to purchase the option position. Figure 11.26 graphs the profits and losses for both options, the stock, and the combined option position.

Investing in the stock costs $100, while the option position costs only $4. Yet the option position profits mimic those of the stock fairly closely. In a sense, the options give very high leverage by simulating the stock's profits and losses with a low investment. Many option traders view this high leverage of options as one of their prime advantages. Thus, a very small investment in the option position gives a position that mimics the profits and losses of a much more costly investment in the stock. In other words, the option position is much more elastic than the similar stock position.

The profit on the stock is always $4 greater than the profit on the option position. However, the stock investment costs $100, while the option position costs only $4. Therefore, the stock

Figure 11.26　Profits and losses at expiration for the elements of a mimicking portfolio

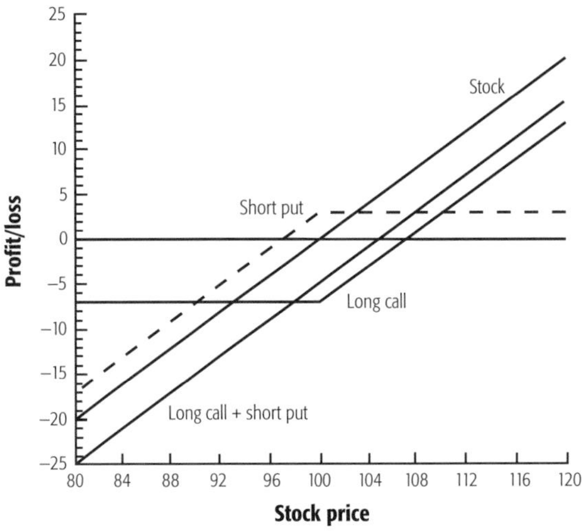

costs $96 more than the option position to guarantee a certain $4 extra profit over the option position. While the long call plus short put option position mimics the profits and losses on the stock, it does not synthetically replicate the stock. As we will see, we can create a synthetic stock by adding investment in the risk-free bond to the option.

Synthetic stock: long call, plus a short put, plus bonds
As we have just seen, a long call combined with a short put can mimic the profit-and-loss pattern at the expiration date for the underlying stock. By adding an investment in the risk-free bond, we can create a portfolio that synthesizes the stock. In this case, the synthetic stock will have the same value as well as an identical profit-and-loss pattern as the stock being synthesized. Therefore, this section shows that a long call, plus a short put, plus the right investment in the risk-free bond can synthesize a stock investment. (Again, we are focusing on European options throughout this discussion, which we denote as c_t and p_t for the values of European calls and puts at time t.) As we will demonstrate, the investment in the risk-free bond should be the present value of the exercise price on the call and the put. Therefore, the formula for a synthetic stock is

$$S_t = c_t - p_t + Xe^{-r(T-t)} \qquad (11.15)$$

where r is the risk-free rate of interest.

At expiration, the value of this portfolio (for both American and European options) will be

$$c_T - p_T + X = \text{MAX}\{0, S_T - X\} - \{0, X - S_T\} + X$$

We know that the stock price can be above, equal to, or below the exercise price. If the stock price at expiration exceeds the exercise price, the call is worth $S_T - X$, and the put is worthless.

The value of the portfolio consists of the value of the call, plus the maturing bond, or $S_T - X + X = S_T$. This is exactly the same value as the stock at the expiration date. If the stock price is below the exercise price on the expiration date of the options, then the call is worthless and the put has a value equal to $X - S_T$. Because the portfolio consists of a short position in the put, the value of the portfolio, including the maturing bond, is $S_T - X + X = S_T$. Again, the value of the long call/short put/long bond is the same as that of the underlying stock. If the terminal value of the stock equals the exercise price, X, then both the call and put are worthless and the value of the synthetic stock portfolio is just X, the value of the maturing risk-free investment. But in this situation, it remains true that the value of the synthetic stock is equal to that of the stock itself, because $S_T = X$.

We can illustrate this synthetic stock by considering the same stock selling for $100 and the same options we considered in the previous section. Comparing just the value of the stock position versus the value of the option position at expiration, the stock position will always be worth $100 more than the option position. For example, assume that the stock price is $120 at expiration. Then, the stock investment is worth $120. The option position will be worth $20, because the call can be exercised for $20 and the put will be worthless. To synthesize the stock, we need to buy a risk-free bond that pays $100 at expiration. We can think of this investment as buying a one-year Treasury bill with a face value of $100. Notice that the payoff on the Treasury bill equals the exercise price for the options. We now have two portfolios that will have identical values at the expiration date:

Investment	Cash flow
Portfolio A	
Long position in the stock	$100
Portfolio B	
Long position in the call	−$7
Short position in the put	+$3
A bond paying the exercise price of $100 at expiration	?

Thus far in the example, we have not said how much the bond should cost. However, we can employ our no-arbitrage principle for guidance. We know that both portfolios will have the same value in one year when the option expires. To avoid arbitrage, the two portfolios must have the same value now as well. This condition implies that the bond must cost $96 and that the interest rate must be 4.17 percent.

To see why the bond must cost $96, we consider the arbitrage opportunity that results with any other bond price. For example, assume that the bond costs $93. With this low bond price, Portfolio A is too expensive relative to Portfolio B. To exploit the arbitrage opportunity, we sell the overpriced Portfolio A and buy the underpriced Portfolio B, transacting as follows:

Transaction	Cash flow
Sell the stock	$100
Buy the call	−7
Sell the put	+3
Buy the bond	−93
Net cash flow	+$3

When the options expire in one year, we can close out all the positions without any additional investment. To close the position, we buy back the stock and honor any obligation we have from selling the put. Fortunately, we will have $100 in cash from the maturing bond we bought. For example, if the stock price at expiration is $90, our call is worthless and the put is exercised against us. Therefore, we use the proceeds from the maturing T-bill to pay the $100 exercise price for the put that is exercised against us. We now have the stock and in return use it to close our short position in the stock. The total result at expiration is that we can honor all obligations with zero cash flow. This is true no matter what the stock price is. Therefore, the cheap price on the bond gave us an arbitrage profit of $3 when we made the initial transaction. The transactions are an arbitrage because they require no investment and offer a riskless profit. With an initial cash inflow of $3, there is clearly no investment. Also, we make a riskless profit immediately when we transact. Any bond price below $96 will permit the arbitrage transactions we have just described.

If the bond is priced higher than $96, Portfolio B is overpriced relative to Portfolio A. We then sell Portfolio B and buy Portfolio A. Again, we have an arbitrage profit. To see how to make an arbitrage profit from a bond price that is too high, assume that the bond price is $98. We then transact as follows:

Transaction	Cash flow
Buy the stock	−$100
Sell the call	7
Buy the put	−3
Sell the bond	+98
Net cash flow	+$2

In one year, the options will expire and the bond will mature. Selling the bond means that we borrow $98 and promise to repa y $100, so we will owe $100 on the bond at expiration. However, no matter what the stock price is at expiration, we can dispose of the stock and close the option positions for a cash inflow of $100. This gives exactly what we need to pay our debt on the bond. For example, assume that the stock price is $93. The call we sold expires worthless, but we can exercise the put. When we exercise the put, we deliver the stock and receive the $100 exercise price. This amount repays the bond debt. Any bond price greater than $96 will permit this same kind of arbitrage transaction.

The synthetic put: the put–call parity relationship
We have just seen that we can buy a call, short a put, and invest in a risk-free bond to create a synthetic stock. In fact, with any three of these four instruments, we can synthesize the fourth. This section illustrates **put–call parity**—the relationship between put, call, stock, and bond prices. Specifically, put–call parity shows how to synthesize a put option by selling the stock, buying a call, and investing in a risk-free bond. Put–call parity asserts that a put is worth the same as a long call, short stock, and a risk-free investment that pays the exercise price on the common expiration date of the put and call. The put–call parity relationship is as follows:

$$p_t = c_t - S_t + Xe^{-r(T-t)} \tag{11.16}$$

To create a put from the other instruments, we use our previous example of a stock selling at $100, a call option worth $7 with a strike price of $100, and a bond costing $96 that will pay $100 in one year. From these securities, we can synthesize the put option costing $3 with an exercise price of $100. To create a synthetic put, we transact as follows:

Investment	Cash flow
Portfolio C	
Buy the call	−$7
Sell the stock	+100
Buy a bond that pays the exercise price at maturity	−96
Net cash flow	$3

In buying Portfolio C, we have the same cash outflow of $3 that buying the put requires. To show that Portfolio C is equivalent to a put with a $3 price and a $100 exercise price, we consider the value of Portfolio C when the stock price equals, exceeds, or is less than $100.

If the stock price is $100 at expiration, the call in Portfolio C is worthless, but we receive $100 from the maturing bond, with which we buy the stock. This disposes of the entire portfolio. The entire portfolio is worth zero, just as the put is worth zero. For any stock price above $100, Portfolio C, like the put itself, is worthless. We can then exercise the call and use the proceeds from the bond to pay the exercise price on the call. This gives us the stock, which we owe to cover our earlier sale of the stock. Thus, we have met all obligations arising from owning Portfolio C. To illustrate this outcome, consider a terminal stock price of $105. In this case, the put would be worthless. Therefore, Portfolio C should be worthless as well. With a stock price of $105, we would exercise the call, paying for the exercise with the proceeds of our maturing bond. We receive a stock worth $105. However, we must repay our short sale of the stock by returning this share. Therefore, there is no net cash flow at the exercise date. Finally, for a stock price less than $100, Portfolio C is worth the difference between the exercise price and the stock price. If the stock price is $95, the call option expires worthless. We receive $100 on the bond investment and use $95 of this to repurchase the stock that we owe. Thus Portfolio C is worth $5, just as the put itself would be.

Considering our profits on Portfolio C, we lose $3 for any stock price of $100 or more, because Portfolio C is then worthless at expiration and it costs $3. For any stock price at expiration less than $100, Portfolio C is worth the exercise price of $100 minus the stock price. Notice that this is an exact description of the profit and losses on the put. Therefore, Portfolio C synthetically replicates the put option with an exercise price of $100 that costs $3.

Put–call parity has another important implication. Assume that $S_t = X$. In this situation, the call will be worth more than the put. To prove this principle, consider the following rearrangement of the put–call parity formula:

$$c_T - p_t = S_t - Xe^{-r(T-t)}$$

If $S_t = X$, the right-hand side of this equation must be positive, because the exercise price X is being discounted. Therefore, the quantity $c_t - p_t$ must also be positive, and this implies that the call price must exceed the put price in this special circumstance.

Using options to manage the effects of dilution caused by stock-based employee compensation programs

Corporations that offer stock options and other forms of stock-based compensation to their employees often find that the newly issued shares for employees lower the value of existing shares traded in the open market. This effect is called "dilution," reflecting the fact that the newly issued shares cause the corporation's earnings to be spread over a larger number of shares. Corporations often use equity options written on their own stock to manage the effects of dilution created by employee stock-based compensation programs.

Of course, the most direct way for a corporation to manage the effects of dilution is to simply repurchase some of the corporation's shares on the open market. This method does not use options at all. With this method, the company buys the same number of shares that it distributes to employees who exercise their options. In other words, the company shrinks the number of available shares at the same time as they add shares by granting options. This method precisely hedges the effects of dilution, but it requires that the company pay the full market price in cash for the shares that are repurchased.

An alternative to outright stock repurchase is for the company to purchase call options written on their own stock. These call options are written by over-the-counter dealers. The call options give the company the right to purchase the number of shares that it needs to offset the dilution effect from the exercise of employee stock options. With a call, the strike price becomes the maximum price the company will possibly pay for the repurchased shares. If the stock price finishes below the strike price, the company simply pays the market price for the repurchased shares. This method is a perfect hedge, but it requires an up-front cash outlay to buy the calls, in addition to the cash required to purchase the shares.

Another way for a company to manage the dilution effect of its stock-based compensation plan is to sell put options. This method is not so much a means of hedging dilution as a means of generating cash (from the premium received by writing the puts) that can be used to fund open market repurchases of stock. The combination of writing put option and repurchasing stock works well if the corporation's stock appreciates. In this case, the rising stock causes employees to exercise their stock options and create dilution. However, the puts will expire unexercised and the corporation retains the option's premium. The corporation can use the put premiums to buy back its shares. Selling puts can be risky. If the stock declines below the put strike price, the corporation has to buy back its shares at an above-market price. For example, in the summer of 2001, Dell Computer Corporation reported that it had sold puts on 96 million shares at an average strike price of $44 per share. As the market for personal computer stocks slumped, Dell found that the price for the company's stock was only $22 per share. The result was that Dell paid $44 per share for stock worth only $22 on the open market.

Finally, corporations can manage dilution risk by simultaneously writing a put on their own shares at one strike price and buying a call on their own shares at a higher strike price. This method is called a **purchased equity collar**. Corporations are attracted to collars because the premium received from the written puts help offset the cost of purchasing the calls. A purchased equity collar sets a maximum cost (the strike price of the call) for repurchasing the corporation's shares if the stock price rises. If the stock price falls, the corporation may end up paying an above-market price for its shares if the puts are exercised. The combination of the sale of puts with the purchase of calls creates a range of forward purchase prices on the stock.

Conclusion

This chapter has explored the value and profits from option positions at expiration. The concept of arbitrage provided a general framework for understanding option values and profits. We began by studying the characteristic payoffs for positions in single options, noting that there are four basic possibilities of being long or short a call or a put.

We then considered how to combine options to create special positions with unique risk and return characteristics. These option combinations included straddles, strangles, bull and bear spreads, butterfly spreads, condors, and a box spread. As we observed, a trader can either buy or sell each of these option combinations, and most can be created using either puts or calls. Each gives its own risk and return profile, which differs from the position in a single option.

We also considered combinations among options, stocks, and bonds. We considered the advantages and disadvantages of covered call writing, and explored how to insure a portfolio by using a put option. We also showed that a combination of options could mimic the profit-and-loss profile of a stock. To create a synthetic stock we used a call, a put, and investment in a risk-free bond. The mimicking portfolio has the same profit-and-loss patterns, while a synthetic instrument has the identical profit-and-loss characteristics and the same value as the instrument being synthesized. We also showed how to create a synthetic put by trading a call, a stock, and the risk-free bond to illustrate the put–call parity relationship. In general, we concluded that put, call, bond, and stock prices are all related and that any one can be synthesized by a combination of the other three.

Exercises

1   Consider a call option with an exercise price of $80 and a cost of $5. Graph the profits and losses at expiration for various stock prices.

2   Consider a put option with an exercise price of $80 and a cost of $4. Graph the profits and losses at expiration for various stock prices.

3   For the call and put in Exercises 1 and 2, graph the profits and losses at expiration for a straddle comprising these two options. If the stock price is $80 at expiration, what will be the profit or loss? At what stock price (or prices) will the straddle have a zero profit?

4   A call option has an exercise price of $70 and is at expiration. The option costs $4, and the underlying stock trades for $75. Assuming a perfect market, how would you respond if the call is an American option? State exactly how you might transact. How does your answer differ if the option is European?

5   A stock trades for $120. A put on this stock has an exercise price of $140 and is about to expire. The put trades for $22. How would you respond to this set of prices? Explain.

6   If the stock trades for $120 and the expiring put with an exercise price of $140 trades for $18, how would you trade?

7   Consider a call and a put on the same underlying stock. The call has an exercise price of $100 and costs $20. The put has an exercise price of $90 and costs $12. Graph a short position in a strangle based on these two options. What is the worst outcome from selling the strangle? At what stock price or prices does the strangle have a zero profit?

8   Assume that you buy a call with an exercise price of $100 and a cost of $9. At the same time, you sell a call with an exercise price of $110 and a cost of $5. The two calls have the same underlying stock and the same expiration. What is this position called? Graph the profits and losses at expiration from this position. At what stock price or prices will the position show a zero profit? What is the worst loss that the position can incur? For what range of stock prices does this worst outcome occur? What is the best outcome and for what range of stock prices does it occur?

9   Consider three call options with the same underlying stock and the same expiration. Assume that you take a long position in a call with an exercise price of $40 and a long position in a call with an exercise price of $30. At the same time, you sell two calls with an exercise price of $35. What position have you created? Graph the value of this position at expiration. What is the value of this position at expiration if the stock price is $90? What is the position's value for a stock price of $15? What is the lowest value the position can have at expiration? For what range of stock prices does this worst value occur?

10   Assume that you buy a portfolio of stocks with a portfolio price of $100. A put option on this portfolio has a strike price of $95 and costs $3. Graph the combined portfolio of the stock plus a long position in the put. What is the worst outcome that can occur at expiration? For what range of portfolio prices will this worst outcome occur? What is this position called?

11   Consider a stock that sells for $95. A call on this stock has an exercise price of $95 and costs $5. A put on this stock also has an exercise price of $95 and costs $4. The call and the put have the same expiration. Graph the profit and losses at expiration from holding the

long call and short put. How do these profits and losses compare with the value of the stock at expiration? If the stock price is $80 at expiration, what is the portfolio of options worth? If the stock price is $105, what is the portfolio of options worth? Explain why the stock and option portfolio differ as they do.

12 Assume that a stock trades for $120. A call on this stock has a strike price of $120 and costs $11. A put also has a strike price of $120 and costs $8. A risk-free bond promises to pay $120 at the expiration of the options in one year. What should the price of this bond be? Explain.

13 In the preceding question, if we combine the two options and the bond, what will the value of this portfolio be relative to the stock price at expiration? Explain. What principle does this illustrate?

14 Consider a stock that is worth $50. A put and call on this stock have an exercise price of $50 and expire in one year. The call costs $5 and the put costs $4. A risk-free bond will pay $50 in one year and costs $45. How will you respond to these prices? State your transactions exactly. What principle do these prices violate?

15 A stock sells for $80 and the risk-free rate of interest is 11 percent. A call and a put on this stock expire in one year and both options have an exercise price of $75. How would you trade to create a synthetic call option? If the put sells for $2, how much is the call option worth? (Assume annual compounding.)

16 A stock costs $100 and a risk-free bond paying $110 in one year costs $100 as well. What can you say about the cost of a put and a call on this stock that both expire in one year and that both have an exercise price of $110? Explain.

17 Assume that you buy a strangle with exercise prices on the constituent options of $75 and $80. You also sell a strangle with exercise prices of $70 and $85. Describe the payoffs on the position you have created. Does this portfolio of options have a payoff pattern similar to that of any of the combinations explored in this chapter?

18 If a stock sells for $75 and a call and put together cost $9 and the two options expire in one year and have an exercise price of $70, what is the current rate of interest?

19 Assume you buy a bull spread with puts that have exercise prices of $40 and $45. You also buy a bear spread with puts that have exercise prices of $45 and $50. What will this total position be worth if the stock price at expiration is $53? Does this position have any special name? Explain.

20 Explain the difference between a box spread and a synthetic risk-free bond.

21 Within the context of the put–call parity relationship, consider the value of a call and a put option. What will the value of the put option be if the exercise price is zero? What will the value of the call option be in the same circumstance? What can you say about potential bounds on the value of the call and put option?

22 Using the put–call parity relationship, write the value of a call option as a function of the stock price, the risk-free bond, and the put option. Consider now a stock price that is dramatically in excess of the exercise price. What happens to the value of the put as the stock price becomes extremely large relative to the exercise price? What happens to the value of the call option?

23 The CBOE is thinking of opening a new market center in London that will trade only European options and has hired you as a consultant. The board of directors for the CBOE believes that there is demand in the market for options contracts that can be used by investors to insure their portfolios. A unique feature of this market is the fact that only put options will be traded.

A   Explain why it will not be necessary to trade call options in this market.
B   Discuss the expected clientele in this market and explain why these traders might not desire to use American options traded in Chicago on the CBOE.
C   The CBOE has asked you as a consultant to identify the important characteristics of the market and the option contracts that will ensure the success of this new market. Identify those characteristics that you feel will contribute to the success of the market.

24 Suppose that an investor purchases a call option on XYZ with a $50 strike price and sells a put option on XYZ with the same strike price. Both options are European options that expire in one month. Describe the investor's position.

25 DRP is currently selling at $58 per share. An American call option written on DRP with six weeks until expiration has a strike price of $50.

A   If DRP does not pay a dividend, explain why it is not economically rational to exercise this American call option prior to expiration. Equivalently, explain why a call option is worth more alive than dead.
B   If DRP pays a quarterly dividend, but the dividend will not be paid for eight weeks, explain why it is not economically rational to exercise this American call option prior to expiration.

26 Call prices are directly related to the volatility of the underlying stock. That is, the more volatile the underlying stock, the more valuable is the call option. However, higher volatility means that the stock price may decrease by a large amount. That is, the probability of a large decrease in the stock price has increased. Explain this apparent paradox.

27 An investor has just obtained the following quotes for European options on a stock worth $30 when the three-month risk-free interest rate is 10 percent per year. Both options have a strike price of $30 and expire in three months:

   European call: $3
   European put: $1³/₄

   A   Given the information above, determine whether the prices conform to the put–call parity rule.
   B   If there is a violation, suggest a trading strategy that will generate riskless arbitrage profits.
   C   Indicate how much profit you will make from the arbitrage transactions, if such an opportunity exists.

28 Suppose that you are an information services professional with contracts throughout the industry. In conversations with colleagues, you get the feeling that Computer Associates International is likely to attempt to acquire Computer Sciences Corporation. You also remember from your finance courses in college that in the course of an acquisition, the share price of the target firm normally increases and the share price of the acquiring firm decreases. (You are confident that trading on the information gleaned in these conversations violates no law and is ethical.)

   A   Discuss the advantages of using options to speculate on the expected stock price changes of the firms involved in an acquisition.
   B   Based on your understanding of option payouts, discuss and explain the option positions that you would establish to speculate on these expected price changes. (Assume that traded options exist for both firms.)

29 After watching a late-night infomercial, a colleague comes to work professing the gospel of income enhancement via covered calls. The pitch man in the infomercial, Mr. Oracle, says that writing covered calls enhances the return on a stock investment with no cost. Discuss the sources of the apparent costless gains and the risks associated with writing covered calls.

30 Late one Friday afternoon in March, an investor receives a call from her broker. Her broker tells her that the March options on Microsoft will expire in ten minutes, that Microsoft is currently trading at $94.50, and that the March 85 call is selling at $8. The investor tells her broker that he is mistaken and must have read his screen incorrectly. Explain which individual, the broker or the investor, is correct. Supposing that the broker is in fact correct, state the transactions that the investor would undertake to take advantage of this situation. Suppose the broker tells the investor that these options are European options. Discuss the impact of the fact that the options are European options on the actions of the investor.

31 As a finance major in college, you were taught the efficient market hypothesis. Because you believe that it is not possible for a mutual fund manager to consistently outperform the market, you hold a portfolio of the 30 stocks that make up the Dow Jones Industrial Average (DJIA). Your broker has just called you with the following offer. He can provide you with insurance that will guarantee that the value of your portfolio will not fall below an indexed level of 8,900. This insurance is evaluated at the end of each quarter and costs $500 per quarter. A quick search of the CBOE web site shows that the Dow is currently trading at an indexed level of 9,005, and that a three-month put option on the DJIA with a strike price of 89 is trading at 2¹/₁₆. The DJIA options traded on the CBOE are quoted at strike prices that are 1/100 of the level of the DJIA. Each premium point is multiplied by $100 to determine the total cost of the option.

   A   Should you accept the insurance contract offered by your broker? Explain.
   B   Explain how you can provide your own insurance for your portfolio. What is the cost of this insurance? What is the maximum loss on your insured portfolio?

32 You own shares of AGH that are currently trading at $100. A European put option written on AGH with a $100 strike price that expires in three months is priced at $4. The equivalent call option is priced at $5.

   A   What is the price of a three-month T-bill that pays par ($100) implied by the prices given above?
   B   What is the continuously compounded three-month interest rate implied by these prices?
   C   A quick check of the price of three-month T-bills on *The Wall Street Journal* web site reveals that this bill is trading at $98.50. Explain your actions upon finding this information.

33 A protective put position is created by combining a long stock position with a long position in a put option written on the stock $(S + P)$. Construct the equivalent position using call options, assuming all the options are European.

34 TMS is currently trading at \$40, which you think is above its true value. Given your knowledge of the firm, its products, and its markets, you believe that \$35 per share is a more appropriate price for TMS. One means of purchasing TMS at \$35 per share would be to write a limit order. A limit order is an order directed to a broker on the floor of the exchange that specifies, among other things, the purchase price of the stock. You also notice that TMS has traded options and that a \$40 put option is selling for \$5. An alternative investment strategy involves purchasing TMS for \$40 and writing a TMS put option for \$5.

  A If at the expiration of the option, TMS's stock is trading at a price above \$40 per share, discuss the benefits of the buy stock/sell put investment strategy.

  B If at the expiration of the option, TMS's stock is trading at a price below \$40 per share, discuss the benefits of this alternative investment strategy.

35 When you purchase property insurance, you must choose the dollar amount of the deductible on the policy. Similarly, when you construct a protective put position, you must choose the strike price on the put option. Discuss the similarities between the choice of the deductible on an insurance policy and the selection of a strike price for the protective put position.

36 A client has recently sold a stock short for \$100. The short sale agreement requires him to cover the short position in one month. The client wants to protect his position against stock price increases. You notice that the stock has puts and calls traded on the CBOE. Explain how your client can use either the put or call option to construct a portfolio that will limit his risk exposure to stock price increases. Compare the two alternative strategies.

Notes

1 Recall that we are ignoring transaction costs. In the options market, both buyers and sellers incur transaction costs. Therefore, the options market is a negative-sum game if we include transaction costs in our analysis.

2 The arbitrage arguments used in this chapter stem from a famous paper by R. C. Merton, "Theory of Rational Option Pricing," *Bell Journal of Economics and Management Science*, 4, Spring 1973, pp. 141–83.

3 For further details, see Mayhew and Vassil Mihov, "How Do Exchanges Select Stocks for Option Listing?" *Journal of Finance*, 59:1, February 2004, pp. 447–71.

4 The buyer of a straddle need not be matched with a trader who specifically sells a straddle. Opposite the buyer of a straddle could be two individuals, one of whom sells a call and the other of whom sells a put.

5 The theoretically maximum loss for the short straddle trader occurs when the stock price goes to zero. In this case, the call cannot be exercised against the short trader, but the put will be exercised. Thus, the trader will lose $X - S = X - 0 = X$ on the exercise. This loss will be partially offset by the funds received from selling the straddle $(C_t + P_t)$, so the total loss will be $X - C_t - P_t$.

6 It is also possible to execute similar strategies with combinations of options and the underlying instrument.

7 The reader should note that the use of terms such as *bear spread* and *bull spread* is not standardized. Although this book uses these terms in familiar ways, other traders may use them differently.

8 Introductory studies of portfolio insurance are: P. A. Abken, "An Introduction to Portfolio Insurance," Federal Reserve Bank of Atlanta, *Economic Review*, 72:6, November/December 1987, pp. 2–25; and T. J. O'Brien, "The Mechanics of Portfolio Insurance," *Journal of Portfolio Management*, 14:3, Spring 1988, pp. 40–47. In his paper "Simplifying Portfolio Insurance," *Journal of Portfolio Management*, 14:1, Fall 1987, pp. 48–51, Fischer Black shows how to insure a portfolio without using option pricing theory, and he shows how to establish an insured portfolio without a definite horizon date.

9 It is possible to create an insured portfolio without using options. These alternative strategies employ stock index futures with continuous rebalancing of the futures position. Because of this continuous rebalancing, these strategies are called "dynamic hedging" strategies. Hayne E. Leland, "Option Pricing and Replication with Transaction Costs," *Journal of Finance*, 40, December 1985, pp. 1283–301, discusses these dynamic strategies. With a dynamic strategy, the insurer must rebalance the portfolio very frequently, leading to a trade-off between having an exactly

insured portfolio and high transaction costs. J. Clay Singleton and Robin Grieves discuss this trade-off in their paper "Synthetic Puts and Portfolio Insurance Strategies," *Journal of Portfolio Management*, 10:3, Spring 1984, pp. 63–9. Richard Bookstaber, "Portfolio Insurance Trading Rules," *Journal of Futures Markets*, 8:1, February 1988, pp. 15–31, discusses some recent technological innovations in portfolio insurance strategies and foresees increasing complexity and sophistication in the implementation of insurance techniques.

10 Several studies have explored the cost of portfolio insurance. Richard J. Rendleman, Jr., and Richard W. McEnally, "Assessing the Cost of Portfolio Insurance," *Financial Analysts Journal*, 43, May/June 1987, pp. 27–37, compare the desirability of an insured portfolio relative to a utility-maximizing strategy. They conclude that only extremely risk-averse investors will be willing to incur the costs of insuring a portfolio. Richard Bookstaber finds similar results in his paper "The Use of Options in Performance Structuring: Modeling Returns to Meet Investment Objectives," in *Controlling Interest Rate Risk: New Techniques and Applications for Money Management*, Robert B. Platt (ed.), New York: Wiley, 1986. According to Bookstaber, completely insuring a portfolio costs about 25 percent of the portfolio's total return. C. B. Garcia and F. J. Gould, "An Empirical Study of Portfolio Insurance," *Financial Analysts Journal*, July/August 1987, pp. 44–54, find that fully insuring a portfolio causes a loss of returns of about 100 basis points. They conclude that an insured portfolio is not likely to outperform a static portfolio of stocks and T-bills. Roger G. Clarke and Robert D. Arnott study the costs of portfolio insurance directly in their paper "The Cost of Portfolio Insurance: Tradeoffs and Choices," *Financial Analysts Journal*, 43:6, November/December 1987, pp. 35–47. Clarke and Arnott explore the desirability of insuring only part of the portfolio, increasing the risk of the portfolio, and attempting to insure a portfolio for a longer horizon. As they conclude, transaction costs are an important factor in choosing the optimal strategy.

11 These synthetic relationships hold exactly only for European options. In Chapter 15, we explore the reasons for this restriction within the context of our discussion of American options.

12

Bounds on Option Prices

Overview

This chapter continues to use no-arbitrage conditions to explore option pricing principles. In the last chapter, we considered the prices that options could have at expiration, consistent with no-arbitrage conditions. In this chapter, we consider option prices before expiration. Extending our analysis to options with time remaining until expiration brings new factors into consideration.

The value of an option before expiration depends on five factors: the price of the underlying stock, the exercise price of the option, the time remaining until expiration, the risk-free rate of interest, and the possible price movements on the underlying stock.[1] For stocks with dividends, the potential dividend payments during an option's life can also influence the value of the option. In this chapter, we focus on the intuition underlying the relationship between put and call prices and these factors. The next chapter builds on these intuitions to specify these relationships more formally.

We first consider how option prices respond to changes in the stock price, the time remaining until expiration, and the exercise price of the option. These factors set general boundaries for possible option prices. Later in the chapter, we discuss the influence of interest rates on option prices, and we consider how the riskiness of the stock affects the price of the option.

The boundary space for call and put options

In Chapter 11, we saw that the value of a call (either European or American) at expiration must be

$$C_T = \text{MAX}\{0, S_T - X\} \tag{12.1}$$

Similarly, the value of a put (either European or American) at expiration is

$$P_T = \text{MAX}\{0, X - S_T\} \tag{12.2}$$

where C_t is the call price at time t; P_t is the put price at time t; S_t is the stock price at time t; X is the exercise price at time t; and T is the expiration date of the option, that is, $t = T$. Corresponding to Equations 12.1 and 12.2, we saw that call and put options had distinctive graphs that specified their values at expiration. Figure 11.4 for a call and Figure 11.6 for a put gave the value of the options at expiration. These two figures simply graph Equations 12.1 and 12.2, respectively. Now we want to consider the range of possible values for call and put options more generally. Specifically, we want to analyze the values that options can have before expiration.[2]

Said another way, we want to explore the values of options as a function of the stock price, S, the exercise price, X, and the time remaining until expiration, $T - t$. In Chapter 11, we only considered options that were at expiration, with $t = T$. Thus, we were considering option values for various ranges of stock price and exercise prices, but with zero time to expiration. Now we want to consider option prices when the stock price, the exercise price, and the time to expiration all vary.

Before expiration, call and put values need not conform to Equations 12.1 and 12.2. Therefore, our first task is to determine the entire possible range of prices that calls and puts may have before expiration. We call this range of possibilities the **boundary space** for an option. Once we specify the largest range of possible prices, we consider no-arbitrage principles that will help us specify the price of an option more precisely.

The boundary space for a call option

To define the boundary space for a call option, we consider extreme values for the variables that affect call prices. Because we first focus on the stock price, the exercise price, and the time remaining until expiration, we consider extremely high and low values for each of these variables. First, the value of a call option will depend on the stock price. We have already seen that a call option at expiration is worth more the greater the price of the stock. Second, the value of a call option depends on the exercise price of the option. Third, the value of a call can depend on the time remaining until the option expires.

The owner of a call option receives the stock upon exercise. The stock price represents the potential benefit that will come to the holder of a call, so the higher the stock price, the greater is the value of a call option. We have already observed this to be true at expiration, as Equation 12.1 shows. Also, the exercise price is a cash outflow if the call owner exercises. As such, the exercise price represents a potential liability to the call owner. The lower the liability associated with a call, the better it is for the call owner. Therefore, the lower the exercise price, the greater is the value of a call. Finally, consider the time remaining until expiration. For clarity, we focus on two American options that differ only because one has a longer time remaining until expiration. Comparing these two options, we see that the one with the longer time until expiration gives every benefit that the one with the shorter time until expiration does. At a given moment, if the shorter-term option permits expiration, so does the option with a longer term until expiration. In addition, the longer-term option allows the privilege of waiting longer to decide whether to exercise. Generally, this privilege of waiting is quite valuable, so the option with the longer life tends to have a higher value. However, no matter what happens, the option with the longer life must have a price at least as great as the option with the shorter life. We will see that the same holds true for European options. The longer the time until expiration, the greater is the value of the option, holding other factors constant.

We have seen that lower exercise prices and longer lives generally increase the value of an option. Therefore, the value of an option will be highest for an option with a zero exercise price and an infinite time until expiration. Similarly, the value will be lowest for an option with a higher exercise price and the shortest time until expiration. A call that is about to expire, with $t = T$, will be the call with the lowest price for a given stock price and a given exercise price. We already know the possible values that such an expiring option can have. This value is simply the call option's price at expiration, which is given by Equation 12.1. At the other extreme, the call with the highest possible value for a given stock price will be the call with a zero exercise price and an infinite time until expiration.

This call option with a zero exercise price and an infinite time until it expires allows us to exercise the option with zero cost and acquire the stock. In short, we can transform this option into the stock any time we wish without paying anything. Therefore, the value of this call must equal the price of the underlying stock. If we can get the stock for zero any time we wish, the price of the call cannot be more than the stock price. Also, the price of the call cannot exceed the stock price, because the call can only be used to acquire the stock. Therefore, we know that

Figure 12.1   The boundary space for a call option

a call on a given stock, with a zero exercise price and an infinite time to expiration, must have a value equal to the stock price. In this special limiting case, $C_t = S_t$.

From this analysis, we have now determined the upper and lower bounds for the price of a call option before expiration. Figure 12.1 depicts the boundaries for the price of a call option as the interior area between the upper and lower bounds. The upper bound for any call option is the stock price. The figure shows this boundary as the 45 degree line from the origin. Along this line, the call option is worth the same as the stock. The lower bound is the value of the call option at expiration. At expiration, if the stock price is at or below the exercise price, the call is worth zero. For any stock price above the exercise price, the expiring call is worth the stock price minus the exercise price. Therefore, the value of a call option must always fall somewhere on or within the bounds given by these lines. Later in this chapter, we develop principles that help us to specify much more precisely where within these bounds the actual option price must lie.

The boundary space for a put option

We now consider the range of possible put prices. We have already considered prices for puts at expiration, and we found the value of a put at expiration to conform to Equation 12.2. That equation gives the lower bound for the value of a put option. To find the upper bound for a put option, we need to consider the best possible circumstances for the owner of a put option.

Upon exercise, the owner of a put surrenders the stock and receives the exercise price. The most the put holder can receive is the exercise price, and he can obtain this only by surrendering the stock. Therefore, the lower the stock price, the more valuable the put must be. This is true before expiration and at expiration, as we have already seen. The owner of an American put can exercise the option at any time. Therefore, the maximum value for an American put is the exercise price. The price of an American put equals the exercise price if the stock is worthless and is sure to remain worthless until the option expires. If the put is a European put, it cannot be exercised immediately, but only at expiration. For a European put before expiration, the maximum possible price equals the present value of the exercise price. The European put price cannot exceed the present value of the exercise price, because the owner of a European put must wait until expiration to exercise.

Figure 12.2   The boundary space for a put option

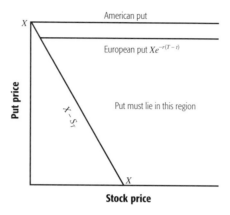

Figure 12.2 shows the bounds for American and European puts. The price of a put can never fall below the maximum of zero or $X - S_T$. This is the put's value at expiration, which Equation 12.2 specifies. For an American put, the price can never exceed X. For a European put, the price can never exceed the present value of the exercise price, $Xe^{-r(T-t)}$. Therefore, the interior of Figure 12.2 defines the range of possible put prices. By developing more exact no-arbitrage conditions, we can say where in this interior area the price of a put can be found.[3]

Relationships between call option prices

In this section, we focus on price relationships between call options. These price differences arise from differences in exercise price and time until expiration. We have already seen in an informal way that the exercise price is a potential liability associated with call ownership. The greater the value of this potential liability, the lower is the value of the call option. In this section, we illustrate this principle more formally by appealing to our familiar no-arbitrage arguments. We use similar no-arbitrage arguments to explicate other pricing relationships. Unless explicitly stated otherwise, all of these relationships hold for both American and European calls.

The lower the exercise price, the more valuable the call
Let us consider a single underlying stock on which there are two call options. The two call options have the same expiration date, but one option has a lower exercise price than the other. In this section, we want to show why the option with the lower exercise price must be worth as much or more than the option with the higher exercise price. For example, assume that two calls exist that violate this principle:

	Time until expiration	Exercise price	Call price
Call A	Six months	$100	$20
Call B	Six months	95	15

These two calls violate our principle, because Call A has a higher exercise price and a higher call price. These prices give rise to an arbitrage opportunity, as we now show. Faced with these prices, the trader can transact as follows:

Transaction	Cash flow
Sell Call A	+$20
Buy Call B	−15
Net cash flow	+$5

Once we sell Call A and buy Call B, we have a sure profit of at least $5. To see this, we consider profits and losses for various stock prices, such as $95 and below and $100 and above. If the stock price is $95, neither option can be exercised. If the stock price stays at $95 or below, both options expire worthless, and we keep our $5 from the initial transactions. If the stock price is greater than $100, say $105, Call A will be exercised against us. When that happens, we surrender the stock worth $105 and receive $100, losing $5 on the exercise against us. However, we ourselves exercise Call B, receiving the stock worth $105 and paying the exercise price of $95. So we can summarize our profits and losses from the exercises that occur when the stock trades at $105:

Surrender stock	−$105
Receive $100 exercise price	+100
Pay $95 exercise price	−95
Receive stock	+105
Net cash flow	+$5

As the calculation shows, if Call A is exercised against us, we exercise Call B and make $5 on the double exercise. Therefore, we make a total of $10, $5 from the initial transaction and $5 on the exercises.

Next, we consider what happens if the stock price lies between $95 and $100, say at $97. This outcome is also beneficial for us, because the option we sold with a $100 strike price cannot be exercised against us. However, we can exercise our option. When we exercise, we pay the $95 exercise price and receive a stock worth $97. We add the $2 profit on this exercise to the $5 we made initially, for a total profit of $7. Figure 12.3 graphs the total profit on the position for all stock prices. With a stock price at or below $95, we make $5 because neither option can be exercised. With a stock price of $100 or above, we make $10—that is, $5 from our initial transaction and $5 from the difference between the two exercise prices. If the stock price is between $95 and $100, we make $5 from our initial transaction plus the difference between the stock price and the $95 exercise price that we face.

These transactions guarantee an arbitrage profit of at least $5, and perhaps as much as $10. Figure 12.3 reflects the arbitrage profit because it shows there is at least a $5 profit for any stock price. If the profit-and-loss graph shows profits for all possible stock prices with no investment, then there is an arbitrage opportunity. In the real world, an investment strategy that requires no initial investment may show profits for some stock price outcomes, but it must also show losses for other stock prices. Otherwise, there is an arbitrage opportunity.

In stating our principle, we said that the call with the lower exercise price must cost at least as much as the call with the higher exercise price. Why doesn't the call with the lower exercise price have to cost more than the call with the higher exercise price? In most real market

Figure 12.3   Arbitrage with Calls A and B

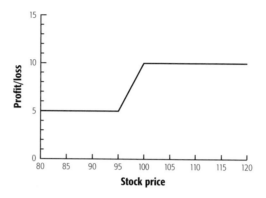

situations, the call with the lower exercise price will, in fact, cost more. However, we cannot be sure that will happen as a general rule. To see why, assume that the stock underlying Calls A and B trades for $5 and there is virtually no chance that the stock price could reach $90 before the two options expire. When the underlying stock is extremely far out-of-the-money, the calls might have the same, or nearly the same, price. In such a situation, both calls would have a very low price. If it is certain that the stock price can never rise to the lower exercise price, both calls would be worthless.

The difference in call prices cannot exceed the difference in exercise prices

Consider two call options that are similar in all respects except that they have exercise prices that differ by $5. We have already seen that the price of the call with the lower exercise price must equal or exceed the price of the call with the higher exercise price. Now we show that the difference in call prices cannot exceed the difference in exercise prices. We illustrate this principle by considering two call options with the same underlying stock:

	Time until expiration	Exercise price	Call price
Call C	Six months	$95	$10
Call D	Six months	100	4

The prices of Calls C and D do not meet our condition, and we want to show that these prices give rise to an arbitrage opportunity. To profit from this mispricing, we trade as follows:

Transaction	Cash flow
Sell Call C	+$10
Buy Call D	−4
Net cash flow	+$6

Selling Call C and buying Call D gives a net cash inflow of $6. Because we sold a call, however, we also have the risk that the call will be exercised against us. We now show that no matter what stock price occurs, we still make a profit.

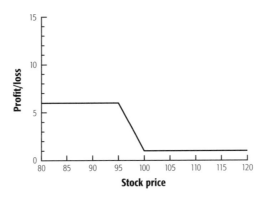

Figure 12.4 Arbitrage with Calls C and D

If the stock price is $95 or below, both options expire worthless, and we keep our initial cash inflow of $6. If the stock price exceeds $100, Call C is exercised against us and we exercise Call D. For example, assume that the stock price is $102. We exercise, pay the $100 exercise price, and receive the stock. Call C is exercised against us, so we surrender the stock and receive the $95 exercise price. Therefore, we lose $5 on the exercise. This loss partially offsets our initial cash inflow of $6. Thus, for any stock price of $100 or more, we make $1. We now consider stock prices between $95 and $100. If the stock price is $98, Call C will be exercised against us. We surrender the stock worth $98 and receive $95, for a $3 loss. The option we own cannot be exercised, because the exercise price of $100 exceeds the current stock price of $98. Therefore, we lose $3 on the exercise, which partially offsets our initial cash inflow of $6. This gives a $3 net profit.

Figure 12.4 shows the profits and losses on this trade for a range of stock prices. As the figure shows, we make at least $1, and we may make as much as $6. Because all outcomes show a profit with no investment, these transactions constitute an arbitrage. The chance to make this arbitrage profit stems from the fact that the call option prices differed by more than the difference between the exercise prices. In real markets, the difference between two call prices will usually be less than the difference in exercise prices. However, the difference in call prices cannot exceed the difference in exercise prices without creating an arbitrage opportunity.[4]

A call must be worth at least the stock price less the present value of the exercise price

We have already noted that a call at expiration is worth the maximum of zero or the stock price less the exercise price. Before expiration, the call must be worth at least the stock price less the present value of the exercise price. That is,

$$C_t \geq S_t - Xe^{-r(T-t)} \tag{12.3}$$

To see why prices must observe this principle, we consider the following situation. Assume that the stock trades for $103 and the current risk-free interest rate is 6 percent. A call with an exercise price of $100 expires in six months and trades for $2. These prices violate our rule, because the call option price is too low: $2 is less than the stock price less the present value of $100. These prices give rise to an arbitrage opportunity. To take advantage, we trade as follows:

Sell the stock	+$103
Buy the call option	−2
Buy a bond with remaining funds	−101
Net cash flow	0

With these transactions, we owe one share of stock. However, with our call option and the money we have left from selling the stock, we can honor our obligations at any time and still have a profit. For example, at the beginning of the transactions, we can exercise our option, pay the $100 exercise price, return the stock, and keep $1.

Alternatively, we can wait until our option reaches expiration in six months. Then the bond we purchased will be worth $101 \times e^{0.06 \times 0.5}$ = $104.08. Whatever the stock is worth at expiration, we can repay with profit. For example, if the stock price is higher than the exercise price, we exercise the option and pay $100 to get the stock. This gives a profit at expiration of $4.08. If the stock price is below the exercise price, we allow our option to expire. We then buy the stock in the open market and repay our debt of one share. For example, if the stock price is $95 at expiration, our option expires, and we pay $95 for the share to repay our obligation. Our profit then is $104.08 − $95 = $9.08. Figure 12.5 graphs the profits from this transaction.

From this analysis, we can see that our option must cost at least $103 − $100e^{-0.06 \times 0.5}$ = $103 − $97.04 = $5.96. Any lower price allows an arbitrage profit. If the call is priced at $5.96, we have $97.04 to invest in bonds after selling the stock at $103 and buying the option at $5.96. At expiration, our bond investment pays $100, which is the exercise price. If the option sold at $5.96, the profit line in Figure 12.5 would shift down to show a zero profit for any stock price of $100 or more. This would eliminate the arbitrage, because there would be some stock prices that would give zero profits. However, in real markets, the price of this call generally would be higher than $5.96. A price of $5.96 ensures against any loss and gives profits for any stock price below $100. If there is any chance that the stock price might be below $100 at expiration, then the call of our example should be worth more than $5.96.

Figure 12.5   Arbitrage of a call against a stock and book

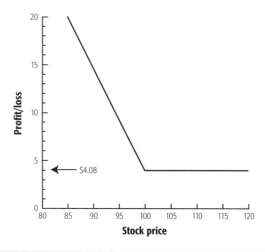

The more time until expiration, the greater the call price

If we consider two call options with the same exercise price on the same underlying good, then the price of the call with more time remaining until expiration must equal or exceed the price of the call that expires sooner. Violating this principle leads to arbitrage, as the following example shows.

Consider two options on the same underlying good:

	Time until expiration	Exercise price	Call price
Call E	Three months	$100	$6
Call F	Six months	100	5

These prices violate our principle, which implies that Call F must cost at least as much as Call E. To capture the arbitrage profits, we trade as follows:

Transaction	Cash flow
Sell Call E	+$6
Buy Call F	−5
Net cash flow	+$1

With a net cash inflow at the time of contracting, the transactions clearly require no investment. Therefore, they meet the first condition for an arbitrage. Next, we need to show that the strategy produces a profit for all stock price outcomes.

First, we show how to protect the arbitrage profit if the options are American options. Any time that Call E is exercised against us, we can exercise Call F to secure the stock to give to the holder of Call E. For example, assume that Call E is about to expire and is exercised against us with the stock price at $105. In that case, we simply exercise Call F and surrender the stock to the holder of Call E, as the following transactions show.

Assuming that Calls E and F are American options

Transaction	Cash flow
Call E is exercised against us	
Receive $100 exercise price	+$100
Surrender stock worth $105	−105
Exercise Call F	
Receive stock worth $105	+105
Pay $100 exercise price	−100
Net cash flow	0

As these transactions show, if the call we sold is exercised against us, we can fulfill all our obligations by exercising our call. There will be no net cash flow on the exercise, and we keep the $1 profit from our original transaction.

Notice that our concluding transactions assumed that both Call E and Call F were American options. This allowed us to exercise our Call F before expiration. Had the options been European options, we could not have exercised Call F when Call E was exercised against us. However, the principle still holds for European options—the European option with more time until expiration must be worth at least as much as the option with a shorter life. We can illustrate this principle for European options with the following transactions.

Assuming that Calls E and F are European options

Transaction	Cash flow
Call E is exercised against us	
Receive $100 exercise price	+$100
Surrender stock worth $105	−105
Sell Call F	
Receive $S - Xe^{-r(T-t)} \geq \$5$	At least +5
Net cash flow	At least 0

As these transactions show, we will receive at least $5 for selling Call F. Earlier, we used no-arbitrage arguments to show that an in-the-money call must be worth at least the stock price minus the present value of the exercise price. The worst situation for these transactions occurs at very low interest rates. However, the arbitrage still works for a zero interest rate. Then, Call F must still be worth at least $S - X = \$105 - \$100 = \$5$. If we get $5 from selling Call F, we still have a net zero cash flow when Call E is exercised against us. If we get more, any additional net cash flow at the time of exercise is just added to the $1 cash inflow we had at the time we initially transacted.

Do not exercise call options on no-dividend stocks before expiration

In this section, we show that a call option on a nondividend-paying stock is always worth more than its mere exercise value. Therefore, such an option should never be exercised. If the trader wants to dispose of the option, it will always be better to sell the option than to exercise it.

For a call option, the **intrinsic value** or the **exercise value** of the option equals $S_t - X$. This is the value of the option when it is exercised, because the holder of the call pays X and receives S_t. We have seen that, prior to expiration, a call option must be worth at least $S_t - Xe^{-r(T-t)}$. Therefore, exercising a call before expiration discards at least the difference between X and $Xe^{-r(T-t)}$. The difference between the call price and the exercise value is the **time value** of the option. For example, consider the following values: $S_t = \$105$; $X = \$100$; $r = 0.10$; and $T - t = 6$ months. The intrinsic value of this call option is $5, or $S_t - X$. However, we know that the market price of the call option must meet the following condition:

$$\begin{aligned} C_t &\geq S_t - Xe^{-r(T-t)} \\ &\geq \$105 - \$100 \times e^{-0.1 \times 0.5} \\ &\geq \$9.88 \end{aligned}$$

Therefore, exercising the call throws away at least $X - Xe^{-r(T-t)} = \$100 - \$95.12 = \$4.88$. Alternatively, it discards the difference between the lower bound on the call price and the exercise value of the call, $9.88 - \$5.00 = \$4.88$. For a nondividend-paying stock, early exercise can never be optimal. This means that the call will not be exercised until expiration. However, this makes an American option on a nondividend-paying stock equivalent to a European option. For a stock that pays no dividends, the American option will not be exercised until expiration, and a European option cannot be exercised until expiration. Therefore, the two have the same price. Notice that this rule holds only for a call option on a stock that does not pay dividends. In some circumstances, it can make sense to exercise a call option on a dividend paying stock before the option expires. The motivation for the early exercise is to capture the dividend immediately and to earn interest on those funds. We explore these possibilities in Chapter 15.

Relationships between put option prices

In Chapter 11, we saw that the value of either an American put or a European put at expiration is given by

$$P_T = \text{MAX}\{0, X - S_T\}$$

Essentially, the put holder anticipates receiving the value of the exercise price and paying the stock price at expiration. Now we want to consider put values before expiration and the relationship between pairs of puts. As we did for calls, we illustrate these pricing relationships by invoking no-arbitrage conditions. Further, the relationships hold for both American and European puts unless explicitly stated otherwise.

Before expiration, an American put must be worth at least the exercise price less the stock price
The holder of an American put option can exercise any time. Upon exercising, the put holder surrenders the put and the stock and receives the exercise price. Therefore, the American put must be worth at least the difference between the exercise price and the stock price:

$$P_t \geq \text{MAX}\{0, X - S_T\}$$

where P_t is the price of an American put at time t.

We illustrate this principle by showing how to reap an arbitrage profit if the principle does not hold. Consider the following data: $S_t = \$95$; $X = \$100$; and $P_t = \$3$. With these prices, the put is too cheap. The put's price does not equal or exceed the $5 difference between the exercise price and the stock price. To take advantage of the mispricing, we transact as shown in the following table:

Transaction	Cash flow
Buy put	−$3
Buy stock	−95
Exercise option	+100
Net cash flow	+$2

With these transactions, we capture an immediate cash inflow of $2. Also, we have no further obligations, so our arbitrage is complete. Notice that these transactions involve the immediate exercise of the put option. Therefore, this kind of arbitrage is possible only for an American put option. To prevent this kind of arbitrage, the price of the American put option must be at least $5. In actual markets, the price of a put generally will exceed the difference between the exercise price and the stock price.

Before expiration, a European put must be worth at least the present value of the exercise price minus the stock price
We have just seen that an American put must be worth at least the difference between the exercise price and the stock price, $X - S_t$. The same rule does not hold for a European put,

because we cannot exercise the European put before expiration to take advantage of the mispricing. However, a similar rule holds for a European put. Specifically, the value of a European put must equal or exceed the present value of the exercise price minus the stock price:

$$p_t \geq Xe^{-r(T-t)} - S_t$$

We can illustrate this price restriction for a European put by using our same stock and option, except that we treat the put as a European put. Also, the risk-free interest rate is 6 percent, and we assume that the option expires in three months. Consider the following data: $S_t = \$95$; $X = \$100$; $p_t = \$3$; $T - t = $ three months; $r = 0.06$—where p_t is the price of a European put at time t. With these values, our principle states that

$$p_t \geq Xe^{-r(T-t)} - S_t = \$100 \times e^{-0.06 \times 0.25} - \$95 = \$98.51 - \$95 = \$3.51$$

Because the put must be worth at least \$3.51 but the actual price is only \$3, we can reap an arbitrage profit by trading as follows:

Transaction	Cash flow
Borrow \$98 at 6 percent for three months	+\$98
Buy put	−3
Buy stock	−95
Net cash flow	0

After making these initial transactions, we wait until the option is about to expire and we transact as follows:

Transaction	Cash flow
Exercise option, deliver stock, and collect exercise price	+\$100.00
Repay debt = \$98 × $e^{0.06 \times 0.25}$	−99.48
Net cash flow	+\$0.52

These transactions give an arbitrage profit of \$0.52 at expiration. Notice that there was a zero net cash flow when we first transacted, so there was no investment. These initial transactions guaranteed the \$0.52 profit at expiration. Therefore, we have an arbitrage—a riskless profit with no investment.

From these two examples, we can see that an American put must be worth at least as much as a European put. The lower bound for the price of an American put is $X - S_t$, but the lower bound for the European put is $Xe^{-r(T-t)} - S_t$. Also, we know that the American put gives all the rights of the European put, plus the chance to exercise early. Therefore, the American put must be worth at least as much as the European put.

The longer until expiration, the more valuable an American put

Consider two American put options that are just alike, except that one has a longer time until expiration. The put with the longer time until expiration must be worth at least as much as the other. Informally, the put with the longer time until expiration offers every advantage of the shorter term put. In addition, the longer-term put offers the chance for greater price increases on the put after the shorter-term put expires. Without this condition, arbitrage opportunities exist.

To illustrate the arbitrage opportunity, assume that the underlying stock trades for $95 and we have two American puts with exercise prices of $100 as follows:

	Time until expiration	Put price
Put A	Three months	$7
Put B	Six months	6

These prices permit arbitrage, because the put with the longer life is cheaper. Therefore, we sell Put A and buy Put B for an arbitrage profit, as shown below:

Transaction	Cash flow
Sell Put A	+$7
Buy Put B	−6
Net cash flow	+$1

After making these transactions, we must consider what happens if Put A is exercised against us. Assume that Put A is exercised against us when the stock price is $90. In this situation, the following events occur:

Transaction	Cash flow
On the exercise of Put A	
Receive stock worth $90	+$90
Pay exercise price of $100	−100
We exercise Put B	
Deliver stock worth $90	−90
Receive exercise price of $100	+100
Net cash flow	0

When the holder of Put A exercises against us, we immediately exercise Put B. No matter what the stock price may be, these transactions give a zero net cash flow. Therefore, the original transaction gave us $1, which represents an arbitrage profit of at least $1. The profit could be greater if Put A expires worthless. Then we have our $1 profit to keep, plus we still hold Put B, which may have additional value. Therefore, the longer-term American put must be worth at least as much as the shorter-term American put. Notice that this rule holds only for American puts. Our arbitrage transactions require that we exercise Put B when the holder of Put A exercises against us. This we could do only with an American option.

For European put options, it is not always true that the longer-term put has greater value. A European put pays off the exercise price only at expiration. If expiration is very distant, the payoff will be diminished in value because of the time value of money. However, the longer the life of a put option, the greater its advantage in allowing something beneficial to happen to the stock price. Thus, the longer the life of the put, the better it is for this reason. Whether having a longer life is beneficial to the price of a European put depends on which of these two factors dominates. We will be able to evaluate these more completely in the next chapter.

The fact that a European put with a shorter life can be more valuable than a European put with a longer life shows two important principles. First, early exercise of a put can be desirable even when the underlying stock pays no dividends. This follows from the fact that a short-term European put can be worth more than a long-term European put. Second, American and European put prices may not be identical, even when the underlying stock pays no dividends. If early exercise is desirable, the American put allows it and the European put does not. Therefore, the American put can be more valuable than a European put, even when the underlying stock pays no dividend.

The higher the exercise price, the more valuable the put

For both American and European put options, a higher exercise price is associated with a higher put price. A put option with a higher exercise price must be worth at least as much as a put with a lower exercise price. Violations of this principle lead to arbitrage.

To illustrate the arbitrage, consider a stock trading at $90 with the following two put options having the same time until expiration:

	Exercise price	Put price
Put C	$100	$11
Put D	95	12

These prices violate the rule, because the price of Put D is higher, even though Put C has the higher exercise price. To reap the arbitrage profit, we transact as follows:

Transaction	Cash flow
Sell Put D	+$12
Buy Put C	−11
Net cash flow	+$1

If the holder of Put D exercises against us, we immediately exercise Put C. Assuming that the stock price is $90 at the time of exercise, we consider the appropriate transactions when we face the exercise of Put D:

Transaction	Cash flow
Exercise of Put D against us	
Receive stock worth $90	+$90
Pay exercise price	−95
Our exercise of Put C	
Deliver stock worth $90	−90
Receive exercise price	+100
Net cash flow	+$5

No matter what the stock price is at the time of exercise, we have a cash inflow of $5 if we both exercise. Further, Put D can be exercised only when it is profitable for us to exercise Put C. Notice that this principle holds for both American and European puts. Put C and Put D can be exercised either before expiration (for an American option) or at expiration only (for a European

Figure 12.6   Arbitrage with Puts C and D

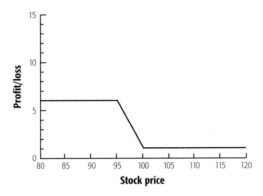

option). Figure 12.6 shows the profits for alternative stock prices. For any stock price of $100 or above, both puts expire worthless and we keep our initial $1 inflow. For a stock price between $95 and $100, we can exercise our option, but Put D cannot be exercised. For example, if the stock is at $97, we exercise and receive $100 for a $97 stock. This $3 exercise profit gives us a total profit of $4. If the stock price is below $95, both puts will be exercised. For example, with the stock price at $90, the exercise profit on Put D is $5, as we have seen. However, our exercise profit on Put C is $10. Thus, we lose $5 on the exercise of Put D against us, but we make $10 by exercising Put C, and we still have our $1 initial inflow, for a net arbitrage profit of $6.

The price difference between two American puts cannot exceed the difference in exercise prices

The prices of two American puts cannot differ by more than the difference in exercise prices, assuming other features are the same. If prices violate this condition, there will be an arbitrage opportunity. To illustrate this arbitrage opportunity, consider the following puts on the same underlying stock:

	Exercise price	Put price
Put E	$100	$4
Put F	105	10

These prices violate our condition, because the price difference between the puts is $6, while the difference in exercise prices is only $5. To exploit this mispricing, we transact as follows:

Transaction	Cash flow
Sell Put F	+$10
Buy Put E	−4
Net cash flow	+$6

Figure 12.7   Arbitrage with Puts E and F

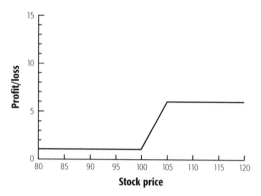

With this initial cash inflow of $6, we have enough to pay any loss we might sustain when the holder of Put F exercises against us. For example, assume the stock trades at $95 and the holder of Put F exercises:

The exercise of Put F against us	
Receive stock worth $95	+$95
Pay exercise price	−105
Our exercise of Put E	
Receive exercise price	+100
Deliver stock worth $95	−95
Net cash flow	−$5

On the exercise, we lose $5. However, we had already received $6 with the initial transactions. This leaves an arbitrage profit of at least $1. As Figure 12.7 shows, we could have larger profits, depending on the stock price. If the stock price equals or exceeds $105, no exercise is possible and we keep the entire $6 of our initial transaction. For stock prices between $100 and $105, the holder of Put F can exercise against us, but we cannot exercise. For example, if the stock price is $103, we must pay $105 and receive a stock worth only $103, for a $2 exercise loss. However, with our initial cash inflow of $6, we still have a net profit of $4. For stock prices below $100, we can both exercise, as in the transactions we showed for a stock price of $95. In this case, we lose $5 on the exercise, but we still make a net profit of $1.

For two European puts, the price difference cannot exceed the difference in the present value of the exercise prices

A similar principle holds for European puts, except that the difference in put prices cannot exceed the difference in the present values of the exercise prices. If Puts E and F are European puts, the interest rate is 10 percent, and the options expire in six months, then the present values of the exercise prices are as follows:

	Exercise price	Present value of exercise price
Put E	$100	$95.12
Put F	105	99.88

According to this principle, the price of Put F cannot exceed the price of Put E by more than $4.76 ($99.88 − $95.12). With prices of $4 and $10 for Puts E and F, there should be an arbitrage profit.

To capture the profit, we sell Put F and buy Put E, as we did with the American puts. This gives a cash inflow of $6, which we invest for six months at 10 percent. The European puts cannot be exercised until expiration, at which time our investment is worth $6 \times e^{0.1 \times 0.5} = \$6.31$. The most we can lose on the exercise is $5, the difference in the exercise prices. As we saw for the American puts, this happens when the stock price is $100 or less. However, we have $6.31 at expiration, so we can easily sustain this loss. If the stock price exceeds $105, neither option can be exercised and we keep our entire $6.31. For the European puts, the graph of the arbitrage profit is exactly like Figure 12.7, except we add $0.31 to every point. If the options had been priced $4.76 apart, our investment would have yielded $5 at expiration ($4.76 \times e^{0.1 \times 0.5}$). This $5 would protect us against any loss at expiration, but it would guarantee no arbitrage profit.

Summary

To this point, we have considered how call and put prices respond to stock and exercise prices and the time remaining until expiration. We have expressed all of these relationships as an outgrowth of our basic no-arbitrage condition: Prevailing option prices must exclude arbitrage profits. For call options, the story is very clear. The higher the stock price, the higher is the call price. The higher the exercise price, the lower is the call price. The longer the time until expiration, the higher is the call price. For put options, the higher the stock price, the lower is the put price. The higher the exercise price, the higher is the put price. For time until expiration, the effects are slightly more complicated. For an American put, the longer the time until expiration, the more valuable is the put. For a European put, a longer time until expiration can give rise to either a lower or higher put price.

We have also seen that no-arbitrage conditions restrict how call and put prices for different exercise prices can vary. For two call options or two American put options that are alike except for their exercise prices, the two option prices cannot differ by more than the difference in the exercise prices. For two European put options with different exercise prices, the option prices cannot differ by more than the present value of the difference in the exercise prices.

Throughout this discussion, we have been trying to tighten the bounds we can place on option prices. For example, Figure 12.1 gave the most generous bounds for call options. There, we noted that the call price could never exceed the stock price as an upper bound. As a lower bound, the call price must always be at least zero or the stock price minus the exercise price, whichever is higher. The price relationships we considered in this section tighten these bounds by placing further restrictions on put and call prices. Figure 12.8 illustrates how we have tightened these bounds for call options. First, we showed that the call price must be at least zero or the stock price minus the present value of the exercise price. Figure 12.8 reflects this restriction by pulling in the right boundary. Now we know that the call price must lie in this slightly smaller area. Also, if we consider a call with a lower exercise price, we know that the call price must be at least as high for the call with the lower exercise price.

Further, we have considered price relationships between pairs of options that differ in some respects. For example, assume that Option X in Figure 12.8 is priced correctly. We want to consider Option Y, which is another call like X, except that it has a longer time until expiration. With its longer time until expiration, the price of Y must equal or exceed the price of X. For example, Y in Figure 12.8 would have to lie on or above the horizontal line *abc* that runs through X. Based on our information, Y in Figure 12.8 has a permissible location.

Figure 12.8   Call price relationships

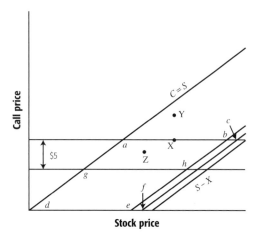

Consider another option, Z, which is just like X except that Z has an exercise price that is $5 higher than X's. The price of Z can never fall below the stock price minus the present value of Z's exercise price. Therefore, the right boundary for the stock price minus the present value of Z's exercise price gives a floor for the price of Z. The price of Z must lie above the line *eb*. With a higher exercise price, the price of Option Z cannot exceed the price of X. Therefore, the price of Z must lie on or below the line *abc*. Combining these two restrictions, we know that the price of Z must lie in the area given by *abed*.

However, we can locate the price of Z more exactly. We know from our discussion that two calls that differ only in their exercise prices must have prices that differ no more than their exercise prices. In our example, the exercise price of Z is $5 more than the exercise price of X. In Figure 12.8, line *gh* is $5 below line *abc*. Therefore, continuing to assume that the price of X is correct, Z must have a price that lies on or above *gh*. If it did not, the price of Z would be too low relative to X. Putting these principles together, we know that the price of Z must lie within the area defined by *abhg*. Z in Figure 12.8 conforms to these rules.

We cannot specify exactly where Z must lie within area *abhg*. Option prices also depend on two additional factors that we must now consider: interest rates and the way in which the stock price moves. After considering these additional factors in this chapter and in Chapter 13, we will be able to pinpoint the price that an option must have.

Option prices and the interest rate

We now apply our no-arbitrage approach to examine the effect of interest rates on option prices. For a call option, the exercise price represents a potential liability the owner of a call option faces at expiration. Before expiration, the lower the present value of the liability associated with owning a call, the better for the call owner. Therefore, as we show in the following section, call option prices increase with higher interest rates. The result may seem counterintuitive, because we generally associate higher asset prices with lower interest rates. This is not so for call options, as our no-arbitrage argument shows. The owner of a put option may exercise and receive the exercise price in exchange for surrendering the stock, so the exercise price represents a potential asset for a put owner. The lower the interest rate, the higher is the present value of that potential asset. Therefore, the lower the interest rate, the higher is the price of a put. This section presents a no-arbitrage argument to show why the price of a put must fall as interest rates rise.

Call prices and interest rates

We have already observed that the price of either an American or a European call must equal or exceed the larger of zero or the stock price minus the present value of the exercise price:

$$C_t \geq \text{MAX}\{0, S_t - Xe^{-r(T-t)}\} \tag{12.4}$$

In Equation 12.4, $Xe^{-r(T-t)}$ is the present value of the exercise price. The larger the interest rate, r, the smaller is that present value, and thus a higher interest rate gives a larger value for $S_t - Xe^{-r(T-t)}$. This makes sense, because the exercise price is a liability that the call owner incurs upon exercise.

We can also show that the call price must rise if interest rates rise by the following no-arbitrage example. Consider a call option on a stock trading at $100. The exercise price of the call is $100. The option expires in six months, and the current interest rate is 10 percent. From Equation 12.4, the price of this call must equal or exceed $4.88:

$$C_t \geq \text{MAX}\{0, \$100 - \$100 \times e^{-0.1 \times 0.5}\} \geq \$4.88$$

For convenience, we assume that the option is correctly priced at $4.88.[5]

Suddenly, interest rates jump from 10 to 12 percent, but the option price remains at $4.88. Now, the option price does not meet the condition in Equation 12.3. The option price is too low, so we want to transact to guarantee an arbitrage profit. Accordingly, we trade as follows:

Transaction	Cash flow
Sell stock	+$100.00
Buy call	−4.88
Buy bond maturing in six months and yielding 12 percent	−95.12
Net cash flow	0

In six months, the option is at expiration and our bond matures. The bond will pay $101.

How we deal with the call and stock depends on the stock price relative to the option price. If the stock trades for $100, the call option is worthless. In this case, we buy the stock for $100 and return it, leaving a profit of $1. If the stock price is less than $100, our profit increases. For example, with a $95 stock price, the option is worthless and we buy the stock for $95. These transactions leave a total profit of $6. If the stock price exceeds $100, we exercise our call and pay the exercise price of $100. After exercising and returning the stock, we still have $1. Therefore, we have a profit at expiration with no investment. This arbitrage opportunity arose because the option price did not increase as the interest rate rose. With our example, the price of the call should have risen to at least $5.82 to exclude arbitrage:

$$C_t \geq \text{MAX}\{0, S_t - Xe^{-r(T-t)}\} \geq \text{MAX}\{0, \$100 - \$100 \times e^{-0.12 \times 0.5}\} \geq \$5.82$$

Because the price did not respond, we were able to reap an arbitrage profit. To exclude arbitrage, the price of a call must be higher the higher the interest rate. Otherwise, a riskless profit without investment will be possible.

Put prices and interest rates

Interest rates also affect put prices. When exercising, the holder of a put receives the exercise price. Therefore, for a put owner, the exercise price is a potential cash inflow. The greater the present value of that potential inflow, the higher will be the value of the put. As a consequence, the put price should be higher the lower is the interest rate. If a put price fails to adjust to changing interest rates, there will be an arbitrage opportunity. This rule holds for both American and European puts.

To show how put prices depend on interest rates, consider a stock trading at $90. A European put option on this stock expires in six months and has an exercise price of $100. Interest rates are at 10 percent. We know that the European put price must meet the following condition:

$$p_t \geq \text{MAX}\{0, Xe^{-r(T-t)} - S_t\} \geq \text{MAX}\{0, \$100 \times e^{-0.1 \times 0.5} - \$90\} \geq \$5.12$$

For convenience, we assume that the put is priced at $5.12.

Let us now assume that interest rates suddenly fall to 8 percent, but that the put price does not change. Our principle asserts that the put should be worth at least $6.08 now. With the put price staying at $5.12, when it should be $6.08, we trade as follows:

Transaction	Cash flow
Borrow $95.12 at 8 percent	+$95.12
Buy stock	−90.00
Buy put	−5.12
Net cash flow	0

With these transactions in place, we wait until expiration in six months to reap our arbitrage profit. At expiration, we owe $99 on our borrowings. From the stock and the put, we must realize enough to cover that payment. Any remaining money will be profit. If the stock price at expiration is $100, we allow our put to expire and we sell the stock. We receive $100, from which we pay $99. This leaves a $1 profit. If the stock price at expiration is below $100, we exercise our put. For example, with a stock price of $95, we exercise our put, deliver the stock, and collect $100. This gives a $1 profit. We make exactly $1 at expiration for any stock price of $100 or less. For any stock price above $100, our put is worthless and our profit equals the difference between the stock price and our $99 debt. From these transactions, we see that we will make at least $1 at expiration. This we achieve with zero investment. Therefore, the failure of the put option price to adjust to changing interest rates generates an arbitrage opportunity. The put price must rise as interest rates fall.

Option prices and stock price movements

Up to this point, we have studied the way in which four factors constrain call and put prices. These factors are the stock price, the exercise price, the time remaining until expiration, and the interest rate. Even with these four factors, we cannot say exactly what the option price must be before expiration. There is a fifth factor to consider—stock price movements before expiration. If we consider a stock with options on it that expire in six months, we know that the stock price can change thousands of times before the options expire. Further, for two stocks, the pattern of changes and the volatility of the stock price changes can differ dramatically. However, if we can develop a model for understanding stock price movements, we can use that model to specify what the price of an option must be.

We now make a drastic, but temporary, simplifying assumption. Between the current moment and the expiration of an option, we assume that the stock price will rise by 10 percent or fall by 10 percent. With this assumption about the stock's price movement, we can use our no-arbitrage approach to determine the exact value of a European call or put. Therefore, knowing the potential pattern of stock price movements gives us the final key to understanding option prices. This chapter illustrates how to determine option prices based on this simplifying model of stock price movements. The next chapter shows how to apply more realistic models of stock price movements to compute accurate option prices.

Let us assume that a stock trades for $100. In the next year, the price can rise or fall exactly 10 percent. Therefore, the stock price next year will be either $90 or $110. Both a put and a call option have exercise prices of $100 and expire in one year. The current interest rate is 6 percent. We want to know how much the put and call will be worth. With these data, the call price is $7.55, and the put is worth $1.89. Other prices create arbitrage opportunities. This section shows that the options must have these prices. Chapter 13 explains why these no-arbitrage relationships must hold. (As we consider a single period in this section, we employ discrete compounding.)

The call price

We have asserted that the call price must be $7.55 given our other data, if the call price is to exclude an arbitrage opportunity. If the option price is lower, we will enter arbitrage transactions that include buying the option. Similarly, if the option price is higher, our arbitrage transactions will include selling the call. We illustrate each case in turn. Let us begin by assuming that the call price is $7.00, which is below our no-arbitrage price of $7.55. If the call price is too low, we transact as follows:

Transaction	Cash flow
Sell one share of stock	+$100.00
Buy two calls	−14.00
Buy bond	−86.00
Net cash flow	0

At expiration, the stock price will be either $110 or $90. If the stock price is $110, the calls will be worth $10 each—the stock price minus the exercise price. If the stock price is $90, the calls are worthless. In either case, the bond will pay $91.16. If the stock price is $90, we repurchase a share with our bond proceeds for $90. This leaves a profit of $1.16. If the stock price is $110, we sell our two options for $20. Adding this $20 to our bond proceeds, we have $111.16. From this amount, we buy a share for $110 to repay the borrowing of a share. This leaves a profit of $1.16. Therefore, we make $1.16 whether the stock price rises or falls. We made this certain profit with zero investment, so we have an arbitrage profit.

Now assume that the call price is $8.00, exceeding $7.55. In this case, the call price is too high, so we sell the call as part of the following transactions:

Transaction	Cash flow
Buy one share of stock	−$100.00
Sell two calls	+16.00
Sell a bond (borrow funds)	−84.00
Net cash flow	0

At expiration, we know we must repay $89.04. If the stock price at expiration is $90, the calls cannot be exercised against us. So we sell our stock for $90 and repay our debt of $89.04. This leaves a profit of $0.96.

If the stock price goes to $110, the calls we sold will be exercised against us. To fulfill one obligation, we deliver our share of stock and receive the exercise price of $100. We then buy back the other call that is still outstanding. It costs $10, the difference between the stock price and the exercise price. This leaves $90, from which we repay our debt of $89.04. Now, we have completed all of our obligations and we still have $0.96. Therefore, with a call priced at $8.00, we will have a profit of $0.96 from these transactions no matter whether the stock price goes up or down. We captured this sure profit with zero investment, so we have an arbitrage profit.

To eliminate arbitrage, the call must trade for $7.55. If that call price prevails, both transaction strategies fail. For example, we might try to transact as follows if the call price is $7.55:

Transaction	Cash flow
Buy one share of stock	−$100.00
Sell two calls	+15.10
Sell a bond (borrow funds)	+84.90
Net cash flow	0

At expiration, we owe $90. If the stock price is $90, our calls are worthless. However, we can sell our share for $90 and repay our debt. Our net cash flow at expiration is zero. If the stock price is $110, the calls will be exercised against us. We deliver our one share and receive $100. From this $100, we repay our debt of $90. This leaves $10, the exact difference between the stock and exercise price. Therefore, we can use our last $10 to close our option position. Our net cash flow is zero. With a call price of $7.55, our transactions cost us zero and they yield zero. This is exactly the result we expect in a market that is free from arbitrage opportunities.[6]

The put price

Based on the same data we have just considered for the call option, the put price must be $1.89 to avoid arbitrage. We can see that this must be the case in two ways. First, we show that put–call parity requires a price of $1.89. Second, we show how any other price leads to arbitrage opportunities similar to those that occurred when the call was priced incorrectly.

From Chapter 11, we know that put–call parity expresses the value of a European put as a function of a similar call, the stock, and investment in the risk-free bond:

$$p_t = c_t - S_t + Xe^{-r(T-t)}$$

where $Xe^{-r(T-t)}$ is the present value of the exercise price. For our example, we know that the correct call price is $7.55 and that the stock trades for $100. With one year remaining until expiration, the present value of the exercise price is \$94.34. According to put–call parity for our example:

$$p_t = \$7.55 - \$100.00 + \$94.34 = \$1.89$$

If the put is not worth \$1.89, arbitrage opportunities arise. This makes sense because the put–call parity relationship is itself a no-arbitrage condition.[7]

We now show how to reap arbitrage profits if the put does not trade for \$1.89. We consider the transactions if the put price is above or below its correct price of \$1.89. First, let us assume that the put price is \$1.50. In this case, the put is too cheap relative to other assets. The other assets that replicate the put are too expensive, taken together. These are the call, stock, and bond combination on the right-hand side of the put–call parity formula. The put–call parity relationship suggests that we should buy the relatively underpriced put and sell the relatively overpriced portfolio that replicates the put. To initiate this strategy, called a **conversion**, we transact as follows:

Transaction	Cash flow
Buy put	−\$1.50
Sell call	+7.55
Buy stock	−100.00
Borrow \$93.95 and invest at 6 percent for one year	+93.95
Net cash flow	0

In one year, our debt is \$99.59 and the put and call are at expiration. The stock price will be either \$90 or \$110. We consider the value of our position for both possible stock prices. If the stock price is \$90, we exercise our put and deliver our share of stock. This gives a cash flow of \$100, from which we repay our debt of \$99.59. We have no further obligations, yet \$0.41 remains. Thus, we make a profit with no initial investment.

If the stock price is \$110, our put is worthless and the stock will be called away from us. When the call is exercised against us, we receive \$100. From this \$100, we repay our debt of \$99.59. Again, this leaves us with \$0.41. No matter whether the stock goes to \$90 or to \$110, we make \$0.41. We have achieved this profit with no initial investment. Consequently, we have a certain profit with zero investment, a sure sign of an arbitrage profit.

We now consider how to transact if the put price is higher than \$1.89. Let us assume that the put trades for \$2.00. With the put being too expensive, we sell the relatively overpriced put and purchase the relatively underpriced portfolio that replicates the put. In this case, our transactions are just the reverse of those we made when the put price was too low. This strategy is called a **reverse conversion** or a **reversal**. We transact as follows:

Transaction	Cash flow
Sell put	+\$2.00
Buy call	−7.55
Sell stock	+100.00
Lend \$94.45 at 6 percent for one year	−94.45
Net cash flow	0

In one year, our loan matures, so we collect $100.12. If the stock price is $90, our call is worthless and the put will be exercised against us. We must accept the $90 stock and pay the $100 exercise price. This leaves one share of stock and $0.12. We use the share to cover our original sale of stock, and we have $0.12 after meeting all obligations.

If the stock price goes to $110, the put we sold will expire worthless. We exercise our call, paying the $100 exercise price to acquire the stock. We now have $0.12 and one share, so we cover our original share sale by returning the stock. Again, we have completed all transactions and $0.12 remains. Therefore, no matter whether the stock goes to $90 or $110 over the one-year investment horizon, we make $0.12. We do this with zero investment, so we have an arbitrage profit.

These transactions illustrate why the put must trade for $1.89 in our example. Any other price allows arbitrage. If the put price is $1.89, both of the transactions we have just considered will cost zero to execute, but they will be sure to return zero when the options expire. In a market free of arbitrage opportunities, this is just what we expect.

Option prices and the riskiness of stocks

As we have seen, option prices depend on several factors, including stock prices. In this section, we explore how stock price changes affect option prices. Specifically, we consider how the riskiness of the stock affects the price of the put or call. We use a simple model of the way a stock price changes to illustrate a very important result: The riskier the underlying stock, the greater is the value of an option. This principle holds for both put and call options. Although it may seem odd for an option price to be higher if the underlying good is riskier, we can use no-arbitrage arguments to show why this must be true.

Essentially, a call option gives its owner most of the benefits of rising stock prices and protects the owner from suffering the full cost of a drop in stock prices. Thus, a call option offers insurance against falling stock prices and holds out the promise of high profits from surging stock prices. The riskier the underlying stock, the greater the chance of an extreme stock price movement. If the stock price falls dramatically, the insurance feature of the call option comes into play. This limits the call holder's loss. However, if the stock price increases dramatically, the call owner participates fully in the price increase. The protection against large losses, coupled with participation in large gains, makes call options more valuable when the underlying stock is risky.

For put options, risk has a parallel effect. Put owners benefit from large stock price drops and suffer from price increases. However, a put protects the owner from the full force of a stock price rise. In effect, a put embodies insurance against large price rises. At the same time, the put allows its owner to benefit fully from a stock price drop. Because the put incorporates protection against rising prices and allows its owner to capture virtually all profits from falling prices, a put is more valuable the riskier is the underlying stock.

In the preceding section, we used a very simple model of stock price movement to show how to price put and call options. In this section, we extend the same model and example to evaluate the effect of riskiness on stock prices. Earlier, we assumed a stock traded for $100 and that its price would go to either $90 or $110 in one year. We assumed that the risk-free rate of interest was 6 percent and that a call and put option both had exercise prices of $100 and expired in one year. Under these circumstances, the call was worth $7.55 and the put was worth $1.89. Any other price for the put or call led to arbitrage opportunities. To explore the effect of risk, we consider two other possible outcomes for the stock price. First, we assume that the stock is not risky. In this case, the stock price increases by the risk-free rate of 6 percent with certainty. Second, we consider stock price movements in which the stock price goes to either $80 or $120.

Option prices for riskless stock

If the stock is risk free, its value grows at the risk-free rate. Otherwise, there would be an arbitrage opportunity between the stock and the risk-free bond.[8] Consequently, we consider prices of our example options assuming that the stock price in one year will be $106 with certainty. Under these circumstances, the call option will be worth $5.66 and the put will be worth zero.

The put will be worth zero one year before expiration because it is sure to be worth zero at expiration. If the stock price is sure to be $106 at expiration, the put only gives the right to force someone to accept a stock worth $106 for $100. Thus, the put is worthless, because there is no chance that the stock price will be below the exercise price of the put.

The call has a certain payoff at expiration, because the stock price is certain. At expiration, the call is worth $\text{MAX}\{0, S_T - X\} = \$6$. With a riskless stock, the call is also riskless. Investment in the call pays a certain return of $6 in one year, so the call must be worth the present value of $6, or $5.66. Any other price for the call creates an arbitrage opportunity. For example, if the option trades at $5.80, we sell the call and invest the $5.80 at 6 percent. In one year, our investment is worth $6.15 and the exercise of the call against us costs us $6. This yields a $0.15 arbitrage profit. For any other price of either the put or the call, our familiar transactions guarantee an arbitrage profit.

Earlier, we placed the following bound on the European call price before expiration:

$$c_t \geq \text{MAX}\{0, S_t - Xe^{-r(T-t)}\}$$

Now we see that this relationship holds exactly if the stock is risk free. In other words, the European call price is on the lower boundary if the stock has no risk. Therefore, holding the other factors constant, any excess value of the call above the boundary is due solely to the riskiness of the stock.

Comparing our two examples of stock price movements, we saw that the risk-free stock implied a call price of $5.66. If the stock price was risky, moving up or down 10 percent in the next year, the call price was $7.55. This call price difference is due to the difference in the riskiness of the stock. As we now show, higher risk implies higher option prices.

Riskier stocks result in higher option prices

In our model of stock price movements, we assumed that stock prices change over a year in a very specific way. When we assumed that stock prices could increase or decrease 10 percent, we found certain option prices. We now consider the same circumstances but allow for more radical stock price movements of 20 percent up or down. All other factors remain the same. In summary, a stock trades today at $100. In one year, its price will be either $80 or $120. The risk-free interest rate is 6 percent. A call and put each have an exercise price of $100 and expire in one year. Under these circumstances, the call price must be $12.26, and the put price must be $6.60. Any other prices create arbitrage opportunities. Therefore, we have observed the price effects of the following three stock price movements on option prices:

Stock price movement	Call price	Put price
Stock price increases by a certain 6 percent	$5.66	$0.00
Stock price rises or falls by 10 percent	7.55	1.89
Stock price rises or falls by 20 percent	12.26	6.60

Table 12.1 Option price response to changes in underlying variables

For an increase in the:	The call price:	The put price:
Stock price	Rises	Falls
Exercise price	Falls	Rises
Time until expiration	Rises	May rise or fall
Interest rate	Rises	Falls
Stock risk	Rises	Rises

In these examples, we held other factors constant. Each example used options with the same exercise price and time to expiration. Also, each example employed the same risk-free rate. As these examples illustrate, greater risk in the stock increases both put and call prices.

Conclusion

In this chapter, we discussed the relationships that govern option prices. We began by considering general boundary spaces for calls and puts. By linking relationships between option features, such as time to expiration and exercise prices, we specified price relationships between options. For example, we saw that the price of a call with a lower exercise price must equal or exceed the price of a similar call with a higher exercise price. We discussed the five factors on which option prices depend: the exercise price, the stock price, the risk-free interest rate, the time to expiration, and the riskiness of the stock. We found that option prices have a definitive relationship to these factors, as summarized in Table 12.1. We will explore these price reactions in detail in Chapter 14.

Understanding these factors helps us place bounds on call and put prices. However, to determine an exact price, we must specify how the stock price can move. To illustrate the important influence of stock price movements on option prices, we considered a very simple model of stock price movements. For example, we assumed that the stock prices can change 10 percent in the next year. With this assumption, we were able to find exact option prices. However, this assumption about the movement of stock prices is very unrealistic. A year from now, a stock may have a virtually infinite number of prices, not just two. With unrealistic assumptions about stock price movements, the option prices we compute are likely to be unrealistic as well. In the next chapter, we work toward more realistic assumptions about stock price movements, and we develop a more exact option pricing model.

Exercises

1 What is the maximum theoretical value for a call? Under what conditions does a call reach this maximum value? Explain.
2 What is the maximum theoretical value for an American put? When does it reach this maximum? Explain.
3 Answer Exercise 2 for a European put.
4 Explain the difference in the theoretical maximum values for an American and a European put.
5 How does the exercise price affect the price of a call? Explain.
6 Consider two calls with the same time to expiration that are written on the same underlying stock. Call 1 trades for $7 and has an exercise price of $100. Call

2 has an exercise price of $95. What is the maximum price that Call 2 can have? Explain.
7 Six months remain until a call option expires. The stock price is $70 and the exercise price is $65. The option price is $5. What does this imply about the interest rate?
8 Assume that the interest rate is 12 percent and four months remain until an option expires. The exercise price of the option is $70 and the stock that underlies the option is worth $80. What is the minimum value the option can have based on the no-arbitrage conditions studied in this chapter? Explain.
9 Two call options are written on the same stock that trades for $70, and both calls have an exercise price

of \$85. Call 1 expires in six months, and Call 2 expires in three months. Assume that Call 1 trades for \$6 and that Call 2 trades for \$7. Do these prices allow arbitrage? Explain. If they do permit arbitrage, explain the arbitrage transactions.

10 Explain the circumstances that make early exercise of a call rational. Under what circumstances is early exercise of a call irrational?

11 Consider a European and an American call with the same expiration and the same exercise price that are written on the same stock. What relationship must hold between their prices? Explain.

12 Before exercise, what is the minimum value of an American put?

13 Before exercise, what is the minimum value of a European put?

14 Explain the differences in the minimum values of American and European puts before expiration.

15 How does the price of an American put vary with time until expiration? Explain.

16 What relationship holds between time until expiration and the price of a European put?

17 Consider two puts with the same term to expiration (six months). One put has an exercise price of \$110, and the other has an exercise price of \$100. Assume the interest rate is 12 percent. What is the maximum price difference between the two puts if they are European, and if they are American? Explain the difference, if any.

18 How does the price of a call vary with interest rates? Explain.

19 Explain how a put price varies with interest rates. Does the relationship vary for European and American puts? Explain.

20 What is the relationship between the risk of the underlying stock and the call price? Explain in intuitive terms.

21 A stock is priced at \$50, and the risk-free rate of interest is 10 percent. A European call and a European put on this stock both have exercise prices of \$40 and expire in six months. What is the difference between the call and put prices? (Assume continuous compounding.) From the information supplied in this question, can you say what the call and put prices must be? If not, explain what information is lacking.

22 A stock is priced at \$50, and the risk-free rate of interest is 10 percent. A European call and a European put on this stock both have exercise prices of \$40 and

expire in six months. Assume that the call price exceeds the put price by \$7. Does this represent an arbitrage opportunity? If so, explain why and state the transactions you would make to take advantage of the pricing discrepancy.

23 Cursory examination of the table below shows a violation of a basic option pricing rule. Which pricing rule has been violated? Discuss the limitations of using a newspaper as the source of prices used to make inferences about pricing.

Option IBM	Strike	Expiration date	Call		Put	
			Volume	Last	Volume	Last
$101^5/_8$	115	Sep	1,632	$^3/_{16}$	10	$13^1/_4$
$101^5/_8$	115	Oct	861	$1^1/_4$	10	$14^1/_4$
$101^5/_8$	115	Jan	225	4	3	14

24 Explain why an American call is always worth at least as much as its intrinsic value. Explain why this is not true for European calls.

25 Give an intuitive explanation of why the early exercise of an in-the-money American put option becomes more attractive as the volatility of the underlying stock decreases, and the risk-free interest rate increases.

26 Suppose that c_1, c_2, and c_3 are the prices of three European call options written on the same share of stock that are identical in all respects except their strike prices. The strike prices for the three call options are X_1, X_2, and X_3, respectively, where $X_3 > X_2 > X_1$ and $X_3 - X_2 = X_2 - X_1$. All options have the same maturity. Assume that all portfolios are held to expiration. Show that

$$c_2 \le 0.5 \times (c_1 + c_3)$$

27 Suppose that p_1, p_2, and p_3 are the prices of three European put options written on the same share of stock that are identical in all respects except their strike prices. The strike prices for the three put options are X_1, X_2, and X_3, respectively, where $X_3 > X_2 > X_1$ and $X_3 - X_2 = X_2 - X_1$. All options have the same maturity. Assume that all portfolios are held to expiration. Show that

$$p_2 \le 0.5 \times (p_1 + p_3)$$

Notes

1   The price of an option depends on these five factors when the underlying stock pays no dividends. As we will discuss in Chapter 14, if the underlying stock pays a dividend, the dividend is a sixth factor that we must consider.

2   Like Chapter 11, the discussion of these rational bounds for option prices relies on a paper by Robert C. Merton, "Theory of Rational Option Pricing," *Bell Journal of Economics and Management Science*, 4, 1973, pp. 141–83.

3   Scholars have tested market data to determine how well puts and calls meet these boundary conditions. Dan Galai was the first to test these relationships in his paper "Empirical Tests of Boundary Conditions for CBOE Options," *Journal of Financial Economics*, 6, June/September 1978, pp. 182–211. Galai found some violations of the no-arbitrage conditions in the reported prices. However, these apparent arbitrage opportunities disappeared if a trader faced a 1 percent transaction cost. Mihir Bhattacharya conducted similar, but more extensive, tests in his paper "Transaction Data Tests on the Efficiency of the Chicago Board Options Exchange," *Journal of Financial Economics*, 1983, pp. 161–85. Like Galai, Bhattacharya found that a trader facing transaction costs could not exploit apparent arbitrage opportunities. However, both studies found that a very low cost trader, such as a market maker, could have a chance for some arbitrage returns.

4   As we discuss in Chapter 14, differences between European and American call options require some slight revisions of these rules. In this section, we have said that the difference in the price of two calls cannot exceed the difference in exercise prices. Our arbitrage arguments for this principle assumed immediate exercise before expiration, thus implicitly assuming that the option is American. For a similar pair of European options, the price differential cannot exceed the present value of the difference between the two exercise prices. The arbitrage profit equals the excess difference between the exercise prices. With European options, this excess differential is not available until expiration, when traders can exercise. Therefore, for European options, the arbitrage profit will be the excess difference in the exercise prices discounted to the present.

5   Assuming that the option is correctly priced at the lower bound implicitly assumes that the stock price has no risk. In other words, we implicitly assume that the stock price will not change before expiration. Making this assumption does not affect the validity of our example, because we are focusing on the single effect of a change in interest rates.

6   The next chapter explains why we need to buy one share of stock and sell two calls in this example. In brief, by combining a bond, a stock, and the right number of calls, we can form a riskless portfolio.

7   The put–call parity relationship was first addressed by Hans Stoll, "The Relationship Between Put and Call Option Prices," *Journal of Finance*, 24, May 1969, pp. 801–24. Robert C. Merton extended the concept in his paper "The Relationship Between Put and Call Option Prices: Comment," *Journal of Finance*, 28, pp. 183–4. Robert C. Klemkosky and Bruce G. Resnick tested the put–call parity relationship empirically with market data. Their two papers are: "An Ex-Ante Analysis of Put–Call Parity," *Journal of Financial Economics*, 8, 1980, pp. 363–72, and "Put–Call Parity and Market Efficiency," *Journal of Finance*, 34, 1979, pp. 1141–55. While they find that market prices do not agree perfectly with the put–call parity relationship, the differences are not sufficiently large to generate trading profits after considering all transaction costs.

8   If the stock earned a riskless rate above the risk-free rate, we would borrow at the risk-free rate and invest in the stock. Later, we could sell the stock, repay our debt, and have a certain return from the difference in the *two* riskless rates. If the stock earned a riskless rate below the risk-free rate, we would sell the stock and invest the proceeds in the higher rate of the risk-free bond. Therefore, for a given horizon, there is only one risk-free rate.

13

European Option Pricing

Overview

In Chapter 12, we showed how to compute call and put prices assuming that stock prices behave in a highly simplified manner. Specifically, we assumed that stock prices could rise by a certain percentage or fall by a certain percentage for a single period. After that single period, we assumed that the option expired. Under these unrealistic and highly restrictive assumptions, we found that calls and puts must each have a unique price; any other price leads to arbitrage. In this chapter, we develop similar option pricing models, but we use more realistic models of stock price movement.

To develop a more realistic option pricing model, this chapter first analyzes option pricing under the simple percentage change model of stock price movements. Now, however, we show how to find the unique prices that the no-arbitrage conditions imply. This framework is the **single-period binomial model**. Analyzing the single-period model leads to more realistic models of stock price movements. One of these more realistic models is the **multi-period binomial model**.

By considering several successive models of stock price changes, we eventually come to one of the most elegant models in all of finance–the **Black–Scholes option pricing model**.

Throughout this chapter, we focus on European options. Later, in Chapter 15, we consider American option pricing and the complications arising from the potential for early exercise. At the beginning of this chapter, we focus on stocks with no dividends. Later in this chapter, we consider the complications that dividends bring in evaluating the prices of European options.

OPTION! provides support for the diverse models that we study in this chapter. With **OPTION!**, we can make virtually all of the computations discussed in this chapter, including the single-period and multi-period binomial model call and put values and Black–Scholes model prices. In each case, use of the software can save considerable computational labor.

The single-period binomial model

In Chapter 12, we considered a stock priced at $100 and assumed that its price would be $90 or $110 in one year. In this example, the risk-free interest rate was 6 percent. We then considered a call and put on this stock, with both options having an exercise price of $100 and expiring in one year. The call was worth $7.55, and the put was worth $1.89. As we showed in Chapter 12, any other option price creates arbitrage opportunities.

Now we want to create a synthetic European call option—a portfolio that has the same value and profits and losses as the call being synthesized. Consider a portfolio comprised of one-half share of stock plus a short position in a risk-free bond that matures in one year and has an initial purchase price of $42.45. In one year, the portfolio's value depends on whether the stock price is $110 or $90. Depending on the stock price, the half-share will be worth $55 or $45. In either event, we will owe $45 to repay our bond. If the stock price rises, the portfolio will be worth $10. If the stock price falls, the portfolio will be worth zero. These are exactly the payoffs for the call option. Therefore, the value of the portfolio must be the same as the value of the call option. Figure 13.1 shows values for the stock, the call, the risk-free bond, and the portfolio value at the outset and one year later. The stock price moves to $110 or $90, and the call moves accordingly to $10 or zero. The risk-free bond increases at a 6 percent rate no matter what the stock does, so borrowing $42.45 generates a debt of $45 due in one year. Likewise,

Figure 13.1   One-period payoffs

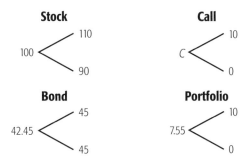

our portfolio of one-half share and a $42.45 borrowing will be worth $10 or zero in one year, depending on the stock price. The diagrams appearing in Figure 13.1 are known as binomial *trees* or *lattices*.

Because our portfolio and the call option have exactly the same payoffs in all circumstances, they must have the same initial value. Otherwise, there would be an arbitrage opportunity. This means that an investment of one-half share of stock, S_t, and a bond, B_t, of $42.45 must equal the value of the call:

$$c_t = 0.5S_t - \$42.45 = \$50 - 42.45 = \$7.55$$

Therefore, the call must be worth $7.55. This is the same conclusion we reached in Chapter 12. This result shows that a combined position in the stock and the risk-free bond can replicate a call option for a one-period horizon.

We now show how to find the replicating portfolio made of the stock and the risk-free investment. At the outset, $T - t = 1$, the value of the portfolio, $PORT_t$, depends on the stock price, the number of shares, N, and the price of the bond, B_t:

$$PORT_t = NS_t - B_t$$

At the end of the horizon, $T - t = 0$, the debt equals the amount borrowed, B_t, plus interest, $B_T = RB_t$. The portfolio's value also depends on the stock price. If the stock price rises, the value of the portfolio will be

$$PORT_{U,T} = NUS_T - RB_t$$

where $PORT_{U,T}$ is the value of the replicating portfolio at time T if the stock price goes up, $U = 1 +$ the percentage of the stock price increase, and $R = 1 + r$. Likewise, if the stock price falls, the value of the portfolio will be

$$PORT_{D,T} = NDS_T - RB_t$$

where $PORT_{D,T}$ is the value of the replicating portfolio at time T if the stock price goes down, and $D = 1 -$ the percentage of the stock price decrease. At expiration, $T - t = 0$, the value of the call also depends on whether the stock price rises or falls. For each circumstance, we represent the call's price as c_U and c_D.

As our example showed, we can choose the number of shares to trade, N, and the amount of funds to borrow, B_t, to replicate the call. Replicating the call means that the portfolio will have the same payoff. Therefore, if the stock price rises,

$$\text{PORT}_{U,T} = NUS_T - RB_t = c_U$$

If the stock price falls,

$$\text{PORT}_{D,T} = NDS_T - RB_t = c_D$$

After these algebraic manipulations, we have two equations with two unknowns, N and B_t. Solving for the values of the unknowns that satisfy the equations, N^* and B_t^*, we find that

$$N^* = \frac{c_U - c_D}{(U - D)S_t}$$

$$B_t^* = \frac{c_U D - c_D U}{(U - D)R}$$

Therefore,

$$c_t = N^* S_t - B_t^* \tag{13.1}$$

This is the single-period binomial call pricing model. It holds for a call option expiring in one period when the stock price will rise by a known percentage or fall by a known percentage. The model shows that the value of a call option equals a long position in the stock, plus some borrowing at the risk-free rate. Applying our new notation to our example, we have

$$c_U = \$10,\ c_D = \$0,\ U = 1.1,\ D = 0.9,\ R = 1.06$$

$$B_t^* = \frac{c_U D - c_D U}{(U - D)R}$$

$$= \frac{10 \times 0.9 - 0 \times 1.1}{(1.1 - 0.9) \times 1.06} = \$42.45$$

$$N^* = \frac{c_U - c_D}{(U - D)S_t} = \frac{10 - 0}{(1.1 - 0.9) \times 100} = 0.5$$

The role of probabilities

In discussing the single-period binomial model, we have not used the concept of probability. For example, we have not considered the likelihood that the stock price will rise or fall. While we have not explicitly used probabilistic concepts, the array of prices does imply a certain probability that the stock price will rise, if we are willing to assume that investors are risk neutral.[1] We assume a risk-neutral economy in this section to show the role of probabilities. The option prices that we compute under the assumption of risk neutrality are the same as those we found from strict no-arbitrage conditions without any reference to probabilities.

Assuming risk neutrality and given the risk-free interest rate and the up and down percentage movements, we can compute the probability of a stock price increase. Using our definitions of N^* and B_t^*, the call is worth

$$c_t = \left(\frac{c_U - c_D}{(U - D)S_t} \right) S_t - \frac{c_U D - c_D U}{(U - D)R}$$

Simplifying, we have

$$c_t = \frac{c_U - c_D}{U - D} - \frac{c_U D - c_D U}{(U - D)R}$$

Isolating the c_U and c_D terms gives

$$c_t = \frac{\left(\dfrac{R - D}{U - D} \right)c_U + \left(\dfrac{U - R}{U - D} \right)c_D}{R}$$

In this equation, the call value equals the present value of the future payoffs from owning the call. If the stock price goes up, the call pays C_U at expiration. If the stock goes down, the call pays C_D. The numerator of this equation gives the expected value of the call's payoffs at expiration. Therefore, the probability of a stock price increase is also the probability that the call is worth C_U. The probability of a stock price increase is $(R - D)/(U - D)$, and the probability of a stock price decrease is $(U - R)/(U - D)$.

For our continuing example, we have the following values: $c_U = \$10$, $c_D = \$0$, $U = 1.1$, $D = 0.9$, and $R = 1.06$. Therefore, the probability of an increase in the stock price (π_U) is 0.8, and the probability of a decrease (π_D) is 0.2. The value of the call in our single period model is

$$c_t = \frac{\pi_U c_U + \pi_D c_D}{R} = \frac{0.8 \times 10 + 0.2 \times 0}{1.06} = \$7.55$$

This result shows that the value of a call equals the expected payoff from the call at expiration, discounted to the present at the risk-free rate, assuming a risk-neutral economy.

Summary

Our single-period model is a useful tool. We have seen how to replicate an option by combining a long position in stock with a short position in the risk-free asset. Also, we used the single-period model to show that the value of a call equals the present value of the call's expected payoffs at expiration. Nonetheless, our single-period model suffers from two defects. First, it holds only for a single period. We need to be able to value options that expire after many periods. Second, our assumption about stock price changes is still unrealistic. Obviously, we do not really know how stock prices can change in one period. In fact, if we define one year as a period, we know that stock prices can take almost an infinite number of values by the end of the period. We now proceed to refine our model to consider these objections.

The multi-period binomial model

The principles that we developed for the single-period binomial model also apply to a multi-period framework.[2] Here, we illustrate the underlying principles by considering a two-period horizon. Over two periods, the stock price must follow one of four patterns. For the two periods, the stock can go up–up, up–down, down–up, or down–down. Assuming fixed down and up

Figure 13.2 Two-period payoffs

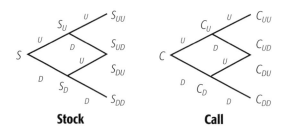

percentages, the up–down and down–up sequences result in the same terminal stock price. For each terminal stock price, a call option has a specific value. Figure 13.2 shows the binomial trees for the stock and call. To clarify the notation, S_{UU} indicates the terminal stock price if the stock price goes up in both periods. C_{UU} is the resulting call price at expiration when the stock price rises in both periods. For the two-period case, the notation π_{UU} indicates the probability of an up–up sequence of price movements, and π_{DD} indicates the probability of a down–down sequence of price movements. We define other patterns accordingly.

We can express the value of a call option two periods before expiration as

$$c_t = \frac{\pi_{UU} C_{UU} + \pi_{UD} C_{UD} + \pi_{DU} C_{DU} + \pi_{DD} C_{DD}}{R^2}$$

In this equation, the call value equals the expected value of the payoffs at expiration discounted at the risk-free rate.

We continue to use our example of a $100 stock that can rise or fall by 10 percent. The probability that the stock price will increase is 0.8, so this gives a 0.2 probability of a price drop. Also, the probability of an increase in one period is independent of the probability of an increase in any other period. We now assume that the call is two periods from expiration and that the stock trades for $100. In the first period, the stock can go up or down, giving $US_t = \$110$, $DS_t = \$90$. After the second period, there are four possible patterns with three actually different stock prices: $UUS_t = \$121$, $DDS_t = \$81$, and $UDS_t = DUS_t = \$99$. The probabilities of these different terminal stock prices are as follows: $\pi_{UU} = 0.8 \times 0.8 = 0.64$, $\pi_{UD} = 0.8 \times 0.2 = 0.16$, $\pi_{DU} = 0.2 \times 0.8 = 0.16$, and $\pi_{DD} = 0.2 \times 0.2 = 0.04$. The call price at expiration equals the terminal stock price minus the exercise price of $100, or zero, whichever is larger. Therefore, we have $C_{UU} = \$21$, $C_{DD} = 0$, and $C_{DU} = C_{UD} = 0$.

To determine the call price two periods before expiration, we apply our formula for a call option two periods before expiration. In doing so, we compute the expected value of the call at expiration and discount for two periods:

$$c = \frac{0.64 \times \$21 + 0.16 \times 0 + 0.16 \times 0 + 0.04 \times 0}{1.06^2} = \frac{\$13.44}{1.06^2} = \$11.96$$

If the call expires in two periods and the stock trades for $100, the call will be worth $11.96. Notice that our sample call pays off at expiration only if the stock price rises twice. Any other pattern of stock price movement in our example gives a call that is worthless at expiration.

With one period until expiration and the stock trading at $100, we saw that the call was worth $7.55. With the same initial stock price and two periods until expiration, the call is worth $11.96. This price difference reflects the difference in the present value of the expected payoffs from the call.

In the single-period binomial model, there are two possible stock price outcomes. With two periods until expiration, there are four possible stock price patterns. In general, there are 2^n possible stock price patterns, where n is the number of periods until expiration. Thus, the number of stock and call outcomes increases very rapidly. For example, if the option is just 20 periods from expiration, there are more than 1 million stock price outcomes and the same number of call outcomes to consider.[3] It quickly becomes apparent that we need a more general formula for the multi-period binomial pricing model. Also, for options with many periods until expiration, we need a computer. **OPTION!** can compute binomial model call and put values.

We have explored the single-period and two-period binomial model in detail, and we have analyzed examples for each. The principles we have developed remain true no matter how many periods we consider. However, the computations become more numerous and cumbersome, as we just saw. Therefore, we now make a mathematical jump to present the formula, which we discuss in intuitive terms.

The multi-period binomial call pricing model

In this section, we begin by introducing the multi-period binomial call pricing model. While it is undeniably complex, a little study will show that the following equation is not really so intimidating:

$$
c_t = \frac{\sum_{j=0}^{n} \left(\frac{n!}{j!(n-j)!} \right) [\pi_U^j \pi_D^{n-j}] \mathrm{MAX}\{0, U^j D^{n-j} S_t - X\}}{R^n} \tag{13.2}
$$

To understand this formula, we need to break it into simpler elements. From our previous discussion, we know that the formula gives the present value of the expected payoffs from the call at expiration. The denominator R^n is the discount factor raised to n, the number of periods until expiration. The numerator gives the expected payoff on the call option. Thus, we need to focus on the numerator.

With the multi-period model, we are analyzing an option that expires in n periods. As a feature of the binomial model, we know that the stock price either goes up or down each period. Let us say that it goes up j of the n periods. Then the stock price must fall $n - j$ periods. Our summation runs from $j = 0$ to $j = n$, which includes every possibility. When $j = 0$, we evaluate the possibility that the stock price never rises. When $j = n$, we evaluate the possibility that the stock price rises every period. The summation considers these extreme possibilities and every intermediate possibility.

For any random number of stock price increases, j, the numerator expresses three things about the call for the j stock price increases among the n periods. First, starting from the right, the numerator gives the payoff on the option if the stock price rises j times. This is our familiar expression beginning with MAX. The value of the call at expiration is either zero, or the stock price minus the exercise price, whichever is greater. The expression $U^j D^{n-j} S_t$ gives the stock price at expiration if the stock price rises j periods and falls the other $n - j$ periods. Second, the numerator expresses the probability of exactly j stock price increases and $n - j$ stock price decreases. Earlier, we saw how to find the probability of up and down movements. Therefore, $\pi_U^j \pi_D^{n-j}$ gives the probability of observing j up movements and $n - j$ down movements. Third, more than one sequence of stock price movements can result in the same terminal stock price. For instance, in the two-period model, we saw that UDS_t gave the same terminal stock price as DUS_t. The numerator also computes the number of different combinations of stock price movements that result in the same terminal stock price. The expression

$$\frac{n!}{j!(n-j)!}$$

computes the number of possible combinations of j rises from n periods. In essence, the combination weights the possibility of exactly n rises and $n-j$ falls by the number of different patterns that result in exactly j rises and $n-j$ falls. For example, only one pattern results in n rises—the stock must rise in every period. By contrast, if $j = n - j$, there will usually be many patterns that can give j rises and $n - j$ falls.

In the expression for the combination, $n!$ is called n-factorial. Its value equals n multiplied by $n - 1$ times $n - 2$ and so on, down to 1:

$$n! = n \times (n - 1) \times (n - 2) \times (n - 3) \times \ldots \times 1$$

To illustrate, if $n = 5$, then $5! = 5 \times 4 \times 3 \times 2 \times 1 = 120$. For example, with the two-period model, we could have the pattern up–down or down–up resulting in the same stock price. Thus, there are two combinations of one increase over two periods. The increase could be first or second. For any j value, the numerator in Equation 13.2 computes the number of combinations of j increases from n periods, times the probability of having exactly j increases times the payoff on the call if there are j increases. The summation ensures that the numerator reflects all possible j values.

In our two-period example, the option pays off at expiration only if the stock price rises both times. In general, many stock price patterns leave the option out-of-the-money at expiration. For valuing the option, stock price patterns that leave the option out-of-the-money are a dead end, because they result in a zero option price. As a consequence, we do not need to fully evaluate stock price patterns that leave the option out-of-the-money at expiration. Instead, we only need to evaluate those values of j for which the option expires in-the-money. In our two-period example, we do not need to compute the entire formula for $j = 0$ and $j = 1$. If the stock price never goes up or goes up only once, the option expires out-of-the-money. For our two-period example, we only need to consider what happens to the option when the stock price rises twice; that is, when $j = 2$. Only then does the option finish in-the-money. Let us define m as the number of times the stock price must rise for the option to finish in-the-money. Thus, when the stock price rises exactly m times, it must fall $n - m$ times. However, this pattern still leaves the option in-the-money, because the stock price rose the needed m times. Then we need only consider values of $j = m$ to $j = n$. In our two-period example, $m = 2$, because the stock price must rise in both periods for the option to finish in-the-money. Therefore, the following formula gives an alternative expression for the value of an option:

$$c_t = \frac{\sum_{j=m}^{n} \left(\frac{n!}{j!(n-j)!} \right) (\pi_U^j \pi_D^{n-j})[U^j D^{n-j} S_t - X]}{R^n} \tag{13.3}$$

Notice that the summation begins with m, the minimum number of stock price increases needed to bring the option into-the-money. Because we consider only the events that put the option in-the-money, we no longer need to worry about the call being worth the maximum of zero or the stock price less the exercise price at expiration. With at least m stock price rises, the option will be worth more than zero, because it necessarily finishes in-the-money. Now we divide the formula into two parts—one associated with the stock price and the other associated with the exercise price:

$$c_t = S_t \left[\sum_{j=m}^{n} \left(\frac{n!}{j!(n-j)!} \right) (\pi_U^j \pi_D^{n-j}) \frac{U^j D^{n-j}}{R^n} \right] - XR^{-n} \left[\sum_{j=m}^{n} \left(\frac{n!}{j!(n-j)!} \right) (\pi_U^j \pi_D^{n-j}) \right]$$ (13.4)

This version of the binomial formula starts to resemble our familiar expression for the value of the call as the stock price minus the present value of the exercise price. If the option is in-the-money and the stock price is certain to remain unchanged until expiration, the call price equals the stock price minus the present value of the exercise price. Our formula has exactly that structure, except for the two complicated expressions in brackets. These two expressions reflect the riskiness of the stock. This uncertainty or riskiness about the stock gives the added value to the call above the stock price minus the present value of the exercise price.

The multi-period binomial model can reflect numerous stock price outcomes if there are numerous periods. Just 20 periods give more than 1 million stock price movement patterns. In our examples, we kept the period length the same and added more periods. This lengthened the total time until expiration. As an alternative, we could keep the same time to expiration and consider more periods of shorter duration. For example, we originally treated a year as a single period. For that year, we could regard each trading day as a period, giving about 250 periods per year. We could evaluate an option with the multi-period model by assuming that the stock price could change once a day.

The binomial model requires that the price move up a given percentage or down a given percentage. Therefore, if we shorten the period, we need to adjust the stock price movements to correspond to the shorter period. While up or down 10 percent might be reasonable for a period of one year, it certainly would not be reasonable for a period of one day. Similarly, a risk-free rate of 6 percent makes sense for a period of one year, but not for a period of one day.

By adjusting the period length, the stock price movement, and the interest rate, we can refine the binomial model as much as we wish. For example, we could assume that the stock price could move one-hundredth of a percent every minute of the year if we wished. Under this assumption, the model would have finer partitions than exist in the market for most stock. However, with the price changing every minute and a time to expiration of one year, we would have trillions of possible stock price outcomes to consider. While having so many periods would be computationally expensive, we could apply the model if we wished. Conceptually, we could make each period so short that the stock price would change continuously. However, if the stock price truly changed continuously, there would be an infinite number of periods to consider. While we cannot compute binomial model values for an infinite number of periods, mathematical techniques do exist to compute option prices when stock prices change continuously.

Binomial put option pricing

In discussing binomial option pricing, we have used call options as an example. However, the model also applies to put options. To value put options, we follow the same reasoning process that we have considered in detail for call options. Rather than detail all of the reasoning leading to the formula, we begin with the formula for the price of a European put option:

$$p_t = \frac{\sum_{j=0}^{n}\left(\frac{n!}{j!(n-j)!}\right)(\pi_U^j \pi_D^{n-j})\text{MAX}\{0, X - U^j D^{n-j} S_t\}}{R^n} \tag{13.5}$$

This formula matches our binomial call formula, except that we substitute the expression for the value of a put at expiration, $X - U^j D^{n-j} S_t$, in place of the value of a call at expiration.

In pricing the call option, we only considered stock price patterns that left the call in-the-money at expiration. The same is true for the put. The put finishes in-the-money if the stock price does not increase often enough to make the stock price exceed the exercise price. We defined m as the number of price increases needed to bring the call into the money. If the price increases $m - 1$ or fewer times, the put finishes in-the-money. Therefore, we can also write the formula for the put as follows:

$$p_t = \frac{\sum_{j=0}^{m-1}\left(\frac{n!}{j!(n-j)!}\right)(\pi_U^j \pi_D^{n-j})[X - U^j D^{n-j} S_t]}{R^n} \tag{13.6}$$

Rearranging terms gives the following:

$$p_t = XR^{-n}\left[\sum_{j=0}^{m-1}\left(\frac{n!}{j!(n-j)!}\right)(\pi_U^j \pi_D^{n-j})\right] - S_t\left[\sum_{j=0}^{m-1}\left(\frac{n!}{j!(n-j)!}\right)(\pi_U^j \pi_D^{n-j})\frac{U^j D^{n-j}}{R^n}\right] \tag{13.7}$$

This formula for the put parallels our familiar expression for the put as equaling the present value of the exercise price minus the stock price. As with the call, the two bracketed expressions account for the risky movement of the stock price.

We can also value the put through put–call parity. We have the value of the call under the binomial model as given in Equation 13.7. Put–call parity tells us that

$$p_t = c_t - S_t + X e^{-r(T-t)}$$

Both approaches must necessarily give the same answer.

Stock price movements

In actual markets, stock prices change to reflect new information. During a single day, a stock price may change many times. From the ticker, we can observe stock prices when transactions occur. When trading ceases overnight, however, we cannot observe the stock price for hours at a time. Where the price wanders during the night, no one can know. Our observations are also limited because stock prices are quoted in eighths of a dollar. The true stock price need not jump from one eighth to the next, but the observed stock price does. Sometimes the observed price remains the same from one transaction to another. But just because we observe the same price twice in succession does not mean it remained at that price between the two observations. From these reflections, we see that we can never know exactly how stock prices change, because we cannot observe the true stock price at every instant. Therefore, any model of stock price behavior deviates from an exact description of how stock prices move. Nonetheless, it is possible to develop a realistic model of stock price movements. In this section, we review a particular model that has been very successful in a wide range of finance applications.

Let us consider the random information that affects the price of a stock. We assume that the information arrives continuously and that each bit of information is small in importance. Under this scenario, we consider a stock price that rises or falls a small proportion in response to each bit of information. We know that finance depends conceptually on the twin ideas of expected return and risk. Thus, we might also think of a stock as having a positive expected rate of return. In the absence of special events, we expect the stock price to grow along the path of its expected rate of return. However, the world is risky. Information about the stock is sometimes favorable and sometimes unfavorable. As this random information becomes known, it pushes the stock away from its expected growth path. When the information is better than expected, the stock price jumps above its growth path. Negative information has the opposite effect; it pushes the stock price below its expected growth path. Thus, we might imagine the stock price growing along its expected growth path just as a drunk walks across a field. We expect the drunk to reach the other side of the field, but we also think he will wander and stumble in unpredictable short-term deviations from the straight path. Similarly, we expect a stock price to rise, because it has a positive expected return, but we also expect it to wander above and below its growth path, due to new information.

Finance uses a standard mathematical model that is consistent with the story of the preceding paragraph. It assumes that the stock grows at an expected rate μ with a standard deviation σ over some period of time Δt:

$$\Delta S = S_{t+1} - S_t = S_t \mu \Delta t + S_t N(0,1)\sigma\sqrt{\Delta t} \tag{13.8}$$

where S_t is the stock price at the beginning of the interval; ΔS is the stock price change during time Δt; $S_t \mu \Delta t$ is the expected value of the stock price change during time Δt; $N(0,1)$ is the normally distributed random variable with $\mu = 0$ and $\sigma = 1$; and σ is the standard deviation of the stock price. Equation 13.8 says that the stock price change during Δt depends on two factors: the expected growth rate in the price and the variability of the growth. First, the expected growth in the stock price over a given interval depends on the mean growth rate, μ, and the amount of time, Δt. Therefore, if the stock price starts at S_t, the expected stock price increase after an interval of Δt equals $S_t \mu \Delta t$. However, this is only the expected stock price increase after the interval. Due to risk, the actual price change can be greater or lower. Deviations from the expected stock price depend on chance and on the volatility of the stock. The equation captures risk by using the normal distribution. For convenience, the model uses the standard normal distribution, which has a zero mean and a standard deviation of 1. The standard deviation represents the variability of a particular stock. We multiply the standard deviation of the stock by a random drawing from the normal distribution to capture the riskiness of the stock. Also, the equation says that the variability increases with the square root of the interval Δt. In other words, the farther into the future we project the stock price with our model, the less certain we can be about what the stock price will be.

Dividing both sides of Equation 13.8 by the original stock price, S_t, gives the percentage change in the stock price during Δt:

$$\frac{\Delta S}{S_t} = \mu \Delta t + N(0,1)\sigma\sqrt{\Delta t}$$

From this equation, it is possible to show that the percentage change in the stock price is normally distributed:

Figure 13.3   Two stock price paths

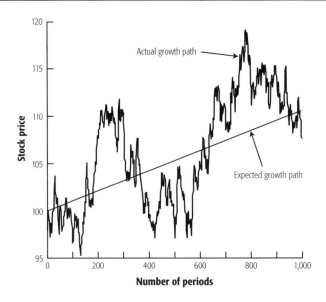

$$\frac{\Delta S}{S_t} \sim N[\mu \Delta t, \sigma \sqrt{\Delta t}\,] \tag{13.9}$$

Figure 13.3 shows two stock price paths over the course of a year, with both stock prices starting at $100. The straight line graphs a stock that grows at 10 percent per year with no risk. The jagged line shows a stock price path with an expected growth rate of 10 percent and a standard deviation of 0.2 per year. We generated the second price path by taking repeated random samples from a normal distribution to create price changes according to Equation 13.8. As the jagged line in Figure 13.3 shows, a stock might easily wander away from its growth path due to the riskiness represented by its standard deviation.

To construct Figure 13.3, we used 1,000 periods per year and a growth rate of 10 percent. To construct the straight line, we assumed that the stock price increased by 0.1/1,000 each period. However, this gives an ending stock price of $110.51, not the $110 we expect if the stock price grows at 10 percent per year. This difference results from using 1,000 compounding intervals during the year.

However, we hypothesize that information arrives continuously, so that the stock price could always change. To avoid worrying about the compounding interval, we now employ continuous compounding. Therefore, we focus on logarithmic stock returns. For example, consider a beginning stock price of $100 and an ending price of $110 a year later. The logarithmic stock return over the year is $\ln(S_t/S_0) = \ln(\$110/\$100) = \ln(1.1) = 0.0953$. The logarithmic stock return is just the continuous growth rate that takes the stock price from its original value to its ending value. Thus, $\$100 \times e^{ut} = \$100 \times e^{0.0953 \times 1} = \$110$. We now need a continuous growth model of stock prices that is consistent with our model for the percentage change stock price model of Equation 13.9. With some difficult math, it is possible to prove the following result:

$$\ln\left(\frac{S_{t+\Delta t}}{S_t}\right) \sim N[(\mu - 0.5\sigma^2)(\Delta t), \sigma\sqrt{\Delta t}]$$ (13.10)

This expression asserts that logarithmic stock returns are distributed normally with the given mean and standard deviation. For a later time, $t + \Delta t$, the expected stock price and the variance of the stock price are as follows:

$$E(S_{t+\Delta t}) = S_t e^{\mu \Delta t}$$
$$VAR(S_{t+\Delta t}) = S_t^2 e^{2\mu \Delta t}(e^{\sigma^2 \Delta t} - 1)$$

Thus, the expected stock price at $t + \Delta t$ depends on the original stock price, S_t, the expected growth rate, m, and the amount of time that elapses, Δt. Similarly, the variance of the stock price depends on the original stock price, the expected growth rate, and the elapsed time as well. The longer the time horizon, the larger will be the variance. The increasing variance reflects our greater uncertainty about stock prices far in the future.

As an example, consider a stock with an initial price of $100 and an expected growth rate of 10 percent. If the stock has a standard deviation of 0.2 per year, we can compute the expected stock price and variance for six months into the future. For this example, we have the following values:

$$S_t = \$100, \mu = 0.1, \sigma = 0.2, \Delta t = 0.5$$
$$E(S_{t+\Delta t}) = \$100 \times e^{0.1 \times 0.5} = \$105.13$$
$$VAR(S_{t+\Delta t}) = \$100 \times \$100 \times e^{2 \times 0.1 \times 0.5}(e^{0.2 \times 0.2 \times 0.5} - 1) = \$223.26$$

The standard deviation of the price over period Δt is $14.94. Figure 13.4 shows stock price realizations that are consistent with this example. We found these prices by drawing random values from a normal distribution and using our example growth rate and standard deviation. Each dot

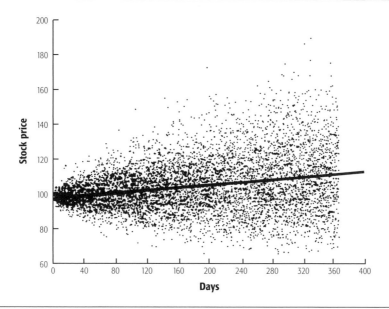

Figure 13.4 Possible stock prices

Figure 13.5 A log-normal distribution

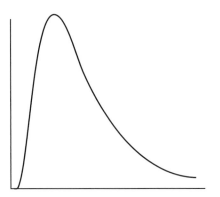

in the figure represents a possible stock price realization. Notice that the price tends to drift higher over time, consistent with a rising expected value. This is shown by the regression line that is fitted through the points. However, there is considerable uncertainty about what the price will be at any future date. The farther we go into the future, the greater that uncertainty becomes.

Research on actual stock price behavior shows that logarithmic stock returns are approximately normally distributed. So we say that, as an approximation, stock returns follow a **log-normal distribution**. Stock returns themselves are not normally distributed. As an example, Figure 13.5 shows a distribution of stock returns with a mean of 1.2 and a standard deviation of 0.6. It is easy to see that this distribution is not normal, because it is skewed to the right. There is a greater chance of larger returns than one would expect with a normal distribution. Figure 13.6 shows the log-normal distribution that corresponds to the values in Figure 13.5. The values graphed in Figure 13.6 are the logarithms of the values used to construct Figure 13.5. The graph in Figure 13.6 shows a normal distribution. We will assume that stock returns are distributed as Figure 13.6 shows, except that the mean and standard deviation differ from stock to stock.

Figure 13.6 The normal distribution

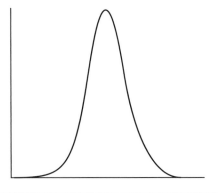

While the log-normal distribution only approximates stock returns, it has two great virtues. First, it is mathematically tractable, so we can obtain solutions for the value of call options if stock returns are log-normally distributed. Second, the resulting call option prices that we compute are very good approximations of actual market prices. In the remainder of this chapter, we treat stock returns as log-normally distributed with a specified mean and variance.

The contribution of options markets to price discovery

One argument in favor of derivative markets is that they contribute to price discovery. As a result of the improved quality of price discovery, the market as a whole does a better job of allocating scarce resources to competing needs. Understanding the contribution of option markets to price discovery has important implications for regulators, exchanges, market makers, and individual investors. Chakravarty, Gulen, and Mayhew parse out the relative share of price discovery occurring in the option market versus the share of price discovery occurring in the stock market. Their study is based on a sample of 60 stocks over five years. Across firms in their sample, the information share attributable to the option market is about 17 percent, with estimates for individual firms ranging from about 12 percent to about 23 percent. They find evidence that the relative share of price discovery in the option market is higher when the relative share of option volume to stock volume is higher, and when the bid–ask spread for options is narrower relative to the bid–ask spread for stocks. They find that price discovery is slightly higher for out-of-the-money options than at-the-money options, and that the relative rate of price discovery across different options is a function of relative trading volume and bid–ask spread.[4]

The binomial approach to the Black–Scholes model

We have seen how to generalize the binomial model to any number of periods. Increasing the number of periods allows for many possible stock price outcomes at expiration, thereby increasing the realism of the results. However, three problems remain. First, as the number of periods increases, computational difficulties begin to arise. Second, increasing the number of periods while holding the time until expiration constant means that the period length becomes shorter. We must adjust the up and down movement factors, U and D, and the risk-free rate to fit the time horizon. Obviously, we cannot use factors with a scale appropriate to a year when the period length is, for example, just one day. Third, we have worked with more or less arbitrarily selected up and down factors. The price that the model gives can only be as good as its inputs. The example inputs we have been considering serve well as illustrations, but they are not appropriate for analyzing real options. Therefore, we need a better way to determine the up and down factors.

Modeling stock returns by a log-normal process solves these three problems simultaneously. If stock returns are log-normally distributed with the mean return given by m and a standard deviation of s for some unit of calendar time Δt, then we define the following binomial inputs as follows:

$$U = e^{\sigma\sqrt{\Delta t}}$$

$$D = \frac{1}{U}$$

$$\pi_U = \frac{e^{\mu \Delta t} - D}{U - D}$$

(13.11)

As the entire analysis takes place within a risk-neutral framework μ, the expected return on the stock must equal the risk-free rate. Therefore, the probability of an upward stock price movement becomes

$$\pi_u = \frac{e^{r\Delta t} - D}{U - D} \tag{13.12}$$

Notice that the values of R, U, and D adjust automatically as the tree is adjusted to include more and more periods during the fixed calendar interval $T - t$. The absolute value of each becomes smaller, exactly as we would expect for a shorter time period. The values for U and D depend on the riskiness of the stock returns. The probability of a stock price increase depends upon the mean return on the stock. Thus, if we can estimate the standard deviation of stock returns, we have reasonable inputs to the binomial model. These can replace the arbitrary example values that we have been using.[5]

To illustrate how the binomial model gives increasingly refined estimates as the number of periods increases, consider a European call option that has one year until expiration and an exercise price of $100. Assume that the underlying stock trades for $100, with a standard deviation of 0.10. The risk-free rate of interest is 6 percent. Figure 13.7 shows how the binomial prices converge to the true option price of $7.46 as the number of periods increases. The binomial prices oscillate around the true price: for a single-period binomial model, the price is $7.76. With two periods, the binomial model gives a price of $6.96. With 20 periods, the binomial price is $7.40, and with 100 periods, the binomial price is $7.45. In general, the greater the number of periods in the lattice, the more accurate is the computed binomial price. **OPTION!** can compute call and put prices for the single-period and multi-period binomial models.

Figure 13.7   The convergence of binomial prices as the number of periods increases

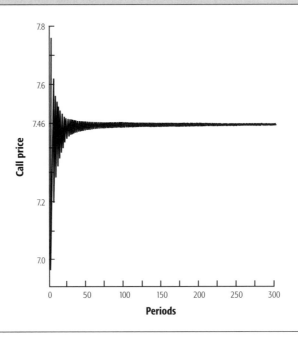

As we show in the next section, using the model of stock returns discussed in this section allows us to compute the value of an option with an infinite number of periods until expiration. With the strict binomial model, we could never employ an infinite number of periods, because it would take forever to add all the individual results.

The Black–Scholes option pricing model

To this point, we have developed the binomial option pricing model. We have discussed the log-normal distribution of stock returns and have presented up and down factors for the binomial model that are consistent with the log-normal distribution of stock returns. Also, we have seen how to adjust the precision of the binomial model by dividing a given unit of calendar time into more and more periods. As we deal with more periods, however, the calculations in the binomial model become cumbersome. As the number of periods in the binomial model becomes very large, the binomial model converges to the famous Black–Scholes option pricing model.

Fischer Black and Myron Scholes developed their option pricing model under the assumptions that asset prices adjust to prevent arbitrage, that stock prices change continuously, and that stock returns follow a log-normal distribution.[6] Also, their model holds for European call options on stocks with no dividends. Further, they assume that the interest rate and the volatility of the stock remain constant over the life of the option. The mathematics they used to derive their result included stochastic calculus, which is beyond the scope of this text. In this section, we present their model and illustrate the basic intuition that underlies it. We show that the form of the Black–Scholes model parallels the bounds on option pricing that we have already observed. In fact, the form of the Black–Scholes model is very close to the binomial model that we have just been considering.

The Black–Scholes call option pricing model

The following expression gives the Black–Scholes option pricing model for a call option:

$$c = S_t N(d_1) - Xe^{-r(T-t)} N(d_2) \tag{13.13}$$

where $N(\cdot)$ is the cumulative normal distribution function, and

$$d_1 = \frac{\ln\left(\dfrac{S_t}{X}\right) + (r + 0.5\sigma^2)(T - t)}{\sigma\sqrt{T - t}} \tag{13.14}$$

$$d_2 = d_1 - \sigma\sqrt{T - t}$$

This model has the general form that we have long considered—the value of a call must equal or exceed the stock price minus the present value of the exercise price:

$$c_t \geq S_t - Xe^{-r(T-t)}$$

To adapt this formula to account for risk, as in the Black–Scholes model, we multiply the stock price and the exercise price by some factors to account for risk, giving the general form

$$c_t = S_t \times \text{risk factor } 1 - Xe^{-r(T-t)} \times \text{risk factor } 2$$

The binomial model shares this general form with the Black–Scholes model. With the binomial model, the risk adjustment factors were the large bracketed expressions of Equation 13.2. With the Black–Scholes model, the risk factors are $N(d_1)$ and $N(d_2)$. In the Black–Scholes model, these risk adjustment factors are the continuous time equivalent of the bracketed expressions in the binomial model.

Computing Black–Scholes option prices

In this section, we show how to compute Black–Scholes option prices. Assume that a stock trades at $100 and the risk-free interest rate is 6 percent. A call option on the stock has an exercise price of $100 and expires in one year. The standard deviation of the stock's returns is 0.10 per year. We compute the values of d_1 and d_2 as follows:

$$d_1 = \frac{\ln\left(\frac{100}{100}\right) + (0.06 + 0.5 \times 0.01) \times 1}{0.1 \times \sqrt{1}} = 0.65$$

$$d_2 = 0.65 - 0.1 \times 1 = 0.55$$

Next, we find the cumulative normal values associated with d_1 and d_2. These values are the probability that a normally distributed variable with a zero mean and a standard deviation of 1.0 will have a value equal to or less than the d_1 or d_2 term we are considering. Figure 13.8 shows a graph of a normally distributed variable with a zero mean and a standard deviation of 1.0. It shows the values of d_1 and d_2 for our example. For illustration, we focus on d_1, which equals 0.65. In finding $N(d_1)$, we want to know which portion of the area under the curve lies to the left of 0.65. This is the value of $N(d_1)$. Clearly, the value we seek is larger than 0.5, because d_1 is above the mean of zero. We can find the exact value by consulting a table of the cumulative normal distribution for this variable. We present this table as Appendix B. Also, we can use **OPTION!** to find these values. For a value of 0.65 drawn from the border of the

Figure 13.8 The standardized normal distribution

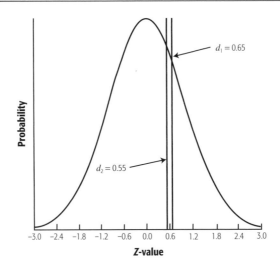

table, we find our probability in the interior: $N(0.65) = 0.7422$. Similarly, $N(d_2) = N(0.55) = 0.7088$. We now have the following:

$$c_t = \$100 \times 0.7422 - \$100 \times 0.9418 \times 0.7088 = \$7.46$$

We chose these values for our example because they parallel the values from our original binomial example. There we also assumed that the stock traded for $100 and that the risk-free rate was 6 percent. We assumed an up factor of 10 percent and a down factor of −10 percent. With a single-period binomial model and these values, we found that a call must be priced at $7.55. The two results are close. However, if we use more periods in the binomial model and use up and down factors that are consistent with a log-normal distribution of stock returns, the binomial model will converge to the Black–Scholes model price. The reader can explore this possibility by using **OPTION!**.

The Black–Scholes put option pricing model

Black and Scholes developed their option pricing model for calls only. However, we can find the Black–Scholes model for European puts by applying put–call parity:

$$p_t = c_t - S_t + Xe^{-r(T-t)}$$

Substituting the Black–Scholes call formula in the put–call parity equation gives the following:

$$p_t = S_t N(d_1) - Xe^{-r(T-t)}N(d_2) - S_t + Xe^{-r(T-t)}$$

Collecting like terms simplifies the equation to the following:

$$p_t = S_t[N(d_1) - 1] + Xe^{-r(T-t)}[1 - N(d_2)]$$

If we consider the cumulative distribution of all values from $-\infty$ to $+\infty$, the maximum value is 1.0. For any value of d_1 that we consider, part of the whole must lie at or below the value and the remainder must lie above it. For example, if $N(d_1)$ is 0.7422, for $d_1 = 0.65$, then 25.78 percent of the total area under the curve must lie at values greater than 0.65. Now we apply a principle of normal distributions. The normal distribution is symmetrical, so the same percentage of the area under the curve that lies above d_1 must lie below $-d_1$. Therefore, for any symmetrical distribution and any arbitrary value, w,

$$N(w) + N(-w) = 1$$

Following this pattern and substituting for $N(d_1)$ and $N(d_2)$ gives the equivalent Black–Scholes value for a put option:

$$p_t = Xe^{-r(T-t)}N(-d_2) - S_t N(-d_1) \tag{13.15}$$

This equation has the familiar form that we have been exploring since Chapter 11. We emphasize that the Black–Scholes model for puts holds only for European puts.

Inputs for the Black–Scholes model

We have seen that the Black–Scholes model for the price of an option depends on five variables: the stock price, the exercise price, the time until expiration, the risk-free rate, and the standard deviation of the stock. Of these, the stock price is observable in the financial press or on a trading terminal. The exercise price and the time until expiration can be known with certainty. We want to consider how to obtain estimates of the other two parameters: the risk-free interest rate and the standard deviation of the stock.

Estimating the risk-free rate of interest

Estimates of the risk-free interest rate are widely available and are usually quite reliable.[7] There are still a few points to consider, however. First, we need to select the correct rate. Because the Black–Scholes model uses a risk-free rate, we can use the Treasury bill rate as a good estimate. Quoted interest rates for T-bills are expressed as discount rates. We need to convert these to regular interest rates and express them as continuously compounded rates. As a second consideration, we should select the maturity of the T-bill carefully. If the yield curve has a steep slope, yields for different maturities can differ significantly. With T-bills maturing each week, we choose the bill that matures closest to the option expiration.

We illustrate the computation with the following example. Consider a T-bill with 84 days until maturity. Its bid yield is 8.83, and its asking yield is 8.77. Letting BID and ASK be the bid and asked yields, the following formula gives the price of a T-bill as a percentage of its face value:

$$P_{TB} = 1 - 0.01 \times \left(\frac{BID + ASK}{2} \right) \left(\frac{\text{days until maturity}}{360} \right)$$

$$= 1 - 0.01 \times \left(\frac{8.83 + 8.77}{2} \right) \left(\frac{84}{360} \right)$$

$$= 0.97947$$

In this formula, we average the bid and asked yields to estimate the unobservable true yield that lies between the observable bid and asked yields. For our example, the price of the T-bill is 97.947 percent of its face value. To find the corresponding continuously compounded rate, we solve the following equation for r:

$$e^{r(T-t)} = \frac{1}{P_{TB}}$$

$$e^{r(0.23)} = 1/0.97947$$
$$0.23r = \ln(1.02096) = 0.0207$$
$$r = 0.0902$$

In the equation, $T - t = 0.23$, because 84 days is 23 percent of a year. Thus, the appropriate interest rate in this example is 9.02 percent. It is fairly easy to secure good estimates of the risk-free interest rate. However, it is not critical to have an exact estimate, as option prices are not very sensitive to the interest rate.

Estimating the stock's standard deviation

Estimating the standard deviation of the stock's returns is more difficult and more important than estimating the risk-free rate. The Black–Scholes model takes as its input the current, instantaneous standard deviation of the stock. In other words, the immediate volatility of the stock is the riskiness of the stock that affects the option price. The Black–Scholes model also assumes that the volatility is constant over the life of the option.[8] There are two basic ways to estimate the volatility. The first method uses historical data, while the second technique employs fresh data from the options market itself. This second method uses option prices to find the option market's estimate of the stock's standard deviation. An estimate of the stock's standard deviation that is drawn from the options market is called an **implied volatility**. We consider each method in turn.[9]

Historical data

To estimate volatility using historical data, we compute the price relatives, the logarithmic price relatives, and the mean and standard deviation of the logarithmic price relatives. Letting PR_t indicate the price relative for day t, so that $PR_t = P_t/P_{t-1}$, we give the formulas for the mean and variance of the logarithmic price relatives as follows:

$$\overline{PR} = \frac{1}{T} \sum_{t=1}^{T} \ln PR_t$$

$$VAR(PR) = \frac{1}{T-1} \sum_{t=1}^{T} (\ln PR_t - \overline{PR})^2$$

As an example, we apply these formulas to data in Table 13.1, which gives 11 days of price information for a stock. With 11 price observations, we compute ten daily returns. The first column tracks the day, while the second column records the stock's closing price for the day. The third column computes the price relative from the prices in the second column. The fourth

Table 13.1 Historical volatility computations

Day	P_t	PR_t	$\ln(PR_t)$	$[\ln PR_t - PR_\mu]^2$
0	100.00			
1	101.50	1.0150	0.0149	0.000154
2	98.00	0.9655	−0.0351	0.001410
3	96.75	0.9872	−0.0128	0.000234
4	100.50	1.0388	0.0380	0.001264
5	101.00	1.0050	0.0050	0.000006
6	103.25	1.0223	0.0220	0.000382
7	105.00	1.0169	0.0168	0.000205
8	102.75	0.9786	−0.0217	0.000582
9	103.00	1.0024	0.0024	0.000000
10	102.50	0.9951	−0.0049	0.000053
		Sums	0.0247	0.004294

Sample μ = 0.0247/10 = 0.00247
Sample σ^2 = 0.004294/9 = 0.000477
Sample σ = 0.021843

column gives the log of the price relative in the third column. The last column contains the result of subtracting the mean of the logarithmic price relatives from each observation and squaring the result. The mean, variance, and standard deviation that we have calculated are all based on our sample of daily data. We use the sample standard deviation as an input to the Black–Scholes model.

Three inputs to the Black–Scholes model depend on the unit of time. These inputs are the interest rate, the time until expiration, and the standard deviation. We can use any single measure we wish, but we need to express all three variables in the same time units. For example, we can use days as our time unit and express the time until expiration as the number of days remaining. Then we must also use a daily estimation of the standard deviation and the interest rate for a single day. Generally, one year is the most convenient common unit of time. Therefore, we need to convert our daily standard deviation into a comparable yearly estimate. We have estimated our daily standard deviation of ten days. However, these are ten trading days, not calendar days. Accordingly, we recognize that we are working in trading time, not calendar time. Deleting weekend days and holidays, each year has about 250–252 trading days. We use 250 trading days per year.

We have already seen that stock prices are distributed with a standard deviation that increases as the square root of time. Accordingly, we can adjust the time dimension of our volatility estimate by multiplying it by the square root of time. For example, we convert from our daily standard deviation estimate to an equivalent yearly value by multiplying the daily estimate times the square root of 250:[10]

$$\text{annualized } \sigma = \text{daily } \sigma \times \sqrt{250} \tag{13.16}$$

For our daily estimate of 0.021843, the estimated standard deviation in annual terms is 0.3454.

In our example, we have used ten days of data. In actual practice, we face a trade-off between using the most recent possible data and using more data. In statistics, we almost always get more reliable estimates by using more data. However, the Black–Scholes model takes the instantaneous standard deviation as an input. This gives great importance to using current data. If we use the last year of historical data, then we have a rich data set for estimating the old volatility. Using just ten days, as we did in our example, emphasizes current data, but it is really not very much data for getting a reliable estimate.

To emphasize the importance of using current data, consider the Crash of 1987. On Black Monday, October 19, 1987, the market lost about 22 percent of its value. If we used a full year of daily data to estimate a stock's historical volatility the next day, our estimate would be too low. In the light of the Crash, the instantaneous volatility had surely increased.

Implied volatility

To overcome the limitations inherent in using historical data to estimate standard deviations, some scholars have turned to techniques of implied volatility. In this section, we show how to use market data and the Black–Scholes model to estimate a stock's volatility. There are five inputs to the Black–Scholes model, which the model relates to a sixth variable, the call price. With a total of six variables, any five imply a unique value for the sixth. The technique of implied volatility uses known values of five variables to estimate the standard deviation. The estimated standard deviation is an implied volatility, because it is the value implied by the other five variables in the model.[11]

To find implied volatilities, we begin with established values for the stock price, the exercise price, the interest rate, the time until expiration, and the call price. We use these to find the implied standard deviation. However, the standard deviation enters the Black–Scholes model through the values for d_1 and d_2, which are used to determine the values of the cumulative normal distribution. As a result, we cannot solve for the standard deviation directly. Instead, we must search for the volatility that makes the Black–Scholes equation hold. To do this, we need a computer. Otherwise, we would have to try an estimate of the standard deviation, make all of the Black–Scholes computations by hand, and adjust the standard deviation for the next try. This would be cumbersome and time-consuming. Therefore, implied volatilities are almost always found using a computer. **OPTION!** has a module for finding implied volatilities.

For most stocks with options, several options with different expirations trade at once. Some researchers have argued that all of these options should be used to find the volatility implied by each. The resulting estimates are then given weights and averaged to find a single volatility estimate. The single estimate is known as a **weighted implied standard deviation**. In principle, this is a good idea because it uses more information. Other things being equal, estimates based on more information should dominate estimates based on less information. However, some options trade infrequently, which makes their prices less reliable for computing implied volatilities. In addition, options way out-of-the-money give somewhat spurious volatility estimates. Virtually all weighting schemes give the highest weight to options closest to-the-money. At-the-money options tend to give the least biased volatility estimates, and many option traders derive implied volatilities by focusing on at-the-money options.[12]

Consider the following example of an implied standard deviation based on a call option. We assume that $X = \$100$ and the option is at-the-money, so that $S = \$100$. We also assume that the option has 90 days remaining until expiration and that the risk-free interest rate is 10 percent, so we have $T - t = 90$ days and $r = 0.10$. The call price is \$5.00. To find the implied standard deviation, we need to find the standard deviation that is consistent with these other values. To do this, we can compute the Black–Scholes model price for alternative standard deviations. We adjust the standard deviation to make the option price converge to its actual price of \$5.00. The sequence of standard deviations and corresponding call prices below shows this relationship. In our example, we first try $\sigma = 0.1$, which gives a call price of \$3.41. This price is too low. Thus, we know the correct standard deviation must be larger, because the call price varies directly with the standard deviation. Next, $\sigma = 0.5$ results in a call price of \$11.03, which is too high. Now we know that the standard deviation must be greater than 0.1, but less than 0.5. The task is to find the standard deviation that gives a call value equal to the specified \$5.00. This happens with $\sigma = 0.187$. Using the implied volatility module of **OPTION!**, we find that the exact standard deviation is 0.186800:[13]

Standard deviation	Corresponding call price	
0.1	$3.41	Too low
0.5	11.03	Too high
0.3	7.16	Too high
0.2	5.24	Too high
0.15	4.31	Too low
0.175	4.78	Too low
0.18	4.87	Too low
0.185	4.97	Too low
0.19	5.06	Too high
0.188	5.02	Too high
0.187	5.00	Success

Beware of a perfect smile

In the world of options, a "volatility smile" refers to the U-shaped pattern that is often seen when plotting an option series' implied standard deviations against the degree to which options within the series are in-, at-, or out-of-the money. The pattern shows that, all else equal, at-the-money options have a lower implied standard deviation than options that are in- or out-of the money. The pattern can differ across option markets and across related options that differ only in their expiration dates. In some markets, the pattern resembles a smirk. Although the volatility smiles are the subject of aggressive investigation by academics and practitioners, no consensus has emerged on the cause. One explanation is that the true distribution of asset prices has fatter tails than the distribution assumed in option pricing models.

Sometimes volatility smiles are an artifact of the exchange settlement procedure. For most listed options, at- or near-the-money options are the most liquid and quotations for these options are representative of market opinion. For deep in- or out-of the money options, trades take place less frequently. For these illiquid options with stale prices, exchange settlement committees may set the price for clearing purposes to reflect the changes in the market that are not reflected in stale option prices. Often, the settlement committee uses an option pricing model to set the price. This means that implied standard deviations obtained from these prices are not reflecting the market consensus, but instead are reflecting the volatility input used in the option pricing model by the exchange settlement committee. If the settlement committee uses a perfect U-shaped volatility smile in selecting the volatility input for the model, the implied standard deviations derived from these prices will reflect this same perfect smile.

European options and dividends

Most of the stocks that underlie stock options pay dividends, yet the Black–Scholes model assumes that the underlying stock pays no dividends. While the Black–Scholes model might be elegant and provide a great deal of insight into option pricing, successful real-world application of the model depends upon resolving the dividend problem. In this section, we consider the impact of dividends on option values and we show how slight adjustments in the Black–Scholes model allow it to apply to options on dividend-paying stocks. We continue to focus on European options.

The effect of dividends on option prices

As we have seen, the value of a call option at expiration equals the maximum of zero or the stock price minus the exercise price, and a put option at expiration is worth the maximum of zero or the exercise price minus the stock price. In our familiar notation,

$$c_T = \text{MAX}\{0, S_T - X\}$$
$$p_T = \text{MAX}\{0, X - S_T\}$$

For both the call and the put, anything that affects the stock price at expiration will affect the price of the option. Dividends that might be paid during the life of the option can obviously affect the stock price. We may regard a dividend as a repayment of a portion of the share's value to the shareholder. As such, we would expect the stock price to fall by the amount of the dividend payment.[14] As a metaphor, we might think of the dividend on a stock as a leakage of value from the stock. As the value of the stock drops due to the leakage of dividends, the changing stock price will affect the value of options on the stock.

A drop in the stock price due to a dividend will have an adverse effect on the price of a call and a beneficial effect on the price of a put. For a call, the stock price at expiration will be lower than it would have been had there been no dividend. Thus, the dividend will reduce the quantity $S_T - X$, thus reducing the value of the call at expiration. For the put, the dividend will reduce the stock price at expiration, and it will therefore increase the quantity $X - S_T$.

We can illustrate the effect of dividends with an example of a call and put that have a common exercise price of $100. Assume that the options are moments from expiration, and that the stock price is $102. Without bringing dividends into consideration, the value of the options would be as follows:

$$c_T = MAX\{0, S_T - X\} = MAX\{0, \$102 - \$100\} = \$2$$
$$p_T = MAX\{0, X - S_T\} = MAX\{0, \$100 - \$102\} = \$0$$

Just before expiration, the stock pays a dividend of $3, causing the stock price to drop from $102 to $99. With a stock price of $99 at expiration, the call option will be worth zero, and the put will be worth $1. Failing to take into account the looming dividend payment could cause large pricing errors from a blind application of the Black–Scholes model. We now turn to adjustments in the Black–Scholes model that reflect dividends.

Adjustments for known dividends

For most stocks, the dividend payments likely to occur during the life of an option can be forecast with considerable precision. If we are looking ahead to a dividend forecasted to occur in three months, we expect the stock price to drop by the amount of the dividend when the stock goes ex-dividend. At the present moment, three months before the ex-dividend date, we can build that looming dividend into our analysis. To do so, we subtract the present value of the dividend from the current stock price. We then apply the Black–Scholes model as usual, except that we use the adjusted stock price as an input to the model instead of the current stock price.

As an example, consider call and put options with a common exercise price of $100 and 150 days until expiration. Assume that the underlying stock trades for $102, and that you expect the stock to pay a $3 dividend in 90 days. The risk-free rate is 9 percent, and the standard deviation for the stock is 0.30. The present value of the $3 dividend is

$$\$3 \times e^{-r(90/365)} = \$2.93$$

According to this technique, we reduce the stock price now by the present value of the dividend, giving an adjusted stock price of $99.07. We then apply the Black–Scholes model in the usual way, except that we use the adjusted stock price of $99.07 instead of the current price of $102. The following table shows the results of applying the adjusted and unadjusted models to the call and the put:

Black–Scholes model price	Call	Put
Adjusted for known dividends	8.91	6.21
Unadjusted	10.74	5.11

Applying the Black–Scholes model, with the adjustment for known dividends that we have just discussed, gives a call value of $8.91 and a put value of $6.21. With no adjustment for dividends, the Black–Scholes prices are $10.74 for the call option and $5.11 for the put option. The difference in prices is substantial, amounting to almost 20 percent. Also, as we hypothesized, subtracting the present value of the dividends from the stock price reduces the value of the call and increases the value of the put.

The same technique applies in situations when there are several dividends. The stock price should be adjusted by subtracting the present value of all dividends that are expected to occur before the expiration date of the option. Dividends expected after the option expires can be ignored, because the option will already have been exercised or allowed to expire before those dividends affect the value of the stock. **OPTION!** can compute the prices of call and put options under the Black–Scholes model adjusted for known dividends.

Adjustments for continuous dividends—the Merton model

Robert Merton has shown how to adjust the Black–Scholes model to account for dividends when the dividend is paid at a continuous rate. Instead of focusing on the quarterly dividends that characterize individual stocks, the Merton model applies when the dividend is paid continuously. Essentially, the adjustment for continuous dividends treats the dividend rate as a negative interest rate. We have already seen that dividends reduce the value of a call option, because they reduce the value of the stock that underlies the option. In effect, we have a continuous leakage of value from the stock that equals the dividend rate. We let the Greek letter delta, δ, represent this rate of leakage.[15]

The Merton model applies particularly well to options on goods such as foreign currency. In such an option, the foreign currency is treated as paying a continuous dividend equal to the foreign interest rate. (We explore options on foreign currency in Chapter 16.) The Merton model also applies fairly well to options on individual stocks if we treat the quarterly dividends as being earned at a continuous rate. Merton's adjustment to the Black–Scholes model for continuous dividends is as follows:

$$c_t^M = e^{-\delta(T-t)}S_t N(d_1^M) - Xe^{-r(T-t)}N(d_2^M)$$

$$d_1^M = \frac{\ln\left(\dfrac{S_t}{X}\right) + (r - \delta + 0.5\sigma^2)(T - t)}{\sigma\sqrt{T - t}}$$

$$d_2^M = d_1^M - \sigma\sqrt{T - t}$$

(13.17)

where δ is the continuous dividend rate on the stock. To adjust the regular Black–Scholes model, we replace the current stock price with the stock price adjusted for the continuous dividend. That is, we replace S_t with

$$e^{-\delta(T-t)}S_t$$

Substituting this expression into the formulas for d_1 and d_2 gives d_1^M and d_2^M as shown above. Merton's adjusted put value is as follows:

$$p_t^M = Xe^{-r(T-t)}N(-d_2^M) - Se^{-\delta(T-t)}N(-d_1^M)$$

(13.18)

When $\delta = 0$, the Merton model reduces immediately to the Black–Scholes model. Thus, the Merton model is a more general model than the original Black–Scholes model, and it will appear repeatedly in the remainder of the text. As an example of how to apply the continuous dividend adjustment, consider the following data: $S_t = \$60$; $X = \$60$; $r = 0.09$; $\sigma = 0.2$; $T - t = 180$ days. The stock will pay a quarterly dividend of $\$2.07$ in 90 days, implying a continuous dividend rate, δ, of 13.75 percent. We compute the call price, c_t^M, as follows:

$$d_1^M = \frac{\ln\left(\dfrac{60}{60}\right) + (0.09 - 0.1375 + 0.5 \times 0.2 \times 0.2)\left(\dfrac{180}{365}\right)}{0.2 \times \sqrt{\dfrac{180}{365}}}$$

$$= \frac{0 - 0.01356}{0.14045} = -0.09656$$

$$d_2^M = -0.09656 - 0.2 \times \sqrt{\frac{180}{365}} = -0.23701$$

$N(d_1^M) = N(-0.09656) = 0.4615$ and $N(d_2^M) = N(-0.23701) = 0.4063$. Therefore, $N(-d_1^M) = 0.5385$ and $N(-d_2^M) = 0.5937$. The call and put values adjusted for continuous dividends are as follows:

$$c_t^M = 60e^{-0.1375 \times (180/365)} \times 0.4615 - 60e^{-0.09 \times (180/365)} \times 0.4063 = \$2.55$$
$$p_t^M = 60e^{-0.09 \times (180/365)} \times 0.5937 - 60e^{-0.1375 \times (180/365)} \times 0.5385 = \$3.88$$

OPTION! allows the direct estimation of European call and put values according to the Merton model.

The binomial model and dividends

The binomial model can evaluate European option prices for options on dividend paying stocks. There are three alternative dividend treatments within the context of the binomial model, and all involve adjusting the lattice to reflect the impact of dividends on the stock price. The first considers options on stocks paying a continuous dividend. This binomial approach is the analog to the Merton model that we considered earlier. The second binomial approach applies to options on a stock that will pay a known dividend yield at a certain time. For example, a stock might pay a dividend equal to some fraction of its value on a certain date, such as a dividend of 3 percent of the stock's value 120 days from now. The third approach applies to a known dollar dividend that will occur at a certain time. For example, 90 days from now, a stock might pay a $1 dividend. The binomial model can accommodate any number of dividend payments between the present and the expiration of the option.

Continuous dividends

To apply the binomial model to options on a stock paying a continuous dividend, we need to adjust the binomial parameters to reflect the continuous leakage of value from the stock that the dividend represents. For the Merton model for European options on a stock paying a continuous dividend, we saw that the adjustment largely involved subtracting the continuous dividend rate, δ, from the risk-free rate, r. This is exactly the adjustment required for the binomial model. For options on a stock paying a continuous dividend δ, the U, D, and π_U factors are as follows:

$$U = e^{\sigma\sqrt{\Delta t}}$$

$$D = \frac{1}{U} \tag{13.19}$$

$$\pi_U = \frac{e^{(r-\delta)\Delta t} - D}{U - D}$$

Figure 13.9   The binomial tree for a stock with a known dividend yield

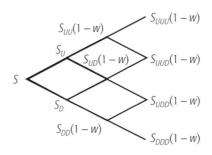

We illustrated the Merton model by considering a call option on a stock with a price of $60, a standard deviation of 0.2, and a continuous dividend rate of 13.75 percent. The call had an exercise price of $60 and expired in 180 days. The risk-free rate was 9 percent. We saw that the price of this option according to the Merton model was $2.5557. According to the binomial model, with 200 periods, the price would be $2.5516, which is almost identical. For the same data, the European put according to the Merton model was worth $3.8845. The binomial model with 200 periods gives a put price of $3.8805.

Known dividend yield

Consider a stock that will pay w percent of its value as a dividend in 55 days. An option on the stock expires in 120 days, and we model the price of the option using a three-period binomial model. In this situation, the dividend will occur in the second period. The binomial tree for the stock will appear as shown in Figure 13.9. At the second period in the binomial tree, the stock price will be reduced to $(1 - w)$ percent of its value. If the stock price rose in each of the first two periods, the stock price at period 2 would be $S_tUU(1 - w)$. Because of the known dividend yield occurring at day 55, the value of the stock is reduced by the w percent dividend. Given that the stock price went up the first two periods, the value of the stock in the third period could be either $S_tUUU(1 - w)$ if the stock price goes up again, or $S_tUUD(1 - w)$ if the stock price falls in the final period. To value either a call or a put in the context of the binomial model with a known dividend yield, we apply the usual technique to work from the terminal stock prices back to the current stock price and current options price. **OPTION!** can compute call and put prices under the binomial model adjusted for known dividend yields.

Extending this example, let us assume that the initial stock price is $80, the exercise price for a call and a put is $75, the standard deviation of the stock is 0.3, and the risk-free rate of interest is 7 percent. The percentage dividend that will be paid is 3 percent, so $w = 0.03$. With 120 days until expiration and a three-period binomial model, $\Delta t = 40/365 = 0.1096$. Therefore,

$$U = e^{0.3 \times \sqrt{0.1096}} = 1.1044$$

$$D = \frac{1}{1.1044} = 0.9055$$

$$\pi_U = \frac{1.0077 - 0.9055}{1.1044 - 0.9055} = 0.5138$$

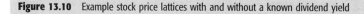

Figure 13.10 Example stock price lattices with and without a known dividend yield

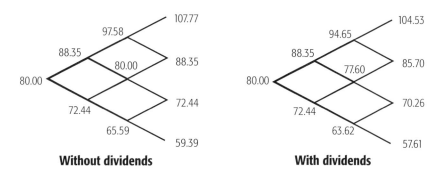

The discounting factor for a single period is $e^{-r\Delta t} = e^{-0.07 \times (40/365)} = 0.9924$. Figure 13.10 shows the binomial tree for the stock of our example. In the left-hand panel, the stock price without dividends appears, while the right-hand tree shows the effect of the 3 percent dividend on the stock price. For example, in the right-hand tree reflecting dividends, the stock price pattern generated by a rise, a rise, and a fall is

$$S_t UUD(1 - w) = \$80 \times 1.1044 \times 1.1044 \times 0.9055(1.0 - 0.03) = \$85.70$$

Figure 13.11 shows two binomial trees for the call option. The left-hand tree in Figure 13.11 does not reflect the dividends and shows that the option's value would be $9.37. The right-hand tree, which does reflect the 3 percent dividend yield, shows that the call is worth $7.94. The difference in the two prices is due entirely to taking account of the dividend.

Figure 13.12 parallels Figure 13.11, except that it shows trees for the put option. The left-hand tree ignores the dividend and shows that the put's value would be $2.67 if there were no dividend. Taking account of the dividend in the right-hand tree gives a put price of $3.64. The effect of the dividend increases the put's value by 36 percent, from $2.67 to $3.64, and decreases

Figure 13.11 Example call price lattices with and without a known dividend yield

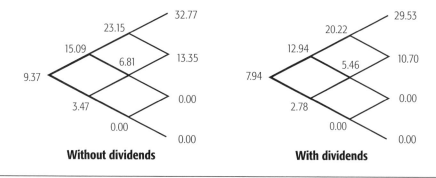

Figure 13.12   Example put price lattices with and without a known dividend yield

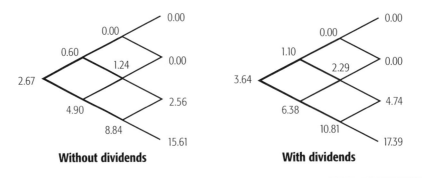

Without dividends   **With dividends**

Figure 13.13   A stock price lattice unadjusted for a known dollar dividend

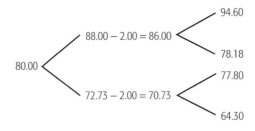

the call's value by 15 percent, from $9.37 to $7.94. Clearly, dividends can have a profound effect on option prices.

Known dollar dividend

Most stocks that underlie stock options pay a fixed dollar dividend, rather than paying a dividend that equals some percentage of their value. This presents a complication, because the tree may develop a tremendous number of branches. For example, assume that the stock price is initially $80 and that $U = 1.1$. Therefore, $D = 0.9091$. After one period, the stock price is either $88 or $72.73, as Figure 13.13 shows. Assume that a $2 dividend is paid just before the first period. Taking the dividend payment into account, the stock price will be either $86 or $70.73 at the first period. In the next period, the stock price will either rise or fall. If it was $86, it will then be $94.60 if the price rises again or $78.18 if the price falls. If the stock price fell in the first period, so that it was $70.73 after the dividend payment, in the second period it will either rise to $77.80 or fall to $64.30. Figure 13.13 shows that there are four possible prices after two periods: $94.60, $78.18, $77.80, or $64.30. In the normal tree, there would be only three prices to consider, because $S_tUD = S_tDU$. That is not the case with known dollar dividends. Letting DIV$ indicate a given dollar dividend, $(S_tU - \text{DIV\$})D$ does not equal $(S_tD - \text{DIV\$})U$. For many periods and multiple dividend payments, the number of nodes to evaluate can explode, making this model very difficult to apply.

We can avoid these difficulties by making a simplifying assumption. We assume that the stock price reflects the dividend, which is known with certainty, and all other factors that might affect the stock price, which are uncertain. We then adjust the uncertain component of the stock price for the impending dividends and model the uncertain component of the stock price with the binomial tree adding back the present value of all future dividends at each node. Specifically, we follow these steps:

(1) Compute the present value of all dividends to be paid during the life of the option as of the present time = t.
(2) Subtract this present value from the current stock price to form $S_t' = S_t - PV$ of all dividends.
(3) Create the binomial tree by applying the up and down factors in the usual way to the initial stock price S_t'.
(4) After generating the tree, add to the stock price at each node the present value of all future dividends to be paid during the life of the option.
(5) Compute the option values in the usual way by working through the binomial tree.

To make this discussion more concrete, consider again the tree that failed to recombine in Figure 13.13. The initial stock price was $80, $U = 1.1$, $D = 0.9091$, and a dividend was to be paid just before the time of the first period. We now additionally assume that one period is 0.25 years and the interest rate is 10 percent. Therefore, the one-period discount factor is

$$e^{-r(\Delta t)} = e^{-0.1 \times 0.25} = 0.9753$$

At the outset, the present value of the dividend is $1.95 = 0.9753($2). To form S_t', we subtract this present value from S_t:

$$S_t' = S_t - PV \text{ of all dividends} = \$80 - \$1.95 = \$78.05$$

Figure 13.14 shows the binomial tree generated from a starting price of $78.05. Notice that the present value of the dividends ($1.95) has been added to the first node only, because only the first node represents a time before the payment of the dividend. Notice also that the tree recombines at the second period, in contrast to that in Figure 13.13. **OPTION!** can compute call and put prices under the binomial model adjusted for known dollar dividends.

Figure 13.14   A stock price lattice adjusted for a known dollar dividend

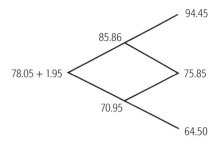

Summary

In this section, we have considered the effect of dividends on European options. In general, a dividend on a stock reduces the value of the stock by the amount of the dividend. Dividends reduce the value of call options because they reduce the stock price. Dividends increase the value of put options because the dividend reduces the price of the stock. The Black–Scholes model as originally developed pertained only to options on nondividend-paying stocks. However, the stocks that underlie most stock options do pay dividends, so the limitation of the Black–Scholes model is potentially serious.

There are several adjustments to the Black–Scholes model to account for dividends. The first one adjusts for known dividends by subtracting the present value of the dividends from the stock price and then applying the Black–Scholes model in the usual way. When the underlying stock pays a continuous dividend, Merton showed how to adjust the Black–Scholes model to account for the dividend.

We also considered adjustments to the binomial model to account for dividends. When the stock pays a known dividend yield at a given date, the binomial model can reflect the impact of this dividend on the stock price and the option quite easily. When the dividend is a given dollar amount, the binomial model requires a more elaborate adjustment, but it too can adjust the stock price and compute option values that reflect the impact of the dividend.

Expensing employee stock options

In October 1995, the Financial Accounting Standards Board (FASB) issued a Statement of Financial Accounting Standard, called SFAS 123, requiring that the hypothetical compensation cost of stock-based employee compensation plans be recognized as an expense in the corporate income statement. SFAS 123 applies to all forms of stock-based compensation, including stock purchase plans, stock options, restricted stock, and stock appreciation rights.

The FASB statement allows companies to choose from two methods to measure the expense of employee stock options. Under the first method, called the fair-value-based method, the compensation cost is measured at the grant date at fair value. FASB defines fair value as the amount at which an option can be exchanged in a current transaction between knowledgeable unrelated willing parties when neither is acting under compulsion. Because employee stock options are not traded in the open market, observable market prices cannot be used as a fair market benchmark. Instead, option pricing models (or possibly dealer quotes) must be used as the fair value benchmark. SFAS 123 specifically mentions the Black–Scholes model and the binomial model as being acceptable option pricing models. The statement also requires disclosure of the general terms of the compensation plan.

Under the second method, called the intrinsic-value-based approach, the company simply records the difference between the option strike price and the value of the underlying shares on the grant date. If an option is at-the-money on the grant date, which is typically the case, the intrinsic-value-based method will yield a compensation cost of zero on the company's financial statements. However, a company using this method must disclose in a footnote the hypothetical effect on earnings using either the Black–Scholes model or the binomial pricing model.

SFAS 123 encourages companies to adopt the fair-value-based method, and perhaps as many as 500 U.S. companies have voluntarily adopted this approach. However, most companies choose to use the intrinsic-value-based method. Because of the collapse of Enron in mid-2001, and other corporate accounting scandals around that time, a number of well-known companies announced plans to change from the intrinsic-value-based approach to the fair-value-based approach. In March 2004, the FASB released an exposure draft of proposed amendments to SFAS 123 that would eliminate the use of the intrinsic-value-based approach and generally require the use of the fair-value-based method for expensing employee stock options. The exposure draft does not specify any particular option pricing model, but gives the company the flexibility to select the model appropriate for the unique characteristics of the company's options.

The proposed elimination of the intrinsic-value-based approach has been controversial. The exposure draft effectively requires the expensing of employee stock options. Critics of the proposal argue that the fair-value-based approach creates legal risks for companies and auditors. By not requiring a specific option pricing model for valuing employee stock options, companies will have to make choices, not only about the model to be used, but the various inputs that the model requires. These choices can have a substantial impact on the reported earnings of a company—and that, in turn, can leave companies open to class action lawsuits by disgruntled shareholders. Critics also argue that expensing stock options will reduce their use and will have an adverse effect on the growth of the U.S. economy.

Tests of the option pricing model

If the Black–Scholes option pricing model correctly captures the factors that affect option prices, the price computed according to the model should correspond closely to the price observed in the market. Otherwise, either the model is inadequate or prices in the market are irrational. Therefore, each of the tests that we will consider in this section evaluates a joint hypothesis— the adequacy of the option pricing model and market rationality. If we find a discrepancy between the two, we can account for this divergence by claiming that the model is inadequate or by allowing that market participants are foolish. Note, however, that the Black–Scholes model was derived under the assumption that prices should not permit arbitrage. Accordingly, any major discrepancy between the model price and the market price would be serious indeed.

The Black–Scholes study

The first empirical study of option pricing was conducted by Black and Scholes.[16] In this 1972 test, they examined over-the-counter option prices, because listed options did not yet trade. Black and Scholes computed a theoretical option price based on their model. If the market price exceeded their theoretical price, they assumed that they sold the option. Similarly, if the market price was below the price they computed, they assumed that they bought the option. In both cases, they assumed that they held a stock position in conjunction with the option that gave a riskless position. (In other words, if they were long the call option, they would hold $-N(d_1)$ shares of stock as well.) This risk-free position should earn the risk-free rate if option prices in the market and their model are identical. They maintained this position until expiration, adjusting the portfolio as needed to maintain its riskless character. Their results showed significant profit opportunities. In other words, actual market prices differed significantly from the theoretical price given by the model. However, while this difference was statistically significant, it was not economically important. When Black and Scholes considered transaction costs, they found that the costs of trading would erode any potential profit. Therefore, option traders could not follow their strategy and make a profit. This result helped to show the strong correspondence between market prices and option prices computed from theoretical models, such as the Black–Scholes model.

The Galai studies

As in the Black–Scholes study, Dan Galai created hedged portfolios of options and stock and used these portfolios to study the correspondence between the Black–Scholes model price and actual market prices for options.[17] In contrast to the Black–Scholes study, Galai used listed option data from the Chicago Board Options Exchange (CBOE). With options trading on an exchange, Galai had access to daily price quotations. Therefore, he was able to compute the rate of return on the hedged option–stock portfolio for each option for each day. He also adjusted the hedge ratio each day to maintain the neutral hedge—neutral in the sense that a change in the stock price would not change the overall value of the combined option–stock position. Comparing market prices to Black–Scholes model prices, Galai assumed that he sold overpriced options and bought underpriced options each day.

Galai's results showed that this strategy could earn excess returns. In other words, his initial results seemed to be inconsistent with an efficient market. However, this apparent result disappeared when Galai considered transaction costs. If transaction costs were only 1 percent, the apparent excess returns disappeared. Most traders outside the market face transaction costs of 1 percent or higher. However, market makers can transact for less than 1 percent transaction costs. This suggests that market makers could have followed Galai's strategy to earn excess returns. Yet even market makers face some additional transaction costs implied by their career choice. For instance, the market maker must buy or lease a seat on the exchange, and the market maker must forego alternative employment. When Galai brought these additional implicit transaction costs into the analysis, the market maker's apparent excess returns diminished or disappeared. At any rate, Galai's results showed that Black–Scholes model prices closely match actual market prices for options.

The Bhattacharya study

Mihir Bhattacharya used an approach similar to that of the Black–Scholes and Galai studies to analyze the correspondence between actual market prices and theoretical prices.[18] Bhattacharya discussed the adherence of market prices to theoretical boundaries implied by no-arbitrage conditions. We focus on one of his three boundaries. As we discussed in Chapter 12, a call option should be worth more than its exercise value if time remains until expiration. Bhattacharya compiled a sample of 86,000 transactions and examined them to determine if immediate exercise was profitable. He found 1,100 such exercise opportunities, meaning that the stock price exceeded the exercise price plus the call price. As we argued in Chapter 12, such a price relationship should not exist. However, these exercise opportunities assumed that the exercise could be conducted without transaction costs. When Bhattacharya considered transaction costs, these apparently profitable exercise opportunities disappeared. The apparent violation of the boundary condition was observed only because transaction costs were not considered. This means that traders could not exploit the deviation from the boundary condition to make a profit.

The MacBeth–Merville study

James MacBeth and Larry Merville used the Black–Scholes model to compute implied standard deviations for the underlying stocks.[19] They assumed that the Black–Scholes model correctly priced at-the-money options with at least 90 days until expiration. Based on these assumptions and the estimated standard deviation, they evaluated how well the Black–Scholes model priced options that were in-the-money or out-of-the-money, and how well the model priced options that had fewer than 90 days until expiration. They found some systematic discrepancies between market prices and Black–Scholes model prices. First, the Black–Scholes prices tended to be less than market prices for in-the-money options, and the Black–Scholes prices tended to be higher than market prices for out-of-the-money options. Second, this first effect was larger the farther the options were from the money. However, it was smaller the shorter the time until expiration. Therefore, we expect to find the greatest discrepancy between market prices and the

Black–Scholes model price for options with a long time until expiration and options that are way in- or way out-of-the-money.

The Rubinstein study

Mark Rubinstein compared market prices with theoretical option prices from the Black–Scholes model and other models of option prices.[20] Some other models outperformed the Black–Scholes model in some respects, yet none did so consistently. Further, Rubinstein confirmed some of the biases noted by MacBeth and Merville for the Black–Scholes model. However, none of the other models were consistently free of bias either. In general, Rubinstein was unable to conclude that there was one single model superior to the others.

Summary

Testing of the option pricing model is far from complete. Recently, attention has turned to the information inherent in option prices that might not be reflected in stock prices, or that might be reflected first in option prices and later in stock prices. For example, Joseph Anthony finds that trading volume in call options leads trading volume in the underlying stock by one day.[21] Although this lead–lag relationship does not necessarily imply any inefficiency in either market, it does seem to suggest that information that reaches the market affects options first.[22] In recent years, the proliferation of many new kinds of options has attracted attention away from options on individual stocks. The kinds of studies on options on individual stocks that were conducted by Black and Scholes and Galai, Bhattacharya, and Rubinstein have recently been conducted for these new kinds of options. In large part, these new results corroborate the earlier results that were found for options on individual stocks. In this section, it has been possible to discuss only some of the most famous studies. There are many other worthwhile studies that have been conducted, and many more still that remain to be conducted.

Long-term Equity AnticiPation Securities (LEAPS)

LEAPS are long-dated options with expiration times out to three years in the future–much longer than traditional options. There are two types of LEAPS, Equity LEAPS and Index LEAPS. Equity LEAPS are available on approximately nearly 500 common stocks, American Depositary Receipts, and exchange-traded funds indexes. Index LEAPS are traded on broad-based, industry-sector, and international indexes.

Equity LEAPS are American-style options, and therefore may be exercised and settled in stock prior to the expiration date. LEAPS currently are listed on the American Stock Exchange, the Chicago Board Options Exchange (CBOE), the Pacific Exchange, and the Philadelphia Stock Exchange. LEAPS are issued and cleared by The Options Clearing Corporation (OCC).

Index LEAPS are long-term index options based either on a fractional value of one-tenth of the value of the underlying index or on the full value of the underlying index. Unlike Equity LEAPS, Index LEAPS are cash-settled based on the difference between the exercise settlement value of the index on the exercise date and the exercise price of the option. Index LEAPS are either European-style options or American-style options.

Conclusion

We began this chapter by developing the binomial model. We showed that the single-period binomial model emerges directly from no-arbitrage conditions that govern all asset prices. We extended the single-period model to the multi-period binomial model. With this model, we found that we could apply our no-arbitrage principles to value options with numerous periods remaining until expiration. Throughout this development, we considered price movements that were somewhat arbitrary.

Researchers have studied the actual price movements of stocks in great detail. We found that logarithmic stock returns are distributed approximately normally and that this model of stock price movements has proven to be very useful as a working approximation of stock price behavior. Using this model of stock price behavior, a binomial model with many periods until expiration approaches the Black–Scholes model. The Black–Scholes model gives an elegant equation for pricing a call option as a function of five variables: the stock price, the exercise price, the risk-free rate, the time until expiration, and the standard deviation

of the stock. Only two of these variables, the interest rate and the standard deviation, are not immediately observable. We showed how to estimate these two parameters.

OPTION! is a useful tool for analyzing the concepts we have developed in this chapter. A module for the binomial model allows the user to specify one or many periods for analysis. In this module, the user specifies the up and down percentage factors. A separate module uses up and down factors that are consistent with the Black–Scholes model. With this module, we can study the convergence of the binomial price to the Black–Scholes price. Another module of OPTION! allows us to compute Black–Scholes call and put values. A separate module finds the implied volatility of the stock based on the Black–Scholes model. A further module computes values of the cumulative normal distribution for input values of d_1 or d_2. Finally, OPTION! also includes a module to generate random price paths consistent with initial values that the user specifies.

Triple witching days

Each year, on the third Friday of March, June, September, and December, the regular quarterly expirations of stock index futures, stock index options, and individual stock options coincide. Traders refer to these four days as "triple witching days," or "freaky Fridays." Because of the concurrent expirations, trading volume on these days has, at times, been unusually high and prices have moved rapidly as traders offset previously established positions, rolled them forward, or attempted last-minute arbitrage transactions among the three expiring contracts. In the late 1980s and the early 1990s, when the triple witching expirations all occurred at the market close, unusual market volatility was blamed on market congestion caused by the concurrent expirations.

In response to complaints about abnormal market volatility on triple witching days, the exchanges trading the different contracts took steps aimed at reducing market volatility. First, the exchanges improved disclosure about expiration day order flow. On the New York Stock Exchange, exchange officials now publicly disclose the 50 stocks with the largest order imbalances on triple witching days (as well as double witching days). This information is provided to the market before the opening of trading, during the day, and shortly before the market close. This information helps attract offsetting orders that can stabilize prices. Second, the Chicago Mercantile Exchange (CME) moved the expiration time of their stock index futures products from the Friday close to the open. The CBOE moved the expiration time of their index options to the close of trading on the Thursday preceding the third Friday of the expiration month. These moves have been successful in reducing public anxiety about expiration day effects, and concern about triple witching days has abated.

Exercises

1 What is binomial about the binomial model? In other words, how does the model get its name?

2 If a stock price moves in a manner consistent with the binomial model, what is the chance that the stock price will be the same for two periods in a row? Explain.

3 Assume that a stock price is $120, and that over the next year it will either rise by 10 percent or fall by 20 percent. The risk-free interest rate is 6 percent. A call option on this stock has an exercise price of $130. What is the price of a call option that expires in one year? What is the chance that the stock price will rise?

4 Based on the data in Exercise 3, what would you hold to form a risk-free portfolio?

5 Based on the data in Exercise 3, what will the price of the call option be if the option expires in two years and the stock price can move up 10 percent or down 20 percent in each year?

6 Based on the data in Exercise 3, what would the price of a call with one year to expiration be if the call has an exercise price of $135? Can you answer this question without making the full calculations? Explain.

7 A stock is worth $60 today. In a year, the stock price can rise or fall by 15 percent. If the interest rate is 6 percent, what is the price of a call option that expires in three years and has an exercise price of $70? What is the price of a put option that expires in three years and has an exercise price of $65? (Use **OPTION!** to solve this problem.)

8 Consider our model of stock price movements given in Equation 13.8. A stock has an initial price of $55 and an expected growth rate of 0.15 per year. The annualized standard deviation of the stock's return is 0.4. What is the expected stock price after 175 days?

9 A stock sells for $110. A call option on the stock has an exercise price of $105 and expires in 43 days. If the interest rate is 0.11 and the standard deviation of the stock's returns is 0.25, what is the price of the call according to the Black–Scholes model? What would be the price of a put with an exercise price of $140 and the same time until expiration?

10 Consider a stock that trades for $75. A put and a call on this stock both have an exercise price of $70 and they expire in 150 days. If the risk-free rate is 9 percent and the standard deviation for the stock is 0.35, compute the price of the options according to the Black–Scholes model.

11 For the options in Exercise 10, now assume that the stock pays a continuous dividend of 4 percent. What, according to the Merton model, are the options worth?

12 Consider a Treasury bill with 173 days until maturity. The bid and asked yields on the bill are 9.43 and

9.37. What is the price of the T-bill? What is the continuously compounded rate on the bill?

13 Consider the following sequence of daily stock prices: $47, $49, $46, $45, $51. Compute the mean daily logarithmic return for this share. What is the daily standard deviation of returns? What is the annualized standard deviation?

14 A stock sells for $85. A call option with an exercise price of $80 expires in 53 days and sells for $8. The risk-free interest rate is 11 percent. What is the implied standard deviation for the stock? (Use **OPTION!** to solve this problem.)

15 For a particular application of the binomial model, assume that $U = 1.09$, $D = 0.91$, and that the two are equally probable. Do these assumptions lead to any particular difficulty? Explain. (Note that these are specified up and down movements, and are not intended to be consistent with the Black–Scholes model.)

16 For a stock that trades at $120 and has a standard deviation of returns of 0.4, use the Black–Scholes model to price a call and a put that expire in 180 days and that have an exercise price of $100. The risk-free rate is 8 percent. Now assume that the stock will pay a dividend of $3 on day 75. Apply the known dividend adjustment to the Black–Scholes model and compute new call and put prices.

17 A call and a put expire in 150 days and have an exercise price of $100. The underlying stock is worth $95 and has a standard deviation of 0.25. The risk-free rate is 11 percent. Use a three-period binomial model and stock price movements consistent with the Black–Scholes model to compute the value of these options. Specify U, D, and π_U, as well as the values for the call and put.

18 For the situation in Exercise 17, assume that the stock will pay 2 percent of its value as a dividend on day 80. Compute the value of the call and the put under this circumstance.

19 For the situation in Exercise 17, assume that the stock will pay a dividend of $2 on day 80. Compute the value of the call and the put under this circumstance.

20 Consider the first tree in Figures 13.10 and 13.12. If the stock price falls in both of the first two periods, the price is $65.59. For the first tree in Figure 13.12, the put value is $8.84 in this case. Given that the exercise price on the put is $75, does this present a contradiction? Explain.

21 Consider the second tree in Figures 13.10 and 13.11. If the stock price increases in the first period, the price is $88.35. For the second tree in Figure 13.11, the call price is $12.94 in this case. Given that the exercise price on the put is $75, does this present a contradiction? Explain.

22 As a cost-cutting measure, your CFO, an accountant, decides to cancel your division's subscription to Bloomberg. You rely on Bloomberg for real-time quotes on Treasury bill prices to value options using the Black–Scholes option pricing model. You discover that you can obtain real-time quotes on commercial paper rates from Reuters, to which you still have a subscription. Discuss the implications of using the yield on AAA rated commercial paper instead of Treasury bill yields to value options using the Black–Scholes model.

23 Assume that stock returns follow a random walk with a drift equal to the expected return on the stock. You are modeling stock returns using a binomial process for the purpose of valuing a European call option. Explain why it is not possible to create an initial position in the stock and the call option that will remain riskless for the entire life of the option.

24 WMM is currently priced at $117.50 per share. The 50-day options on WMM are currently being traded at three different strike prices, $110, $115, and $120. The 50-day Treasury bill is priced to yield an adjusted annual return of 6 percent compounded continuously. The prices and implied volatilities for the three different options are shown below:

Strike	Call	Implied volatility
$110	$8.50	0.16
115	5.375	0.21
120	3.75	0.26

If the WMM options are priced by the Black–Scholes model, then the implied volatility of each of the 50-day option contracts would be the same.

A Which of the three implied volatilities would you use as an estimate for the true volatility?

B If you knew that the true volatility of the stock was 0.20, what could you say about the value of the call options? What action would you take upon observing the implied volatilities shown in this table?

25 The dominant asset pricing models in finance maintain that the price of a share of stock depends on the amount of nondiversifiable covariation risk intrinsic in a stock. That is, the market only prices covariation risk that cannot be costlessly diversified away by

shareholders. Only the nondiversifiable segment of total risk is priced by the market. The Black–Scholes model argues that the value of an option contract depends on the total variability of a stock's return. Reconcile these apparent inconsistencies in pricing theory. Should option prices depend only on the level of nondiversifiable risk? If not, explain.

26 Solving for the implied volatility of an option "by hand" is a laborious and time-consuming process of trial and error. The process requires you to choose a value for the option's implied volatility and calculate the value of the option using this guess. You compare the calculated value of the option with the value of the option observed in the market and, based on the direction and magnitude of the error, you develop another guess as to the value of the implied volatility. You repeat this process until the calculated value of the option is equal to the observed value of the option. Modern spreadsheets available on desktop computers have taken the labor out of the process of solving for implied volatility. Explain the process that would be used to solve for the implied volatility of an option using the Black–Scholes call option pricing model in a spreadsheet program.

27 We generally assume that the price of a share of stock decreases by the dollar amount of a dividend on the day when the stock goes ex-dividend, at least approximately. The ex-dividend date is the date on which the purchaser of a share of stock is not entitled to the next dividend paid by the firm. That is, the stock does not carry the right to the next dividend. Develop an arbitrage-based argument why, in a competitive market without frictions, the price of a stock must fall by the dollar amount of the dividend on the day the stock goes ex-dividend.

28 A quick check of the wire reveals that TMS is trading at $50 per share. Earlier in the day, you were having lunch with a colleague and her husband Will, the CFO of TMS. During the lunch discussion, you talked about TMS's recently introduced new products. Will made it clear that if the products are well received by the market, TMS will be trading at $60 in six months, and if the market does not respond to the products, TMS will be trading at $42 in six months. The current six-month risk-free interest rate is 6 percent. Calculate the price of a six-month European call option written on TMS with a $50 strike price. Show that the price calculated using the one-period risk-neutral pricing model, $c = (c_U \pi_U + c_D \pi_D)/R$, is the same as the price calculated using the single-period no-arbitrage binomial pricing model, $c = N*S - B*$.

29 You are paired with the president of NYB to play golf in a tournament to raise money for the local children's

hospital. After playing golf in the tournament, you learn that the president of NYB expects the price of his firm to increase by 6 percent per quarter if their new stores are successful in Seattle. If the stores are unsuccessful, he expects the stock price of NYB to decrease 5 percent per quarter. Checking Quote.com you find NYB trading at $30 per share. The current three-month risk-free interest rate is 3 percent, and you expect this rate to remain unchanged for the next six months.

A   Calculate the price of a six-month European call and put option written on NYB with $31 strike prices using the two-period risk-neutral pricing model.

B   Confirm that the put–call parity relationship generates the same price for the put option.

C   Construct the two-period stock price tree. Working backward through the stock price tree, use the one-period risk-neutral pricing model, $c = (c_U \pi_U + c_D \pi_D)/R$, to calculate the value of a one-period call option, given that the stock price has increased in period one, c_{up}. Calculate the value of a one-period call option, given that the stock price has decreased in period one, c_{down}. Calculate the current value of a one-period call option that has a value of c_{up} if the stock price increases or a value of c_{down} if the stock price decreases. (This process of valuing an option is known as the recursive valuation process.) Compare the price of the call option calculated using the recursive process with the price of the call option calculated using the two-period risk-neutral pricing model. Do the same for a put.

D   Repeat the process of part C for a call using the single-period no-arbitrage binomial pricing model, $c = N*S - B*$, to calculate the price of the single-period call option. Discuss what happens to $N*$ at each branch in the tree.

30   Both put and call options on HWP are traded. Put and call options with an exercise price of $100 expire in 90 days. HWP is trading at $95 and has an annualized standard deviation of 0.3. The three-month risk-free interest rate is 5.25 percent per annum.

A   Use a three-period binomial model to compute the value of the put and call options using the recursive procedure (single-period binomial option pricing model). Be sure to specify the values of U, D, and π_U.

B   What is the risk-neutral probability of a stock price increase in period one, period two, and period three?

31   Consider a stock, ABM, trading at a price of $70. Analysis of ABM's recent returns reveals that ABM has an annualized standard deviation of return of 0.4. The current risk-free rate of interest is 10 percent per annum.

A   What is the price of a European call written on ABM with a $75 strike price that expires in 180 days? Price the option according to the Black–Scholes model.

B   What is the price of a European put written on ABM with a $75 strike price that expires in 180 days? Price the option with the Black–Scholes model. Calculate the price of the put using put–call parity and compare it with the price calculated using the Black–Scholes model.

32   Consider a stock with a price of $72 and a standard deviation of 0.4. The stock will pay a dividend of $2 in 40 days and a second dividend of $2.50 in 130 days. The current risk-free rate of interest is 10 percent per annum.

A   What is the price of a European call written on this stock with a $70 strike price that expires in 145 days? Price the option with the Black–Scholes model.

B   What is the price of a European put written on this stock with a $70 strike price that expires in 145 days? Price the option with the Black–Scholes model.

33   Consider a stock that trades for $75. A put and a call on this stock both have an exercise price of $70, and they expire in 145 days. The risk-free rate is 9 percent per annum, and the standard deviation of the stock is 0.35. Assume that the stock pays a continuous dividend of 4 percent.

A   What, according to the Merton model, is the price of a European call written on this stock?

B   What, according to the Merton model, is the price of a European put written on this stock?

34   Your broker has just told you about TXF. He describes the firm as the real innovator in the entertainment industry. You search the web and discover that TXF has both put and call options trading on the exchange. Put and call options with an exercise price of $70 expire in 145 days. TXF is currently trading at $75, and has an annualized standard deviation of 0.35. The three-month risk-free interest rate is 9 percent per annum. A quick, back-of-the-envelope calculation

reveals that TXF is paying dividends at a continuous rate of 4 percent.

A   Use a four-period binomial model to compute the value of both the put and call options using the recursive procedure (single-period binomial option pricing model).

B   Compare the values of the put and call options calculated in this problem with the values of the put and call options calculated using then Merton model. Explain the source of the differences in the calculated values of the options.

35   CSM is trading at $78 and has an annualized standard deviation of return of 30 percent. CSM is expected to pay a dividend equal to 3 percent of the value of its stock price in 70 days. The current risk-free rate of interest is 7 percent per annum. Options written on this stock have an exercise price of $80 and expire in 120 days.

A   Using a four-period binomial model, calculate the value of a European put option written on CSM using the recursive procedure (single-period binomial option pricing model).

B   Using a four-period binomial model, calculate the value of a European call option written on CSM using the recursive procedure (single-period binomial option pricing model).

36   One year later than the time of the previous exercise, the management of CSM announces that they are changing their dividend policy. CSM will now pay a fixed dollar dividend each quarter. CSM's management declares that the payout for the current year will be $6.00 to be paid equally each quarter. CSM now trades at $85. However, the firm's risk has increased. CSM's annualized standard deviation of return is now 40 percent. CSM will pay the first quarterly dividend in 10 days with the second quarterly dividend coming 90 days after the first dividend. The current risk-free rate of interest is 5.5 percent per annum. Options written on CSM have an exercise price of $80 and expire in 120 days.

A   Using a four-period binomial model, calculate the value of a European put option written on CSM using the recursive procedure (single-period binomial option pricing model).

B   Using a four-period binomial model, calculate the value of a European call option written on CSM using the recursive procedure (single-period binomial option pricing model).

37   Consider the following data, which are used in all the various parts of this exercise:

Today's date:	Friday, December 5, 2006
Option's expiration date:	January 16, 2007
Treasury bill yields:	Bid: 5.09 percent
	Ask: 5.05 percent

Date	HCJ closing price
October 22, 2006	135.6875
October 23, 2006	135.6250
October 24, 2006	135.3750
October 27, 2006	128.7500
October 28, 2006	133.3750
October 29, 2006	131.1250
October 30, 2006	128.6250
October 31, 2006	130.0000
November 3, 2006	134.1250
November 4, 2006	134.2500
November 5, 2006	133.5625
November 6, 2006	132.0625
November 7, 2006	131.5625
November 10, 2006	130.1875
November 11, 2006	130.6250
November 12, 2006	129.1875
November 13, 2006	131.5625
November 14, 2006	133.3125
November 17, 2006	134.8750
November 18, 2006	134.0000
November 19, 2006	135.0625
November 20, 2006	136.8750
November 21, 2006	137.8750
November 24, 2006	135.5000
November 25, 2006	139.0000
November 26, 2006	141.5625
November 28, 2006	141.5000
December 1, 2006	143.8125
December 2, 2006	142.2500
December 3, 2006	144.6875
December 4, 2006	142.5625

The calculations required to solve these problems can be done in a spreadsheet, or by hand, for the masochist.

A   Determine the number of days until the January HCJ options expire.

B   Determine the continuously compounded interest rate on the Treasury bill.

C   Calculate the annualized standard deviation of return on HCJ's stock using the time series of HCJ stock returns. Assume that there are 252 trading days in a typical year.

D Using the Black–Scholes option pricing model, calculate the current price of the January 140 call and put options written on HCJ. The stock price is 143.125.

E Use the following information, as of December 4, to calculate the implied standard deviations for the January 135 and 145 HCJ call options.

Stock price	142.5625	142.5625
Exercise price	135	145
Days until expiration	43	43
Risk-free rate	5.15%	5.15%
Call price	$12.00	$4.75

F Use the equally weighted average of the implied standard deviation on the January 135 and 145

call options in the Black–Scholes option pricing model to calculate the current price on the January 140 call and put options. Compare the option prices calculated using the historical volatility and the implied volatility.

G Assume that stock prices follow a random walk with a drift. Use the weighted average of the implied volatilities on the January 135 and 145 call options and the continuously compounded return on the Treasury bill calculated in part B above to calculate the parameters in a binomial process, $U = e^{\sigma \sqrt{\Delta t}}$, $D = 1/U$, and $\pi_U = e^{r \Delta t} - D/U - D$. Use a four-period binomial model to calculate the value of the January 140 call and put options written on HCJ. Compare the option prices calculated using the binomial model with option prices calculated using the Black–Scholes model. Explain the source of the differences in the option prices.

Notes

1   A risk-neutral investor considers only the expected payoffs from an investment. For such an investor, the risk associated with the investment is not important. Thus, a risk-neutral investor would be indifferent between an investment with a certain payoff of $50 or an investment with a 50 percent probability of paying $100 and a 50 percent probability of paying zero.

2   The development of the binomial model stems from two seminal articles: R. Rendleman and B. Bartter, "Two-State Option Pricing," *Journal of Finance*, 34, December 1979, pp. 1093–110, and J. Cox, S. Ross, and M. Rubinstein, "Option Pricing: A Simplified Approach," *Journal of Financial Economics*, 7, September 1979, pp. 229–63. J. Cox and M. Rubinstein develop and discuss the binomial model in their book *Option Pricing*, Englewood, Cliffs, NJ: Prentice-Hall, 1973, and their paper "A Survey of Alternative Option Pricing Models," which appears in M. Brenner (ed.), *Option Pricing*, Lexington: D. C. Heath, 1983, pp. 3–33.

3   Not every one of these stock price outcomes will be unique. Even in the two-period model, we saw that *UDS = DUS*. Strictly speaking, with 20 periods, there are more than 1 million stock price paths.

4   For further details, see Sugato Chakravarty, Huseyin Gulen, and Steward Mayhew, "Informed Trading in Stock and Option Markets," *Journal of Finance*, 59:3, June 2003, pp. 1235–58.

5   To this point, we have considered the binomial model in some detail, and we have considered the

log-normal model of stock prices. In essence, each different assumption about stock price movements leads to a different class of option pricing models. For instance, we have already observed that assuming stock prices can either rise or fall by a given amount in a period leads to the binomial model. The log-normal assumption that we have just been considering assumes that the stock price path is continuous. In other words, for the stock price to go from $100 to $110, the price must pass through every value between the two. Another entire class of assumptions about stock price movements assumes that the stock price follows a jump process—the stock price jumps from one price to another without taking on each of the intervening values. A quick test to distinguish these two models is to determine whether the stock price path can be drawn without lifting pen from paper. If so, then the stock price path is continuous. The following papers analyze option pricing under alternative assumptions about stock price movements: J. Cox and S. Ross, "The Valuation of Options for Alternative Stochastic Processes," *Journal of Financial Economics*, 3, January–March 1976, pp. 145–66; R. Merton, "Option Pricing When Underlying Stock Returns Are Discontinuous," *Journal of Financial Economics*, 3, January–March 1976, pp. 125–44; F. Page and A. Saunders, "A General Derivation of the Jump Process Option Pricing Formula," *Journal of Financial and Quantitative Analysis*, 21:4, December 1986, pp. 437–46; C. Ball and W. Torous, "On

Jumps in Common Stock Prices and Their Impact on Call Option Pricing," *Journal of Finance*, 40:1, March 1985, pp. 155–73; and E. Omberg, "Efficient Discrete Time Jump Process Models in Option Pricing," *Journal of Financial and Quantitative Analysis*, 23:2, June 1988, pp. 161–74.

6   F. Black and M. Scholes, "The Pricing of Options and Corporate Liabilities," *Journal of Political Economy*, May 1973, pp. 637–59, provide the classic statement of the model. In his paper "Fact and Fantasy in the Use of Options," *Financial Analysts Journal*, 31:4, May/June, 1975, pp. 36–41 and 61–72, Fischer Black develops many of the same ideas in a more intuitive manner. More recently, Fischer Black has told the story of how Myron Scholes and he discovered the option pricing formula. See F. Black, "How We Came Up with the Option Formula," *Journal of Portfolio Management*, Winter 1989, pp. 4–8.

7   In imperfect markets, there may not be a single interest rate, but traders may face a borrowing rate and a lending rate. J. Gilster and W. Lee consider this possibility in their paper "The Effects of Transaction Costs and Different Borrowing and Lending Rates on the Option Pricing Model: A Note," *Journal of Finance*, 39:4, September 1984, pp. 1215–21. They also consider transaction costs and show that considering both imperfections in the debt market and transaction costs results in two offsetting influences. As such, they conclude, neither has a strong effect on the estimation of the option price, and Black–Scholes option prices conform well to actual prices observed in the market. Thus, neither market imperfection is too important because the two imperfections tend to cancel each other.

8   Of course, it is possible that the stock volatility could change over the life of the option, but shifting volatilities present difficulties in finding an option pricing model. J. Hull and A. White, "The Pricing of Options on Assets with Stochastic Volatilities," *Journal of Finance*, 42:2, June 1987, pp. 281–300, address this issue. While Hull and White acknowledge that no formula for an option price assuming changing volatility has been found, they develop techniques for approximating the value of an option with changing volatility. In doing so, they assume that changes in volatility are correlated with changes in the stock price. This problem has also been studied by L. Scott, "Option Pricing When the Variance Changes Randomly: Theory, Estimation, and an Application," *Journal of Financial and Quantitative Analysis*, 22:4, December 1987, pp. 419–38. Scott uses simulation techniques to approximate option prices, but concedes that no formula for an option price

under shifting volatilities has been found. Finally, James Wiggins explores this problem as well in his paper "Option Values Under Stochastic Volatility: Theory and Empirical Estimates," *Journal of Financial Economics*, 19:2, December 1987, pp. 351–72. He also acknowledges that an actual formula for the price of an option under shifting volatilities is lacking. Wiggins applies a numerical estimation technique to develop estimates of option prices assuming that volatility follows a continuous process. Under this assumption, Wiggins is able to compute estimated option prices.

9   There is a third potentially useful method that we do not consider in this book. M. Parkinson, "The Random Walk Problem: Extreme Value Method for Estimating the Variance of the Displacement," *Journal of Business*, 53, January 1980, pp. 61–5, showed that focusing on high and low prices for a few days could give as good an estimate as using historical data for five times as many days. His model assumes that stock prices are distributed log-normally. Compared with the use of historical data on the closing price for a given day, Parkinson's method uses both the high and low prices for the day. This method would allow a good estimate from more recent historical data than simply focusing on the history of closing prices. M. Garman and M. Klass, "On the Estimation of Security Price Volatilities from Historical Data," *Journal of Business*, 53:1, 1980, pp. 67–78, pointed out some difficulties with Parkinson's approach. First, his method is very sensitive to any errors in the reported high and low prices. Further, if trading during the day is sporadic, Parkinson's method will generate biased estimates of volatility. In particular, with discontinuities in the trading, the reported high will almost certainly be lower than the high that would have been observed with continuous trading. Similarly, the reported low will be higher than the value that would have been achieved under continuous trading. Garman and Klass also show how to improve Parkinson's type of estimate.

10   Similarly, assume that we estimate the standard deviation with weekly data. We would convert this raw data to annualized data by multiplying the weekly standard deviation times the square root of 52. Similarly, if we begin with monthly data, we annualize our monthly standard deviation by multiplying it times the square root of 12.

11   In principle, we can take any five of the values as given and solve for the sixth. For example, Menachem Brenner and Dan Galai, "Implied Interest Rates," *Journal of Business*, 59, July 1986, pp. 493–507, find that interest rates implied in the options market correspond to other short-term rates of interest.

These implied rates are nearer to the borrowing rate than to the lending rate. Further, in situations where early exercise is imminent, the interest rates implied in the option markets can differ widely from short-term rates on other instruments. Steve Swidler takes this approach a step further in his paper "Simultaneous Option Prices and an Implied Risk-Free Rate of Interest: A Test of the Black–Scholes Model," *Journal of Economics and Business*, 38:2, May 1986, pp. 155–64. Swidler uses two options, which allow him to estimate two parameters simultaneously— two equations in two unknowns. Swidler estimates the implied interest and the implied standard deviation. Although the standard deviation can differ from stock to stock, there should be a common interest rate for all options on a given date. For most of the stocks he examines, Swidler finds that a single interest rate can be found. Accordingly, he regards his evidence as supporting the reasonableness of the Black–Scholes model.

12 For a discussion of these weighting techniques, see H. A. Latane and R. J. Rendleman, Jr., "Standard Deviations of Stock Price Ratios Implied in Option Prices," *Journal of Finance*, 31, 1976, pp. 369–82; D. P. Chiras and S. Manaster, "The Information Content of Option Prices and a Test of Market Efficiency," *Journal of Financial Economics*, 6, 1978, pp. 213–34; and R. E. Whaley, "Valuation of American Call Options on Dividend Paying Stocks: Empirical Tests," *Journal of Financial Economics*, 10, 1982, pp. 29–58. In his paper, Stan Beckers, "Standard Deviations Implied in Option Prices as Predictors of Future Stock Price Variability," *Journal of Banking and Finance*, 5, 1981, pp. 363–82, concludes that using the option with the highest sensitivity to the standard deviation provides the best estimate of future volatility. For a review of the literature on implied volatility, see Stewart Mayhew, "Implied Volatility," *Financial Analysts Journal*, 51:4, July/August 1995, pp. 8–20.

13 **OPTION!** searches for the correct standard deviation in a way similar to the sequence of standard deviations and prices shown here. However, it uses a somewhat more sophisticated procedure for choosing the next standard deviation to try.

14 In fact, considerable research shows that the stock price falls when a stock goes ex-dividend, but the drop in the stock price does not equal the full amount of the dividend. In this text, we make the simplifying assumption that the stock price falls by the amount of the dividend. Alternatively, the reader may regard the dividend as being equal to the amount

of the fall in the stock price occasioned by the dividend payment.

15 This is not the same as capital delta, Δ, which stands for the sensitivity of the call option price to a change in the stock price.

16 F. Black and M. Scholes, "The Valuation of Option Contracts and a Test of Market Efficiency," *Journal of Finance*, 27:2, 1972, pp. 399–417.

17 D. Galai, "Tests of Market Efficiency of the Chicago Board Options Exchange," *Journal of Business*, 50:2, April 1977, pp. 167–97, and "Empirical Tests of Boundary Conditions for CBOE Options," *Journal of Financial Economics*, 6:2/3, June–September 1978, pp. 182–211.

18 M. Bhattacharya, "Transaction Data Tests on the Efficiency of the Chicago Board Options Exchange," *Journal of Financial Economics*, 12:2, 1983, pp. 161–85.

19 J. D. MacBeth and L. J. Merville, "An Empirical Examination of the Black–Scholes Call Option Pricing Model," *Journal of Finance*, 34:5, 1979, pp. 1173–86.

20 M. Rubinstein, "Nonparametric Tests of Alternative Option Pricing Models Using All Reported Trades and Quotes on the 30 Most Active CBOE Option Classes from August 23, 1976 through August 31, 1978," *Journal of Finance*, 40:2, 1985, pp. 455–80. The other models tested were extensions of the Black–Scholes model based on changing assumptions about how stock prices move. For instance, they included option models based on the assumption that stock prices jump from one price to another, rather than moving continuously through all intervening prices as the stock price moves from one price to another. Rubinstein tested the following models: the Black–Scholes model, the jump model, the mixed diffusion jump model, the constant elasticity of variance model, and the displaced diffusion model.

21 J. H. Anthony, "The Interrelation of Stock and Options Market Trading-Volume Data," *Journal of Finance*, 43:4, September 1988, pp. 949–64.

22 Option prices may react before stock prices due to the trading preferences of informed traders. We have already seen that option markets often offer lower transaction costs than the market for the underlying good. For traders with good information, the options market may be the preferred market to exploit their information. On this scenario, we would expect to see option prices and volume change before stock prices and volume. The trading of the informed traders would move option prices, and the arbitrage linkages between options and stocks would lead to an adjustment of the corresponding stock prices.

14

Option Sensitivities and Option Hedging

Overview

Chapter 13 developed the principles of pricing for European options. There, we analyzed option pricing within the framework of the binomial model and extended the discussion to encompass the Black–Scholes model, which gives a closed-form solution for the price of a European option on a nondividend stock. We also considered the Merton model, which provides a solution for the price of a European option on a stock paying a continuous dividend.

In this chapter, we continue our exploration of these models by focusing on the response of option prices to the factors that determine the price. Specifically, we noted in Chapter 13 that the price of a European option depends on the price of the underlying stock, the exercise price, the interest rate, the volatility of the underlying stock, and the time until expiration. This chapter analyzes the sensitivity of option prices to these factors and shows how a knowledge of these relationships can direct trading strategies and can improve option hedging techniques.

With OPTION!, we can compute all of the sensitivity measures that we consider in this chapter. Also, OPTION! can graph the response of the option price to the different factors.

Option sensitivities in the Merton and Black–Scholes models

Throughout this chapter, we focus on the Merton model (given in Equations 13.17 and 13.18) and the sensitivity of option prices in this model to the underlying factors. This approach embraces the Black–Scholes model (presented in Equations 13.13–13.15), as we may regard the Merton model simply as the Black–Scholes model extended to account for stocks that pay continuous dividends. As we saw in Chapter 13, the Merton model simplifies to the Black–Scholes model if we assume that the underlying stock pays no dividends. Similarly, the sensitivities of option prices in the Merton model reduce to those for the Black–Scholes model if we assume that the underlying stock pays no dividends.

The option price sensitivities that we consider in this chapter all derive from calculus. For example, the sensitivity of the option price with respect to the stock price is simply the first derivative of the option pricing formula with respect to the stock price. For readers unfamiliar with calculus, we illustrate this basic idea in two ways. The first derivative of the call price with respect to the stock price is just the change in the call price for a change in the stock price:

$$\frac{\Delta c}{\Delta S}$$

This change in the call price is measured for an extremely small change in the stock price. In fact, in terms of calculus, the change in the call price is measured for an infinitesimal

Table 14.1   Call prices for various stock prices

Call price	Stock price	$N(d_1)$
$9.1111	$98.00	0.5780
9.4024	98.50	0.5874
9.6984	99.00	0.5967
9.9991	99.50	0.6060
10.1512	99.75	0.6105
10.3044	100.00	0.6151
10.3660	100.10	0.6169
10.4587	100.25	0.6196
10.6142	100.50	0.6241
10.9284	101.00	0.6330
11.2472	101.50	0.6418
11.5702	102.00	0.6505

change in the stock price. As a second illustration, consider a European call option on a stock priced at $100 with a standard deviation of 0.3. The option expires in 180 days, has a strike price of $100, and the current risk-free rate of interest is 8 percent. Table 14.1 shows the value of this call for stock prices in the neighborhood of $100. It also shows the value of $N(d_1)$ computed at each price. Consider a change in the stock price from $100.00 to $102.00. For this change of $2.00 in the stock price, the call price changes from $10.3044 to $11.5702. Therefore,

$$\frac{\Delta c}{\Delta S} = \frac{1.2658}{2.00} = 0.6329$$

Next, consider a change in the stock price from $100.00 to $100.10. In this case, the call price changes from $10.3044 to $10.3660, giving the following:

$$\frac{\Delta c}{\Delta S} = \frac{0.0616}{0.10} = 0.6160$$

For these two cases, we now compare the relative change in call prices to $N(d_1)$. For a stock price of $100.00, $N(d_1) = 0.6151$, and our $\Delta c/\Delta S$ term has a value in that neighborhood. We also note that for a $2.00 stock price change, $\Delta c/\Delta S$ is 0.6329, but for a $0.10 change, $\Delta c/\Delta S$ = 0.6160. As the change becomes smaller, the value for $\Delta c/\Delta S$ approaches the value of $N(d_1)$ for a stock price of $100.00, which is 0.6151. For an infinitesimally small change in the stock price, the change in the value of the call option will exactly equal $N(d_1)$. In fact, $N(d_1)$ is the first derivative of the call price with respect to the stock price for a nondividend stock. The line for the call in Figure 14.1 shows how the value of our example option changes as a function of the stock price. The straight-line tangent to the option price curve in the left-hand panel of Figure 14.1 shows the instantaneous rate of change in the call price for a change in the stock price. The slope of this straight line is the first derivative of the call price with respect to the stock price. As the figure shows, the straight line indicates the slope of the call price curve at a stock price of $100.00, which is 0.6151.

Figure 14.1   Call and put prices as a function of the stock price

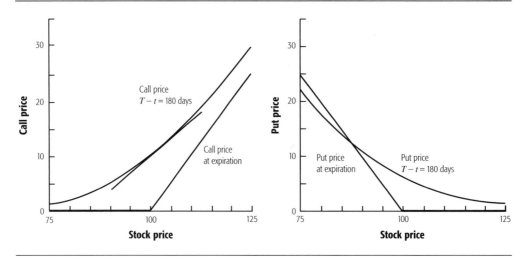

Note: $X = \$100$; $\sigma = 0.3$; $r = 0.08$; $T - t = 180$ days.

Table 14.2   Call sensitivities for the Merton model

Name	Sensitivity
DELTA$_c$	$\dfrac{\partial c}{\partial S} = e^{-\delta(T-t)}N(d_1^M)$
THETA$_c$	$-\dfrac{\partial c}{\partial (T-t)} = -\dfrac{SN'(d_1^M)\sigma e^{-\delta(T-t)}}{2\sqrt{T-t}} + \delta SN(d_1^M)e^{-\delta(T-t)} - rXe^{-r(T-t)}N(d_2^M)$
VEGA$_c$	$\dfrac{\partial c}{\partial \sigma} = S\sqrt{T-t}\,N'(d_1^M)e^{-\delta(T-t)}$
RHO$_c$	$\dfrac{\partial c}{\partial r} = X(T-t)e^{-r(T-t)}N(d_2^M)$
GAMMA$_c$	$\dfrac{\partial \text{DELTA}_c}{\partial S} = \dfrac{\partial^2 c}{\partial S^2} = \dfrac{N'(d_1^M)e^{-\delta(T-t)}}{S\sigma\sqrt{T-t}}$

Note: $N'(d_1^M) = \dfrac{1}{\sqrt{2\pi}}e^{-0.5(d^M)^2}$.

All of the sensitivity measures we consider in this chapter are similarly conceived and derived. They all derive from calculus, and they all express the sensitivity of an option price to a change in one of the underlying parameters. In the common calculus notation for our example, the first derivative of the call price with respect to the stock price is denoted as $\partial c/\partial S$. Table 14.2 presents the standard sensitivities used in option analysis for the Merton model as it applies to

Table 14.3 Put sensitivities for the Merton model

Name	Sensitivity
DELTA$_P$	$\dfrac{\partial p}{\partial S} = e^{-\delta(T-t)}[N(d_1^M) - 1]$
THETA$_P$	$-\dfrac{\partial p}{\partial(T-t)} = -\dfrac{SN'(d_1^M)\sigma e^{-\delta(T-t)}}{2\sqrt{T-t}} - \delta SN(-d_1^M)e^{-\delta(T-t)} + rXe^{-r(T-t)}N(-d_2^M)$
VEGA$_P$	$\dfrac{\partial p}{\partial\sigma} = S\sqrt{T-t}\,N'(d_1^M)e^{-\delta(T-t)}$
RHO$_P$	$\dfrac{\partial p}{\partial r} = -X(T-t)e^{-r(T-t)}N(-d_2^M)$
GAMMA$_P$	$\dfrac{\partial\text{DELTA}_p}{\partial S} = \dfrac{\partial^2 p}{\partial S^2} = \dfrac{N'(d_1^M)e^{-\delta(T-t)}}{S\sigma\sqrt{T-t}}$

Note: $N'(d_1^M) = \dfrac{1}{\sqrt{2\pi}}e^{-0.5(d_1^M)^2}$.

Table 14.4 Call sensitivities for the Black–Scholes model

Name	Sensitivity
DELTA$_c$	$\dfrac{\partial c}{\partial S} = N(d_1)$
THETA$_c$	$-\dfrac{\partial c}{\partial(T-t)} = -\dfrac{SN'(d_1)\sigma}{2\sqrt{T-t}} - rXe^{-r(T-t)}N(-d_2)$
VEGA$_c$	$\dfrac{\partial c}{\partial\sigma} = S\sqrt{T-t}\,N'(d_1)$
RHO$_c$	$\dfrac{\partial c}{\partial r} = X(T-t)e^{-r(T-t)}N(d_2)$
GAMMA$_c$	$\dfrac{\partial\text{DELTA}_c}{\partial S} = \dfrac{\partial^2 c}{\partial S^2} = \dfrac{N'(d_1)}{S\sigma\sqrt{T-t}}$

Note: $N'(d_1) = \dfrac{1}{\sqrt{2\pi}}e^{-0.5(d_1)^2}$.

calls, while Table 14.3 gives the same equations for puts. (See Chapter 13 for the equations for the two models and other terms.)

As we saw in Chapter 13, the Black–Scholes model is the same as the Merton model in the special case of there being no dividends on the stock. Similarly, we can derive the sensitivities for the Black–Scholes model from those of the Merton model if we assume that the stock pays no dividends. Tables 14.4 and 14.5 parallel Tables 14.2 and 14.3 and give the sensitivities for the Black–Scholes model.

Table 14.5   Put sensitivities for the Black–Scholes model

Name	Sensitivity
DELTA$_P$	$\dfrac{\partial p}{\partial S} = N(d_1) - 1$
THETA$_P$	$-\dfrac{\partial p}{\partial (T - t)} = -\dfrac{SN'(d_1)\sigma}{2\sqrt{T - t}} + rXe^{-r(T-t)}N(-d_2)$
VEGA$_P$	$\dfrac{\partial p}{\partial \sigma} = S\sqrt{T - t}N'(d_1)$
RHO$_P$	$\dfrac{\partial p}{\partial r} = -X(T - t)e^{-r(T-t)}N(-d_2)$
GAMMA$_P$	$\dfrac{\partial \text{DELTA}_p}{\partial S} = \dfrac{\partial^2 p}{\partial S^2} = \dfrac{N'(d_1)}{S\sigma\sqrt{T - t}}$

Note: $N'(d_1) = \dfrac{1}{\sqrt{2\pi}}e^{-0.5(d_1)^2}$.

Table 14.6   Option sensitivities

	Black–Scholes model, $\delta = 0.0$		Merton model, $\delta = 0.03$	
	Call	Put	Call	Put
Option prices	$10.3044	$6.4360	$9.4209	$7.0210
DELTA	0.6151	−0.3849	0.5794	−0.4060
THETA	−12.2607	−4.5701	−10.3343	−5.5997
VEGA	26.8416	26.8416	26.9300	26.9300
RHO	25.2515	−22.1559	23.9250	−23.4823
GAMMA	0.0181	0.0181	0.0182	0.0182

Note: $S = \$100$; $X = \$100$; $r = 0.08$; $\sigma = 0.3$; $T - t = 180$ days.

Earlier, we considered a call option on a stock priced at $100 with a standard deviation of 0.3 and no dividend. The call had 180 days until expiration, and we assumed a risk-free rate of 8 percent. Table 14.6 shows all of the sensitivities for calls and puts for both the Black–Scholes model (assuming no dividend) and for the Merton model (assuming a continuous dividend of 3 percent). **OPTION!** computes all of these sensitivity measures. We now consider each of the measures in turn.

DELTA

DELTA is the first derivative of an option's price with respect to a change in the price of the stock. As such, DELTA measures the sensitivity of the option's price to changing stock prices. $DELTA_c$ is always positive, while $DELTA_p$ is always negative. Thus, the value of a call increases with a stock price increase, while the value of a put decreases if the stock price increases. In Table 14.6 for the options on a nondividend stock, $DELTA_c = 0.6151$ and $DELTA_p = -0.3849$. These sensitivities can be interpreted as follows. If the stock price rises by $1, the price of the call will rise by approximately $0.6151, while the price of the put will fall by about $0.3849.

These estimations of the change in the option price are only approximate. If the change in the stock price were infinitesimal, the DELTAs would give us an exact price change for the options. Because a $1 change in the stock price is discrete, our computed prices remain estimates. If the stock price is $101, we have $c = 10.9284 and $p = 6.0601. Thus, the call price increases by $0.6240 (compared to the predicted $0.6151) and the put price falls by $0.3759 (compared to the predicted fall of $0.3849).

The right-hand panel of Figure 14.1 shows how the put price of our example varies with the stock price. Notice that the price of a European put can be less than its intrinsic value, as we discussed in Chapter 13. As the two panels of Figure 14.1 indicate, option prices are extremely dependent upon stock prices, and the price of the underlying stock is the key determinant of an option price. Therefore, DELTA is the most important of all of the sensitivity measures that we consider in this chapter.

DELTA-neutral positions

Consider a portfolio, P, of a short position of one European call on a nondividend stock combined with a long position of DELTA units of the stock. The portfolio would have the following value:

$$P = -c + N(d_1)S \qquad (14.1)$$

Continuing to use our sample options of Table 14.6, the cost of the portfolio, assuming a current stock price of $100.00, would be

$$P = -c + N(d_1)S = -$10.3044 + 0.6151 \times $100.00 = $51.2056$$

If the stock price were to suddenly change to $100.10, the portfolio's value would be

$$P = -c + N(d_1)S = -$10.3660 + 0.6151 \times $100.10 = $51.2055$$

Thus, the value of the portfolio would change by only $0.0001 for a $0.10 change in the stock price. If the change in the stock price were infinitesimal, the price of the portfolio would not change at all. If the change in the stock price were larger, the change in the value of the portfolio would be larger, but it would still be quite small relative to the change in the stock price. For example, if the stock price rose from $100 to $110, the portfolio's value would be

$$P = -c + N(d_1)S = -$17.2821 + 0.6151 \times $110.00 = $50.3789$$

In this case, a change of $10 in the stock price caused a change of $0.8267 in the value of the portfolio. Figure 14.2 shows how the value of this portfolio changes for changes in the stock price.

A portfolio such as the one we are considering, and described by Equation 14.1, is known as a **DELTA-neutral portfolio**. It is DELTA-neutral because an infinitesimal change in the price

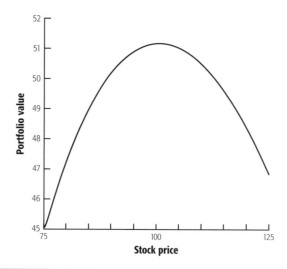

Figure 14.2   The value of a DELTA-neutral portfolio as a function of the stock price (portfolio includes −1 call and 0.6151 shares)

Note: $X = \$100$; $\sigma = 0.3$; $r = 0.08$; $T - t = 180$ days.

of the stock does not affect the price of the portfolio. Put another way, we could say that the DELTA of this portfolio is zero; the value of the portfolio is insensitive to the value of the stock.

As we saw in Chapter 13, the Black–Scholes model assumes that the stock price changes continuously. Imagine now that we can trade shares and options continuously as the stock price changes. We see from the equation for DELTA in Table 14.2 that DELTA changes when the stock price changes. (DELTA also changes when other factors, such as the standard deviation and the time remaining until the option expires, change as well.) Assume now that we trade continuously to rebalance our portfolio as the stock price changes. In rebalancing, we seek to maintain the condition of Equation 14.1. In particular, we trade continuously to maintain our portfolio as a DELTA-neutral portfolio. By trading continuously, the portfolio is DELTA-neutral at every instant and never loses or gains value in response to changes in the stock price. By following this strategy of continuously rebalancing our portfolio, we know that it has zero price risk as a function of changing stock prices. In effect, by continuously rebalancing, we create a risk-free portfolio. Further, if the portfolio is risk-free, it must earn the risk-free rate of return.

This is the key intuition of the Black–Scholes model. Black and Scholes realized that continuous trading could maintain a DELTA-neutral portfolio as a risk-free portfolio earning the risk-free rate. This was an important step that enabled them to find a solution for their option pricing model.

As a practical matter, creating a DELTA-neutral portfolio in the manner described appears to be a difficult way of buying a risk-free security. Why not just buy a Treasury bill? Later in this chapter, we explore the extremely valuable practical consequences of using DELTA oriented hedging technologies. At the present, however, we can easily see how the idea of a DELTA-neutral portfolio can be very useful in adjusting the riskiness of a stock trading strategy.

Figure 14.3   The value of a DELTA-neutral portfolio as a function of the stock price (one portfolio includes −1 call and 0.6151 shares, and one portfolio includes −0.5 calls and 0.6151 shares)

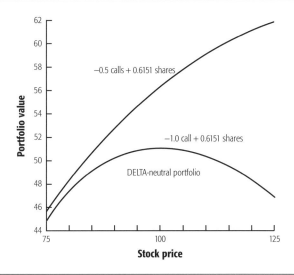

Note: $X = \$100$; $\sigma = 0.3$; $r = 0.08$; $T - t = 180$ days.

For the call option and the stock that we have been considering, assume that an outright investment in the stock is too risky. An investor in this position could use the idea of DELTA-neutrality to shape the risk characteristics of the investment to her particular needs. For example, assume that a trader holds a portfolio as follows:

$$-0.5c + N(d_1)S = -0.5 \times \$10.3044 + 0.6151 \times \$100.00 = \$56.3578$$

This portfolio is similar to the DELTA-neutral portfolio that we considered earlier, except instead of selling a call, the investor sells only one-half of a call. In considering the DELTA-neutral portfolio, we saw that selling the call in conjunction with investing in the stock gave a risk-free portfolio. Now, by selling one-half of a call, the investor diminishes the risk, but does not totally eliminate it. Figure 14.3 shows how the value of the DELTA-neutral portfolio and this new portfolio will vary as the stock price changes. This new portfolio has some risk exposure to changing stock prices, but it is much less risky than the stock itself. Later in this chapter, we consider a variety of strategies for using options to accept, avoid, or transform various investment risks.

As we noted earlier, DELTA changes as the stock price and other parameters of the option pricing model change. For our continuing example, Figure 14.4 shows how the DELTAs of the call and put vary with changing stock prices. DELTA_c tends to approach 1.0 when the call option is deep-in-the-money. Similarly, when the call is deep-out-of-the-money, DELTA_c approaches zero. When the stock price is near the exercise price, DELTA_c is most sensitive to a change in the stock price. For DELTA_p, similar principles apply. DELTA_c is always greater than zero, while DELTA_p is always less than zero. The DELTA of a deep-in-the-money put approaches −1, while the DELTA of a deep-out-of-the-money put approaches zero. **OPTION!** can make graphs similar to those of Figure 14.4.

Figure 14.4   Call and put DELTAs as a function of the stock price

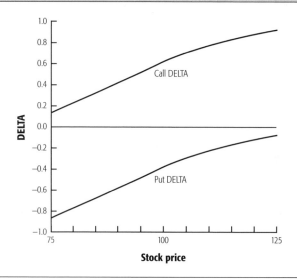

Note: $X = \$100$; $\sigma = 0.3$; $r = 0.08$; $T - t = 180$ days.

An Option's Beta

Although the "Greeks" describe the sensitivity of option prices to changes in the underlying variables influencing option price, some traders are interested in the relationship between an individual equity option and changes in the overall market. In other words, these traders are interested in the systematic risk of the option, best characterized by another Greek letter, beta. An call option's beta is equal to the option's elasticity times the stock's beta:

$$\beta_c = \eta \beta S$$

where η is the option's elasticity, defined as

$$\eta = (\delta c/\delta S)S/c = N(d_1)(S/c)$$

in which $N(d_1)$ is the call's DELTA.

For example, take the call option for the nondividend-paying stock shown in Table 14.6. The DELTA of this option is 0.6151, the call price is $10.3044, and the underlying stock price is given as $100 per share. Using this information to evaluate the call's elasticity yields the following:

$$\eta = 0.6151 \times (100/10.3044) = 5.9693$$

If the stock's beta is 1.30, then the call's beta can be calculated as

$$\beta_c = \eta \beta S = 5.9693 \times 1.30 = 7.7601$$

Consistent with intuition on the riskiness of calls, the call's beta will always be greater than the stock's beta. Notice also that the option's beta changes over the life of the option even if the stock's beta remains constant.

THETA

If the stock price and all other parameters of the option pricing model remain constant, the price of options will still change with the passage of time. THETA is the negative of the first derivative of the option price with respect to the time remaining until expiration. Depending upon the circumstances, $THETA_c$ and $THETA_p$ can be greater or less than zero. However, $THETA_c$ and $THETA_p$ are generally less than zero.[1]

The tendency for option prices to change due merely to the passage of time is known as **time decay**. To see how the passage of time affects option prices, consider our continuing example of call and put options with $S = \$100$, $X = \$100$, $\sigma = 0.3$, $r = 0.08$, and $T - t = 180$ days. For these values, we noted earlier that $c = \$10.30$ and $p = \$6.44$. For these values, $THETA_c = -12.2607$, and $THETA_p = -4.5701$. These values of THETA are expressed in terms of years. Suppose that the time to expiration changes by 0.1 years (37 days) from 180 days until expiration to 143 days. Recalling that THETA is the negative of the first derivative of the option price with respect to time until expiration, we would expect the call and put prices to be $c = \$10.30 + 0.1 \times (-12.2607) = \$9.07$, and $p = \$6.44 + 0.1 \times (-4.5701) = \$5.98$. Recalling that all of these computed prices are approximations, the actual prices would be $c = \$9.01$ and $p = \$5.92$.

If all parameters remain constant, except the expiration date draws nearer, both options will have to fall in value. Both the call and the put will be worthless at expiration, because $S = X = \$100$. Therefore, the call and put options will lose their entire value through time decay. Figure 14.5 illustrates time decay for our sample options.

$THETA_c$ and $THETA_p$ both vary with changing stock prices and with the passage of time. For the options of our continuing example, Figure 14.6 shows how the call and put THETAs vary with the stock price. (Notice that the graph shows how a put that is deep-in-the-money can have a positive THETA.) $THETA_c$ and $THETA_p$ also both change with the passage of time.

Figure 14.5   Call and put prices as a function of the time until expiration

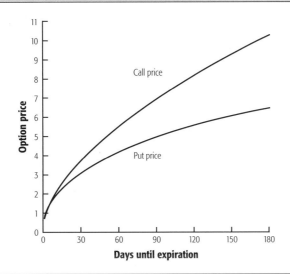

Note: $S = \$100$; $X = \$100$; $\sigma = 0.3$; $r = 0.08$.

Figure 14.6   Call and put THETAs as a function of the stock price

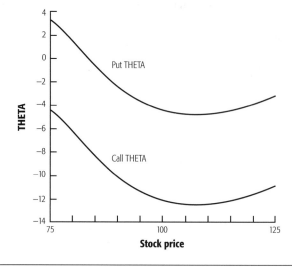

Note: $X = \$100$; $\sigma = 0.3$; $r = 0.08$; $T - t = 180$ days.

Figure 14.7   Call and put THETAs as a function of the time until expiration

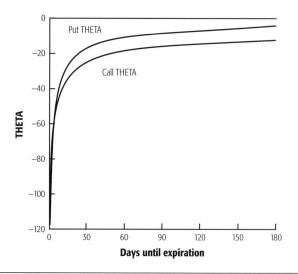

Note: $X = \$100$; $\sigma = 0.3$; $r = 0.08$.

If the stock price is near the exercise price, THETA$_c$ and THETA$_p$ will become quite negative as expiration nears, as Figure 14.7 shows. However, this is not true for options that are deep-in-the-money or deep-out-of-the-money. Figure 14.6 shows how THETA$_c$ and THETA$_p$ change in very different manners depending upon whether the options are in-the-money or out-of-the-money. For example, a European put that is in-the-money will have a positive THETA as expiration nears.

VEGA

VEGA is the first derivative of an option's price with respect to the volatility of the underlying stock. $VEGA_c$ and $VEGA_p$ are identical and are always positive. (VEGA is sometimes known as kappa, lambda, or sigma as well. We use the term VEGA throughout.)

The VEGA is an important determinant of option prices. A sudden substantive change in the standard deviation of the underlying stock can cause a dramatic change in option values. As we noted for our example options, $c = \$10.30$ and $p = \$6.44$ when $\sigma = 0.3$. If volatility were to suddenly increase by 0.2 so that $\sigma = 0.5$, we would expect new prices of $c = \$10.30 + 0.2 \times 26.8416 = \$15.67$, and $p = \$6.44 + 0.2 \times 26.8416 = \$11.81$.

The actual call and put prices with $\sigma = 0.5$ would be $c = \$15.69$ and $p = \$11.82$, causing a price increase of 52 percent for the call and 84 percent for the put. During and immediately following the Crash of 1987 (when the stock market lost 20–25 percent of its value in one day), the perceived volatility for stocks increased tremendously, causing an increase in option values. (Of course, calls generally lost value due to falling prices, and puts increased in value for the same reason.) Figure 14.8 shows how call and put prices vary with the standard deviation for our example options.

VEGA tends to be greatest for an option near-the-money. When an option is deep-in-the-money or deep-out-of-the-money, the VEGA is low and can approach zero. Figure 14.9 shows how VEGA varies with respect to the stock price for the call and put of our continuing example. Because the two example options are at-the-money, VEGA is at its maximum. For calls or puts in-the-money or out-of-the-money, the VEGA will be lower.

Figure 14.8   Call and put prices as a function of the standard deviation

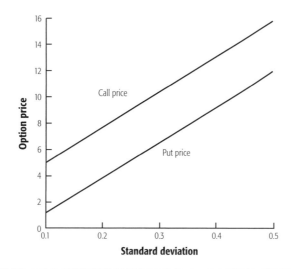

Note: $S = \$100$; $X = \$100$; $r = 0.08$; $T - t = 180$ days.

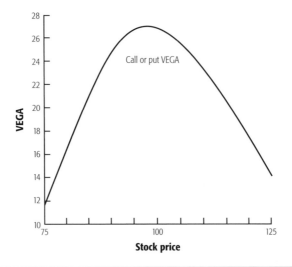

Figure 14.9 Call and put VEGA as a function of the stock price

Note: $X = \$100$; $r = 0.08$; $T - t = 180$ days.

RHO

RHO is the first derivative of an option's price with respect to the interest rate. RHO_c is always positive, while RHO_p is always negative. In general, option prices are not very sensitive to RHO. In Table 14.6, $RHO_c = 25.2515$, and $RHO_p = -22.1559$. If the interest rate were to increase by 1 percent, then the call price should increase by $0.01 \times 25.2515 = \$0.2525$, while the price of the put should fall by $0.01 \times (-22.1559) = -\$0.2216$. Figure 14.10 shows how the prices of our example options would change given varying interest rates. Large changes in the interest rate have relatively little effect on the option prices.

RHO changes as a function of both the stock price and the time until expiration. RHO_c tends to be low for an option that is deep-out-of-the-money and high for a deep-in-the-money call. RHO_c tends to be sensitive to the stock price when a call is near-the-money. For a deep-in-the-money put, RHO_p is generally low, and RHO_p is generally large for a deep-out-of-the-money put. When the put is near-the-money, RHO_p tends to be more sensitive to the stock price. Figure 14.11 illustrates the sensitivity of RHO_c and RHO_p to the stock price for the options in our continuing example.

RHO_c and RHO_p change as time passes, with both tending toward zero as expiration approaches. The interest rate affects the price of an option in conjunction with the time remaining until expiration mainly through the time value of money. If little time remains until expiration, the interest rate is relatively unimportant, and the price of an option becomes less sensitive to the interest rate. For our example options, Figure 14.12 shows how RHO_c and RHO_p tend to zero as expiration approaches.

Figure 14.10   Call and put prices as a function of the interest rate

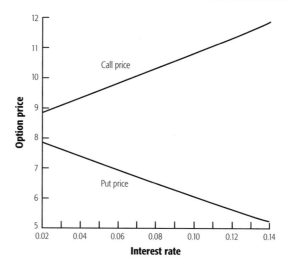

Note: $S = \$100$; $X = \$100$; $\sigma = 0.3$; $T - t = 180$ days.

Figure 14.11   Call and put RHOs as a function of the stock price

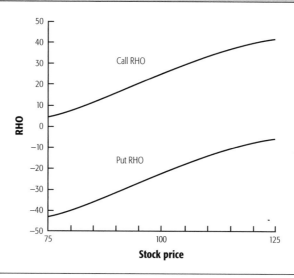

Note: $X = \$100$; $\sigma = 0.3$; $r = 0.08$; $T - t = 180$ days.

Figure 14.12   Call and put RHOs as a function of the time until expiration

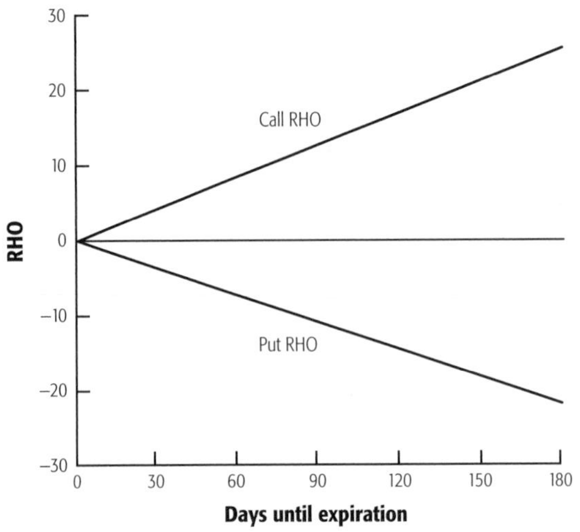

Note: $S = \$100$; $X = \$100$; $\sigma = 0.3$; $r = 0.08$.

GAMMA

Unlike the other sensitivity measures we have considered thus far, GAMMA does not measure the sensitivity of the price of an option to one of the parameters. Instead, GAMMA measures how DELTA changes with changes in the stock price. The GAMMA of a put and a call are always identical, and GAMMA can be either positive or negative. (In terms of calculus, GAMMA is the second derivative of the option price with respect to the stock price.) GAMMA is the only second-order effect that we consider, but it is an important one.

From our example computations in Table 14.6, we see that $GAMMA_c = GAMMA_p = 0.0181$. The table also shows $DELTA_c = 0.6151$, and $DELTA_p = -0.3849$. If the stock price were to increase by \$1 from \$100 to \$101, we would expect the two DELTAs to change. The new expected $DELTA_c = 0.6151 + 1 \times 0.0181 = 0.6332$, and the new expected $DELTA_p = -0.3849 + 1 \times 0.0181 = -0.3668$. With a stock price of \$101, the actual values are $DELTA_c = 0.6330$, and $DELTA_p = -0.3670$.

GAMMA tends to be large when an option is near-the-money. A large GAMMA for a given stock price simply means that the DELTA is highly sensitive to changes in the stock price around its current level. For our sample options, Figure 14.4 shows that $DELTA_c$ and $DELTA_p$ are sensitive to the stock price when the price is near the exercise price of \$100. When an option is deep-in-the-money, the DELTA is near 1.0 and is not very sensitive to changing stock prices. Because of DELTA's low sensitivity to stock prices, the GAMMA for a call or a put that is deep-in-the-money must be low. A similar principle applies for a call or a put that is deep-out-of-the-money. In such a situation, the DELTA of either a call or a put will be quite low, and it will be insensitive to changing stock prices. Due to this low sensitivity, the GAMMA will be small for either a call or a put that is deep-out-of-the-money.

Figure 14.13   GAMMA as a function of the stock price

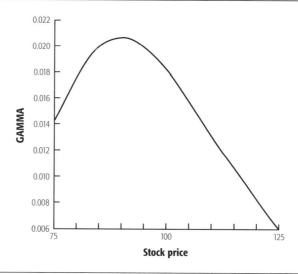

Note: $X = \$100$; $\sigma = 0.3$; $r = 0.08$; $T - t = 180$ days.

Figure 14.4 shows how $DELTA_c$ and $DELTA_p$ vary with the stock price for our sample options. GAMMA essentially measures the slope of the graphs in Figure 14.4. Because the slopes of the graphs in Figure 14.4 are near zero for calls or puts that are deep-in-the-money or deep-out-of-the-money, GAMMA must be low as well. When the calls or puts are near-the-money, the rate of change in the DELTA as a function of the stock price is high—that is, the slope of the graph in Figure 14.4 is high. Therefore, for near-the-money options, GAMMA must be large.

Figure 14.13 shows how GAMMA varies with the stock price for our sample options. The figure applies to both the put and the call, because the GAMMAs are the same for a put and call with the same underlying instrument, time to expiration, and strike price. As the figure shows, GAMMA is large when the option is near-the-money and small when the option is deep-in-the-money or when it is deep-out-of-the-money.

GAMMA also varies with the time remaining until expiration. For an option that is near-the-money, GAMMA increases as expiration approaches. This large GAMMA reflects the heightened sensitivity of the DELTA to the stock price when the option is near-the-money and expiration is near. For an option that is deep-out-of-the-money or deep-in-the-money, GAMMA will fall dramatically as expiration becomes very close. For in-the-money or out-of-the-money options, with expiration distant, the GAMMA will tend to rise as time passes. However, it is difficult to make solid generalizations about how GAMMA will change without actually calculating the effects of the passage of time. Both our example options are at-the-money, so the GAMMAs of the call and put will rise as expiration nears. Figure 14.14 shows how GAMMA varies with time remaining until expiration for options at-the-money, in-the-money, and out-of-the-money.

Positive and negative GAMMA portfolios

Earlier in this chapter, we created an example of a DELTA-neutral portfolio. For our sample call option, we saw that we could create a DELTA-neutral portfolio consisting of a long

Figure 14.14   Gamma as a function of the time until expiration

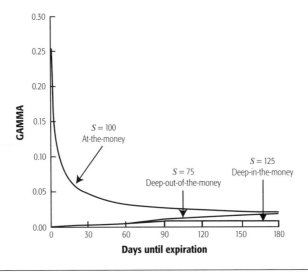

Note: $X = \$100$; $\sigma = 0.3$; $r = 0.08$; $T - t = 180$ days.

position of 0.6151 shares of the underlying stock and a short position of one call. Figure 14.2 shows how the value of this portfolio changes as the stock price changes. As the price of the stock moves away from $100, the value of the portfolio decreases.

The underlying stock has a DELTA of 1.0, which never changes. The change in the value of the stock is always 1 : 1 for changes in the value of the stock. Because the DELTA of the stock never changes, its GAMMA must be zero; the DELTA of the stock is completely insensitive to changes in the stock price. For our example call, the GAMMA is 0.0181. Because we have sold one call with a GAMMA of 0.0181 and 0.6151 shares with a GAMMA of zero, the GAMMA of this portfolio must be 2.0181. Because the portfolio has a negative GAMMA, the DELTA of the portfolio must decrease if the stock price changes.

For small changes in the stock price, we know that the price of the portfolio of −1 call and 0.6151 shares will not change, because the portfolio was constructed to be DELTA-neutral. For large changes in the stock price, however, the value of this portfolio will fall. The following data show the value of the elements of the portfolio and the total portfolio for stock prices of $90, $100, and $110:

Stock price	Call price	0.6151 Shares	Portfolio value (−1 call + 0.6151 shares)
$90	$5.12	$55.36	$50.24
100	10.30	61.51	51.21
110	17.28	67.66	50.38

The negative GAMMA of this portfolio ensures that large changes in the stock price will make the portfolio lose value. This is true whether the stock price rises or falls.

By contrast, consider a DELTA-neutral portfolio with a positive GAMMA. We can construct such a portfolio by combining our example put with the underlying stock to form a new portfolio. From Table 14.6, $p = \$6.4360$, $DELTA_p = -0.3849$, and $GAMMA_p = 0.0181$. A portfolio of one put and 0.3849 shares of stock will be DELTA-neutral, will be worth $44.926, and will have a GAMMA of 0.0181. The following table shows how the value of this positive GAMMA portfolio will vary with large changes in the stock price:

Stock price	Put price	0.3849 Shares	Portfolio value (1 put + 0.3849 shares)
$90	$11.25	$34.64	$45.89
100	6.44	38.49	44.93
110	3.41	42.34	45.75

These examples of a negative GAMMA portfolio and a positive GAMMA portfolio show the desirability of positive GAMMAs. If a trader holds a position with a positive GAMMA, large changes in the stock price will cause the portfolio value to increase. We have explored this within the context of a DELTA-neutral portfolio, but the principle holds for all portfolios.

Creating neutral portfolios

We have seen that a trader can create a DELTA-neutral portfolio from a stock and a call or from a stock and a put. In some situations, a trader might like to create a position that is neutral with respect to some other parameter, such as the THETA or VEGA of a portfolio. We now focus on stock plus option portfolios, and show how to ensure various types of neutrality for these portfolios.

We saw that a stock plus call or a stock plus put portfolio could be created as a DELTA-neutral portfolio. In general, a stock plus a single option portfolio can be made neutral with respect to just one parameter. For example, when we created the DELTA-neutral portfolios analyzed earlier, we found that the resulting portfolios were not GAMMA-neutral. A portfolio comprising a stock and a single option can never be DELTA-neutral and GAMMA-neutral unless the GAMMA of the option happens to be zero. However, we can control both the DELTA and the GAMMA of a stock plus option portfolio by creating a portfolio of a stock and two different options.

To illustrate this idea, we introduce another call option on the same underlying stock that we have been considering throughout this chapter. This call option has the same time to expiration, but its exercise price is $X = \$110$. For this call, we have $c = \$6.06$, $DELTA_c = 0.4365$, and $GAMMA_c = 0.0187$. To create a portfolio that is DELTA-neutral and GAMMA-neutral using our stock and these two calls, we create a portfolio that meets the two following conditions:

$$N_s + DELTA_s + N_1 DELTA_1 + N_2 DELTA_2 = 0$$
$$N_s + GAMMA_s + N_1 GAMMA_1 + N_2 GAMMA_2 = 0$$

where N_s, N_1, and N_2 are the number of shares, the number of the first call (with $X = \$100$), and the number of the second call (with $X = \$110$) to be held in the portfolio. We choose to create the portfolio with one share of stock, so $N_s = 1$. This leaves two equations with two unknowns, N_1 and N_2. We must choose these values to meet the two neutrality conditions.

For our example stock and options, we have the following:

$$1 \times 1 + N_1 \times 0.6151 + N_2 \times 0.4365 = 0$$
$$1 \times 0 + N_1 \times 0.0181 + N_2 \times 0.0187 = 0$$

If $N_1 = -5.1917$ and $N_2 = 5.0251$, the conditions will be met. Therefore, we create a DELTA-neutral and GAMMA-neutral portfolio by buying one share, selling 5.1917 calls with $X = \$100$, and buying 5.0251 calls with $X = \$110$. The resulting portfolio will be both DELTA-neutral and GAMMA-neutral.

This portfolio may be DELTA-neutral and GAMMA-neutral, but its value will still be sensitive to other parameters, such as the standard deviation of the underlying stock or the time until expiration. If we wanted to make the portfolio neutral with respect to DELTA, GAMMA, and VEGA, for example, we would need to add a third option to the portfolio. In general, we need to use one option for each sensitivity parameter that we want to control.

"Pin Risk" and "Getting Gamma'd"

As Figure 14.14 shows, the GAMMA for an option increases at an increasing rate as an at-the-money option approaches expiration. In practical terms, this increase in gamma means that traders face increasing GAMMA risk as the expiration date approaches and the stock price is "pinned" to the option's exercise price. Traders refer to this risk as "pin risk." Coping with pin risk is known in the trade as "getting gamma'd." Pin risk means that the value of the option is very sensitive to extremely small changes in the value of the underlying asset. As the expiration date approaches, changes in the value of the underlying asset from below to above the exercise price causes the option's DELTA to abruptly change from zero to one, meaning that the option's GAMMA is extremely large. Forming an effective hedge in the presence of pin risk can be extremely challenging, if not impossible.

Perhaps the best way illustrate pin risk is to consider a digital (or binary) call option. Such an option expires worthless if the stock finishes below the strike price and pays a fixed amount (say, $5 per share) if the stock finishes above the strike price. In other words, the option pays $5 per share to the holder of the call whether the option finishes in the money by a little bit or by a whole lot. If the stock price equals the exercise price as the call approaches expiration, even a one penny change in the stock price can tip the option's value from zero to $5 per share. Hedging such an outcome is difficult (i.e., costly) because the hedge construction must be perfect to counter the effects of even small changes in the price of the underlying.

For conventional puts and calls, pin risk poses problems for both option holders and option writers. If the option finishes in-the-money, it will most likely be exercised. But if the stock price is pinned to the option strike price as expiration approaches, neither the option holder nor the option writer can anticipate what their position will be after the option expires. For example, a trader may sell a covered call on PQR stock. Assume that the call has an exercise price of $100 per share. As expiration approaches the stock price is fluctuating between $98 and $102 per share. This means the trader has no idea whether the option will finish in-, at-, or out-of-the money. If the option finishes in-the-money and the option is called by the holder, the call writer is assigned and he delivers the 100 shares covering the call, leaving the call writer with a flat position in the stock. If the option finishes out-of-the-money and the call writer is not assigned, the trader remains long 100 shares of stock and is exposed to market risk until the market opens and the stock can be sold.

Option sensitivities and option trading strategies

Thus far in this chapter, we have seen that a trader can use a knowledge of option sensitivities to control risk. By the same token, this knowledge can be used to guide speculative trading strategies as well. By knowing the sensitivities of the various positions, a trader can create strategies to exploit certain expectations efficiently. Further, a trader should be aware of the various sensitivities of a position so she does not suffer unpleasant surprises.

In Chapter 11, we considered a wide variety of strategies, such as straddles, strangles, butterfly spreads, and condors, and we evaluated the profitability of these trades at expiration. Now, armed with the Black–Scholes model and the Merton model, we can understand how the value of these positions will behave prior to expiration. Further, given a knowledge of the sensitivities, we can analyze how a given trading strategy is likely to behave when the stock price changes, when volatility changes, or when the option approaches expiration. To explore the characteristics of option strategies, we consider the sample options shown in Table 14.7, which we use to illustrate some of the typical strategies.

The straddle

Consider a long straddle consisting of call C_2 and put P_2 from Table 14.7. The cost of this position is $16.74. If the stock price at expiration is $100, which is the common exercise price

Table 14.7 Sample options

	Calls			
	C_1 $X = \$90$ $T - t = 180$ days	C_2 $X = \$100$ $T - t = 180$ days	C_3 $X = \$110$ $T - t = 180$ days	C_4 $X = \$100$ $T - t = 90$ days
Price	16.33	10.30	6.06	6.91
DELTA	0.7860	0.6151	0.4365	0.5820
GAMMA	0.0138	0.0181	0.0187	0.0262
THETA	−11.2054	−12.2607	−11.4208	−15.8989
VEGA	20.4619	26.8416	27.6602	19.3905
RHO	30.7085	25.2515	18.5394	12.6464

	Puts			
	P_1 $X = \$90$ $T - t = 180$ days	P_2 $X = \$100$ $T - t = 180$ days	P_3 $X = \$110$ $T - t = 180$ days	P_4 $X = \$100$ $T - t = 90$ days
Price	2.85	6.44	11.80	4.95
DELTA	−0.2140	−0.3849	−0.5635	−0.4180
GAMMA	0.0138	0.0181	0.0187	0.0262
THETA	−4.2839	−4.5701	−2.9612	−8.0552
VEGA	20.4619	26.8416	27.6602	19.3905
RHO	−11.9582	−22.1559	−33.6087	−11.5295

Note: $S = \$100$; $r = 0.08$; $\sigma = 0.3$; $\delta = 0$.

Figure 14.15   The profit/loss of a straddle as a function of the stock price with various times remaining until expiration

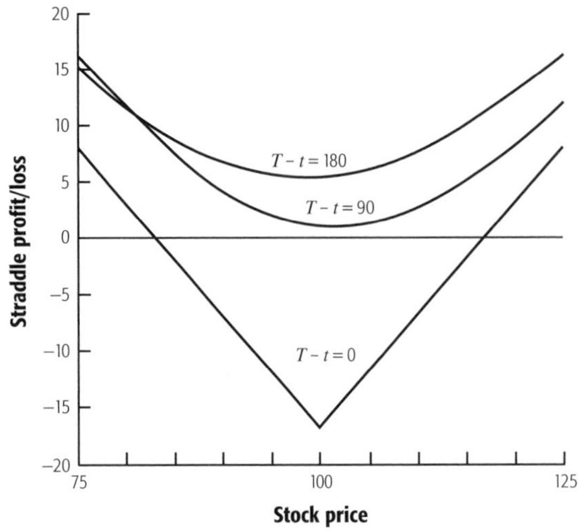

Note: $X = \$100$; $\sigma = 0.3$; $r = 0.08$.

for the two options, the position will expire worthless. At expiration, the value of the straddle will equal the intrinsic value of the call if the stock price exceeds $100, or it will equal the intrinsic value of the put if the stock price is below $100.

At the present, 180 days before expiration, the straddle has a DELTA of 0.2302, so the value of the straddle will vary directly with the stock price, but at a much reduced rate. The GAMMA of the straddle is 0.0362, so large shifts in the stock price will be beneficial. The VEGA of the straddle is 53.6832, indicating that any increase in volatility will increase the value of the position. The THETA of the straddle is −16.8308, emphasizing that the passage of time will reduce the value of the position. In fact, if the stock price remains at $100 for the 180 days that remain until expiration, the value of the straddle will decay from $16.74 to zero over this period. A single day is 0.00273973 years. Therefore, with a THETA of −16.8308, we would expect a loss in the value of the straddle from day 180 to day 179 of −$0.046, assuming the stock price remains steady at $100. While the straddle might lose only about $0.05 of its value per day due to time decay, it will decay to just $11.86 in 90 days. Figure 14.15 shows how the profit and loss from this straddle varies for 180, 90, and zero days to expiration as a function of the stock price.

Time decay works to the benefit of the seller of this straddle, reducing the potential liability each day. By the same token, the seller is exposed to volatility risk. If the volatility of the underlying stock increases, both option values will rise and the short straddle position will lose. Finally, the positive GAMMA on the straddle is unfortunate from the point of view of the seller.

The strangle

As we saw in Chapter 11, a strangle is similar to a straddle because it involves the purchase of a put and a call. Unlike a straddle, however, the strike prices of the put and call are not identical. To purchase a strangle, the trader buys a call with a lower exercise price and purchases

Figure 14.16   The profit/loss of two strangles as a function of the stock price

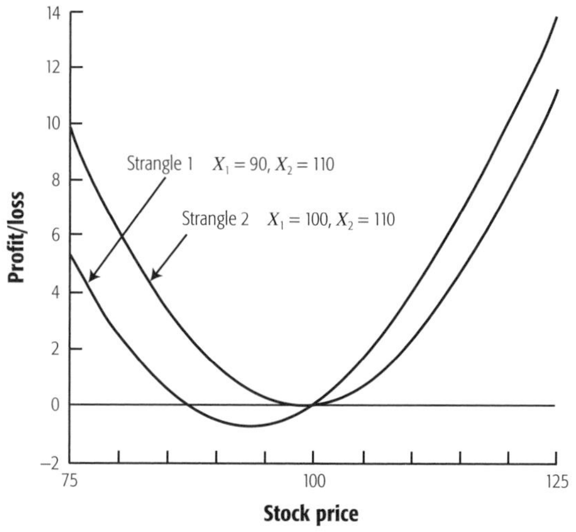

Note: $\sigma = 0.3$; $r = 0.08$; $T - t = 180$ days.

a put with a higher exercise price. Here, we consider two different strangle purchases, using the example options detailed in Table 14.7.

The first strangle covers the exercise price range from $90 to $110. To purchase the strangle, the trader buys C_1 with an exercise price of $90 and buys P_3 with an exercise price of $110. For C_1, we have $c = \$16.33$, DELTA $= 0.7860$, GAMMA $= 0.0138$, THETA $= -11.2054$, VEGA $= 20.4619$, and RHO $= 30.7085$. For P_3, $p = 11.80$, DELTA $= -0.5635$, GAMMA $= 0.0187$, THETA $= -2.9612$, VEGA $= 27.6602$, and RHO $= -33.6087$. Because both options are $10 into-the-money, they are fairly expensive, and the total cost of this strangle is $28.13. C_1 has a large DELTA, due to its being well into-the-money. For C_1 RHO is positive, but RHO is negative for P_3. As a result, the strangle is not very sensitive to interest rates.

As a second strangle, we focus on an exercise price range from $100 to $110. This strangle requires the purchase of C_2 and P_3. For C_2, $c = 10.30$, DELTA $= 0.6151$, GAMMA $= 0.0181$, THETA $= -12.2607$, VEGA $= 26.8416$, and RHO $= 25.2515$. P_3 is the same put we considered in the preceding paragraph, as it is used in both strangles that we consider. This second strangle costs $22.10. The DELTA of the call (0.6151) and put (-0.5635) almost offset each other, so this strangle is almost DELTA-neutral. However, the strangle has a positive GAMMA, and a high positive sensitivity to volatility. The RHOs of C_2 (25.2515) and P_3 (-33.6087) have different signs and largely offset each other. Therefore, the strangle has a low sensitivity to interest rates.

Figure 14.16 shows the profit-and-loss profiles for both strangles as a function of the current stock price. At the current stock price of $100, the profit or loss on the two positions is equal. For any stock price below $100, the second strangle has a greater profit (or a smaller loss). If the stock price moves above $100, the first strangle has a greater profit.

Notice that the two strangles have quite different risk profiles. As we noted earlier, the second strangle (with $X_1 = \$100$ and $X_2 = \$110$) is almost DELTA-neutral. The first strangle (with $X_1 = \$90$ and $X_2 = \$110$) is much more sensitive to changes in the stock price around

$S = \$100$. The VEGA for the first strangle is 48.1221, while the VEGA for the second strangle is 54.5018. As both strangles employ the same put (P_3), this difference in VEGA is due to the difference in VEGA between C_1 and C_2, and demonstrates the greater sensitivity to risk of the first strangle.

The butterfly spread with calls

In a butterfly spread, a purchaser employs calls with three different exercise prices with the same underlying good and the same expiration. To illustrate the investment characteristics of this position, we use calls C_1–C_3 from Table 14.7. To purchase a butterfly spread, the trader would buy C_1 (with $X = \$90$), buy C_3 (with $X = \$110$), and sell two C_2 (with $X = \$100$). Thus the position is long C_1, long C_3, and short two C_2. This position costs $1.79:

$$16.33 - 2 \times 10.30 + 6.06 = \$1.79$$

At a price of $1.79, we might expect future payoffs to be unlikely and small, and we should be aware of potential risks. From Chapter 11, we know that a butterfly spread with calls has the greatest payoff at expiration if the stock price equals the exercise price of the calls that were sold. For our example, that price would be $100. If the stock price at expiration were $100, C_1 (with $X = \$90$) would be worth $10, and all other options in the spread would expire worthless.

The DELTA of this butterfly spread is

$$0.7860 - 2 \times 0.6151 + 0.4365 = -0.0077$$

Thus, the DELTA of the spread is almost zero, but just slightly negative. Any change in the stock price will cause a slight fall in the value of the position. Further, the GAMMA is near zero, but also slightly negative:

$$0.0138 - 2 \times 0.0181 + 0.0187 = -0.0037$$

There is also little to hope for from a change in volatility, because the VEGA for the spread is negative:

$$20.4619 - 2 \times 26.8416 + 27.6602 = -5.5611$$

Therefore, the position is not very sensitive to volatility, but an increase in volatility would cause some loss in value.

The butterfly spread has a RHO of -1.2551:

$$30.7085 - 2 \times 25.2515 + 18.5394 = -1.2551$$

The value of the butterfly spread will vary inversely with interest rates, but the position is not very sensitive to interest rates.

The THETA for the butterfly spread is

$$-11.2054 - 2 \times (-12.2607) - 11.4208 = 1.8952$$

The positive THETA indicates that time decay will increase the value of the position.

These relationships are clear from Figure 14.17. As we noted, DELTA for the spread is slightly negative. In Figure 14.17, this leads to a shallow curve for the figure, but with a downward slope

Figure 14.17   The profit/loss of a butterfly spread as a function of the stock price

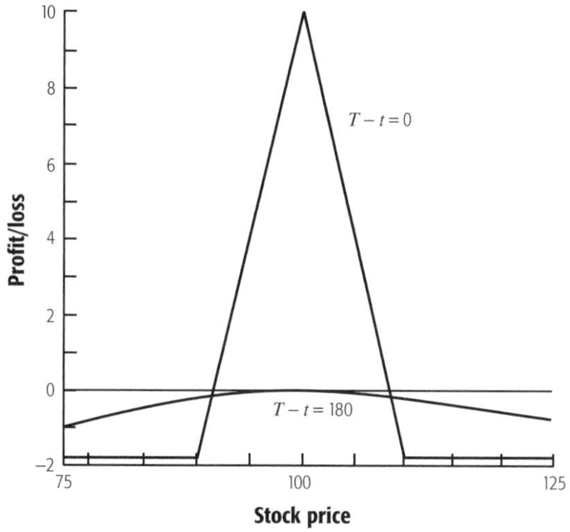

Note: $\sigma = 0.3$; $r = 0.08$; $T - t = 180$ days; $X_1 = \$90$; $X_2 = \$100$; $X_3 = \$110$.

for stock prices greater or less than $100. The negative GAMMA is shown in the figure as the increasing downward curvature of the line. Figure 14.17 also shows the profit and loss on the butterfly spread as a function of the stock price at expiration. If the stock price remains at $100, time decay will cause the value of the butterfly spread to rise to $10 at expiration. Thus, time decay increases the value of this position, consistent with the positive THETA noted earlier.

The bull spread with calls

To create a bull spread with calls, a trader purchases a call with a lower exercise price and sells a call with a higher exercise price. The two calls have the same underlying good and same term to expiration. We illustrate the bull spread with calls by considering options C_1 and C_2 from Table 14.7. These calls have exercise prices of $90 and $100, respectively. Option C_1 costs $16.33, and Option C_2 costs $10.30. Therefore, the spread will cost $6.03.

The sensitivities for the spread are as follows: DELTA = 0.7860 − 0.6151 = 0.1709; GAMMA = 0.0138 − 0.0181 = −0.0043; THETA = −11.205 + 12.2607 = 1.0553; VEGA = 20.4619 − 26.8416 = −6.3797; and RHO = 30.7085 − 25.2515 = 5.4570. Therefore, we see that a stock price increase will cause an increase in the value of the spread, which will be partially offset for large stock price changes by the negative GAMMA. Time decay will cause an increase in the value of the spread, as shown by the positive THETA. The spread has a negative VEGA, indicating that an increase in the stock's volatility will cause a decrease in the value of the spread. Finally, the RHO is positive, so an increase in interest rates will cause the spread to increase in value.

Figure 14.18 shows the profit-and-loss profile for the spread as a function of the price of the underlying stock. The graph shows that the value of the spread is positively related to the stock price. Further, Figure 14.18 illustrates that time decay will cause an increase in profits on the position. If no other parameters change, the profit-and-loss profile for the spread will collapse to its value at expiration, as shown in the graph.

Figure 14.18   The profit/loss of a bull spread with calls at a function of the stock price

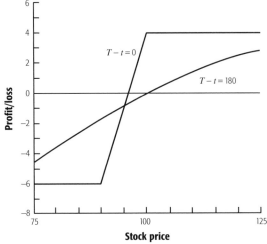

Note: $\sigma = 0.3$; $r = 0.08$; $T - t = 180$ days; $X_1 = \$90$; $X_2 = \$100$.

The VEGA of the option with the higher exercise price (C_2 with $X = \$100$) is larger than that of C_1 (with $X = \$90$). Because the position is long C_1 and short C_2, the spread's VEGA is negative. Therefore, an increase in volatility will cause the price of the spread to fall. Figure 14.19 shows the profitability of the spread as a function of the standard deviation.

A ratio spread with calls

As discussed in Chapter 11, there are infinitely many possible ratio spreads, because a new position can be created merely by changing the ratio between the options that comprise the spread. Therefore, we illustrate the general technique of ratio spreads with a fairly simple ratio spread using just two options.

Earlier, we considered the straddle composed of call C_2 and put P_2 from Table 14.7. We noted that the straddle costs \$16.74 and has a DELTA $= 0.6151 - 0.3849 = 0.2302$. The straddle had a VEGA $= 26.8416 + 26.8416 = 53.6832$. Thus, the straddle is essentially a volatility strategy with a relatively low DELTA and a high VEGA.

Consider now a trader's desire to create a position with most of the characteristics of a straddle, but to make it more purely a volatility strategy. In other words, the trader anticipates a volatility increase for the underlying stock, but does not wish to take a position on whether stock prices might rise or fall. Therefore, this trader would like to create a DELTA-neutral position with a high VEGA. The trader can create such a position by using a ratio spread that is similar to the straddle. However, instead of buying one C_2 and one P_2, the trader decides to buy one C_2 and to buy enough puts (P_2) to create a DELTA-neutral position. Therefore, the trader buys one C_2 and 1.5981 P_2, which costs \$10.301 + 0.5981(6.44) = \$20.59. This position is DELTA-neutral because the DELTA of the spread is

$$\text{DELTA} = 0.6151 + 1.5981 \times (-0.3849) = 0.0$$

Figure 14.19 The profit/loss of a bull spread with calls as a function of the standard deviation

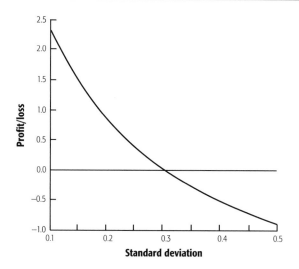

Note: $S = \$100$; $r = 0.08$; $T - t = 180$ days; $X_1 = \$90$; $X_2 = \$100$.

The other sensitivities for the ratio spread are as follows: GAMMA $= 0.0181 + 1.5981 \times 0.0181$ $= 0.0470$; THETA $= -12.2607 + 1.5981 \times (-4.5701) = -19.5642$; VEGA $= 26.846 + 1.5981$ $\times 26.8416 = 69.7372$; and RHO $= 25.2515 + 1.5981 \times (-22.1559) = -10.1558$. Therefore, this ratio spread has zero DELTA, and a high VEGA. The value of the spread will suffer from time decay and will fall if interest rates rise.

Figure 14.20 shows the profitability of the straddle and the ratio spread as a function of the stock price. The ratio spread is much less sensitive to changing stock prices. This is consistent with its creation as a DELTA-neutral position. Both the straddle and the spread are essentially a bet on increasing volatility. However, the ratio spread is a purer bet on volatility, because it is insensitive to stock price changes. Figure 14.21 shows how the profitability of the straddle and the ratio spread change with changing volatility. Clearly, the ratio spread is more sensitive to changing volatility, as is shown by its greater slope in Figure 14.21.

One of the advantages of ratio spreads is the ability to avoid risk exposure to one parameter and to accept risk exposure to another. For example, one could use a ratio spread of the form we have considered to create a position that is VEGA-neutral but has a large DELTA, indicating a high sensitivity to changes in the stock price. This VEGA-neutral position could be created by buying C_2 and selling P_2 in a ratio of $1 : 1$. The resulting spread would have a DELTA $= 1.0$. Thus, with a ratio spread of two options, one can maintain neutrality with respect to one parameter and accept sensitivity with respect to a second parameter.

The calendar spread

All of the option strategies we have considered thus far have employed options with the same expiration date. A **calendar spread** or a **time spread** is an option combination that employs options with different expiration dates but a common underlying stock. These spreads all have a horizon that terminates by the time the near-expiration option expires.

Figure 14.20   The profit/loss of a straddle and a ratio spread as a function of the stock price

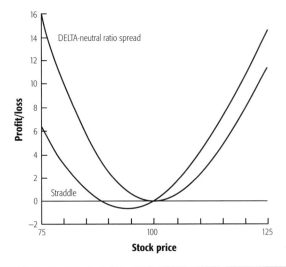

Note: $\sigma = 0.3$; $r = 0.08$; $T - t = 180$ days; $X_1 = \$100$.

Figure 14.21   The profit/loss of a straddle and a ratio spread as a function of the standard deviation

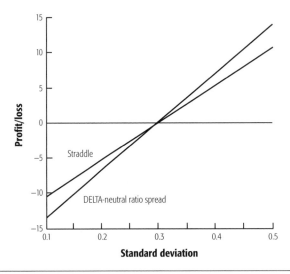

Note: $S = \$100$; $r = 0.08$; $T - t = 180$ days; $X_1 = \$100$.

Figure 14.22   The value of a calendar spread with calls as a function of the stock price

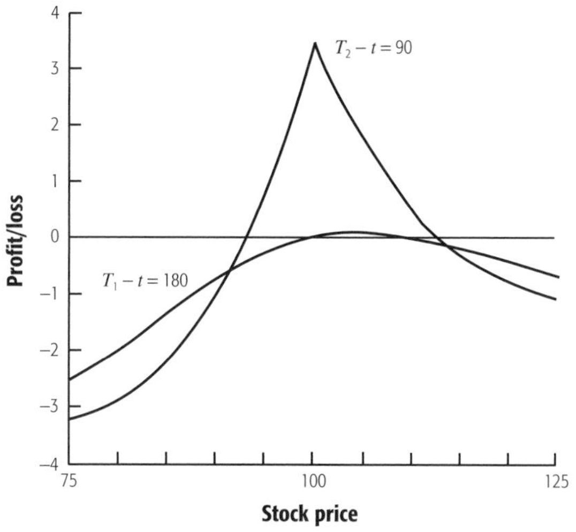

Note: $r = 0.08$; $T_1 - t = 180$ days; $T_2 - t = 90$ days; $X_1 = X_2 = \$100$.

By using calendar spreads, a trader can adopt speculative strategies designed to exploit beliefs about future stock prices. Bullish and bearish calendar spreads are both possible. The trader can also exploit differential sensitivities to create positions that are neutral with respect to some option parameter, while selecting exposure to others. For example, a trader might create a DELTA-neutral calendar spread that will profit with time decay.

A calendar spread with calls

As a first example of a calendar spread, consider calls C_2 and C_4 in Table 14.7. These calls are identical, except that call C_2 expires in 180 days, while C_4 expires in 90 days. Assume that a trader creates a calendar spread by buying C_2 and selling C_4. The cost of this position is $\$10.30 - \$6.91 = \$3.39$. The sensitivities for the spread are as follows: DELTA = 0.6151 − 0.5820 = 0.0331; GAMMA = 0.0181 − 0.0262 = −0.0081; THETA = −12.2607 − (−15.8989) = 3.6382; VEGA = 26.8416 − 19.3905 = 7.4511; and RHO = 25.2515 − 12.6464 = 12.6051. In purchasing this position, the trader has obtained a position that will gain value for an increase in the stock price, volatility, and interest rate. Further, the position will increase in value with time decay.

Figure 14.22 shows the profitability of the calendar spread at the time it is initiated (with 180 days until C_2 expires and 90 days until C_4 expires). It also shows the value of the spread in 90 days (when C_4 expires and C_2 has 90 days remaining until expiration). We first consider the value profile of the spread at the time it is initiated. At $S = \$100$, the spread is worth $\$3.39$, the price the trader paid. As we have seen, it is essentially DELTA-neutral and GAMMA-neutral, with a relatively low sensitivity to the standard deviation and the interest rate. The spread does have a positive THETA, however, indicating that time decay will increase the value of the position.

Figure 14.23   The value of a calendar spread with puts as a function of the stock price

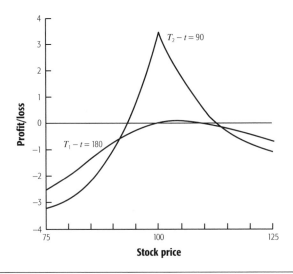

Note: $r = 0.08$; $T_1 - t = 180$ days; $T_2 - t = 90$ days; $X_1 = X_2 = \$100$.

This positive time decay is also shown in Figure 14.22, because the figure shows the profitability of the position in 90 days, when C_4 expires. If the stock price is at $100, C_4 will expire worthless, but C_2 will be worth $6.91. Therefore, the price of the spread will rise from $3.39 to $6.91 over 90 days if the stock price does not change. This increase in profits is due strictly to time decay. Therefore, this type of calendar spread with calls is essentially an attempt to take advantage of time decay.

A calendar spread with puts
Consider the spread in which a trader buys a put with a distant expiration and sells a put with a nearby expiration. We illustrate this spread by considering puts P_2 and P_4 from Table 14.7. The trader buys P_2 for $6.44 and sells put P_4 for $4.95, for a total cost of $1.49.

The sensitivities for the spread are as follows: DELTA $= -0.3849 - (-0.4180) = 0.0331$; GAMMA $= 0.0181 - 0.0262 = -0.0081$; THETA $= -4.5701 - (-8.0552) = 3.4851$; VEGA $= 26.8416 - 19.3905 = 7.4511$; and RHO $= -22.1559 - (-11.5295) = -10.6264$. The most important features of this spread are its low DELTA and its significantly positive THETA. The position is not very sensitive to changes in stock prices, but it should appreciate with time decay. Figure 14.23 shows the profitability of this spread as a function of the stock price at the time it is initiated (when P_2 has 180 days until expiration and P_4 has 90 days until expiration). The figure also shows the profitability of the spread at the expiration date of the nearby put. Notice that this graph is almost (but not quite) identical to Figure 14.22. Implementing a calendar spread with puts or calls gives virtually the same profit-and-loss profile. If the stock price remains constant at $S = \$100$, the value of the spread will rise from $1.49 to $4.95 over the 90 days until P_4 expires. Thus, this calendar spread with puts is essentially an attempt to exploit time decay.

Conclusion

This chapter has explored the sensitivity of option prices to the key para-meters that determine the price of an option–the stock price, the standard deviation of the stock's returns, the interest rate, and the time remaining until expiration. We explored these measures within the context of the Merton model, and showed that the Merton model embraces the Black–Scholes model. Given a knowledge of these sensitivities, a trader can use options more effectively, both for hedging and for speculating.

We have seen that DELTA measures the sensitivity of the price of an option to the price of the underlying stock. GAMMA measures the tendency for DELTA to change as the stock price changes, providing a measure of a second order for the key sensitivity DELTA. VEGA gauges the sensitivity of an option's price to the volatility of the underlying stock, while RHO measures the sensitivity of the option price to the interest rate. Finally, THETA measures the sensitivity of the option price to the time to expiration of the option.

By combining options with the underlying stock, or by combining options into portfolios, the trader can create positions with exactly the desired risk exposures. For example, we saw that a trader could use a stock and a call to create a portfolio that is DELTA-neutral. A DELTA-neutral portfolio does not change in value as the stock price changes infinitesimally. We also saw how to use two options in conjunction with a stock to make a portfolio both DELTA-neutral and GAMMA-neutral.

In many instances, a trader will seek exposure to one or more of the option parameters as a speculative technique. For example, we saw how traders can use straddles to accept exposure to volatility while minimizing exposure to changes in the stock price. Such a strategy is essentially a bet on increasing volatility, if the trader buys a straddle. We also observed that strangles created with different pairs of exercise prices could have substantially different DELTAs, even when all other factors are equal. A speculator interested in making money is well advised to master these relationships. A hedger needs to know how a given posi-tion responds to changing parameters to understand a hedge completely and to create more effective hedges. Given a knowledge of these sen-sitivities, a speculator or a hedger can understand the full spectrum of risk entailed by a position.

Exercises

1 Consider Call A, with $X = \$70$, $r = 0.06$, $T - t = 90$ days, $\sigma = 0.4$, and $S = \$60$. Compute the price, DELTA, GAMMA, THETA, VEGA, and RHO for this call.

2 Consider Put A, with $X = \$70$, $r = 0.06$, $T - t = 90$ days, $\sigma = 0.4$, and $S = \$60$. Compute the price, DELTA, GAMMA, THETA, VEGA, and RHO for this put.

3 Consider a straddle comprised of Call A and Put A. Compute the price, DELTA, GAMMA, THETA, VEGA, and RHO for this straddle.

4 Consider Call A. Assuming that the current stock price is $60, create a DELTA-neutral portfolio consisting of a short position of one call and the necessary number of shares. What is the value of this portfolio for a sudden change in the stock price to $55 or $65?

5 Consider Call A and Put A from above. Assume that you create a portfolio that is short one call and long one put. What is the DELTA of this portfolio? Can you find the DELTA without computing? Explain. Assume that a share of stock is added to the short call/long put portfolio. What is the DELTA of the entire position?

6 What is the GAMMA of a share of stock if the stock price is $55 and a call on the stock with $X = \$50$ has a price $c = \$7$ while a put with $X = \$50$ has a price $p = \$4$? Explain.

7 Consider Call B written on the same stock as Call A, with $X = \$50$, $r = 0.06$, $T - t = 90$ days, $\sigma = 0.4$, and $S = \$60$. Form a bull spread with calls from these two instruments. What is the price of the spread? What is its DELTA? What will the price of the spread be at expiration if the terminal stock price is $60? From this information, can you tell whether THETA is positive or negative for the spread? Explain.

8 Consider again the sample options, C_2 and P_2, of the chapter discussion as given in Table 14.7. Assume now that the stock pays a continuous dividend of 3 percent per year. See if you can tell how the sensitivities will differ for the call and a put without computing. Now compute the DELTA, GAMMA, VEGA, THETA, and RHO of the two options if the stock has a dividend.

9 Consider three calls, Calls C, D, and E, all written on the same underlying stock, with $S = \$80$, $r = 0.07$, and $\sigma = 0.2$. For Call C, $X = \$70$ and $T - t = 90$ days. For Call D, $X = \$75$ and $T - t = 90$ days. For Call E, $X = \$80$ and $T - t = 120$ days. Compute the price, DELTA, and GAMMA for each of these calls. Using Calls C and D, create a DELTA-neutral portfolio assuming that the position is long one Call C. Now use Calls C, D, and E to form a portfolio that is DELTA-neutral and GAMMA-neutral, again assum-ing that the portfolio is long one Call C.

10   Your largest and most important client's portfolio includes option positions. After several conversations, it becomes clear that your client is willing to accept the risk associated with exposure to changes in volatility and stock price. However, your client is not willing to accept a change in the value of her portfolio resulting from the passage of time. Explain how the investor can protect her portfolio against changes in value due to the passage of time.

11   Your newest client believes that the Asian currency crisis is going to increase the volatility of earnings for firms involved in exporting, and that this earnings volatility will be translated into large stock price changes for the affected firms. Your client wants to create speculative positions using options to increase his exposure to the expected changes in the riskiness of exporting firms. That is, your client wants to prosper from changes in the volatility of the firm's stock returns. Discuss which "Greek" your client should focus on when developing his options positions.

12   A long-time client, an insurance salesperson, has noticed the increased acquisition activity involving commercial banks. Your client wishes to capitalize on the potential gains associated with this increased acquisition activity in the banking industry by creating speculative positions using options. Your client realizes that bank cash flows are sensitive to changes in interest rates, and she believes that the Federal Reserve is about to increase short-term interest rates. Realizing that an increase in the short-term interest rates will lead to a decrease in the stock prices of commercial banks, your client wants the value of her portfolio of options to be unaffected by changes in short-term interest rates. Explain how the investor can use option contracts to protect her portfolio against changes in value due to changes in the risk-free rate, and to capitalize on the expected price changes in bank stocks.

13   Your brother-in-law has invested heavily in stocks with a strong Asian exposure, and he tells you that his portfolio has a positive DELTA. Give an intuitive explanation of what this means. Suppose that the value of the stocks that your brother-in-law holds increases significantly. Explain what will happen to the value of your brother-in-law's portfolio.

14   Your mother-in-law has invested heavily in the stocks of financial firms, and she tells you that her portfolio has a negative RHO. Give an intuitive explanation of what this means. Suppose that the Federal Reserve increases short-term interest rates. Explain what will happen to the value of your mother-in-law's portfolio.

15   Your brother, Daryl, has retired. With the free time necessary to follow the market closely, Daryl has established large option positions as a stock investor.

He tells you that his portfolio has a positive THETA. Give an intuitive explanation of what this means. Daryl is also a big soccer fan, and is heading to France to watch the World Cup for a month. He believes that there is not sufficient liquidity in the market to close out his open option positions, and he is going to leave the positions open while he is in France. Explain what will happen to the value of your brother's portfolio while he is in France.

16   Consider the following information for a call option written on Microsoft's stock:

$S = \$96$	DELTA = 0.2063
$X = \$100$	GAMMA = 0.0635
$T - t = 5$ days	THETA = −48.7155
$\sigma = 0.4$	VEGA = 3.2045
$r = 0.1$	RHO = 0.2643
	Price = \$0.5

If in two days Microsoft's stock price has increased by \$1 to \$97, explain what you would expect to happen to the price of the call option.

17   Consider a stock, CVN, with a price of \$50 and a standard deviation of 0.3. The current risk-free rate of interest is 10 percent. A European call and put on this stock have an exercise price of \$55 and expire in three months (0.25 years).

A   If $c = \$1.61057$ and $N(d_1) = 0.3469$, then calculate the put option price.

B   Suppose that you own 3,000 shares of CBC, a subsidiary of CVN Corporation, and that you plan to go Christmas shopping in New York City the day after Thanksgiving. To finance your shopping trip, you wish to sell your 3,000 shares of CBC in one week. However, you do not want the value of your investment in CBC to fall below its current level. Construct a DELTA-neutral hedge using the put option written on CVN. Be sure to describe the composition of your hedged portfolio.

18   An investor holds a portfolio consisting of three options, two call options and a put option, written on the stock of QDS Corporation with the following characteristics:

	C_1	C_2	P_1
DELTA	0.8922	0.2678	−0.6187
GAMMA	0.0169	0.0299	0.0245
THETA	−5.55	−3.89	−3.72

The investor is long 100 contracts of option C_1, short 200 contracts of option C_2, and long 100 contracts of option P_1. The investor's options portfolio has the following characteristics:

$$\text{DELTA} = 0.8922 \times 100 - 0.2678 \times 200 - 0.6187 \times 100 = -26.21$$

$$\text{GAMMA} = 0.0169 \times 100 - 0.0299 \times 200 + 0.0245 \times 100 = -1.84$$

$$\text{THETA} = -5.55 \times 100 + 3.89 \times 200 - 3.72 \times 100 = -149$$

The investor wishes to hedge this portfolio of options with two call options written on the stock of QDS Corporation with the following characteristics:

	C_a	C_b
DELTA	0.5761	0.6070
GAMMA	0.0356	0.0247
THETA	−9.72	−7.04

A How many contracts of the two options, C_a and C_b, must the investor hold to create a portfolio that is DELTA-neutral and has a THETA of 100?

B If QDS's stock price remains relatively constant over the next month, explain what will happen to the value of the portfolio created in part A of this question.

C How many of the two options, C_a and C_b, must the investor hold to create a portfolio that is both DELTA- and GAMMA-neutral?

D Suppose that the investor wants to create a portfolio that is DELTA-, GAMMA-, and THETA-neutral. Could the investor accomplish this objective using the two options, C_a and C_b, that have been used in the previous exercises? Explain.

19 Both put and call options trade on HWP. Put and call options with an exercise price of $100 expire in 90 days. HWP is trading at $95, and has an annualized standard deviation of return of 0.3. The three-month risk-free interest rate is 5.25 percent per year.

A Use a four-period binomial model to compute the value of the put and call options using the recursive procedure (single-period binomial option pricing model).

B Increase the stock price by $0.25 to $95.25 and recalculate the value of the put and call options using the recursive procedure (single-period binomial option pricing model).

C For both the call and put options, calculate DELTA as the change in the value of the option divided by the change in the value of the stock.

D Decrease the stock price by $0.25 to $94.75 and recalculate the value of the put and call options using the recursive procedure (single-period binomial option pricing model).

E For both the call and put options, calculate DELTA as the change in the value of the option divided by the change in the value of the stock.

F For both the call and put options, calculate GAMMA as the difference between the DELTA associated with a stock price increase and the DELTA associated with a stock price decrease, divided by the change in the value of the stock.

G Increase the risk-free interest rate by 20 basis points to 5.45 percent per year and recalculate the value of the put and call options using the recursive procedure (single-period binomial option pricing model).

H For both the call and put options, calculate RHO as the change in the value of the option divided by the change in the risk-free interest rate.

I Increase the volatility of the underlying stock to 33 percent and recalculate the value of the put and call options using the recursive procedure (single-period binomial option pricing model).

J For both the call and put options, calculate VEGA as the change in the value of the option divided by the change in the volatility of the stock.

K Notice that each branch in the binomial tree represents the passage of time. That is, as one moves forward through the branches in a binomial tree, the life of the option wastes away. Also notice that the initial stock price of $95 reappears in the middle of the second branch of the tree. Using the parameter values for U, D, π_U, π_D, Δt, and $e^{-r\Delta t}$ calculated using the initial information given, recalculate the value of the call and put options using a **two-period** model. That is, calculate the option prices after 45 days, assuming the stock price is unchanged.

L For both the call and put options, calculate THETA as the difference in the value of the option with two periods to expiration less the value of the option with four periods to expiration, divided by twice the passage of time associated with each branch in the tree; that is, $2 \times \Delta t$.

20 Consider a stock, ABM, trading at a price of $70. Analysis of ABM's recent returns reveals that ABM has an annualized standard deviation of return of 0.4. The current risk-free rate of interest is 10 percent per year.

A What is the price of a European call and put written on ABM with a $75 strike price that expires in 180 days? Price the options using the Black–Scholes model.

B Increase the stock price by $0.25 to $70.25 and recalculate the value of the put and call options.

C For both the call and put options, calculate DELTA as the change in the value of the option divided by the change in the value of the stock.

D Decrease the stock price by $0.25 to $69.75 and recalculate the value of the put and call options.

E For both the call and put options, calculate DELTA as the change in the value of the option divided by the change in the value of the stock.

F For both the call and put options, calculate GAMMA as the difference between the DELTA associated with a stock price increase and the DELTA associated with a stock price decrease divided by the change in the value of the stock.

G Increase the risk-free interest rate by 25 basis points to 10.25 percent per year and recalculate the value of the put and call options.

H For both the call and put options, calculate RHO as the change in the value of the option divided by the change in the risk-free interest rate.

I Increase the volatility of the underlying stock to 44 percent and recalculate the value of the put and call options.

J For both the call and put options, calculate VEGA as the change in the value of the option divided by the change in the volatility of the stock.

K Decrease the life of the option by 10 percent to 162 days and recalculate the value of the put and call options.

L For both the call and put options, calculate THETA as the difference in the value of the option with 162 days to expiration less the value of the option with 180 days to expiration divided by the passage of time.

21 Consider a stock that trades for $75. A put and a call on this stock both have an exercise price of $70, and they expire in 145 days. The risk-free rate is 9 percent per year and the standard deviation of return for the stock is 0.35. Assume that the stock pays a continuous dividend of 4 percent.

A What, according to the Merton model, are the prices of a European call and put option written on this stock?

B Increase the stock price by $0.25 to $75.25 and recalculate the value of the put and call options.

C For both the call and put options, calculate DELTA as the change in the value of the option divided by the change in the value of the stock.

D Decrease the stock price by $0.25 to $74.75 and recalculate the value of the put and call options.

E Calculate DELTA for both the call and put options as the change in the value of the option divided by the change in the value of the stock.

F Calculate GAMMA for both the call and put options as the difference between the DELTA associated with a stock price increase and the DELTA associated with a stock price decrease divided by the change in the value of the stock.

G Increase the risk-free interest rate by 25 basis points to 9.25 percent per year and recalculate the value of the put and call options.

H Calculate RHO for both the call and put options as the change in the value of the option divided by the change in the risk-free interest rate.

I Increase the volatility of the underlying stock to 38.5 percent and recalculate the value of the put and call options.

J Calculate VEGA for both the call and put options as the change in the value of the option divided by the change in the volatility of the stock.

K Decrease the life of the option by 20 percent to 116 days and recalculate the value of the put and call options.

L Calculate THETA for both the call and put options as the difference in the value of the option with 116 days to expiration less the value of the option with 145 days to expiration divided by the passage of time.

22 CSM is trading at $78 and has an annualized standard deviation of return of 30 percent. CSM is expected to pay a dividend equal to 3 percent of the value of its stock price in 70 days. The current risk-free rate of interest is 7 percent per year. Options written on this stock have an exercise price of $80 and expire in 120 days.

A Using a four-period binomial model, calculate the values of European put and call options written on CSM.

B Increase the stock price by $0.25 to $78.25 and recalculate the value of the put and call options using the recursive procedure (single-period binomial option pricing model).

C   Calculate DELTA for both the call and put options as the change in the value of the option divided by the change in the value of the stock.

D   Decrease the stock price by $0.25 to $77.75 and recalculate the value of the put and call options using the recursive procedure (single-period binomial option pricing model).

E   Calculate DELTA for both the call and put options as the change in the value of the option divided by the change in the value of the stock.

F   Calculate GAMMA for both the call and put options as the difference between the DELTA associated with a stock price increase and the DELTA associated with a stock price decrease divided by the change in the value of the stock.

G   Increase the risk-free interest rate by 20 basis points to 7.20 percent per year and recalculate the value of the put and call options using the recursive procedure (single-period binomial option pricing model).

H   Calculate RHO for both the call and put options as the change in the value of the option divided by the change in the risk-free interest rate.

I   Increase the volatility of the underlying stock to 33 percent and recalculate the value of the put and call options using the recursive procedure (single-period binomial option pricing model).

J   Calculate VEGA for both the call and put options as the change in the value of the option divided by the change in the volatility of the stock.

K   Notice that each branch in the binomial tree represents the passage of time. That is, as one moves forward through the branches in a binomial tree, the life of the option wastes away. Also notice that the initial stock price of $78 reappears in the middle of the second branch of the tree. Using the parameter values for U, D, π_U, π_D, Δt, and $e^{-r\Delta t}$ calculated using the initial information given, recalculate the value of the call and put options using a **two-period** model. Assume that the dividend will be paid before period one and make the appropriate adjustments to the stock price tree. That is, calculate the option prices after 60 days, assuming that the stock price is unchanged.

L   Calculate THETA for both the call and put options as the difference in the value of the option with two periods to expiration less the value of the option with four periods to expiration divided by twice the passage of time associated with each branch in the tree; that is, $2 \times \Delta t$.

23   DCC exports high-speed digital switching networks, and their largest and most important clients are in Asia. A recent financial crisis in Asia has diminished the prospects of new sales to the Asian market in the near term. However, you believe that DCC is a good investment for the long term. A quick check of Quote.com reveals that DCC is trading at $78.625 per share. Your previous calculation of the historical volatility for DCC indicated an annual standard deviation of return of 27 percent, but examining the implied volatility of several DCC options reveals an increase in annual volatility to 32 percent. There are two traded options series that expire in 245 days. The options have $75 and $80 strike prices, respectively. The current 245-day risk-free interest rate is 4.75 percent per year, and you hold 2,000 shares of DCC.

	X = 75		X = 80	
	Call	Put	Call	Put
DELTA	0.6674	−0.3326	0.574	−0.426
GAMMA	0.0176	0.0176	0.019	0.019
THETA	−7.5372	−4.0865	−7.7495	−4.0687
VEGA	23.4015	23.4015	25.2551	25.2551
RHO	27.6835	−21.0792	24.4395	−27.574

A   Construct a portfolio that is DELTA- and GAMMA-neutral using the call options written on DCC.

B   Construct a portfolio that is DELTA- and GAMMA-neutral using the put options written on DCC.

C   Construct a portfolio that is DELTA- and THETA-neutral using the call options written on DCC.

D   Construct a portfolio that is DELTA- and THETA-neutral using the put options written on DCC.

E   How effective do you expect the DELTA- and GAMMA-neutral hedges to be? Explain.

24   Consider a stock, PRN, that trades for $24. A put and a call on this stock both have an exercise price of $22.50, and they expire in 45 days. The risk-free rate is 5.5 percent per year, and the standard deviation of return for the stock is 0.28.

A   Calculate the price of the put and call option using the Black–Scholes model.

Note: Use the following information for the remaining parts of this problem.

Suppose that you own 1,500 shares of PRN and you wish to hedge your investment in PRN using the traded PRN options. You are going on vacation in 45 days and want to use your shares to finance your vacation, so you do not want the value of your PRN shares to fall below $22.50.

B Construct a hedge using a covered call strategy. In a covered call strategy, the investor sells call options to hedge against the risk of a stock price decline.

C Construct a hedge using a protective put strategy. In a protective put strategy, the investor purchases put options to hedge against the risk of a stock price decline.

D If PRN is trading at $19 in 45 days, analyze and compare the effectiveness of the two alternative hedging strategies.

E If PRN is trading at $26 in 45 days, analyze and compare the effectiveness of the two alternative hedging strategies.

25 A friend, Audrey, holds a portfolio of 10,000 shares of Microsoft stock. In 60 days, she needs at least $855,000 to pay for her new home. You suggest to Audrey that she can construct an insured portfolio using Microsoft stock options. You explain that an insured portfolio can be constructed several different ways, but the basic notion is to create a portfolio that consists of a long position in Microsoft's stock and a long position in put options written on Microsoft. If at the end of the hedge period Microsoft's stock is trading at a price below the strike price on the put option, Audrey has the right to sell her Microsoft stock to the owner of the put option for the strike price. Thus, at the end of the hedge period, Audrey has sufficient assets to cover her needs or obligations. This hedging strategy can be implemented using traded options. However, Audrey may not be able to find an option with the desired strike price or expiration date. Dynamic hedging permits Audrey to overcome these limitations associated with traded option contracts. In dynamic hedging, Audrey constructs a portfolio that consists of a long position in stock and a long position in Treasury bills. As the underlying stock price changes, Audrey dynamically alters the allocation of assets in the portfolio between stock and Treasury bills. Therefore, we can view dynamic hedging as an asset allocation problem in which Audrey determines how much of her resources are allocated to the stock, and how much of her resources are allocated to Treasury bills. The amount of resources available for investment is simply the current cash value of Audrey's stock position. The proportion of resources committed to the stock, w, is calculated as

$$\frac{SN(d_1)}{S + P} = w$$

where S is the current stock price, P is the price of the relevant put option, and $N(d_1)$ comes from the Black–Scholes model. The proportion of resources committed to the Treasury bill is $1 - w$.

A Microsoft is currently trading at $90. The annualized risk-free interest rate on a 60-day Treasury bill is 5 percent. The current volatility of Microsoft's stock is 0.32. Audrey wishes to create an insured portfolio. Since she needs $855,000 in 60 days, she decides to establish a position in a 60-day Microsoft put option with an $85.50 strike price. Audrey calls her broker, who informs her that there is no 60-day Microsoft put option with a strike price of $85.50. Thus, Audrey must construct a dynamic hedge to protect the value of her investment in Microsoft stock. Using the Black–Scholes model, calculate the value of a put option with an $85.50 strike price with 60 days to expiration. Dètermine the allocation of assets in Audrey's insured portfolio. That is, find the proportion of resources committed to Microsoft stock, w, and the proportion of resources committed to Treasury bills, $1 - w$. Determine the dollar amount of her resources committed to Microsoft stock, and the dollar amount of her resources committed to Treasury bills.

B Twenty days later, Microsoft is trading at $92. The annualized risk-free interest rate on a 40-day Treasury bill is 5 percent, and the volatility of Microsoft's stock is 0.32. Using the Black–Scholes model, calculate the value of a put option with an $85.50 strike price with 40 days to expiration. Determine the allocation of assets in Audrey's insured portfolio. That is, find the proportion of resources committed to Microsoft stock, w, and the proportion of resources committed to Treasury bills, $1 - w$.

C Twenty days later, Microsoft is trading at $86. The annualized risk-free interest rate on a 20-day Treasury bill is 5 percent, and the volatility of

Microsoft's stock is 0.32. Using the Black–Scholes model, calculate the value of a put option with an $85.50 strike price with 20 days to expiration. Determine the allocation of assets in Audrey's insured portfolio. That is, find the proportion of resources committed to Microsoft

stock, w, and the proportion of resources committed to Treasury bills, $1 - w$.

D Discuss the adjustments that Audrey has made in the allocation of resources between Microsoft stock and Treasury bills as Microsoft's stock price has changed.

Note

1 THETA_p could be positive for a put that is deep-in-the-money. For example, if $S = \$50$, $X = \$100$, $r = 0.08$, $\sigma = 0.3$, and $T - t = 180$ days, then $p = \$46.1354$, and $\text{THETA}_p = 7.6377$. Notice that the put is worth less than $X - S$, because the put is European and the owner cannot exercise. However, if none of the parameters change over the life of the option, the put price must rise to $50 at the expiration date.

15

American Option Pricing

Overview

Chapter 13 considered the principles of pricing for European options—those that can be exercised only at the expiration of the option. There we considered the binomial model and saw how it could be extended logically to the Black–Scholes model. Strictly speaking, the Black–Scholes model holds only for European options on nondividend-paying stocks. However, we saw that it is possible to extend the Black–Scholes model to account for dividends by several adjustment procedures, such as the known dividend adjustment and the Merton model, which accounts for continuous dividends. In addition, we saw that the binomial model can price options on stocks that pay dividends, either in the form of a proportional dividend or an actual dollar dividend. Therefore, the tools for pricing European options are quite robust. However, all of the models considered in Chapter 13 pertain strictly to European options.

This chapter focuses on American options—those that can be exercised at any time during the option's life. Most options that are publicly traded are American options, so it is important to develop techniques for pricing these instruments. However, the early exercise feature of American options brings with it substantial complexity. As we will see, there are no general closed-form pricing models for American options that would parallel the Black–Scholes model for European options.

This chapter begins by analyzing the differences between American and European options. It then turns to consider some attempts to estimate the value of American options. Also, we consider a special case in which there is an exact option pricing formula. Later in the chapter, we return to the binomial model and show how it can be used to price American options with a high degree of accuracy. **OPTION!** can compute prices for all of the option models considered in this chapter.

American versus European options

Consider two calls or two puts that are just alike in terms of having the same underlying good, the same exercise price, and the same time to expiration, but one option is American and the other is European. In this context, American options are just like European options, except that the American option allows the privilege of early exercise. Because of this parallel between the two kinds of options, we analyze American options by contrasting them with the simpler European options that we have already considered, under the assumption that the options are parallel; that is, have the same underlying good, the same exercise price, and the same time until expiration. The difference in price between parallel American and European options must stem from the early exercise feature of the American option. Thus, if we know the price of a European option, we can price the parallel American option by determining the impact of the early exercise privilege. The value of the right to exercise before expiration is the **early exercise premium**. Much of our analysis of American options will concentrate on valuing the early exercise premium.

Because an American option affords every benefit of a parallel European option, plus the potentially valuable benefit of early exercise, we know that, for parallel options,

$$C_t \geq c_t \quad \text{and} \quad P_t \geq p_t$$

where American options are denoted by uppercase C or P, and European options are indicated by lowercase c or p. While the American option must be worth at least as much as the parallel European option, it may not actually be worth more—the early exercise premium may have no value in some circumstances. In some situations, however, the early exercise premium may be extremely valuable, and the American option can be worth much more than the parallel European option.

American versus European puts

In Chapter 12, we considered various boundary conditions that limited the arbitrage-free range of option prices. Due to its early exercise feature, an American put can always be converted into its exercise value $X - S_t$. Therefore,

$$P_t \geq X - S_t$$

For a European put, we saw in Chapter 12 that

$$P_t \geq Xe^{-r(T-t)} - S_t$$

The difference in prices of parallel American and European options depends largely on the extent to which the option is in-the-money, the interest rate, and the amount of time remaining until expiration. The early exercise of an American put discards the value of waiting to see how stock prices evolve. On the other hand, by exercising immediately, the owner of an American put captures the exercise value, $X - S_t$, and can invest those proceeds from the time of exercise until the expiration date of the option. The greater this amount of time, and the higher the interest rate, the greater is the incentive for early exercise.

To illustrate this idea, consider a European put option with an exercise price of $100 and 180 days until expiration. The underlying stock has a standard deviation of 0.1, and the risk-free rate is 10 percent. If the stock price is $100, the European put is worth $0.9749, well above its immediate exercise value of zero. However, if the stock price is $85, the European put is worth $10.33, well below $X - S_t = \$15$. With a stock price of $85, we know that the parallel American put would be worth at least $15. Figure 15.1 graphs the value of this European put and the quantity $X - S_t$ for various stock prices. As the graph shows, for stock prices near $85, the value of the European put approaches its lower bound of $Xe^{-r(T-t)} - S_t$ and changes almost 1 : 1 for changes in the stock price. Figure 15.1 suggests why American puts can be worth considerably more than their parallel European puts—the American put gives its owner the right to capture the exercise value immediately. With lower interest rates or a shorter time to expiration, the difference $X - S_t$ would be lower relative to the value of the European put. For example, for this option with a stock price of $85 and only 20 days until expiration, the European put would be worth $14.45, much closer to the exercise value of $15.

Notice that this substantial difference in the value of American and European puts arises without any consideration of dividends, because the stock considered in our previous example had no dividends. As Figure 15.1 shows, the difference between $X - S_t$ and the value of a European put is larger when the put is deep-in-the-money. For a put, large dividends reduce the value of the underlying stock substantially and tend to push a put deeper into-the-money. Thus, dividends can also increase the difference in value between European and American puts.

For an American put on a dividend paying stock, the optimal time to exercise is generally immediately after a dividend payment. Certainly, exercising just before a dividend payment would not make sense; it would be much better to wait for the dividend payment to reduce the stock price and push the put further into-the-money.

Figure 15.1   The boundary space for European and American puts

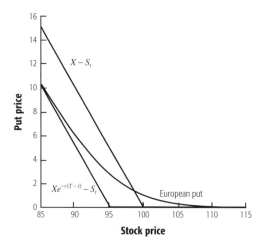

In this discussion of early exercise of American puts, the critical point to realize is that a substantial difference between European and American puts can arise even when there are no dividends. Further, it can be quite rational to exercise an American put before expiration on a nondividend-paying stock. Later in this chapter, we will see exactly when it is rational to exercise an American put before expiration.

American versus European calls

In understanding the differences between American and European calls, we begin with the simpler situation in which the underlying stock pays no dividends. For calls on a nondividend-paying stock, early exercise is never rational, and the price of an American and European call will be the same.

In Chapter 12, we explored boundary conditions for European call options and showed that before expiration the call must be worth at least as much as the stock price minus the present value of the exercise price. That is,

$$c_t \geq S_t - Xe^{-r(T-t)}$$

The immediate exercise value of a call is only $S_t - X$. As long as there is some time remaining until expiration and the interest rate is not zero, the European call will be worth more than the immediate exercise value.

Relative to its parallel European call, an American call gives benefits from the right to exercise early. However, the boundary condition on the call shows that early exercise is never desirable if the underlying stock pays no dividend. Therefore, the right to exercise early that is inherent in the American call can have no value, and for calls on a nondividend-paying stock, the price of an American call is the same as the price of a parallel European call.

We now consider the importance of dividends on call values. If the underlying stock pays a dividend, it can be rational to exercise early, and an American call can be worth more than its parallel European call. We emphasize this point by considering a radical situation. Assume that a stock trades for $80 and the firm has announced that it will pay a liquidating dividend of $80 one minute before the options on this stock expire. Assume that American and European calls on this share have an exercise price of $60 and the present time is two minutes before expiration. (The time is just before expiration in this example, so that we can ignore the time value of money.) What would be the value of the American and European calls?

For the owner of the American call, the strategy is clear. The owner should exercise the option immediately, paying the exercise price of $60 and receiving the liquidating dividend of $80. This gives a cash flow of +$20, so the value of the American call must be $20. The European call cannot be exercised until expiration. But, under the terms of this example, the stock will be worth zero at the expiration of the option due to the payment of the liquidating dividend one minute before expiration. Therefore, the European call must be worth zero.

Another way to see that the European call is worth zero is from the adjustment for known dividends, discussed in Chapter 13. There, we saw that one could adjust the stock price by subtracting from the stock price the present value of all dividends to be paid during the life of the option. The Black–Scholes model could then be applied as usual if we substituted this dividend-adjusted stock price for the current stock price as an input to the model. In our present example, we would subtract the $80 dividend from the $80 stock price, giving an adjusted stock price of zero. Because the call is at expiration, it will be worth the maximum of zero or the adjusted stock price minus the exercise price. Therefore, the European call will be worth zero in the extreme circumstance we are considering.

In less extreme circumstances—when the dividend is smaller relative to the value of the stock and when there is more time remaining until expiration—it can still be rational to exercise before expiration. The decision to exercise early depends mainly on the amount of the dividend, the interest rate, and the time remaining until expiration. Our extreme example shows a general principle about early exercise. If there is to be early exercise of a call, it should occur immediately before a dividend payment. Later in this chapter, we will explore more fully the conditions that lead to the early exercise of calls. We now turn to models for pricing American options.

Dividend capture strategies

Experienced traders use a strategy known as "dividend capture" to take advantage of the small set of option holders who fail to exercise their options even when it is profitable to do so. Experienced traders know that if a call option is to be exercised, the optimal time to exercise is immediately before the ex-dividend date. To construct a dividend capture strategy, a trader will (prior to the ex-dividend day) simultaneously sell a deep in-the-money call and purchase an in-the-money call with a higher exercise price. Both options are sufficiently in-the-money to be exercised just before the ex-dividend day. Because both options are in-the-money, the option's prices will be highly correlated and the combined position will be essentially hedged. On the day before the stock goes ex-dividend, the trader exercises the call option that he holds and hopes that the call he sold will not be exercised against him. If the call he sold is not exercised, the trader makes a profit because the stock price, and therefore the call price, will fall by the amount of the dividend on the ex-dividend day. The trader sells the stock he received in the exercise of his long call and buys back the unexercised short call. In this case, the trader profits by the amount of the dividend he will receive.

If the call the trader sold is exercised before the ex-dividend instant, the trader delivers the shares he received from the exercise of his call. In this case, the trader makes no money, but does not lose any either (other than transaction costs). To enhance the chances of a dividend capture strategy, a trader should choose to sell a call option that is sufficiently deep-in-the-money to be exercised just prior to the ex-dividend instant. In addition, the trader must have reason to believe that the traders holding this call will fail to exercise it when they should. As a rule of thumb, traders expect retail traders to be the most likely to fail to exercise their calls. Professional traders believe that these retail traders are most likely to purchase short-maturity calls that are not too deep-in-the-money. Therefore, in constructing a spread position to capture the dividend, professional traders will sell the calls they believe retail traders are holding.

For example, assume that today's date is May 15, the day before the ex-dividend date for XYZ stock. The stock is priced at $38.75 on this date and the holder of the stock on the ex-dividend date will be entitled to receive a 75 cent per share dividend. A June call with an exercise price of $35 is priced at $3.75. A June call with an exercise price of $30 sells for a price of $8.75. Both calls are clearly in-the-money. To construct a dividend spread, a trader simultaneously sells the call with the $35 exercise price and purchases the call with the $30 strike price. The trader's net cost at the outset is $5.00. At the end of the day, the investor exercises the $30 call, receiving proceeds of $S_{t-1} + 0.75 - 30$. (Day $t - 1$ is the day before ex-dividend, and the notation S_{t-1} is the stock price net of the value of the escrowed dividend). If the $35 call option is exercised against the investor before the ex-dividend (which will not be known until the next day before market opening), the investor's obligation is $-(S_t + 0.75 - \$35)$, and the net terminal value is $S_t + 0.75 - \$30 - S_t - 0.75 + 35$ or $+\$5$, exactly a wash, considering that $5 was paid up front. However, if the $35 call option is not exercised, the investor goes into the next morning with a long position in the stock (acquired from exercising the $30 call) and a short position in the $35 call, which has a value of $S_t + 0.75 - 30 - C_t$. For all intents and purposes, this position is offset by that of the short-in-the-money call. The outstanding call, being deep-in-the-money, is selling for about its floor value of $S_t - 35$, so the net value of the position is $0.75 - 30 + 35$ or about $+5.75$. The net initial cash outlay in initiating this strategy was $5, so the profit is $0.75, exactly the amount of the dividend.

Dividend capture strategies have been impaired in recent years by a clearinghouse rule that automatically exercises expired options if they finish three to four points or more in-the-money, unless instructed otherwise by the option holder. Automatic exercise rules were implemented partly to protect retail investors from professional traders engaged in dividend capture strategies.

Assignment risk

Assignment risk is the risk borne by the option writer resulting from the exercise decision of the option holder. For every option exercised by an option holder, there is an exercise assignment for the option writer. An option writer may be assigned an exercise at any time during the period the option is exercisable. Once an exercise is assigned, the option writer must deliver (in the case of a call) or purchase (in the case of a put). This means that the theory of rational exercise is equally important for both option holders and option writers.

Many trading strategies requiring the use of a short option and the underlying stock rely on some assessment of the risk of assignment. For this reason, option writers carefully monitor the probability of exercise and assignment. A surprise assignment can be costly. For example, if the holder of a call option unexpectedly exercises his option, the writer must perform on his obligation and deliver the stock. A surprise assignment may cause the option writer to scramble to locate the stock.

Many option strategies require the use of short options. These combination strategies are vulnerable to assignment risk. For example, a short straddle position is a combination of writing uncovered calls and puts. If either option is assigned, a leg of the combined position disappears. Either the assigned leg must be replaced or the unassigned leg must be closed out. If the unassigned leg is not closed out, subsequent market fluctuations may cause this leg to be assigned as well, causing a loss on both of the original short option positions.

Pseudo-American call option pricing

The **pseudo-American call option pricing model** was created by Fischer Black.[1] It does not provide an exact pricing technique for American calls, but does provide an estimated call price that draws on the intuitions of the Black–Scholes model. Later, we explore more exact methods for pricing American calls, but the pseudo-American model is important because it clearly shows the factors that lead to early exercise, and it highlights the differences between European and American calls. Essentially, the valuation technique requires four steps:

(1) From the current stock price, subtract the present value of all dividends that will be paid before the option expires. So far, this is the same as the procedure that we followed for the known dividend adjustment for European calls.
(2) For each dividend date, reduce the exercise price by the present value of all dividends yet to be paid, including the dividend that is about to go ex-dividend.
(3) Taking each dividend date and the actual expiration date of the option as potential expiration dates, compute the value of a European call using the adjusted stock and exercise prices.
(4) Select the highest of these European call values as the estimate of the value of the American call.

Each step has a clear rationale. In the first step, we adjust the stock price to reflect its approximate value after it pays the dividends. In the second step, we effectively add back the value of dividends to be received from the stock if we exercise. This is accomplished by reducing the liability of the exercise price by the present value of the dividends we will capture if we exercise. In the third step, we evaluate different exercise decisions. If we exercise, we will do so just before a dividend payment to capture the dividend from the stock. Thus, in the third step we consider the payoffs from each potential exercise date. Finally, in the fourth step, we compare the different payoffs associated with each exercise strategy that we computed in the third step. Assuming that we plan to follow the best exercise strategy, we approximate the current American call price as the highest of these computed European call prices. As an example, consider the following data: $S_t = \$60$; $X_t = \$60$; $T - t = 180$ days; $r = 0.09$; $\sigma = 0.2$; $D_1 = \$2$, to be paid in 60 days; $D_2 = \$2$, to be paid in 150 days.

What is the pseudo-American call worth? The present value of the dividends is as follows:

$$D_1 e^{-rt} + D_2 e^{-rt} = \$2 \times e^{-0.09 \times (60/365)} + \$2 \times e^{-0.09 \times (150/365)} = \$3.90$$

We subtract this present value from the stock price, so we use \$56.10 as our stock price in all subsequent calculations. We will use this adjusted stock price to compute call values, assuming the option expires at three different times: the actual expiration date, the date of the last dividend, and the date of the first dividend. Three inputs remain constant for each computation: $S = \$56.10$, $r = 0.09$, and $\sigma = 0.2$. The time until expiration will vary, and we must adjust the exercise price for different dividend amounts.

We begin with the actual expiration date. Applying the Black–Scholes model with $T - t = 180$ days and $X = \$60$ gives a call value of \$2.57. (This is the same as the known dividend adjustment for European calls discussed in Chapter 13.) Next, we deal with each dividend date, starting with the final dividend. The dividend is just about to be paid, so we adjust the exercise price by subtracting \$2. Thus, for $X = \$58$ and $T - t = 150$ days, the call value is \$2.97. Next, we consider the date of the first dividend. The present value of the dividends at that time consists of the dividend that is just about to be paid, \$2, plus the present value of the second dividend that will be paid in 90 days, $\$2 \times e^{-0.09 \times (90/365)} = \$1.96$. Together, these dividends have a present value of $3.96, so we adjust the exercise price to $56.04. Therefore, for $X = \$56.04$ and $T - t = 60$ days, the call price is $2.28.

Now we have three estimated call prices corresponding to two dividend dates and the actual expiration date of the option. The estimates are $2.28 for the first dividend date, $2.97 for the second date, and $2.57 for the actual expiration date. Therefore, we take the largest value, $2.97, as the estimate of the pseudo-American call value. According to Whaley, the average error for this pseudo-American model is about 1.5 percent.[2]

The strategy behind the pseudo-American option technique is to realize that an American call on a dividend paying stock can be analyzed as consisting of a series of options. Given that early exercise is only optimal just prior to a dividend payment, we may think of the American call as consisting of a portfolio of European options that expire just before each dividend and at the actual exercise date. In the pseudo-American technique, we evaluate each of those European options, and treat the American option as being worth the maximum of all of the European options.

Expiration day wildcard options: the case of Farmers Group, Inc.

The OCC sets rules for its clearing members governing the exercise of option contracts. OCC rules require that a clearing member tender an exercise notice to the OCC between 9:00 a.m. and 7:00 p.m. Central Standard Time (CST) on any business day prior to the expiration date of the option. Separate rules apply on the expiration date.

In addition, exchange rules set exercise deadlines after the close of trading but before the OCC deadline. For example, the Philadelphia Stock Exchange closes at 3:00 p.m. CST, and the exchange's exercise deadline is 4:30 p.m. CST. On the expiration day, the right to exercise after the close of the market can create extra value to the option holder if important news comes to the market after the market close but before the exercise deadline. This extra value is referred to by traders as a "wildcard option."

Holders of equity options have been known to enhance the value of their expiration-day wildcard option by simply ignoring the exercise deadline set by the exchange. For example, at 6:00 p.m. CST on Friday June 17, 1988, an option expiration day, the California Insurance Department issued a ruling barring a takeover of Farmers Group, Inc.–news that was expected to cause a substantial decline in Farmers Group stock at the opening the following Monday. Farmers Group stock had closed at $62 per share, the June 60 calls closed at $2^7/_{16}$ and the June 60 puts closed at $^3/_8$. The fact that the out-of-the money put finished at $^3/_8$ and the call finished at $^7/_{16}$ more than its intrinsic value is consistent with the hypothesis that the wildcard option is valued by the option holder. Acting on this news, several option holders ignored the Philadelphia Exchange's 4:30 p.m. CST deadline, but exercised their put options ahead of the OCC's 7:00 p.m. CST deadline. As a result, 10,418 of the 10,667 apparently worthless puts were exercised, while only 2,793 of the 9,341 apparently in-the-money calls were exercised. In essence, put holders used the settlement procedure to collect $60 per share from option writers on stock known by nearly all to be worth considerably less. Several put writers sued, claiming that put holders had fraudulently exercised their contracts, but the court denied the fraud claim and ruled that any remedy resided at the exchange. Exchange rules imposed only a modest bookkeeping fine for failure to meet the exchange's exercise deadline. The price of Farmers Group stock did, in fact, fall to $56 at the open the following Monday, making the maneuver worthwhile for the option holders.

Exact American call option pricing

In general, there is no closed-form solution to the value of an American call option on a dividend-paying stock. However, an exact pricing formula is possible in one special case. It is

Figure 15.2   Decision points for options on a dividend-paying stock

possible to compute the exact price for an option on a stock that pays a single dividend during the life of the option.[3] The model is also known as the **compound option model**.

As discussed in the previous section on the pseudo-American model, an American call option really consists of a series of options that expire just before the various dividend dates and at the actual expiration of the option. We now focus on the situation in which there is just one dividend between the present and the expiration date of the option, time T. We assume that the dividend occurs at time t_1. The time line in Figure 15.2 shows the decision points that we must consider. As t_1 approaches, the owner of the call must decide whether to exercise. If she exercises, she does so the instant before t_1, receives the stock with dividends and pays the exercise price. If she does not exercise, the stock pays the dividend and she continues to hold a call on the stock, now without the dividend. The instant after the dividend payment occurs, the call is effectively a European call, because there are no more dividend payments and early exercise on a European call is never rational. Letting S_1 be the stock price just after the dividend, D_1, is paid, and letting C_1 be the call price just after the dividend is paid, her choice is as follows:

Exercise   Receive stock with dividend; pay the exercise price:
                    $S_1 + D_1 - X$
Do not exercise   Own call on the stock with the stock's value reduced by the dividend
                    amount:
                    C_1

Considering the American call before the dividend date, we can see that it is really a compound option, or an option on an option. It is an option on an option because the owner of the call has the option to refrain from exercising and to own a European option.

The exercise decision as t_1 approaches depends principally on the stock price. If the stock reaches some critical level, the owner should exercise. If it is below that level, the call owner will be better off not exercising and owning the resulting (effectively European) call. The critical stock price, S^*, is the stock price at which the owner is indifferent about the exercise decision, and the owner will be indifferent if the exercise decision leaves her wealth unchanged. The critical stock price is the stock price that makes the two outcomes equal:

$$S^* + D_1 - X = C_1 \tag{15.1}$$

For example, assume that the dividend date t_1 is at hand and that 90 days remain until the option expires. The exercise price is $100, the standard deviation of the stock is 0.2, the risk-free rate is 10 percent, and the dividend that is to be paid is $5. If the stock price immediately after the dividend is paid is $100.67, the call option is worth $5.67. For these data, $S^* = 100.67, because

$100.67 + $5.00 − $100.00 = $5.67

If the stock price is higher than $100.67 the instant before t_1, the call owner should exercise. If the stock price is less than $100.67, she should not exercise.

We now turn to the valuation of the American call before the dividend date. In this case, the value of the call is as follows:

$$C_t = (S - D_1 e^{-r(t_1-t)})N(b_1) - (X - D_1)e^{-r(t_1-t)}N(b_2)$$

$$+ (S - D_1 e^{-r(t_1-t)})N_2\left(a_1; b_1; -\sqrt{\frac{t_1 - t}{T - t}}\right) - Xe^{-r(T-t)}N_2\left(a_2; b_2; -\sqrt{\frac{t_1 - t}{T - t}}\right) \qquad (15.2)$$

where

$$a_1 = \frac{\ln\left(\dfrac{S - D_1 e^{-r(t_1-t)}}{X}\right) + (r + 0.5\sigma^2)(T - t)}{\sigma\sqrt{T - t}}$$

$$a_2 = a_1 - \sigma\sqrt{T - t}$$

$$b_1 = \frac{\ln\left(\dfrac{S - D_1 e^{-r(t_1-t)}}{S^*}\right) + (r + 0.5\sigma^2)(t_1 - t)}{\sigma\sqrt{t_1 - t}}$$

$$b_2 = b_1 - \sigma\sqrt{t_1 - t}$$

The function $N_2(a; b; \rho)$ is the standardized cumulative bivariate normal distribution. For two variables, x and y, that are distributed according to the standardized bivariate normal function and have a correlation of p, $N_2(a; b; \rho)$ is the probability that $x \leq a$ and that $y \leq b$. N_2 is like the standard normal function used in the Black–Scholes model, except that it takes into account two variables that are correlated. Considered singly, variables x and y are distributed normally with a mean of zero and a standard deviation of 1.0. Assume for the moment that $a = 0$, $b = 0$, and the correlation between x and y is zero, so that $\rho = 0$. In that case, N_2 would give the probability of both x and y being less than or equal to zero. Considered alone, the chance that $x \leq 0$ is 50 percent, and the same is true of y considered by itself. Because we assume that the correlation between the two is zero, the joint probability of both x and y being less than 0 is just the product of the two individual probabilities, or 25 percent. **OPTION!** can compute these bivariate probabilities.

We now turn to a close examination of the formula, which bears close similarities to the Black–Scholes model. At time t, the value of the call must equal the present value of the expected payoffs on the option. We have already seen that these are somewhat complex. First, at the dividend date, if the stock price exceeds the critical stock price, the call owner will exercise. In that case, the payoff is the stock with dividend minus the exercise price, and this payoff occurs at t_1. If the stock price is less than the critical price at t_1, she will not exercise. The payoffs from the option then become either zero, if the exercise price equals or exceeds the stock price at expiration, or the stock price less the exercise price, if the stock price exceeds the exercise price at expiration. In the exact American call pricing formula, the cumulative normal (N) and the bivariate cumulative normal (N_2) express various probabilities of certain stock price outcomes. These probabilities give different weights to possible outcomes from the option investment. For example, the term

$$N_2\left(a_2; b_2; -\sqrt{\frac{t_1 - t}{T - t}}\right) \tag{15.3}$$

measures the probability that $S^* + D_1 \leq S_t$ and that $S_T \geq X$. This probability would be associated with the payoff that arises when the owner does not exercise the option at the dividend date, but the option is in-the-money at expiration. Thus, without exploring all of the mathematics, we see that the call price is a function of the payoffs that arise in the various possible circumstances, such as not exercising and having the call finish in-the-money, coupled with the probability of those circumstances arising.

We now show how to compute the exact value of an American call on a stock with one dividend according to this model. Continuing with our example, we have an American call with an exercise price of $100 on a stock with a standard deviation of 0.2. The risk-free rate is 10 percent. The stock will pay a $5 dividend when the option has 90 days remaining until expiration. We will find the price of the call when it has 180 days remaining until expiration and the stock price is $110.

The first step is to compute the value of the stock less the present value of the dividend:

$$S - D_1 e^{-r(t_1-t)} = \$110 - 5e^{-0.1\times(90/365)} = \$105.12$$

Other terms are as follows:

$$a_1 = \frac{\ln\left(\dfrac{110.00 - 4.88}{100.00}\right) + (0.1 + 0.5 \times 0.2 \times 0.2) \times (180/365)}{0.2\sqrt{180/365}}$$

$$= \frac{0.0499 + 0.0592}{0.1404} = 0.7771$$

$$a_2 = 0.7771 - 0.2 \times \sqrt{180/365} = 0.6367$$

$$b_1 = \frac{\ln\left(\dfrac{110.00 - 4.88}{100.67}\right) + (0.1 + 0.5 \times 0.2 \times 0.2) \times (90/365)}{0.2\sqrt{90/365}}$$

$$= \frac{0.0433 + 0.0296}{0.0993} = 0.7341$$

$$b_2 = 0.7341 - 0.2 \times \sqrt{90/365} = 0.6348$$

$$\sqrt{\frac{t_1 - t}{T - t}} = \sqrt{\frac{90}{180}} = 0.7071$$

Given these values, we now compute the cumulative normal and cumulative bivariate normal terms:

$$N(b_1) = N(0.7341) = 0.768556$$

$$N(b_2) = N(0.6348) = 0.737221$$

$$N_2\left(a_1; -b_1; -\sqrt{\frac{t_1 - t}{T - t}}\right) = N_2(0.7771; -0.7341; -0.7071) = 0.099098$$

$$N_2\left(a_2; -b_2; -\sqrt{\frac{t_1 - t}{T - t}}\right) = N_2(0.6367; -0.6348; -0.7071) = 0.101320$$

We now compute the value of the American call, as follows:

$$
\begin{aligned}
C_t &= 105.12 \times 0.768556 + 105.12 \times 0.099098 - 100e^{-0.1 \times (180/365)} \times 0.101320 \\
&\quad - (100.00 - 5.00)e^{-0.1 \times (90/365)} \times 0.737221 \\
&= 80.79 + 10.42 - 9.64 - 68.33 \\
&= \$13.24
\end{aligned}
$$

Thus, with 180 days until expiration, this American call should be worth $13.24. This compares with a pseudo-American value in the same circumstances of $12.91. **OPTION!** can compute the value of a call under the exact American call option pricing model.

Strictly speaking, this model holds only for an American call on a stock paying a single dividend before the option's expiration date. However, when there is more than one dividend, exercise is normally rational only for the final dividend. Therefore, we can use the exact pricing model if we subtract the present value of all dividends other than the final one from the stock price and then use the adjusted stock price in all computations. (Notice that this parallels the logic of the known dividend adjustment to the Black–Scholes model.)

As we have just noted, it is only for this special case of a call with one dividend that we can compute an exact American option price. For all other circumstances, we must use a variety of approximation techniques. Fortunately, these techniques work very well, and we turn now to a consideration of them.

Early exercise behavior: empirical evidence

A critical element of the theory of option valuation is the early exercise privilege attached to American-style options. A 1994 study by Overdahl and Martin found that early exercise commonly occurs in the equity options market.[4] During their sample period, approximately 30 percent of all exercised calls and 60 percent of all exercised puts were exercised before expiration, with over 80 percent of all early exercises occurring at least one week prior to expiration.

Overdahl and Martin found that fewer than 1 percent of exercised options fail to conform to the exercise boundaries of the theory of option valuation. Perhaps surprisingly, a small set of calls written on nondividend-paying stocks were exercised early. These call options were thinly traded where the transaction costs of selling the calls exceeded the cost of extinguishing the option early.

This evidence is potentially bad news for those engaged in dividend capture strategies. A successful dividend spread strategy requires that some call option holders fail to exercise in accordance with the theory. This evidence is potentially good news for those engaged in trading strategies where assignment risk must be managed. The evidence shows that the risk of unanticipated assignment–that is, the probability that exercise occurs when the theory says it should not–is rare.

In a separate study, Poteshman and Serbin analyzed the early exercise of options by different classes of investors.[5] Traders at large investment houses exercised their options in precise accordance with the theory of rational option exercise. However, for customers of discount brokers and customers of full-service brokers, a significant number of options were not exercised in accordance with the theory.

Analytic approximations of American option prices

In Chapter 13, we considered the Merton model, which extended the Black–Scholes model to European options on stocks that pay a continuous dividend at a constant rate. The analytic approximations that we now consider apply to American options on an underlying instrument that pays a continuous dividend at a constant rate. The Merton model provides a closed-form solution to the problem of European options on stocks with continuous dividends. For American options, no closed-form solutions are available. The analytic approximations for American options considered in this section are extremely accurate and computationally inexpensive. **OPTION!** can compute both call and put values according to the analytic approximation presented in this section.

To understand the incentive for early exercise of an option on a stock with a continuous dividend, consider again the Merton model developed in Chapter 13:

$$c_t^M = Se^{-\delta(T-t)}N(d_1^M) - Xe^{-r(T-t)}N(d_2^M)$$

The difference in value between this European option and a parallel American option arises from the potential benefits of early exercise. Thus, we focus on an option that is deep-in-the-money. In such a situation, d_1^M will be large, and d_2^M will be large as well. Consequently, $N(d_1^M)$ and $N(d_2^M)$ will approach 1.0. In the limit, then, for an option that is extremely deep-in-the-money, the Merton model approaches the following:

$$c_t = S_t e^{-\delta(T-t)} - Xe^{-r(T-t)}$$

By contrast, an American option would have to be worth at least its immediately available exercisable proceeds:

$$C_t \geq S_t - X$$

If a trader owns the American option, she has a choice between these two quantities. Which is preferable depends upon how deep-in-the-money the option is, the dividend rate on the stock, δ, the interest rate, r, and the time remaining until the option expires, $T - t$. If the stock price reaches a critical level, S^*, such that

$$S_t^* - X = c(S_t^*, X, T - t) + \text{early exercise premium} \tag{15.4}$$

the owner of an American option is indifferent about exercising. If the stock price exceeds S^*, she will exercise immediately to capture the exercise proceeds $S_t - X$. If the stock price is below S^*, she will not exercise. Figure 15.3 presents a graph of these relationships. Notice that the European call in Figure 15.3 can be worth less than $S_t - X$, because of the dividend. (As we noted above, a deep-in-the-money European call will tend to its lower bound of $S_t e^{-\delta(T-t)} - Xe^{-r(T-t)}$.) At the critical stock price, S^*, the European call is worth exactly $S^* - X$. For any stock price greater than S^*, the European call will be worth less than the exercisable proceeds for the American call. This explains why the owner of the American call is indifferent about exercise at a stock price of S^*; at that stock price, the American and European calls are worth the same: $S^* - X$. For higher stock prices, the value of the European call falls below that of the American call, and the value of the American call becomes equal to its exercisable proceeds. Thus, the owner of the American call should exercise to capture the quantity $S_t - X$. Those funds can then be invested from the exercise date to the expiration date to earn a return that will be lost if the option is not exercised.

Figure 15.3   American calls and the incentive for early exercise

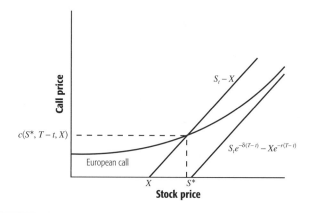

A similar argument applies to American put options. As the stock price falls well below the exercise price, there comes a point at which

$$X - S^{**} = p(S^{**}, X, T - t) + \text{early exercise premium} \tag{15.5}$$

where S^{**} is the critical stock price for an American put. If the stock price falls below S^{**}, the American put should be exercised to capture the exercised proceeds of $X - S_t$. Figure 15.4 presents a graph of this relationship for the European and American puts. As the graph shows, for any stock price less than S^{**}, the American put should be exercised immediately.

Although a complete discussion of the mathematics is beyond the scope of this text, we present the formulas for an analytic approximation of the American call and put options, and we discuss the computation of call and put values under the terms of the model.

Figure 15.4   American puts and the incentive for early exercise

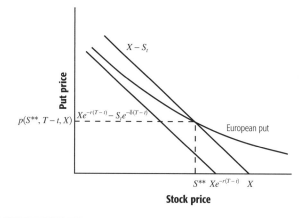

The analytic approximation for an American call is as follows:

$$C_t = c_t + A_2 \left(\frac{S_t}{S^*} \right)^{q_2} \quad \text{if} \quad S_t < S^* \tag{15.6}$$

$$= S_t - X \qquad \text{if} \quad S_t \geq S^*$$

where

$$A_2 = \frac{S^*[1 - e^{-\delta(T-t)}N(d_1)]}{q_2}$$

and S^* is the solution to

$$S^* - X = c_t(S^*, X, T - t) + \{1 - e^{-\delta(T-t)}N(d_1)\}(S^*/q_2) \tag{15.7}$$

$N(d_1)$ and $p(S^*, X, T - t)$ are evaluated at S^*. To find S^* requires an iterative search for the value that makes the equation balance. Other terms are as follows:

$$q_2 = \frac{1 - n + \sqrt{(n-1)^2 + 4k}}{2}$$

$$n = \frac{2(r - \delta)}{\sigma^2}, \quad k = \frac{2r}{\sigma^2(1 - e^{-r(T-t)})}$$

For an American put, the analytic approximation is as follows:

$$P_t = p_t + A_1 \left(\frac{S_t}{S^{**}} \right)^{q_1} \quad \text{if} \quad S_t > S^{**} \tag{15.8}$$

$$= X - S_t \qquad \text{if} \quad S_t \leq S^{**}$$

where

$$A_1 = \frac{S^{**}[1 - e^{-\delta(T-t)}N(-d_1)]}{q_1}$$

$$q_1 = \frac{1 - n - \sqrt{(n-1)^2 + 4k}}{2}$$

S^{**} is found by an iterative search to make the following equation hold:

$$X - S^{**} = p_t(S^{**}, X, T - t) - [1 - e^{-\delta(T-t)})N(-d_1)](S^{**}/q_1) \tag{15.9}$$

$N(-d_1)$ and $p_t(S^{**}, X, T - t)$ are evaluated at the critical stock price S^{**}.

To illustrate the application of this model, consider an American call option on an underlying stock that is currently priced at $60, has a standard deviation of 0.2, and pays a continuous dividend of 13.75 percent. The call has a strike price of $60 and 180 days until expiration. The risk-free rate is 9 percent. In Chapter 13, we illustrated the Merton model with a European call having the same terms and found that the price of the European call was $2.5557.

The first step in computing the value of this American call is to find the values of the inter-mediate terms n, k, and q_2. They are as follows:

$$n = \frac{2 \times (0.09 - 0.1375)}{0.2 \times 0.2} = -2.375$$

$$k = \frac{2 \times 0.09}{0.2 \times 0.2 \times [1 - e^{-0.09 \times (180/365)}]} = 103.6555$$

$$q_2 = \frac{1 - (-2.375) + \sqrt{(-2.375 - 1)^2 + 4 \times 103.6555}}{2} = 12.007537$$

We next search for the critical stock price, S^*, and find that $S^* = 70.2336$. (This search must be done by trial and error until the correct one is discovered.) If the actual stock price equaled the critical price, the European call would be worth $9.0152. Then, d_1 and $N(d_1)$, computed at that critical stock price of $70.2336, would be 1.024716 and 0.847251, respectively. Based on these values, we calculate A_2 as follows:

$$A_2 = \frac{70.2336 \times [1 - e^{-0.1375 \times (180/365)} \times 0.847251]}{12.007537} = 1.218344$$

We can now compute the American call price. Because the current stock price of $60 lies below the critical price of $70.2336, the value of the American call is as follows:

$$C_t = 2.5557 + 1.218344 \times \left(\frac{60}{70.2336}\right)^{12.007537} = 2.5557 + 0.183878 = 2.7395$$

Thus, the early exercise premium is $0.18. Because this computation involves an iterative search for S^*, it is quite tedious to perform without a computer. **OPTION!** solves for the critical stock price and the price of American calls and puts directly using this analytic approximation.

The binomial model and American option prices

Thus far in this chapter, we have considered various option pricing models for finding the value of American options on dividend paying stocks. As we have seen, there is no general exact solution for this problem. In fact, only for the case of an American call on a stock paying a single dividend during the option's life is it possible to compute an exact price. In all other cir-cumstances, we must rely on estimation techniques. The analytic approximation method we have studied in this chapter applies only to continuous dividends. With stocks typically paying dis-crete dividends, the need for other estimation techniques is particularly important.

The binomial model is particularly important for American options because it applies to both American calls and puts on stocks with all kinds of dividend payments. These include the case of no dividends, continuous dividends, known dividend yields, and known dollar dividends. There is a common strategy for applying the binomial model that applies to all types of dividend pat-terns, and we begin our discussion by analyzing the underlying strategy for the binomial model for American options. We then consider each of the different dividend strategies in turn.

No dividends

In Chapter 12, we explored the boundary conditions on the pricing of European options on stocks paying no dividends. For nondividend stocks, we saw that it can never be optimal to exercise a call before expiration. This means that the American call and the European call on a non-dividend stock must have the same value. Therefore, for the case of a call on a nondividend stock, we can price the American call as if it were a European call. It can often be advantageous to exercise puts on nondividend stocks, so the value of European and American puts can differ substantially. We illustrate this point for an American put and explicate the basic strategy for applying the binomial model to American options.

The basic strategy

In Chapter 13, we explored the binomial model for European options on stocks with and without dividends. For European options on nondividend stocks, we derived the possible stock prices at expiration and determined the value of the option (call or put) at expiration from our no-arbitrage condition. We then computed the value of an option one period before expiration as the expected value of the option at expiration discounted for one period. We continued this strategy, working through the binomial lattice, until we found the value of the option at the current time.

For options on stocks with dividends, we applied the binomial model by creating a lattice for the stock that reflected the timing and amount of dividend payments that the stock would make. These adjustments affected the distribution of possible stock values at the expiration date. We then computed the option values in the usual way by working from the exercise date back to the present.

To apply the binomial model for American options, we follow the same basic valuation strategy as for European options. There is, however, one important difference. For the option lattice for an American option, the option value is set equal to the maximum of:

(1)   the expected option value in one period discounted for one period at the risk-free rate; and
(2)   the immediate exercise value of the option, $S_t - X$ for a call, or $X - S_t$ for a put.

Except for this treatment of each node in the lattice for an American option, the binomial model for an American option is applied in exactly the same way as it is for a European option.

We illustrate this technique by considering an American put on a stock that pays no dividend. We assume the following data: $S_t = \$80$; $X = \$75$; $r = 0.07$; $\sigma = 0.3$; $T - t = 120$ days. Assuming a three-period binomial model, a single period is 40 days, or 0.1096 years. This gives a discount factor of 0.9924 per period, and the following parameter values: $U = 1.1044$; $D = 0.9055$; $\pi_U = 0.5138$. Figure 15.5 shows the stock price tree consistent with these data. (The careful reader may recall the same example from Figure 13.10.) The left-hand tree of Figure 15.6 repeats the left-hand tree from Figure 13.12, which is the binomial tree for a European put option on this stock. As the tree shows, the value of the European put is \$2.67 at node c. The right-hand tree in Figure 15.6 is the binomial tree for an American put. Aside from the left-hand tree's being for a European put and the right-hand tree's pertaining to an American put, all other circumstances are the same. An examination of the two trees shows that they are identical except for the prices at nodes a, b, and c.

Before turning to the differences at nodes a, b, and c, we first consider why the other nodes are identical. First, consider the nodes at expiration. At expiration, European and American options are identical. Both can be exercised and both have the same payoffs from the exercise decision.

Figure 15.5   The three-period stock price lattice

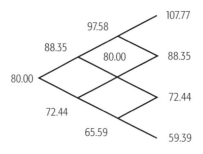

Figure 15.6   Three-period price lattices for a European and an American put

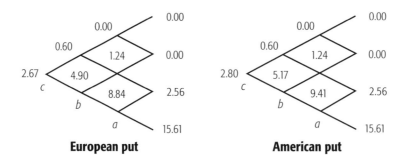

European put   **American put**

Therefore, European and American options at expiration must have the same value. Second, consider a node one period before expiration, such as the middle node of the tree, at which the stock price is $80 and both the European and American put prices are $1.24. If the stock price one period prior to expiration is $80, the American put cannot be exercised because the put is out-of-the-money. Therefore, it offers no advantage over the parallel European put. Consequently, the value must be the same.

These reflections lead us to see a condition for an American and a European option to have identical prices at a given node: If the option cannot be exercised at the given node, and if all nodes that can be reached subsequent to the node under consideration have identical prices for American and European options, then the price of the American and European options must be identical at the node in question. We can illustrate this point from the same tree by considering the node two periods before expiration in which the stock price is $88.35 and the value of the put (either European or American) is $0.60. The American put cannot be exercised at that node, because it is out-of-the-money with a stock price of $88.35. Further, all subsequent nodes have identical prices for the American and European puts. Therefore, the price of the European and American puts must be the same at that node.

We now turn to consider those nodes at which prices differ for the European and American put. At node a, the stock price is $65.59, the European put price is $8.84, and the American put price is $9.41. The European put price is just the expected value of the put's expiration values contingent upon the stock's rising or falling. The value at node a for the American put is as follows:

$$P = MAX(X - S, p) = MAX(\$75 - \$65.59, \$8.84) = \$9.41$$

If the stock price reaches node a, the holder of an American put should exercise and capture the exercise value of $9.41. This is higher than the present value of the expected payoff at expiration, which is the price of the European put: $8.84. As this example shows, the American put derives its higher value from its right to exercise early when conditions warrant.

At node b, the stock price is $72.44, and the European put is worth $4.90. The owner of the American put could exercise immediately for an exercise value of $75.00 − $72.44 = $2.56, but this would be foolish. One period later, the put will be worth $1.24 if the stock price rises or $9.41 if the stock price falls. Given that the probability of a stock price rise is 0.5138, the present value of the put's expected value in one period is

$$[0.5138 \times \$1.24 + 0.4862 \times \$9.41]e^{-0.07 \times (40/365)} = \$5.21 \times 0.9924 = \$5.17$$

The value of the put at node b is therefore

$$MAX\{\$2.56, \$5.17\} = \$5.17$$

Therefore, at node b, the put should not be exercised, and it is worth $5.17—the present value of the expected put value in one period.

At node c, the present time at which we want to value the option, the same rule applies. The American put cannot be exercised rationally, because it is out-of-the-money with $75 − $80 = −$5. The present value of the expected value of the put in one period is

$$[0.5138 \times \$0.60 + 0.4862 \times \$5.17]e^{-0.07 \times (40/365)} = \$2.80$$

The value of the American put at node c, which represents the present time, is

$$MAX\{-\$5.00, \$2.80\} = \$2.80$$

Because the exercise value (−$5.00) is negative, the value of the American put equals the present value of the expected value in one period ($2.80), and the American put should not be exercised.

This example illustrates the basic principle of applying the binomial model to American options. As we work back through the tree, discounting the next period's expected option values, we must ask at every node whether the immediate exercise value or the computed present value is greater. The value at the node is the maximum of those two quantities. Further, we may note that the stock tree is unaffected by whether the option we are analyzing is an American or a European option. We now consider how to apply the binomial model to American options on dividend paying stocks.

Continuous dividends

In Chapter 13, we explored the Merton model, which adjusts the Black–Scholes model to price European options on stocks that pay a continuous dividend. We also showed how to use the binomial model to price European options on stocks that pay continuous dividends. There we saw that the parameters for the binomial model for a stock paying a continuous dividend are as follows:

$$U = e^{\sigma\sqrt{\Delta t}}$$

$$D = \frac{1}{U}$$ (15.10)

$$\pi_U = \frac{e^{(r-\delta)\Delta t} - D}{U - D}$$

As we have discussed in this chapter, the stock price tree is identical whether we are pricing European or American options. Therefore, these parameters apply to generating the binomial tree of stock prices for American options on stocks paying a continuous dividend. As an examination of these parameters shows, the stock price tree will be identical in both cases. However, the probability of a stock price increase varies inversely with the level of the continuous dividend rate, δ.

To illustrate the binomial model for pricing options on stocks with continuous dividends, consider the following data: $S_t = \$60$; $X = \$60$; $T - t = 180$ days; $\sigma = 0.2$; $r = 0.09$. Based on these data, consider a European and an American call option on this stock in the context of a two-period binomial model:

$$U = e^{\sigma\sqrt{\Delta t}} = e^{0.2\times\sqrt{(90/365)}} = 1.104412$$

$$D = \frac{1}{U} = 0.905460$$

$$\pi_U = \frac{e^{(r-\delta)\Delta t} - D}{U - D} = \frac{e^{(0.09-0.1375)\times(90/365)} - 0.905460}{1.104412 - 0.905460} = 0.416663$$

The single-period discount factor is $e^{-0.09\times(90/365)} = 0.978053$. Figure 15.7 gives the two-period stock price tree for these data, while Figure 15.8 shows the trees for a European and an American call. At expiration, the call will be in-the-money only if the stock price rises twice to a terminal price of \$73.18. In this case, both the European and American calls are worth \$13.18. One period before expiration, the present value of the expected terminal call value is

$$\$13.18 \times 0.416663 \times 0.978053 = \$5.37$$

This is the value of the European call at the node with a stock price of \$66.26. For the American call, the same expected value prevails, but the owner of the American call could exercise. The

---

Figure 15.7   The two-period stock price lattice

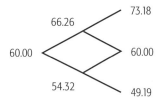

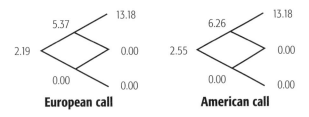

Figure 15.8   Two-period price lattices for a European and an American call

exercise value of the American call is $66.26 − $60.00 = $6.26. Therefore, the value of the American call is

$$C = \text{MAX}\{S - X, c\} = \text{MAX}\{\$6.26, \$5.37\} = \$6.26$$

If the stock price reaches $66.26 in one period, then the holder of the American call should exercise. In terms of the binomial tree for the American call, the value at this node becomes $6.26. At the present time, the present values of the expected call values one period hence are $2.19 for the European call and $2.55 for the American call. Thus, the current price of the European call is $2.19. At the present, the stock price and exercise price are both $60, so the American option cannot be exercised rationally. This means that the current American call price is $2.55, based on a two-period tree. With 200 periods, the European call value is $2.55 and the American call price is $2.73. Table 15.1 shows how the two call prices converge to their true values as the number of periods in the binomial tree ranges from one to 200. For comparison, the Merton model price for the European option is $2.5557 and the American analytic approximation is $2.7395. Thus, the binomial method provides estimates that are extremely close to other model prices that we have explored.

Table 15.1   The convergence of European and American call prices

Number of periods	European call	American call
1	3.3129	3.3129
2	2.1894	2.5530
3	2.8139	2.9399
4	2.3625	2.6380
5	2.7099	2.8517
10	2.4763	2.6909
25	2.5861	2.7554
50	2.5396	2.7216
100	2.5476	2.7256
200	2.5516	2.7275

Known dividend yields

In Chapter 13, we considered options on a stock that pays a known dividend yield at a certain date. For example, a stock might pay a dividend equal to 1 percent of its value in 90 days. The dividend payment obviously affects the stock price tree for the binomial model, and the loss of value from the stock will affect the value of calls and puts. This is true for both European and American options. Although the existence of dividends will affect the value of European calls and puts, it does not call for European option owners to make any special decisions, as they cannot exercise even if they wished. For the holder of an American call or put, there is an exercise decision, because the American option owner can exercise immediately before the dividend payment (in the case of a call), exercise immediately after the dividend payment (in the case of a put), or not exercise. While the dividend will affect the stock price tree, we note again that the stock price tree will be identical whether we are considering a European or an American option.

To apply the binomial model for an American call or put, we begin with the terminal stock price and the value of the option at expiration and work from expiration back to the present in the normal way. However, at each node, we must take account of the potential for early exercise. As we have seen, we take early exercise into account by finding the value of a European option at each node and comparing this value with the exercise value of the American option. If the exercise value exceeds the European value, the option price at the node should be the exercise value. Otherwise, the price at the node should be the European option price.

To see how to apply the binomial model to compute American option prices on a stock with a known dividend yield, consider the following data. A stock is currently priced at $80, and it will pay a dividend equal to 3 percent of its value in 55 days. The standard deviation of the stock is 0.3, and the risk-free rate is 7 percent. A call option on this stock has 120 days until expiration and an exercise price of $75. Based on these data, and with a three-period binomial model, $\Delta t = 40/365 = 0.1096$. Therefore,

$$U = e^{0.3 \times \sqrt{0.1096}} = 1.1044$$

$$D = \frac{1}{1.1044} = 0.9055$$

$$\pi_U = \frac{1.0077 - 0.9055}{1.1044 - 0.9055} = 0.5138$$

The discounting factor for a single period is $e^{-r\Delta t} = e^{-0.07 \times (40/365)} = 0.9924$. Figure 15.9 shows the stock price tree for this example. (This same example was considered in Chapter 13 for European calls.) In terms of Figure 15.9, the dividend occurs between time 1 (day 40) and time 2 (day 80). The call owner might exercise at time 1 before the dividend is paid, but if she waits until time 2, the dividend will already be paid, and the dividend's value will be lost from the stock.

Figure 15.10 shows option price trees for European and American calls consistent with the stock price tree of Figure 15.9. At expiration and the period prior to expiration, the European and American call option trees are identical. This is because the exercise value for the American option never exceeds the value of the European call. In the first period, if the stock price rises from $80.00 to $88.35, the owner of an American call should exercise. We can see the desirability of exercise in this case as follows. At the node with a stock price of $88.35, the present value of the expected value of the call in the next period is $12.94, the value of the European call. With a stock price of $88.35 and an exercise price of $75.00, the American call

Figure 15.9   The three-period stock price lattice

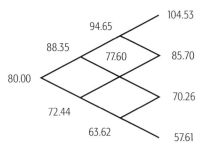

Figure 15.10   Three-period price lattices for a European and an American call

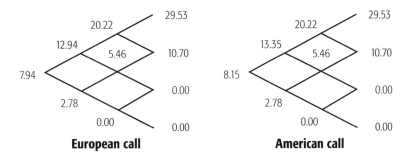

can (and should) be exercised for an exercise value of $13.35. Thus, in the tree for the American call, the value at this node is the exercise value of $13.35. This difference in the two trees affects the current values of the European and American calls, which are $7.94 and $8.15, respectively. With 200 periods, the European and American calls are worth $7.61 and $8.04, respectively. The binomial model applies to options on stocks with any number of dividend yields during the life of the option.

For these options, none of the other models we have considered apply. From the valuation date, the dividend amount is uncertain, as it will be 3 percent of whatever stock price prevails in 55 days. Therefore, the exact American option pricing model does not apply. Further, the analytic approximation method for American options does not apply, because the dividend is not continuous. For European options, we cannot apply the known dividend adjustment, because the dollar amount of the dividend is unknown. Similarly, we cannot apply the Merton model because the dividend is not continuous. Of all the methods we have studied, only the binomial model can deal with the known dividend yield for an American option. **OPTION!** can compute prices for American call and put options on stocks with as many as three known dividend yields by using the binomial model.

Known dollar dividends

For options on stocks with known dollar dividends, the binomial model can be applied in a manner almost identical to that appropriate for known dividend yields. The first step is to generate the tree describing the potential stock price movements. As we saw in Chapter 13 when we considered the pricing of European options on stocks with known dollar dividends, there can be a problem with the tree failing to recombine after the dividend has been paid. In this situation, the number of nodes can increase dramatically, particularly when there are many periods and several dividends. (For details on why the tree fails to recombine, see Chapter 13.)

We can solve this problem as we did in Chapter 13 by making a simplifying assumption. We assume that the stock price reflects the dividend, which is known with certainty, and all other factors that might affect the stock price, which are uncertain. We then adjust the uncertain component of the stock price for the impending dividends and model the uncertain component of the stock price with the binomial tree, adding back the present value of all future dividends at each node. Specifically, we follow these steps:

(1)   Compute the present value of all dividends to be paid during the life of the option as of the present time t.
(2)   Subtract this present value from the current stock price to form $S'_t = S_t - \text{PV}$ of all dividends.
(3)   Create the binomial tree by applying the up and down factors in the usual way to the initial stock price S'_t.
(4)   After generating the tree, add to the stock price at each node the present value of all future dividends to be paid during the life of the option.
(5)   Compute the option values in the usual way by working through the binomial tree.

These are exactly the steps we used in Chapter 13 to resolve this difficulty.

The application of this procedure to American options is exactly the same as with European options, with one exception. In working through the tree to generate the option price tree, we must compare the present value of next period's expected option value with the exercise value of the option. The option price at the node is the higher of the present value or the exercise value. The computation of the value at a node is exactly the same as in other cases we have already considered, such as the application of the binomial model to options on stocks with known dividend yields.

We illustrate the application of the binomial model to options on stocks with a known dollar dividend by considering a comprehensive example. A stock now trades for $50, has a standard deviation of 0.4, and will pay a dividend of $2 in 90 days. An American call and put on this stock expire in 120 days, and both have an exercise price of $50. The risk-free rate of interest is 9 percent, and we will model the price of the options with a five-period binomial model.

According to the five steps outlined earlier, we begin by subtracting the present value of the dividends to be paid during the life of the option from the current stock price. The present value of the dividend is $1.96, so the adjusted stock price, S' is $48.04. A single period is 24 days, and the discount factor for one period is 0.9941. The parameters for the binomial model with five periods are as follows:

$$\Delta t = \frac{24}{365} = 0.065756 \text{ years}$$

$$U = e^{\sigma\sqrt{\Delta t}} = e^{0.4\times\sqrt{0.065753}} = 1.108015$$

$$D = \frac{1}{U} = 0.902515$$

$$\pi_U = \frac{e^{r\Delta t} - D}{U - D} = \frac{e^{0.09 \times (0.065753)} - 0.902515}{1.108015 - 0.902515} = 0.503262$$

The top panel of Figure 15.11 shows the stock price lattice generated with a starting price of $48.04 and the up and down factors shown above. This upper lattice does not reflect the dividend. Having generated this lattice, we account for dividends by adding the present value of all future dividends to be paid during the life of the option to each node. The bottom lattice of Figure 15.11 shows the adjusted stock prices. As the dividend will be paid in 90 days, the dividend falls between the third and fourth periods. This means that for periods 4 and 5, there are no dividends to consider, and the two lattices have identical stock prices in periods 4 and 5. For all periods before the dividend, the stock price at each node is adjusted by adding the present value of the dividend. For example, the node for the second period represents a time that is 48 days from now. At that time, the dividend will be 42 days away, and the present

---

Figure 15.11   Five-period stock price lattices unadjusted and adjusted for a known dollar dividend

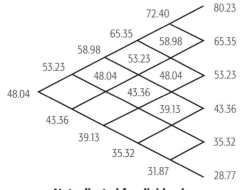

Not adjusted for dividends

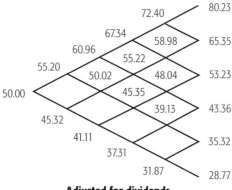

Adjusted for dividends

Figure 15.12 Five-period price lattices for an American call and put on a stock with a known dollar dividend

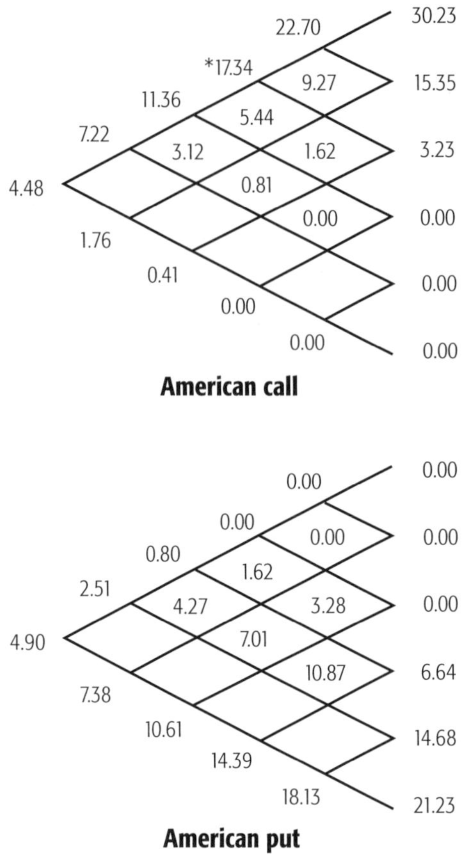

American call

American put

value of the dividend at that point is $1.98. Therefore, if we compare the stock prices in the two lattices for period 2, the prices in the bottom lattice will exceed their counterparts in the upper lattice by $1.98. All other stock prices in periods 1–3 are adjusted similarly. The bottom stock price lattice in Figure 15.11 is the lattice that we will use to compute the option prices.

In Figure 15.12, the upper lattice pertains to the American call, while the lower lattice prices the American put. Some prices are preceded by an asterisk, indicating that the price represents the exercise value of the option at that node. For example, the call lattice has a price of $17.34 in period 4. The present value of the two option values in period 4 is $15.93. However, the stock price at that node is $67.34, implying an exercise value of $17.34. Because the exercise value exceeds $15.93, the call value at that node is $17.34. Working back through the lattice to the present shows an American call value of $4.48 and an American put value of $4.90. With the five-period lattice, the European call and put are worth $4.31 and $4.81, respectively. For the same data, except using a lattice with 200 periods, the American call is worth $4.59, and the American put is $4.78. With a 200-period lattice, the European call and put are $4.17 and $4.66, respectively. We also note that this example can be solved using the exact American call option pricing model, which gives a call price of $4.59, the same as the binomial model with 200 periods.

Conclusion

This chapter explored the pricing of American options. We began by reviewing the differences between American and European options. For nondividend stocks, the American and European calls have the same value, as early exercise is never desirable. For puts, however, we showed that there are incentives to early exercise even when there are no dividends. Therefore, the price of an American put can exceed that of a European put even in the absence of dividends. When the underlying stock pays dividends, circumstances can arise in which it would be desirable to exercise a call and a put before expiration, and the prices of American and European options diverge.

The discussion then turned to models for pricing American options, beginning with Black's pseudo-American option pricing model. We then considered the exact pricing model for an American call with a single dividend before the option's expiration. We noted that this is the only situation in which an exact pricing formula exists for American options. In all other pricing situations, we must use approximation techniques.

When the underlying stock pays a continuous dividend, an approximation for American options applies. This analytic approximation is analogous to the Merton model for European options, and it accurately estimates the prices of American calls and puts when the underlying instrument pays a continuous dividend.

Most stocks pay discrete dividends, so the analytic approximation does not apply. Accordingly, we turned to the binomial model and showed how it can apply to American options when the underlying good pays dividends in a variety of different ways. We considered the binomial model for American options when the underlying good pays a continuous dividend, when it pays a known dividend yield, and when it pays a known dollar dividend. In the last two cases, the binomial model can accommodate any number of dividends.

Many of the calculations of this chapter are quite tedious and time-consuming. (Imagine, for instance, the tedium of computing the binomial model price for a lattice of 100 periods.) OPTION! computes option prices for all of the models considered in this chapter.

Exercises

1 Explain why American and European calls on a non-dividend stock always have the same value.

2 Explain why American and European puts on a non-dividend stock can have different values.

3 Explain the circumstances that might make the early exercise of an American put on a nondividend stock desirable.

4 What factors might make an owner exercise an American call?

5 Do dividends on the underlying stock make the early exercise of an American put more or less likely? Explain.

6 Do dividends on the underlying stock make the early exercise of an American call more or less likely? Explain.

7 Explain the strategy behind the pseudo-American call pricing strategy.

8 Consider a stock with a price of $140 and a standard deviation of 0.4. The stock will pay a dividend of $2 in 40 days and a second dividend of $2 in 130 days. The current risk-free rate of interest is 10 percent. An American call on this stock has an exercise price of $150 and expires in 100 days. What is the price of the call according to the pseudo-American approach?

9 Could the exact American call pricing model be used to price the option in Exercise 8? Explain.

10 Explain why the exact American call pricing model treats the call as an "option on an option."

11 Explain the idea of a bivariate cumulative standardized normal distribution. What would be the cumulative probability of observing two variables both with a value of zero, assuming that the correlation between them was zero? Explain.

12 In the exact American call pricing model, explain why the model can compute the call price with only one dividend.

13 What is the critical stock price in the exact American call pricing model?

14 Explain how the analytic approximation for American option values is analogous to the Merton model.

15 Explain the role of the critical stock price in the analytic approximation for an American call.

16 Why should an American call owner exercise if the stock price exceeds the critical price?

17 Consider the binomial model for an American call and put on a stock that pays no dividends. The current stock price is $120, and the exercise price for both the put and the call is $110. The standard deviation of the stock returns is 0.4, and the risk-free rate is 10 percent. The options expire in 120 days. Model the price of these options using a four-period tree. Draw the stock tree and the corresponding trees for the call and the put.

Explain when, if ever, each option should be exercised. What is the value of a European call in this situation? Can you find the value of the European call without making a separate computation? Explain.

18 Consider the binomial model for an American call and put on a stock whose price is $120. The exercise price for both the put and the call is $110. The standard deviation of the stock returns is 0.4, and the risk-free rate is 10 percent. The options expire in 120 days. The stock will pay a dividend equal to 3 percent of its value in 50 days. Model and compute the price of these options using a four-period tree. Draw the stock tree and the corresponding trees for the call and the put. Explain when, if ever, each option should be exercised.

19 Consider the binomial model for an American call and put on a stock whose price is $120. The exercise price for both the put and the call is $110. The standard deviation of the stock returns is 0.4, and the risk-free rate is 10 percent. The options expire in 120 days. The stock will pay a $3 dividend in 50 days. Model and compute the price of these options using a four-period tree. Draw the stock tree and the corresponding trees for the call and the put. Explain when, if ever, each option should be exercised.

20 Consider the analytic approximation for American options. A stock sells for $130, has a standard deviation of 0.3, and pays a continuous dividend of 3 percent. An American call and put on this stock both have an exercise price of $130, and they both expire in 180 days. The risk-free rate is 12 percent. Find the value of the call and put according to this model. Demonstrate that you have found the correct critical stock price for both options.

21 An American call and put both have an exercise price of $100. An acquaintance asserts that the critical stock price for both options is $90 under the analytic approximation technique. Comment on this claim and explain your reasoning.

22 Consider a stock with a price of $80 and a standard deviation of 0.3. The stock will pay a $5 dividend in 70 days. The current risk-free rate of interest is 10 percent. Options written on this stock have an exercise price of $80 and expire in 120 days. Model and compute the price of these options using a four-period tree.

   A Draw the stock price trees.
   B Calculate the values of European and American call and put options written on this stock. Value the options using the recursive procedure. Construct the price trees for each option.
   C Compare the prices of the European and American options. How much value does the right to

exercise the option before expiration add to the value of the American options?
   D Explain when, if ever, each option should be exercised.

23 Consider a stock with a price of $70 and a standard deviation of 0.4. The stock will pay a dividend of $2 in 40 days and a second dividend of $2 in 130 days. The current risk-free rate of interest is 10 percent. An American call on this stock has an exercise price of $75 and expires in 180 days. What is the price of the call according to the pseudo-American approach?

24 Consider a stock with a price of $140 and a standard deviation of 0.4. The stock will pay a dividend of $5 in 40 days and a second dividend of $5 in 130 days. The current risk-free rate of interest is 10 percent. An American call on this stock has an exercise price of $150 and expires in 100 days.

   A What is the price of the call according to the pseudo-American approach?
   B What is the price of the call according to the compound option pricing model?
   C What is the critical stock price, S^*? Discuss the implications of this finding on the likelihood of exercising the call option early.
   D Compare the prices calculated using the three option pricing methods.

25 Consider the binomial model for an American call and put on a stock that pays no dividends. The current stock price is $120, and the exercise price for both the put and the call is $110. The standard deviation of the stock returns is 0.4, and the risk-free rate is 10 percent. The options expire in 120 days. Model the price of these options using a four-period tree.

   A Draw the stock price tree and the corresponding trees for the call and the put options.
   B What is the value of each of the two options? Value the options using the recursive procedure.
   C Explain when, if ever, each option should be exercised.
   D What is the value of a European call written on this stock? Can you find the value of the European call without making a separate computation? Explain.

26 Consider the binomial model for an American call and put on a stock whose price is $50. The exercise price for both the put and the call is $55. The standard deviation of the stock returns is 0.35, and the risk-free rate is 10 percent. The options expire in 160 days. The stock will pay a dividend equal to 4 percent of its value

in 65 days. Model and compute the price of these options using a four-period tree.

A   Draw the stock price tree.

B   What is the value of each of the two options? Value the options using the recursive procedure. Draw the tree for each option.

C   Explain when, if ever, each option should be exercised.

Notes

1   Fischer Black first proposed this idea in his paper "Fact and Fantasy in the Use of Options," *Financial Analysts Journal*, July/August 1975, pp. 36–72.

2   R. E. Whaley, "Valuation of American Call Options on Dividend Paying Stocks: Empirical Tests," *Journal of Financial Economics*, 10, March 1982, pp. 29–58.

3   This model was developed in a series of papers. R. Roll, "An Analytical Formula for Unprotected American Call Options on Stocks with Known Dividends," *Journal of Financial Economics*, 5, 1977, pp. 251–58; R. Geske, "A Note on an Analytic Valuation Formula for Unprotected American Call Options on Stocks with Known Dividends," *Journal of Financial Economics*, 7, 1979, pp. 375–80; R. Whaley, "On the Valuation of American Call Options on Stocks with Known Dividends," *Journal of Financial Economics*, 9, 1981, pp. 207–11; R. Geske, "Comments on Whaley's Note," *Journal of Financial Economics*, 9, 1981, pp. 213–15.

4   See J. Overdahl, "The Exercise of Equity Options: Theory and Empirical Evidence" (with Peter Martin), *Journal of Derivatives*, Fall, 1994, pp. 38–51.

5   A. M. Poteshman and V. Serbib, "Clearly Irrational Financial Market Behavior: Evidence from the Early Exercise of Exchange Traded Stock Options," *Journal of Finance*, 58:1, 2003, pp. 37–70.

16

Options on Stock Indexes, Foreign Currency, and Futures

Overview

This chapter considers three different kinds of options: options on stock indexes, options on foreign currency, and options on futures. We consider these different types of options together because the principles that determine the price of these options are almost identical. In essence, the three types of options considered in this chapter are united by the fact that the good underlying each option can be treated as paying a continuous dividend. The pricing of these options is further unified by the conceptual connections among the different options. For example, we will consider options on stock index futures as well as options on stock indexes themselves, and we analyze options on foreign currency futures as well as options on foreign currencies alone.

While there may be common principles for the pricing of these three types of options, the markets for each of these options are quite large and have their own features. These were explored in Chapter 10. Consequently, this chapter begins by analyzing the pricing principles for these options. As noted above, the underlying instruments may all be treated as paying a continuous dividend—particularly when we think of a dividend as a leakage of value from the instrument paying the dividend. For a stock index, the continuous dividend really is a dividend—the aggregate dividends on the stocks represented in the index. For a foreign currency, we may treat the foreign interest rate as a continuous dividend. For a futures option, the cost of financing and storing the underlying good (a bond, 5,000 bushels of wheat, or the proverbial pork bellies) is a leakage of value from the commodity.

Because the underlying good pays a continuous dividend, we know that the Merton model, which was discussed in Chapter 13, pertains directly to pricing these three types of European options. Also, the binomial model directly applies as well. For American options, discussed in Chapter 15, two approaches are clearly applicable. First, the analytic approximation technique works extremely well in pricing the types of options discussed in this chapter. Second, we can also apply the binomial model under the assumption of continuous dividends.

European option pricing

In Chapter 13, we considered the Merton model, which extends the Black–Scholes model to provide an exact pricing model for European options on stocks that pay dividends at a continuous rate. We also discussed the binomial model and saw that it can apply to European option pricing on stocks that pay a continuous dividend. In this section, we extend both of these models to the pricing of European options on stock indexes, foreign currency, and futures.

The Merton model

The Merton model extends the Black–Scholes model by treating continuous dividends as a negative interest rate. In Chapter 13, we saw how dividends reduce the value of a call option, because they reduce the value of the stock that underlies the option. In effect, a continuous dividend implies a continuous leakage of value from the stock that equals the dividend rate. We let the Greek letter delta, δ, represent this rate of leakage.[1] Merton's adjustment to the Black–Scholes model for continuous dividends is as follows:

$$c_t^M = e^{-\delta(T-t)}S_t N(d_1^M) - Xe^{-r(T-t)}N(d_2^M)$$

$$d_1^M = \frac{\ln\left(\dfrac{S_t}{X}\right) + (r - \delta + 0.5\sigma^2)(T - t)}{\sigma\sqrt{T - t}} \tag{16.1}$$

$$d_2^M = d_1^M - \sigma\sqrt{T - t}$$

where δ is the continuous dividend rate on the stock.

To adjust the regular Black–Scholes model, we replace the current stock price with the stock price adjusted for the continuous dividend. That is, we replace S_t with

$$e^{-\delta(T-t)}S_t \tag{16.2}$$

Substituting this expression into the formulas for d_1 and d_2 gives d_1^M and d_2^M as shown above. Merton's adjusted put value is as follows:

$$p_t^M = Xe^{-r(T-t)}N(-d_2^M) - Se^{-\delta(T-t)}N(-d_1^M) \tag{16.3}$$

When $\delta = 0$, the Merton model reduces immediately to the Black–Scholes model.

We can determine the price of options on stock indexes, foreign currency, and futures if we can determine the correct term to substitute for Equation 16.2 in the Black–Scholes model.

The binomial model

In Chapter 13, we saw that the price at time t of a European call, c_t, and a European put, p_t, could be expressed as follows under the terms of the binomial model:

$$c_t = \frac{\displaystyle\sum_{j=m}^{n}\left(\frac{n!}{j!(n-j)!}\right)(\pi_U^j \pi_D^{n-j})[U^j D^{n-j}S_t - X]}{R^n} \tag{16.4}$$

$$p_t = \frac{\displaystyle\sum_{j=0}^{n}\left(\frac{n!}{j!(n-j)!}\right)(\pi_U^j \pi_D^{n-j})\text{MAX}[0, X - U^j D^{n-j}S_t]}{R^n} \tag{16.5}$$

where $U = 1 +$ the percentage increase in a period if the stock price rises; $D = 1 -$ the percentage decrease in a period if the stock price falls; $R = 1 +$ the risk-free rate per period; π_U is the probability of a price increase in any period; and π_D is the probability of a price decrease in any period. These pricing models apply for any time span divided into n periods, where m is the minimum number of price increases to bring the call into-the-money at expiration.

To apply the binomial model to options on goods paying a continuous dividend, we need to adjust the binomial parameters to reflect the continuous leakage of value from the stock that the dividend represents and to accurately reflect the price movements on the stock. For the Merton model for European options on a stock paying a continuous dividend, we saw that the adjustment largely involved subtracting the continuous dividend rate, δ, from the risk-free rate, r. This is exactly the adjustment required for the binomial model. For options on a good paying a continuous dividend δ, the U, D, and π_U factors are as follows:

$$U = e^{\sigma\sqrt{\Delta t}}$$

$$D = \frac{1}{U}$$

$$\pi_U = \frac{e^{(r-\delta)\Delta t} - D}{U - D}$$

(16.6)

We can apply this binomial model to options on stock indexes, foreign currency, or futures by determining the appropriate δ and the correct price of the instrument to take the place of S_t in the binomial model.

Options on stock indexes

The Merton model and the binomial model apply directly to pricing options on stock indexes. Because a stock index merely summarizes the performance of some set of stocks, we may think of the stock index as representing a portfolio of stocks, some of which pay dividends. Because we are pricing an option on this portfolio of stocks, we are concerned only with the dividends on the entire portfolio—we need to consider the dividends on individual stocks only insofar as they determine the overall dividend for the portfolio. Almost all individual stocks pay periodic discrete dividends (usually following a quarterly payment pattern). However, for stock indexes, including many stocks, the assumption of a continuous dividend payment is fairly realistic. In general, the greater the number of stocks represented in a stock index, the more realistic is the assumption of continuous dividends.[2]

To illustrate the application of the Merton model to pricing options on stock indexes, consider a stock index that has a current value of 350.00. The standard deviation of returns for the index is 0.2, the risk-free rate is 8 percent, and the continuous dividend rate on the index is 4 percent. European call and put options on this stock index expire in 150 days and have a strike price of 340.00. Therefore, the dividend rate of 4 percent takes the role of δ in the Merton model, and the index value of 350.00 takes the role of S_t. For these data, we find the value of the call and put in index units as follows:

$$d_1^M = \frac{\ln\left(\dfrac{350}{340}\right) + [0.08 - 0.04 + 0.5 \times 0.2 \times 0.2]\left(\dfrac{150}{365}\right)}{0.2\sqrt{\dfrac{150}{365}}}$$

$$= \frac{0.028988 + 0.024658}{0.128212} = 0.418413$$

$$d_2^M = 0.418413 - 0.2\sqrt{\frac{150}{365}} = 0.290201$$

$N(d_1^M) = N(0.418413) = 0.662177$, $N(d_2^M) = N(0.290201) = 0.614169$, $N(-d_1^M) = N(-0.418413) = 0.337823$, and $N(-d_2^M) = N(-0.290201) = 0.385831$. Therefore, the call and put are worth the following:

$$c_t^M = e^{-0.04\times(150/365)}350.00 \times 0.662177 - 340.00e^{-0.08\times(150/365)} \times 0.614169 = \$25.92$$
$$p_t^M = 340.00e^{-0.08\times(150/365)} \times 0.385831 - 350.00e^{-0.04\times(150/365)} \times 0.337823 = \$10.63$$

For a five-period binomial model price on the same options, the call is worth $26.37, while the put is worth $11.08. With 200 periods, the call price is $25.94, and the put price is $10.65. (The calculations for the binomial model are not shown here, but similar calculations for other options appear later in this chapter.)

Flexible Exchange (FLEX) Options

In contrast to conventional options that are listed by exchanges, FLEX options are established through a special procedure that allows investors, within certain constraints, to specify the contract terms of the listed option. A FLEX option is created when an investor, meeting certain eligibility criteria, posts a "request for quote" for the option containing the specific characteristics she desires. The procedure for creating FLEX options permits investors to customize key contract terms, such as the option's strike price, exercise style, and expiration date. Index FLEX options first appeared in 1993 as a way for the option exchanges to compete with the over-the-counter index option and warrant market, where all contract terms can be customized.

There are constraints on the types of options eligible for FLEX trading. For equity FLEX options, the request cannot specify an expiration date more than five years into the future. In addition, a minimum size threshold for a quote request is 250 contracts (where each contract covers 100 shares of the underlying stock) must be met. For index FLEX options, the request for quote cannot specify an expiration date exceeding ten years into the future. Index FLEX options must also meet a minimum size threshold of $10 million in notional value for the underlying index covered by the requested options. The requests are further constrained by the fact that only a small set of indexes and a broader set of individual stocks are eligible for the FLEX option trading procedure.

Once the request for quote is posted and is disseminated to trader screens and the trading floor, responding quotes can be submitted. The trader requesting the quote can then decide whether to accept the responding quote, or to revise the terms of the quote. Once the quote is accepted, a trade occurs and a FLEX option is created. No FLEX series, whether new or established, is continuously quoted, as would be the case for conventional options. To trade an established FLEX option, the investor uses the same procedure for creating the FLEX option. FLEX options are issued and guaranteed by the Options Clearing Corporation, which eliminates the counterparty credit risk that would exist for an equivalent trade in the over-the-counter market.

Options on foreign currency

We now explore the application of the Merton model to pricing options on a foreign currency. We assume that we are looking at the issues from the point of view of a U.S. option trader. In terms of the Merton model, the dollar value of the foreign currency takes the role of the stock price, S_t, and the foreign risk-free interest rate takes the role of the continuous dividend rate, δ. The standard deviation in the Merton model is that of the underlying asset, so the correct standard deviation to use in the model is the standard deviation of the foreign currency.

As an example, consider a European call and a European put option on the British pound. The pound is currently worth $1.40, and has a standard deviation of 0.5, reflecting difficulties in the European Monetary System (EMS). The current British risk-free rate is 12 percent, while the U.S. rate is 8 percent. The call and put both have a strike price of $1.50 per pound, and they both expire in 200 days.

According to the Merton model, the call is worth $0.1452, while the put value is $0.2700. Both of these prices are the dollar price for an option on a single British pound. We illustrate

Figure 16.1 A five-period binomial lattice for the British pound

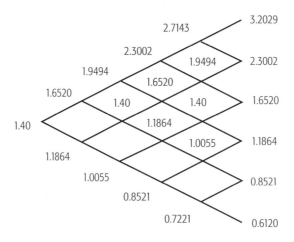

the computation of the price of the currency options using a five-period binomial model. The binomial parameters are as follows:

$$U = e^{\sigma\sqrt{\Delta t}} = e^{0.5\times\sqrt{0.1096}} = 1.1180$$

$$D = \frac{1}{U} = 0.847452$$

$$\pi_U = \frac{e^{(r-\delta)\Delta t} - D}{U - D} = 0.445579$$

The one-period discount factor is $e^{-0.08\times(40/365)} = 0.9913$. Figure 16.1 shows the five-period binomial lattice for the foreign currency price, while Figure 16.2 shows the lattices for the call and the put. The price of the call is \$0.1519, and the put is worth \$0.2766. For a 200-period lattice, the call is worth \$0.1454 and the put is worth \$0.2702. These 200-period binomial estimates are extremely close to the values from the Merton model.

Options on futures

Consider a good such as gold that has a large stock relative to consumption, is easily storable, does not have a seasonal production pattern (like wheat), and does not have a seasonal consumption pattern (like gasoline). Further, assume that it is possible to sell gold short and to obtain the use of the proceeds from the short sale.[3] When these conditions hold, the futures price at time t, F_t, for delivery of the good at time T is given by

$$F_t = \text{SPOT}_t\, e^{r(T-t)} \tag{16.7}$$

Figure 16.2   The five-period lattices for foreign currency call and put prices

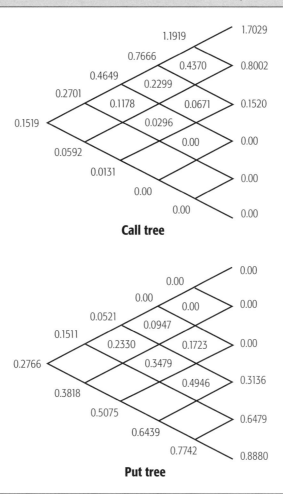

Call tree

Put tree

If this relationship between the spot, or cash, price and the futures price did not prevail, there would be immediate arbitrage opportunities, as we have seen in Chapter 3. In general, all precious metals (gold, silver, platinum, and palladium) and all financial instruments (equities and debt) conform almost perfectly to this relationship. To the degree that a commodity fails to conform to the cost-of-carry model, the pricing techniques discussed in this chapter do not pertain to pricing futures options on that commodity.

In terms of the Merton model, the rate at which the spot price grows, r, takes the place of δ, and the futures price takes the place of the stock price in Equation 16.1. In other words, for futures on commodities that conform to the cost-of-carry model, $\delta = r$.[4] When we make this substitution in Equation 16.1, the formula becomes considerably simpler due to the equivalence of δ and r. Fischer Black first applied this model to options on futures, and this application is often known as the Black model.[5] For European futures options, the price of the futures call, c_t^F, and put, p_t^F, are as follows:

The Black model

$$c_t^F = e^{-r(T-t)}[F_t N(d_1^F) - X N(d_2^F)]$$

$$p_t^F = e^{-r(T-t)}[X N(-d_2^F) - F_t N(-d_1^F)]$$

$$d_1^F = \frac{\ln\left(\dfrac{F_t}{X}\right) + (0.5\sigma^2)(T-t)}{\sigma\sqrt{T-t}} \tag{16.8}$$

$$d_2^F = d_1^F - \sigma\sqrt{T-t}$$

Equation 16.8 employs the standard deviation of the futures price.

The binomial model also applies to options on futures, and the parameters of Equations 16.4 and 16.5 can be applied directly. Notice that the probability of a futures price increase becomes

$$\pi_U = \frac{e^0 - D}{U - D} = \frac{1 - D}{U - D}$$

As an example, consider European options on a stock index futures that expires in one year. The current cash market price of the index is 480.00, and the risk-free rate is 7 percent. Therefore, according to the cost-of-carry model, the futures price must be

$$F_t = 480.00 e^{0.07 \times (365/365)} = 514.80$$

European call and put options on this futures contract have an exercise price of 500.00, and the standard deviation of the futures price is 0.2. The price of the call and put according to the Merton/Black model must be as follows:

$$d_1^F = \frac{\ln\left(\dfrac{514.80}{500.00}\right) + 0.5 \times 0.2 \times 0.2}{0.2} = 0.245852$$

$$d_2^F = 0.245852 - 0.2 = 0.045852$$

$N(d_1^F) = 0.597102$ and $N(d_2^F) = 0.518286$. Therefore, the call and put prices are as follows:

$$c_t^F = e^{-0.07}[514.80 \times 0.597102 - 500.00 \times 0.518286] = \$44.98$$
$$p_t^F = e^{-0.07}[500.00 \times 0.481714 - 514.80 \times 0.402898] = \$31.18$$

For a binomial model with five periods, the call and put prices are $46.49 and $32.69, respectively. With 200 periods, the binomial model gives prices of $44.95 and $31.15 for the call and put, respectively.

Using interest rate futures options to hedge mortgage pipeline risk

Many banks package together mortgage loans and "securitize" them. Specifically, loans are placed in a trust, and securities representing shares in the trust's assets are sold to public investors.

The money raised by the securitization can be used to make mortgage loans and the process is repeated.

Mortgage lenders face interest rate risk throughout the securitization process. However, one of the greatest risks occurs during the loan origination stage when lenders are exposed to "pipeline risk." Pipeline risk occurs when the lender offers the borrower a guarantee, or lock, on the borrowing rate prior to the loan actually closing. This "rate lock" exposes the lender to the risk of rising interest rates before the loan actually closes. To cope with pipeline risk, lenders have developed hedging strategies using interest rate futures and futures options.

To hedge against pipeline risk, lenders must take into account not only the risk directly associated with changes in interest rates, but also the second-order effects. The most significant second-order effect results from "fallout"; that is, the risk that the borrower may walk away from the loan before closing. Fallout is related to interest rates. In general, as rates rise, the percentage of loans that go to closing tends to rise, and the opposite happens when rates fall, since borrowers hold the option to walk away from a rate lock if better rates are available elsewhere. In essence, fallout results from borrowers exercising the interest rate put option the lender gives the borrower as part of any rate lock. The value of this put option increases as rates fall, and decreases as rates rise. The value of the put increases with the length of time between the loan commitment and closing and vice versa. As a result of fallout risk, lenders must estimate the quantity of loans that are going to close, and therefore do not know the amount of loans that need to be hedged. Loans that close under the rate lock guarantee expose the lender to a risk of rising rates because the value of the loan declines when rates rise.

The propensity of a loan to fall out of the pipeline depends largely on the responsiveness of the borrower to interest rate changes. A healthy portion of the loans in the pipeline will be unresponsive to interest rate changes, meaning that these loans are expected to close. Other loans will fall out no matter what happens to interest rates and will not close. Other loans will be responsive to interest rates. If rates rise, they will close. If rates fall, the loans will fall out of the pipeline. Experienced lenders rigorously monitor the level of fallout in their pipelines, and know the likely effects of interest rate changes on fallout for various types of borrowers.

To hedge those loans subject to fallout risk, lenders can purchase European-style put options in interest rate futures. These puts will offset the puts provides to borrowers with the rate lock. If interest rates rise, more loans are likely to go through to closing (the "pull-through," in trader jargon). By exercising the futures puts, the lender receives a short futures position at a futures price established at the time the put was purchased (assuming the put is at-the-money at the time of purchase). From the perspective of the lender the purchased put option makes sense. If rates rise, and the loan closes, the lender must be able to hedge the value of the loan. The purchased futures put option allows the lender to implement a futures hedge for the value of the pipeline loans only if it is needed, that is, when the likelihood of fallout diminishes. Of course, this type of hedging is costly because it entails a premium that must be paid to purchase the puts. The cost of this hedge will increase with the maturity of the option, the volatility of interest rates, and the degree to which the purchased put is in-the-money.

If interest rates drop, and fallout becomes more likely, there is no need to hedge the value of these loans since they will not close. In this case, the put option expires worthless. The cost of this hedging strategy is the premium paid to purchase the put options. However, the lost premium must be compared to the alternative. If the lender had used futures, instead of using options, to hedge this portion of the pipeline, fallout would have required the lender to liquidate the hedge at a loss. This loss would have been much greater than the lost premiums.

Forecasting with Options

One useful application of option pricing models is for forecasting. If the option market is informationally efficient and if the model of the market's pricing of options is properly specified, then observed option prices can be used to "back out" the market's assessment of the probability distribution of future spot prices or rates. The main advantage of this "efficient-markets method" of forecasting is that it is a cheap route to informative short-term forecasts. Forecasting methods differ by the degree to which they are informative and their cost. Generally, the most informative forecasts are also the most expensive. The information-to-cost ratio is very high for this method relative to the alternatives. This method is now frequently used in both government and business as a check on other forecasting methods, if nothing else. With a laptop computer, a listing of option prices, and an option pricing routine, any person off the street can free ride off the informed market participants.

The method works by estimating the parameters that describe the log-normal distribution from which future spot prices are drawn. It turns out that there are only two parameters that we need to characterize the log-normal distribution: the mean and the variance. Using crude oil as an example, we can use the crude oil futures contract as the expected spot price. The weighted implied standard deviation from crude oil options can be used to determine the variance estimate. Armed with this information, we can estimate the probability that the future spot rate will lie within any arbitrary range of prices. Consider a sample forecast based on information available on October 24, 2006, showing a December 2006 futures price of $59.35 per barrel and a WISD across all December futures options of 31.31 percent per year. The forecaster is asked to use this information to estimate the probability that spot crude oil prices in December 2006 will be between $55 and $60 per barrel. The area under the log-normal distribution, characterized with the parameters we have obtained from futures and futures option prices, is 0.365; that is, there is a 36.5 percent chance that spot crude oil prices in December will be between $55 and $60 per barrel.

Options on futures versus options on physicals

For some goods, such as foreign currencies, options trade on the futures contract and on the good itself. For example, in Chapter 10 we saw that the Philadelphia Stock Exchange trades options on foreign currencies, while the Chicago Mercantile Exchange trades options on foreign currency futures. The differences between options on futures and options on the underlying good itself depend critically on whether the option is a European or an American option.

At the expiration of a futures contract, the futures price must equal the spot price. This is necessary to avoid arbitrage. For example, in the gold market, if the spot price is $400 per ounce and the futures contract is at expiration, the futures contract price must also be $400. If it were not, there is a simple and immediate arbitrage opportunity. If the futures price at expiration exceeded the spot price, a trader would buy the physical good and deliver it in the futures market to capture the higher futures price. By contrast, if the futures price was below the spot price, the arbitrageur would buy a futures contract, take delivery of gold, and sell the gold for the higher spot price. To avoid both of these potential arbitrage plays, the spot price and the futures price must be equal at the expiration of the futures contract.

The no-arbitrage condition has important implications for pricing European futures options. Because a European option can be exercised only at expiration, a European futures option can be exercised only when the futures price and the spot price are identical. This restriction on exercise means that the payoffs on European futures options and options on physicals are identical. Therefore, the price of a European futures option and a European option on the physical must always be identical.

For American options, the analysis is more complex, because the trader can exercise an American option at any time. The relationship between prices of American options on futures and physicals depends on the relationship between the futures price and the spot price prevailing at a given time prior to expiration. For precious metals and financials, the futures price before expiration almost always exceeds the spot price. In the markets for some commodities, the spot price often exceeds the futures price. This happens in markets for industrial metals such as copper, in markets for agricultural goods, and in the energy market. Although a complete explanation for why these price relationships arise lies beyond the scope of this book, we offer a very brief explanation. In essence, the futures price will lie above the spot price if supplies of the underlying good are large relative to consumption, if the underlying good is easily storable and transportable, if the market for the underlying good is well developed, if supply of and demand for the underlying good are free of seasonal fluctuations, and if it is easy and cheap to effect short sales for the underlying good. These conditions prevail for precious metals and financials. By contrast, industrial metals, agricultural commodities, and energy products are strongly affected by supply and demand seasonalities, by poorly developed cash markets, and by costly transportation and storage. These factors allow the spot price to exceed the futures price on occasion.[6]

Without regard for the economic factors that cause the futures price or the spot price to be higher, the relationship between the futures and spot price determines the relationship between prices for American futures options and American options on the physical. When the futures price exceeds the spot price, the price of an American futures call must exceed the price of an American call on the physical, and the price of an American futures put must be less than the price of an American put on the physical. When the spot price exceeds the futures price, the price of an American futures call must be below the price of an American call on the physical and the price of an American futures put must exceed the price of an American put on the physical.

Agricultural Price Supports as Options

One application of option pricing models that has received a lot of attention from policy-makers over the past decade has been to value agricultural price supports (and other government guarantees) as put options. Government price supports work as nonrecourse loans, with the crop pledged as collateral. The nonrecourse loans are available from the Commodity Credit Corporation (CCC). Farmers who take out the loan may choose at any time to sell the crop in the market and repay the loan with interest, or they may close the loan by turning the crop pledged as collateral to the CCC at the established loan rate; for example, $2.50 per bushel. The loan rate thus places a floor on the effective price at which the farmer can sell the crop. If the market price is below the loan rate, the government pays the difference between the loan rate and the market price on each unit of output.

In recognition of the possibility that commodity price stabilization programs and crop insurance programs offered by the federal government compete with the products offered by futures exchanges, the 1996 Federal Agricultural Improvement and Reform (FAIR) Act authorized the U.S. Department of Agriculture to determine whether futures and futures options could provide producers with reasonable protection from the financial risks of fluctuations in price, yield, and income inherent in the production and marketing of agricultural commodities.

Option sensitivities

In Chapter 14, we considered the sensitivity of option prices to changes in the underlying parameters. Our exploration focused on the Merton model, and we analyzed the DELTA, GAMMA, THETA, VEGA, and RHO of European calls and puts. In this section, we extend that analysis to options on stock indexes, options on foreign currencies, and options on futures. The principles are virtually identical, but we must make slight substitutions in the definitions of the sensitivities to account for differences in the underlying instruments. Tables 16.1 and 16.2 present the call and put sensitivities for the Merton model. These are the same tables as discussed in Chapter 14. These same sensitivities apply to options on stock indexes, options on foreign currencies, and options on futures with the following substitutions.

Sensitivities of options on stock indexes
Interpret S_t as the price of the stock index, and interpret δ as the continuous dividend yield on the stock index. Adjust the computation of d_1 and d_2 by making these same substitutions.

Sensitivities of options on foreign currency
Interpret S_t as the price of the foreign currency, and interpret δ as the continuous interest rate on the foreign risk-free instrument. Adjust the computation of d_1 and d_2 by making these same substitutions.

Sensitivities of options on futures
Interpret S_t as the price of the futures contract, and interpret δ as being equal to the risk-free rate, so that $r - \delta = 0$. Adjust the computation of d_1 and d_2 by making these same substitutions.

Because these sensitivities are so similar, we illustrate all with an example of a European option on the British pound. The current value of a British pound is \$1.56. The U.S. risk-free rate of interest is 8 percent, while the risk-free rate on the British pound is 11 percent. The standard deviation of the British pound is 0.25, and the option expires in 90 days. The

---

Table 16.1   Call sensitivities for the Merton model

Name	Sensitivity
DELTA$_c$	$\dfrac{\partial C}{\partial S} = e^{-\delta(T-t)}N(d_1^M)$
THETA$_c$	$-\dfrac{\partial C}{\partial(T-t)} = -\dfrac{SN'(d_1^M)\sigma e^{-\delta(T-t)}}{2\sqrt{T-t}} + \delta SN(d_1^M)e^{-\delta(T-t)} - rXe^{-r(T-t)}N(d_2^M)$
VEGA$_c$	$\dfrac{\partial C}{\partial \sigma} = S\sqrt{T-t}\,N'(d_1^M)e^{-\delta(T-t)}$
RHO$_c$	$\dfrac{\partial C}{\partial r} = X(T-t)e^{-r(T-t)}N(d_2^M)$
GAMMA$_c$	$\dfrac{\partial \text{DELTA}_C}{\partial S} = \dfrac{\partial^2 C}{\partial S^2} = \dfrac{N'(d_1^M)e^{-\delta(T-t)}}{S\sigma\sqrt{T-t}}$

Note: $N'(d_1^M) = \dfrac{1}{\sqrt{2\pi}}e^{-0.5(d_1^M)^2}$.

Table 16.2   Put sensitivities for the Merton model

Name	Sensitivity
DELTA$_p$	$\dfrac{\partial p}{\partial S} = e^{-\delta(T-t)}N[(d_1^M) - 1]$
THETA$_p$	$-\dfrac{\partial p}{\partial(T - t)} = -\dfrac{SN'(d_1^M)\sigma e^{-\delta(T-t)}}{2\sqrt{T - t}} - \delta SN(-d_1^M)e^{-\delta(T-t)} + rXe^{-r(T-t)}N(-d_2^M)$
VEGA$_p$	$\dfrac{\partial p}{\partial \sigma} = S\sqrt{T - t}\,N'(d_1^M)e^{-\delta(T-t)}$
RHO$_p$	$\dfrac{\partial p}{\partial r} = -X(T - t)e^{-r(T-t)}N(-d_2^M)$
GAMMA$_p$	$\dfrac{\partial \mathrm{DELTA}_p}{\partial S} = \dfrac{\partial^2}{\partial S^2} = \dfrac{N'(d_1^M)e^{-\delta(T-t)}}{S\sigma\sqrt{T - t}}$

Note: $N'(d_1^M) = \dfrac{1}{\sqrt{2\pi}}e^{-0.5(d_1^M)^2}$.

Table 16.3   Foreign currency option sensitivities

	Merton model	
	Call	Put
Option prices	$0.1002	$0.0526
DELTA	0.6082	−0.3650
THETA	−0.1085	−0.1578
VEGA	0.2859	0.2859
RHO	0.2093	−0.1534
GAMMA	1.9058	1.9058

Note: $S = \$1.56$; $X = \$1.50$; $\sigma = 0.25$; $T - t = 90$ days; $r = 0.08$; $\delta = 0.11$.

exercise price of the options we consider is $1.50. In terms of the Merton model, our inputs would be $S = \$1.56$, $X = \$1.50$, $\sigma = 0.25$, $T - t = 90$ days, $\delta = 0.11$, and $r = 0.08$. With these values, a European call is worth $0.1002, and a European put is worth $0.0526. Table 16.3 shows the sensitivity values for this option.

Pricing American options

Chapter 15 explored the pricing of American stock options. There, we saw that exact solutions for pricing American-style options are generally not available. Further, we noted that the key feature that made American call option pricing distinct from European call option pricing was the payment of dividends by the underlying good. In this section, we explore the pricing of American options on stock indexes, foreign currency, and futures.

As we have discussed earlier in this chapter, we may regard futures, foreign currencies, and stock indexes as goods that pay continuous dividends. This makes them particularly well suited to analysis by the Barone-Adesi and Whaley analytic approximation. Therefore, we begin our analysis of American options on stock indexes, foreign currency, and futures by applying the analytic approximation to these instruments.

The binomial model also applies to these instruments, and we consider it in detail later in this chapter. The binomial model has special applicability to options on stock indexes, because stock indexes actually have dividend payment patterns that are discrete. As we will see later in this chapter, there are certain periods of the year when stocks tend to pay dividends. This seasonality in dividend payments from stocks implies that stock indexes will also exhibit a seasonal dividend pattern. The binomial model is particularly well suited to handling this type of dividend pattern.

Analytic approximations

As we discussed in Chapter 15, we may analyze the value of an American option as consisting of the value of a corresponding European option, plus an early exercise premium. The value of an American option must always be at least the amount of its immediately available exercisable proceeds. For a call,

$$C_i \geq S_t - X$$

If a trader owns the American option, she has a choice between the exercisable proceeds or the value of the European call. Which is preferable depends upon how deep-in-the-money the option is, the dividend rate on the stock, δ, the interest rate, r, and the time remaining until the option expires, $T - t$. If the stock price reaches a critical level, S^*, such that

$$S_t^* - X = c(S^*, X, T - t) + \text{early exercise premium} \tag{16.9}$$

the owner of an American call option is indifferent about exercising. If the stock price exceeds S^*, she will exercise immediately to capture the exercise proceeds $S_t - X$. If the stock price is below S^*, she will not exercise. At the critical stock price, S^*, the European call is worth exactly $S^* - X$. For any stock price greater than S^*, the European call will be worth less than the exercisable proceeds for the American call. This explains why the owner of the American call is indifferent about exercise at a stock price of S^*; at that stock price, the American and European calls are worth the same: $S^* - X$. For higher stock prices, the value of the European call falls below that of the American, and the value of the American call becomes equal to its exercisable proceeds. Thus, the owner of the American call should exercise to capture the quantity $S - X$. Those funds can then be invested from the exercise date to the expiration date to earn a return that will be lost if the option is not exercised.

A similar argument applies to American put options. As the stock price falls well below the exercise price, there comes a point at which

$$X - S^{**} = p(S^{**}, X, T - t) + \text{early exercise premium} \tag{16.10}$$

where S^{**} is the critical stock price for an American put. If the stock price falls below S^{**}, the American put should be exercised to capture the exercised proceeds of $X - S_t$. From Chapter 15, the analytic approximation for an American call on a stock is as follows:

$$C_t = c_t + A_2 \left(\frac{S_t}{S^*}\right)^{q_2} \quad \text{if} \quad S_t < S^*$$
$$\quad\quad = S_t - X \quad\quad\quad \text{if} \quad S_t \geq S^*$$

(16.11)

where

$$A_2 = \frac{S^*[1 - e^{-\delta(T-t)}N(d_1)]}{q_2}$$

and S^* is the solution to

$$S^* - X = c_t(S^*, X, T - t) + \{1 - e^{-\delta(T-t)}N(d_1)\}(S^*/q_2)$$

(16.12)

$N(d_1)$ and $p(S^*, X, T - t)$ are evaluated at S^*. To find S^* requires an iterative search for the value that makes the equation balance. Other terms are as follows:

$$q_2 = \frac{1 - n + \sqrt{(n-1)^2 + 4k}}{2}$$

$$n = \frac{2(r - \delta)}{\sigma^2}, \quad k = \frac{2r}{\sigma^2(1 - e^{-r(T-t)})}$$

For an American put, the analytic approximation is as follows:

$$P_t = p_t + A_1 \left(\frac{S_t}{S^{**}}\right)^{q_1} \quad \text{if} \quad S_t > S^{**}$$
$$\quad\quad = X - S_t \quad\quad\quad \text{if} \quad S_t \leq S^{**}$$

(16.13)

where

$$A_1 = \frac{S^{**}[1 - e^{-\delta(T-t)}N(-d_1)]}{q_1}$$

$$q_1 = \frac{1 - n - \sqrt{(n-1)^2 + 4k}}{2}$$

S^{**} is found by an iterative search to make the following equation hold:

$$X - S^{**} = p_t(S^{**}, X, T - t) - [1 - e^{-\delta(T-t)}N(-d_1)](S^{**}/q_1)$$

(16.14)

$N(-d_1)$ and $p_t(S^{**}, X, T - t)$ are evaluated at the critical stock price S^{**}. We now consider how this model can apply to options on stock indexes, foreign currency, and futures.

The analytic approximation for options on stock indexes

To apply the Barone-Adesi and Whaley model to options on stock indexes, we merely need to reinterpret certain parameters in the model. Specifically, we interpret S in the model to indicate the price of the stock index in question, and we interpret δ as the aggregate dividend rate on all of the stocks represented in the index. S^* and S^{**} are the critical levels of the stock index that would trigger exercise.

As an example, assume that a stock index has a current value of 400.00, that the risk-free rate of interest is 7 percent, that the continuous dividend rate on the stocks comprising the index is 3.5 percent, that the standard deviation of the stock index is 0.18, that the time to expiration is 140 days, and that the exercise price is 380.00. For these values, the Barone-Adesi and Whaley model gives a call price $C = 32.14$ and a put price $P = 7.41$, where these option values are expressed in index units. For the call, the critical price is $S^* = 822.31$, while for the put the critical price is $S^{**} = 328.50$. Because the current index value is below S^* and above S^{**}, there is no incentive to exercise. **OPTION!** solves for the critical stock index value and the price of American calls and puts on stock indexes using this analytic approximation. It also can graph the value of American options as a function of the underlying parameter values.

The analytic approximation for options on foreign currencies

As with options on stock indexes, we can apply the Barone-Adesi and Whaley model to American options on foreign currencies by reinterpreting Equations 16.11 and 16.13. To apply these equations to options on foreign currency, we interpret S as the current value of the foreign currency. The dividend rate, δ, is interpreted as the risk-free rate of interest on the foreign currency.

Earlier in this chapter, we considered an example of a British pound in the context of the Merton model. In that example, the pound was currently worth \$1.40 and had a standard deviation of 0.5. The British risk-free rate is 12 percent, while the U.S. rate is 8 percent. The exercise price for both a call and a put is \$1.50, and the two options expire in 200 days. Using the Merton model, we found that the European option values would be $c = \$0.1452$ and $p = \$0.2700$. For these same parameter values, American options would be worth: $C = \$0.1498$ and $P = \$0.2718$. The critical prices are $S^* = \$2.52$ and $S^{**} = \$0.69$. Thus, it would be unwise to exercise either the call or the put. These values were found by letting the spot value of the pound (\$1.40) take on the role of S in the analytic approximation formula, while the British interest rate (12 percent) played the role of the dividend, δ. **OPTION!** can compute and graph American foreign currency option values under the Barone-Adesi and Whaley model.

The analytic approximation for options on futures

The Barone-Adesi and Whaley model applies with equal facility to options on futures. In Equations 16.11–16.13, we interpret S as the futures price, and we assume that the rate of return on the underlying asset equals the risk-free rate. That is, we assume that $r = \delta$. This assumption is valid if the futures contract is a financial asset or a precious metal.

To apply this model to futures, consider an American call and put on platinum. The cost-of-carry model holds very well for this precious metal, justifying our assumption that $r = \delta$. Assume that the current spot price of platinum is \$500.00 per ounce, that the risk-free rate of interest is 11 percent, that an American futures call and put expire in 75 days, and that the two options have an exercise price of \$500.00. If platinum conforms to the cost of carry, the futures price must be

$$F = Se^{r(T-t)} = \$500 \times e^{0.11 \times (75/365)} = \$511.43$$

The volatility of the futures price is 0.25. In applying Equations 16.11–16.13, we replace S with the futures price of \$511.43, and replace δ with the risk-free rate of 11 percent. For these data, the American option prices are $C = \$28.5323$ and $P = \$17.2875$, with critical futures prices $S^* = \$622.98$ and $S^{**} = \$401.2984$. For the corresponding European options, the prices are

$c = \$28.37$ and $p = \$17.1955$. The early exercise premium on the call is about $0.16, and for the put the premium is about $0.09.

Earlier, we noted that the value of an American call on a futures contract would be higher than the value of an American call on the physical good if the futures price exceeded the spot price. We also said that the American put on the futures would be worth less than the corresponding American put on the physical if the futures price exceeded the cash price. This example confirms that point, because the prices of options on physical platinum (given the spot price of $500 and assuming the same standard deviation of 0.25 pertains to the futures price and to the spot price) are $C = \$22.09$ and $P = \$22.09$. Thus, the call price on the physical good is lower and the put price on the physical good is higher than the corresponding option on the futures.[7]

Summary

In this section, we have seen that the Barone-Adesi and Whaley analytic approximation applies not only to options on stocks, but to options on stock indexes, options on foreign currency, and options on futures. To apply the model to these disparate instruments, we merely need to reinterpret some of the parameters in the model in the way we have explored in this section.

It is worth emphasizing that the Barone-Adesi and Whaley model assumes that the underlying good in each case pays at a continuous rate, whether it be dividends on a stock index, the foreign interest rate for foreign currency options, or the cost-of-carry rate on the good underlying a futures contract. This assumption is virtually without flaw for options on foreign currency and options on futures, and it is quite reasonable for options on stock indexes. However, we must note that the dividend flow from stock indexes is not really continuous. To deal with discontinuous dividend flows, we now turn to a consideration of the binomial model and its applications to options on stock indexes, foreign currency, and futures.

The binomial model

In Chapter 15, we considered the application of the binomial model to pricing American options when the underlying good paid no dividend, a continuous dividend, a known dividend yield, or a known dollar dividend. Because this chapter considers options on stock indexes, foreign currency, and futures, we are most interested in applying the binomial model to a dividend payment stream that is continuous or that pays known dividends. As Chapter 15 has already shown how to apply the binomial model to the nondividend case and to the case of known dividend yields, we focus on the dividend patterns of greatest interest, continuous dividends and known dollar dividends.

Review of the basic strategy for the binomial model

As we have seen in Chapters 13 and 15, we follow a common strategy for computing option prices under the binomial model. For options on stocks with dividends, we applied the binomial model by creating a lattice for the stock that reflected the timing and amount of dividend payments that the stock would make. These adjustments affected the distribution of possible stock values at the expiration date. We then computed the option values in the usual way by working from the exercise date back to the present.

To apply the binomial model for American options, we follow the same basic valuation strategy, with one important difference. For the option lattice for an American option, the option value is set equal to the maximum of:

(1)   the expected option value in one period discounted for one period at the risk-free rate; and
(2)   the immediate exercise value of the option, $S_t - X$ for a call, or $X - S_t$ for a put.

Except for this treatment of each node in the lattice for an American option, the binomial model for an American option is applied in exactly the same way as it is for a European option. As we work back through the tree, discounting the next period's expected option values, we must ask at every node whether the immediate exercise value or the computed present value is greater. The value at the node is the maximum of those two quantities. Further, we may note that the stock tree is unaffected by whether the option we are analyzing is an American or a European option.

Review of the binomial model and continuous dividends

In Chapter 13, we explored the Merton model, which adjusts the Black–Scholes model to price European options on stocks that pay a continuous dividend. We also showed how to use the binomial model to price European options on stocks that pay continuous dividends. There we saw that the parameters for the binomial model for a stock paying a continuous dividend are as follows:

$$U = e^{\sigma\sqrt{\Delta t}}$$

$$D = \frac{1}{U}$$

$$\pi_U = \frac{e^{(r-\delta)\Delta t} - D}{U - D}$$

(16.15)

As we have discussed in this chapter, the stock price tree is identical whether we are pricing European or American options. Therefore, these parameters apply to generating the binomial tree of stock prices for American options on stocks paying a continuous dividend. As an examination of these parameters shows, the stock price tree will be identical in both cases. However, the probability of a stock price increase varies inversely with the level of the continuous dividend rate, δ.

Review of the binomial model and known dollar dividends

To apply the binomial model to options on goods with known dollar dividends, the first step is to generate the tree describing the potential stock price movements. As we saw in Chapter 13 when we considered the pricing of European options on stock with known dollar dividends, there can be a problem with the tree failing to recombine after the dividend has been paid. In this situation, the number of nodes can increase dramatically, particularly when there are many periods and several dividends. (For details on why the tree fails to recombine, see Chapter 13.)

We can solve this problem as we did in Chapter 13 by making a simplifying assumption. We assume that the stock price reflects the dividend, which is known with certainty, and all other factors that might affect the stock price, which are uncertain. We then adjust the uncertain component of the stock price for the impending dividends and model the uncertain component of the stock price with the binomial tree adding back the present value of all future dividends at each node. Specifically, we follow these steps:

(1) Compute the present value of all dividends to be paid during the life of the option as of the present time t.
(2) Subtract this present value from the current stock price to form $S'_t = S_t -$ PV of all dividends.
(3) Create the binomial tree by applying the up and down factors in the usual way to the initial stock price S'_t.

Figure 16.3   The seasonal pattern of dividends in the S&P 500® stock index

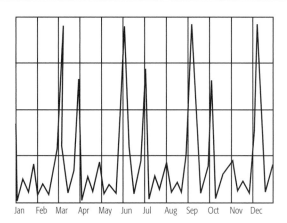

Jan Feb Mar Apr May Jun Jul Aug Sep Oct Nov Dec

(4)   After generating the tree, add to the stock price at each node the present value of all future dividends to be paid during the life of the option.

(5)   Compute the option values in the usual way by working through the binomial tree.

These were exactly the steps that we used in Chapter 13 to resolve this difficulty.

The application of this procedure to American options is exactly the same as with European options, with a single exception. In working through the tree to generate the option price tree, we must compare the present value of next period's expected option value with the exercise value of the option. The option price at the node is the higher of the present value or the exercise value. The computation of the value at a node is exactly the same as in other cases we have already considered.

The binomial model for options on stock indexes

As we have just discussed, the binomial model can apply to options on stock indexes for both a continuous dividend on the stock index and for specific dividends at certain times. Stock indexes in fact tend to pay dividends in a discrete manner, with higher dividend payments coming at certain times of the year. Figure 16.3 shows the typical dividend pattern on the S&P 500® index, which is a function of the tendency of firms to pay dividends at the end of each calendar quarter.

In this section, we explore how to apply the binomial model to options on stock indexes with discrete dividend patterns of the type shown in Figure 16.3. Later in this chapter, we show how to apply the binomial model to continuous payments on futures options and foreign currency.

To make the discussion more concrete, let us consider a stock index with a current value of 1,200.00. An American call and put option on the index expire in 125 days and have a common exercise price of 1,250.00. The volatility of the index is 0.2. The current risk-free interest rate is 8 percent. During the life of these options, the index will pay two dividends. The first dividend occurs on day 15 and will be 15 index units, while the second falls on day 120 and will be 20 index units. The present value of the two dividends at the present date is as follows:

$$PV = 15.00\,e^{-0.08\times(15/365)} + 20.00\,e^{-0.08\times(120/365)} = 34.4316$$

The next step is to subtract this value from the current index, to form

$$S'_t = 1,200.00 - 34.4316 = 1,165.5684$$

We now compute the up and down factors and apply them to S'_t to form the stock index tree. We will form a tree with five periods, so that each period consists of 25 days:

$$\Delta t = \frac{25}{365} = 0.0685 \text{ years}$$

$$U = e^{\sigma\sqrt{\Delta t}} = e^{0.2\times\sqrt{0.0685}} = 1.0537$$

$$D = \frac{1}{U} = 0.9490$$

$$\pi_U = \frac{e^{r\Delta t} - D}{U - D} = \frac{e^{0.08\times0.0685} - 0.9490}{1.0537 - 0.9490} = 0.5396$$

The upper panel in Figure 16.4 shows the stock index lattice for this example. However, we must still adjust this lattice by adding to each node the present value of all dividends to be received from that point to the expiration date of the option. The nodes occur at 0, 25, 50, 75, 100, and 125 days from the present. The first dividend occurs in 15 days, so it will affect only the node representing the present. The second dividend occurs in 120 days, so it will affect all nodes, except those at expiration. The lower panel of Figure 16.4 shows the stock index lattice adjusted for the present value of the dividends. For the present, we already know that the present value of both dividends is 34.43. All later periods occur after the first dividend, so we need to consider only the second dividend for subsequent nodes. At the first period, 25 days from now, the present value of the final dividend is

$$20.00e^{-0.08\times(120-25)/365} = 19.59$$

The other present values (19.70, 19.80, and 19.91) are found similarly, and are included in the stock index lattice in the bottom panel of Figure 16.4.

To compute the price of an option, we create a parallel lattice, starting at the expiration date. Figure 16.5 shows the call and put lattices for the American options we are considering. For the option, the value at expiration is simply the intrinsic value of the option at that point. We then consider the nodes representing one period before expiration, and compute the expected value of the payoffs one period later and discount that expected payoff for one period. For example, if the stock index value falls in four periods, it will be at 996.29 at expiration, while if it falls every period, it will be at 897.33. For a put at expiration, the payoffs will be 253.71 and 352.67, respectively, as the adjusted lattice for the stock index shows. One period earlier, the discounted expected value of these two payoffs is

$$\{0.5396 \times 253.71 + 0.4604 \times 352.67\} \times 0.9945 = 297.63$$

In terms of the adjusted lattice for the stock index, this corresponds to a stock index price at time four of 965.32.

Because we are working with American options, the holder of the put has the right to exercise at any time. At the fourth period, if the stock index price is 965.32, the immediate

Figure 16.4   The five-period stock index price lattice

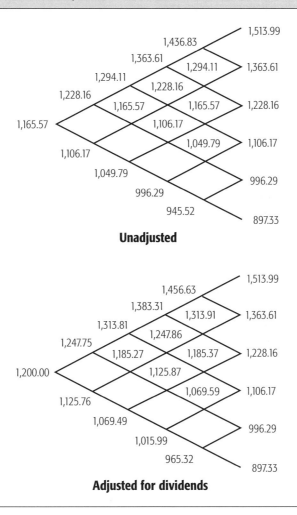

Unadjusted

Adjusted for dividends

exercise value is 1,250.00 − 965.32 = 284.68. The holder of the put faces the following choice at the node we are considering. She may exercise the option for an immediate cash inflow of 284.68 index units, or continue to hold the put, with its expected present value of 297.63 index units. A rational trader would hold at this point. The node in the put lattice that we are considering must have the maximum of the immediate exercise value (284.68) or the discounted expected value of the payoffs in one period (297.63). Thus, the node in the put lattice in Figure 16.5 has the value 297.63. Asterisks in the option lattices indicate an entry resulting from an exercise. For example, if the stock price falls in both of the first two periods, the put holder should exercise. Figure 16.5 shows that the value of an American call on the stock index would be 35.23 index units, while the American put is worth 84.01 index units. As the figure also shows, early exercise of either option is unlikely.

Figure 16.5 The five-period lattice for an American call and put on the stock index

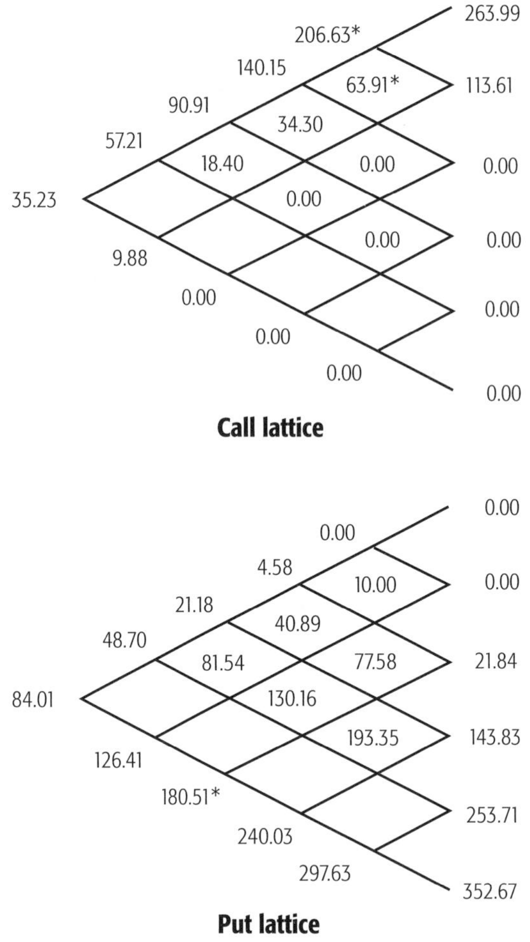

Call lattice

Put lattice

The binomial model for options on foreign currency

We now illustrate how the binomial model applies to options on foreign currency by considering the binomial model with continuous dividends. This continuous dividends approach applies to stock index options and options on futures as well.

We illustrate the application of the binomial model to American options on foreign currency with the same example considered earlier in this chapter, except that we now allow the option to be an American option. Earlier, we analyzed a European call and put option on the British pound. The pound is currently worth \$1.40, and has a standard deviation of 0.5. The current British risk-free rate is 12 percent, while the U.S. rate is 8 percent. The call and put both have a strike price of \$1.50 per pound, and they both expire in 200 days.

With a five-period binomial model, we found that the parameters were $U = 1.1800$; $D = 0.847452$; and $\pi_U = 0.445579$. The one-period discount factor is $e^{-0.08 \times (40/365)} = 0.9913$. All of these values are the same whether the option under consideration is European or American. Consequently, the lattice for the foreign currency remains the same as well. As we saw for the European options, the five-period lattice gave a call price of $0.1519 and a put price of $0.2766. For a 200-period lattice, the call was $0.1454 and the put was $0.2702. For comparison, the Merton model gave a call price of $0.1452 and a put price of $0.2700.

To compute the price of American options on the foreign currency, we apply our familiar technology of constructing and evaluating lattices for the call and the put. For each node, we compute the expected value of the payoffs one period later and discount them for one period. Because we are now analyzing American options, we must check each node to determine whether the intrinsic value or our discounted expected value is greater. The node in question takes on the maximum of these two values.

Figure 16.6 gives the call and put lattices for these American options. An asterisk indicates a node at which early exercise is optimal. Because early exercise is optimal in some instances

Figure 16.6 The five-period lattice for an American call and put on the British pound

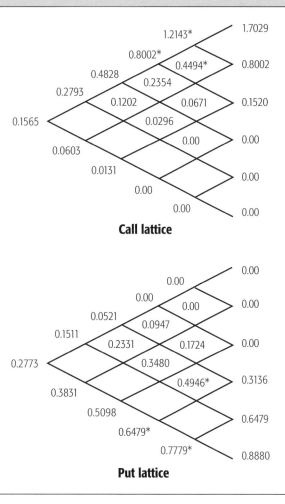

Call lattice

Put lattice

for both the call and the put, the price of these American options must be greater than their European counterparts. The price of the American call is $0.1565, and the American put is $0.2773. This gives an early exercise premium of $0.0046 on the call and $0.0007 for the put.

The binomial model for options on futures

We now apply the binomial model to options on futures. Generally, the goods underlying futures contracts may be thought of as paying a rate of return that equals the cost of carry. Earlier, we saw that this rate must equal the risk-free rate of interest to avoid arbitrage—at least if markets were sufficiently perfect. Equation 16.6 gave the parameters for the binomial model as it applies to options on goods paying a continuous return. For futures, we assume that $r = \delta$. The parameters for the binomial model are the same whether we consider a European or an American option.

As an example, we consider again the option on the stock index futures contract that we analyzed previously. A stock index stands at 480.00, and the risk-free rate of interest is 7 percent. A call and a put on the stock index futures contract expire in one year. Therefore, the futures prices must be 514.80, as we saw above. If the standard deviation of the futures contract is 0.2 and the exercise price on both the call and put is 500.00, we saw that the five-period binomial prices for the European call and put are 46.49 and 32.69, respectively.

For these options, the binomial parameters are as follows:

$$U = e^{\sigma\sqrt{\Delta t}} = e^{0.2 \times \sqrt{0.2}} = 1.093565$$

$$D = \frac{1}{U} = 0.914441$$

$$\pi_U = \frac{e^{(r-\delta)\Delta t} - D}{U - D} = 0.477652$$

Figure 16.7   The five-period lattice for the stock index futures price

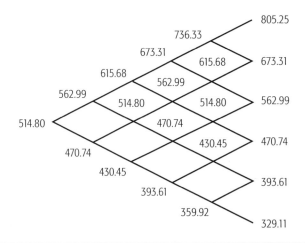

Figure 16.8   The five-period lattice for the American call and put futures options

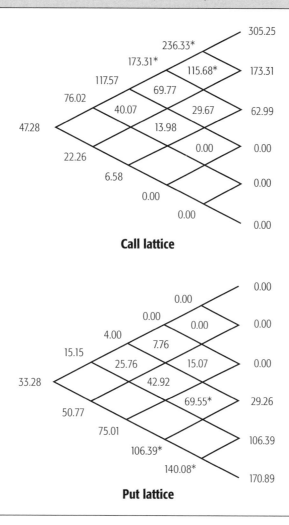

305.25

236.33*

173.31*   173.31

117.57   115.68*

76.02   69.77

40.07   29.67   62.99

47.28   13.98

22.26   0.00   0.00

6.58

0.00   0.00

0.00

0.00

0.00

Call lattice

0.00

0.00

0.00   0.00

4.00   0.00

15.15   7.76

25.76   15.07   0.00

33.28   42.92

50.77   69.55*   29.26

75.01

106.39*   106.39

140.08*

170.89

Put lattice

The discount factor per period is 0.9861. Figure 16.7 shows a five-period binomial lattice for the futures price. At the end of one year, the futures price will range between \$329.11 and \$805.25. Figure 16.8 shows the American call and put lattices for options on this futures contract. The asterisks indicate nodes at which the exercise value was substituted for the computed present value of the next period's expected payoffs. As we saw earlier in this chapter, the five-period binomial prices for European options were \$46.49 and \$32.69 for the call and put, respectively. As Figure 16.8 shows, the American option prices from a five-period binomial analysis are \$47.28 and \$33.28 for the call and put, respectively.

The volatility index (VIX) of the Chicago Board Options Exchange

In 1993, the Chicago Board Options Exchange (CBOE) introduced an index based on the implied volatility of options. The index has been revised since its original incarnation, but has always been known as the VIX. It has become a widely used benchmark for measuring expected near-term stock market volatility. The original index was based on the implied volatility of a hypothetical at-the money option on the S&P 100 index. The new version, rolled out in September 2003, is based on a weighted average of implied volatility derived from a wide range of options traded on the S&P 500. The VIX index provides a real-time measure of expected stock market volatility over the next 30 days. The index reflects the consensus view of market participants about expected near-term market volatility. The index has been called a "fear gauge," because during times of market stress, when investors are fearful, the VIX tends to rise, and as investor fear subsides, the VIX tends to decline. The index is calculated continuously throughout the trading day from real-time options prices and is widely disseminated to market participants. The VIX index is used as the reference index for a variety of derivative products, including VIX futures, VIX options, and volatility swaps. The precise method for calculating the VIX index is given on the CBOE's web site (www.cboe.com).

Conclusion

This chapter has applied familiar ideas to new instruments—options on stock indexes, options on foreign currency, and options on futures contracts. We considered both European and American options. We saw that European options on stock indexes, foreign currency, and futures can be priced by the Merton model or by the binomial model. For American options, we analyzed the analytic approximation of Barone-Adesi and Whaley, and we considered the binomial model.

In essence, the Merton model applies directly, given a slight reinterpretation of the parameters of the model. The reinterpretation requires that we substitute the stock index value, the foreign currency value, or the futures price for the stock price in the Merton model. We also substitute the dividend rate on the stock index, the foreign interest rate on the foreign currency, or the cost of carry on the futures, which we presume to equal the risk-free rate. With these substitutions, we can apply the Merton model to price the options considered in this chapter. The binomial model applies in a straightforward way to European stock index options, options on foreign currency, and options on futures.

For American options, we saw that both the Barone-Adesi and Whaley model and the binomial model are well suited to analyzing the options considered in this chapter. It is extremely reasonable to regard foreign currencies and futures as paying a continuous yield, and it is a reasonable assumption for stock indexes as well. Thus, the analytic approximation works quite well for the types of options considered in this chapter.

The binomial model applies to all of the American options discussed in this chapter as well. It is particularly well suited to pricing options on stock indexes. Although it may be reasonable to assume that stock indexes pay a continuous dividend, we saw that there are significant discontinuities in the dividend stream for many real-world stock indexes. The binomial model is ideal for pricing options on goods that pay discrete dividends.

Exercises

1 Explain why interest payments on a foreign currency can be treated as analogous to a dividend on a common stock.

2 Why do we assume that the cost of carry for a futures option is the same as the risk-free rate?

3 Explain how to adjust a price lattice for an underlying good that makes discrete payments.

4 If a European and an American call on the same underlying good have different prices when all of the terms of the two options are identical, what does this difference reveal about the two options? What does it mean if the two options have identical prices?

5 Consider an option on a futures contract within the context of the binomial model. Assume that the futures price is 100.00, that the risk-free interest rate is 10 percent, that the standard deviation of the futures is 0.4, and that the futures option expires in one year. Assuming that a call and a put on the futures option

also expire in one year, compute the binomial parameters U, D, and π_U. Now compute the expected futures price in one period. What does this reveal about the expected movement in futures prices?

6 For a call and a put option on a foreign currency, compute the Merton model price, the binomial model price for a European option with three periods, the Barone-Adesi and Whaley model price, and the binomial model price with three periods for American options. Data are as follows: The foreign currency value is 2.5; the exercise price on all options is 2.0; the time until expiration is 90 days; the risk-free rate of interest is 7 percent; the foreign interest rate is 4 percent; the standard deviation of the foreign currency is 0.2.

7 Consider a call and a put on a stock index. The index price is 500.00, and the two options expire in 120 days. The standard deviation of the index is 0.2, and the risk-free rate of interest is 7 percent. The two options have a common exercise price of 500.00. The stock index will pay a dividend of 20.00 index units in 40 days. Find the European and American option prices according to the binomial model, assuming two periods. Be sure to draw the lattices for the stock index and for all of the options that are being priced.

8 Consider two European calls and two European put options on a foreign currency. The exercise prices are $0.90 and $1.00, giving a total of four options. All options expire in one year. The current risk-free rate is 8 percent, the foreign interest rate is 5 percent, and the standard deviation of the foreign currency is 0.3.

The foreign currency is priced at $0.80. Find all four option prices according to the Merton model. Compare the ratios of the option prices to the ratio of the exercise prices. What does this show?

9 You work for the Treasury Department of a large Midwestern soap company and your job is to evaluate proposals from OTC dealers. Your company currently has an equity-index swap that pays your company $250 times the difference between the prevailing S&P 500 stock index price one month from now and the index level of 1,000 (if the difference is positive) or zero (if the difference is negative). You want to restructure the deal so as to extend the life of the option to a year past the original expiration date (13 months from today). You want to restructure the deal without paying any additional cash over and above what has been agreed to for the 30-day contract. If current volatility is 30 percent (annual), the current S&P 500 price is 1,200, the current short-term interest rate is a constant 6 percent (annual), and the annual dividend yield is 3 percent, how much would you expect the dealer to alter the option's strike price in consideration for extending the option's life by one year? Assume 30 days per month and 360 days per year.

10 In the analytic approximation model for the pricing of American-style futures options, futures volatility and spot volatility are assumed to be equal. Is this a reasonable assumption?

Notes

1 Again, this is not the same as capital delta, Δ, which stands for the sensitivity of the call option price to a change in the stock price.

2 Even large indexes, such as the S&P 500, exhibit a distinct seasonal pattern in their index payments. Therefore, continuous dividends for a stock index represent something of an assumption.

3 When these conditions are not met, the pricing relationships discussed in this section do not hold. Slight deviations from these idealized conditions lead to slight pricing discrepancies, while some commodities do not obey the pricing rule at all. This issue was discussed in Chapter 3. For more details, see R. Kolb and J. Overdahl, *Understanding Futures Markets*, 6th edn, Malden, MA: Blackwell, 2006, Chapters 1–3.

4 Notice that this equivalence of δ and r implies that the expected change in the futures price is zero. As the futures requires no investment and we are employing risk-neutrality arguments, the expected payoff from all investments is the risk-free rate. The risk-free rate applied to zero investment gives a zero expected profit.

5 Fischer Black, "The Pricing of Commodity Contracts," *Journal of Financial Economics*, 3, March 1976, pp. 167–79.

6 For a detailed explanation of these pricing relationships, see Chapter 3 of R. Kolb and J. Overdahl, *Understanding Futures Markets*, 6th edn, Malden, MA: Blackwell, 2006.

7 Notice that the call and put on the physical have the same price of $22.09. This will always be the case if the price of the spot good equals the exercise price.

17

The Options Approach to Corporate Securities

Overview

In this chapter, we apply the concepts developed in this book to the analysis of corporate securities such as stocks and bonds. We will see that virtually all securities have option features, and the options approach to corporate securities can help us understand these securities more fully.

Since the Black–Scholes model first appeared in the early 1970s, research on options has expanded rapidly. Option theory has given insight into several areas of finance, one of the most fruitful being corporate finance. In this chapter, we explore the insights that option theory brings to understanding corporate securities. By thinking of corporate securities as embracing options, we can build a deeper understanding of the value of securities such as stocks and bonds.[1]

The chapter begins by considering a firm with a simple capital structure of equity and a single pure discount bond. We show that the equity of the firm can be regarded as a call option on the entire firm with an exercise price equal to the obligation to the bondholders. Similarly, we can analyze the bond as involving an option as well. For this simple case, we show that the corporate bond can be regarded as consisting of a risk-free bond plus a short position in a put option. Of course, most firms have a more complex financial structure, but considering this simple case introduces the option dimension of most corporate securities.

In more realistic situations, the options embedded in corporate securities are more complex. In many firms, some debt is subordinated to more senior debt, meaning that the firm pays on the junior debt only after the senior debt claims have been satisfied. We show that the options approach to junior and senior debt analyzes these bonds as involving different exercise prices. When a firm has equity and coupon bonds, the analysis of the equity shows that the stock owners have a series of options. As another example, convertible debt includes a specific option—the option to convert the debt instrument into shares of the firm. The option to convert debt to equity is an option purchased by and held by the bond owner. Most corporate bonds are callable, so the issuer of the bond is entitled to retire the bond under specified circumstances. This call feature gives the issuer of the bond options with specified exercise prices. Understanding the option features of these different debt instruments gives a clearer understanding of their pricing. As we will see, these option features of corporate bonds have value, and they definitely affect the value of the bonds in which they are embedded.

A **warrant** is a security that gives the owner the option to convert the warrant into a new share of the issuing firm by paying a stated exercise price. This definition shows that a warrant is very similar to an option. However, there is an important difference. An option has an existing share as its underlying good. By contrast, the exercise of a warrant requires that the firm issue a new share of stock. As we will see, this difference leads to a slight difference in the valuation of options and warrants.

Equity and a pure discount bond

We begin our analysis of corporate securities by focusing on a firm with an extremely simple capital structure. This firm has common stock and a single bond for its financing. The bond is a pure discount bond that matures in one year. In this section, we want to understand these securities from the options point of view.

Common stock as a call option

For this firm financed by common stock and a single pure discount bond, we assume the bond issue is a pure discount bond, with face value FV. Let the current time be $t = 0$, and let the maturity date of the bond be $t = m$. Between the present and $t = m$, the firm operates, generating cash flows. We further assume that the firm is operated by agents of the shareholders for the benefit of the shareholders. Also, during this period, new information about the prospects of the firm becomes available. At any time, the value of the firm equals the present value of the firm's future cash flows. The firm value also equals the total value of its outstanding securities. At $t = 0$, the firm's value, V_0, is as follows:

$$V_0 = S_0 + B_0 \tag{17.1}$$

where S_0 is the entire value of all stocks outstanding at time zero and B_0 is the entire value of all bonds outstanding at time zero. The value of the bonds equals the present value of the face value, discounted at the appropriate risky discount rate r' for m periods:

$$B_0 = \text{FV}e^{-r'm} \tag{17.2}$$

When the bond matures, the firm can either pay the indebtedness, FV, or default. If the firm defaults, the bondholders take over the firm to salvage whatever they can. If the firm has a value greater than its indebtedness, FV, the firm will pay the bondholders, and the firm will then belong entirely to the stockholders. Thus, the stockholders' payoff at $t = m$, S_m, is either zero (if they default) or the value of the firm minus the debt to the bondholders ($V_m - \text{FV}$). In other words, the stock is just like a European call, with the following payoff:

$$S_m = \text{MAX}\{0, V_m - \text{FV}\} \tag{17.3}$$

Therefore, the stock is a call option on the firm with an exercise price equal to the debt obligation, FV. Figure 17.1 shows the position of the stockholders. If the firm value at expiration is less than or equal to FV, then the stockholders do not have enough to pay the bondholders. Accordingly, they default and receive nothing. If the firm value exceeds FV, the stockholders pay the bondholders and keep any excess value.

From our analysis of stock options, we know the call value must equal or exceed the stock price minus the present value of the exercise price. Applying that principle to our treatment of stock itself as an option, we have the following:

Figure 17.1   The option analysis of corporate debt

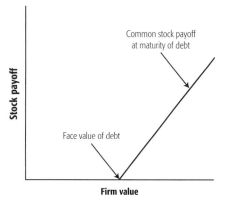

$$S_0 \geq V_0 - \mathrm{FV}e^{-r't} \tag{17.4}$$

This formula emphasizes another principle of option pricing. We know that call prices increase for higher risk in the underlying good. In analyzing common stock as an option on the value of the firm, we see that increasing the risk of the firm will make the stock more valuable. This is true even if the increasing risk does not increase the expected value of the firm at the expiration of the bond. The reason for this increase in value is the same that we saw for stock options. The stockholders have an incentive to increase risk. If the higher risk pays off, the stockholders keep all the benefits. If the risk does not pay off, the limited liability feature of stock protects the stockholders from losing more than their investment. Therefore, increasing risk gives a better chance for a very positive outcome for the stockholders, while the option protects against very negative outcomes. However, increasing the risk of the firm without increasing its expected value cannot increase the value of the firm as a whole. The increase in the value of the stock must come at the expense of the bondholders. Increasing the risk of the firm without increasing the firm's expected value transfers wealth from bondholders to stockholders. Bondholders are aware of this incentive for the stockholders. As a result, bond covenants often prevent the borrower from increasing the risk of the firm.

The option analysis of corporate debt

Let us now examine the same simple firm from the perspective of the debt holder. The stockholders have promised to pay FV to the debt holders at $t = m$. However, the stockholders will pay only if the firm's value exceeds FV at the maturity of the debt. Otherwise, they will let the bondholders have the firm. Therefore, the payoff for the bondholders at $t = m$, B_m, will be the lesser of the firm's value or FV. Figure 17.2 graphs the payoffs that the bondholders receive. As the figure shows, the bondholders receive the entire value of the firm if the firm value at the maturity of the debt is less than the debt obligation, FV. However, the bondholders never receive more than the promised payment of FV. Thus, the payoff to the bondholders, B_m, is the lesser of the firm's value, V_m, or FV:

$$B_m = \mathrm{MIN}\{V_m, \mathrm{FV}\} \tag{17.5}$$

We have already seen the payoff to the stockholders at $t = m$, and we know that the value of the bonds and stocks must equal the value of the firm. Therefore,

---

Figure 17.2   The option analysis of corporate debt

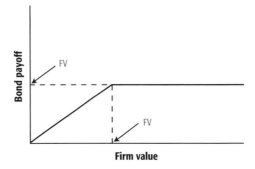

$$B_m = V_m - \text{MAX}\{0, V_m - \text{FV}\} \qquad (17.6)$$

This equation shows that the bondholders have effectively purchased the entire firm and written a European call option to the stockholders. The call option is on the entire firm. The face value of the debt, FV, is the exercise price. This conclusion exactly complements our analysis of the stock as a call option on the value of the firm.

A closer analysis of Figure 17.2 shows that it has the same payoff shape that we studied in Chapter 11. In essence, the bondholders' payoff consists of two embedded positions. The general shape matches that of a short position in a put. However, the entire position can never be worth less than zero. The bondholders effectively hold a short position in a put with an exercise price of FV, in addition to a long position in a risk-free bond paying FV. To see why this is so, assume that the firm's value at maturity exactly matches the obligation to the bondholders, $V_m = \text{FV}$. From Figure 17.2, we see that the bondholders receive FV for this terminal firm value. With $V_m = \text{FV}$, the put option that the bondholders issued expires worthless.

Consider now any lower value for the firm at maturity. If the firm value is lower than FV, the stockholders exercise their put option, forcing the firm upon the bondholders. Now, the bondholders receive their risk-free payment of FV, but they lose an amount equal to the shortfall in the firm's value below FV. In our notation, the bondholders receive FV. They also lose either zero, if the firm's value exceeds FV, or they lose $\text{FV} - V_m$, if the debt obligation exceeds the value of the firm:

$$B_m = \text{FV} - \text{MAX}\{0, \text{FV} - V_m\} \qquad (17.7)$$

As this equation shows, the bondholders receive a payoff equal to a long position in a riskless bond and a short position in a put with an exercise price of FV.

Thus, we have seen that we can analyze the position of the bondholders in two ways:

(1)   The bond consists of ownership of the entire firm with a short position in a call on the entire firm given to the shareholders. The exercise price of the call possessed by the shareholders is FV.
(2)   The bond consists of a risk-free bond paying FV combined with a short position in a put option sold to the shareholders, which allows the shareholders to put the entire firm to the bondholders for an exercise price of FV.

From our exploration of put–call parity in Chapter 11, we know that the following relationship must hold:

$$S_t - c_t = Xe^{-r(T-t)} - p_t \qquad (17.8)$$

We can apply put–call parity to our present situation by recalling that the value of the entire firm, V_o, plays the role of the stock and that the exercise price equals the promised payment to the bondholders, FV:

$$V_o - S_o = B_o \quad \text{or} \quad V_o - c_t = \text{FV}e^{-r(T-t)} - p_t \qquad (17.9)$$

In Equation 17.9, notice that the promised payment on the bond, FV, is discounted at the risk-free rate of interest, r, not the risky rate of interest r'. This difference reflects the analysis of the risky bond as consisting of a risk-free bond with a promised payment of FV plus a short position in the put option on the entire firm. The difference in price between the risk-free and risky bond equals the short position in the put.

The KMV default prediction model

One application of the options approach to corporate securities is to generate analytic models that predict default. These models treat default as an option, meaning the value of the default option can be estimated from a small set of variables. As we have seen in Equation 17.3, stock is just like a European call with an exercise price equal to the face value of the debt obligation (FV). The stockholder's payoff is zero in the event of default, or the value of the firm less the debt to bondholders in the absence of default. From the perspective of bondholders, they effectively hold a short position in a put with an exercise price of FV, in addition to a long position in a risk-free bond paying FV.

KMV is a firm that has pioneered the use of option pricing theory to generate a forward-looking market assessment of the probability of default for public companies. Moody's acquired KMV in the 1990s and the company became known as Moody's KMV. Banks and holders of traded debt rely on Moody's KMV Credit Monitor product to manage the credit risk in their portfolios. The value of the default option can be written as a function of five variables: the market value of the firm's assets, AV; the face value of the firm's debt, FV, the volatility of the firm's assets, σ_{AV}; the risk-free rate of interest, r; and the time to maturity of the debt, $T - t$.

The variables AV and σ_{AV} must be estimated. Moody's KMV uses a proprietary method to estimate these variables. The variable AV is estimated from a model of the relationship between the market value of the firm's equity and the market value of the firm's assets. This requires knowledge of the company's capital structure. The variable σ_{AV} is estimated from a model of the relationship between the volatility of the firm's assets and the volatility of the firm's equity. Once these variables are estimated, the Moody's KMV model estimates the value of the default option, which can be used to estimate the probability of default.

Senior and subordinated debt

Many firms have two or more debt issues in their capital structure. Thus, we now consider a firm with three securities: stock, senior debt, and subordinated debt. Subordinated debt is a bond issue that receives payment only after the firm fully meets senior debt obligations. Let the two debt issues be pure discount bonds that both mature at $t = m$. The face values on the two obligations are FV_s for the senior debt and FV_j for the junior or subordinated debt. We want to analyze the subordinated debt in option terms.

The holders of the subordinated debt receive payment only after the firm fully meets the claims of the senior debtholders. Therefore, for any firm value V_m that is less than FV_s, the junior debtholders receive zero. If the firm value exceeds FV_s, the junior debtholders receive at least some payment. The subordinated debtholders receive full payment if the firm's value equals or exceeds the entire amount due on both debt issues: $V_m \geq FV_s + FV_j$. Figure 17.3 shows the payoffs for the senior and junior debt. The payoffs on the junior debt match a portfolio of a long call with a strike price of FV_s and a short call with a strike price of FV_j, as Figure 17.4 shows. The stockholders in this firm own a call on the value of the firm with a strike price equal to $FV_s + FV_j$. For the call option represented by the stock to come into-the-money, the value of the firm must exceed the total payoff of the two debt issues. Therefore, the payoff on the call in this situation is as follows:

$$S_m = \text{MAX}\{0, V_m - (FV_s + FV_j)\}$$

Figure 17.3   Payoffs on junior and senior corporate debt

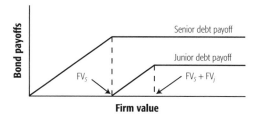

Figure 17.4   Junior debt analyzed as a portfolio of calls

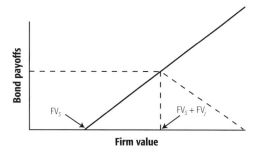

As always, the value of the firm must equal the value of all outstanding securities. However, the different classes of securities offer different ways to create various options and provide different divisions of the corporate pie when the bonds mature.

Callable bonds

The typical corporate bond is a callable bond. A **callable bond** is a bond that can be redeemed at the will of the issuer by the payment of a specified amount. Usually, the bond is not callable until a specified number of years after its issuance. Thereafter, the issuer may call the bond at any time. As an example, a firm might issue a bond today that is callable in five years (and thereafter), with a required payment equal to 110 percent of the face value of the bond. Typical call provisions allow this required payment to decline in subsequent years. In some cases, the bond is callable only on certain dates.

The issuer of the bond has an incentive to call the bond if the coupon rate exceeds the current market rate of interest. For example, if the callable bond were issued at 11 percent and current rates for similar debt are 6 percent, the issuer might wish to call the 11 percent bond and issue new debt at the prevailing market rate of 6 percent.

When it issues a callable bond, the firm itself retains a valuable option to require the bondholder to surrender the bond in return for the payment of a certain amount. Therefore, the call feature of a corporate bond means that the issuing firm has a call option on the outstanding bond. The exercise price of this call option is the call price that the firm must pay to call the bond.

For the bondholder, a callable bond is less desirable than a bond with no call feature. The bondholder knows that the issuer will exercise the call feature only when it benefits the issuing firm. In our example, the bondholder receiving an 11 percent coupon payment in a 6 percent interest rate environment certainly would prefer that the issuer not call the bond. Therefore, in accepting a callable bond, the bondholder realizes that he is implicitly buying a (noncallable) bond and selling a call option on the bond to the issuer. As we have seen, this call option held by the issuer has greater value when market rates of interest lie below the coupon rate on the bond.

The value of the noncallable bond varies inversely and smoothly with interest rates over the entire range of rates. By contrast, the value of a callable bond parallels the value of the noncallable bond for higher interest rates. For low interest rates, however, the value of the callable bond remains constant at a lower level.

To understand the difference in the values of callable and noncallable bonds, consider the following example of two similar bonds. One is noncallable while the other is callable on a single date in five years at a call price of $1,100.[2] We assume that both bonds have an initial maturity of 30 years and that both have an 8 percent coupon and a $1,000 face value. We further assume that the noncallable bond has an 8 percent yield at issuance, so it is priced at its face value of $1,000. The callable bond is identical in its promised coupon payments and maturity and differs from the noncallable bond only in its call feature. As we have seen, this means that the buyer of the callable bond grants the issuer a call option that has some value. Therefore, we know that the price of the callable bond at issuance must be less than the otherwise identical noncallable bond.

Figure 17.5 illustrates the values of the two bonds five years after issuance, when both bonds have 25 years remaining until maturity. If market rates of interest are 8 percent, the noncallable bond will still be worth $1,000. The callable bond will be priced below $1,000 because of the call feature. If interest rates are higher, at 10 percent for example, the price of the noncallable bond will be $817, and the price of the callable bond will still be somewhat lower. If interest rates are substantially lower than 8 percent—say 6 percent, for example—the price of the noncallable bond will be $1,257. At this point, we can see that there will be a substantial divergence between the price of the callable and noncallable bond. The call price for the bond of $1,100 is effectively the upper bound on the price of the callable bond, even in a low interest rate

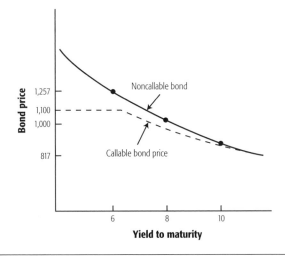

Figure 17.5 Callable versus noncallable bonds

environment. Investors will not be willing to pay more than \$1,100 for the callable bond, because they know it can be called away from them at that price.

The issuing firm holds a call option on the bond and a short position in the underlying bond. If interest rates fall, the value of bonds will rise in general. However, the callable bond is a single security, meaning that the bond and the call option on the bond are inextricably bound together. To capture the value of the call option, the issuer must exercise the call feature of the bond. This union of the call and the underlying bond in a single security helps to explain why the value of the callable bond cannot rise significantly above its call price. The resulting pricing is depicted in Figure 17.5. To summarize, for prices at or below the call price on the callable bond, the two bonds will behave similarly. However, the callable bond will always be worth somewhat less than an otherwise similar bond due to the presence of the call feature. For higher prices on the noncallable bond, the price of the callable bond will be capped at or near the call price of the bond.

Figure 17.5 does not show the exact price of the callable bond, because it does not attempt to exactly price the call that is embedded in the callable bond. However, we know that the price of the embedded call will depend on the time until expiration, the prevailing interest rate, the price of the otherwise similar bond, the call price, and the volatility of the price of the otherwise similar bond.

Convertible bonds

Many corporate bonds are convertible into shares of the issuing firm. The holder of the bond has the option to convert the bond into shares under the terms specified in the bond indenture. For example, a firm might issue a \$1,000 face value convertible bond with a 20-year maturity and a coupon rate of 9 percent. The bond could be converted into eight shares of stock by surrendering the bond.[3] We assume that a share of the issuing firm was worth \$100 at the time of issuance. We can analyze this type of convertible bond as consisting of two elements: a regular bond with no-conversion feature, plus a call option on eight shares of stock with the exercise price of the option being the value of the bond. The number of shares received for the bond upon conversion is the conversion ratio. Because the purchase of a convertible bond receives a call option on the shares of the issuing firm, the convertible bond sells for more than an otherwise similar nonconvertible bond. This means that the issuing firm can issue a convertible bond at a lower interest rate than an otherwise similar nonconvertible bond. However, the firm gives a call option to secure this lower interest rate.

At any time during its life, the bond must be worth at least its conversion value. In our example, we assume that the conversion ratio was eight shares, so the bond must be worth at least eight times the current share price. If this condition were not met, there would be an immediate arbitrage opportunity, because a trader could buy the bond, exercise the conversion feature to secure the shares, and sell the shares for more than the price of the bond. Of course, the bond can sell for more than its conversion value, because the bond always has all of the features of a straight bond.

At the maturity of the bond, the bond will pay its face value, will be converted, or the firm will default. The firm will default if the face value exceeds the value of the firm. In the case of default, the owners of the convertible bond will take over the entire firm. Assuming the firm does not default, the convertible bond will be worth the maximum of the face value or the conversion ratio times the stock price.

In many instances, the bond indenture prohibits the issuing firm from paying a dividend during the life of the convertible bond. In this case, the bond will not be converted prior to its maturity date. This is clear by analogy to a call. Exercising a call or converting a convertible bond on a nondividend stock terminates the option in favor of its intrinsic value. As we saw for a call, the owner is better off selling the call and buying the stock in the open market. Similarly, the holder of a convertible bond on a nondividend stock will not exercise, because doing so discards the excess value of the call option over and above its intrinsic value.

Some convertible bonds are also callable. For convertible callable bonds, both the issuer and the bondholder hold an option associated with the bond. As we have seen, the issuer has a call option on the underlying bond, and the owner of a convertible bond has a call option on the firm's shares. Consider a convertible bond that could be profitably converted, and assume that the underlying shares pay no dividend. As we have just seen, the bondholder will not willingly convert prior to the maturity of the bond, because converting the bond discards the time value that is inherent in the option. However, the issuer would like the holder of the convertible bond to convert as soon as possible for the same reason. Therefore, the issuer of a convertible callable bond can force conversion by calling the bond. As soon as the convertible callable bond can be converted, the issuer should call the bond to force conversion. This is clear, because if it behooves the bondholder to delay conversion, it must benefit the issuer to force conversion. After all, the bond is an asset to the bondholder, but a liability to the issuer. Therefore, forcing conversion eliminates the time premium associated with the conversion option.

Tax-timing options

One application of option pricing models is to value the tax-timing option accompanying the ownership of stocks. The purchase of any taxable security confers on its owner a tax-timing option to recognize capital gains and losses in an optimal fashion. The tax-timing option will be reflected in the market price of securities. When an investor purchases shares in a mutual fund, he acquires a tax-timing option on the shares of the fund that he purchases, but he gives up the tax-timing options on the individual securities that comprise the fund. Therefore, the tax-timing value of owning shares in a mutual fund is likely to be less than the tax-timing value of direct ownership of the securities that comprise the fund. This result is an illustration of a more general principle related to options: a portfolio of options is more valuable than an option on the corresponding portfolio.

Warrants

A typical warrant allows the owner to pay a stated price for a share of common stock of the firm that issues the warrant. Usually, warrants are created with three to seven years to expiration. As such, a warrant is very much like a call option on the stock of the issuing firm. However, a call option has as its underlying instrument an existing share. By contrast, the exercise of a warrant requires the issuing firm to create a new share and deliver it to the exerciser of the warrant. Therefore, the exercise of a warrant involves a dilution of ownership because a new share is created. Warrants are often attached to bonds as a "sweetener" to make the bonds more saleable. Often, these warrants are detachable and can even trade in a separate market. However warrants are issued, they are valuable instruments, with all of the features of a call option, except for the fact that they command a newly created share upon exercise rather than an existing share.

At the expiration date of the warrant, exercise would make sense only if the resulting share value from exercise exceeded the exercise price. Let V_B be the share price before exercise, let X be the exercise price of the warrant, let n be the number of shares outstanding before exercise, and let q be the number of warrants. The value of the firm after exercise will be $nV_B + qX$, because the total exercise price on the warrants is qX, and the firm's value increases due to the influx of cash from the exercise of the warrants. There will be $n(1 + q/n)$ shares outstanding after exercise. Therefore, the value of a share after exercise will be

$$\frac{nV_B + qX}{n + q} \tag{17.10}$$

As an example, consider a firm with 100 outstanding shares priced at $48 per share, and assume that the shares pay no dividend. The firm has warrants for ten shares outstanding with an exercise price on the warrants of $50. If the warrants are exercised, the firm will be worth $5,300, the present value of the firm plus the $500 exercise price of the warrants. The firm will then have 110 shares outstanding after it issues the ten shares to meet the exercise of the warrants. Consequently, each share after exercise would be worth $48.18. With an exercise price of $50 and a post-exercise share price of $48.18, exercise is not feasible. Thus, exercise will only be feasible if the stock price equals or exceeds the exercise price.

As with a call option, a warrant should not be exercised until expiration. The reasoning is the same; early exercise discards the time premium associated with the option. Instead of exercising the call or warrant, the owner should sell the call or warrant and purchase the underlying good.

The value of a European warrant equals the value of a parallel European call after adjustment for the dilution of ownership caused by the exercise of the warrant. If q warrants are exercised and n shares are outstanding before exercise, there will be $n(1 + q/n)$ shares outstanding after exercise. The European warrant gives title to one of those shares. Therefore, the value of a European warrant at time t, W_t, must be

$$W_t = \frac{c_t}{1 + \dfrac{q}{n}}$$

In other words, the value of a European warrant equals the value of a European call option divided by one plus the proportion of shares created in response to the exercise of the warrant.

Using option pricing theory to value offshore petroleum leases

James Paddock, Daniel Siegel, and James Smith, in a 1988 study, use option pricing theory to value leases for offshore petroleum.[4] The holder of an offshore petroleum lease receives the right to explore and develop a tract during the life of the lease. They value a lease on an unexplored tract as a compound option, where the unexplored tract is an option on the development option.

Using the option pricing approach is not a silver bullet for valuation. Even though the approach has advantages over the traditional discounted cash flow analysis in terms of the data and computational requirements, modelers will still encounter many practical implementation problems. However, perhaps the biggest advantage of the option valuation approach is the fact that the model generates the "Greeks"— that is, the analytic measures of the option's sensitivity to changes in the values of the underlying variables. The model can also be used to determine when it makes sense to exercise the option to develop a lease, as opposed to selling the lease rights to someone else. Petroleum exploration, development, and extraction has proven to be a fruitful application of the option pricing approach. The approach is also useful for determining when to abandon a producing property; that is, to exercise the abandonment option.

Conclusion

In this chapter, we have explored how various corporate securities can be analyzed in terms of the option concepts developed throughout this book. We began by considering an extremely simple firm drawing its capital only from common stock and a single pure discount bond. For such a firm, we saw that the common stock can be treated as a call option on the entire firm. In this case, the call option has an exercise price equal to the payment promised to the bondholders, and the expiration date for the option is the maturity of the bond. The bond itself can be analyzed in option terms as well. We used put–call parity to show that the bond can be analyzed in two equivalent ways. First, the bond represents ownership of the entire firm coupled with a short position in a call on the entire firm given to the shareholders. The exercise price of the call possessed by the shareholders is the payment promised to the bondholders. As a second and equivalent analysis, the bond consists of a risk-free bond paying the face value of the bond combined with a short position in a put option sold to the shareholders, which allows the shareholders to put the entire firm to the bondholders for an exercise price of the face value of the bond.

Next, we considered a firm with stock, senior debt, and subordinated debt in its capital structure. The stock owners have essentially the same position as in the simplest case. They own a call on the entire firm, and the exercise price of the call is the total set of payments promised to both the senior and subordinated debtholders. The subordinated debtholder essentially holds a long call on the firm with an exercise price equal to the payment promised to the senior bondholders coupled with a short call on the entire firm with an exercise price equal to the payment promised to the junior bondholders. If the shareholders decide not to exercise their call, it will be because the value of the firm is less than the exercise price that the stockholders face–the payments promised to the junior and senior debtholders. The junior debtholders can then claim the firm by exercising their call on the senior debtholders; they merely must pay the senior debtholders as promised. However, the junior debtholders have also issued a call, because the stockholders may call the firm away from them by making the promised payment.

Both callable and convertible bonds have options embedded in them. As we saw, a callable bond consists of a straight bond, but the issuer of the bond retains a call option on the bond. Thus, the issuer is long this call, and the bondholder has sold the call to the issuer. This call gives the issuer of the bond the right to purchase the bond and avoid any further payments by paying the call price. In a bond convertible into common stock, the owner of the bond has a call option on the shares of the firm. The bondholder in this case can convert a bond into shares by surrendering the bond and paying the stipulated price to acquire the shares permitted by the bond covenant. In the case of both the callable bond and the convertible bond, the embedded options have value, and this value can be a considerable proportion of the total value of the bond.

Finally, we considered the pricing of warrants. We noted that a warrant is similar to a call option. However, a call option gives the holder the right to buy an existing share, while a warrant gives the holder the right to buy a newly issued share from the firm. The exercise of the warrant thus involves a dilution of ownership in the firm; therefore, a warrant is slightly less valuable than an otherwise similar call option.

Exercises

1 Explain why common stock is itself like a call option. In the option analysis of common stock, what plays the role of the exercise price and what plays the role of the underlying stock?

2 Consider a firm that issues a pure discount bond that matures in one year and has a face value of $1 million. Analyze the payoffs that the bondholders will receive in option pricing terms, assuming that the only other security in the firm is common stock.

3 Consider a firm with common stock and a pure discount bond as its financing. The total value of the firm is $1 million. There are 10,000 shares of common stock priced at $70 per share. The bond matures in ten years and has a total face value of $0.5 million. What is the interest rate on the bond, assuming annual compounding? Would the interest rate become higher or lower if the volatility of the firm's cash flows increases?

4 A firm has a capital structure consisting of common stock and a single bond. The managers of the firm are considering a major capital investment that will be financed from internally generated funds. The project can be initiated in two ways, one with a high fixed-cost component and the other with a low fixed-cost component. Although both technologies have the same expected value, the high fixed-cost approach has the potential for greater payoffs. (If the product is successful, the high fixed-cost approach gives much lower total costs for large production levels.) What does option theory suggest about the choice the managers should make? Explain.

5 In a firm with common stock, senior debt, and subordinated debt, assume that both debt instruments mature at the same time. What is the necessary condition on the value of the firm at maturity for each security holder to receive at least some payment? With two classes of debt, does option theory counsel managers to increase the riskiness of the firm's operations? Would there be any difference on this point between a firm with a single debt issue and two debt issues?

Which bondholders would tend to be more risk averse as far as choosing a risk level for the firm's operations is concerned? Explain.

6 Consider a firm financed solely by common stock and a single callable bond issue. Assume that the bond is a pure discount bond. Is there any circumstance in which the firm should call the bond before the maturity date? Would such an exercise of the firm's call option discard the time premium? Explain.

7 Consider a firm financed only by common stock and a convertible bond issue. When should the bondholders exercise? Explain. If the common shares pay a dividend, could it make sense for the bondholders to exercise before the bond matures? Explain by relating your answer to our discussion of the exercise of American calls on dividend-paying stocks.

8 Warrants are often used to compensate top executives in firms. Often, these warrants cannot be exercised until a distant expiration date. This form of compensation is used to align the manager's incentives with the maximization of the shareholders' wealth. Explain how the manager's receiving warrants might thwart the efforts to change his or her incentives.

9 In preparation for the CFA exam, you have been watching *Trading Places*. During your most recent viewing of the movie, you were struck by the notion that creating a call option on frozen concentrated orange juice would be possible. Describe the process of creating a synthetic call option on frozen concentrated orange juice using the frozen concentrated orange juice futures contract. Be sure to discuss the information necessary to create the synthetic option.

10 In automobile lease arrangements, the lessee has the right to buy the car from the manufacturer for a fixed price at the expiration of the lease. Assume that the lease in question matures in three years, and there are no tax advantages to leasing the car.

A Describe the positions of the automobile manufacturer and the car owner.

B Explain how such an option could be valued. Explain how you might estimate the parameters necessary to value this option. Be sure to discuss the factors complicating the valuation of this option.

C Explain why automobile manufacturers would bundle this right with the automobile lease.

D Does the presence of the right to purchase the car at the expiration of the lease increase the price of the lease? Explain.

11 A developer has purchased 60 acres of rural property just north of Augusta, Georgia, to develop a golf course. The golf course project will also include a housing development. To generate operating capital, the developer is selling rights. The rights give the holder of the contract the right to purchase lots in the housing development for a fixed price. Each lot in the housing development is half an acre. The agreements expire six months after they are signed. The developer is offering the following inducement. A potential homeowner can purchase a lot for $25,000 at the end of six months if the homeowner enters the contract this week. The purchase price for a lot increases to $40,000 on all contracts signed after this week. The developer has asked you to price the rights to purchase property in the development. Explain how you would value these options. Discuss the factors that make the valuation of this contract difficult.

12 Kevin is employed by Farm State Insurance. It is Kevin's job to develop a pricing model to price automobile insurance. Farm State Insurance will offer accident insurance policies to drivers of all ages, in all states. The insurance policies will be renewable semiannually. The policies only cover accidents and do not cover the theft of the vehicle. Several different deductibles will be offered to prospective policyholders. Model the auto insurance as an option. Discuss the pricing of this type of insurance policy and the construction of the insurance policies offered to drivers.

13 Your bank is thinking of offering a new product to small businesses. This product will allow a customer to borrow up to $50,000 at a fixed rate of interest. This line of credit has a life span of two years. The customer can draw against the credit line as many times as he or she wants over the life of the contract. However, the minimum amount that may be borrowed is $5,000. Once the customer has borrowed funds, he or she has up to one year to repay the loan. This contract has a fixed life and a fixed interest rate. The small business person gains access to the line of credit by paying an up-front fee. It is your job to price the contract and determine the amount of the up-front fee. Model the fixed rate line of credit as an option. Explain when an investor is likely to use this line of credit.

14 The local junior service league is organizing a fundraiser for the local homeless shelter. The owner of the Hallmark card shop in town has donated the grand prize of four Beanie Babies®. These are not just any Beanie Babies. They are Garcia, Peace, Erin, and Princess Bear, the most famous and valuable retired Beanie Babies. However, in your state, it is a felony to operate a raffle. So rather than raffling off the grand prize, the junior service league must sell rights to the public that permit the "winner" of the raffle to purchase the grand prize at a retail price of $6.99 per baby. The "winner" will be randomly selected from among all entrants. It is your job to price the raffle

tickets to be offered for sale. Explain how you would value these tickets.

15 Debt contracts represent fixed claims against the cash flows of a firm, while an equity contract entitles the shareholder to claim against the residual cash flows of the firm. The small firm in question has one shareholder, the entrepreneur who started and runs the firm. The firm's debt consists of loans from the local commercial bank. The firm's primary source of revenues is exports to Singapore. Because of the Asian financial crisis, the firm is facing a considerable reduction in cash flows. The manager/entrepreneur has two investment projects. One is a safe project that will only generate sufficient cash flows to cover the firm's debt obligations. The other project is considerably more risky, but if successful will generate twice the firm's normal annual revenue. Which project do you expect the entrepreneur to undertake? Explain.

16 You have just been hired as CFO for a medium-sized manufacturing firm. The SEC requires your firm to report the value of the stock option contracts awarded to employees in your annual 10K report. Your firm has issued stock options to its executives. The options generally have a strike price that is slightly higher than the firm's stock price when they are offered. The options can be exercised anytime during the life of the option. If the options are exercised, the firm issues new Treasury stock. Executives often exercise these options well before the expiration date of the option. The options issued to executives cannot be sold to any other party, and the options automatically expire if the executive leaves the firm. The majority of the options awarded to executives have had a life of three years. It is your job to value the options awarded by your firm. Explain why the firm would choose to compensate its executives with options. Explain how you would value these options. Discuss the possible reasons why an executive might choose to exercise these options early.

17 WCS has enjoyed massive growth in the past decade and is in the process of constructing a new 80-story corporate headquarters building. This construction project is early in the planning stage. The management of WCS has a choice between two technologies for the heating and cooling plant for the building. The choice is between a heating and cooling plant that burns only oil and one that burns either oil or natural gas. That is, the latter heating and cooling plant can be converted from oil burning to a natural gas fueled facility after a fixed-cost expenditure of $50,000. Although the dual fuel plant has greater initial cost, it offers management greater flexibility in the future. In making the choice between the two heating and cooling plants, the firm's managers must assess the value of this operating option. Evaluate this investment decision facing the managers of WCS as an option. Assume that natural gas comes from domestic suppliers and heating oil is supplied in the global oil market.

18 You are evaluating DOG as a potential target for acquisition. DOG has capital structure that consists of common stock and a convertible bond. The bond matures in ten years and, upon conversion by a bondholder, the firm must issue additional shares of stock. Describe the bondholders' position. Discuss the valuation of the convertible bond. Explain when the bondholders should exercise their option. If DOG pays a dividend, would it be rational for the bondholders to exercise their option before the bond matures? Explain by relating your answer to the decision to exercise an American call option on a dividend-paying stock.

Suppose that the bond also has a call provision. The call provision gives the firm's managers the right to call the bond after five years at a premium to par. Discuss the impact of the introduction of the call provision to the bond contract on the decision by the owners of the bond to convert the bond to stock prior to expiration of the bond contract.

Notes

1 Of course, the original Black–Scholes paper, "The Pricing of Options and Corporate Liabilities," *Journal of Political Economy*, 81, 1973, pp. 637–59, already focused on the option characteristics of stocks and bonds.

2 Generally, bonds are not callable until their first call date, and they are then callable at any time thereafter.

3 Other features are possible. For example, some bonds can be converted to preferred stock. Some convertible bonds can be converted only by surrendering the bond and making a cash payment. Some convertible bonds can be converted only on certain dates. Further, some convertible securities are preferred stock that can be converted into common stock.

4 James L. Paddock, Daniel R. Siegel, and James L. Smith, "Option Valuation of Claims on Real Assets: The Case of Offshore Petroleum Leases," *Quarterly Journal of Economics*, August 1988, 103:3, pp. 479–508.

18

Exotic Options

Overview

In recent years, financial engineers have created a variety of complex options that are collectively known as **exotic options**. The payoffs on these options are considerably more diverse than the payoffs on the straightforward options that we have considered to this point. For example, the payoff on a **lookback call option** depends on the minimum stock price experienced during some past period. Other exotic options have different and more complicated payoff structures. This chapter explores the pricing and uses of these exotic options.

We approach these exotic options by contrasting them with the plain vanilla options explored earlier in this book. For a **plain vanilla option**, the value of an option at any particular moment depends only upon the current price of the underlying good, the exercise price, the risk-free rate of interest, the volatility of the underlying good, the time until expiration, and the dividend rate on the underlying good. Further, there is a fixed underlying good, a fixed and stated exercise price, and a known time to expiration, and there are no special conditions on any of the option parameters.

With respect to the price of the underlying good, it is important to emphasize that the price of a plain vanilla option depends only on the current price of the underlying good, so the price of the option is independent of the price path followed by the underlying good. As we will see in this chapter, many exotic options exhibit **path dependence**–the price of the option today depends on the previous or future price path

followed by the underlying good. For example, the price of a lookback call option depends on the minimum price reached by the underlying good over some past period. Further, the price of an average price option depends upon the future average price of the underlying good. Thus, to price a path-dependent option, it is not enough to know the current price of the underlying good. Instead, we must have information about the previous path that the price of the underlying good traversed.[1]

This chapter considers nine classes of exotic options: forward-start options, compound options, chooser options, barrier options, binary options, lookback options, average price options, exchange options, and rainbow options. Because of the complexity of these options, we focus on European options, emphasizing cases in which closed-form solutions are available. Thus, all of the exotic options are analyzed as extended instances of the Merton continuous dividend model. In their working paper "Exotic Options," Mark Rubinstein and Eric Reiner have presented a unified and comprehensive treatment of these exotic options, and this chapter relies largely on their excellent work.[2] We also refer to other studies and original contributions for each of the types of exotic options.

This chapter explores each type of exotic option in a separate section that discusses the payoff structure of the option, presents the valuation formula for the option, and shows a calculation example. The **OPTION!** software available on the web site that accompanies this book can compute the value of all of the exotic options discussed in this chapter.

Assumptions of the analysis and the pricing environment

In this chapter, we focus exclusively on European exotic options for which closed-form solutions exist. For most American exotic options, and for some European exotic options, there is no exact pricing formula. For these options, simulation or approximation methods must be used to estimate the price. This process adds considerable complexity. By focusing on European exotic options with closed-form solutions, we can gain a rich understanding of exotic options, while avoiding much mathematical complexity.

In our analysis, we make the usual assumptions underlying the Black–Scholes model and the Merton model. In particular, we assume that the price of the asset underlying the exotic option follows a log-normal random walk, that there are no arbitrage opportunities, and that the price of the underlying asset is expected to appreciate at the risk-free rate of interest, less any payouts from the asset, such as dividends. These assumptions allow us to evaluate options in a risk-neutral framework. As we explored in Chapter 13, these assumptions lead to the Black–Scholes model and the Merton model. Because we will refer to it often in this chapter, we repeat the Merton model here for convenience:

$$c_t^M = e^{-\delta(T-t)}S_t N(d_1^M) - Xe^{-r(T-t)}N(d_2^M)$$

$$p_t^M = Xe^{-r(T-t)}N(-d_2^M) - e^{-\delta(T-t)}S_t N(-d_1^M)$$

$$d_1^M = \frac{\ln\left(\dfrac{S_t}{X}\right) + (r - \delta + 0.5\sigma^2)(T - t)}{\sigma\sqrt{T - t}} \tag{18.1}$$

$$d_2^M = d_1^M - \sigma\sqrt{T - t}$$

Forward-start options

In a forward-start option, the price of the option is paid at the present, but the life of the option starts at a future date. Further, the exercise price is typically specified to be the current price at the beginning of the option's life—that is, the option contract specifies that the option will be at-the-money when the option's life begins. Forward-start call options are often used in executive compensation packages. An executive might receive a forward-start call option on the firm's shares with an exercise price to equal the firm's share price at the time the option life starts.

For a forward-start option, there are three dates to consider: the valuation date, t, the date on which the option life begins, which is called the **grant date**, tg, and the date on which the option eventually expires, T. Thus it must be the case that

$$t \leq tg \leq T$$

Accordingly, the time until the option life begins will be $tg - t$, and when the option's life begins, the time until expiration will be $T - tg$.

The value of a forward-start option is simply the value of an option with the current stock price, an exercise price equal to the current stock price, and a time to expiration of $T - tg$, with this value being discounted by the dividend rate on the underlying good over the period until the option is granted, $tg - t$:

$$\text{forward-start call} = e^{-\delta(tg-t)}C_{tg}^M$$
$$\text{forward-start put} = e^{-\delta(tg-t)}P_{tg}^M \tag{18.2}$$

where C_{tg}^M and P_{tg}^M are the values of the call and put options, respectively, according to the Merton model, with a time to expiration of $T - tg$. The idea here is that the price of the underlying good and the exercise price on the forward-start option will change proportionally. (For a forward-start option specified to be at-the-money on the grant date, the stock and exercise price at that time will be equal.) Therefore, a forward-start option today is essentially a deferred granting of an option with a stock and exercise price equal to today's stock price and a time to expiration that equals the period from the grant date to the final expiration date.[3]

To illustrate the value of these forward-start options more fully, consider the following data: $S = 100$; $X = 100$; $T - t = 1$ year; $\sigma = 0.2$; $r = 0.1$; $\delta = 0.05$; $tg = 0.5$ years. Using these data, we will price a call option. Notice that the time to expiration as of the grant date is $T - tg = 0.5$

years, so this is the time to expiration that will be used in the Merton model. We first compute d_1^M and d_2^M:

$$d_1^M = \frac{\ln\left(\dfrac{100}{100}\right) + [0.1 - 0.05 + 0.5 \times 0.2 \times 0.2] \times 0.5}{0.2 \times \sqrt{0.5}} = 0.247487$$

$$d_2^M = 0.247487 - 0.141421 = 0.106066$$

With these values for d_1^M and d_2^M, $N(d_1^M) = 0.597734$ and $N(d_2^M) = 0.542235$. So the value of the underlying call option is

$$
\begin{aligned}
C_{tg}^M &= e^{-\delta(T-tg)} S_t N(d_1^M) - X e^{-r(T-tg)} N(d_2^M) \\
&= e^{-0.05 \times 0.5} \times 100 \times 0.597734 - 100 e^{-0.1 \times 0.5} \times 0.542235 \\
&= 6.7186
\end{aligned}
$$

The value of the forward-start call is

$$\text{forward-start call} = e^{-\delta(tg-t)} C_{tg}^M = e^{-0.05 \times 0.5} \times 6.7186 = 6.5527$$

With the same input values, the forward-start put is worth 4.2042.

Compound options

A compound option is an option on an option; in other words, when one option is exercised, the underlying good is another option. In this section, we consider the pricing of the four types of possible compound European options: a call on a call, a call on a put, a put on a call, and a put on a put. For example, consider the owner of a call on a call. The owner of the compound call has until the expiration date of the compound option (the call on a call) to decide whether to exercise the compound option. If so, she will receive the underlying call option with its own exercise price and time until expiration. If that underlying option is exercised, she will receive the underlying good.

For the underlying option, we will use our familiar notation, letting X be the exercise price, and letting T be the expiration date. For the compound option, let x be the exercise price and let te be the time at which the compound option expires. Because these are European options, the owner of the compound option cannot exercise until the expiration date of the compound option, te. If she exercises the compound option, she will immediately receive the underlying call in the case we are considering. Therefore, when the compound option is at expiration, the choice is really very simple: pay x and receive the underlying option or do nothing and allow the option to expire worthless. Thus, when the compound option reaches expiration, the trader will exercise the compound call if the price of the underlying call is worth more than the exercise price of the compound option, x. At the expiration date of the compound option, the underlying call (or underlying put) can be priced according to the Merton model with inputs S_{te} for the price of the underlying good, X for the exercise price, $T - te$ for the time remaining until expiration, σ for the volatility of the underlying good, r for the risk-free rate, and δ for the dividend rate on the underlying good.

Before the expiration date of the compound option—that is, from t until te—the value of the compound option depends on the value of the underlying good in a compound manner. First, the value of the underlying option is largely a function of the value of the underlying good, as we have studied throughout this book. Second, the value of the compound option also depends on the price of its underlying good, which is the option underlying the compound option.

The valuation of these compound options is highly analogous to the valuation of an American option with a dividend payment between the valuation date and the expiration date that we studied in Chapter 15. There, we saw that the value depends on the critical stock price, S^*, that made the owner of the underlying call indifferent between exercising and allowing the option to expire worthless. In the case of an option on an underlying call, the critical stock price will be the stock price that leaves the owner of the underlying call indifferent between exercising or not. Therefore, for a compound option on an underlying call, the critical price is the stock price at which the value of the underlying call equals the cost of acquiring it, which is x. Thus, the critical stock price for an underlying call (a call on a call or a put on a call) is the value of S^* that makes the following equation hold:

$$S^* e^{-\delta(T-te)} N(z) - X e^{-r(T-te)} N(z - \sigma\sqrt{T - te}) - x = 0 \tag{18.3}$$

where

$$z = \frac{\ln\left(\dfrac{S^*}{X}\right) + (r - \delta + 0.5\sigma^2)(T - te)}{\sigma\sqrt{T - te}}$$

For a compound option on an underlying put (a call on a put or a put on a put), the critical stock price satisfies the following relationship:

$$-S^* e^{-\delta(T-te)} N(-z) - X e^{-r(T-te)} N(-z - \sigma\sqrt{T - te}) - x = 0 \tag{18.4}$$

Before we can write the valuation formula for a call on a call, we must define three additional variables:

$$w_1 = \frac{\ln\left(\dfrac{S}{S^*}\right) + (r - \delta + 0.5\sigma^2)(T - t)}{\sigma\sqrt{te - t}}$$

$$w_2 = \frac{\ln\left(\dfrac{S}{X}\right) + (r - \delta + 0.5\sigma^2)(te - t)}{\sigma\sqrt{te - t}}$$

and

$$\rho = \sqrt{\frac{te - t}{T - t}}$$

With these definitions, the value of a call on a call, CC_t, is as follows:

$$
\begin{aligned}
CC_t = {} & Se^{-\delta(T-t)} N_2(w_1; w_2; \rho) \\
& - X e^{-r(T-t)} N_2(w_1 - \sigma\sqrt{te - t}; w_2 - \sigma\sqrt{T - t}; \rho) \\
& - x e^{-r(te-t)} N(w_1 - \sigma\sqrt{te - t})
\end{aligned}
\tag{18.5}
$$

In Equation 18.5, the three terms correspond to the key factors that determine the value of the compound option, S, k, and K. The function N_2 is the bivariate normal cumulative probability already discussed in Chapter 15.[4]

To apply this formula, consider the following data: $S = 100$; $\sigma = 0.2$; $r = 0.1$; $\delta = 0.05$; $X = 100$ (the exercise price on the underlying option); $x = 8$ (the exercise price on the compound option); $T - t = 1$ year (the expiration date of the underlying option); $te = 0.25$ years (the expiration date of the compound option). With these data, we must first find the critical value that would make the option owner indifferent between exercising the compound option and allowing it to expire. The critical price depends on the value of z, which in turn depends on S^*. This means that the values of S^* and z must be solved simultaneously. This can be done by an iterative search over potential values of S^*. This is best done by computer. For these data, the critical value is 99.235871. This can be verified by computing z and the resulting value of zero in the equation for finding S^*.

Having found S^*, the values of w_1 and w_2 are given by the following:

$$w_1 = \frac{\ln\left(\dfrac{100}{99.235871}\right) + (0.1 - 0.05 + 0.5 \times 0.2 \times 0.2) \times 0.25}{0.2 \times \sqrt{0.25}}$$

$$= \frac{0.007671 + 0.0175}{0.1}$$

$$= 0.251706$$

$$w_2 = \frac{\ln\left(\dfrac{100}{100}\right) + (0.1 - 0.05 + 0.5 \times 0.2 \times 0.2) \times 1.0}{0.2 \times 1.0} = \frac{0 + 0.07}{0.2} = 0.35$$

The correlation coefficient is

$$\rho\sqrt{\frac{0.25}{1.0}} = 0.5$$

With these values of w_1, w_2, and ρ, we can compute all of the values for the unit and bivariate cumulative normal probabilities:

$N_2(w_1; w_2; \rho) = N_2(0.251706; 0.35; 0.5) = 0.458898$

$N_2(w_1 - \sigma\sqrt{te - t}; w_2 - \sqrt{T - t}; \rho) = N_2(0.151706; 0.15; 0.5) = 0.395366$

$N(w_1 - \sigma\sqrt{te - t}) = N(0.251706 - 0.1) = 0.560291$

These probabilities can be found and verified by using **OPTION!** We can now use these intermediate results to compute the value of our compound option:

$$CC_t = 100 \times e^{-0.05 \times 1.0} \times 0.458898 - 100 \times e^{-0.1 \times 1.0} \times 0.395366 - 8 \times e^{-0.1 \times 0.25} \times 0.560291$$
$$= 3.5059$$

This result can be verified by using these input values and the **OPTION!** software.

Using the appropriate definition for the critical stock price, given in Equation 18.3 for compound calls or Equation 18.4 for compound puts, the following formulas give the value of a call on a put (CP_t), a put on a call (PC_t), and a put on a put (PP_t):

$$
\begin{aligned}
CP_t = &-Se^{-\delta(T-t)}N_2(-w_1; -w_2; \rho) \\
&+ Xe^{-r(T-t)}N_2(-w_1 + \sigma\sqrt{te-t}; -w_2 + \sigma\sqrt{T-t}; \rho) \\
&- xe^{-r(te-t)}N(-w_1 + \sigma\sqrt{T-t})
\end{aligned}
\tag{18.6}
$$

$$
\begin{aligned}
PC_t = &-Se^{-\delta(T-t)}N_2(-w_1; -w_2; -\rho) \\
&+ Xe^{-r(T-t)}N_2(-w_1 + \sigma\sqrt{te-t}; w_2 - \sigma\sqrt{T-t}; -\rho) \\
&+ xe^{-r(te-t)}N(-w_1 + \sigma\sqrt{te-t})
\end{aligned}
\tag{18.7}
$$

$$
\begin{aligned}
PP_t = &Se^{-\delta(T-t)}N_2(w_1; -w_2; -\rho) \\
&- Xe^{-r(T-t)}N_2(w_1 - \sigma\sqrt{te-t}; -w_2 + \sigma\sqrt{T-t}; -\rho) \\
&+ xe^{-r(te-t)}N(w_1 - \sigma\sqrt{te-t})
\end{aligned}
\tag{18.8}
$$

With the same input values used for the call on a call, the resulting compound option values are as follows:

$$CP_t = 0.6490, \quad PC_t = 1.3675, \quad \text{and} \quad PP_t = 3.1498$$

Figure 18.1 shows how compound option values vary as a function of the underlying stock price. Panels a–d correspond to call on a call, call on a put, put on a call, and put on a put compound options, respectively. For each graph, we use the same parameters as our example calculation. As Figure 18.1a shows, the value of a call on a call is an increasing function of the stock price, while Figure 18.1b shows that the value of a call on a put is a decreasing function of the stock price. Both of these compound calls vary in price, as would the underlying options. However, as Figures 18.1c–d show, the value of a put on a call is a decreasing function of the stock price, while the price of a put on a put increases with an increasing stock price.

Chooser options

The owner of a chooser option has the right to determine whether the chooser option will become a call or a put option by a specified choice date. After the choice date, the option becomes a plain vanilla call or put, depending on the owner's choice. Chooser options are also known as an **as-you-like-it option**. Bankers Trust offers several types of chooser options in the over-the-counter market.[5] Chooser options are useful for hedging a future event that might not occur. For example, while Congress considered the North American Free Trade Agreement (NAFTA) in 1993, there was considerable uncertainty about the bill's passage. Passage was expected to be beneficial to the value of the Mexican peso; rejection of the bill was expected to send the peso tumbling. Traders could hedge this uncertainty with a chooser option on the Mexican peso. If NAFTA passes, one can choose to let the option be a call; if the bill fails, the owner can choose to let the option be a put.[6]

In considering chooser options, there are three dates to consider: the valuation date, t; the choice date, when the owner of the chooser must choose for the option to be a call or put, tc; and the expiration of the option, T. The dates must have the following relative values:

Figure 18.1   (a) A call on a call price, (b) a call on a put price, (c) a put on a call price, and (d) a put on a put price, each as a function of the stock price

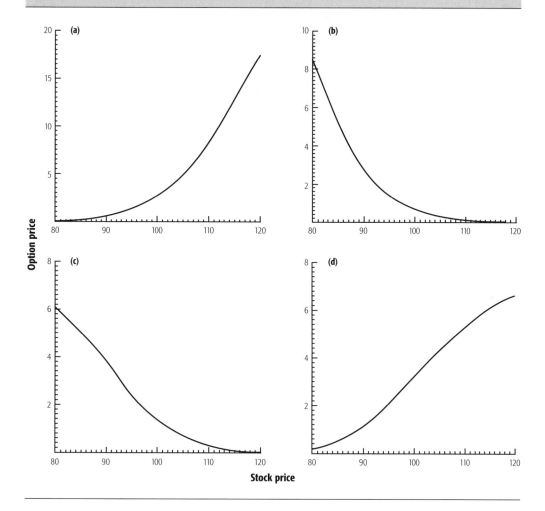

$$t \leq tc \leq T$$

The problem is to evaluate the option at time t, before the choice date. After the choice date, the value of the option will simply be the value of the plain vanilla call or put given by the Merton model. In our treatment of chooser options, we will focus on simple chooser options, in which the potential put and call have a common exercise price and expiration date. Complex choosers allow the potential call and put to have different exercise prices, different expiration dates, or both different exercise prices and expiration dates.

For a simple chooser, there are two extreme values for the choice date, tc, to consider. If the choice must be made immediately, $t = tc$, then the owner of the chooser will choose that the option be a call or a put, whichever has a greater value:

$$\text{If } t = tc, \text{ then } Chooser_t = \text{MAX} \begin{Bmatrix} C(S, X, T - t, \sigma, r, \delta) \\ P(S, X, T - t, \sigma, r, \delta) \end{Bmatrix}$$

If the choice date is at the expiration of the option, $tc = T$, then the chooser is really a straddle. Viewed from the valuation date, t, the value of the straddle is the value of the call and the put:

If $t = T$, then $Chooser_t = C(S, X, T - t, \sigma, r, \delta) + P(S, X, T - t, \sigma, r, \delta)$

Thus, these extreme values for the choice date determine the upper and lower bounds for the value of a simple chooser. If the choice date is now, $t = tc$, then the chooser value is at the lower bound and equals the maximum of the call or put value. If the choice can be deferred until the expiration date, $tc = T$, then the value of the chooser is the same as a straddle and equals the combined value of the plain vanilla call plus the plain vanilla put.

In the normal event, when the choice date, tc, is after t but before T, one will not want to choose whether the option is a call or put until the choice date. Therefore, the payoff on a chooser comes on the choice date, and it will be as follows:

$$Chooser_{tc} = \text{MAX} \begin{Bmatrix} C(S_{tc}, X, T - tc, \sigma, r, \delta) \\ P(S_{tc}, X, T - tc, \sigma, r, \delta) \end{Bmatrix}$$

Applying put–call parity, the value of the chooser at tc is as follows:

$$Chooser_{tc} = \text{MAX} \begin{Bmatrix} C(S_{tc}, X, T - tc, \sigma, r, \delta) \\ C(S_{tc}, X, T - tc, \sigma, r, \delta) + Xe^{-r(T-tc)} - S_{tc}e^{-\delta(T-tc)} \end{Bmatrix}$$

This is equivalent to the following:

$$Chooser_{tc} = C(S_{tc}, X, T - tc, \sigma, r, \delta) + \text{MAX}\{0, Xe^{-r(T-tc)} - S_{tc}e^{-\delta(T-tc)}\}$$

Viewed from the present valuation date, t, this payoff at tc means that the value of the chooser will be the same as the following portfolio:

$$C(S, X, T - t, \sigma, r, \delta) + P(Se^{-\delta(T-tc)}, Xe^{-r(T-tc)}, tc - t, \sigma, \delta)$$

Therefore, the value of a simple chooser at time t is as follows:

$$\begin{aligned} Chooser_t = {} & Se^{-\delta(T-t)}N(w_1) - Xe^{-r(T-t)}N(w_1 - \sigma\sqrt{T - t}) \\ & + Xe^{-r(T-t)}N(-w_2 + \sigma\sqrt{tc - t}) - Se^{-\delta(T-t)}N(-w_2) \end{aligned} \tag{18.9}$$

where the values of w_1 and w_2 are as follows:

$$w_1 = \frac{\ln\left(\dfrac{S}{X}\right) + (r - \delta + 0.5\sigma^2)(T - t)}{\sigma\sqrt{T - t}}$$

$$w_2 = \frac{\ln\left(\dfrac{S}{X}\right) + (r - \delta)(T - t) + 0.5\sigma^2(tc - t)}{\sigma\sqrt{tc - t}}$$

In Equation 18.9, the value of the chooser has two parts. The first portion, with the form $S - X$, corresponds to the value of the potential call, while the second portion, with the form $X - S$, corresponds to the value of the potential put.

As a calculation example, consider the following data: $S = 100$; $X = 100$; $T - t = 1$ year; $\sigma = 0.25$; $r = 0.10$; $\delta = 0.05$; $tc = 0.5$ years. With these values, we first compute w_1 and w_2, finding that $w_1 = 0.3250$ and $w_2 = 0.371231$. The cumulative normal values required are as follows:

$$N(w_1) = N(0.3250) = 0.627409$$
$$N(-w_2) = N(-0.371231) = 0.355233$$
$$N(w_1 - \sigma\sqrt{T - t}) = N(0.3250 - 0.25) = 0.529893$$
$$N(-w_2 + \sigma\sqrt{tc - t}) = N(-0.371231 + 0.17678) = 0.422910$$

Applying these values to Equation 18.9, we find that

$$
\begin{aligned}
Chooser_t =\ & 100 \times 0.951229 \times 0.627409 - 100 \times 0.904837 \times 0.529893 \\
& + 100 \times 0.904837 \times 0.422910 - 100 \times 0.951229 \times 0.355233 \\
=\ & 16.2100
\end{aligned}
$$

We can verify that the value of this chooser lies between the lower and upper bounds by computing the value of the corresponding plain vanilla call and put. With the same parameter values, the call is worth 11.7343 and the put is worth 7.0951. We noted that the lower bound for the price of the chooser would be the maximum value of either the plain vanilla call or the put. The upper bound for the price of the chooser is the combined value of the call and put, which is equivalent to the following straddle:

$$\text{MAX}\{\text{plain vanilla call or put}\} \le Chooser \le \text{plain vanilla call} + \text{plain vanilla put}$$
$$\text{MAX}\{11.7343, 7.0951\} \le Chooser \le 11.7343 + 7.0951$$
$$11.7343 \le Chooser = 16.21 \le 18.8294$$

Figure 18.2 shows how the value of a chooser option varies with the stock price, by using the same parameter values as our example chooser and allowing the stock price to vary. The parabolic shape of the graph reflects the characteristic graph of a straddle, such as that shown in Figure 11.9. Figure 18.3 shows more specifically how the value of our example chooser will vary with the time until the choice must be made. If the choice must be made immediately, Figure 18.3 shows that the value of the chooser will be 11.73, which equals the value of the plain vanilla call. If the choice can be deferred until expiration, Figure 18.3 shows that the value of the chooser is the same as the value of the straddle, which is 18.83.

Barrier options

Barrier options can be "in" options or "out" options. An "in" barrier option has no value until the price of the underlying good touches a certain barrier price. When that happens, the option becomes a plain vanilla option. Accordingly, an "out" option is initially like a plain vanilla option, except if the price of the underlying good penetrates the stated barrier, the option immediately expires worthless. Barrier options can be either calls or puts, permitting eight types of barrier options:

Figure 18.2   The price of a simple chooser option as a function of the stock price

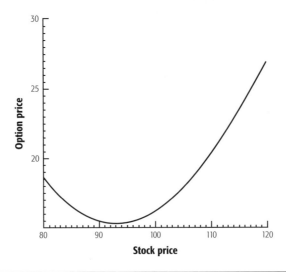

Figure 18.3   The price of a chooser option as a function of the days until the choice date

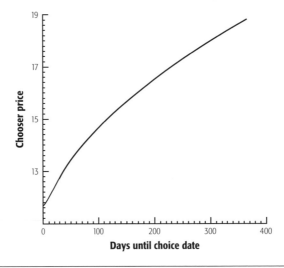

down-and-in call
up-and-in call
down-and-in put
up-and-in put
down-and-out call

up-and-out call
down-and-out put
up-and-out put

Barrier options may also pay a rebate, which is a booby prize. For an "out" barrier option, the rebate is paid immediately when the barrier is hit and the option passes out of existence. For an "in" barrier option, the rebate is paid if the option expires without ever hitting the barrier price. Barrier options are also known as **knock-in** and **knock-out** options. Barrier options exhibit path dependence. The value of a barrier option at the present depends on the previous sequence of stock prices, particularly on whether the stock price has already hit the barrier for an "in" option. The present price of a barrier option can also depend on the future price path of the underlying stock: Will the price hit the barrier between now and expiration?

Barrier options may be viewed as conditional plain vanilla options. "In" barrier options become plain vanilla options if the barrier is hit. "Out" barrier options are plain vanilla options, with the condition that they may pass out of existence if the barrier is hit. These conditions make barrier options inferior to unconditional plain vanilla options, so barrier options will be cheaper than otherwise identical plain vanilla options. This cheapness gives barrier options a special usefulness in hedging applications. For example, a portfolio manager may expect the value of her portfolio to increase, but wishes to protect against the possibility of a large drop in value. Accordingly, she might buy a put option with an exercise price slightly below the present price of the portfolio. As we have seen previously in Chapter 11, this is essentially a portfolio insurance strategy. By buying a down-and-in put instead of a plain vanilla put, the portfolio manager can get the same protection, but at a cheaper price.

Figure 18.4 shows how payoffs arise for a down-and-in option. As mentioned earlier, the stock price must be above the barrier for such an option to be interesting; if the stock price is

Figure 18.4   Alternative stock price paths for down-and-in barrier options

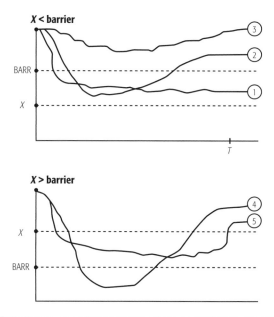

below the barrier, the barrier has been touched and the barrier option has already become a plain vanilla option. Thus, the initial stock price will exceed the barrier, but the exercise price may be either higher or lower than the barrier. The top panel of Figure 18.4 shows a situation in which the barrier, BARR, exceeds the exercise price, X. Three stock price paths are shown in this panel. First, the stock price may penetrate the barrier, and terminate above the exercise price but below the barrier. Second, the stock price may penetrate the barrier, and the terminal price might exceed the barrier. (We distinguish these two cases, because the probabilities associated with these two price paths are different, even though they have the same payoff.) Third, the stock price may never penetrate the barrier and the payoff is the rebate amount, REBATE. The bottom panel shows a similar situation, except in this case the exercise price exceeds the barrier. In price path 4, the stock price penetrates the barrier, but terminates above the exercise price. Finally, in price path 5, the barrier is never hit, so the payoff is REBATE. As Figure 18.4 pertains only to down-and-in options, we must also consider down-and-out options, particularly the fact that the rebate is paid immediately upon the barrier being pierced. This gives a sixth payoff possibility.

As an example, we focus on the payoffs from a down-and-in call. For this option, there are three possible payoff outcomes: if the barrier is never touched, the payoff is REBATE; if the barrier is touched, and $S_T > X$, the payoff is $S_T - X$; and if the barrier is touched, and $S_T \leq X$, the payoff is zero. There are alternative ways in which these various payoffs may be earned, particularly when we realize it is possible for the exercise price to be either above or below the barrier price. To price a down-and-in call, we must consider these five price paths and their associated payoffs, for a stock price at expiration of S_T:

(1)   BARRIER $\geq S_T \geq X$; payoff is $S_T - X$.
(2) $S_T \geq$ BARRIER $\geq X$, and the barrier was touched; payoff is $S_T - X$.
(3) $S_T \geq$ BARRIER $\geq X$, and the barrier was never touched; payoff is REBATE.
(4) $S_T \geq X \geq$ BARRIER, and the barrier was touched; payoff is $S_T - X$.
(5) $S_T \geq X \geq$ BARRIER, and the barrier was never touched; payoff is REBATE.

The value of a down-and-in call is the present expected value of these payoffs. In addition, for an "out" option, there is a sixth price path and payoff to consider, which is presented later. For each type of option, we need expressions for these possible payoffs and price paths.

We define some intermediate values prior to considering the six payoff/probability expressions that cover both "in" and "out" barrier options:

$$\lambda = \frac{r - \delta + 0.5\sigma^2}{\sigma^2}$$

$$\mu = r - \delta + 0.5\sigma^2$$

$$a = \frac{\mu}{\sigma^2}, \quad b = \frac{\sqrt{\mu^2 + 2r\sigma^2}}{\sigma^2}$$

Letting BARR indicate the barrier price, we define the following:

$$w_1 = \frac{\ln\left(\dfrac{S}{X}\right)}{\sigma\sqrt{T - t}} + \lambda\sigma\sqrt{T - t}$$

$$w_2 = \frac{\ln\left(\dfrac{S}{\mathrm{BARR}}\right)}{\sigma\sqrt{T-t}} + \lambda\sigma\sqrt{T-t}$$

$$w_3 = \frac{\ln\left(\dfrac{\mathrm{BARR}^2}{SX}\right)}{\sigma\sqrt{T-t}} + \lambda\sigma\sqrt{T-t}$$

$$w_4 = \frac{\ln\left(\dfrac{\mathrm{BARR}}{S}\right)}{\sigma\sqrt{T-t}} + \lambda\sigma\sqrt{T-t}$$

$$w_5 = \frac{\ln\left(\dfrac{\mathrm{BARR}}{S}\right)}{\sigma\sqrt{T-t}} + b\sigma\sqrt{T-t}$$

Tables 18.1–18.4 present expressions for the present values of payoffs resulting from particular price paths with their associated probabilities. Table 18.5 shows the value of each possible barrier option in terms of the expressions in Tables 18.1–18.4.

As an example, let us consider a down-and-in call with the exercise price lying above the barrier ($X > \mathrm{BARR}$). According to Table 18.1, the value of this call will be DC4 + DC5. This analysis corresponds to the bottom panel of Figure 18.4. The value of this down-and-in call (given that $X > \mathrm{BARR}$) is the present value of the two payoffs, $S_T - X$ or REBATE, multiplied by their associated probabilities.[7]

Pursuing this same example, we will compute the value of a down-and-in call (with $X > \mathrm{BARR}$) using the following data: $S = 100$; $X = 100$; $T - t = 1$ year; $\sigma = 0.2$; $r = 0.1$; $\delta = 0.05$; BARR = 97; REBATE = 2—where BARR is the barrier price and REBATE is the rebate amount. The value of this down-and-in call will be DC4 + DC5, so we will need the intermediate values of

Table 18.1   Valuation expressions for down calls

DC1	$Se^{-\delta(T-t)}N(w_1) - Xe^{-r(T-t)}N(w_1 - \sigma\sqrt{T-t})$
DC2	$Se^{-\delta(T-t)}N(w_2) - Xe^{-r(T-t)}N(w_2 - \sigma\sqrt{T-t})$
DC3	$Se^{-\delta(T-t)}\left(\dfrac{\mathrm{BARR}}{S}\right)^{2\lambda}N(w_4) - Xe^{-r(T-t)}\left(\dfrac{\mathrm{BARR}}{S}\right)^{2\lambda-2}N(w_4 - \sigma\sqrt{T-t})$
DC4	$Se^{-\delta(T-t)}\left(\dfrac{\mathrm{BARR}}{S}\right)^{2\lambda}N(w_3) - Xe^{-r(T-t)}\left(\dfrac{\mathrm{BARR}}{S}\right)^{2\lambda-2}N(w_3 - \sigma\sqrt{T-t})$
DC5	$\mathrm{REBATE}\, e^{-r(T-t)}\left\{N(w_2 + \sigma\sqrt{T-t}) - \left(\dfrac{\mathrm{BARR}}{S}\right)^{2\lambda-2}N(w_4 - \sigma\sqrt{T-t})\right\}$
DC6	$\mathrm{REBATE}\left\{\left(\dfrac{\mathrm{BARR}}{S}\right)^{a+b}N(w_5) + \left(\dfrac{\mathrm{BARR}}{S}\right)^{a-b}N(w_5 - 2b\sigma\sqrt{T-t})\right\}$

Table 18.2	Valuation expressions for down puts

DP1 $\qquad Xe^{-r(T-t)}N(-w_1 + \sigma\sqrt{T-t}) - Se^{-\delta(T-t)}N(-w_1)$

DP2 $\qquad Xe^{-r(T-t)}N(-w_2 + \sigma\sqrt{T-t}) - Se^{-\delta(T-t)}N(-w_2)$

DP3 $\qquad Xe^{-r(T-t)}\left(\dfrac{\text{BARR}}{S}\right)^{2\lambda-2} N(w_4 - \sigma\sqrt{T-t}) - Se^{-\delta(T-t)}\left(\dfrac{\text{BARR}}{S}\right)^{2\lambda} N(w_4)$

DP4 $\qquad Xe^{-r(T-t)}\left(\dfrac{\text{BARR}}{S}\right)^{2\lambda-2} N(w_3 - \sigma\sqrt{T-t}) - Se^{-\delta(T-t)}\left(\dfrac{\text{BARR}}{S}\right)^{2\lambda} N(w_3)$

DP5 $\qquad \text{REBATE } e^{-r(T-t)}\left\{ N(w_2 + \sigma\sqrt{T-t}) - \left(\dfrac{\text{BARR}}{S}\right)^{2\lambda-2} N(w_4 - \sigma\sqrt{T-t})\right\}$

DP6 $\qquad \text{REBATE}\left\{ \left(\dfrac{\text{BARR}}{S}\right)^{a+b} N(w_5) + \left(\dfrac{\text{BARR}}{S}\right)^{a-b} N(w_5 - 2b\sigma\sqrt{T-t})\right\}$

Table 18.3	Valuation expressions for up calls

UC1 $\qquad Se^{-\delta(T-t)}N(w_1) - Xe^{-r(T-t)}N(w_1 + \sigma\sqrt{T-t})$

UC2 $\qquad Se^{-\delta(T-t)}N(w_2) - Xe^{-r(T-t)}N(w_2 + \sigma\sqrt{T-t})$

UC3 $\qquad Se^{-\delta(T-t)}\left(\dfrac{\text{BARR}}{S}\right)^{2\lambda} N(-w_4) - Xe^{-r(T-t)}\left(\dfrac{\text{BARR}}{S}\right)^{2\lambda-2} N(-w_4 + \sigma\sqrt{T-t})$

UC4 $\qquad Se^{-\delta(T-t)}\left(\dfrac{\text{BARR}}{S}\right)^{2\lambda} N(-w_3) - Xe^{-r(T-t)}\left(\dfrac{\text{BARR}}{S}\right)^{2\lambda-2} N(-w_3 + \sigma\sqrt{T-t})$

UC5 $\qquad \text{REBATE } e^{-r(T-t)}\left\{ N(-w_2 + \sigma\sqrt{T-t}) - \left(\dfrac{\text{BARR}}{S}\right)^{2\lambda-2} N(-w_4 - \sigma\sqrt{T-t})\right\}$

UC6 $\qquad \text{REBATE}\left\{ \left(\dfrac{\text{BARR}}{S}\right)^{a+b} N(-w_5) + \left(\dfrac{\text{BARR}}{S}\right)^{a-b} N(-w_5 + 2b\sigma\sqrt{T-t})\right\}$

l, w_2, w_3, and w_4. These values are $\lambda = 1.75$, $w_2 = 0.502296$, $w_3 = 0.045408$, and $w_4 = 0.197704$. The needed cumulative normal values are as follows:

$$N(w_3) = 0.518109$$
$$N(w_2 - \sigma\sqrt{T-t}) = 0.618787$$
$$N(w_3 - \sigma\sqrt{T-t}) = 0.438571$$
$$N(w_4 - \sigma\sqrt{T-t}) = 0.499084$$

Table 18.4   Valuation expressions for up puts

UP1	$Xe^{-r(T-t)}N(-w_1 + \sigma\sqrt{T-t}) - Se^{-\delta(T-t)}N(-w_1)$
DP2	$Xe^{-r(T-t)}N(-w_2 + \sigma\sqrt{T-t}) - Se^{-\delta(T-t)}N(-w_2)$
UP3	$Xe^{-r(T-t)}\left(\dfrac{\text{BARR}}{S}\right)^{2\lambda-2}N(-w_4 + \sigma\sqrt{T-t}) + Se^{-\delta(T-t)}\left(\dfrac{\text{BARR}}{S}\right)^{2\lambda}N(-w_4)$
UP4	$Xe^{-r(T-t)}\left(\dfrac{\text{BARR}}{S}\right)^{2\lambda-2}N(-w_3 - \sigma\sqrt{T-t}) - Se^{-\delta(T-t)}\left(\dfrac{\text{BARR}}{S}\right)^{2\lambda}N(-w_3)$
UP5	$\text{REBATE}\, e^{-r(T-t)}\left\{N(-w_2 + \sigma\sqrt{T-t}) - \left(\dfrac{\text{BARR}}{S}\right)^{2\lambda-2}N(-w_4 + \sigma\sqrt{T-t})\right\}$
UP6	$\text{REBATE}\left\{\left(\dfrac{\text{BARR}}{S}\right)^{a+b}N(-w_5) + \left(\dfrac{\text{BARR}}{S}\right)^{a-b}N(-w_5 + 2b\sigma\sqrt{T-t})\right\}$

Table 18.5   Valuation of barrier options

	$X > \text{BARR}$	$X < \text{BARR}$
Down-and-in call (DIC)	DC4 + DC5	DC1 − DC2 + DC3 + DC5
Up-and-in call (UIC)	UC1 + UC5	UC2 − UC4 + UC3 + UC5
Down-and-in put (DIP)	DP2 + DP3 − DP4 + DP5	DP1 + DP5
Up-and-in put (UIP)	UP1 − UP2 + UP3 + UP5	UP4 + UP5
Down-and-out call (DOC)	DC1 − DC4 + DC6	DC2 − DC3 + DC6
Up-and-out call (UOC)	UC6	UC1 − UC2 − UC3 + UC4 + UC6
Down-and-out put (DOP)	DP1 − DP2 − DP3 + DP4 + DP6	DP6
Up-and-out put (UOP)	UP2 − UP3 + UP6	UP1 − UP4 + UP6

With these intermediate values, we can compute the values of DC4 and DC5 from Table 18.1:

$$\text{DC4} = 100 \times 0.951229 \times \left(\frac{97}{100}\right)^{3.5} \times 0.518109 - 100 \times 0.904837 \times \left(\frac{97}{100}\right)^{1.5} \times 0.438571$$

$$= 44.300383 - 37.911247$$

$$= 6.389136$$

$$\text{DC5} = 2 \times 0.904837 \times \left\{0.618787 - \left(\frac{97}{100}\right)^{1.5} \times 0.499084\right\} = 0.256960$$

The value of the down-and-in call with an exercise price above the barrier, $\text{DIC}_{X>\text{BARR}}$, is the sum of the two portions, DC4 for the present value of the $S_T - X$ payoff, plus DC5 for the

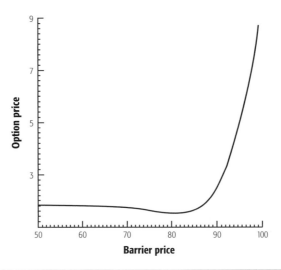

Figure 18.5   The down-and-in call price as a function of the barrier price

present value of the rebate payoff, where the payoffs are weighted by the probability that they will be received:

$$DIC = DC4 + DC5 = 6.3891 + 0.2570 = 6.6461$$

Figure 18.5 shows how our sample down-and-in call price varies as a function of the barrier price. If the barrier price is 50, the option is worth little, because the stock price stands at 100 and the chance of its falling to 50 within the next year is small. By contrast, if the barrier is near 100, the chance of hitting the barrier is much greater, so the barrier option price is closer to that of a plain vanilla call. With these same parameter values, a plain vanilla call would be worth 9.94.

For our particular barrier option, with BARR = 97 and REBATE = 2, the computed price was 6.6461. Only 0.26 of this price was attributable to the barrier, which was DC5. For the same barrier option with BARR = 97 and REBATE = 0, the price of the option is 6.3891. By focusing on this same option, but assuming that REBATE = 0, we can see how the price of the barrier option approaches the price of a plain vanilla call as the barrier is set closer to the current stock price of 100. Assuming that REBATE = 0, our option would be worth 6.39 with BARR = 97, 7.46 with BARR = 98, 8.64 with BARR = 99, and 9.94 (the same as the plain vanilla call) with BARR = 99.9999.

Binary options

Binary options have payoffs that are discontinuous, either paying nothing or a considerable amount, depending on the satisfaction of some condition. For example, a **cash-or-nothing call** is a type of binary option that pays a fixed cash amount if the stock price terminates above the exercise price or pays nothing if the terminal stock price is below the exercise price. Other types of binary options that we will consider in this section are **asset-or-nothing options**, **gap options**, and **supershares**. These binary options are also known as **digital options**, a name that reflects the all-or-nothing character of their payoffs.[8]

Cash-or-nothing options

A cash-or-nothing call pays a fixed cash amount, Z, if the terminal stock price, S_T, exceeds the exercise price, X; otherwise the call pays nothing. Similarly, a cash-or-nothing put pays a fixed cash amount, Z, if the terminal stock price is below the exercise price. These options require no payment of an exercise price. Instead, the exercise price merely determines whether the option owner receives a payoff. Viewed from the perspective of the valuation date, t, the value of a cash-or-nothing call will simply be the present value of the fixed cash payoff multiplied by the probability that the terminal stock price will exceed the exercise price. Let $CONC_t$ and $CONP_t$ indicate cash-or-nothing calls or puts, respectively. From the Merton model, the probability of the option finishing in the money is $N(d_2^M)$. The present value of the fixed cash payoff, Z, is $Ze^{-r(T-t)}$. Therefore, the value of a cash-or-nothing call is as follows:

$$CONC_t = Ze^{-r(T-t)}N(d_2^M) \tag{18.10}$$

By analogous reasoning, the value of a cash-or-nothing put is as follows:

$$CONP_t = Ze^{-r(T-t)}N(-d_2^M) \tag{18.11}$$

Consider now a cash-or-nothing call and put with the following parameter values: $S = 100$; $X = 105$; $T - t = 0.5$ years; $\sigma = 0.2$; $r = 0.1$; $\delta = 0.05$; $Z = 100$—where Z is the fixed cash amount that the option owner receives if the option finishes in-the-money. For these values,

$$d_2^M = \frac{\ln\left(\frac{S_t}{X}\right) + (r - \delta + 0.5\sigma^2)(T - t)}{\sigma\sqrt{T - t}} - \sigma\sqrt{T - t}$$

$$= \frac{\ln\left(\frac{100}{105}\right) + (0.1 - 0.05 + 0.5 \times 0.2 \times 0.2) \times 0.5}{0.2 \times \sqrt{0.5}} - 0.2 \times \sqrt{0.5}$$

$$= -0.238933$$

and $N(d_2^M) = N(-0.238933) = 0.405579$. For the put $N(-d_2^M) = N(0.238933) = 0.594421$. The values of the two options are as follows:

$$CONC_t = Ze^{-r(T-t)}N(d_2^M) = 100 \times e^{-0.1\times0.5} \times 0.405579 = 38.5799$$
$$CONP_t = Ze^{-r(T-t)}N(-d_2^M) = 100 \times e^{-0.1\times0.5} \times 0.594421 = 56.5431$$

Notice that a portfolio consisting of a cash-or-nothing call and put (with the same payoff and term to expiration) has a certain payoff. Specifically, the portfolio will pay the common amount Z. Therefore,

$$CONC_t + CONP_t = Ze^{-r(T-t)}, \text{ for a common expiration and a common } Z$$

Figure 18.6 shows how the values of these options vary as a function of the stock price. The value of the two options together equals the present value of Z no matter what the stock price might be.

Figure 18.6   The value of cash-or-nothing options as a function of the stock price

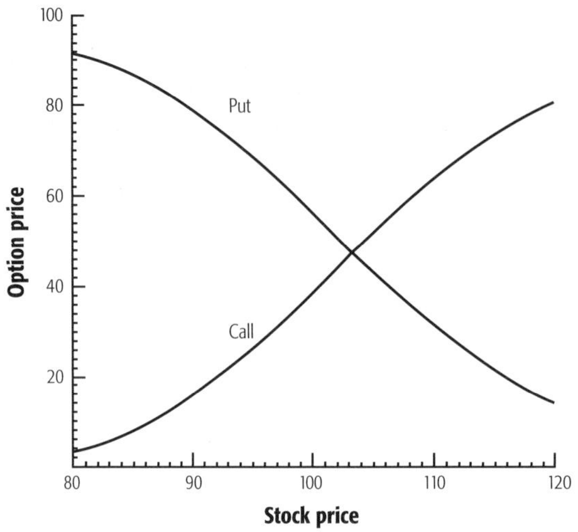

Event markets

In August 2003, a furor erupted in Washington, D.C. over the disclosure that the Pentagon intended to operate an experimental market that would have allowed online traders to trade on the probability of future terrorist attacks and the occurrence of future political events in the Middle East. For a few days, it was the best-known market in America, even though it was dissolved before trading actually commenced. Formally, it was called the Policy Analysis Market (PAM), but many news accounts referred to the market as the "turmoil exchange." The market would have traded 24 hours a day, seven days a week. The Pentagon wanted to create the PAM in order to gather information that would help validate other sources of intelligence that could be used to stop terrorism and reduce political instability.

The PAM was inspired by the Iowa Electronic Markets (IEM), where investors trade contracts on election outcomes. In over 15 years of experience, research has demonstrated that IEM markets do a better job of predicting actual election results than polls do. PAM was supposed to harness the power of markets to aggregate the knowledge and information of thousands of investors. Markets do a good job of aggregating information. Because traders are using real money to back their opinions, they have an incentive to use cold, hard, honest logic and reliable information in basing their trades. This feature mitigates the so-called "yes man" effect within an organization, whereby an analyst may be tempted to tell the boss what she wants to hear. News reports cited this feature as one reason why the Pentagon was contemplating a market to aggregate intelligence information.

The PAM and IEM are part of a broader set of markets called "event markets." Event markets allow participants to profit from the occurrence of a specific event. These markets go by a variety of names: nonprice markets, prediction markets, decision markets, proposition markets, opinion markets, information markets, and nontraditional markets.

Several facilities offer contracts on various types of events. For example, TradeSports, based in Ireland, offers over 1,300 contracts on everything from sporting events to elections, to the probability of key terrorists being "neutralized" by a particular date. During the furor about the PAM in August 2003, they even listed a contract on the resignation of the Pentagon official in charge of the market. Other event markets, such as the Hollywood Stock Exchange, offer contracts on the box-office success of new film releases.

Event contracts are more often styled as options. The contracts are typically crafted with a fixed pay-out if the event occurs and zero payout if the event does not occur. A payoff structure of this sort resembles a binary option. For example, a contract may be structured so that it pays $1.00 if a Republican is elected president and zero otherwise. If the contract is currently trading at 60 cents, this means that an investment of 60 cents today could yield $1.00 if a Republican is elected. If one ignores for the moment the time value of money, the price can be interpreted as the market's assessment of the odds of the event occurring. In this case, the contract price of 60 cents can be interpreted as a 60 percent chance that a Republican will be elected.

Asset-or-nothing options

Asset-or-nothing options are similar to cash-or-nothing options, with one major difference. Instead of paying a fixed cash amount as cash-or-nothing options do, the payoff on an asset-or-nothing option is the underlying asset. If the terminal asset price exceeds the exercise price, the owner of a call receives the asset, but if the terminal asset price is below the exercise price, the call expires worthless. For a put, if the terminal asset price is less than the exercise price, the put owner receives the asset, but if the terminal asset price exceeds the exercise price, the put expires worthless. As with cash-or-nothing options, the exercise price is never paid. Instead, the value of the asset relative to the exercise price determines whether the option pays off or is worthless.

For an asset-or-nothing call (AONC), the value is simply the present value of the asset, depreciated for dividends between the present and expiration, multiplied by the probability that the terminal asset price will exceed the exercise price. Similarly, the asset-or-nothing put (AONP) is worth the present value of the asset, discounted for the dividends between the present and expiration, multiplied by the probability that the terminal asset price will be below the exercise price. Thus, the values of the options are as follows:

$$\text{AONC}_t = e^{-\delta(T-t)}S_t N(d_1^M)$$
$$\text{AONP}_t = e^{-\delta(T-t)}S_t N(-d_1^M)$$

(18.12)

A portfolio of an asset-or-nothing call and put, with the same term to expiration and underlying asset, is worth the present value of the asset discounted for the dividends to be paid over the life of the option:

$$\begin{aligned}\text{AONC}_t + \text{AONP}_t &= e^{-\delta(T-t)}S_t N(d_1^M) + e^{-\delta(T-t)}S_t N(-d_1^M) \\ &= e^{-\delta(T-t)}S_t [N(d_1^M) + N(-d_1^M)] \\ &= e^{-\delta(T-t)}S_t\end{aligned}$$

As an example, consider asset-or-nothing options with the following parameters: $S = 100$; $X = 90$; $T - t = 0.5$ years; $\sigma = 0.2$; $r = 0.1$; $\delta = 0.05$. With these values, $d_1^M = 0.992499$, $N(d_1^M) = N(0.992499) = 0.839523$, and $N(-d_1^M) = N(-0.992499) = 0.160477$. The option values with these parameters are as follows:

$$\text{AONC}_t = e^{-\delta(T-t)}S_t N(d_1^M) = e^{-0.05 \times 0.5} \times 100 \times 0.839523 = 81.8795$$
$$\text{AONP}_t = e^{-\delta(T-t)}S_t N(-d_1^M) = e^{-0.05 \times 0.5} \times 100 \times 0.160477 = 15.6515$$

Figure 18.7   The value of asset-or-nothing options as a function of the stock price

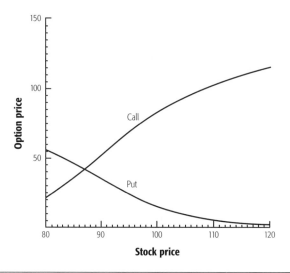

Figure 18.7 graphs the values of our two sample options as a function of the stock price. Notice that the shapes of the value curves in this figure are quite similar to those for the cash-or-nothing options in Figure 18.6. When the stock price is high, say around 120, the asset-or-nothing put is worth very little, reflecting the slight chance that the terminal stock price will be below the exercise price of 90. With a high stock price, the call is worth very nearly the same as the stock. For example, with a stock price of 100, the call is worth 81.88, as we have seen, and the present value of the asset is 97.53, so the call is worth 82.93 percent of the asset. For a stock price of 120, with a present value of 117.04, the call is worth 115.72, or 98.87 percent of the present value of the asset. Finally, if the stock is at 150, the call is worth 146.29, which equals the present value of the stock.

Gap options

Gap options are similar to plain vanilla options, except that the payoff is determined as a function of the exercise price. The payoff on a gap option depends on the usual factors in a plain vanilla option, but it also affected by the gap amount, which may be negative or positive. Letting the value of the gap be indicated by g, the value of a gap call (GAPC_t) and a gap put (GAPP_t) are as follows:

$$\text{GAPC}_t = e^{-\delta(T-t)}S_t N(d_1^M) - (X + g)e^{-r(T-t)}N(d_2^M)$$
$$\text{GAPP}_t = (X + g)e^{-r(T-t)}N(-d_2^M) - e^{-\delta(T-t)}S_t N(-d_1^M)$$

$$(18.13)$$

These formulas are very similar to those for plain vanilla options according to the Merton model, with the values for d_1^M and d_2^M being identical to those from the Merton model. In the valuation formulas, the gap amount is added to the exercise price so the quantity $X + g$ replaces X in the valuation formulas (but not in the formulas for d_1^M and d_2^M).

Figure 18.8   Gap call prices as a function of the stock price

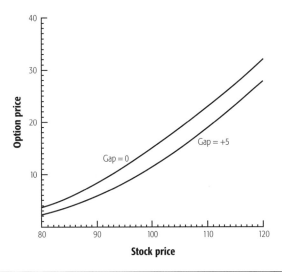

As an example of gap options, consider the following parameters: $S = 100$; $X = 90$; $T - t = 0.5$ years; $\sigma = 0.3$; $r = 0.1$; $\delta = 0.05$. With these values, we will compute the value of a gap call with a positive gap, $g = 5$, and a gap put with a negative gap, $g = -5$. Both options have common values for d_1^M and d_2^M:

$$d_1^M = \frac{\ln\left(\dfrac{100}{90}\right)(0.1 + 0.05 - 0.5 \times 0.3 \times 0.3) \times 0.5}{0.3 \times \sqrt{0.5}} = 0.720591$$

$$d_2^M = d_1^M - \sigma\sqrt{T - t} = 0.720591 - 0.3 \times \sqrt{0.5} = 0.508459$$

Corresponding cumulative values are $N(d_1^M) = 0.764420$, $N(d_2^M) = 0.694434$, $N(-d_1^M) = 0.235580$, and $N(-d_2^M) = 0.305566$. With $g = +5$ for the gap call and $g = -5$ for the gap put, the option values are as follows:

$$\text{GAPC}_t = 100 \times e^{-0.05 \times 0.5} \times 0.764420 - (90 + 5)e^{-0.1 \times 0.5} \times 0.694434 = 11.8008$$
$$\text{GAPP}_t = (90 - 5)e^{-0.1 \times 0.5} \times 0.305566 - 100 \times e^{-0.05 \times 0.5} \times 0.235580 = 1.7300$$

Figure 18.8 focuses on the gap call of this example, in which the call had a positive gap of 5. As Equation 18.13 makes clear, a positive gap for a call effectively increases the exercise price, which is a liability from the point of view of the call's owner. Therefore, a positive gap for a call decreases the value of the call relative to an otherwise identical plain vanilla call. In Figure 18.8, the lower line graphs the value of the gap call of our computational example. The upper line graphs the value of the otherwise similar call with a zero gap, $g = 0$. When $g = 0$, the gap option becomes a plain vanilla option.

Supershares

A supershare is a financial instrument whose value depends on an underlying portfolio of other financial assets. A supershare represents a contingent claim on a fraction of the underlying portfolio. The contingency is that the value of the underlying portfolio must lie between a lower and an upper bound on a certain future date. If the value of the underlying portfolio lies between the bounds, the supershare is worth a proportion of the portfolio. If the value of the portfolio lies outside the bounds, the supershare expires worthless.[9]

The basic idea behind supershares is the creation of a financial intermediary that holds a portfolio of securities and issues two kinds of claims against that portfolio. The first kind of claim is a supershare, which has an uncertain payoff depending on the performance of the portfolio. The second kind of claim is a purchasing power bond that pays a given rate of real interest. In our analysis, we are concerned with the claim that has an uncertain payoff—the supershare.

Letting X_L indicate the lower bound and X_U represent the upper bound, the payoffs for the supershare on the expiration date, T, are as follows:

$$S_T/X_L \text{ if } X_L \leq S_T \leq X_H; \ 0 \text{ otherwise}$$

A supershare is essentially like a portfolio of two asset-or-nothing calls, in which the owner of a supershare purchases an asset-or-nothing call with an exercise price of X_L and sells an asset-or-nothing call with an exercise price of X_H. This is quite similar to the bull spread with calls that we considered in Chapter 11. As such, the price of a supershare is as follows:

$$SS = \frac{Se^{-\delta(T-t)}}{X_L}[N(w_L) - N(w_H)] \tag{18.14}$$

where

$$w_L = \frac{\ln\dfrac{S}{X_L} + (r - \delta + 0.5\sigma^2)(T - t)}{\sigma\sqrt{T - t}}$$

and

$$w_H = \frac{\ln\dfrac{S}{X_H} + (r - \delta + 0.5\sigma^2)(T - t)}{\sigma\sqrt{T - t}}$$

As a calculation example, consider the following data: $S = 100$; $X_L = 100$; $X_H = 105$; $T - t = 0.5$ years; $\sigma = 0.2$; $r = 0.1$; $\delta = 0.05$. With these input values, $w_L = 0.247487$, $w_H = 20.097511$, $N(w_L) = 0.597734$, and $N(w_H) = 0.461160$. The value of this supershare is as follows:

$$SS = \frac{100 \times e^{-0.05 \times 0.5}}{100}(0.597734 - 0.461160) = 0.1332$$

Figure 18.9 shows how the price of this supershare varies with the stock price. The higher, more sharply curved line in the figure is the graph of our example supershare. Notice that the

Figure 18.9 Supershare prices as a function of the stock price

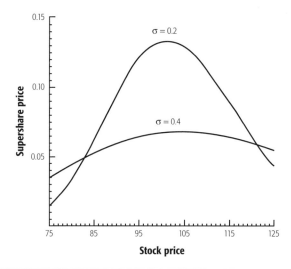

price of the supershare is $0.1332 when the stock price is 100. The value of the supershare reaches its highest value for stock prices in the neighborhood of 100–105. This neighborhood is exactly the range of the lower and upper bounds that determine the payoff. Notice also that the shape of this line is quite similar to that of a short position in a strangle, as in Figure 11.11.

The flatter curve in Figure 18.9 is for the same supershare, except that it assumes that the underlying stock has a standard deviation of 0.4. With a higher standard deviation, there is less chance that the terminal stock price will fall in the range of 100–105, so the supershare written on a higher risk stock has a lower value.

Lookback options

For a plain vanilla option, the payoff depends only on the terminal stock price, not the price at any other time. For a lookback option, the exercise price and the option's payoff are functions of the price of the underlying good up to the expiration of the option. For lookback calls, the exercise price is the minimum stock price experienced over the life of the option. For lookback puts, the exercise price is the maximum stock price over the same period. Thus it is said of lookback options that they allow the option owner to "buy at the low and sell at the high." Of course, this opportunity will be priced in a rational market.

Consider the decision to purchase a lookback at time t with expiration at time T. The payoffs on the lookback call (LBC) and put (LBP) would be as follows:

LBC: $MAX\{0, S_T - MIN[S_t, S_{t+1}, \ldots, S_T]\}$
LBP: $MAX\{0, MAX[S_t, S_{t+1}, \ldots, S_T] - S_T\}$

In effect, a lookback call allows the purchaser to acquire the asset at its minimum price over the life of the option, while the lookback put allows the owner to sell the asset at its maximum price over the relevant interval. Of course, the option to make these transactions has considerable value. Notice that lookbacks should always be exercised. For a call, the terminal stock price will always exceed some price experienced on the asset during its life. For a put, the terminal stock price will always be less than some stock price during the interval. Lookback options are clearly path-dependent options, because the value ultimately depends on the minimum or maximum stock price reached over the life of the option, not merely on the terminal price when the option expires.[10]

Assuming that the stock price is observed continuously, the value of a lookback call is as follows:

$$LBC = Se^{-\delta(T-t)} - MINPRIe^{-r(T-t)}N\left(\frac{-b + \mu(T-t)}{\sigma\sqrt{T-t}}\right)$$

$$+ MINPRIe^{-r(T-t)}\lambda e^{b(1-1/\lambda)}N\left(\frac{-b + \mu(T-t)}{\sigma\sqrt{T-t}}\right) \qquad (18.15)$$

$$- Se^{-\delta(T-t)}(1 + \lambda)N\left(\frac{-b + \mu(T-t) - \sigma^2(T-t)}{\sigma\sqrt{T-t}}\right)$$

where MINPRI is the minimum price of the underlying asset experienced during the life of the option and

$$b = \ln\left(\frac{S}{MINPRI}\right); \mu = r - \delta - 0.5\sigma^2; \lambda = \frac{0.5\sigma^2}{r - \delta}$$

$$LBP = Se^{-\delta(T-t)} - MAXPRIe^{-r(T-t)}N\left(\frac{-b - \mu(T-t)}{\sigma\sqrt{T-t}}\right)$$

$$- MAXPRIe^{-r(T-t)}\lambda e^{b(1-1/\lambda)}N\left(\frac{b - \mu(T-t)}{\sigma\sqrt{T-t}}\right) \qquad (18.16)$$

$$+ Se^{-\delta(T-t)}(1 + \lambda)N\left(\frac{b + \mu(T-t) + \sigma^2(T-t)}{\sigma\sqrt{T-t}}\right)$$

where MAXPRI is the maximum price experienced during the life of the option. The variables λ and μ are the same as defined for the lookback call, but the definition of b for the lookback put is as follows:

$$b = \ln\left(\frac{S}{MAXPRI}\right)$$

As an example of lookback call pricing, consider the following values: $S = 100$; $MINPRI = 90$; $T - t = 0.5$ years; $\sigma = 0.3$; $r = 0.1$; $\delta = 0.05$. Using these data, we will compute the value of the lookback call. The intermediate values that we need are as follows:

$$b = \ln\left(\frac{100}{90}\right) = 0.105361$$

$$\lambda = \frac{0.5 \times 0.3 \times 0.3}{0.10 - 0.05} = 0.9$$

$$\mu = 0.1 - 0.05 - 0.5 \times 0.3 \times 0.3 = 0.005$$

The value for the lookback call, taking into account all of the discounting and showing the value of the arguments for the cumulative normal function, is as follows:

$$\begin{aligned}
\text{LBC} = \ & 97.5310 - 85.6106 \times N(0.508462) \\
& + 85.6106 \times 0.9 \times e^{0.105361\times(-0.1111)}N(-0.484891) \\
& - 9705310 \times 1.9 \times N(-0.720594)
\end{aligned}$$

Thus, the value of the lookback call is

$$\text{LBC} = 97.5310 - 59.4510 - 23.9027 - 43.6551 = 18.3275$$

Because lookbacks offer cheap exercise prices for calls and high payoffs for puts, lookbacks are worth considerably more than their plain vanilla counterparts. For a plain vanilla call with the same parameters, including the exercise price of 90, the price would be 15.10. Thus the lookback call has a price that is 3.23 higher than the corresponding plain vanilla call. The difference could be even more severe. For example, consider the same input values used for the lookback call, but assume that the minimum price to date is 100. The price of this lookback would be 16.4920. The corresponding plain vanilla call, with $X = 100$, would be 9.3970.

Figure 18.10 graphs our sample option using the same parameters. The upper line of Figure 18.10 shows the value of the lookback call. The lower line shows the value of an otherwise similar plain vanilla call option with an exercise price $X = 90$. Notice that the volatility of these options is $\sigma = 0.3$. For higher-volatility stocks, the value of both the lookback call and the plain vanilla call will be higher. Figure 18.11 shows the value of a lookback call and a corresponding plain vanilla call with the same parameter values as our sample option—except the volatility of the options is $\sigma = 0.9$. A comparison of Figures 18.10 and 18.11 shows that the higher the volatility of the underlying stock, the greater will be the difference between the lookback

Figure 18.10   The value of a lookback call and a plain vanilla call as a function of the stock price

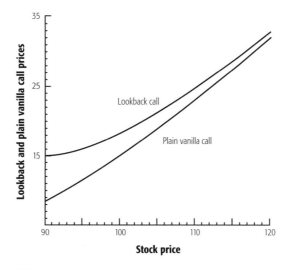

Figure 18.11 The value of a lookback call and a plain vanilla call as a function of the stock price

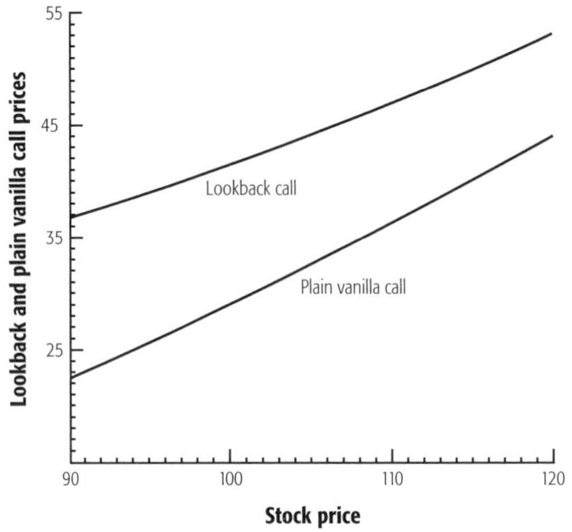

and plain vanilla calls. The large percentage difference in the price of the lookback and plain vanilla calls emphasizes the costliness of lookbacks.

The high premiums on lookback options have hindered their popularity in actual markets. This limitation has led to the creation of **partial lookback options**. These partial lookbacks restrict the minimum or maximum used in computing the payoff in some way.[11]

Backdated options

In the Fall of 2005, *The Wall Street Journal* reported that the United States Securities and Exchange Commission was investigating executive and employee stock options that were often granted immediately prior to a run-up in the stock of the company underlying the option. The article suggested that companies were retroactively setting, that is backdating, the option's grant date to coincide with a recent low in the company's stock price. Typically, the strike price of the option is set at the market price of the underlying stock on the day an option is granted. By setting the strike price to correspond with a favorable backdated stock price, executives and employees would receive options that were effectively in-the-money at the grant date. In essence, companies were granting lookback options to their executives and employees. Although granting backdated options is not illegal in itself, the practice can create disclosure and accounting issues. For example, shareholders may be told that the date of the grant is when the directors vote on the award, but then a different date is selected to correspond to a date with a lower stock price. In addition, accounting rules may be violated if the full value of the backdated option is not included as employee compensation. In July of 2006, the first criminal and civil complaints were filed with respect to the alleged illegal backdating of executive and employee stock options. The United States Internal Revenue Service also announced a probe into the practice, including the practice of backdating option exercises, to see whether tax laws were violated.

Average price options

An **Asian option** is an option whose payoff depends on the average of the price of the under-lying good or the average of the exercise price. (These options are called "Asian options" because Bankers Trust was the first to offer such products and they offered them initially in their Tokyo office.[12]) In this section, we consider one type of Asian option, an average price option. In an average price option, the average price of the underlying good essentially takes the place of the terminal price of underlying good in determining the payoff.

Asian options are extremely useful in combating price manipulations. For example, consider a corporate executive given options on the firm's shares as part of her compensation. If the option payoff were determined by the price of the firm's shares on a particular day, the exec-utive could enrich herself by manipulating the price of her shares for that single day. However, if the payoff of the option depended upon the average closing price of the shares over a six-month period, it would be much more difficult for her to profit from a manipulation. Asian options were first used in this kind of application. As a further example, commodity-linked bonds have two forms of payoffs, the payoffs from a straight bond plus an option on the average price of the linked commodity. By making the payoff depend on the average price of the com-modity, such as oil, the chance of a manipulation is lessened.[13]

The average price may be computed as either a geometric average or as an arithmetic aver-age. Unfortunately, there is no closed-form solution for the price of an arithmetic average price option, even though most actual average price options are based on an average price. These options must be valued by simulation techniques. It is possible, however, to compute the value of a geometric average price option, and this section focuses exclusively on a geometric aver-age price call option.

A fundamental concern is the frequency with which the price will be observed over the aver-aging period. If the price is observed at the close each day, then the geometric average price will be computed by multiplying the available n daily price observations together and then tak-ing the nth root of the product. An average price option may exist with some of the averaging period already under way. Alternatively, the time for averaging may lie in the future. Therefore, there are three time variables to consider:

t_0 = the time until the averaging period begins
t_1 = the time since the averaging period began
t_2 = the time remaining for averaging

It is typical for the averaging period to last until the option expires, and this typical case is assumed in this analysis. Therefore, $t_2 = T - t$, where the option expires at time T and the option is being valued at time t. Thus, there are three possibilities to consider:

(1) The averaging period has already begun prior to the present time t. In this case, $t_0 = 0$ and $t_1 > 0$.
(2) The averaging period begins immediately at time t. In this case, $t_0 = t_1 = 0$.
(3) The averaging period will begin sometime later, after time t but before time T. In this case, $t_0 > 0$ and $t_1 = 0$.

If the averaging period has already started, there is an average price A available to compute. If the averaging period starts in the future, the average price, A, is 1.

We begin the presentation of the pricing formula by defining several intermediate variables:

$$W = A^{[t_1/(t_1+t_2+h)]} S^{[(t_2+h)/(t_1+t_2+h)]}$$

$$M = \left(t_0 + t_2 \frac{t_0 + h}{2(t_1 + t_2 + h)} \right) [r - \delta - 0.5\sigma^2]$$

$$\Sigma^2 = \left(t_0 + \frac{t_2(t_2 + h)(2t_2 + h)}{6(t_1 + t_2 + h)^2} \right) \sigma^2$$

$$w_1 = \frac{\ln\left(\dfrac{W}{X}\right) + M}{\Sigma} + \Sigma$$

where h is the frequency of price observations used to compute the average price. For example, if the price is observed daily, $h = 1/365$ years. The price of the geometric average price call, AVGPRI, is as follows:

$$AVGPRI = We^{-r(T-t)}e^{(M+0.5\Sigma^2)}N(w_1) - Xe^{-r(T-t)}N(w_1 - \Sigma) \tag{18.17}$$

As a calculation example, consider a geometric average price option for which averaging has been under way for one half-year; the option expires in a half-year. For this option, the price is observed daily to compute the average price. The data are as follows: $S = 100$; $X = 90$; $\sigma = 0.2$; $r = 0.1$; $\delta = 0.05$; $t_0 = 0.0$; $t_1 = 0.5$ years; $t_2 = 0.5$ years; $h =$ each day, or $1/365$ years; $A = 95$. For these data, we have $W = 97.474774$, $M = 0.00376$, $\Sigma^2 = 0.001671$, and $w_1 = 2.084497$. The value of the option is as follows:

$$
\begin{aligned}
AVGPRI &= 97.474774 \times e^{-0.1 \times 0.5} e^{(0.00376 + 0.5 \times 0.001671)} \times 0.981443 - 90 \times e^{-0.1 \times 0.5} \times 0.979504 \\
&= 91.419406 - 83.855912 \\
&= 7.5634
\end{aligned}
$$

Figure 18.12 shows the relationship between the value of our example average price call and the average price of the underlying good.

Exchange options

We now consider an option to exchange one asset for another. Upon exercising, the owned asset is exchanged for the acquired asset. The valuation of an exchange option depends upon the usual parameters for the individual assets—price, risk, and dividend rate. In addition, the time until expiration and the correlation of returns between the assets also affect the valuation. We will treat the owned asset as asset 1 and the asset to be acquired as asset 2. Thus, an exchange option may be regarded as a call on asset 2, with the exercise price being the future value of asset 1.

Although exchange options were first priced in 1978, these options have existed for quite some time in the form of incentive fee arrangements, margin accounts, exchange offers, and standby commitments.[14] As an example, consider an example from the merger market. A target firm is offered the opportunity to exchange shares from the target firm for shares in the acquiring firm. The shareholders in the target firm now hold an exchange option to exchange their shares for those of the acquirer. The value of this option can range from zero to the quite valuable. To know how valuable this kind of option is, we need a pricing formula.

Figure 18.12   The price of an average price call as a function of the average stock price

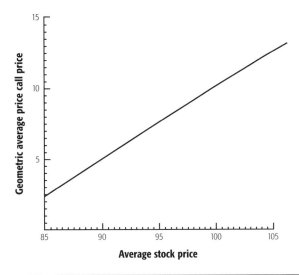

The value of a European exchange option is as follows:

$$\text{EXOPT} = S_2 e^{-\delta_2(T-t)} N(w_1) - S_1 e^{-\delta_1(T-t)} N(w_2) \tag{18.18}$$

where

$$\Sigma^2 = \sigma_1^2 + \sigma_2^2 - 2\rho\sigma_1\sigma_2$$

$$w_1 = \frac{\ln\left(\dfrac{S_2}{S_1}\right) + (\delta_1 - \delta_2 + 0.5\Sigma^2)(T - t)}{\Sigma\sqrt{T - t}}$$

$$w_2 = \frac{\ln\left(\dfrac{S_2}{S_1}\right) + (\delta_1 - \delta_2 + 0.5\Sigma^2)(T - t)}{\Sigma\sqrt{T - t}}$$

This formula is quite similar to the Merton model, except that the volatility of the portfolio of the two assets, Σ, takes the place of the volatility of the underlying stock, σ, and the price of the asset to be sacrificed, S_1, takes the place of the exercise price, X. As a computational example, consider the following data: $S_1 = 100$; $S_2 = 100$; $\sigma_1 = 0.3$; $\sigma_2 = 0.2$; $\delta_1 = 0.05$; $\delta_2 = 0.05$; $T - t = 0.5$ years; $\rho = 0.5$. According to our convention, asset 1 is the owned asset that may be exchanged for asset 2. With these values, we have $\Sigma^2 = 0.07$, $w_1 = 0.093541$, $w_2 = -0.093541$, $N(w_1) = 0.537263$, and $N(w_2) = 0.462737$. The value of the option to exchange asset 1 for asset 2 is as follows:

$$\begin{aligned}
\text{EXOPT} &= 100 \times e^{-0.05 \times 0.5} \times 0.537263 - 100 \times e^{-0.05 \times 0.5} \times 0.462737 \\
&= 52.399840 - 45.131198 \\
&= 7.2687
\end{aligned}$$

Figure 18.13   The value of an exchange option as a function of individual asset volatilities

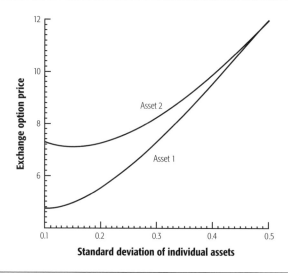

Figure 18.14   The value of an exchange option as a function of correlation between assets

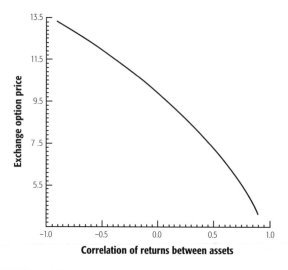

For our sample exchange option, Figure 18.13 shows how the price of the option varies with the volatilities of the individual assets. The bottom line shows how the value of the option varies with the volatility of asset 1, while the upper line pertains to the volatility of asset 2. Each line shows the sensitivity of the option's value to changes in the volatility of one asset, holding the volatility of the other asset constant. For our example option, $\sigma_1 = 0.3$ and $\sigma_2 = 0.2$. The bottom line shows that the option is worth 6.04 at that level of volatility. As σ_1 varies (and σ_2 remains constant) the value of the exchange option varies directly. The upper line shows the same relationship for asset 2. For the same sample exchange option, Figure 18.14 shows that the value of the option varies inversely with the correlation between the two assets.

Rainbow options

This section considers a class of exotic options known as rainbow options. The discussion here is limited to "two-color" rainbow options—options on two risky assets, where the number of risky assets is the number of colors in the rainbow. This section distinguishes and analyzes five types of two-color rainbow options: the best of two risky assets and a fixed cash amount, the better of two risky assets, the worse of two risky assets, the maximum of two risky assets, and the minimum of two risky assets. We consider each of these in turn, starting with an option on the best of two risky assets and cash. As we will see, the other rainbow options can be understood largely in terms of this first option.

As an example of a two-color rainbow option, consider a zero-coupon bond that pays a stated rate of interest, but allows the owner of the bond to choose the currency in which the interest is paid. The value of the bond upon maturity will differ depending on the exchange rate. The right to choose the currency of repayment gives the holder of the bond a call on the maximum of two assets—the repayment in one currency or another. By contrast, consider the same type of bond, but assume that the firm may choose the currency of repayment.[15]

Call on the best of two risky assets and cash

The owner of this option has a choice among three payoffs at expiration: risky asset 1, risky asset 2, or a fixed cash amount. There is no exercise price. Letting S_{1T} be the terminal value of asset 1, S_{2T} be the terminal value of asset 2, and X be the fixed cash amount, the present value of each payoff is as follows:

Q1. $e^{-r(T-t)}E(S_{1T})$, conditional on $S_{1T} > S_{2T}$ and $S_{1T} > X$

Q2. $e^{-r(T-t)}E(S_{2T})$, conditional on $S_{2T} > S_{1T}$ and $S_{2T} > X$

Q3. $e^{-r(T-t)}X$, conditional on $X > S_{1T}$ and $X > S_{2T}$

Prior to exercise, the value of the option will equal the sum of the present value of these expected payoffs. Thus, the evaluation of the option turns on assessing how high the stock prices are likely to go, and which asset is likely to have the highest price at expiration. The performance of the two assets will depend in part on the degree to which they are correlated.

To present the pricing formula, we begin with some preliminary variable definitions:

$$\Sigma^2 = \sigma_1^2 + \sigma_2^2 - 2\rho\sigma_1\sigma_2 \qquad \rho_1 = \frac{\rho\sigma_2 - \sigma_1}{\Sigma} \qquad \rho_2 = \frac{\rho\sigma_1 - \sigma_2}{\Sigma}$$

$$w_1 = \frac{\ln\left(\dfrac{S_1}{X}\right) + (r - \delta_1 + 0.5\sigma_1^2)(T - t)}{\sigma_1\sqrt{T - t}}$$

$$w_2 = \frac{\ln\left(\dfrac{S_2}{X}\right) + (r - \delta_2 + 0.5\sigma_2^2)(T - t)}{\sigma_2\sqrt{T - t}}$$

$$w_3 = \frac{\ln\left(\dfrac{S_1}{S_2}\right) + (\delta_2 - \delta_1 + 0.5\Sigma^2)(T - t)}{\Sigma\sqrt{T - t}}$$

$$w_4 = \frac{\ln\left(\dfrac{S_2}{S_1}\right) + (\delta_1 - \delta_2 - 0.5\Sigma^2)(T - t)}{\Sigma\sqrt{T - t}}$$

With these preliminary definitions, the values of the potential payoffs are as follows:

Q1. $S_1 e^{-\delta_1(T-t)}\{N(w_3) - N_2(-w_1; w_3; \rho_1)\}$

Q2. $S_2 e^{-\delta_2(T-t)}\{N(w_4) - N_2(-w_2; w_4; \rho_2)\}$ (18.19)

Q3. $X e^{-r(T-t)} N_2(-w_1 + \sigma_1\sqrt{T-t}; -w_2 + \sigma_2\sqrt{T-t}; \rho)$

The value of a call on the best of two risky assets and cash, BEST3, equals the sum of these three quantities:

$$\text{BEST3} = Q1 + Q2 + Q3 \qquad\qquad (18.20)$$

As a computational example, consider the following data: $S_1 = 100$; $S_2 = 95$; $X = 110$; $T - t = 1$ year; $\sigma_1 = 0.2$; $\sigma_2 = 0.3$; $r = 0.08$; $\delta_1 = 0.04$; $\delta_2 = 0.03$; $\rho = 0.4$. Since the owner of the option will receive the best of two assets or the cash payment, the value should be at least the present value of the largest quantity, which is the cash payment of 110. However, there is also a chance that one of the two assets will exceed 110 when the option expires in one year, so we must take into account the potential payoff of these other assets.

With our sample data, we have the following intermediate results:

$\Sigma^2 = 0.082$; $\rho_1 = -0.279372$; $\rho_2 = -0.768273$
$w_1 = -0.176551$; $w_2 = -0.172012$; $w_3 = 0.287381$; $w_4 = -0.001024$
$N(w_3) = 0.613090$; $N(w_4) = 0.499591$
$N_2(-w_1; w_3; \rho_1) = 0.307309$; $N_2(-w_2; w_4; \rho_2) = 0.147242$
$N_2(-w_1 + \sigma_1; -w_2 + \sigma_2; \rho) = 0.496938$

Using these intermediate results, the three partial results for asset 1, asset 2, and the fixed cash payment are as follows:

Q1. $100 \times e^{-0.04} \times 0.305781 = 29.3787$
Q2. $95 \times e^{-0.03} \times 0.352349 = 32.4833$
Q3. $110 \times e^{-0.08} \times 0.496938 = 50.4605$

The value of the option, BEST3, equals the sum of these three parts:

$$\text{BEST3} = Q1 + Q2 + Q3 = 29.3787 + 32.4833 + 50.4605 = 112.3224$$

Figure 18.15 shows how the value of this sample option varies inversely with the correlation between the two risky assets.

Call on the maximum of two risky assets

In this section, we consider calls on the maximum of two risky assets. This is similar to the option on the maximum of two risky assets and cash that we just considered. However, for this option, there is no potential cash payoff. Further, these options have an exercise price. To exercise the call, the owner pays the exercise price and selects the better of the two risky assets.

The valuation of this option is quite straightforward once we have valued a call on the maximum of two assets and cash. The payoff on a call on the maximum of two assets is the same as that of a call on two risky assets and cash minus the payment of the exercise price:

$$\text{MAX}\{S_{1T}, S_{2T}, X\} - X$$

Figure 18.15 The value of a call on the best of two risky assets and cash as a function of the correlation between the two risky assets

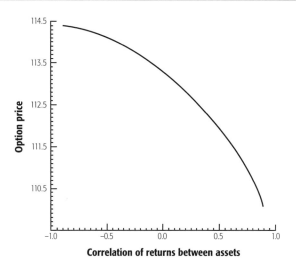

As we have already seen in the preceding section, the value of an option with payoffs of MAX$\{S_{1T}, S_{2T}, X\}$ is simply BEST3 = Q1 + Q2 + Q3. The future liability X has a present value of $Xe^{-r(T-t)}$. Therefore, the value of a call on the maximum of two risky assets, CMAX, is as follows:

$$\text{CMAX} = \text{BEST3} - Xe^{-r(T-t)}Q1 + Q2 + Q3 - Xe^{-r(T-t)} \quad (18.21)$$

Using the same data from the previous section, the value of this option will be as follows:

$$\text{BEST3} - Xe^{-r(T-t)} = 112.3224 - 110 \times e^{-0.08 \times 1} = 10.7796$$

Later in this chapter, we will see how to value a put on the maximum of two risky assets.

Figure 18.16 shows that the value of the option on the maximum of two assets varies inversely with the correlation between the two assets. A comparison of Figures 18.15 and 18.16 shows that the value of a call on the best of two risky assets and cash and the value of a call on the maximum of the same two assets have exactly the same sensitivity to the correlation between the two assets.

Call on the better of two risky assets

A call on the better of two risky assets, CBETTER, is a special case of a call on two risky assets and cash. To form the special case, just specify that the exercise price is zero, $X = 0$. The call on two risky assets and cash is now just a call on two risky assets. With $X = 0$, w_1 and w_2 become arbitrarily large. Therefore,

$$\text{CBETTER} = \text{BEST3, given that } X = 0 \quad (18.22)$$

Using the same inputs as those for a call on two risky assets and cash, the value of this call is CBETTER = 104.9635.

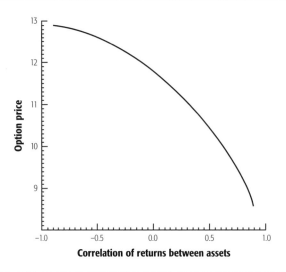

Figure 18.16   The value of a call on the maximum of two risky assets as a function of the correlation between the two risky assets

Put on the maximum of two risky assets

The valuation of a put on the maximum of two risky assets can be derived as a function of the value of the options we have just been studying. To exercise a put on the maximum of two risky assets, the owner surrenders the more valuable of the two risky assets and receives the exercise price. Thus, the payoff on this put is

$$\text{MAX}\{0, X - \text{MAX}(S_{1T}, S_{2T})\}$$

This payoff can be replicated by the following portfolio:

Replicating portfolio
Lend the present value of the exercise price.
Buy a call on the maximum of the two risky assets with exercise price X.
Sell a call on the better of the two risky assets.

At expiration (*assume asset 1 is more valuable than asset 2*)
Receive X as loan matures.

If asset 1 is worth more than X
Exercise option on the maximum, pay X, and receive asset 1.
Deliver asset 1.
Net result: 0

If X is greater than value of asset 1
Let call on the maximum expire worthless.
Purchase asset 1 in market.
Net result: $X = S_{1T}$

Figure 18.17 The value of a put on the maximum of two risky assets as a function of the correlation between the two risky assets

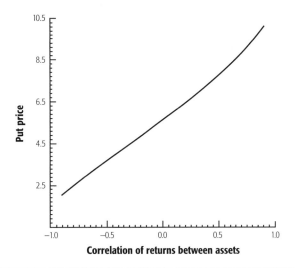

Thus the payoff from this portfolio will be exactly like the payoff from the put on the maximum of two risky assets. Therefore, the put and this portfolio must have the same value. Therefore, the value of a put on the maximum of two assets, PMAX, is as follows:

$$PMAX = CMAX - CBETTER + Xe^{-r(T-t)} \tag{18.23}$$

Using the data given above in the rainbow option section, we have

$$PMAX = 10.7796 - 104.9635 + 101.5428 = 7.3589$$

Figure 18.17 shows that the value of our sample put varies directly with the correlation between the two assets. A comparison of Figure 18.16, for a call on the maximum of our two sample assets, and Figure 18.17 shows that calls vary inversely with the correlation, while puts vary directly.

Call on the minimum of two risky assets

A call on the minimum of two risky assets pays the value of the inferior risky asset upon payment of the exercise price X. This call has the payoff

$$MAX\{0, MIN(S_{1T}, S_{2T}) - X\}$$

This call can be replicated by a portfolio of three options we have considered already:

Buy a plain vanilla option on the first asset with exercise price X.
Buy a plain vanilla option on the second asset with exercise price X.
Sell a call on the maximum of the two assets with exercise price X.

Upon expiration, the portfolio owner exercises the call on the more valuable asset and uses this asset to satisfy the call on the maximum that was sold to form the portfolio. These transactions have a net zero cash flow, because the portfolio owner receives X and pays X. The portfolio owner still holds the call on the inferior asset. If the inferior asset is worth X or less, the option expires worthless. If the inferior asset is worth more than X, the portfolio owner exercises for a profit equal to the difference. Therefore, the value of a call on the minimum of two assets, CMIN, with exercise price X is as follows:

$$\text{CMIN} = C_t^M(S_1) + C_t^M(S_2) + \text{CMAX} \tag{18.24}$$

where $C_t^M(S_j)$ indicates a plain vanilla call on asset S_j. Using our data, we have the following:

$C_t^M(S_1) = 5.4369$
$C_t^M(S_2) = 7.4635$
CMAX = 10.7796 (as solved above)

Therefore, the value of a call on the minimum of two assets is

CMIN = 5.4369 + 7.4635 − 10.7796 = 2.1208

We show how to price a put on the minimum of two assets below.

Call on the worse of two risky assets

A call on the worse of two risky assets has a payoff equal to the inferior asset, but without the payment of any exercise price. In this case, $X = 0$, so the call payoff is

$$\text{MAX}\{0, \text{MIN}(S_{1T}, S_{2T}) - 0\} = \text{MIN}(S_{1T}, S_{2T})$$

We have already seen that CBETTER is the same as CMAX, if $X = 0$. Therefore, we can find the value of a call on the worse of two risky assets, CWORSE, by finding the value of plain vanilla calls with $X = 0$ for the two assets and subtracting the value of CBETTER:

$$\text{CWORSE} = C_t^M(S_1) + C_t^M(S_2) - \text{CBETTER}, \text{ given that } X = 0 \tag{18.25}$$

Using the same example values:

$C_t^M(S_1) = 96.0789$, if $X = 0$
$C_t^M(S_2) = 92.1923$, if $X = 0$
CBETTER = 104.9635 (as calculated above)
CWORSE = 96.0789 + 92.1923 − 104.9635 = 83.3077

Put on the minimum of two risky assets

A put on the minimum of two risky assets pays X and requires the delivery of the inferior asset. Therefore, the payoff on this put is

$$\text{MAX}\{0, X - \text{MIN}(S_{1T}, S_{2T})\}$$

To value this put, we create a replicating portfolio:

Replicating portfolio
Buy call on the minimum of two risky assets with exercise price X.
Sell call on the worse of two risky assets.
Lend the present value of the exercise price X.

At expiration (assume asset 2 has the lower value)
Receive X.

If $S_{2T} \geq X$
Exercise call on minimum, paying X.
Deliver inferior asset to complete obligation on sale of call on the worse of two assets.
Net result: 0

If $S_{2T} \geq X$
Buy inferior asset in market.
Deliver inferior asset to complete obligation on sale of call on the worse of two assets.
Net result: $X - S_{2T}$

As this portfolio exactly replicates the payoffs on the put, it must have the same value as the put on the minimum of two risky assets, PMIN. Therefore,

$$\text{PMIN} = \text{CMIN} - \text{CWORSE} + Xe^{-r(T-t)} \tag{18.26}$$

From our previous solutions, we have the following:

CMIN = 2.1201
CWORSE = 83.3077

Therefore,

PMIN = 2.1201 − 83.3077 + 101.5428 = 20.3552

Conclusion

In this chapter, we have explored a large variety of exotic options. The analysis has focused on European options, for which closed-form solutions exist. As we have seen, many of these exotic options can be understood in terms of the familiar plain vanilla options priced in the Merton model.

This chapter considered nine classes of exotic options: forward-start options, compound options, chooser options, barrier options, binary options, lookback options, average price options, exchange options, and rainbow options. For each of these options, the payoffs are more complicated than those of plain vanilla options. We have seen that these specialized payoffs can be used to manage risks or to shape a speculative position more exactly. Many of these options exhibit path dependence, with the price of the option at a given time depending upon the price history or the price future of the underlying asset.

The **OPTION!** software that accompanies this book can compute the value of all of the exotic options discussed in this chapter and can price all of the example options considered in this chapter.

Exercises

For all of the following problems, compute the answers by hand, being sure to show intermediate results. After making the computations, use **OPTION!** to check the accuracy of your computations.

1 Using the following parameter values, find the price of a forward-start put: $S = 100$; $X = 100$; $T - t = 1$ year; $\sigma = 0.2$; $r = 0.1$; $\delta = 0.05$; $tg = 0.5$.

2 Price all four types of compound options assuming the following parameter values: $S = 100$; $\sigma = 0.4$; $r = 0.1$; $\delta = 0.05$; $X = 100$; $x = 8$; $T = 1$ year; $te = 0.25$ years.

3 Price a simple chooser option based on the following parameter values: $S = 100$; $X = 100$; $T - t = 1$ year; $\sigma = 0.5$; $\rho = 0.1$; $\sigma = 0.05$; $tc = 0.5$ years. By comparing this result with that of the example chooser in the sample text, what can you conclude about the influence of the stock's risk on the value of the chooser?

4 Find the value of a down-and-in put with: $S = 100$; $X = 100$; $T - t = 1$ year; $\sigma = 0.3$; $\rho = 0.1$; $\delta = 0.05$; BARR = 97; and REBATE = 2.

5 Consider a cash-or-nothing call and put, with common parameter values: $S = 100$; $X = 110$; $T - t = 0.5$ years; $\sigma = 0.4$; $r = 0.1$; $\delta = 0.0$; and $Z = 200$. What is the value of each option? What is the value of a long position in both options? Which items of information given above are not needed to value the portfolio of the two options?

6 Consider an asset-or-nothing call and put, with common parameter values: $S = 100$; $X = 110$; $T - t = 0.5$ years; $\sigma = 0.4$; $r = 0.1$; and $\delta = 0.0$. What is the value of each option? What is the value of a long position in both options? Which items of information given above are not needed to value the portfolio of the two options?

7 Value a gap call with: $S = 100$; $X = 100$; $T - t = 0.5$ years; $\sigma = 0.5$; $r = 0.1$; $\sigma = 0.03$; and $g = 7$.

8 Value a supershare with: $S = 100$; $X_L = 95$; $X_H = 110$; $T - t = 0.5$ years; $\sigma = 0.2$; $r = 0.1$; $\delta = 0.05$. By com-

paring this calculation with the sample supershare of the text, what can you conclude about the value of supershares and the value $X_H - X_L$?

9 Find the value of a lookback call and put with the common parameters: $S = 110$; $T - t = 1$ year; $\sigma = 0.25$; $r = 0.08$; and $\delta = 0.0$. For the call, MINPRI = 80. For the put, MAXPRI = 130.

10 Find the value of an average price option with these common parameters: $S = 100$; $X = 90$; $\sigma = 0.2$; $r = 0.1$; $\delta = 0.05$; $t_0 = 0.0$; $t_1 = 0.5$; $t_2 = 0.5$; and $A = 95$. Compute the value of the option with observations every two days, $h = 2/365$. Now compute the value of the option assuming continuous observation; that is, $h = 0$. Compare these results with the sample option of the chapter. What does this suggest about the value of the option and the frequency of observation?

11 Consider an exchange option with the following common parameter values: $S_1 = 100$; $S_2 = 100$; $\sigma_1 = 0.3$; $\sigma_2 = 0.2$; $\delta_1 = 0.05$; $\delta_2 = 0.05$; $T - t = 0.5$ years. Compute the value of this exchange option with $\rho = 0.0$ and $\rho = 0.7$. Compare your results with those for the sample exchange option in the chapter. What do these results suggest about the value of exchange options as a function of the correlation between the two assets?

For rainbow options, consider these parameter values: $S_1 = 100$; $S_2 = 100$; $X = 95$; $T - t = 0.5$ years; $\sigma_1 = 0.4$; $\sigma_2 = 0.5$; $r = 0.06$; $\delta_1 = 0.02$; $\delta_2 = 0.03$; and $\rho = 0.2$. (Interpret $X = 95$ as the exercise price or as the cash payment depending on the type of option.) Use this information for Exercises 12–18.

12 Find the value of an option on the best of two assets and cash.

13 Find the value of an option on the better of two assets.

14 Find the value of a call on the maximum of two assets.

15 Find the value of a put on the maximum of two assets.

16 Find the value of a call on the minimum of two assets.

17 Find the value of a call on the worse of two assets.

18 Find the value of a put on the minimum of two assets.

Notes

1 For a good introduction to the idea of path dependence in option pricing, see W. Hunter and D. Stowe, "Path-Dependent Options: Valuation and Applications," *Economic Review*, Federal Reserve Bank of Atlanta, July/August 1992, pp. 30–43.

2 Mark Rubinstein and Eric Reiner, "Exotic Options," Working paper, University of California at Berkeley, 1995.

3 For more on the pricing and applications of forward-start options, see: Mark Rubinstein, "Pay Now,

Choose Later," *Risk*, February 1991; Rubinstein and Reiner, "Exotic Options"; and Peter G. Zhang, *Exotic Options: A Guide to the Second-Generation Options*, River Edge, NJ: World Scientific Press, 1997.

4   For the original paper on pricing compound options, see R. Geske, "The Valuation of Compound Options," *Journal of Financial Economics*, 7, March 1979, pp. 63–81. See also Mark Rubinstein, "Double Trouble," *Risk*, December 1991 – January 1992; Rubinstein and Reiner, "Exotic Options"; Alan Tucker, "Exotic Options," Working paper, Pace University, New York, 1995; and Zhang, *Exotic Options*.

5   See Mark Rubinstein, "Options for the Undecided," *Risk*, April 1991, and Rubinstein and Reiner, "Exotic Options."

6   This peso example is drawn from Zhang, *Exotic Options*. For pricing of chooser options, see also Tucker, "Exotic Options."

7   For more detailed discussion of the pricing of barrier options, see: Mark Rubinstein, "Breaking Down the Barriers," *Risk*, September 1991; Rubinstein and Reiner, "Exotic Options"; Tucker, "Exotic Options"; and Zhang, *Exotic Options*. See also Emanuel Derman and Iraz Kani, "The Ins and Outs of Barrier Options," *Derivatives Quarterly*, 3:2, Winter 1996, pp. 55–67.

8   For a discussion of the pricing of binary options, see: Mark Rubinstein, "Unscrambling the Binary Code," *Risk*, October 1991; Rubinstein and Reiner, "Exotic Options"; Tucker, "Exotic Options"; Zhang, *Exotic Options*.

9   Supershares were created by Nils Hakansson, "The Purchasing Power Fund: A New Kind of Financial Intermediary," *Financial Analysts Journal*, 32, November/December 1976, pp. 49–59.

10 The first paper on lookback options appeared in 1979, long before such options actually existed. See Barry Goldman, Howard Sosin, and Mary Ann Gatto, "Path Dependent Options: Buy at the Low, Sell at the High," *Journal of Finance*, 34, December 1979, pp. 1111–27. The results of Goldman, Sosin, and Gatto were generalized to embrace a dividend paying underlying asset by Mark Garman, in his paper,

"Recollection in Tranquility," *Risk*, March 1989, pp. 16–18. For more on the pricing of lookbacks, see also Rubinstein and Reiner, "Exotic Options"; Tucker, "Exotic Options"; and Zhang, *Exotic Options*.

11 For a discussion of partial lookback options, see Zhang, *Exotic Options*.

12 Zhang, *Exotic Options*.

13 For a discussion of Asian options, see: A. Kemna and A. Vorst, "A Pricing Method for Options Based on Average Asset Values," *Journal of Banking and Finance*, 14, March 1990, pp. 113–29; Rubinstein and Reiner, "Exotic Options"; S. Turnbull and L. Wakeman, "A Quick Algorithm for Pricing European Average Options," *Journal of Financial and Quantitative Analysis*, 26, September 1991, pp. 377–89; Tucker, "Exotic Options"; and Zhang, *Exotic Options*. Kemna and Vorst give examples of several commodity-linked bonds.

14 The first paper on exchange options was by William Margrabe, "The Value of an Option to Exchange One Asset for Another," *Journal of Finance*, March 1978. Margrabe distinguished the four applications just mentioned. For additional insights on pricing exchange options, see: Mark Rubinstein, "One for Another," *Risk*, July 1991; Rubinstein and Reiner, "Exotic Options"; Tucker, "Exotic Options"; and Zhang, *Exotic Options*.

15 The original paper on rainbow options, by Rene Stulz, was "Options on the Minimum or the Maximum of Two Risky Assets," *Journal of Financial Economics*, 10, July 1982, pp. 161–85. Thus, Stulz was pricing two-color rainbow options. Stulz's work was extended to multicolored rainbow options by Herb Johnson, "Options on the Maximum or the Minimum of Several Assets," *Journal of Financial and Quantitative Analysis*, 22, September 1987, pp. 277–83. The name "rainbow option" was originated by Mark Rubinstein, "Somewhere Over the Rainbow," *Risk*, November 1991. For additional discussion of rainbow options, see: Mark Rubinstein, "Return to Oz," *Risk*, November 1994; Rubinstein and Reiner, "Exotic Options"; Tucker, "Exotic Options"; and Zhang, *Exotic Options*.

19

Interest Rate Options

Overview

This chapter explores interest rate options–options on financial assets whose prices are sensitive to changing interest rates. Prior to this chapter, we have assumed that interest rates are constant in the application of our various pricing models. For instance, the Black–Scholes model explicitly assumes that interest rates are constant over the life of the option. This assumption has worked well on the whole, allowing us to value options while keeping mathematical complexity under control. However, the value of many instruments is tied very directly to interest rates, and for some instruments, prices have fluctuated primarily due to changes in interest rates.

We begin by examining the market for interest rate options. As we will see, the main classes of interest rate options are options on interest rate futures contracts, over-the-counter options that are traded on a wide variety of instruments, and interest rate options that are embedded in debt instruments, such as bonds and mortgages.

Key to pricing interest rate options is a basic understanding of the term structure of interest rates and the yield curve. We discuss the relationship between the yield curve for coupon-bearing instruments, the zero-coupon yield curve, and the forward yield curve. These three measures of the relationship between maturity and yield are intimately connected, and we show how to move from one kind of yield measure to another using a method called bootstrapping. We also consider an explicit market in forward rates of interest.

After surveying the yield curve, we explore some analytic tools for valuing interest rate options. The first of these is the option-adjusted spread (OAS). In this kind of spread analysis, an instrument with an embedded interest rate option is compared to a similar instrument with no such option. The difference in yields between the instruments, the yield spread, provides a measure of the value of the embedded option.

Central to the evaluation of interest rate options is the Black model. We have already introduced the Black model in Chapter 16. There we saw how to use the Black model to value options on futures, including interest rate futures. In this chapter, we show why the Black model works even for options on interest rate futures. We also evaluate the Black model in more detail and show how to use it to value more explicit interest rate options. For example, the Black model can be used to value European options on coupon-bearing bonds. In addition, we explore the active market in interest rate options based on LIBOR (the London Interbank Offered Rate).

These options based on LIBOR are known as "calls on LIBOR" and "puts on LIBOR." We explore the application of the Black model to these options and show how these options can be used to create interest rate caps, floors, and collars. These are powerful interest rate risk management tools that can also be valued using the Black model.

Interest rate options: markets and instruments

Of all the instruments analyzed in this book so far, interest rate options are traded in the most diverse forms and the most varied markets. This section surveys the different kinds of interest rate options and the markets in which they trade. We may separate interest rate options into three groups: those that are traded on exchanges, those that trade over-the-counter, and those that are embedded in some other financial instrument.

Exchange-traded options

The dominant form of exchange-traded interest rate option is an option on a futures contract in which the futures contract has an interest-sensitive asset as its underlying good. In addition, there is a small market for the direct trading of options on bonds. In Chapter 16, we considered options on futures in general and included a discussion of options on interest rate futures. In this chapter, we examine techniques for pricing these instruments more closely.

The leading options on interest rate futures contracts are traded on the Chicago Board of Trade (CBOT), the Chicago Mercantile Exchange (CME), and Euronext.liffe. Figure 19.1 presents quotations from *The Wall Street Journal* for exchange-traded options on interest rate futures. As the quotations indicate, there are relatively few really successful contracts, but some of these are very successful. The figure also indicates that some instruments have a high ratio of volume to open interest, while others do not. Essentially, the contracts with a high ratio of volume to open interest are those that are traded frequently and have a high speculative interest, such as options on T-bond futures. Virtually all of the others have a relatively low ratio of volume to open interest. This is due to the importance of the Eurocurrency-based contracts and the shorter-term Treasury contracts as hedging vehicles for the swaps market.[1]

Over-the-counter options

For interest rate options that are explicitly traded, in contrast to options embedded in other instruments, the over-the-counter (OTC) market is the source of real growth and innovation. Because the OTC market is almost exclusively a private market, complete and accurate statistics on market size and activity are not available. However, it is possible to place a lower bound on the size of this market. To do so, we rely on two sources. The first of these is the Bank for International Settlements (BIS). Also, the Office of the Comptroller of the Currency (OCC) reports on the derivatives trading activity of United States banks and their affiliates.

The BIS conducts a regular survey of its membership regarding the size of their activity and the extent of their outstanding commitments. In the OTC market, the concept of a **notional principal** is critical. The notional principal may best be understood by analogy with the futures market and the futures options market. For example, a Eurodollar futures contract (or an option on a Eurodollar futures) is based on an underlying instrument with a principal of $1 million. However, the million dollars in no way represents the actual investment in or risk exposure involved in a one-contract position in Eurodollar futures or futures option. This $1 million is analogous to the notional principal reported for OTC derivatives. The notional principal is the principal amount used for computing the size of interest payments. It is not an amount actually at risk, nor is it an amount that is actually exchanged. Instead, it provides a basis for computing interest flows.

Table 19.1 presents the recent growth of the OTC interest rate options market. By 2005, OTC interest rate options with nearly $28 trillion of notional principal were outstanding. Based on outstanding notional principal, the OTC interest rate options market has grown seven times the size it was a decade ago.

The Comptroller of the Currency (OCC) reports that the 882 banks and trust companies with derivatives positions have a substantial position in both exchange-traded and OTC options, which are concentrated heavily in interest rate options. In 2006, these banks had outstanding positions of $110.2 trillion in all derivative contracts measured in terms of notional principal.[2] These bank figures are not independent of the BIS figures. Every option has a buyer and seller, so probably some of the bank positions are also counted in the BIS report. Further, some of these option positions could be counted twice. These considerations indicate how difficult it is to assess the full size of the OTC interest rate options market exactly. However, we can conclude that the size of the interest rate options market is tremendous, with many trillions of dollars in outstanding notional principal and trillions of dollars in annual activity. The OTC interest rate options market includes a rich diversity of different kinds of option contracts.

Figure 19.1 Quotations for exchange-traded options on interest rate futures

INTEREST RATE

T-BONDS (CBT)
$100,000; points – 64ths of 100%

STRIKE PRICE	CALLS-SETTLE Mar	Apr	May	PUTS-SETTLE Mar	Apr	May
101	2–00	....	....	0–26	....	0–61
102	1–21	....	....	0–47	1–24	....
103	0–51	1–14	....	1–13	1–57	2–12
104	0–29	0–54	....	1–55	2–32	....
105	0–16	0–37	....	2–42	3–14	....
106	0–08	0–24	....	3–33	...	....

Est vol 34,000; Mn vol 16,234 calls 13,604 puts
Op int Mon 225,074 calls 220,713 puts

T-NOTES (CBT)
$100,000; points – 64ths of 100%

STRIKE PRICE	CALLS-SETTLE Mar	Apr	May	PUTS-SETTLE Mar	Apr	May
102	2–27	....	....	0–09	0–30	....
103	1–39	....	....	0–21	0–50	....
104	0–60	1–13	....	0–42	....	....
105	0–31	0–50	....	1–13	1–51	....
106	0–15	0–32	....	1–61	2–32	....
107	0–07	0–19	....	2–52	....	....

Est vol 61,000 Mn 11,669 calls 20,887 puts
Op int Mon 344,934 calls 302,826 puts

5 YR TREAS NOTES (CBT)
$100,000; points – 64ths of 100%

STRIKE PRICE	CALLS-SETTLE Mar	Apr	May	PUTS-SETTLE Mar	Apr	May
10250	1–07	....	....	0–13	....	....
10300	0–49	....	....	0–23	....	....
10350	0–32	....	....	0–38	....	....
10400	0–19	0–45	....	0–57	....	....
10450	0–10	0–33	....	1–17	1–16	....
10500	0–15	0–23	....	....	1–38	....

Est vol 9,100 Mn 12,067 calls 3,850 puts
Op int Mon 126,959 calls 103,309 puts

EURODOLLAR (CME)
$ million; pts of 100%

STRIKE PRICE	CALLS-SETTLE Feb	Mar	Apr	PUTS-SETTLE Feb	Mar	Apr
9400	6.55	6.55	....	0.00	0.00	....
9425	4.10	4.10	....	0.05	0.10	....
9450	1.85	2.10	4.85	0.30	0.55	0.50
9475	0.65	0.95	3.00	1.60	1.90	....
9500	0.22	0.40	1.75	....	3.85	2.35
8525	....	0.17	1.05	....	....	4.10

Est vol 157,148 Mn vol 105,575 calls 48,968 puts
Op int Mon 1,408,775 calls 1,358,234 puts

1 YR. MID-CURVE EURODLR (CME)
$1 million contract units; pts of 100%

STRIKE PRICE	CALLS-SETTLE Feb	Mar	Apr	PUTS-SETTLE Feb	Mar	Apr
9425	4.45	4.75	....	0.15	0.45	....
9450	2.35	2.95	2.35	0.55	1.15	2.35
9475	1.05	1.65	1.40	1.75	2.35	3.90
9500	0.42	0.80	....	3.60	4.00	....
9525	0.15	0.35	0.45	....	6.00	....
9550	0.05	0.20	....	....	....	....

Est vol 62,575 Min 26,982 calls 14,484 puts
Op int Mon 443,648 calls 282,109 puts

2 YR. MID-CURVE EURODLR (CME)
$1 million contract units; pts of 100%

STRIKE PRICE	CALLS-SETTLE Mar	Jun	PUTS-SETTLE Mar	Jun
9375	4.55	....	0.55	1.50
9400	2.80	3.35	1.30	2.50
9425	1.45	2.25	2.45	....
9450	0.65	1.35	....	5.45
9475	....	0.80	....	....
9500	...	...	...	....

Est vol 0 Mn 0 calls 1,500 puts
Op int Mon 13,658 calls 12,688 puts

EURLBOR (LIFFE)
Euro 1,000,000

STRIKE PRICE	CALLS-SETTLE Feb	Mar	Apr	PUTS-SETTLE Feb	Mar	Apr
95125	0.30	0.30	0.57	....	0.00	....
95250	0.18	0.19	0.45	0.00	0.02	0.00
95375	0.08	0.11	0.34	0.03	0.06	0.01
95500	0.02	0.05	0.24	0.09	0.13	0.04
95625	0.00	0.02	0.15	0.20	0.22	0.07
95750	....	0.01	0.08	0.32	0.33	0.13

Vol Tu 14,175 calls 18,572 puts
Op int Mon 658,554 calls 626,134 puts

10 YR. GERMAN EURO GOVT BD
(Eurobund) (Eurex) 100,000; pts in 100%

STRIKE PRICE	CALLS-SETTLE Feb	Mar	Apr	PUTS-SETTLE Feb	Mar	Apr
10750	0.91	1.11	1.08	0.01	0.20	0.54
10800	0.42	0.76	0.79	0.01	0.35	0.75
10850	0.09	0.49	0.56	0.18	0.58	1.02
10900	0.01	0.29	0.37	0.59	0.88	1.33
10950	0.01	0.16	0.25	1.09	1.25	1.71
11000	0.01	0.08	0.16	1.59	1.67	2.12

Vol Tu 60,348 calls 42,504 puts
Op int Mon 651,571 calls 601,238 puts

Source: *The Wall Street Journal*, January 24, 2001, p. C19. Reprinted by permission of *The Wall Street Journal*, © 2001 Dow Jones & Company, Inc. All rights reserved worldwide

Table 19.1   The growth of the interest rate options market ($ billions)

Year	Notional outstanding (year-end)
1988	$327.3
1989	537.3
1990	561.3
1991	577.2
1992	634.5
1993	1,397.6
1994	1,572.8
1995	3,704.5
1996	4,722.6
1997	4,920.0
1998	7,997.0
1999	9,380.0
2000	9,476.0
2001	10,933.0
2002	13,746.0
2003	20,012.0
2004	27,082.0
2005	27,885.0

Source: Through 1998 data are from the International Swaps and Derivatives Association web site (www.isda.org). Later data are from the Bank for International Settlements

Embedded options

In addition to the explicit interest rate options traded on exchanges and the OTC market, there is a large class of interest rate options that are embedded in other securities. Broadly speaking, these embedded interest rate options can be found in callable corporate coupon bonds and in mortgage obligations.

In the United States, long-term corporate bonds are typically issued as coupon bonds with a call provision. The call provision allows the issuing firm to retire the bond at a specific date and price. Therefore, the issuing firm has an option that is embedded in the bond contract. This call provision is essentially an interest rate option, because the value of the call provision depends on the price of the bond, which depends in turn on the level of interest rates. Until recently, many U.S. Treasury bonds were also issued with call provisions. Now, however, U.S. Treasury bonds are issued without a call provision.[3] The widespread presence of call features on existing Treasuries and both existing and future corporate bonds means that trillions of dollars of bonds exist with embedded options. For most of these bonds, the presence of these embedded options has a significant effect on the market value of the bonds. As we will also see, the option feature of these bonds affects the way in which the prices of the bonds respond to changes in interest rates.

Real estate mortgages constitute another major class of securities with embedded interest rate options. Almost all home mortgages contain a prepayment provision, which allows the borrower to prepay the mortgage balance before the maturity of the mortgage. This prepayment provision is an option granted by the lender to the borrower. There are trillions of dollars of these mortgages outstanding, and most mortgages are prepaid before maturity, meaning that this prepayment option is generally exercised at some point.

In the United States, home mortgages are typically bundled by mortgage bankers to form the basis of securities known as mortgage-backed securities. In essence, a **mortgage-backed security** (**MBS**) is a portfolio or pool of real estate mortgages. Investors in an MBS invest in the entire portfolio of mortgages constituting the MBS and participate in all of the cash flows from the portfolio on a *pro rata* basis. As a consequence, these pooled mortgages are often called **pass-throughs**. Once these mortgages are assembled into pools, they are often guaranteed against default by the Government National Mortgage Association (GNMA) or Federal National Mortgage Association (FNMA). As a result, these instruments trade at a yield that is just a little higher than Treasury issues, once the MBS yield has been adjusted for the prepayment option.

Of the many mortgages constituting an MBS, some will be paid in each period through exercise of the borrower's prepayment option. Prepayments are driven by two main incentives. First, some mortgages are prepaid because the owner sells the home. Second, a mortgage might be prepaid to take advantage of more favorable refinancing rates. From the point of view of the investor in an MBS, this second prepayment incentive is more important.

Refinancing tends to occur when current interest rates are substantially lower than the rate at which the mortgage was initiated. When prepayment occurs on a mortgage in an MBS, the MBS investor receives a share of that prepayment. From the point of the MBS investor, this return of principal is unwelcome, coming as it generally does when interest rates are low. The MBS investor now finds herself with cash that must face reinvestment at the lower prevailing rate.

Valuation of prepayments is complex, because prepayments depend not only on movements in interest rates, but also on demographics. Some mortgage pools tend to experience higher prepayment rates because the mortgages in the pool are issued by borrowers who are more likely to sell their homes, due to upward mobility, job transfers, and so on. Therefore, the prepayment option feature of home mortgages is complex and financially important to understanding MBS valuation. MBS specialists spend considerable resources to understand the likely prepayments on various mortgage pools.[4]

In addition to pass-throughs, another type of MBS is a **collateralized mortgage obligation** (**CMO**). A CMO is created by breaking up the cash flows from a pool of mortgages into packages intended to appeal to investor groups with different needs. Such a package is called a **tranche**. The various tranches may differ regarding the coupon rate (the contracted rate of interest when the mortgage is initiated) and maturity. These tranches are then sold to investors. In addition, mortgages can also be stripped into their interest components and principal components. In a typical mortgage, part of each monthly payment repays interest for the month, and the remainder of the payment reduces the principal balance. An **interest only** (**IO**) is an MBS that consists of only the interest portion of the payments from the mortgage pool. Similarly, a **principal only** (**PO**) consists of only the principal repayment portions.

For both callable bonds and mortgages, understanding the value and investment character depends on understanding the effect that the embedded option has on the investment vehicle. Efforts to price instruments with embedded options typically analyze the security as consisting of two parts. The **host** is the underlying security without the option. The value of the entire security can then be approached by pricing the two parts, host and embedded option, separately:

$$\text{value of instrument with embedded option} = \text{host} \pm \text{value of option} \qquad (19.1)$$

The presence of the embedded option may either add additional value to the host or reduce the value of the host. For example, the call feature on a callable bond is a call option retained by the issuer of the bond and, therefore, granted by the bond investor. Because the bond investor must grant this option in the purchase of the bond, the bond has less value than it otherwise would. For a mortgage, the borrower also possesses the prepayment option. For both dominant types of securities with embedded options, callable bonds and home mortgages, the borrower possesses the option, so the option feature generally reduces the value of, and raises the yield on, the investment vehicle.

Summary

This section has surveyed the various kinds of interest rate options available in the marketplace. The variety is limited only by human ingenuity. Nonetheless, certain types of interest rate options dominate the market and claim our special attention. These are options on interest rate futures contracts, OTC options on bonds, OTC calls and puts on LIBOR, and the home mortgages, with a special emphasis on the prepayment options they contain. An understanding these kinds of interest rate options provides a foundation for tackling some of the more complex and obscure interest rate options.

The term structure of interest rates

In this section, we explore the **term structure of interest rates**—the relationship between term-to-maturity of bonds and their respective yields. Analyzing the term structure of interest rates requires focusing on bonds that are as similar as possible, except with respect to maturity. Consequently, term structure analysis avoids attention to bonds that differ in their tax status, default risk, callability, and coupon levels. Figure 19.2 shows yield curves for the period 1975–92. The variation in level and shape of the curves is striking. Table 19.2 shows similar data for a different period in tabular form, based on bonds selling at par. Therefore, these data express the **par yield curve**—the relationship between yield and maturity for bonds selling at par.

Starting with data based on the term structure of par bonds, which are published daily in sources such as *The Wall Street Journal*, it is possible to derive other yield measures that will be important in understanding interest rate options. We are particularly interested in the zero-coupon yield curve and in the implied forward yield curve. The **zero-coupon yield curve** expresses the relationship between yield and maturity for bonds paying no coupon payments over the life of the bond. A **forward rate of interest** or **forward rate** is a rate of interest for a period that begins at some date in the future and extends to a more distant date. For example, a forward

---

Figure 19.2   U.S. Treasury spot yield curves, 1975–92

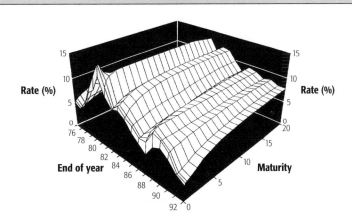

Source: From T. Coleman, L. Fisher, and R. Ibbotson, *Historical US Treasury Yield Curves, 1993 Edition* (New York: Moody's Investors' Service, Inc., 1993), p. 7. © 1993. Reprinted by permission of Moody's Investors Service.

Table 19.2	Estimated par bond U.S. Treasury yields, year-end									
Year	Maturity (years)									
	1	1.5	2	3	4	5	7	10	15	20
1949	1.08	1.19	1.24	1.401	1.20	1.40	1.63	1.80	1.94	–
1959	4.84	5.06	5.18	5.07	5.01	5.02	5.03	4.89	4.68	4.56
1969	8.19	8.48	8.63	8.51	8.46	8.20	7.90	7.77	7.74	7.33
1979	11.83	11.54	10.39	10.79	10.49	10.46	10.43	10.39	10.36	10.20
1989	8.00	7.95	7.92	7.95	7.96	8.08	8.00	8.08	8.17	8.11

Source: From T. Coleman, L. Fisher, and R. Ibbotson, *Historical U.S. Treasury Yield Curves, 1993 Edition* (New York: Moody's Investors Service, Inc., 1993), Table 9-2.

rate might cover a period beginning two years from today and extending for three years to a time five years from today. The **implied forward yield** curve expresses the relationship between term to maturity and rates for forward rates as implied by the par yield curve. All of these interest rate relationships, the par yield curve, the zero-coupon yield curve, and the implied forward yield curve, form a single system of mutually consistent interest rates. Given one set of rates, it is possible to find the others, as we now show.

We begin by considering the zero-coupon yield curve. The zero-coupon yield curve, or **zero curve**, captures the relationship between zero-coupon spot yields and term to maturity as of a particular date. The zero curve, as opposed to other kinds of yield curves, represents a set of yields unencumbered by complicating assumptions about reinvestment rates for coupons received before bond maturity. As a result, practitioners can be confident that the discount factors and expected forward rates derived from the zero curve do not depend on any reinvestment rate assumptions. Because of the desirable properties that it possesses, the zero curve has become a key ingredient to the valuation of many financial instruments, including swaps.

A zero curve can be based on any class of interest rates and denominated in any type of currency. Therefore, there are many different types of zero curves. However, we focus on the U.S. dollar LIBOR zero curve. The zero curve must be constructed—as opposed to observed—because directly observable, and reliable, zero rates are available for only a limited number of maturities. For other maturities, zero rates must be constructed using a combination of bootstrapping and interpolation techniques.

Any coupon bond may be regarded as a portfolio of zero-coupon bonds. Each cash flow on the coupon bond is considered to be the payoff from a zero-coupon bond. Therefore, we can express the value of a coupon bond as follows:

$$P_0 = \sum_{t=1}^{M} \frac{C_t}{Z_{0,t}} \tag{19.2}$$

where P_0 is the price of the bond at $t = 0$, C_t is the cash flow from the bond occurring at time t, and $Z_{x,y}$ is the zero-coupon factor for a payment to be received at time y measured from time x. Equation 19.2 is the same as the familiar bond pricing formula, except that it allows a different interest rate to be applied to each payment on the bond. Table 19.3 presents U.S. Treasury bonds from the par yield curve, all with an assumed par value of 100. Table 19.4 shows the cash flows from each of the bonds in Table 19.3. From these, we show how to compute the zero-coupon yield curve and the implied forward yield curve. Based on Table 19.4, we have the following:

Table 19.3 Illustrative Treasury instruments, par = 100

Instrument	Maturity	Annual coupon rate (% of par)	Price (% of par)
A	6 months	5.8	100
B	1 year	6.0	100
C	1.5 years	6.4	100
D	2 year	6.8	100
E	3 year	7.0	100

Table 19.4 Cash flows from illustrative Treasury bonds

Bond	Cash flow (years)					
	0.5	1.0	1.5	2.0	2.5	3.0
A	102.9					
B	3.0	103.0				
C	3.2	3.2	103.2			
D	3.4	3.4	3.4	103.4		
E	3.5	3.5	3.5	3.5	3.5	103.5

$$P_A = \frac{102.9}{Z_{0,0.5}}$$

$$P_B = \frac{3.0}{Z_{0,0.5}} + \frac{103.0}{Z_{0,1}}$$

$$P_C = \frac{3.2}{Z_{0,0.5}} + \frac{3.2}{Z_{0,1}} + \frac{103.2}{Z_{0,1.5}}$$

$$P_D = \frac{3.4}{Z_{0,0.5}} + \frac{3.4}{Z_{0,1}} + \frac{3.4}{Z_{0,1.5}} + \frac{103.4}{Z_{0,2}}$$

$$P_E = \frac{3.5}{Z_{0,0.5}} + \frac{3.5}{Z_{0,1}} + \frac{3.5}{Z_{0,1.5}} + \frac{3.5}{Z_{0,2}} + \frac{3.5}{Z_{0,2.5}} + \frac{103.5}{Z_{0,3}}$$

where the subscripts $A–E$ on the price indicate the bond, since we are finding all prices at time zero, and the subscripts on Z are expressed in years.

Our first task is to find the six-month zero-coupon factor $Z_{0,0.5}$:

$$P_0 = \frac{C_{0,5}}{Z_{0,0.5}}$$

$$100 = \frac{102.9}{Z_{0,0.5}}$$

$$Z_{0,0.5} = 1.029$$

With a six-month zero-coupon factor of 1.029, the implied annualized yield, assuming semi-annual compounding, is 5.88 percent.

We next find the one-year zero-coupon factor by treating the one-year coupon bond as a portfolio of zero-coupon instruments. The one-year bond consists of a payment in six months of 3 (half the annual coupon rate) plus a second payment in one year of 103 (the par value, plus the final semiannual coupon payment):

$$P_0 = \frac{C_{0.5}}{Z_{0,0.5}} + \frac{C_1}{Z_{0,1}}$$

$$100 = \frac{3}{1.029} + \frac{103}{Z_{0,1}}$$

$$Z_{0,1} = \frac{103}{100 - \dfrac{3}{1.029}} = 1.06093$$

In essence, we have begun with a short-term zero-coupon instrument, found the zero-coupon factor, and used this initial factor to find the factor for the next shortest term. This process is called **bootstrapping**—the sequential process of using a short-term rate to find a longer-term rate. Continuing the process of bootstrapping gives $Z_{0,1.5} = 1.099346$ and $Z_{0,2} = 1.143826$. Notice that we are stymied at this point with respect to the instruments in Tables 19.3 and 19.4. Our next desired factor would be $Z_{0,2.5}$. However, we do not have the price of a bond maturing at $t = 2.5$. Also, we cannot use the bond maturing at $t = 3$, because it has an intervening payment at $t = 2.5$. Therefore, bootstrapping requires an instrument maturing at each date up to and including the longest maturity date for which we wish to compute the zero-coupon factor. Note also that all of the bonds in Tables 19.3 and 19.4 traded at par. The bootstrapping technique could be applied to bonds that are not at par, due to a diversity of coupon rates. However, differing coupon rates can affect bond yields, so it is best to use par bonds only.

The set of bond yields we have been considering also implies a set of forward rates of interest. Let $FR_{x,y}$ indicate a forward rate of interest to cover the period that begins at future time x and ends at a later time y. Also, let $FR_{x,y}$ be the forward rate zero-coupon factor to cover the period that begins at future time x and ends at a later time y. Given the relevant zero-coupon factors, any FRF can be found as

$$FRF_{x,y} = \frac{Z_{0,y}}{Z_{0,x}} \tag{19.3}$$

Using the data of Tables 19.3 and 19.4, along with the zero-coupon factors already computed, we have the following:

$$FRF_{0.5,1} = \frac{Z_{0,1}}{Z_{0,0.5}} = \frac{1.060931}{1.029} = 1.031031$$

$$FRF_{1,1.5} = \frac{Z_{0,1.5}}{Z_{0,1}} = \frac{1.099346}{1.060931} = 1.036209$$

$$FRF_{1.5,2} = \frac{Z_{0,2}}{Z_{0,1.5}} = \frac{1.143826}{1.099346} = 1.040460$$

$$FRF_{0.5,1.5} = \frac{Z_{0,1.5}}{Z_{0,0.5}} = \frac{1.099346}{1.029} = 1.068363$$

$$FRF_{0.5,2} = \frac{Z_{0,2}}{Z_{0,0.5}} = \frac{1.143826}{1.029} = 1.111590$$

$$FRF_{1,2} = \frac{Z_{0,2}}{Z_{0,1}} = \frac{1.143826}{1.060931} = 1.078134$$

Given the various FRFs, the forward rates, the FRs, are the interest rates implied by the forward rate factors. By using FRFs, we can make computations based strictly on cash flows and then move to forward rates under various compounding assumptions.

In the example data of Tables 19.3 and 19.4, the yield curve is upward sloping, with longer maturity bonds having higher yields than short maturity bonds. In this situation, the zero-coupon rates are higher than the rates on the coupon bonds. For example, assuming annual compounding, the zero-coupon interest rate on a two-year zero-coupon bond is 6.9498 percent, compared to the yield of 6.8 percent on the coupon bond. Forward rates map onto these spot yield measures only approximately, but for the same example, the forward interest rate to cover from year 1 to year 2 is 7.8134 percent. This leads to the following rule:

For upward-sloping yield curves:

> forward rate > zero-coupon rate > coupon bond rate

For downward-sloping yield curves:

> forward rate < zero-coupon rate < coupon bond rate

We will use the bootstrapping technique and the various yield measures in pricing interest rate options. As we will see in later chapters, bootstrapping is also important in pricing swap agreements.

Using options to anticipate changes in the Federal Funds rate

The Federal Open Market Committee (FOMC) is the main policy-making arm of the Federal Reserve System. The FOMC meets every six weeks to set the target for the Federal Funds rate until the next meeting. The Federal Funds rate, which represents the interest rate paid on overnight loans between banks, is a widely watched benchmark interest rate. Market analysts carefully examine market data and statements by Federal Reserve members for clues as to whether the Federal Funds rate will rise or fall. Option contracts on Federal Funds futures, traded at the CBOT, provide a way to "back out" the market's assessment of the future distribution of the Federal Funds rate. By setting the market price of the option to the model price, an analyst can determine the implied standard deviation of the distribution assumed by the model. The mean of the distribution can be found from the corresponding price of Federal Funds futures. By recovering this distribution, it is possible to estimate the likelihood of each outcome to be considered by the FOMC. FOMC minutes reveal that FOMC members consider the option-implied distribution in their deliberation to gauge market expectations.[5]

Stripped Treasury securities and forward rate agreements (FRAs)

In the previous section, we saw how to compute zero-coupon factors and rates along with forward rate factors and rates from the par yield curve. Explicit markets for zero-coupon instruments and forward rates also exist.

Treasury strips

Figure 19.3 presents quotations from *The Wall Street Journal* for U.S. Treasury strips. A stripped T-bond is created when a normal T-bond is decomposed into a series of zero-coupon bonds corresponding to the various coupon and principal payments that constitute the bond. For example, a 30-year semiannual coupon T-bond could be stripped to give 60 zero-coupon instruments that pay the original coupon payment of the bond, plus one zero-coupon bond that corresponds to the principal repayment on the bond. If the T-bond were issued as a callable bond, the stripping of T-bonds would not be feasible. In fact, the desire to accommodate the strips market largely led the Treasury to cease issuing callable bonds. The yields in Figure 19.3 give the entire zero-coupon yield curve. This information is very useful, as it sometimes is not possible to find suitable par bonds for all maturities to allow the computation of the zero-coupon yield curve.

Forward rate agreements (FRAs)

There is also an explicit market for forward rates. A contract based on the forward rate is known as a **forward rate agreement** (**FRA**). Forward rate agreements are typically based on **LIBOR**, which stands for "London Interbank Offered Rate," a rate at which large international banks lend funds to each other. Typically, an FRA calls for the exchange of a payment based on LIBOR at a future date in return for a payment based on a fixed rate of interest agreed on the contracting date. One can contract to either pay-fixed and receive floating or to receive-fixed and pay floating. Typically, an FRA market maker will have a spread on the fixed side of the deal to provide a profit margin.[6]

For example, consider an FRA market maker who agrees today to pay six-month LIBOR in six months in exchange for a fixed interest payment at an annual rate of 5 percent and a notional principal of $20 million. (If the market maker is willing to take the receive-fixed side of the deal at 5.00 percent, she might be willing to take the pay-fixed side at only 4.96 percent. Spreads of four basis points are typical in this market.) When the FRA expires in six months, assume that six-month LIBOR stands at 5.8 percent. Payments on the FRA would be the interest rate times the fraction of the year times the notional principal:

Receive-fixed: $0.050 \times 0.5 \times \$20,000,000 = \$500,000$
Pay-floating: $-0.058 \times 0.5 \times \$20,000,000 = -\$580,000$
Net payment: $-\$80,000$

In this case, the market maker would be obligated to make a net payment of $80,000. In the FRA market, it is customary for settlement amounts to be "determined in advance and paid in arrears." The payment based on the FRA in our example would be due six months after the date of determination, because six months was the maturity of the interest rate being used in the FRA. Thus, FRAs based on three-month LIBOR are paid three months after the determination date, FRAs based on six-month LIBOR are paid six months after the determination date, and so on.

Figure 19.3 Quotations for U.S. Treasury strips

U.S. Treasury Strips

MATURITY		TYPE	BID	ASKED	CHG	ASK YLD	MATURITY		TYPE	BID	ASKED	CHG	ASK YLD
Aug	06	ci	99:23	99:24	...	4.49	Aug	10	np	81:29	81:30	...	4.97
Aug	06	np	99:23	99:24	...	4.57	Aug	10	bp	81:27	81:28	...	4.99
Nov	06	ci	98:16	98:17	...	4.87	Nov	10	ci	81:06	81:07	...	4.89
Nov	06	np	98:14	98:15	1	5.09	Nov	10	bp	80:28	80:28	...	4.99
Nov	06	np	98:14	98:15	...	5.11	Feb	11	ci	79:31	80:00	...	4.96
Feb	07	ci	97:07	97:08	...	5.06	Feb	11	np	80:00	80:01	...	4.95
Feb	07	bp	97:05	97:06	...	5.20	May	11	ci	79:17	79:18	...	4.81
Feb	07	np	97:05	97:05	...	5.22	Aug	11	ci	77:30	77:31	...	4.98
May	07	ci	96:00	96:01	...	5.10	Aug	11	np	78:02	78:03	...	4.95
May	07	np	95:29	95:30	...	5.20	Nov	11	ci	77:27	77:28	2	4.77
May	07	np	95:30	95:30	...	5.20	Feb	12	ci	76:01	76:01	...	4.99
Aug	07	ci	94:25	94:26	...	5.11	Feb	12	np	76:02	76:03	...	4.98
Aug	07	np	94:22	94:23	...	5.19	May	12	ci	75:19	75:20	...	4.87
Aug	07	np	94:23	94:23	...	5.18	Aug	12	ci	74:09	74:09	...	4.97
Aug	07	np	94:23	94:24	...	5.18	Aug	12	np	74:06	74:07	...	4.99
Nov	07	ci	93:20	93:21	...	5.08	Nov	12	ci	73:07	73:08	...	5.00
Nov	07	np	93:17	93:18	...	5.16	Nov	12	np	73:06	73:06	...	5.01
Feb	08	ci	92:17	92:18	...	5.03	Feb	13	ci	72:07	72:07	1	5.02
Feb	08	np	92:15	92:16	...	5.08	Feb	13	np	72:10	72:10	1	5.00
Feb	08	np	92:14	92:15	...	5.10	May	13	ci	71:09	71:10	1	5.03
Feb	08	np	92:13	92:13	...	5.13	May	13	np	71:14	71:14	1	5.00
May	08	ci	91:12	91:13	...	5.04	Aug	13	ci	70:21	70:21	1	4.98
May	08	bp	91:09	91:10	...	5.09	Aug	13	np	70:17	70:18	1	5.01
May	08	np	91:09	91:10	...	5.09	Nov	13	ci	69:19	69:20	1	5.02
May	08	np	91:09	91:10	...	5.10	Nov	13	np	69:18	69:19	1	5.03
Aug	08	ci	90:08	90:09	...	5.04	Feb	14	ci	68:16	68:17	1	5.06
Aug	08	np	90:06	90:06	...	5.08	Feb	14	np	68:22	68:23	1	5.03
Aug	08	bp	90:09	90:09	...	5.02	May	14	ci	67:19	67:20	1	5.07
Nov	08	ci	89:02	89:03	...	5.07	May	14	np	67:27	67:28	1	5.03
Nov	08	np	89:02	89:03	...	5.07	Aug	14	ci	66:24	66:24	1	5.08
Nov	08	np	89:02	89:03	...	5.07	Aug	14	np	67:00	67:01	1	5.03
Nov	08	bp	89:03	89:03	...	5.07	Nov	14	ci	65:26	65:27	1	5.09
Feb	09	ci	88:01	88:02	...	5.03	Nov	14	np	66:05	66:06	1	5.03
Feb	09	np	88:00	88:00	−1	5.06	Feb	15	ci	64:31	64:31	1	5.10
Feb	09	bp	88:00	88:00	...	5.05	Feb	15	bp	65:06	65:07	1	5.06
May	09	ci	86:30	86:30	−1	5.05	Feb	15	np	65:11	65:12	1	5.03
May	09	np	87:01	87:02	−1	5.00	May	15	ci	64:07	64:08	1	5.09
May	09	np	86:31	87:00	−1	5.02	May	15	np	64:16	64:17	1	5.04
May	09	np	86:31	87:00	−1	5.03	Aug	15	ci	63:10	63:10	1	5.11
Aug	09	ci	85:30	85:31	−1	5.01	Aug	15	bp	63:17	63:18	1	5.07
Aug	09	np	85:29	85:30	−1	5.02	Aug	15	np	63:23	63:24	2	5.03
Aug	09	bp	85:29	85:30	−1	5.02	Nov	15	ci	62:12	62:12	1	5.13
Nov	09	ci	84:26	84:27	−1	5.03	Nov	15	bp	62:19	62:20	1	5.09
Nov	09	bp	84:28	84:28	−1	5.02	Nov	15	np	62:27	62:28	1	5.05
Nov	09	np	84:28	84:29	−1	5.01	Feb	16	ci	61:18	61:18	...	5.14
Feb	10	ci	83:31	84:00	...	4.96	Feb	16	bp	61:29	61:29	1	5.08
Feb	10	bp	83:27	83:28	...	5.01	Feb	16	np	62:03	62:04	...	5.04
Feb	10	np	83:28	83:28	...	5.00	May	16	ci	60:24	60:25	...	5.14
May	10	ci	83:00	83:01	...	4.95	May	16	np	61:10	61:11	...	5.05
May	10	np	82:28	82:28	...	4.99	May	16	bp	61:01	61:01	...	5.10
Aug	10	ci	82:03	82:04	...	4.91							

Source: *The Wall Street Journal*, July 25, 2006, p. B9. Reprinted by permission of *The Wall Street Journal*, © 2006 Dow Jones & Company, Inc. All rights reserved.

FRAs are quoted in the following manner:

term to expiration in months × term to end of period covered by agreement rate

For example, the FRA we considered above, with six months to expiration for six-month LIBOR and a fixed rate of 5 percent, would be quoted as

6 × 12   5.00%

The first number indicates the months until the FRA expires, the second indicates the number of months until the instrument presumed to underlie the FRA matures, while the difference between the two numbers shows the maturity of the presumed underlying instrument. There is no actual instrument that is delivered; instead, the presumed underlying instrument is simply an instrument of the underlying maturity that pays LIBOR. Instead of exchanging instruments, the profit or loss is settled in cash, as in our preceding example. The 5 percent in the quotation is the fixed rate of interest to be paid in exchange for LIBOR.

The rates on FRA agreements also tie in with the zero-coupon yield curve. Assume that the current six-month spot rate is 4.95 percent, and consider now the following FRA quotations that imply a rising yield curve:

6 × 12	5.00%
12 × 18	5.10
18 × 24	5.20

We adopt the following notation:

$FRA_{x,j}$ is the rate of interest on an FRA for a period beginning at time x and ending at time y
$FRA_{0,y}$ indicates a spot rate from time zero to time y

On the basis of this notation, we have the following:

$FRA_{0,6} = 0.0495$
$FRA_{6,12} = 0.0500$
$FRA_{12,18} = 0.0510$
$FRA_{18,24} = 0.0520$

Note the following equivalences:

$FRA_{x,y} = FR_{x,y} = FRF_{x,y} - 1$

We will use $FR_{x,y}$ to refer to forward rates generically and $FRA_{x,y}$ to refer to a rate on a forward rate agreement. To avoid arbitrage, the two must be equal. We also define the following:

$FRAC$ is the fraction of the year covered by the FRA
NP is the notional principal

We now want to integrate the quotation and payment mechanism of the FRA market with our technique of bootstrapping to find zero-coupon factors. In particular, we need to take into account the fact that payments occur in arrears and that the dollar amount of the payment depends on the part of the year covered by the FRA multiplied times the notional principal.

Based on the first FRA, $FRA_{0,6} = 0.0495$, to cover the period from the present to six months, the fixed-side payment would be

$$FRA_{0,6} \times FRAC \times NP = 0.0495 \times 0.5 \times \text{notional principal}$$

We have not defined the notional principal for this example because the notional principal does not affect the rates on FRAs, just the dollar amount of the payment. Therefore, in general, we may ignore the notional principal in our computations of FRA rates. We can compute the value for the first zero-coupon factor, $Z_{0,6}$, as follows:

$$Z_{0,6} = 1 + 0.5 \times 0.0495 = 1.024750$$

where $FRAC = 0.5$ reflects the half-year between payments and $FRA_{0,6} = 0.0495$ is the current LIBOR six-month spot rate. Note that the payment actually occurs at the end of the period covered by the FRA, but is based on the observation of LIBOR at the beginning of the period covered by the FRA.

The zero-coupon factor for the second payment covers 12 months, and given the value of $Z_{0,6}$, we can compute the value of $Z_{0,12}$ as

$$Z_{0,12} = Z_{0,6} \times (1 + 0.5 \times 0.0500) = 1.050369$$

where 0.5 reflects the half-year between payments and 0.0500 is the rate on the 6×12 FRA. Values for $Z_{0,18}$ and $Z_{0,24}$ follow similarly:

$$Z_{0,18} = Z_{0,12} \times (1 + 0.5 \times 0.0510) = 1.050369 \times 1.0255 = 1.077153$$
$$Z_{0,24} = Z_{0,18} \times (1 + 0.5 \times 0.0520) = 1.077153 \times 1.0260 = 1.105159$$

Starting with $Z_{0,6}$ and using the bootstrapping technique, we have found all of the zero-coupon factors that we need. As we will see later in this chapter, FRA agreements tie in closely with interest rate options, as do the pricing conventions for the FRA market that we have just discussed. These zero-coupon factors and FRA rates are also important for understanding the swaps market, which is explored in later chapters.

The option-adjusted spread (OAS)

With the background presented above on the market for interest rate options and the term structure of interest rates, we now turn to analytic techniques for valuing options. The first of these is the option-adjusted spread. The **option-adjusted spread (OAS)** is the yield differential between a corporate bond (or mortgage instrument) with an embedded option and a Treasury bond. The Treasury bond is chosen so that the two instruments will have essentially similar maturity and coupon characteristics. So defined, the yield spread provides a measure of the option's value and the default risk differential between the Treasury and the bond (or mortgage instrument). Sometimes the OAS is defined between two securities of the same default risk, coupon, and maturity. In this case, the OAS would embrace only the yield differential due to the option feature inherent in one of the two securities. Because it is difficult to find comparable bond or mortgage instruments, it is more common to compute the OAS relative to a Treasury instrument.

The OAS is often applied to corporate bonds with call provisions and to home mortgages with the option for the home-owner to prepay the mortgage. In each case, the spread is typically calculated as a spread between the yield on the instrument with the embedded option and a Treasury instrument with similar cash flows. The OAS is the number of basis points that must be added to the yield on the Treasury instrument so that the spread-adjusted Treasury and the corporate bond or mortgage will have the same price.

As an illustration of this technique, consider a 20-year corporate semiannual coupon bond with a coupon rate of 10 percent. The bond is callable in five years and is currently priced at 97.25 percent of par. The corresponding yield to maturity for this bond is 10.3278 percent. The call feature embedded in this bond obviously has a value to the issuer, but the value of that option is unclear. Under the OAS technology, a spread to Treasury is computed to provide a metric of that value. Consider also a T-bond with a 10 percent coupon and a 20-year remaining maturity. The T-bond is priced at 108.533 percent of par and yields 9.0681 percent. Thus we have the following:

Instrument	Price	Yield to maturity
Callable corporate bond	97.250	10.3278%
Treasury bond	108.533	9.0681%

The promised cash flows on the two instruments are the same. The difference in the yield to maturity stems from two sources: the difference in default risk and the presence of the call feature on the corporate bond.

Table 19.5 presents detailed information on these two bonds. The first column of the table lists the 40 periods of the life of each bond, while the second column sets out the semiannual cash flows that are common to each bond. The third column shows the zero-coupon annual rate appropriate to each period, which reflects a term structure assumed for this example. The short-term rate is 8 percent, rising to a rate of 10.7 percent over the 20 years of remaining maturity on the bonds. Column 4 shows the zero-coupon factor for each semiannual period, while column 5 presents the zero-coupon factor appropriate to the cash flow for each period. The zero-coupon rates in column 3 give a unique discounting rate for each period's cash flow. This reflects the shape of the yield curve, instead of discounting flows from various times at a single yield to maturity. The zero-coupon factors of column 5 are the $Z_{0,t}$ terms for this particular term structure environment that we saw how to find earlier in this chapter.

Column 6 shows the present values of each of the cash flows from the T-bond, which total 108.533. (Each element in column 6 is just the corresponding cash flow from column 2 divided by the appropriate factor from column 5.) Given the first six columns of information in Table 19.5, we are now prepared to find the OAS. Specifically, we need to find the number of basis points to add to each zero-coupon semiannual factor in column 4 that will equate the price of the T-bond and the price of the corporate bond.

This is found by an iterative search. When 64.46 basis points are added to the zero-coupon semiannual discount rate for each period, the present value of the Treasury cash flows will be 97.25, which is the same price as the corporate bond. Column 7 of Table 19.5 shows the zero-coupon factor that results from adding the 64.46 basis points to each semiannual discount rate, while column 8 shows the resulting present values of each cash flow. With 64.46 basis points

Table 19.5   Data for the callable corporate bond and the Treasury bond

(1) Period	(2) Cash flow	(3) Zero-coupon Treasury rate	(4) Zero-coupon semiannual Treasury discount factor	(5) Zero-coupon Treasury discount factor	(6) Present value of T-bond cash flows	(7) OAS-adjusted discount factor	(8) Present value of AS-adjusted Treasury cash flows
1	5	0.080000	1.0400	1.0400	4.8077	1.046446	4.7781
2	5	0.081631	1.0408	1.0824	4.6192	1.095902	4.5625
3	5	0.082096	1.0410	1.1269	4.4370	1.147950	4.3556
4	5	0.083242	1.0416	1.1738	4.2597	1.203129	4.1558
5	5	0.084439	1.0422	1.2233	4.0872	1.261679	3.9630
6	5	0.084882	1.0424	1.2753	3.9208	1.323359	3.7783
7	5	0.085351	1.0427	1.3297	3.7603	1.388364	3.6014
8	5	0.086052	1.0430	1.3869	3.6052	1.457049	3.4316
9	5	0.087164	1.0436	1.4473	3.4546	1.529942	3.2681
10	5	0.087926	1.0440	1.5110	3.3091	1.607064	3.1113
11	5	0.089075	1.0445	1.5783	3.1680	1.688998	2.9603
12	5	0.090063	1.0450	1.6493	3.0315	1.775943	2.8154
13	5	0.090536	1.0453	1.7240	2.9002	1.867783	2.6770
14	5	0.091434	1.0457	1.8028	2.7735	1.965212	2.5443
15	5	0.092050	1.0460	1.8858	2.6514	2.068328	2.4174
16	5	0.092425	1.0462	1.9729	2.5343	2.177243	2.2965
17	5	0.092640	1.0463	2.0643	2.4221	2.292127	2.1814
18	5	0.093304	1.0467	2.1606	2.3142	2.413835	2.0714
19	5	0.093427	1.0467	2.2616	2.2109	2.542153	1.9668
20	5	0.094332	1.0472	2.3682	2.1113	2.678442	1.8668
21	5	0.095423	1.0477	2.4812	2.0151	2.823499	1.7709
22	5	0.096137	1.0481	2.6005	1.9227	2.977420	1.6793
23	5	0.096262	1.0481	2.7256	1.8344	3.139918	1.5924
24	5	0.096791	1.0484	2.8576	1.7497	3.312116	1.5096
25	5	0.097595	1.0488	2.9970	1.6683	3.495088	1.4306
26	5	0.098334	1.0492	3.1443	1.5902	3.689460	1.3552
27	5	0.099000	1.0495	3.3000	1.5152	3.895870	1.2834
28	5	0.099261	1.0496	3.4638	1.4435	4.114336	1.2153
29	5	0.100178	1.0501	3.6373	1.3747	4.346940	1.1502
30	5	0.100982	1.0505	3.8209	1.3086	4.594440	1.0883
31	5	0.101899	1.0509	4.0156	1.2451	4.858140	1.0292
32	5	0.102798	1.0514	4.2220	1.1843	5.139157	0.9729
33	5	0.103538	1.0518	4.4406	1.1260	5.438332	0.9194
34	5	0.103917	1.0520	4.6713	1.0704	5.755954	0.8687
35	5	0.104388	1.0522	4.9151	1.0173	6.093481	0.8205
36	5	0.105145	1.0526	5.1735	0.9665	6.453108	0.7748
37	5	0.105323	1.0527	5.4459	0.9181	6.834534	0.7316
38	5	0.105691	1.0528	5.7337	0.8720	7.239762	0.6906
39	5	0.106441	1.0532	6.0389	0.8280	7.671733	0.6517
40	105	0.106995	1.0535	6.3620	16.5044	8.131603	12.9126

Figure 19.4   Yield curves for the Treasury bond and the callable bond

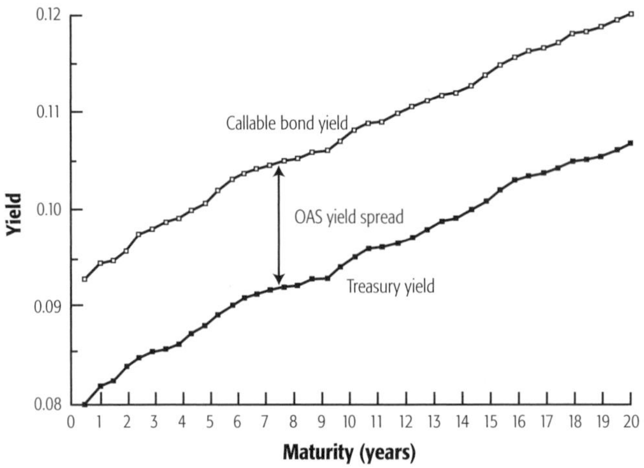

being the semiannual OAS, the annualized OAS is just twice that, or 128.92 basis points. Figure 19.4 shows the yield curves for the Treasury and the callable corporate bonds. They have the same shape, but the callable bond yield curve lies 128.92 basis points above the T-bond curve.

The basic procedure for finding OAS can be elaborated more fully. For example, one might consider the effect of varying interest rate environments on the instruments, such as a steepening yield curve or a downward-sloping yield curve. Also, the potential exercise of the embedded option under different interest rate scenarios can affect the relative spread of the instrument with the embedded option versus Treasuries. For home mortgages, prepayment can occur at any time, so the incentives to prepay under different interest rate regimes can be analyzed. These problems are often tackled using various kinds of simulation analysis. For example, one might specify a probability distribution for possible changes in short-term interest rates and then conduct Monte Carlo analyses to generate numerous interest rate paths and the corresponding price paths for the bonds. In fact, there is quite an active industry in analyzing instruments with embedded options, particularly in the mortgage arena.[7]

The Black model

In addition to options embedded in debt instruments, a number of different types of "free-standing" interest rate options exist, and these can be valued directly. This section explores the Black model, which serves as an industry benchmark for the valuation of many types of interest rate options. As we will see, it is a direct extension of the Black–Scholes–Merton model and our previous discussion of options on futures. Chapter 13 introduced Merton's extension of the Black–Scholes model to pertain to options on underlying goods paying a dividend at a continuous rate:

The Merton model

$$c_t^M = e^{-\delta(T-t)}S_t N(d_1^M) - Xe^{-r(T-t)}N(d_2^M)$$

$$d_1^M = \frac{\ln\left(\dfrac{S_t}{X}\right) + (r - \delta + 0.5\sigma^2)(T - t)}{\sigma\sqrt{T - t}}$$

$$d_2^M = d_1^M - \sigma\sqrt{T - t}$$

(19.4)

where δ is the continuous dividend rate on the stock.

In Chapter 16, we noted that Fischer Black extended the Black–Scholes–Merton model to options on futures contracts. The rate at which the spot price grows, r, takes the place of δ, and the futures price takes the place of the stock price in Merton's model. In other words, for futures on commodities that conform to the cost of carry model, $\delta = r$.[8] When we make this substitution in Equation 16.1, the formula becomes considerably simpler due to the equivalence of δ and r. For European futures options, the prices of the futures call, c_t^F, and put, p_t^F, are given by the Black model:

The Black model

$$c_t^F = e^{-r(T-t)}[F_t N(d_1^F) - XN(d_2^F)]$$

$$p_t^F = e^{-r(T-t)}[XN(-d_2^F) - F_t N(-d_1^F)]$$

$$d_1^F = \frac{\ln\left(\dfrac{F_t}{X}\right) + 0.5\sigma^2(T - t)}{\sigma\sqrt{T - t}}$$

$$d_2^F = d_1^F - \sigma\sqrt{T - t}$$

(19.5)

Equation 19.5 employs the standard deviation of the futures price. If we compare the Merton model and the Black model carefully, we see that there are only two differences. The first difference is that the futures price F_t takes the place of the stock price, S_t. The second difference concerns the interest rate. We consider each difference in turn.

In Chapter 3, we saw that futures and forward prices are not necessarily identical. Differences in the two prices are due to varying interest rate patterns and their effect on the daily settlement cash flows of futures. These differences tend to be statistically significant, but economically small. In the Black model, the futures price appears as a proxy for the forward price of the good at the expiration date of the futures. This is tantamount to assuming one of two things. First, it may be regarded as assuming that interest rates are nonstochastic, so that futures and forward prices are strictly equal. Second, it may be regarded as assuming that the difference between the futures price and forward price is not economically significant, so that the futures price is a good proxy for the forward price. In practical terms, the assumptions are not onerous; the Black model works extremely well for many interest rate options.

The Black model, as developed and as specified above, pertains specifically to options on futures. However, because the futures price is being interpreted as a forward price, the model holds equally well for any forward price. For example, a forward rate of interest or the forward price of a bond could take the role of F_t in the Black model. When the terminal price of the underlying good at the expiration of the option is distributed log-normally, the Black model applies.

We will consider a variety of applications and extensions of the Black model. Because the good underlying the futures contract is assumed to obey the cost-of-carry relationship, the interest rate principally drops out of the equation. Comparing Equations 19.4 and 19.5, we see that r appears in both the d_1^M and the d_2^M terms. In the Black model, r does not appear in either the d_1^F term or the d_2^F term. In fact, r appears in the Black model only in the discounting of the payoffs from the option expiration to the present.

The second difference between the Merton model and the Black model concerns the interest rate term, r. In the Black model, r is still assumed to be constant, but this assumption has little effect on the model's applicability to options on interest rate futures. The payoffs on the option depend largely on the $N(d_1^F)$ and $N(d_2^F)$ terms, but the interest rate has dropped out of these terms. Assuming that r is constant for the purposes of discounting the payoffs from expiration to the present, it is a small matter that is unlikely to affect the model value of the option to any significant degree. We may also use the zero-coupon factor for computing the present value of the option payoff. In that case, $1/Z_{t,T}$ would replace the term $e^{-r(T-t)}$ in Equation 19.5, giving the following:

$$c_t^F = \frac{1}{Z_{t,T}} [F_t N(d_1^F) - X N(d_2^F)]$$

$$P_t^F = \frac{1}{Z_{t,T}} [X N(-d_2^F) - F_t N(-d_1^F)]$$

(19.6)

Because of its wide applicability, accuracy in matching market prices, and relative mathematical simplicity, the Black model is widely used in industry to price options on interest rate futures as well as other interest rate options. In fact, it provides an industry benchmark against which more complicated models are measured. However, we should bear in mind that the Black model, as an outgrowth of the Black–Scholes–Merton model, is a model for European options.

Applications of the Black model

In this section, we apply the Black model to a variety of interest rate options. As discussed earlier in this chapter, a large market exists for options on interest rate futures, so we consider an application of the Black model to options on T-bond futures. The Black model also applies directly to a European option on a bond. Earlier in this chapter, we discussed forward rates and the market for FRAs. In this section, we also evaluate options on FRAs, which are known as calls and puts on LIBOR. All of these applications are well suited to the Black model.

Options on T-bond futures

As discussed above, and as elaborated in Chapter 16, there is a robust market for options on interest rate futures. T-bond futures and options on T-bond futures trade on the CBOT. The T-bond futures contract has $100,000 of bond principal as the underlying good, with the specification that the deliverable bonds are of a maturity greater than or equal to 15 years. Prices are quoted as a percentage of the par value of the underlying bonds. (Chapters 5 and 6 provide considerable detail on the institutional features and pricing of T-bond futures.) T-bond futures options trade with expirations tied to each futures expiration and have prices expressed as a percentage of par. Futures options generally expire in the latter part of the month before the corresponding futures expires.

As an example, assume that today is February 20, and consider an option on the September T-bond futures. The option will expire in six months on August 20. (As we are not interested presently in day count conventions, we treat the expiration as 0.5 years.) The current T-bond futures price is 115–11 (that is, $115 + 11/32$ percent of par = 115.34375). The standard deviation of the futures price is 0.15. This standard deviation could be determined from an analysis of recent T-bond futures prices or as an implied volatility (for details on volatility estimation, see Chapter 13). The current short-term interest rate is 6.05 percent. The yield curve is slightly upward sloping, so we assume that the six-month zero-coupon factor is $Z_{0,6} = 1.031746$. We will price a call and a put, each with a strike price of 110.

Applying the Black model from Equation 19.5, we first compute d_1^F and d_2^F:

$$d_1^F = \frac{\ln\left(\dfrac{F_t}{X}\right) + 0.5\sigma^2(T-t)}{\sigma\sqrt{T-t}} = \frac{\ln\left(\dfrac{115.34375}{110}\right) + (0.5 \times 0.15^2) \times 0.5}{0.15 \times \sqrt{0.5}} = 0.500268$$

$$d_2^F = d_1^F - \sigma\sqrt{T-t} = 0.500268 - 0.106066 = 0.394202$$

Finding the cumulative normal values for the put and call, we have $N(d_1^F) = 0.691557$, $N(d_2^F) = 0.653284$, $N(-d_1^F) = 0.308443$, and $N(-d_2^F) = 0.346716$.

Assuming continuous discounting at the short-term rate of 6.05 percent, we have the following:

$$c_t^F = e^{-r(T-t)}[F_t N(d_1^F) - X N(d_2^F)]$$
$$= e^{-0.0605 \times 0.5}(115.34375 \times 0.691557 - 110 \times 0.653284)$$
$$= 7.6700$$

$$p_t^F = e^{-r(T-t)}[X N(-d_2^F) - F_t N(-d_1^F)]$$
$$= e^{-0.0605 \times 0.5}(110 \times 0.346716 - 115.34375 \times 0.308443)$$
$$= 2.4855$$

If we wanted to take account of the shape of the term structure in pricing these options, we would use our zero-coupon factor, $Z_{0,6} = 1.031746$:

$$c_t^F = \frac{1}{1.031746}[F_t N(d_1^F) - X N(d_2^F)]$$
$$= 0.9623 \times (115.34375 \times 0.691557 - 110 \times 0.653284)$$
$$= 7.6623$$

$$p_t^F = \frac{1}{1.031746}[X N(-d_2^F) - F_t N(-d_1^F)]$$
$$= 0.969231 \times (110 \times 0.346716 - 115.34375 \times 0.308443)$$
$$= 2.4830$$

Because the term structure is upward sloping, the prices reflecting the shape of the term structure are slightly lower than the prices based on the short-term rate. In our example, the term structure was only modestly upward sloping, so the price difference was quite small—less than one cent on each option. This outcome illustrates that, in general, option prices are not very sensitive to the discounting of the payoff back to the present.

European bond options

We now explore the application of the Black model to European bond options. A bond option is simply an option with a bond as the underlying good. For example, the underlying good might be a Treasury bond or note.

Applying the Black model to value an option on a bond presents three complications. First, the input price to the model should be the forward price of the bond. Second, the application of the model must account for accrued interest and any coupon payments between the valuation date and the expiration of the option. Third, the input volatility should be the volatility of the forward bond price. We consider each of these issues in turn.

The forward price of the bond

In our discussion of the Black model, we noted that the input price for the underlying good is the forward price of that good for the expiration date of the option. In applying the Black model to futures, this was not a particular problem, because the futures price is immediately observable and is closely analogous to a forward price anyway. For typical bonds, there is no quoted forward price. Therefore, application of the Black model to value options on bonds must address the issue of finding the forward price of the underlying bond. We could find the forward price of the bond by looking to the term structure of interest rates. There are two ways of dealing with this problem. First, we could use the zero-coupon yield curve to value the bond as of the expiration date of the option. Second, we could take the present bond price and compound it forward to the expiration date of the option using the term structure of interest rates between the present date and the expiration date of the option. If the bond pays any coupon payments between the valuation date of the option and the option's expiration, we will have to take these into account.

Accrued interest and coupon payments

Bond prices are typically quoted without accrued interest. To apply the Black model successfully, we need to focus on the actual cash flows that are at stake. Therefore, if the bond price is quoted without accrued interest, we will have to take the accruals into account. When the underlying bond is a coupon bond, there will likely be coupon payments between the time the option is being valued and the option expiration. This will affect the estimation of the forward price of the underlying good. This situation is really analogous to pricing an option on a dividend paying stock. Payments of intervening dividends on a stock or intervening coupons on a bond both represent a "leakage of value" from the underlying good that must be considered. If we use the term structure to value the bond as of the expiration date of the option, we can ignore the intervening coupons, because we are valuing the bond at a date beyond any of these intervening coupon payments. However, if we use the present price of the bond and compound it forward to the expiration date of the option to find the forward bond price, we will need to reduce the present price of the bond by the present value of the intervening coupons. This adjusted bond price—the current cash price of the bond minus the present value of any intervening coupon payments—can be compounded to the expiration date of the option to find the forward price of the bond. These two techniques should give exactly the same forward price.

The input volatility

The correct volatility for the model is the volatility of the forward bond price. Like the forward price of the bond, the volatility of the forward price is not immediately observable. It will require estimation. Usually, data on bond yields are available, and we can use bond yield volatility to estimate the volatility of the forward bond price by considering how the forward bond price would respond to a change in yields. That bond yield can be used to estimate the volatility of the forward bond price.

A comprehensive European bond option example

All of the complications associated with applying the Black model to value a European bond option can be illustrated by working through an extended example. Consider a European bond option that expires in seven months on a T-note that matures in 28 months and has a semi-annual coupon rate of 8 percent. The exercise price on the option is 1,020.00. This note has two months of accrued interest and the following remaining cash flows, assuming a par value of $1,000:

Months	Cash flow (assuming par value of 1,000)
4	40
10	40
16	40
22	40
28	1,040

Table 19.6 presents information on two term structure environments for a 48-month horizon. For this example, we will use the upward-sloping yield curve, presented in column 2 of Table 19.6. The third column of the table shows the appropriate zero-coupon factor for each month, and we will use monthly compounding for all calculations in this example. Based on the cash flows stated above and the yield curve data of Table 19.6, the actual value of the bond is as follows:

$$P_0 = \frac{40}{1.0190} + \frac{40}{1.0493} + \frac{40}{1.0818} + \frac{40}{1.1166} + \frac{1,040}{1.1538} = \$1,051.54$$

With two months having elapsed since the last coupon payment, the accrued interest on the bond is $0.3333 \times \$40 = \$13.33$. The corresponding quoted price of the bond should be $1,038.21, the present value of the future cash flows minus the accrued interest of 13.33.

The forward price of the bond

We need the forward price of the bond seven months from now. During that seven months, the bond will pay a coupon. This is directly analogous to a dividend on the stock. Both the coupon payment on the bond and the dividend payment on the stock reduce the future value of both instruments from what they would have been without the payment. Therefore, in projecting the forward price of the bond, we need to take that coupon payment into account.[9] We can use the current cash price to find this forward price by subtracting the present value of the intervening coupons and compounding this result forward for seven months:

forward bond price = (current cash price − PV of intervening coupons) × $Z_{0,7}$
$$= (1,051.54 - 39.25) \times 1.0339$$
$$= \$1,046.61$$

As an alternative, we can find the forward bond price for the expiration date of the option, by using the term structure to compute the bond price as of that date. Seven months from now, the bond will be between coupon dates, with three months having elapsed since the last coupon

Table 19.6 Sample upward and downward yield curve data (monthly compounding)

Term to maturity (months)	Upward-sloping curve		Downward-sloping curve	
	Annualized par yield	Zero-coupon discount factor	Annualized par yield	Zero-coupon discount factor
1	0.055200	1.0046	0.078000	1.0065
2	0.055670	1.0093	0.078343	1.0131
3	0.056528	1.0142	0.077895	1.0196
4	0.056594	1.0190	0.077842	1.0262
5	0.056814	1.0239	0.077711	1.0328
6	0.057108	1.0289	0.077542	1.0394
7	0.057278	1.0339	0.077516	1.0461
8	0.057513	1.0390	0.077295	1.0527
9	0.057665	1.0441	0.077195	1.0594
10	0.057870	1.0493	0.077069	1.0661
11	0.058113	1.0546	0.076923	1.0728
12	0.058291	1.0599	0.076854	1.0796
13	0.058504	1.0653	0.076678	1.0863
14	0.058742	1.0708	0.076571	1.0931
15	0.058856	1.0762	0.076378	1.0998
16	0.059072	1.0818	0.076248	1.1066
17	0.059244	1.0874	0.076108	1.1134
18	0.059439	1.0931	0.076016	1.1203
19	0.059652	1.0989	0.075858	1.1271
20	0.059827	1.1047	0.075745	1.1340
21	0.060020	1.1106	0.075623	1.1409
22	0.060227	1.1166	0.075493	1.1478
23	0.060402	1.1226	0.075357	1.1547
24	0.060590	1.1287	0.075256	1.1617
25	0.060750	1.1348	0.075108	1.1686
26	0.060962	1.1411	0.074993	1.1756
27	0.061144	1.1474	0.074872	1.1826
28	0.061337	1.1538	0.074746	1.1896
29	0.061537	1.1603	0.074615	1.1966
30	0.061713	1.1668	0.074481	1.2036
31	0.061896	1.1734	0.074343	1.2106
32	0.062116	1.1802	0.074230	1.2177
33	0.062311	1.1870	0.074113	1.2248
34	0.062511	1.1939	0.073966	1.2318
35	0.062663	1.2007	0.073842	1.2389
36	0.062872	1.2078	0.073716	1.2460
37	0.063035	1.2148	0.073586	1.2531
38	0.063227	1.2220	0.073477	1.2603
39	0.063399	1.2292	0.073343	1.2674
40	0.063576	1.2365	0.073207	1.2745
41	0.063755	1.2439	0.073090	1.2817
42	0.063937	1.2514	0.072970	1.2889
43	0.064122	1.2590	0.072849	1.2961
44	0.064308	1.2667	0.072725	1.3033
45	0.064496	1.2745	0.072600	1.3105
46	0.064666	1.2823	0.072473	1.3177
47	0.064856	1.2903	0.072362	1.3250
48	0.065030	1.2983	0.072232	1.3322

payment. The forward bond price will be the present value of the remaining cash flows valued at that date seven months from now:

$$\text{forward bond price} = \frac{C_{10}}{Z_{10}/Z_7} + \frac{C_{16}}{Z_{16}/Z_7} + \frac{C_{22}}{Z_{22}/Z_7} + \frac{C_{28}}{Z_{28}/Z_7}$$

$$= \frac{40}{1.0493/1.0339} + \frac{40}{1.0818/1.0339} + \frac{40}{1.1166/1.0339} + \frac{1,040}{1.1538/1.0339}$$

$$= \$1,046.61$$

Either of these equivalent methods may be used to find the appropriate forward bond price to serve as the price input to the model.

The volatility of the forward bond price

We also need the volatility of the forward bond price. As mentioned above, the volatility of the forward bond price is not immediately available. Furthermore, there is not even a series of forward bond prices that we could use to compute an estimated volatility from historical data. (This contrasts with the futures market, in which futures price quotations are available each day and can be used to estimate the volatility of the futures price.) However, there is a variety of time series for yields on bonds of various types, such as Treasury issues of various maturities and AAA bond yields, as well as many others. At the expiration of the option, the underlying T-bond will have a maturity of 21 months. This is fairly close to a two-year maturity. Let us assume that the annualized standard deviation of the two-year Treasury bond yield is 0.20. To emphasize, this is the volatility of the yield, not the bond itself. We can use this yield volatility to estimate the volatility of the bond price to serve as the volatility input for the Black model.

Macaulay's duration (D) and Macaulay's modified duration (MD) of a bond are as follows:

$$D = \left\{ \sum_{t=1}^{M} t \left[\frac{C_t}{(1 + YTM)^t} \right] \right\} \Big/ (\text{bond price})$$

$$MD = \left\{ \sum_{t=1}^{M} t \left[\frac{C_t}{(1 + YTM)^t} \right] \right\} \Big/ \left(\frac{\text{bond price}}{1 + r_t} \right) \tag{19.7}$$

where C_{tr} is the cash flow from the bond at time t and YTM is the bond's yield to maturity expressed in the same time unit as t. (Note that the modified duration is just duration divided by $1 + r$.) Then, the resulting duration measure will be expressed in the same time units as t.[10] The duration price change formula is as follows:

$$\Delta P \approx -MDP\Delta AYTM \tag{19.8}$$

where $AYTM$ in Equation 19.8 is the yield to maturity expressed in annual terms. This holds for a parallel shift in the yield curve, and results in an approximate price change that is quite close to the actual price change. From the price change formula, it follows that

$$\frac{\Delta P}{P} \approx -MD \times AYTM \times \frac{\Delta AYTM}{AYTM} \tag{19.9}$$

$$\sigma_P \approx MD \times AYTM \times \sigma_{AYTM}$$

Thus, given the annual yield to maturity of the forward bond (*AYTM*), we can compute the modified duration (*MD*). Then, given the standard deviation of the forward bond yield (σ_{AYTM}), we can approximate the standard deviation of the forward bond price (σ_P).

For our forward bond, the monthly yield to maturity is 0.005231, which satisfies the forward bond pricing equation:

$$\text{forward bond price} = \frac{40}{(1 + YTM)^3} + \frac{40}{(1 + YTM)^9} + \frac{40}{(1 + YTM)^{15}} + \frac{1{,}040}{(1 + YTM)^{21}}$$

$$YTM = 0.005231$$

and the annualized yield to maturity, continuing to assume monthly compounding, is 0.064607. Next, we find the *MD*:

$$MD = \left[\frac{3 \times 40}{(1 + YTM)^3} + \frac{9 \times 40}{(1 + YTM)^9} + \frac{15 \times 40}{(1 + YTM)^{15}} + \frac{21 \times 1{,}040}{(1 + YTM)^{21}}\right] \Big/ \left(\frac{\text{forward bond price}}{1 + YTM}\right)$$

$$= 20{,}590.07/(1{,}046.61/1.005231)$$

$$= 19.78$$

The *MD* measured in months is 19.78, so the annualized *MD* = 19.78/12 = 1.6483.[11] Recalling that we are assuming a standard deviation of 0.20 for the two-year Treasury yields, we have, in annual terms,

$$\sigma_P \approx MD \times AYTM \times \sigma_{AYTM} = 1.6483 \times 0.064607 \times 0.20 = 0.021298$$

We now have all of the required inputs for the Black model. The forward price is 1,046.61; the time to expiration is seven months, or 0.5833 years; the exercise price is 1,020.00; the standard deviation of the forward price is 0.021298; and the seven-month factor is 1.0339. We begin by computing the d_1^F and d_2^F terms:

$$d_1^F = \frac{\ln\left(\dfrac{F_t}{X}\right) + 0.5\sigma^2(T - t)}{\sigma\sqrt{T - t}}$$

$$= \frac{\ln\left(\dfrac{1{,}046.61}{1{,}020.00}\right) + (0.05 \times 0.021298^2) \times 0.5833}{0.021298 \times \sqrt{0.5833}}$$

$$= 1.591339$$

$$d_2^F = d_1^F - \sigma\sqrt{T - t}$$

$$= 1.591339 - 0.016266$$

$$= 1.575072$$

The cumulative normal terms that we require for both the put and the call are as follows:

$$N(d_1^F) = N(1.591339) = 0.944233$$
$$N(d_2^F) = N(1.575072) = 0.942380$$
$$N(-d_1^F) = N(-1.591339) = 0.055767$$
$$N(-d_2^F) = N(-1.57072) = 0.057620.$$

The values of the call and put are as follows:

$$c_t^F = \frac{1}{1.0339} [F_t N(d_1^F) - X N(d_2^F)]$$

$$= 0.967212 \times (1{,}046.61 \times 0.944233 - 1{,}020 \times 0.942380)$$
$$= 26.13$$

$$p_t^F = \frac{1}{1.0339} [X N(-d_2^F) - F_t N(-d_1^F)]$$

$$= 0.967212 \times (1{,}020 \times 0.057620 - 1{,}046.61 \times 0.055767)$$
$$= 0.392785$$

Therefore, the call is worth $26.13 and the put is worth $0.39.

Calls and puts on LIBOR

Earlier in this chapter, we discussed the active market in forward interest rates based on LIBOR. Market makers are active in FRAs with one-month, three-month, six-month, and one-year maturities, and will provide quotations on other maturities as well. A parallel options market exists in which calls on LIBOR and puts on LIBOR trade. For example, there is a market for calls on three-month LIBOR and for puts on one-month LIBOR. These options are generally European in form.

Payoffs for options on LIBOR
The payoff on calls and puts on LIBOR depends on the maturity of LIBOR being quoted and the notional principal. Consider first a call on three-month LIBOR with a notional principal of $1 million and an exercise price, or strike rate, of 9 percent. The call pays off if the observed three-month LIBOR rate on the expiration date of the option exceeds the strike rate. In that case, the payoff on this call equals the difference between the observed rate and the strike rate multiplied by the quarter of a year maturity of the rate, times the notional principal. For our example call option, if the observed rate is 10.5 percent, the payoff will be

$$(0.1050 - 0.0900) \times 0.25 \times \$1{,}000{,}000 = \$3{,}750$$

Let *FRAC* be the fraction of the year covered by the maturity of the underlying LIBOR instrument, let *NP* be the notional principal, and let *SR* be the strike rate. A general expression for the payoff on a call on LIBOR will be

$$\text{MAX}\{0, (\text{Observed LIBOR} - SR) \times FRAC \times NP\} \tag{19.10}$$

where Observed LIBOR is the rate observed at the expiration of the option for LIBOR of the appropriate maturity. A put on LIBOR pays off when the observed rate at expiration is less than the strike rate. The payoff for a put on LIBOR is

$$\text{MAX}\{0, (SR - \text{Observed LIBOR}) \times FRAC \times NP\} \tag{19.11}$$

For example, consider a put on one-month LIBOR with a strike rate of 8.5 percent and a notional principal of $25 million. At the expiration of the option, assume that the one-month

LIBOR rate stands at 7.03 percent and Observed LIBOR = 0.0703. The payoff on this put would be

$$(0.0850 - 0.0703) \times (1/12) \times \$25,000,000 = \$30,625$$

Determination in advance; settlement in arrears
In our discussion of FRAs, we noted that they are generally "determined in advance and settled in arrears." Thus, the payment on a six-month FRA generally occurs six months after the determination date. Calls and puts on LIBOR are generally structured in a parallel manner. The payoffs are determined at the expiration date, but the payment is made at a date that lags the determination date by the maturity of the LIBOR quotation. (When the lag between determination and payment equals the maturity of the LIBOR quotation, the lag is said to be the **natural time lag**.) Thus, the actual payoffs on our sample call and put would be three months and one month after the determination dates, respectively. In pricing calls and puts on LIBOR, we will need to take this settlement in arrears into account.

Convexity

Convexity is to bond pricing what GAMMA is to option pricing. In bond pricing, duration provides a reasonable estimate of bond price changes due to small changes in yield. But for larger changes in yield, duration does not completely describe a bond's price responsiveness because the value of duration changes with yield. Convexity describes the way in which duration changes in response to changes in yield. In other words, duration is equal to the slope of the curve describing the relationship between a bond's price and yield, whereas convexity measures the degree of curvature of the price/yield relationship. If a bond did not display any convexity, then duration alone would provide a good estimate of the sensitivity of bond prices to changes in yield.

Convexity can be either positive or negative. For a bond with positive convexity, as yields fall, the bond's price will increase at an increasing rate. As yields rise, the bond's price will fall at a decreasing rate. In other words, positive convexity implies that the value of the bond decreases slower and increases faster relative to a linear approximation. The greater the convexity, the greater is the effect. For a bond with negative convexity, as yields fall, the bond's price will increase at a decreasing rate and as yields rise, the bond's price will fall at an increasing rate.

The degree of positive or negative convexity influences the market price and yield of the bond. Compared to an identical bond with no convexity, a bond with positive convexity will sell for a higher price and lower yield. Likewise, a bond with negative convexity will have a lower price and higher yield than a bond with no convexity, all else equal. The amount of a bond price that is attributable to convexity can be thought of as the market price of convexity. Managers of bond portfolios must consider the price of convexity when evaluating the purchase or sale of a bond. The price of convexity will depend on the volatility in yields. If yields are stable, then the market price for convexity will be low. If yields are volatile, then the market price for convexity will be high.

A bond without embedded options will always display positive convexity. A bond with embedded options can display either positive or negative convexity. If the embedded option is equivalent to a long call or put position, positive convexity will result. If the embedded option is equivalent to a short call or put position, negative convexity will result. Thus, the option premium can be viewed as the price of convexity. In addition, the option's DELTA and GAMMA will assist a bond portfolio manager in controlling the duration and convexity of the overall portfolio.

The Black model and options on LIBOR

The Black model applies quite directly to calls and puts on LIBOR. The currently observed forward LIBOR (*FLIBOR*) plays the role of the futures price. Specifically, $FLIBOR_t$ is observed at time t, when the option is being valued. It is the forward LIBOR with a maturity corresponding to the maturity of the option and it is the forward rate with a time horizon that matches the expiration date of the option. Notice that $FLIBOR_t$ should be identical to the FRA rates for the same period in the future.

Using $FLIBOR_t$ in the Black model is tantamount to assuming that the forward LIBOR is log-normally distributed. The strike rate plays the role of the exercise price, while the standard deviation of the LIBOR forward rate (*FLIBOR*) of the requisite maturity is the volatility measure for the model:

$$c_t^{FLIBOR} = NP \times FRAC \times e^{-r(T+FRAC-t)}[FLIBOR_t \times N(d_1^{FLIBOR}) - SR \times N(d_2^{FLIBOR})]$$

$$p_t^{FLIBOR} = NP \times FRAC \times e^{-r(T-FRAC-t)}[SR \times N(-d_2^{FLIBOR}) - FLIBOR_t \times N(-d_1^{FLIBOR})]$$

$$d_1^{FLIBOR} = \frac{\ln\left(\dfrac{FLIBOR_t}{SR}\right) + 0.5\sigma^2(T-t)}{\sigma\sqrt{T-t}} \qquad (19.12)$$

$$d_2^{FLIBOR} = d_1^{FLIBOR} - \sigma\sqrt{T-t}$$

In this equation, we have the Black model with the following substitutions. $FLIBOR_t$ takes the role of the futures price and *SR* substitutes for the exercise price. The payoff on each option is discounted for a longer period, the time to expiration plus *FRAC*, to account for the delayed payment, and the values of each option are multiplied by *NP* (*FRAC*) to convert the values to dollar amounts.

The following equation is identical to Equation 19.12, except that it uses the zero-coupon factor instead of the continuously compounded rate to discount the payoff on the option from the payoff date (the expiration of the option plus *FRAC*) to the present:

$$c_t^{FLIBOR} = NP \times FRAC \times \frac{1}{Z_{t,T+FRAC}}[FLIBOR_t \times N(d_1^{FLIBOR}) - SR \times N(d_2^{FLIBOR})]$$

$$p_t^{FLIBOR} = NP \times FRAC \times \frac{1}{Z_{t,T+FRAC}}[SR \times N(-d_2^{FLIBOR}) - FLIBOR_t \times N(-d_1^{FLIBOR})]$$

$$\qquad (19.13)$$

$$d_1^{FLIBOR} = \frac{\ln\left(\dfrac{FLIBOR_t}{SR}\right) + 0.5\sigma^2(T-t)}{\sigma\sqrt{T-t}}$$

$$d_2^{FLIBOR} = d_1^{FLIBOR} - \sigma\sqrt{T-t}$$

Applying the Black model to options on LIBOR

As an example, consider a call and put on one-month LIBOR that both expire in eight months. The strike rate on the call and put is 7 percent. The notional principal is $10 million. From the FRA market, the historical standard deviation of the one-month LIBOR rate has been 0.23, which is our estimate of the standard deviation of *FLIBOR*. The yield curve is downward sloping, as illustrated in the last two columns of Table 19.6, which assumes monthly compounding. The one-month forward rate for a period from month eight to month nine is the value we need for $FLIBOR_t$. From Table 19.6, we see that the eight- and nine-month zero-coupon factors are 1.0527 and 1.0594. The one-month forward rate is, therefore, $1.0594/1.0527 - 1 = 0.006365$. With monthly compounding, the annualized rate is 7.9106 percent. Therefore, $FLIBOR_t = 0.079106$.

We first find the d_1^{FLIBOR} and d_2^{FLIBOR} values:

$$d_1^{FLIBOR} = \frac{\ln\left(\dfrac{FLIBOR_t}{SR}\right) + 0.5\sigma^2(T-t)}{\sigma\sqrt{T-t}}$$

$$= \frac{\ln\left(\dfrac{0.079106}{0.0700}\right) + 0.5 \times (0.23)^2 \times 0.6667}{0.23 \times \sqrt{0.6667}}$$

$$= 0.745104$$

$$d_2^{FLIBOR} = d_1^{FLIBOR} - \sigma\sqrt{T-t}$$
$$= 0.745104 - 0.187794$$
$$= 0.557310$$

The relevant cumulative probabilities are $N(d_1^{FLIBOR}) = N(0.745104) = 0.771896$, $N(d_2^{FLIBOR}) = N(0.557310) = 0.711342$, $N(-d_1^{FLIBOR}) = N(-0.745104) = 0.228104$, and $N(-d_2^{FLIBOR}) = N(-0.557310) = 0.288658$. The one-month maturity corresponds to 0.0833 years. Using our zero-coupon factor of 1.0594 to cover the nine months until payment on the options would be received, the option values according to Equation 19.13 are as follows:

$$c_t^{FLIBOR} = NP \times FRAC \times \frac{1}{Z_{0,9}}[FLIBOR_t \times N(d_1^{FLIBOR}) - SR \times N(d_2^{FLIBOR})]$$

$$= 10,000,000 \times 0.0833 \times \frac{1}{1.0594} \times (0.079106 \times 0.771896 - 0.07 \times 0.711342)$$

$$= 8,863.333$$

$$p_t^{FLIBOR} = NP \times FRAC \times \frac{1}{Z_{0,9}}[SR \times N(-d_2^{FLIBOR}) - FLIBOR_t \times N(-d_1^{FLIBOR})]$$

$$= 10,000,000 \times 0.0833 \times \frac{1}{1.0594} \times (0.07 \times 0.288658 - 0.079106 \times 0.228104)$$

$$= 1,700.8333$$

As we will see shortly, these calls and puts on LIBOR are important elements in controlling interest rate risk on loans and investments.

Term structure models

Term structure option pricing models (also called "lattice," "tree," or "whole yield curve" models) have advantages over "closed-form" option pricing models (such as the Black model). One shortcoming of closed-form models is their inability to handle discrete cash flows and early exercise decisions. To account for these features, a number of term structure models have been developed over the past 20 years that explicitly model discrete cash flows and allow for the possibility of early exercise. The simplest models assume that the movements in yield curves are related to a single rate, such as a short-term T-bill rate. These models are referred to as "one-factor models." The best known of these models are the Ho–Lee model, the Hull–White model, the Black–Derman–Toy model, and the Black–Karasinski model.

One shortcoming of one-factor models is that they assume that the entire term structure is driven by the short-term interest rate. This assumption drastically abstracts from reality. If literally true, all yields would be perfectly correlated. By implication, one could safely hedge a 30-year bond with a three-month T-bill or vice versa. However, broad movements in yields are highly correlated. A parallel shift of yields accounts for roughly 85 percent of the total variation in all yields. This is one reason for the popularity of single factor models.

To improve on single-factor models, two-factor models have been developed that, according to numerous empirical academic studies, offer a significantly better fit to the term structure. Unfortunately, valuation using such models takes much longer to compute and the models are more difficult to calibrate to the data.[12]

Forward put–call parity

In Chapter 11, we considered the put–call parity relationship for European options. For a put and call with the same expiration date and a common exercise price equal to the price of the common underlying stock, the price of the call equals the price of the put. As we saw there, the purchase of a call, the sale of a put, and the purchase of a risk-free bond paying the exercise price at the expiration of the options gives a portfolio that has exactly the same value as the underlying stock.

Put–call parity for European options, where $X = S_t$

$$c_t - p_t + Xe^{-r(T-t)} = S \tag{19.14}$$

In this section, we explore **forward put–call parity** to see how the purchase of a call and the sale of a put on an interest rate can exactly replicate a forward contract on the interest rate.

As we have observed, there is an explicit forward rate market for interest rate contracts based on LIBOR. This is the market for forward rate agreements, or FRAs, that we have already considered. We also have noted the equivalence between forward LIBOR rates ($FLIBOR_t$) and the rate for an FRA to cover the same future period. Consider now a call and a put on LIBOR with a common strike rate, SR, and underlying instrument, and the same notional principal. For a long call/short put portfolio, the payoff will be as follows:

$\text{MAX}\{0, (\text{Observed LIBOR} - SR) \times FRAC \times NP\}$
$- \text{MAX}\{0, (SR - \text{Observed LIBOR}) \times FRAC \times NP\}$
$= (\text{Observed LIBOR} - SR) \times FRAC \times NP$

where Observed LIBOR is the rate observed at the expiration of the option for the appropriate maturity, *FRAC* is the fraction of the year for the underlying instrument, and *NP* is the notional principal.

For an FRA to cover the same time period and with the same notional principal, the payoff will be

$$(\text{Observed LIBOR} - FRA) \times FRAC \times NP$$

where *FRA* is the rate on the forward rate agreement, and Observed LIBOR is the observed rate on the determination date for the forward rate agreement, for LIBOR of the appropriate maturity. For identical time periods, it must be the case that

$$FLIBOR_t = FRA_{x,y}$$

as a no-arbitrage condition. Consider now the special case in which the strike rate for the long call/short put portfolio is chosen such that

$$SR = FLIBOR_t = FRA_{x,y}$$

where the time periods for all three measures are the same.

In this special case, when the strike rate on the options is the same as the forward LIBOR rate or the rate on an FRA, the payoff on the long call/short put portfolio will be the same as the payoff on the forward rate agreement. Therefore, the long call/short put portfolio is equivalent to the forward rate agreement. This is the principle of forward put–call parity.

Forward put–call parity

$$c_t^{FLIBOR} - p_t^{FLIBOR} = 0 \tag{19.15}$$

when the common strike rate on the put and call options equals the currently prevailing forward rate, $SR = FRA_{x,y}$, and the time periods covered by the options and the forward rate agreement are the same.

This result makes sense considering that the cost of entering an FRA, negotiated at the current forward rate prevailing in the market and reflecting the current term structure, is zero, and it will pay off at the expiration date based on the observed LIBOR at that date relative to the contract rate.

To illustrate forward put–call parity, recall the previous section, where we saw that the one-month LIBOR rate eight months forward was 0.079106, based on the downward-sloping yield curve of Table 19.6. Consider now an FRA entered for that forward rate. We also consider a put and a call entered on the same terms: eight-month expiration, one-month underlying LIBOR, and a strike rate on the options equal to the forward LIBOR rate of 0.079106. Thus this example meets the condition that

$$SR = FLIBOR_t = FRA_{x,y}$$

Figure 19.5 shows the payoffs for a long call plus a short put on LIBOR for a common strike rate of 0.079106 in the upper panel. The lower panel shows the payoffs for a long position in the corresponding FRA. They are identical. Therefore, the long call/short put portfolio exactly replicates the FRA payoffs, and the option portfolio must have the same price as the FRA. Since

Figure 19.5   Payoffs for calls and puts on LIBOR and an FRA

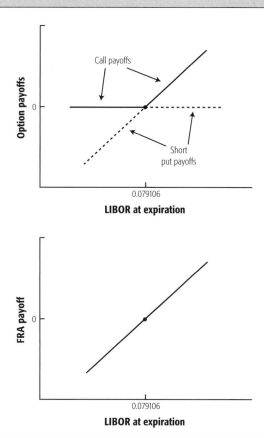

the FRA is costless, the option portfolio also must be costless. The option portfolio can be costless only when the call and put have the same price, since the portfolio is constructed by buying the call and selling the put.

To see this in yet another way, let us return to Equations 19.12 and 19.13, the equations for calls and puts on LIBOR. In the special case we are considering, the strike rate on the options equals the forward LIBOR rate. In terms of our notation, the special case is $SR = FLIBOR_t$. We first evaluate the d_1^{FLIBOR} and d_2^{FLIBOR} terms in this special circumstance. When $SR = FLIBOR_t$, replace $FLIBOR_t$ with SR:

$$d_1^{FLIBOR} = \frac{\ln\left(\dfrac{SR}{SR}\right) + 0.5\sigma^2(T - t)}{\sigma\sqrt{T - t}}$$

$$= \frac{0 + 0.5\sigma^2\sqrt{T - t}\sqrt{T - t}}{\sigma\sqrt{T - t}}$$

$$= 0.5\,\sigma\sqrt{T - t}$$

$$d_2^{FLIBOR} = d_1^{FLIBOR} - \sigma\sqrt{T-t}$$
$$= 0.5\sigma\sqrt{T-t} - \sigma\sqrt{T-t}$$
$$= -0.5\sigma\sqrt{T-t}$$
$$d_2^{FLIBOR} = -d_1^{FLIBOR}$$

In this special circumstance, when the call and put have the same underlying instrument, expiration, and strike rate, we now see that $SR = FLIBOR_t$ and $d_2^{FLIBOR} = -d_1^{FLIBOR}$. Therefore, replacing $FLIBOR_t$ with SR, and replacing d_2^{FLIBOR} with $-d_1^{FLIBOR}$, we have the following:

$$c_t^{FLIBOR} = NP \times FRAC \times e^{-r(T+FRAC-t)}[SR \times N(d_1^{FLIBOR}) - SR \times N(-d_1^{FLIBOR})]$$
$$p_t^{FLIBOR} = NP \times FRAC \times e^{-r(T+FRAC-t)}[SR \times N(d_1^{FLIBOR}) - SR \times N(-d_1^{FLIBOR})]$$

From this, it follows that the long call/short put portfolio must be worth zero:

$$c_t^{FLIBOR} - p_t^{FLIBOR} = NP \times FRAC \times e^{-r(T+FRAC-t)} \times SR$$
$$\times [N(d_1^{FLIBOR}) - N(-d_1^{FLIBOR}) - N(d_1^{FLIBOR}) + N(-d_1^{FLIBOR})]$$
$$= 0$$

because the sum of the cumulative normal probabilities in the bracketed expression is zero.

However, even though the long call/short put portfolio costs zero, the individual options may have value. They just have to have the same value. To illustrate this, we compute the value of the call and put, when the strike rate equals the forward rate of 0.079106. First, the d_1^{FLIBOR} and d_2^{FLIBOR} terms are as follows:

$$d_1^{FLIBOR} = 0.5\sigma\sqrt{T-t} = 0.5 \times 0.23 \times \sqrt{0.6667} = 0.093897$$
$$d_2^{FLIBOR} = -d_1^{FLIBOR} = -0.093897$$

The cumulative normal probabilities are $N(d_1^{FLIBOR}) = N(0.093897) = 0.537405$, $N(d_2^{FLIBOR}) = N(-0.093897) = 0.462595$, $N(-d_1^{FLIBOR}) = N(-0.093897) = 0.462595$, and $N(-d_2^{FLIBOR}) = N(0.093897) = 0.537405$. The call and put prices are as follows:

$$c_t^{FLIBOR} = NP \times FRAC \times \frac{1}{Z_{0.9}} [FLIBOR_t \times N(d_1^{FLIBOR}) - SR \times N(d_2^{FLIBOR})]$$

$$= 10,000,000 \times 0.0833 \times \frac{1}{1.0594} \times (0.079106 \times 0.537405 - 0.079106 \times 0.462595)$$

$$= 4,655.04$$

$$p_t^{FLIBOR} = NP \times FRAC \times \frac{1}{Z_{0.9}} [SR \times N(-d_2^{FLIBOR}) - FLIBOR_t \times N(-d_1^{FLIBOR})]$$

$$= 10,000,000 \times 0.0833 \times \frac{1}{1.0594} \times (0.079106 \times 0.537405 - 0.079106 \times 0.462595)$$

$$= 4,655.04$$

We now turn to applications of calls and puts on LIBOR in controlling interest rate risk.

Caps, floors, and collars

In this section, we introduce caps, floors, and collars, all of which are combinations of calls and puts on LIBOR that can be used to control interest rate risk. We begin the analysis by considering a single future period for a loan and how the cost of the loan over that period can be constrained with a single call on LIBOR or a single put on LIBOR. As we will see, these applications involve the same logic as forward put–call parity.

A caplet

Assume that a firm needs to borrow $10 million for a three-month period beginning four months from now. Assume also that today the three-month forward LIBOR for a period starting four months from now is 8 percent. In terms of our notation, $FRA_{4,7} = 0.08$. Given this financing need, there are at least two ways that the firm could arrange now to borrow these funds at a fixed rate of 8 percent:

(1) With $FRA_{4,7} = 0.08$, the firm could enter a loan agreement at a fixed rate of 8 percent for the period in question.
(2) With $FRA_{4,7} = 0.08$, the firm could enter a floating rate loan by purchasing a call and selling a put for the same period, both with a strike rate of 8 percent. From our discussion of forward put–call parity, the price of the call and put would be equal, so the long call/short put combination would be costless and the borrowing cost would be fixed at 8 percent.

Instead of pursuing either of these alternatives, the firm might merely wait to see what rate prevails for three-month LIBOR in four months. If the firm does this, it might result in paying a higher or lower rate than the 8 percent that the firm might reasonably expect to pay for its loan based on the prevailing forward rate. Whatever rate prevails, the actual interest cost of the loan will be

Observed LIBOR $\times$ 1/4 $\times$ $10,000,000

where in our example the Observed LIBOR is the three-month rate prevailing at month four, and the interest payment will be due at month seven.

Rather than bearing the full interest rate risk associated with its financing need, the firm decides that it would like to limit the maximum interest rate it has to pay to 8.5 percent. Given the prevailing forward rate of 8 percent, it should be possible to transact to guarantee that the actual loan rate will not exceed the desired 8.5 percent. To place an upper bound on the actual cost of the loan at 8.5 percent, the firm purchases a call on three-month LIBOR with a notional principal of $10 million to expire in four months, which is the same time that the loan commences. The payoff on this call will occur at month 7 and will be

MAX{0, (Observed LIBOR $-$ 0.085) $\times$ 1/4 $\times$ $10,000,000}

We now evaluate the total financial result of the loan and the call on LIBOR. Assume that the Observed LIBOR at month four for a three-month maturity is 9 percent. The interest cost of the loan will be

$0.09 \times 1/4 \times \$10,000,000 = \$225,000$

and the payoff on the call will be

$(0.09 - 0.085) \times 1/4 \times \$10,000,000 = \$12,500$

Thinking of the loan cost of $225,000 diminished by the $12,500 payoff on the call, the outcome is the same as if the firm had entered a loan at 8.5 percent, for which the interest would have been

$$0.085 \times 1/4 \times \$10,000,000 = \$212,500$$

From this, we can see that the firm has put an upper bound on the cost of the loan at 8.5 percent through the purchase of the option. In market parlance, we can say that the firm has capped the loan at 8.5 percent through the purchase of the call on LIBOR. A **caplet** is a call on LIBOR purchased in conjunction with a floating rate loan to cover a single period. An **interest rate cap** is a sequence of calls on LIBOR organized to correspond to a multi-period floating rate loan based on LIBOR. Note that the 8.5 percent rate on the loan does not include the cost of the call in the caplet or the sequence of calls in the cap.

To review our example, consider the following facts. The firm initiated a floating rate loan for a three-month period to begin in four months. At the time the firm initiated the loan, the relevant FRA rate was 8 percent, $FRA_{4,7} = 0.08$. In conjunction with this loan, the firm purchased a call on three-month LIBOR to cover the same period with a strike rate of 8.5 percent. As we have seen, combining the floating rate loan with the purchase of the call effectively capped the loan rate at the strike rate of the call, or 8.5 percent, plus the purchase price of the call. This capped loan also allows the possibility for the loan cost to fall below the anticipated cost of 8 percent. If the observed three-month LIBOR at month four is 7 percent, for example, the loan cost will be the 7 percent market rate, plus the cost of the call. To evaluate the cost of the call, let us assume that the yield curve is flat at 8 percent, and that the annualized standard deviation of the three-month forward LIBOR is 0.25. According to Equation 19.12, with these data, the call will cost $6,342.45.

Let us now assume that the firm also decides to sell a put on LIBOR to go with the capped loan, choosing a strike rate of 7.75 percent. As we will see, this effectively places a lower bound, or floor, on the interest cost at 7.75 percent. A **floorlet** is a put on LIBOR sold in conjunction with a floating rate loan to cover a single period. An **interest rate floor** is a sequence of puts on LIBOR organized to correspond to a multi-period floating rate loan based on LIBOR. For the firm of our example, the effective rate of interest cannot fall below the floor level of 7.75 percent, plus the effect of the options. For example, assume that the three-month Observed LIBOR in four months is 7.0 percent. The call expires worthless. The firm then pays the 7 percent rate on the loan:

$$0.07 \times 1/4 \times \$10,000,000 = \$175,000$$

The put is exercised against the firm, for an outlay of

$$MAX\{0, (0.0775 - 0.07) \times 1/4 \times \$10,000,000\} = \$18,750$$

The total effective cost of the loan, not counting the options, is $193,750. This is equivalent to an interest cost of 7.75 percent:

$$0.0775 \times 1/4 \times \$10,000,000 = \$193,750$$

Given the flat term structure at 8 percent and a volatility of 0.25 as the standard deviation of the three-month forward LIBOR on an annualized basis, Equation 19.12 gives the value of the put as $8,087.73.

Figure 19.6 The collared loan example

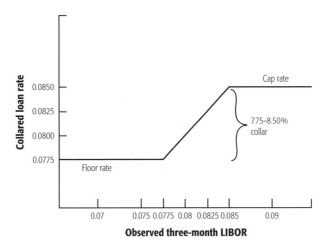

The purchase of the call and the sale of the put, together, place bounds on the cost of the loan. The upper bound is the strike rate of the call, and the lower bound is the strike rate on the put. The portfolio of a cap and a floor used in this way is called a collar. A **collar** may be defined as a combination of a call and put on LIBOR, with the same expiration and underlying good, with a long position in one instrument and a short position in the other. Thus, if the firm adds a collar to its floating rate loan, the rate on our example loan is collared between 7.75 percent and 8.5 percent. A collar is referred to as a floor rate – cap rate percent collar, so our example loan has a 7.75–8.50 percent collar. Figure 19.6 shows the possible rates for our collared loan. For any observed LIBOR of 7.75 percent or below, the rate on the collared loan will be the floor rate of 7.75 percent. For any observed LIBOR from 7.75 to 8.5 percent, the loan rate will be the same as the observed LIBOR rate. For any observed LIBOR rate greater than 8.50 percent, the loan rate will be the capped rate of 8.5 percent.

Figure 19.6 and our discussion to this point do not take into account the cost of buying the call nor the proceeds from selling the put that form the collar. We may view the addition of a collar to the loan as part of the final cost of the loan. To review, our collared loan consists of three parts: the determination to borrow $10 million for three months at the three-month LIBOR rate prevailing in four months; the purchase of a call (caplet) to parallel this loan at a cost of $6,342.45; and the sale of a put (floorlet) to parallel this loan for an inflow of $8,087.73. The purchase of the collar (purchase of a call for $6,342.45 and sale of a put for $8,087.73) actually generates a cash inflow of $1,745.28 when the options positions are instituted. We may think of this inflow from the collar as reducing the rate on the loan. To evaluate all of the different loan opportunities in similar terms, the future value of this inflow at the date when the interest must be repaid in seven months is

$$e^{0.08\times(7/12)} \times \$1,745.28 = \$1,828.66$$

The addition of the collar to the loan terms reduces the resulting rate by 7.3 basis points, because

$$\$10,000,000 \times 0.25 \times 0.00073146 = \$1,828.66$$

This reduction will arise no matter what the actual interest rate on the loan is. Therefore, in Figure 19.6, the final interest rate of the loan would be depicted if the entire graph were shifted down by 7.3 basis points, so the effective cost of the loan runs from 7.677 to 8.427 percent, depending on the rate observed in four months for three-month LIBOR.

For our example, we have considered only some of the many possible ways to cap the loan rate, to put a floor under the loan rate, or to collar the loan rate. The upper panel of Table 19.7 presents the Black model prices for a variety of options that might be combined with the floating rate loan of our example. All have a four-month expiration and a $10 million notional principal, pertain to a three-month loan, are based on a flat yield curve at 8 percent, and assume that the forward rate has a standard deviation of 0.25 per year. The lower panel presents various financing alternatives, including capped rates and rates with a floor, as well as several collars.

As a first comment on Table 19.7, we may note that the borrower could secure a floating rate loan at the three-month LIBOR rate that prevails in four months, or a fixed rate loan at an interest rate of 8 percent. These can be achieved without using options. The borrower could also obtain a capped rate of 8 percent by buying a call on LIBOR at 8 percent for a dollar outlay of $10,981.33 (corresponding to a future value of $11,505.94). This call purchase would add 46 basis points to the interest rate, because each basis point on the loan is worth $250:

$$\$10,000,000 \times \frac{1}{4} \times 0.0001 = \$250$$

For the loan capped at 8 percent, the true cost would be the observed LIBOR plus 46 basis points to a maximum of 8.46 percent. All of the other financing alternatives are presented in similar terms. Notice that it is cheap to cap the loan at 10 percent or to establish a 6 percent floor rate. This reflects the slight chance that the observed LIBOR would exceed 10 percent or be less than 6 percent. While Table 19.7 presents 11 different financing possibilities, the real range of possibilities is endless given all the possible cap rates, floor rates, and collars that could be devised. Finally, note that no one opportunity is absolutely superior to others. They are all consistent with the existing term structure and other information. Therefore, the financing choice depends on preferences and beliefs about the future course of interest rates.

So far, we have considered a caplet, a floorlet, and a collar on a single-period loan. Caps and floors really pertain to multi-period loan agreements. For example, one might enter a five-year floating rate loan to pay three-month LIBOR. This loan would have 20 payments, each dependent on an observation of three-month LIBOR on different dates. It is possible to cap this loan, to put a floor rate under it, or to put a collar on it. For example, to cap this loan, one would need a portfolio of 20 call options, with maturities that match each of the observation dates for LIBOR. Each option would be priced using the Black model, and the total cost of the options would be combined into a single fee that would cap the rate at the selected common strike price for the options. The analysis for the multi-period case is identical to our extended example of the caplet and floorlet. It must simply be repeated for each of the payment dates on the multi-period loan. It is common for lenders, such as commercial banks, to offer capped, floored, or collared loans for a specified rate plus a single fee. The fee represents the value of the portfolio of options that constitute the cap, floor, or collar, and would be paid at the inception of the loan. Note also that it is possible to offer capped, floored, or collared loans without an explicit fee. This could be done by offering terms that are somewhat above the market rate, with the excess rate on the loan covering the cost of the associated options.

Table 19.7   (a) Option values and (b) financing alternatives for the three-month loan example

(a) Black model option prices for various strike rates ($10 million notional principal; four-month expiration; three-month loan; 0.25 standard deviation on loan rate; yield curve flat at 8 percent)

Strike rate	Call price	Put price
0.0600	$47,926.27	$205.87
0.0700	26,327.13	2,466.93
0.0725	21,752.05	3,856.89
0.0750	17,647.13	5,717.03
0.0775	14,052.27	8,087.22
0.0800	10,981.33	10,981.33
0.0825	8,422.45	14,387.50
0.0850	6,341.95	18,272.05
0.0875	4,690.31	22,585.46
0.0900	3,408.96	27,269.16
0.1000	810.51	48,530.91

(b) Financing alternatives and the effect of options on the resulting loan rate

Description	Call cash flow	Put cash flow	Option effect on loan rate in basis points*	Resulting loan rate (to the nearest basis point)
Floating	0	0	0	Observed LIBOR
Fixed at 8%	0	0	0	8% fixed
Cap at 8%	−10,981.33	0	+46.02	Observed LIBOR + 46 b.p. up to maximum of 8.46%
Cap at 10%	−810.51	0	+3.40	Observed LIBOR + 3 b.p. up to maximum of 10.03%
Floor at 6%	0	+$205.87	−0.86	Observed LIBOR − 1 b.p. down to minimum of 5.99%
Floor at 7%	0	+2,466.93	−10.34	Observed LIBOR − 10 b.p. down to minimum of 6.90%
Floor at 8%	0	+10,981.33	−46.02	Observed LIBOR − 46 b.p. down to minimum of 7.54%
7.75–8.5 percent collar	−6,341.95	+8,087.22	−7.31	Observed LIBOR − 7 b.p. from minimum of 7.68% to maximum of 8.43%
6–10 percent collar	−810.51	+205.87	+2.53	Observed LIBOR + 3 b.p. from minimum of 6.03% to maximum 10.03%
7–9 percent collar	−3,408.96	+2,466.93	+3.95	Observed LIBOR + 4 b.p. from minimum of 7.04% to maximum of 9.04%
8–8 percent collar	−10,981.33	+10,981.33	0	8% fixed

*The option effect in basis points is the future value of the option cash flows at the termination of the loan, divided by the value of one basis point = $250. *Example*: For the 7.75–8.5 percent collar, the net cost of the options is $1,745.27. The loan terminates in seven months, and the yield curve is flat at 8 percent. The future value is $1,828.65. Because the option cash flow is a net inflow, the effect on the interest rate is a reduction of the rate by $1,828.65/$250 = 7.31 basis points.

Conclusion

This chapter has explored the basics of interest rate options. We began by considering the variety of interest rate options and the markets in which they trade. We noted that exchange-traded interest rate options are dominated by options on interest rate futures. In the over-the-counter market, a variety of options trade, including options on coupon bearing bonds, as well as calls and puts on LIBOR. In addition to interest rate options traded explicitly on futures exchanges and over-the-counter, there are embedded options. These embedded options are elements of interest-sensitive financial obligations. We considered the call option inherent in a callable bond and the prepayment option that is typical of most home mortgages.

We explored the term structure of interest rates, and studied the relationship between the par yield curve, the zero-coupon yield curve, and the implied forward yield curve. These three expressions of the term structure of interest rates form an integrated system of yield and price relationships that are crucial for interest rate option pricing. The market for U.S. Treasury strips directly reflects the zero-coupon yield curve, as Treasury strips are essentially U.S. Treasury bonds and notes that have been decomposed into zero-coupon bonds corresponding to various coupon and principal obligations. There is also a well-developed market that corresponds to forward rates. This is the market for forward rate agreements, or FRAs, which are essentially agreements in which one transacts for forward rates of LIBOR, the London Interbank Offered Rate. FRA payoffs depend on the contract rate compared to the subsequently observed spot LIBOR rate.

Turning to analytic techniques, we saw that the option-adjusted spread (OAS) was a technique for evaluating the value of options embedded in bonds. The OAS is the yield differential between an instrument with an embedded option and the yield on a Treasury security with essentially similar cash flows.

The Black model is the principal analytic and pricing technique studied in this chapter. Originally devised for options on futures, it also applies, as we saw, to a wide class of interest rate options. We specifically examined the application of the Black model to T-bond interest rate futures, to options on coupon bonds, and to calls and puts on LIBOR.

The market for calls and puts on LIBOR, in conjunction with the FRA market, makes explicit the no-arbitrage condition of forward put–call parity. This parity relationship basically states that a long call/short put portfolio is equivalent to an FRA if certain conditions are met: the time period covered by the options must correspond to the time period covered by the FRA, and the common strike rate on the options must equal the FRA rate. In such a case, the long call/short put portfolio will have the same payoffs as the FRA. As the FRA, entered at prevailing market rates, is an initially costless agreement, the long call/short put portfolio must have a zero value as well.

Building on the idea of forward put–call parity, we explored interest rate caps, floors, and collars. A long call on LIBOR in conjunction with a floating rate loan provides a cap (upper bound) on the loan rate equal to the strike rate on the call. A short put on LIBOR in conjunction with a floating rate loan provides a floor (lower bound) on the loan equal to the strike rate on the put. A floating rate loan in conjunction with a long call and a short put on LIBOR provides a collared loan with a cap equal to the strike rate on the call and a floor equal to the strike rate on the put, presuming that the call strike rate lies above and the put strike rate lies below the floating rate on the loan. We also saw how caps, floors, and collars can produce a wide variety of loan terms by their use singly and in combination.

Exercises

1 Explain the relationship among mortgage-backed securities, mortgage pass-throughs, and collateralized mortgage obligations.

2 Explain the similarities and differences between the zero-coupon yield curve and the implied forward yield curve.

3 Given the zero-coupon yield curve, explain how to find the implied forward yield curve.

4 Given the implied forward yield curve, explain how to find the zero-coupon yield curve.

5 Given the par yield curve, explain how to find the zero-coupon yield curve.

6 How does Equation 19.2 differ from the usual bond pricing formula?

7 Explain how to create a forward rate agreement for Treasuries using Treasury strips. Specifically, how would you create a forward rate agreement to cover a period from five to eight years in the future? Assume the five-year zero-coupon rate is 7 percent and the eight-year zero-coupon rate is 7.3 percent. Assume also that you wish to take a long position in the FRA, with a transaction amount of $1 million (that is, the market value of the strips traded will be $1 million).

8 Assume that you wish to conduct an OAS analysis of a callable corporate bond with an 18-year maturity that is callable in seven years. You cannot find any Treasury bond that matches the cash flows of the callable bond. Explain how you might proceed with your analysis.

9 In various incarnations of the Black model in this chapter, we saw that the role of the stock price in the Black–Scholes–Merton model could be played alternately by the futures price, the forward bond price, and the forward LIBOR interest rate. What underlying

assumptions unite these various proxies for the stock price and allow the application of the Black model?

10   What does it mean for an interest rate agreement to be "determined in advance and settled in arrears"?

11   You are examining a horizon extending from six through nine months in the future. For this period, an FRA is available, as well as calls and puts on LIBOR. Assume that you enter an FRA to receive-fixed and pay LIBOR. You also buy a call on LIBOR and sell a put on LIBOR for the same period, with strike rates equal to the rate on the FRA. All instruments have the same notional amount. Explain the economic import of your transactions. Can the totality of your transactions be analyzed as some simpler instrument? If so, what?

12   For a future period, the FRA rate is 8 percent. Consider the following varieties of a "collarlet" (caplet plus floorlet) for this loan. Assume that the periods and notional amounts of the options match the terms of the FRA.

A   A collarlet gives an 8–8 percent collar on the loan. How much should the collarlet cost?

B   A 7.8–7.9 percent collarlet is costless. How should you respond as an arbitrageur?

C   A 8.2–8.5 percent collarlet is fairly priced. What can you infer about its cost?

D   A 7.5–7.8 percent collarlet is fairly priced. What can you infer about its cost?

Maturity (years)	Yield curve #1 (par annual yields)	Yield curve #2 (par annual yields)
1	0.0500	0.1200
2	0.0540	0.1196
3	0.0545	0.1191
4	0.0552	0.1171
5	0.0564	0.1130
6	0.0594	0.1105
7	0.0652	0.1070
8	0.0666	0.1035
9	0.0714	0.0992
10	0.0772	0.0953

13   Using the yield data in the table above, interpret Yield curve #1 as the par yield curve. Complete the following table by finding all zero-coupon factors and by finding all one-year forward rate factors. Also, find all four-year forward rates. Assume annual compounding throughout.

Maturity (years)	Par yield	Zero-coupon factor	One-year forward rate factors
1			
2			
3			
4			
5			
6			
7			
8			
9			
10			

14   Using the yield data in the table above, interpret Yield curve #2 as the zero-coupon yield curve. Find all zero-coupon factors. Find the par yield curve. Assume annual compounding throughout.

15   Using the yield data in the table above, interpret Yield curve #1 as the zero-coupon yield curve. Find the price of an 8 percent annual coupon bond that matures in eight years. A callable bond with a price of 98.75 percent of par matures in eight years and has a coupon of 8 percent. Find the OAS between these bonds.

16   A T-bond futures contract matures in five months, and the corresponding T-bond futures option expires in four months. The current futures price is 103.50. The yield curve is flat at 7 percent. Assume continuous compounding. The standard deviation of the T-bond futures price is 0.2835. The strike price for both a call and a put is 100.00. Using the Black model, find the price of the call and the put.

17   Consider European call and put options on a Treasury bond with a coupon of 6 percent paid semi-annually that matures in 40 months and has a par value of $1,000. The current term structure environment is given by the downward-sloping yields of Table 19.6. Use these yields and monthly compounding throughout. Both the call and put expire in three months. The call has an exercise price of $970, and the put has an exercise price of $1,010. The standard deviation of Treasury yields is given as follows: one-year maturity, 0.30; two-year maturity, 0.28; three-year maturity, 0.25; and five-year maturity, 0.19. (Use linear interpolation to find the appropriate yield volatility for the maturity of this bond.) Find the prices of the call and put options.

18   A call and put on three-month LIBOR expire in seven months. The yield curve environment is given by the upward-sloping yield curve of Table 19.6.

The notional principal for the option is $100 million. The standard deviation of the three-month forward rate is 0.24. Assuming the strike rate on both the put and the call is 5.6 percent, price the two options. What would the prices be if the options were determined and paid in advance? Assume monthly compounding throughout.

19 Consider the downward-sloping yield curve of Table 19.6. Find $FRF_{11,17}$. Find $FRA_{11,17}$ assuming monthly compounding. For a call and put on six-month LIBOR that both expire in eleven months, what is the value of a long call/short put portfolio with a strike rate of 6.00 percent and a notional principal of $20 million? Assume that the standard deviation of the six-month forward rate is 0.27. How would you construct

a riskless bond from the put, call, and FRA? How does this relate to forward put–call parity?

20 The upward-sloping term structure of Table 19.6 prevails. Consider a loan based on six-month LIBOR with a maturity of 24 months and a loan amount of $100 million. The loan is to start immediately. Assume that the standard deviation of all relevant interest rates is 0.23.

A What is the cost of capping this loan at 7 percent?

B What is the cost of a floor for this loan at 6 percent?

C What is the cost of a 5.0–7.5 percent collar for this loan?

Notes

1 The rationale and importance of these option hedging vehicles for the swaps market are explored in some detail in our treatment of the swaps market.

2 See the Comptroller of the Currency, *OCC Bank Derivatives Report, First Quarter 2006*.

3 The basic reason for the removal of call provisions from U.S. Treasury bonds is a desire to facilitate the trading of stripped T-bonds, which we discuss later in this chapter.

4 The MBS market is extensive and complex. For much more on the institutional aspects of the MBS product, see William W. Bartlett, *Mortgage-Backed Securities*: *Products, Analysis, Trading*, New York: New York Institute of Finance, 1989.

5 For more information on this method, see John B. Carlson, William R. Melick, and Erkin Y. Sahinoz, "An Option for Anticipating Fed Action," *Economic Commentary*, Federal Reserve Bank of Cleveland, September 1, 2003.

6 Like most money market instruments, LIBOR interest payments are based on a 360-day year. For simplicity, we abstract from market day count conventions in our presentation. Day count conventions are addressed specifically in the final section of Chapter 22.

7 For more on option-adjusted spreads, see Chapter 11, "Option-Adjusted Spread Approach to the Valuation of Corporate Bonds," in Richard S. Wilson and Frank J. Fabozzi, *The New Corporate Bond Market*, Chicago: Probus Publishing, 1990; William W. Bartlett, *Mortgage-Backed Securities: Products, Analysis, Trading*, New York: New York Institute of Finance, 1989; and Si Chen, "Understanding Option-

Adjusted Spreads: The Implied Prepayment Hypothesis," *Journal of Portfolio Management*, Summer 1996, pp. 104–13. These works also discuss computing OAS between Treasuries and the instrument with the embedded option versus using two instruments with similar default risks.

8 Notice that this equivalence of δ and r implies that the expected change in the futures price is zero. As the futures requires no investment and we are employing risk-neutrality arguments, the expected payoff from all investments is the risk-free rate. The risk-free rate applied to zero investment gives a zero expected profit.

9 See the discussion of the adjustment of the Black–Scholes model for known dividends in Chapter 13. Our treatment of the coupon payment is the same as the treatment of the known dividend.

10 For more on duration measures, see Robert W. Kolb, *Investments*, 4th edn, Malden, MA: Blackwell, 1995, Chapters 7 and 8.

11 Duration is a major topic in its own right. There are numerous more complicated duration estimation techniques. For example, one could compute duration using the various zero-coupon rates instead of a single yield to maturity. Also, various techniques exist for annualizing duration. For a comprehensive discussion of duration, see Gerald O. Bierwag, *Duration Analysis: Managing Interest Rate Risk*, Cambridge, MA: Ballinger, 1987.

12 For more information on the pricing of interest rate options, see R. Rebonato, *Modern Pricing of Interest-Rate Derivatives*, Princeton, NJ: Princeton University Press, 2002.

20

The Swaps Market: An Introduction

Overview

This chapter provides a basic introduction to the swaps market.[1] As we will see, the swaps market has grown rapidly in the past few years because it provides firms that face financial risks with a flexible way to manage that risk. We will explore the risk management motivation that has led to this phenomenal growth in some detail.

In essence, a swap is an agreement between two parties, called counterparties, to exchange a sequence of cash flows in the same or different currencies. There are five basic kinds of swaps: interest rate swaps, foreign currency swaps, equity swaps, commodity swaps, and credit swaps. In an interest rate swap, one party might pay interest based on a floating rate, while the other party would pay at a fixed rate. In a foreign currency swap, one party might pay in dollars at a floating rate, while the other would pay in Japanese yen at a fixed rate. Changes in interest rates determine the winners and losers in an interest rate swap. For a foreign currency swap, changes in interest rates in both countries and changes in the exchange rate between the two currencies determine the winners and losers, as we will see in some detail. Similar fixed-for-floating structures are also common in equity, commodity, and credit swaps.

Participants in the swaps market have various motivations, covering the game from speculation and arbitrage to hedging. However, the basic motivation for swaps, and the basic purpose of the swap market, is for businesses to shape and manage the interest rate and foreign currency risk inherent in their commercial operations.

A significant industry has arisen to facilitate swap transactions. This chapter considers the role of **swap facilitators**–economic agents who help counterparties to consummate swap transactions. Swap facilitators may serve as brokers or dealers. In the early days of the swap market, brokers were much in evidence, functioning as agents who identified and brought prospective counterparties into contact with each other without participating in the swap itself. **Swap dealers** are in the business of making a market in swaps and serving as counterparties to those seeking to complete swaps. In today's swap market, swap dealers predominate.

The chapter focuses largely on simpler interest rate and currency swaps known as plain vanilla swaps. We briefly consider how prices for these swaps are set and how they can be employed for business purposes. Chapters 21 and 22 extend the discussions of pricing and applications, respectively.

By taking part in swap transactions, swap dealers expose themselves to financial risk. This risk can be serious, because it is exactly the risk that the swap counterparties are trying to avoid. Therefore, the swap dealer has two key problems. First, the swap dealer must price the swap to provide a reward for his services in bearing risk. Second, the swap dealer essentially has a portfolio of swaps that results from his numerous transactions in the swaps market. Therefore, the swap dealer has the problem of managing a swap portfolio. We explore how swap dealers price their swap transactions and how swap dealers manage the risks inherent in their swap portfolios.

The chapter concludes with a survey of swaps that go beyond plain vanilla interest rate and currency swaps. These include many more complicated interest rate and foreign currency swap structures. Also, there are other types of swaps based on commodity and equity indexes. In summary, this chapter provides an overview of the swap market and indicates how swaps are priced and used to manage business risk.

Swaps

A **swap** is an agreement between two or more parties to exchange a sequence of cash flows over a period in the future. For example, Party A might agree to pay a fixed rate of interest on $1 million each year for five years to Party B. In return, Party B might pay a floating rate of interest on $1 million each year for five years. The parties that agree to the swap are known as **counterparties**. The cash flows that the counterparties make are generally tied to the value of

Table 20.1   The value of outstanding swaps ($ billions of principal)

Year	Total interest rate swaps	Total currency swaps
1987	$682.9	$182.8
1988	1,010.2	316.8
1989	1,539.3	434.8
1990	2,311.5	577.5
1991	3,065.1	807.2
1992	3,850.8	860.4
1993	6,177.8	899.6
1994	8,815.6	914.8
1995	12,810.7	1,197.4
1996	19,170.9	1,559.6
1997	22,115.4	1,584.8
1998	36,262.0	2,253.0
1999	43,936.0	2,444.0
2000	48,768.0	3,194.0
2001	58,897.0	3,942.0
2002	79,120.0	4,503.0
2003	111,209.0	6,371.0
2004	150,631.0	8,223.0
2005	172,869.0	8,501.0

Source: Through 1997 from the International Swaps and Derivatives Association web site (www.isda.org).
From 1998 forward from the Bank for International Settlements (www.bis.org). Year-end values

debt instruments or to the value of foreign currencies. Therefore, the two basic kinds of swaps are **interest rate swaps** and **currency swaps**.

The origins of the swap market can be traced to the late 1970s, when currency traders developed currency swaps as a technique to evade British controls on the movement of foreign currency. The first interest rate swap occurred in 1981, in an agreement between IBM and the World Bank. Since that time, the market has grown rapidly. Table 20.1 shows the amount of swaps outstanding from 1987 to 2005. By 2005, interest rate swaps with $172 trillion in underlying value were outstanding, and currency swaps totaled another $8.5 trillion. The total swaps market exceeded a notional amount of $180 trillion, with about 95 percent of the swaps being interest rate swaps and the remaining 5 percent being primarily currency swaps.[2] The growth in this market has been phenomenal; in fact, it has been the most rapid for any financial product in history.

The swaps market

In this section, we consider the special features of the swaps market. For purposes of comparison, we begin by summarizing some of the key features of futures and options markets. Against this background, we focus on the most important features of the swap product. The section concludes with a brief summary of the development of the swaps market.

A review of futures and options market features

In Chapters 2–19, we explored the futures and options markets. We noted that futures contracts trade exclusively in markets operated by futures exchanges and regulated by the Commodity

Futures Trading Commission (CFTC). In our discussion of options, we focused primarily on exchange-traded options. This portion of the options market, regulated by the Securities Exchange Commission (SEC), is highly formalized with the options exchanges playing a major role in the market.

Futures markets trade highly standardized contracts, and the options traded on exchanges also have highly specified contract terms that cannot be altered. For example, the S&P 500® futures contract is based on a particular set of stocks, for a particular dollar amount, with only four fixed maturity dates per year. In addition, futures and exchange-traded options generally have a fairly short horizon. In many cases, futures contracts are listed only about one to two years before they expire. Even when it is possible to trade futures for expiration in three years or more, the markets do not become liquid until the contract comes much closer to expiration. For exchange-traded stock options, the longest time to maturity is generally less than one year. These futures and options cannot provide a means of dealing with risks that extend farther into the future than the expiration of the contracts that are traded. For example, if a firm faces interest rate risk for a ten-year horizon associated with a major building project, the futures market allows risk management only for the horizon of futures contracts currently being traded, which is about three years.[3] In recent years, over-the-counter (OTC) markets for options have become more important. For example, the exotic options discussed in Chapter 18 trade only OTC, and OTC trading is important for the interest rate options analyzed in Chapter 19.

The characteristics of the swaps market

On futures and options exchanges, major financial institutions are readily identifiable. For example, in a futures pit, traders can discern the activity of particular firms, because traders know who represents which firm. Therefore, exchange trading necessarily involves a certain loss of privacy. In the swaps market, by contrast, only the counterparties know that the swap takes place. Thus, the swaps market affords a privacy that cannot be obtained in exchange trading.[4]

We have noted that futures and options exchanges are subject to considerable government regulation. By contrast, the swaps market has virtually no government regulation. As we will see later, swaps are similar to futures. The Commodity Futures Modernization Act of 2000 (CFMA) excluded swaps on financial products from regulation under the Commodity Exchange Act, the law governing futures trading in the United States. The CFMA exempted by statute swaps on energy and metals, while retaining the government's anti-fraud and anti-manipulation authority in these markets. The CFMA provided legal certainty about the enforceability of swap agreements. The International Swaps and Derivatives Association, Inc. (ISDA) is an industry organization that provides standard documentation for swap agreements and keeps records of swap activity.

The swaps market also has some inherent limitations. First, to consummate a swap transaction, one potential counterparty must find another counterparty that is willing to take the opposite side of a transaction. If one party needs a specific maturity, or a certain pattern of cash flows, it could be difficult to find a willing counterparty. In the early days of the swap market, counterparties generally faced this problem as end-users of the swaps market transacted directly with each other. As we see later in this chapter, the swaps market is now served by swap dealers who make markets in swaps. Second, because a swap agreement is a contract between two counterparties, the swap cannot be altered or terminated early without the agreement of both parties. Third, for futures and exchange-traded options, the exchanges effectively guarantee performance on the contracts for all parties. By its very nature, the swaps market has no such guarantor. As a consequence, parties to the swap must be certain of the creditworthiness of their counterparties.

As we will see later in this chapter, the swaps market has developed mechanisms to deal with these three limitations. The problem of potential default is perhaps the most important. Assessing the financial credibility of a counterparty is difficult and expensive. Therefore, participation in the swaps market is effectively limited to firms and institutions that either engage in frequent swap transactions or have access to major swap dealers that assess creditworthiness. In effect, the swaps market is virtually limited to firms and financial institutions, and there are only a few individual transactors in the market. Appendix A discusses the new rules for accounting for derivatives, including swaps.

Plain vanilla swaps

In this section, we analyze the two basic kinds of swaps that are available. The basic swap is known as a **plain vanilla swap**, which can be an interest rate swap or a foreign currency swap. We begin by considering the mechanics of these plain vanilla swaps. Later in this chapter, we consider more complicated swaps called flavored swaps.

Interest rate swaps

In a plain vanilla interest rate swap, one counterparty agrees to pay a sequence of fixed-rate interest payments and to receive a sequence of floating-rate interest payments. This counterparty is said to have the **pay-fixed** side of the deal. The opposing counterparty agrees to receive a sequence of fixed-rate interest payments and to pay a sequence of floating-rate payments. This counterparty has the **receive-fixed** side of the deal.

The swap agreement specifies a time over which the periodic interest payments will be made, which is the **tenor** of the swap. The amount of the periodic interest payments is a fraction of a dollar amount specified in the swap agreement, which is called the **notional principal**. The notional principal is a nominal quantity used as a scale factor to determine the size of the interest payments in the swap agreement. Later, we explore the motivation that these counterparties might have for taking their respective positions. First, however, we need to understand the transactions.

To see the nature of the plain vanilla interest rate swap most clearly, we use an example. We assume that the swap covers a five-year period (a five-year tenor) and involves annual payments on a $1 million notional principal amount. Let us assume that Party A is the pay-fixed counterparty and agrees to pay a fixed rate of 9 percent to Party B. In return, Party B, the receive-fixed counterparty, agrees to pay a floating rate of LIBOR to Party A. As we have seen in Chapter 19, LIBOR is the London Interbank Offered Rate and represents the rate at which large international banks lend to each other. LIBOR-based loans are essentially privately negotiated business loans that may have a variety of maturities. Most of the maturities range from one month to a year. Quotations of LIBOR rates appear daily in the "Money Rates" column of *The Wall Street Journal*. Floating rates in the swaps market are most often set as equaling LIBOR, which is also called **LIBOR flat**.

In our example swap agreement, Party A pays 9 percent of $1 million, or $90,000, each year to Party B. Party B makes payments to Party A in return, but the actual amount of the payments depends on movement in LIBOR. The LIBOR maturity for this plain vanilla swap will be the one-year LIBOR rate, because there is one year between each of the payments on the swap. We assume that one-year LIBOR stands at 8.75 percent at the time the swap agreement is negotiated, a rate that may differ substantially from the fixed rate on the swap.

Conceptually, the two parties also exchange the principal amount of $1 million. However, actually making the transaction of sending each other $1 million would not make practical sense. As a consequence, principal amounts are generally not exchanged. Instead, the notional

Table 20.2   Cash flows for a plain vanilla interest rate swap

Year	$LIBOR_t$	Floating-rate obligation: Party B pays Party A	Fixed-rate obligation: Party A pays Party B
0	8.75%		
1	$LIBOR_1 = ?$	$LIBOR_0 \times \$1,000,000 =$ $0.0875 \times \$1,000,000 = \$87,500$	\$90,000
2	$LIBOR_2 = ?$	$LIBOR_1 \times \$1,000,000$	\$90,000
3	$LIBOR_3 = ?$	$LIBOR_2 \times \$1,000,000$	\$90,000
4	$LIBOR_4 = ?$	$LIBOR_3 \times \$1,000,000$	\$90,000
5	N/A	$LIBOR_4 \times \$1,000,000$	\$90,000

principal is used to determine the amount of the interest payments. Because the principal is not actually exchanged, it is only a notional principal, an amount used as a base for computations, but not an amount that is actually transferred from one party to another. In our example, the notional principal is \$1 million, and knowing that amount lets us compute the actual dollar amount of the cash flows that the two parties make to each other each year.

Generally, the determination of LIBOR occurs at one settlement date, with payment occurring at the next settlement date. The payment is said to be determined in advance and paid in arrears. Table 20.2 shows what is known about the cash flows on this swap agreement at $t = 0$, the time at which the swap is negotiated. As mentioned above, LIBOR at the time of negotiation is 8.75 percent, but the future course of LIBOR is unknown. In each period, the fixed-rate payment will be \$90,000. In general, the floating-rate payment at a given time t depends on the level of LIBOR at period $t - 1$. Thus, at the inception of the swap agreement, LIBOR is observed and this determines the floating-rate payment that occurs in the first period. In our example, with LIBOR at 8.75 percent when the swap is negotiated, the first floating-rate payment will be \$87,500. The second payment, which occurs at $t = 2$, depends on LIBOR at $t = 1$, and this is unknown when the swap is negotiated. The table shows LIBOR at the end of the swap's tenor as "N/A." This rate is nonapplicable, because it does not determine any of the cash flows associated with the swap. This convention of determining the floating-rate payment in advance and actually making the payment in arrears matches the conventions that prevail in the market for floating-rate notes and bank loans.

Figure 20.1 parallels Table 20.2 and shows the cash flows on the swap from the perspective of each party. In this time line, an up-arrow indicates a cash inflow, while a down-arrow indicates a cash outflow. The upper panel of Figure 20.1 pertains to Party A, the pay-fixed counterparty. In each year, Party A will pay a fixed amount of \$90,000. In return, Party A receives a payment that depends on LIBOR. At year 1, Party A will receive \$87,500, because LIBOR stands at 8.75 percent when the swap is negotiated; that is, $LIBOR_0 = 8.75$ percent. Party A's receipt in subsequent years is not known when the swap is negotiated, because those payments depend on the unknown future of LIBOR. The lower panel shows the same swap from the perspective of Party B, the receive-fixed counterparty. Each year, Party B will receive a fixed payment of \$90,000, and make a payment based on LIBOR. From the figure, it is clear that Parties A and B have "mirror-image" cash flows. The receipts for one are the payments for the other. This emphasizes the fact that a swap is a zero-sum game—one party's gain is the other's loss. In general, we can show everything about a swap by just looking at it from the perspective of a single party.

Figure 20.1   A plain vanilla interest rate swap

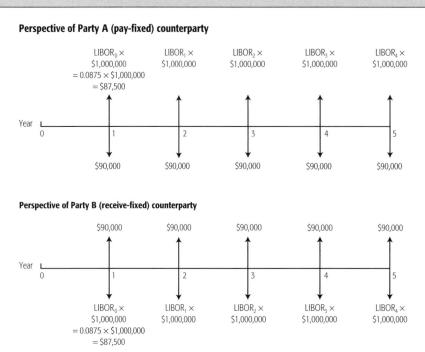

Perspective of Party A (pay-fixed) counterparty

Perspective of Party B (receive-fixed) counterparty

Continuing with our example of a plain vanilla interest rate swap, let us now assume that LIBOR is 10 percent at $t = 1$. This rate will determine the floating-rate payment to occur at $t = 2$, assuming that the swap is paid in arrears. This means that Party A will be obligated to pay $90,000 to Party B, while Party B will owe $100,000 to Party A. Offsetting the two mutual obligations, Party B owes $10,000 to Party A. Generally, only the net payment, the difference between the two obligations, actually takes place in interest rate swaps. Again, this practice avoids unnecessary payments.[5]

For our example swap, the payments are annual and the tenor is five years. Consequently, the swap has five determination dates, the dates at which the amount of payments due from each party are determined. There are also five payment dates, the actual dates on which each net payment is made. The determination dates occur at years 0, 1, 2, 3, and 4. The corresponding payment dates occur one year later than their respective determination dates. In general, the payment date occurs one period after the determination date. For example, on a swap with quarterly payments, the payment date follows its corresponding determination date by one quarter.

While most swaps are "determined in advance and paid in arrears," some swap agreements specify payment in advance. These swaps are called **in-advance swaps**. For a swap with payments in advance, the payment due is the present value of the in-arrears obligation, discounted at LIBOR. This is the marketwide convention for in-advance swaps. If our sample plain vanilla swap had been an in-advance swap, the first payment would occur at $t = 0$. The fixed-rate payment would be the present value of $90,000, while the floating-rate payment would be the present value of $87,500, each discounted at the LIBOR of 8.75 percent. Thus, the floating-rate payment would be $80,459.77, and the fixed-rate payment would be $82,758.62. Since only net payments are made, the actual payment would be from the fixed-rate to the floating-rate payer (from Party A to Party B) for $82,758.62 − $80,459.77 = $2,298.85.

For the same plain vanilla interest rate swap, which we now interpret as an in-advance swap, let us now assume that the time is $t = 1$ and that one-year LIBOR now stands at 10 percent. For this in-advance swap, the payments at $t = 1$ will be as follows. The floating-rate payer must pay the present value of its obligation (0.10 × $1,000,000 = $100,000) discounted at the prevailing LIBOR of 10 percent. This equals $100,000/1.10 = $90,909.09. The fixed-rate payment is the present value of $90,000, or $90,000/1.1 = $81,818.18. This means that the floating-rate payer, Party B, will make a net payment of $9,090.91 to Party A.

Foreign currency swaps

In a plain vanilla currency swap, one party typically holds one currency and desires a different currency. The swap arises when one party provides a certain principal in one currency to its counterparty in exchange for an equivalent amount of a different currency. Each party will then pay interest on the currency it receives in the swap, and this interest payment can be made at either a fixed or a floating rate.

For example, Party C may have European Union euros and be anxious to swap those euros for U.S. dollars. Similarly, Party D may hold U.S. dollars and be willing to exchange those dollars for euros. With these needs, Parties C and D may be able to engage in a currency swap. There are four possibilities for making interest payments:

(1)   Party C pays a fixed rate on dollars received, and Party D pays a fixed rate on euros received.[6]
(2)   Party C pays a floating rate on dollars received, and Party D pays a fixed rate on euros received.
(3)   Party C pays a fixed rate on dollars received, and Party D pays a floating rate on euros received.
(4)   Party C pays a floating rate on dollars received, and Party D pays a floating rate on euros received.

Although all four patterns of interest payments are observed in the market, the predominant quotation is of the second type: pay floating on dollars/pay fixed on the foreign currency, and this is known as the plain vanilla currency swap.[7]

Before analyzing the cash flows on the plain vanilla swap (floating rate on dollars/fixed rate on a foreign currency), we begin with a simpler case. The simplest kind of currency swap arises when each party pays a fixed rate of interest on the currency it receives. The fixed-for-fixed currency swap involves three different sets of cash flows. First, at the initiation of the swap, the two parties actually exchange cash. Typically, the motivation for the currency swap is the actual need for funds denominated in a different currency. This differs from the interest rate swap in which both parties deal in a single currency and can pay the net amount. Second, the parties make periodic interest payments to each other during the life of the swap agreement, and these payments are made in full without netting. Third, at the termination of the swap, the parties again exchange the principal.

As an example of the fixed-for-fixed currency swap, let us assume that the current spot exchange rate between euros and U.S. dollars is €0.8 per dollar. Thus, the euro is worth $1.25. We assume that the U.S. interest rate is 10 percent and the EU interest rate is 8 percent. Party C holds €25 million and wishes to exchange those euros for dollars. In return for the euros, Party D would pay $31.25 million to Party C at the initiation of the swap. We also assume that the tenor of the swap is seven years and the parties will make annual interest payments. With the interest

Figure 20.2   A fixed-for-fixed currency swap

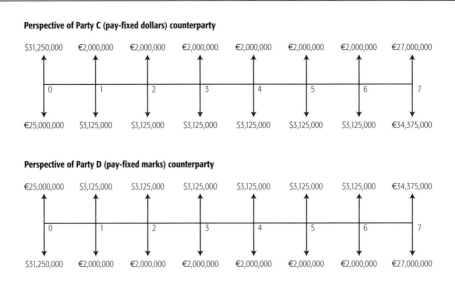

Perspective of Party C (pay-fixed dollars) counterparty

$31,250,000	€2,000,000	€2,000,000	€2,000,000	€2,000,000	€2,000,000	€2,000,000	€27,000,000
0	1	2	3	4	5	6	7
€25,000,000	$3,125,000	$3,125,000	$3,125,000	$3,125,000	$3,125,000	$3,125,000	€34,375,000

Perspective of Party D (pay-fixed marks) counterparty

€25,000,000	$3,125,000	$3,125,000	$3,125,000	$3,125,000	$3,125,000	$3,125,000	€34,375,000
0	1	2	3	4	5	6	7
$31,250,000	€2,000,000	€2,000,000	€2,000,000	€2,000,000	€2,000,000	€2,000,000	€27,000,000

rates in our example, Party D will pay 8 percent interest on the €25 million it received, so the annual payment from Party D to Party C will be €2 million. Party C receives $31.25 million and pays interest at 10 percent, so Party C will pay $3.125 million each year to Party D. As the payments are made in different currencies, netting is not a typical practice. Instead, each party makes the full interest payment.

At the end of seven years, the two parties again exchange principal. In our example, Party C would pay $31.25 million and Party D would pay €25 million. This final payment terminates the currency swap. Figure 20.2 shows the cash flows on this fixed-for-fixed currency swap from the perspective of each party. At time $t = 0$, the principal amounts are exchanged. At the end of each of the seven years, the fixed interest payments are exchanged. Finally, at the end of the swap, $t = 7$, the principal amounts are again exchanged.

When this fixed-for-fixed currency swap is negotiated at $t = 0$, the entire sequence of cash flows is known for the entire tenor of the swap. Which set of cash flows is more desirable, only time will tell, because interest rates for the dollar and the euro will fluctuate, as will the dollar/euro exchange rate. Like the plain vanilla interest rate swap we have considered, the fixed-for-fixed currency swap is a zero-sum game. One set of cash flows will turn out to be better than the other. The party that gains does so at the other party's expense.

As noted above, the fixed-for-floating currency swap is the prevalent type of currency swap, and is considered to be the plain vanilla currency swap. In this type of swap, parties typically exchange principal at the outset of the swap, but one party pays a fixed rate of interest on the foreign currency it receives, while the other pays a floating rate on the currency it receives.

As an example of a fixed-for-floating (plain vanilla) currency swap, consider a swap arranged between a U.S. and a Japanese firm, assuming that $1 is worth ¥120 when the swap is negotiated. Let the notional amounts be $10 million and ¥1.2 billion, with a tenor of four years based on annual payments. The Japanese four-year fixed interest rate is 7 percent, and the U.S. firm promises to pay this fixed rate. For its part, the Japanese firm promises to pay one-year LIBOR flat, which is currently 5 percent. Table 20.3 shows the anticipated cash flows.

Table 20.3   Cash flows for a plain vanilla currency swap

Year	$LIBOR_t$	Dollar obligation: Japanese firm pays U.S. firm	Yen obligation: U.S. firm pays Japanese firm
0	5.00%	¥1,200,000,000	$10,000,000
1	$LIBOR_1 = ?$	$LIBOR_0 \times \$10,000,000 =$ $0.0500 \times \$10,000,000 = \$500,000$	¥84,000,000
2	$LIBOR_2 = ?$	$LIBOR_1 \times \$10,000,000$	¥84,000,000
3	$LIBOR_3 = ?$	$LIBOR_2 \times \$10,000,000$	¥84,000,000
4	N/A	$LIBOR_3 \times \$10,000,000 + \$10,000,000$	¥84,000,000 + ¥1,200,000,000

Figure 20.3   A plain vanilla currency swap

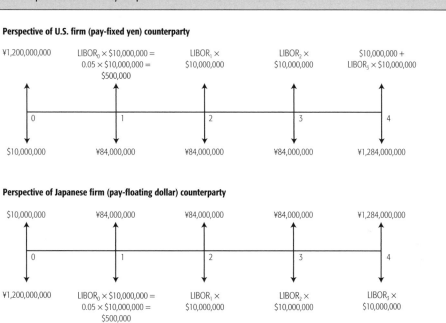

Customarily, foreign currency swaps are determined in advance and paid in arrears, just as we have seen with interest rate swaps. However, foreign currency swaps can sometimes be in-advance swaps as well. Figure 20.3 parallels Table 20.3 and shows the cash flows on the plain vanilla currency swap from the perspective of each counterparty.

Summary

In this section, we have considered the transactions involved in plain vanilla interest rate and currency swaps. As we saw for an interest rate swap, the essential feature is a contract that requires the pay-fixed party to make a sequence of fixed-rate interest payments and to receive a sequence of floating-rate interest payments. The opposing counterparty, the receive-fixed party, agrees to receive a sequence of fixed-rate interest payments and to pay a sequence of floating-rate payments. All of these payments are based on a common notional principal. In a currency swap, the two parties exchange currencies to obtain access to a foreign currency that better meets their business needs. Each party pays interest on the currency received, which can be paid at a fixed or floating rate. The plain vanilla currency swap assumes a fixed foreign rate and a floating U.S. rate. To this point, we have only focused on the elementary transactions involved in simple swaps, but we have not considered the motivation that leads to swap agreements.

Motivations for swaps

Historically, there have been two basic motivations for swap agreements. In the early years of the market, during the 1980s, some parties entered the swap market in an effort to exploit perceived market inefficiencies. For example, the swap market was seen as a means of obtaining fixed-rate financing at a cheaper rate than was otherwise available. If identical financing were available at different rates through different instruments, this would imply an informationally inefficient market. These differential rates would mean that a lender would provide the same financing at two different rates via a swap agreement and a conventional instrument. While this claim of arbitrage profits remains controversial, most observers agree that the swaps market has now matured and such opportunities are no longer available. In this section, we consider an example of a swap that relies on the motivation of arbitrage.

Today, the swaps market is a mature market that is well understood by many sophisticated practitioners. Therefore, there are likely to be few, if any, arbitrage opportunities available. Instead, the swaps market has succeeded because it offers more operationally efficient and flexible means of packaging and transforming cash flows than other instruments, such as exchange-traded options and futures. These uses of the swaps market are not motivated by perceived informational inefficiencies. Instead, the motivation turns on reducing transaction costs, lowering hedging costs, avoiding costly regulations, and maintaining privacy. These business applications in an informationally efficient market will be the primary focus of our discussion of swaps.

However, we begin by considering a swap transaction designed to exploit a market inefficiency, which turns on the comparative advantage in borrowing costs between two firms. We then turn to understanding the motivations for swaps for risk management purposes in an operationally efficient market. We consider two simple examples of how firms might use the swaps market to manage interest rate risk. The motivation for these latter swap transactions is operational efficiency and cost-effectiveness, rather than an effort to exploit an informational inefficiency.

Comparative advantage

In some situations, one firm may have better access to the capital market than another firm.[8] For example, a U.S. firm may be able to borrow easily in the United States, but it might not have such favorable access to the capital market in Germany. Similarly, a German firm may have good borrowing opportunities domestically but poor opportunities in the United States. Notice that this comparative advantage implies an inefficiency in the financial market, because the differential access to the markets implies that lenders evaluate the firms differently in different countries.

Table 20.4 presents borrowing rates for Parties C and D, the firms of our fixed-for-fixed currency swap example. In the previous example, we assumed that, for each currency, both parties faced the same rate. We now assume that Party C is a German firm with access to euros at a rate of 7 percent, while the U.S. firm, Party D, must pay 8 percent to borrow euros. On the other hand, Party D can borrow dollars at 9 percent, while the German Party C must pay 10 percent for its dollar borrowings.

Table 20.4   Borrowing rates for two firms in two currencies

Firm	U.S. dollar rate	Euro rate
Party C	10%	7%
Party D	9%	8%

Figure 20.4   The comparative advantage fixed-for-fixed currency swap (exchange of currencies at initiation)

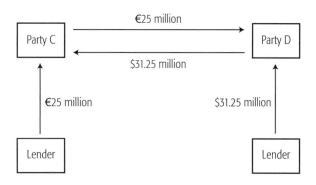

As the table shows, Party C enjoys a comparative advantage in borrowing euros and Party D has a comparative advantage in borrowing dollars. (Again, notice the market inefficiency that these rates imply: in one currency, Party C is regarded as a better credit risk; in the other currency, Party D is the better credit risk.) These rates raise the possibility that each firm can exploit its comparative advantage and share the gains by reducing overall borrowing costs. This possibility is shown in Figure 20.4, which parallels Figures 20.2, but focuses just on the exchange of currencies at the initiation of the swap.

Figure 20.4 shows that Party C borrows €25 million from a third-party lender at its borrowing rate of 7 percent, while Party D borrows $31.25 million from a fourth party at 9 percent. After these borrowings, both parties have the funds to engage in the fixed-for-fixed currency swap that we have already analyzed. To initiate the swap, Party C forwards the €25 million it has just borrowed to Party D, which reciprocates with the $31.25 million it has borrowed. In effect, the two parties have made independent borrowings and then exchanged the proceeds. For this reason, a currency swap is also known as an **exchange of borrowings**.

Figure 20.5 shows the annual interest cash flows for the loans and the fixed-for-fixed currency swap. Party C annually receives €2 million from Party D and pays interest of €1.75 million on its loan. This gives a net inflow of €250,000 per year. Valuing these euros at the exchange rate of $1 = €0.8, the net flow has a value of $312,500. Party C also pays $3.125 million annually to Party D, giving Party C a net annual cash outflow of $2,812,500 for the use of $31.25 million, for an effective interest rate of 9 percent. This compares favorably with the 10 percent rate at which Party C can borrow dollars, as shown in Table 20.4, for a net savings of 1 percent financing cost to Party C.

Each year, Party D receives $3.125 million from Party C and pays $2,812,500 on its loan, for an annual inflow of $312,500. At the exchange rate of $1 = €0.8, this inflow is worth €250,000. Party D also pays €2 million to Party C, for a net annual cash outflow of €1.75 million. This

Figure 20.5 The comparative advantage fixed-for-fixed currency swap (interest payments with lenders)

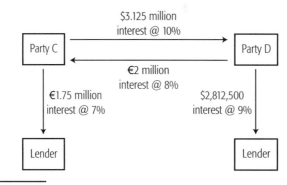

Assuming that $1 = €0.8:

Party C borrows dollars at an effective interest rate of 9 percent as follows, with all values expressed ultimately in dollars:

Interest payment $= \$3,125,000 - €2,000,000 \times 1.25 + €1,750,000 \times 1.25$

$= \$2,812,500$ on $31.25 million

Party D borrows euros at an effective interest rate of 7 percent as follows, with all values expressed ultimately in euros:

Interest payment $= €2,000,000 - \$3,125,000 \times 0.8 + \$2,812,500 \times 0.8$

$= €2,000,000 - €2,500,000 + €2,250,000$

$= €1,750,000$ on €25 million

outflow pays for the use of €25 million, for an effective interest rate of 7 percent. This is better than the EU interest rate that is available to Party D of 8 percent, as shown in Table 20.4. Thus, Party D also saves 1 percent on its financing costs. By using the swap, both parties achieve an effective borrowing rate that is much lower than they could have obtained by borrowing the currency they needed directly. Parties C and D share equally in this example. By engaging in the swap, both firms can use the comparative advantage of the other to reduce their borrowing costs. Figure 20.6 shows the termination cash flows for the swap, when both parties repay the principal.

Converting a fixed-rate asset into a floating-rate asset

As we noted above, the comparative advantage fixed-for-fixed swap was predicated on a market imperfection—conflicting credit risk assessments of the two counterparties in two countries. We now focus on two examples of using swaps that do not rely on the presence of market imperfections. These examples are more closely related to current market conditions and the actual business practices of firms.

As an example of a prime candidate for an interest rate swap, consider a typical savings and loan association. Savings and loan associations accept deposits and lend those funds for long-term mortgages. Because most deposits are short term, deposit rates must adjust to changing interest rate conditions. Most mortgagors wish to borrow at a fixed rate for a long time. As a result, the savings and loan association can be left with floating-rate liabilities and fixed-rate

Figure 20.6 The comparative advantage fixed-for-fixed currency swap (repayment of principal with lenders)

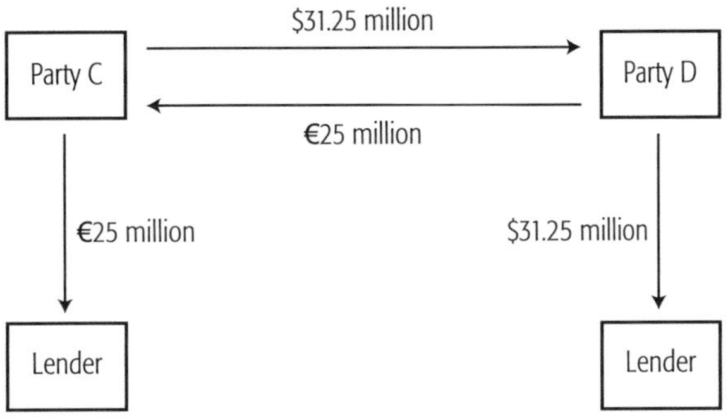

assets. This means that the savings and loan is vulnerable to rising rates. If rates rise, the savings and loan will be forced to increase the rate it pays on deposits, but it cannot increase the interest rate it charges on the mortgages that have already been issued.

To escape this interest rate risk, the savings and loan might use the swaps market to transform its fixed-rate assets into floating-rate assets or transform its floating-rate liabilities into fixed-rate liabilities. Let us assume that the savings and loan wishes to transform a fixed-rate mortgage into an asset that pays a floating rate of interest. In terms of our plain vanilla interest rate swap example, the savings and loan association is like Party A—in exchange for the fixed-rate mortgage that it holds, it wants to pay a fixed rate of interest and receive a floating rate of interest. Thus, the savings and loan wants to be a pay-fixed counterparty in a swap. Engaging in a swap as Party A did will help the association to resolve its interest rate risk.

To make the discussion more concrete, we extend our example of the plain vanilla interest rate swap. We assume that the savings and loan association has just loaned $1 million for five years at 9 percent with annual payments, and we assume that the savings and loan pays a deposit rate that equals LIBOR minus 1 percent. With these rates, the association will lose money if LIBOR exceeds 10 percent, and it is this danger that prompts the association to consider an interest rate swap.

Figure 20.7 shows our original plain vanilla interest rate swap with the additional information about the savings and loan that we have just elaborated. In the figure, Party A is the savings and loan association, and it receives payments at a fixed rate of 9 percent on the mortgage. After it enters the swap, the association also pays a fixed rate of 9 percent on a notional principal of $1 million. In effect, it receives mortgage payments and passes them through to Party B under the swap agreement. Under the swap agreement, Party A receives a floating rate of LIBOR flat. From this cash inflow, the association pays its depositors LIBOR minus 1 percent. This leaves a periodic inflow to the association of 1 percent, which is the spread that it makes on the loan.

In our example, the association now has a fixed-rate inflow of 1 percent, and it has succeeded in avoiding its exposure to interest rate risk. No matter what happens to the level of interest rates, the association will enjoy a net cash inflow of 1 percent on $1 million. This example clarifies how the savings association has a strong motivation to enter the swaps market. From the very nature of the savings and loan industry, the association finds itself with a risk exposure to rising interest rates. However, by engaging in an interest rate swap, the association can secure a fixed-rate position.[9]

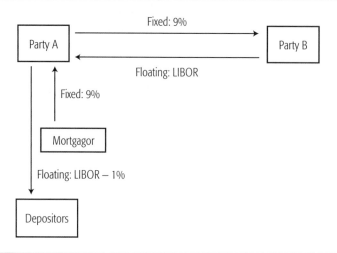

Figure 20.7   Motivation for the plain vanilla interest rate swap

Notice that the savings and loan could have achieved the same result in other ways if it were free from regulatory constraint and were willing to radically alter its business operations. For example, the savings and loan could achieve the same reduction in interest rate risk by paying off all of its depositors and issuing a fixed-rate bond to fund its mortgage lending. Obviously, this approach is not available to a savings and loan institution, because such a course of action would mean that the firm would cease to be a depository institution altogether. For the firm in this example, the swaps market is attractive because it provides a means of altering its interest rate risk without changing its business operations. The motivation is business efficiency, not the pursuit of an arbitrage profit.

Creating hybrid fixed/floating debt

Consider an industrial firm with an outstanding FRN (floating-rate note) paying LIBOR plus 2 percent semiannually, a remaining term to maturity of six years, and a par value of $30 million. The issuer has decided that it would like to fix its financing cost for the first three years of the remaining maturity, while allowing the rate to float for the remaining three years. A "brute force" approach to this need would be to purchase all of the existing bonds in the open market, and issue a new bond that has the desired characteristics of a fixed rate for three years followed by a floating rate for three years. This course of action would be quite expensive and difficult. First, a bond buyback is an expensive undertaking in itself. Second, the firm would have to register and issue the new bond, incurring substantial registration fees and flotation costs. Third, the firm might have difficulty finding investors who would want a hybrid fixed/floating bond. Through the swaps market, however, the firm can realize its desire efficiently and at low cost.

The firm can change the structure of its debt by leaving its existing FRN intact and entering a pay-fixed interest rate swap. Specifically, the firm initiates a swap to pay a fixed rate on $30 million with semiannual payments with a tenor of three years and to receive LIBOR. Assuming the fixed rate for such a swap is 6 percent, the firm will have fixed its financing cost at

8 percent for the first three years while allowing the rate it pays on the bond to float for the last three years of the FRN's life. The firm's fixed-rate financing cost is 8 percent, because with the swap agreement, the firm pays LIBOR 12 percent on its FRN, receives LIBOR on the swap agreement, and pays 6 percent fixed on the swap agreement. We illustrate this transaction by focusing on a single payment, since all six of the semiannual payments have the same structure:

Initial position:

Semiannual cash flow on outstanding FRN:	$-(\text{LIBOR } 12\%) \times 1/2 \text{ year} \times \$30,000,000$
Pay-fixed swap semiannual cash flows:	$-6\% \times 1/2 \text{ year} \times \$30,000,000$ $+ \text{ LIBOR} \times 1/2 \text{ year} \times \$30,000,000$
Net semiannual cash flow (swap flows plus outstanding FRN):	$-(\text{LIBOR} + 2\%) \times 1/2 \text{ year} \times \$30,000,000$ $-6\% \times 1/2 \text{ year} \times \$30,000,000$ $+ \text{ LIBOR} \times 1/2 \text{ year} \times \$30,000,000$ $= -8\% \times 1/2 \text{ year} \times \$30,000,000$ $= -\$1,200,000$

Compared with the difficulty and expense of a bond buyback and a reissuance, the swap agreement can be arranged quickly and cheaply to achieve the same financial results for the firm. This example illustrates the real current motivation for the swaps market. Swaps provide a cost-effective and operationally efficient means of altering a financial position that could probably also be achieved in a more expensive and cumbersome manner. Today, the popularity of the swaps market depends much more on the operational efficiencies that it offers, rather than on attempts to exploit informational inefficiencies.

Summary

In this section, we have explored three simple examples of using swaps. The first example focused on exploiting a comparative advantage in borrowing costs between two countries. This example depended on a market inefficiency, a differential credit assessment of two firms in two countries. Today, the swaps market should be reckoned as highly efficient and the arbitrage-based opportunities of the comparative advantage example are unlikely to be found.

Instead, utilization of the swaps market turns on the desire of firms to shape their interest rate risk and foreign currency exposure. The swaps market has grown so fast and become so large because swaps provide an efficient and cost-effective means of allowing firms to transform their risk exposures, as the last two examples of this section illustrated. The transformations in risk exposure and cash flow patterns that firms achieve by using swaps can generally be accomplished in other ways. In fact, Chapter 21 shows how swaps can be analyzed in terms of more familiar financial instruments, such as bonds, options, and forward contracts. The swaps market has succeeded because it allows these same objectives of altering risk and transforming cash flows to be accomplished cheaply and efficiently. The examples considered in this section merely hint at the full usefulness of the swaps market. Chapter 22 provides a series of more realistic and extended examples.

Swap facilitators

A swap facilitator is a firm that assists in the completion of swaps, and may be classified as a swap broker or a swap dealer. When a swap facilitator acts strictly as an agent, without taking any financial position in the swap transaction, the facilitator acts as a **swap broker**. In some instances, a swap facilitator may actually transact for its own account to help complete the swap. In this case, the swap facilitator acts as a **swap dealer** or **swap bank**.

In the early development of the swap market, swap brokers played a prominent role in finding two appropriate swap parties and bringing them together to complete the swap. The swap broker essentially played an informational role. In today's swap market, the swap dealer predominates. A variety of swap dealing firms stand ready to serve as a counterparty to virtually any desired swap transaction. We briefly consider swap brokers and then concentrate on swap dealers.

Swap brokers

For a swap transaction to occur without a swap dealer, two counterparties with matching needs must find each other. As we have seen, a firm with a short-term and fairly standard risk exposure might use futures or exchange-traded options to manage that risk. Special risk exposures often lead firms to look beyond futures and exchange-traded options to the swaps market for the management of that special exposure. For example, even with the plain vanilla interest rate and currency swaps examples that we considered, the risks faced by the parties could not be managed completely with futures or exchange-traded options. As the risk exposure goes beyond the plain vanilla variety, futures and exchange-traded options are even less adequate for managing these more complex risks.

For a potential swap participant with a specific need, finding a counterparty can be very difficult. In the previous example of a plain vanilla currency swap, Party C must find another firm that meets a number of conditions. The firm that will act as a counterparty to Party C must have the following: preferential borrowing access to $31.25 million, a need for euros, a requirement that matches Party C in size ($31.25 million versus €25 million), a time horizon of seven years, a willingness to transact at the time desired by Party C, and an acceptable credit standing. For Party C to find this potential counterparty is a daunting task.

The difficulty of finding counterparties creates an opportunity for a swap broker. A swap broker has a number of firms in her client base and stands ready to search for swap counterparties upon demand. In the example of the plain vanilla currency swap, Party C might approach a swap broker and seek assistance in finding a counterparty. In effect, Party C would rely on the swap broker's specialized knowledge of the swap needs of many firms.

After Party C solicits the assistance of a swap broker, the broker contacts potential counterparties. In general, a firm such as Party C will desire privacy, so the broker will not identify Party C until she finds a very likely counterparty. (This is another reason why firms use swap brokers. By having a swap broker conduct the search, Party C in our example can preserve its anonymity.) Once the swap broker finds a suitable counterparty, which turns out to be Party D in our plain vanilla currency swap example, the broker brings the two parties together. The broker then helps to negotiate and complete the swap contract. For her services, the swap broker receives a fee from each of the counterparties.

In summary, the swap broker serves as an information intermediary. The broker uses her superior knowledge of potential swap participants to find the right counterparty. The broker exercises discretion by protecting the identity of the potential counterparties until the swap partners are found. Notice that the swap broker is not a party to the swap contract. As a broker, the swap facilitator does not bear financial risk, but merely assists the two counterparties in completing the swap transaction. The operations of the swap broker described above are somewhat cumbersome, depending on an active search and trying to match counterparties. As the swaps market has matured, the swap broker has diminished in importance. Today, well-established swap dealers perform the informational role of swap brokers, and stand ready to act as a counterparty in a swap agreement.

Swap dealers

Our discussion of swap brokers shows the limitations of their services. The swap broker can only complete a swap by finding two parties with matching needs. The search for matching counterparties is cumbersome and destined to fail in many instances. This situation provides an opportunity for a swap dealer.

In essence, the swap dealer stands ready to serve as a counterparty in any swap. In the plain vanilla interest rate swap example, we noted that Party A was a savings and loan association that paid a floating rate of LIBOR – 1 percent to its depositors and made a five-year fixed-rate mortgage loan at 9 percent. This initial business position left Party A exposed to rising interest rates, and Party A wanted to avoid this risk by converting the fixed rate it received on its mortgage loan to a floating rate. Party A's ability to complete this swap depended on finding a suitable counterparty with a matching need, such as Party B in our example.

If there is no swap dealer and a firm like Party B cannot be found, Party A is left unable to complete the swap. In today's market with a number of swap dealers, Party A can simply initiate its desired swap with a swap dealer as a counterparty. Party A no longer needs to worry about a Party B at all. Figure 20.8 shows the plain vanilla interest rate swap example as before, except the swap dealer acts as the counterparty to Party A. The availability of swap dealers makes it extremely easy for firms to complete swaps without searching for an appropriate counterparty.

The swap dealer hopes to make a profit on each swap she enters. Therefore, the swap dealer charges a spread between the two sides of the swap that is analogous to a bid–ask spread in the stock market. As a swap dealer engages in a series of swaps, she accumulates a **swap book**, a portfolio of swaps. This swap book has its own risks that the swap dealer must manage. Therefore, we need to consider the basic economics of swap pricing, how the dealer sets her prices to be consistent with the economics of pricing yet still make a profit, and how the dealer can manage the risk of her swap portfolio. We consider each of these issues in turn.

Figure 20.8   A plain vanilla interest rate swap with a swap dealer

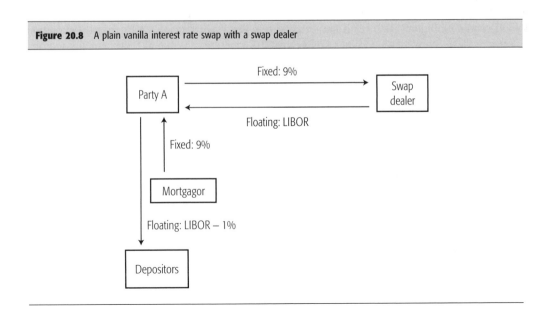

Inter-dealer brokers

Swap dealers, such as Goldman Sachs, are important players in the OTC market because they construct swaps for their end-user counterparties, such as a corporate treasury department or a money manager. Another important player in the OTC market is the **inter-dealer broker**.

Inter-dealer brokers have gained in importance as the swap market has matured. When swaps first arrived on the financial scene, they were highly customized deals constructed to meet the precise needs of the swap counterparties. As the market has matured, swaps have become more standardized and bid–ask spreads have narrowed. To fill the needs of the changing swap market, the inter-dealer broker business evolved as a specialist intermediary between swap dealers. An inter-dealer broker acts much like an exchange for OTC swaps, where bids and offers are posted electronically on a trading screen or through voice brokerage (that is, the telephone). The inter-dealer market provides price discovery and trade execution services for dealers. Trade execution takes place in two steps. In the first step a bid or offer is matched by two dealers, based solely on the price and the size of the transaction. In the second step, the identity of the opposing dealer is revealed and each side determines whether the trade fits within each dealer's counterparty credit limit for the opposing dealer.

The inter-dealer market offers one avenue for a dealer to hedge. For example, a swap dealer contemplating a "customer facilitation" transaction with an end-user can hedge the residual risk resulting from that transaction either in either the futures market or in the inter-dealer market. A dealer servicing an end-user with a $100 million U.S. dollar LIBOR-based pay-fixed (to the dealer) swap at one tenor can offset this position with a similar swap that is pay-floating to the dealer, or the dealer can establish a short position in a strip of Eurodollar futures. Firms such as ICAP (formerly Intercapital) dominate the inter-dealer swaps market.

Pricing of swaps

This section illustrates the bare basics of swap pricing by focusing on the intuition behind the pricing of plain vanilla interest rate swaps. Chapter 21 explores the pricing of interest rate and currency swaps in detail. For now, we seek to convey the basic principle. Consider the three yield curves of Figure 20.9. Each curve has a two-year spot rate of 5.40 percent. One curve slopes modestly upward to 6.20 percent by year 10. One curve is flat at 5.40 percent, and one slopes modestly downward to 4.6 percent at year 10. We want to consider how a plain vanilla interest rate swap would be priced in each environment. In every case, the plain vanilla interest rate swap requires the pay-floating party to pay LIBOR each period in return for a fixed-rate payment.

If we compare the upward- and downward-sloping yield curves, we can ask which environment would justify a higher fixed-rate payment in exchange for LIBOR for a vanilla swap with a ten-year tenor. To answer this question, consider the forward rates of interest that prevail in each environment. The forward rates are clearly higher in the upward-sloping yield curve environment, as we explored in some detail in Chapter 19.

When the forward rates are higher, the fixed rate on the swap should be higher. Without attempting to prove this proposition here, there are two intuitive justifications for this claim. First, forward rates are often taken as a forecast of future expected spot interest rates. Thus, one would expect higher spot rates over the ten-year horizon in the upward-sloping term structure environment. If those higher rates were to materialize, the LIBOR payments would rise over time and this would require a higher fixed-rate payment on the swap. Second, the upward-sloping yield curve requires a higher fixed-rate payment on the swap to avoid arbitrage. With the ready

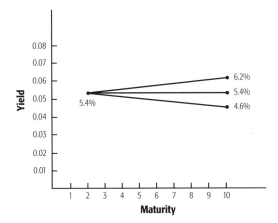

Figure 20.9   Three sample yield curves

availability of forward rate agreements (FRAs), one could hedge the various payments on the swap at rates consistent with the shape of the term structure. Therefore, the fixed rate on the swap must reflect both the level and shape of the term structure. This is the essential factor that determines swap pricing:

> The no-arbitrage fixed rate on an interest rate swap agreement depends principally on the level of interest rates and the shape of the term structure.

Chapter 21 demonstrates this principle in detail and illustrates the mathematics of interest rate swap pricing. By analogy with our intuitive consideration of the term structure for interest rate swap pricing, we state an analogous principle for foreign currency swap pricing without attempting proof at this point:

> The no-arbitrage fixed rate on a foreign currency swap agreement depends principally on the term structure of interest rates for the two currencies in the swap (which together also define the term structure of foreign exchange rates between the two currencies).

Chapter 21 also demonstrates this principle of pricing for foreign currency swaps and illustrates it with several examples. For the present, we accept as given that the yield curve principally determines interest rate swap pricing, and go on to explore how the dealer sets prices to be consistent with the existing term structure of interest rates in a way to yield a profit.

The indication swap pricing schedule

In the early to mid-1980s, swap banks were often able to charge a front-end fee for arranging a swap. As the market has matured, efficiency has increased, and that ability has been competed away. (For some very complicated swaps that require substantial analysis, front-end fees are still charged, however.) Therefore, the swap dealer today generally receives her total compensation by charging a bid–ask spread between the rates she is willing to pay and the rate she demands on swap transactions. With a maturing market, this spread has also narrowed. Whereas in the mid-1980s spreads might have been 50 basis points, two to four basis points is much more

Table 20.5   Sample swap indication pricing

Maturity (years)	Bank's fixed rates (T-note rate plus indicated basis points)		T-note yields (%)
	Bank pays	Bank receives	
2	43	45	2.95
3	74	76	3.38
4	79	81	3.80
5	69	71	4.23
7	80	82	4.51
10	70	72	4.94

common today. This tightening spread reflects the increasing liquidity, sophistication, and pricing efficiency of a maturing financial market.

Table 20.5 shows a sample indication pricing schedule for an interest rate swap. It is consistent with the upward-sloping yield curve of Figure 20.9. The table assumes that the customer of the swap bank will offer LIBOR flat; that is, a rate exactly equal to LIBOR without any yield adjustment, which is the typical pricing arrangement for interest rate swaps. Prices are quoted as a spread to Treasury issues. This spread is called the **swap spread** (a spread separate from the bid–ask spread). There are two important features of Table 20.5. First, the rate the bank pays or receives increases with the maturity in question. This increase reflects the upward-sloping term structure revealed by the column of current T-note yields. Second, the swap bank makes a gross profit that equals the spread between what the bank pays and what it receives. For example, the bid–ask spread for a two-year swap is two basis points. The narrowness of all of these spreads is representative of today's swap market.

As an example of how the pricing schedule in Table 20.5 functions, assume that the customer wishes to take the receive-fixed side of a swap with a seven-year tenor. Based on the pricing schedule of Table 20.5, the customer would pay the LIBOR rate on the notional amount in each period and would receive a fixed rate from the swap bank that equals the seven-year T-note rate of 4.51 percent plus 80 basis points for a total rate of 5.31 percent. By contrast, if the customer wishes to take the pay-fixed side of a seven-year swap, the customer would pay the seven-year T-note rate of 4.51 percent plus 82 basis points for a fixed rate of 5.33 percent. In return, the bank would pay the customer LIBOR in each period.[10] As the swap market has developed in recent years, it has become much more competitive, and the spread available to swap dealers has dwindled.[11] In this example, the swap dealer earns a gross spread of just two basis points.

The pricing schedule of Table 20.5 is fully consistent with the existing term structure. As interest rates change, the swap dealer will revise the schedule. This is done on a daily basis. Failure to offer rates consistent with the term structure will immediately subject the swap dealer to arbitrage losses. The dealer must also offer a spread that is competitive with other swap dealers. Too large a spread will mean no customers; too narrow a spread will mean no profits. We might say that the term structure determines the fixed rate on the swap, and swap dealer competition determines the spread around that fixed rate.

In addition to the term structure, there are at least two minor factors that affect pricing. These are the creditworthiness of the potential counterparty and the current risk exposure of the dealer's swap book. Poor credit risks expose the swap dealer to the risk that a counterparty will default. The current risk exposure of a swap book can make a particular kind of swap look more or less attractive as an addition to the book, depending on whether the potential swap increases or reduces the overall risk of the swap portfolio. We consider these issues in the context of how a swap dealer can manage the various risks inherent in a swap portfolio.[12]

Swap portfolios

In this section, we briefly consider the principal risks that a swap dealer faces in managing a swap portfolio. These risks range from default risk to interest rate risk. We then illustrate how the swap dealer can manage some of these risks, with a particular focus on interest rate risk.

Risks in managing a swap portfolio

In managing a portfolio of many swaps, the swap dealer faces a number of different risks. First, there is **default risk**, the risk that one of its counterparties might fail to perform according to the swap agreement. Therefore, the swap dealer must appraise the creditworthiness of the swap partner. As we have seen earlier in this chapter, there is no clearinghouse in the swaps market to guarantee performance on a contract if one of the counterparties defaults. If the swap dealer suffers a default by one of its counterparties, the dealer must either absorb the loss or institute a lawsuit to seek recovery on the defaulted obligation.

In most swaps, the timings of cash flows between the counterparties are matched fairly closely. For example, in the plain vanilla interest rate swap of Figure 20.8, the fixed and floating cash flows occur at similar times, and we noted that only the net amount is actually exchanged. Thus, default on a swap seldom could involve failure to pay the notional amount or even an entire periodic payment. In this sense, default on an interest rate swap is not as critical as default on a corporate bond, in which an investor might lose the entire principal. Instead, a swap default would generally imply a loss of the change in value due to shifting interest rates. While this amount can be quite significant, such a default would not be as catastrophic as a bond default in which the entire principal could be lost.

As we explore in more detail later in this chapter, the swap dealer seeks to build a swap portfolio in which the risks of individual swaps offset each other. When a swap dealer suffers a default, the elaborate structure of offsetting risks can be upset. This leaves the swap dealer in a riskier position, and the dealer must struggle to reestablish the risk control that was upset by the default. Because of the potential costs associated with default, the swap dealer will adjust the pricing on the fixed side of the swap to reflect the risk of default. Parties that have a high risk of default are likely to be excluded from the market. For example, airlines under bankruptcy protection probably have very limited access to the swaps market. As we noted earlier, the swaps market is mainly a market for financial institutions and corporations due to the importance of default considerations and the need for one party to be able to confirm the creditworthiness of a prospective counterparty.[13]

A swap dealer also faces **basis risk**—the risk that the normal relationship between two floating rates might change. To illustrate this risk, assume that a bank engages in an interest rate swap to make floating payments based on a Euribor and to receive floating payments based on U.S. LIBOR. After this agreement is reached, assume that market disturbances (such as bank defaults) in Europe cause Euribor rates to rise relative to U.S. LIBOR. The swap dealer must still pay the higher Euribor rates, but will receive only the lower U.S. LIBOR. Therefore, the swap dealer suffers a loss due to basis risk, as the normal relationship between European and U.S. floating rates has changed.

The swap dealer also faces mismatch risk. When he acts as a counterparty in a swap, the swap dealer accepts a risk position that he is anxious to offset by engaging in other swaps. **Mismatch risk** refers to the risk that the swap dealer will be left in a position that he cannot offset easily through another swap. This arises if there is a mismatch in the needs between the swap dealer and other participants.

Mismatches among the swaps in a portfolio leave the dealer with **interest rate risk**, the risk of a change in the swap portfolio's value due to a change in interest rates. This is the most serious risk that the swap dealer faces. For example, the swap dealer may have promised to pay a floating rate and to receive a fixed rate. If the general level of interest rates rises, the swap dealer's cash outflows will rise as well. However, the dealer continues to receive the stipulated fixed rate. The swap dealer incurs a loss due to a shift in interest rates. In Figure 20.8, for example, the swap dealer is left to receive $900,000 annually and to pay LIBOR on a notional principal of $10 million in each year. If rates rise, the payments that the dealer must make will increase, while the dealer's cash inflows will remain the same. Such a rise in interest rates would generate a loss for the swap dealer, so the dealer faces interest rate risk.

Swap dealers as financial intermediaries

Swap dealers are generally firms that produce multiple products, in addition to acting as swap dealers. For example, investment banks and the derivatives units of commercial banking firms are typical swap dealers. These firms engage in many activities, from helping corporations to issue securities, to lending, to speculating. We want to focus on the swap dealer as a financial intermediary—a firm that seeks to offer financial services to other firms and receive a profit for this service. The financial intermediary can function because it has special expertise that its customers lack, such as greater financial sophistication, greater knowledge of financial markets, and the capital inherent in being able to perform a specialized task. As a financial intermediary, the swap dealer seeks the quiet life of reasonable profits in exchange for a valuable service to its customers and wishes to avoid speculation and interest rate risk. From this perspective, we approach the swap dealer as a firm that finds itself exposed to interest rate risk in the ordinary conduct of making a market in swaps and wishes to control and avoid that risk.

Managing interest rate risk in a swap portfolio

To explore how a swap dealer manages interest rate risk, we assume that the dealer begins with its optimal set of investments. Therefore, acting as a counterparty exposes the dealer to an unwanted risk that was accepted only to help complete the swap transaction and to earn a profit. Against this background, we return to our example of the plain vanilla interest rate swap of Figure 20.8 to explore how the swap dealer can manage this unwanted risk. For simplicity, we assume that the yield curve is flat.

After acting as a counterparty in the swap of Figure 20.8, the swap dealer is obligated to receive a fixed rate of 9 percent and to pay LIBOR on a notional amount of $10 million annually for the next five years. The swap dealer will want to offset the risk that she has undertaken, but she needs to offset that risk on better terms than she undertook as a counterparty to Party A. Otherwise, the profit she hoped to capture will disappear.

Let us assume that Party E contracts with our swap dealer to pay-floating for a tenor of three years, with annual payments, and a notional principal of $10 million. As we have already seen in Figure 20.8, the dealer contracted with Party A to receive fixed at 9 percent. Now the dealer contracts with Party E to pay fixed at a rate of 8.9 percent. This implies a ten basis point spread for the dealer between the pay-fixed and receive-fixed swaps.

By entering this second swap with Party E, the swap dealer offsets a substantial portion of the risk she accepts by transacting with Party A in the initial swap. Figure 20.10 shows the

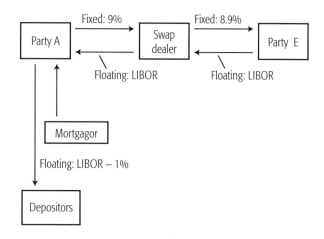

Figure 20.10   The swap dealer as intermediary in a plain vanilla interest rate swap

transactions involving Parties A and E, along with the swap dealer. After completing these transactions, we see that the swap dealer has some profits to show for her efforts. Specifically, the dealer breaks even on the floating-rate side of the transaction because she both receives and pays LIBOR. At the same time, the dealer receives a fixed rate of 9 percent ($900,000) from Party A and pays a fixed rate of 8.9 percent ($890,000) to Party E. However, the swap dealer still has considerable risk as a result of the transaction.

Table 20.6 shows the swap dealer's cash flows resulting from the two swaps. The first two columns of the table show the cash flows that result from the swap dealer's transactions with Party A. To serve the needs of Party A, the swap dealer receives a 9 percent fixed-rate payment and pays LIBOR on a $10 million notional amount. Based on the portion of the transaction with Party A, the swap dealer will receive $900,000 each year and pay LIBOR on $10 million each year. Which set of cash flows is better is uncertain, because the future course of interest rates is not known. For example, if LIBOR stays constant at 8 percent over the five years, the swap dealer will make 1 percent per year for five years on $10 million. However, if LIBOR jumps to 11 percent and remains constant, the swap dealer will lose 2 percent on $10 million each year. As a result, the swap dealer will receive $900,000 but must pay $1.1 million each year, for an annual net loss of $200,000. Thus, the riskiness of acting as a counterparty to Party A is clear. Table 20.6 also shows the swap dealer's cash flows that result from transacting with Party E. For each of the first three years, the dealer will pay a fixed interest

Table 20.6   The swap dealer's cash flows

Year	From Party A	To Party A	From Party E	To Party E	Dealer's net cash flow
1	$900,000	LIBOR	LIBOR	$890,000	$10,000
2	$900,000	LIBOR	LIBOR	$890,000	$10,000
3	$900,000	LIBOR	LIBOR	$890,000	$10,000
4	$900,000	LIBOR	0	0	$900,000 − LIBOR × $10 million
5	$900,000	LIBOR	0	0	$900,000 − LIBOR × $10 million

rate of 8.9 percent on $10 million, or $890,000. In addition, the dealer will receive LIBOR on a notional amount of $10 million.

Table 20.6 shows the swap dealer's net cash flows in the last column. During the first three years, the dealer receives LIBOR from Party E and pays LIBOR to Party A, both on notional amounts of $10 million. On this portion of the transaction, the dealer has a net zero cash flow. The dealer also receives $900,000 from Party A each year and pays $890,000 to Party E each year. Considering all parts of the transaction, the dealer receives a net spread of ten basis points on a $10 million notional amount. Taking all of the dealer's cash flows during the first three years into account, we see that the dealer has a net cash inflow of $10,000 per year.

Even after transacting with both Parties A and E, the swap dealer has a residual risk that is evident from her net cash flows. In years 4 and 5, the dealer will receive $900,000 from Party A, but she must pay LIBOR. Whether this will create a profit or loss for the dealer depends on future interest rates. However, in Table 20.6 we can see that the dealer has substantially reduced her risk by trading with Party E. The dealer may hope to enter other swaps to reduce this risk or may use the futures market to hedge the remaining risk for years 4 and 5, although this hedge is likely to be imperfect, as we discuss below.

Table 20.6 also shows that the swap dealer is making a profit as a financial intermediary. Because of her superior market knowledge and position, the dealer was able to complete the second swap with Party E. By transacting with Party E, instead of just transacting with Party A, the swap dealer secures a ten basis point spread on the notional amount for three years. In addition to earning a profit on the spread, the dealer's transaction with Party E offsets a substantial portion of the risk inherent in acting as a counterparty to Party A in the initial swap transaction.

In our example of the swap dealer's transactions, we assumed that the swap dealer had an initial portfolio of assets that met her needs in terms of risk and diversification. By acting as a counterparty to Party A, the swap dealer assumed a risk in pursuit of profit. The dealer could have taken this position as a speculation on interest rates. However, the swap dealer preferred to act as a financial intermediary, making a profit by providing informational services. In our example, the swap dealer is able to capture a spread of ten basis points and reduce risk by transacting with Party E. Ideally, the swap dealer acting as a financial intermediary would also like to avoid the remaining risk exposure in years 4 and 5. Being able to do so requires that the dealer find another swap partner.

Because we are assuming that the swap dealer wishes to act only as a financial intermediary, the swap dealer will be very concerned about how the risk involved in a prospective swap can be offset by participating in other swaps. For example, in the dealer's swap of Figure 20.10, the readiness of the swap dealer to enter the transaction with Party A may well depend on the dealer's expectation of completing swaps with other counterparties like Party E. If the dealer considers transacting with Party A and does not know of Party E, the dealer may require more favorable terms to transact with Party A. However, if the dealer knows about Parties A and E from the outset, the dealer may accept less favorable terms with Party A, because she knows she can offset some of the risk of acting as Party A's counterparty by engaging in a second swap with Party E.

As we noted, the swap dealer faces the net cash flows shown in the last column of Table 20.6 after engaging in the two interest rate swaps with Parties A and E. Assume now that another potential swap participant, Party F, is available to swap the cash flows in years 4 and 5. In other words, Party F would be willing to pay LIBOR rate on a $10 million notional amount for years 4 and 5 and to receive a fixed rate of 9 percent. The swap dealer would find Party F to be a very attractive counterparty. The dealer might be quite willing to swap with Party F on even terms (9 percent fixed versus LIBOR) just to offset the risk that remained after swapping with

Parties A and E. In summary, the swap dealer will be very pleased to create a structure of swaps that leaves no interest rate risk and still provides a decent profit.

As a practical means of dealing with an imbalanced swap book, the dealer might shade her quotations slightly to attract the most beneficial swap partners. In our example, the dealer's net position is slightly tilted toward the received-fixed side of the market in years 4 and 5, while being balanced in years 1–3. In years 4 and 5, the anticipated cash flow for the dealer is $900,000 – LIBOR × $10 million. To offset this receive-fixed residual position, the dealer might shift her bid–ask spread to generate more swaps in which she takes the pay-fixed side of the deal. For example, if the term structure indicates an appropriate fixed rate of 8.95 percent and she has been operating with a spread of 8.90 to 9.00 percent, she might offer terms of 8.91 to 9.01, in which she would pay-fixed at 8.91 percent and receive-fixed of 9.01 percent. This slight shift in rates would have the effect of attracting customers who want to receive-fixed and allow her to engage in more pay-fixed swaps. In actual practice, a swap dealer is engaging in numerous swaps, so the problem of rebalancing the interest rate risk exposure is a constant one.

In most events, the swap dealer will be left with a swap book that contains residual interest rate risk, leaving the dealer with either a pay-fixed or receive-fixed net position. Let us assume that the swap dealer is left with the residual risk shown in the last column of Table 20.6 after all swaps are taken into account. Specifically, the swap bank is still committed to receiving $900,000 and paying LIBOR on a notional amount of $10 million in years 4 and 5.

This residual risk position reflects both mismatch risk and interest rate risk. The mismatch risk occurs because the dealer has been unable to offset the risks associated with the swap with Party A. The transaction with Party E offsets most of the risk arising from the swap with Party A, but some risk remains due to the mismatch between the needs of Parties A and E. The transactions of Table 20.6 also reflect a continuing interest rate risk. As we noted, if rates rise, the dealer suffers a loss, as she must pay the higher floating rates that result.

As a consequence, the swap dealer will be anxious to offset these two remaining risks associated with her commitments in periods 4 and 5 in Table 20.6. When the swap dealer faces a risk such as that in Table 20.6, she can use the inter-dealer market to obtain a position in an offsetting swap. Or the swap dealer can use the futures market as a temporary means of offsetting the risk. For example, the swap dealer might sell Eurodollar futures with a distant expiration, as Eurodollar futures rates are essentially the same as LIBOR. With this transaction, the swap dealer would offset a considerable portion of the risk that remains in Table 20.6. When the swap dealer executes the futures transaction properly, she will be left only with an obligation to pay a fixed amount.

However, even after this transaction, some risk remains. Eurodollar futures may be a close substitute for the unavailable swap, but they are unlikely to provide a perfect substitute. In our example, the dealer will probably not be able to match the futures expiration dates with the cash flows in years 4 and 5. Consequently, there is likely to be some imperfection in setting the quantity of futures to trade, and there is still some basis risk between the LIBOR rate of the cash flows in years 4 and 5 and the rate on the Eurodollar futures. Because of these imperfections in substituting for the unavailable swap, the swap dealer will likely continue to seek a swap that meets the risk needs exactly. However, until that is available, the Eurodollar futures position can act as an effective risk-reducing position.

Beyond plain vanilla swaps

In this section, we explore the additional features that swaps may possess to make them more varied, more flexible, and more efficiently designed for particular risk management situations.[14]

Currently, there is a bewildering variety of swap structures being used in the market, and new features are constantly being created. Therefore, the catalog of this section is incomplete, but it provides some insight into the basic enhancements that can extend swaps beyond the plain vanilla structure that we have explored. We consider interest rate swaps and foreign currency swaps in turn.

Flavored interest rate swaps

A plain vanilla interest rate swap has a constant notional principal for the life of the swap. Further, each interest payment on the fixed side is for the same dollar amount, being calculated on the same notional principal at the same rate of interest. While the floating payment may vary due to fluctuating interest rates, it is computed on the same notional principal in each period. It is possible to extend interest rate swaps beyond the plain vanilla structure by altering the characteristics of the notional principal or the payments derived from that principal.

In an **amortizing swap**, the notional principal is reduced over time. This means that the fixed interest payment becomes smaller during the life of the swap, and the floating payment does as well, at least if interest rates are stable. Because mortgage principal is generally amortized, an amortizing swap provides a useful instrument for managing the interest rate risk associated with mortgages.

While the notional principal diminishes in an amortizing swap, it can also be scheduled to increase. In an **accreting swap**, the notional principal becomes larger during the life of the swap. This kind of swap matches the cash flows often encountered in construction finance. For example, consider a construction project in which the builder will draw down $10 million of additional financing at the end of each of the seven years of the life of a particular building project as interim construction objectives are achieved. Typically, this kind of financing is committed at the outset of the project, and the additional loans are promised at a floating rate. These flows could be converted to a fixed rate through an accreting swap designed with a principal that increases $10 million each year and has a fixed interest rate.

By combining features of amortizing and accreting swaps, it is possible to create interest rate swaps with quite variable notional principals that increase and decrease over the life of the swap. In a **seasonal swap**, the notional principal varies according to a fixed plan. This kind of swap can be useful in matching the financing needs of retailers. For example, the swap could be structured on a seasonal basis to match the typically heavy fourth-quarter cash needs of retailing firms. When the notional principal on the swap first increases and then amortizes to zero over the life of the swap, the swap is called a **roller coaster** swap. Thus, the notional principal can be structured to conform to any financing or risk management need.

In addition to allowing the notional principal of an interest rate swap to vary, swaps can be created with variations on coupon payments. In a plain vanilla swap, the fixed and floating payments are typically established at the prevailing rates when the swap is initiated. For example, consider a five-year swap with annual payments on a notional principal of $25 million initiated when the yield curve is flat at 8 percent. In this situation, one might create an **off-market swap** by setting the fixed payment at 9 percent and the floating payment equal to LIBOR. In this example, the pay-fixed party has agreed to pay a higher rate over the life of the swap. To compensate for this series of extra payments, the pay-floating party must make an additional cash payment to the pay-fixed party. With a fixed rate of interest at 1 percent above the market on a notional principal of $25 million, the pay-fixed party will be paying an excess $250,000 each year. With the yield curve flat at 8 percent, the appropriate payment from the pay-floating party to the pay-fixed party would be the present value of those five payments of $250,000 discounted at 8 percent, which is $998,178.

In this example, the pay-fixed party receives $998,178 at the initiation of the swap and pays $2.25 million annually. The pay-floating party pays on a notional principal of $25 million. Thus, this example includes features of a loan and an interest rate swap, with the pay-floating party providing approximately $1 million of financing to the pay-fixed side of the deal as part of the swap agreement.

A **forward swap** is a swap agreement in which the parties agree that the cash flows will begin at a date in the future. Forward swaps may be interest rate, currency, commodity, or equity swaps. For example, two counterparties might agree to exchange LIBOR for a fixed rate beginning in two years, with the tenor of the swap being five years from that date. If the contractual rates are based on the forward rate for the two instruments at the planned initiation date, there should be no exchange of cash at the initiation of the agreement. If the rates specified do not conform to the forward rates for the planned inception of the cash flows, then the swap is an off-market swap and one party will be obligated to pay the other.

An **extension swap** is a swap agreement designed to extend the tenor of an existing swap. As such, an extension swap is a special type of forward swap. For example, in the middle of the tenor of an interest rate swap in which one party pays LIBOR and receives a fixed rate, the parties might agree to extend the tenor of the swap by an additional three years. If the agreement is initiated based on the forward rates for the date of inception (that is, at the termination of the current swap agreement), there should be no payment at the time the agreement is made.

As we have seen for a plain vanilla interest rate swap, one party pays a fixed rate of interest, while the second pays a floating rate. In a **basis swap**, both parties pay a floating rate of interest, but the payments are computed on different indexes. Let us assume that the three-month LIBOR currently stands at 6 percent, while the three-month T-bill rate is 5.25 percent. In a basis swap with a notional principal of $100 million based on these two rates, one party might pay the T-bill rate plus 75 basis points, while the second party would pay LIBOR. Although the T-bill rate and LIBOR tend to move together, the spread between the two rates does change with the perceived differential in default risk between bank obligations and U.S. Treasury issues.

If the rate widens, the party paying the T-bill rate plus 75 basis points will win; if the rate narrows, the party paying LIBOR will win. For example, assuming annual payments on the $100 million notional principal, both parties expect to pay $6 million annually. If rates rise, but LIBOR rises more due to political unrest, perhaps, rates might change to a T-bill rate of 5.50 percent and a LIBOR rate of 6.40 percent. With these new rates, the LIBOR payment would be $6.4 million, while the T-bill payer would be obligated for $6.25 million, leaving a net payment of $150,000 per year from the LIBOR payer.

Another kind of basis swap is a yield curve swap. In a **yield curve swap**, both parties pay a floating rate, but the indexes differ in yields. For example, one party might pay based on the three-month T-bill rate, while the other party might pay based on a 30-year bellwether bond. Assuming that long-term rates are initially above short-term rates, a flattening yield curve would benefit the party paying based on the 30-year bond, while a steepening yield curve would benefit the payer basing payment on the short-term index.

These yield curve swaps are sometimes implemented as a **constant-maturity swap** (CMS). The Federal Reserve Board maintains yield series for Treasury issues of various constant maturities, such as a five-year or ten-year constant maturity T-note. A yield curve swap could be implemented by using a constant-maturity series as an index for the rates in a yield curve swap. For example, one could swap three-month LIBOR against the ten-year constant-maturity Treasury index.

A yield curve swap represents a technique that might appeal to financial institutions, particularly those with long-term assets and short-term liabilities, such as a savings and loan association.

For example, assume that a savings and loan holds short-term deposits and long-term assets. Such an institution is subject to losses if short-term rates rise relative to long-term rates. The savings and loan might enter a yield curve swap in which it makes payments based on a long-term index and receives payments based on a short-term index. This swap arrangement could help protect the institution from the yield curve risk that it faces in its core S&L business.

A **rate-differential swap**, or **diff swap**, has payments tied to interest rate indexes in two different currencies, but all payments are in a single currency. For example, a diff swap might be structured with all payments in U.S. dollars, with one party paying three-month U.S. LIBOR and the other party paying three-month Euribor, but with payments in dollars. Assume that both the LIBOR and the Euribor yield curves are flat, that the dollar rate is 7 percent, and that the euro rate is 6.75 percent. The payment based on U.S. LIBOR might be LIBOR flat, and the payment based on Euribor would also be Euribor flat, but paid in dollars. (Chapter 21 explores currency swap pricing and shows why both parties would pay LIBOR flat, even though the rates are 7 percent in the United States and 6.75 percent in the EU. Chapter 22 shows how to price diff swaps.) This kind of swap would exploit changes in U.S. versus EU interest rates over the tenor of the swap.

The interest rate swaps considered so far all focus on differences in levels of interest rates, whether those rates are of the same or different maturities, or in the same or different currencies. A **corridor swap** is structured so that payment obligations occur only when the reference rate is within some specified range or corridor. For example, one might contract to receive a fixed rate and pay six-month LIBOR only when LIBOR is greater than 5 percent but less than 7 percent. In this situation, the fixed rate would be lower than that on a comparable plain vanilla interest rate swap. The corridor swap is essentially a speculation on the volatility of LIBOR.

Flavored currency swaps

A currency swap calls for the two counterparties to exchange currencies at the outset of the swap and to make a series of interest payments for the currency that is received. At the end of the swap tenor, the counterparties repay the currencies that they have received. In the plain vanilla currency swap, one party generally pays a floating rate, while the other pays a fixed rate. Currency swaps are subject to many of the same elaborations as those we have considered for interest rate swaps.

As we observed in discussing interest rate swaps, more complicated swap structures can be created by allowing the notional principal to vary over the tenor of the swap. In the context of interest rate swaps, we considered amortizing, accreting, seasonal, and roller coaster swaps based on prenegotiated changes in the notional principal. Currency swaps are subject to the same variations. For example, a U.S. firm might import clothes from Hong Kong, with much higher imports in the winter, and pay for these in Hong Kong dollars. The firm might structure a currency swap with a seasonal notional principal to match its greater anticipated need for funds in winter months.

Two fixed-for-floating swaps can be combined to create a fixed-for-fixed currency swap. As an example, consider a firm that has entered into a plain vanilla currency swap to receive fixed Swiss franc payments and to pay in U.S. dollars based on LIBOR. By pairing this swap with another fixed-for-floating agreement, the firm can create a fixed-for-fixed swap. For example, assume that the second swap agreement obligates the firm to make fixed payments in euros and to receive floating payments in U.S. dollars. Figure 20.11 shows the two fixed-for-floating swaps.

As Figure 20.11 shows, the firm both makes and receives floating U.S. dollar payments. Thus, assuming equal notional principal amounts for the two swaps, these payments offset each other.

Figure 20.11 A pair of fixed-for-floating currency swaps

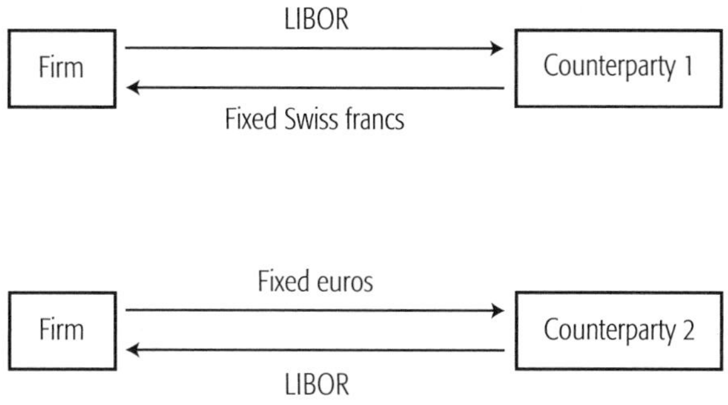

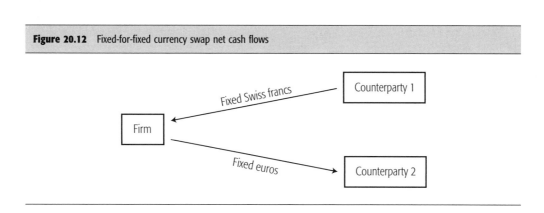

Figure 20.12 Fixed-for-fixed currency swap net cash flows

Figure 20.12 shows the net cash flows resulting from this swap for the firm. Given the offset of the U.S. dollar flows, the firm is left receiving fixed Swiss franc payments and paying fixed euro payments. This construction of a fixed-for-fixed currency swap by combining two plain vanilla (fixed-for-floating) currency swaps illustrates how swaps can be combined to transform cash flows.

A **CIRCUS swap** is a fixed-for-fixed currency swap created by combining a plain vanilla interest rate swap with a plain vanilla currency swap. (CIRCUS stands for "combined interest rate and currency swap.") As an example, consider another firm that enters a plain vanilla currency swap. In this swap, the firm receives fixed-rate euro payments and pays LIBOR. The firm also enters a U.S. dollar plain vanilla interest rate swap to pay-fixed/receive-floating. Figure 20.13 shows the periodic interest payments on these two plain vanilla swaps.

Assuming that the two swaps have the same tenor and notional principal, the firm has combined these two plain vanilla swaps to create a fixed-for-fixed currency swap. Figure 20.14 shows the net periodic cash flows that the firm faces from the two combined swaps.

Commodity swaps

In a **commodity swap**, the counterparties make payments based on the price of a specified amount of a commodity, with one party paying a fixed price for the good over the tenor of the swap,

Figure 20.13   Two plain vanilla swaps to constitute a CIRCUS swap (periodic payments)

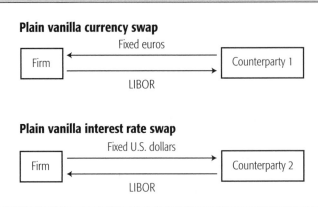

Plain vanilla currency swap

Plain vanilla interest rate swap

Figure 20.14   The firm's net cash flows in a CIRCUS swap (periodic payments)

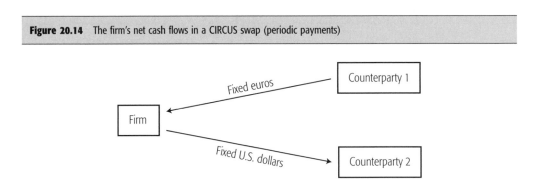

while the second party pays a floating price. In general, the commodity is not actually exchanged, and the parties make only net payments. Chase Manhattan Bank created the first commodity swap in 1986.[15]

As an example, consider a rice farmer producing 200 tons of rice annually. The farmer is anxious to avoid the price fluctuations of the spot rice market, particularly as import restrictions in Japan and Korea wax and wane. However, the farmer is uncomfortable trying to use the futures market in rice due to its low liquidity and uncertain future. Therefore, the farmer seeks a swap arrangement in which she takes the receive-fixed side of the deal. For example, she might agree to receive a fixed payment per ton for each of the next five years and promise to pay the actual market price of rice each year. Figure 20.15 shows the cash flows associated with this swap agreement. Each year, the farmer pays the actual price of rice based on the nominal amount of 200 tons, while the counterparty pays a fixed price negotiated when the swap agreement was established. With this arrangement, the farmer knows that she will receive a certain price for her rice for each of the next five years.

If we consider a single annual crop, this swap agreement has a structure that is very similar to the classic hedging example with agricultural futures. In the classic short hedge, the farmer anticipates a harvest and sells futures to establish a fixed price for her crop. In fact, a commodity

Figure 20.15   A commodity swap for rice

swap is so similar to a futures contract that the CFTC restricted the permissible range of commodity swap agreements to ensure that they remained sufficiently distinct from the futures contracts that the Commission regulates. Specifically, the CFTC stipulated that such agreements cannot be canceled by one party alone, that they are not supported by a system of margins or marking-to-market, that the agreements be related to the parties' normal line of business, and that the transactions be restricted to commercial firms and not the retail trade.[16]

The form of a commodity swap is very similar to that of an interest rate swap. Neither type of swap employs an exchange of notionals. In a commodity swap, one party takes the receive-fixed/pay-floating side of the deal, while the other takes the pay-fixed/receive-floating side, just as in an interest rate swap. Further, only net payments are actually made, as in interest rate swaps. The basic difference is simply that the underlying good in an interest rate swap is cash, while the underlying good in a commodity swap is some physical good.

The size of the commodity swap market is small relative other contract types. At year-end 2005, commodity swaps outstanding had a notional value of $2.6 trillion, according to the BIS survey, with OTC commodity contracts of all types having an outstanding notional value of $3.6 trillion. The market for commodity swaps grew rapidly in the period between 2000 and 2005 as pension funds, university endowments, and hedge funds allocated portions of their investment portfolios to commodity-linked investments as a hedge against inflation and to achieve long-term diversification objectives. For example, a pension fund manager may want to allocate a portion of the fund's assets allocated to commodities to track the Goldman Sachs Commodity Index (GSCI). The fund manager can gain exposure to the GSCI by entering into a commodity index swap with a swap dealer in which the fund takes the receive-floating side of a fixed-for-floating swap. The fund manager agrees to receive a floating payment linked to the GSCI and promises to pay a fixed amount each year. The swap dealer then hedges its exposure using the inter-dealer market or commodity futures markets. Hedging the GSCI in the futures market requires managing the so-called **Goldman Roll**, in which the index is rebalanced by rolling from an expiring futures contract into the next nearby contract as prescribed by the rebalancing algorithm of the index.

Equity swaps

In an **equity swap**, the counterparties exchange payments based on a notional principal specified as a stock portfolio. Like a commodity swap, the equity swap is quite similar to an interest rate swap, because there is an underlying notional principal, a fixed tenor, and one party has a receive-fixed/pay-floating commitment, while the other has a pay fixed/receive-floating position.

Consider an institutional investor with a $100 million portfolio of stocks invested in an index fund that tracks the S&P 500. If the manager of this portfolio becomes bearish, she has several

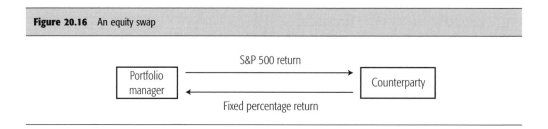

Figure 20.16   An equity swap

choices for avoiding the risk of a stock market decline. She could sell the stocks in the portfolio, hedge the stock market risk in the futures market, or hedge the risk by using index options. She could also use an equity swap.

For her situation, the portfolio manager could enter an equity swap agreement in which she pays the S&P 500 return each period and receives a fixed percentage payment, with both payments being based on the $100 million notional principal of her portfolio. For example, each quarter the portfolio manager might pay the total return earned by the S&P 500 and receive a quarterly payment of 2.5 percent, both payments being based on the $100 million notional principal. Figure 20.16 illustrates these cash flows. This arrangement would insulate the value of the portfolio against any drop in the stock market and guarantee the portfolio manager a quarterly return of 2.5 percent.

For example, if the S&P 500 enjoyed a return of 3 percent in a given quarter, her undisturbed portfolio would rise in value by 3 percent and she would pay this to the counterparty, so this would leave the portfolio value unchanged. However, the portfolio manager would also receive a payment of 2.5 percent. If the S&P 500 had a return of −5 percent, the portfolio manager would make no payment and would receive a payment of 7.5 percent. This inflow of 7.5 percent, combined with the drop in the value of the portfolio of 5 percent, would still give a net return on the portfolio of 2.5 percent.

As with the other swap structures we have considered in this chapter, the equity swap can be elaborated by allowing variations in the notional principal or the periodic payment. For example, one variant of the equity swap might be for one counterparty to pay the S&P 500 return and receive the Russell 2000 return, creating a swap agreement to speculate on the differential return between large and small stocks.

The notional amount outstanding of equity swaps and equity index swaps was $1.1 trillion at year-end 2005, according to the BIS survey. Total OTC equity-linked derivatives totaled just over $5 trillion in notional amounts outstanding at the same time.

Credit swaps

A credit swap is a privately negotiated, over-the-counter derivative, designed to transfer credit risk from one counterparty to another. The payoff of a credit swap is linked to the credit characteristics of an underlying reference asset, also called a reference credit. Credits swaps enable financial institutions and corporations to manage credit risks. The market for credit swaps has been growing rapidly in recent years. The ISDA survey of the market shows that the size of the market, which was less than $1 trillion in notional amounts as of December 2001, grew to exceed $17 trillion by the end of 2005.

Credit swaps take many forms. In a **credit default swap**, two parties enter into a contract whereby Company A pays Company B a fixed periodic payment for the life of the agreement.

Company B makes no payments unless a specified credit event occurs. Credit events are typically defined to include a failure to make payments when due, bankruptcy, debt restructuring, a change in external credit rating, or a rescheduling of payments for a specified reference asset. If such a credit event occurs, the party makes a payment to the first party, and the swap then terminates. The size of the payment is usually linked to the decline in the reference asset's market value following the credit event.

In a **total return swap**, two companies enter an agreement whereby they swap periodic payment over the life of the agreement. Company C (called the protection buyer) makes payments based upon the total return—coupons plus capital gains or losses—of a specified reference asset or group of assets. Company C (the protection seller) makes fixed or floating payments as with a plain vanilla interest rate swap. Both companies' payments are based upon the same notional amount. The reference asset can be almost any asset, index or group of assets. Among the underlying assets of a total return swap are loans and bonds.

Total return swaps have numerous applications. For example, total return swaps enable banks to manage the credit exposure resulting from their lending activities. Consider a Milwaukee bank that lends $10 million to a local brewing company at a fixed interest rate of 7 percent. This interest rate charged by the bank includes a built-in risk premium to account for expected credit risk over the life of the loan. However, the bank still faces exposure to an unexpected increase in the brewing company's credit risk over the life of the loan. If credit risk unexpectedly increases, the market value of the loan (an asset to the bank) will fall. To hedge this credit risk, the bank can enter into a total return swap. Assume that the life of the swap is one year, with a single exchange of cash flows at maturity and a notional principal of $10 million. Assume also that the swap is structured so that the bank pays the swap dealer a fixed rate of 9 percent plus the change in the loan's market value. In return, the bank receives one-year U.S. dollar LIBOR. Assume that over the course of the following year an increase in credit risk causes the market value of the loan to fall so that on the swap's maturity date the loan is worth only 95 percent of its initial value. Under the terms of the swap, the bank owes the swap dealer the fixed rate of 9 percent minus the 5 percent capital loss on the market value of the loan, for a net total of 4 percent. In return, the bank receives a floating payment of one-year LIBOR, assumed to be 8 percent, from the swap dealer. Thus, the net inflow to the bank is 4 percent (8 percent minus 4 percent) multiplied by the swap's notional principal. This gain can be used to offset the loss of market value on the loan over the period.

Total return swaps provide protection against loss in value of the underlying asset irrespective of cause. For example, if the interest rate changes, then the net cash flows of the total return swap will also change even though the credit risk of the underlying loans has not necessarily changed. In other words, the swap's cash flows are influenced by market risk as well as credit risk. The credit default swap enables the bank to avoid the interest-sensitive element of total return swaps. A key difference between a credit default swap and a total return swap is the fact that the credit default swap provides protection against specific credit events while the total return swap provides protection against loss due to market risk and credit risk. Finally, either credit default swaps or total return swaps entail two sources of credit exposure: one from the underlying reference asset and another from possible default by the counterparty to the transaction.

When does a credit event occur?

Precisely specifying in swap contracts when a credit event occurs can pose problems. In September 2000, controversy erupted in two instances over just what exactly constitutes a "triggering event" in a standard credit default swap. In one instance, a large debt restructuring by Indianapolis-based life insurer Conseco caused some lenders, who had bought protection with credit default swaps written with Conseco as the reference asset, to exercise the default triggers in the swap agreements. Some protection sellers cried foul, alleging that certain protection buyers had a conflict of interest resulting from their dealings with Conseco. These protection buyers were the same lenders whose actions allegedly forced the triggering event in the first place. In the second instance, AT&T's announcement that it planned to split into four separate companies generated controversy because the standard master agreements for credit default swaps had not contemplated an event involving a split into more than two separate companies. The International Association of Swaps and Derivatives Dealers (ISDA), which drafts the standard master agreements, has tried to clarify the language in the standard agreements. At issue is whether the aforementioned types of credit events should be included as standard triggering events in credit default swaps, or whether they should be contracted for separately by swap counterparties.[17]

Swaptions

A **swaption** is an option on a swap that can be either American or European in form. A **receiver swaption** gives the holder the right to enter a particular swap agreement as the fixed-rate receiver. A **payer swaption** gives the holder the right to enter a particular swap agreement as the fixed-rate payer. As with all options, ownership gives a right but not an obligation. The swap agreement underlying the swaption is defined with respect to all of its terms, such as its tenor, notional principal, and fixed-rate and floating-rate index. For the swaption, there is a stated expiration date.

We may think of a receiver swaption as being a call option on a bond that pays a fixed rate of interest. If the owner of a receiver swaption exercises, she will be in the position of the owner of a bond who receives fixed interest payments. The floating payments that she makes play the role of the exercise price. Similarly, a payer swaption is analogous to a put option on a bond. When the owner of a payer swaption exercises, he will be in the position of an issuer of a fixed-rate bond, because the exercise of the payer swaption requires a sequence of fixed-rate interest payments in exchange for inflows at a floating rate.

To understand these features more clearly, consider a payer swaption. The purchaser of the payer swaption pays an agreed premium to the seller at the inception of the transaction. Usually, the premium is stated as some number of basis points on the notional principal of the swap underlying the option. It is typical for this premium to lie in the range of 20–40 basis points, but the premium depends upon the exercise price, the time to expiration, and the volatility of the underlying rates.[18] The exercise price of the payer swaption is a fixed rate specified in the swaption agreement. Assuming that the swaption is European, the owner will exercise the payer swaption if the contractual fixed rate (the exercise price) is lower than the fixed rate prevailing in the open market for swaps with the same tenor as that underlying the payer swaption. Upon exercise by the owner of the payer swaption, the seller of the payer swaption is obligated to make the series of floating-rate payments specified in the swap agreement.

The receiver and payer swaptions come into-the-money in different circumstances. A receiver swaption pays off when interest rates fall, and a payer swaption pays off when interest rates rise. The owner of a receiver swaption will want to exercise when interest rates fall, because the owner of the receiver swaption will then receive a sequence of fixed interest payments stipulated in the swaption contract in exchange for making a sequence of floating-rate payments at the new lower rate of interest. By contrast, the owner of a payer swaption will exercise when interest rates rise. Upon the exercise of a payer swaption, the owner of the payer swaption will be obligated to make a sequence of fixed interest payments at the old lower rate stipulated in the swaption contract and will receive a sequence of floating-rate payments at the now higher rate.

As an example, consider a European payer swaption on a five-year swap with annual payments and a notional principal of $10 million. Let us assume that the fixed rate specified in the swap agreement is 8 percent and the floating rate is LIBOR. For this payer swaption, the premium might be 30 basis points. With a principal of $10 million, the premium would then be $30,000. Six months after contracting, at the expiration date of the option, the owner of the payer swaption can either exercise or let the option expire worthless. If the owner exercises, he will pay a fixed rate of 8 percent and receive a floating rate of LIBOR for the five years of the swap. The owner of the payer swaption will exercise if the fixed rate on swaps of the type underlying the option is greater than 8 percent. For example, at expiration assume that the market for this type of swap calls for a fixed-rate payment of 8.5 percent in exchange for LIBOR for a five-year tenor. The holder of the payer swaption will exercise because he can enter the swap agreement at terms more favorable than those prevailing in the market. Conversely, if the market fixed rate for such a swap is less than 8 percent, say 7.75 percent, the owner of the payer swaption will allow the swaption to expire because it is worthless. The swaption is worthless because it is at expiration and gives the owner the right to enter a swap to pay 8 percent and receive LIBOR. However, the prevailing market rate allows anyone to enter a swap to pay 7.75 percent and receive LIBOR.

Consider now the choices facing the holder of a European receiver swaption. To acquire this swaption, the owner pays a premium to purchase the swaption. At the expiration date, the owner may exercise. If she exercises, she will enter a swap to receive-fixed and pay-floating. The owner should exercise if the fixed rate on the swap underlying the swaption exceeds the market fixed rate on swaps of the same type as that underlying the swaption. For example, assume that the swap underlying this receiver swaption has a seven-year tenor with semiannual payments, a notional principal of $50 million, and a fixed rate of 6.5 percent in exchange for LIBOR. At expiration, assume that the market fixed rate for this type of swap is 7 percent. In this circumstance, the receiver swaption is worthless and its holder will allow it to expire. The swaption is worthless because it allows the holder to enter a swap to receive 6.5 percent, but the market rate for this type of swap is to receive a fixed rate of 7 percent. By contrast, if the prevailing fixed rate for this type of swap is 6 percent at the expiration of the swaption, the holder of the receiver swaption should exercise, because the swaption entitles her to enter a swap to receive a 6.5 percent fixed rate when the prevailing market offers only a 6 percent fixed rate on this type of swap.

A corporate application of a swaption

Swaptions offer the same kinds of speculative and hedging opportunities as all other options, as we have studied in previous chapters. As an example, consider a firm that has issued a callable bond. From the perspective of the issuer, we may analyze a bond with a call provision as consisting of a noncallable bond plus the purchase of a call option on the bond. From the issuing firm's point of view, the firm has paid for the option by promising a higher coupon rate for the callable bond than the rate necessary for a noncallable bond. We assume that the first call date for this bond lies in the future and the firm has decided that it will not want to call the bond, because the firm anticipates a continuing need for funds and does not particularly wish to incur the transaction costs of calling the bond and going through the registration procedures to issue another bond to meet its financing requirements. Having made this determination, the call feature of the bond represents an unwanted option in the firm's portfolio that will be losing value through time decay as expiration approaches. Yet the call provision has a real value. The firm's problem is to find a way to capture the value of the call provision without actually calling the bond. To capture the value of the call provision, the firm could sell a receiver swaption with terms that match the call feature of the bond. In effect, this transaction would unwind the call feature inherent in the original bond, because the firm receives a swaption premium that equals the value of the call provision on the firm's bond.

For the firm in this situation, consider the following data. The call date is one year away, the semiannual coupon rate on the bond is 9 percent, the principal amount of the bond issue is $150 million, and the present maturity of the bond is seven years. To implement its strategy, the firm sells a European receiver swaption with an expiration of one year. The swap that underlies the swaption has a tenor of six years, a notional principal of $150 million, calls for semiannual payments, a fixed rate of 9 percent, and a floating rate equal to LIBOR. The price of this swaption depends on the current fixed swap rates relative to the terms specified for the swap underlying the swaption. The lower rates are today, when the firm sells the swaption, the greater is the value of the call provision on the bond and the greater is the value of the swaption that the firm sells. After selling the swaption, the swaption premium belongs to the firm, but the firm has a potential obligation in one year.

At expiration, the holder of this receiver option will make its exercise decision depending on prevailing market rates for this kind of swap. At expiration, if the fixed rate for this kind of swap is above the fixed rate specified in the swap agreement, say 11 percent, the owner of the swaption will not exercise and the swaption will expire worthless. The swaption holder will not exercise, because exercising entails entering a swap to receive a fixed rate of 9 percent and pay LIBOR, when it could simply go to the market and enter an analogous swap to receive a fixed rate of 11 percent and pay LIBOR. In this case, the obligation of the firm is extinguished without performance, and the firm has simply gained the swaption premium. Note also, that with current fixed interest rates of 11 percent, the firm has no incentive to call its bonds.

By contrast, if market interest rates at expiration are lower than the fixed rate specified for the swap underlying the swaption, say 7 percent, the owner of the swaption will exercise. By exercising, the owner of the swaption can enter a swap to receive a fixed rate of 9 percent and pay LIBOR at a time when the market only offers a fixed rate of 7 percent in exchange for LIBOR. If the swaption is exercised against the firm, it will be obligated to make a sequence of interest payments at 9 percent and to receive LIBOR. In this situation, the firm will also call its bond, because market rates are at 7 percent and the coupon rate on its bond is 9 percent. The firm then might issue a floating-rate note for its financing need. Assuming that it issues a floating-rate note at LIBOR for a term of six years to match the tenor of the swap, the firm's cash flows for the life of the swap are as follows:

Swap:	Pay 9 percent fixed rate on $150 million notional principal; receive LIBOR on $150 million notional principal
Debt financing:	Issue a $150 million floating-rate note with a maturity of six years at LIBOR; use the proceeds of the $150 million floating-rate note to call the existing bond and repay the $150 million principal

Netting out the receipt and payment of LIBOR and the call and refinancing of the original bond, the firm's net position is to continue paying the fixed rate of 9 percent, equal to the coupon rate on its original bond. However, the firm has captured the value of its call provision by the receipt of the swaption premium.[19]

In our discussion of flavored interest rate swaps, we noted that an extension swap is a swap agreement that extends the tenor of an existing swap. Thus an extension swap is a firm commitment. By contrast, extendible and cancelable swaps are swap agreements with embedded swaptions, and they may be either pay-fixed or receive-fixed in form. Thus, the owner of an extendible swap has the right, but not the obligation, to enter into an extension swap. Both extendible and cancelable swap agreements may be analyzed as consisting of a plain vanilla swap plus a swaption.

Extendible and cancelable swaps

In an extendible pay-fixed swap, the pay-fixed counterparty has the option to extend the tenor of the swap. If she exercises that option, the existing swap agreement remains in force for the additional time specified in the agreement. The swap underlying the payer swaption has the same form as the existing pay-fixed swap. Upon exercise of the payer swaption, a new swap is created on which payments would begin at the end of the existing swap. We may analyze this extendible pay-fixed swap as consisting of two distinct elements—a plain vanilla pay-fixed swap plus a payer swaption. The plain vanilla pay-fixed swap portion of the extendible swap has a tenor that extends to the expiration date of the embedded payer swaption. The swaption gives the holder the right to extend the swap agreement for an additional period.

A cancelable swap gives a party the right, but not the obligation, to cancel an existing plain vanilla swap at a specific time during the originally contemplated tenor of the swap. The embedded swaption has an exercise date falling some time during the tenor of the underlying plain vanilla swap, and the swap underlying the swaption would have a tenor that covers the period from the exercise date through the tenor of the original plain vanilla swap. For example, a cancelable receive-fixed swap agreement consists of a plain vanilla receive-fixed swap plus a pay-fixed swaption. The plain vanilla swap has a tenor that extends over a given period. The swaption has an expiration date during the tenor of the plain vanilla swap, and the swap underlying the swaption extends from the expiration date of the swaption to the end of the tenor of the plain vanilla swap. Exercise of the swaption creates a new swap that exactly offsets the remaining payments on the plain vanilla swap.

To make this more concrete, consider the following example of a cancelable receive-fixed swap. A firm enters a cancelable receive-fixed swap with a notional amount of $20 million, a tenor of seven years, receipt of annual interest payments of 6.60 percent, and payments of LIBOR. The agreement also includes a swaption, the right to cancel the swap immediately after the fourth payment. This cancelable receive-fixed swap may be analyzed as consisting of two elements: a plain vanilla receive-fixed swap with a tenor of seven years and a European payer swaption that expires in four years and has a tenor of three years. If the owner of the cancelable swap cancels the swap, this is equivalent to exercising the payer swaption, because the swap underlying the payer swaption would have exactly the cash flows that offset the remaining tenor of the original plain vanilla swap.

Analyzing the extendible and cancelable swaps as plain vanilla swaps plus swaptions makes pricing these complex swaps simpler, because it is relatively easy to price plain vanilla swaps and swaptions. Thus, there are four possible extendible and cancelable swap forms that may be analyzed as follows:

extendible pay-fixed swap = plain vanilla pay-fixed swap plus a payer swaption
extendible receive-fixed swap = plain vanilla receive-fixed swap plus a receiver swaption
cancelable pay-fixed swap = plain vanilla pay-fixed swap plus a receiver swaption
cancelable receive-fixed swap = plain vanilla receive-fixed swap plus a payer swaption

Thus the extendible swaps have an embedded swaption of the same type as the swap itself. An extendible pay-fixed swap has an embedded payer swaption, and an extendible receive-fixed swap has an embedded receiver swaption. Cancelable swaps have embedded swaptions of the opposite type that offset the terms of the swap itself. A cancelable pay-fixed swap has an embedded receiver swaption, and a cancelable receive-fixed swap has an embedded payer swaption.

Conclusion

This chapter has introduced the swaps market. From its origins in the late 1970s and early 1980s, the swaps market has grown to enormous proportions, with notionals exceeding $180 trillion. Most of the market is concentrated in interest rate swaps, but there are billions of dollars of outstanding notional amounts in foreign currency swaps, equity swaps, commodity swaps, and credit swaps as well. During this period of rapid growth, the swaps market has matured and has become more competitive and more informationally efficient.

In contrast with futures and exchange-traded options, we noted that swap agreements are extremely flexible in amount, maturity, and other contract terms. As further points of differentiation between futures and exchange-traded options versus swaps, the swaps market does not utilize an exchange and is virtually free of governmental regulation.

The chapter also analyzed plain vanilla interest rate and currency swaps. We saw that an interest rate swap essentially involves a commitment by two parties to exchange cash flows tied to some principal, or notional, amount. One party takes the pay-fixed/receive-floating side of the swap, while the opposing counterparty takes the receive-fixed/pay-floating position. In a foreign currency swap, both parties acquire funds in different currencies and exchange those principal amounts. Each party pays interest to the other in the currency that was acquired, with these interest payments taking place over the term of the swap agreement. To terminate the agreement, the parties again exchange foreign currency. Early in the development of the swaps market, some traders sought profits by exploiting market inefficiencies. In today's mature market, market inefficiencies are extremely rare. As a consequence, swap transactions are motivated by a desire to transform the cash flows patterns of financial assets and liabilities. The growth of the swaps market reflects the flexibility, low cost, and operational efficiency of the swaps form of contracting.

In today's swaps market, swap dealers have largely supplanted swap brokers, reflecting the growth and maturation of the market. The swap dealer stands ready to act as a counterparty in a swap agreement, thereby accepting a financial risk. For the swap dealer, we considered the factors that influence pricing, and we discussed the techniques that swap dealers use to manage the risk associated with their portfolios of swaps.

The chapter concluded with a survey of the many varieties of swaps. These include many enhancements that take both interest rate swaps and currency swaps beyond plain vanilla. In addition, we considered equity and commodity swaps.

Exercises

1   Explain the differences between a plain vanilla interest rate swap and a plain vanilla currency swap.
2   Explain the role that the notional principal plays in understanding interest rate swap transactions. Why is this principal amount regarded as only notional? How does it compare with a deliverable instrument in the interest rate futures market?
3   Consider a plain vanilla interest rate swap. Explain how the practice of net payments works.
4   Assume that you are a money manager seeking to increase the yield on your portfolio and that you expect short-term interest rates to rise more than the yield curve would suggest. Would you rather pay a fixed long-term rate and receive a floating short rate, or the other way around? Explain your reasoning.
5   Assume that the yield curve is flat, that the swaps market is efficient, and that two equally creditworthy counterparties engage in an interest rate swap. Who should pay the higher rate, the party that pays a floating short-term rate or the party that pays a fixed long-term rate? Explain.
6   In a currency swap, counterparties exchange the same sums at the beginning and the end of the swap period. Explain how this practice relates to the

custom of making interest payments during the life of the swap agreement.

7 Explain why a currency swap is also called an "exchange of borrowings."

8 What are the two major kinds of swap facilitators? What is the key difference between the roles that they play?

9 In the context of interest rate swaps, "basis risk" is the risk arising from an unanticipated change in the yield relationship between the two instruments involved in the swap. Explain how basis risk affects a swap dealer. Does it affect a swap broker the same way? Explain.

10 Assume that a swap dealer attempts to function as a pure financial intermediary, avoiding all interest rate risk. Explain how such a dealer may yet come to bear interest rate risk.

11 Two parties enter an interest rate swap paid in arrears on the following terms: a seven-year tenor, annual payments, $100 million notional principal, and a fixed rate of 6.75 percent, with LIBOR as the floating rate. Assume that the following LIBOR spot rates are observed at each of the following dates:

Year (date of observation)	One-year LIBOR (rate actually observed)	Receive-fixed cash flow
0	0.0680	
1	0.0575	
2	0.0875	
3	0.0674	
4	0.0600	
5	0.0700	
6	0.0655	
7	0.0685	

From the perspective of the receive-fixed side of the deal, what is the cash flow at each payment date of the swap? What role does the swap rate observed at the termination of the swap (year 7) play in the analysis?

12 A plain vanilla foreign currency swap has just been arranged between Parties ABC and XYZ. ABC has agreed to pay dollars based on LIBOR, while XYZ will pay British pounds at a fixed rate of 7 percent. The current exchange rate is £1 = $1.65. The notional principal is £100 million = $165 million. The tenor of the swap is seven years, and the swap has annual payments paid in arrears. Complete the following table showing the **periodic** cash outflows only for each party at each relevant period of the swap (ignore the exchange of principal):

Year of observation	LIBOR rate observed (%)	XYZ Sterling pay outflows	ABC dollar pay outflows
0	6.580		
1	5.870		
2	6.745		
3	6.550		
4	6.100		
5	6.800		
6	6.350		
7	6.450		

13 A swap dealer holds the following portfolio of interest rate swaps, all with annual payments, all with floating payments equal to LIBOR:

Swap	Notional principal ($ million)	Tenor (years)	Fixed rate (%)	Dealer's position
A	20	3	7.000	Receive-fixed
B	30	5	6.500	Pay-fixed
C	25	4	7.250	Pay-fixed
D	50	7	7.300	Receive-fixed
E	10	2	6.750	Receive-fixed

A Complete the following table showing the dealer's position for each payment in each year—for example, the entry for a given year t and a given swap with a fixed rate of 8 percent, and a notional principal of $15 million, would be of the form $(LIBOR_{t-1} - 8.00) \times \$15,000,000$:

Year	The swap dealer's anticipated cash flows					Dealer's net position
	Swap A	Swap B	Swap C	Swap D	Swap E	
1						
2						
3						
4						
5						
6						
7						

B Appraise the dealer's net risk position.

C Recommend transactions that the dealer might use to reduce the net risk.

14 Consider the swap indication schedule shown in the table below. Two parties, A and B, arrange a plain vanilla interest rate swap, with the bank as intermediary. In effect, A and B are counterparties to each other as described below, but their individual swaps are actually negotiated with the bank. Party A enters a receive-fixed plain vanilla swap, while Party B enters a pay-fixed plain vanilla swap. Both swaps have a notional principal of $50 million and a five-year tenor. Both swaps have annual payments made in arrears:

Sample swap indication pricing

Maturity (years)	Bank's fixed rates (T-note rate plus indicated basis points)		T-note yields (%)
	Bank pays	Bank receives	
1	23	27	5.74
2	29	33	5.67
3	33	37	5.60
4	37	40	5.55
5	40	44	5.49

A For each of the parties, state exactly the commitment that they undertake in their swap agreements.

B What net cash flows will the bank anticipate at each relevant date? What interest rate risk does the bank face?

C In the event of default by either party, analyze the interest rate risk position of the bank.

15 What is the difference between a seasonal and a roller coaster swap?

16 Compare and contrast an accreting and an amortizing swap.

17 "An equity swap is nothing but a commodity swap." Do you agree or disagree with this statement? Explain.

18 Consider two plain vanilla interest rate swaps that have the same notional principal, the same fixed rate, and the same initial floating rate. One swap has a tenor of five years, while the second has a tenor of ten years. Assume that you take a pay-fixed position in the ten-year swap and a receive-fixed position in the five-year swap. What kind of instrument do these transactions create? Explain, assuming that the term structure is flat. What difference would it make if the term structure were not flat?

19 "A swaption is essentially a portfolio of options on futures or options on forwards." Is this statement correct? Explain.

20 Generally, political unrest in Europe is accompanied by an increase in the yield differential between Eurocurrency deposit rates and U.S. T-bill rates. Explain how to construct a basis swap to profit from such a development. Explain how this might be related to a TED spread in futures.

21 Using interest rate swaps based on U.S. Treasury instruments, explain how to create a yield curve swap that will profit if the yield curve has an upward slope and the curve steepens. Explain how this might be related to the NOB spread in futures.

22 Explain how two fixed-for-floating foreign currency swaps might be combined to create a fixed-for-fixed foreign currency swap.

23 What is mismatch risk? Why is mismatch risk an important concern of swap dealers?

Notes

1 We wish to acknowledge the special contribution to these swaps chapters (Chapters 20–22) made by Gerald W. Buetow of James Madison University and Donald J. Smith of Boston University. Both Jeff and Don read and commented on earlier versions of these chapters. Of course, we are responsible for any remaining deficiencies. The material for this chapter and the next draws heavily from *Interest Rate and Currency Swaps: A Tutorial*, by Keith C. Brown and Donald J. Smith, Charlottesville, VA: The Research Foundation of the Institute of Chartered Financial Analysts, 1995.

2 These figures are based on a survey of members of the International Swaps and Derivatives Association (ISDA) until 1997. After that time, the Bank for International Settlements has been maintaining these statistics. The statistics are for swap contracts only. Total OTC derivatives contracts exceeded $284 trillion by notional amounts in December 2005. As we will also see, terms such as *outstanding swap amounts* and *futures open interest* require a special interpretation. As we discuss shortly, these dollar amounts are notional principals. Swap payments are a function of these notional principals.

3   One exception to this general rule about the available maturities of futures contracts is the Eurodollar
futures contract, which currently trades quite distant
expirations. As we will see in Chapter 21, the distant
maturity of Eurodollar futures is tied to the swap
market itself. Even in the swap market, it is often not
feasible to contract for as far into the future as some
parties desire.

4   This does not mean to imply that exchange trading
sacrifices all anonymity. However, traders watch the
activities of major institutions. When these institutions
initiate major transactions, it is not possible to maintain complete privacy. It is somewhat ironic that
individual traders can trade on futures and options
markets with a discretion that is not available to
multi-billion dollar financial institutions.

5   The practice of net payments and not actually
exchanging principal also protects each counterparty
from default by the other. For example, it would be
very unpleasant for Party A if it paid the principal
amount of $1 million in our example and Party B failed
to make its payment to Party A. Making only net payments greatly reduces the potential impact of default,
and it reduces transaction costs.

6   As the next chapter discusses, this fixed-for-fixed
currency swap can be created as a CIRCUS swap (combined interest rate and currency swap) by combining
a plain vanilla currency swap with a plain vanilla interest rate swap. We will also see how the fixed-for-fixed
currency swap can be constructed as a pair of plain
vanilla currency swaps.

7   Chapter 21 shows that having a floating leg facilitates
the pricing of swaps, because there are other instruments in the market with floating payments, such as
futures and interest rate forward contracts.

8   This discussion of comparative advantage draws on
the analysis by K. Kapner and J. Marshall in *The Swaps
Handbook*, New York: New York Institute of Finance,
1990.

9   In our example, the savings and loan is still subject
to the risk that the mortgagor might repay the loan
early if rates fall. More complicated swap structures
are available to address this issue. For example, it is
possible to enter a swap arrangement in which the
notional principal varies as interest rates fluctuate.

10 In actual market practice, the participants must carefully consider the actual way in which yields are
calculated on Treasury securities versus the money

market computations that govern LIBOR. We
abstract from these technicalities.

11 See Keith C. Brown, W. V. Harlow, and Donald J.
Smith, "An Empirical Analysis of Interest Rate
Swap Spreads," *Journal of Fixed Income*, 3:4, March
1994, pp. 61–78. These authors find that the spreads
have narrowed considerably.

12 The swap dealer will also consider some other issues
in setting final pricing terms. If the swap is very complicated, the swap dealer may charge a higher price
than otherwise. Similarly, if the swap is to involve
cross-border currency flows, the dealer may be concerned with regulatory constraints that might impede
the flow of funds.

13 The problem of default risk is receiving active attention. See, for example, Eric H. Sorensen and Thierry
F. Bollier, "Pricing Swap Default Risk," *Financial
Analysts Journal*, 50:3, May/June 1994, pp. 23–33,
for a model of swap default risk. Some swap agreements allow a party to terminate a swap agreement if a counterparty receives a credit downgrade.
Douglas J. Lucas explores this issue in his paper "The
Effectiveness of Downgrade Provisions in Reducing
Counterparty Credit Risk," *Journal of Fixed Income*,
5:1, June 1995, pp. 32–41.

14 This section draws on an article by Peter A. Abken,
"Beyond Plain Vanilla: A Taxonomy of Swaps,"
Federal Reserve Bank of Atlanta, *Economic Review*,
March/April 1991. Reprinted in R. Kolb, *The
Financial Derivatives Reader*, Miami, FL: Kolb
Publishing, 1993.

15 J. Marshall and K. Kapner, *The Swaps Market*, 2nd
edn, Miami, FL: Kolb Publishing, 1993, p. 120.

16 K. R. Kapner and J. F. Marshall, *The Swaps Handbook*, New York: New York Institute of Finance, 1990,
pp. 288–9.

17 For more information on this subject, see "Splitting
Headaches," *Risk*, July 2001, pages 36–7.

18 See P. A. Abken, "Beyond Plain Vanilla: A Taxonomy
of Swaps," Federal Reserve Bank of Atlanta, *Economic Review*, March/April 1991. Reprinted in R.
Kolb, *The Financial Derivatives Reader*, Miami, FL:
Kolb Publishing, 1993.

19 This example is adapted from Keith C. Brown and
Donald J. Smith, *Interest Rate and Currency Swaps:
A Tutorial*, Charlottesville, VA: The Research
Foundation of the Institute of Chartered Financial
Analysts, 1995, pp. 109–10.

21

Swaps: Economic Analysis and Pricing

Overview

In this chapter, we explore two closely related themes, the economic analysis of swaps and the principles of swap pricing. The economic analysis of swaps shows how swaps may be interpreted in terms of other financial instruments. In a number of instances, this chapter shows that a portfolio of nonswap instruments can exactly replicate the cash flows on a swap. When that exact replication is possible, we have a greater insight into swap pricing. The price of a swap must be identical to a portfolio of other instruments with cash flows that exactly replicate the cash flows on the swap.

The chapter begins by showing how a plain vanilla interest rate swap can be replicated by two bonds, one of which is a regular coupon bond while the other is a bond that pays a floating rate. A fixed-for-fixed currency swap and a plain vanilla currency swap are also shown to be equivalent to two-bond portfolios. The same principles of analyzing plain vanilla swaps apply to more complicated swaps, as we demonstrate for a forward and a seasonal interest rate swap. Interest rate swaps are also shown to be analyzable as a portfolio of forward interest rate contracts, while

a fixed-for-fixed currency swap is equivalent to a portfolio of foreign exchange forward contracts. An interest rate swap is also closely related to a portfolio of Eurodollar futures contracts. Finally, an interest rate swap is shown to be equivalent to a portfolio of calls and puts on LIBOR.

Having explored the relationship between swaps and other financial instruments, the chapter turns to the pricing of swaps, considering interest rate and currency swaps in turn. The plain vanilla interest rate swap always pays LIBOR as the floating rate, so pricing an interest rate swap essentially requires finding the correct fixed rate for the swap. The chapter shows how to find the one fixed rate that prevents arbitrage, which is also the one fixed rate that does not disadvantage either party. Pricing currency swaps is closely related to pricing interest rate swaps, except that a currency swap involves two currencies. Therefore, currency swap pricing must be responsible to the term structure of interest rates in the two currencies and the term structure of exchange rates as well. The chapter concludes by showing how to find the no-arbitrage fixed rate for a variety of currency swaps.

The economic analysis of swaps

In this section, we consider swaps from a variety of economic viewpoints. By understanding how to analyze swaps in terms of more familiar financial instruments, we can deepen our understanding of the swaps market in general and lay a foundation for understanding how prices of swap contracts are determined.

We begin by analyzing interest rate and foreign currency swaps in terms of bonds. As we will see, swaps can be interpreted as a combination of buying and selling a pair of bonds. We then show that it is possible to view an interest rate swap as a collection of forward or futures contracts. The analysis of swaps as a portfolio of forwards is critical in the marketplace for the pricing of swaps. As a final type of analysis, we show that a swap agreement can be interpreted as a portfolio of option contracts.

If a swap is shown to have identical cash flows to another portfolio of securities, this information can be helpful in pricing a swap. If two instruments, or portfolios of instruments, have identical cash flows, they must have the same price. In some cases, it is easy to find a price for one package of securities but not the other. Being able to price one portfolio reveals the price of the other equivalent package of cash flows. For example, we will see that an interest rate swap is equivalent to a portfolio of bonds, in the sense that the swap and the portfolio of bonds have identical cash flows. If we know the prices of the bonds in the portfolio, then we know the price of the swap.

An interest rate swap as a combination of capital market instruments

In this section, we show how four different types of interest rate and foreign currency swaps can be interpreted as a pair of bond transactions. In each case, a swap is equivalent to the simultaneous purchase of one bond and the sale of another. Key to this analysis is a bond that pays a floating rate of interest, known as a **floating-rate note (FRN)**.

Plain vanilla receive-fixed interest rate swap

A plain vanilla receive-fixed interest rate swap may be constructed from a long position in a bond coupled with the issuance of an FRN, as the following example illustrates. Consider a 6 percent corporate bond with an annual coupon payment, a remaining maturity of four years, and a market value of $40 million. For convenience, we assume that this bond trades at par. A corresponding FRN has a $40 million principal that pays LIBOR annually and has a four-year maturity. Figure 21.1 shows the cash flows associated with buying the corporate bond and issuing the FRN.

The net flows from this pair of bond transactions are as follows. At the outset, the firm buys a bond for $40 million and issues an FRN with a principal balance of $40 million, for a net zero cash flow. Similarly, at the end of the four-year period, both bonds will mature. At maturity, the firm will be repaid its $40 million principal on the corporate bond, and it will repay

Figure 21.1   A receive-fixed interest rate swap as a pair of bond transactions

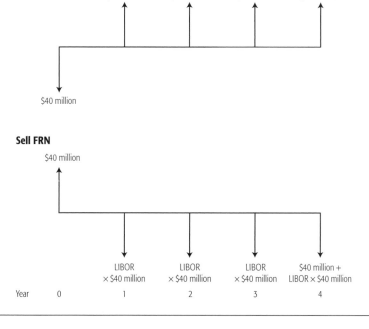

the $40 million on the FRN, for a net zero cash flow on the principal amounts. This leaves the four annual coupons to consider on both the corporate bond and the FRN. Each annual coupon payment net cash flow will consist of a $2.4 million inflow on the corporate bond and an outflow on the FRN equal to LIBOR times $40 million:

$2.4 million − LIBOR × $40 million

Whether this net flow will be positive or negative depends on movements in interest rates. The important point to notice about the net cash flows is that they are identical to a receive-fixed plain vanilla interest rate swap with annual payments and a four-year tenor. Thus, the bond portfolio is financially equivalent to an interest rate swap.

Plain vanilla pay-fixed interest rate swap
From Figure 21.1, it is also clear that a similar strategy can be used to create a plain vanilla pay-fixed interest rate swap. To create the pay-fixed swap, one would issue a corporate fixed-coupon bond and buy an FRN. Using the same bond and FRN described in Figure 21.1, issuing a fixed-coupon bond and buying an FRN would result in no net principal cash flows and four annual flows equal to

LIBOR × $40 million − $2.4 million

Other more complex interest rate swaps can be interpreted as more complex bond portfolios by following the same basic strategy.

Fixed-for-fixed currency swap
To create a fixed-for-fixed currency swap, one can buy a bond denominated in one currency and issue a bond denominated in a second currency. For example, assume that one wishes to create a fixed-for-fixed currency swap with a notional principal of €50 million and a tenor of five years with annual payments to pay U.S. dollars and receive euros. Assume that the spot exchange rate is $1 = €0.8, the prevailing euro interest rate (Euribor) is 7 percent, and the U.S. dollar rate is 6 percent.

In the example, one wishes to receive euros and pay dollars, so the fixed-for-fixed swap is created by buying the euro-denominated bond and issuing a dollar-denominated bond. With a desired notional amount of €50 million and an exchange rate of €1 = $0.8, the issuance will be for a dollar-denominated bond with a principal amount of $40 million. The upper panel of Figure 21.2 shows the separate cash flows from buying the euro-denominated bond and issuing the dollar-denominated bond. The lower panel shows the overall cash flows from the combined purchase and sale. In the lower panel at the outset, the net flow is to receive $40 million and pay €50 million. At the end of five years, the principal payments will be to receive €50 million and pay $40 million. In addition, there will be five annual coupon payments of $2.4 million and a coupon receipt of €3.5 million. The cash flows in the lower panel that we have been describing are the same cash flows as a fixed-for-fixed currency swap to receive euros and pay U.S. dollars with a notional principal of €50 million and a tenor of five years with annual payments. Thus, we may analyze a fixed-for-fixed currency swap as being equivalent to purchasing a bond in one currency and issuing a bond in another currency.

Plain vanilla currency swap
A plain vanilla currency swap may be analyzed also in terms of a two-bond portfolio. To create a plain vanilla currency swap (pay-floating U.S. dollars and receive-fixed foreign currency),

Figure 21.2   A fixed-for-fixed currency swap as the sale and purchase of bonds in different currencies

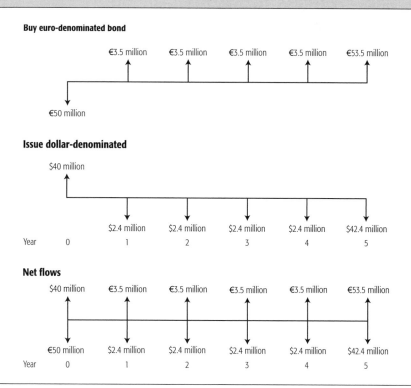

one would issue a dollar-denominated FRN and buy a foreign bond. Consider a party that issues at par an annual coupon FRN for $20 million with a maturity of three years to pay LIBOR. With an exchange rate of $1 = ¥120, this same party also buys a yen-denominated bond at par with a market value of ¥2.4 billion, a maturity of three years, and annual coupon payments of 5 percent. The upper panel of Figure 21.3 shows the cash flows associated with each bond, while the lower panel shows the combined flows from the two bonds. In combination, these two bonds have the same cash flows as a plain vanilla currency swap to pay LIBOR and receive-fixed yen with a notional principal of $20 million, annual payments, and a tenor of three years.

Forward interest rate swap
In addition to the simple swaps considered already in this section, many more complicated swap structures can be analyzed in terms of bonds. Consider the following four bond transactions:

(1)   Purchase an eight-year annual coupon FRN based on one-year LIBOR at par with a face value of $30 million.
(2)   Issue an eight-year 8 percent annual coupon bond at par with a face value of $30 million.
(3)   Issue a three-year annual coupon FRN based on one-year LIBOR at par with a face value of $30 million.
(4)   Purchase a three-year 8 percent annual coupon bond at par with a face value of $30 million.

Figure 21.3   A plain vanilla currency swap as the issuance of an FRN and the purchase of a bond

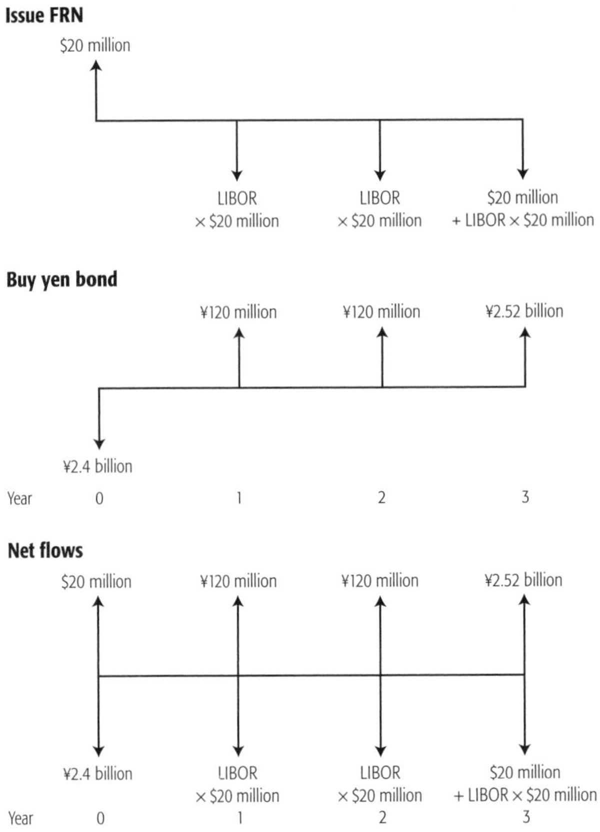

Figure 21.4 presents a cash flow diagram for each bond transaction in the upper panel. The final time line of the figure shows the net cash flows. The cash flows on bonds 3 and 4 together exactly cancel out the cash flows on bonds 1 and 2 for the first three years. The resulting cash flow pattern is that of a pay-fixed forward swap to begin in three years, to have annual payments, and to have a tenor of five years. Therefore, the four-bond portfolio and the forward swap are equivalent.

Seasonal interest rate swap

A typical seasonal interest rate swap might have quarterly payments with one payment each year being based on a substantially larger notional principal. The paradigm here is a retailer with the last quarterly flow of the year being larger to reflect the Christmas retailing surge. Consider the following portfolio of bonds:

(1)   Issue a semiannual coupon FRN based on six-month LIBOR at par with a face value of $10 million with payment dates in May and November and a maturity of seven years.

(2)   Issue a semiannual coupon FRN based on six-month LIBOR at par with a face value of $10 million with payment dates in February and August and a maturity of seven years.

Figure 21.4   A forward interest rate swap as a four-bond portfolio

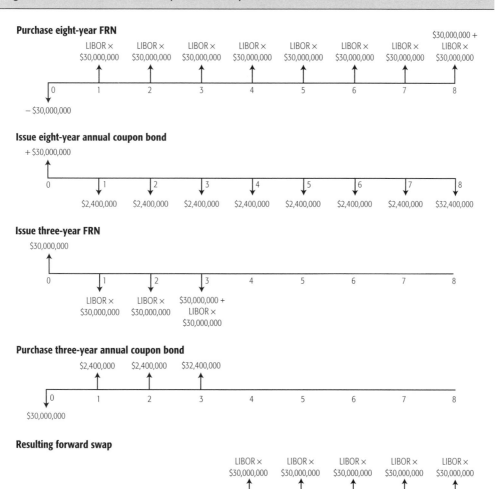

(3)   Purchase a semiannual 6.5 percent coupon bond at par with payment dates in May and November and a maturity of seven years, with a face value of $10 million.

(4)   Purchase a semiannual 6.5 percent coupon bond at par with payment dates in February and August and a maturity of seven years, with a face value of $10 million.

(5)   Issue an annual coupon seven-year FRN at par based on one-year LIBOR with a face value of $20 million, with each annual payment date in November.

(6)   Purchase a 6.5 percent annual coupon bond at par with a face value of $20 million, with each annual payment date in November and a maturity of seven years.

Together, these six bonds create a bond portfolio that is equivalent to a quarterly payment receive-fixed seasonal interest rate swap with a tenor of seven years. The February, May, and August

Figure 21.5   Annual cash flows from the six-bond portfolio

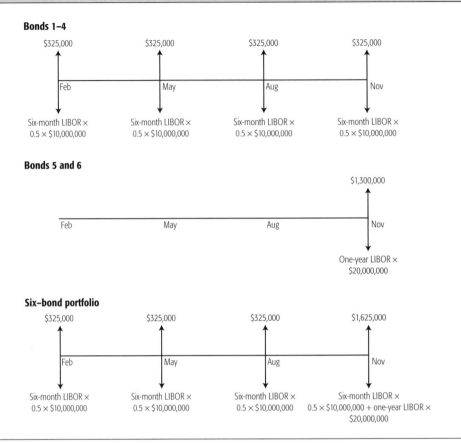

payments in the swap will be based on a notional principal of $10 million, while the November payment will be based on a notional principal of $30 million.

At the initiation of the bond portfolio, the net cash flow is zero, as the bond issuances offset the bond purchases. The same is true when the bonds mature: the repayment of principal on a bond that was issued is funded by the maturity of a bond that was purchased. Figure 21.5 shows the cash flows that would result for a single year of the bond portfolio. The cash flows have the same form as those of a swap.

In a typical quarterly payment swap, the floating-rate payments would normally be based on three-month LIBOR. In our bond portfolio, they are based on six-month LIBOR for the first four bonds, and the additional November payment from bonds 5 and 6 is based on one-year LIBOR.

Comparing the bond portfolio to a seasonal swap, we see that the bond portfolio is cumbersome relative to the swap. The bond portfolio requires six bonds to replicate (or almost replicate) a swap that can be described fairly completely as:

Receive-fixed at 6.5 percent quarterly with a notional principal of $10 million in February, May, and August, and with a notional principal of $30 million in November for a tenor of seven years, with floating payments based on three-month LIBOR.

Notice that the bond portfolio is not exactly equivalent to the swap just described, because the floating payments are based on either six-month or one-year LIBOR in the bond portfolio, and based on three-month LIBOR in the swap description. As a swap becomes slightly more complicated, the replicating bond portfolio quickly becomes extremely complicated. Constructing a bond portfolio that matches the swap cash flows and interest calculations exactly would be difficult. One would need the semiannual payment FRNs in the portfolio to be based on three-month LIBOR, which would be unusual. Alternatively, one might seek a quarterly payment FRN with payments based on three-month LIBOR. Either of these strategies would still leave the larger annual November payment, which would need to be based on three-month LIBOR as well. This kind of bond also would be rare.

Even ignoring the problem with the quarterly payments in the bond portfolio being based on nonquarterly LIBOR, the bond portfolio is a cumbersome and costly way of securing the cash flow obligations that can be achieved inexpensively and easily through the swap directly. The operational efficiency of this kind of swap relative to the bond portfolio illustrates one of the reasons for the swap market's stunning success.

Summary

In this section, we have seen how plain vanilla and other simple interest rate and currency swaps can be replicated by a simple two-bond portfolio. Because the two-bond portfolio and the corresponding swap have identical cash flows, the swap and the bond portfolio must have the same value. Thus, the equivalence between the swap and the bond portfolio heightens our understanding of the swap product and also provides insight into price determination for swaps.

We have also seen that more complicated swaps can be replicated by more elaborate bond portfolios. For example, we saw that a forward interest rate swap could be replicated exactly by a four-bond portfolio. A seasonal swap can be replicated by a six-bond portfolio, except that problems arise in the maturity of the floating-rate calculation between the swap and the bond portfolio. Consideration of this seasonal swap shows that as swaps become slightly more complicated, the corresponding bond portfolio becomes much more complicated and costly to construct, highlighting the operational efficiency of the swap market.

An interest rate swap as a portfolio of forward rate agreements

In this section, we analyze an interest rate swap in terms of a portfolio of interest rate forward contracts. In the interest rate market, these forward contracts are known as **forward rate agreements (FRA)**. We introduced FRAs in Chapter 19, with our discussion of interest rate options. We briefly review the key features of FRAs here, before showing how an interest rate swap can be analyzed as a portfolio of FRAs.

Key features of FRAs

Typically, an FRA calls for the exchange of LIBOR at a future date in return for a payment based on a fixed rate of interest agreed on the contracting date. For example, consider an FRA market maker who agrees today to pay six-month LIBOR in six months in exchange for a fixed interest payment at an annual rate of 5 percent and a notional principal of $20 million. When the determination date on the FRA arrives, assume that LIBOR stands at 5.8 percent. Payments on the FRA would be the interest rate times the fraction of the year times the notional principal:

Receive-fixed:	$0.050 \times 0.5 \times \$20,000,000 = \$500,000$
Pay-floating:	$0.058 \times 0.5 \times \$20,000,000 = -\$580,000$
Net payment:	$-\$80,000$

In this case, the market maker would be obligated to make a net payment of $80,000. In essence, this FRA agreement is a one-date swap agreement. Therefore, we may analyze an interest rate swap agreement as a sequence of FRAs.

FRAs are quoted in the following manner:

term to expiration in months × term to end of period covered by agreement

For example, the FRA we considered above, with six months to expiration for six-month LIBOR, would be quoted as

6 × 12   5%

The first number indicates the months until the FRA expires, the second indicates the number of months until the instrument presumed to underlie the FRA matures, while the difference between the two numbers shows the maturity of the presumed underlying instrument. There is no actual instrument that is delivered; instead, the presumed underlying instrument is simply an instrument of the underlying maturity that pays LIBOR. Instead of exchanging instruments, the profit or loss is settled in cash as in our preceding example. The 5 percent is the fixed rate of interest to be paid in exchange for LIBOR. FRAs are normally "determined in advance and settled in arrears," as discussed in Chapter 19. In our example of the 6 × 12 FRA, the determination date would be at month 6, and the actual payment would occur at month 12.

On-market and off-market FRAs

As we have seen, FRA market makers offer to make a market in FRAs for a variety of maturities at stated rates. An FRA agreement entered at the prevailing market-determined rate is an **on-market FRA**. For the example we have just been considering, the on-market rate for a six-month FRA with a determination date in six months and a payment date in 12 months would be 5 percent. Entering an on-market FRA is costless, as it is simply a forward contract initiated at the prevailing rate. An **off-market FRA** is an FRA entered at a rate that differs from the prevailing market-determined rate. Because the terms for an off-market FRA differ from those prevailing in the market, a payment is required to enter the FRA. For example, let us assume that the prevailing rate on an FRA is

6 × 12   5%

An off-market receive-fixed FRA for this period is entered at a rate of 7 percent with a notional principal of $10 million. For this agreement, the on-market rate is 5 percent, so the on-market fixed payment would be

$0.05 \times 1/2 \times \$10,000,000 = \$250,000$

while the off-market fixed payment would be

$0.07 \times 1/2 \times \$10,000,000 = \$350,000$

Both payments would occur in one year at month 12, and both FRAs call for the same dollar payment on the floating side. From this example, it is clear that entering the off-market receive-fixed FRA will pay $100,000 more than the on-market FRA in one year. Therefore, this receive-fixed off-market FRA will require the payment of the present value of the $100,000 when the

FRA is initiated or the payment of $100,000 at month 12. As we now show, off-market FRAs play a critical role in analyzing an interest rate swap as a portfolio of FRAs.

Interest swaps and FRAs

With this background, we can now see how a plain vanilla interest rate swap can be analyzed as a portfolio of FRAs. Consider the following FRA quotations:

6 × 12	5%
12 × 18	5%
18 × 24	5%

These quotations offer a fixed rate of interest for six-month LIBOR 6, 12, and 18 months from now, and these rates are consistent with a flat yield curve. Faced with these rates, a firm enters all three FRAs to receive-fixed and pay six-month LIBOR.

A sequence of evenly spaced instruments with the same notional principal is called a **strip**. (We explored Eurodollar strips in Chapter 6.) By entering these three FRA agreements at a notional principal of $20 million, the firm has entered a strip of FRAs and is obligated to receive a fixed rate of 5 percent and pay six-month LIBOR on a notional principal of $20 million each six months over the next two years. The determination dates will be at months 6, 12, and 18, and the corresponding payment dates will be at months 12, 18, and 24.

This sequence of three FRAs is equivalent to a receive-fixed interest rate swap at 5 percent with semiannual payments on a notional principal of $20 million and a tenor of two years. From the point of view of the receive-fixed party, the periodic cash flow will be

$$0.05 \times 1/2 \text{ year} \times \$20 \text{ million} - \text{LIBOR} \times 1/2 \text{ year} \times \$20 \text{ million}$$

Therefore, when the yield curve is flat, a plain vanilla interest rate swap is equivalent to a sequence of FRAs.

We now consider the more realistic case of a yield curve with shape. Assume that the current six-month spot rate is 4.95 percent, and consider now the following FRA quotations that imply a rising yield curve:

6 × 12	500%
12 × 18	5.10%
18 × 24	5.20%

These spot and FRA yields cover a range from 4.95 percent to 5.20 percent. A plain vanilla interest rate swap calls for a single fixed rate for the entire tenor of the swap. With these varying FRA rates, it is not clear how the equivalence between the strip of FRAs and the plain vanilla swap can be maintained.

Intuitively, the fixed rate on the swap must be greater than 4.95 percent, but less than 5.20 percent. However, the fixed swap rate is unlikely to match any of the four rates. Instead, the fixed rate on the swap must be a function of the spot rate and the three rates on the FRA, such that the fixed rate on the swap implies payments with the same present value as the sequence of FRAs. If this pricing rule were not maintained, arbitrage would be possible. The arbitrage would result because the cash flows on an interest rate swap can be replicated by a sequence of FRAs. This no-arbitrage principle enforces an equality between the present value of the fixed payments and the present value of the floating payments viewed from the initiation of the swap. It also provides a way to find the no-arbitrage fixed rate for the swap given the FRA quotations.

Later in this chapter, we show exactly how to find the fixed rate for this swap. For now, let us simply assume that the no-arbitrage fixed rate for this swap is 5.075 percent. We select this rate as it is the midpoint between the high and low rates. Notice that it does not match any of the four FRA rates actually available. This will generally be the case in any term structure environment when the yield curve has shape. Thus, for a swap in this situation with a fixed rate of 5.075 percent, the swap may be replicated by a strip of off-market FRAs:

Quarter	FRA rate (%)	Fixed rate (%)	Fixed-rate bias
1	4.95	5.075	Too high
2	5.00	5.075	Too high
3	5.10	5.075	Too low
4	5.20	5.075	Too low

In the rising yield curve environment of our example, the fixed rate on the swap is first too high, for periods 1 and 2, and then too low for periods 3 and 4. In general, we would expect the fixed rate on the swap to be about the average of the FRA rates covering the tenor of the swap. The first two payments on this swap have a present value that is beneficial to the receive-fixed counterparty, while the last two payments benefit the pay-fixed party, assuming that the FRA rates materialize as the actual rates to cover the various periods.

In summary, we may interpret an interest rate swap as a strip of FRAs. In the rare event of a flat yield curve, all FRA rates will be the same and the fixed rate for the swap will be the same as the common FRA rate. In the more usual case, when the yield curve has shape, the fixed rate on the swap will not equal any of the FRA rates. Instead, it will be the unique fixed rate that makes the present values of all the individual payments sum to zero. This is the one fair fixed rate for the swap that does not disadvantage either party. The strip of FRAs will then be a strip of off-market FRAs, and it is this strip of off-market FRAs that is equivalent to a plain vanilla interest rate swap.

Negative interest rates?

Just contemplating the idea of negative interest rates can be a brain-teaser. In the upside-down world of negative rates, a lender would actually be willing to pay a borrower to take the lender's loan. Savers would be willing to pay banks to keep their money on deposit. The concept seems impossible to imagine, yet in a deflationary economy, it is possible for a lender to lose less paying someone to take his money than to leave the money idle and let it fall even further in value. Deflationary economies in Asia briefly produced negative short-term interest rates during the late 1990s. For example, in November 1998, rates on three-month Japanese Treasury bills fell to −0.05 percent, and euro/yen rates fell to −0.06 percent. Historically, negative interest rates have been observed for brief periods in Switzerland and the United States.

A negative interest rate environment poses a special problem for counterparties to currency and interest rate swaps. For example, in a fixed-for-floating interest rate swap, a negative floating amount means that the fixed-rate payer may have to pay a net amount in excess of the fixed amount. To see this, recall that in this type of swap, the fixed-rate payer is also the floating-rate receiver. If the reference interest rate used to set the floating becomes negative, the fixed-rate payer is "owed" a negative amount by the floating-rate payer. This means that the net exchange of cash flows will result in the fixed-rate payer paying an amount in excess of the fixed rate. In response to this peculiar situation, the International Swaps and Derivatives Association (ISDA) issued a memorandum to its members urging swap counterparties to include in their contracts specific language to cover the possibility of negative interest rates. One way of handing the situation is to equate a negative interest rate with zero, effectively flooring the floating rate at zero. In this case, the net amount the fixed-rate payer would pay would be the fixed rate. The other way to handle the situation is to give full effect to a negative floating amount. Under this approach, it is assumed that the information available to the counterparties at the initiation of the swap results in a fixed rate that factors in the probability of negative interest rates. In this case, the net exchange of cash flows will include the effect of negative rates. ISDA recommends that this second approach be included as the standard approach in swap master agreements.

Interest rate parity

Consider two countries with debt instruments issued in the currencies of each country and the spot and forward currency exchange rates between the two currencies. The **interest rate parity theorem** asserts that the interest rates in the two countries and the exchange rates between the two currencies form an integrated system. There must be parity in this system of interest and exchange rates to avoid arbitrage. Specifically, interest rate parity asserts that investment in one currency must yield the same proceeds as the following alternative strategy over a given investment horizon:

(1)   Convert funds into a foreign currency at the spot rate at the outset.
(2)   Invest in the foreign currency.
(3)   Reconvert the proceeds to the original currency via a foreign exchange forward contract initiated at the outset of the investment horizon to convert the investment proceeds into the original currency at the investment horizon.

Let

$_{x,y}FX_{t,T}$ = for a foreign exchange forward contract initiated at time t with delivery at time T, the value of one unit of the x-currency in terms of the y-currency

Thus,

$_{\$,euro}FX_{0,3}$ = the forward exchange value of \$1 in terms of euros for a contract initiated at time $t = 0$, with delivery at time $T = 3$, and
$_{\$,¥}FX_{0,0}$ = the spot price of \$1 in terms of Japanese yen for immediate delivery, because $t = T$

In Chapter 19, we introduced the notation of zero-coupon factors, such that $Z_{t,T}$ is the factor for a payment to be received at time T measured from time t. Where necessary, we will indicate currencies by a prescript for the factor.

In terms of this notation, we can express the interest rate parity theorem as follows:

Interest rate parity

$$_{x}Z_{t,T} = {}_{x,y}FX_{t,t} \times {}_{y}Z_{t,T} \times {}_{y,x}FX_{t,T} \tag{21.1}$$

Again, in English this theorem says that:

> Investment in currency x from time t until time T must have the same proceeds as converting funds from currency x to currency y at the foreign exchange spot rate, investing in currency y from time t until time T, and converting the proceeds of the investment in currency y back into currency x via a forward contract initiated at time t with payoff at time T.

To illustrate this parity condition, assume that the foreign exchange spot rate between the dollar and the euro is $\$1 = €0.8$, the one-year U.S. interest rate is 9 percent, and the one-year European EMU interest rate is 12 percent, all with annual compounding. Interest rate parity asserts that the one-year foreign exchange forward rate must be $€1 = \$1.216518$, or $\$1 = €0.822018$, because only this forward foreign exchange rate meets the parity condition, given the spot exchange rate and the two interest rates:

$$_x Z_{t,T} = {}_{x,y}FX_{t,t} \times {}_y Z_{t,T} \times {}_{y,x}FX_{t,T}$$
$$_\$ Z_{0,1} = {}_{\$,euro}FX_{0,0} \times {}_{euro} Z_{0,1} \times {}_{euro,\$}FX_{0,1}$$
$$1.09 = 0.8 \times 1.12 \times 1.216518$$

If interest rate parity did not hold, arbitrage would be possible. For example, if $_{euro,R}FX_{0,1} <$ 1.216518 in this situation, investment in dollars would be clearly superior. If $_{euro,R}FX_{0,1} > 1.216518$, investment in euros would yield a higher return. Arbitrage would proceed by borrowing in the currency in which funds are relatively cheap, and investing in the currency where the return is relatively high, with a forward contract to convert funds to the currency that was borrowed originally. For example, assume that the forward exchange rate is $€1 = \$1.3$ and the other variables are as given. One would transact as follows:

$t = 0$
Borrow $\$1,000,000$ million in the United States for one year at 9 percent.
Exchange $\$1,000,000$ million for $€800,000$ at the spot exchange rate.
Invest $€800,000$ in Europe for one year at 12 percent.
Sell $€896,000$ one year forward at $€1 = \$1.3$ for a total of $\$1,164,800$.
Net cash flow = 0

$t = 1$ year
Collect proceeds of European investment: $€800,000 \times 1.12 = €896,000$.
Deliver $€896,000$ against forward contract; collect $\$1,164,800$.
Repay U.S. loan: $\$1,000,000 \times 1.09 = \$1,090,000$.
Net cash flow = +$\$74,800$

This is a clear example of arbitrage, as it produces a riskless profit without investment. It should be borne in mind that interest rate parity expresses a relationship among interest rates in two countries, the spot exchange rate and the forward exchange rate. All four elements must be mutually consistent to avoid arbitrage.

Consistent with interest rate parity, there is a term structure of foreign exchange rates. The term structure of interest rates in two countries and the term structure of exchange rates between the two countries form an integrated system that must be consistent with interest rate parity to avoid arbitrage. For example, assume that the term structure of interest rates in the United States is strongly upward sloping, while the term structure of interest rates in Europe is more gently upward sloping and at a lower level. Table 21.1 shows this situation in a simplified form, along with the term structure of dollar/euro exchange rates that is consistent with interest rate parity. Because the U.S. term structure of interest rates lies above the European term structure of interest rates, the value of the mark in terms of dollars must rise as maturities lengthen.

Table 21.1   Term structures of dollar and European interest rates and the dollar/euro exchange rate

Maturity (years)	U.S. dollar interest rate par yields	U.S. dollar interest rate zero-coupon factors	European EMU interest rate par yields	European EMU interest rate zero-coupon factors	Forward exchange rate euro value of $1
0	N/A	N/A	N/A	N/A	0.800000
1	0.080	1.080000	0.050	1.050000	0.777778
2	0.085	1.177688	0.052	1.106814	0.751855
3	0.088	1.289411	0.054	1.171394	0.726778
4	0.091	1.420766	0.055	1.239756	0.698078
5	0.093	1.567391	0.056	1.314914	0.671135

Interest rates are yield to maturities. Annualized compounding throughout.
Example with five-year maturity:
Dollar proceeds of U.S. investment = dollar proceeds of European investment
1.567391 = 0.8 × 1.314914/0.671135
1.567391 = 1.567391

A fixed-for-fixed currency swap as a strip of foreign exchange forward contracts

With this background on interest rate parity, we can now see how to interpret a fixed-for-fixed currency swap as a strip of foreign exchange forward contracts. Consider a five-year fixed-for-fixed currency swap with annual payments negotiated in the context of the interest rate and exchange rate environment shown in Table 21.1, and assume that determination dates occur at years 0, 1, 2, 3, and 4, with payment dates falling one year later. Assume that the notional principal is $100 million, equivalent to €80 million, and that the dollar payer promises to pay a fixed rate of 8.5 percent, while the European payer promises to pay a fixed rate of 5.3 percent. (These rates are arbitrarily set at roughly the midpoints of the two yield curves for the tenor of the swap. Later in this chapter, we show how to find the no-arbitrage rates for this kind of swap.) The first time line in Figure 21.6 shows the cash flows from the perspective of the dollar payer. In each year, 1–5, the dollar payer pays $8.5 million and receives €4,240,000. The time line also shows the exchanges of principal at the inception of the swap and at year 5.

The cash flows shown in the upper time line of Figure 21.6 essentially express the cash flows from the following portfolio of foreign exchange contracts:

Sell €80,000,000 spot at a rate of $1 = €0.8 for $100,000,000.
Sell $8,500,000 one year forward at a rate of $1 = €0.498824 for €4,240,000.
Sell $8,500,000 two years forward at a rate of $1 = €0.498824 for €4,240,000.
Sell $8,500,000 three years forward at a rate of $1 = €0.498824 for €4,240,000.
Sell $8,500,000 four years forward at a rate of $1 = €0.498824 for €4,240,000.
Sell $8,500,000 five years forward at a rate of $1 = €0.498824 for €4,240,000.
Sell $100,000,000 five years forward at a rate of $1 = €0.8 for €80,000,000.

The cash flows for the fixed-for-fixed currency swap in the upper time line of Figure 21.6 are equivalent to this portfolio of one spot foreign exchange transaction and six forward exchange transactions. Notice that the foreign exchange rates for each year are the same (except for the last exchange of principal) and that they do not equal any of the forward exchange rates in

Figure 21.6 Cash flows on the five-year fixed-for-fixed currency swap

Perspective of dollar payer

	$100,000,000	€4,240,000	€4,240,000	€4,240,000	€4,240,000	€84,240,000
0	1	2	3	4	5
	€80,000,000	$8,500,000	$8,500,000	$8,500,000	$8,500,000	$108,500,000

Dollar perspective

	$100,000,000	$5,451,428	$5,639,383	$5,833,972	$6,073,825	$125,518,703
0	1	2	3	4	5
	$100,000,000	$8,500,000	$8,500,000	$8,500,000	$8,500,000	$108,500,000

Euro perspective

	€80,000,000	€6,611,113	€6,390,768	€6,177,613	€5,933,663	€72,818,148
0	1	2	3	4	5
	€80,000,000	€4,240,000	€4,240,000	€4,240,000	€4,240,000	€84,240,000

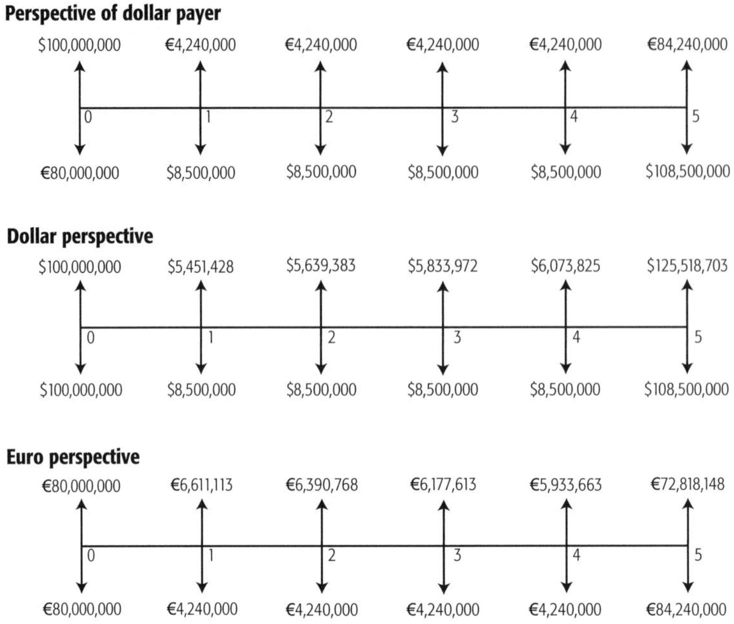

Table 21.1. Therefore, we see that a fixed-for-fixed currency swap may be viewed as a portfolio of off-market foreign exchange transactions.

This perspective also provides guidance to the pricing of this kind of currency swap. The second time line of Figure 21.6 shows the dollar equivalents of the cash flows in the upper time lines. All of the euro cash flows have been translated into dollars using the respective forward rates. For example, the euro inflow at year 3 is €4,240,000, and the three-year forward currency rate is 0.726778 from Table 21.1. Therefore, the dollar value of that flow is €4,240,000/0.726778 = $5,833,972. In the second time line, the exchange of principal is a wash. The dollar payer loses by at least $2,000,000 on each of the annual coupon payments in years 1–5. The reexchange of principal at year 5 (€80 million for $100 million) implies an exchange rate of $1 = €0.8, which was the original spot rate. On the reexchange of principal, the dollar payer recoups much of the losses on the individual coupon payments. For this fixed-for-fixed currency swap to be fairly priced, the present value of all of the cash flows in the second time line must be zero, when these cash flows are discounted based on the U.S. dollar zero-coupon term structure. Otherwise, one side gains at the expense of the other.

Similarly, we can view the entire transaction from the perspective of one concerned with euros. To do so, we convert all of the dollar flows into marks at the respective exchange rates. For example, at year four, the euro payer receives $8.5 million. The four-year forward rate is $1 = €0.698078, so the euro value of that payment would be €5,933,663. The cash flows in the third time line must have a zero present value when discounted according to the European zero-coupon discount rates (Euribor). Otherwise, one party gains at the other's expense. As we show later in this chapter, this equivalence between a fixed-for-fixed currency swap and a portfolio of off-market foreign exchange transactions provides a valuable guide to pricing currency swaps.

Figure 21.7   Cash flows on the five-year plain vanilla currency swap

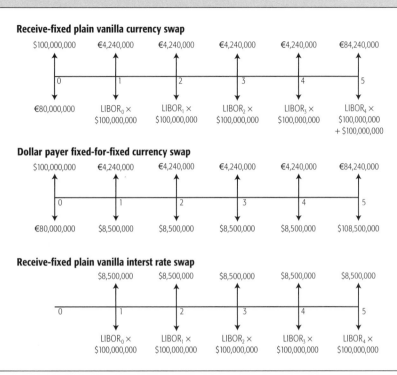

Receive-fixed plain vanilla currency swap

Dollar payer fixed-for-fixed currency swap

Receive-fixed plain vanilla interst rate swap

A plain vanilla currency swap as a fixed-for-fixed currency swap plus a plain vanilla interest rate swap

In this section, we explore the equivalences between a plain vanilla currency swap, on the one hand, and a fixed-for-fixed currency swap plus a plain vanilla interest rate swap, on the other. The plain vanilla currency swap calls for the dollar payer to pay LIBOR against a fixed rate on a foreign currency. Consider a plain vanilla currency swap in the rate environment of Table 21.1. Assume that the swap has a five-year tenor, and annual payments determined in advance and paid in arrears based on one-year LIBOR. The notional principal is $100 million, equivalent to €80 million. The euro fixed rate is 5.3 percent. Determination dates occur at years 0, 1, 2, 3, and 4, with settlement dates one year later. $LIBOR_t$ indicates the one-year LIBOR rate prevailing at time t. This swap is the plain vanilla analog of the fixed-for-fixed swap that we explored in the previous section. The first time line of Figure 21.7 shows the cash flows for the plain vanilla currency swap just described from the perspective of the receive-fixed party.

We now want to show that this plain vanilla currency swap is equivalent to a fixed-for-fixed currency swap plus a plain vanilla interest rate swap. The second time line of Figure 21.7 shows the cash flows for the fixed-for-fixed currency swap analyzed in the preceding section. It consists of the same notional principal of $100 million, equivalent to €80 million, with the dollar payer paying 8.5 percent fixed and the euro payer paying 5.3 percent. (The second time line of Figure 21.7 is identical to the first time line of Figure 21.6.) The third time line of Figure 21.7 shows the cash flows for a plain vanilla interest rate swap with a notional principal of $100 million, a five-year tenor, annual payments, and a fixed rate of 8.5 percent. If we add the cash flows for the dollar payer fixed-for-fixed currency swap and the cash flows for the receive-fixed plain vanilla interest rate swap, the combined cash flows are exactly the same as the cash flows for the receive-fixed plain vanilla currency swap. Therefore, we can conclude as follows:

> receive-fixed plain vanilla currency swap
>   = dollar payer fixed-for-fixed currency swap   (21.2)
>   + receive-fixed plain vanilla interest rate swap

> pay-fixed plain vanilla currency swap
>   = FOREX payer fixed-for-fixed currency swap   (21.3)
>   + pay-fixed plain vanilla interest rate swap

We have already seen that a plain vanilla interest rate swap can be analyzed as a pair of bonds or as a strip of FRAs. Similarly, we noted that a fixed-for-fixed currency swap can be analyzed as a portfolio of foreign exchange contracts. Therefore, it is possible to decompose the plain vanilla currency swap into these more basic elements. In Chapter 20, we discussed a CIRCUS swap, a combined interest rate and currency swap. A CIRCUS swap is a fixed-for-fixed currency swap created by combining a plain vanilla currency swap and a plain vanilla interest rate swap.

Rearranging terms in Equation 21.2 gives the following:

> dollar payer fixed-for-fixed currency swap
>   = receive-fixed plain vanilla currency swap
>   − receive-fixed plain vanilla interest rate swap
>   = receive-fixed plain vanilla currency swap
>   + pay-fixed plain vanilla interest rate swap

and a similar rearrangement of Equation 21.3 gives

> FOREX payer fixed-for-fixed currency swap
>   = pay-fixed plain vanilla currency swap
>   − pay-fixed plain vanilla interest rate swap
>   = pay-fixed plain vanilla currency swap
>   + receive-fixed plain vanilla interest rate swap

Summary

In the last few sections, we have seen that plain vanilla interest rate swaps, fixed-for-fixed currency swaps, and plain vanilla currency swaps can be analyzed as portfolios of FRAs and foreign exchange forward contracts. By considering foreign exchange rates and interest rate parity, we see that the term structure of interest rates in two countries and the term structure of foreign exchange rates form a unified system of prices that must obey parity conditions to avoid arbitrage. Interest rates and currency swaps also must fit into this system to avoid arbitrage opportunities. The decomposition of interest rate and currency swaps into these interest rate and foreign exchange forward contracts shows how the entire system is constructed and also provides guidance to the determination of no-arbitrage pricing of swaps that we pursue later in this chapter.

An interest rate swap as a strip of Eurodollar futures contracts

As we learned in Chapter 2, futures contracts are a type of forward contract with specific additional institutional features. A futures contract is distinguished from other forward contracts by the margining and daily resettlement feature, along with the presence of exchange trading and clearinghouse guarantees. Aside from these institutional considerations, an interest rate futures contract is essentially like an interest rate forward contract. Therefore, an interest rate swap can be viewed as a portfolio of successively maturing interest rate futures contracts. In terms of our earlier example, we might think of an interest rate swap as being similar to a strip of interest rate futures contracts.[1] Because interest rate swap agreements so often use LIBOR as the floating rate in the contract, a strip of Eurodollar futures contracts is highly analogous to an interest rate swap agreement.

One of the main reasons for the development of the swaps market was the need for custom-tailored instruments with a tenor that exceeded the maturities available in the futures market. Typically, futures contract maturities do not extend for more than two years or so, but swap agreements can have a considerably longer tenor. Further, most futures contracts have very limited volume and open interest in the more distant maturities. As we have seen in Chapter 20, a swap dealer who participates in an interest rate swap may be left with a risk position that is undesired. As we saw in our earlier discussion, the swap dealer accepts this risk position to complete the swap agreement and earn a profit, but the dealer would typically like to avoid this risk.

If a strip of futures contracts could be regarded as a substitute for an interest rate swap, the swap dealer might be able to use Eurodollar strips to hedge unwanted interest rate risk that arises in the swap business. However, such a strategy would require an active market in distant Eurodollar maturities. In the earlier days of the swaps market, the Eurodollar futures contract certainly did not possess the depth or liquidity to allow Eurodollar strips to serve this role. For example, at the end of 1986, total open interest in all Eurodollar contract expirations was 214,000 contracts, and the most distant listed Eurodollar futures was the December 1988 contract, which was only two years distant. Figure 21.8 shows recent quotations for the Eurodollar contract with an extremely high level of open interest and with contract expirations extending for ten years. This extended maturity range and deep liquidity is unparalleled for any other futures contract of any type. The main reason for these special features is the interest of swap dealers in using Eurodollar strips to offset risk inherent in the interest rate swap positions that they undertake. Note, however, that market depth remains a problem for the very distant expirations.

For swap market operations, a strip of FRAs is a closer substitute for a swap than a strip of Eurodollar futures. Eurodollar futures contracts have just four main expiration dates per year, one each in March, June, September, and December, although there is a less liquid market for other upcoming months, as Figure 21.8 shows. Because of these limited expiration dates, a strip of Eurodollar futures will not match the timing of swap payments as closely as a strip of FRAs. Also, the futures market calls for daily settlement cash flows, and these daily cash flows can cause futures and forward prices to be unequal, as we have studied in Chapter 3. Swaps, like FRAs, but unlike futures, do not have daily settlement cash flows, so a strip of FRAs is a closer substitute for a swap than a strip of Eurodollar futures. These minor issues aside, a strip of Eurodollar futures is conceptually very similar to an interest rate swap.

A review of interest rate options

This section provides a capsule review of the features of interest rate options that are important for understanding swaps. All of the material of this section is presented in detail, with calculation examples, in Chapter 19. Here we briefly consider calls and puts on LIBOR, the Black model for these options, forward put–call parity, as well as caps, floors, and collars. The reader familiar with Chapter 19 may skip this section without loss.

Figure 21.8 Quotations for Eurodollar futures

	OPEN	HIGH	LOW	SETTLE	CHG	YIELD	OPEN INTEREST
Aug06	94.540	94.590	94.540	94.590	+.037	5.41	35,688
Sep06	94.525	94.575	94.520	94.570	+.035	5.43	1,602,202
Oct06	-----	-----	-----	94.530	+.030	5.47	2,925
Nov06	94.515	94.515	94.515	94.545	+.020	5.45	631
Dec06	94.540	94.580	94.525	94.570	+.020	5.43	1,569,494
Mar07	94.635	94.675	94.620	94.665	+.020	5.33	1,222,739
Jun07	94.745	94.800	94.730	94.795	+.035	5.20	1,024,899
Sep07	94.835	94.890	94.825	94.885	+.040	5.11	1,044,195
Dec07	94.860	94.925	94.860	94.915	+.035	5.08	893,948
Mar08	94.870	94.930	94.865	94.920	+.035	5.08	563,333
Jun08	94.860	94.915	94.855	94.910	+.035	5.09	377,625
Sep08	94.840	94.890	94.840	94.885	+.030	5.11	280,004
Dec08	94.800	94.850	94.800	94.845	+.030	5.15	272,839
Mar09	94.780	94.825	94.775	94.815	+.025	5.18	242,854
Jun09	94.745	94.785	94.735	94.775	+.025	5.22	181,112
Sep09	94.705	94.735	94.695	94.730	+.020	5.27	128,291
Dec09	94.660	94.690	94.650	94.680	+.015	5.32	116,371
Mar10	94.640	94.665	94.625	94.655	+.015	5.34	104,074
Jun10	94.605	94.630	94.590	94.620	+.015	5.38	88,126
Sep10	94.565	94.595	94.555	94.580	+.010	5.42	94,719
Dec10	94.525	94.555	94.515	94.540	+.010	5.46	73,493
Mar11	94.510	94.535	94.500	94.525	+.010	5.47	55,744
Jun11	94.480	94.510	94.475	94.500	+.010	5.50	37,766
Sep11	94.470	94.475	94.460	94.470	+.005	5.53	25,334
Dec11	94.430	94.435	94.420	94.430	+.005	5.57	19,920
Mar12	94.415	94.420	94.405	94.415	+.005	5.58	15,298
Jun12	94.390	94.395	94.380	94.390	+.005	5.61	12,171
Sep12	94.355	94.365	94.350	94.360	+.005	5.64	9,372
Dec12	94.325	94.330	94.315	94.320	-----	5.68	6,830
Mar13	94.310	94.315	94.300	94.305	-----	5.69	6,037
Jun13	-----	94.290	94.275	94.280	-----	5.72	5,610
Sep13	94.255	94.265	94.245	94.250	-----	5.75	1,911
Dec13	94.225	94.235	94.215	94.220	-----	5.78	1,459
Mar14	94.210	94.220	94.200	94.205	-----	5.79	1,733
Jun14	-----	94.195	94.175	94.180	-----	5.82	1,517
Sep14	-----	94.165	94.145	94.150	-----	5.85	3,251
Dec14	-----	94.135	94.115	94.120	-----	5.88	1,197
Mar15	-----	94.125	94.105	94.110	-----	5.89	715
Jun15	-----	94.105	94.085	94.110	-----	5.91	593
Sep15	-----	94.075	94.055	94.060	-----	5.94	704
Dec15	-----	94.045	94.025	94.030	-----	5.97	403
Mar16	-----	94.040	94.020	94.025	-----	5.97	506
Jun16	-----	94.025	94.005	94.010	-----	5.99	1560

Source: Excerpted from the 2006 *Daily Price Bulletin* published by the Chicago Mercantile Exchange, available at
www.cme.com/prices/bulletinindex.cfm. © 2006 by the Chicago Mercantile Exchange. Reprinted by permission of the Chicago Mercantile
Exchange

Calls and puts on LIBOR

Paralleling the FRA market, there is an active market for options on LIBOR. For example, there is a market for calls on three-month LIBOR and for puts on one-month LIBOR. These options are generally European in form.

The payoff on calls and puts on LIBOR depends on the maturity of LIBOR being quoted and the notional principal. Consider first a call on three-month LIBOR with a notional principal of $1 million and an exercise price, or strike rate, of 9 percent. The call pays off if the observed three-month LIBOR rate on the expiration date of the option exceeds the strike rate. In that case, the payoff on this call equals the difference between the observed rate and the strike rate multiplied by the quarter of a year maturity corresponding to the rate, times the notional principal. For our example call option, if the observed rate is 10.5 percent, the payoff will be

$$(0.1050 - 0.0900) \times 0.25 \times \$1,000,0000 = \$3,750$$

Let *FRAC* be the fraction of the year covered by the maturity of the underlying LIBOR instrument, *NP* be the notional principal, and *SR* be the strike rate. A general expression for the payoff on a call on LIBOR will be as follows:

$$\text{MAX}\{0, (\text{Observed LIBOR} - SR) \times FRAC \times NP\} \tag{21.4}$$

where Observed LIBOR is the rate observed at the expiration of the option for LIBOR of the appropriate maturity. A put on LIBOR pays off when the observed rate at expiration is less than the strike rate. The payoff on a put on LIBOR is

$$\text{MAX}\{0, (SR - \text{Observed LIBOR}) \times FRAC \times NP\} \tag{21.5}$$

For example, consider a put on one-month LIBOR with a strike rate of 8.5 percent and a notional principal of $25 million. At the expiration of the option, assume that the one-month LIBOR rate stands at 7.03 percent, and Observed LIBOR = 0.0703. The payoff on this put would be

$$(0.0850 - 0.0703) \times (1/12) \times \$25,000,000 = \$30,625$$

In our discussion of FRAs, we noted that they are generally "determined in advance and settled in arrears." Thus, the payment on a six-month FRA generally occurs six months after the determination date. Calls and puts on LIBOR are generally structured in a parallel manner. The payoffs are determined at the expiration date, but the payment is made at a date that lags the determination date by the maturity of the LIBOR quotation. Thus, the actual payoffs on our sample call and put would be three months and one month after the determination dates, respectively. In pricing calls and puts on LIBOR, we will need to take this settlement in arrears into account.

The Black model and options on LIBOR

As discussed in detail in Chapter 19, the Black model was developed to apply to options on futures. However, it applies to calls and puts on LIBOR as well. The currently observed forward LIBOR (*FLIBOR*) plays the role of the futures price. Specifically, $FLIBOR_t$ is observed at time t, when the option is being valued. It is the forward LIBOR with a maturity corresponding to the maturity of the option, and it is the forward rate with a time horizon that matches the expiration date of the option. Notice that $FLIBOR_t$ should be identical to the FRA rates for the same period in the future. The strike rate plays the role of the exercise price, while the standard deviation of the LIBOR forward rate (*FLIBOR*) of the requisite maturity is the volatility measure for the model. Therefore, the Black model for calls and puts on LIBOR is as follows:

$$c_t^{FLIBOR} = NP \times FRAC \times e^{-r(T+FRAC-t)}[FLIBOR_t \times N(d_1^{FLIBOR}) - SR \times N(d_2^{FLIBOR})]$$
$$p_t^{FLIBOR} = NP \times FRAC \times e^{-r(T+FRAC-t)}[SR \times N(-d_2^{FLIBOR}) - FLIBOR_t \times N(-d_1^{FLIBOR})]$$

$$d_1^{FLIBOR} = \frac{\ln\left(\dfrac{FLIBOR_t}{SR}\right) + 0.5\sigma^2(T-t)}{\sigma\sqrt{T-t}} \tag{21.6}$$

$$d_2^{FLIBOR} = d_1^{FLIBOR} - \sigma\sqrt{T-t}$$

In this equation, we have the Black model with the following substitutions. *FLIBOR_t* takes the role of the futures price, and *SR* substitutes for the exercise price. The payoff on the options is discounted for a longer period, the time to expiration plus *FRAC*, to account for the delayed payment, and the values of the options are multiplied by *NP(FRAC)* to convert the values to dollar amounts.

The following equation is identical to Equation 21.6, except that it uses the zero-coupon factor instead of the continuously compounded rate to discount the payoff on the option from the payoff date (the expiration of the option plus *FRAC*) to the present:

$$c_t^{FLIBOR} = NP \times FRAC \times \frac{1}{Z_{t,T+FRAC}}[FLIBOR_t \times N(d_1^{FLIBOR}) - SR \times N(d_2^{FLIBOR})]$$

$$p_t^{FLIBOR} = NP \times FRAC \times \frac{1}{Z_{t,T+FRAC}}[SR \times N(-d_2^{FLIBOR}) - FLIBOR_t \times N(-d_1^{FLIBOR})]$$

$$\tag{21.7}$$

$$d_1^{FLIBOR} = \frac{\ln\left(\dfrac{FLIBOR_t}{SR}\right) + 0.5\sigma^2(T-t)}{\sigma\sqrt{T-t}}$$

$$d_2^{FLIBOR} = d_1^{FLIBOR} - \sigma\sqrt{T-t}$$

Chapter 19 presents examples of how to calculate the values of puts and calls on LIBOR according to the Black model of Equations 21.6 and 21.7.

Forward put–call parity

We noted the equivalence between forward LIBOR rates (*FLIBOR_t*) and the rate for an FRA to cover the same future period. Consider now a call and a put on LIBOR with a common strike rate *SR*, underlying instrument, and the same notional principal. For a long call/short put portfolio, the payoff will be as follows:

MAX{0, (Observed LIBOR − SR) × FRAC × NP}
− MAX{0, (SR − Observed LIBOR) × FRAC × NP}
= (Observed LIBOR − SR) × FRAC × NP

where Observed LIBOR is the rate observed at the expiration of the option for the appropriate maturity, *FRAC* is the fraction of the year for the underlying instrument, and *NP* is the notional principal. The payoff on this long call/short put portfolio is exactly the same as the payoff on an FRA to cover the same time period and with the same notional principal, when the strike rate on the options equals the FRA rate. Therefore, the long call/short put portfolio is equivalent to the forward rate agreement. This is the principle of forward put–call parity.

$$c_t^{FLIBOR} - p_t^{FLIBOR} = 0 \qquad (21.8)$$

when the common strike rate on the put and call options equals the currently prevailing forward rate, $SR = FRA_{x,y}$, and the time periods covered by the options and the forward rate agreement are the same. This result makes sense, considering that the cost of entering an FRA negotiated at the current forward rate prevailing in the term structure is zero, and it will pay off at the expiration date based on the observed LIBOR at that date relative to the contract rate.

Caps, floors, and collars

A **caplet** is a long call on LIBOR combined with an FRA. The call provides a cap on the effective rate for the FRA that equals the strike rate on the call. A **floorlet** is a short put on LIBOR combined with an FRA. The floorlet provides a lower bound, or floor, on the effective rate for the FRA that equals the strike rate on the put. The option terms must match the FRA terms, such as time period covered and notional principal, as the following example illustrates.

Consider an FRA for a period covering from four to seven months in the future, such that $FRA_{4,7} = 6.5$ percent with a notional principal of $10 million. A firm planning to borrow under these terms purchases a call on LIBOR with matching terms and a strike rate of 7 percent. Not counting the cost of the call, the maximum rate that the firm will have to pay for its loan of $10 million is 7 percent. If rates in four months are less than 7 percent, the call expires worthless and the firm borrows at the prevailing rate. If the prevailing rate is above 7 percent, the call pays off an amount that exactly offsets the cost of the loan in excess of 7 percent, thereby capping the rate at 7 percent.

Similarly, a short put combined with an FRA puts a lower bound on the effective borrowing rate. For example, assume that a firm planning to borrow as just described sells a put with a strike rate of 6 percent in conjunction with its loan. Not counting the price received for selling the put, the lower bound on the effective borrowing rate is 6 percent. In four months, if the prevailing rates exceed 6 percent, the put will expire worthless and the firm will borrow at the prevailing rate. If rates are below 6 percent, the firm will borrow at the prevailing rate, but the short put will be exercised against the firm. The loss on the exercise will exactly offset the benefit of rates lower than the floor rate of 6 percent, effectively putting a floor on the firm's borrowing rate at the 6 percent strike rate on the put. For a multi-period loan, a sequence of caplets is called a **cap**, and a sequence of floorlets is called a **floor**.

For the same example, assume the firm buys the call and sells the put. This places a **collar** on the loan rate. The loan rate has an upper bound at the strike rate on the call (7 percent) and a lower bound at the strike rate on the put (6 percent). This particular collar would be referred to as a 6–7 percent collar. Between these two bounds, the effective rate of the loan matches the prevailing market rate at year 4. A collar can also cover a multi-period loan.

The cap rate, floor rate, and collar rates on a loan do not take account of the cash flows from the purchase or sale of the options. These cash flows will affect the final effective cost of the loan. One special case of interest is a **zero-cost collar**, a collar in which the price paid for the call is exactly offset by the price received for the put. For example, in a collar for a single period, if the call and put have the same strike rate, and the strike rate equals the FRA rate, the total cost of the collar will be zero. This is essentially the result of forward put–call parity.

An interest rate swap as a portfolio of options

We have already seen that an interest rate swap may be analyzed as a strip of off-market FRAs, and that a single FRA can be analyzed as a long call/short put portfolio with a common strike rate that equals the FRA rate. Therefore, an interest rate swap may be analyzed as a strip of off-market FRAs, each of which is created by an option position that consists of a long call and a short put on LIBOR, with all of the options having the same strike rate. This is equivalent to showing that an interest rate swap can be analyzed as a portfolio of calls and puts on LIBOR. We now explore this principle in detail and show more specifically that an interest rate swap is equivalent to a zero-cost collar, subject to the condition that the cap rate, floor rate, and the fixed rate on the swap are all the same.

We have seen that an interest rate swap can be analyzed as a strip of off-market FRAs with a common fixed rate and that an interest rate swap negotiated at the market rate is costless. A collar having the same tenor and settlement dates as an interest rate swap, and a common cap and floor rate equal to the prevailing rate on interest rate swaps, will also be costless and will provide the same payoffs as the interest rate swap on each date. We illustrate this principle with an example.

Consider a pay-fixed interest rate swap with a tenor of four years, annual settlement dates, a fixed rate of 7.30 percent, and a notional principal of $80 million. A long collar with a tenor of four years, annual settlement dates, a common cap and floor rate of 7.30 percent, and a notional principal of $80 million will have exactly the same payoffs as the pay-fixed interest rate swap and, like the swap, will be costless. To see this more fully, consider the following outcomes on both the swap and the collar for two settlement dates, one when LIBOR exceeds the swap/collar rate of 7.3 percent and one when LIBOR is less than 7.3 percent:

LIBOR = 7.7 percent:
  Swap:

  Pay fixed at 7.3 percent = $-0.073 \times \$80,000,000 = -\$5,840,000$
  Receive floating at 7.7 percent = $0.077 \times \$80,000,000 = \$6,160,000$
  Net = +$320,000

  Collar:

  Cap: MAX{0, (0.077 − 0.073) × $80,000,000 × 1 year}
         = MAX{0, $320,000} = $320,000
  Floor: −MAX{0, (0.0732 − 0.077) × $80,000,000 × 1 year}
         = −MAX{0, −$320,000} = 0
  Net = +$320,000

LIBOR = 6.8 percent:
  Swap:

  Pay fixed at 7.3 percent = $-0.073 \times \$80,000,000 = -\$5,840,000$
  Receive floating at 6.8 percent = $0.068 \times \$80,000,000 = \$5,440,000$
  Net = −$400,000

  Collar:

  Cap: MAX{0, (0.068 − 0.073) × $80,000,000 × 1 year}
         = MAX{0, −$400,000} = 0
  Floor: −MAX{0, (0.073 − 0.068) × $80,000,000 × 1 year}
         = −MAX{0, $400,000} = −$400,000
  Net = −$400,000

From this example, we see that the pay-fixed interest rate swap has the same payoffs as owning the interest rate collar (long cap/short floor) for every settlement date, no matter how LIBOR stands in relationship to the cap and floor rate. Since the interest rate swap and the interest rate collar have the same cash flows in every period, they must have the same value. Because an on-market interest rate swap is costless, an interest rate collar with the same terms and a cap and floor rate equal to the fixed rate on the swap also must be costless. Therefore, we see that the following equivalencies must hold, assuming the same tenor and settlement dates on both the swap and the collar:

> pay-fixed interest rate swap = long interest rate collar (buy cap/sell floor)
> receive-fixed interest rate swap = short interest rate collar (sell cap/buy floor)

Summary

In the first part of this chapter, we have seen that interest rate and currency swaps may be analyzed in terms of a variety of other instruments. We began by showing that a plain vanilla interest rate swap provides the exact same sequence of cash flows as a suitably constructed bond portfolio. We presented a similar analysis for a fixed-for-fixed and a plain vanilla currency swap as well. We analyzed a plain vanilla interest rate swap as a portfolio of FRAs and as a close, but not exact, match for a strip of Eurodollar futures contracts. Similarly, a fixed-for-fixed currency swap was shown to have the same cash flows as a sequence of forward foreign exchange contracts. We also showed that a plain vanilla interest rate swap has cash flows that are identical to a collar with a common cap and floor rate that equals the fixed rate on the swap.

In addition to providing greater insight into the economic meaning of swaps, these various analyses have two further important benefits. First, swaps are not instruments that provide new cash flow possibilities that are unattainable with other instruments. The fact that swap cash flows can be replicated by other instruments means that the economic benefits of swaps do not arise because they create new cash flow patterns. Instead, the swaps market must have achieved its success by providing a more efficient means of contracting for desirable cash flow patterns. For example, a plain vanilla interest rate swap turns out to be a more efficient financial instrument than an equivalent package of numerous calls and puts on LIBOR. Second, by seeing how swaps can be analyzed as other instruments, we gain great insight into the principles that determine swap pricing. For example, if a plain vanilla interest rate swap is equivalent to a strip of FRAs, it is possible to use the robust FRA market to determine the appropriate price for a swap. We turn now to the pricing of swaps.

Interest rate swap pricing

The term structure of interest rates is the key to pricing interest rate swaps; the term structure of interest rates and the term structure of foreign exchange rates are the keys to pricing currency swaps. We have seen that bonds, FRNs, FRAs, calls and puts on LIBOR, foreign exchange forward contracts, interest rate futures, and swaps are all related instruments. If they are not priced properly relative to each other and relative to the existing term structures, arbitrage will be possible. Thus, we approach swap pricing in a no-arbitrage environment that focuses on the term structure of interest and currency rates.

The term structure of interest rates and foreign exchange rates

In Chapter 19, we discussed three related term structures or yield curves in detail: the **par yield curve**, the zero-coupon yield curve, and the implied forward yield curve. The par yield curve expresses the relationship between the yield on a coupon bond selling at par and bond maturity. The **zero-coupon yield curve** shows the relationship between yield and maturity for single future payments. The **implied forward yield curve** shows the relationship between forward rates of interest for various future periods as implied by the par yield curve and the zero-coupon yield curve. These three term structures form an integrated system—one set of rates implies another. For example, the zero-coupon yield curve can be found by using the data of the par yield curve in conjunction with the technique of **bootstrapping**, as discussed in detail in Chapter 19. Rather than reviewing the discussion of these yield curves, we recall the key notation introduced in Chapter 19:

$Z_{x,y}$ = the zero-coupon factor for an investment initiated at time x and extending until time y

$FR_{x,y}$ = the forward rate of interest for a period beginning at time x and extending until time y

$FRA_{x,y}$ = the interest rate on an FRA for a period beginning at time x and extending until time y

$FRF_{x,y}$ = the forward rate factor for a period beginning at time x and extending until time y

We also note the following equivalencies:

$$FR_{x,y} = FRA_{x,y} = FRF_{x,y} - 1$$

$$FRF_{x,y} = \frac{Z_{0,y}}{Z_{0,x}}$$

Pricing a plain vanilla interest rate swap

In a plain vanilla interest rate swap, the receive-fixed party will pay a floating rate equal to LIBOR flat in each period. Determining a price for the plain vanilla interest rate swap requires finding the fixed rate that will be received in exchange for making the sequence of floating-rate payments. This is called the swap fixed rate, or *SFR*. At the time the swap is negotiated, the agreed *SFR* must not give an arbitrage opportunity to either side. This no-arbitrage condition means that the agreed *SFR* must be consistent with the term structure of interest rates. One way of determining the *SFR* is to use FRA quotations as representative of the term structure. Based on these FRA quotations, we use the no-arbitrage equivalence of the present value of the strip of FRAs and the present value of the fixed payments to find the no-arbitrage fixed rate for the swap that is consistent with the FRA quotations. Actual market pricing of swaps relies on money market yield and day counting conventions. We can abstract from these technicalities.[2]

We begin by using an example of a plain vanilla interest rate swap with a notional principal of $20 million, a tenor of two years, and payments every six months. The following table shows the relevant quotations for a strip of FRAs and their associated payments with a notional principal of $20 million:

6 months	$0.0495 \times 0.5 \times \$20,000,000 = \$495,000$
12 months	$0.0500 \times 0.5 \times \$20,000,000 = \$500,000$
18 months	$0.0510 \times 0.5 \times \$20,000,000 = \$510,000$
24 months	$0.0520 \times 0.5 \times \$20,000,000 = \$520,000$

Each payment on the fixed side would be the unknown swap fixed rate, *SFR*, times the half-year between payments times the notional principal of $20 million. Each fixed payment would be:

$SFR \times 0.5 \times \$20{,}000{,}000$

According to our no-arbitrage principle, the sequences of fixed and floating payments must have the same present value at the initiation of the swap. We see that these rates range from 4.95 percent to 5.20 percent, so it seems intuitively reasonable that the fixed rate must be in that range and that it should be some kind of average of these various floating rates.

Recalling that $Z_{0,t}$ is the zero-coupon factor for a horizon starting at the present, time zero, and ending at time t, we will express time in months, so $Z_{0,18}$ is the zero-coupon factor to cover the period from the present until the end of the eighteenth month. In our example, the no-arbitrage condition becomes

$$\frac{0.0495 \times 0.5 \times \$20{,}000{,}000}{Z_{0,6}} + \frac{0.0500 \times 0.5 \times \$20{,}000{,}000}{Z_{0,12}}$$
$$+ \frac{0.0510 \times 0.5 \times \$20{,}000{,}000}{Z_{0,18}} + \frac{0.0520 \times 0.5 \times \$20{,}000{,}000}{Z_{0,24}}$$
$$= \frac{SFR \times 0.5 \times \$20{,}000{,}000}{Z_{0,6}} + \frac{SFR \times 0.5 \times \$20{,}000{,}000}{Z_{0,12}}$$
$$+ \frac{SFR \times 0.5 \times \$20{,}000{,}000}{Z_{0,18}} + \frac{SFR \times 0.5 \times \$20{,}000{,}000}{Z_{0,24}}$$

(21.9)

In this no-arbitrage condition, it appears that we have four unknown zero-coupon factors ($Z_{0,6}$, $Z_{0,12}$, $Z_{0,18}$, and $Z_{0,24}$) plus the unknown swap fixed rate (SFR). However, we actually do have the information to find $Z_{0,6}$, and we can use $Z_{0,6}$ to find the other factors through a technique known as bootstrapping, as described in detail in Chapter 19.

Applying the bootstrapping technique, we use an initially known zero-coupon factor and forward rates to find successive factors. We illustrate the technique for our example swap by noting that we can compute the value for the first factor, $Z_{0,6}$, as follows:

$$Z_{0,6} = 1 + 0.5 \times 0.04950 = 1.024750$$

where the 0.5 reflects the half-year between payments and 0.04950 is the current LIBOR spot rate. The factor for the second payment covers the first 12 months of the swap. Given the value of $Z_{0,6}$, we can compute the value of $Z_{0,12}$ as follows:

$$Z_{0,12} = Z_{0,6} \times (1 + 0.5 \times 0.0500) = 1.050369$$

where 0.5 reflects the half-year between payments and 0.0500 is the rate on the 6×12 FRA. Values for $Z_{0,18}$ and $Z_{0,24}$ follow similarly:

$$Z_{0,18} = Z_{0,12} \times (1 + 0.5 \times 0.0510) = 1.050369 \times 1.0255 = 1.077153$$
$$Z_{0,24} = Z_{0,18} \times (1 + 0.5 \times 0.0520) = 1.077153 \times 1.0260 = 1.105159$$

Starting with $Z_{0,6}$ and using the bootstrapping technique, we have found all of the zero-coupon factors that we need.

We can now use these factors in Equation 21.9 to find the swap fixed rate, SFR:

$$\frac{0.0495 \times 0.5 \times \$20,000,000}{1.024750} + \frac{0.0500 \times 0.5 \times \$20,000,000}{1.050369}$$

$$+ \frac{0.0510 \times 0.5 \times \$20,000,000}{1.077153} + \frac{0.0520 \times 0.5 \times \$20,000,000}{1.105159}$$

$$= \frac{SFR \times 0.5 \times \$20,000,000}{1.024750} + \frac{SFR \times 0.5 \times \$20,000,000}{1.050369}$$

$$+ \frac{SFR \times 0.5 \times \$20,000,000}{1.077153} + \frac{SFR \times 0.5 \times \$20,000,000}{1.105159}$$

Solving for *SFR*, we have the following:

$$(0.5 \times \$20,000,000) \times \left(\frac{0.0495}{1.024750} + \frac{0.0500}{1.050369} + \frac{0.0510}{1.077153} + \frac{0.0520}{1.105159}\right)$$

$$= SFR \times (0.5 \times \$20,000,000) \times \left(\frac{1}{1.024750} + \frac{1}{1.050369} + \frac{1}{1.077153} + \frac{1}{1.105159}\right)$$

$$SFR = \frac{\left(\dfrac{0.0495}{1.024750} + \dfrac{0.0500}{1.050369} + \dfrac{0.0510}{1.077153} + \dfrac{0.0520}{1.105159}\right)}{\left(\dfrac{1}{1.024750} + \dfrac{1}{1.050369} + \dfrac{1}{1.077153} + \dfrac{1}{1.105159}\right)} = 0.050598$$

Thus, this swap fixed rate of 5.0598 percent is the rate on the fixed side of the swap that prevents arbitrage.

We can generalize this example to provide a more general expression for finding the swap fixed rate. To do so, we introduce the following notation:

PART = fraction of the year between swap payments

Substituting this notation into Equation 21.9 gives the following:

$$\frac{FRA_{0,6} \times PART \times NP}{Z_{0,6}} + \frac{FRA_{6,12} \times PART \times NP}{Z_{0,12}} + \frac{FRA_{12,18} \times PART \times NP}{Z_{0,18}}$$

$$+ \frac{FRA_{18,24} \times PART \times NP}{Z_{0,24}} = \frac{SFR \times PART \times NP}{Z_{0,6}} + \frac{SFR \times PART \times NP}{Z_{0,12}} \tag{21.10}$$

$$+ \frac{SFR \times PART \times NP}{Z_{0,18}} + \frac{SFR \times PART \times NP}{Z_{0,24}}$$

which simplifies to

$$PART \times NP\left(\frac{FRA_{0,6}}{Z_{0,6}} + \frac{FRA_{6,12}}{Z_{0,12}} + \frac{FRA_{12,18}}{Z_{0,18}} + \frac{FRA_{18,24}}{Z_{0,24}}\right)$$

$$= PART \times NP \times SFR\left(\frac{1}{Z_{0,6}} + \frac{1}{Z_{0,12}} + \frac{1}{Z_{0,18}} + \frac{1}{Z_{0,24}}\right) \tag{21.11}$$

which in turn reduces to the following equation:

$$SFR = \left(\frac{FRA_{0,6}}{Z_{0,6}} + \frac{FRA_{6,12}}{Z_{0,12}} + \frac{FRA_{12,18}}{Z_{0,18}} + \frac{FRA_{18,24}}{Z_{0,24}}\right) \Bigg/ \left(\frac{1}{Z_{0,6}} + \frac{1}{Z_{0,12}} + \frac{1}{Z_{0,18}} + \frac{1}{Z_{0,24}}\right) \quad (21.12)$$

Equation 21.12 still pertains to our example in terms of the specific number and timing of payments. Otherwise, it is a general expression for the swap fixed rate.

By generalizing the number and timing of payments even further, we can transform Equation 21.12 into a general formula for the fixed rate on a swap. Any plain vanilla interest rate swap can be characterized as having a total of N payments, occurring at a regular interval of MON months apart. The example swap we have been considering has four payments ($N = 4$) spaced six months apart ($MON = 6$). Therefore, the following equation provides a generalized expression for the swap fixed rate on a plain vanilla interest rate swap:

$$SFR = \left(\sum_{n=1}^{N} \frac{FRA_{(n-1)\times MON, n\times MON}}{Z_{0,n\times MON}}\right) \Bigg/ \left(\sum_{n=1}^{N} \frac{1}{Z_{0,n\times MON}}\right) \quad (21.13)$$

Equation 21.13 follows directly from our no-arbitrage approach to analyzing a swap. As such, it reflects the actual timing of each payment on the swap and allows a different discount rate to be applied to each payment, as reflected by the term structure.

The subscripts in Equation 21.13 are necessarily cumbersome. To ensure that the meaning and application of the equation are clear, we show how Equation 21.13 fits our example swap. We have noted that the example swap has a total of four payments spaced six months apart. So, in terms of Equation 21.13, $N = 4$ and $MON = 6$. The following table shows the value of each subscript for each of the four payments:

n	$n - 1$	$(n - 1) \times MON$	$n \times MON$
1	0	$0 \times 6 = 0$	$1 \times 6 = 6$
2	1	$1 \times 6 = 6$	$2 \times 6 = 12$
3	2	$2 \times 6 = 12$	$3 \times 6 = 18$
4	3	$3 \times 6 = 18$	$4 \times 6 = 24$

Applying these subscripts to a four-payment swap with a six-month interval between payments will return us to Equation 21.12, illustrating how our general expression, Equation 21.13, applies to individual swaps.

When we approached the issue of swap pricing, we began with the intuition that the swap fixed rate for our example swap should have been greater than 4.95 percent, but less than 5.2 percent. As our pricing showed, this intuition was correct. We might hope to generalize this intuition somewhat to say that the swap fixed rate should be the same as the average of the floating rates. In fact, this will not be exactly the case. Instead, the geometric average of the floating rates on a swap will be near, but not equal to, the swap fixed rate. It is worth understanding why this is the case.

The following equation expresses the approximate swap fixed rate ($APPROXSFR$) as the geometric average of the floating rates on a swap:

$$(1 + APPROXSFR)^T = \prod_{n=1}^{N} (1 + FRA_{(n-1)\times MON, n\times MON})^{PART} \quad (21.14)$$

where T is the number of years covered by the swap agreement, and the other terms are as defined previously. In Equation 21.14, the time period covered by the swap agreement on the left-hand side of the equation must be the exact time period covered by the spot and FRA rates on the right-hand side of the equation. In essence, Equation 21.14 says that the approximate swap fixed rate (APPROXSFR) is a geometric average of the rates covering each of the subperiods of the swap's tenor. On the floating side of the swap, these subperiods include the initial period covered by the spot rate, followed by a number of forward rate periods to the end of the swap's tenor.

Using Equation 21.14 and our example swap with a tenor of two years and semiannual periodic payments, we see that the APPROXSFR is 5.0625 percent as follows:

$$
\begin{aligned}
(1 + APPROXSFR)^{2.0} &= 1.0495^{0.5} \times 1.0500^{0.5} \times 1.0510^{0.5} \times 1.0520^{0.5} \\
&= 1.024451 \times 1.024695 \times 1.025183 \times 1.025671 \\
&= 1.103812
\end{aligned}
$$

Therefore, APPROXSFR = 5.0625 percent.

For our example swap, we have found:

$$SFR = 5.0598\%$$
$$APPROXSFR = 5.0625\%$$

What accounts for this difference? In our no-arbitrage approach to the swap, we considered the actual transactions that one could enter for each FRA. The market rate for each FRA differs, reflecting the exact shape of the term structure. The floating side of the swap consists of one payment based on the spot rate prevailing at the initiation of the swap, plus a portfolio of FRAs, each with its own rate. As such, the rate on each FRA reflects the exact shape of the term structure. The APPROXSFR is merely the geometric average, or IRR, of the individual rates on the floating side of the swap. As such, it implicitly assumes that all payments on the floating side are discounted at a single rate. Further, the geometric average is the same no matter what the order of the constituent rates turns out to be. This is not true of the SFR.

In general, the SFR and APPROXSFR will be equal only when the term structure is flat. For a rising term structure, such as the term structure for our example swap, the APPROXSFR will exceed the SFR. If the term structure is falling, the SFR will exceed the APPROXSFR. For example, consider our same swap with a falling term structure but the same rates (that is, SPOT = 5.20 percent, FRA 6 × 12 = 5.10 percent, FRA 12 × 18 = 5.00 percent, and FRA 18 × 24 = 4.95 percent). In this situation, the SFR would be 5.0651 percent, and the APPROXSFR would be the same as before, 5.0625 percent. For the APPROXSFR calculation of Equation 21.14, the falling term structure merely changes the order of rates that are multiplied together, so the product does not change. Because the term structure is falling in this new example, the SFR exceeds the APPROXSFR. In general, the APPROXSFR gives a close indication of the true SFR, and the closer the term structure is to being flat, the better the approximation. Of course, for actual pricing of swap agreements, one requires the true SFR.

Since we have described an FRA as a one-date swap, we see that the swap agreement of our example consists of a strip of off-market FRAs. In our example, the 18 × 24 FRA rate is 5.20 percent, but the off-market FRA implied by the analysis of the interest rate swap is 5.0598 percent. Given the FRA rates available in the market, the single rate chosen for the swap fixed rate equates the present value of the floating and fixed payments in the swap agreement. With the off-market rate, one would expect that sometimes each party will receive a net payment.

In our pricing example, we began with quotations for a strip of FRA agreements and used these to find the zero-coupon factors for each period. Given the zero-coupon yield curve, we

Table 21.2	A plain vanilla swap as a zero-cost collar					
Time period (x,y months)	$Z_{x,y}$	$FRA_{x,y}$	Term to expiration (years)	Call value	Put value	Collar value (call-put)
0,6	1.024750	0.0495	0.0	0	10,717.39	−10,717.39
6,12	1.050369	0.0500	0.5	30,956.08	36,651.84	−5,695.76
12,18	1.077153	0.0510	1.0	48,801.79	45,072.19	+3,729.60
18,24	1.105159	0.0520	1.5	63,043.81	50,360.25	+12,683.56
						Total = $0.01

could have found the *SFR* for this swap without the FRA quotations. Similarly, given the par yield curve, we could have found the zero-coupon yield curve without the FRA quotations. In general, one set of quotations (par, zero, or FRA) is sufficient to price a swap, because all instruments are priced in the same yield curve environment.

Pricing a plain vanilla interest rate swap as a zero-cost collar

Earlier in this chapter, we saw that a plain vanilla interest rate swap could be analyzed as a zero-cost collar where the strike rate on all of the options comprising the collar equals the *SFR*. To illustrate this pricing technique, we show that the equivalent option portfolio would indeed have a zero cost, using the two-year swap of the preceding section as an example. There we saw that the *SFR* was 0.050598 (actually, 0.05059826504, which we use in the calculations of this section to minimize rounding errors). The swap has four semiannual payments and a notional principal of $20 million.

From an options perspective, we have a cap and floor comprising the collar. The cap and the floor each have expirations at months 0, 6, 12, and 18, with corresponding payments at months 6, 12, 18, and 24. Table 21.2 summarizes the relevant information. The first option is at expiration when the swap is initiated. As the *SFR* exceeds the current FRA, the call expires worthless. In six months, the put will pay

$$(0.05059826504 - 0.0495) \times 0.5 \times \$20,000,000 = \$10,982.65$$

The collar has a negative position in the put, so with $Z_{0,6} = 1.024750$, the present value of that obligation is −$10,714.81. All other options are priced according to the Black model assuming a standard deviation of 0.25 for all forward rates and discounting the payoffs at the Z factor corresponding to the payoff timing. As Table 21.2 illustrates, the total cost of the collar is zero.

As noted, the option values assume a standard deviation of 0.25 for all forward rates. What if the true standard deviation had been different? What if the standard deviation had varied across different forward periods? A different standard deviation would change the value of the individual options in any case. However, for each option pair, the long call/short put for any given period, the difference in value does not change with a change in the standard deviation.

Currency swap pricing

As we have seen for interest rate swap pricing, the basic pricing strategy is to find the *SFR* that is consistent with the term structure and gives a zero net present value to both counterparties to the swap. Any other solution would allow arbitrage. The same intuition applies to currency swap pricing.

In Chapter 20, we considered four different patterns of simple currency swaps as follows, and identified the second of these as the standard plain vanilla currency swap:

(1)   Party A pays a fixed rate on dollars received, and Party B pays a fixed rate on foreign currency received.
(2)   Party A pays a floating rate on dollars received, and Party B pays a fixed rate on foreign currency received.
(3)   Party A pays a fixed rate on dollars received, and Party B pays a floating rate on foreign currency received.
(4)   Party A pays a floating rate on dollars received, and Party B pays a floating rate on foreign currency received.

Key to the pricing of these foreign currency swaps is the *SFR* from the plain vanilla interest rate swap. In each instance, a party paying a fixed rate simply pays the *SFR* from a plain vanilla interest rate swap, while the party paying a floating rate pays LIBOR flat in dollars or the foreign currency, as the situation requires. Thus, the pricing rules for these four possible simple currency swaps are as follows:

(1)   Party A pays the dollar *SFR* on dollars received; Party B pays the foreign currency *SFR* on foreign currency received.
(2)   Party A pays U.S. LIBOR; Party B pays the foreign currency *SFR* on foreign currency received.
(3)   Party A pays the dollar *SFR* on dollars received; Party B pays foreign currency LIBOR on foreign currency received.
(4)   Party A pays U.S. LIBOR; Party B pays foreign currency LIBOR on foreign currency received.

We illustrate and explain these pricing principles by considering a fixed-for-fixed currency swap and a plain vanilla currency swap.

Pricing a fixed-for-fixed currency swap

According to the first pricing principle for a fixed-for-fixed currency swap, each party should pay the *SFR* for the currency it receives. Thus, in a fixed-for-fixed currency swap, the *SFR* for each party is the same as the *SFR* on a plain vanilla interest rate swap in the home currency for the same tenor.

To illustrate the pricing technique, we will price the fixed-for-fixed currency swap considered earlier in this chapter. That swap had a notional principal of $100 million, equivalent to €80 million, implying a spot exchange rate of $1 = €0.8. The swap had a tenor of five years with annual payments. Determination dates occurred at years 0, 1, 2, 3, and 4, with corresponding settlement dates one year later. Table 21.1 presents full term structure information for both currencies. In our earlier example, we arbitrarily assumed as a temporary measure that the dollar payer paid a fixed rate of 8.5 percent, while the euro payer paid 5.3 percent. We now want to find the correct *SFR* for each party and show why this is the no-arbitrage solution.

Using the zero-coupon factors from Table 21.1, we find the FRA rates as follows:

	U.S. dollar	Euro
$FRA_{0,1}$	0.080000	0.050000
$FRA_{1,2}$	0.090452	0.054109
$FRA_{2,3}$	0.094866	0.058348
$FRA_{3,4}$	0.101872	0.058360
$FRA_{4,5}$	0.103202	0.060623

From Equation 21.13, the two SFRs are:

Dollar *SFR* = 0.093000
Euro *FRA* = 0.056000

Given that these swaps have a tenor of five years, the *SFR*s simply equal the par yield for a five-year bond.

Table 21.3 details the cash flows for this fixed-for-fixed currency swap, first for the dollar payer and then for the euro payer. For the dollar payer, all of the dollar cash flows are converted to euros at the spot or forward exchange rate. The net euro cash flows are discounted at the zero-coupon discount rates for the euro. The last column shows the present value of the euro cash flows for each year. They sum to zero. The bottom part of Table 21.3 presents the same information from the perspective of the euro payer. The cash flows are converted into dollars at the respective foreign exchange rates, and the present value of the cash flows for the euro payer sum to zero.

A close consideration of Table 21.3 reveals the essential structure of a fixed-for-fixed currency swap. Each party pays a fixed rate that is based on the maturity of the swap and the par yield for the currency received. These rates can be quite different, as in our example, but the term structure of exchange rates exactly offsets the difference in the par yields between the two currencies, in accordance with interest rate parity.

Pricing a plain vanilla currency swap

We now turn to the pricing of a plain vanilla currency swap, fixed payments in a foreign currency in exchange for floating dollar payments at U.S. dollar LIBOR flat. We illustrate the pricing of this swap by using the same data that we explored in the fixed-for-fixed swap. Table 21.4 is similar to Table 21.3, except that Table 21.4 pertains to a comparable plain vanilla currency swap (floating U.S. LIBOR versus fixed foreign currency payments). The fixed euro cash flows are at the same rate of 5.6 percent. The dollar cash flows are unknown after the present and will depend on the one-year LIBOR rate that prevails at determination dates 0, 1, 2, 3, and 4. Table 21.4 shows the dollar flows based on the FRA rates from the U.S. dollar term structure. As in Table 21.3 for the fixed-for-fixed currency swap, the present value of the cash flows sum to zero.

Summary of currency swap pricing

In the last two sections, we have explored two examples of currency swap pricing in some detail. The first example was a fixed-for-fixed currency swap, while the second example was a closely related plain vanilla currency swap. In the fixed-for-fixed swap, we saw that each party would pay an *SFR* that equaled the par yield for a maturity that matched the tenor of the swap. In the case of a plain vanilla currency swap, the *SFR* also equals the par yield for a maturity matching the tenor of the swap in exchange for U.S. dollar LIBOR. Based on these examples, we can state general pricing rules for the following four types of currency swaps:

(1) **Fixed-for-fixed**
    Each party pays an *SFR* equal to the *SFR* on a plain vanilla currency swap.
(2) **Plain vanilla (dollar LIBOR—foreign currency fixed)**
    The floating payer pays U.S. LIBOR; the fixed payer pays an *SFR* equal to the *SFR* on a plain vanilla currency swap.
(3) **Dollar fixed/foreign currency floating**
    The dollar payer pays an *SFR* equal to the *SFR* on a plain vanilla currency swap; the foreign currency payer pays LIBOR in the foreign currency.

Table 21.3 Cash flow analysis for fixed-for-fixed currency swap

U.S. dollar payer—euro perspective

Settlement date (year)	Euro cash flow	Dollar cash flow	FOREX rate (euro per dollar)	Euro value of dollar cash flow	Net euro cash flow	Euro zero-coupon factor	Present value of euro cash flow
0	−80,000,000	100,000,000	0.800000	80,000,000	0	1.000000	0
1	4,480,000	−9,300,000	0.777778	−7,233,335	−2,753,335	1.050000	−2,622,224
2	4,480,000	−9,300,000	0.751855	−6,992,252	−2,512,252	1.106814	−2,269,805
3	4,480,000	−9,300,000	0.726778	−6,759,035	−2,279,035	1.171394	−1,945,575
4	4,480,000	−9,300,000	0.698078	−6,492,125	−2,012,125	1.239756	−1,623,001
5	84,480,000	−109,300,000	0.671135	−73,355,056	11,124,945	1.314914	8,460,587
							Total −€18 ≈ 0

Euro payer—U.S. dollar perspective

Settlement date (year)	Euro cash flow	Dollar cash flow	FOREX rate (euro per dollar)	Dollar value of euro cash flow	Net dollar flow	U.S. dollar zero-coupon factor	Present value of dollar cash flow
0	80,000,000	−100,000,000	0.800000	100,000,000	0	1.000000	0
1	−4,480,000	9,300,000	0.777778	−5,760,000	3,540,000	1.080000	3,277,778
2	−4,480,000	9,300,000	0.751855	−5,958,592	3,341,408	1.177688	2,837,261
3	−4,480,000	9,300,000	0.726778	−6,164,195	3,135,805	1.289411	2,431,967
4	−4,480,000	9,300,000	0.698078	−6,417,625	2,882,375	1.420766	2,028,747
5	−84,480,000	109,300,000	0.671135	−125,876,285	−16,576,285	1.567391	−10,575,718
							Total $34 ≈ 0

Table 21.4 Cash flow analysis for plain vanilla currency swap

U.S. dollar payer—euro perspective

Settlement date (year)	Euro cash flow	U.S. one-year FRA	Dollar cash flow	FOREX rate (euro per dollar)	Euro value of dollar cash flow	Net euro flow cash	Euro zero-coupon factor	Present value of euro cash flow
0	-80,000,000	0.080000	100,000,000	0.800000	80,000,000	0	1.000000	0
1	4,480,000	0.090452	-8,000,000	0.777778	-6,222,222	-1,742,222	1.050000	-1,659,259
2	4,180,000	0.094866	-9,045,226	0.751855	-6,800,703	-2,320,703	1.106814	-2,096,742
3	4,480,000	0.101872	-9,486,630	0.726778	-6,894,671	-2,414,671	1.171394	-2,061,366
4	4,480,000	0.103202	-10,187,139	0.698078	-7,111,413	-2,631,413	1.239756	-2,122,525
5	84,480,000	N/A	-110,320,196	0.671135	-74,039,762	10,440,238	1.314914	7,939,864
								Total -€27 ≈ 0

Euro payer—U.S. dollar perspective

Settlement date (year)	Euro cash flow	U.S. one-year FRA	Dollar cash flow	FOREX rate (euro per dollar)	Dollar value of euro cash flow	Net dollar cash flow	U.S. dollar zero-coupon factor	Present value of dollar cash flow
0	80,000,000	0.080000	-100,000,000	0.800000	100,000,000	0	1.000000	0
1	-4,480,000	0.090452	8,000,000	0.777778	-5,760,000	2,240,000	1.080000	2,074,074
2	-4,480,000	0.094866	9,045,226	0.751855	-5,958,596	3,086,630	1.177688	2,620,922
3	-4,480,000	0.101872	9,486,630	0.726778	-6,164,198	3,322,432	1.289411	2,576,704
4	-4,480,000	0.103202	10,187,139	0.698078	-6,417,626	3,769,513	1.420766	2,653,157
5	-84,480,000	N/A	110,320,196	0.671135	-125,876,332	-15,556,135	1.567391	-9,924,857
								Total $1 ≈ 0

(4) **Floating-for-floating**

The dollar payer pays U.S. LIBOR; the foreign currency payer pays LIBOR in the foreign currency.

Swap counterparty credit risk

Counterparty credit risk is a significant concern of end-users and dealers in the swaps market. Credit risk arises from the possibility of a default by the swap counterparty when the value of the swap is positive (i.e., in-the-money). Current credit exposure is measured by the swap's current **replacement cost**; that is, the amount required to replace the swap in the event of a counterparty default today. Only positive swap values are of interest in determining swap credit exposure. This is because with negative- or zero-value swaps (i.e., out-of-the-money or at-the-money swaps), the counterparty owes nothing in the event of a default. In other words, the only time money is at risk is when the default occurs with a counterparty owing money.

Current replacement cost represents current credit exposure. However, current replacement cost alone does not accurately portray the potential credit risk over the life of the swap. A counterparty might default at some future date with swap values significantly different than current swap values. The potential loss is larger because the replacement cost can potentially become larger over the life of the swap.

As a first step to managing counterparty credit risk, end-users and swap dealers estimate the potential replacement cost for each of the swaps that they hold with individual swap counterparties. Estimating the potential replacement cost is essential for being able to monitor, manage, and allocate counterparty credit line usage relative to the counterparty credit limits. Dealers and end-users are particularly interested in monitoring the incremental effect on credit line usage resulting from an additional transaction with a counterparty.

Measuring the potential replacement cost relies on simulation techniques. Simulation techniques rely on probability distributions to project the range of potential values of the swap over the swap's remaining life. Of interest are only the positive values that the swap can potentially take on. For simulations far out into the future, there can be much uncertainty about potential swap value, resulting in a wide range of estimates.

It is common for swap participants to characterize counterparty credit risk with a single number. Projecting potential exposures over the life of the swap will produce many numbers. For example, a swap with a remaining life of five years will have credit exposures measured for various potential default dates; for example, one year in the future, two years in the future, and so on. When the series of credit exposure measures is plotted against tenor, a time-varying **exposure profile** for the counterparty is produced. To reduce credit exposure to a single number, swap market participants frequently choose the maximum exposure; that is, the greatest amount that would potentially be lost in the event of a counterparty default. The maximum exposure is a probability estimate of the "true" maximum exposure.

A contentious issue in the evaluation of credit risk concerns what is known as netting. Most swap contracts, called **master agreements**, state that if a counterparty defaults on one swap, it must default on all swaps. Therefore, swaps with a negative replacement cost will offset swaps with a positive replacement cost when the defaulting counterparty is the same in the two cases. Under such a netting arrangement, counterparty credit exposure is defined as the net positive replacement cost after netting.

To be effective, simulation methods must account for netting effects and bankruptcy rules. In addition, the method must account for what a bankruptcy court would do in the event of a default. For example, in one legal scenario a bankruptcy court may determine the replacement cost of each swap in the portfolio and simultaneously close out all positions. In an alternate legal scenario, a bankruptcy court may allow each swap to run until its settlement, maturity, or expiration date, and then close out only those swaps that have a positive replacement cost. Selectively closing out only those swaps with positive value is called **cherry picking**. The possibility of cherry picking is a scenario that must be accounted for in measuring potential counterparty credit exposure.

There is no reason why all swaps between dealers and end-users will be subject to the same legal rules. Some swaps may be covered by a legally binding netting agreement and others may not. The simulation method must apply the appropriate legal rules to each contract.

Conclusion

This chapter has explored the economic analysis of swaps and the principles of swap pricing. We have seen that the cash flows on a plain vanilla interest rate swap can be exactly replicated in at least three ways. First, a plain vanilla interest rate swap is equivalent to a two-bond portfolio. Second, a plain vanilla interest rate swap has exactly the same cash flows as a suitably constructed portfolio of forward rate agreements (FRAs). Third, an interest rate swap is equivalent to a zero-cost collar, which is a portfolio of calls and puts on LIBOR. A plain vanilla interest rate swap is also very closely related to, but not identical to, a strip of Eurodollar futures contracts. Currency swaps can be analyzed in terms that are similar to those for interest rate swaps. For example, the chapter shows that a fixed-for-fixed currency swap is equivalent to a two-bond portfolio, as is a plain vanilla currency swap. The chapter also shows that

a fixed-for-fixed currency swap is equivalent to a portfolio of foreign exchange forward contracts.

The chapter has also shown how to price interest rate and currency swaps. For a plain vanilla interest rate swap, the floating payment is always LIBOR, so pricing the swap means finding the no-arbitrage fixed rate for the swap, which becomes the *SFR*. The *SFR* depends on the term structure and is essentially found by a present value technique. The *SFR* is the one rate that gives the pay-fixed and receive-fixed payers the same zero net present value cash flows when all of the swap cash flows are discounted at rates from the current term structure. The same basic technique applies to pricing currency swaps. In currency swaps, however, there are the term structures of interest rates for both countries to consider, along with the term structure of exchange rates.

Exercises

1 A trader buys a bond that pays an annual coupon based on LIBOR with a principal amount of $10 million. The actual payment in each year depends on the level of LIBOR observed one year previously. The same trader simultaneously sells a $10 million bond that pays a fixed rate of 7 percent interest and also has an annual coupon. Both bonds have a maturity of five years and are priced at par. The trader also enters a pay-fixed interest rate swap with annual payments, a tenor of five years, and a notional principal of $10 million. For the swap, the fixed rate is 7 percent and the floating rate is LIBOR. The swap also pays in arrears.

A Construct a time line for each bond showing the payments associated with the bond.

B Construct a time line showing the net payments resulting from the two bonds.

C Construct a time line showing the payments for the swap.

D Based on the two time lines from parts B and C, what conclusion can you draw regarding the relationship between swaps and bond portfolios?

2 Assume that today is December 17, 2003. A firm enters a plain vanilla interest rate swap as the receive-fixed party on a swap with a tenor of one year, quarterly payments at the end of the next four quarters, and a notional principal of $25 million. At the same time, this firm buys a strip of Eurodollar futures for the next four contracts, with 25 contracts per expiration. (Ignore daily settlement; in other words, assume that all futures-related cash flows occur at the expiration of the futures contract, which occurs at the end of each quarter.) At present, $t = 0$, the LIBOR yield curve is flat at 8 percent, and the fixed rate on the swap is also 8 percent.

A Complete the following table using our familiar $LIBOR_t$ notation. Assume that the Eurodollar futures rate converges to LIBOR at expiration.

Quarter	Net receive-fixed swap cash flow	Net long futures cash flow
0		
1		
2		
3		
4		

B If this swap had been a determined-in-advance/paid-in-advance swap, what would be the payment at $t = 3$ on the swap?

C What conclusion can you draw regarding the relationship between a plain vanilla interest rate swap and a strip of Eurodollar futures?

3 Consider a plain vanilla swap from the point of view of the pay-fixed counterparty. The swap has a tenor of five years with annual payments, a notional principal of $50 million, payments in arrears, a floating rate of LIBOR, and a fixed rate of 7 percent. Assume that the pay-fixed counterparty buys a call option with an expiration date of two years. If the call is in-the-money, it pays the observed LIBOR on that date minus 7 percent on a notional principal of $50 million. The pay-fixed party also sells a similar put option: two-year expiration, $50 million notional principal. If the put is in-the-money, the payoff equals 7 percent minus observed LIBOR times the notional principal. In each case, the rate is observed in two years, with the payment date actually occurring one year later. Bearing in mind that the rates observed at year 2 determine the actual cash flow at year 3 on the swap, put, and call:

A Complete the following table showing the pay-fixed side of the swap, the long call, and the short put for the payment at year 3 as a function of LIBOR observed at year 2.

Payment at year 3

$LIBOR_2$	Pay-fixed net swap payment	Long call payoff	Short put payoff
0.05			
0.06			
0.07			
0.08			
0.09			

B What does this table show about the relationship between a single swap payment and the call/put portfolio of options?

C What does the table show about an entire swap and a possible portfolio of options?

D If the swap had been a receive-fixed swap, what option position would have replicated the swap payment at year 3?

4 Explain how an interest rate swap can be analyzed as a strip of futures. What are some limitations of this analysis?

5 Today, the following percentage rates may be observed: $FRA_{0,3} = 0.0600$, $FRA_{3,6} = 0.0595$, $FRA_{6,9} = 0.0592$, $FRA_{9,12} = 0.0590$, $FRA_{12,15} = 0.0590$, $FRA_{15,18} = 0.0588$, $FRA_{18,21} = 0.0587$, and $FRA_{21,24} = 0.0586$, where the subscripts pertain to months. Consider a plain vanilla swap with a tenor of two years, quarterly payments, and a notional principal of $10 million.

A Compute the discount rates for each payment date on the swap.

B Find the *SFR* for this swap.

C Find the *APPROXSFR* for this swap.

D Assume that the same swap is to be negotiated as an off-market swap in which the receive-fixed party will receive 7 percent. What payment at the initiation of the swap will make the transaction a fair deal?

6 Today in the market, you observe the following discount rates, where the subscripts indicate months: $Z_{0,3} = 1.0240$, $Z_{0,6} = 1.0475$, $Z_{0,9} = 1.0735$, $Z_{0,12} = 1.0976$, $Z_{0,15} = 1.1193$, $Z_{0,18} = 51.1472$, $Z_{0,21} = 1.1655$, and $Z_{0,24} = 1.1872$. Compute all possible three-month FRA rates.

7 A zero-coupon swap is a swap in which the fixed rate is zero. Instead of making periodic coupon payments, the fixed-rate payer makes a single large payment at the termination of the swap. Zero-coupon swaps may be either interest rate swaps in any currency (with no exchange of principal) or foreign currency swaps (with the customary exchange of principal). Using one zero-coupon swap (either an interest rate or a foreign currency swap), and one bond of any type, construct a synthetic zero-coupon bond that pays euros, and has a principal amount of €100 million and a maturity of five years. The euro yield curve is flat at 6.3 percent. Assume annual payments throughout.

A Find the cash flows associated with the European zero and draw a time line for this instrument.

B Draw time lines for the two instruments that will replicate the European zero, showing the cash flow amounts at each time, under the assumption of constant interest rates.

C State the transactions necessary to replicate the European zero.

D Explain how the replication you have created still works if interest rates change.

8 Consider an already existing fixed-for-fixed foreign currency swap that was negotiated at an exchange rate of $1 = ¥111 with a notional principal of $100 million = ¥11.1 billion yen. The swap has quarterly payments and a remaining tenor of one year. The dollar fixed rate is 7 percent, and the yen fixed rate is 6.8 percent. Assume that the following foreign exchange rates are observed now, where $_{s,\text{¥}}FX_{x,y}$ is the value of the dollar in terms of yen for a contract initiated at month x with delivery at month y: $_{s,\text{¥}}FX_{0,3} = 115$, $_{s,\text{¥}}FX_{0,6} = 117$, $_{s,\text{¥}}FX_{0,9} = 119$, and $_{s,\text{¥}}FX_{0,12} = 120$.

A Prepare a time line showing the remaining payments on the swap from the point of view of the dollar payer.

B Calculate the present value of the swap from the point of view of the dollar payer if the following U.S. percentage interest rates hold: $FRA_{0,3} = 0.0635$, $FRA_{3,6} = 0.0640$, $FRA_{6,9} = 0.0642$, and $FRA_{9,12} = 0.0645$.

C How does the solution of this problem relate to the interest rate parity theorem?

9 Today, you observe the following U.S. interest rates: $FRA_{0,3} = 0.0650$, $FRA_{3,6} = 0.0655$, $FRA_{6,9} = 0.0659$, and $FRA_{9,12} = 0.0661$, where the subscripts pertain to months. Consider a plain vanilla interest rate swap with quarterly payments and a tenor of one year with a notional principal of $50 million and a zero-cost collar that parallels this swap, having four payments and a remaining life of one year, with a notional principal of $50 million. The collar has a common strike rate of 6.5 percent for the put (floor) and the call (cap).

A Without computation, determine whether the collar is fairly priced. Explain.

B Find the *SFR* for a plain vanilla swap.

C Explain an arbitrage strategy based on the facts presented, being sure to state the transactions you would make to exploit the arbitrage.

D Compute the present value of your arbitrage transactions.

10 For a fairly priced plain vanilla swap with annual payments and a tenor of five years, the fixed rate is 6.44

percent. The yield curve is flat. You also are aware of two bonds available in the marketplace, each with annual coupon payments and maturities of five years. The first is a coupon bond with a coupon rate of 8.25 percent. The second is an FRN paying LIBOR 12 percent. Assume zero default risk for all instruments.

A Without computation, but by inspecting the information given, which bond should be worth more?

B Compute the no-arbitrage price difference between the two bonds.

C Explain what arbitrage transactions you would enter if the price difference between the bonds were 6 percent of par. (Assume that the truly more valuable bond is priced higher than the truly less valuable bond, but the price difference is 6 percent instead of the no-arbitrage price difference that you found in part B of this question.) Draw a time line for each instrument assuming a par value of 100. Hint: You will need a third instrument, some kind of interest rate swap, to ensure that the transaction is an arbitrage opportunity rather than a speculation.

11 Consider two term structure environments, one in which the yield curve rises and one in which the yield curve falls by the same amount, as shown in the following table:

Maturity (subscripts pertain to years)	FRA rates (%)	
	Environment #1	Environment #2
$FRA_{0,1}$	0.0600	0.0600
$FRA_{1,2}$	0.0610	0.0590
$FRA_{2,3}$	0.0620	0.0580
$FRA_{3,4}$	0.0630	0.0570
$FRA_{4,5}$	0.0640	0.0560

A For a plain vanilla interest rate swap with a five-year tenor, annual payments made in arrears, and a notional principal of $30 million, find the *SFR* for this swap in each yield curve environment.

B Find the present value of each payment from the point of view of the pay-fixed party in each environment. Find the sum of the present value of the payments in each environment.

C Evaluate the default risk on these two swaps from the point of view of a swap bank in which the swap bank pays fixed, assuming a relatively stable yield curve environment.

D   Explain how any observed difference in default risk from the point of view of the bank might affect the bank's pricing of the swap.

Note: The remaining questions all use the same interest rate data, the same foreign exchange data, the same notional principal, and the same tenor.

Interest Rate Data: Exercise 12
Foreign Exchange Data: Exercise 13
Swap Terms: Semiannual payments; $100,000,000 = ¥13,350,000,000 notional principal
Tenor: five years

12   The following data pertain to U.S. and Japanese interest rates over the next five years for semiannual periods. Complete the following tables.

U.S. rates

Maturity (semiannual periods)	Annualized par yield	Zero-coupon factor	Forward rate factor
1	0.067700		
2	0.068504		
3	0.069367		
4	0.070146		
5	0.070294		
6	0.071231		
7	0.071893		
8	0.071988		
9	0.072105		
10	0.072293		

Japanese rates

Maturity (semiannual periods)	Annualized par yield	Zero-coupon factor	Forward rate factor
1	0.048327		
2	0.049302		
3	0.049428		
4	0.050119		
5	0.050766		
6	0.051651		
7	0.052546		
8	0.053157		
9	0.053170		
10	0.053356		

13   Find the foreign exchange rates between the U.S. dollar and the Japanese yen for the next ten semi-annual periods consistent with the interest rates of Exercise 12, and complete the following table.

Dollar/yen exchange rates

Maturity (semiannual periods)	Dollar per yen	Yen per dollar
0		
1		
2		
3		
4		
5		
6		
7		
8		
9		
10		

14   Based on the U.S. rates of Exercise 12, find the *SFR* for a plain vanilla U.S. interest rate swap with a tenor of five years, semiannual payments, and a notional principal of $100 million.

15   Based on the Japanese rates of Exercise 12, find the *SFR* for a plain vanilla Japanese interest rate swap with a tenor of five years, a notional principal of ¥13,350,000,000, and semiannual payments.

16   Complete the following tables, based on the U.S. and Japanese interest rates of Exercise 12, the foreign exchange rates of Exercise 13, and the *SFR*s computed in Exercises 14 and 15. The following letters correspond to column labels in the tables.

A   Cash flows on a U.S. semiannual coupon bond with a five-year maturity, a par value of $100 million, which trades at par.

B   The cash flows consistent with the term structure of Exercise 12 for a semiannual U.S. dollar floating-rate bond with a par value of $100 million and a maturity of five years.

C   The cash flows on the receive-fixed side of the U.S. dollar interest rate swap computed in Exercise 14.

D   The cash flows consistent with the term structure on the pay-floating side of the U.S. dollar interest rate swap computed in Exercise 14.

E   The cash flows on a Japanese semiannual coupon bond with a five-year maturity, a par value of ¥13,350,000,000, which trades at par.

F   The cash flows consistent with the term structure of Exercise 12 on a semiannual Japanese yen floating-rate bond with a par value of ¥13,350,000,000 and a maturity of five years.

G   The cash flows on the pay-fixed side of the Japanese yen interest rate swap computed in Exercise 15.

H   The cash flows on the pay-floating side of the Japanese yen interest rate swap computed in Exercise 15.

U.S. instruments

Maturity (semiannual periods)	A Buy semiannual bond	B Sell FRN	C Receive-fixed interest rate swap	D Pay-floating interest rate swap
0				
1				
2				
3				
4				
5				
6				
7				
8				
9				
10				
Present value of cash flows				

Japanese instruments

Maturity (semiannual periods)	E Buy semiannual bond	F Sell FRN	G Receive-fixed interest rate swap	H Pay-floating interest rate swap
0				
1				
2				
3				
4				
5				
6				
7				
8				
9				
10				
Present value of cash flows				

U.S. rates

Maturity floating (semiannual payment periods)	Forward rate $FRA_{t-1,t}$	Floating payment $FRA_{t-1,t} \times NP$
1		
2		
3		
4		
5		
6		
7		
8		
9		
10		

Japanese rates

Maturity (semiannual periods)	Forward rate $FRA_{t-1,t}$	Floating payment $FRA_{t-1,t} \times NP$
1		
2		
3		
4		
5		
6		
7		
8		
9		
10		

17   Based on the tables of the preceding question, explain how a U.S. dollar plain vanilla receive-fixed interest rate swap is equivalent to a portfolio of bonds. Show how to replicate the swap position with a bond portfolio.

18   Explain the transactions necessary to replicate a U.S. dollar plain vanilla receive-fixed swap as a portfolio of FRAs.

19   Based on the previous calculations, complete the following tables detailing the cash flows for a fixed-for-fixed currency swap. What is the expected present value benefit or loss on the periodic payments for the dollar payer? What is the expected present value benefit or loss on the reexchange of principal for the dollar payer? Explain the portfolio of capital market instruments that would replicate this fixed-for-fixed swap from the point of view of the dollar payer.

Fixed-for-fixed currency swap—dollar payer perspective

Date (semiannual periods)	Actual cash flows		Dollar value of cash flows	
	Receipts	Payments	Receipts	Payments
0				
1				
2				
3				
4				
5				
6				
7				
8				
9				
10				
10				

Fixed-for-fixed currency swap—dollar payer perspective

Date (semiannual periods)	Present value of cash flows		
	Receipts	Payments	Net
0			
1			
2			
3			
4			
5			
6			
7			
8			
9			
10			
10			
Sums			

20 Consider again the fixed-for-fixed currency swap of the preceding question. Explain how this swap could be replicated in the foreign exchange forward market, detailing the FOREX forward contracts necessary to replicate the swap.

21 Explain how a plain vanilla dollar-pay currency swap can be replicated using capital market instruments as the key elements of the replicating portfolio. Illustrate the replicating cash flows in a table.

22 Explain how a yen fixed-pay plain vanilla currency swap can be replicated by combining two other swaps. Prepare a table showing the replicating cash flows.

23 Why are only positive swap values used to measure counterparty credit risk?

24 What is "cherry picking"? Why does cherry picking complicate the scenario analysis of swap counterparty credit risk?

25 What is replacement cost? Why is potential replacement cost an important consideration for measuring swap counterparty credit risk?

26 What is the key difference between a credit default swap and a total return swap?

27 Explain how an interest rate swap can be viewed as a portfolio of forward rate agreements.

Notes

1 See I. G. Kawaller, "Interest Rate Swaps versus Eurodollar Strips," *Financial Analysts Journal*, September/October 1989, for a discussion of the relationship between swaps and strips.

2 For details of day count and exact market pricing conventions, see Keith C. Brown and Donald J. Smith, *Interest Rate and Currency Swaps: A Tutorial*, Charlottesville, VA: The Research Foundation of the Institute of Chartered Financial Analysts, 1995, Chapter 4. The basic day count conventions are discussed at the end of Chapter 22.

22

Swaps: Applications

Overview

In this chapter, we explore a variety of applications and extensions to the discussion of swaps in the preceding two chapters. We have already briefly considered some possible simple applications of swaps in these earlier chapters; this chapter extends those examples to more realistic situations. The swap applications presented in this chapter range from the relatively simpler examples to more complex ones. The application examples include pricing applications and solutions to more practical business problems for interest rate and currency swaps, as well as some more esoteric swap structures.

We begin by considering a parallel loan—a loan, designed to evade currency restrictions, that was popular in the late 1970s and early 1980s and that led directly to the development of the swaps market. We then show how to create a variety of synthetic securities by using swaps. A useful technique for comparing complex financing alternatives is the all-in cost. This technique considers all of the cash flows on two or more financing alternatives and uses internal rate of return techniques to find the cheapest alternative. We next consider a historical interest rate swap example—a swap between B. F. Goodrich and a Dutch bank, Rabobank. This provides an opportunity to use the all-in cost to compare the alternatives that these companies faced.

In discussing hedging with interest rate futures earlier in this text, we saw that duration was an important concept. This chapter explores the duration of interest rate swaps and shows how to apply duration tech-

niques with swaps to manage the interest rate risk that firms face. As we will see, the firm can take a duration-based approach to eliminating, decreasing, or increasing interest rate risk, to suit the firm's risk preferences.

Structured notes are debt instruments with peculiar payoff characteristics, such as a floating rate that moves inversely with market rates. Firms typically issue structured notes to appeal to investor tastes, and then combine those notes with swaps to give the issuer a simpler and more traditional total debt obligation. This chapter shows how to hedge structured notes and how to create them synthetically from simple securities combined with swaps.

The chapter also shows how to price flavored interest rate and currency swaps. This discussion extends the pricing techniques introduced in Chapter 21. This chapter shows how to price equity swaps and how to use equity swaps to control equity market risk. We considered swaptions in Chapter 20. This chapter explains how to price swaptions using the Black model of Chapter 19. The chapter gives examples of pricing and using swaptions to create cancelable and extendable swaps.

Finally, the chapter explains day count conventions that are used in actual market pricing of swaps. Money market instruments and bonds are priced under varying assumptions about the number of days in a year. These assumptions affect actual cash flows on swaps. The chapter concludes by showing how to take these conventions into account, and illustrates swap pricing under realistic day count conventions.

The parallel loan—how swaps began

Today, there are no officially imposed restrictions on the movement of most major currencies. In the not too recent past, central banks in many industrialized countries imposed active restrictions on the flow of currency. The parallel loan market developed to circumvent restrictions imposed by the Bank of England on the free flow of British pounds. British firms wishing to invest abroad generally needed to convert pounds into U.S. dollars. The Bank of England required these firms to buy dollars at an exchange rate above the market price. The purpose of this policy was to defend the value of the pound in terms of other currencies. Firms, naturally, were not interested in subsidizing the Bank of England by paying the above-market rate for dollars required by the Bank of England's policies. Attempts to evade these currency controls led directly to the development of the market for currency swaps.

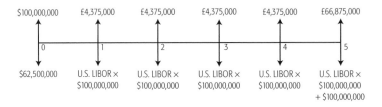

Figure 22.1 Cash flows for a parallel loan

Consider two similar firms, one British and one American, each with operating subsidiaries in both countries. Assume that the free-market value of the pound is £1 = $1.60 and that the officially required exchange rate for British firms to acquire dollars is £1 = $1.44. In this environment, the British firm would like to exploit an investment opportunity in the United States that requires an outlay of $100 million. The free-market value of the needed $100 million is £62.5 million (100,000,000/1.60). If the British firm complies with the Bank of England's regulations, it will have to pay £69,444,444 for the needed dollars (100,000,000/1.44). From the firm's point of view, this regulation would require the firm to pay a subsidy of almost £7 million.

By cooperating with a U.S. firm that has operations in England, the firm can evade the currency controls. The British firm lends pounds to the U.S. subsidiary operating in England, while the U.S. firm lends a similar amount to the British subsidiary operating in the United States. This is a **parallel loan**—two multinational firms lend each other equivalent amounts of two different currencies on equivalent terms in two countries. A parallel loan is also known as a **back-to-back loan**.

Let us suppose that the U.S. subsidiary of the British firm borrows $100 million from the parent of the U.S. firm for five years at one-year U.S. LIBOR, while the British subsidiary of the U.S. firm borrows £62.5 million from the British parent for five years at a fixed rate of 7 percent interest. Figure 22.1 shows the cash flows from the perspective of the British firm, integrating the cash flows of the British parent and subsidiary. These are exactly the cash flows from a plain vanilla receive-fixed currency swap. In creating this parallel loan, the British firm would be careful to record these loans as two unrelated transactions, keeping the Bank of England in the dark. In this example, the British firm got the free-market exchange rate. In practice, the U.S. and British firms might share the gains from evading the currency controls by an exchange rate value of the pound between $1.44 and $1.60. Alternatively, the two firms might share the gains from currency evasion by having the U.S. firm pay a fixed rate that is somewhat lower.

The development of swaps stemmed directly from these incentives to create parallel loans. Although the projected cash flows from the parallel loan and the plain vanilla currency swap are identical, there are still some subtle but important differences. In the parallel loan, both parties need to pretend that the transactions are completely distinct. If so, default on one of the loans would not justify default by the other party. In an interest rate swap agreement, there are cross-default clauses. (The parallel loan cannot contain those cross-default clauses, because the two parties are trying to pretend that the parallel loans are distinct.) Also, a swap agreement would have lower transaction costs than arranging two separate loans.[1]

Creating synthetic securities with swaps

In earlier chapters, we saw that certain securities could be synthesized from combinations of derivatives. For example, in Chapter 11, we explored the put–call parity relationship, which shows how any three of four instruments (a put, a call, the underlying good, a risk-free bond) can synthesize the fourth instrument. In Chapter 21, we saw that swaps could be analyzed as a portfolio of other instruments, such as a portfolio of bonds, a portfolio of floating-rate agreements (FRAs), or a portfolio of options.

Exploring the creation of synthetic securities has two motivations. First, it provides a deeper analysis of swaps and an understanding of how to use swaps to change the form of existing instruments. In Chapter 21, we showed how to deconstruct swaps in terms of other instruments; now we show how to construct other instruments using swaps. Second, by seeing that an existing security is equivalent to a synthetic security, we learn how to compare financing and investment alternatives in the search for cheaper financing costs and higher investment returns. The synthetic securities discussed in this section are quite simple in character. As we will see later in the chapter, they are akin to fundamental building blocks that can be combined to create more complex and flexible financial structures.

Synthetic fixed-rate debt

Consider a firm with an existing floating-rate debt obligation that wishes to eliminate the uncertainty inherent in floating debt. A firm in this position could create a synthetic fixed-rate debt instrument by combining its existing floating-rate obligation with an interest rate swap. Assume that a firm has an outstanding issue of $50 million on which it pays a floating-rate annual coupon and that the debt matures in six years. The firm wishes to transform this obligation into a fixed-rate instrument with the same maturity.

Figure 22.2 shows the firm's existing obligation in the upper time line. To transform this existing obligation into a fixed-rate instrument, the firm can engage in a swap agreement to receive-floating/pay-fixed, with a tenor and payment timing to match its existing debt, as shown in the bottom time line of Figure 22.2. The combination of the existing debt and the pay-fixed/receive-floating interest rate swap gives the firm a synthetic fixed-rate obligation instead of its current floating-rate debt.

Figure 22.2   Elements of synthetic fixed-rate debt

Existing debt

Pay floating coupon payments

Principal repayment and last coupon

Interest rate swap

Receive-floating

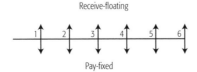

Pay-fixed

Figure 22.3   Elements of synthetic floating-rate debt

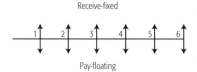

Synthetic floating-rate debt

An existing fixed-rate obligation can be transformed into floating-rate debt by reversing the technique used to create synthetic fixed-rate debt. Assume that a firm has an existing fixed-rate debt obligation with a maturity of six years that requires annual interest rate payments. The upper time line of Figure 22.3 shows the cash flows associated with this obligation. (This example parallels that of Figure 22.2, except that the initial obligation has fixed-rate coupons.)

By combining this fixed-rate obligation with a receive-fixed/pay-floating interest rate swap, the instrument can be transformed from a fixed-rate to a synthetic floating-rate obligation. The lower time line of Figure 22.3 shows the cash flows on a receive-fixed/pay-floating interest rate swap. By combining this swap with the existing obligation, the firm transforms its existing fixed-rate obligation into a synthetic floating-rate debt with the same maturity.

Synthetic callable debt

Consider a firm with an outstanding fixed-rate obligation that possesses no call feature. The issuing firm would like to be able to call this debt in three years, but does not want the obligation to retire the issue. In essence, the firm wishes that the existing noncallable debt had a call provision allowing a call in three years.

When a firm calls an existing debt instrument, it repays the debt. We may view that repayment as creating a new financing need that the firm will meet from floating-rate obligations. After all, in calling the debt, it retired the existing fixed-rate obligation. From this perspective, we may see that the decision to call an existing fixed-rate obligation is like creating a synthetic floating-rate debt obligation using a call. As we have just seen, a fixed-rate debt obligation, combined with an interest rate swap to receive fixed payments and pay floating, transforms the fixed-rate instrument into a floating-rate obligation.

However, in the present instance, the issuer wishes to have the option, but not the obligation, to make this transformation. Therefore, the firm can create a synthetic callable bond by using a swaption. Because the firm wants to possess the call option feature of a callable bond,

| Table 22.1 | Transforming callable into noncallable debt | | |
Call date scenario	Swap	Issuer	Result
Interest rates higher	Swaption not exercised	Does not call the bond	Issuer has fixed-rate financing
Interest rates lower	Swaption exercised; issuer pays fixed and receives floating for remainder of bond's life	Calls the bond and funds with floating for remainder of bond's life	Issuer has fixed-rate financing

Source: Adapted from L. S. Goodman, "Capital Market Applications of Interest Rate Swaps," Chapter 7 of C. R. Beidleman, *Interest Rate Swaps*, Homewood, IL: Business One Irwin, 1991. © 1991. Reprinted by permission from the McGrow-Hill Companies

we know that the firm must purchase a swaption, because only buying a swaption—an option on a swap—gives that flexibility. The swap that underlies the desired swaption must allow the firm to receive-fixed/pay-floating. Therefore, the firm needs to purchase a receiver swaption with an expiration of three years.

At the expiration of the swaption, the firm can simulate a callable bond by exercising its swaption. Upon exercise, the firm will continue to pay fixed on its existing bond (which is not callable), receive fixed on the swap, and pay floating on the swap. Netting out the fixed payment and fixed receipt, the firm is left with a pay-floating obligation, which is analogous to having been able to call the bond.

Synthetic noncallable debt

A firm with outstanding callable debt can use interest rate swaps to eliminate the call feature and capture its value. When it issued the callable debt, the firm essentially purchased a call option from the bondholders. If the firm is sure that it will not wish to call the debt, it may wish to recapture the value represented by that call option. We considered this situation from the perspective of corporate financial management in our discussion of swaptions in Chapter 20. In essence, we now regard the example firm of the swaption discussion in Chapter 20 as having created synthetic noncallable debt by using swaptions. Table 22.1 shows how the firm maintains fixed-rate noncallable debt whether or not the swaption is exercised.

Synthetic dual-currency debt

A **dual-currency bond** has principal payments denominated in one currency, with coupon payments denominated in a second currency. For example, an issuing firm might borrow dollars and pay coupon payments on the instrument in euros.[2] When the bond expires, the firm would repay its principal obligation in dollars. This dual-currency bond can be synthesized from a regular single-currency bond with all payments in dollars (a dollar-pay bond) combined with a fixed-for-fixed currency swap.

The upper time line in Figure 22.4 shows the cash flows from owning a typical dollar-pay bond. The purchaser of the bond invests at the outset and then receives coupon inflows and the return of principal upon maturity. The second time line in Figure 22.4 shows the cash flows for a fixed-for-fixed foreign currency swap in which the party receives fixed euro inflows and pays fixed dollar amounts. Notice that there is no exchange of borrowings in this swap. (A

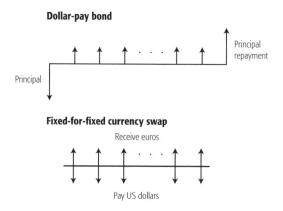

Figure 22.4   Elements of synthetic dual-currency debt

Dollar-pay bond

Principal repayment

Principal

Fixed-for-fixed currency swap

Receive euros

Pay US dollars

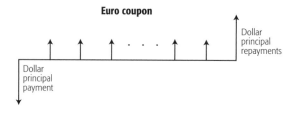

Figure 22.5   Cash flows on synthetic dual-currency debt

Euro coupon

Dollar principal repayments

Dollar principal payment

currency swap with no exchange of borrowings is known as a **currency annuity swap**. Later in this chapter, we show how to price such a swap.) The amounts of the cash flows in the currency swap are constructed to equal the coupon payments.

Figure 22.5 shows the effect of combining the dollar-pay bond with the foreign currency swap. The dollar coupon payments on the dollar-pay bond and the dollar payments on the fixed-for-fixed currency swap perfectly offset each other. This leaves euro inflows from the swap that take the place of the coupon payments. As Figure 22.5 shows, the principal payment and repayment are in dollars; all of the coupon cash flows are in euros. Thus, a dollar-pay bond combined with the appropriate fixed-for-fixed currency swap with no exchange of borrowings produces a dual-currency bond.

The all-in cost

As we have seen in the preceding section, it is possible to use swaps to create a variety of synthetic securities. In a perfect market without taxes, all securities with the same cash flow should have the same value. However, it must also be acknowledged that an early impetus to the development of the swaps market was the difference in net costs of various financial structures that were equivalent in terms of their underlying cash flows. These cost differences emerged from various market imperfections and inefficiencies. These market imperfections included taxes, transaction costs, illiquidity in some markets, and similar factors. In the early development of the swaps market, it may also have been possible to exploit inefficiencies in the market when instruments with the same cash flows sold for different prices. According to considerable anecdotal evidence, these inefficiencies resulted from investor ignorance of techniques for creating synthetic securities and from a failure to recognize that various securities had synthetic equivalents.

In a financial market that functions well, the same asset must sell for the same price in two different locations. For example, in Chapter 1 we considered a hypothetical example of a share of IBM trading at two different prices on the New York Stock Exchange and the Pacific Stock Exchange. Clearly, a single share of stock is such a simple security that all parties recognize that it should have a single price on two exchanges. However, when securities become more complex and cash flows are extended in time, these equivalences may not be so obvious. Therefore, a tool to compare financing alternatives can be quite useful.

The **all-in cost** is the internal rate of return (IRR) for a given financing alternative. It is called the all-in cost because it includes all costs associated with the alternative being evaluated, such as flotation costs and administrative expenses, as well as the actual cash flows for the instrument being evaluated. As such, the all-in cost represents an effective annual percentage cost and provides a comprehensive basis for comparing different financing alternatives. As we will see in some more complicated applications later in this chapter, the all-in cost is a useful technique in a variety of situations.

We illustrate the concept of the all-in cost by comparing two financing alternatives available to the firm that are different in structure but that have very similar actual cash flows. The first instrument is a ten-year semiannual payment bond with a principal amount of \$40 million and a coupon rate of 7 percent. This instrument is priced at par:

$$P = \sum_{t=1}^{M} \frac{C_t}{(1 + y)^t} \tag{22.1}$$

where M is the maturity date of the bond; C_t is the cash flow from the bond at time t, which could be principal or interest; and y is the yield to maturity. In Equation 22.1, y is the yield to maturity on the bond, which is also the IRR that equates the price and the present value of the cash flows associated with the bond. Therefore, the yield to maturity meets the definition of the all-in cost for this bond. Because the bond pays a coupon of 7 percent and is priced at par, the yield on the bond and the all-in cost are both 7 percent. Therefore, the firm can secure its fixed-rate financing at an all-in cost of 7 percent by issuing a straight bond.

As a second financing alternative, the firm can borrow \$40 million for ten years at a floating rate of LIBOR plus 30 basis points, with the rate being reset each six months. LIBOR currently stands at 6.5 percent. Because the firm currently faces a floating financing rate of 6.8 percent, it looks attractive compared to the 7 percent fixed-rate financing vehicle. However, the firm has determined to secure fixed-rate financing. As we saw earlier in this chapter, issuing a floating-rate bond combined with a pay-fixed/receive-floating interest rate swap is equivalent to a fixed-rate bond. Upon inquiry, the firm learns that it can enter a pay-fixed/receive floating interest rate swap, to pay 6.5 percent and receive LIBOR. The fee for arranging the swap and the associated administrative costs is an immediate payment of \$400,000.

In summary of this second financing alternative, the firm would borrow \$40 million at a floating rate of 6.8 percent, and it would enter a swap agreement to pay-fixed at 6.5 percent and receive LIBOR. The firm must also pay a \$400,000 fee for the swap, so it will net only

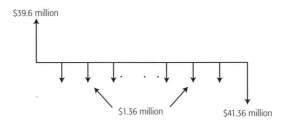

Figure 22.6   Cash flows for the second financing alternative

$39.6 million of actual financing. The two financing alternatives have very similar cash flows and both imply a fixed-rate financing of about $40 million. The choice of financing, therefore, reduces to comparing the all-in costs of the two deals. Figure 22.6 shows the net cash flow line for the second financing alternative, reflecting the effect of the swap. The firm receives $39.6 million at inception, makes 20 semiannual payments of $1.36 million, and repays the principal of $40 million at the end of ten years. The all-in cost for the second alternative is simply the IRR that equates the present cash inflow of $39.6 million with all of the cash outflows. For these flows, the IRR is 0.034703 on a semiannual basis, or 0.069406 in annual terms. This is slightly lower than the 7 percent IRR on the straight bond financing, so the firm prefers the floating-rate instrument coupled with the interest rate swap. Being able to compute the IRR on the two deals and compare the all-in costs leads to the correct decision. However, the firm should also be aware that the six basis point differential might simply reflect an additional credit risk on the swap if the market is fully efficient. If so, the firm would be indifferent between the two financing alternatives.

The B. F. Goodrich – Rabobank interest rate swap

This section discusses an actual swap from early in the development of the swap market.[3] In early 1983, B. F. Goodrich, a large producer of automobile tires, was in trouble. Following the recession of 1982, Goodrich's cash flow had been adversely affected and its credit rating had been downgraded from BBB to BBB–. Losses for 1982 totaled $33 million. Nonetheless, Goodrich needed $50 million in new financing to fund its ongoing operations. Goodrich could have borrowed from its bankers, but it wanted to preserve those credit lines and preferred longer-term financing in the 8–10 year range or, ideally, at a 30-year maturity. Goodrich also wanted fixed-rate financing. At this time, 30-year Treasury rates were about 10.30 percent. With a BBB– credit rating, Goodrich anticipated a financing rate of 13 percent for 30-year funds. Medium-term U.S. Treasuries were yielding about 10.10 percent, with medium-term BBB rates standing at 12–12.50 percent.

Salomon Brothers, the investment banking firm, suggested that Goodrich borrow in the United States at a floating rate tied to LIBOR. Then Goodrich could arrange a swap to convert the financing to a fixed rate. At this time, there had never been a public debt offering tied to LIBOR in the United States. Salomon felt confident that a floating-rate financing would succeed, because depository institutions were receiving enormous deposit inflows as a result of financial deregulation. Many of these new deposits paid a floating rate of interest, which made floating assets particularly desirable from the point of view of the depository institutions.

Rabobank was a large Dutch banking organization, consisting of more than 1,000 agricultural cooperative banks. These "ag" banks served the credit needs of small communities, with an emphasis on farm financing. Total assets exceeded 110 billion Dutch guilders, or $42 billion. Rabobank enjoyed a AAA rating, but had never borrowed in the Eurobond market. Rabobank had moved beyond agricultural financing into commercial lending and other banking activities, and was contemplating a $50 million medium-term issuance in the Eurobond market. However, Rabobank ultimately sought floating-rate financing. Through communications with its financing partners in London, it became known that Rabobank was potentially willing to issue a fixed-rate Eurobond and engage in an interest rate swap to secure floating-rate financing. At this time, in early 1983, 7–10 year Eurobond dollar yields were about 11 percent for AAA issuers. AAA banks were able to borrow at LIBOR plus 1/4 to 3/8 percent for 7–10 year FRNs, and three-month LIBOR was 8.75 percent. Foreign governments were issuing fully guaranteed loans at LIBOR plus 25 basis points.

Through representations by Salomon Brothers, Rabobank became interested in B. F. Goodrich as a swap partner, but it was concerned about the creditworthiness of Goodrich. At this early point in the swap market, swap dealers had not yet come into prominence, so swaps were often arranged directly between the counterparties. A direct swap between Rabobank and Goodrich would leave both sides exposed to default risk by the other party. Given the difference in credit ratings, this was obviously much more of a concern for Rabobank.

The transactions

Against this background, both Goodrich and Rabobank issued debt and two swaps were created to solve the financing needs and credit concerns of the various parties:

(1)   With Salomon acting as underwriter, B. F. Goodrich issued an eight-year FRN in the U.S. bond market. The principal amount was $50 million, the bond was noncallable, and the rate was three-month LIBOR plus 0.50 percent, with interest paid semiannually.

(2)   Rabobank issued a $50 million noncallable eight-year Eurobond with annual coupons at a rate of 11 percent.

(3)   B. F. Goodrich executed a swap with Morgan Guaranty Bank. Goodrich promised to pay $5.5 million each year for eight years. This matched the coupon payment on the Rabobank issuance. Morgan Bank promised to pay B. F. Goodrich a semiannual floating rate tied to three-month LIBOR for eight years. The semiannual payment was equal to

$$1/2 \text{ year} \times \$50,000,000 \times (\text{three-month LIBOR} - x)$$

The x represents a discount from LIBOR, and the size of this discount was undisclosed.

(4)   Morgan Bank promised to pay Rabobank $5.5 million each year for eight years. Rabobank promised to pay Morgan semiannual payments over eight years at LIBOR $- x$, the same undisclosed discount from LIBOR.

The two swap agreements were independent of each other in their legal terms. Each was a separate bilateral swap with Morgan Guaranty Bank. This structure insulated Rabobank from the potential default by B. F. Goodrich. In all of the financing arrangements detailed above, Rabobank and B. F. Goodrich actually have no obligations to each other. Morgan effectively interposed itself between the two swap counterparties and acted as a swap dealer. With Morgan's AAA credit rating, fears of default were considerably eased. Each swap agreement was entered as a "two-way or no-way" agreement. If one party failed to pay, the other party was released from an obligation to pay as well. For serving as this intermediary, Goodrich paid Morgan Guaranty a one-time fee of $125,000 and an undisclosed annual fee for each of the next eight years. This fee was probably in the range of 8–37 basis points. Apparently, Goodrich secured very favorable financing terms from this arrangement. One commercial banker was quoted as saying "There is no way Goodrich could have gotten that pricing from their banks." Against this description of the transactions, let us consider the position of each of the parties, Goodrich, Rabobank, and Morgan Guaranty. We begin with Morgan, as its position is the simplest.

Morgan Guaranty's position

Morgan's two swap agreements had exactly offsetting cash flows. As long as neither party defaulted, Morgan simply received payments from Rabobank or B. F. Goodrich and passed them along to the other party. Upon default by either Goodrich or Rabobank, Morgan Guaranty would suddenly be exposed to interest rate risk. In exchange for the service of forwarding funds and bearing a potential exposure to interest rate risk, Morgan received the one-time fee of $125,000 plus the unknown annual fee of 8–37 basis points, or $40,000–185,000, in each of the eight years of the swap's tenor.

B. F. Goodrich's position

B. F. Goodrich could probably have issued a fixed-rate medium-term note for 12–12.5 percent, given rates in early 1983. Against this direct financing alternative, B. F. Goodrich:

(1)   issued a medium-term semiannual payment FRN at LIBOR plus 0.50 percent;
(2)   received floating semiannual payments on the swap at LIBOR − x percent;
(3)   paid fixed on the swap at 11 percent, with annual payments;
(4)   paid Morgan a one-time fee of $125,000; and
(5)   paid Morgan eight annual payments, each probably in the range of 8–37 basis points, or $40,000–$185,000.

Because we do not know the discount from LIBOR in step (2) of Goodrich's financing and because we do not know the annual payment in step (5), we cannot determine exactly how well Goodrich did with this financing. However, we can explore this issue further by making some reasonable assumptions. Let us assume that the discount from LIBOR that Goodrich received was 50 basis points and that the eight annual payments it made to Morgan were at the midpoint of the 8–37 basis point range, or 22.5 basis points. Table 22.2 details the cash flows for Goodrich under these assumptions. The all-in cost for Goodrich under these assumptions is 5.9744 percent semiannually, or 11.9488 percent in annual terms. Under these assumptions, it seems that the swap financing arrangement compares favorably with the anticipated 12–12.5 percent fixed-rate financing alternative. However, this pleasing result is largely an artifact of our assumptions. For example, if the discount from LIBOR that Goodrich received in step (2) was 75 basis points and the annual fee in step (5) was 37 basis points, the semiannual all-in cost would be 6.16502 percent, for an annualized all-in cost of 12.33004 percent, which is about the same as the fixed-rate financing alternative.

Rabobank's position

Based on market conditions at the time, Rabobank could probably have issued a fixed-rate Eurobond at 11 percent or an FRN at LIBOR plus 25–50 basis points, probably closer to LIBOR plus 50 basis points. In the actual transactions, Rabobank:

Table 22.2 B. F. Goodrich's cash flows

Semiannual period	Principal cash flows	Annual interest payments	Fifty basis points over LIBOR	Discount from LIBOR[1]	Fees to Morgan[2]	Net cash flow
0	$50,000,000				−$125,000	$49,875,000
1			−$125,000	−$125,000		−250,000
2		−$5,500,000	−125,000	−125,000	−112,500	−5,862,500
3			−125,000	−125,000		−250,000
4		−5,500,000	−125,000	−125,000	−112,500	−5,862,500
5			−125,000	−125,000		−250,000
6		−5,500,000	−125,000	−125,000	−112,500	−5,862,500
7			−125,000	−125,000		−250,000
8		−5,500,000	−125,000	−125,000	−112,500	−5,862,500
9			−125,000	−125,000		−250,000
10		−5,500,000	−125,000	−125,000	−112,500	−5,862,500
11			−125,000	−125,000		−250,000
12		−5,500,000	−125,000	−125,000	−112,500	−5,862,500
13			−125,000	−125,000		−250,000
14		−5,500,000	−125,000	−125,000	−112,500	−5,862,500
15			−125,000	−125,000		−250,000
16	−50,000,000	−5,500,000	−125,000	−125,000	−112,500	−55,862,500

[1]Discount from LIBOR on swap floating receipts assumed to be 50 basis points.
[2]Annual fee to Morgan assumed to be 22.5 basis points: $0.00225 \times \$50,000,000 = \$112,500$.

(1) issued an eight-year fixed-rate noncallable annual coupon bond at 11 percent;
(2) promised to pay Morgan eight years of semiannual payments at LIBOR − x through a swap; and
(3) received from Morgan eight annual payments of $5.5 million.

The result of these three financings was a floating-rate loan at LIBOR − x for Rabobank. Rabobank paid no fees and there were no other complications. Thus, Rabobank appears to be a clear winner. At a time when sovereign debt was being issued at LIBOR plus 25 basis points, Rabobank apparently secured financing at a rate lower than LIBOR, LIBOR − x.

Summary

In this actual swap, there are a number of interesting features. First, we see Morgan Guaranty operating in the early environment of swaps, when swaps were arranged directly between counterparties. However, Morgan actually served as a swap dealer, acting as the counterparty to both Goodrich and Rabobank. As the swap market has matured, firms such as Morgan have become increasingly willing to serve as counterparties without having to pre-arrange a matched set of swaps. Second, we see that the interposition of Morgan in creating two swaps solved Rabobank's problems with Goodrich's poor credit. Third, Goodrich and Rabobank considered together apparently secured cheaper financing through this arrangement than was possible without the swap agreements. It seems clear that Rabobank was considerably better off, and Goodrich may have secured cheaper financing as well. In today's more mature swap market, it would be more difficult to find superior financing alternatives such as these. Finally, Table 22.2 shows how the all-in cost provides an effective means for comparing financing costs in these kinds of swap arrangements. The analysis in Table 22.2 is the kind of work that Goodrich needed to do in evaluating its financing alternatives.

The duration of interest rate swaps

In our discussion of hedging with interest rate futures in Chapter 6, we saw that duration is an important tool for controlling interest rate risk. There, we saw that futures could be used to immunize a balance sheet against fluctuations in interest rates. Similar hedging techniques apply with interest rate swaps. Therefore, we need to understand the duration of an interest rate swap. In the next section, we show how to apply interest rate swaps to control the duration of a balance sheet.

We saw in Chapter 21 that an interest rate swap could be analyzed as a portfolio of two bonds. In essence, a receive-fixed swap consists of a short position in a floating-rate instrument combined with a long position in a fixed-rate coupon bond. Conversely, a pay-fixed swap consists of a short position in a coupon bond, coupled with a long position in a floating-rate instrument. Therefore, an interest rate swap has a duration that equals the duration of the bond portfolio that is equivalent to the swap. The duration of a swap can be either positive or negative, depending on whether the swap is a receive-fixed or a pay-fixed swap. Based on these reflections, we can state the following rules:

duration of a receive-fixed swap = duration of the underlying coupon bond
− duration of the underlying floating-rate bond
> 0

duration of a pay-fixed swap = duration of the underlying floating-rate bond
− duration of the underlying coupon bond
< 0

The duration of a floating-rate instrument equals the time between reset dates for the interest rate. Thus an FRN with semiannual payments would have a duration equal to six months, or one half-year. The calculation of the duration of the swap, then, really depends on finding the duration of the fixed-rate coupon bond underlying the swap. As an example, consider an interest rate swap with an SFR of 7 percent, a tenor of seven years, and semiannual payments. Table 22.3 shows the calculation of the Macaulay duration for the coupon bond portion of the swap. As the table shows, the duration of the fixed side of the swap is 11.302738 semiannual periods, or 5.651369 years. For the floating side of the swap, the duration is six months, or one half-year. Therefore, for this swap,

duration of a receive-fixed swap = 5.651369 − 0.5 = 5.151369 years
duration of a pay-fixed swap = 0.5 − 5.651369 = −5.151369 years

As this example shows, receive-fixed swaps can be quite useful in lengthening the duration of an existing position, while pay-fixed swaps can be used effectively to decrease the duration of an existing position.

Table 22.3   Calculation of duration for the fixed-rate side of an interest rate swap

Semiannual period	Cash flows	Discount factor	Present value of cash flow	Weighted present value of cash flow
1	35	1.035000	33.82	0.033816
2	35	1.071225	32.67	0.065346
3	35	1.108718	31.57	0.094704
4	35	1.147523	30.50	0.122002
5	35	1.187686	29.47	0.147345
6	35	1.229255	28.47	0.170835
7	35	1.272279	27.51	0.192568
8	35	1.316809	26.58	0.212635
9	35	1.362897	25.68	0.231125
10	35	1.410599	24.81	0.248122
11	35	1.459970	23.97	0.263704
12	35	1.511069	23.16	0.277949
13	35	1.563956	22.38	0.290929
14	1,035	1.618695	639.40	8.951658
			Sum = bond price = $1,000	Sum = bond duration = 11.302738

Note: Duration is expressed in semiannual periods. Duration = 5.651369 years.

Interest rate immunization with swaps

We now turn to an application of swaps to manage the duration of ongoing business operations. Consider FSF, a financial services firm with the stylized balance sheet shown in Table 22.4. All dollar values are market values. Most assets are held as amortizing loans with a ten-year average maturity. On the liability side, FSF relies largely on money market obligations and an

Table 22.4   FSF, Financial Services Firm, stylized balance sheet—market values

Assets		Liabilities and net worth	
A: Cash	$7,000,000	D: Six-month money market obligations (average yield 6%)	$75,000,000
B: Marketable securities (six-month maturity; yield 7%)	18,000,000	E: FRN (five-year maturity; 7.3% current yield; semiannual payments)	40,000,000
C: Amortizing loans (ten-year average maturity; semiannual payments; 8% average yield)	130,467,133	F: Coupon bond (ten-year maturity; semiannual payments; 6.50% coupon; par value $25,000,000, annual *YTM* = 7%)	24,111,725
		Total liabilities	$139,111,725
		Net worth	$16,355,408
Total assets	$155,467,133	Total liabilities and net worth	$155,467,133

FRN issue with a five-year maturity. FSF has also issued a coupon bond that has ten years remaining until maturity.

The interest rate risk of FSF

The interest rate risk of FSF can be analyzed by using the concept of duration. Most of the balance sheet items have a duration that is evident and requires no computation. Cash has a duration of zero years. The marketable securities and the six-month money market obligations are zero-coupon instruments that mature in six months, so their duration is one half-year. The duration of the FRN is also one half-year, because it has annual payments. This leaves the amortizing loan on the asset side and the coupon bond on the liability side with durations that require computation. Table 22.5 presents detailed computations of the durations for the amortizing loan

Table 22.5 Duration calculation for FSF balance sheet items

Semiannual period	Amortizing loan (asset item C)				Coupon bond (liability item F)			
	Cash flow	Discount factor	Present value	Weighted present value	Cash flow	Discount factor	Present value	Weighted present value
1	$9,600,000	1.040000	$9,230,769	0.070752	$812,500	1.035000	$785,024	0.032558
2	9,600,000	1.081600	8,875,740	0.136061	812,500	1.071225	758,477	0.062914
3	9,600,000	1.124864	8,534,365	0.196242	812,500	1.108718	732,828	0.091179
4	9,600,000	1.169859	8,206,120	0.251592	812,500	1.147523	708,047	0.117461
5	9,600,000	1.216653	7,890,500	0.302394	812,500	1.187686	684,103	0.141861
6	9,600,000	1.265319	7,587,019	0.348916	812,500	1.229255	660,969	0.164477
7	9,600,000	1.315932	7,295,211	0.391413	812,500	1.272279	638,618	0.185400
8	9,600,000	1.368569	7,014,626	0.430124	812,500	1.316809	617,022	0.204721
9	9,600,000	1.423312	6,744,833	0.465278	812,500	1.362897	596,156	0.222523
10	9,600,000	1.480244	6,485,416	0.497092	812,500	1.410599	575,997	0.238886
11	9,600,000	1.539454	6,235,977	0.525770	812,500	1.459970	556,518	0.253889
12	9,600,000	1.601032	5,996,132	0.551507	812,500	1.511069	537,699	0.267604
13	9,600,000	1.665074	5,765,511	0.574487	812,500	1.563956	519,516	0.280101
14	9,600,000	1.731676	5,543,761	0.594883	812,500	1.618695	501,948	0.291446
15	9,600,000	1.800944	5,330,539	0.612860	812,500	1.675349	484,974	0.301704
16	9,600,000	1.872981	5,125,518	0.628574	812,500	1.733986	468,574	0.310935
17	9,600,000	1.947900	4,928,383	0.642173	812,500	1.794676	452,728	0.319196
18	9,600,000	2.025817	4,738,830	0.653796	812,500	1.857489	437,418	0.326544
19	9,600,000	2.106849	4,556,567	0.663575	812,500	1.922501	422,626	0.333029
20	9,600,000	2.191123	4,381,315	0.671635	25,812,500	1.989789	12,972,482	10.760310
			Total: $130,467,133	Total—duration in semiannual periods: 9.209125 Duration—years: 4.604562			Total: $24,111,725	Total—duration in semiannual periods: 14.906737 Duration—years: 7.453369

Note: The weighted present values are the present value of each cash flow, divided by the value of the instrument, multiplied by the time (in semiannual periods) until the cash flow is received. Example: The cash flow received at the 15th semiannual period on the amortized loan has a present value of $5,330,539. It represents 0.040857 of the value of the loan ($5,330,539/$130,467,133). Multiplying this fraction times the 15 semiannual periods until this cash flow is received gives: 15 × 0.040857 = 0.0612860. The duration in semiannual periods is the sum of these weighted present values.

Table 22.6   Summary of durations for FSF balance sheet items

Item	Assets		Item	Liabilities	
	Market value	Duration (years)		Market value	Duration (years)
A: Cash	$7,000,000	0.000000	D: Money market obligations	$75,000,000	0.500000
B: Marketable securities	$18,000,000	0.500000	E: FRN	$40,000,000	0.500000
C: Amortizing loans	$130,467,133	4.604562	F: Coupon bond	$24,111,725	7.453369

(asset item C) and the coupon bond (liability item F) from the balance sheet for FSF. The amortizing loans throw off $9.6 million per semiannual period for a market value of $130,467,133. The duration of these loans is 9.209125 semiannual periods, or 4.604562 years. The coupon bond has a market value of $24,111,725 and a duration of 14.906737 semiannual periods, or 7.453369 years.

Table 22.6 summarizes the market value and durations of the balance sheet items. Based on the information, we can compute the duration of the assets and liabilities. The durations are weighted averages of the duration of the individual items, weighted by the fraction of assets or liabilities. Letting D_A represent the duration of the assets and D_L the duration of the liabilities, we have

$$D_A = \frac{\$7,000,000}{\$155,467,133} \times 0.000000 + \frac{\$18,000,000}{\$155,467,133} \times 0.5000000 + \frac{\$130,467,133}{\$155,467,133} \times 4.604562$$

$$= 3.922013$$

$$D_L = \frac{\$75,000,000}{\$139,111,725} \times 0.500000 + \frac{\$40,000,000}{\$139,111,725} \times 0.5000000 + \frac{\$24,111,725}{\$139,111,725} \times 7.453369$$

$$= 1.705202$$

Hedging the asset and liability portfolios individually

Armed with this duration analysis of its balance sheet, FSF can use the swaps market to protect itself against unanticipated changes in interest rates. We first consider how the asset and liability portfolios can be protected against changing interest rates individually. In the next section, we show how to synthesize the entire analysis into an integrated solution. For both the asset and liability portfolios, we use the swap of the preceding section as a hedging instrument. That swap had a seven-year tenor, semiannual payments, and an SFR of 7 percent. As discussed in the preceding section, and computed in Table 22.3, the duration of the fixed side of the swap is 5.651369 years. With semiannual payments, the duration of the floating side is one half-year. So the duration of the received-fixed position in the swap is 5.151369 years, and the duration of the pay-fixed position in the swap is just the negative, or −5.151369 years.

In general, the solution for hedging an existing asset or portfolio, X, with hedging vehicle, H, using the duration approach is given by

$$D_X \times MV_X + D_H \times MV_H^* = 0 \qquad (22.2)$$

where D_X is the duration of the position to be hedged, D_H is the duration of the hedging instrument, MV_X is the market value of the position to be hedged, and MV_H^* is the market value (or notional principal) of the hedging vehicle. The market value of a swap, in the sense of Equation 22.2, equals the notional principal. To completely immunize a position from changes in value due to changes in interest rates, the desired duration should be zero. Given the existing position and the choice of a hedging instrument, the problem is to find the amount of the hedging instrument, MV_H^*, that satisfies Equation 22.2.

Therefore, FSF can protect the market values of the asset and liability sides of its balance sheet by combining each with the interest rate swap of the preceding section. For the asset portfolio, the duration is 3.922013 years, so we need a pay-fixed swap with its duration of 25.151369. We apply Equation 22.2 to find the correct notional principal for the swap, MV_H^*, and have the following:

$$3.922013 \times \$155,467,133 - 5.151369 \times MV_H^* = 0$$

MV_H^* for the assets = \$118,365,451 in a pay-fixed swap. Therefore, we can hedge the asset side of the FSF balance sheet by entering a pay-fixed swap with a notional principal of \$118,365,451.

Similarly, we can use the same swap to hedge the liability side of the balance sheet. The total liabilities are \$139,111,725. Because these are liabilities, FSF has a short position in these instruments. Therefore, considering the liabilities on their own, FSF will need a receive-fixed swap to complete the hedge. Again, applying Equation 22.2 to the liabilities, we have the following:

$$1.705202 \times (-\$139,111,725) + 5.151369 \times MV_H^* = 0$$

MV_H^* for the liabilities is \$46,048,651 in a receive-fixed swap.

Duration gap hedging

In the preceding section, we showed how to eliminate the interest rate risk in the asset and liability portfolios separately. As we saw, the assets required a pay-fixed swap with a notional principal of \$118,365,451, and the liability portfolio required a receive-fixed swap with a notional principal of \$46,048,651. These two swaps are partially offsetting. Combined, the two swaps really equal a pay-fixed swap with a notional principal of \$118,365,451 − \$46,048,651 = \$72,316,800. This section shows how to reach this same solution by using an integrated approach to the entire risk position of FSF.

As we have noted for FSF, the value of the assets is \$155,467,133 with a duration of 3.922013 years, while the value of the liabilities is \$139,111,725 with a duration of 1.705202 years. The difference in durations is 2.286999 years, but the assets exceed the liabilities by the net worth of the firm. We need an integrated measure of the duration difference, or duration gap, between the assets and liabilities that reflects the difference in market value between the assets and liabilities. This measure is called the **duration gap**, D_G, which is defined as follows:

$$D_G = D_A - \frac{\text{total liabilities}}{\text{total assets}} \times D_L \qquad (22.3)$$

The ratio of total liabilities to total assets acts as a scale factor to reflect the difference in market value between the assets and liabilities. For FSF, the duration gap is as follows:

$$D_G = 3.922013 - \frac{\$139,111,725}{\$155,465,133} \times 1.705202 = 2.396201$$

The duration gap is greater than the difference in durations because the market value of the assets exceeds the market value of the liabilities. Because the duration gap embraces both the assets and liabilities and reflects the difference in market value between the two, it summarizes the entire risk position of the firm. Because the duration gap of FSF is 2.396201, the entire firm has an interest rate risk that behaves like a long position in a bond with a duration of 2.396201 years.

To hedge the entire value of the firm, FSF could use a pay-fixed swap to set the duration gap of the entire firm, including the swap, so that it equals zero. Using the duration gap that we just computed and our sample pay-fixed swap, we have

$$2.396201 \times \$155,467,133 - 5.151369 \times MV_H^* = 0$$

MV_H^* for hedging the entire firm is $72,316,800 in a pay-fixed swap. This is the same result that we found by hedging the asset portfolio with a pay-fixed swap and the liability portfolio with a receive-fixed swap and noting the offsetting positions that were created.

Setting interest rate sensitivity with swaps

So far, we have seen how to immunize FSF against changing interest rates, which amounted to setting the duration gap to zero. Let us now assume that FSF wants to reduce, but not eliminate, the interest rate risk inherent in the firm's operations. FSF management decides to make the firm behave like a bond with a duration of one year, instead of behaving like a bond with a duration equal to the firm's duration gap of 2.396201.

In general, we can use swaps to set the duration gap of the firm to any desired level as follows:

$$D_G^* = D_G + D_S\left(\frac{MV_H^*}{\text{total assets}}\right) \tag{22.4}$$

where D_G^* is the desired duration gap, D_S is the duration of the swap, and MV_H^* is the required market value (notional principal) for the swap. To set the duration gap of the firm's interest-sensitive assets to one year, the required solution is as follows:

$$D_G^* = 1.0 = D_G + D_S\left(\frac{MV_H^*}{\text{total assets}}\right)$$

$$= 2.396201 + 5.151369\left(\frac{MV_H^*}{\$155,467,133}\right)$$

$$MV_H^* = -\$42,137,025$$

The negative sign on MV_H^* indicates that a pay-fixed swap is required. (If one were sure that a pay-fixed swap would be required, the sign for D_S could be shown as a negative, reflecting the duration of the pay-fixed position.)

This result makes intuitive sense, given what we have already seen. The duration gap of the firm was 2.396201 initially, and this position combined with a pay-fixed swap having a notional principal of $72,316,800 moved the duration gap of the firm to zero. Changing the duration gap from 2.267558 to 1.0 alters it by 58.2673 percent (1.396201/2.396201). Not surprisingly, the necessary swap position is 58.2673 percent as large ($42,137,025/$72,316,800) as the swap necessary to move the duration gap to zero.

With a duration gap greater than zero, the firm's value is exposed to the danger of rising interest rates. If the firm expects rates to rise and wishes to speculate on that eventuality, it might wish to set its duration gap to be less than zero. For instance, a modest speculative position could be achieved with a duration gap of −0.5 years. The swap position to achieve this exposure would be as follows:

$$D_G^* = -0.5 = D_G + D_S\left(\frac{MV_H^*}{\text{total assets}}\right)$$

$$= 2.396201 + 5.151369\left(\frac{MV_H^*}{\$155,467,133}\right)$$

$$MV_H^* = -\$87,406,681$$

So, a pay-fixed swap with a notional principal of $87,406,681 is required to change the duration gap to 20.5 years. This procedure moves the duration gap of the firm from its original positive value of 2.396201, indicating an exposure to rising rates, beyond the risk-neutral duration gap of zero, to a negative duration gap of 20.5. Now, if rates rise, the firm will benefit. However, it is exposed to losses if rates fall.

Finally, we consider how swaps could be used to take an extreme speculative position for FSF. A duration of ten years would be an extremely large duration for any bond in the market, indicating a large sensitivity to rising interest rates. FSF could use a swap to create this position with startling ease. Applying Equation 22.4, the solution would be as follows:

$$D_G^* = 10.0 = D_G + D_S\left(\frac{MV_H^*}{\text{total assets}}\right)$$

$$= 2.396201 + 5.151369\left(\frac{MV_H^*}{\$155,467,133}\right)$$

$$MV_H^* = \$229,480,907$$

To change the duration gap for the firm from 2.396201 to ten years, the firm would enter a receive-fixed swap with a notional principal of $229,480,907. We have seen that a pay-fixed swap of modest proportions reduces the interest rate risk of FSF. A receive-fixed swap increases the duration gap for FSF.

These examples emphasize the power and flexibility of swaps for changing the interest rate exposure of a firm. The risk of extreme positions should not be neglected either. A formula for the approximate price change of an interest-sensitive asset is as follows:

$$\Delta P \approx -D\frac{\Delta AYTM}{1 + AYTM}P$$

where D is expressed in years, $AYTM$ is the annual yield-to-maturity on the asset, and P is the current price of the asset. If FSF were to set its duration gap to ten years, its net worth would be extremely vulnerable to interest rate risk. Taking the average rate on all of FSF's positions at 7 percent for convenience, we see that an interest rate increase of only ten basis points would cost FSF almost $152,854, which is about 1 percent of its net worth of $16,355,408:

$$\Delta P = -D\left(\frac{\Delta AYTM}{1 + AYTM}\right)P = -10 \times \frac{+0.0010}{1.07} \times \$16,355,408 = -\$152,854$$

A major rise in rates, say an increase of five percentage points, would cost FSF $7,642,714, or about 46.7 percent of its net worth, if FSF's duration gap were set to ten years:

$$\Delta P = -D\left(\frac{\Delta AYTM}{1 + AYTM}\right)P = -10 \times \frac{+0.005}{1.07} \times \$16,355,408 = -\$7,642,714$$

Swaps, like other powerful tools, require caution in their use.[4]

China Aviation Oil

In November 2004, China Aviation Oil (CAO) announced that it had lost up to $550 million through trading in crude oil swaps, futures, and options. CAO's trading losses followed a year-long surge in crude oil prices. The company, which took the view that oil prices would fall, was eventually unable to meet margin calls on its contracts before winding down its open positions and turning unrealized paper losses into real losses.

CAO, which has a state monopoly on importing jet fuel into China, began speculating in the direction of oil prices in the fall of 2003. It started out with short derivatives positions covering 2 million barrels of oil. By March of 2004 this position had generated $5.8 million in mark-to-market losses. In the company's prospectus, CAO had promised that if the company's trading losses exceeded $5 million, the open positions would be closed out unless an exception was authorized by CAO's chief executive office. Rather than close out the money-losing open positions, CAO instead increased the size of its trades, in the hope that falling oil prices in the future would offset the as-yet unrecognized trading losses that had accumulated. The company amended its soon-to-expire positions into later-dated positions, in an attempt to buy time to allow its bet on lower-priced oil to come true. By June, CAO's losses had climbed to $30 million. The company again increased the size of its positions, so that by October they covered 52 million barrels.

As oil prices rose and losses continued to mount, CAO started to face margin calls from counterparties. However, the company was unable to meet margin payment demands. As a result, several of CAO's counterparties unilaterally closed out positions with CAO. In aggregate, the margin demands and close-out settlement demands resulted in a realized loss of $390 million by November 2004. At that point, CAO asked its counterparties to close out the remaining derivatives positions, resulting in the recognition of an additional $160 million loss. CAO was bankrupt, offering to settle with creditors for 41 cents on the dollar.

In an auditors' report issued in March 2005, the debacle was blamed on several factors. First, CAO's trading losses resulted from a bad bet on crude oil prices. Second, the company valued its crude-oil options positions incorrectly, a fact that led it to misunderstand the true magnitude of its losses until it was too late. Third, CAO employed inadequate internal controls and risk management practices. Internal controls and risk management guidelines that were supposed to be in place were simply ignored. In the end, the CAO debacle is similar to other derivatives trading debacles. However, the CAO case had one unusual twist. One month prior to the company's public disclosure of its losses, CAO's parent company, China Aviation Oil Holding Company (CAOHC), sold $108 million in CAO stock to investors. Proceeds from the sale were loaned to CAO to help meet the company's margin calls. At the time of the sale, CAO's trading losses were not disclosed to investors, although the stock was sold at a 14 percent discount to the current market price, and investors were required to sign a letter confirming that they were aware that limited due diligence was conducted by the investment bank handling the sale. Because the CAO shares are listed on the Singapore exchange, the Securities Investment Association of Singapore (SIAS) has been investigating the matter.

Most of CAO's losses were in off-exchange, privately negotiated, over-the-counter derivatives. One consequence of the role that OTC derivatives played in the CAO debacle is that Chinese market regulators gained fresh appreciation for the daily mark-to-market feature of futures markets. The daily marking-to-market of futures positions forces daily recognition of gains and losses, and would have reduced the likelihood of losses of the scale incurred by CAO. In the future, the CAO debacle may have the effect of indirectly encouraging the growth of futures markets in China.

Structured notes

A structured note is a debt instrument with special features designed to appeal to investors, created in conjunction with a derivative position taken by the issuer. The special features inherent in the security give investors payoff characteristics on the structured note that are generally unavailable in the market. A typical example of a structured note is an **inverse floater**, a floating-rate note with a yield that varies inversely with movements in interest rates. The issuer of an **inverse floater** would promise the purchaser of the note a return that varies inversely with interest rates, but the issuer would typically take a position in the swaps market to protect itself from the interest rate risk inherent in such a payoff pattern. With a structured note, the issuer offers an unusual but desirable payoff pattern, but uses derivatives to ensure that its own obligations are of a simple and traditional character.

The investor in a structured note obtains a payoff pattern that could be created by combining a traditional debt instrument with the appropriate derivatives position, as we will see. However, there are good reasons for some investors to prefer the purchase of a structured note to the creation of their own structured note through transacting in the swaps market. First, structured notes are available in small quantities from issuers. Creating a structured note requires specific analysis and derivatives contracting that would not be feasible for a small investment. Second, structured notes are often issued by federal agencies, so the purchase of a structured note can involve much less credit evaluation and credit risk than the creation of a homemade structured note. Third, structured notes issued by a recognizable entity are much more marketable than a homemade structured note. Finally, some investors might like to obtain the payoff pattern available in a structured note, but face restrictions on the use of derivatives markets.[5] As we will see with the examples described below, structured notes give investors the opportunities to act on their beliefs about future movements in interest rates, to trade off current yield against future higher yields, to act on specific market views, and to increase or decrease risk to taste.

The inverse floater

An **inverse floating-rate note**, or **inverse floater**, has a payoff pattern that is inversely related to a floating reference rate. An inverse floater is also known as a **reverse floater**, or a **bull FRN**. (It is called a "bull" FRN because it is attractive to those who are bullish on bond prices, expecting lower interest rates.) For example, assume that six-month LIBOR now stands at 7 percent. An inverse floater might promise to pay a floating rate of interest equal to 14 percent minus six-month LIBOR. The initial yield on the inverse floater would be 7 percent. As LIBOR rises, however, the interest paid on the inverse floater would fall. If six-month LIBOR rose to 9 percent, for example, the note would only pay 5 percent, 14 percent minus the six-month LIBOR of 9 percent. If LIBOR fell from its initial level of 7 percent, the rate paid on the inverse floater would rise. For example, a six-month LIBOR of 5 percent would require a payment on the inverse floater of 9 percent, which equals 14 percent minus the six-month LIBOR of 5 percent.

Consider this same floater if LIBOR rises to a level above 14 percent—say, 17 percent. The terms specified so far would require the purchaser of the bond to pay the issuer, because the payment on the bond is supposed to be 14 percent minus LIBOR. Almost all inverse floaters include the stipulation that there will be no interest payment if LIBOR exceeds the stipulated fixed rate, which is 14 percent in our example. This amounts to the inclusion of an option with the inverse floater. It also explains why the fixed rate should be set quite high relative to LIBOR at the time of issuance, and it also indicates a reason for favoring shorter maturities on inverse floaters—so that LIBOR will be unlikely to exceed the fixed rate during the life of the bond.

An inverse floater could be an attractive investment if one anticipates falling interest rates. For the issuer, offering the inverse floating rate might attract investors to the issue in pursuit of a payoff pattern that is not widely available in the market. The issuer might hope to reduce its borrowing costs by a few basis points. (Note that the savings in financing cost to the issuer assumes some kind of market imperfection. As we see in detail below, the investor could create the same payoff pattern by her own transactions. The issuer's ability to reduce its financing cost must turn on the issuer's greater efficiency in creating the instrument—which implies a market imperfection.)[6]

As an example of an inverse floater, consider a firm that issues a $100 million inverse floater that has a maturity of five years, and pays annual interest equal to 14 percent minus one-year LIBOR. The issuer can create this instrument without using the derivatives market, but in the creation of structured notes, it is common for the issuer to use derivatives to maintain a traditional interest rate exposure for itself, while offering a nontraditional payoff pattern to the investor. Thus, we begin the analysis of this inverse floater by assuming that the firm issues the inverse floater and uses the swaps market to avoid the inverse pattern of interest expenses. Later, we show how to create the issuance and purchase of a synthetic inverse floater from the same elements.

Assume that the issuer of the inverse floater also initiates a receive-fixed swap with terms that match the inverse floater. Specifically, the receive-fixed swap has a tenor of five years and floating-rate payments equal to one-year LIBOR. The notional principal for the swap is $200 million, which is twice as large as the principal on the inverse floater. (We refer to this kind of swap as being "double-sized" because the notional principal on the swap is twice as large as the loan principal.) Assuming that the yield curve is flat at 7 percent, the swap fixed rate will also be 7 percent.

Figure 22.7 presents three cash flow time lines pertaining to various features of this inverse floater. The first time line of Figure 22.7 shows the cash flow obligations associated with the inverse floater. Each period, the issuer must pay $14 million, less LIBOR × $100 million. It is useful to think of the issuer as paying $14 million and receiving LIBOR × $100 million under the terms of the inverse floater. The second time line shows the cash flows for the "double-sized" receive-fixed swap. The inflow is the SFR of 7 percent on $200 million, or $14 million per year. The outflow is one-year LIBOR times the notional principal of $200 million. The third time line shows the combined cash flows from the issuance of the inverse floater and the receive-fixed swap. Except for the cash flows involving the principal on the loan, the annual cash flows

Figure 22.7   Cash flows for issuing an inverse floater

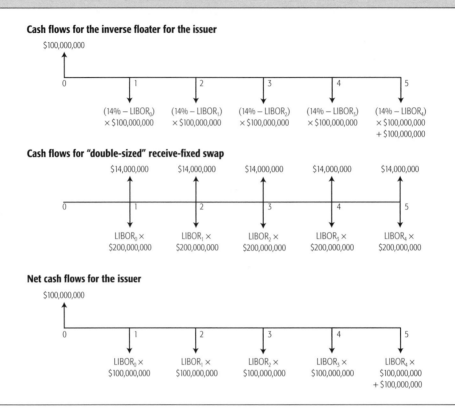

Cash flows for the inverse floater for the issuer

Cash flows for "double-sized" receive-fixed swap

Net cash flows for the issuer

are all the same. Therefore, we consider the cash flow at year 3 in detail as representative of the cash flows on the entire financing arrangement.

Year 3 cash flow on inverse floater

Inverse floater	$(-14\% + \text{LIBOR}_2) \times 100,000,000 =$
	$-\$14,000,000 + \text{LIBOR}_2 \times \$100,000,000$
"Double-sized" receive-fixed swap	$+\$14,000,000 - \text{LIBOR}_2 \times \$200,000,000$
Result—net cash flow for issuer	$-\text{LIBOR}_2 \times \$100,000,000$

As the preceding analysis shows, for each year the fixed cash flows net to zero. This leaves only floating cash flows. The inverse floater gives the issuer a cash inflow tied to LIBOR that offsets the 14 percent fixed rate. The receive-fixed swap requires a floating cash flow tied to LIBOR on $200 million. The net result is an annual interest payment equal to LIBOR on $100 million. In sum, the issuer has issued an inverse floater, but combined with a receive-fixed interest rate swap, with a notional principal twice as large as the debt issuance principal, the net result is the same as the issuer having issued an FRN with the original desired principal. The final time line of Figure 22.7 reflects this result—it is exactly the cash flow pattern for issuing a straight FRN with a principal of $100 million.

Still viewing matters from the point of view of the issuer, we may view these transactions in two ways. We have just seen that issuing an inverse floater plus initiating a "double-sized" receive-fixed swap is equivalent to issuing an FRN with a principal that is the same as the principal of the inverse floater. For a common notional or principal amount, Figure 22.7 effectively says the following:

Decomposition of inverse floater:

issuing inverse floater + "double-sized" receive-fixed swap = issuing FRN   (22.5)

or

issuing FRN − "double sized" receive-fixed swap = issuing inverse floater   (22.6)

or, because being short a receive-fixed swap is the same as being long a pay-fixed swap, the equivalent position is as follows:

Synthesizing issuance of inverse floater:

issuing FRN + "double sized" pay-fixed swap = issuing inverse floater   (22.7)

This gives a formula for synthesizing the issuance of an inverse floater. We consider the year 3 cash flow for the issuance of the inverse floater synthesized by issuing an FRN and initiating a pay-fixed swap with a larger notional principal:

Year 3 cash flow on synthetic inverse floater issuance

Issued FRN	$-\text{LIBOR}_2 \times \$100,000,000$
"Double-sized" pay-fixed swap	$+\$14,000,000 + \text{LIBOR}_2 \times \$200,000,000$
Result—synthetic inverse floater issuance	$-\$14,000,000 + \text{LIBOR}_2 \times \$100,000,000$

We now consider the inverse floater from the point of view of the investor. If firms or agencies issue inverse floaters, the investor can simply purchase one. Alternatively, the investor can also create an inverse floater for herself. As we have seen, the issuer can synthesize the issuance, so the investor must be able to synthesize the purchase. A synthetic purchase will be just the opposite of a synthetic issuance. If we reverse all of the positions for the synthetic issuance in Equation 22.7, we will have the formula for the synthetic purchase of an inverse floater:

Synthetic purchase of inverse floater:

−issuing FRN − "double-sized" pay-fixed swap = −issuing inverse floater

or

purchasing FRN + "double-sized" receive-fixed swap
= purchasing inverse floater   (22.8)

Equation 22.8 gives the formula for the purchase of a synthetic inverse floater. To see this in detail, we again consider the year 3 cash flow for the purchase of this synthetic inverse floater:

Year 3 cash flow on synthetic inverse floater purchase

Purchase FRN	$+\text{LIBOR}_2 \times \$100,000,000$
"Double-sized" receive-fixed swap	$+\$14,000,000 - \text{LIBOR}_2 \times \$200,000,000$
Result—synthetic inverse floater purchase	$+\$14,000,000 - \text{LIBOR}_2 \times \$100,000,000$

As we have seen, any investor with access to the swaps market can make her own inverse floater investment by buying an FRN and entering a double-sized receive-fixed plain vanilla interest rate swap. Nonetheless, the market for issuing inverse floaters is fairly large, with billions of dollars of principal being issued each year. This continuing issuance apparently reflects the greater operational efficiency of larger firms and agencies in creating this kind of instrument.

The bear floater

A bear floater is a floating-rate note designed to allow the investor to profit from rising interest rates. Thus, the investor in a bear floater would be bearish on bond prices. Like an inverse floater, the bear floater can be issued as a stand-alone security with its peculiar payoff characteristics. Alternatively, the issuer may conceive the bear floater in conjunction with a derivatives position that gives the issuer a more conventional interest rate exposure.

A bear floater is constructed with a high floating rate, less a fixed rate. Assume that the yield curve today is flat at 6 percent. In this environment, a bear floater might have an interest rate equal to

$$2 \times \text{one-year LIBOR} - 6\%$$

With a flat yield curve at 6 percent, the initial yield on this bear floater would be 6 percent. This is the same rate that would prevail on a straight FRN, which would yield 6 percent in this environment.

The special feature of a bear floater comes into play as interest rates rise. A straight FRN will have its yield rise in a 1 : 1 ratio with market rates. By contrast, the interest rate on the bear floater specified above would have to rise twice as fast as market rates. For example, if one-year LIBOR rises to 9 percent, the yield on the bear floater would rise to 12 percent. If one-year LIBOR fell below 3 percent, the computed rate on the note would be negative. However, a bear floater will typically specify that the interest rate paid on the note cannot be less than zero.

The issuer of the bear floater may simply issue the security and bear the interest rate exposure associated with rising rates. More typically, the bear floater will be issued in conjunction with a derivatives position as a structured finance transaction. The first time line of Figure 22.8 shows the cash flows for this bear floater assuming a five-year maturity with annual payments and a principal amount of $50 million. The issuer's annual payment is as follows:

$$(2 \times \text{one-year LIBOR} - 6\%) \times \$50,000,000$$

It is convenient to think of the issuer's payment as paying $2 \times \text{LIBOR}$ and receiving 6 percent each year.

If the issuer combines the bear floater with a plain vanilla interest rate swap, the issuer can choose the ultimate form of its financial obligation. The second time line of Figure 22.8 shows the cash flows for a pay-fixed plain vanilla interest rate swap. The swap has a notional principal

Figure 22.8 Cash flows for issuance and transformation of a bear floater to an FRN

Cash flows on a bear floater for the issuer

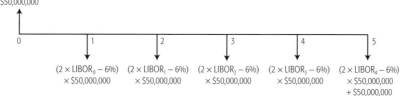

Cash flows on a pay-fixed swap

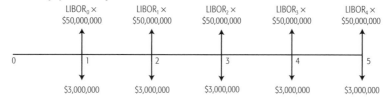

Net cash flows for the issuer

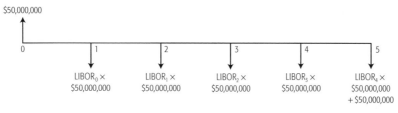

of \$50 million, a fixed rate of 6 percent, a five-year tenor, and annual payments. Combining this swap with the bear floater gives the issuer an annual interest rate cash flow equal to

$$[-(2 \times \text{one-year LIBOR} - 6\%) + (\text{one-year LIBOR} - 6\%)] \times \$50,000,000$$

This complicated cash flow simplifies to

$$-\text{one-year LIBOR} \times \$50,000,000$$

so the issuer's exposure is simply that of a standard FRN. The third time line of Figure 22.8 shows the resulting cash flows for the issuer from issuing the bear floater and entering a pay-fixed swap as just described. Therefore, we may analyze the issuance of a bear floater as follows:

Decomposition of issuing bear floater:

$$\text{issuing bear floater} + \text{pay-fixed swap} = \text{issuing FRN} \qquad (22.9)$$

This analysis also shows how an issuer can create a synthetic bear floater, if the issuer wants to have the exposure inherent in issuing a bear floater:

Synthesizing issuance of bear floater:

issuing FRN − pay-fixed swap = issuing bear floater

or

issuing FRN + receive-fixed swap = issuing bear floater   (22.10)

As we have just seen, the issuer of a bear floater can easily arrange for its ultimate exposure to be simply the issuance of a straight FRN. Similarly, the issuer of a bear floater can use swaps to convert its exposure to that of a fixed-rate bond. The first time line in Figure 22.9 shows the cash flows on the bear floater and is identical to the first time line of Figure 22.8. The issuer can use a pay-fixed swap with a notional principal twice that of the bear floater to convert its total exposure to that of a fixed-rate bond. In our example, the issuer would enter a pay-fixed swap with a notional principal of $100 million, a five-year tenor, annual payments based on one-year LIBOR, and a fixed rate of 6 percent. The cash flows for this pay-fixed swap appear in the second time line of Figure 22.9. These are just twice as large as the cash flows for the pay-fixed swap in Figure 22.8. The last time line shows the result of combining the issuance of the bear floater with a "double-sized" pay-fixed swap. The resulting cash flows in the third time line are just the cash flows from the issuance of a fixed-rate bond. Therefore, we have a second potential decomposition of the bear floater issuance:

Figure 22.9   Alternative cash flows for issuance and transformation of a bear floater to an FRN

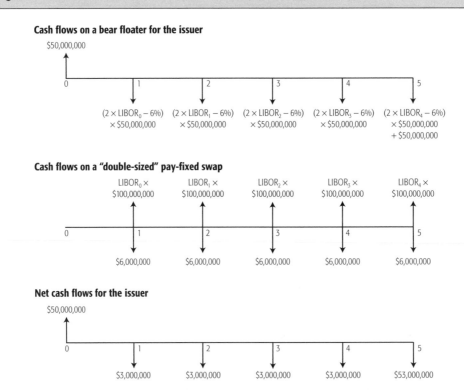

Decomposition of issuing bear floater:

issuing bear floater + "double-sized" pay-fixed swap = issuing fixed-rate note   (22.11)

This analysis also shows how an issuer can create a synthetic bear floater, starting with the issuance of a fixed-rate note:

Synthesizing issuance of bear floater:

issuing fixed-rate note – "double-sized" pay-fixed swap = issuing bear floater

or

issuing fixed-rate note + "double-sized" receive-fixed swap   (22.12)
= issuing bear floater

What the issuer may synthesize, the investor may also construct. In the same market environment we have been considering, assume that no bear floaters are available and an investor desires the interest rate exposure inherent in the bear floater. Based on our preceding analysis of the bear floater from the point of view of the issuer, we can see how the investor can create a synthetic bear floater. Equation 22.10 showed how the issuer can synthesize a bear floater from an FRN and a receive-fixed swap. The investor can create the same synthetic security, starting with the purchase of an FRN, by taking a position that is the opposite of that shown in Equation 22.10:

Synthesizing purchase of bear floater:

purchase FRN + pay-fixed swap = purchase of bear floater   (22.13)

Alternatively, the investor can synthesize the purchase of a bear floater by starting with a fixed-rate bond:

purchase fixed-rate note + "double-sized" pay-fixed swap   (22.14)
= purchase of bear floater

As we noted at the outset of our discussion, the bear floater usually provides that the interest rate on the instrument cannot be less than zero. That is, the bear floater normally also includes an interest rate floor set to zero. The equivalencies in Equations 22.9–22.14 do not reflect this extra condition. As discussed in Chapter 19, an interest rate floor is an option granted to the purchaser of a debt obligation by the debtor, and has obvious value. In our example of the bear floater, the value of the implicit interest rate floor depends on the likelihood that the specified rate on the floater will reach zero, which equals the probability that LIBOR will fall to 3 percent during the life of the bond.

As we have seen in this discussion, the interest rate exposure of the bear floater issuer does not need to resemble the exposure inherent in the floater itself. By using swaps, the issuer can transform its interest rate exposure. The same principles apply, at least in theory, to the purchaser. The purchaser can obtain the exposure inherent in the purchase of a bear floater by purchasing ordinary debt instruments and combining them with swaps. However, the continuing large issuances of both inverse and bear floaters bear witness to the greater operational efficiency of some market participants in creating these financial structures.

The cross-index basis note

In a **cross-index basis note**, or **quanto note**, the investor receives a rate of interest that is based on a floating-rate index for a foreign short-term rate, but is paid in the investor's domestic currency. For example, a U.S. investor might buy a note with an interest rate based on European interest rates, but with all payments on the note being made in U.S. dollars. From the investor's point of view, the quanto note allows exposure to foreign interest rates without currency exposure. Also, the quanto note allows the investor to speculate on relative changes in the foreign and domestic yield curves. From the point of view of the issuer, the quanto note can offer investors attractive investment opportunities that might not be available elsewhere. Also, the issuer can issue a quanto note, but use swaps to transform its risk exposure to a perhaps more congenial form.

As an example, consider Figure 22.10, which shows yield curves for one-year LIBOR in both U.S. dollars and British pounds sterling.[7] Current rates are 5 percent in dollars and 8 percent in pounds. However, the U.S. yield curve is strongly upward sloping, while the British yield curve is even more strongly downward sloping.

In this environment, a firm might issue a quanto note that pays a floating rate equal to one-year British LIBOR plus or minus a spread, with a maturity of five years, annual payments, a principal of $30 million, and with all payments being made in U.S. dollars. The spread on British LIBOR would reflect the difference between the U.S. dollar and British pound term structures. From Figure 22.10, it seems clear that British yields are expected to be below U.S. yields for most of the five years, even though the initial yield on the British pound is higher. In this environment, the quanto note will have to pay British LIBOR plus a spread to attract dollar investments.

Given that the quanto note will pay British LIBOR plus a spread, the initial yield on the quanto will be more than 3 percent higher than the floating rate available on a straight U.S.

Figure 22.10   U.S. and British yield curves

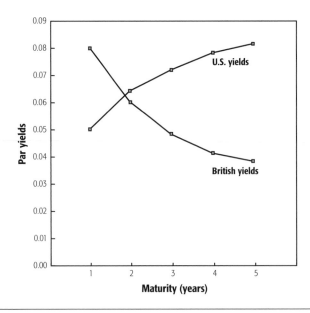

Figure 22.11 Issuing and hedging a quanto note

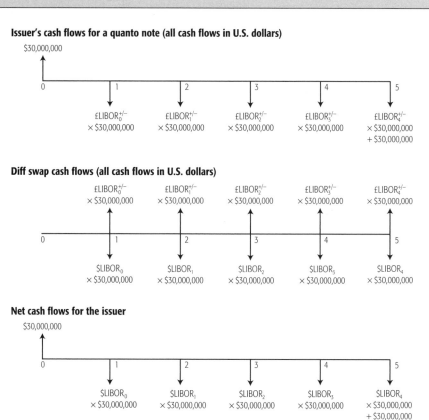

Issuer's cash flows for a quanto note (all cash flows in U.S. dollars)

Diff swap cash flows (all cash flows in U.S. dollars)

Net cash flows for the issuer

dollar FRN. However, the yield curves in Figure 22.10 suggest that this yield differential is expected to narrow quickly with British rates even becoming lower than U.S. rates. If the future interest rates correspond to the forward rates implied by the yield curves in Figure 22.10, the U.S. investor will soon receive less on the quanto note than a purely domestic U.S. FRN. Therefore, the investor in this quanto note has an implicit speculation that the interest rates will not converge as quickly or fully as the market seems to expect.

On the other side, the issuer of the quanto note has an implicit speculation that rates will narrow more quickly than the market expects. However, the issuer may wish to offset this risk by engaging in a swap. The first time line of Figure 22.11 shows the cash flows from issuing this quanto note. The principal is paid in dollars. The amount of each interest payment is determined by the level of British LIBOR, but the actual payment is made in U.S. dollars. As it stands, the issuer of the quanto note is exposed to interest rate risk in the United States and the United Kingdom.

As discussed in Chapter 20, a **rate-differential swap**, or **diff swap**, has payments tied to interest rate indexes in two different currencies, but all payments are in a single currency. For example, a participant in a diff swap might receive British LIBOR, plus or minus a spread, and pay U.S. dollar LIBOR, with all payments being made in U.S. dollars. The spread would reflect the differences in the yield curves for the two currencies.

The issuer of our example quanto note might find a diff swap an attractive hedging vehicle. The second time line of Figure 22.11 shows the cash flows on a diff swap in which the issuer receives British LIBOR plus or minus a spread and pays U.S. LIBOR. The spread in the diff swap and the quanto note are the same. The diff swap has a notional principal of $30 million, annual payments, and a tenor of five years. (The determination of the exact spread on the British pound interest rate requires more information on the exact shape of the two yield curves. Later in this chapter, we show how to price this quanto note and its accompanying diff swap.)

The third time line of Figure 22.11 shows the cash flows from combining the issuance of the quanto note plus a diff swap to receive payments based on British LIBOR and pay based on U.S. LIBOR. By combining the quanto note and the diff swap, the issuer has the net position of having issued a straight U.S. dollar FRN.

The Dispute Between Bankers Trust and Gibson Greetings

On April 19, 1994, Gibson Greetings, Inc., a manufacturer of seasonal cards, wrapping paper, and related products announced that it had taken a $16.7 million charge resulting from losses on two swap transactions with BT Securities Corporation, a subsidiary of Bankers Trust New York Corporation ("BT"). BT is now part of Deutsche Bank. The announcement stated that this loss was in addition to a $3 million charge announced earlier, related to the same swap transactions. A lawsuit filed by Gibson against BT was settled out of court in November 1994, with Gibson paying BT only $6.2 million out of $20.7 million owed under the terms of its swap agreements with BT. In addition to this private lawsuit, three different government regulatory actions resulted from the Gibson–BT dispute.

Although the Gibson–BT dispute revolved around two swap contracts, Gibson and BT had engaged in 27 previous transactions. The two contracts in dispute represented the cumulative position resulting from the earlier transactions. The relationship between Gibson and BT began innocently enough, with simple plain vanilla fixed-for-floating interest rate swaps. Over time, the transactions between Gibson and BT evolved to more complex, customized structures. The dispute centered around the duties of the two parties in determining the value of these complex structures. Gibson claimed that BT had breached the fiduciary duty it owed Gibson as its financial advisor by dispensing advice that advantaged BT at Gibson's expense. BT claimed that its relationship with Gibson was purely arm's length, without any fiduciary or advisory role. As we will see, characterizing the nature of the relationship between BT and Gibson was an important element of the dispute.

Gibson entered into its first interest rate swaps with BT on November 12, 1991. These plain vanilla interest rate swaps were, according to Gibson, intended to "reduce its interest costs" related to a $50 million fixed-rate (9.33 percent) borrowing completed in May 1991. Attracted to the low short-term rates at the time, Gibson transformed its fixed obligation into a floating obligation by entering into two fixed-for-floating interest rate swaps on this date, each with a notional amount of $30 million.

By transmuting its fixed interest rate expense into a floating-rate expense, the swaps allowed Gibson to offset a portion of its fixed interest expense on its borrowing during 1992 and 1993. In each of those years, Gibson would have received a net payment equal to 1.21 percent of $30 million from BT. Based on expectations about LIBOR at the initiation of the swap agreements, Gibson's overall interest rate expense during 1994–6 was expected to rise above its initial fixed-rate obligation. Of course, this is reasonable, since, when all the swap payments are taken together, the swaps initially had zero value. *Ex ante*, Gibson had only succeeded in shifting its anticipated interest expense from one period to another.

However, if future interest rates were to be below the rates initially expected to prevail, then Gibson would have profited from the swap; that is, Gibson would have received a value of fixed payments higher than the value of the floating payments made. Further, if future rates were to be low enough relative to expectations, then Gibson's interest rate expense could be lower during this period as well. Of course, achieving this reduction in interest rate expense was dependent on winning what was, in effect, a bet on the future direction of rates.

Gibson did not hold these swaps to term but, after amending the contracts in January 1992, terminated them on July 7, 1992, receiving a payment from BT of $260,000, which represented the value of the swaps at that time. This payment reflected the fact that Gibson had profited under its swaps from falling interest rates during the first half of 1992.

On October 1, 1992, Gibson entered into another swap with BT, called a "ratio swap." In this swap, the payment to Gibson from BT was to be as follows:

$$\text{net payment from BT} = 5.5\% - (\text{LIBOR}^2)/6.0\%$$

This swap increased Gibson's exposure to increases in the level of short-term interest rates. Under the new swap, the future net payments to Gibson would become negative more rapidly than under the original swaps, and the difference would become exponentially greater the greater the rate.

This swap was amended three times to shorten the agreement before being terminated on April 21, 1993, with BT making a payment to Gibson of $978,000. In one of the amendments, the termination date of the swap was shortened by a year in exchange for Gibson entering into another swap. Through March 4, 1994, Gibson entered into several additional swaps with BT. When interest rates spiked upward sharply beginning in February 1994, Gibson had two outstanding swaps with BT, and it was still exposed to interest rate increases. According to Gibson, between February 25 and March 3, 1994, the present value of Gibson's two outstanding swaps fell by $9.5 million, for a cumulative loss of $17.5 million. On March 4, Gibson rolled its existing swaps into two final swaps that became the subject of the company's suit.

Although the plain vanilla and ratio swap transactions described above were not at the center of the Gibson–BT dispute, it is important to understand the process by which these transactions became intertwined with more complex future transactions. It is this process of terminating a swap, or a portion of a swap (a so-called **tear-up agreement**), in consideration for entering into a new or amended swap agreement, that ultimately triggered the dispute. Of the 29 transactions between Gibson and BT, many involved the termination of one position in exchange for entering into another position. This process of rolling from one position to another (what some practitioners call **morphing**) requires agreement between the parties as to the terms that will equate the tear-up value of the existing swap (or swap portion) to the value of the new position (or amendment) received in exchange for the tear-up. The dispute between Gibson and BT centered around the duties of the two parties in determining the value of the positions involved in tear-ups and rollovers. Because of the complex nature of the customized deals, valuation of the deals relied on model prices since comparable market quotes were not observable, as would be the case with a less-complex, less-customized, plain vanilla transaction. Gibson, and the government, alleged that BT knew of Gibson's reliance upon information provided by BT to value Gibson's swap positions. In addition, Gibson, and the government, alleged that BT had misled Gibson about the value of Gibson's swap positions. Gibson alleged that BT had provided it with valuations that significantly understated the magnitude of Gibson's losses, leaving Gibson unaware of the actual extent of its losses from its swap transactions. Moreover, Gibson, and the government, alleged that an advisory relationship existed between BT and Gibson. Under this legal theory, BT owed Gibson a duty not to misrepresent valuation information. BT argued that their transactions with Gibson were strictly arm's length deals and that the master swap agreement did not establish any advisory or fiduciary relationship. BT argued that tear-up values they quoted were simply that–quotations at which BT stood ready to transact a tear-up.

BT was certainly aware of Gibson's reliance on BT's models. A taped conversation between a BT managing director and his supervisor includes the following passage: "From the very beginning, [Gibson] just, you know, really put themselves in our hands like 96 percent . . . And we have known that from day one . . . these guys have done some pretty wild stuff. And you know, they probably did not understand it quite as well as they should. I think that they have a pretty good understanding of it, but not perfect. And that's like perfect for us." The SEC alleged that on two occasions BT provided Gibson with valuations that differed by more that 50 percent from the value generated by BT's models and recorded on BT's books.

We can characterize the factual background to the dispute between Gibson and BT as follows:

• The swap transactions between Gibson and BT exposed Gibson to increases in short-term interest rates.

- Gibson and BT frequently amended existing swap positions or tore up existing swap positions in exchange for rolling into new swap positions.
- Market prices about the tear-up values and the value of new customized swap positions were not observable. Instead, valuation models were used and positions were "market to model."
- The dispute between Gibson and BT centered around the extent of Gibson's reliance on BT to determine the value of the positions involved in tear-ups and rollovers.

The Gibson–BT case has led to changes in the way swap agreements are structured. Swap contracts today explicitly detail the roles and responsibilities of swap counterparties. Also, swap dealers are careful not to offer advice unless an advisory relationship is acknowledged to exist.

Pricing flavored interest rate and currency swaps

To price a flavored interest rate swap, we apply the same technique used to price the plain vanilla interest rate swap: we find the swap fixed rate (SFR) that equates the present values of the cash flows from the pay-fixed and receive-fixed sides of the swap. The zero-coupon factors for the present value calculations are derived from the yield curve in effect when the swap is initiated. In using these discount rates, no assumption is made about the future course of interest rates. Instead, this pricing approach finds the swap terms that prevent arbitrage.

In Chapter 21, we found that the SFR on a plain vanilla swap was given by Equation 21.13, reproduced here as follows:

$$SFR = \left(\sum_{n=1}^{N} \frac{FRA_{(n-1) \times MON, n \times MON}}{Z_{0, n \times MON}} \right) \Big/ \left(\sum_{n=1}^{N} \frac{1}{Z_{0, n \times MON}} \right) \qquad (22.15)$$

For convenience, we repeat key definitions presented in Chapter 21:

$PART$ = the fraction of the year between swap payments
$FRA_{x,y}$ = the rate of interest on an FRA for a period beginning at time x and ending at time y; also $FRA_{0,t}$ indicates a spot rate from time = 0 to time = t
NP = the notional principal on the swap
$Z_{x,y}$ = the zero-coupon factor for an investment initiated at time x and extending until time y
$FR_{x,y}$ = the forward rate of interest for a period beginning at time x and extending until time y
N = the total number of payments
$FRF_{x,y}$ = the forward rate factor for a period beginning at time x and extending until time y
MON = the number of months between payments on the swap

We also note the following equivalencies:

$$FR_{x,y} = FRA_{x,y} = FRF_{x,y} - 1$$

$$FRF_{x,y} = \frac{Z_{0,y}}{Z_{0,x}}$$

In this section, we apply these general principles of swap pricing to four different flavored swaps: a forward interest rate swap, a seasonal swap, a diff swap, and a currency annuity swap. In each case, the pricing solution is to find the terms of the swap that make it arbitrage free. This means that the present values for each party must be equal, given the structure of interest rates and exchange rates that prevail when the swap is initiated. The principles illustrated for the swaps in this section provide a model for pricing any kind of flavored swap.

The forward swap

In Chapter 21, we saw that a forward swap could be replicated as a portfolio of four bonds, as shown in Figure 21.4. The forward swap would have to have the same price as the four-bond portfolio. It is also possible to price the forward swap directly, using the same approach that we applied to find the SFR for a plain vanilla interest rate swap. The pay-fixed forward swap synthetically duplicated by the four-bond portfolio in Figure 21.4 had a notional principal of $30 million and annual payments, was set to begin in three years, and had a tenor of five years. For that swap, the yield curve was flat at 8 percent. Therefore, the SFR for the forward swap also had to be 8 percent. We will now show how to price this kind of forward swap in a more typical yield curve environment.

As the following analysis shows, a forward swap is really just a plain vanilla interest rate swap with a deferred starting date. Because of this, the principles of plain vanilla pricing apply quite directly to the forward swap. Figure 22.12 shows the cash flows on this forward swap from the receive-fixed perspective. The actual LIBOR rates that will prevail are, of course, unknown from our perspective at time zero when the forward swap is initiated. However, the no-arbitrage rates for our contracting purposes are the forward rates from the yield curve that correspond to the various one-year LIBOR rates. Given the necessary yield curve information, our pricing problem is to find the *SFR* that makes the present values of the fixed and floating cash flows equal from the perspective of time zero.

If we look at the time line of Figure 22.12 from the vantage point of a potential counterparty at time 3, the cash flows on the forward swap have exactly the same form as the cash flows on a receive-fixed plain vanilla swap. Therefore, we can price the forward swap from time zero or time 3.

We begin by pricing this forward swap from the perspective of time zero. Table 22.7 presents the necessary information on the yield curve at the time the swap is to be initiated. The zero-coupon factors and forward rate factors have been computed from the par yields by bootstrapping, as discussed in Chapters 19 and 21. As Table 22.7 shows, the yield curve is humped, with the par yields initially rising and then falling. Figure 22.13 shows the humped par yield curve corresponding to the data in Table 22.7. The floating rates implied by the yield curve, and shown in Table 22.7, are as follows:

$LIBOR_3$	$FR_{3,4}$	0.091347
$LIBOR_4$	$FR_{4,5}$	0.086299
$LIBOR_5$	$FR_{5,6}$	0.071005
$LIBOR_6$	$FR_{6,7}$	0.066356
$LIBOR_7$	$FR_{7,8}$	0.042257

Figure 22.12 Cash flows for the forward swap (receive-fixed perspective)

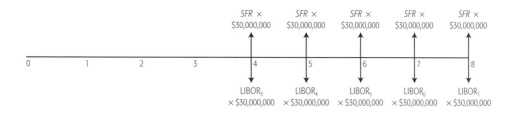

Table 22.7   Term structure information for pricing the forward swap

Maturity (years)	Par yield	Zero-coupon factor	Forward rate factor
1	0.0503	1.050300	1.050300
2	0.0635	1.131936	1.077726
3	0.0704	1.229247	1.085969
4	0.0750	1.341535	1.091347
5	0.0769	1.457308	1.086299
6	0.0761	1.560784	1.071005
7	0.0750	1.664352	1.066356
8	0.0718	1.734682	1.042257

Figure 22.13   The par yield curve for pricing the forward swap

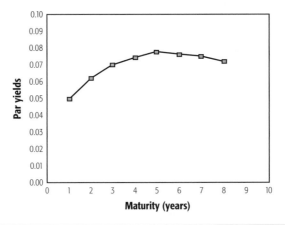

The fixed-rate payments will occur at times 4, 5, 6, 7, and 8, and will equal the *SFR* times the notional principal of $30 million.

Table 22.8 details the cash flows, zero-coupon factors, and present values for each payment. Consistent with Table 22.8, the present value of the floating-rate cash flows is given by the following:

$$PV_{FLOAT} = \frac{FR_{3,4} \times NP}{Z_{0,4}} + \frac{FR_{4,5} \times NP}{Z_{0,5}} + \frac{FR_{5,6} \times NP}{Z_{0,6}} + \frac{FR_{6,7} \times NP}{Z_{0,7}} + \frac{FR_{7,8} \times NP}{Z_{0,8}}$$

$$= \frac{0.091347 \times \$30,000,000}{1.341535} + \frac{0.086299 \times \$30,000,000}{1.457308} + \frac{0.071005 \times \$30,000,000}{1.560784}$$

$$+ \frac{0.066356 \times \$30,000,000}{1.664352} + \frac{0.042257 \times \$30,000,000}{1.734682}$$

$$= 2,042,742 + 1,776,541 + 1,364,793 + 1,196,076 + 730,797$$

$$= \$7,110,949$$

Table 22.8 Cash flows for forward swap, time-zero perspective

Date (year)	Floating-rate cash flow	Fixed-rate cash flow	Zero-coupon factor	Present value of floating-rate cash flow	Present value of fixed-rate cash flow
1	0	0	1.050300	0	0
2	0	0	1.131936	0	0
3	0	0	1.229247	0	0
4	0.091347 × $30,000,000	SFR × $30,000,000	1.341535	2,042,742	SFR × 22,362,443
5	0.086299 × $30,000,000	SFR × $30,000,000	1.457308	1,776,541	SFR × 20,585,902
6	0.071005 × $30,000,000	SFR × $30,000,000	1.560784	1,364,793	SFR × 19,221,109
7	0.066356 × $30,000,000	SFR × $30,000,000	1.664352	1,196,076	SFR × 18,025,033
8	0.042257 × $30,000,000	SFR × $30,000,000	1.734682	730,797	SFR × 17,294,236
				Total: 7,110,949	Total: SFR × 97,488,724

On the fixed-rate side, the present value of the fixed-rate flows is as follows:

$$PV_{FIXED} = \frac{SFR \times NP}{Z_{0,4}} + \frac{SFR \times NP}{Z_{0,5}} + \frac{SFR \times NP}{Z_{0,6}} + \frac{SFR \times NP}{Z_{0,7}} + \frac{SFR \times NP}{Z_{0,8}}$$

$$= \frac{SFR \times \$30,000,000}{1.341535} + \frac{SFR \times \$30,000,000}{1.457308} + \frac{SFR \times \$30,000,000}{1.560784}$$

$$+ \frac{SFR \times \$30,000,000}{1.664352} + \frac{SFR \times \$30,000,000}{1.734682}$$

$$= SFR \times 22,362,443 + SFR \times 20,585,902 + SFR \times 19,221,109$$

$$+ SFR \times 18,025,033 + SFR \times 17,294,236$$

$$= SFR \times 97,488,724$$

We complete the calculation of the SFR by equating the present value of the cash flows on the floating-rate and fixed-rate sides and solving for the SFR:

$$PV_{FLOAT} = PV_{FIXED}$$
$$7,110,949 = SFR \times 97,488,724$$
$$SFR = 0.072941$$

We now show that the forward swap can also be priced from the standpoint of the time at which the comparable plain vanilla swap would be initiated. In general, this is one period before the first cash flow; for our example, that would be at time 3. The cash flows are not affected by this change in perspective. The discounting does change, however, because we are discounting to time 3 instead of to time zero. The zero-coupon factors for each cash flow are obtained from the forward rate factors or the zero-coupon factors in Table 22.7, as follows:

$$Z_{3,4} = Z_{0,4}/Z_{0,3} = 1.341535/1.229247 = 1.091347$$
$$Z_{3,5} = Z_{0,5}/Z_{0,3} = 1.457308/1.229247 = 1.185529$$
$$Z_{3,6} = Z_{0,6}/Z_{0,3} = 1.560784/1.229247 = 1.269707$$
$$Z_{3,7} = Z_{0,7}/Z_{0,3} = 1.664352/1.229247 = 1.353961$$
$$Z_{3,8} = Z_{0,8}/Z_{0,3} = 1.734682/1.229247 = 1.411174$$

$$PV_{FLOAT} = \frac{FR_{3,4} \times NP}{Z_{3,4}} + \frac{FR_{4,5} \times NP}{Z_{3,5}} + \frac{FR_{5,6} \times NP}{Z_{3,6}} + \frac{FR_{6,7} \times NP}{Z_{3,7}} + \frac{FR_{7,8} \times NP}{Z_{3,8}}$$

$$= \frac{0.091347 \times \$30,000,000}{1.091347} + \frac{0.086299 \times \$30,000,000}{1.185529} + \frac{0.071005 \times \$30,000,000}{1.269707}$$

$$+ \frac{0.066356 \times \$30,000,000}{1.353961} + \frac{0.042257 \times \$30,000,000}{1.411174}$$

$$= 2,511,035 + 2,183,810 + 1,677,671 + 1,470,264 + 898,337$$

$$= \$8,741,116$$

Also, from the perspective of time 3, the present value of the fixed-side cash flows is as follows:

$$PV_{FIXED} = \frac{SFR \times NP}{Z_{3,4}} + \frac{SFR \times NP}{Z_{3,5}} + \frac{SFR \times NP}{Z_{3,6}} + \frac{SFR \times NP}{Z_{3,7}} + \frac{SFR \times NP}{Z_{3,8}}$$

$$= \frac{SFR \times \$30,000,000}{1.091347} + \frac{SFR \times \$30,000,000}{1.185529} + \frac{SFR \times \$30,000,000}{1.269707}$$

$$+ \frac{SFR \times \$30,000,000}{1.353961} + \frac{SFR \times \$30,000,000}{1.411174}$$

$$= SFR \times 27,488,965 + SFR \times 25,305,159 + SFR \times 23,627,498$$

$$+ SFR \times 22,157,211 + SFR \times 21,258,895$$

$$= SFR \times 119,837,728$$

We complete the solution by equating the present values of the fixed and floating sides of the swap and solving for the SFR:

$$PV_{FLOAT} = PV_{FIXED}$$
$$8,741,116 = SFR \times 119,837,728$$
$$SFR = 0.072941$$

This is the identical solution that we reached from the time-zero perspective. In sum, a forward swap can be priced by finding the SFR that equates the present value of the cash flows on the two sides of the swap from the time of contracting (time zero) or one period before the first cash flow.

The seasonal swap

In Chapter 21, we saw that a seasonal swap could be synthesized by a six-bond portfolio. The resulting seasonal swap explored in Chapter 21 had quarterly payments in February, May, August, and November. The notional principal was $10 million for payments in February, May, and August, and $30 million for the November payment. The swap had a tenor of seven years. Pricing this swap uses the same technology that we have explored for plain vanilla swaps; that is, we need to find the SFR that equates the present value of the floating-rate and fixed-rate cash flows. However, we must take account of the varying notional principal. We can allow the notional principal to vary by including a different potential notional principal in each element of Equation 22.15. Let NP_n be the notional principal for the nth time period. In that case, the formula for the SFR on a seasonal swap is as follows:

Figure 22.14   The term structure for the seasonal swap

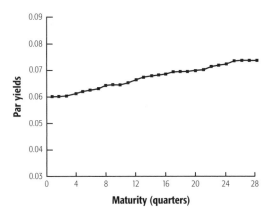

$$SFR = \left(\sum_{n=1}^{N} \frac{NP_n \times FRA_{(n-1) \times MON, n \times MON}}{Z_{0,n \times MON}} \right) \Bigg/ \left(\sum_{n=1}^{N} \frac{NP_n}{Z_{0,n \times MON}} \right) \tag{22.16}$$

The only difference between Equation 22.15, for the *SFR* of a plain vanilla swap, and Equation 22.16, for the *SFR* on a seasonal swap, is the inclusion of a varying notional principal in Equation 22.16. Therefore, Equation 22.15 is a special case of Equation 22.16 that arises when the notional principal is constant in all periods. We can use Equation 22.16 to price our seasonal swap. Figure 22.14 shows the gently rising term structure over the 28 quarters that comprise the tenor of the seasonal swap. The yields in Figure 22.14 are par yields. As our swap has quarterly payments, we must take account of quarterly compounding.

Table 22.9 presents information on the term structure environment and the cash flows on this seasonal swap. The second column shows the annualized par yields, while the third column shows the notional principal for each of the 28 quarterly periods covered by the swap. Columns 4–6 show the quarterly par yields, the zero-coupon factor for each quarter, and the forward rate factor for each quarter. The quarterly par yield is just the annualized par yield divided by four. The zero-coupon factors were found by the bootstrapping method, and the forward rate factors were computed from the zero-coupon factors.

To complete the calculation of the *SFR* on this swap, we need to find the present value of the floating-rate cash flows (the numerator of Equation 22.16) and the present value of the notional principals (the denominator of Equation 22.16). In both the numerator and denominator of Equation 22.16, there will be one term corresponding to each period of the swap. As an example, we show how the numerator and denominator elements for the 15th period were found. The notional principal for period 15 is $10 million. The forward rate for this period is 0.017726, and the zero-coupon factor is 1.288071. Therefore, the corresponding element from the present value of the floating cash flow in the numerator is

$$\frac{\$10,000,000 \times 0.017726}{1.288071} = \$137,617$$

This value appears along with the 27 other present values in the seventh column of Table 22.9.

Table 22.9   Term structure and cash flow data for the seasonal swap

Quarter	Par yield	Notional principal	Quarterly par yield	Zero-coupon factor	Forward rate factor	Present value of floating payments	Value of NP_t/Z_t
1	0.0600	$10,000,000	0.015000	1.015000	1.015000	$147,783	$9,852,217
2	0.0601	10,000,000	0.015025	1.030276	1.015050	146,077	9,706,137
3	0.0605	10,000,000	0.015125	1.046070	1.015330	146,549	9,559,590
4	0.0611	30,000,000	0.015275	1.062534	1.015739	444,381	28,234,391
5	0.0619	10,000,000	0.015475	1.079861	1.016307	151,010	9,260,451
6	0.0626	10,000,000	0.015650	1.097752	1.016568	150,927	9,109,526
7	0.0631	10,000,000	0.015775	1.115940	1.016569	148,476	8,961,055
8	0.0641	30,000,000	0.016025	1.135911	1.017895	472,616	26,410,520
9	0.0644	10,000,000	0.016100	1.154933	1.016747	145,004	8,658,511
10	0.0645	10,000,000	0.016125	1.173839	1.016370	139,457	8,519,056
11	0.0653	10,000,000	0.016325	1.195580	1.018521	154,912	8,364,141
12	0.0659	30,000,000	0.016475	1.217465	1.018305	451,060	24,641,365
13	0.0668	10,000,000	0.016700	1.241484	1.019729	158,915	8,054,876
14	0.0675	10,000,000	0.016875	1.265636	1.019455	153,717	7,901,166
15	0.0677	10,000,000	0.016925	1.288071	1.017726	137,617	7,763,547
16	0.0686	30,000,000	0.017150	1.315198	1.021060	480,384	22,810,254
17	0.0693	10,000,000	0.017325	1.342301	1.020608	153,527	7,449,894
18	0.0694	10,000,000	0.017350	1.366265	1.017853	130,670	7,319,224
19	0.0695	10,000,000	0.017375	1.390738	1.017912	128,795	7,190,427
20	0.0697	30,000,000	0.017425	1.416564	1.018570	393,276	21,178,005
21	0.0702	10,000,000	0.017550	1.445745	1.020600	142,487	6,916,849
22	0.0712	10,000,000	0.017800	1.480883	1.024304	164,118	6,752,728
23	0.0714	10,000,000	0.017850	1.509355	1.019227	127,386	6,625,347
24	0.0722	30,000,000	0.018050	1.545419	1.023893	463,816	19,412,211
25	0.0731	10,000,000	0.018275	1.584434	1.025245	159,331	6,311,402
26	0.0732	10,000,000	0.018300	1.614720	1.019115	118,380	6,193,024
27	0.0733	10,000,000	0.018325	1.645692	1.019181	116,553	6,076,471
28	0.0736	30,000,000	0.018400	1.680413	1.021098	376,657	17,852,754
						Total: $6,103,881	Total: $327,085,139

The present value of the 15th notional principal is as follows:

$$\frac{\$10,000,000}{1.288071} = \$7,763,547$$

This element appears in the last column of Table 22.9.

The sum of the present value of all of the floating payments is shown at the bottom of column 7 in the table, and equals $6,103,881. This is the value of the numerator of Equation 22.16 as applied to our seasonal swap. The sum of the present value of all of the notional principals appears at the bottom of column 8 and equals $327,085,139. This is the value of the denominator of Equation 22.16.

Given this information, the swap fixed rate on a quarterly basis is as follows:

$$SFR = \frac{\$6,103,881}{\$327,085,139} = 0.01866144$$

In annualized terms, the $SFR = 0.074646 = 4 \times 0.01866144$.

The rate-differential (diff) swap

Earlier in this chapter, we explored the issuance of a quanto note and saw how it could be hedged with a diff swap. In that discussion, we saw that the quanto note would have to carry an interest rate equal to British LIBOR plus some undetermined yield spread. The diff swap used as a hedging vehicle had payments that were equal to British LIBOR plus the yield spread versus U.S. dollar LIBOR flat. In this section, we show how to find the yield spread given the interest rate environment depicted in Figure 22.10. Table 22.10 presents the term structure information for this environment, along with the zero-coupon and forward rate factors.

We begin by pricing the quanto note, but—as we will see—pricing the quanto note gives us our swap pricing solution as well. We want to find the fair price for the quanto note given the term structure environment. As shown in the first time line of Figure 22.11, the cash flows for the issuer consist of an inflow of $30 million at time zero, followed by five annual payments of British LIBOR plus a spread, with the payment in dollars. In addition, the issuer must repay the $30 million principal at year 5. Because the quanto note is a floating note, it is issued at par, so the cash flows in years 1–5 must have a total present value of $30 million at the time of issuance. The only unknown in this situation is the spread on British LIBOR. Therefore, our problem is to find the spread ($SPRD$) that satisfies the following equation:

$$\$30,000,000 = \sum_{t=1}^{5} \frac{(\pounds LIBOR_t + SPRD) \times \$30,000,000}{Z_{0,t}} + \frac{\$30,000,000}{Z_{0,5}}$$

Solving for $SPRD$ gives a value of 0.041527. Therefore, the quanto note should pay £LIBOR + 415.27 basis points to be fairly priced.

We now turn to pricing the diff swap. As with all swap pricing, the key is to find the terms that equate the present values of the two sides of the swap, consistent with the prevailing term structure. In this diff swap, one party will pay British LIBOR plus a spread, while the other

Table 22.10 Interest rate data for rate-differential (diff) swap (for annual coupon bonds)

Maturity (years)	U.S. dollar			British pound			
	Par yield	Future value factor	One-year forward rate factor	Par yield	Future value factor	One-year forward rate factor	Forward value of £1
1	0.0500	1.050000	1.050000	0.0800	1.080000	1.080000	1.555556
2	0.0650	1.135279	1.081218	0.0600	1.122353	1.039216	1.618427
3	0.0720	1.235012	1.087849	0.0480	1.148130	1.022967	1.721076
4	0.0780	1.357937	1.099533	0.0420	1.174603	1.023057	1.849731
5	0.0820	1.496762	1.102232	0.0390	1.205378	1.026200	1.986779

will pay U.S. LIBOR, with all the payments on both sides of the swap being denominated in dollars. As the second time line in Figure 22.11 indicates, the present values of the cash flows based on British LIBOR and U.S. LIBOR are as follows:

$$PV_{£LIBOR} = \sum_{t=1}^{5} \frac{(£LIBOR_t + SPRD) \times \$30,000,000}{Z_{0,t}}$$

$$PV_{\$LIBOR} = \sum_{t=1}^{5} \frac{\$LIBOR_t \times \$30,000,000}{Z_{0,t}}$$

The pricing solution is to find the value of $SPRD$ that makes these two present values equal:

$$\sum_{t=1}^{5} \frac{(£LIBOR_t + SPRD) \times \$30,000,000}{Z_{0,t}} = \sum_{t=1}^{5} \frac{\$LIBOR_t \times \$30,000,000}{Z_{0,t}}$$

Solving for $SPRD$ gives the following:

$$SPRD = \left(\sum_{t=1}^{5} \frac{\$LIBOR_t}{Z_{0,t}} - \sum_{t=1}^{5} \frac{£LIBOR_t}{Z_{0,t}} \right) \bigg/ \left(\sum_{t=1}^{5} \frac{1}{Z_{0,t}} \right)$$

$$= \frac{0.331891 - 0.163815}{4.047451} \tag{22.17}$$

$$= 0.041527$$

Equation 22.17 shows that the appropriate spread of the diff swaps is 415.27 basis points, which is the same as the spread on the quanto note. Equation 22.17 also provides a general equation for the appropriate spread on a diff swap.

The currency annuity swap

A currency annuity swap is similar to a plain vanilla currency swap without the exchange of principal at the initiation or the termination of the swap. It is also known as a **currency basis swap**. For example, one party might make a sequence of payments based on British LIBOR while the other makes a sequence of payments based on U.S. LIBOR. As we will see, the currency annuity swap generally requires one party to pay an additional spread to the other or to make an up-front payment at the time of the swap. Variations of this structure can be created by allowing one, or both, parties to pay at a fixed rate. In pricing these swaps, the key is to specify a spread or up-front payment that makes the present value of the cash flows incurred by each party equal.

As an example, we consider a swap of British LIBOR versus U.S. LIBOR made in the context of the interest rate environment of Figure 22.10 and Table 22.10, which we have already explored for the diff swap. The spot exchange rate at time zero is £1 = $1.60, and the corresponding forward exchange rates are shown in the final column of Table 22.10. The notional principal is £50 million, equivalent to $80 million. The specific terms of the swap require one party to pay a floating rate equal to one-year British LIBOR on a notional principal of £50 million for five years, plus or minus a spread. Unlike the diff swap, these payments will be made in British pounds. The other party will pay U.S. LIBOR on a notional principal of $80 million.

The time line in Figure 22.15 shows the cash flows on this swap from the point of view of the dollar payer. For the dollar payer, the present value of the outflows is as follows:

Figure 22.15 Cash flows for the currency annuity swap

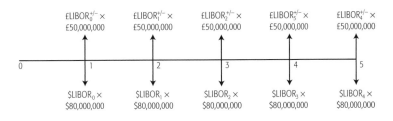

$$PV_{OUTFLOWS} = \$80,000,000 \times \sum_{t=1}^{5} \frac{\$LIBOR_t}{Z_{0,t}} = \$80,000,000 \times 0.331891 = \$26,551,280$$

Recall that $_{£,\$}FX_{0,t}$ indicates the dollar value of a forward contract for £1 initiated at time zero for payment at time t. Then, also from the perspective of the dollar payer, the U.S. dollar value of the British pound inflows is as follows:

$$PV_{INFLOWS} = £50,000,000 \times \sum_{t=1}^{5} \frac{(£LIBOR_t + SPRD) \times {_{£,\$}FX_{0,t}}}{Z_{0,t}}$$

$$= £50,000,000 \times \sum_{t=1}^{5} \frac{£LIBOR_t \times {_{£,\$}FX_{0,t}}}{Z_{0,t}} + £50,000,000 \times SPRD \times \sum_{t=1}^{5} \frac{{_{£,\$}FX_{0,t}}}{Z_{0,t}}$$

$$= £50,000,000 \times 0.272614 + £50,000,000 \times SPRD \times 6.990144$$

$$= \$13,630,700 + \$349,507,200 \times SPRD$$

Now equating the values of the inflows and outflows from the point of view of the dollar payer, we have the following:

$$PV_{INFLOWS} = PV_{OUTFLOWS}$$
$$\$13,630,700 + \$349,507,200 \times SPRD = \$26,551,280$$
$$SPRD = 0.036968$$

The payer of British pounds should pay British LIBOR plus 3.6968 percent versus U.S. LIBOR flat.

Alternatively, the swap could be structured such that the five annual payments are British LIBOR flat versus U.S. LIBOR flat. In this case, the payer of pounds would have to make a payment to the dollar payer that equals the present value of the spread payments:

$$PV_{SPRD} = SPRD \times £50,000,000 \sum_{t=1}^{5} \frac{{_{£,\$}FX_{0,t}}}{Z_{0,t}}$$

$$= 0.036968 \times £50,000,000 \times 6.990144$$

$$= \$12,920,580$$

Summary

In this section, we have explored the pricing of flavored interest rate and currency swaps. Specifically, we have priced a forward interest rate swap, a seasonal swap, a diff swap, and a currency annuity swap. In every instance, the general strategy was the same. The present value of the cash flows for both counterparties must be the same, and these cash flows must be consistent with the relevant term structure or structures that prevail when the swap is initiated. These general principles apply to the pricing of all swaps, and the illustrations of this section provide a guide to implementing those principles.

Equity swap pricing and applications

In this section, we consider the pricing of equity swaps and some of their potential applications. To price an equity swap, we follow our familiar pricing strategy. We find the terms of the swap that prevent arbitrage and that are consistent with the existing term structure information. In an equity swap, however, we need to attend to the term structure of equity prices.

In Chapter 7, we saw that the no-arbitrage price of a stock index futures contract is given by Equation 7.5, reproduced here as follows:

$$F_{0,t} = S_0(1 + C) - \sum_{i=1}^{N} D_i(1 + r_i) \tag{22.18}$$

where $F_{0,t}$ is the stock index futures price at $t = 0$ for a futures contract that expires at time t; S_0 is the value of the stocks underlying the stock index at $t = 0$; C is the percentage cost of carrying the stocks from $t = 0$ to the expiration at time t; D_i is the ith dividend; and r_i is the interest earned on carrying the ith dividend from its time of receipt until the futures expiration at time t. This equation does not consider the effects of daily settlement, so it pertains to forward contracts on the underlying stock index as well as the futures. If we assume that the index of Equation 22.18 pays a dividend that is some fraction, δ, of the value of the index, Equation 22.18 simplifies to the following:

$$F_{0,t} = S_0(1 + C - \delta) \tag{22.19}$$

where δ is the dividend yield on the index for the period from 0 to t.

In this context, consider the market information for stock index forward contracts and interest rates presented in Table 22.11. The current value of the stock index is 1,107.10. The data in the table pertain to the next four quarters. Values of the stock index extend from the present value of 1,107.10 to 1,170.00 one year from now. The stocks in the index are estimated to pay dividends that will give a dividend yield of 0.96 percent of the value of the index in each of the first three quarters. The dividend yield for the fourth quarter is 1.02 percent. The implied cost of carry is computed from Equation 22.19 for each quarter. Table 22.11 also gives information on interest rates. The yield curve is modestly upward sloping from 6.12 percent for maturities of one quarter to 6.29 percent for a maturity of one year. The table also shows the zero-coupon and forward-rate factors commensurate with these par rates. The zero-coupon factors were found by bootstrapping.

In a typical equity swap, one party pays a floating rate based on the equity index, while the counterparty pays an interest rate that may be either floating or fixed. We show how to price each kind of equity swap.

Table 22.11 Equity index and interest rate data

Quarter	Stock index forward price	Estimated quarterly dividend yield	Implied cost of carry of stock index	Annualized par yield	Par yield (quarterly)	Zero-coupon factor	Forward rate factors
1	1,123.0000	0.0096	0.023962	0.0612	0.015300	1.015300	1.015300
2	1,140.5000	0.0096	0.025183	0.0618	0.015450	1.031141	1.015602
3	1,156.2000	0.0096	0.023366	0.0623	0.015575	1.047465	1.015831
4	1,170.0000	0.0102	0.022136	0.0629	0.015725	1.064423	1.016190

An equity swap with a fixed interest payment

As an example of an equity swap with a fixed interest payment, consider a swap with a notional principal of \$10,000 times the spot value of the equity index, 1,107.10, with quarterly payments and a tenor of one year. The equity party pays the quarterly return on the index, while the party paying an interest rate pays a fixed rate of interest. To price this swap, we note that the terms are analogous to those of a plain vanilla interest rate swap, except that the floating payments are determined from the term structure of equity prices instead of the term structure of interest rates. We find the solution to the pricing problem by equating the present value of the floating flows from the equity side with the fixed interest payment promised by the debt side of the swap.

Letting C_t be the cost of carry for period t, the present value of the cash flows for the equity payer in a swap with T periods is as follows:

$$PV_{EQUITY} = NP \times \sum_{t=1}^{T} \frac{C_t}{Z_{0,t}} \qquad (22.20)$$

The present value of the cash flows for the debt side of the swap with fixed interest payments is as follows:

$$PV_{FIXED\ DEBT} = NP \times SFR \sum_{t=1}^{T} \frac{1}{Z_{0,t}} \qquad (22.21)$$

Equating the present values of the debt and equity sides and solving for SFR gives the following:

$$SFR = \left(\sum_{t=1}^{T} \frac{C_t}{Z_{0,t}} \right) \Big/ \left(\sum_{t=1}^{T} \frac{1}{Z_{0,t}} \right) \qquad (22.22)$$

Equation 22.22 has the same form as Equation 21.13, the equation for the SFR in a plain vanilla swap. The only difference is that the cost of carry replaces the forward rate of interest in the numerator.

Completing the solution for our sample equity swap, the SFR, based on Equation 22.22, is as follows:

$$SFR = \frac{\left(\dfrac{0.023962}{1.015300} + \dfrac{0.025183}{1.031141} + \dfrac{0.023366}{1.047465} + \dfrac{0.022136}{1.064423} \right)}{\left(\dfrac{1}{1.015300} + \dfrac{1}{1.031141} + \dfrac{1}{1.047465} + \dfrac{1}{1.064423} \right)}$$

$$= \frac{0.091127}{3.848892} = 0.023676$$

This is the quarterly fixed rate, so the annualized *SFR* is 0.094704 = 430.023676. The fixed-side quarterly payment will be the notional principal of $10,000 times the spot index of 1,107.10 times the quarterly SFR:

$$\$10,000 \times 1,107.10 \times 0.023676 = \$262,117$$

An equity swap with a floating interest payment

A second typical kind of equity swap involves floating payments on the equity side against a floating rate of interest. The equity-side payments equal the return on the equity index, as in our previous example. The debt-side payments would be set equal to a floating interest rate index plus or minus a spread. The pricing principle remains the same: the present value of the equity and debt payments must be equal and must be consistent with the term structure of equity rates and interest rates. The floating-side debt payments will have a present value equal to the following:

$$PV_{FLOATING\ DEBT} = NP \times \sum_{t=1}^{T} \frac{FRA_{t-1,t} + SPRD}{Z_{0,t}} \qquad (22.23)$$

where *SPRD* is the spread to be paid in addition to (or subtraction from) the forward rate for the period ($FRA_{t-1,t}$). The equity-side payments are the same as before, with the total present value as given by Equation 22.20. The pricing problem is to find the value of *SPRD* that equates the present value of the equity payments (Equation 22.20) with the floating interest payments (Equation 22.23):

$$PV_{EQUITY} = PV_{FLOATING\ DEBT}$$

$$NP \times \sum_{t=1}^{T} \frac{C_t}{Z_{0,t}} = NP \times \sum_{t=1}^{T} \frac{FRA_{t-1,t} + SPRD}{Z_{0,t}}$$

$$NP \times \sum_{t=1}^{T} \frac{C_t}{Z_{0,t}} = NP \times \sum_{t=1}^{T} \frac{FRA_{t-1,t}}{Z_{0,t}} + NP \times SPRD \times \sum_{t=1}^{T} \frac{1}{Z_{0,t}}$$

Solving for *SPRD* gives the interest rate differential that the payer of the floating interest rate must pay in addition to the forward rate of interest:

$$SPRD = \left(\sum_{t=1}^{T} \frac{C_t}{Z_{0,t}} - \sum_{t=1}^{T} \frac{FRA_{t-1,t}}{Z_{0,t}} \right) \Big/ \left(\sum_{t=1}^{T} \frac{1}{Z_{0,t}} \right) \qquad (22.24)$$

Using the data of Table 22.11, consider an equity swap in which the floating payer pays LIBOR plus a spread against the return on the index. The swap has quarterly payments, a tenor of one year, and a notional principal equal to $25,000 times the spot index of 1,107.10. Based on the values in Table 22.11, we have the following:

$$\sum_{t=1}^{T} \frac{C_t}{Z_{0,t}} = 0.091127$$

$$\sum_{t=1}^{T} \frac{FRA_{t-1,t}}{Z_{0,t}} = 0.060524$$

$$\sum_{t=1}^{T} \frac{1}{Z_{0,t}} = 3.848892$$

Therefore, the floating interest rate payer should agree to pay LIBOR plus a spread equal to the following:

$$SPRD = \left(\sum_{t=1}^{T} \frac{C_t}{Z_{0,t}} - \sum_{t=1}^{T} \frac{FRA_{t-1,t}}{Z_{0,t}} \right) \Big/ \left(\sum_{t=1}^{T} \frac{1}{Z_{0,t}} \right)$$

$$= \frac{0.091127 - 0.060524}{3.848892} = 0.07951$$

The spread is, therefore, 79.51 basis points per quarter. Stated in annualized terms, the arbitrage-free floating interest rate should be LIBOR + 3.1804 percent (LIBOR + 4 × 0.007951).

Hedging equity risk with an equity swap against a fixed interest rate

Consider an equity portfolio manager who is bearish for stocks over the near term, but who expects current values to prevail within a year. The portfolio consists of a well-diversified equity portfolio, similar to the stock index that we have been considering. The current value of the portfolio is $150 million. The manager decides to avoid the risk of short-term fluctuations by entering a swap to pay a floating rate on the equity side and to receive a fixed interest payment for each quarter over the next year. Table 22.11 gives information on the current equity and debt market environments.

The manager enters a swap to pay the return on the stock index times $135,000 each quarter in return for a fixed interest payment. With the index standing at 1,107.10, this gives a notional principal on the swap of $149,458,500, which is almost the same as the value of the portfolio. In return, the portfolio manager will receive a fixed interest rate of 2.3676 percent per quarter on the same notional principal, giving a quarterly inflow of $3,538,579. The portfolio itself is undisturbed, so the portfolio manager continues to receive the dividends. With the dividend forecasts in Table 22.11, the dividend receipts over the next year should be $5,850,000 = (0.0096 × 3 + 0.0102) × $150,000,000.

Table 22.12 shows two possible outcomes for this swap. In the upper panel, the portfolio manager's expectations are essentially realized. Starting from an index value of 1,107.10, the index first falls, and then returns to its original level by the end of the year at a value of 1,108.50. The table shows the four fixed interest receipts of $3,538,579 for a total interest inflow of $14,154,316. Because the manager is obligated to make payments based on the return

Table 22.12   Possible outcomes for the equity swap

Quarter	Interest received	Index values	Index return	Equity-side cash outflow	Net cash flow on swap
Manager's expectations realized					
0		1,107.10			
1	3,538,579	1,043.06	−0.057845	−8,645,400	12,183,979
2	3,538,579	1,056.03	0.012435	1,858,452	1,680,127
3	3,538,579	1,110.10	0.051201	7,652,454	−4,113,875
4	3,538,579	1,108.50	−0.001441	−215,416	3,753,995
	Total: $14,154,316			Total: $650,090	Total: $13,504,226
Alternative scenario					
0		1,107.10			
1	3,538,579	1,123.45	0.014768	2,207,250	1,331,329
2	3,538,579	1,157.09	0.029943	4,475,307	−936,728
3	3,538,579	1,215.02	0.050065	7,482,677	−3,944,098
4	3,538,579	1,232.00	0.013975	2,088,694	1,449,885
	Total: $14,154,316			Total: $16,253,929	Total: −$2,099,613

of the portfolio, the equity-side payments can be either positive or negative. The fifth column of Table 22.12 shows the equity-side cash outflows on the swap. A negative value in this column indicates that the equity side of the swap will *receive* a payment based on the portfolio return in addition to the interest payment for the debt side of the swap. For example, in the first quarter, the index falls from 1,107.10 to 1,043.06 for a return of 20.057845. The corresponding equity-side *outflow* is really an *inflow* in this circumstance of 8,645,400 = 0.057845 × $149,458,500. The final column of Table 22.12 shows the net cash flow from the swap in each period. In the upper panel, the total equity-side outflows were $650,090, and the swap generated a net cash inflow of $13,504,226.

Without the swap, the terminal value of the portfolio would be the result of the change in the value of the stocks plus the dividends received:

$$\text{terminal portfolio value without swap} = \$150,000,000 \times \frac{1,108.50}{1,107.10} + \$5,850,000$$

$$= \$156,039,685$$

The total return on the portfolio would have been 4.03 percent. With the swap, the terminal portfolio value equals the terminal portfolio value without the swap, plus the interest payments received, less the equity-side payments made. From the upper panel of Table 22.12,

$$\text{terminal portfolio value including swap} = \$156,039,685 + \$14,154,316 - \$650,090$$
$$= \$169,543,911$$

With the terminal portfolio value of $169,543,911, the total return on the portfolio was 13.03 percent, making the portfolio manager a hero.

Things might have gone differently, however. The bottom panel of Table 22.12 shows the results of an alternative scenario—the stock market enjoys a bull rally over the next year. In this scenario, the index rises from 1,107.10 to 1,232.00:

$$\text{terminal portfolio value without swap} = \$150,000,000 \times \frac{1,232.00}{1,107.10} + \$5,850,000$$

$$= \$172,772,591$$

This gives a total return on the portfolio of 15.18 percent.

In this alternative market environment, the swap would still yield the quarterly interest receipts of \$3,538,579, for a total of \$14,154,316. However, with the market rising every period, the equity side of the swap has substantial outflows each quarter. These outflows total \$16,253,929. Therefore, the portfolio value with the swap would be as follows:

$$\text{terminal portfolio value including swap} = \$172,772,591 + \$14,154,316 - \$16,253,929$$
$$= \$170,672,978$$

With the swap, the terminal value is \$2.1 million less than it would have been otherwise, and the return on the portfolio is only 13.78 percent instead of the 15.18 percent that the undisturbed portfolio would have enjoyed.

Swaption pricing and applications

This section extends and completes our analysis of swaptions by drawing on the capital we have developed previously in several different chapters of this text. First, we introduced swaptions in Chapter 20. A swaption is an option on a swap. A **receiver swaption** gives the owner the right to enter a swap at a specified future date as the receive-fixed party. A **payer swaption** gives the owner the right to enter a swap at a specified future date as the pay-fixed party. We continue to focus on European-style swaptions. Second, because a swaption is an option on a swap to begin at a future date, the swap underlying the swaption is a forward swap. Earlier in this chapter, we explored the pricing of forward swaps and saw that pricing a forward swap is very similar to pricing a plain vanilla swap. Finally, we draw on the discussion of the pricing of calls and puts on LIBOR from Chapter 19, where we saw that the Black model could be used to price these kinds of interest rate options. In this section, we show how to find the price of a swaption and explore the ways in which swaptions and swaps can be used together for financial risk management.

The exercise decision

When a swaption expires, the owner can exercise and enter a swap. If the owner of a payer swaption exercises, she will make fixed payments at the strike rate on the swaption, *SR*, and receive floating payments on the swap. If the owner of a receiver swaption exercises, she will receive fixed payments at the strike rate on the swaption, *SR*, and make floating payments. In both cases, the exercise decision depends on the value of the payments to be made at the strike rate compared to the anticipated value of the floating-rate payments.

The most basic principle of swap pricing is that the present value of the fixed and floating payments must be equal, when the fixed payments are discounted at the *SFR* and the floating payments are discounted at the forward rates implied by the yield curve. Since these two sides are equal, the *SFR* summarizes the present value of the floating-side payments in a single number. Therefore, the exercise decision on the swap can be made by comparing the strike rate on the swaption with the fixed rate on the underlying swap. (In other words, the *SFR* serves as a proxy for the value of the floating-rate payments on the swap.)

Upon exercise of a payer swaption, the swaption owner will enter the swap to pay the strike rate on the swap, *SR*, and receive the floating-rate payments on the swap, whose value is reflected by the *SFR* on the swap. Similarly, upon exercise of a receiver swaption, the swaption owner will enter the swap to receive the strike rate on the swap and make the floating payments, with a value reflected by the *SFR* on the underlying swap. Summarizing, we can give the appropriate exercise rules as follows:

Payer swaption: exercise if *SFR* > *SR*
Receiver swaption: exercise if *SR* > *SFR*

Swaption valuation at expiration

In this section, we briefly explore the value of a payer and receiver swaption at expiration. As we will see, if a swaption is in-the-money, the benefit is essentially an interest savings on each payment that is a function of the difference between the *SFR* on the swap and the *SR* on the swaption. We also use this discussion to lay the foundation for the pricing of swaptions prior to expiration.

The value of a payer swaption at expiration

Upon exercising a European swaption at its expiration, the underlying swap will commence. We know from our study of swap pricing that, at inception, the floating-rate payments and the fixed-rate payments must have the same present value. By exercising a payer swaption, the holder of the swaption enters a swap and pays the strike rate on the swaption, *SR*, instead of the currently prevailing swap fixed rate, *SFR*. On each payment in the swap initiated by exercising the swaption, the cash outflow is reduced by the difference between the *SFR* and the *SR*:

payoff on each swap payment = $(SFR - SR) \times NP \times FRAC$

where *FRAC* is the fraction of the year covered by the maturity of the underlying LIBOR instrument and *NP* is the notional principal. Because the payer swaption will be exercised only when *SFR* > *SR*, it is also the case that the payoff from the option on any payment in the swap equals the following:

payoff on each swap payment = $\text{MAX}\{0, (SFR - SR) \times NP \times FRAC\}$ (22.25)

We will use the fact expressed by Equation 22.25 when we turn to pricing the option before expiration.

Viewed from the expiration of the swaption and the initiation of the swap, the present value of all of the payoffs from the *T* payments in the swap is as follows:

$$\text{value of payer swaption at expiration} = \sum_{t=1}^{T} \frac{1}{Z_{0,t}} \times (SFR - SR) \times NP \times FRAC \qquad (22.26)$$

Assuming no default on the swap, this is a risk-free value. As we see by comparing Equations 22.26 and 22.25, the value of the swaption at expiration is just the value of the portfolio of payoffs on all of the individual payments.

The value of a receiver swaption at expiration

The holder of a receiver swaption will exercise at expiration if the strike rate on the swaption, *SR*, exceeds the swap fixed rate, *SFR*. Exercising allows the holder to receive a cash flow each period that is larger than it otherwise would be. The additional periodic cash flow is a function of the difference between *SR* and *SFR*, and is as follows:

$$\text{payoff on each swap payment} = (SR - SFR) \times NP \times FRAC \tag{22.27}$$

Because the holder of the swaption will exercise only if the strike rate on the option exceeds the swap fixed rate, it must also be the case that

$$\text{payoff on each swap payment} = \text{MAX}\{0, (SR - SFR) \times NP \times FRAC\} \tag{22.28}$$

At the expiration of the swaption and the initiation of the swap, the present value of all of the payoffs from the *T* payments in the receiver swap is as follows:

$$\text{value of receiver swaption at expiration} = \sum_{t-1}^{T} \frac{1}{Z_{0,t}} \times (SR - SFR) \times NP \times FRAC \tag{22.29}$$

Swaption valuation before expiration

We now show that a swaption can be understood as a portfolio of calls or puts on LIBOR. In Chapter 19, we saw that the payoff at expiration for a call and put on LIBOR is given by Equations 19.10 and 19.11:

$$\text{MAX}\{0, (\text{Observed LIBOR} - SR) \times FRAC \times NP\} \tag{19.10}$$

$$\text{MAX}\{0, (SR - \text{Observed LIBOR}) \times FRAC \times NP\} \tag{19.11}$$

Equation 19.10 gives the payoff for a call on LIBOR, while Equation 19.11 gives the payoff for a put on LIBOR. The payoff for a payer swaption (Equation 22.25) has the same form as the payoff for a call on LIBOR (Equation 19.10). Similarly, the payoff for a receiver swaption (Equation 22.28) has the same form as the payoff for a put on LIBOR (Equation 19.11). As we have seen, a payer swaption consists of one payoff of the form of Equation 22.25 (or 19.10) for each swap payment date; similarly, a receiver swaption consists of one payoff of the form of Equation 22.28 (or 19.11) for each swap payment date. Therefore, a payer swaption is a portfolio of calls on LIBOR, while a receiver swaption is a portfolio of puts on LIBOR.

In Chapter 19, we saw that the Black model could be used to value options on LIBOR, assuming the LIBOR rate at the expiration of the option is log-normally distributed. In pricing a swaption, we apply the identical technique to value each call or put that pertains to a single payment on the swaption and that together constitute the value of a payer or receiver option.

We first focus on a single payment on a swap that underlies a swaption. Assume that the swaption is being valued at time *t* and that the option expires at time *T*. We consider the *n*th payment on the swap, which occurs at time T_n, which occurs some time after time *T*. Thus, at the time the swaption is being valued, the swaption has time *T* − *t* remaining until expiration and time $T_n - t$ remaining until the *n*th payment on the swap. This difference between the time to expiration and the time until the payment is received is important for pricing. For example, in pricing calls and puts on LIBOR, we took account of the fact that payments are determined in advance and paid in arrears. This required taking into account the full amount of time from the present valuation date until the time the payment is actually received. Keeping in mind the distinction between times $T - t$ and $T_n - t$, the values of the call and put pertaining to a single payment on the swap are as follows:

$$c_t = NP \times FRAC \times e^{-r(T_n-t)}[SFR \times N(d_1) - SR \times N(d_2)]$$
$$p_t = NP \times FRAC \times e^{-r(T_n-t)}[SR \times N(-d_2) - SFR \times N(-d_1)]$$

(22.30)

where

$$d_1 = \frac{\ln\left(\dfrac{SFR_t}{SR}\right) + 0.5\sigma^2(T - t)}{\sigma\sqrt{T - t}}$$

$$d_2 = d_1 - \sigma\sqrt{T - t}$$

As Equation 22.30 shows, the d_1 and d_2 terms use the time period $T - t$. This time period pertains to the expiration on the swaption, which determines the probability that the swaption will finish in-the-money. By contrast, the discounting runs over the period $T_n - t$, because this is the time from the valuation date to the payment on the underlying swap.

Because a swaption is simply a portfolio of calls or puts, the value of a payer swaption is simply a portfolio of calls of the form of Equation 22.30, and a receiver swaption is a similar portfolio:

$$\text{payer swaption}_t = \sum_{n=1}^{N} NP \times FRAC \times e^{-r(T_n-t)}[SFR \times N(d_1) - SR \times N(d_2)]$$

(22.31)

$$\text{receiver swaption}_t = \sum_{n=1}^{N} NP \times FRAC \times e^{-r(T_n-t)}[SR \times N(-d_2) - SFR \times N(-d_1)]$$

where d_1 and d_2 are as defined in Equation 22.30, t is the valuation date, and T_n is the time at which the nth payment will be received. In addition to using the continuous discounting at a constant rate of Equation 22.31, we can also value the options using the zero-coupon factors that reflect the shape of the term structure:

$$\text{payer swaption}_t = NP \times FRAC \times [SFR \times N(d_1) - SR \times N(d_2)]\sum_{n=1}^{N} \frac{1}{Z_{t,T_n}}$$

(22.32)

$$\text{receiver swaption}_t = NP \times FRAC \times [SR \times N(-d_2) - SFR \times N(-d_1)]\sum_{n=1}^{N} \frac{1}{Z_{t,T_n}}$$

A swaption pricing example

Table 22.13 presents term structure information that we will use for several swaption examples. Consider the yield curve environment for the point of view of time zero. A forward swap begins in four years and has semiannual payments, a tenor of three years, and a notional principal of $75 million. The *SFR* for this forward swap is as follows:

Table 22.13   Term structure data for swaption valuation and examples

Semiannual period	Par yield (annual terms)	Par yield (semiannual terms)	Zero-coupon factor	Forward rate factor
1	0.0609	0.030450	1.030450	1.030450
2	0.0633	0.031650	1.064341	1.32889
3	0.0657	0.032850	1.101993	1.035376
4	0.0671	0.033550	1.141445	1.035801
5	0.0691	0.034550	1.185882	1.38930
6	0.0701	0.035050	1.230758	1.037842
7	0.0703	0.035150	0.035150	1.035832
8	0.0717	0.035850	1.327830	1.041551
9	0.0719	0.035950	1.376825	1.036898
10	0.0724	0.036200	1.430414	1.038922
11	0.0734	0.036700	1.491779	1.042900
12	0.0741	0.037050	1.554339	1.041937
13	0.0745	0.037250	1.617077	1.040363
14	0.0758	0.037900	1.696634	1.049198
15	0.0762	0.038100	1.767774	1.041930
16	0.0776	0.038800	1.862638	1.053663
17	0.0776	0.038800	1.934908	1.038800
18	0.0788	0.039400	2.040646	1.054647
19	0.0795	0.039750	2.141559	1.049451
20	0.0803	0.040150	2.253429	1.052237
21	0.0805	0.040250	2.351470	1.043508
22	0.0813	0.040650	2.480371	1.054817
23	0.0827	0.041350	2.650501	1.068591
24	0.0828	0.041400	2.765752	1.043483
25	0.0837	0.041850	2.937885	1.062237
26	0.0850	0.042500	3.157790	1.074851
27	0.0850	0.042500	3.291996	1.042500
28	0.0859	0.042950	3.518782	1.068890
29	0.0872	0.043600	3.817729	1.084957
30	0.0875	0.043750	4.023761	1.053967

$$SFR = \left(\sum_{t=9}^{14} \frac{FRA_{(t-1),t}}{Z_{0,t}} \right) \Big/ \left(\sum_{t=9}^{14} \frac{1}{Z_{0,t}} \right)$$

Treating the numerator and denominator separately for convenience, we have the following:

$$\text{numerator} = \frac{0.036898}{1.376828} + \frac{0.042900}{1.430414} + \frac{0.038922}{1.491779} + \frac{0.041937}{1.554339} + \frac{0.040363}{1.617077} + \frac{0.049198}{1.696634}$$

$$= 0.163706$$

$$\text{denominator} = \frac{1}{1.376828} + \frac{1}{1.430414} + \frac{1}{1.491779} + \frac{1}{1.554339} + \frac{1}{1.617077} + \frac{1}{1.696634}$$

$$= 3.946910$$

Based on these calculations: $SFR = 0.163706/3.946910 = 0.041477$ on a semiannual basis, or 0.082954 in annual terms.

Consider now a payer and receiver swaption on this forward swap from the point of view of time zero. The payer swaption has a strike rate of 8 percent in annual terms, and the receiver swaption has a strike rate of 9 percent. The standard deviation of the forward swap rate is 0.11. First, for the payer swaption, the d_1 and d_2 terms are as follows:

$$d_1 = \frac{\ln\left(\dfrac{SFR_t}{SR}\right) + 0.5\sigma^2(T - t)}{\sigma\sqrt{T - t}} = \frac{\ln\left(\dfrac{0.082954}{0.08}\right) + 0.5 \times 0.11^2 \times 4}{0.11 \times \sqrt{4}} = 0.274816$$

$$d_2 = d_1 - \sigma\sqrt{T - t} = 0.274816 - 0.11 \times 2 = 0.054816$$

The cumulative normal values are $N(d_1) = N(0.274816) = 0.608271$ and $N(d_2) = N(0.054816) = 0.521858$. In finding the SFR for the forward swap, we have already determined that

$$\sum_{n=1}^{N} \frac{1}{Z_{t,T_n}} = 3.946910$$

Applying Equation 22.32, the value of the payer swaption is as follows:

$$\text{payer swaption}_t = NP \times FRAC \times [SFR \times N(d_1) - SR \times N(d_2)] \sum_{n=1}^{N} \frac{1}{Z_{t,T_n}}$$

$$= \$75,000,000 \times 0.5 \times [0.082954 \times 0.608271 - 0.08 \times 0.521858] \times 3.946910$$

$$= \$1,289,142$$

The cost of the payer swaption is $1,289,142. The cost of swaptions is often expressed in basis points of the notional principal. This swaption costs 171.89 basis points = $1,289,142/$75,000,000.

We turn now to the receiver swaption, which has its own d_1 and d_2 terms. For the receiver swaption,

$$d_1 = \frac{\ln\left(\dfrac{SFR_t}{SR}\right) + 0.5\sigma^2(T - t)}{\sigma\sqrt{T - t}} = \frac{\ln\left(\dfrac{0.082954}{0.09}\right) + 0.5 \times 0.11^2 \times 4}{0.11 \times \sqrt{4}} = -0.266044$$

$$d_2 = d_1 - \sigma\sqrt{T - t} = -0.266044 - 0.11 \times \sqrt{4} = -0.486044$$

The cumulative normal terms are $N(-d_1) = N(0.266044) = 0.604897$ and $N(-d_2) = N(0.486044) = 0.686532$. Applying Equation 22.32 for a receiver swaption, we have the following:

$$\text{receiver swaption}_t = NP \times FRAC \times [SR \times N(-d_2) - SFR \times N(-d_1)] \sum_{n=1}^{N} \frac{1}{Z_{t,T_n}}$$

$$= \$75,000,000 \times 0.5 \times [0.09 \times 0.686532 - 0.082954 \times 0.604897] \times 3.946910$$

$$= \$1,718,276$$

For this forward swap, the option to receive 9 percent instead of the market swap rate of 8.2954 percent costs $1,718,276 or 229.11 basis points.

A swaption application

Continuing with the term structure environment of Table 22.13, we now consider a swaption application. Viewing the term structure data of Table 22.13 from time zero, a bond portfolio manager is considering entering a pay-fixed plain vanilla interest rate swap with a tenor of five years, a notional principal of $50 million, and semiannual payments. The manager is somewhat uneasy about the tenor of the swap and would like to know how much it would cost to have the option to cancel the swap after three years or extend it for another two years at the same rate as the plain vanilla swap.

As we discussed in Chapter 20, extendable and cancelable swaps can be created by combining a plain vanilla swap and the appropriate swaption. Our manager will enter a pay-fixed swap. The relevant rules for this situation from Chapter 20 are as follows:

extendable pay-fixed swap = plain vanilla pay-fixed swap + a payer swaption
cancelable pay-fixed swap = plain vanilla pay-fixed swap + a receiver swaption

Specifically, to extend the swap for two additional years, the manager needs a payer swaption with a maturity of five years, an underlying swap of two years, and a strike rate equal to the rate on the initial five-year plain vanilla swap that she is contemplating. To cancel the swap after three years, the manager will need a receiver swaption with a maturity of three years, an underlying swap with a tenor of two years, and a strike rate that equals the fixed rate on the five-year plain vanilla swap.

To evaluate the issue fully, the manager needs to know the swap rate for three swaps: the five-year plain vanilla swap, the two-year swap to begin in three years that underlies the swaption for the cancelable swap (ranging from year 3 to year 5), and the two-year swap to begin in five years that underlies the swaption for the extendable swap (ranging from year 5 to year 7). Based on the data in Table 22.13, where the subscripts range over the semiannual periods, we have the following:

$$\sum_{t=1}^{10} \frac{1}{Z_{0,t}} = 8.312206, \quad \sum_{t=7}^{10} \frac{1}{Z_{0,t}} = 2.962917, \quad \sum_{t=11}^{14} \frac{1}{Z_{0,t}} = 2.521503$$

$$\sum_{t=1}^{10} \frac{FRA_{t-1,t}}{Z_{0,t}} = 0.300901, \quad \sum_{t=7}^{10} \frac{FRA_{t-1,t}}{Z_{0,t}} = 0.113409, \quad \sum_{t=11}^{14} \frac{FRA_{t-1,t}}{Z_{0,t}} = 0.109696$$

Based on these values, the fixed rates on the various swaps in the analysis are as follows:

$$\text{five-year plain vanilla } SFR = \left(\sum_{t=1}^{10} \frac{FRA_{t-1,t}}{Z_{0,t}} \right) \bigg/ \left(\sum_{t=1}^{10} \frac{1}{Z_{0,t}} \right) = \frac{0.300901}{8.312206} = 0.0362000$$

$$\text{forward swap (years 3–5) } SFR = \left(\sum_{t=7}^{10} \frac{FRA_{t-1,t}}{Z_{0,t}} \right) \bigg/ \left(\sum_{t=7}^{10} \frac{1}{Z_{0,t}} \right) = \frac{0.113409}{2.962917} = 0.038276$$

$$\text{forward swap (years 5–7) } SFR = \left(\sum_{t=11}^{14} \frac{FRA_{t-1,t}}{Z_{0,t}} \right) \bigg/ \left(\sum_{t=11}^{14} \frac{1}{Z_{0,t}} \right) = \frac{0.109696}{2.521503} = 0.043504$$

These are semiannual rates and they correspond to annual rates of 0.072400 for the five-year plain vanilla swap, 0.076552 for the forward swap covering years 3–5, and 0.087008 for the forward swap covering years 5–7. The key rate is the $SFR = 0.072400$ for the five-year plain vanilla swap, because this is the rate on the swap that the manager would like to be able to either cancel at year 3 or extend from year 5 to year 7.

To make the plain vanilla swap extendable, we have seen that the manager will require a payer swaption. Given her situation, the necessary payer swaption will have a maturity of five years, a strike rate equal to the SFR on the plain vanilla swap of 0.072400, an underlying swap with a tenor of two years, semiannual payments, and a notional principal of $50 million. We have seen that for this forward swap, the swap rate is 0.087008, and we assume that the volatility of this forward rate is 0.15. This gives the information necessary to value the payer swaption. The d_1 and d_2 terms are as follows:

$$d_1 = \frac{\ln\left(\dfrac{SFR_t}{SR}\right) + 0.5\sigma^2(T-t)}{\sigma\sqrt{T-t}} = \frac{\ln\left(\dfrac{0.087008}{0.072400}\right) + 0.5 \times 0.15^2 \times 5}{0.15 \times \sqrt{5}} = 0.715672$$

$$d_2 = d_1 - \sigma\sqrt{T-t} = 0.715672 - 0.15 \times \sqrt{5} = 0.380262$$

The corresponding cumulative normal values are $N(d_1) = N(0.715672) = 0.762903$ and $N(d_2) = N(0.380262) = 0.648125$. The value of the swaption is as follows:

$$\text{payer swaption}_t = NP \times FRAC \times [SFR \times N(d_1) \times SR \times N(d_2)] \sum_{n=1}^{N} \frac{1}{Z_{t,T_n}}$$

$$= \$50{,}000{,}000 \times 0.5 \times (0.087008 \times 0.762903 - 0.072400 \times 0.648125) \times 2.521503$$

$$= \$1{,}226{,}359$$

This value of $1,226,359 is 245.27 basis points of the $50 million notional principal.

To make the swap cancelable after three years, the manager will require a receiver swaption with a maturity of three years and a strike rate equal to the rate of 0.072400 on the plain vanilla swap. The underlying swap will have a notional principal of $50 million, semiannual payments, and a tenor of two years. We assume that the standard deviation of this forward swap rate is 0.13. For the receiver swaption, the d_1 and d_2 terms are as follows:

$$d_1 = \frac{\ln\left(\dfrac{SFR_t}{SR}\right) + 0.5\sigma^2(T-t)}{\sigma\sqrt{T-t}} = \frac{\ln\left(\dfrac{0.076552}{0.072400}\right) + 0.5 \times 0.13^2 \times 3}{0.13 \times \sqrt{3}} = 0.360240$$

$$d_2 = d_1 - \sigma\sqrt{T-t} = 0.360240 - 0.13 \times \sqrt{3} = 0.135073$$

The corresponding cumulative normal values are $N(-d_1) = N(-0.360240) = 0.359334$ and $N(-d_2) = N(-0.135073) = 0.446277$. The value of the receiver swaption is as follows:

$$\text{receiver swaption}_t = NP \times FRAC \times [SR \times N(-d_2) - SFR \times N(-d_1)] \sum_{n=1}^{N} \frac{1}{Z_{t,T_n}}$$

$$= \$50,000,000 \times 0.5 \times (0.072400 \times 0.446277 - 0.076552 \times 0.359334) \times 2.962917$$

$$= \$355,751$$

This value of the receiver swaption of \$355,751 is 71.15 basis points of the \$50 million notional principal.

In sum, our manager plans to enter a five-year plain vanilla swap at a swap rate of 7.24 percent with a notional principal of \$50 million. She would like to be able to cancel the swap after three years. The swaption to make this possible is a receiver swaption with a maturity of three years, which will cost \$355,751, or 71.15 basis points. She would also like to be able to extend the swap for two additional years at the end of the five-year tenor of the plain vanilla swap. The payer swaption necessary to meet this desire will cost \$1,226,359, or 245.27 basis points. Together, these two swaptions will cost \$1,582,110, or 316.42 basis points.

Paying over 3 percent of the notional principal of a swap is expensive insurance for not being able to make up your mind about the necessary tenor of the swap. Both options cannot be used, as they are mutually exclusive.[8] The manager might be able to salvage some value from the (at least) one swaption that will not be exercised, but it might be better for her to rethink the strategy of the swap and the flexibility that is really necessary in canceling or extending the swap.

Day count conventions

Throughout our discussion of swaps, we have abstracted from the technicalities of the exact interest calculation that is used in actual market transactions. This choice has allowed us to avoid some tedious arithmetic to focus on the economics of the swap market. This section provides a brief overview of the actual conventions employed. The basic interest rate swap involves a series of fixed-rate payments associated with a long-term instrument against a series of floating-rate payments tied to the money market. The bond market and money market use fundamentally differing assumptions about day counts and interest computations.

In the money market, interest payments are generally computed on the assumption that the year has 360 days and that interest accrues each calendar day. For example, a LIBOR rate of 8.30 percent on a notional principal of \$10 million, over a quarterly period of 91 days, would generate an interest payment of

$$\$10,000,000 \times 0.0830 \times \frac{91}{360} = \$209,805.56$$

As this example indicates, money market yields are computed according to a day count convention of actual/360.

In the bond market, two different day count conventions are common. One is actual/365, the other is 30/360, assuming that the year has 360 days and that each month has 30 days. For most bonds, the actual/365 convention applies. For example, a \$100,000 par value Treasury bond with a yield of 8.30 percent for a semiannual period with 182 days would generate an interest payment of

$$\$10{,}000{,}000 \times 0.0830 \times \frac{182}{365} = \$4{,}138.63$$

Because these conventions differ, it is important to take their effects into account in swap contracting and cash flow computations. For example, consider a two-year plain vanilla interest rate swap with semiannual payments. The terms are an unknown *SFR* against six-month LIBOR. The notional principal is $100 million. The four six-month periods covered by the swap have 182, 183, 181, and 182 days, respectively. The fixed-side cash flows are computed on an actual/365 basis, while the floating-side cash flows are computed on an actual/360 basis. The basic no-arbitrage pricing condition requires equality in the present value of the fixed-side and floating-side cash flows. On this swap, the first fixed cash flow is

$$\$10{,}000{,}000 \times SFR \times \frac{182}{365}$$

and the first floating cash flow is

$$\$10{,}000{,}000 \times LIBOR_0 \times \frac{182}{360}$$

Differences in day count conventions affect each cash flow, the present values of the two sides of the swap, and the swap rates.

As an example, we price this four-period swap in the term structure environment of Table 22.13. First, we price it according to our simplified Equation 22.15; then we price the same swap considering the day count conventions. For the simplified Equation 22.15, the numerator and denominator are as follows:

$$
\begin{aligned}
\text{numerator} &= \frac{FRA_{0,1}}{Z_{0,1}} + \frac{FRA_{1,2}}{Z_{0,2}} + \frac{FRA_{2,3}}{Z_{0,3}} + \frac{FRA_{3,4}}{Z_{0,4}} \\[2mm]
&= \frac{0.030450}{1.030450} + \frac{0.032889}{1.064341} + \frac{0.035376}{1.101993} + \frac{0.035801}{1.141445} = 0.123917
\end{aligned}
$$

$$
\begin{aligned}
\text{denominator} &= \frac{1}{Z_{0,1}} + \frac{1}{Z_{0,2}} + \frac{1}{Z_{0,3}} + \frac{1}{Z_{0,4}} \\[2mm]
&= \frac{1}{1.030450} + \frac{1}{1.064341} + \frac{1}{1.101993} + \frac{1}{1.141445} = 3.693528
\end{aligned}
$$

The *SFR* is as follows:

$$SFR = \frac{\text{numerator}}{\text{denominator}} = \frac{0.123917}{3.693528} = 0.033550$$

This *SFR* of 0.033550 is expressed in semiannual terms. The corresponding annualized *SFR* is 0.067100.

We now compute the *SFR* taking the day count conventions into account. The four semiannual periods have 182, 183, 181, and 182 days, respectively. The fixed-rate payments are computed on an actual/365 basis, while the floating payments are based on an actual/360 day assumption. The basic computation is the same as in Equation 22.15, except the fraction of the year cannot be factored out, as it differs for each payment and differs between the numerator (for the floating payments) and the denominator (for the fixed payments). Taking the day count conventions into account, the present value of the floating payments is as follows:

$$PV_{FLOATING} = NP \left(\frac{FRA_{0,1} \times \frac{182}{360}}{Z_{0,1}} + \frac{FRA_{1,2} \times \frac{183}{360}}{Z_{0,2}} + \frac{FRA_{2,3} \times \frac{181}{360}}{Z_{0,3}} + \frac{FRA_{3,4} \times \frac{182}{360}}{Z_{0,4}} \right)$$

$$= \$100,000,000$$

$$\times \left(\frac{0.060900 \times \frac{182}{360}}{1.030450} + \frac{0.065778 \times \frac{183}{360}}{1.064341} + \frac{0.070752 \times \frac{181}{360}}{1.101993} + \frac{0.071602 \times \frac{182}{360}}{1.141445} \right)$$

$$= \$100,000,000 \times 0.125288$$

$$= \$12,528,800$$

The present value of the fixed-rate payments is as follows:

$$PV_{FIXED} = NP \left(\frac{SFR \times \frac{182}{365}}{Z_{0,1}} + \frac{SFR \times \frac{183}{365}}{Z_{0,2}} + \frac{SFR \times \frac{181}{365}}{Z_{0,3}} + \frac{SFR \times \frac{182}{365}}{Z_{0,4}} \right)$$

$$= \$100,000,000 \times SFR \times \left(\frac{\frac{182}{365}}{1.030450} + \frac{\frac{183}{365}}{1.064341} + \frac{\frac{181}{365}}{1.101993} + \frac{\frac{182}{365}}{1.141445} \right)$$

$$= \$100,000,000 \times SFR \times 1.841792$$

$$= SFR \times \$184,179,200$$

Because we are not factoring out the expression for the fraction of the year, as it differs for each payment, note that the FRA rates that appear above are the annualized rates.

To compute the *SFR*, we equate the present values for the fixed and floating payment streams, and solve for the *SFR*:

$$PV_{FLOATING} = PV_{FIXED}$$

$$\$12,528,800 = SFR \times \$184,179,200$$

$$SFR = \frac{\$12,528,800}{\$184,179,200} = 0.068025$$

This *SFR* is already in annualized terms. The annualized *SFR* according to the simplified Equation 22.15 is 0.067100, compared to an *SFR* = 0.068025 taking the day count conventions into account. This is a difference of 9.25 basis points—a significant difference that needs to be considered in actual swap pricing.

Conclusion

This chapter has considered some important refinements in understanding the swaps market that extend the discussions of Chapters 20 and 21. We began by seeing how parallel loans helped British firms to evade currency controls and created financial structures that led directly to the emergence of the swaps market.

For the financial manager, the existence of the swaps market gives many additional financing opportunities, and comparing these financing alternatives becomes complex. The all-in cost provides a way to use internal rate of return techniques to compare financing alternatives with very different terms. A study of the swap between B. F. Goodrich and the Dutch bank, Rabobank, provided a historical example of how to use the all-in cost technique.

We next introduced the concept of the duration of an interest rate swap. As with interest rate futures, swap duration provides a powerful technique for managing interest rate risk. We showed how the financial manager can use a duration-based approach to swaps to eliminate, reduce, or even increase the interest rate risk that the firm faces.

Structured notes have become important financing tools. In essence, a structured note is a security offering the lender an unusual payoff pattern. By coupling these instruments with swaps, the issuer can offer the unusual payoff pattern and maintain a traditional interest rate exposure for itself. This chapter also showed how to hedge these structured notes and how to create them synthetically by using swaps.

Chapter 21 showed how to price plain vanilla interest rate and currency swaps. This chapter extended the pricing analysis to flavored swaps. Specifically, we showed how to price forward swaps, seasonal swaps, diff swaps, and currency annuity swaps. These pricing examples also provide models for pricing virtually any kind of complex swap. The chapter also showed how to price equity swaps, and how these swaps can be used to manage equity market risk.

Swaptions were introduced in Chapter 20. This chapter showed how to price swaptions in realistic yield curve environments and showed how to use swaptions to transform swaps. Specifically, we showed how to use swaptions to create cancelable and extendable swaps.

Finally, we took note of the day count conventions employed in the market. The money market and bond markets utilize different assumptions regarding the number of days in the year. These assumptions affect each cash flow in a swap and the pricing of swaps. This chapter explained these conventions and illustrated their application in a swap pricing example.

Exercises

1 At present, you observe the following rates: $FRA_{0,1} = 5.25$ percent and $FRA_{1,2} = 5.70$ percent, where the subscripts refer to years. You also observe prices on calls and puts on one-year LIBOR that expire in one year, with payment the following year. For a call on LIBOR with a strike rate of 5.70 percent, the price is 150 basis points. The corresponding put has a strike rate of 5.70 percent, and a cost of 143 basis points.

    A Explain how these prices represent an arbitrage opportunity. Draw a diagram illustrating the arbitrage opportunity.

    B Assuming a notional principal of $100 million, state the transactions that you would enter to secure the arbitrage profit.

    C Compute the present value of the arbitrage profit.

2 An inverse floating-rate note, or inverse floater, is a debt instrument with a floating rate that moves inversely with market rates. Generally, an inverse floater pays a fixed rate minus LIBOR. Consider an FRN with a principal amount of $50 million paying LIBOR with a five-year maturity. Consider also a plain vanilla interest rate swap with a fixed rate of 7 percent, a floating rate equal to LIBOR, a notional principal of $100 million, and a tenor of five years. For both instruments, assume annual payments.

    A Explain how to construct the inverse floater from the instruments described above. Assume that there is no floor rate on the inverse floater. What is the net annual payment on the inverse floater?

    B Compute the value of a net annual payment if LIBOR is 5.5 or 6.5 percent.

    C What happens to this instrument if LIBOR exceeds 14 percent?

    D Explain how to construct an inverse floater from a fixed-rate bond and a plain vanilla swap.

    E What modifications to the analysis would be required to replicate an inverse floater with a floor rate?

3 A portfolio manager handles a Japanese equity portfolio for her clients, who are principally long-term dollar-based investors seeking exposure to the Japanese economy. The current value of the portfolio is $1.5 billion, and the spot exchange rate is $1 = ¥125. The portfolio pays an annual dividend of 3 percent. However, the quarterly distributions are weighted heavily toward the last quarter, with a mix of approximately 20–20–20–40 percent across the four quarters. The manager feels that her clients, many of whom rely on dollar income from the portfolio, would appreciate a dollar income stream less subject to foreign exchange risk. Therefore, the portfolio manager would like to reduce the exchange rate risk associated with the dividend payments while retaining the equity exposure to the Japanese market and while retaining the foreign exchange exposure on the principal. For the purpose of this analysis, we assume that the dividend payments are made on the last day of each quarter and that we are presently approaching year-end. The manager has invited you to make proposals for avoiding this exchange rate risk over a horizon of three years. Note that the problem is not the uneven amounts of the dividends across quarters, but the foreign exchange risk of those payments.

A Briefly compare and contrast the merits of using futures, FOREX forwards, or a swap to solve this problem.

B Explain how you would address this problem by using at least one swap among the instruments you would recommend.

4 Assume you can borrow at a fixed rate for ten years for 11 percent or that you can borrow at a floating rate of LIBOR plus 40 basis points for ten years. Assume also that LIBOR stands at 10.60 percent. Under these circumstances, your financial advisor states: "The all-in cost is the same on both deals—11 percent. Therefore, the two are equivalent, and one should be indifferent between these two financing alternatives." How would you react? Explain.

5 A firm needs to secure fixed-rate financing of $40 million for a horizon of five years. It is considering two alternatives that seem equally attractive to management in terms of the instruments involved. Thus, the choice revolves solely around the relative cost. Alternative A is to issue a straight bond with annual coupon payments. The bond would sell at par, the firm would net 98 percent of the sale proceeds, and the coupon rate would be 7 percent. Administrative costs would be $30,000 for each coupon payment, and would be payable on the payment date. Under Alternative B, the firm would engage in a sequence of one-year financings, obtained at the prevailing rate each year, with each annual financing in the amount of $40 million. The firm would pair this financing with a pay-fixed interest rate swap. The firm's investment bank has guaranteed to make this sequence of loans at LIBOR, but would charge a fee of 15 basis points on each loan amount, payable at

each loan date. The investment bank would also take the receive-fixed side of the swap that the firm needs with a fixed rate of 7.3 percent. The two alternatives differ slightly in the dollar amount of funds that they would provide, but this difference can be ignored. What is the all-in cost for each alternative?

6 Today the following rates may be observed: $FRA_{0,3}$ = 0.0600, $FRA_{3,6}$ = 0.0595, $FRA_{6,9}$ = 0.0592, $FRA_{9,12}$ = 0.0590, $FRA_{12,15}$ = 0.0590, $FRA_{15,18}$ = 0.0588, $FRA_{18,21}$ = 0.0587, and $FRA_{21,24}$ = 0.0586, where the subscripts pertain to months. Consider a two-year plain vanilla interest rate swap with quarterly payments, and also consider a forward interest rate swap to be initiated in 12 months, with quarterly payments, a notional principal of $20 million, and a tenor of 12 months.

A Without computing the *SFR* for the forward swap, compare and contrast the *SFR* for the plain vanilla swap of the previous exercise with the *SFR* for the forward swap. What should the relationship be between the two *SFR*s?

B Find the *SFR* for the forward swap.

C Assume that today the following rates are observed: $FRA_{0,3}$ = 0.0590, $FRA_{3,6}$ = 0.0588, $FRA_{6,9}$ = 0.0587, and $FRA_{9,12}$ = 0.0586, where the subscripts pertain to months. What would be the *SFR* for a plain vanilla swap based on these rates, assuming a tenor of one year and quarterly payments? Explain.

7 Consider an amortizing interest rate swap with an initial notional principal of $50 million, annual payments, and a tenor of five years that is negotiated today. The notional principal is $50 million for the first payment, and then drops $10 million per year. FRA rates covering the tenor of this swap are as follows, where the subscripts indicate years: $FRA_{0,1}$ = 0.0600, $FRA_{1,2}$ = 0.0615, $FRA_{2,3}$ = 0.0623, $FRA_{3,4}$ = 0.0628, and $FRA_{4,5}$ = 0.0633.

A Assuming that Equation 22.15 does not pertain to an amortizing swap, which numbered equation from the chapter is best suited to computing the *SFR* for this amortizing swap? Explain.

B Find the relevant zero-coupon factors for each of the payments in the swap.

C Compute the *SFR* for this swap.

Note: The following interest rate data for the United States and the United Kingdom are used in almost all of the remaining exercises. These data cover the next ten years by semiannual periods.

8 Complete the following table for U.S. interest rates.

U.S. interest rates

Semiannual period	Annualized par yield	Semiannual par yield	Zero-coupon factor	Forward rate factor
1	0.055329			
2	0.055682			
3	0.056260			
4	0.057375			
5	0.057944			
6	0.057961			
7	0.059389			
8	0.059813			
9	0.059910			
10	0.060649			
11	0.060982			
12	0.061214			
13	0.061532			
14	0.061702			
15	0.062721			
16	0.063835			
17	0.064431			
18	0.064785			
19	0.066198			
20	0.066626			

9 Complete the following table for British interest rates.

British interest rates

Semiannual period	Annualized par yields	Semiannual par yield	Zero-coupon	Forward rate
1	0.053832			
2	0.054334			
3	0.056197			
4	0.057242			
5	0.058987			
6	0.059890			
7	0.061010			
8	0.062106			
9	0.062947			
10	0.064515			
11	0.064558			
12	0.066683			
13	0.067310			
14	0.068090			
15	0.069823			
16	0.069891			
17	0.070146			
18	0.070253			
19	0.071105			
20	0.071393			

10 Consider a forward interest rate swap on British rates from the perspective of time zero. The forward swap has semiannual payments, and the first payment will be made in three years. The swap has a tenor of five years and a notional principal of £100 million. From the perspective of time zero, find the *SFR* for this forward swap. If we were to treat the forward swap as an immediate swap, at what time would the swap be valued? From that point in time, treat the forward swap as an immediate swap and determine the *SFR*. Show that the two *SFR*s computed are the same.

11 In the United States, a retailer is faced with a seasonal cash flow pattern over the next five years. The retailer has determined to enter a pay-fixed seasonal swap with a tenor of five years. In the first part of each year, the notional principal will be $50 million. In the second half of each year, the notional principal will be $75 million. Determine the *SFR* for this seasonal swap, and complete the following table:

Seasonal swap cash flows

Semiannual period	Notional principal	Fixed payment	Implied floating payment
1	$50,000,000		
2	75,000,000		
3	50,000,000		
4	75,000,000		
5	50,000,000		
6	75,000,000		
7	50,000,000		
8	75,000,000		
9	50,000,000		
10	75,000,000		

12 In the United Kingdom, the manager of a fixed-rate mortgage portfolio at a building society is quite satisfied with the composition of her portfolio, but she would like to protect the value of the portfolio from rising interest rates. The current market and principal value of the portfolio is £200 million. The mortgages in the portfolio are somewhat unusual in that they do not allow prepayment. However, the principal on the mortgages is being repaid over the next five years consistent with the schedule in the following table. The manager is considering two possible swaps to hedge the interest rate risk of the portfolio. First, the manager might initiate a plain vanilla interest rate swap with a notional principal of £100 million and a tenor of five years. Alternatively, the manager is wondering if she might prefer an amortizing swap with a notional principal schedule that matches the table below and a tenor of five years.

Semiannual period	Notional principal
1	£200,000,000
2	175,000,000
3	133,000,000
4	127,000,000
5	107,000,000
6	85,000,000
7	77,000,000
8	65,000,000
9	45,000,000
10	22,000,000

A By inspecting the British interest rates, but without computation, which swap would have the higher *SFR*? Explain.

B Find the *SFR* for the plain vanilla swap.

C Find the *SFR* for the amortizing swap.

D Which of the two swaps would you recommend to the manager? Which side of the swap should the manager take? Explain.

13 At time zero, the five-year forward FOREX rate is $1 = £0.580024. What is the current spot exchange rate to the nearest cent? Rounding the spot exchange rate to the nearest full cent, complete the following table.

U.S. and British foreign exchange rates

Semiannual period	Pound per dollar	Dollar per pound
0		
1		
2		
3		
4		
5		
6		
7		
8		
9		
10		
11		
12		
13		
14		
15		
16		
17		
18		
19		
20		

14 At time zero, a British exporter has just entered a contract to supply Princess Diana memorabilia to a U.S. customer. The contract calls for the purchase of $50 million worth of material each six months over the next four years. The U.S. customer will pay in dollars. The British exporter would like to avoid the foreign exchange risk inherent in this transaction, but is unsure whether to accept exposure to British interest rates. The exporter also needs additional financing to cope with this increase in business, and is considering issuing a quanto note to provide the financing and to cope with the interest rate risk and possibly the foreign exchange risk inherent in the large new order. The quanto note that the exporter is considering would be based on British LIBOR, would have payments in U.S. dollars, and would have terms that match the Princess Diana order. Specifically, the issue would be for $400 million, with semiannual interest-only payments, and would have a maturity of four years. The spot exchange rate is £1 = $1.760000.

A Explain the interest rate and currency exposure that the British borrower would face if he issued the quanto note in conjunction with the Princess Diana cash flows.

B By visually comparing the British and U.S. yield curves, what can you infer about the likely spread? Price the quanto note. What spread should the exporter expect on the issuance?

C Complete the following table, identifying the implied dollar cash flows on the quanto note. How closely do these match the dollar inflows? What do you think of the proposed issuance size as a means of offsetting the foreign exchange risk?

Quanto note cash flow comparison

Semiannual period	Dollar inflow from sales	Implied quanto note outflow	Net dollar flow
1	$50,000,000		
2	50,000,000		
3	50,000,000		
4	50,000,000		
5	50,000,000		
6	50,000,000		
7	50,000,000		
8	50,000,000		

D The exporter is uncertain that the quanto note approach is correct, but is convinced that the U.S. provides the best capital pool for achieving his financing. An alternative approach is to issue a four-year, semiannual payment, amortizing note in the U.S. for $350 million at the fixed U.S. rate. Find the rate for this issuance that is compatible with the U.S. term structure, and complete the following table for the issuance amount of $350 million. Discuss the suitability of this approach in terms of avoiding the foreign exchange risk inherent in the Princess Diana project.

Amortizing note cash flow comparison—$350 million principal

Semiannual period	Dollar inflow from sales	Implied quanto note outflow	Net dollar flow
1			
2			
3			
4			
5			
6			
7			
8			

E As another alternative, the British exporter may just finance in England and confront the financial risk of the dollar inflows with a swap; that is, the British exporter is interested in swapping the eight $50 million inflows against British pounds. Propose two alternative currency swaps in which the exporter pays his dollar receipts in exchange for British pounds. One swap gives the exporter a fixed British pound payment, while the other gives a floating payment. Price the fixed-rate swap, and complete the following table detailing the cash flows on the floating-rate swap.

British exporter's currency annuity cash flow analysis

Semiannual period	$FR_{t-1,t}$	Implied British pound cash inflow on floating-rate swap
1		
2		
3		
4		
5		
6		
7		
8		

15 A U.S. oilfield equipment manufacturer, DrillBit, is currently negotiating a contract with a Houston-based oil exploration firm, FindIt, for a medium-term contract to deliver equipment each six months for two years. The present is time zero. If the deal goes through, the first equipment will be delivered in six months, with payment for the equipment being made six months following delivery. The contract calls for four deliveries spaced six months apart, with equipment valued at $60 million for each delivery. Most of DrillBit's financing is at a floating rate, so DrillBit is considering initiating a pay-fixed interest rate swap to match the cash flows on the FindIt deal. By entering this pay-fixed swap, DrillBit would agree to pay a sequence of four payments of $60 million in return for a sequence of four payments tied to LIBOR of equal present value. The floating-rate inflows on the swap would approximately match DrillBit's current floating-rate debt obligations (not described here). So the swap would effectively convert DrillBit's existing financing position for a floating-rate obligation to a fixed-rate obligation. However, it is presently uncertain whether the deal with FindIt will be completed.

A Describe the swap being proposed in detail with regard to its timing and cash flows. What is the implicit notional principal on which the floating payments must be computed? Complete the following table showing the cash flows on the swap consistent with the existing U.S. term structure.

Annuity swap cash flow analysis

Semiannual period	Fixed payment	$FR_{t-1,t}$	$FR_{t-1,t}/Z_{0,t}$	Implied floating payment
2				
3				
4				
5				

B What is the *SFR* on this swap?

C Explain how DrillBit might structure a swaption now to match its needs described above if the deal goes through.

D Price the swaption, assuming that the standard deviation of all interest rates is 0.22 and the strike rate is 6 percent.

16 A U.S. industrial firm, Sterling Industries, with a less than sterling credit rating, seeks new financing to upgrade its manufacturing facilities. Sterling has determined that it wants fixed-rate financing without any foreign exchange exposure. Sterling needs to arrange its financing in two steps. First, it needs $175 million at present in the form of a semiannual coupon bond with a maturity of six years. Second, as its modernization plans proceed, Sterling will need another $50 million in financing at year 4. This too will be a semiannual coupon bond, and it will have a maturity of four years. Sterling has been exploring the possibilities for meeting its financing needs with investment bankers in both the United States and the United Kingdom and is considering several alternatives. It is now time zero, which is when Sterling will issue first financing. Although Sterling is sure that it wants its ultimate interest rate exposure to be as just described, Sterling's management remains open to alternative ways of achieving that exposure. Assuming, for the moment, that Sterling could issue at the rates shown in the U.S. yield curve, at what rates would it expect to issue its two financings? Unfortunately, given its credit rating, Sterling is unable to issue at the rates in the interest rate tables completed in exercises 8 and 9. Instead, Sterling faces the following three alternatives for meeting its financing needs:

A   Issue a six-year semiannual coupon bond at prevailing rates plus 135 basis points with a principal of $175 million. Wait until year 4 and issue the second semiannual coupon bond. Sterling's U.S. investment banker indicates that Sterling can reasonably expect similar terms on its second financing, but that the spread will probably be only about 125 basis points, as the loan amount is substantially less. Flotation costs on both alternatives are estimated to be 120 basis points, payable at the time of flotation on each issue. This alternative involves some interest rate risk, but Sterling is willing to consider this alternative seriously if it is truly price-effective.

B   Issue an FRN with a principal amount of $175 million and a six-year maturity at a spread of 110 basis points over the LIBOR rates in the table. Sterling's U.S. investment banker is also willing to commit to financing Sterling's residual needs itself for a commitment fee of 90 basis points for a second issuance of an FRN at year 4 in the amount of $50 million with a maturity of four years. (This commitment would not be structured as an option, but as a firm commitment by both parties.) The FRN from the investment banker would also have the same 110 basis point spread over LIBOR, and the commitment fee would be payable at time zero. Flotation costs for any FRN

will be 85 basis points, which is in addition to the spread and any commitment fee. Sterling is determined to have a fixed interest rate position. The investment banker agrees to act as counterparty for any necessary swap or swaps at the rates implied by the U.S. yield curve of the table for a fee of 45 basis points of the entire financing package ($175,000,000 + $50,000,000) payable immediately. Except for the fee, the swap will be fairly priced according to the term structure.

C   Through its British investment advisers, Sterling is also considering financing in England. Sterling can issue a British FRN with a six-year maturity at British LIBOR, from the table, plus 85 basis points. The flotation costs for the service of the British investment banking firm would be 80 basis points on an FRN. The British investment banker is willing to act as a counterparty to Sterling for any desired swap that it might need in conjunction with this financing. Sterling is interested in this financing alternative but concerned about how it will plan for and meet the second part of its financing need. The British advisor is unwilling to predict Sterling's access to British markets for the second part of its financing need. Sterling discusses the entire matter fully with its U.S. investment banker; the U.S. investment banker is willing to allow Sterling to have the commitment for the second tranche described in alternative B above, without going through the U.S. investment banker for the immediate financing. The terms would be the same as described in alternative B, except the commitment fee would be 105 basis points and the swap initiation fee would be 55 basis points if Sterling only takes that part of the deal. The U.S. investment banking firm is still willing to provide a swap for the entire deal, so the swap initiation fee would apply to the entire financing package that Sterling contemplates ($175,000,000 + $50,000,000).

For each of the three financing plans, describe in detail the instruments that Sterling would issue and the swaps that it would enter. For each alternative, prepare a table showing the cash flows for each period and determine the all-in cost of each alternative. (For simplicity, ignore any swap cash flows in determining the all-in cost.) Which alternative would you adopt if you were Sterling's CEO? Explain.

Use the following data on Mid-Continent National Bank for the remaining exercises. Use the U.S. interest rate data from Exercise 8 above.

The asset/liability committee at Mid-Continent National Bank (MCNB) has recently been reconstituted and is beginning its analysis of the bank's financial position. The ALCO (asset/liability committee) is interested in using swaps and a duration-based approach to manage the bank's interest rate exposure. The following balance sheet shows MCNB's current position in market value terms:

Mid-Continent National Bank stylized balance sheet—market values

Assets		Liabilities and net worth	
A: Cash	$73,000,000	E: Demand deposits	$225,000,000
B: Marketable securities (six-month maturity; yield 7%)	135,000,000	F: Three-month money market obligations (average yield 6.2%)	175,000,000
C: Amortizing loans (ten-year average maturity; semiannual payments; 8% average yield)	475,000,000	G: Six-month money market obligations (average yield 6.8%)	85,000,000
D: Commercial loans (five-year average maturity; semiannual payments; 7.4% average yield; par value $235,000,000)	$248,415,824	H: FRN (four-year maturity; semiannual payments)	130,000,000
		I: Coupon bond (seven-year maturity; semiannual payments; 8.5% coupon; par value $180,000,000)	203,670,556
		Total liabilities	$818,670,556
		Net worth	$112,745,268
Total assets	$931,415,824	Total liabilities and net worth	$931,415,824

17 Using the zero-coupon factors for the United States from exercise 8, find the payment on the amortizing loan. For balance sheet items C, D, and I, find the semiannual and annualized yield-to-maturity, and compute the Macaulay duration based on the yield-to-maturity (not the zero-coupon rates). For each of these items, set out the computations in a table of the form shown below:

Duration computation worksheet

Semiannual period	Cash flow	Present value of cash flow	Weighted present value of cash flow
1			
2			
.			
.			
Maturity			
Sums			

18 Complete the following table summarizing the durations for all of the balance sheet items for MCNB:

Summary of durations for MCNB balance sheet items

Assets			Liabilities		
Item	Market value	Duration (years)	Item	Market value	Duration (years)
A: Cash			E: Demand deposits		
B: Marketable securities			F: Three-month money market		
C: Amortizing loans			G: Six-month money market		
D: Commercial loans			H: FRN		
			I: Coupon Bond		

19 Compute the duration of the asset portfolio and the liability portfolio for MCNB individually.

20 Find the duration gap for MCNB.

21 Find the durations for the fixed-rate side and floating-rate side of an eight-year plain vanilla interest rate swap in terms of semiannual periods and years. What are the durations of the receive-fixed and pay-fixed plain vanilla swap?

22 Explain how to hedge the asset portfolio alone using this swap to give the combined asset portfolio/interest rate swap a duration of zero. Show your calculations.

23 Explain how to hedge the liability portfolio alone using this swap to give the combined liability portfolio/interest rate swap a duration of zero. Show your calculations.

24 Using the duration gap already computed, explain how to hedge the interest rate risk of the entire bank so that the bank plus swap position has a duration of zero.

25 Using the duration gap approach, show how to set the duration of the entire bank plus swap position so that it has a duration of 2.0 years.

26 Using the duration gap approach, show how to set the duration of the entire bank plus swap position so that it has a duration of 8.0 years. Compute the effect on MCNB's net worth if the yield curve shifted up or down by 50, 100, and 500 basis points, assuming that the average yield-to-maturity for the entire bank is 6.50 percent.

Notes

1 This parallel loan example and discussion is adapted from Mehraj Mattoo, *Structured Derivatives: A Handbook of Structuring, Pricing, and Investor Applications*, London: Pitman, 1997, pp. 139–41.

2 This example is adapted from John F. Marshall and Kenneth R. Kapner, *The Swaps Market*, 2nd edn, Miami, FL: Kolb Publishing, 1993, pp. 143–6.

3 This discussion of the B. F. Goodrich–Rabobank swap is adapted and condensed from Scott Mason, Robert Merton, André Perold, and Peter Tufano, *Cases in Financial Engineering*, Englewood Cliffs, NJ: Prentice-Hall, 1995, pp. 499–509.

4 For more on duration and swaps, see Keith C. Brown and Donald J. Smith, *Interest Rate and Currency Swaps: A Tutorial*, Charlottesville, VA: The Research Foundation of the Institute of Chartered Financial Analysts, 1995, pp. 41–7; and George C. Eliopoulos, "Applications of Interest Rate Swaps," in Ravi E. Dattatreya, *The Handbook of Derivative Instruments*, Chicago: Probus Publishing, 1991, pp. 525–64.

5 This discussion of structured notes draws on Leland E. Crabbe and Joseph D. Argilagos, "Anatomy of the Structured Note Market," *Journal of Applied Corporate Finance*, 7:3, Fall 1994, pp. 85–98. See also Christopher L. Culp, Dean Furbush, and Barbara T. Kavanagh, "Structured Debt and Corporate Risk Management," *Journal of Applied Corporate Finance*, 7:3, Fall 1994, pp. 73–84.

6 Inverse floaters have been quite popular in Europe, due to the sharply downward sloping yield curves that predominated in the early to mid-1990s, particularly in Germany. For example, in January of 1993, more than DM 2.7 billion was issued in the German market alone, according to the Globecon Group, Ltd., *Derivatives Engineering*, Irwin Professional Publishing, 1995, p. 208. Issuers include General Electric Capital Corporation, Deutsche Bank, and the Republic of Austria, for the first sovereign issue of an inverse floater.

7 This quanto note example and discussion is adapted from Mattoo, *Structured Derivatives*, pp. 287–8.

8 These two swaptions are mutually exclusive if we view them as both applying to the same underlying swap. Obviously, if one swaption is used to cancel the swap, the other cannot be used to extend the same swap. However, the manager might use one swaption to cancel at year 3, and then keep the other swaption until its expiration at year 5. Conditions then might favor exercise.

APPENDIX A

A Summary of Accounting Rules for Derivative Instruments

Introduction

In 1998, the Financial Accounting Standards Board (FASB) issued a comprehensive set of regulations governing accounting for derivative instruments as its Statement of Financial Accounting Standards No. 133, "Accounting for Derivative Instruments and Hedging Activities" (FAS 133). The entire document is 245 pages long. This appendix provides a brief summary of the most important concepts in FAS 133, but it is only a summary. Application of the principles of FAS 133 will require familiarity with the statement itself.

Before the issuance of FAS 133, accounting rules for derivatives transactions were not as clear and uniform as might have been desired. The issuance of FAS 133 supersedes many previous FAS statements pertaining to derivatives (FAS 80, FAS 105, and FAS 119). FAS 133 also amends FAS 80 ("Foreign Currency Translation") and FAS 107 ("Disclosures about Fair Value of Financial Instruments"). As such, FAS 133 provides a new and uniform treatment of accounting for derivatives. Originally scheduled to go into effect in 1999, implementation of FAS 133 was delayed due to protests by affected firms. The FASB also issued FAS 138 to modify the terms of implementation in response to complaints, but FAS 138 does not significantly modify the principles of FAS 133. In 2000, FAS 133/FAS138 became fully operational and now form the basic framework for derivatives accounting in the United States.

Instruments covered by FAS 133

FAS 133 governs accounting for derivative instruments of all types, and FAS 133 gives a detailed definition of what constitutes a derivative. In essence, the FAS 133 definition parallels the concept of derivatives developed in this text and definitely embraces futures, options, and swaps. The statement also distinguishes between freestanding derivative instruments (such as futures, options, and swaps contracts) and embedded derivative instruments, such as call provisions (see Chapter 19 of this text), mortgage participations (see Chapter 19 of this text), structured notes (see Chapter 22 of this text), and equity-indexed notes (see Chapter 22 of this text). These last instruments are regarded as hybrid instruments by FAS 133 because they may be analyzed as a host instrument plus a derivative instrument. The accounting treatment of freestanding derivative instruments and embedded derivatives can be different in some circumstances, as discussed later in this appendix.

The basic accounting strategy

FAS 133 utilizes the concept of the fair value of a derivative instrument as the key measure for applying its accounting rules. Fair value is essentially the market value of the instrument.

Quoted market prices are to be used to assess fair value where possible. When a quoted price is not available, estimates of fair value can be used. These estimates can be based on discounted cash flows, option pricing models, option-adjusted spread models, and other similar techniques as appropriate.

All material derivatives positions must be recognized as assets or liabilities in the entity's statement of financial position at their fair value. Changes in the fair value of derivatives receive different accounting treatment depending on the purpose for which the derivatives position was entered. The intended use of the derivative can be either nonhedging or hedging. If the derivatives position was entered for a nonhedging purpose, the change in fair value of the derivative is reflected in the earnings for the immediate period. For example, if an option bought for a nonhedging purpose was worth $100,000 at the beginning of a given quarter and worth $115,000 at the end of that quarter, the firm's earnings would reflect the $15,000 gain in the value of the instrument as a contribution to earnings for that quarter.

Alternatively, if a firm enters a derivatives position for a hedging purpose, the change in the fair value of the derivative instrument may receive an accounting treatment that does not immediately affect earnings in the same way.

Designation of a derivatives position as a hedging instrument

FAS 133 very explicitly requires three conditions that must be met for a derivative position to receive accounting treatment as a hedge. First, any derivatives position must be designated as a hedging position at the time the derivatives position is initially entered, and the position being hedged also must be identified and documented at the time the hedging derivatives position is initiated. Second, the use of the derivative must meet the standards for a type of hedge recognized by FAS 133. There are three basic types of hedges recognized by FAS 133: a fair value hedge, a cash flow hedge, and a foreign currency hedge, as discussed below. Third, the entity must document that the derivatives position has a high effectiveness as a hedge of the hedged position and must continue to monitor that effectiveness over the life of the hedge.

The FASB wanted to ensure that any derivatives position qualifying for hedge accounting be conceived initially as a hedge:

> The Board decided that concurrent designation and documentation of a hedge is critical; without it, an entity could retroactively identify a hedged item, a hedged transaction, or a method of measuring effectiveness to achieve a desired accounting result. The Board also decided that identifying the nature of the risk being hedged and using a hedging derivative consistent with an entity's established hedging policy for risk management are essential components of risk management and are necessary to add verifiability to the hedge accounting model. (FAS 133, para. 385)

Thus, the board wants to avoid accounting gimmickry in which an entity hides derivatives losses to avoid disclosure or trumpets derivatives gains to puff up reported earnings.

To qualify for hedge accounting treatment, the derivatives position must be an effective means of hedging the risk specified in the hedging documentation. For example, interest rate futures might reasonably be considered an effective hedging vehicle for a bond portfolio, but not a stock portfolio. FAS 133 does not specify how an entity should assess effectiveness. However, the method must be reasonable and consistent: "The Board considers it essential that an entity document at the inception of the hedge how effectiveness will be assessed for each hedge and then apply that effectiveness test on a consistent basis for the duration of the designated hedge" (FAS 133, para. 386).

Recognized types of hedges

FASB recognizes three types of hedges: a fair value hedge, a cash flow hedge, and a foreign currency hedge. Qualifications for each type of hedge are different, as are the rules for accounting for derivatives used in such hedges. The following summary attempts to capture the basic idea of the accounting rules, but does not reflect the full nuance of FAS 133.

The fair value hedge

For a fair value hedge, there is a hedging instrument (the derivatives instrument) and a hedged instrument (the bond, stock, or other instrument). For a fair value hedge, the gain or loss on the derivatives instrument (the change in fair value) is reflected in earnings in the current period. The gain or loss on the hedged instrument can be separated conceptually into two parts. First, there is a gain or loss on the hedged instrument attributable to the hedged risk. Second, there is (potentially) a gain or loss on the hedged instrument attributable to factors other than the hedged risk. For the hedged instrument, we focus first on the change in fair value attributable to the hedged risk, such as interest rate risk. The entire change in the fair value of the hedged instrument due to the hedged risk must be reflected in earnings in the period in which the change in value occurs, and the carrying amount of the hedged instrument is adjusted by the same amount. In a completely effective fair value hedge, the change in the derivative's fair value and the change in the hedged instrument's fair value attributable to the hedged risk would exactly offset each other. If the hedge is not completely effective, the derivative and the hedged instrument will change in value by unequal amounts. In any event, the entire change in fair value of the hedged instrument due to the hedged risk must be reflected in current earnings. "Any hedge ineffectiveness directly affects earnings because there will be no offsetting adjustment of a hedged item's carrying amount for the ineffective aspect of the gain or loss on the related hedging instrument" (FAS 133, para. 22).

To qualify as a fair value hedge, "At inception of the hedge, there is formal documentation of the hedging relationship and the entity's risk management objective and strategy for undertaking the hedge, including identification of the hedging instrument, the hedged item, the nature of the risk being hedged, and how the hedging instrument's effectiveness in offsetting the exposure to changes in the hedged item's fair value attributable to the hedged risk will be assessed" (FAS 133, para. 20a). The firm also must expect the hedge to be effective at its inception, and the effectiveness must be monitored over the life of the hedge.

The cash flow hedge

A cash flow hedge involves a derivatives instrument used as a hedging instrument. The derivative instrument hedges the exposure to variability in expected future cash flows attributable to a particular risk. The risk comes in two possible forms. First, the risk may be associated with an existing asset or liability, such as future interest payments on a variable rate debt instrument. Second, the risk may be associated with a forecasted transaction, such as a forecasted purchase or sale of an asset. As an example of an existing asset or liability, consider a portfolio of variable rate debt instruments. One might institute a cash flow hedge to reduce the riskiness of the cash flows from the portfolio resulting from changing interest rates. As an example of a forecasted transaction, consider the plan to purchase equities in three months. One might use a cash flow hedge to reduce the uncertainty about the future purchase price of the equity portfolio.

To qualify for treatment as a cash flow hedge, there must be the usual formal documentation of the hedging relationship, statement of the risk management objective and strategy, and identification of the hedged and hedging instruments and of the risk being hedged. There also must be a reasonable expectation that the hedge will be highly effective and a plan for assessing the ongoing effectiveness of the hedge. For a cash flow hedge of existing assets or liabilities, there must be a close link between the cash flow variability of the hedging and hedged instruments. For a forecasted transaction hedge, the forecasted transaction must be clearly identified and probable to occur, and the transaction contemplated must be with a party external to the hedging entity.

Accounting for a cash flow hedge divides the gain or loss on a derivative into an effective and ineffective portion, related to the risk being hedged. The effective portion of the gain or loss is reported in other comprehensive income. The ineffective portion is reported in earnings. In addition, part of the change in the fair value of a derivative may be excluded from the hedging consideration. As such, those changes in value are neither effective nor ineffective, because they are not related to the hedge. These changes in fair value are recognized in current earnings. If a forecasted transaction is abandoned or ceases to be probable, the net gain or loss in accumulated other comprehensive income shall be immediately reclassified into earnings (FAS 133, para. 33).

The foreign currency hedge

There are three types of foreign currency hedges. First, there is a fair value foreign currency hedge of an unrecognized firm commitment or an available-for-sale security. As an example of an unrecognized firm commitment, consider a U.S. firm that has promised to purchase Japanese machine tools in six months at a price specified in Japanese yen. The U.S. firm is exposed to foreign currency risk because the dollar value of that commitment might change. It might use a foreign currency hedge to control that risk. As an example of an available-for-sale security, consider a U.S. firm that holds a security denominated in Swiss francs. Upon sale, the firm will receive Swiss francs, exposing it to changes in the U.S. dollar – Swiss franc exchange rate. Second, there is a cash flow foreign currency hedge, which is virtually identical to the cash flow hedges described above. Third, there is a hedge of the foreign currency exposure of a net investment in a foreign operation.

To qualify as a foreign currency fair value hedge, the hedge must meet the fair value hedge requirements already discussed and should be accounted for in the same manner. In hedging an available-for-sale security, the foreign currency hedge pertains to changes in fair value of the hedged security due to changes in foreign exchange rates, not due to other causes.

To qualify as a foreign currency cash flow hedge, the hedge must meet the same qualifications previously summarized for cash flow hedges. In addition, the hedging instrument must be a derivative financial instrument. The contemplated transaction can be between two operating units of the same reporting entity (for example, a parent and a foreign subsidiary). A qualifying foreign currency cash flow hedge receives the same accounting treatment as the cash flow hedges already discussed.

For a hedge of foreign currency exposure of a net investment in a foreign operation, the hedging instrument can be a derivative or nonderivative financial instrument. The gain or loss on the hedging instrument shall be reported as a translation adjustment consistent with FAS 52, "Foreign Currency Translation."

Accounting for embedded derivative instruments

When a host instrument contains an embedded derivative instrument, which is not being used as a hedging instrument under FAS 133, the entire instrument (host plus derivative) is to be accounted for under pre-FAS 133 rules. If the embedded derivative instrument is being used as a hedging instrument under FAS 133, the embedded derivative must be formally distinguished from the host instrument. In this alternative case, the host instrument would be accounted for under generally accepted accounting principles for instruments of that type in accordance with pre-FAS 133 rules, and the embedded derivative instrument would be accounted for under the rules specified in FAS 133.

Special provisions for not-for-profit organizations

FAS 133 applies to all types of entities, including corporations and not-for-profit organizations. However, the accounting rules for not-for-profits are somewhat specialized, as these entities do not report earnings. These entities should report the gain or loss on a hedging instrument as a change in net assets in the period of change, unless the hedge is a hedge of foreign currency exposure. For foreign currency hedges, the for-profit rules apply to not-for-profit organizations. These not-for-profit entities should recognize changes in the carrying amount of the hedged item as a change in net assets in the period of change for a fair value hedge. Not-for-profit organizations are not permitted to use cash flow hedge accounting.

Disclosure requirements

FAS 133 requires that entities report their derivatives positions, whether used for hedging purposes or not. For derivatives not used in a hedging strategy, the disclosure must indicate the purpose of the derivative activity.

For derivatives transactions qualifying as hedging activity under FAS 133, the disclosure requirements are more exacting. This disclosure must reveal the objectives for holding the instruments, the situation that motivates those objectives, and the firm's strategies for achieving the objectives. The disclosure must specify the type of hedge implemented by each derivatives position and the firm's risk management policy for each type of hedge. For example, the disclosure for a fair value hedge must reveal the net gain or loss recognized in earnings due to the hedge's ineffectiveness, the gain or loss excluded from the assessment of hedge effectiveness, and a description of where the net gain or loss is reported in the statement of financial performance. Similar requirements pertain to cash flow and foreign currency hedges as well.

Summary

FAS 133 attempts to bring increased structure and rationality to reporting derivatives positions, particularly those intended as hedges. First, for derivatives positions to receive accounting treatment, the statement requires that the position be conceived and documented as a hedge at the time of the initial derivatives transaction. Second, to qualify for hedge accounting, the derivatives transaction and its associated hedge instrument must fall under one of three stringent definitions of a hedge (a fair value hedge, a cash flow hedge, or a foreign currency hedge). Third, the hedging entity must have a reasonable expectation that the hedge will be highly effective, and the hedging entity must test and monitor the effectiveness of the hedge throughout the life of the hedge. Finally, the hedging entity must disclose its strategies and objectives in hedging and clearly specify the outcome of the hedge and its impact on the firm's earnings.

APPENDIX B

The Cumulative Distribution Function for the Standard Normal Random Variable

z-value	Cumulative probability									
	0.00	0.01	0.02	0.03	0.04	0.05	0.06	0.07	0.08	0.09
0.0	0.5000	0.5040	0.5080	0.5120	0.5160	0.5199	0.5239	0.5279	0.5319	0.5359
0.1	0.5398	0.5438	0.5478	0.5517	0.5557	0.5596	0.5636	0.5675	0.5714	0.5753
0.2	0.5793	0.5832	0.5871	0.5910	0.5948	0.5987	0.6026	0.6064	0.6103	0.6141
0.3	0.6179	0.6217	0.6255	0.6293	0.6331	0.6368	0.6406	0.6443	0.6480	0.6517
0.4	0.6554	0.6591	0.6628	0.6664	0.6700	0.6736	0.6772	0.6808	0.6844	0.6879
0.5	0.6915	0.6950	0.6985	0.7019	0.7054	0.7088	0.7123	0.7157	0.7190	0.7224
0.6	0.7257	0.7291	0.7324	0.7357	0.7389	0.7422	0.7454	0.7486	0.7517	0.7549
0.7	0.7580	0.7611	0.7642	0.7673	0.7704	0.7734	0.7764	0.7794	0.7823	0.7852
0.8	0.7881	0.7910	0.7939	0.7967	0.7995	0.8023	0.8051	0.8078	0.8106	0.8133
0.9	0.8159	0.8186	0.8212	0.8238	0.8264	0.8289	0.8315	0.8340	0.8365	0.8389
1.0	0.8413	0.8438	0.8461	0.8485	0.8508	0.8531	0.8554	0.8577	0.8599	0.8621
1.1	0.8643	0.8665	0.8686	0.8708	0.8729	0.8749	0.8770	0.8790	0.8810	0.8830
1.2	0.8849	0.8869	0.8888	0.8907	0.8925	0.8944	0.8962	0.8980	0.8997	0.9015
1.3	0.9032	0.9049	0.9066	0.9082	0.9099	0.9115	0.9131	0.9147	0.9162	0.9177
1.4	0.9192	0.9207	0.9222	0.9236	0.9251	0.9265	0.9279	0.9292	0.9306	0.9319
1.5	0.9332	0.9345	0.9357	0.9370	0.9382	0.9394	0.9406	0.9418	0.9429	0.9441
1.6	0.9452	0.9463	0.9474	0.9484	0.9495	0.9505	0.9515	0.9525	0.9535	0.9545
1.7	0.9554	0.9564	0.9573	0.9582	0.9591	0.9599	0.9608	0.9616	0.9625	0.9633
1.8	0.9641	0.9649	0.9656	0.9664	0.9671	0.9678	0.9686	0.9693	0.9699	0.9706
1.9	0.9713	0.9719	0.9726	0.9732	0.9738	0.9744	0.9750	0.9756	0.9761	0.9767
2.0	0.9772	0.9778	0.9783	0.9788	0.9793	0.9798	0.9803	0.9808	0.9812	0.9817
2.1	0.9821	0.9826	0.9830	0.9834	0.9838	0.9842	0.9846	0.9850	0.9854	0.9857
2.2	0.9861	0.9864	0.9868	0.9871	0.9875	0.9878	0.9881	0.9884	0.9887	0.9890
2.3	0.9893	0.9896	0.9898	0.9901	0.9904	0.9906	0.9909	0.9911	0.9913	0.9916
2.4	0.9918	0.9920	0.9922	0.9925	0.9927	0.9929	0.9931	0.9932	0.9934	0.9936
2.5	0.9938	0.9940	0.9941	0.9943	0.9945	0.9946	0.9948	0.9949	0.9951	0.9952
2.6	0.9953	0.9955	0.9956	0.9957	0.9959	0.9960	0.9961	0.9962	0.9963	0.9964
2.7	0.9965	0.9966	0.9967	0.9968	0.9969	0.9970	0.9971	0.9972	0.9973	0.9974
2.8	0.9974	0.9975	0.9976	0.9977	0.9977	0.9978	0.9979	0.9979	0.9980	0.9981
2.9	0.9981	0.9982	0.9982	0.9983	0.9984	0.9984	0.9985	0.9985	0.9986	0.9986
3.0	0.9987	0.9987	0.9987	0.9988	0.9988	0.9989	0.9989	0.9989	0.9990	0.9990
3.1	0.9990	0.9991	0.9991	0.9991	0.9992	0.9992	0.9992	0.9992	0.9993	0.9993
3.2	0.9993	0.9993	0.9994	0.9994	0.9994	0.9994	0.9994	0.9995	0.9995	0.9995
3.3	0.9995	0.9995	0.9995	0.9996	0.9996	0.9996	0.9996	0.9996	0.9996	0.9997
3.4	0.9997	0.9997	0.9997	0.9997	0.9997	0.9997	0.9997	0.9997	0.9997	0.9998

Index